**HANDBOOK OF THE ECONOMICS OF GIVING,
ALTRUISM AND RECIPROCITY
VOLUME 1**

HANDBOOKS IN ECONOMICS

23

Series Editors

KENNETH J. ARROW
MICHAEL D. INTRILIGATOR

AMSTERDAM · BOSTON · HEIDELBERG · LONDON
NEW YORK · OXFORD · PARIS · SAN DIEGO
SAN FRANCISCO · SINGAPORE · SYDNEY · TOKYO
North-Holland is an imprint of Elsevier

HANDBOOK OF THE ECONOMICS OF GIVING, ALTRUISM AND RECIPROCITY
FOUNDATIONS

VOLUME 1

Edited by

SERGE-CHRISTOPHE KOLM
Paris, France

and

JEAN MERCIER YTHIER
University of Metz

AMSTERDAM · BOSTON · HEIDELBERG · LONDON
NEW YORK · OXFORD · PARIS · SAN DIEGO
SAN FRANCISCO · SINGAPORE · SYDNEY · TOKYO
North-Holland is an imprint of Elsevier

North-Holland is an imprint of Elsevier
Radarweg 29, PO Box 211, 1000 AE Amsterdam, The Netherlands
The Boulevard, Langford Lane, Kidlington, Oxford OX5 1GB, UK

First edition 2006

Copyright © 2006 Elsevier B.V. All rights reserved

No part of this publication may be reproduced, stored in a retrieval system or transmitted in any form or by any means electronic, mechanical, photocopying, recording or otherwise without the prior written permission of the publisher

Permissions may be sought directly from Elsevier's Science & Technology Rights Department in Oxford, UK: phone (+44) (0) 1865 843830; fax (+44) (0) 1865 853333; email: permissions@elsevier.com. Alternatively you can submit your request online by visiting the Elsevier web site at http://elsevier.com/locate/permissions, and selecting *Obtaining permission to use Elsevier material*

Notice
No responsibility is assumed by the publisher for any injury and/or damage to persons or property as a matter of products liability, negligence or otherwise, or from any use or operation of any methods, products, instructions or ideas contained in the material herein. Because of rapid advances in the medical sciences, in particular, independent verification of diagnoses and drug dosages should be made

Library of Congress Cataloging-in-Publication Data
A catalog record for this book is available from the Library of Congress

British Library Cataloguing in Publication Data
A catalogue record for this book is available from the British Library

ISBN-13: 978-0-444-50697-9
ISBN-10: 0-444-50697-7

ISSN: 0169-7218 (Handbooks in Economics series)
ISSN: 1574-0714 (Handbook of the Economics of Giving, Altruism and Reciprocity series)

For information on all North-Holland publications
visit our website at books.elsevier.com

Printed and bound in the United Kingdom

Transferred to Digital Print 2010

To the memory of Louis-André Gérard-Varet

To the memory of Patricia Anita Lingard Wise

INTRODUCTION TO THE SERIES

The aim of the *Handbooks in Economics* series is to produce Handbooks for various branches of economics, each of which is a definitive source, reference, and teaching supplement for use by professional researchers and advanced graduate students. Each Handbook provides self-contained surveys of the current state of a branch of economics in the form of chapters prepared by leading specialists on various aspects of this branch of economics. These surveys summarize not only received results but also newer developments, from recent journal articles and discussion papers. Some original material is also included, but the main goal is to provide comprehensive and accessible surveys. The Handbooks are intended to provide not only useful reference volumes for professional collections but also possible supplementary readings for advanced courses for graduate students in economics.

KENNETH J. ARROW and MICHAEL D. INTRILIGATOR

CONTENTS OF THE HANDBOOK

VOLUME 1

Chapter 1
Introduction to the Economics of Giving, Altruism and Reciprocity
SERGE-CHRISTOPHE KOLM

PART I: FOUNDATIONS

1A: Social view

Chapter 2
The Empirical Analysis of Transfer Motives
ERIK SCHOKKAERT

Chapter 3
Altruistic Behavior and Altruistic Motivations
JON ELSTER

Chapter 4
The Gift and Reciprocity: Perspectives from Economic Anthropology
CHRIS HANN

1B: Overall views

Chapter 5
The Economic Theory of Gift-Giving: Perfect Substitutability of Transfers and Redistribution of Wealth
JEAN MERCIER YTHIER

Chapter 6
Reciprocity: Its Scope, Rationales, and Consequences
SERGE-CHRISTOPHE KOLM

1C: Experimental social psychology

Chapter 7
The Formation of Social Preferences: Some Lessons from Psychology and Biology
LOUIS LÉVY-GARBOUA, CLAUDE MEIDINGER AND BENOÎT RAPOPORT

Chapter 8
The Economics of Fairness, Reciprocity and Altruism – Experimental Evidence and New Theories
ERNST FEHR AND KLAUS M. SCHMIDT

1D: Human nature

Chapter 9
The Economics of Human Relationships
PIER LUIGI SACCO, PAOLO VANIN AND STEFANO ZAMAGNI

Chapter 10
Human Nature and Sociality in Economics
NICHOLAS BARDSLEY AND ROBERT SUGDEN

1E: Special topics

Chapter 11
Natural Kantian or *Zoo Economicus*? Evolutionary Theories of Selfishness and Altruism among Men and Beasts
THEODORE C. BERGSTROM

Chapter 12
Solidarity Norms and Institutions in Village Societies: Static and Dynamic Considerations
JEAN-PHILIPPE PLATTEAU

VOLUME 2

PART II: FAMILY TRANSFERS

Chapter 13
Microeconomic Models of Family Transfers
ANNE LAFERRÈRE AND FRANÇOIS-CHARLES WOLFF

Chapter 14
Altruism, Exchange or Indirect Reciprocity: What Do the Data on Family Transfers Show?
LUC ARRONDEL AND ANDRÉ MASSON

Chapter 15
Intergenerational Altruism and Neoclassical Growth Models
PHILIPPE MICHEL, EMMANUEL THIBAULT AND JEAN-PIERRE VIDAL

Chapter 16
Wealth Transfer Taxation: A Survey of the Theoretical Literature
HELMUTH CREMER AND PIERRE PESTIEAU

Chapter 17
The Economics of Migrants' Remittances
HILLEL RAPOPORT AND FRÉDÉRIC DOCQUIER

PART III: THIRD SECTOR AND LABOR

Chapter 18
Philanthropy
JAMES ANDREONI

Chapter 19
Donative Nonprofit Organizations
MARC BILODEAU AND RICHARD STEINBERG

Chapter 20
The Economics of Organ Transplantation
EMANUEL D. THORNE

Chapter 21
Altruism, Reciprocity and Cooperation in the Workplace
JULIO J. ROTEMBERG

Chapter 22
Reciprocity, Altruism, and Cooperative Production
LOUIS PUTTERMAN

PART IV: THE POLITICAL ECONOMY OF VOLUNTARY TRANSFERS

Chapter 23
Strong Reciprocity and the Welfare State
CHRISTINA M. FONG, SAMUEL BOWLES AND HERBERT GINTIS

Chapter 24
Selfishness, Altruism and Normative Principles in the Economic Analysis of Social Transfers
DIDIER BLANCHET AND MARC FLEURBAEY

Chapter 25
The Political Economy of Intergenerational Cooperation
ALESSANDRO CIGNO

Chapter 26
The Economics of International Aid
RAVI KANBUR

PREFACE TO THE HANDBOOK

Field and methods

The field of the Handbook is the analysis of non-market voluntary transfers of scarce resources, of the reasons for their existence including notably the motives of the agents involved, and of their relations and interactions with market allocation and public finance. It includes the measurement of the magnitude and share of non-market voluntary transfers and their evolution over time; and the assessment of the importance of moral conducts in market exchange for the good functioning of markets. It also includes the developing, and systematic use for the purposes of economic analysis, of descriptions and abstract representations of the "social man" significantly more realistic, accurate and complete than the conventional representation of the "economic man" often assumed in the economics of the nineteenth and twentieth centuries. From this latter aspect, the Handbook extends and renews a continuous tradition of economic science, notably represented in the works of most of the founders, from the late eighteenth century (Adam Smith) to the early twentieth (notably Pareto). Applications include family transfers, gift-giving and volunteering in charities and other non-profit organizations, cooperation and reciprocity in labor relations, social transfers, public redistribution and international aid. Methods cover a wide spectrum, in relation to the variety of considered phenomena, notably: psychological and normative analysis, including the relevant branches of moral and political philosophy; models of economic equilibrium and growth; game theory, including its evolutionary variants; laboratory experiments in psychology and game interactions; and econometric and statistical assessment of transfers and transfer motives.

Purpose

The *Handbook of the Economics of Giving, Altruism and Reciprocity* aims to provide a definitive source, reference guide, and teaching supplement for its field. It surveys, as of the early 2000's, the state of the art of the economic theory and of the econometric and statistical study of its object, and it also provides extensive reviews of the contemporary contributions of the other disciplines concerned by the domain, such as anthropology, psychology, philosophy, political science, sociology, biology and socio-biology. In addition to its use as a reference guide, the Editors hope that this Handbook will assist researchers and students working in a particular branch of this vast field to become acquainted with other branches. Each of the chapters can be read independently.

Organization

The Handbook includes 26 chapters on various topics in the field. Chapter 1 introduces the subject and proposes a first overview of the field. The following chapters are arranged into four parts. *Part I* treats *Foundations*, including reviews of economic theories and empirical findings relative to gift-giving, reciprocity and their motives, and also surveys of similar contributions from within anthropology, philosophy, psychology and evolutionary theory. The next three parts concentrate on applications to the three sectors of society where non-market voluntary transfers are particularly significant: the family, with *Part II* relative to *Family Transfers*, including microeconomic and macroeconomic theories of family transfers and of their taxation, and corresponding econometric analyses; the third sector, with *Part III* on *Third Sector and Labour*, including theoretical and empirical analyses of philanthropy, non-profit organizations, cooperatives and co-operation in labor relations, and organ donations; and the State, with *Part IV* covering *The Political Economy of Voluntary Transfers*, including reviews of the theoretical and empirical analyses of the welfare state and of international aid.

Level

All the topics presented are treated at an advanced level, suitable for use by economists and social scientists working in the field, or by graduate students in both economics and the social sciences.

Acknowledgements

First of all, we would like to make a special mention of gratitude to Louis-André Gérard-Varet, who participated as editor to the initial conception of the Handbook, and who unfortunately died shortly after the launching of the project. These two volumes would not have existed without him. They are dedicated to his memory. Our other principal acknowledgements are to Kenneth Arrow and Michael Intriligator for their friendly advice as general editors of the series, and to the authors of chapters in the present Handbook, who not only prepared their own chapters but also provided advice on the organization and content of the volumes and reviewed other chapters. We are also most grateful to Valerie Teng, senior publishing editor in charge, and her team, for their very helpful assistance and their patience. The authors' conference that we organized at Marseilles in January 2002 was an important step in the preparation of the volumes. We are indebted to the Institut d'Economie Publique, the Université de la Méditerranée, and the Ecole des Hautes Etudes en Sciences Sociales for providing us with the necessary financial and organizational support on this occasion. Finally, we are grateful to the Université de Metz and the Equipe de Recherche en Anthropologie et Sociologie de l'Expertise for providing us with financial support for the editing of substantial parts of the volumes.

The editors

CONTENTS OF VOLUME 1

Introduction to the Series	vii
Contents of the Handbook	ix
Preface to the Handbook	xiii

Chapter 1
Introduction to the Economics of Giving, Altruism and Reciprocity
SERGE-CHRISTOPHE KOLM 1

Abstract	4
Foreword	5
Part I: **General overview**	7
1. The economics of moral sentiments	7
2. Motives for altruism and altruistic giving	8
3. Structures of altruism	10
4. Altruism and democracy: Altruistic joint giving and its public implementation	16
5. Motives and reasons for nonaltruistic giving	18
6. The structure of nonaltruistic giving	20
6.1. From motives to forms	20
6.2. Contradiction and possibilities in the logic of motives	22
7. The inefficiency of individual giving when joint or public giving is possible: The perplexing joint giving theorem	23
8. Reciprocities	25
8.1. An overview	25
8.2. "Human rocks on which societies are built"	27
8.3. The special games of reciprocity	30
9. Importance and scope of giving, altruism, and pro-social conducts	32
9.1. Overview	32
9.2. Families	32
9.3. The political and public sector	34
9.4. Giving in philanthropy, solidarity, and charity	37
9.5. General respect, civility, sociality, and help	40
9.6. The correction of "failures" of exchanges and organizations	41
9.7. Associations, clubs, cooperatives	42
9.8. The workplace and labour relations	43
9.9. Social giving: Relation, symbol, status	43
9.10. Normative economics and the good society	45

10. Giving reactions — 47
  10.1. About two particular issues that caught the fancy of economists: Intertemporal giving and the internalization of the gift externality — 47
  10.2. Interferences with altruistic giving: General view — 49
11. Solving "Adam Smith's problem" — 50
12. The causes of and reasons for altruism — 52

Part II: Altruisms and giving — 54

13. Altruisms: Types and causes or reasons — 54
  13.1. General presentation — 54
  13.2. Natural or hedonistic altruism — 57
  13.3. Normative altruisms — 60
14. Altruism and justice; impartial altruism — 71
  14.1. Altruism and justice — 71
  14.2. Impartial altruism — 74
  14.3. History — 77
  14.4. Altruism and justice: Consistency or conflict, force or freedom — 78
15. Giving: An abundance and variety of motives and reasons — 80
  15.1. An overview — 80
  15.2. Social effects — 81
  15.3. Intrinsically normative (non-altruistic) giving — 84
  15.4. Self-interested giving — 84
  15.5. Giving in social relations and communities — 89

Part III: Values and history — 90

16. The normative economics of altruism and giving — 90
  16.1. The ethics of economics — 90
  16.2. The intrinsic value of altruism and giving — 92
  16.3. Giving as improving fairness in freedom — 92
  16.4. Altruism, giving, reciprocity, and failures of economic interactions — 93
  16.5. Liberal social contracts and joint giving — 94
  16.6. Retro-gifts and the process-liberal public debt — 98
  16.7. Selfish altruism: The situation of the other person may be your own — 99
  16.8. Justice from altruism, and distribution as a public good: The distributive or moral surplus — 101
17. Historical landmarks — 103
  17.1. Economics and altruism — 103
  17.2. Interdependent utilities and social choice — 104
  17.3. Altruism and uncertainty — 105
  17.4. Interdependent utilities and interdependent giving — 106
  17.5. A notable debate: Blood and the efficiency of giving — 107
  17.6. Volumes in the economics of giving, altruism and reciprocity — 108
Appendix: The joint giving theorem — 108
References — 110
Further reading — 114

PART 1: FOUNDATIONS

1A: Social view

Chapter 2
The Empirical Analysis of Transfer Motives
ERIK SCHOKKAERT   127
Abstract   128
Keywords   128
  1. Introduction   129
  2. Some basic insights from the psychological literature   130
    2.1. A list of motivations   131
      (a) self-interest   131
      (b) reciprocity   132
      (c) norms and principles   133
      (d) pure altruism and empathy   134
    2.2. Some broader questions   135
  3. Tastes and motivations: Why are economists interested? Why should they be interested?   137
    3.1. The empirical predictions of the pure public goods model   138
    3.2. Other consequences for government policy   140
    3.3. The analysis of philanthropic markets and non-profit organizations   141
    3.4. Rationality and egoism: The homo economicus   142
  4. Charitable giving and volunteering   144
    4.1. Giving as a private good: Tax prices and income   144
    4.2. Crowding out and the warm-glow of giving   153
    4.3. Status of sociological and demographic variables 157
    4.4. Direct evidence on preferences   159
  5. Interhousehold and intrafamily transfers of money and time   165
    5.1. Altruism versus exchange or reciprocity: A sketch 166
    5.2. Motives for interhousehold transfers   168
    5.3. Gifts: The deadweight loss of Christmas?   171
  6. Conclusion   174
Acknowledgements   176
References   176

Chapter 3
Altruistic Behavior and Altruistic Motivations
JON ELSTER   183
Abstract   184
Keywords   184
  1. Introduction   185
  2. The nature and sources of altruistic motivations   185

3. Can interest mimic altruism? ... 187
  4. Can passion mimic altruism? ... 192
  5. Transmutation of motivations ... 200
  6. Is altruism possible and knowable? ... 202
References ... 205

Chapter 4
The Gift and Reciprocity: Perspectives from Economic Anthropology
CHRIS HANN ... 207
Abstract ... 208
Keywords ... 208
  1. Introduction ... 209
  2. History and theory ... 210
    2.1. Malinowski and Mauss ... 210
    2.2. Polanyi and Sahlins ... 213
    2.3. Recent contributions ... 214
  3. Ethnographic examples ... 216
    3.1. Food sharing ... 216
    3.2. Socialist and postsocialist networking ... 218
  4. Cross-cultural experiments ... 220
  5. Conclusions ... 221
References ... 221

1B: Overall views

Chapter 5
The Economic Theory of Gift-Giving: Perfect Substitutability of Transfers and Redistribution of Wealth
JEAN MERCIER YTHIER ... 227
Abstract ... 228
Keywords ... 229
  1. Introduction ... 230
  2. Gift-giving in social equilibrium theory: A preliminary overview ... 232
    2.1. Preferences and rights ... 232
    2.2. Four characteristic properties ... 236
    2.3. Theory and facts ... 241
  3. Perfectly substitutable transfers in a pure distributive social system ... 243
    3.1. Pure distributive social system and equilibrium ... 244
    3.2. Diagrammatic representation ... 247
    3.3. Three studies of pure distributive equilibrium ... 251
    3.4. Existence, determinacy ... 261
  4. Perfectly substitutable transfers in a competitive market economy ... 267
    4.1. Interdependent preferences ... 269

4.2. General equilibrium with benevolent gift-giving and competitive market exchange	275
4.3. Perfectly substitutable transfers and the transfer problem	282
5. The effectiveness of public redistribution with perfectly substitutable transfers	283
5.1. Neutrality in general Pareto social systems	285
5.2. Neutrality in BBV distributive social systems	288
6. Efficient redistribution with perfectly substitutable transfers	296
6.1. General theory	297
6.2. Free-riding and population size in BBV distributive social systems	318
6.3. Mechanism design in BBV distributive social systems	328
7. Imperfectly substitutable transfers	329
7.1. Logical tests of the perfect substitutability of transfers	329
7.2. Empirical tests of the perfect substitutability of transfers	336
8. Conclusion	341
Appendix A	341
A.1. Proofs	341
A.2. Mechanisms for private contributions to public goods	354
References	361

Chapter 6
Reciprocity: Its Scope, Rationales, and Consequences
SERGE-CHRISTOPHE KOLM

	371
Abstract	375
Part I: Facts and forms	376
1. Introduction	376
1.1. Evidence, scope, and motives of reciprocity	376
1.2. Social scope and values of reciprocity	378
1.3. Equality and fraternity: The two, three or four types of reciprocity	380
1.4. Reciprocity and the general motives for giving	382
1.5. Reciprocity and reciprocating good or bad	384
1.6. Understanding and explaining reciprocity	385
1.7. Organisation	386
2. The evidence, scope, and pervasiveness of the reciprocity relationship	387
2.1. Society as reciprocity and general respect	387
2.2. Relations of reciprocity	388
2.3. Extended reciprocities	389
2.4. Reciprocity and exchange and markets	391
2.5. Reciprocity and organizations and labour	392
2.6. Established groups, cooperatives, associations	393
2.7. Reciprocity and community	393
2.8. Public aid	394
2.9. Intergenerational reciprocities	395
2.10. Evidence and history	395

3. Reciprocity as the quintessential sociality and social bond — 397
4. Definitions, givings and exchanges — 398
   4.1. Concepts and distinctions — 398
   4.2. Motives for giving, notably in reciprocity — 400
   4.3. Sequential exchange — 408
5. Reciprocities: Forms and structures — 411
   5.1. Facts and relations — 411
   5.2. Reciprocal structures — 411
   5.3. Larger reciprocities — 416
   5.4. Reciprocity as social or economic system — 417
   5.5. Reciprocity, revenge, reciprocation — 418
   5.6. Reciprocity as giving or as reciprocation — 420

Part II: Motives — 421
6. Motives: The three worlds of reciprocity — 421
   6.1. Three basic reasons — 421
   6.2. An outlook of the general structure — 423
   6.3. Comparative, matching, compensatory, or balance reciprocity — 424
   6.4. Liking reciprocities — 429
   6.5. Continuation reciprocity — 439
   6.6. Comparing the three polar motives of reciprocity — 441
   6.7. Relational, process, status, or symbolic reciprocities — 441
   6.8. Imitation and conforming — 442
   6.9. The graph of reciprocity — 442
   6.10. The six basic reciprocations — 443
   6.11. The motives of extended reciprocations — 443
7. Reciprocity and other social sentiments — 444
   7.1. Fairness, equity, justice — 444
   7.2. The principle of universalization: the categorical imperative — 448
   7.3. Other social sentiments — 449
8. Reciprocity in the modes of economic realization — 449

Part III: Values and reasons — 453
9. The values of reciprocity — 453
   9.1. The issues — 453
   9.2. General respect and sociability from reciprocity — 455
   9.3. Reciprocal corrections of market failures — 456
   9.4. Reciprocity in trust, relational capital, and efficiency — 465
   9.5. The intrinsic values of reciprocity — 467
10. Normative uses of reciprocity — 468
    10.1. The values of reciprocity — 468
    10.2. Cooperatives — 469
    10.3. General rules of society — 469
    10.4. Putative reciprocities — 470

10.5. Macrojustice	470
10.6. The Good Society: The classical scientific directing utopia	471
11. How and why? Understanding and explaining reciprocity	472
11.1. Understanding	472
11.2. Biology?	475
11.3. Social and cultural evolution	478
Part IV: Formal analysis and interaction	482
12. Formal analysis of reciprocity	482
12.1. Methodology	482
12.2. Comparative, matching, or balance reciprocities	486
12.3. Liking-reciprocity	492
13. Strategic interaction and process preferences: Games of reciprocity and their consequences	504
13.1. Presentation	504
13.2. General properties about processes	508
13.3. Solutions of the return-gift and reciprocity games	513
13.4. Comparison of reciprocities with other processes	520
Part V: Reciprocity in economics	521
14. Reciprocity in economics	522
14.1. A short overview and a corrected bias	522
14.2. Completing economics	526
References	529
Further reading	534

1C: Experimental social psychology

Chapter 7
The Formation of Social Preferences: Some Lessons from Psychology and Biology
LOUIS LÉVY-GARBOUA, CLAUDE MEIDINGER AND BENOÎT RAPOPORT 545

Abstract	546
Keywords	547
1. Introduction	548
2. The evolutionary emergence of social types	550
2.1. The problem of selection of social behavior in non-cultural species	550
2.2. From animal societies to human societies	555
3. Social learning	561
3.1. Theoretical perspectives	561
3.2. Empirical findings: The role of the family	563
3.3. The role of other socializers	564
3.4. Cross-cultural differences	565
3.5. Conclusion	565
4. Cognitive theories of moral and pro-social development	566
4.1. How children use the rules of a game and how conscious of these rules they are	566

4.2. How children form moral judgements	566
4.3. Other theories of stages	570
4.4. Cognitive correlates of pro-social development	572
5. Social cognition	573
5.1. Perspective-taking, identification with, and projection of self onto others	573
5.2. Identification with a known other and self-projection onto unknown others	575
5.3. Social cognition and the stages of pro-social development	578
5.4. Choosing and valuing an income distribution	579
6. Social norms and reciprocity	581
6.1. The fairness heuristic	581
6.2. Social norms of fairness in proposal-response games	583
6.3. Some evidence on social norms	585
6.4. The working of a social norm: Homans' "cash posters"	586
7. In-group favoritism and self-anchored altruism	589
7.1. Categorization and the preference for similarity	589
7.2. In-group favoritism and out-group discrimination in minimal groups	591
7.3. Self-anchored altruism	593
7.4. Comparing behavior in social dilemmas and in social choices	595
8. Social drives and emotions	597
8.1. Social comparison	597
8.2. Reducing inequity	599
8.3. Helping others in need: Is the motivation truly altruistic?	600
9. Some lessons from psychology and biology: A summary	603
References	604

Chapter 8
The Economics of Fairness, Reciprocity and Altruism – Experimental Evidence and New Theories
ERNST FEHR AND KLAUS M. SCHMIDT

	615
Abstract	616
Keywords	616
1. Introduction and overview	617
2. Empirical foundations of other-regarding preferences	621
2.1. Other-regarding behavior in simple experiments	621
2.2. Other-regarding preferences or irrational behavior	628
2.3. Neuroeconomic foundations of other-regarding preferences	631
3. Theories of other-regarding preferences	636
3.1. Social preferences	637
3.2. Interdependent preferences	644
3.3. Models of intention based reciprocity	647
3.4. Axiomatic approaches	652
4. Discriminating between theories of other-regarding preferences	653
4.1. Who are the relevant reference actors?	654

4.2.	Equality versus efficiency	656
4.3.	Revenge versus inequity reduction	660
4.4.	Does kindness trigger rewards?	662
4.5.	Maximin preferences	664
4.6.	Preferences for honesty	666
4.7.	Summary and outlook	667

5. Economic applications   669
    5.1. Cooperation and collective action   669
    5.2. Endogenous formation of cooperative institutions   673
    5.3. How fairness, reciprocity and competition interact   676
    5.4. Fairness and reciprocity as a source of economic incentives   680

6. Conclusions   683

References   684

1D: Human nature

Chapter 9
The Economics of Human Relationships
PIER LUIGI SACCO, PAOLO VANIN AND STEFANO ZAMAGNI   695

Abstract   696
Keywords   696
1. Introduction   697
2. 'Communicative' aspects of reciprocity and altruism and the concept of 'socially provided goods'   698
3. The positional side of economic interaction   700
    3.1. Positional competition and labor issues   701
    3.2. Positional competition and growth   702
4. The relational side of economic interaction   704
    4.1. Relational orientation and labor issues   706
    4.2. Relational orientation and economic growth   708
    4.3. The case of private growth and social impoverishment   711
5. Cultural and economic selection: The evolutionary foundations of altruism and pro-sociality   717
6. Back to the basics in the economic analysis of human interaction?   723
References   726

Chapter 10
Human nature and sociality in economics
NICHOLAS BARDSLEY AND ROBERT SUGDEN   731

Abstract   732
Keywords   732
1. Hobbes's asocial model of man   736
2. Convention   738

3. Rousseau and the 'most remarkable change in man'	742
4. Fellow-feeling	745
5. Other-oriented motivations in modern economics	748
5.1. Rational choice altruism	749
5.2. Warm glow	751
5.3. Inequality aversion	752
5.4. Rabin's theory of reciprocity	754
6. Expressive rationality	756
7. Team reasoning	758
8. Sociality and the 'private language' argument	761
9. Conclusions	764
Acknowledgements	765
References	765

1E: Special topics

Chapter 11
Natural Kantian or *ZOO ECONOMICUS*? Evolutionary theories of selfishness and altruism among men and beasts
THEODORE C. BERGSTROM

	771
Abstract	772
Keywords	772
1. Selfishness and group selection	774
2. Games and social interactions	777
2.1. What is the game and who is playing?	777
2.2. Prisoners' dilemma games	778
2.3. Stag hunt games	779
2.4. Evolutionary dynamics and altruism	780
3. Haystack models	781
3.1. Maynard Smith's mice	781
3.2. General haystack models and assortative matching	783
3.3. Cohen and Eshel's generalized haystack models	784
3.4. The iron rule of selfishness	787
3.5. Haystacks and the iron rule	788
3.6. Migration and stochastic extinction	789
3.7. Relative and absolute payoffs	790
3.8. "Too stringent to be realistic?"	791
4. Assortative matching	794
4.1. Measures of assortativity	794
4.2. Hamilton's kin selection theory	795
4.3. Evolutionary dynamics with assortative mating	798
4.4. Assortative matching with partner choice	801
4.5. Assortative matching induced by spatial structure	803

5. Repeated games and group selection	806
5.1. Group selection from multiple Nash equilibria	806
5.2. How can costly punishment survive?	807
5.3. Evidence from psychology and anthropology	811
6. Conclusion	813
6.1. Further reading	813
References	814

Chapter 12
Solidarity Norms and Institutions in Village Societies: Static and Dynamic Considerations
JEAN-PHILIPPE PLATTEAU

	819
Abstract	820
Keywords	820
1. Introduction	821
2. Other-regarding norms in agrarian societies	823
3. The customary system of land tenure	829
3.1. Land access and guaranteed livelihoods	829
3.2. The commons as embodiment of the community	833
4. Erosion of the social security function of customary land tenure	835
4.1. The transformation of the commons	836
4.2. Individualization of land tenure rights	846
5. Voluntary reciprocal contingent transfers	854
5.1. General considerations	854
5.2. A short survey of the economic theory of informal insurance mechanisms	856
5.3. Empirical evidence	863
6. Conclusion: Institutional change and solidarity mechanisms in village societies	874
References	878
Author Index of Volume 1	I-1
Subject Index of Volume 1	I-19

Chapter 1

INTRODUCTION TO THE ECONOMICS OF GIVING, ALTRUISM AND RECIPROCITY

SERGE-CHRISTOPHE KOLM

Institute of Public Economics, School for Advanced Studies in the Social Sciences

Contents

Abstract	4
Foreword	5
Part I: **General overview**	7
1. The economics of moral sentiments	7
2. Motives for altruism and altruistic giving	8
3. Structures of altruism	10
4. Altruism and democracy: Altruistic joint giving and its public implementation	16
5. Motives and reasons for nonaltruistic giving	18
6. The structure of nonaltruistic giving	20
6.1. From motives to forms	20
6.2. Contradiction and possibilities in the logic of motives	22
7. The inefficiency of individual giving when joint or public giving is possible: The perplexing joint giving theorem	23
8. Reciprocities	25
8.1. An overview	25
8.2. "Human rocks on which societies are built"	27
8.3. The special games of reciprocity	30
9. Importance and scope of giving, altruism, and pro-social conducts	32
9.1. Overview	32
9.2. Families	32
9.3. The political and public sector	34
9.3.1. Public services and general political motives	34
9.3.2. Actors of the political and public system	36
9.4. Giving in philanthropy, solidarity, and charity	37
9.4.1. Social situation	37
9.4.2. Motives	38

Handbook of the Economics of Giving, Altruism and Reciprocity, Volume 1
Edited by Serge-Christophe Kolm and Jean Mercier Ythier
Copyright © 2006 Elsevier B.V. All rights reserved
DOI: 10.1016/S1574-0714(06)01001-3

9.5. General respect, civility, sociality, and help	40
9.6. The correction of "failures" of exchanges and organizations	41
9.7. Associations, clubs, cooperatives	42
9.8. The workplace and labour relations	43
9.9. Social giving: Relation, symbol, status	43
9.10. Normative economics and the good society	45
10. Giving reactions	47
10.1. About two particular issues that caught the fancy of economists: Intertemporal giving and the internalization of the gift externality	47
10.1.1. Intertemporal giving, both ways: Bequest and the retro-gift public debt	47
10.1.2. Economic internalization of helping externalities	48
10.2. Interferences with altruistic giving: General view	49
11. Solving "Adam Smith's problem"	50
12. The causes of and reasons for altruism	52
Part II: Altruisms and giving	54
13. Altruisms: Types and causes or reasons	54
13.1. General presentation	54
13.1.1. Introduction	54
13.1.2. The twelve basic types of altruism	56
13.1.3. The objects of reasons for giving and altruisms	56
13.2. Natural or hedonistic altruism	57
13.2.1. Emotional contagion	58
13.2.2. Empathies	58
13.2.3. Affection and sympathy	59
13.2.4. Compassion and pity	59
13.2.5. Relations and nature of hedonistic altruism	60
13.3. Normative altruisms	60
13.3.1. The three types of normative altruism: moral, social, and rational	60
13.3.2. Moral and social normative altruism	61
13.3.3. Rational altruism	67
14. Altruism and justice; impartial altruism	71
14.1. Altruism and justice	71
14.2. Impartial altruism	74
14.3. History	77
14.4. Altruism and justice: Consistency or conflict, force or freedom	78
15. Giving: An abundance and variety of motives and reasons	80
15.1. An overview	80
15.2. Social effects	81
15.2.1. Opinion	81
15.2.2. Situation	83
15.2.3. Relation	83
15.3. Intrinsically normative (non-altruistic) giving	84

15.4. Self-interested giving	84
15.4.1. Introduction	84
15.4.2. Gifts and interests	85
15.4.3. Giver's benefit from the gift's effect on processes and their outcome	86
15.5. Giving in social relations and communities	89

Part III: **Values and history** 90

16. The normative economics of altruism and giving 90

- 16.1. The ethics of economics — 90
- 16.2. The intrinsic value of altruism and giving — 92
- 16.3. Giving as improving fairness in freedom — 92
- 16.4. Altruism, giving, reciprocity, and failures of economic interactions — 93
    - 16.4.1. Causing market failures — 93
    - 16.4.2. Curing market failures — 93
- 16.5. Liberal social contracts and joint giving — 94
    - 16.5.1. Liberal social contracts — 95
    - 16.5.2. Public goods and joint giving — 95
    - 16.5.3. The core with interdependent coalitions — 96
- 16.6. Retro-gifts and the process-liberal public debt — 98
- 16.7. Selfish altruism: The situation of the other person may be your own — 99
- 16.8. Justice from altruism, and distribution as a public good: The distributive or moral surplus — 101

17. Historical landmarks 103

- 17.1. Economics and altruism — 103
- 17.2. Interdependent utilities and social choice — 104
- 17.3. Altruism and uncertainty — 105
- 17.4. Interdependent utilities and interdependent giving — 106
- 17.5. A notable debate: Blood and the efficiency of giving — 107
- 17.6. Volumes in the economics of giving, altruism and reciprocity — 108

Appendix: The joint giving theorem 108

References 110
Further reading 114

Abstract

Altruism, giving and pro-social conduct, and reciprocity, are the basis of the existence and performance of societies, through their various occurrences: in families; among the diverse motives of the political and public sector; as the general respect and moral conduct which permit life in society and exchanges; for remedying "failures" of markets and organizations (which they sometimes also create); and in charity and specific organizations. Altruism has various origins: it can be hedonistic or natural altruism in empathy, affection, sympathy, emotional contagion, pity, and compassion; or normative altruism of the moral, non-moral social, and rational types. Giving can be altruistic, aimed at producing some social effect in the fields of social sentiments, situations or relations, an intrinsic norm, or self-interested. Reciprocity, in which a gift elicits another gift, is a pervasive social relation due to either a desire of balance (and possibly fairness), or to liking a benevolent giver (moreover, self-interested sequential exchanges look like it). Joint giving for alleviating poverty and need makes giving a contribution to a pure public good for which efficient public transfers crowd out private gifts. Yet, private giving can be an intrinsic norm or a demand of reason, or it can be motivated by the non-moral concern about judgments of others or of oneself. Families – the institutions for love and giving – are networks of reciprocities. Intertemporal giving includes gifts to future generation through bequests, and to earlier generations through the relevant public indebtedness ("retro-gifts"). Normative opinions about societies, and in particular about justice, imply and require altruism and constitute a form of it. Moreover, altruism is the mark of good social relations and good persons. Altruism and giving have always been analysed by economics, notably by all great economists, with an upsurge of studies in the last third of the 20th century.

Keywords

altruism, giving, reciprocity, transfers, family, charity

JEL classification: A13, B10, C71, D30, D31, D61, D62, D63, D64, E62, H21, H23, H41, H53, H62, I31, J41, P35, Z13

> *First think, then compute*
> (A teacher of mathematics)

Foreword

Love, justice, and compassion move people, allocate goods, and structure societies. Families – the institutions for love – form and endow children, thus creating most of accumulation and growth. Exchange and markets rest on the respect of rights and rules, much of which is spontaneous. Compassion alleviates miseries collectively through the support of public aid, and individually through private and organized charity. Voting and political action are importantly motivated by views of the common good, the public interest, and fairness, and they determine the high level of taxes paid. All organizations require some mutual aid and trust among their members. Various associations are created with the main or sole purpose of acting together or enjoying each other. Life in society and its quality require the respect of others and their rights, basic fairness, and readiness to help. The quest for self-interest is often in fact that of means to give to one's family, secure the respect of others, and sometimes help others or support causes. Without the required concerns for others, self-interested interactions would produce miseries, fail to work through exchange, and degenerate into wars of all against all. If "you cannot make good literature with good sentiments", as André Gide wrote, you can hardly make good economics with only poor ones. "Man is neither angel nor beast". Altruism, giving or respecting, and reciprocities – i.e., answering a gift with another gift – are "human rocks on which societies are built" (Marcel Mauss).[1] This includes their economy.

This topic would have to become the new frontier of economics, were it not, in fact, its oldest concern and tradition. Economics has always studied altruism and giving, with landmarks in works of Adam Smith, John Stuart Mill, Ysidro Edgeworth, Vilfredo Pareto, Léon Walras, or Philip Wicksteed, for instance. These studies incurred an upsurge in the last third of the 20th century, notably with analyses of "interdependent utilities" motivated by affection, compassion, or a sense of justice, and of reciprocities. Altruism also relates to the field of normative economics and "social choice" since caring about the quality or fairness of society implies caring about other persons. These studies seem to have proved that the general concepts and methods of economic analysis can be very helpful for the study of altruism, giving, and reciprocity, provided that the relevant motives, sentiments, and types of relations are adequately considered.

The present introductory chapter aims at providing the necessary basis for the economic analysis of altruism, giving, and reciprocity. Its core is the second of its three parts, which presents the various types of altruism and of giving, whose specification is

---

[1] *Essay on the Gift* (1924).

necessary for understanding the phenomena under consideration. The third part focuses on the normative implications of altruism, giving, and reciprocity, and on historical landmarks of their analysis. The first part presents main issues about the economics of altruism, giving, and reciprocity.

This first part presents, in particular, the social importance and the scope of the various kinds of relations of giving and altruism (Section 9); the various structures of altruistic concerns for others and of their interdependences (Section 3); the motives and structures of non-altruistic giving (Sections 5 and 6); an outline of the question of reciprocities (Section 8); the issue of the efficient crowding out of altruistic joint giving by transfers of public aid (Section 7); the reactions of giving to transfers, and in particular the questions of intergenerational transfers through bequests and the public debt, and of giving induced by redistribution (Section 10); the relation between selfish and altruistic motives and conducts (Section 11); and the origin of altruism (Section 12).

Altruism and giving have many different types which, however, divide into main categories. Altruism is hedonistic (or natural), or normative. Hedonistic or natural altruism includes affective altruism (affection and the milder sympathy), pure hedonistic altruism which is either empathy or emotional contagion, and moral hedonistic altruism which includes compassion and pity. Normative altruism refers to "intuitive" moral values and norms, to non-moral social values and norms, and to rational moral principles (e.g., impartiality and justice, universalization such as Kant's, or putative reciprocity).

All types of altruism can motivate giving and helping. Yet, giving and helping can also result from other motives, which are to follow intrinsic norms or to induce various social effects, or are more purely self-interested. The social effects of giving can consist of judgments or sentiments (praise, esteem, status of virtuousness, gratitude, affection), social situations (giving can result from or create both a higher or lower status), and social relations (peace, goodwill, agreement, friendship, liking, and enjoying the social intercourse). Giving can also favour the self interest of the giver through various effects which can be return-gifts, rewards of various origins, consequences of status, or indirect effects through markets or political or other social processes.

The most important effect of altruism is probably the respect of other persons and their rights and properties, which could not sufficiently and well be secured only by self-defence and the police. This permits peace, social freedom defined by this respect – it is the basic social ethic of our societies –, and the general amenity of society. This respect is in particular a condition of a working market system. Moreover, further norms of conduct and reciprocities provide the spontaneous correction of various market failures and of similar potential deficiencies of organizations (yet, giving, benevolent collusions, and reciprocities also sometimes constitute market failures). Families constitute of course a prominent field of display of the sentiments and conducts under consideration. The economic effects of bequests and family-induced education are particularly important. Finally, altruistic care for alleviating misery leads to charity, which is important in some societies, and also to political support of the large fiscal transfers where this motive associates with a sense of justice (and the large number of uncoordinated givers makes public transfers a priori the efficient means).[2]

Part I: General overview

1. The economics of moral sentiments

One of the best known and most often quoted of all texts is the first lines of the first book about society of the founding father of economics, Adam Smith:

> *Chap. I*
>
> *Of Sympathy*
>
> *How selfish soever man may be supposed, there are evidently some principles in his nature, which interest him in the fortune of others, and render their happiness necessary to him, though he derives nothing from it except the pleasure of seeing it. Of this kind is pity or compassion, the emotion which we feel for the misery of others, when we either see it, or are made to conceive it in a very lively manner. That we often derive sorrow from the sorrow of others, is a matter of fact too obvious to require any instances to prove it; for this sentiment, like all the other original passions of human nature, is by no means confined to the virtuous and humane, though they perhaps may feel it with the most exquisite sensibility. The greatest ruffian, the most hardened violator of the laws of society, is not altogether without it.*

(*The Theory of Moral Sentiments*, 1759, Part 1, Section 1, Chapter 1.)

Smith would probably want his remark to apply even to economists. However, later economists would prefer to express it in a "spirit of geometry" rather than in Smith's "spirit of *finesse*" or subtlety (as Blaise Pascal puts it). They would represent the higher or lower level of happiness of individual i by the value of an ordinal utility function u_i, and write the influence emphasized by Smith as

$$u_i = u_i(u_{-i}, x_i), \qquad (1)$$

---

[2] Many questions considered in this introductory chapter have been discussed with Jean Mercier Ythier, sometimes for a long time. Jean also read in detail and commented the text, in proposing many improvements always relevant and often adopted. Remaining imperfections of all kinds can only show my own limitations. I also want to express my gratitude to all contributors of these volumes, for giving me the exceptional opportunity to read and comment their chapters, and for discussions during the two meetings which prepared this work and a previous research volume on the same topic (*The Economics of Reciprocity, Giving and Altruism*, 2000, London, Macmillan, for the International Economic Association).

where $u_{-i} = \{u_j\}_{j \neq i}$ is the set of the levels u_j for all individuals $j \neq i$, and x_i denotes other factors of individual i's happiness, including her own consumption.[3] The universal sentiment described by Smith makes each u_i be an increasing function of each u_j for all $j \neq i$, particularly for low levels of u_j representing individual j's misery. Smith even says that sufficiently high levels of u_j for $j \neq i$ are "necessary" to individual i, which can probably be translated as necessary for u_i to have a sufficient level. The specific sentiment Smith has in mind does not even allow that some u_i does not depend on some u_j, but the influence may have various magnitudes. Malevolence, malice, *schadenfreude*, envy, and even plain indifference to others' pain or joy, are other topics and are probably suitably considered as pathologies of human sentiments.[4] However, we should never forget that, as history teaches us, it is also a fact that practically any human being can very easily kill others if he has been sufficiently persuaded that they are different from him and noxious to his society. Man is capable, towards his fellow men, of the deepest love and the most admirable sacrifice, as well as entrenched hatred and the most atrocious cruelty, and anything in between. This volume, fortunately, restricts its concern to altruism and giving – including reciprocity that the social science classically defines as a set of related gifts.

The main importance of altruism, giving, and reciprocity, is that they constitute essential facts of societies, which keep them together, are basic aspects of them, provide some of their main properties, and influence all other aspects. They appear in general sociality and the general respect of people and their rights, in families, in all groups or communities, in works of charity, and in and through political life and public policy. They are importantly and sometimes crucially enlightened by their economic analysis, and they are essential in the working and performance of the economic system. They both permit exchanges and remedy their various failures. Even in keeping to the most superficial aspect – numbers –, private charity transfers some 5% of GNP in the US. However, this joint giving to the poor and needy people is a public good and we will see that efficiency, democracy, consistency, and morals demand that it be realized by public transfers: this is indeed the case for several times this amount in most countries. Moreover, gifts to children in education and bequest account for about 80% of savings, and hence of investment, capital accumulation, technical progress, and growth.[5]

2. Motives for altruism and altruistic giving

Altruism is the preference for the good of some other people in itself, and it also denotes acting in favour of this good for this motive. It has more causes or reasons than noted in Smith's introduction. Smith notes *compassion* and *pity*. He later mentions a

---

[3] See Kolm 1966a.
[4] The economics of envy and other comparative social sentiments is presented in Kolm 1995.
[5] See Kotlikoff and Summers (1981), and Gale and Scholtz (1994).

sentiment which is a kind of what we now call – after Max Scheler – *empathy* from imagining oneself in the place of the other person. He also suggests a *contagion of emotions* (Spinoza's *imitatio affectuum*). The term *sympathy* he uses rather means nowadays a weak kind of *affection* or *liking* (although it is etymologically quite close to compassion). The induced emotions are generally of a different nature and lower intensity than those of the observed ones, yet in being similarly agreeable or disagreeable and similarly more or less intense. These effects constitute *hedonistic* (or *natural*) *altruism*. However, if these sentiments make you desire the good of other people because this augments your pleasure or diminishes your displeasure, as Smith has it, this is not a moral reason; in particular this is not a moral motive for helping other people. Yet, there also exist *morals* that makes you desire the good of other people, as some non-moral social norms can also do (the difference between both is in particular revealed by the sentiment induced by failure to abide by the rule: guilt in one case and shame in the other); these two types of motives constitute *normative altruism*. All these sentiments induce you to help the other person or to give something to her when the cost is compensated by the relief, pleasure, or sense of moral or social properness that these sentiments induce in you as a consequence of the resulting relief or pleasure of the beneficiary, or of other improvements in her situation.

However, although empathy, compassion, pity, sympathy, or affection, as causes of altruism and giving, are not moral causes, they nevertheless are commonly considered as moral in themselves. Indeed, morals demand not only that you help others but also, if possible, that you feel the corresponding altruistic sentiment. They demand that you feel compassion or pity and value that you show sincere sympathy. They occasionally demand that you practice empathy. They demand that you both help and like other people in a way and intensity that depends on the proximity and type of your relation, in particular in the family and in communities of various types. In a more demanding version, however, morals demand, on the contrary, that you both treat and like other people equally, meaning that you should behave justly towards them. They also sometimes demand that you help and like some others, or all others, "as yourself" (which is again justice), or even more than yourself – as Auguste Comte understood the terms "altruism" and "altruist" when he introduced them. And many groups socially value that you indulge in emotional contagion.

Morals include justice and fairness – although non-moral social rules also include various norms of fairness. Giving and exchange are the two kinds of free transfers, but giving also affects the distribution of wealth, income, or consumption in society. Giving thus elicits judgments of distributive justice, and also the most acute conflicts among them. Giving to your children, notably through bequests and education, results from your affection and your right to freely use your resources, and your parental love, your right, and your support are all praised or approved of by basic social and moral values. Yet, from the point of view of the beneficiaries, these grants are not allocated according to need, merit, or equality. Your children "only took the pain to be born", as Beaumarchais puts it. This is the main source of inequality, and the paragon of inequality of opportunity. By contrast, giving to the needy people or to the poor satisfies basic needs and tends to reduce inequality thanks to a free choice of the giver.

Any sense of justice or fairness implies caring about the good of other persons, that is, altruism. And any consistent altruism towards several persons in a world of scarcities faces the question of distributive justice. Conversely, a sense of justice necessarily implies altruism, even if you use it to defend your interest. Indeed, since justice is impartial by nature and definition, if you claim it for yourself it has to be for some "objective" reason which also applies or could apply to other people (note that if you make up this argument for the sole purpose of defending your interest, that is, you are a *pharisian*, this implies that you believe that it may have an influence, and hence that some other people have the corresponding altruism). This structure is basic for Adam Smith, who emphasizes that impartiality implies altruism – and empathy favours impartiality. He describes our capacity to be impartial by the successful image or concept of the "impartial spectator" that each of us harbours "in her breast". John Stuart Mill even sees all altruism as the result of impartiality (which, however, he sees as the restricted and problematic form of a utilitarian valuation of the sum of utilities). Yet, you apply your opinions about justice or fairness sometimes in individual giving, but often in attempts to persuade by discussion and to influence public constraints through political participation. Indeed, justice or fairness often implies a constraint on some people and, in a state of law, the public sector has the monopoly of the legitimate constraint on adults (apart from self-defence).

3. Structures of altruism

The set of relations (1) for all individuals i has very important consequences and a few possible variants, which will shortly be considered. Individual i wants to give to individual j in transferring goods from x_i to x_j if this sufficiently increases u_j (plus other indirect effects) for overcompensating, in u_i, the decrease of i's goods in x_i. The "interdependence of utilities" shows that each individual's "happiness" (or utility level) or consumption is, in economic parlance, an "externality" for each other, and a collective concern or "public good" for all others. A priori, this suggests that it should be a concern of the social, collective, political and public level and sphere of action. There is also mutual concern between individuals (but this is not the standard concept or reciprocity – shortly considered – which relates either the gifts both ways or the functions $u_i(u_j)$ and $u_j(u_i)$, rather than the levels of utility, income or consumption). The set of equations (1) can be solved for the u_i in giving $u_i = v_i(x)$ where $x = \{x_j\}$ is the set of the x_j for all j.[6] Low levels of altruism (u_i depends little on u_j) induce a unique solution. However, high mutual concerns (dependence between the u_i) can lead to multiple solutions such

---

[6] This solution of the set of interdependent utilities is discussed in detail in Kolm 1966a (see also Kolm 1984a).

that some are worse for everyone than others, including among stable states when a dynamics of adjustment is considered – this relates classical situations in groups such as couples or families which are stuck with mutually induced misery or are engaged in dynamics of worsening interactions (for instance with $u_i(u_j)$ and $u_j(u_i)$ for a couple).[7]

Other reasons for the concern for others sometimes lead to different structures. Moral "paternalistic" conceptions see the good of an individual in something other than her happiness, and conceptions of justice also often consider as relevant other items concerning an individual than her happiness. These reasons make u_i depend directly on individual j's consumption or situation, say x_j, and one can have $u_i = u_i(u_{-i}, x)$ where $x = \{x_j\}$ is the set of x_j for all j. This can even become $u_i(x)$ if individual i is no longer directly concerned with others' "utilities" or happiness u_{-i}. Yet, a sentiment of comparative justice about the distribution of happiness – or of the social value of some eudemonistic aggregate – can make individual i be concerned with the set u of all u_j, including u_i, thus leading to the forms $u_i = u_i(u, x_i)$ or $u_i = u_i(u, x)$.

Finally, what may be relevant, concerning x_i, is some concept of individual welfare of individual i, represented by an index $w_i = w_i(x_i)$ – Pareto's "ophelimity" –, or the income y_i of individual i with which she freely buys the goods she uses.

Possibly resulting forms are $u_i = u_i(u_{-i}, w_i)$ solved as $u_i = v_i(w)$ where $w = \{w_j\}$ denotes the set of the w_j for all j, or directly $u_i(w)$. These are particular forms.[8] Yet, the latter is proposed by Vilfredo Pareto in his article of 1913 "*Il Massimo di utilità per una collettività in sociologia*" (also reprinted as a long footnote in his *Treatise of Sociology* and in *Mind and Society*), and Ysidro Edgeworth had considered in *Mathematical Psychic* (1881) the particular case of two individuals and linear utilities, $u_1 = w_1 + \lambda w_2$ and $u_2 = w_2 + \mu w_1$.[9] Both authors note that, with increasing such functions u_i, Pareto efficiency relative to the utilities u_i implies Pareto-efficiency relative to the ophelimities w_i, but there are ophelimity-Pareto-efficient states that are not utility-Pareto-efficient. This is described by Edgeworth as a "shrinking of the contract curve" in the space of the goods in the x_i. Now, competitive markets secure Pareto efficiency with ophelimities only, whereas the ethically meaningful property is Pareto efficiency with utilities. Hence, competitive markets secure this latter property solely with some restriction on the distribution of resources, and they may have to be accompanied by the appropriate redistribution.[10] The redistributions that can have this effect can be favoured at unanimity, thanks to altruism. Compassion, pity, or a sense of justice usually make them redistribute towards the poorer and diminish inequality. People could a priori decide

---

[7] These multiplicities, dynamics, and stability, are analysed in Kolm 1984a.

[8] The function $u_i(u_{-i}, x_i)$ can be replaced by $u_i(u_{-i}, w_i)$ when the ordering of instances of x_i by function u_i does not depend on the levels u_j for $j \neq i$. The functions $u_i(x)$ can be replaced by $u_i(w)$ when the ordering of instances of x_j for each j by function u_i depends neither on the x_k for $k \neq j$ nor on i.

[9] Pareto writes the relation in differential form $du_i = \sum a_{ij} dw_j$. However he notes that the coefficients a_{ij} are not constant and depend on the situation. Moreover, he doubtlessly considered these differential forms as integrable (you cannot "climb up the – smooth – hill of pleasure" along non-integrable paths).

[10] See also Kolm (1963), Winter (1969), Collard (1975), Archibald and Donaldson (1976).

this by direct agreement between themselves, but, generally, their number precludes this solution and, therefore, the redistribution has to be made by the public sector (see Sections 4 and 7).

Pareto's altruism with $u_i = u_i(w)$, or more general altruistic forms $u_i = u_i(w_{-i}, x_i)$ where $w_{-i} = \{w_j\}_{j \neq i}$ is the set of the w_j for $j \neq i$, differ from the forms $u_i = u_i(u_{-i}, x_i)$ or $u_i = u_i(u_{-i}, w_i)$ by the assumption that individual i derives no pleasure from the pleasure that other people derive from the pleasure of other people, or that she finds this pleasure of hers or of other people to be irrelevant for her choice maximizing u_i. This is at odds with the view of the apostle of the morality of pleasure, Jeremy Bentham, who asserts that the pleasure that other individuals derive from the pleasure of others exists and should be counted. That is, however, for the social ethical purpose of maximizing the utilitarian sum which Bentham thus takes as $\sum u_i$ (whereas most modern utilitarians would prefer the other alternative in using $\sum w_i$). Yet, Pareto also considers a social ethical maximand above individuals' utilities or ophelimities. However, he rejects the sum of utilities because "we can neither compare nor add them, because we ignore the ratio of units in which they are expressed".[11] He thus considers more general non-linear "social welfare functions" of the form $W(u)$, thus assuming the moral value of the pleasure that people derive from the welfare of other people, if not from their pleasure (yet, Pareto had used a form $V(w)$ in his *Cours d'Economie Politique* (1897), but this can be reconciled with his later view as being $V(w) = W[u(w)]$).

Largely quoting Pareto, Abram Bergson considers "social welfare functions" in insisting on the fact that they represent the social ethical views of specific individuals, be they "advisors", "officials", or "the economist", and which are, with the previous notations, $V_i(w)$ (1954) or $W_i[u(x)]$ (1966) where i is the index of one such individual (this index is explicit in the first reference and implicit in the second). The first formulation is also formally akin to the Paretian utility of individual i. However, the surest thing about Bergson's maximands is that they intend to describe moral views. Nothing is said about the place of individual i's particular satisfaction that she derives from her own consumption or from her children's. Nevertheless, these functions are increasing in all their arguments, which implies a type of altruism of individual i. This altruism is of the moral kind, contrary to the altruism described by Adam Smith as deriving from empathy or emotional contagion (that which he calls "sympathy") and is of a "hedonistic" or "natural" kind – yet, Smith also later analyses duty.[12]

Finally, one can consider preferences about income distribution. However, this has to be justified, notably with respect to two essential issues (see Kolm 1966a). First, the incomes in question should be defined when resource uses are variable and notably in the common case where they include earned incomes and labour can vary. Second, the set of Pareto-efficient income distributions is very large when most altruisms are

---

[11] *Cours d'Economie Politique*, II, p. 20. The issue of the strong limitation of the logical possibility of using a utilitarian sum is presented in Kolm 1996a, Chapter 14.

[12] All the reasons for being concerned with other people can be jointly present in Kolm 1966a.

weak, which is the case in a large society (nations for instance). Hence this concept is of little usefulness in itself for specifying the socially desirable distributions. Therefore, one should consider more finely individuals' preferences about the distributive structure and their possible scope of consensus, and normative solutions for specifying the desired distribution.

If individual i buys her bundle of consumption goods with income y_i and a given price vector p_i (which may a priori depend on individual i, for instance if one good is leisure bought in working less at a price which is individual i's wage rate), then relation (1) can be written as $u_i = \tilde{u}_i(u_{-i}, y_i, p_i)$, and if this holds for all i a solution of this system (with the same discussion as above) can be $u_i = v_i(y, p)$, where $y = \{y_j\}$ is the set of the y_j, and p is the set of the price vectors p_i. One may also have directly $u_i = \tilde{u}_i(y, p)$ if individual i considers that each other individual j is responsible, and hence accountable, for the goods she buys with her income y_j, and is accountable for her tastes which enable her to derive satisfaction from her consumption. Similar final forms can also result from derived $u_i = v_i(w)$ or direct $u_i = u_i(w)$ in writing the indirect (Roy) ophelimity functions $w_i = \tilde{w}_i(y_i, p_i)$. In all cases, with constant prices p, one has $u_i = U_i(y)$. (The issue of the interdependence of individuals' choices has been analysed, but vanishes with perfect markets.)

If earned income is included, the income y_i can for instance be that which, associated with a notional given labour, is considered by individual i to be as good as her actual pair of income and labour. It can be, in particular, the "leisurely equivalent income" where the reference given labour is zero; or, rather, this reference labour can be around average labour. Furthermore, in a large society where most of the corresponding altruisms are weak (most willingnesses to pay for others' incomes $(\partial U_i/\partial y_j)/(\partial U_i/\partial y_i)$ are small – although nonnegative), the set of Pareto-efficient distributions y is very large. Hence the interest of this property is quite limited. Therefore, other criteria of the social value of distributions y are necessary. These criteria belong to principles of distributive justice. Hence, the forms $U_i(y)$ led to the theory of the comparison and measures of inequalities based on such distributional preferences, with the presentation of the meaningful properties of redistributions, of their relations, and of people's preferences about them. Another solution resulted from the treatment of the distribution y as a public good for the individuals (see Section 16).[13] The simple fact of functions $U_i(y)$ and of unanimously preferred redistributions was also considered by Hochman and Rodgers (1969) and other studies.[14]

All the specific motives and reasons to be concerned with other people give specific structures to the functions defined above. These structures have often remarkable properties and consequences. Some of these motives and reasons are beyond the scope of the present volume, such as the hostile sentiments of malevolence, malice, spite, and

---

[13] All these topics and other related ones are throughly analysed in Kolm 1966a.
[14] Musgrave (1970), Goldfarb (1970), Bergstrom (1999), Olsen (1971), Zeckhauser (1971), von Furstenberg and Mueller (1971), Thurow (1971), Mishan (1972), Daly and Giertz (1972), Scott (1972), and others.

schadenfreude, and the comparative sentiments which are negative with envy, jealousy, and sentiments of inferiority or superiority, and more neutral with preference for conforming or on the contrary for distinction for oneself or for other persons, or preference for social uniformity or diversity *per se*.[15] Other social sentiments are on the contrary closely related to the present topic, such as the sense of justice or fairness, whose structure has given rise to a particularly abundant literature.[16] In fact, a basic method in social ethics (called "endogenous social choice") consists of the determination of the structures of individuals' preferences about social states that are common to all members of a society.[17] An important point is that individuals' judgments of various types – such as self-interested preferences and social ethical views – are sometimes independent and disjoint in a structure of multiple selves with various possible types of relations between them, and sometimes incorporated in the same overall evaluation. As an example of the second case, for social ethical judgments that deem individuals to be both responsible for spending their income in free exchange and accountable for their capacities to be satisfied and other needs, the relevant variables are incomes y_j, one can write $U_i(y) = \tilde{U}_i(y_i, y)$ where the second (vector-) argument y is the object of the social ethical evaluation, and $\tilde{U}_i$ as function of this argument y is increasing for expressing benevolence, and, when people face the same prices (for instance with the same given notional labour noted above for erasing differences in wages), symmetrical for expressing impartiality, possibly augmented by transfers from rich to poor of less than half the difference in their incomes (i.e. "rectifiant", hence Schur-concave with the symmetry), varying in specific ways under specific changes of y, and so on. The retained set of properties determines a specific structure for U_i, for use in applications.[18]

The above noted interdependences apply to sets of individuals constituting various groups or societies, of all possible type and size, from the dyad (sometimes a couple), small groups (families or others), larger groups (e.g., some organization or category of people), nations (in which a large part of redistributions motivated by overall justice take place), or the whole world. A specific model can describe pure sentiments or mixed ones. In the latter case, the functions incorporate the effect of the synthesis of their various sentiments by the individuals (this can be smooth associations with compromises or priorities among desires or duties or the outcome of "a tempest under a skull" as Victor Hugo puts it). The functions can be used for evaluating the state of the society under

---

[15] The comparative normative principle of "equity" analysed in Kolm 1971a is related to envy and jealousy. Envy, jealousy, and sentiments of superiority and inferiority constitute a basis of the taxation of conspicuous consumption (Kolm 1971b). Yet, the full analysis of the economics of comparative sentiments is presented (about the case of envy) in Kolm 1995. It is in particular shown how individual preferences can be "laundered" or "cleansed" from these sentiments in replacing notionally, in utility functions for instance, the items of other people on which this sentiment bears by the individual's own corresponding item – thus leading to "envy-free preferences or utility functions".

[16] See Kolm 1966a, Sections 6 and 7, and a general survey in Silber, ed. 2000.

[17] See Kolm 2004.

[18] Studies that use specific structures of functions U_i without justification, hence arbitrary structures, *prima facie* transmit this shortcoming to their conclusions.

consideration – possibly for choosing public action about distribution –, or for providing a step in explaining or forecasting the conduct of people, including in interactions, giving, or voting.

However, the models constituted by the noted functions expressing individuals' concerns about others are limited when taken by themselves, and should be completed or incorporated in other models, in two essential respects concerning evaluation and action, respectively. First, individuals' evaluation of the distribution (of goods, incomes, welfare, or happiness) often depends on specific facts or acts, and often on the past, and the relevant variables or parameters have then to be introduced or made explicit when a more advanced analysis is sought or required. For instance, an individual may be thought to deserve or merit some good, income, or satisfaction because of specific acts or choices of hers (e.g., labour, effort). Individual needs may be relevant and may have to be more explicit than only incorporated in the structure of utility or welfare functions (e.g., family size, health, age). An individual may be entitled to an income or a good because she has earned it, or because it has been given to her (basic social freedom or process liberalism). An individual's concern about others generally depends on their social relation to her; it is in particular more intense when the "social distance" between them is shorter (e.g., family, extended family, belonging to the same group of various possible kinds, in particular to the same nation).

The second issue is that individuals act in different contexts, each of which mobilises a particular set of sentiments and motives, with often a dominant (sometimes unique) sentiment. For instance, self-centeredness is dominant in market exchanges (this is Philip Wicksteed's "non-tuism" – see Section 11 below) although fairness, promise-keeping and truth-telling also have important roles in these interactions. Families are the institutions for love and giving, although they display also all other possible kinds of social sentiments. Charity is supposed to be motivated by pity, compassion, and solidarity although we will see that if they were the only motives, private charity should be replaced by public transfers. The variety of motives at work in the political and public sectors include some altruism and sense of justice, notably in militancy and to some degree in voting (see Section 9.3). Solidarity is often particularly important within clubs and associations. Hence, the effects of the various types of sentiments and attitudes towards other people and society are in a large part segmented among various attitudes and types of relations, although in each case other, possibly second-order, sentiments often also play important roles.

This more or less segmented aspect of human life into various activities, and of questioning about the world into diverse issues, gives practical relevance to the question whether an individual is – or is better represented as – a single, integrated self, or several selves, one for each activity or question. Each such self can be considered as endowed with one preference ordering or utility function. Economists tend to have a preference for the single, integrated self, who in particular chooses among different alternatives possibly in choosing or compromising among various interests or values. However, individuals' social ethical values are often considered separately, by a specific ordering of evaluation function. This is probably the meaning of Bergson's social welfare function, and what the field of social choice calls individual values. John Stuart Mill and Léon Walras see the individual as either self-interested or altruistic and moral according to the moments. And various models focus on specific sentiments for analysis or application.

4. Altruism and democracy: Altruistic joint giving and its public implementation

An improvement in individual j's situation x_j, for instance an increase in her consumption or income, increases u_j or w_j, and hence also altruistic u_i for $i \neq j$, possibly with indirect effects in the first formulation (u_i depending on u_{-i}), and it may also increase u_i directly. This makes individual i give to individual j if this effect overcompensates for her the corresponding loss and the worsening of x_i. However, as Smith emphasises in the second paragraph of the *Theory*, the increase in satisfaction that an individual derives from an improvement in another's situation is generally lower than the increase in satisfaction she would incur if this improvement were in her own situation.[19] Hence, this altruism does not generally lead to gift giving, or it does only when the other person is sufficiently miserable – and in a rather small amount – or for the few people particularly close to the giver such as the members of her family. Yet, an individual's happiness (u_j), welfare (w_j), or situation (x_j), and gifts that improve them, are a priori favoured by all other individuals. They are "public goods" for them. Hence, if these others could agree that each gives to individual j, each could find that her own contribution is worth the overall improvement in x_j (or u_j or w_j). This individual contribution may be small if the individuals are numerous. Actually, individuals are very numerous, and hence only very low degrees of altruism suffice. The set of transfers would then be favoured unanimously.

The givers can implement this result in making a collective agreement about their gifts. As for any other contract, this agreement would be enforced by the legal system and the public force. However, when they are numerous they cannot, practically, enter into the necessary contact and bargaining. Then, a role of the public sector is to realize nevertheless this set of transfers unanimously desired. As in the implementation of any contract, each individual is forced to yield her contribution, although she prefers the whole set of transfers to its absence – if the contributions of the other individuals are given, she prefers to yield less or not at all. But since there is no actual contract, this forced contribution appears as a tax. In this choice, the public sector can either try to make out what the collective agreement would have been if it were possible (this is a "liberal social contract"), or introduce other conceptions of distributive justice (since this is another of its functions) (see Section 16).

Hence, such a system of redistributive taxes can be unanimously preferred to its absence. That is, its absence is not Pareto efficient. Now, a democratic political system

---

[19] Smith interestingly explains that individual i tends to consider the function $u_i[u_j(x_j)]$ as $\alpha \cdot u_i(x_j)$ with $\alpha < 1$, in "putting herself in the other's shoes" concerning her situation (rather than also her propensity to enjoy or suffer), and in discounting the intensity of the effect.

normally secures Pareto efficiency. For instance, even with the imperfect democracy of our electoral competition, any political program that is not Pareto efficient can be defeated by other possible programs at the unanimity of expressed votes, by the very definition of this property. Hence, a democratic political system will realize a system of redistributive taxes manifesting unanimously desired altruistic joint giving.

The necessary public implementation of joint giving has been noticed for a long time. For instance, "Private charity is insufficient because the benefits from it accrue to people other than those who made the gift ... We might all of us be willing to contribute to the relief of poverty, *provided* everyone else did. We might not be willing to contribute the same amount without such assurance ..." And this justifies "government action to alleviate poverty" (Milton Friedman, *Capitalism and Freedom*, 1962). Logic, in fact, goes further than that, as we will shortly see, since it concludes that only the government should alleviate poverty in a democratic, efficient, and altruistic society (Section 7).

Hence, when private giving to the poor is observed, either the motives are not altruistic, or the society is not democratic and is inefficient (and the waste concerns aid to the neediest).

None of these alternatives is ruled out a priori, which shows a scope for both political and moral progress. In particular, there are many other possible reasons for giving to people in need than to alleviate poverty and suffering. Some of these motives lead to exactly the same conclusion: efficiency and democracy require public aid (for instance if the giver cares about having the aura of an altruist in her eyes or in the eyes of other people and hence behaves like one, or if she cares specifically about her own total contribution – private gift plus redistributive tax – because it constitutes her sacrifice for the poor, as we will see). Yet, other motives permit private giving in democracy but, then, they are often rather immoral and inconsistent.

All these possible motives are, indeed, varied. There can simply be a norm for giving in itself, without specific regard for the beneficiary's welfare provided the gift goes this way. This norm can be moral, or only social in bowing to public opinion. Giving may even be a tradition or a habit. The individual may care about judgments about herself by other people or by herself. This judgment can build an image of the person. This judgment, however, can focus on various items. The full moral judgment is the praise for being an altruist. Yet, this may not suffice for sufficiently influencing the person's motive, and thus inducing her to actually become an altruist. Then, the judgment can withdraw to the praise of behaving like an altruist, which induces the same behaviour and effects as if the person were actually an altruist. The judgment may also focus on more partial items, and then it is rather inconsistent as a moral judgment. In particular, it can appreciate the individual's sacrifice in favour of the poor, that is her full contribution through private giving and taxation – we have seen that this fails to induce giving. Yet, the judgment can also emphasize the responsibility of the giver, and hence only her private gift, except if the tax represents an implicitly desired contribution to the joint giving – and then it again has to be added to the gift. Moreover, people may be motivated by comparisons about the private gifts or the total contributions of themselves and of other people for several possible reasons such as doing one's fair share if others do theirs, keeping up with others, imitation, conforming, distinction, competition in giving or contributing, sentiments of inferiority or superiority, envy, or jealousy. These comparisons can be the direct view of the person or that of other people's judgments about which she cares. Finally, genuine altruism can be associated with principles of conduct which avoids the "free riding" of the joint giving which makes taxation the efficient solution. A classical such principle is universalization in the family of Kant's categorical imperative – give in imagining that everybody does like you. Another case is that of altruism motivated by "putative reciprocity", that is the reasoning "I help her because she would have helped me if our situations were permuted".

5. Motives and reasons for nonaltruistic giving

More generally, giving is voluntarily incurring a cost for the good of someone else, but this may only be a means for another end. In particular, one may give for eliciting self-satisfaction, praise, gratitude, esteem, admiration, liking, or love (Adam Smith emphasizes the difference between the moral desire to be praiseworthy and the immoral or at best amoral desire to be praised); for gaining an aura of generosity in one's own eyes and in the eyes of other persons whose judgment one values; hence for acquiring or maintaining such a reputation or status valued in itself or for the various other advantages it may bestow or permit one to obtain. One may give for showing and proving one's friendship, affection, liking or love, which tends to elicit or reinforce the desired friendship, affection, liking or love of the other person in return. People also often give in given circumstances simply because they feel they have to do it, possibly because it is a tradition, in considering more or less the judgment of their conscience or of other people, but also sometimes by pure habit and inertia.

Yet, one also sometimes gives or helps in order to obtain tangible advantages by indirect effects through many possible types of social processes including rewards from an organization (possibly a firm) or the family – when the aid is within such a group – or from an institution (possibly an official one); effects of induced redistribution; political (for instance electoral) advantage; indirect market effects (such as through the effects of transfers on terms of trade classically discussed in international trade); and so on. In particular, one may give for eliciting a return-gift in a reciprocity; or for obtaining return-gifts from actors other than the initial receiver in a "reverse reciprocity" which is often presented as vastly overcompensating the cost of the initial gift (by René Descartes and Adam Smith, for instance). In any event, "give and you will be given to" (Luke). One may also give as a return-gift for eliciting a further gift from the initial giver or from someone else; for maintaining a social balance or fairness by comparison with an initial gift; for showing gratitude; or for rewarding generosity or a deserving giver. More generally, one may give to any giver or benefactor, as an incentive to reiterate her action or as a reward for her merit or deservingness; and therefore one may also give knowing that one may be remunerated in this way for these reasons.

Yet, one may also simply give as a piece of information for showing and proving peaceful intentions, or sentiments of friendship, affection, liking, love or gratitude, or a desire to enter in a relation of any kind – and the gift may show and prove the generosity, wealth or ability of a possible partner, or the quality of a supply (sample). The gift can also only be a way of drawing information from the reaction, concerning the receiver's attitude, intention, or means. People thus give to put an end to a dispute, conclude a bargaining, seal an agreement, an alliance, or a union, and establish or maintain good social relations. These gifts can be mere symbols of the intention of the giver or be tangible in proving, by their cost, the sincerity of the giver. The acceptance of the gift means accepting the relationship. Such gifts are often both ways, and then sometimes materially identical. These gifts are varied, from pens and pins to wives and cities, in passing by the mutual gifts of identical rings, drinks, or receptions. People also sometimes give for the mere interest of the relationship in the process of giving and receiving.

A gift can also soften a hostile attitude. Yet, one classically gives both for showing a superiority over the receiver and on the contrary for manifesting one's submission towards her; and for glorifying the receiver or on the contrary for humiliating her (for instance in suggesting that she is unable to take care of her needs or of her family's). Other gifts intend to make the receiver morally indebted towards the giver (for the status in itself or for the possibility of demanding some service in return later on), or they intend on the contrary to redeem and erase a pending moral debt.

One may finally give for doing one's fair share in giving given that other contributors do theirs; for conforming to others' giving in a similar situation of the giver and of the circumstances; for keeping up with other givers; for not being humiliated or ashamed by giving less or not at all; or on the contrary for eliciting the admiration, possibly the envy, or even the shame or humiliation of those who give less or not at all; and for maintaining or conquering a relative status in generosity or wealth, hence possibly in engaging in conspicuous competitive giving (where the gifts are either used as in public fund-raising operations or Papuan pig-feasts, or destroyed as in the potlatch).

Hence, the variety of forms of the giving way of allocating resources is bewildering. Gifts are provided with very different aims, and sometimes strictly opposite ones. They range from the most generous sacrifice to being the instrument of social sentiments and relations among the most odious, in passing by the plain service of the giver's self-interest. They also range from the most spontaneous and even almost unconscious act to resulting from the most elaborate pondering and strategies. They are both the proof of sincerity and the classical vector of hypocrisy and treacherous lies. They are the free single transfers, but are also sometimes insistently demanded by strong social norms. They a priori concern two persons, but they are often imbedded in networks of social relations. They look plainly material, but their real nature is often in fact, rather, affection, demand of affection, gratitude, query, acquiescence, confirmation, promise, vainglory, or spite. The variety of the giving relationship is matched by its pervasiveness and crucial importance in society, as Section 9 will show.

Even the main field of economics, markets and exchange, when carefully analysed, reveals the essential role of motives that are not self-interest, and hence consciously favour other people, often as the result of moral or social normative conducts. Indeed, first, many relations of market, exchange, agreement, and cooperation thrive in spite of the presence of classical causes of market failures which should have inhibited them, thanks to the role of various moral conducts such as honesty, truth telling, promise keeping, fairness, reciprocity, trust and trustworthiness, respect, and benevolence. This permits them to overcome costs and impossibilities in information and communication, exclusion and constraining, bargaining and transaction, and establishing and enforcing contracts, which induce imperfect contracts, incomplete markets, missing agreements, and free-riding public goods (bargaining is often concluded only thanks to a fair compromise, or is replaced by fair arbitration, and you often prefer a fair deal to a good deal; various contributions to public goods and collective action are much higher than pure self-interest leads one to expect; most opportunities to steal and cheat are not seized; and so on). Similar virtues are essential in the life of firms and other organizations, between members and between them and the firm, and they are powerful factors of their efficiency. Second, on the contrary, these behaviours also interfere with the efficient price system; for instance, various issues of fairness in the labour market, among employees or between employees and employer, constitute a main cause of wage rigidities and hence of macroeconomic problems. Other behaviours influenced by norms and status, or seeking status or relative positions, also depart from standard economic models. Third, voluntary altruistic respect of property and rights is a condition *sine qua non* of the very existence and working of markets (self-defence is costly and often impossible, and the police is costly and could not be sufficiently present, informed, and effective).

6. The structure of nonaltruistic giving

6.1. From motives to forms

Nonaltruistic giving is giving for a final reason other than the receiver's good, or not only for this motive. The choice of the gift by the giver can again be described by the maximization of a utility function (or, more generally, by finding the best possible element of a preference ordering), although the interesting part is often the psychological, social or philosophical analysis of the motives and of their properties and relations with other facts.[20] Let u_i denote an ordinal utility level and function of individual i, X_i the initial endowment of goods of individual i, and g_{ij} a gift from individual i to individual j. X_i and g_{ij} are defined as vectors of quantities of goods (or services) in the space

---

[20] In particular, norm following can be represented in this way. A practically imposed norm shows by a priority structure of the preference ordering. Moreover, most norms can be more or less obeyed, and this choice can be represented with the ordering. Social opinion can be an explicit or implicit factor of the ordering. The preference can also bear on the types of social relations and modes of interaction (this is for instance a central feature in the theory of reciprocity).

of the quantities of goods (they can in particular be one-dimensional, notably measured in money as an income or wealth and an income transfer, but this does not fit for all the cases). After the transfer of the gift g_{ij}, individual i has the allocation $x_i = X_i - g_{ij}$, and individual j has the allocation $x_j = X_j + g_{ij}$. If individual i is concerned about her gift g_{ij} only because she has altruistic sentiments (in addition to self-interest), she chooses g_{ij} that maximizes $u_i(x_i, x_j, \ldots) = u_i(X_i - g_{ij}, X_j + g_{ij}, \ldots)$ where u_i depends on x_j for the more or less direct or indirect reasons noted in Section 3. If individual i may give to individual j for other reasons, she chooses g_{ij} that maximizes

$$u_i(X_i - g_{ij}, g_{ij}, S_i),$$

where S_i is the set of all relevant variables and parameters other than the first two arguments of the function. If individual i has also some altruistic motives towards individual j, S_i includes $x_j = X_j + g_{ij}$. The various motives for giving g_{ij} are related to various elements of the set S_i.

For instance, if g_{ij} is a return-gift of a reciprocity, S_i includes a gift g_{ji} from individual j to individual i. "Extended reciprocities" make S_i include g_{ki} for some $k \neq i$ or j in the case of a "generalized reciprocity" (you tend to help if you have been helped, even by someone else, which is the classical "helping behaviour" of social psychologists), or g_{jk} for some $k \neq i$ or j in the case of a "reverse reciprocity" (you tend to help meritorious people who help others, a case emphasized by the philosopher René Descartes and by Adam Smith).

The noted motives of comparative fairness in contribution, conforming, or comparative status in generosity and competitive giving, make S_i include g_{kj} (or $g_{k\ell}$ if ℓ is another receiver) for at least one $k \neq i$ or j.

Note that u_i is a priori an increasing function of g_{kj} if individual i has altruistic sentiments towards individual j and hence appreciates higher endowments of individual j $X_j + g_{kj}$ or $X_j + g_{ij} + g_{kj}$, but that u_i tends to be a decreasing function of g_{kj} if individual i is motivated by giving g_{ij} for conformity, comparative status, or competitive giving in comparison with g_{kj}.

In all cases, what may matter are gifts in relation to the wealth of givers or receivers (which can express a relative sacrifice of the giver or a relative contribution to the receiver's wealth), and the formulation allows this in including the relevant wealths in the set S_i.

Individual i is sometimes also motivated by her image as giver, in the eyes of other people or in her own eyes, and by the associated judgment and status. Adam Smith explains this own evaluation of oneself by empathy of the view of other people judging oneself (or of the view of the impartial spectator). A priori, one may praise or criticize oneself without this detour. However, we will see that in the present case it practically happens to be necessary – which shows the depth of Smith's insights. At any rate, one can denote as I_k^i the image of individual i in the eyes of individual k, and as $I^i = \{I_k^i\}_k$ the set of the I_k^i for all individuals k. For $k = i$, I_i^i is individual i's image of herself. Individual i's images as giver to individual j depend on the gift g_{ij}, $I^i = I^i(g_{ij})$. One particular such image of individual i is that of the receiver j, I_j^i, related to the beneficiary's gratitude (or resentment if she finds that g_{ij} does not match her expectations). A concern of individual i about her relative status as giver can be represented either by the inclusion of g_{kj} (or $g_{k\ell}$) for other individuals k among the factors of the images of herself I^i, or directly by the inclusion of I^k for $k \neq i$ as arguments of individual i's utility function. This function then is $u_i(X_i - g_{ij}, I^i, S_i)$ or $u_i(X_i - g_{ij}, I, S_i)$ where $I = \{I^i\}$ is the set of the images I^i of all individuals i, and S_i is the set of other relevant arguments (one of them is $x_j = X_j + g_{ij}$ or $X_j + \sum_k g_{kj}$, according to the case, if individual i also has some altruistic sentiment towards individual j).

In some cases, the gift g_{ij} has indirect effects providing an extra allocation $y_k(g_{ij})$ to individual k (which can notably be i or j). These indirect effects can have a number of origins – economic, social of various types, etc. – discussed in forthcoming Section 15.3 (notably concerning $y_i(g_{ij})$). The y_k are again vectors of quantities of goods, possibly reduced to a one-dimensional money or income, and with the possibility of negative coordinates for describing a loss. Then, in the foregoing formula, $X_i - g_{ij}$ has to be replaced by $X_i - g_{ij} + y_i(g_{ij})$ (and $X_j + g_{ij}$ by $X_i + g_{ij} + y_j(g_{ij})$). The various possible origins of the y_k includes the well-studied effects through markets, rewards of various origins, and so on, but $y_i(g_{ij})$ can also be (or include) a return-gift provided by individual j, $y_i(g_{ij}) = -y_j(g_{ij}) = g_{ji}(g_{ij})$ where the last notation denotes the return gift. In a number of cases, y_i can overcompensate the loss of the gift g_{ij} and thus make giving profitable for the giver from a strictly self-interested point of view.

6.2. *Contradiction and possibilities in the logic of motives*

However, you cannot give only to be praised or praiseworthy as an altruist, or for a moral action, or in order to have an image or a status as a moral person, because objectives of being praised or being praiseworthy are not moral in themselves, whereas a moral action requires a moral intent, and any altruism requires seeking the good of the receiver in itself. Even simply giving in order to be a moral person – and not only to act like one – may not be possible because this is not a moral objective in itself (you should, also, manage to direct your intention towards a moral aim). Yet, acting with a result that helps someone when this is not the final objective can nevertheless deserve some praise, but with a lower status and intensity. This approval can be stronger if this action is costly to the actor, as with giving. Indeed, even if it is not its final intent, a sacrifice that entails benefits for others can elicit positive consideration. Moreover, there are values and norms of giving that attach to the gift or help in itself, rather than to the beneficiary's situation, although it should be favourable to it. These values or norms can be of a moral, or other social, psychological nature. Yet, the attachment to the gift in itself prevents this motive from being genuinely moral. The nonmoral social norms or values induce the kind of conduct the breach of which elicits shame rather than guilt. Then, the judgment of other people is of primary importance ("you should be ashamed of not helping your brother"), although it may sometimes be only imagined (this is the case in Smith's conception of empathizing the imagined judgment of other individuals – or of the impartial spectator – about oneself). Finally, you may try to deceive other people in pretending to have genuinely moral motives, but this is specifically against morals, and it requires again other people (in a personal, not anonymous, gift, there is at least the receiver, but this is only one person and often of too low a status to be of importance in this role). In all these cases, the contradiction may be soften if genuine moral altruism is one of your motives, along with seeking praiseworthiness, praise, image, or status. However, cognitive dissonance may tend to make this coexistence of opposite motives psychologically unstable, and this can have drastic consequences (for instance sincere benevolence tends to deteriorate the possibility of efficient joint giving – as we will now see).

7. The inefficiency of individual giving when joint or public giving is possible: The perplexing joint giving theorem

Joint altruism where several individuals want the good of the same individual(s) is notably important for helping the people in need or poor. We have seen in Section 4 that in these cases efficiency requires joint coordinated giving which, when the givers are numerous, is achieved by transfers of the public sector. As we recalled, Milton Friedman has admitted that this is a case where public transfers can be justified. Yet, a simple theorem says, more precisely, that Pareto efficiency precludes the very existence of individually chosen givings, such as private charity, and all the transfers should be through public taxes and subsidies. This also holds when the potential givers are not only altruists in caring for the welfare of the aided people, but care also, or only, about their own total contribution to them (gift and tax) in itself, for any of the motives noted in the previous section, such as seeking praise or praiseworthiness, or image or status in one's eyes or in the judgment of other people. (This also holds when givers care for all poverty but specialize in the aid of some persons – they "have their poor".) The Appendix at the end of this chapter shows this "joint giving theorem", and its various results which are simply mentioned here.[21]

This theorem should be compared to facts. Privately decided charitable giving accounts for about 5% of GNP in the USA. It is very much lower in Europe. In both places, public transfers of aid are substantial. They are clearly higher in Europe. We have remarked above that democracy implies Pareto efficiency (Section 4). Hence, the joint giving theorem, by itself, suggests the starting and startling conclusion that – possibly contrary to appearances – Western European societies are less wasteful and more democratic than the US. And the waste is first of all in the aid to the poor and needy.

Fortunately, however, a next section of the theorem has it that an individual privately chosen giving can be consistent with Pareto efficiency (and hence democracy) if this

---

[21] A fuller analysis is provided in Kolm 2005.

individual cares for her private gift specifically, and not only because it is a part of her contribution (along with her taxes that aid the needy) which she would value in itself or because it helps the needy or both. However, we will see that this solution is in fact not possible in a large society. Yet, let us first remark that if this person is to be appreciated because of her sacrifice (in favour of the needy), it is her whole sacrifice that counts, her tax plus her individual gift. Then, to single out the private gift is irrational, and the alternative to lack of efficiency and of democracy is irrationality. Moreover, distinguishing one's own gesture for boosting one's image in one's own eyes – Jim Andreoni's "warm glow" –, or in the eyes of other people – that is, for showing off and vainglory – is hardly moral. This would also hold for distinguishing one's own total contribution (tax included) from its effect on the overall welfare of the beneficiaries, but private giving may be singled out because one's taxes are less visible to other people, distributive taxes are most often mixed with general taxes for all purposes, or private responsibility is valued in itself (whereas it is the total contribution that helps the needy). At any rate, high private giving reveals either shameful waste and a lack of democracy, or irrationality and immorality. And this waste, again, is notably in the aid to the poor and needy. Moreover, the degree of immorality is suggested by still another result of the joint giving theorem: on average, an extra gift should be provided N million times more for the glory of the giver than for the relief of the poor, where N millions is the population of the country. Now, this condition does not hold in a large society, even if the average individual concern for the needy is low. Hence, again, there cannot be both private giving and social efficiency (and democracy). Note also that if the distributive taxes are computed as the amount that the payer would have agreed to pay in an agreement with her co-givers, then the payer is also putatively responsible for its amount, there is no reason to distinguish it from the private individual gift (see Section 16.5), and then the existence of private giving implies waste and absence of democracy.

However, the individuals are sometimes concerned not only about their own specific gifts, but also about those of other people, notably for comparison. They would for instance envy the generosity of people who give more than they do, or feel inferior to them, or on the contrary they would feel superior to those who give less than they do. These are hardly nicer sentiments, and hence it is reassuring that this concern makes no difference for the above results. Yet, there is a difference if such concerns are not about the specific gifts of the individuals but are about their specific contribution (gift plus tax), which is more rational – in so far as envy and sentiments of superiority are rational. Then, indeed, another piece of the joint giving theorem says that an individual can give in efficiency if envy (or sentiments of inferiority or superiority) towards an extra contribution of hers exceeds the altruism it satisfies.

Of course, other facts can intervene, three categories of which can be noted here. First, there are other sentiments comparing individuals' contributions or gifts, which have the same effect as those noted but not the same moral implications. Indeed, these comparisons can be motivated by sheer imitation or desire to conform (desire for distinction takes up back to the previous cases), or by the desire to do one's share if other people do theirs. In these cases also, higher contributions or gifts by the others is costly for the person. Second, altruism can be associated with or result from other moral reasons which lead one to give irrespective of others' contributions, such as the noted universalization and putative reciprocities (see Section 13.3.3).[22] Third, fiscal modes can intervene. Taxes are generally not lump-sum (with the resulting disincentive effects and the waste of the "burden of taxation" which jeopardizes Pareto efficiency). Private donations can be deductible from taxes (the part so recovered can be considered as belonging to the public transfer) or matched by public subsidies. Taxes for aid can be singled out or public aid can be financed out of general taxation. All these issues are the object of specific analyses.

8. Reciprocities

8.1. An overview

A gift or favour motivated by another gift, for instance the return gift of an initial gift, constitutes the very important social relation of *reciprocity*. This is very different from a self-interested exchange where each transfer (or favour) is provided under the condition that the other is provided, and hence is not a gift (in the proper sense of the term).

Reciprocity has three types of motives, which can be mixed. "Balance reciprocity" aims at maintaining a balance between both gifts (sometimes from a sentiment of fairness), or at avoiding moral indebtedness. In "liking reciprocity" the return-gift is provided because the initial receiver likes the initial giver, either because she receives this gift provided with benevolence, or because she is liked by the initial giver (then this is a reciprocity of sentiments). However, the return gift may also aim at inducing a further gift – this is "continuation reciprocity". Yet, this latter motive leads to a sequence of recurring transfers both ways, each of which aims at inducing the continuation of the relation, and which can be self-interested: this *sequential exchange* is in fact a type of exchange rather than reciprocity proper (however, the last transfer cannot be self-interested if it is well foreseen).

Moreover, beyond the basic reciprocity where – letters denoting agents – A gives to B entails B gives to A, one can observe and explain "extended reciprocities" such as "generalized reciprocity" where A gives to B entails B gives to C (as in the classical "helping behaviour" of social psychology), "reverse reciprocity" where A gives to B entails C gives to A (emphasized, as we have recalled, by the philosopher René Descartes and by Adam Smith), "chain reciprocity" where A gives to B who gives to C who gives to D, etc., and "general reciprocity" which is a reciprocity between an agent and society in general or the set of others (perhaps G.H. Mead's "generalized other").

In replacing giving (or favouring) by its opposite, harming, balance reciprocity and continuation reciprocity have counterparts in revenge and in retaliation for deterrence (although deterrence stops the relation rather than extending it). However, liking

---

[22] And, for a full presentation, Kolm 2005.

reciprocities have no such counterparts since you do not tend to hurt someone because you dislike her, or even to dislike someone only because she dislikes you. Reciprocity, and revenge and retaliation, are called "reciprocation" – the understanding of the term reciprocity retained here is that which has for long been classical and standard in the social science.

Relationships of reciprocity are pervasive and often essential.

The general spontaneous respect of others and their property that is necessary to the existence of a free and peaceful society (with the aid of self-defence and the police), and in particular to the existence of property rights and of a market, is in fact a reciprocity since people would not so respect others if they were not so respected themselves (this is a general reciprocity).

Families, which have been successively modelled as a *pater familias* (Becker) and as an exchange (Chiappori), are in fact essentially a network of reciprocities – as they are now modelled – with relations of other types being more moments of this complex.[23] Between generations, in particular, people give to their children given that their children will give to them and to their own children, and given that they have received gifts from their parents; and they give to their aging parents given that their parents have given to them and to their own parents, and their children will give to them. This builds intergenerational reciprocities which are direct, or generalized and reverse chain reciprocities, with reactions which are either delayed or anticipating the motivating gift – each individual thus reciprocates in six such reciprocities between contiguous generations. Other intergenerational chain reciprocities are found in the general acceptance, in many societies, of pay-as-you-go pension systems (the young, who will be financed by the younger, finance the old who have financed the older), and of the public funding of education (taxpayers, whose education has been financed by the older, finance that of the young who will finance that of the younger) – in both cases, there jointly is a generalized and a reverse reciprocity, which are anticipating and delayed, with a reversal of the association of these properties (and there can also be a direct reciprocity of pension for education).

The presence of reciprocity constitutes both a motivational and relational "failure" of systems of market and of command solely based on self-interest, and the most common cause of spontaneous remedy to the other "failures" of these systems due to difficulties in information, communication, or coercion of all types, as we will see. Reciprocity is also typical of communities of all kinds where they occur both between members and between each member and the community as such or its institutions.

Voluntary contributions to non-excludable public goods are often favoured by the knowledge that the other beneficiaries also contribute and do their fair share (in particular, this often happens for joint giving). Sequential mutual aid or transfers – which can depend, in particular, on the specific needs of the receiver or means of the giver – are

---

[23] See Chapter 14 by Luc Arondel and André Masson in this Handbook. Yet, in the intrafamily reciprocitarian motives, affection predominates over balance (and continuation).

often possible only because balance (or liking) reciprocity motivates the last transfer (and, hence, it also certainly is one of the motives of previous acts). Reciprocity in trust – which is favoured by the fact that trustworthy people tend to be trustful (they tend to judge others from the sample of mankind they know best, themselves) – has been shown to be a strong factor of economic efficiency and productivity at the level of firms or of cultural areas. Bargaining is often concluded and sealed by reciprocal concessions. Reciprocity of mutual help at the workplace is widespread and often necessary for its working and efficiency. Labour relations are conspicuous for occasional conflicts but are more often the seat of reciprocities in goodwill, benevolence, effort, and loyalty. All these relations entail reciprocity equilibria which differ from the competitive market model. For instance, reciprocity among workers checks competition among them and creates downward wage rigidities. However, sociopsychologists have for long analysed the fact that people often want to provide their pay's worth of labour (the experiments of Adam (1963, 1965) and Adam and Rosenbaum (1964) have given rise to much discussion, but there were others before, and there has been numerous others later). This conduct is the logical opposite of tipping: a return gift of labour for pay rather than a return gift of money for good service. This conduct leads to an appearance of involuntary subemployment – this is George Akerlof's (1982) theory of "efficiency wages".[24]

Reciprocity also constitutes an economic system in itself, with various possible scopes and extensions. Motives and relations of reciprocity constitute the ideal of the social movement of cooperatives. Traditional economies are essentially systems of reciprocity, and socially successful development depends largely on keeping and relying upon specific relations and motives of reciprocity. Perceptive analysts of economic systems classically retain the threefold division into market exchange, command, and reciprocity. Actual societies are a mix of all three, in characteristic and varied proportions. Reciprocity has been the central topic and concept of economic anthropology from its inception.

Finally, the political system, and the vast allocation of resources it commands, rests on important aspects of reciprocity. People receive freely the vast amount of benefits provided by public services. They support politicians and vote for large taxes. Statesmen are supposed to act for the good of the people whose reciprocal support rests on liking and gratitude. Yet, this is a smaller part of the story for political men of lower ambition.

8.2. "Human rocks on which societies are built"

The fact, the importance, the nature, and the various types of reciprocity could not have escaped Adam Smith:

> "Of all the persons, however, whom nature points out for our peculiar beneficence, there are none to whom it seems more properly directed than to those whose beneficence we have ourselves already experienced. Nature, which formed men for that

---

[24] The various effects of this family on wages and employment are more generally analysed in Kolm 1990.

mutual kindness, so necessary for their happiness, renders every man the peculiar object of kindness, to the persons to whom he himself has been kind. Though their gratitude should not always correspond to his beneficence, yet the sense of his merit, the sympathetic gratitude of the impartial spectator, will always correspond to it."

(*The Theory of Moral Sentiments*, Part VI, Section 2, Chapter 1.)

This giving to someone because she has given to you was labelled reciprocity in Smith's time (by Morelly 1755).[25] This pervasive social conduct[26] was claimed to be "the vital principle of society" by L.T. Hobhouse (1906), and "one of the human rocks on which societies are built" by Marcel Mauss in his highly influential *Essay on the Gift* of 1924, and it has been since then a central explanatory concept of the social science.[27] This pair of favours both ways thoroughly differs from an exchange in the strict and proper sense – for instance a market exchange – because the two transfers are gifts, they are given, hence, by definition, each results from an act that is free in isolation, whereas the transfers of an exchange are mutually conditional, that is, each has to be performed, by external obligation if necessary (or promise keeping), when the other is performed.[28]

Smith sees several motives as explaining reciprocity. Tangible reciprocity is of "beneficence", but it rests on a reciprocity of kindness. This refers to both the action and the sentiment that motivates it. The reciprocity in sentiment can be described as "I like people who like me". Smith also notes both the gratitude of the beneficiary of the gift or kindness towards the first giver, and the merit of the latter. He also mentions the "sympathetic gratitude of the impartial spectator"; the reference to the "impartial spectator" suggests a reason of fairness.

This includes most of the motives for genuine reciprocity. They fall into two categories. As we have seen, in *liking reciprocity* the return gift is motivated by liking the initial giver because she provided a benevolent gift, and/or because she likes the initial receiver. The latter reason is *reciprocal liking*, a reciprocity in sentiment based on affection altruism. Smith emphasizes that reciprocal liking is particularly appreciated because "*nothing pleases us more than to observe in other men a fellow-feeling with all the emotions of our own breast*".[29] The initial gift can have the role of revealing the

---

[25] Smith also occasionally used the term reciprocity. However, whether he uses it in this sense or only for describing self-centered exchange is a classical debate in "smithology" (see, e.g., Danner, 1973). Later proper uses include Proudhon (*Le manuel du spéculateur à la bourse*, 1853/1857), L.T. Hobhouse (1906), the anthropologist student of Karl Menger Thurnwald (e.g., *Die Gemeinde der Banaro*, 1932), and many anthropologists (Malinowski, Mauss, Firth, etc.) and sociologists (Simmel, H. Becker, Homans, Gouldner, etc.).

[26] Conduct is behaviour plus its motives.

[27] For a general analysis, see Kolm 1984a.

[28] Although the definition of reciprocity in the social science is unambiguous, some other discourses have used this vocabulary in all directions. Some have seen exchange in the strict sense (as with market exchange) as a type of reciprocity, while others have called reciprocity a type of exchange. The basic issue is that distinguishing the motivations is essential.

[29] *The Theory of Moral Sentiments*, 10.

liking or of proving its intensity (even if the initial giver gives in order to be liked as a result of her gift or of her liking, her gift reveals how much she wants to be liked, and *ipso facto* how much she likes, because you want more to be liked by someone the more you like her).[30]

The second type of genuine reciprocity is *balance reciprocity* where the motive of the return gift is to maintain some social balance with the initial gift, sometimes for a reason of fairness. This motive often includes a desire to avoid moral indebtedness. The desire of balance or the preference for it is quite primitive and basic, although people are more or less sensitive to it, depending on personality, culture, education, and social setting. It is to be compared with revenge and the desire for it, its counterpart in conducts of negative reciprocation. The judgment of other people sometimes matter, but not always and not necessarily. The motive has an aspect of a norm for reciprocating or for avoiding moral indebtedness. It then belongs to normative altruism.[31] This also includes the desire of fairness when it is present. This norm can have dimensions of inner demand or obligation, of a nonmoral social norm, and, more or less, of a moral norm.[32] The social aspect is related to the judgment of other people, but this judgment can be imagined or become internalized.

Gratitude towards the giver both elicits or favours liking her, and favours providing a return gift with a sense of balance.

The giver's merit, for her voluntary sacrifice on behalf of the receiver, is a reason for providing her with a corresponding reward. However, this remuneration can be provided by the initial receiver or by someone else (including an institution). Indeed, Adam Smith continues with: "*No benevolent man ever lost altogether the fruits of his benevolence. If he does not always gather them from the persons from whom he ought to have gathered them, he seldom fails to gather them from other people*". He even specifies, quite optimistically, "*and with a tenfold increase*", before concluding generally that "*Kindness is the parent of kindness; and if to be beloved by our brethren be the great object of our ambition, the surest way of obtaining it is, by our conduct to show that we really love them*".

This giving to a giver by agents who are not beneficiaries of the initial gift – the "reverse reciprocity" of the modern theory of reciprocity – had been emphasized, in almost the same terms, by the philosopher René Descartes one century earlier, with the same belief that, in the end, the initial giver will turn out to be better off.[33] This relates to classical promises of religions, for next lives or for this one (e.g., Luke: "give and you will be given to"). If a giver is aware of this result, she may be tempted to give to obtain this final benefit. In this case, however, the gift would no longer result from liking and be the acting part of kindness.

---

[30] A full analysis of these motives, relations, and sentiments is provided in Chapter 6 on reciprocity in this volume.
[31] "The norm of reciprocity" is the title of a renowned study of this topic by Alvin Gouldner (1960).
[32] See the distinctions in Section 13.3.
[33] Descartes, *Letter to the Queen Christina of Sweden*, Works, IV.

Yet, among "extended reciprocities", this reverse reciprocity is probably less important than the opposite "generalized reciprocity" by which someone who has been helped tends to help others, even those who have not helped her in the first place. This is the "helping behaviour" of social psychology, one of the most studied and documented of human conducts (these studies were especially motivated by the intense debate following a much publicized crime where none of the numerous onlookers intervened or called for help).[34]

An individual also sometimes gives or helps in return to his receiving a gift or help, in order to be given to or helped again, by the initial giver or by another agent, who then would be motivated, at least in part, by the hope to receive again a further return gift or help. This leads to a recurrent sequence of gifts or helping both ways, which occur by themselves or in answer to the occurrence of some specific need of the receiver or means of the giver. The motivations can be purely self-interested or at least partially so. When they are purely self-interested, the relation is but a *sequential exchange*, where each gives in order that the sequence continues. This relation, however, is better classified as exchange than as reciprocity, as far as the crucial issue of motivation is concerned.

8.3. The special games of reciprocity

Consider two individuals i and j engaged in a simple reciprocity where they respectively give g_{ij} and g_{ji} to the other, where these two items denote vectors of quantities of goods or services. Individual i's utility function is

$$u_i = u_i(X_i - g_{ij} + g_{ji}, g_{ij}, g_{ji}, X_j + g_{ij} - g_{ji}),$$

where X_i and X_j denote the initial endowments of goods or services of individuals i and j, respectively (they are vectors of their quantities). The first argument manifests individual i's self interest. The last argument can describe individual i's altruism towards individual j – then u_i increases with quantities of goods in this vector –, but it may also not exist (or again it can support descriptions of individual i's envy, sense of inferiority or superiority, desire of distinction or of conformity, and so on). The pair of central arguments, g_{ij} and g_{ji}, can describe preferences about the comparison of both gifts for reasons of balance, fairness, gratitude, resentment (if the gift received is lower than expected), comparative status, or competitive giving. The presence of the second argument g_{ij} in itself can represent individual i's duty, sense of propriety, or status-seeking. However, if the reason for the duty or for the status were genuinely moral or virtuous, it should in fact refer to the receiver's benefit, hence to the last argument $X_j + g_{ij} - g_{ji}$. When g_{ji} is given, the function $g_{ij}(g_{ji})$ denotes the (a) g_{ij} that maximizes u_i. Similar concepts are defined for individual j.

If individual i is the first to give, she (more or less) foresees individual j's return gift $g_{ji}(g_{ij})$. If she does not question this order of the givings, she chooses the (a)

---

[34] The Kitty Genovese case, 1964.

gift g_{ij} that maximizes u_i with $g_{ji} = g_{ji}(g_{ij})$. She is a "Stackelberg leader" in the reciprocity game. She can be said to "exploit" the reciprocal reaction of the other person. In so doing, she is purely self-interested if u_i depends only on its first argument, $u_i = u_i[X_i - g_{ij} + g_{ji}(g_{ij})]$. But she is not in the other cases (in particular, she can be also altruistic). This is a *domination reciprocity*.

However, reciprocity has a flavour of egalitarianism in actions towards the other person. Now, there being a first and a second player constitutes a strong inequality, if they act as described above. If the actors extend their reciprocitarian sentiments to the orders of the moves in time, they seek a solution that does not depend on this issue, that is, on who is first or second to give or even whether they give simultaneously. Then, a first giver chooses a gift that could be her return-gift if she were the return-giver receiving the actual return-gift as initial gift. Hence, the chosen gifts satisfy the two relations $g_{ij} = g_{ij}(g_{ji})$ and $g_{ji} = g_{ji}(g_{ij})$. The solution has the *form* of a Cournot–Nash solution, but it has a full and rational explanation which is lacking in other cases of one or two-shot games. It is a moral Cournot–Nash solution realizing the "ordering equity" relative to the order of the moves. The result is an *equilibrium reciprocity*.

The classically known structures of these two solutions show that it generally seems that other pairs of gifts can make both individuals better off: they seem not to be Pareto efficient (the individuals' indifference loci are generally not tangent to each other). However, the individuals have to choose these other pairs of gifts. For instance, they would make an agreement in this respect. Or, alternatively, an external benevolent power would impose the solution on them. In both cases, however, the transfers would no longer be gifts in the proper sense of the term. In the case of an agreement, the transfers would be parts of an exchange, since they would be mutually conditional on each other by external obligation or promise-keeping once the agreement is accepted. In the other process, the transfers would be imposed on the agents. In both cases, the related attitudes, meanings, and hence motives, would be different. Hence, the preferences about these transfers, and the structure of the utility functions, would a priori be different. The choice of the agreement or of the imposed transfers would have to be made with these new preferences. And the individuals may not end up happier or more satisfied in the end, even if one can make such comparisons when preferences change. In particular, they may lose intrinsic qualities of the relationship of reciprocity which they may appreciate, such as mutual kindness, consideration or respect; fellow feeling; and not being considered only as a means but also – at least in part – as an end (good reciprocity – there are others – is exchange that places the partner "in the kingdom of ends").[35]

---

[35] A large part of what goes on in the process of so-called "development" consists of replacing relations of reciprocity by market exchanges, thus changing the society and, in the end, the personality of people, in a way that they generally cannot foresee or even conceive at the onset of the transformation.

9. Importance and scope of giving, altruism, and pro-social conducts

9.1. Overview

Altruism, giving, and reciprocity have an overwhelming importance in society, its economy, and the allocation of resources. They permit their existence, performance, and quality in various ways. Not only do they rule the life and the economy of families and the sector of charity, and capital accumulation through gifts to children, but they are a main factor of political life and of the role of the public sector and public finance through the effects of conceptions of justice and of the common good in addition to joint giving. They permit the very existence of a free and peaceful society and of a free market through the respect of others and of their rights and property. They underlie most of the spontaneous and decentralized corrections of the various shortcomings and "failures" of the market and of organizations (including firms). Therefore, they are an essential factor of economic efficiency, productivity and growth through various ways. They have an important role in labour relations and at the workplace. They are a basic objective of many cooperatives, associations, and clubs. They are crucial in general sociability and hence for the essential amenity of life in society. They constitute a most basic social bond. Finally, they are the most universal criterion for judging the intrinsic quality of social relations and of individuals.

9.2. Families

The allocation of resources should first have people to whom to allocate; and persons also provide the main economic resource, the stock of human capacities. Hence, there should first be procreation, which usually results from love, a particularly strong type of altruistic sentiment and of liking reciprocity.[36] Moreover, no society can survive without someone feeding children and taking care of them – gifts which again essentially result from love (and a little from duty). The first social relations and sentiments a human being is aware of and experiences, and the only ones for several years, are kinds of very strong, warm and reciprocal altruism. The first social relations and sentiments mankind has observed and experienced, in the family, the extended family, and small groups, are mostly giving, strong altruism, and reciprocities.

Moreover, people tend to mate with altruists, notably because they are likeable and prone to protect them and their common offspring, which favours the spread of genetic configurations favourable both to altruism and to being attracted by altruists (and hence again to the reproduction of altruists).[37] This selection of the "altruistic gene" is

---

[36] Adam Smith, a life-long bachelor, finds this "passion by which nature unites the two sexes" to be "always, in some measure, ridiculous" and holds that this "passion appears to every body, but the man who feels it, entirely disproportionate to the value of its object" (*The Theory of Moral Sentiments*, 39).
[37] See Section 12.

complemented by the "selfish gene" which makes you help people who *might* be genetic relatives, and possibly by the selection of cooperative societies among competing groups as conceived by Darwin and Kropotkin.

Nowadays, "more than one half of the American population depend for their security and material satisfactions not upon the sale of their services but rather upon their relationships to others" (Edmund Phelps, 1975).

Moreover, we have noted the impressive fact that gifts to children through bequests and education produce about 80% of savings and capital accumulation, and hence of investment, technical progress, and per capita economic growth – the rest of growth being due to loving procreation – (Kotlikoff and Summers, 1981, Gale and Scholtz, 1994).

Even economists who scorn altruism and cherish the selfish *homo economicus* live in families where they themselves probably love and give. They can hardly fail to notice the presence of altruistic sentiments and behaviour there – or so it seems. Indeed, a number of economists have emphasized for long the contrast between the motives in the market and in the family. This was implied by Philip Wicksteed's notion of *non-tuism*, shortly discussed, or in our days by Gary Becker's "altruism in the family, egoism outside of the family". Becker (1974) sees indeed the family as dominated by an altruistic distributing *pater familias*. Yet, a number of other economists, on the contrary, push the consistency to the point of seeing even the family as a self-interested exchange, and this model was theoretically developed (Chiappori's initial work). This acknowledges the effects of interactions and the multipolarity of a family, but with a surprising view of motivations. Then, a new new economics of the family reconciled interactive multipolarity with giving and positive affects in basing a theory of the family on reciprocity (Arrondel and Masson).[38] In fact, families display all forms of relations – giving, exchange, and constraint –, but are better seen as a network of reciprocities where relations of other types are in fact moments in this broader framework. And reciprocity of the liking type dominates other types in the family.

Yet, the family also manifests all the noted types of direct and chain intergenerational reciprocities, since one gives to one's children and to one's aging parents, given that one's children will give to oneself and to their children, and one's parents have given to oneself and to their parents.

However, giving to children is more important than supporting one's parents in families in developed economies. Indeed, people not only save for their retirement but, in addition, give much to their children in the form of raising, education, gifts and bequests. This voluntary transmission in fact accounts for most of savings and hence of capital formation nowadays (in countries with pay-as-your-go pension systems, this collective scheme makes the young finance the retirees and saving for one's retirement is still lower).

---

[38] See their Chapter 14 in this Handbook.

9.3. The political and public sector

9.3.1. Public services and general political motives

You receive vast amounts of free public services. You benefit from numerous public goods with free access and free of charge. If you are poor, you are granted public subsidies, aids in kind, the assistance of social services, and again free public services and goods; this is by far the largest amount of aid to people in need or poor nowadays (and if you are rich you manage to have your area receive the best public services and your firm receive public subsidies). On the whole, the public sectors give between one third to more than one half of GNP in our time. You freely choose to vote for the very high taxes that finance these services (you may have to choose among high levels only, but if sufficiently many of us wanted low levels, some politicians would propose it). What are, however, the motivations? What are, more generally, the motivations of all the actors who can influence the public choice individually or collectively? Are these people egoistic and self-interested, as they often seem, or are they altruistic and aiming at the common good, as they often say? Indeed, a school of scholarship, notably in economics, assumes the first alternative, whereas the actors themselves assert most of the time that their choice is motivated by the defence or promotion of the general good, including the realization of justice in society, or at least that it conforms to this objective.

Before pointing out the main issue, specific to the political/public sector, in this respect, let us notice that the various actors commonly want to help other people in need through public regulation, public action and public finance even if they have to contribute themselves, to some degree, for reasons of compassion, pity, moral duty, solidarity, justice, or putative reciprocity (i.e., the reason expressed as: "I help them, given that they would have helped me if our situations were reversed").[39] This is notably related to the situation of joint altruism, joint giving, and its realization by the public sector (see Sections 4 and 7). In particular, taxpayers choose as voters this aspect of public finance.

Moreover, in most political/public choices of all kinds, a characteristic feature of this sector is that the two types of motives – self-interested and altruistic – can lead to the same choice and cannot be disentangled. The reason is clear and inherent to the nature of this sector. Indeed, many of the issues in question concern general aspects of society (e.g., moral, national, historical, aesthetic, environmental, etc.), and preferences about them express both individual tastes and concern about the common good and about what is good for the other people. Other issues concern more ordinary public goods or regulation, that you generally want both for yourself and for others: the latter aspect is

---

[39] The term "putative" means that the reverse situation is purely notional. An application of putative reciprocity is that of "fundamental reciprocity" where the reason for aid is some given relative handicap from birth (e.g. poor health) or family and social environment (for instance concerning education).

an altruism. Still other issues affect specific personal interests that are best defended in joining with the other people having similar interests, in political actions of all types (votes, parties, other forms of expression, lobbying, revolution, etc.). Then, you jointly defend your interest and that of the other people in a similar situation. You favour and help them as they favour and help you – this is solidarity. Your interest becomes an "objective" cause, and it should not be too difficult neither to find a conception of justice that shows that the defence or promotion of this interest is right, just, or fair, nor for you to adopt and possibly to believe these arguments.

Indeed, apart from the issues of public aid noted above, people rarely defend views of justice that oppose their own interests. This is puzzling and worrying on the grounds of human rationality, since ethics is supposed to be an exercise in end or value rationality and its conclusion should have no reason to be correlated with the reasoner's interests. Yet, in ethicizing their interests in this way, people ipso facto transmute them into an altruism towards people having the same interests. However, these moral arguments defending one's own interests may not be sincere. They may be just "noise" as a school of economists is fond to say. They would be mere *pharisianism* – that is, defending one's interests with moral arguments in which one does not believe.

However, the existence of pharisianism does not support a conception of man as exclusively self-interested but, on the contrary, it proves it to be false. Why, indeed, would people care to argue in favour of their interests with moral arguments? If it is for actually defending or promoting their interests, this assumes that these arguments influence the behaviour of some other people. Hence, these other people are influenced by morals, at a cost for their own self-interest. Since their action serves the people who present the argument, this reaction is a moral altruism. Moreover, pharisians believe that other people may react in this way from their experience and observations, and possibly also from introspection and a hypothesis of analogy of other people with themselves (or from empathy for these others). Therefore, pharisianism, a homage that vice pays to virtue, implies some virtue and proves its existence. Even if people present the moral argument in order not to appear purely greedy, this implies that other persons appreciate the moral reason (this is also inferred as just noted). And even if they entertain a view of the righteousness of their interest in order not to see themselves as purely acquisitive individuals, then they themselves attach some value to this moral reason – contrary to the hypothesis.

Hence, the fact that moral arguments are sincere or are not is beyond the point. In any case, their simple use a priori implies that they are influential, or expected to be from experience or introspection, and therefore that some people are influenced by such arguments. These people then are moral altruists if these arguments favour the interests of other people. And even arguments that only aim at softening the image of some people imply this kind of recognition.

In fact, the issue of sincerity is ambiguous. People often present or emphasize arguments in order to counterbalance other arguments presented with opposite conclusions, so as to make a fair judgment possible. In these cases, these people can be sincere and yet present biased arguments – for a justifiable reason. Moreover, when they defend their interest with moral arguments, people are often not clear to themselves whether they really believe the reason they give or not. This does not matter, however: as we have seen, the simple use of moral reasons proves their influence and, a priori, that of moral altruism.

Finally, for example, the fact that freedom of exchange may be more defended by the rich and inequality more criticized by the poor does not imply that only self-interest matters. It implies, on the contrary, that both conceptions of justice can influence actual political choices. This implies in turn that influential actors are to some degree moral altruists motivated by these opposite conceptions of justice. Moreover, in a democracy where the ultimate political power rests in the population – e.g., the electorate –, these moral altruists have to be very numerous. The upshot is well epitomized by Jean-Jacques Rousseau's remark that "morals and politics cannot be separated, and he who wants to study one without the other is bound to misunderstand both".

Indeed, the abundant and pervasive political discourse speaks of nothing else than the good for society and justice – corresponding to the two problems politics has to solve, collective concern and sharing. Both topics imply kinds of altruism. This has been noted for the common good. For justice, it results from the property of impartiality inherent to the concept, whatever the specific form it takes. Indeed, this implies that the values defended attach to "objective" characteristics which can be those of various persons (for justice towards individuals). Hence, a position of justice that favours the interests of a person also defends those of others, a priori. Moreover, the simple fact of taking an impartial view of individuals' interests constitutes a general altruism in itself.

Conversely, altruism towards several persons, and in particular the altruism towards all humans emphasized by Adam Smith, implies and requires definitions of the limits between the interests of people when they oppose one another. Yet, setting an arbitrary limit to the interests of someone would not be altruistic. Hence these borders of interests have to be defined from justified, objective, and impartial reasons, that is, from criteria and principles of justice. Finally, the implementation of justice and of the chosen common good generally requires constraints which, in a state of law, are the prerogative of the public sector.

9.3.2. *Actors of the political and public system*

The noted close relations between self-interest and aspects of altruism affect all actors of the political and public process. In addition, for each type of actors there are more or less specific relations between their interested and altruistic motives. These actors are of four types: voters; supporters, militants, activists and party members; the political personnel; and civil servants.

No voter, party member, militant, activist or supporter has a decisive influence in a large election, and yet they spend time, effort, and money in these activities. Hence, they are not motivated by their self-interest. They say that they do this because it serves other people, or also serves them, which is an altruistic motive. Other moral reasons that they may give are specific reasons for moral altruism. And, in fact, their actions serve the other people having the interests they defend or holding the values they promote. They also serve many people in permitting the functioning of a political system if it is better than possible alternatives.

In addition to these actors, the political and public process has two other categories of actors: politicians or statesmen, and civil servants, at all levels. Contrary to the other categories, they are professional (at least for a part of their life). Hence they can have an interest in their own career. This polarizes most of the self-interest that there is in their motivations. Even if they had no other motivations, this one would suffice to transmit and implement the objectives of the voters and supporters of all kinds, notably their altruistic intents of all types. However, as the other actors, they also have other motivations, and they have various effective ways to translate them into acts and facts.

Political men seek fame, power, and income. Yet, most of them also want the good of their society and of their co-citizens and want to do something about it. They see these objectives as much more complementary than opposed, since more power by election or promotion enables them to better serve and promote their view of the good; and seeing the good as congruent with the positions whose defence and implementation will make them elected or re-elected avoids the uneasiness caused by cognitive dissonance. Yet, although political ideals may adjust to political interests, they also often determine the choice of a political career and the basic choices in it. Disentangling these two kinds of motives is therefore not easy or even not possible, even for their holders themselves. Moreover, political men are not only implementers; they also have a major role of influence and in the formation of public opinion. When they are in power, poor information of voters and the distance between elections leaves them a large scope for promoting their own objectives, moral or immoral (Jean-Jacques Rousseau remarked that the English are free only one day every seven years, the election day; and a President in his last term is free from electoral threats).[40]

Finally, there is, in a number of societies, a special ethic of the civil service (or public service), at work from the bottom to the top of the hierarchy. This is supported to some extent by promotions which favour agents who display such a "spirit of the public service", thus providing them with both a reward in self-interest and an enlarged field of public responsibility. This ethos and ethics includes strongly altruistic motivations. The problems that this attitude leads one to pose have been a major impetus for the development of public economics and normative economics.

9.4. Giving in philanthropy, solidarity, and charity

9.4.1. Social situation

Private giving outside of the family has a notable importance. For instance, we noted that it takes up about 5% of GNP in the USA. It displays a large variety of forms: it is to

---

[40] This view of Jean-Jacques Rousseau is still nowadays commonly proposed by his Swiss compatriots for praising their system of referendums.

people in need or as support of various specific causes that benefit many people, direct or through various organizations, in money, in kind, or in giving the labour, effort, or body parts of the human person. Private giving has, with both public giving and the market, close relations which are associations, complementarities, substitutions, or competition.

Private giving is tied to public contributions through tax deductions and deductibilities, and joint or matching contributions. Yet, a given support can also often be provided either by private voluntary contributions or by the public sector. Different countries often choose different solutions in this respect, with a global tendency in each country, so that the sharing between private and public aid is very different from one country to the other. As a result, the size of the private philanthropic sector varies widely across countries, as does the size of the public sector in an inverse relation.[41] Section 7 has shown how this sharing can depend on the individuals' motives to give and on political efficiency in the different countries. This is notably manifested in the traditions and political and social culture of the country, and hence in its social, political, institutional, and ideological history. For instance, the historically large role of the public sector in Europe jointly results from the ethics (or ideology) of the Welfare State, monarchical traditions (even in Republics), the presence of a professional civil service, and, essentially, the opportunity provided by the fact that public budgets increased tremendously during the World Wars and could, when military expenditures subsided after the wars, be largely redirected towards social aid – particularly needed at these times –, while the wars had created a sentiment of interclass national solidarity which hardly existed before. Practically, each type of aid tends to occupy fields where the other is absent or insufficient.

Private giving is also sometimes an alternative to relying on the market. For instance, the economic profession was impressed by Richard Titmuss's (1971) findings that the English system of giving blood for transfusion is much superior – notably in terms of the quality of blood – to the American system of buying it, and by Kenneth Arrow's (1974) discussion of this issue and consequently of the role of giving and of moral behaviour in the economy.

9.4.2. Motives

An individual, indeed, cares about another's pain more, and wishes its relief more, the larger the pain, the more she knows it, and generally the more she knows the other person, relates to her, and likes her. This basic and obvious fact can mobilize various types of sentiments (shortly presented in full). Sentiments of compassion and pity rest on an emotion and are commonly supported by a moral demand. In most cases, their object is the pain of another person. The emotion is then influenced by empathy about this pain (with the possible assistance of some emotional contagion). Yet, pity and compassion

---

[41] A recent important study by Alesina and Glaeser (2004) compares the modalities of the relief of poverty in the U.S. and in Europe.

can also attach to an act or a situation of the other person that are deemed improper and not only to pain. At any rate, pity and compassion require having a priori some emotional distance from the object: the more you a priori like the other person, the more you suffer from her pain, but the less this is due to compassion or pity (and the more this results from direct empathy). The intensity of the brute sentiment that induces compassion and pity varies like that of the pain that elicits it (*ceteris paribus*) but is usually lower than it. Compassion and pity lead to wishing an alleviation of this pain, notably by the observer, and also by others and hence by joint giving and by public aid, and moral altruism also induces this desire and action. Moral and (other) social altruism also demand both affection and support among members of the same communities, with an intensity parallel to the degree of closeness and proximity. This includes family relationships and other solidarities. Moreover, justice and fairness, which are other aspects of social ethics, can also demand the alleviation of the pain. Their comparative dimension may then also specify who should pay for this relief.

Moreover, all the various noted normative (moral and social) values entail praise or blame for the acts of aid and the sentiments that induce them, and hence of the persons who give or should give and experience the sentiments, by other people, by the person herself, by society in general, or as abstract intrinsic judgment made up by the person. This often influences helping behaviour, and it occasionally also influences the evaluated sentiments. The judgment of sentiments may foster benevolence, and hence the resulting propensity to give. Caring about the judgment about oneself as actor is not a properly moral motive. However, it can induce giving in cases where actual benevolence does not suffice.

Therefore, the motives of aid to the people in need are compassion or pity, sense of justice or fairness, and other moral or normative altruisms, supported by a sense of community with various possible extensions, plus, possibly, a quest for praise or favourable self-image. These motives are largely different from and incompatible with those of the other main field of giving, the family, because affection has emotional precedence over both compassion or pity, and moral or other social normative altruism. You take care of your children when they need it because you love them, and you neither really pity them nor have to help them because it is your duty or the proper thing to do. The comparison between these two kinds of altruism is, of course, more complex and subtle. A sense of community favours both sympathy (somehow a mild affection) and compassion. Empathy associates naturally with affection and is, to some degree, an ingredient of compassion. Fairness plays some roles in the family. Yet, the most striking fact of the comparison is the difference and incompatibility, and the responsible sentiment is affection, the feeling that blurs the border between self and other.

Finally, supporting people in need directly or through causes is a priori a case of joint giving with many participants. We have seen in Section 7 that democracy or efficiency, and altruism and a number of other motives, lead to the realization of all this aid through taxation and public aid. Hence, private giving realizes the transfers when the political system is deficient (notably in democracy and efficiency), or when the motives attach to particular variables, such as the giver's private gift or a comparison with the full contribution (tax plus gift) of other people. These particular sentiments can be reinforced by others' judgments, but all these evaluations are not altruistic and have a limited rationality and morality.

9.5. General respect, civility, sociality, and help

The first altruism is restraint from harming. The first gift is restraint from stealing. The first reciprocity is answering respect with respect.

Most of the time, most people neither harm nor steal nor lack respect, and – it seems – nor even feel like doing it.

The general a priori benevolence and altruism towards our fellow humans jointly results from morals and norms, empathy, sympathy in all senses, and a priori affection for what is similar to oneself. This feeling is something very important. Even if it is moderate, each applies it to many people and benefits from this attitude of many people. It makes people a priori respect others and be respected by them. It makes "spontaneous order" a priori differ from the "war of all against all". It makes normal societies differ from the Hobbesian Iks described by the anthropologist Turnbull. Between two people, this sentiment establishes a presumption of mutual help if needed, rather than war. This feeling and attitude permit peace without a police state, and, hence, a free and peaceful society. They induce respecting rights and property, and hence permit exchange and markets, with a tolerable level of private defence and public protection. They pave the way to providing help to other people when they need it. In particular and most importantly, much below the level of need that induces assistance by some other person, the large number of a priori benevolent others makes joint giving a requirement of unanimity (a priori implemented by public aid and transfers).

In fact, no society can exist without a large extent of voluntary altruistic respect for others and for their rights and properties. Peace and security can result from restraint or constraint, and the latter can be due to self-defence or to the police force. Relying on self-defence alone amounts to a detestable and untenable "war of all against all". Relying on the police alone is impossible if there is not one policeman behind each of us, and it makes for an execrable police state. In fact, there would even have to be two policemen behind each policeman for preventing him from self-interestedly using his force. Solely relying on both these solutions is a mixture of two evils and would seriously misallocate resources towards the weapon industry. These effects can be avoided only if voluntary respect solves a notable part of the question, as is the case in normal societies in normal times (although both other means are generally also more or less required for prevention by deterrence).

In particular, this common general respect of other people, their rights, and in particular their properties is indispensable to the normal functioning of an extensive and efficient system of exchange. This basic altruism is a requirement of a working market.

Moreover, this respect, accompanied by politeness, menial help, and larger help when needed, in all or most encounters, provides the social amenity necessary to a normal and sufficiently smooth and even agreeable life in society. The closer the relationship between people, the larger this necessity. This is indispensable to the general quality of life and to the efficiency of activity in society. Altruism is the lubricant of social relations, as necessary to the working of society as oily lubricant is to that of engines.

9.6. The correction of "failures" of exchanges and organizations

The efficiency of markets is fettered by a number of "market failures" including externalities, non-excludable public goods, transaction costs, missing markets, incomplete contracts or impossibilities of establishing or enforcing contracts, and so on. Organizations, notably hierarchical ones, are hampered by difficulties in information, transmitting orders, reporting, imposing decisions, and so on. All these vices have two basic causes: difficulties, costs, or impossibilities in *information* and in *constraining* people. Impediments in constraining can be remedied by the corresponding voluntary action or restraint of the concerned individuals, and those concerning information can largely be remedied by voluntary transmission of information. When the actor sees these acts as not being the most favourable ones to her interest, they constitute gifts. Concerning information, this leads to truth-telling, sincerity, and voluntary disclosure. Concerning actions, this leads to giving, helping, promise-keeping, trustworthiness, loyalty, abstention from cheating, solidarity in an organization, reciprocal action or contribution, and so on. The motives are often moral. They are also often normative and social of a non-moral kind – like following a social norm whose violation elicits shame rather than guilt which is specific to moral failure. These motives, or at least and particularly the social non-moral ones, can be reinforced by a quest for image or status in the eyes of oneself or of others. In the case of an organization, the motives can be loyalty or devotion to the group or to its direction, sympathy or affection towards the other members, or solidarity towards them. Sympathy, affection and solidarity leading to such behaviour can also occur in an exchange, especially when it takes place within a community. Finally, these conducts may be reciprocal and motivated by a concept of balance, possibly supported by a sense of fairness – such as helping, contributing to a public good, telling the truth, not cheating, keeping one's promises, being trustworthy and trusting, and so on, given that other participants do the same. Even if someone so acts in order that the other(s) continue to act in this way in the future, this can work only if the last action has another – not self-interested – motive and hence is a gift, and then this motive doubtlessly also existed before (uncertainty about the end of the process or the motives of other participants can also solve this problem, but the very steadiness of a mutually profitable relation often elicits positive affective mutual sentiments).

In improving social efficiency, these various non-strictly-self-interested conducts and motives often end up favouring the strict self-interests of these actors.[42] Then, disinterested conduct favours one's strict interest in the end, as if by a kind of immanent justice.

---

[42] Self-interest is "strict" when it excludes satisfactions from status, image in the eyes of others or of oneself, and the like.

People may be aware of this, but if they conclude that they will act this way for favouring this interest, then this motive induces them to act differently, the magic of normed and moral action is broken, and the underlying inefficiency surfaces. This occurs in a framework of actions of several people, where each person benefits from this behaviour of a number of other people, and the very original agreement failure prevents that they choose to behave this way in a collective binding agreement. However, these conducts are very often maintained by reciprocities: people behave in the proper way given that others do too.[43] Moreover, the fact that all or many people benefit from these behaviours have often led to their becoming social norms, by a process involving many interacting individual judgments rather than conscious individual decisions. In such situations, furthermore, the individual choice tends to be supported by a "generalization ethics" of the Kantian type.

Market failures are also commonly corrected by public intervention. Yet, this has limits due to difficulties in obtaining the necessary decentralized and local information, to costs and impossibilities of constraining, and to general problems of the public and political sector caused by issues of motivation in addition to, again, questions of information and of constraining. Hence, the decentralized corrections of all these "failures", due to different motivations including altruistic and normative ones, are essential factors of economic and social efficiency.

9.7. Associations, clubs, cooperatives

In addition to these altruistic, giving, and reciprocitarian aspects of exchanges and organizations having other objectives, people create a number of social forms where these types of relations purposefully have a particular importance. Setting aside the case of marriage already noted, they are associations, clubs, and various groups. Their aims are varied. Sharing among members and socializing are sometimes the only aims. Yet, these relations are often important although there is another objective. This can be an activity of the members in culture or leisure, mutual help which then becomes more than only mutual insurance in terms of social relations, working for a cause or philanthropy, and so on. Many instances of cooperation share this spirit. Cooperatives have specific aims, but they are often set up with the ideal of maintaining, among their members, positive relations that go beyond mutual self-interest. Cooperative movements emphasize this aspect, which is sometimes lost in the course of time, but also survives in important cases (notably when they are related to a political cause). The network of associations with altruistic mutual cooperation or help – be they traditional or more recent – which exist in a society, often constitutes a major aspect of this society, usually as a sign and a vector of its quality in essence and achievements.

---

[43] The chapter on reciprocity in this volume analyses extensively the efficiency effects of reciprocities.

9.8. The workplace and labour relations

Some economists, who wanted to explain all behaviour by selfishness but lived in a family, adhered to the view that there is "altruism within the family, egoism outside of the family". The above remarks show how erroneous this simplistic view is. Yet, let us consider the social insertion of the individual which is in a sense the antithesis of the family, the workplace and labour relations where the rule is self-interest organized by command and hierarchy. For simplicity, let us forget about family firms and about how many families started at the workplace. The latter fact, however, says something. People spend at work most of their time outside of the family. They find there most of their social relations, and therefore most of their friends. To begin with, the general sociality of respect, menial help, and larger help if necessary, applies there. These relations are particularly important because of the time and fraction of life they occupy. Moreover, this duration, especially when the same people are met, or simply because the relations occur in the same social framework which develops uses and traditions, tends to make this sociality more intense. People working together know each other. Empathy, sympathy, emotional contagion, and reciprocities have a large field of opportunities for developing. The help includes issues relative to the work itself, including in providing information. All relations are reinforced by the fact that they tend to be reciprocal. These non-strictly self-interested conducts lead to the behaviours, noted above, that permit the organization to overcome its inherent "failures" in information and constraining. In addition, co-workers have common interests in working conditions and wages, with regard to the external conditions of the organization – including competition –, or in opposition to other parts of the organization – such as the management. This elicits and reinforces solidarity, while raising the public-good and free-riding problems of joint interest, and their solutions by normed behaviour and altruistic and reciprocitarian sentiments. Reciprocity develops even across hierarchical relations. Even if bonuses are more incentives than gifts, there also is the more surprising but much studied behaviour of working in order to match and deserve the pay received (as noticed above, this was applied by G. Akerlof for explaining involuntary unemployment). In the end, labour relations include strict command, hierarchical constraint, and exploitation, but they by no means reduce to that, and assuming they do prevents understanding and explaining what happens in this essential part of the economy.[44]

9.9. Social giving: Relation, symbol, status

Gift giving is a voluntary unconditional act in favour of someone else. In its various forms, it constitutes the positive social relation. Being in general more or less costly for

---

[44] See Chapter 21 of this Handbook by Julio Rotemberg. Rotemberg (1994) analyzed mutual altruism at the workplace (different from full liking reciprocity).

the giver, it is a voluntary sacrifice of the giver in favour of the beneficiary. Hence, it can a priori constitute a strong relation. It is therefore bound and apt to carry meaning about the giver's sentiments and intentions, and to be a particularly meaningful act in a social relationship. Its cost can indicate and measure the intensity of these sentiments and intentions. Yet, even when the cost is low, the act and the gift can keep their meaning and be symbols sending a signal or acting as a reminder of the giver's sentiments or promises or of the relationship. Accepting a gift is also sometimes an option meaning acceptance of the relationship proposed by the gift. The various meanings can be for the giver, the receiver, or other observers of the relationship. All these functions of the gift are very different from its direct improvement of the receiver's situation and from any satisfaction derived from creating this improvement. They manifest other-regarding sentiments, social relations, and social bonds, and are sometimes important in their existence. The instances of this role of the gift are very varied. The gifts can be of all size and value. The symbolic and relational meaning can be essential or minute, and durable or occasional. The relation and the gift can be fortuitous or institutionalized. The setting can be the family, business relations, and all types of social relations. The motivating sentiments and intentions can be those expressed or other ones. They can be benevolent, self-interested, or malevolent.

Gifts can thus show, manifest, express, confirm, and prove by their cost, various sentiments and intentions towards the receiver. They can mean peace, friendliness, acceptance, friendship, liking, or love. Gifts seal, celebrate, or confirm an agreement or an exchange. They show goodwill in a relation. They can manifest consideration and respect. Gifts, indeed, can mean things which are opposite to each other. They can initiate a relationship, maintain it, or put an end to it. They can manifest submission or obedience, as well as superiority or domination shown by generosity, and also brotherly friendliness between equals. They can express gratitude, pay back a moral debt, or intend to bind the receiver by a moral debt. Giving and receiving, and the relation they constitute or manifest, are thus often related to the social status of the giver or of the receiver, often to a hierarchical status. Various statuses imply obligation to give or to receive or result from such acts. You may give because you have a status, to maintain a status, to acquire a status, or to get rid of a status.

More generally, gift-giving can have many important social roles, functions, and intentions, other than only benefiting the receiver, and this latter effect is sometimes negligible or absent. Giving and accepting provide information about sentiments and intentions, constitute symbols of relations and of promises, and are the occasion of festive encounters, in social situations of various types and of all degrees of importance. People sometimes find it important to transfer to each other identical rings. Others alternately treat each other with identical drinks up to more than they wish or ought. Gifts seal deals and agreements. They are used to confirm hierarchical relations of all types: a domination with a gift to a subordinate, a submission by a gift to a superior, and even an equality in a brotherly gift or reciprocity. As we have seen, gifts can have as their only aim the promotion of the image or status of the giver in the eyes of other people or in her own eyes – although this cannot be the true image of a moral person –, but other gifts are still worse when they aim at morally or socially enslaving the receiver by a moral debt, or at humiliating her in showing that she is not capable to cater for her own need or her family's. Yet, other gift-givings, on the contrary, permit one to redeem a moral debt or to erase or compensate an inferior status. The Inuit people, who have little else to watch but their relationships and whose wisdom is expressed in sayings, have two of them about giving, both concerning its effect on social relations: the gentle "friends make gifts and gifts make friends" is matched by another view devoid of illusion, "the gift makes the slave as the whip makes the dog".

Finally, the most important consequence of the attitude and act of giving may be the easiest to forget about precisely because it is ubiquitous and basic. Freely bowing to another person's will is a kind of gift whose pervasiveness, even in moderate degrees and in reciprocity, constitute the condition of a viable society in a world where scarcities make individuals' desires oppose one another. Giving, yielding, accepting, acquiescing, or endorsing constitute the essence of the multifarious acts and attitudes that make life in society possible. This often goes with a sense of fairness and, to some degree, of fellow-feeling.

9.10. Normative economics and the good society

Hence, even though giving can be motivated by self-interest, negative sentiments, and vicious intentions, it essentially also has all the noted effects crucial to the quality and even the existence of society, whereas altruism underlies the various social sentiments that are the main source of human satisfaction, and altruistic giving is unanimously considered the most valuable of social relations and the most praiseworthy of social actions. Now, the good society is made of good relations, not only of profitable exchange, and of good persons, not only of sybaritic consumers. One discipline which cannot forget this is normative economics.

Normative economics is more traditionally concerned with the quality of society concerning the efficiency (notably Pareto wise) and the fairness and justice of the economic system. As for efficiency, its central topic concerns the "failures" of markets, agreements, and organizations. Hence, the very important effects of giving, altruism, and pro-social and moral conducts for remedying these failures are a prime concern of these studies – as is, similarly, the responsibility of such conducts in creating such failures.

Giving in all its forms also has important effects on the distribution of resources and hence on its justice or fairness. When one helps poorer people, a free act both has this valuable effect and generally diminishes inequality. However, the essential giving and support within families are both usually praised and the major source of inequalities in opportunities, non-earned incomes, and earning capacities created by education. Finally, spontaneous respect of people and properties is an essential condition for the protection of social freedom, the fundamental value of our societies.

Normative economics considers social ethical conceptions with the intention that they be applied. This application, however, implies that these conceptions are endorsed by some people who want, approve, or accept their realization. Indeed, a social ethical view, principle, or set of principles is a priori three things: an ethical logic in itself – that normative economics studies –; a sociological phenomenon of morals and opinion when this view has at least some social importance; and an individual opinion for people who hold this view. Realization – and, hence, the usefulness of the analysis – imply that the last two aspects exist or arrive. If this view takes as end value a concept of what is good for individuals, its endorsement by an individual constitutes an altruism of the latter. Conversely, any altruism towards several people – and in particular the general a priori altruism – implies a conception of the best sharing among them, that is, of distributive justice, which is a basic part of a social ethical view.

These close relations between altruism and giving on the one hand and normative economics, social ethics, justice, and fairness on the other hand hold at all social levels, from the overall view of societies with often an implementation by politics and the public sector, to issues of local justice and direct interactions among agents. The latter case occurs in particular in one of the basic types of reciprocity.[45]

*

In the end, "altruism is expressed in varied forms. It may be individual, interpersonal, and unilateral, as within the family. It may also be cooperative and multilateral, being institutionalized in agencies of government, voluntary associations or private philanthropies. If a task of economists is to illuminate the allocation of resources, then the analysis of altruistic resource use is a bridge to be crossed" (Phelps, 1975). This is to say the least. Yet, those among economists who are so fond of quoting Robertson's proposition that the role of economists is to economize on love – the scarcest resource –, miss a basic point that they could read in an alternative reference, Aristotle. Altruism, like the capacity to love, is a virtue, and this type of resource has the particularity that it is more augmented than eroded by use, that the more you use it, the more you have of it, because it is perfected by training and habit. One economist who emphasized this is Alfred Marshall (1890) who, after noticing that "men are capable of more unselfish service than they generally render", adds that "the supreme aim of the economist is to discover how this latent asset can be developed more quickly and turned to account more wisely".[46]

---

[45] The relations between normative economics and altruism and giving will be fully considered in Sections 14.3, 15 and 16.
[46] See Stephano Zamagni (1995, Introduction).

10. Giving reactions

10.1. *About two particular issues that caught the fancy of economists: Intertemporal giving and the internalization of the gift externality*

10.1.1. *Intertemporal giving, both ways: Bequest and the retro-gift public debt*

Giving can go through time, in both directions. Downstream through bequests, and upstream by the appropriate public debt. Both are essential social and economic issues.

You love your grand-daughter, and your grand-daughter loves you. You want to help her when you will no longer be here, and you do this by bequest. She herself will want to have helped you when you need it. She cannot do it by herself, but the government can do it for her thanks to public expenditures financed by issuing public debt that will be later redeemed thanks to taxes paid by your grand-daughter. Hence, a present government serving the people should foresee and anticipate this desire of your granddaughter as well as possible, and obey and realize it in this way (this has been called a *retro-gift*).[47] Although your grand-daughter approves of the whole operation, when the redeeming time comes she generally has to be forced to pay because the helping first part of the operation has already taken place.

Note that your grand-daughter will generally be richer than you are, because of economic growth and technical progress, and of the bequest she received from you.

When you suffer from a situation of economic slump, she will wants to help you out, thanks to debt-financed public expenditures. You accept her benevolent gift. You have a way to refuse it, which is to augment correspondingly your bequest to her; this cancels out both her sacrifice and the present effect of the public expenditure in increasing your savings and decreasing your consumption. Yet, a priori you accept her benevolent gift. This gift is also, in fact, a return-gift for the gift of bequest she receives from you. In addition, she also provides this gift in her own interest, since maintaining the economic activity also maintains the formation of capital from which she will benefit, and part of your maintained income will be saved and transmitted to her as bequest.

Financing the public expenditure by a tax is forcing you to spend, whereas financing the appropriate expenditure by a public debt is making you benefit from a gift of your descendents which you do not want to refuse and know you should not reject. Hence, the so-called "Ricardian equivalence" between tax and public debt (Robert Barro, 1974) does not hold a priori, as facts show. Its theory thinks about your liking your granddaughter, but not about your grand-daughter liking you.

In fact, of course, many other things happen. People do not actually consider taxes on their descendents for obvious reasons. They do not know the amount of the public borrowing. At any rate, the global amounts say nothing to them. They do not know if a part will be paid by their own descendents, and which one and when. In fact, the public

---

[47] See Kolm 1985 (and also 1996a).

debt can never be redeemed and grow as the interests paid (with the proper economic growth). At any rate, public finance is subject to many other effects. People do not know them, and nobody can foresee the future factors. Public finance other than what they directly see of it is opaque to them. The future at the distance of a generation is very uncertain. Moreover, gifts to descendents are joint gifts with those of other relatives of the beneficiaries. These relatives can be in diverse generations. Some of them are not yet determined (future marriages) and cannot be known. Hence, agreements of joint giving are not possible. In addition, the motives for bequest are often not pure altruism. There is a "warm glow" of bequest leading the giver to value the bequest per se. In fact, a large part of the volume of bequest probably results from uncertainty about the date of death – in this respect, bequest is more accident than gift. Finally, the public policy normally takes people's reaction into account. And, at any rate, taxation, and notably the large tax on bequests, limits the possible effects on the beneficiaries.

10.1.2. Economic internalization of helping externalities

When an agent helps another at a cost that falls short of the value of the aid, this help can be induced by buying it. However, this is not possible in a number of cases. For instance, the service can be an externality. The relation can also happen between members of a society where such buying does not occur. For example, the two protagonists are members of an organization, for instance a firm, and the aid increases the productivity of the beneficiary. Or they can be members or the same family. In these cases, the buying, through some material incentive, can be performed by a dominating agent, who can, for instance, use for this purpose something withdrawn from the beneficiary or from what she would have received otherwise. This agent can for instance be a government who so internalizes the externality, possibly in taxing the beneficiary. Or it can be the management of the organization (firm) who can remunerate the helper with a bonus financed with the extra gain. Or, again, this compensation can be performed within a family. The same outcome can result from the authority pursuing its objectives in choosing, in particular, financial transfers. For example, the government maximizes some social welfare function and chooses taxes and subsidies. Or the firm maximizes its profit and chooses the wages of its employees. Or, again, a family head maximizes a function of the utility, consumption, or income of the members of the family and distributes or redistributes among them. This maximization has the noted effect of overcompensating the helper if it follows the rule that an increase in the wealth of the group benefits all its members. Indeed, the helping increases the wealth of the group by assumption, and the maximization with the distribution or redistribution makes the helper better off on the whole (as it makes all other members better off). The principle that an increased wealth benefits everyone has been a national political ideal.[48] This notion that an increase in

---

[48] For instance, the French statesman Edgar Faure opposed redistribution of wealth but proposed that everyone benefits from new benefits (a lawyer, he was inspired by the classical form of the marriage contract called "community reduced to acquisitions").

any resource should benefit everyone is a classical principle of fairness, called for instance "solidarity" by William Thomson. The condition says also that each individual welfare is a "superior good" for the overall wealth. This is an implicit assumption in Gary Becker's (1974) conception of intra-family redistribution by a benevolent *pater familias* with the noted effect (the so-called "rotten kid theorem").

10.2. Interferences with altruistic giving: General view

The cases of the two foregoing paragraphs, and those of the effects of public transfers on private giving discussed in Section 7, are particular cases of the effects on giving of other transfers – or their equivalent – between the giver and the receiver, and, more generally, of the interaction between giving and some interference with the donor, the beneficiary, or both. Various types of phenomena intervene in these situations which, for simplicity, are restricted here to cases of altruistic giving – that is, the donor cares only about the receiver's situation in addition to her own – (other important cases were also considered in Section 7). The interference is often that of a public policy, but it can notably also be that of any of the other distributing dominant agents considered in the previous section. The gift can notably be aid to poor and needy people in charity, or intrafamily gifts and notably bequest. The interference can affect one of the two parties of the giving or both of them. It can be giving to or taking from the giver or the receiver, or a transfer between them, in both possible directions. The type of interaction between the giver and the interfering agent is a crucial determinant. The general case is that they play a "game" which can be cooperative or non-cooperative. In the latter case, the solution can notably be a Cournot–Nash or a Stackelberg equilibrium, and, in the latter case, either the giver or the interfering agent can be the leader. The interference can also simply be considered as given exogenously, but this is a priori a weak and imperfect model, and there can be a fuller consideration of this agent's objective.

An exogenous variation of the giver's means (a decrease can result from a tax) induces her to vary her gift in the same direction and of a lower amount if the receiver's situation is a normal good for her. An exogenous gift to the beneficiary leads the giver to reduce her gift (in the same condition), and the final result should be the same as if this amount were given to the giver – if she continues to give. However, the situation often turns out to be an agreement between the two givers – with, for instance, a public subsidy (or a tax rebate) for the initial giver.

As a gift can more or less "crowd out" another gift to the same person, it can also deter the beneficiary from helping herself in self-care or effort. The standard solution consists of providing conditional gifts, such as charity to the "deserving poor" rather than also to the "undeserving poor" in 19th century England, the present restriction of unemployment subsidies to people actively seeking a job, or aid tied to own contribution or subsidies to effort. This effect is James Buchanan's (1975) "Samaritan dilemma".

The cases of transfers imposed between the donor and the beneficiary has a number of applications. The transfers have been considered as exogenously given. The gift then a priori adjusts so as to exactly compensate the transfer and it erases its effects, if there remains a gift. In this way, lower private charity compensates public transfers. A decrease in bequests erases the effects of government taxes to finance expenditures in favour of future generations. Conversely, an increase in bequests compensates the effects of public expenditures financed by borrowing (Barro, 1974). Similarly, the actions of the dominating agents of Section 10.1.2 amount to transferring from the beneficiary to the giver, but the transfer considered now is explicitly chosen. Actually, of course, the transfers are usually chosen in considering the giver's reactions and various types of game-theoretic relations can take place, and a number of other aspects are also important in each case (see, e.g., Section 10.1.1).

11. Solving "Adam Smith's problem"

As Blaise Pascal wrote, "man is neither angel nor beast" (he added "he who wants to play angel plays beast"). Adam Smith seems to have been obsessed by the idea that people serve the interests of other people. However, he relied, for this purpose, on two opposite assumptions about motivations in his two main works. Indeed, the universal altruist of the *Theory of Moral Sentiments* stands in a striking contrast with the selfish exchanger of the *Wealth of Nations* (1776). The vivid description of the former may lead one to think that she is ready to help other people, and yet Smith later says that you would do better to rely on the other person's egoism (in exchange) to obtain something from her. The possible contradiction was even made a topic of scholarship by German scholars under the name *Das Adam Smith Problem*. It is said that Smith reversed his view about human nature after his visit to France where he met economists. In any event, he certainly read the argument of the *Wealth of Nations* in the *Essays on Moral* of the Jansenist Pierre Nicole, written one century earlier and translated into English by John Locke.[49] In fact, Smith was probably ready to welcome the reversal of perspectives about motivations. Indeed, the altruist of the *Theory of Moral Sentiments* is only limitedly moral. Much of his altruism is of the hedonistic kind. He largely favours the other person's pleasure because, by spontaneous empathy and somewhat by spontaneous emotional contagion, it fosters his own pleasure. Kant would sternly deny that this is moral, or even good (however, Smith also introduces both impartiality and duty).

At any rate, Smith praises both the altruistic and the selfish characters because they serve other individuals. For the selfish person, this is in the framework of market exchange. The idea was developed by Pareto into the Pareto efficiency of competitive markets. This, however, is for individuals maximizing their ophelimities w_i rather than their altruistic utilities u_i, whereas the highest utility is what they in fact want. Hence, there is also a *Pareto Problem*. It is striking, in fact, that the economists who analysed

---

[49] This is likely because some passages of the *Wealth of Nations* are very close to passages of *Essays on Moral*, for instance those marveling about the very large number of persons whose work ultimately serve a single one (and of those who ultimately benefit from a person's work). Smith also read Mandeville and his presentation of the "public virtue of private vices".

the efficiency of selfish exchange the most perceptively are those who also emphasised altruism (Smith, John Stuart Mill, Edgeworth, Léon Walras for solidarity, Pareto). This raises two questions: the relations between altruism and markets, and the motives of individuals.

The most important fact is that there is no contradiction between the altruism and the selfishness of humans, but, on the contrary, essential complementarities in their manifestations and effects, for three reasons:

(1) Although the market rests on selfish behaviour, some altruism is indispensable to its working, for preventing generalized stealing and cheating that self-defence and the police alone could not check (moreover, who would prevent purely self-interested police and armed forces from robbing at gunpoint?).

(2) Altruism could jeopardize the efficient working of the price system through lack of competition, price rebates, overpayments or overprovision.[50] However, most of the altruism that exists in society beyond family circles and can lead to transfers is joint altruism towards people in need or poor. It requires joint giving with many contributors, which cannot occur spontaneously, and has essentially to be performed by the fiscal system if this giving is socially efficient, rational, and moral (see Section 7). Hence it is or should be performed by the public sector, outside of the market. This permits the efficient working of the market not to be jeopardized by intrusive giving (the public transfers can avoid such effects).

(3) Market exchange, giving, and voting for transfers occur in different circumstances, at different times, and among people with different relations – the market, the family, charity, the polity.

Altruistic conduct in markets that would induce price rebates, overpayments or, for a given payment, providing more goods or labour or accepting less of them, or again abstaining from competing in supplying or demanding items or labour, would destroy the economic efficiency of the price system as informing agents about relative scarcities and desires. However, self-interest alone induces one to take rather than to exchange, when the other person's self-defence and the fear of the police are not sufficient. And, in fact, a minimum of voluntary respect of others' property and of spontaneous honesty is necessary to a normal working of an extensive market system. Hence, exchange, which is neither giving nor stealing, implies and requires an altruism low enough to limit interfering giving and high enough to limit disruptive stealing. Low altruism could also lead to some joint giving where contributors share the cost, but free riding checks it (hence an agreement failure can prevent a market failure), and public realization takes *ipso facto* the issue out of the market.

More generally, individuals commonly have different motives depending on whom they relate to and the circumstances and moments. They can be selfish – yet, respectful

---

[50] See Kolm (1984a) and Lawrence Kranish (1998) for a general analysis of these effects. A particular instance is the reciprocitarian labour supply creating apparent subemployment (considered by Akerlof as noted above).

– in markets, and altruistic in the family, in giving to charity, in approving of joint gifts implemented by public transfers (while preferring not to pay themselves), or in letting their vote about public policy or a constitution be influenced by their sense of justice. Indeed, we have noted that both John Stuart Mill and Léon Walras point out that people can be selfish or concerned about other people or a common good according to their state of mind, the latter case occurring in their moments of calm reflection – although supporting the common good in choosing a constitution, in crucial votes, or in case of collective danger is rather done in collective excitement – (remember that John Stuart Mill calls altruism favouring the highest utilitarian sum of individual utilities). And Pareto distinguishes the sphere of the economy where people seek to maximize their ophelimity w_i from the higher sphere of "sociology" where the concerns are individuals' utility u_i.

Yet, the most elaborate answer to the challenge posed by "Adam Smith's problem" came from the most subtle and perceptive of English economists, Philip Wicksteed (1888, 1906, 1933).[51] In addition to his early contributions to economic choice theory (transitivity and its limits, priorities, revealed preferences, marginal inequalities, bounded rationality, allocation of time, effort and attention, intrafamily economics, group preferences in "communal sense", etc.), Wicksteed, also a methodist clergyman and a profound commentator of Auguste Comte and Vilfredo Pareto, was particularly interested in altruism. For him, choice theory (refined one) applies to this motive of allocation no less and no more than to others. He is, of course, well aware of "economic" exchanges by which each participant takes the other as only a means, and yet serves the other's ends in seeking only her own. He emphasizes, however, that these ends need not be selfish in themselves. They only need to be selfish towards the partner in exchange, not towards the rest of the world. You may want to benefit in order to support your family or give to charity or other causes. For Wicksteed, there exist such *economic relations*, but no *economic man* in the classical sense. "What makes it an economic transaction is that I am not considering you except as a link in the chain, or considering your desires except as the means by which I may gratify those of someone else – not necessarily myself. *The economic relation does not exclude from my mind every one but me, it potentially includes everyone but you*" (emphasis added). Wicksteed labels this attitude *non-tuism*. He also notes that motives depend on the moment, and that business relations, and especially employment relations, are sometimes not purely non-tuistic.

12. The causes of and reasons for altruism

Information about the causes of and reasons for altruism can be useful for two reasons: for foreseeing altruism and its consequences such as respect for other people or helping

---

[51] An interesting recent presentation of the essence of Wicksteed's *Common Sense of Political Economy* is proposed by Ian Steedman (1989, Chapter 10).

them, and for trying to influence altruism – essentially to promote it because of its mostly favourable consequences and intrinsic value. Altruism is the main concern of moral education, and the topic of the penal system can be said to be its absence or misplacement. Hence, the causes of altruism and of its absence have been the object of intense reflection and debate at all times and in all societies (as far as we know). A standard and main issue concerns the relative importance of social influence and education and of the underlying biological material, with a particular place for influence during infancy. This question has taken prominence because the answer is supposed to tell us what can and what cannot be changed and influenced. As far as mere explanation is concerned, however, this question is not correctly posed because culture is not more recent than other aspects of humans and it influences biological selection by mating and survival rates (human "natural" genetic selection, as well as "human nature", are largely culture). Moreover, the very anatomy of the brain is influenced by culture which acts in creating connections and neurons and not only influx. Neurobiologists have found with relative precision the areas of the brain, neuronic circuits, and hormones "responsible" for social emotions and attachments, but no useful conclusion have been derived yet (such as finding out someone's anti-social propensity).

The main information about the cause of altruism or lack of it is to be found in studies in psychology, notably the psychology of the child and generic psychology (with the landmark study of Jean Piaget's (1932) *The Birth of the Moral Sentiment in the Child* and the work of Kohlberg), social psychology, sociology, psychoanalysis (*cum grano salis*), and history and anthropology. These contributions of other disciplines are, of course, beyond our present topic.[52]

Some adepts of the "dismal science", faced with the sad evidence that human character is not so sad after all, tried to save selfishness in displacing it from *homo economicus* to her genes, and hence became interested in the sociobiological selection of altruism towards kin. Another selectional cause of altruism can be found in group selection – groups of altruistic co-operators outperform others –, which is as old as selection theory since it is Darwin's own theory of competing tribes. Yet, a third mechanism of genetic selection explains altruism much more straightforwardly.

Indeed, you (that is, any animal) have an interest in mating with altruists since they will protect you and your common offspring. This makes the "altruistic gene" (genetic configurations favourable to altruism) spread more than alternatives. Moreover, since your mate's altruism helps you survive more, the character of being attracted by altruists is also selected and spreads, in addition to consciously seeking protection. The altruist protects your common offspring because of his/her altruism and because they are his/her offspring – and you both care for your offspring (would it only be as a result of the selection of altruism towards kin). People who give gifts in courtship may not do it in order to pretend that they are altruists, but this behaviour of theirs may have been selected for this very reason. Of course, altruism also can be a handicap for self-survival, and an equilibrium obtains.

---

[52] For a discussion of this literature, with synthesis and conclusions, see Kolm 1984a.

Yet, I do not hope that any biological consideration will provide any conclusion sufficiently specific, subtle, and to the point to be useful for understanding human altruism. They only present hypotheses about very rough psychological features which do not match, by far, the variety revealed by reflective and analytical observation. I regret it, but, for example, the mere variety of types of altruisms pointed out in the next section seems to vindicate this conclusion. However, the biological approach seems to be appreciated by some people, notably in economics, and it seems helpful for them to be convinced of the possibility of altruism.

Part II: Altruisms and giving

13. Altruisms: Types and causes or reasons

13.1. General presentation

13.1.1. Introduction

Understanding, explaining, and forecasting altruism, giving, and their consequences requires having a clear view of the nature of these phenomena, each of which has a variety of types and of causes or reasons. This is the objective of the remarks presented in this section.

The very definitions of altruism and of giving are tricky, and can only really be presented after the consideration and analysis of the various cases. For a start, an altruistic view of a person is a view that values positively and for itself what is good for another person or what it deems to be so.[53] And giving is an unconditional action of a person, purposefully favourable in some way to another and costly in some way for the actor. Note that, apart from this cost, the giver may benefit from other effects of her action and give for this reason. The noted persons can be individuals – as it will be the case here – or any other relevant social entities. An altruistic view leads its holder to give when this person finds that the valuable consequences according to this view more than compensate the costs for her. An altruist may be someone who holds altruistic views, but it more commonly means someone who gives for this reason. Similarly, altruism may refer to the existence of altruistic views (not far from benevolence), but it more commonly also requires the resulting givings (not far from beneficence) – yet, since giving will often be a variable of the analysis, these distinctions of vocabulary would not be fruitful here. Altruistic views are of various types distinguished by their causes or reasons. These types can more or less be jointly present. They divide into two categories, *hedonistic* or *natural altruism*, and *normative altruism*. The social psychological phenomena of affection, sympathy, empathy, emotional contagion, fellow feeling, compassion, and pity,

---

[53] This "good" is the happiness, pleasure, satisfaction, or welfare of this other person only as a particular case. The other cases are what economists call "paternalism".

make a person feel happy or sad as a consequence of the happiness or pain, or good or bad situation, of another person. They induce "natural" or "hedonistic" altruism. On the other hand, normative altruism is induced by *moral intuition*, non-moral *social* norms, or various applications of *reason* or rationality. Moral intuition and moral reason induce the two kinds of *moral altruism*.

There are, of course, many other reasons to give than altruism. They do not focus on and value the improvement of the beneficiary's situation *in itself*. The most direct such conduct is following a simple norm or value of giving with this property. This norm or value is psychologically of a moral kind without referring to an altruistic intention (for this reason, one can validly deny that this conduct is actually moral in an ethical sense). This norm of giving is a priori supported by a social view, and by the corresponding opinion of some people (voiced or implicit). More generally, however, judgments about giving elicit a number of motives that induce it. They are made by other people, by some social opinion, and by the actor herself. They lead to seeking praise and approval, absolute or relative status, and a good image, from the judgments of other people but including self-approval and image of oneself in one's own eyes (that Adam Smith takes to be an empathy of other persons' views of oneself). Both moral sentiments and social judgments induce social norms or values of the two kinds relevant here: a norm or value for giving per se, and a norm or value for caring about the beneficiary, and hence, possibly, for giving for her sake. Giving because of non-moral social norms or values is in between giving from an intuitively moral motive and giving because of the judgment of other people or of society, since it is close to the former and yet generally requires the consideration of the judgments of other people (or the imagination of this judgment). Yet, failing to abide by moral values and by non-moral social values elicits respectively guilt and shame, two very different sentiments. Moreover, some moral norms of giving are derived from specific reasonings such as universalization of Kant's type, hypothetical substitution or reciprocity, etc. We have also seen the central role of giving in a variety of types of social relations. Finally, various social or economic effects of giving can provide strictly self-interested benefits to the giver. This includes effects through markets, return gifts for reasons of balance, fairness, gratitude, or liking, and other social rewards provided either for rewarding merit or for inducing further gifts. The motives of such actions lose all social dimension.

The present part shows the various types of altruism (Section 13) and of non-altruistic giving (Section 15), with special consideration of the relations between altruism and justice (Section 14). The varieties of altruism and of non-altruistic giving are summarized in Tables 1 and 3, respectively. Motives for giving can focus on the beneficiary or on the giver, and the former case can be "paternalistic" or not. Section 13.2 presents the various types of natural or hedonistic altruism, whereas Section 13.3 analyses the three kinds of normative altruism and their relations and effects. Non-altruistic giving can aim at eliciting social effects concerning judgments, the giver's and the receiver's situation, or social relations (Section 15.2), or at favouring self-interest through various possible ways (Section 15.3) – including indirect economic or social effects, reward, or a return gift.

13.1.2. The twelve basic types of altruism

Table 1 summarizes the structure of altruism and its twelve basic types.

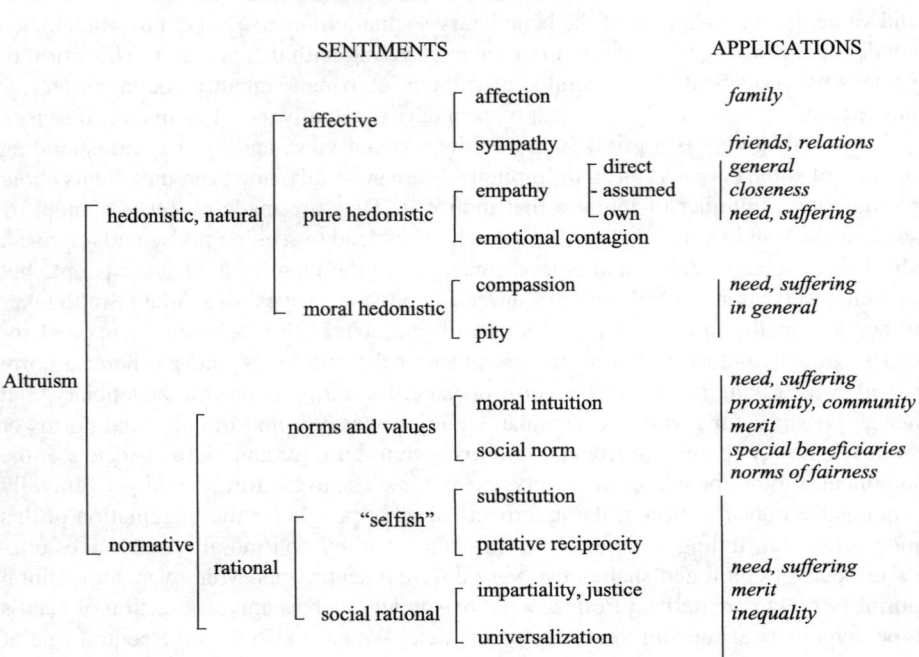

Table 1
Types and structure of altruism

	SENTIMENTS	APPLICATIONS
Altruism — hedonistic, natural — affective	affection	family
	sympathy	friends, relations
Altruism — hedonistic, natural — pure hedonistic	empathy — direct / assumed / own	general / closeness / need, suffering
	emotional contagion	
Altruism — hedonistic, natural — moral hedonistic	compassion	need, suffering in general
	pity	
Altruism — normative — norms and values	moral intuition	need, suffering proximity, community merit
	social norm	special beneficiaries norms of fairness
Altruism — normative — rational — "selfish"	substitution	
	putative reciprocity	need, suffering merit inequality
Altruism — normative — rational — social rational	impartiality, justice	
	universalization	

13.1.3. The objects of reasons for giving and altruisms

13.1.3.1. Gift or receiver's situation The relevant issue for evaluating a gift can be either the resulting situation of the beneficiary, or the gift in itself. This distinction practically identifies with the two families of reasons for giving: altruism values the situation of the receiver, and various other effects of the gift are generally based on the gift in itself. Norms or values and opinions of all types can attach to these two types of items. From Sections 4 and 7, appreciation of the gift in itself can result from valuing the sacrifice or the responsibility of the giver (the issue of distributive taxes was also discussed there). Some instances may seem to belong to a case but actually belong to the other. For example, if someone makes a conspicuous gift to someone else in order to enhance the receiver's social status, then this status is the aspect of the receiver's situation she values.

13.1.3.2. "Paternalism" In altruism, favouring what is good for the beneficiary of a gift can be either according to the receiver's judgment, or according to another conception. The former case corresponds to economists' classical "respect of the preferences" of the receiver. It is then usually taken to mean valuing the receiver's satisfaction. It is also classically related to the more tangible meaning of valuing the receiver's happiness, pleasure, or joy, or the relief of her pain, suffering, misery, or dissatisfaction. The other case is usually called "paternalism", although this term is ambiguous in itself since a benevolent "father" may also value his children's satisfaction or happiness rather than his own conception of what is good for them if it would lead to another choice. Altruism resulting from empathy or emotional contagion favours the other person's joy, happiness, pleasure, or lesser pain. Normative altruisms and altruism resulting from affection or compassion can be of both types.

Moreover, the dichotomy between the two cases is not simplistic, notably for reasons concerning aspects of the beneficiary with respect to information, weakness of the will, compulsion, addiction, and multiple self simultaneously or over time. The preferences of a person are not always a unique well defined system. There often are oppositions between her short-term and her long-term interests or desires, her greed and her desire to be a good person or to behave properly, her choice and what she thinks she should choose or what she thinks ex post she should have chosen. This raises issues of prudence, moral behaviour, weakness of the will, compulsion, addiction, and regret. An altruist who wants the good of the other person as this person conceives it may therefore have values which oppose some desires, manifestations or expressions of this person. The altruist and the person in question may have different relevant information, and one piece of information, or the other, may be better. A person may even wish to be constrained in her actions in the name of better information, in her short-term pleasure in the name of her long-term interest or prudence, and in her greed in the name of good or proper behaviour. This can be both economists' "paternalism", and obedience to one of the person's desires. An altruistic sailor on Ulysses' boat should forcefully tie him to the mast in the name of Ulysses' medium-term interest. The altruistic spanking justified by the dictum *qui bene amat bene castigat* can be both drilling into the father's ideal (in a sense the extreme form of so-called "paternalism"), or promotion of the victim's long-term interest or moral ideal (or future moral ideal).

13.2. Natural or hedonistic altruism

When you are happier because someone is happier, or because she is in a situation that you think is better for her, then your own eudemonism or hedonism makes you value the pleasure or lesser pain of the other, or the relevant improvement in her situation. This is natural or hedonistic altruism. It has several types of causes (which can be jointly present).

13.2.1. Emotional contagion

Emotional contagion makes you have emotions that you observe in others. This is well known and also present in animal societies (particularly for fear and anger). This constitutes the *imitatio affectuum* (imitation of affects) so central in Spinoza's *Ethics* and for David Hume. It is also a main factor of crowd psychology (Gustave Le Bon). The induced emotion is generally of lower intensity than the original one (but it is higher in appropriate conditions, and there can be feedbacks and phenomena of resonance).

13.2.2. Empathies

You can imagine yourself being in the place of some other person. This thought can be called *substitution*. Yet, you can apply this to various characteristics of this other person. Besides the other person's material, social, or physical situation, you can also imagine endorsing various mental characteristics of hers, such as understanding, intentions, tastes and preferences, or some of them or aspects of them. When this mental operation affects your emotions or feelings in the direction of those of the other person, one speaks of *empathy* (a term due to Max Scheler). However, there are three types of empathy, or three aspects of it. (1) In *direct empathy*, you imagine directly endorsing the other person's emotional state, or state of her feeling, which you infer from her expression (verbal, physical, written, etc.). (2) In *assumed empathy*, you imagine having emotions or feelings that you infer to be those of the other person from what you know about her situation, tastes, sensibility, and so on. (3) In *own empathy*, you imagine what would be your own emotions and feelings if you were in the other person's place for the non-emotional characteristics for which you imagine the substitution. For instance, the empathy described by Adam Smith (without the name) is own empathy. These three types of empathy can be mixed and associated. In particular, you will want a consistency between direct and assumed empathy, that is, between the emotions and feelings that the other person seems to experience and their causes or reasons (including the other person's tastes, sensibility, etc.). Own empathy would amount to assumed empathy if there were full substitution for all characteristics that can affect the considered emotions or feelings (including tastes, sensibility, etc.), but this may not be possible. Direct empathy can easily be associated with emotional contagion.

Then, these imagined emotions and feelings of yours, induced from the other person's emotions or feelings or from their causes, induce in you derived empathy-emotions which differ from the imagined feeling – and a fortiori from the actual ones – in being in the same way agreeable or painful, and with an intensity which varies in the same direction but is generally lower. These empathy-emotions then induce acting, such as giving or helping that pleases the other person or improves her situation, and hence has parallel effects on the empathy-emotion, if they appear to be worth the cost. We have thus noticed that empathy implies three levels of emotions, feelings or sentiments: the original ones of the other person, those imagined for yourself, and the resulting empathy-emotions. The first and the last are real, whereas the intermediate ones are imagined. Moreover, empathy can be more or less voluntary or involuntary.

13.2.3. Affection and sympathy

A priori *affection* towards someone, liking her, directly implies liking what is good for her, and notably her joy or the alleviation of her pain. Affection can be associated with empathy (notably when one knows the liked person well), and with emotional contagion (notably if one is close to her, in frequent contact where she falls under one's attention), but it is a proper cause of altruism by itself. Affective altruism can value the pleasure of the liked person, but it can also wish aspects of the person's situation that one deems to be good for her and that are not the most conducive to her pleasure (a "paternalism" that can even lead to *qui bene amat bene castigat*).

Feeling *sympathy* towards someone a priori entails enjoying her pleasure and feeling sorrow for her grief. The induced sentiments are generally of lower intensity than the original ones. Sympathy is favourable to empathy and emotional contagion, but it is a cause of altruism in itself. Sympathy is relatively close to a mild form of affection, but there may also be some difference in nature. In particular, sympathy does not entail so close an involvement with the other person's good, and sense of responsibility for it, as affection generally does. As a consequence, sympathy can lead one to value and favour, in addition to the other person's pleasure, her long-term prudential interest, but probably not other aspects of her situation for themselves in a classical "paternalistic" fashion.

Apart from this present-day meaning, the term sympathy has meant different things. Adam Smith uses it to mean empathy and, secondarily, emotional contagion. The etymological sense of sympathy is about the same as compassion, and it applies well to emotional contagion and to empathy.

13.2.4. Compassion and pity

Compassion and *pity* are altruistic sentiments towards people in poor situation. The misery that elicits them can be material, but also purely mental in relation to some expectation or habit. These sentiments need no a priori positive sentiment towards the other, such as affection and sympathy. On the contrary, affection precludes pity in crowding it out, since the pain you feel from the pain of someone you like much or love a priori leaves no room for a sentiment of pity. Less intense liking produces this effect only to some extent. However, notwithstanding the apparent purity of the concepts of compassion and pity, they are in fact cocktails of the other views and feelings. Indeed, they mobilize elements of empathy and of emotional contagion, and they also have a dimension of intuitive moral altruism – or are closely associated with it. They induce sadness from the other person's grief, usually with a much lower intensity (except for saints), and they sometimes are motivated by specific aspects of the other's situation and not only her pain, in a kind of paternalism. Pity can also have an element of condescension.

13.2.5. *Relations and nature of hedonistic altruism*

The various forms of natural altruism have relations between themselves. They can more or less be jointly present, some favouring others or the converse. Affection and sympathy favour empathy and emotional contagion because of the knowledge of the other person they imply and of the focus of attention on her they induce. Empathy is also favoured by the interest in and curiosity about the other person induced by affection and sympathy. Compassion and pity are restricted to poor situations of the other person, we have seen that they contain some empathy and emotional contagion, but that they rather tend to be excluded or limited by the presence of affection or sympathy which tend to mobilize – in a sense – the sentiment towards the suffering person.

Natural altruism can easily be seen as genuine and proper altruism, but it can also be seen, on the contrary, as an extension of egoism, because it rests on one's pleasure, notably in the case of empathy and emotional contagion, and because it is, in the case of affection and to some extent of sympathy, in essence an extension of the ego to one's family or friends. This reduction of natural altruism to egoism would notably oppose it to moral altruism. Along this line, Kant would doubtlessly classify natural altruism along with other tastes among the individual's "inclinations" which morals should fight (in the name of reason in his view).

13.3. *Normative altruisms*

13.3.1. *The three types of normative altruism: moral, social, and rational*

Normative altruism of an individual is her seeing the good of some other people as a value in itself, a final or end value. This view can thus conceive of norms about this good. It can motivate giving or helping in spite of the costs. There is also normative giving concerned with the gift or help in itself rather than as improving the beneficiary's situation, although it has to have this latter effect. Such action can be induced by moral advice on indictment or by non-moral social norms or values. It will be classified as a type of non-altruistic giving.

Normative altruism divides into three categories, which can be called respectively *intuitively moral*, *social*, and *rational*. Two are moral in nature: the intuitively moral and the rational types. Yet, intuitively moral and social normative altruism refer directly to values or norms, in opposition to rational normative altruism in which some reasoning of a moral and logical nature is basic (although it is sometimes quite short). The names used require a few precisions. The adverb "intuitively" is meant to distinguish "intuitively moral" from "rational moral". It is chosen because of the very common use of the term "moral intuition" for describing the nature of the values in question (this traditional use extrapolates the normal sense of the term intuition which refers to a kind of cognition about facts, and in this sense it treats values as if they were truths, which they are not). Moreover, these intuitive moral values are doubtlessly no less social in origin than the other values to which we restrict the term "social" for the sake of brevity and convenience, and whose full name should more exactly be "non-moral social". Yet, these two categories are a priori neatly distinct. A moral value or obligation is felt as intrinsic – even if it applies in specific social contexts –, it can entail a duty, and failing in this respect entails guilt. A (non-moral) social value or norm basically refers to a judgment "of society", or "of other people", it says what is proper or correct, or what is to be done, and failing in this respect elicits uneasiness or shame. However, a few remarks are required. A social value or norm may have become internalized, or it may have become a personal habit – and this is in fact the most common case, in addition to the social judgment. The judgment of other people or of society may be only imagined. Moral values are also acquired by internalization of judgments "of society" or of others, but they are hypostaziated and acquire an autonomous status. Moreover, moral values are generally also social in the sense that they are praised by "society" or by "other people". Yet, this is not necessary for them. The criterion is the judgment of your conscience. Indeed, there are cases, often remarkable, of moral values that oppose general opinion. In fact, in all these cases, "society" may be a sub-society whose views may oppose that of other people or societies. These distinctions and relations are summarized as follows:

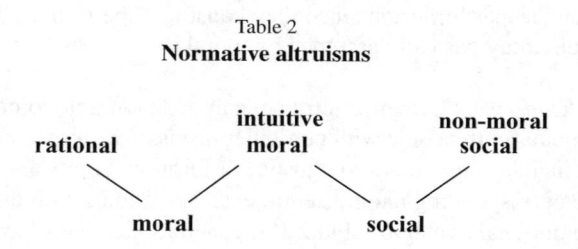

Table 2
Normative altruisms

```
                    intuitive              non-moral
   rational          moral                  social
        \           /    \                  /
          moral              social
```

13.3.2. Moral and social normative altruism

13.3.2.1. Nature and distinction Giving and helping are *prima facie* the paragon of actions praised by morals. Benevolence as disposition to help, attitudes favourable to other persons, and the corresponding sentiments, are the paragon of moral attitudes or sentiments – where "moral" is taken in its ethical sense. Moral judgments, indeed, bear not only on acts but also on intentions, attitudes, and sentiments. In particular, they do not only praise helping per se in general, but also judge its motives. They discuss, endorse or criticize various moral values and norms. In fact, moral judgments hold an action to be moral – and praise it for this – only if its intention is, but they can also approve of some acts that are not properly moral acts in this sense. In giving in order to show off, they approve of giving but regret the motive. And they even condemn the motive when giving aims at humiliating the receiver. Moral judgments even judge the motives of natural and hedonistic altruism, in spite of the fact that they are bare psychological phenomena: these judgements can hold that you ought to love your family or "your neighbour", that you should not be insensitive to other people's pain, and that you should practice empathy. They see favourably that you let yourself be emotionally contaminated when the sentiment is love but they condemn it when it is hatred. A particular religious tradition has emphasized the value, and developed the concept, of charity in acts, sentiments, or judgments, towards persons in an unfortunate situation of some kind (other traditions are content with compassion or with general solidarity).

This moral altruism is one kind of normative altruism. Another kind – social altruism – refers to judgments "of society" or "in society" of praise or blame, that are not moral in the strict sense of ethical. They refer to "properness", to what "is done" or "is not done", often to custom, tradition, or uses (when not to fashion). A major difference between these two categories of normative judgments is that social normative judgments focus essentially on acts and attitudes, whereas moral judgments evaluate also the inner facts of motives and intentions, which even constitute their most basic reference. This is due to the fact that the judgment of other people is essential or at least important in social normative evaluation: the actor judges herself through the judgment of others, whether it is actual or imagined by her. Hence, essentially visible facts matter, that is, acts and attitudes. Morals, on the other hand, consider more intentions and motives, and even take them as the deepest criterion since they constitute the primary cause with respect to the moral autonomy basically assumed by moral evaluations of conduct.

13.3.2.2. Applications Normative altruism can be favourable to other people in general, more particularly to people with particular needs or with special social relations to oneself, and it includes opinions about justice or fairness. In pity and compassion, it accompanies the corresponding natural sentiments, sometimes with the addition of some sympathy or emotional contagion; indeed, it generally demands having pity or feeling compassion to begin with.

Essential moral judgments (and possibly social normative ones) favour what is deemed to be good for people in general, especially the relief of their misery or of various aspects of it, and of their pain. When held by an individual, this judgment favours what is good for others in this way, and hence it is an altruism. Such judgments have two types of application. Normative (notably, moral) altruistic judgments constitute one motive for giving, notably for helping people in need. Moreover, a complete general benevolent judgment must also choose when scarcities or other reasons create an opposition among what is deemed to be good for various people, for instance their interests or well-being. When it is a normative judgment, this implies that this choice belongs to questions of distributive justice or fairness. The solutions refer to issues of impartiality and equality about various possible items, of merit or deservingness, needs, various types of rights, responsibility, and tradition and custom. The implementation of these principles is sometimes realized by giving, but it is more often achieved by more or less coercive public action. Morals includes principles of justice and fairness, but some rules of fairness belong to (other) social values and norms.

Moreover, social normative and moral judgments also hold that you should particularly give to and help people who are in a particular social relation with you, notably members of your family and of various groups to which you belong. This is often made redundant by affection (you certainly have a duty to take care of your children but you generally do not take care of your children because it is a duty). Yet, these judgments also praise this affection and make it a duty (you should also love your children).

13.3.2.3. Comparisons: natural, normative, moral, social Normative judgments are of a nature thoroughly different from that of natural altruism, although there are relations between them since the former evaluate not only acts but also sometimes sentiments, including some sentiments that induce natural altruism, namely compassion, pity, affection, and empathy. Normative judgments refer to values which can belong to morals and ethics, or to social norms or customs. In this sense, they are transcendent to their holders who see them as "objective" and, generally for social norms and sometimes for moral norms, as "external" to themselves – in contrast to the case of tastes –; they constitute Freud's *superego*. These judgments refer to what is proper, right, intrinsically good, or to what should intrinsically be the case (which becomes a duty when a moral judgment refers to a person's choice). In fact, the psychological situation of moral values with respect to *ego* is paradoxical, since they can be seen as both the most inner and intimate of sentiments, and as fully external higher commands and indictments. However, all these judgments may be more chosen by their holders than their ordinary tastes are. Yet, this choice usually consists of adopting some position that already exists in the society, held by some smaller or larger part of its members. And moral *metanoia* is sometimes a particularly deep experience. Finally, the effects of education and other social influences are clear. Normative judgments are *de facto* cultural. Moreover, those considered here are social not only by their nature and their origin, but also by their object.

Moral and social normative judgments thus have important common aspects, but they also have important psychological and social differences. And they can both coincide and support one another, and enter into conflict. The psychological and social differences are of five types.

(1) Moral values are seen as more "transcendent" than social ones. Social values "transcend" the individual but not society, whereas moral values are felt as "transcending" both.

(2) Moral values attach more importance to motives of action, whereas social judgments principally consider acts.

(3) Social normative motives often require the judgment "of society" or of other people, whereas this is not necessary for properly moral motives. However, this "social judgment" may be "internalized" by the actor, imagined by her, presented by her and to her in a division of personality, or sclerosed into habit or tradition.

(4) "Propriety" essentially refers to social judgments, whereas "duty" refers to moral values.

(5) Failing to behave (and sometimes think or feel) properly elicits *shame* for social norms and values, whereas failing to behave and feel as required elicits *guilt* for moral norms and values.[54]

Of course, a person sees moral and social values as judging not only her own actions and sentiments, but also those of other people, actions of institutions (in particular those concerned with social aid and issues of justice), and states of society (notably concerning the situations of individuals and fairness towards them). In the case of normative altruism, both the actor and the object of the conduct can be not only individuals but also, by extension, groups of them, institutions, or other social entities (e.g., patriotism can be ranked along both normative altruisms, and also affective altruism).

13.3.2.4. The ambiguous status of social normative motives Social normative judgments can lead to giving, but their role with respect to altruism is in fact ambiguous. On the one hand, they are sometimes close to moral judgments, or even confounded with them. On the other hand, respecting a social norm in order that other people have a good opinion of yourself – or that they do not have a bad one – is not a morally motivated act since this objective is not moral. In particular, taking care of the good of someone else, and as a consequence helping her or giving to her, with such an objective, is not moral altruism (this is a fortiori the case when the gift or aid in itself aims at eliciting this favourable or not unfavourable opinion). This is not the directly hedonistic or natural altruism described above either. In fact, it is not altruism at all. Two aspects participate to this ambiguous status: the types of manifestations of "society's views" and the intrinsic praiseworthiness of giving.

First, although social norms always require that a judgment "by society" is present somewhere, its enactment may more or less put this aspect between parentheses. Following the norm may have become a habit, a mechanistic behaviour. However, if this behaviour is seen by other people, notably if it concerns interpersonal relations, one should consider what would happen if the habit is not followed: would there be some disapproval or blame or not? Social norms can be simply justified by tradition or custom – whereas when a moral norm is justified in this way, this implies a kind of hypostasis of the corresponding social entity. Frequently, also, the individual has "internalized" the social norm. This does not make it a moral norm although moral norms come into people's mind largely in this way. Such an individual has "society in her head". If she does not respect the norm, the individual may feel ill at ease, even sometimes embarrassed, and even possibly ashamed, even when nobody else relevant knows it (yet, she does not feel guilty as it would be the case for a moral norm). The individual may also want to be praiseworthy rather than praised, or, if she is praised, she wants to deserve it. This is also common for moral norms. This motive does not seek image or status in the eyes of others. A next step is that the individual values her image of herself in her own view, in itself or by comparison with other people, and she may also value a resulting status

---

[54] See the discussion in Chapter 3 by Jon Elster in this volume.

(in her view). This involves a dissociation of personality. Adam Smith argues that self judgment is an empathy of the judgment of oneself or of one's acts by other people or by an "impartial spectator". Yet, this is not necessarily the case: taking some distance for evaluating oneself may suffice. Then, the individual may care for the judgment of other people, but only in imagining it. This may be a dim view of the opinion "of society" or of a part of it, or it may refer to the potential judgment of specific other people. Finally, only, the actual judgment of other people may come into play. The basic point is that there is a large spectrum of cases between what seems to be an own, intrinsic motivation, and the desire to be favourably judged by other people, in avoiding reproof or blame, eliciting approval or praise, building one's image in others' eyes, and seeking to maintain or acquire some social status in this way.

The second issue is that there obviously are non-moral social norms, but when the evaluated act is giving, this is an act which is *prima facie* morally praiseworthy in itself, and is a classical result of moral altruism. Hence, the association and confusion of motives occurs easily.

As we have seen in Section 7, a crucial issue is whether a giver cares about the good of the beneficiary – and this is altruism –, or whether she cares about her gift in itself. Both may result from social norms or values. The most standard case is valuing the act, which is external and visible. Yet, there may also be social values of aiming at the good of some other people, and of actually caring about this good (full altruism).

13.3.2.5. A society is more altruistic than its members   You approve people who give to others whose good you value (including to yourself), and you may admire moral or empathic altruism in itself. Now, the opinion of other people about oneself is one of the main motives for action, and for satisfaction or dissatisfaction, in all societies, and for all types of issues (including concerning one's own consumption and way of life). Hence, giving can be fostered by approval or by trying to avoid disapproval. Added to other motives, this can elicit the act or induce giving more. It can even be the sole motive present for some giving.

Adam Smith emphasizes that the desire to be praised and the desire to be praiseworthy are very different in nature, although they are related and are often jointly present. In particular, seeking approval, or trying to avoid disapproval, are not moral motives in themselves. However, approval or disapproval, and praise or blame, can be made in the name of some moral reason. In this case, acts motivated by them are determined by moral judgments in the end. Moreover, someone who judges others in this way may not give herself, because she finds it too costly or, possibly, because people influenced by these judgments – notably hers – give sufficiently. Then, there may be people who give without moral motives, and people who judge morally without acting morally, in a nice social division of labour where some are "moral" in act and not in mind, and others are moral in judgment but not in action, and yet, collectively, there are both the moral judgments and the corresponding moral acts determined by them (the type of economists who enjoy expressing scepticism or cynicism about human motives would thus like these two kinds of individuals, the hypocritical moralist and the self-centred status seeker, and yet giving ultimately caused by morals can actually occur). Someone may even both give because of the judgment of others and judge others in this way: then, she both "acts morally" and judges morally but she does not act for a moral motive. And this may be the case of everyone in the society, where there then are moral acts and moral judgments that determine them but no moral motive. More generally, however, people would jointly judge their own acts and the acts of others, and be sensitive to the judgments of others (and of themselves) about themselves. Mutual approval can thus be a powerful factor of giving in the society, inducing it or increasing it as a multiplier of individual altruism.

13.3.2.6. Self-image These praises or blames, when they judge moral acts (or sentiments), have three noteworthy aspects. First, you often judge yourself also in the same way, as if by an external observer, in addition to other sentiments concerning your own acts or sentiments. You "are satisfied when you look at yourself in the mirror", or you "dare not look at yourself". You may be under the scrutiny of the "eye of your conscience". This reinforces the direct moral motive for action. Second, you may be concerned by the hypothetical judgment of the fact by people who do not know it (sometimes more or less particular people such as a member of your family or your guru, and they can be deceased persons). Imagining such a hypothetical judgment can merely become a way of trying to determine the right action. This judgment can also become depersonalized. It then is only a way of reflecting about the right conduct for choosing it, in looking at it from some distance, so to speak. Third, these judgments "crystallize" into an image of yourself as a more or less well-behaved or virtuous person. Caring about this image of yours in the eyes of other people is not a moral motive in itself, but caring about this image in your own eyes or as it is built by the depersonalized and abstract judgment can be seen as an aspect of moral reflection.

13.3.2.7. Moral akrasia An individual may act morally, she may be forced to act morally, and she may also welcome being forced to act morally because she regrets the weakness of her moral will – her moral *akrasia*. In particular, giving is a free act by definition, but an individual may regret her own excessive meanness without being able to overcome it as she would like to. This kind of mental duality and conflict is a common situation, which leads, for instance, to self-commitment for prudence (long term interest) – as with Ulysses and the call of the sirens. The person may then welcome to be forced to do what she thinks she ought to do but cannot do by herself. This can notably be giving to people in need or whom she ought to support. The person then welcomes to be forced to be as generous and good as she thinks she should be or she really is. This constraint has to come from the public sector – in a state of law where it has the monopoly of legitimate coercion of adults. And the individual may favour this situation by supporting it on political grounds. Voting in favour of the corresponding laws or taxes is then a form of self-commitment. The government becomes Ulysses' mast against the sirens of selfishness. A similar situation is very common for prudential issues, leading to safety regulation and compulsory insurance or saving. People are "forced to be free" (to do what they really want to), as Rousseau says,[55] and they may be free to be forced to be free in voting for it.[56] This can add to the issue of joint giving for demanding forced distributive transfers for implementing individual freedom.

13.3.3. Rational altruism

13.3.3.1. General principle One of the three categories of normative altruism is rational altruism. It is moral as is also intuitive moral altruism. It opposes the two other categories, intuitively moral and social normative altruisms, in that its various forms each rest on a reasoning using more or less counterfactuals. The reasoning can go from the simplest one – such as imagining oneself in the situation of someone else – to the most sophisticated theories of justice, fairness, or social ethics (because they have applications in altruistic conducts, and altruism and giving imply issues of justice or fairness). A counterfactual is a situation that does not exist and yet can influence reality because it is imagined by people and, in this way, influences their preferences, attitudes, and possibly choices. For example, a person may imagine being in the situation of another, or that their situations are permuted, or again that she is an "impartial spectator", or possibly that all the other people act as she does or follow the rule that guides her. From the reasoning, the person derives a moral obligation, or a reason to follow a course of action, which can lead her to help or give. We will consider three categories of rational altruism describing respectively substitution, permutation, and putative reciprocity for one, impartiality and justice for the other, and universalization (including Kant's categorical imperative) for the third.

The use of reasons and of rationality differs neatly from intuitive moral values and from social norms and values. However, they are in fact used jointly with these other values. On the one hand, these values and their application use, of course, aspects of rationality such as basic requirements of logic, consistency, equal treatment of equals, and so on. On the other hand, the use of reason and of reasonings usually requires at some point the use of a value of another type in order to be complete and applicable. This value determines, for instance, which characteristics of the persons and their situations are considered for substitution, permutation, or equality among individuals, or what are the desired properties of a society where everybody follows the same rule for applying Kant's "categorical imperative". In fact, and more generally, Kant's ultimate general value, considering each person "in the kingdom of ends", or "always treating others also as an end and not only as a means", is a moral altruism presented as being of the "intuitive" kind (although reasoning using impartiality and substitution can help supporting it).

---

[55] Probably rather about the free riding issue.
[56] Moreover, voting is compulsory in some countries, where people are then forced to be free to be forced to be free.

13.3.3.2. Substitution "Imagine you were in her situation" is commonly proposed for inducing someone to help. This is an exhortation to some kind of empathy with the other person, for inducing the corresponding altruism, possibly with an extension to compassion or pity. Yet, the conceptual experiment of such a substitution can, more generally, provide information about the other person, and this information can be used in various types of moral altruism. This can lead to the application of intuitive moral or social values, or of the adequate principles of justice or fairness (notably concerning impartiality or equality). Imagining oneself in the place of the other person is also sometimes associated with imagining herself in one's place, thus leading to the important reasoning of "putative reciprocity".

13.3.3.3. Putative reciprocities Indeed, "we should help them because they would help us if this had happened to us" is a remark I heard from an 8-year-old French girl after the tsunami in the Indian ocean. This assumption was definitively a counterfactual given the place where she lives (the Alps). This reasoning appears not to be infrequent. The help then is motivated as notionally being a reciprocity. The nature of this reciprocity is a balance reciprocity, with an aspect of fairness, which focuses more on the need of the helped person than on the gift or service provided – a distinction that has crucial consequences in the case of joint giving.[57] This object of the reciprocity is related to the fact that this view also includes a reciprocity in sentiments: we feel compassion towards them notably because, and all the more that, they would have felt compassion towards us if our situations were reversed.

Putative reciprocity is also sometimes extended: the belief that you would be helped if you needed it may make you more prone to help others, even if they are not those who would help you (a generalized putative reciprocity); and you may be all the more prone to help someone if you know that she would help others if they needed it, even if they are other persons than yourself (a reverse putative reciprocity).

13.3.3.4. Justice Another reasoning invites you to take an objective view. That is, rather than imagining yourself in the place of a person who needs help, you imagine yourself in the place of what classical thought calls the "impartial spectator" (you take what the philosopher Thomas Nagel calls the "view from nowhere"). Then, if you consider what is relevantly good for people, which implies a solution to the question of sharing between them, your view refers to a notion of justice. It may demand that you transfer something from your holdings to some other person, or that you help her. This is a main conception in Adam Smith's *Theory of Moral Sentiments*. A priori, any conception or principle of justice can lead to the conclusion that you ought to give to someone else or help her.[58] In particular, the general respect of basic rights (or "social

---

[57] Balance reciprocity a priori focusses on the gift or help, but it can be the gift given the need of the receiver (or the means of the giver).
[58] The literature about the concepts or principles of justice is very large. General analytical surveys are provided in Kolm 1996a and in Part 5 of Kolm 2004.

freedom") induces you to respect the security and the properly acquired property of other people. Such a general principle and its consequence for the overall distribution of resources constitutes the "macrojustice" part of the general realization of justice in society. Social freedom, Pareto efficiency, and the relevant facts, imply that this overall distributive justice demands that you hand out to the other people the excess of your wage for a given labour over the average wage for this labour in society (each individual being endowed with her proper given productivity), or give to each other person the product of a given labour of yours, these notional "distribution labours" depending on the degree in which the society in question constitutes a community.[59] Other principles and criteria in "microjustice" (and "mesojustice") can demand gifts and help from you.

Following this aspect of Smith's thought, John Stuart Mill sees, in the conception of the impartial spectator, the only reason for altruism. However, being also strongly influenced by Jeremy Bentham, he considers more specifically that this impartial spectator is a moral utilitarian maximizing a sum of individual utilities (which cannot be accepted in its classical presentation of a universal principle adding utilities, for reasons that refer to meaning, logic, and also morals).[60] Yet, one may find interest in the notion of an impartial spectator practicing empathy with every individual at once, and hence aggregating their various interests or values and balancing among them when scarcities or logic require it, within her own psychology, feelings, emotions, and judgments.

There have been attempts to give more precision to the concept of the impartial spectator and to the interindividual synthesizing and aggregating operation it implies. You may, for instance, imagine that you are in the situation of each individual successively for the same duration, or that you incur the risk of becoming each individual with the same probability – these reasonings are *moral time-sharing* and *moral risk*, respectively.[61] However, even if you consider that "being" a particular individual implies this fact in all respects (including all aspects of the person, notably her tastes and preferences), the overall view still depends on the observer for two reasons: (1) individuals have various preferences about "being" various persons (people who fancy glory dream that they are Napoleon, while altruistic people wish they were Mother Theresa); (2) people have different risk-aversion or preferences about variability in time (for the theories of moral risk and moral time-sharing, respectively). These points have been missed by John Harsanyi in his moral-risk theory of the "original position". That is, because of these two aspects of individual preferences, there is one specific original position for each individual. Then, a consistent solution consists of considering these original positions for each of the actual individuals, and then, similarly, the original positions of these original positions, and so on recursively in a process of infinite regress which is con-

---

[59] See Kolm 2004. In the first formulation, people less productive than average receive an analogous subsidy.
[60] See Kolm 1996a, Chapter 14.
[61] The notions presented in this paragraph are fully developed in Kolm 2004, Chapter 21.

verging.[62] However, the very reduction of a choice of justice to a self-interested choice in uncertainty is problematic because the individual is responsible for her evaluation of the risks she takes, whereas a choice of justice is accountable towards morals or society.

Another family of classical theories of social ethics or justice consists of the theories of the social contract. A social contract is an imaginary, hypothetical, and putative agreement among people, whose result is taken as the social ethical principle to be implemented. Many instances of applications can be found. In fact, John Rawls (1971) presented his theory of the original position as a theory of the social contract – although he sees people in the original position as having the same preferred choice of principles of justice, and hence their agreement is not one with exchange and compromise. We will also see how a theory of the "liberal social contract" can determine the various individual contributions in a joint giving (Section 16.6).

Yet, one of the most important instances of normative putative exchanges nowadays is that of *fundamental insurance*. When people differ by characteristics that are given to them, one can imagine that, at a hypothetical and notional time "before" these characteristics are attributed to them, they agreed about a mutual insurance against the risk of finding oneself with such characteristics of poor quality and their consequences. Then, the implementation of this insurance constitutes transfers which compensate more or less for this poor situation and for the inequality, and it provides a rationale for these compensatory transfers. These characteristics can for instance be earning capacities influenced by natural endowments and by family influence notably on education, or having a natural poor health. The role of individual choices in uncertainty in the putative insurance agreement raises the same problem as that noted earlier. However, if actual individuals unanimously agree with such a theory, this justifies it. Moreover, there can be, about these items, sentiments of putative reciprocity, which become *fundamental reciprocity*; the outcome would be rather similar, but there is no (hypothetical) selfish choice in uncertainty any longer. In these cases, people who pay for helping others agree, in the end, with this transfer.

A notable example concerns health insurance in Europe. This insurance is public, and a practically unanimous opinion rejects its privatization with the argument: "with private insurance, people who have a higher propensity to be sick will pay higher premia or receive lower coverage for given premia; now it is already bad that they have a poor health, and in addition they would have to pay more, or they would receive less care whereas they need more". The compensation for given health handicaps comes under the heading of insurance because it is associated with the standard insurance against health risk. In particular, the people with a lower propensity to be sick endorse this

---

[62] However, the result is no longer a utilitarian-like sum of individual utilities. Now this theory of the impartial spectator of Harsanyi is commonly taken to be the central justification of a utilitarian form (although the added utilities are the risk-relevant von Neumann–Morgenstern ones rather than those that could represent happiness as classical utilitarianism has it). That is, the idea was in fact that Harsanyi had established an impartial spectator who should be utilitarian as assumed by John Stuart Mill, and in this way had vindicated utilitarianism. Hence the foregoing remarks have a major importance in the history of economic and philosophical thought.

reasoning, and therefore their corresponding extra payment is in fact a gift. The amounts of transfers in question are very important.

Fundamental insurance results in joint giving to the people in need, but it avoids the pitfalls of both insurance – the "moral hazard" – and of joint giving – free riding and mutual crowding out. Moral hazard does not occur because the (notionally) insured fact is in reality a priori given and does not depend of the agent's acts. The difficulty of joint giving does not occur because the relevant variables are the transfers from each giver to each receiver supposedly implementing the insurance contract between them, rather than the receiver's overall welfare (each contract takes account of the simultaneous contracts with other people when they are – notionally – agreed upon). Yet, for issues covering a large population, questions of information and practicality lead to a public implementation.

13.3.3.5. Universalization The imagined actions can also be those of other people only. For example, people contribute to the support of causes when their own action makes no practical difference because they are small in a large number. When asked why they do it nevertheless, a common answer is "what if nobody contributed?" The same answer is the most common one when people are asked why they care to vote in a large election given that their vote makes no actual difference – a most important issue since without vote, de facto there is no democracy. These conducts obey the moral injunction: "you should act as if everybody acted similarly". This is individually illogical or irrational if the other people do not act in this way. This conduct becomes rational only if all people follow the moral injunction and this leads them to the same act – then, the assumption becomes true. Hence, this principle has a kind of social rationality. An obvious application is to the voluntary provision of public goods, where this "universalization principle" can check free riding. This applies in particular to joint giving. Another application is the general respect of the rights of other people and general sociality. Of course, Immanuel Kant hypostasiated this common and spontaneous principle into his "categorical imperative": "act in such a way that you can want the maxim of your action to become a universally followed principle" (it is not the place, here, to discuss the specificities of this formulation).

14. Altruism and justice; impartial altruism

14.1. Altruism and justice

If you come from a family with several children, you probably discovered the pinch of unfairness and the peace of fairness in your mother's benevolence towards you and your siblings. More broadly, parents' altruism providing bequests and education is the main source of inequality in society. It is the very essence of inequality of opportunity. And education is a main factor of earnings. Moreover, the situation of elderly people depends much on the care and support of their children. Therefore, family altruism is an essential cause of injustice as tangible inequality. However, these results are perfectly just from the point of view of another social ethical conception that defends the legitimacy of free transfers and of their consequences, since gifts are such transfers, along with free exchanges. These are the two basic and opposed principles of justice in our societies. Their judgments about family altruism are thoroughly opposed. On the contrary, the other main application of altruism, charity, miraculously reconciles the two enemy conceptions of justice: it alleviates poverty, satisfies basic needs, and diminishes the inequality between the giver and the receiver, and it is a free transfer. The conflicts can be moral and normative: you should help you nephew from normative community altruism, and yet condemn nepotism from impartial universal justice.

The scarcity of desired items – the subject matter of economics – and the resulting opposition of the self-interest of individuals, are the reason for both altruism and giving on the one hand, and questions of distributive justice or fairness on the other. The two issues are therefore intrinsically interfering and closely related. Your gifts, or their absence, influence the distribution in society and hence its fairness. This also holds for any other influence of your altruism on the distribution (e.g., through public actions, such as in implementing joint giving or resulting from the political process). Distribution is affected by your sharing your gift or your benevolence between two people, or by your giving to some and not to others. The simple fact of your giving affects the distribution between yourself and the beneficiary. Symmetrically, an opinion about justice in society implies a favourable concern about what is good for other people, which is an altruism.

The issue of justice refers to social ethics and therefore belongs to morals, as moral normative altruism does. There are, however, a number of rules of fairness that belong, rather, to social norms, as social normative altruism does. Moreover, emotions are raised both by indignation against injustice and by the causes of hedonistic or natural altruism, and the former can be among the strongest. Finally, empathy, a cause of altruism, and impartiality, a necessary property of principles of justice, have close relations. The psychological conditions of the application of the logical rule of impartiality require at least some capacity for empathy, and empathy is in itself a kind of impartiality or at least a step in this direction.

Altruism and justice or fairness are the two types of non-egoistic and non-instrumental judgments about the allocation of goods in society, the topic of economics (an instrumental judgment can for instance value the distribution for its effect on national output valued for a reason of national power). Each of these judgments can influence this distribution, by gifts for altruism, and, for justice, notably by coercive public actions of transfers or of defence of property. Hence, the judgments of each type judge the effects of the judgments of the other type. Conceptions of justice can blame family gifts because they promote inequality, or accept them as free acts, as we have seen; and they can praise charity because it satisfies needs or reduces inequality, or accept it because it is a free act. Family altruism can judge forced transfers affecting relatives or gifts to them as egoism does, whereas pity can approve of redistributive justice that alleviates misery – whether this is the aim of this policy or whether this only intends to diminish inequality. The means of the implementation of the two types of judgments – altruism and justice – are essentially opposed to each other about the essential issue of freedom, since gifts are free by definition, whereas distributive transfers and the enforcement of rights constitute constraints. However, the relations are more varied even in this respect only, since protecting a right to do something or a right acquired by free exchange or action is also protecting freedom, a sense of justice can motivate some benevolent acts or gifts, altruism can lead to some spontaneous respect of rights, and joint giving often has to take the form of forced transfers.

In spite of their differences and oppositions, altruism and judgments of justice require each other. Indeed, a sense of fairness or justice towards persons implies caring about something which is assumed to be favourable for them (according to some conception), that is, it implies altruism. Note that claiming justice or fairness for oneself is not an exception to this conclusion. Indeed, justice has to be impartial, as we will see, hence it can only be justified by "objective" properties – rather than because you are the beneficiary –, and therefore it applies also to anyone in the same relevant situation (even if, in a given case, you happen to be the only person to which it applies).

Conversely, altruism does not a priori require or imply considerations of fairness or justice, but it is closely associated with them. One type of altruism results from some sense of justice, "impartial altruism" considered in the next section (and, historically, all of justice has been considered as a moral altruism, as we shall recall). For the rest, altruism per se does not require considerations of justice. In particular, everyone can a priori love everyone and wish her good without limit (except concerning limited cognitive and affective capacities for attention to others or affection). However, when altruism translates into giving, it meets the constraints of the actual allocation. The most common case concerns scarcities when someone wants to give to several others. Yet, there also exists, for instance within families and between friends, cases of excess of generosity where each wants to give to the other more than she receives from her. In the latter case, the solution necessarily belongs to the field of fairness because it resolves an opposition between opposite desires. In the other case of a giver who gives to several people, a priori the choice could be seen as proceeding from ordinary preferences or tastes of the giver concerning the set of beneficiaries. However, since the altruistic giver cares about what she deems to be relevantly good for the receivers and there is a conflict in this respect, the choice falls by definition in the domain of distributive justice or fairness. For instance, a mother does not only allocate her love, care, and other means among her children in equating marginal love. She importantly cares about rules of fairness, as is demanded by the children themselves – and would it only be for avoiding jealousy among them.[63] Generally, when nothing relevant distinguishes beneficiaries, the gift is equally shared, a solution characteristic of the field of justice. In cases where this is not possible or there are strong economies of scale in the benefit, and the situation is not a part of a continuing relationship, the solution consists of using a chance draw with an equal probability that each person wins – again an egalitarian solution. The incorpora-

---

[63] There is a limit to Victor Hugo's contention that motherly love is a pure public good ("a mother's heart is like a bread that a god partakes and multiplies . . . each has her share and all have the whole").

tion of considerations of justice in altruism also occurs naturally, without the pressure of conflicting choices. For instance, it is remarkable that the concept of justice restricting charity to the "deserving poor" occurred notably in Victorian ethics which wanted transfers to the poor as charity from a sentiment of benevolent pity and certainly not for a reason of distributive justice, since desert is a concept of justice. This case is an example of a remarkable asymmetry between the two polar references of justice, namely need, satisfaction, welfare or happiness, on the one hand, and desert or merit, on the other hand: whereas the former can be the objects of both benevolence and criteria of justice, the latter belong essentially to the field of justice.

Since a sense of justice or fairness requires altruism, such views can be seen as constituting one type of altruism, as we have seen. However, let us make it precise that this concerns the most common type of justice or fairness but not the whole field. This is justice and fairness whose end-value is the good of individuals (some conception of it) – indeed, there can also be justice and fairness for other social entities (firms, regions, countries, and so on), and justice can evaluate the situation of individuals or other entities as they relate to other values taken as ends (e.g., national independence or influence). Hence, there is a common ground for altruism and justice or fairness, which constitutes a rather limited part of altruism and most of justice or fairness. This is the field of justice or fairness which is considered henceforth. Moreover, when a concept of justice favours equality between individual items and each solution with equality is dominated by other possible but unequal states where the item is better for all individuals, altruism endorsing such a concept of justice should certainly lead one to choose a second-best egalitarian solution, which is not so dominated but where the inequality is minimal in some sense.

14.2. Impartial altruism

The characteristic property of justice is its impartiality among individuals for the chosen characteristics of their situation. These characteristics can be of various types. Someone who gives to several other persons can be impartial among them. But if someone considers justice in a society to which she belongs, she has to make abstraction of her own specific place in the evaluated state. Notably, the judgment should consider her own self-interest and the interests of people she favours because of their particular relation to her (kin, friends, members of specific groups to which she belongs) or because of characteristics she likes and are irrelevant to the conception of justice in question, as if they were the interests of anybody else. Hence, a main difference between altruism and justice is one of viewpoint: the person caring for others is *ego* in the case of altruism and some imagined external observer in the case of justice. Presenting a judgment of justice implies taking the observer's viewpoint. Hence, people can a priori agree about such a view, whereas self-interest and self-centred favouritism are irremediably opposed in questions of distribution. A judgment of justice is that of an altruistic external observer. In this sense, one can say that *justice is the altruism of society*. The philosopher Thomas Nagel calls this perspective the "view from nowhere". Yet, the classical image is the "impartial spectator" of Hume, Hutcheson, Adam Smith, and others. In this respect, justice is opposed to both individual altruism and egoism, since they are views of society by a specific individual, for favouring others in one case and caring for oneself only in the other – malevolence, mischievousness and sadism equally belong to this category. Justice becomes individual altruism solely when specific individuals take this viewpoint in their moral judgments, either in times when they are morally minded, or in association or compromises with a specific valuation of their self-interest, of their favouritism, or of other kinds of altruism. Adam Smith describes this internalization of the point of view of justice as an empathy for the impartial spectator or as "having an impartial spectator in one's breast". However, the property of impartiality does not suffice for determining the judgment. There remains the choice of the relevant individual items, and the structure of the judgment in addition to its impartiality (this structure shows, notably, when the actual constraints on the distributional choice prevent reaching the relevant equality and forces one to resort to a second-best allocation in this sense). That is, there are a priori several possible impartial spectators, and a particular conception of justice chooses a specific one. A spectator is "nowhere" but she still has a specific view.

Denote again as x_i a set of relevant parameters describing the situation of individual i, $x_{-i} = \{x_j\}u_{j \neq i}$ the set of x_j for all individuals $j \neq i$, $x = \{x_j\} = (x_i, x_{-i})$ the set of x_j for all individuals, and u_i an ordinal utility function of individual i. If individual i is egoistic, $u_i = u_i(x_i)$. If she is altruistic in the usual sense, $u_i = u_i(x_i, x_{-i})$ where u_i increases when the x_j of some individuals $j \neq i$ improve according to some conception. Note that Auguste Comte, who introduced the terms altruist and altruism, meant by it $u_i(x_{-i})$, that is, the individual's full devotion to others. He forgot that Saint Martin gave only one half of his coat to the poor in the cold, not all of it. This equality seems to result from impartiality. Consider, therefore, an impartial judgment expressing a conception of justice. Choose parameters x_i that permit its representation. These parameters may have to include commodities, individuals' welfare w_i, the larger satisfaction or happiness of the individuals (see the discussion in Section 3, and this u_i may therefore in fact be the v_i of this section), descriptions of needs, freedoms or rights of the individuals, and relations to their previous acts for describing merit or deservingness. As a result, some of the considered utility functions are, or are in part, classical (Roy) indirect utility functions when the relevant characteristics include means of individuals choices and actions. Assume that this impartial judgment can compare the states of society and say if one is preferable to the other from its point of view (or if they are equivalent in this respect), in leading to a corresponding ordering of these states representable by an ordinal function $s(x)$. This function can be seen as the "utility function" of the impartial spectator. Impartiality is described by the fact that function $s(x)$ is symmetrical in the relevant parameters of the x_i (i.e., its value does not change when these sets of relevant parameters are permuted among the individuals). This moral evaluation or evaluator is better seen as benevolent, that is, the value of s increases when a x_i becomes better according to the retained conception. Orderings of justice are often not representable by such maximand functions because they include priorities. Yet, any such ordering can be approximated as closely as one wants by such a function. Moreover, the approximation is often actually the priority rather than the function, because some degree of compromise is often admitted, even if it is a very limited one.

Then, the choice of justice maximizes $s(x)$ over possible x. For instance, Saint Martin's utility function would be $s(x)$, or $u_i[s(x)]$, where x_j is the surface of cloth allocated to individual j. It is not even $u_i[x_i, s(x)]$ where u_i increases with s, probably because he is a saint (or, rather, he was declared one for this reason).[64] More ordinary people can have such utility functions $u_i[(x_i, s(x)]$. This is a particular case of altruism that can be called *impartial altruism*. Adam Smith proposes that individual i "empathizes" the view of the impartial spectator, or that function s is, in some sense, "in the breast" of function u_i. John Stuart Mill thinks that altruism is only impartial altruism (although he also urged Comte to distinguish benevolence from concern for justice). Note that impartial altruism cannot be the Comte altruism noted earlier.

However, there are several possible conceptions of justice. In the foregoing representation, they differ from one another about two aspects: the choice of the relevant parameters in x_i and the structure of function $s(x)$. Individual i can choose one of these conceptions, represented by the particular function $s_i(x)$, and her utility function becomes $u_i[x_i, s_i(x)]$. Then, individuals can be opposed about the allocation of goods, and about their conceptions of justice.

A classical mistake met in the history of thought is the – implicit – belief that impartiality suffices for determining the principle of justice or fairness. Even Adam Smith seems not to have avoided this pitfall. Yet, it appears most clearly with John Stuart Mill because he added, to the impartial spectator inherited from Adam Smith, Bentham's influence which convinced him that social ethics – of which justice is an aspect – is the utilitarian highest sum of individual utilities. His impartial spectator was therefore a utilitarian, and she chooses $s(x) = \sum w_i$ or $\sum u_i$ (see Section 3). The impartiality is described by Bentham's famous redundant dictum: "each is to count for one and nobody is to count for more than one". Of course, Mill also advocated social freedom – a different conception of justice – and he could not derive it from utilitarianism. If utilities or welfare indexes are so added, then function u_i can have a linear form, say, with w_i for simplicity (see Section 3) and with numbers $\alpha_i > 0$ and $\beta_i > 0$, $u_i = \alpha_i w_i + \beta_i \sum w_j = w_i + \beta_i \sum u_{j \neq i} w_j$ if one takes $\alpha_i + \beta_i = 1$. With only two individuals, this is the form used by Edgeworth (1881). Yet, with a larger number of individuals, this differs from a linear form of Pareto's utility $u_i = w_i + \sum_{j \neq i} a_{ij} w_j$ because the a_{ij} can differ for different j. The difference results from the fact that the altruism in question is a form of impartial altruism, which is not a priori Pareto's assumption. For instance, you can particularly favour your kin over other people with Pareto's form but not with the other form. Yet, both types of altruism can jointly coexist with a utility function of the form $u_i = u_i[x_i, x_{-i}, s_i(x)]$.

---

[64] Did the pope who declared him a saint know the truth, namely that Martin was in fact a Comte altruist – and hence still more a saint – since half his coat is all he could give because officers of the Roman army owned only half of their equipment, the other half belonging to the Emperor? Only this structure of property rights prevented Martin from becoming not only a saint but also a martyr.

However, as we have remarked, both John Stuart Mill and Léon Walras (not a utilitarian) considered that individuals are both egoistic and moral, yet not in the noted synthetic form of a compromise, but in being either one or the other according to the moment. They would be moral in their moments of calm and reflection. This sequencing of individuals' states of mind have doubtlessly some realism, although the adoption of impartial constitutions, or self-sacrifice for saving someone or for a public cause, happen more often in times of collective or individual excitement. Then, people can get out of their everyday self. They can in particular join some non-self-centred "group mind".

14.3. History

The relations between justice and altruism are put to the forefront by a historical transformation of the nature of the concept of justice in Western thought. Justice is for us a property of a state of society, whereas it used to be a property of actions towards others and of their actors, and, in fact, a type of altruism. In Antiquity, for instance in the perceptive analyses of Plato (*The Laws*) and Aristotle (*Nicomachean Ethics* and *Eudemian ethics*), justice is a virtue of people who practice it. In contrast, but with this history in mind, John Rawls calls justice "the virtue of institutions". The ancient meaning lasted for a long time. For instance, Adam Smith in *The Theory of Moral Sentiments* sees justice as a virtue. It is, for him, motivated by the "impartial spectator" who rests "in the breast" of each of us. This impartiality leads to seeing oneself as any other of one's fellow human beings. This leads one to want the good of other persons as one wants one's own self-interest, and hence, possibly, to act favourably towards others. It thus is an altruism. This is complementary to empathy where you imagine your feelings if you were in the place of the other person. It could indeed result from sufficient empathy practiced equally towards all others. The impartial spectator can also in fact be imagined as a person specialist in the exercise of multi-empathy, that is, of empathizing the feelings of all people simultaneously and with the same care. Then, your empathy of such an imagined external impartial spectator produces your sentiment of impartial altruism. We have seen how John Stuart Mill, influenced by Bentham, gives a utilitarian form to this conception. This impartial altruism can lead one to give. Yet, it does not lead one to give enough according to Auguste Comte who – as we have seen – introduced the term altruism as meaning self-sacrifice giving priority to others, hence as the full opposite of egoism, rather than as only favouring balanced equity (and who, incidentally, happened to be seeking Mill's financial support).[65]

---

[65] A remnant of the ancient meaning of the concept of justice is found in Roman languages with the rare use of the term "a just" for denoting a person endowed with this virtue. Note that the above historical remarks have focussed on Western thought. In many other thoughts, the concept of justice as we understand it is altogether inexistent – and yet these people survive. There are, of course, norms of fairness or local justice for sharing chores or crops – say –, and occasional applications of the rationality of equality, but no general conception of the property of justice as we understand it. Social rules can take this place in communitarian ethics. In the very few other systems, the place of the concept of justice is occupied by a virtue in the family of altruism, for instance compassion in Buddhism.

14.4. Altruism and justice: Consistency or conflict, force or freedom

These numerous close relations between altruism and justice on the grounds of logic, psychology and history contrast with the immediate evidence of a strong opposition concerning their realization. Indeed, giving is by definition a free act, whereas conceptions of justice are largely implemented by public coercion (even though some of them inspire some individual private actions). The interest of a person induces her to want more for herself. Her benevolence induces her to be ready to pay something for some other person having something. Her sense of justice can induce her, in addition, to favour transfers from some other person to another one. Hence, both altruism and a sense of justice constitute externalities in preferences, which can induce interferences with other people, but the latter only can a priori imply constraints – including that of simply protecting rights (constraints for implementing joint giving are something else). However, judgments of benevolent justice value the interests of individuals, even of those they want to constrain – for instance, they can recommend a transfer from some person to another while favouring an improvement in the former's situation if it costs nothing (preferring a lower endowment of a better endowed, without any gain for someone else, because it reduces an unjust inequality, is most often a perversion of the sense of justice: benevolent justice a priori implies a priority of benevolence over equality). Views of justice would not exist without this concern for the interests of individuals, and in particular of others. Hence, these judgments of justice differ from benevolence, altruism and concern for others, *per se*, but they require them for their existence, they rest on them, and they specify them.

Distributive justice, more generally, draws the line between people's interests. If necessary, it demands transfers of money or goods, or services, from one to the other. At any rate, it opposes people who want to take more than what it deems to be their share – that is, it defines theft. This a priori requires the coercion of the persons who want more or who want to yield nothing or less than justly demanded. Yet, in a "state of law", coercion of adults is a monopoly of the public sector. This sector is therefore in charge of this very important part of the implementation of justice. Its actions are determined by the political and institutional setting.

Justice is realized without coercion, hence by voluntary gifts or respect, only when its demand coincides with the free choice of the relevant agents. This happens when the principle of justice endorses the agents' free choices in question, when agents endorse this principle as a value inspiring their individual conduct, or when a different motive leads nevertheless to an act favoured by the principle.

The former case is that of "process-liberal" justice which values "social freedom". This ethic states that the agents are fully free, except, necessarily, to violate the freedom of others, that is, to interfere forcefully with them – hence, it amounts to freedom from forceful interference. Exchanges and giving are the two kinds of transfers that respect this rule.

However, these two kinds are also often distinguished by judgments about justice because giving affects the distribution of the value of wealth in society – contrary, a priori, to exchange – and there may be a value of justice other than process-liberalism concerned with this aspect. Then, giving constitutes a private interference with this public issue, as in the cases of intra-family and charity transfers discussed above. The freedom of the giver may oppose the distributive justice of the outcome. However, the coincidence is kept when the gift improves the justice of the resulting distribution as it is conceived. This is frequent when helping the poor and needy, which may both alleviate suffering and reduce inequality. Yet, the levels of transfers chosen by the giver and favoured by the principle of justice may not a priori be the same, and the tax regime of donations is often used to try to make them closer to one another. In particular, both effects of satisfying needs and reducing inequality can motivate both private giving and a public value, but the mix of motives may differ, with a gift motivated mainly by compassion and a public value leaving a larger place for the reduction of inequality.

In other cases, people freely apply rules of fairness that are seen as properly left to their choice and not interfering with overall values of justice. This often occurs when there are mutual gifts or favours, hence with little overall impact on the overall distribution. For instance, the return gifts of balance-reciprocity are often more or less motivated by a consideration of egalitarian fairness. This category also includes rules of fairness adopted to conclude an agreement (for instance an equal split of a difference is the simplest case). People also often choose, accept, or settle for a "fair price" (the history of the concept of the "just price" could be recalled here). They sometimes prefer a fair deal to a good deal.

The distributive effects of public policy result from three issues, each of which has a relation with altruism. (1) The political fight between groups of persons defending their interests and those of the persons they like or think they should support. (2) The implementation of principles of justice, which also results from conflicts between the alternative principles and their supporters. These ethical – or ideological – conflicts parallel those among interests, but they do not coincide with them, because people are not fully pharisians (as proved by the very existence of pharisianism which assumes that moral reasons have an influence), and because the means are very different – they are threats for conflicts of interest and arguments for ethical debates. (3) The implementation of joint giving with the appropriate distribution of the contributions (see Section 7). Joint giving is unanimously desired, by definition, although each individual contribution may have to be imposed, and givers' interests are opposed in the choice of their contribution (Section 16.6 will take up this question).

In contrast, individuals' interests are opposed in the application of a distributive policy. Even if the policy focuses on some aid, someone has to pay the tax financing it. This policy may be the political outcome of the conflict of interests. However, it is always presented as the application of reasons concerning justice, and the very insistence on this justification proves that ethical arguments have at least some influence. In fact, people are not uncommonly "of two minds" in admitting that "there is something" in a rule that they oppose on any ground. No one is thoroughly devoid of some "impartial spectator" sleeping "in her breast". Ideally, politics should be the social process inducing the manifestation of people's inner "spectator", the argumented dialogue of their ethics, and hence the synthesis of syntheses of interests rather than their conflict. This shows once more the perceptive relevance of Rousseau's aphorism that "politics and morals cannot be separated, and he who wants to study them separately is bound to misunderstand both". In fact, this best part of politics commonly comes from a large acceptance of the rule of the political process, a large agreement at the constitutional level. Now each such free acceptation, full or partial, direct or indirect, of a rule, principle, or policy that does not fully coincide with one's interest implies the corresponding moral altruism.

15. Giving: An abundance and variety of motives and reasons

15.1. An overview

Giving is voluntarily favouring someone else or a public cause at a cost for oneself without requiring a counterpart. It occurs when the giver's desire for it overcompensates the cost (and when it is accepted, when this is relevant). This desire results from one or several motives among a large number of different possible ones. Any analysis of giving for explaining, forecasting, or evaluating, crucially rests on understanding and distinguishing these motives. Observation shows that the motives for giving are both very numerous and very varied in many respects. A simple taxonomy of types of motives shows at least fifty of them, and this is not the most detailed distinction, by far. However, they group together in various categories, and, to begin with, into a few broad ones.

The first distinction is probably between *altruistic* giving motivated by altruistic sentiments of the giver and giving from other motives. The twelve broad types of altruistic motives have been presented in Section 13. Each motive leads to giving to or helping particular beneficiaries in particular circumstances.

In *natural* or *hedonistic altruism*, affection leads to giving in the family. Sympathy elicits giving to friends and acquaintances. Empathy and emotional contagion lead to helping in general, but particularly people in need or pain, and they are favoured by closeness. Compassion and pity focus on need and suffering in general.

Normative altruism has four main dimensions of application: the relief of the *needs and suffering of other persons*, a part of *justice and fairness*, giving to people in *close social proximity* with the giver, and *general benevolence*. In particular, all types of normative altruism can induce helping people in need or who suffer. Moral altruism supports pity and compassion. Intuitively moral and social altruisms lead one to give to people with whom one has particular relations, as in the family or in solidarity between members of the same communities of various types. They also sometimes lead to giving to particular people in the society, distinguished by a special status, in following a tradition. Finally, all types of normative altruism favour certain principles of justice or fairness, which can lead to private giving and to demanding or accepting public actions. For all types, these principles can lead to providing various kinds of rewards of merit or desert, and of relief of needs. Rational altruism emphasizes impartiality and equality.

The other types can value rules provided by tradition. In the end, moral altruisms can make giving a duty.

The other motives for giving, leading to non-altruistic giving, can be classified into three main categories focussing respectively on the *social effects* of the gift, on *normative non-altruistic giving*, and on *self-interest* more strictly conceived. Social effects can themselves be divided into the three categories of the *opinion* of other people, the resulting *social situation* of the giver and sometimes of the receiver, and questions of *social relations*. Giving is also sometimes a norm or value without full altruism of the giver, yet which she can feel as moral or simply social, as a duty or as proper action, and which can induce praise (or blame) by the giver herself or by other people. This latter effect is an aspect of social opinion. Such giving can also reduce to tradition or habit. Finally, giving can favour the giver's self-interest in various ways, through indirect effects of various types – either economic through markets or otherwise social (for instance political) –, in inducing a return gift or maintaining a sequential exchange, in inducing a reward, or in inducing or maintaining a social situation or status that provide some tangible advantage. If these benefits are the sole motive, an essential dimension of giving is absent, but these benefits can also be associated with other motives.

Table 1 of Section 13, in presenting the various types of altruism, has also presented the various types of altruistic giving. Table 3 completes Table 1 in summarizing the types of giving in the other categories.

15.2. Social effects

15.2.1. Opinion

The *social effects* of giving that induce it concern *opinion*, *situation*, and *relation*.

When you give something to someone, or help her, this has two kinds of effects. You improve the situation of this person, and this is a priori appreciated by her and by people who are altruistic towards her, including possibly yourself (with the effects of possible paternalistic altruism). This is what is described in Section 3. The people who so value the situation of the beneficiary value *ipso facto* indirectly your action because of this effect. However, this action is also bound to arouse other sentiments and judgements in them: praise, approval, or esteem; gratitude in the case of the beneficiary and people who are strongly altruistic towards her; possibly liking; and avoidance of disapproval, blame, criticism, or contempt, when the gift or help was expected. These judgments and sentiments have as object the giver – yourself. They are often appreciated by the giver, and this may be a motive for giving. This motive can be at work even when you are not altruistic towards the beneficiary. It may induce giving by itself or in association with any other motive.

A priori, these judgments and sentiments are attached to the gift in itself and directly, rather than to its effect on the situation of the beneficiary and in addition to the possible direct evaluation of this effect, even though they require the existence of this effect for the beneficiary (or, alternatively, the intention to produce this benefit), and even though

Table 3
Motives for non-altruistic giving

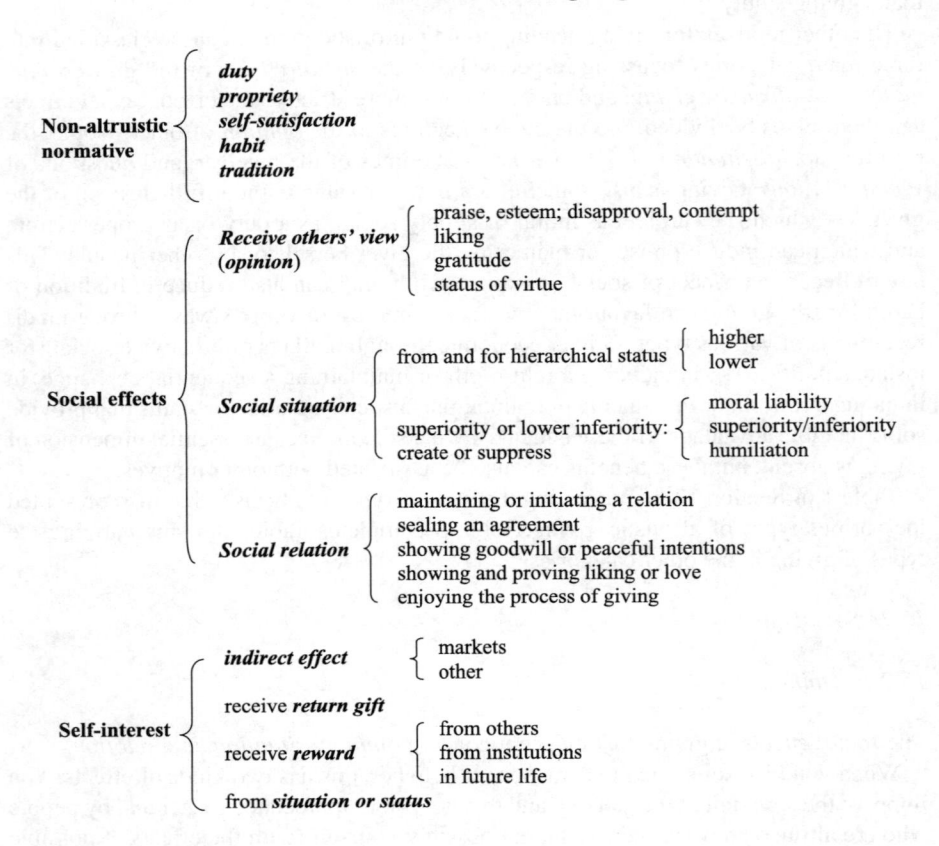

- **Non-altruistic normative**
  - *duty*
  - *propriety*
  - *self-satisfaction*
  - *habit*
  - *tradition*

- **Social effects**
  - *Receive others' view* (*opinion*)
    - praise, esteem; disapproval, contempt
    - liking
    - gratitude
    - status of virtue
  - *Social situation*
    - from and for hierarchical status
      - higher
      - lower
    - superiority or lower inferiority: create or suppress
      - moral liability
      - superiority/inferiority
      - humiliation
  - *Social relation*
    - maintaining or initiating a relation
    - sealing an agreement
    - showing goodwill or peaceful intentions
    - showing and proving liking or love
    - enjoying the process of giving

- **Self-interest**
  - *indirect effect*
    - markets
    - other
  - receive *return gift*
  - receive *reward*
    - from others
    - from institutions
    - in future life
  - from *situation or status*

this evaluation of the gift and the giving is bound to depend on this benefit. Hence, your appreciation of these judgments and sentiments also depends on these items, and so is your resulting incentive to give. We have seen in Section 7 how important this issue is in the widespread case of joint giving. The main reason for this structure of these judgments and sentiments is that they appreciate that you took the decision to give, and hence that you are responsible for the gift or help. This structure also generally results, in addition, from an appreciation of the cost you incur (in considering the items relevant for appreciating this cost). These judgments are something else than a possible appreciation of the fact that you are an altruist towards the beneficiary. They may also depend on other items, such as, by comparison, gifts by other people or other gifts of yours, or a social norm.

In fact, the approval, non-disapproval, or esteem may not be judgements of specific individuals, but of a general abstract social opinion that you imagine.

These judgments about the giver by altruists are those that lead to the separation between the act of giving or helping and the altruistic evaluator discussed in Section 13.3.2, with the conclusion that they can make society as a whole more altruistic than its members are. Note that the praise aims at the gift or aid in itself, but that it is motivated by an altruistic concern for the beneficiary's situation.

15.2.2. Situation

These judgments can provide the giver with a social status, and existing statuses may demand giving. Thus, you may give to acquire or maintain a status. This aspect acquires a particular dimension when the receiver enters into the consideration of statuses, and relative status is emphasized. Giving and receiving are then often important with respect to the relative *social situations* of the giver and of the receiver. However, it is remarkable that such givings may be from the person of higher status to the person of lower status, or the reverse. Giving to a superior can manifest submission or confirm its acceptance. It can also be a reward for benevolence, or in fact a price for protection. Yet, it sometimes also is de facto extortion under threat, disguised in the more amiable relationship of giving (and the superior may indeed protect this source of revenue from external threats). However, giving is also often from the superior, as a proof or manifestation of superiority, and its acceptance can be an acknowledgement of this status; it can then be a display of generosity, possibly creating a moral indebtedness, or just in fact a reward for inducing obedience.

In all kinds of encounters, giving can aim at creating a social superiority over the receiver or over other people, or at erasing or diminishing a similar inferiority. It can create moral indebtedness of the receiver, or, on the contrary, erase or diminish a pending moral debt. Giving also sometimes aims at creating and displaying an advantage in the comparison of the quality of the persons: the giver appears to be generous and disinterested, while in contrast the receiver may seem self-interested and greedy. As we have noted, the aim can even be to humiliate the receiver (for instance in suggesting that she is incapable of catering for her needs or for those of her family).

All aspects of social situation and status can be judged by the giver, by the receiver, and by other people, and the giver is often sensitive to the corresponding social opinion. The anonymity, or its absence, of the giver, the receiver, and the relation between them, can thus be an important factor.

15.2.3. Relation

Finally, as emphasized earlier (Section 9.9), the very nature of giving as a voluntary sacrifice for the good of the other person gives it a crucial function of information and demonstration, inducing its widespread role for establishing or maintaining a relationship, in showing and proving goodwill, peaceful intentions, liking, or love, in sealing an agreement, and so on. In fact the simple pleasure of the social relation of the process of giving is a motive in a number of cases, and occasionally the only one.

15.3. Intrinsically normative (non-altruistic) giving

People often feel they have to give without much consideration of the situation of the beneficiary. The gift should be useful, but the focus of intention is on the giving rather than on the relief or benefit. This is not altruism since the motive is not an altruistic intention. This motive is in the nature of a mental obligation or valuation, with various possible intensities. It can be a duty or other social norm, rule, value or injunction, and it can degenerate into a habit or a benign tradition. This motive for giving is normative and deontic, and not consequentialist (as are, for instance, altruism or the desire to have some social effect).[66] Hence, as for all motives of this kind, describing it by a utility function is awkward, although possible in describing "the satisfaction of following the norm" or the dissatisfaction of failing to do so – this permits one to take account of the sentiment about more or less following a norm. This motive is not moral in the sense of moral altruism, and yet some other sentiment of moral value, norm, or duty can be attached to an act of giving in itself. The motive may be felt as a social norm or value or not. It can be conceived of as essentially personal. But it can also be seen as a social norm or value, and, then, it can relate to actual or imagined praise. Finally, this motive is not, in itself, being satisfied of oneself, although this sentiment can accompany it. Seeing such an intrinsically normative giving as valued because it would provide a "warm-glow" is drawing it to a consequentialist intention, which is not its intrinsic nature. Yet, one has also to consider what happens when the agent fails to behave as required. Even if there is no "warm-glow" when she obeys the norm, there may come a "cold-glow" of guilt or shame – and possibly reproof – when she does not.

However, the normative character of such a gift or help implies its approval in itself, or by any people, in particular the actor herself in self-approval and self-esteem, and, possibly, other people whose opinion may count for the giver (who may only imagine their judgement). Others' evaluations may be altruistic or may solely value the respect of the norm in question.

15.4. Self-interested giving

15.4.1. Introduction

Giving can also favour the strict self-interest of the giver, in various ways. These advantages may induce her to give because they overcompensate the cost of the gift, or they can have this effect in being associated with other motives for giving. A most obvious case is that of giving inducing a return gift in a reciprocity. If receiving this benefit is the only motive, giving is an exploitation of the return gift, and the relation is

---

[66] Normative altruism is both deontic and consequentialist. Favouring the good of the other person is consequentialist, but doing this is a moral or social norm or value, a duty or proper feeling or behaviour. This is deontology demanding concern for a consequence.

a "half-reciprocity". Yet, the return gift may come from a third agent (this is a "reverse reciprocity"). A number of authors have pointed out this tendency to give to people who give, from agents other than the receiver, and they often propose that the giver will be better off in the end (René Descartes and Adam Smith are cases in point). One reason for this gift to the giver is to reward her merit. This reward can be from private agents or from institutions, and one cannot avoid noting here the beliefs in a reward in the next life in various religions. The material benefits can also be attached to, or result from, a status acquired thanks to giving, helpfulness, or generosity. Yet, the giver can also receive benefits irrespective of particular specific motives, as a result of various possible indirect effects. These effects can for instance be of an economic, political, or social nature (or a combination of such effects). The consideration of economic effects of this type have a long and famous history, with the debates about the welfare effects of international transfers (the problem of "German compensations" after the first World War). The conditions of the existence of such effects through changes in prices or otherwise have been the object of intensive studies.

15.4.2. Gifts and interests

Self-interested giving may have to be excluded from the category of *genuine* giving characterized by other motivations. This would in particular imply excluding sequential exchange from reciprocities. Yet this conduct exists, and its motives are often mixed in various ways with other, nonselfish motivations. First of all, reciprocity in general is intrinsically such a mixed mode, and people often derive a purely personal and material benefit from the set of transfers, in addition to the other types of sentiments, emotions, and motivations. But there are also specific forms of selfish givings or selfish reciprocities (possibly more appropriately named pseudo-gifts and pseudo-reciprocities). Yet, the term selfish itself can cover various attitudes. "Strict self-interest" will refer to exclusive attachment, in the actions considered, to one's own consumption in the most standard sense ("material" self-interest also expresses this idea but is awkward since one may have to include various "intangible" goods or services, and some "intangible" valued effects of consumption or possession). Yet, a number of "social" interests are in fact also "selfish", such as seeking, as ends in themselves, nonreproof, approval, fame, reputation, good image, others' consideration or respect, domination, status, good relations, friendship, and so on. Of course, the meaning of words oppose selfishness to altruism, and hence it would not be serious to suggest that all gifts would be "selfish" because, being free and voluntary by definition, they are desired by their author, or could be *ipso facto* considered as providing her with satisfaction or even pleasure. This holds for normative altruism – one could speak of the satisfaction of following a norm –, but also for natural or hedonistic altruism although the corresponding giving decidedly makes the giver happier or less unhappy (by the effects of emotional contagion, empathy, affection, or pity). Many reasons can lead to selfish giving of various types, such as the

following ones:
- The gift's effect on some social process favours the giver sufficiently to overcompensate the cost of the gift. This process can be economic, political, made of intra-family relations, etc.
- A gift or a reciprocity can show and prove goodwill and hence permit a relation that is beneficial to the giver, such as a concession to conclude a bargaining, a favour to seal an agreement, a service or a gift to induce trust, and so on.
- The gift can have various informational effects favourable to the giver, such as informing the receiver of a giver's offer (as with gifts of samples), signalling some other action of the giver, or eliciting a reaction that usefully informs the giver.
- In particular, a gift may in fact constitute a demand for establishing a relation of various possible types (personal, commercial, political, and so on), and its value, or the sacrifice it entails for the giver, may indicate the intensity of the desire for this relation (as well as the means and the generosity of the partner).
- A strictly self-interested sequence of two-way gifts can constitute a mutually beneficial sequential exchange.
- A giver may self-interestedly exploit the receiver's return-gift reaction (a "half-reciprocity").
- A giver can receive gifts from third parties motivated by a reverse reciprocity, and a classical moral view is that this will overcompensate the cost of the initial gift.
- A gift can elicit a variety of social opinions and sentiments, or of social statuses, that not only can be favoured in themselves by the giver, but may also entail a number of other advantages.
- And so on.

15.4.3. Giver's benefit from the gift's effect on processes and their outcome

15.4.3.1. The general property A gift a priori influences the processes and interactions in which the giver or the receiver are engaged, and indirectly other processes and interactions, and hence the results of these processes. These effects may be favourable to the giver or unfavourable to the receiver, or both. And it may be that the global, overall effects make gift giving favourable to the giver, and/or unfavourable to the receiver, from the point of view of their own strict self-interest. If the giver gains in the end and is aware of these induced effects and of this consequence, then her strict self-interest induces her to give. By the same token, if the indirect effects lead to an overall decrease of the receiver's welfare, giving is deterred by altruism and induced by malevolence, and the receiver will refuse the gift if she can and if this can prevent the effect (since simple destruction of goods by the would-be giver may suffice for some types of effects). Various cases will differ by the nature of the mechanism influenced by the gift and influencing the welfare of the people concerned. These mechanisms can involve markets of various types, other interactions, public and political or family redistributions (see Section 10.1.2), and so on. A number of discussions that have developed in economics are about instances of this general phenomenon.

15.4.3.2. The "transfer paradox" through effects on prices, markets, or exchange For example, the gift can affect supplies or demands and hence prices, and this can induce the indirect effect. Since resource owners sometimes benefit from a partial destruction of the resource that boosts its price, they also benefit from giving this amount or its product away to a distant country (as the European Community gave butter to Russia for supporting Western European farmers or the US support their farmers in giving away farm products as foreign aid).

Contrary effects of transfers have gained historical fame in the discussion of the "problem of transfers" in international economics, that is, the effects of international transfers on the terms of trade. The first debate concerned a "tribute" rather than a gift, but the logic is the same. In the debates about the effects of the German war compensations after the first world war, it was argued that the transfers could, by their effects on supplies and demands in international markets, alter the terms of trade so as to diminish the actual amount of wealth transferred. Leontief (1936, 1967) then presented a numerical example where this effect is so large that, in the end, the giver is better off and the receiver is worse off. However, this "first Leontief paradox" (as I called it)[67] is exhibited in a competitive market, and Samuelson (1947) suggested that it can only refer to unstable equilibria – hence it could not be observed in real life with competitive markets. However, when there is monopolistic exploitation notably by tariffs (which affect prices of internationally traded goods), the welfare of the exploiting nation always varies in the direction of the transfer, while that of the exploited nation can a priori vary either way (Kolm 1969a, 1970). Yet, when this exploitation is only partial, notably because there are other trading countries, then the giver can again benefit on the whole (id.). This was applied to the analysis of foreign aid. Actually, of course, agents may or may not be aware of such perverse effects through market interaction.

These results concerning this "transfer paradox" and its application to selfish giving apply to any markets. With a Cournot monopolistic domination, the paradox cannot happen for the dominant (price setting) agent but it can for the dominated one who, hence, can have a strict self-interest in giving to the dominant agent. With competitive markets, the relation of the transfer paradox to the instability of equilibria depends on the concept of stability, and standardly vanishes for more than two traders [Chichilnisky (1980, 1983), Brecher and Bhagwati (1981), Jones (1982), Geanakoplos and Heal (1983), Polemarchakis (1983), Bhagwati, Brecher and Hatta (1983), Dixit (1983), Yano (1983), Postlewaite and Webb (1984)]. Balasko (1978) and Safra (1983) consider occurrences of the transfer paradox in the large due to multiple equilibria. Advantageous transfers where both parties gain, with competitive equilibria and more than two traders, are shown by Gale (1974) in an example and by Guesnerie and Laffont (1978) more generally, and by Leonard and Manning (1983). Postlewaite (1979) showed that the paradox

---

[67] The second Leontief paradox (often just called the Leontief paradox) is the finding that the exports of the US were more labor intensive and less capital intensive than their imports.

can occur in any efficient and individually beneficial reallocation scheme, and Sertel (1989, 1990, 1994) exhibited selfish giving in a number of types of interaction.[68]

15.4.3.3. Redistribution Section 10.2 has discussed situations where an aid or a gift benefits more the receiver than it costs the giver, and yet cannot be bought because it is an externality or because this is not done between these agents who are members of the same organization or family, and where a superior agent (government, firm, family head) realizes transfers that overcompensate the giver, specifically or in general distribution.

15.4.3.4. Exploiting the return gift, sequential exchange, reverse reciprocity In many instances, indeed, giving can be favourable to the strict self-interest of the giver in a rather direct way by a reaction of some agent. This reaction may be sufficiently large to overcompensate the cost of the gift. Reactions in the family of reciprocity provide a number of instances of this situation.

An agent may give in order to receive a return gift from the receiver, whatever the motive of this reaction. Many instances of this effect can be observed. For example, in a number of cases employees want to match the pay they receive, or an increase in it, by sufficient work and productivity. This is shown by numerous observations in studies of labour relations (reviewed and used in Kolm 1990) and by classical experiments initiated by Adam (1963, 1965) and Adam and Rosenbaum (1964). This leads employers to exploit this return gift in choosing pay. This is the basis of the noted proposal by Akerlof of an explanation of apparently involuntary unemployment, generalized to other reciprocitarian relations in later studies (Kolm 1990).

The aim of the return gift, however, may be to elicit another gift from the initial giver who may then expect a new return gift. The relation then develops into a sequential exchange. Both parties may be strictly self-interested in this process. This is what Peter Hammond (1975) and Mordechai Kurz (1977, 1978) call "altruism". The motive of the last transfer raises a problem, but sufficient uncertainty about the end of the process or about the other agent suffices to sustain it.[69]

The reward for giving may also be provided by other agents, in a reverse reciprocity. A classical moral assertion is that altruistic giving will be overcompensated by such benefits, leaving the giver with a net advantage in self-interest in the end – the almost identical formulations of this view by René Descartes and Adam Smith have been noted (if this is true, this may be a pity, because this benefit may undermine the intrinsically praiseworthy altruistic motivation in the long run, and if the giving becomes self-interested, the reward may cease to be provided).

---

[68] The transfer paradox (and selfish giving) for competitive equilibria naturally also applies to a situation of "Lindahl equilibrium" with public goods, as it appears in the diagrams in Kolm (1970) for the simplest case of two persons and two goods. But the receiver can reject the gift, an objection that Sertel (1994) waved in considering three agents and a receiver who also gains.

[69] See Basu (1977, 1987), Radner (1980), Smale (1980), Axelrod (1984), Kreps et al. (1982).

15.4.3.5. Reputation, social effects, image, status   Giving often induces a favourable judgment of the giver by other people, which the giver often appreciates in itself, and which can also lead these people to act in ways that provide self-interested and notably material advantages to the giver. This occurs in many forms. Giving can elicit trust and permit a number of desired or profitable actions or interactions. It can provide a status which may entail many advantages of all kinds. It can elicit gratitude or liking from which the giver may derive various side-benefits. Firms give, most often to enhance their public image and have more customers. Politicians give to attract votes.

15.5. Giving in social relations and communities

We have pointed out the essential relational, informational and symbolic role of giving (Section 9.9). Indeed, sacrificing one's interest for the good of someone else – true giving – is a priori a strong social relation. It relates to other social relations and social bonds with influences both ways. Notably, when it results from a relation, it often manifests, actualizes, shows, proves and activates it, and thus makes it exist or last. In particular, giving $x\%$ of one's wealth to someone else can be seen as voluntarily submitting $x\%$ of one's economic self to the disposition of someone else. This is a relation with a priori a strongly integrative nature. In fact, genuine, altruistic giving is closely related to the notion of community, as a privileged relation between members. This is clear for the family and various solidarities, and shown by the fact that the volume of private and public aid or redistribution in larger societies is closely correlated to the prevailing sense of community.

Mankind is no less a set of communities than a collection of individuals, and this fact structures the relations of altruism and giving. Communities include notably, below mankind as a whole, national, cultural, political, labour, local, and kin communities. Each individual relates to the other members of each of the communities she belongs to, and to the community as a whole or its institutions. These relations include altruisms of various kinds, and more or less gift-giving for various motives. These altruisms and giving are induced by the sentiment of common belonging, but they also intrinsically more or less constitute and maintain the community. In particular, various kinds of gifts, support or aid between members or between members and the group manifest the community, prove its existence and effectiveness, and contribute to the existence and duration of this social structure and its institutions.

The various types of altruisms and of reasons for giving, and of communities, have specific relations. Solidarity denotes the potentially mutual aid characteristic of communities in general. Comparative justice, leading to impartial altruism (see Section 14), is defined among members of some narrower or broader community. Pity, compassion, empathy, and emotional contagion require a minimum sentiment of commonness and similarity with the observed person (being another human person should suffice but unfortunately does not always, and some people extend these feelings to some animals). The general altruism noted by Adam Smith, and the a priori respect and common help noted above, manifest the general community of mankind. Aid within communities is commonly demanded by moral altruism, and still more by nonmoral social norms. The intensity of these sentiments, and hence the importance and frequency of the resulting help and giving, correlate with the intensity of the sense of community. This intensity is due to several factors, including culture, interests, tradition, actual closeness, and size. Fiscally implemented joint giving manifests solidarity in the national community. The closest community takes us back to the family and its mutual and reciprocal love and support. The tighter the community, a priori the more intense the altruisms of various kinds and the larger the resulting giving. However, the nature of these motives changes in the comparison, since the tighter the community, the more affection is likely to play a role, and this sentiment tends to check those of pity and compassion, and to make that of moral duty superfluous.

Part III: Values and history

16. The normative economics of altruism and giving

16.1. The ethics of economics

Improving society has always been the basic motive of economics, from its beginnings and permanently (even the rather recent economists who did not want to emphasize this aspect endorsed it by their injunctions which were more assertive the less they were derived from analysis – and implicit or summary moral positions have little chance to be sound ethics). This concern of economics implies that some people have ethical concerns – those to whom these reflexions are addressed and those who would implement the recommendations. This is a priori in contradiction with any hypothesis of purely selfish individuals. However, economics has endorsed various moral values. These values turn out to all have an important relation with issues of altruism and giving. One can begin with efficiency, in the modern form of Pareto efficiency, based on the social value of unanimity. Then come the twin values of freedom and welfare. The basically relevant freedom is *social freedom*, that is, an absence of forceful interference with individuals' actions, including the intended consequences of these actions, by individuals alone, in groups, or in institutions. Individuals' actions are thus only constrained not to forcefully interfere with others' actions. Both free exchange and gift giving are non-forceful interferences,[70] and a free transfer is either a gift or one part of an exchange or agreement. The ban on forceful interference applies in particular to consequences of previous free acts respecting social freedom, such as rights acquired by free exchange or agreement (or received as gifts). Social freedom is classically presented in various ways, depending on the emphasis put on various aspects, such as the classical

---

[70] Let us discard here the cases where the beneficiary of a gift both wishes to refuse it and cannot refuse it for material or social reasons.

basic rights presenting the general principle and main fields of application, "process-freedom" with emphasis on free exchange and markets, or the "negative freedom" of Isaiah Berlin and others (Kant, J.S. Mill, etc.). The moral endorsement of social freedom is "process liberalism".[71] Historically, most economists have so endorsed social freedom as an end value. Yet, a number of them only see its instrumental value, notably through the economic efficiency of the competitive market for "welfare" – this latter emphasis is rather recent, although it follows Adam Smith and Vilfredo Pareto. Social freedom is a balance of rights between private agents, which a priori differs from the balance of force and threats between them. Although maintaining it is the object of law, courts, public coercion, and self defense, it is also commonly implemented by voluntary restraint from harming and stealing. Compared with the sole use of force and threat, this respect constitutes an altruistic gift from the agents who would benefit from the confrontation.

Yet, with social freedom, there remains to allocate the given resources. The main ones are human capacities, notably productive capacities which account for most of the value of the economic output.[72] The value of the disposition of these capacities (i.e., their rent), can be left to their holders or more or less redistributed. Then, equalization with the proper measures leads to an equal sharing of the proceeds of an equal labour of each individual (with different given capacities), or "equal labour income equalization". Each individual keeps the proceeds of the rest of her freely chosen labour. This redistribution also amounts to each individual yielding to each other the proceeds of the same labour. This aspect of balance or fairness of these bilateral transfers may induce their more or less voluntary acceptance, in a kind of pervasive reciprocity.

Social freedom and this distribution implement "macrojustice", which defines the bulk of the proper distribution. Yet, there remains many other issues of fairness, for which a number of criteria can be applied. The analysis of these criteria developed in economics since the mid-60's, and it occupies most of the field of normative economics nowadays. Its central concerns are issues of equality and inequality, of various items in various circumstances, and provisioning needs, rewarding merit and desert, and satisfying legitimate rights. These criteria are worthy of study and may be implemented only if there is sufficient relevant altruism. Finally, economics has even not forgotten what is obvious to everybody, namely that the good society is made of good people and good social relations,[73] although the "dismal science" brand of economists are prompt to brandish the *Wealth of Nations*, the possible efficiency of markets, and perhaps Mandeville to argue that "private vices make public virtues" (with relations of exchange).

---

[71] Called simply liberalism in other European languages and in English before some moment in the early 20th century.
[72] The questions raised in this paragraph are presented in Kolm 2004.
[73] Kolm 1984a.

16.2. The intrinsic value of altruism and giving

In fact, almost all cultures, moral systems, and people see in giving and altruism the paragon of moral conduct and sentiments, a main – often the main – moral value and virtue (especially if one includes helping one's kin or group). Hence, if economics consistently applies its usual preference for "respecting individuals' preferences" to all the domain of individuals' evaluations, it should endorse this intrinsic value of giving and altruism. It should value, as people do, acts and sentiments of compassion, benevolence, solidarity, charity, fraternity, favouring the common good, or fairness, and the quality of good social relations that result from them. In fact, it can hardly avoid directly endorsing this judgment.

16.3. Giving as improving fairness in freedom

Moreover, giving and reciprocity improve allocative fairness in provisioning the needy, attributing to some people what is due to them (according to some criterion), securing fair balance, and diminishing inequality between donor and beneficiary. They do this in respecting social freedom and thanks to it, by decentralized actions without coercion. In particular, giving to alleviate need or poverty constitutes a normative blessing since it has one basic value, liberty, realize a number of others: it alleviates pain, reduces poverty, diminishes inequality between the giver and the receiver and – generally – overall inequality, and it is desired by the two people directly concerned and – generally – by some people while nobody regrets it. Specifically, giving to a poorer individual (without making her richer than the giver) constitutes a "progressive transfer" which unambiguously diminishes the inequality between the incomes or wealths of these two people, and hence also all the measures of overall income or wealth inequality that respect this "transfer principle".[74] The unanimous ("Pareto") improvement obtains if everyone either approves of these free act and reduction of pain, poverty, and inequality, or, at least, is indifferent about them. Joint giving that benefits someone poorer than all the givers and in need has the same properties if it results from a free agreement between the givers or if it is realized by a public authority in such a way that everyone prefers the whole set of transfers, and if the beneficiary remains poorer than the givers (concerning inequality, this redistribution amounts to a set of progressive transfers). On the other hand, the much-praised solidarity or support among members of families or other communities are the main source of inequality of opportunity and oppose ideals of broader impartiality, equality, and justice.

---

[74] That is, measures of inequality that are *rectifiant*. Rectifiance plus symmetry in the considered wealths or incomes – symmetry is justified by the absence of relevance of individual characteristics that differ across the individuals in question – is *isophily*, which mathematically amounts to Schur convexity. See Kolm 1966a, 1966b.

16.4. Altruism, giving, reciprocity, and failures of economic interactions

16.4.1. Causing market failures

Altruism and giving are no less both the worst and the best of things in the second main field of normative economics, the question of the various inefficiencies induced by "market failures".

Giving violates the mode of behaviour that constitutes competitive markets. Hence, when it intervenes in a framework of exchange, a priori it undermines the efficiency of such markets and of the price system. Important examples are found in collusions that block competition and are sustained by conducts of solidarity, norms of fairness, or promise keeping. These motives can prevent an agent from competitively undercutting a supply price or overbidding in buying, when it would be her self-interest to do it. Yet, these agents may finally gain from their collusive behaviour, although the means are often these non-selfish conducts, normative and often achieved in reciprocity with other agents in the similar situations. The resulting price rigidities jeopardize market efficiency. Notably, these conducts in the labour market lead to downward wage rigidities inducing unemployment, and, in this field and others, to behaviours conducive to inflation.

The non-purely-self-interested conduct can also take place between the parties of an exchange. The competitive model and, a priori, the resulting efficiency of the price system, can be upset by altruistic price rebates, overpayments, overprovision, accepting underprovision, or settling for a "just price" or "fair price" that is not the competitive price. Employees providing labour from a sense of reciprocity for the pay they receive apply a conduct analysed for a long time by social psychology (with the landmark analyses and experiments of Adam and others in the early 1960's), and which is the basis of the noted possible cause of unemployment pointed out by Akerlof (1982, a case of the general effects of labour relations presented in Kolm 1990).

However, such disruptions of efficiency in markets are more or less qualified by two aspects. First, as Wicksteed emphasized that people are more non-tuistic than egoists as individuals (see Section 11), they are also more non-tuistic than altruists in exchanges. That is, they largely keep their altruistic and selfish conducts for different relations. Second, altruists enjoy what is good for the other, notably her welfare or means, and both the donor and the beneficiary may enjoy the relation in itself. These benefits may overcompensate possible costs in economic efficiency in a narrow sense. At any rate, individual preferences are no longer those that produce the selfish behaviour, and this is to be taken into account notably for considering the Pareto-efficiency of the relation (this issue is discussed in Section 8.2 in the case of reciprocity).

16.4.2. Curing market failures

On the other hand, altruism and reciprocity are also essential causes of economic efficiency. A most basic reason rests in the spontaneous respect of people and of their rights and properties. This is an indispensable complement to self-defence and to the role of the police, and society is better and more efficient the larger the importance of this spontaneous respect. This respect can be extended to that of truth in truth-telling and of one's word in promise-keeping, and no market can function without a large minimum of such normed conducts.

Economists have often been surprised to see working interactions where the model assuming selfish motives predicts complete failure. This occurred for instance, for the reasons noted in Section 9.6, in voluntary contributions to public goods, collective actions, voting, the implementation of incomplete contracts, doing without missing markets, to which one can add many cases of truth-telling and revelation of private information, promise-keeping, and spontaneous respect of persons, rights, and properties. The main motives responsible for these conducts are moral values and norms. They are generally "intuitively" moral, but rational moral values sometimes have an important influence, notably with universalizations (popular "Kantianism") or putative reciprocities (see Section 13.3.3). Non-moral social values or norms also often play an important role. There are also desires for reputation – possibly for deriving future benefits but often valued in itself –, and for being praised or praiseworthy, and simple self-satisfaction (see Section 13.3.2). Moral and (other) social values or norms manifest the corresponding normative altruism. A number of these motives are norms of fairness of various types. Many of these relations are reciprocities, notably balance reciprocities which can have a dimension of fairness, in various types of applications. Indeed, these reciprocities lead the agents to more or less duplicate the result of an exchange without the selfish motivation: one gives not under the condition that the other people give, but simply given that they also give (yet, we have seen in Section 8 that, in fact, the goods or services transferred are not a priori in the same quantities or proportions as they would have been in the selfish exchange if it had taken place). These behaviours permit the partial or full remedy to the basic causes of these failures of exchanges or agreements: difficulties, costs, or impossibilities in information or constraining, and transaction costs. They lead to giving given that one is given to, or to contributing given that other people contribute, where these gifts or contributions can be transferring objects, providing services, or revealing information and truth-telling, keeping one's promises, respecting others and their rights and properties, and so on.

16.5. *Liberal social contracts and joint giving*

Joint giving, notably to poor people, is a case of non-excludable public good, and hence of "market failure", of major importance by the large number of possible contributors and by its objective. Its realization and the determination of each person's contribution can follow the general principles and methods for dealing with such "failures" and in particular public goods.

16.5.1. Liberal social contracts

Social freedom (including free exchange) meets the various classical causes of "market failures" due to difficulties in information, coercion or exclusion, and agreement. Specific conducts that are not purely selfish remedy these problems, but only in part. Adequate coercion is another mode of solution, notably by the public sector. The result should be Pareto efficient given all available means (information, coercion, and so on). Yet, there remains the choice of the distribution among the individuals that results from this action. If the distribution that results from social freedom (with the appropriate distribution of given resources) is morally endorsed, the solution consists of determining the outcome that would result from free action or agreement in the hypothetical case where the cause of the "failure" is absent. Such solutions are "liberal social contracts" (a social contract is, by definition, a theory in social ethics stating that the government should do what would have resulted from a hypothetical free agreement in specified circumstances).[75] Such an agreement would achieve Pareto efficiency among its parties in its setting if not reaching it is considered an agreement failure, and hence is assumed away for this hypothetical agreement. Moreover, the resulting distribution is that resulting from social freedom. A liberal social contract can thus be said to protect social freedom from the impediments causing the "failure", in enforcing what its result would be in their absence. Note that even when an agreement is actually achieved, the enforcement of the contract is secured by public constraint if necessary. More generally, even if a right is actually acquired (possibly by labour, first occupancy, or discovery, and not only exchange or agreement), its protection from the encroachment of other people is secured by public constraint towards others if necessary. Hence, the actual state with "failure" adds the constraints constituted by the cause of this failure (ignorance, non-coercion, non-exclusion, transaction costs, etc.) to the ideal process-free state; the liberal social contract adds the constraint of its implementation to this actual state; but, to the ideal state without impediment, whose outcome it enforces, it adds no constraint but only the hypothetical character of the agreement.

16.5.2. Public goods and joint giving

A main "market failure" is the case of joint concerns or "public goods" and of voluntary payments for them. In general, purely self-concerned individuals will not pay, or pay sufficiently, in an individual decision. (They will be "free riders" of the contribution of other people if there is any.) This "failure" has two causes. The individuals could sign a collective agreement about their contributions. The agreement can then be enforced by the public sector, as any other contract. This agreement can make any

---

[75] The putative contract is between the citizens (sometimes their ancestors in some theories), or between them and the government – both contracts are classically seen as jointly present. The particular "liberal social contracts" between citizens are a main topic of Kolm 1985 and also the object of a general presentation in Kolm 1987a and 1987b.

beneficiary-contributor better off than its absence. Then, each individual signs the agreement because if she does not sign or if any other person does not sign the other situation prevails, whereas if she signs she is in a better situation if all others also sign. However, if the people concerned are too numerous or dispersed, this voluntary agreement may not occur because of difficulties, costs, or impossibilities of transaction, information, contact, etc. Then, if people can be excluded from the benefit of the good, any agent can produce the good in making them pay for access. In this case, however, this seller will not know well which prices to charge. And exclusion is not possible in a class of cases. In these situations, the hypothetical existence of such an agent in a liberal social contract is not a possible solution notably because this would not say what to do with the profit (in addition there may be other necessary characteristics of this agent which are undetermined, such as her risk-aversion for choosing in uncertainty when choosing which prices to charge). Hence, the solution is the hypothetical collective agreement in a liberal social contract, essentially implemented by the public sector.

Joint giving is, for altruistic givers, a case of a public good which is the receiver's situation or total receipt. Transfers decided by a collective agreement about joint giving are twice free: as gifts and as objects of a free agreement with co-givers. An altruistic giver benefits simply from knowing the situation of the receiver (yet, hiding information about this situation is not exclusion from this benefit but only introducing uncertainty about it: the altruist does not basically want to know but only that the receiver's situation improves). There generally are many possible contributors, notably when giving to people in need (the situation is the same if some givers specialize in giving to some needy people, since there should nevertheless be an agreement among all givers when they are also concerned by gifts to other people than "their poor"). Therefore, the solution implementing the distributive ethic of social freedom is the implementation of the liberal social contract assuming the possibility of a direct collective agreement. The next paragraph considers this agreement (for public goods in general).

16.5.3. The core with interdependent coalitions

There is a set of individuals. Each is free to act, given the possibilities, in the sense of social freedom. The individuals of a group of this set are also free to agree to perform acts which they can do. It is assumed that reaching the agreement and making it binding for the people who agree is possible and costless – this is the hypothesis of the liberal social contract (the obligation to abide by the agreement can be seen as enforcement by the public force as for any lawful contract). Not making an agreement is a priori a particular possible outcome for the group. If the group has to choose between two states that it can realize, such that all members prefer one to the other, then it certainly chooses the former. Let us consider, in addition, the assumption that a group does not realize a state that it can realize if it can also realize another state that all members prefer to the former one. If these two states are the only possible ones, this amounts to the previous remark. But the assumption is something new in the other cases. This assumption can be called one of collective rationality (the history of thought also suggests calling it the

Coase hypothesis – rather than "theorem" or conjecture – and it is, in fact, the basic assumption of cooperative game theory). The unanimous preference in question in the group can be with indifference for some members, but not all (this definitional property will not be repeated). A consequence of the assumption is that each group chooses a state that is Pareto efficient for its members among the states that its cooperation can realize (by definition of this property of a state: it is possible and no other possible state is unanimously preferred). A cooperating group is classically called a "coalition". A consequence of the situation is that the achieved state is such that no coalition can induce another state that is preferred by all its members. This is a theory of the "core", but we will see that it has to differ from classical such theories. It has in common with other theories of the core that considering the "grand coalition" consisting of all agents in question implies that the achieved state is Pareto efficient. Which of these states prevails results more or less from the consideration of more restricted coalitions. Then, the situation is quite different from that of other notions of the core or related concepts.

Indeed, when a (partial) coalition decides that its members provide contributions different from those of a considered set of contributions, the other individuals concerned by the public good are affected by this choice, their preferences lead them to react in choosing other contributions that are the best for them, and this change influences in turn the members of the coalition in question. This holds whether each individual action is chosen collectively in some coalition or individually (an individual is a particular singleton coalition). That is, the relevant concept of the core is that of the "core with externality" or the "core with interdependent coalitions".[76]

In contrast, in the other theories, a coalition takes the actions of other people as either not affecting its members (core for private goods and Foley's theory of the core for public goods) or as given to them, as not reacting to their choice different from the allocation in question ("strong Nash equilibrium"). In the core for private goods, the members of a coalition allocate their own resources among themselves, and the other individuals are not affected by this operation (they are only by the absence of a larger cooperation). By analogy with the case of private goods, Duncan Foley's (1970) theory of a core for public goods assumes that the members of a coalition receive no benefit from contributions (gifts for joint giving) from individuals who are not members of this coalition. However, these other individuals could in fact contribute (give) individually or in forming other coalitions. Hence, for a non-excludable public good, this assumption a priori does not hold (this is the case of joint giving). If exclusion is possible, it should be explained why agents who are not members of the coalition in question choose to exclude the members of this coalition from the benefits of their contributions; it could be in order to raise the cost of not accepting the allocation (contributions) under consideration; however, these non-members could, or not, benefit from the contributions of this coalition, depending on a decision of the coalition if it can also exclude others from the benefits of its contributions; hence there is an exclusion game which should

---

[76] See Kolm 1987c, 1987d, 1987e, 1987f, 1987g, 1989.

be explicit. The exclusion is necessarily the case only in particular types of material situations, for instance if a coalition produces one quantity of the public good and there materially cannot be two such quantities (but, then, which coalition produces the good has to be determined), or if the public good is local and a partial coalition has to emigrate; these are the types of situations where Foley's concept applies, and it is not the case of joint giving. In still another theory in the family of the core, that of "strong Nash equilibrium", the individuals outside of the coalition do not react to the coalition acting differently from the situation under consideration (a proposed set of contributions). However, with non-exclusion, this absence of reaction will not be the case in general. Agents outside of the dissenting coalition have an interest to react, hence they will do it, and the coalition has to take this reaction into account. Moreover, a strong Nash equilibrium is both Pareto efficient (the case of the "grand coalition" noted above) and a Cournot–Nash equilibrium (the case of singleton coalitions). Now, in the standard cases a Cournot–Nash equilibrium is not Pareto efficient and, hence, no strong Nash equilibrium exists. However, the assumption that other people do not react to the choice of a person also holds for ordinary Cournot–Nash equilibria and they are commonly considered, and Pareto efficiency may be desired for its normative value.[77]

Therefore, the obtained state (set of individual contributions or gifts) is such that there is no coalition whose members become all more satisfied in acting differently, and this takes into account that this change will a priori induce changes in the acts (contributions, gifts) of the other persons. In this respect, these other persons can act individually, or cooperate among themselves, or again be partitioned into coalitions with cooperation within each coalition but not across coalitions. A coalition may consist of a single individual, either for the initial, dissenting coalition, or for any induced one among other people. The non-cooperative relations among coalitions may a priori be of any type, such as Cournot–Nash or Stackelberg.

Notable properties of the result are revealed by particular structures that may be the case or be sufficient approximations. With quasilinear utilities, usually only one coalition of a partition of people into non-cooperating coalitions gives, and the other individuals and coalitions are free riders (with a Cournot–Nash interaction, this is the coalition that gives the largest amount when it alone gives). The case of a large number of small contributors also shows remarkable properties (and is realistic for aid to people in need).

16.6. Retro-gifts and the process-liberal public debt

In a society where social freedom is fully respected, the only possible justification of a public debt is to realize transfers to earlier generations desired a priori by the pay-

---

[77] The only case where Cournot–Nash equilibria have a full justification in one- or two-shot games is a game of reciprocity presented in the chapter on reciprocity.

ers of the taxes that redeem the debt.[78] Of course, the public sector determining such a borrowing estimates these preferences of future generations. These transfers can in particular be gifts to earlier generations. A notable consequence of this optimum public debt policy has been shown in Section 10.

You give to your children and your children give, or will give, to you. You can give to your great-grand children by leaving sufficient capital for them. A priori, however, in our growing economies, they will need help much less than your great-grand mother did (during the great depression). In fact, wise governments of the time provided public aid financed by a public deficit that is now redeemed thanks to the taxes we pay. In addition to contributing to reflate the economy, this achieved exactly what you want: you give to your great-grand mother.

This is a *retro-gift*, which can also benefit someone of the past unrelated to you, notably because of her needs and poverty. Retro-gifts are particular cases of *retro-transfers*, which also include *retro-payments* in which you pay a previous generation for a service it provides to you (for instance, they have planted a forest from which you benefit, and this forest has been financed by public borrowing now reimbursed thanks to your taxes).[79] A retro-gift can also be a part of an intergenerational reciprocity. The whole operation of a retrogift, and of a retro-payment for a unanimously desired intertemporal exchange, is desired by the corresponding taxpayers. However, at the time of the payment of the tax, the other part has already been performed – it is the subsidy to the earlier generations or the service they provide that will benefit later generations –, and hence taxpayers would a priori prefer not to pay. This is akin to any compulsory implementation of a contract, but more original for gift giving, although this is similar to the case of joint giving implemented by the public sector.

Retro-transfers constitute the only process-liberal justification of the public debt. They remedy the "failure" of free transfers created by the "arrow of time". Of course, a retro-gift may also be a joint gift, when several persons want to help the same one(s) in previous generations. The givers may be of the same or of different generations. For instance, a person may have several descendents who want to help her.

16.7. Selfish altruism: The situation of the other person may be your own

In collective decisions that will affect an uncertain future, you often care about various individual situations for a purely self-interested motive, because you do not know which of these situations will be your own, into which possible individual situation you will happen to fall. Hence, you may also take care of individual situations which will be those of other people, and then you are de facto an "altruist", that is, you are one in your choice if not in your sentiments. A shift in time transferring this view to the later

---

[78] However, if market imperfections create involuntary unemployment and cannot be directly corrected, macroeconomic effects of the public debt can justify it by an extended and second-best application of a liberal social contract (see above).

[79] See Kolm 1985.

situation transforms this viewpoint into a common reason provided for helping another person in need, that described by the argument that "it could have happened to you". This notion is the basis of one of the most famous theories of social ethics or justice of recent times, the theory of the "original position" notably proposed by John Rawls and John Harsanyi. Both these authors propose that the moral choice or policy is the one that an individual would have chosen in an "original position" where "it" does not know what "it" will have in all respects in actual life, including "its" own tastes (and, of course, "its" sex). Their two theories differ, but we have noticed above a basic issue that they do not face (Section 13.3.3.4). A choice in the original position is made with preferences which have to have two given features: the preference about risk and the corresponding risk-aversion, and the preferences about "being" various persons (and in particular having their preferences in actual life). Hence, if actual individuals are imagined back in an original position, they have to keep these two aspects of their preferences for their choice in this position, and hence these individuals in the original position are generally not identical and a priori do not make the same choice. Moreover, the individuals can be imagined as keeping still other features of their actual preferences and situation for their imagined hypothetical choice in uncertainty. These are theories of the "partially original position".[80]

Since the individuals in this hypothetical uncertain situation are not identical, their preferred choices do not a priori present the unanimity that would result from this identity. Then, inspired by the theories of the social contract, one can propose to replace this lacking unanimity of preferences by the unanimity of a free agreement among these different persons (Rawls proposes this reference to the social contract, although he assumes that all individuals in the original position have the same preferred choice). The advantage of this agreement over an agreement between actual individuals is that these hypothetical individuals are more similar among themselves, and, hence, the scope of a priori possible agreements is more restricted. Therefore, these individuals are assumed to make a unanimous agreement about what should be done when any of the a priori possible situations prevails. Such an a priori possible situation is defined by the fact that the a priori uncertain (in the considered hypothetical situation) aspect of each individual's preferences and situation receives a specification. Then, the decision of this hypothetical agreement for the case where the actual preferences and situation occur is applied. Taking a hypothetical agreement as a social ethical norm is by definition a theory of a social contract. The present theory differs from other social contracts by the nature of the state in which the agreement is made (called the "state of nature" in classical contractarian theory). The notionally randomized items, that is, all that the individuals do not keep and hence are uncertain about in this partially original position, can in fact be specific and restricted. The theory then is a theory for compensating inequalities in this respect in actual life. For example, this item may be given productive capacities, depending on genetic endowment and education provided by the family, given health as the propensity (not) to become sick, or any other characteristics of individuals. The

---

[80] See Kolm 1985, 1998a.

agreement then is in fact a mutual insurance against the risk of being poorly endowed in the characteristic, and the actual result consists of compensations from the individuals better endowed to the individuals poorly endowed. This is notably considered for items that are given to the individuals before they could take out an actual insurance, such as given individual characteristics, family influence, education received, and given social advantages or handicaps. This theory then is a "fundamental insurance" defining actual compensatory transfers.

However, this choice wants to be about justice but is determined by what would be the individuals' selfish conduct in uncertainty and in exchange. This raises a problem because justice and selfish conduct have different rationales. In particular, an individual's selfish choice in uncertainty has no reason to represent a choice of justice among the various persons that she could be in the different realizations. The relevant justice may focus on aspects of the individuals' situation different from their utility (relevant for the self-interested choice). Moreover, when they can be compared, the moral inequality aversion tends to exceed individual risk aversion. However, the situation is different if selfish exchange is replaced by benevolent reciprocity. The motive becomes: "I help this person, given that, if our situations were reversed, she would have helped me". This is the putative reciprocity whose actual importance and consequences have been noted above (Section 13.3.3.3). Reciprocity is based on sentiments of balance or fairness or of mutual liking. These seem to be morally acceptable bases of distributive fairness. Moreover, we have also seen that fundamental insurance is the practically unanimously endorsed justification of public health insurance – rather than private one – in many societies, which implies large basically voluntary transfers (beyond actuarial insurance) for helping people with poor given health (Section 13.3.3.4).

16.8. *Justice from altruism, and distribution as a public good: The distributive or moral surplus*[81]

If all individuals care about what they have only, any redistribution makes someone worse off, in the absence of particular indirect effects.[82] When some people care about what some others have, the same property often holds. Yet, if some such concerns for the situation of other people are sufficiently large, there may exist redistributions that nobody regrets and some value. The social states from which such redistributions do not exist have, by definition, a Pareto efficient distribution. Pareto efficiency is a property of a social state that is certainly to be valued, because it means that there is no unanimously preferred deviation from it (with the possibility of indifference for some people). However, in a large society where most of the altruism that exists is only moderate, the set of the Pareto efficient distributions is very large. Therefore, this property does not help much in the quest of the Graal of normative economics, the optimum distribution. Something else should be added, and this is the important ingredient.

---

[81] See Kolm 1966a.
[82] Notably in an economic surrounding of perfectly competitive markets.

When some people care about what some others have, the distribution becomes a collective concern, a public good in this sense. Hence, one proposal consists of applying to it the standard principle used for the choice of public goods, in benefit–cost analysis, the criterion of the surplus. This principle, however, should be properly applied as follows.[83] By definition, the surplus of a state B over a state A is the algebraic sum of individuals' money equivalent of having state B rather than state A (the m-surplus), or of individuals' willingness to pay for having state B rather than state A (the p-surplus). The difference between both concepts and measures results from the fact that, for the m-surplus, the individuals are in state A when their money equivalent is notionally given to them for obtaining a state equivalent to state B; whereas, for the p-surplus, the individuals are in state B when their willingness to pay is taken out from them for obtaining a state equivalent to state A. Then, the surplus principle chooses a possible state A such that no surplus for having any other possible state B rather than state A is positive, both for the m-surplus and for the p-surplus. This condition also amounts to the fact that no surplus for having state A rather than state B is negative, for both the m-surplus and the p-surplus (the condition for one of the two surplus concepts amounts to that for the other in inverting the states).[84]

---

[83] See Kolm 1966a (see also 2004).
[84] Calling y_i individual i's wealth, $y = \{y_i\}$, $y_{-i} = \{y_j\}_{u_{j \neq i}}$, and $U^i(y)$ individual i's ordinal utility as a function of the distribution y, the money equivalent and the willingness to pay of individual i for having distribution y' rather than distribution y are respectively $m_i(y', y)$ and $p_i(y', y)$ defined by

$$U^i[y_i + m_i(y', y), y_{-i}] = U^i(y')$$

and

$$U^i(y) = U^i[y'_i - p_i(y', y), y'_{-i}].$$

Clearly, $m_i(y, y') = -p_i(y', y)$, and $p_i(y, y') = -m_i(y', y)$. Define as $m(y', y) = \sum m_i(y', y)$ and $p(y', y) = \sum p_i(y', y)$ the m-surplus and the p-surplus, respectively. One has

$$m(y', y) + p(y, y') = m(y, y') + p(y', y) = 0.$$

If P is the set of possible distributions, the chosen distribution is $y \in P$ such that, for all $y' \in P$,

$$m(y', y) \leq 0, \quad m(y, y') \geq 0, \quad p(y', y) \leq 0, \quad p(y, y') \geq 0$$

(these inequalities constitute only two conditions).

When y' is close to y, say $y' = y + dy$, and the U^i are differentiable, these conditions imply $\sum_{i,j} v^i_j \cdot dy_j \leq 0$ where $v^i_j = U^i_j / U^i_i$ and $U^i_j = \partial U^i / \partial y_j$. For a pure redistribution, $\sum y'_i = \sum y_i$ and $\sum dy_i = 0$. Then, since $v^i_i = 1$ for all i, $\sum_{i,j} v^i_j \cdot dy_j = \sum_{i,j \neq i} v^i_j \cdot dy_j = \sum v_i \cdot dy_i$ with $v_i = \sum_{j \neq i} v^j_i$. Hence, the conditions are effective even when the v^i_j for $i \neq j$ are very low (lexical egoism). If distribution y is a moral (distributive) surplus distribution, then $\sum v_i(y) \cdot dy_i \leq 0$ for all possible $y' = y + dy$ in the neighbourhood of y. If, in particular, transfers both ways between y_i and y_j are possible, then $v_i = v_j$. Considering both surpluses (m and p) gives second-order conditions. Various meanings and properties of this solution, second-order conditions, existence, and uniqueness, are discussed in Kolm 1966a.

If all people are purely selfish, this principle specifies no distribution. But if they care about what others have, no matter how little, the principle gives a solution, most of the time a unique one. This holds in particular when people value their own wealth very much more than that of others, say with priority ("lexical egoism"). This results from the basic logic of the surplus method, namely the following. An individuals' self-interested money value of, or willingness to pay for, a dollar for herself is a dollar. Hence, for a redistribution without indirect effects, where the sum of incomes remains the same by definition, the values measuring the self-interests of all individuals cancel out in the sums of the surplus. Therefore, these sums depend only on the individuals' values of the amounts transferred for other reasons, notably because of their altruisms if they are the social sentiments present (including the resulting conceptions of justice). In fact, the basic justification of the described distributive surplus principle derives from this property: if you want a distributive criterion that is derived from the opinions of the members of the society about the justice of this distribution and from their altruism only, hence discarding their own self-interest, the solution is the distributive surplus. The basic reason is that cancelling out the self-interested values of a redistribution implies using the algebraic sums of money equivalents or willingnesses to pay. The idea of deriving the solution form the opinions of the members of the society only, called "endogenous social choice", can be considered as unavoidable, since where else could we find such information for the comprehensive society (and for a smaller society, imposition from outside would be intrusion).

17. Historical landmarks

17.1. Economics and altruism

Almost all major economists in history made important contributions to the analyses of altruism and giving, often in specialized books (Adam Smith, John Stuart Mill, Léon Walras, Vilfredo Pareto, in particular). In recent times, the list of economists' works on this issue contains several hundred entries. Of course, economists have mainly studied non-altruistic exchange, but the famous *homo economicus* they used for this purpose describes a non-altruistic *relation* and cannot be assumed to represent the full conception of man of these authors. Its self-interestedness describes the *non-tuism* of the relation rather than the egoism of the person, using Philip Wicksteed's perceptive distinction. Moreover, observation showed that self-interested exchanges or cooperation could not work without important inputs of a different, other-regarding kind, based on morals, respect, and, importantly, reciprocity. Why, indeed, is there exchange rather than theft, why are many promises kept, why do people engage in collective action, why do they sometimes tell the truth, etc.? Only part of these behaviours can be explained by the fear of punishment or of retaliation. Furthermore, the topic of economics is more broadly defined as the allocation of resources. Then, altruism sprang to the face of anyone who opened the boxes of the other main allocative systems, the family, charity and donations, and the vast redistributive political and public sector with its complex of diverse motivations – from the most cruel to the most altruistic and the whole spectrum in between.

It is an embarrassing situation, for a field of study, when the culminating work happens to be the first one, especially if it is over two centuries old. One strategy is to forget about it – apart from paying lip-service. This has largely been the fate of Adam Smith's *Theory of Moral Sentiments*, certainly one of the major works in thinking about society of all times.[85] We have seen that much is in this work – including reciprocity, self-image and praise-seeking.

Giving a Benthamite specification to the "impartial spectator" of Hutcheson, Hume and Smith led John Stuart Mill to his utilitarian altruist (in her moments of calm reflection). Since Mill was both reflective and a person living by his ideals, this theory made him a tempting target. This was not bypassed by Auguste Comte who, fond of new terms as he was, concluded that altruists should give money to sociologists – as he called these two categories of people – in a letter to John Stuart Mill where he explained his financial difficulties (1844).[86] Mill then had two businessmen friends of his help Comte out. However, when Comte repeated his demand one year later, Mill refused and pointed out that altruism should mean an impartial balance of interest rather than self-sacrifice for the other fellow as Comte understood it. Comte angrily answered that, in any event, businessmen have the duty to support philosophers.[87]

17.2. Interdependent utilities and social choice

From Mill's utilitarian altruism (altruistic because utilitarian), economic studies concerned with such issues divide into two branches. One of them considers individuals who are jointly self-interested and altruistic, in a single utility function. Yet, since these individuals also have a particular interest in themselves, it is natural to consider that the intensity of their altruism can depend on who are the other individuals who can be the objects of this sentiment. For instance, the representation of their preferences should be able to admit that they make their children "count for more than others", in Bentham's terms. Then, after the formulation of Edgeworth, restricted to only two individuals and additive "welfares" (but with the notice of the "shrinking contract curve" property), this leads to the more complete formulation of Pareto, with individuals' "utilities" which can depend on all individuals' "ophelimities". The second branch considers separately

---

[85] It is advised to read *The Theory of Moral Sentiments* in its French translation, because it has three more chapters than the English original. They were added by the French translator, Sophie de Condorcet (Antoine's wife) after Adam Smith's stay in Paris – where he was converted, by their economist friends, to acknowledging the magic of exchange which transmutes the private vice of "selfishness" into the public virtue of apparent "altruism".

[86] Comte may have borrowed the term "altruism" from the poet Andrieux who was his professor at the Ecole Polytechnique.

[87] This put an end to their interesting correspondence. See Mill's *Unpublished Correspondence* (1828–1871) [Mill (1898)]. Yet, Comte continued to survive thanks to other gifts which became labelled "the positivist subsidy".

the individuals' concern for others, in focussing on its moral reason in social ethics (this is not far from Mill's view – and Walras's non-welfarist conception – who see this as people's judgments "in their moments of calm reflection"). Yet, utilitarianism meets the difficulty of the lack of general meaning of the operation of addition of utility functions which can describe something like individual's "happiness". This led to Bergson's more general "social welfare function" representing an individual's social ethics. However, since this function is no longer the unique utilitarian sum, what should it be for representing what is better for society? These two branches thus led respectively to the two fields of "interdependent utilities" on the one hand and of classical "social choice theory" on the other hand. Finally, endogenous social choice leads to finding solutions to the social ethical problem of the latter field in individuals' "embodied" social ethical view described by the former field.[88]

17.3. Altruism and uncertainty

The logical problem in adding individuals' utilities can result notably from their ordinal structure. This structure was pointed out simultaneously by Pareto and by the mathematician Henri Poincaré in a famous letter in answer to Léon Walras. This answer adds the further remark: "you consider individuals with perfect foresight and fully egoistic; the second property may be acceptable, but the former one is demanding too much". Poincaré may not have known about Walras's intense concern about positive social sentiments, notably expressed in his lectures and book about workers' cooperatives and associations. Yet, his remark points out the two issues of uncertainty and altruism, which have logical and psychological similarities, and actual and theoretical interactions, and have been considered and analysed by economics in parallel successive steps (with a merging in theories of the original position and fundamental insurance).

Both concern for uncertainty and altruism consist, for an individual, of being concerned with several individuals, who are herself in several possible prospects in selfish uncertainty, and also other individuals in altruism. In fact, empathy, one of the main sources of altruism, consists of imagining oneself in the place of someone else, as one imagines oneself in the various prospects when facing an uncertainty that concerns oneself. We have also seen that a main theory in social ethics, the "original position" and "fundamental insurance", consists of building a rational altruism from a notional uncertainty. Moreover, interactions among agents can jointly involve giving and uncertainty, and notably, at the deepest level of interaction, reciprocity and game-theoretic strategy.

The analyses of both domains developed in four parallel steps, concerning views and acts, and single and interacting individuals. Table 4 shows these steps. Individual views are those of uncertain prospects and altruism. They can lead to the individual acts of a choice in uncertainty and of giving. With several interacting individuals, uncertainty leads notably to contingent and insurance markets, while agents' altruism and giving

---

[88] See Section 16.8, more fully Kolm 1966a, and more generally Kolm 2004.

Table 4
Uncertainty and altruism

	Uncertainty	*Altruism*
individual view	uncertain prospects	altruism
individual acts	choice in uncertainty	giving
interdependent acts	contingent and insurance markets	interfering giving
interdependent views	games of strategy	reciprocities

interfere in various notable ways with the choices of similar or different agents. More deeply, the very views of various agents interfere with each other epistemically in games of strategy and as regards motives for giving in reciprocity.

17.4. Interdependent utilities and interdependent giving

A main distinction is between concern for the good of other people, that is, altruism, and other concerns about gifts and sentiments. The former phenomenon leads to the question of "interdependent utilities" in a broad sense. Section 3 has recalled the history and the various specific structures of this concept. This concept can explain or justify transfers and notably gifts. The application has been in three fields, corresponding to three types of institutions: the public sector, charity, and the family. The public sector is notably concerned with two consequences of altruism, efficiency and distributive justice. It is ruled by the political system where self-interests and different social ethical views find their equilibrium. This application of interdependent utilities begun in the mid 1960's. With joint giving, private charity met the problem of public goods analysed notably in the late 1960's. These gifts interfere with public redistribution, and, with an efficient public action, private charity can only be explained by motives different from the only concern with the beneficiary's welfare, notably specific ethical principles (universalization, putative reciprocity, fundamental insurance), or direct concern for the gifts (demonstration effects, or specific moral or social norms or values, or specific self-esteem, that attach to the gift in itself). The third application of interdependent utilities is the economics of the family, notably with the analyses of G. Becker (1974), and applications such as Barro's "Ricardian equivalence" (1974, see Section 10.1.2). However, families manifest many other relations than simple altruism, notably the intrisic value and interdependence of sentiments, and diverse reciprocities.

In reciprocity, a gift elicits another gift for a reason of balance, sometimes associated with fairness (which includes merit), or because a benevolent gift elicits liking the giver – in addition to the different phenomenon of sequential exchange. Reciprocity has constituted a central concept in the social science for one century, and a topic of economic analysis for several decades. This was accompanied by applications of the economic theory of reciprocity to a number of issues such as distributive justice, labour relations, the family, intergenerational transfers, intergenerational financing of pensions and education, bargaining and the settlement of conflicts, voluntary contributions to public goods, voluntary restraint in the use of natural resources, non-market economies, and economic development and social change.[89]

17.5. A notable debate: Blood and the efficiency of giving

For many epigones of Adam Smith's second thoughts, market exchange is the most efficient way of transferring things. Later development of economics emphasized notably the virtue of the price system for efficiently carrying the needed information. In some cases, however, one can compare modes of transfers, notably market exchange and giving, as they actually work. For instance, blood for medical purposes is given in a number of countries and sold and bought in others. In 1971, Richard Titmuss compared these two modes, in the cases of the UK and US, respectively. His conclusion is that the giving system of the UK is superior to the buying system of the US in all respects, for the quality of the blood, the situation of the donors, and the general attitude of persons towards others and society. The issue of quality refers in particular to a question of information in which the market is much inferior to giving. The reason is clear: some infections, and notably hepatitis, were undetectable in blood samples. The altruistic people who give their blood abstain from giving when they know they have had the disease. The purely self-interested sellers of their blood lack this motive and practice. This is a classical situation of asymmetric information. Titmuss also intrinsically favours the general motive and action that leads to giving, in particular to giving to society or others in general rather then to specific known others, that is, *general giving*.[90] Moreover, he holds that it is not possible to have both systems in the same place.

This work launched a notable debate. Robert Solow (1971) proposed that its results constitute "a devastating and unanswerable indictment of the American system". Kenneth Arrow's (1974) review turned into a much noticed, perceptive and pioneering discussion of the role of altruism and morality for securing economic efficiency in remedying market failures. Notably, altruism and a sense of responsibility prevent exploiting advantages of asymmetric information, all commercial transactions imply an element of trust, and, in general, "ethical behaviour can be regarded as a socially desirable institution which facilitates the achievement of economic efficiency". Moreover, Arrow notices that people who give are motivated by the result, and also by their gift in itself, and, for joint giving, by some implicit social contract with co-givers (suggested by T. Nagel). However, Arrow suggests that Titmuss's contention that there cannot be both

---

[89] See, notably, Adam (1963), Kolm (1973, 1984a, 1984b, 1990), Akerlof (1982), Sugden (1984), Swaney (1990), Rabin (1993), for various lines of study. In sociology, after Hobhouse (1906), reciprocity is studied by Simmel, Gouldner, Howard Becker, Homans, and others. Reciprocity is central for many anthropologists such as Thurnwald, Mauss, Malinowski, Firth, Lévi-Strauss, Sahlins, and others. See Chapter 6 of this volume for other ancient and more recent references. The "pseudo-reciprocity" of self-interested sequential exchanges has also been the object of a number of investigations and applications.

[90] See Kolm 1984a.

giving and a market for blood in the same place – and hence that buying blood crowds out the superior giving (in a kind of Gresham's law) – lacks a theoretical explanation. The analysis of this issue requires that of the various specific motives, but let us only remark here that, if we believe Kant, in acquiring a price blood looses its dignity.

17.6. Volumes in the economics of giving, altruism and reciprocity

Although the analysis of altruism and giving by economists has, as we have seen, a long and glorious history, it became rather rare around the middle of the 20th century. The revival of this field of studies in the last third of the 20th century, notably with the consideration of "interdependent utilities" (see Section 3), was in particular marked by the publication of a few volumes dealing with the economics of altruism, giving, and reciprocity at a general level. Three of them are collective books, with a general presentation or introduction. Two gather papers of conferences; they are edited by Phelps (1975) and by Gérard-Varet, Kolm and Mercier Ythier (2000). The third volume, edited by Zamagni (1995), gathers a number of notable articles about altruism, mostly by economists. Two volumes, by Collard (1978) and Margolis (1981) present models of microeconomic interactions with altruism, and a number of applications. A different approach, with more philosophical considerations, is followed by Steedman (1989). An ambitious movement aimed at studying the "grant economy", with the humanistic vision of Boulding (1973) as programmatic presentation, and collective volumes (edited by Boulding and Pfaff 1972 and Boulding and Wilson 1978). "Grants" are taken to mean transfers other than exchanges, including gifts and things taken by force, private or public. The association of giving and taking may raise a difficulty for analysis, but we have seen that the important public transfers can associate both modes. Kolm (1984a) analyses reciprocity and giving, with an interest in the general quality of society. Reciprocity and giving, exchange, and the use of force, are the three modes of social interaction and economic transfers, present in various proportions in all societies, with various performances with respect to efficiency, and very different consequences for the quality of society, of its members, and of relations between them. Comparison and evolution in this threefold partition of social interactions are particularly revealing for comparing societies and analyzing their social progress.

Appendix: The joint giving theorem

The properties noted in Section 7 are shown here. The notations are as follows. Indices i or j denote the individuals who may contribute. For individual i, consider her free individual gift $g_i \geqslant 0$, the distributive tax she pays $t_i \geqslant 0$, her own total contribution $c_i = g_i + t_i$, her initial wealth X_i, and her final wealth $x_i = X_i - c_i$. The total transfer is $c = \sum c_i$. The beneficiary has initial wealth X, final wealth $x = X + c$, and an increasing ordinal utility function $u = u(x)$ with derivative $u' > 0$. Individual i's utility function u^i increases with x_i, it also increases with x or $u(x)$ if individual i is an altruist, and, for the noted reasons, it may increase with c_i or g_i, and decrease when c_j or g_j increases for some $j \neq i$. Hence, denoting $c_{-i} = \{c_j\}_{j \neq i}$ and $g_{-i} = \{g_j\}_{j \neq i}$ the sets of the c_j and g_j for $j \neq i$, respectively,

$$u^i = u^i(x_i, x, c_i, g_i, c_{-i}, g_{-i})$$

with the respective partial derivatives $u^i_{x_i} > 0$, $u^i_x \geqslant 0$, $u^i_{c_i} \geqslant 0$, $u^i_{g_i} \geqslant 0$, $u^i_{c_j} \leqslant 0$ and $u^i_{g_j} \leqslant 0$ for $j \neq i$ (writing a derivative implies the assumption of its existence). Nothing is changed if x is replaced by $u(x)$. The chosen g_i and t_i make c_i a relatively small part of X_i and hence no constraint $x_i \geqslant 0$ is relevant.

Individual i individually chooses her gift g_i that maximizes u^i (hence, given the other variables g_j for $j \neq i$ and t_j for all j). Therefore, if $g_i > 0$,

$$-u^i_{x_i} + u^i_x + u^i_{c_i} + u^i_{g_i} = 0. \tag{1}$$

Pareto efficiency for this society of potential givers and receivers implies that there exist coefficients $\lambda_i > 0$ such that $U = \sum \lambda_j u^j + u$ is maximal (without loss of generality). Public policy chooses taxes t_i. When it implements a Pareto efficient social state, this choice maximizes such a function U. This implies, for tax t_i,

$$\lambda_i \cdot \left(-u^i_{x_i} + u^i_x + u^i_{c_i}\right) + \sum_{j \neq i} \lambda_j \cdot \left(u^j_x + u^j_{c_i}\right) + u' \leqslant 0, \tag{2}$$

with $= 0$ if $t_i > 0$ and $\leqslant 0$ if $t_i = 0$.

Conditions (1) and (2) entail

$$-\lambda_i u^i_{g_i} + \sum_{j \neq i} \lambda_j \cdot \left(u^j_x + u^j_{c_i}\right) + u' \leqslant 0. \tag{3}$$

Since $u' > 0$, and $u^j_x \geqslant 0$ and $\lambda_j > 0$ for all j, the condition can hold only if $u^i_{g_i} > 0$ and/or $u^j_{c_i} < 0$ for some j. Therefore, Pareto efficiency implies the following conditions for individual gifts g_i:
- If the individuals are only altruists (no direct effects of the c_i or g_i on utilities), there is no private giving g_i.
- If, in addition, or instead, they may care about their own specific contribution ($u^i_{c_i} \neq 0$), the same result holds.
- If, in addition, or instead, they may care about the specific gifts of other people ($u^i_{g_j} \neq 0$), the same result holds.
- There can be a gift $g_i > 0$ only if individual i cares for her own gift and/or her contribution c_i is envied by some other individuals (or they enjoy feeling that they contribute more).

Moreover, if condition (3) is satisfied thanks to the envy or sentiment of superiority of the other people ($u^j_{c_i} < 0$, and $u^i_{g_i}$ is zero or small), then, the $|u^j_{c_i}|$ should be on average higher than the u^j_x, that is, *individuals should be more envious or domineering than altruistic*, on average.

In the other case of satisfaction of the condition, due to $u^i_{g_i} > 0$ with $|u^j_{c_i}|$ low or zero, the condition shows that $u^i_{g_i}$ should be higher than the average u^j_x by an order of magnitude at least equal to that of the population of the fiscal constituency. Hence, in a country with a population of N millions, *an extra gift is valued at least N million times more for the glory of the giver than for the relief of the needy*, on average. With a large population, this condition will not hold, and, hence, caring about one's own gift cannot explain giving in an efficient society (in particular a democratic one).

Yet, private giving can be compatible with Pareto efficiency when it is motivated by other, more specific, moral reasons, such as the principle of universalization (e.g., Kant's categorical imperative) or putative reciprocity, noted in Section 13.3.3 (see Kolm 2005).

The welfare $u(x)$ of the aided people is an end-value of society before being a public good for the givers. This shows by the fact that $u(x)$ is a term of the social ethical maximand U. This makes this issue formally different from that of ordinary public goods. Yet, the foregoing analysis translates into that of financing ordinary public goods by voluntary contributions or taxes in writing $u = u' = 0$ in the formulas. Results similar to those obtained above also hold. This can in particular apply to the present issue if the efficiency in question is not that of the whole society but only that of an actual or putative agreement among the givers. One difference is that, with a pure public good or pure altruism – the u^i depend only on x_i and x –, condition (3) can be satisfied with $u^j_x = 0$ for all $j \neq i$; but this cannot occur for more than one i, and hence there is at most one individual concerned with x (or altruist) in the society, and hence there is no public good (or joint altruism) – at least at the margin.

The foregoing results are presented for public goods in general in Kolm (1970), and for giving with an analysis of the motivations in Kolm (1984a). A specific concern for one's gift or "writing the gifts in the utility function" was suggested notably by Arrow (1974) and Becker (1974), and also worked out by Steinberg (1987) and Andreoni (1989, 1990).

References

Adam, J.S. (1963). "Wage inequalities, productivity and work quality". Industrial Relat. 3, 9–16.
Adam, J.S. (1965). "Inequity in social exchange". In: Berkowitz (Ed.), In: Advances in Experimental Social Psychology, vol. 2. Academic Press, New York.
Adam, J.S., Rosenbaum, W.E. (1964). "The relationship of worker productivity to cognitive dissonance about wage inequalities". Journal of Abnormal and Social Psychology 69, 19–25.
Akerlof, G. (1982). "Labor contract as partial gift exchange". Quarterly Journal of Economics 97, 543–569.
Alesina, A., Glaeser, E. (2004). Fighting Poverty in the US and in Europe. A World of Difference. Oxford University Press, Oxford.
Andreoni, J. (1989). "Giving with impure altruism: Applications to charity and Ricardian equivalence". Journal of Political Economy 97, 1447–1458.
Andreoni, J. (1990). "Impure altruism and donations to public goods: a theory of warm-glow giving". Economic Journal 100, 464–477.
Archibald, G.C., Donaldson, D. (1976). "Non-paternalism and the basic theorems of welfare economics". Canadian Journal of Economics 9, 492–507.

Arrow, K.J. (1974). "Gift and exchanges". Philosophy and Public Affairs 1 (4), 343–362.
Axelrod, R. (1984). The Evolution of Cooperation. Academic Press, New York.
Balasko, Y. (1978). "The transfer problem and the theory of regular economies". International Economic Review 19, 687–694.
Barro, R.J. (1974). "Are government bonds net wealth?". Journal of Political Economy 82 (6), 1095–1117.
Basu, K. (1977). "Information and strategy in iterated prisoners' dilemma". Theory and Decision 8, 293–298.
Basu, K. (1987). "Modelling finitely repeated games with uncertain termination". Economic Letters 23, 147–151.
Becker, G.S. (1974). "A theory of social interaction". Journal of Political Economy 82 (6), 1063–1093.
Bergson A. (1954). "On the Concept of Social Welfare". Quarterly Journal of Economics; Reprinted in: Essays in Normative Economics, 1966.
Bergson, A. (1966). Essays in Normative Economics. Harvard University Press, Cambridge, MA.
Bergstrom, T.C. (1999). "Systems of benevolent utility functions". Journal of Public Theory 1, 71–100.
Bhagwati, J.N., Brecher, R., Hatta, T. (1983). "The generalized theory of transfer and welfare: Bilateral transfers in a multilateral world". American Economic Review 83, 606–618.
Boulding, K. (1973). The Economics of Love and Fear, a Preface to Grants Economics. Wadsworth, Belmont, CA.
Boulding, K., Pfaff, M. (Eds.) (1972). Redistribution to the Rich and to the Poor. Wadsworth, Belmont, CA.
Boulding, K., Wilson, T.F. (Eds.) (1978). Redistribution Through the Financial System. Praeger, New York.
Brecher, R., Bhagwati, J.N. (1981). "Foreign ownership and the theory of trade and welfare". Journal of Political Economy 89, 497–518.
Buchanan, J.M. (1975). "The Samaritan dilemma". In: Phelps, E.S. (Ed.), Altruism, Morality and Economic Theory.
Chichilnisky, G. (1980). "Basic goods, the effects of commodity transfers and the international economic order". Journal of Development Economics 7, 505–519.
Chichilnisky, G. (1983). "The transfer problem with three agents once again: Characterization, uniqueness and stability". Journal of Development Economics 13, 237–248.
Collard, D. (1975). "Edgeworth's proposition on altruism". Economic Journal 85, 355–360. Reprinted in Zamagni (Ed.), 1995.
Collard, D. (1978). Altruism and the Economy. A Study in Non-Selfish Economics. Martin Robertson, Oxford.
Daly, G., Giertz, F. (1972). "Welfare economics and welfare reform". American Economic Review 62, 131–138.
Danner, P.L. (1973). "Sympathy and exchangeable value: Keys to Adam Smith's social philosophy". Review of Social Economy 34 (3), 317–331.
Dixit, A. (1983). "The multi-country transfer problem". Economics Letters 13, 49–54.
Edgeworth, F.Y. (1881). Mathematical Psychics: An Essay on the Application of Mathematics to the Moral Sciences. London School of Economics. New editions 1888, 1932, 1967, 1981.
Foley, D. (1970). "Lindahl's solution and the core of an economy with public goods". Econometrica 38, 66–72.
Friedman, M. (1962). Capitalism and Freedom. Chicago University Press, Chicago, IL.
von Furstenberg, G.M., Mueller, D.C. (1971). "The Pareto optimal approach to income redistribution: a fiscal application". American Economic Review 61, 628–637.
Gale, D. (1974). "Exchange equilibrium and coalitions: An example". Journal of Mathematical Economics 1, 63–66.
Gale, W.G., Scholtz, J.K. (1994). "Intergenerational transfers and the accumulation of wealth". Journal of Economic Perspectives 8 (4), 145–160.
Geanakoplos, J.D., Heal, G. (1983). "A geometric explanation of the transfer paradox in a stable economy". Journal of Development Economics 13, 223–236.
Gérard-Varet, L.-A., Kolm, S.-Ch., Mercier Ythier, J. (Eds.) (2000). The Economics of Reciprocity, Altruism, and Giving. MacMillan, London.

Goldfarb, R.S. (1970). "Pareto optimal redistribution: comment". American Economic Review 60, 994–996.
Gouldner, A. (1960). "The norm of reciprocity: A preliminary statement". American Sociological Review 25, 161–178.
Guesnerie, R., Laffont, J.-J. (1978). "Advantageous reallocations of initial resources". Econometrica 46, 835–841.
Hammond, P. (1975). "Charity: altruism or egoism ?". In: Phelps, E. (Ed.), Altruism, Morality, and Economic Theory. Russel Sage Fundation, New York.
Hobhouse, L.T. (1906). Morals in Evolution: A Study in Comparative Ethics. Second edition, 1951. Chapman and Hall, London.
Hochman, H.M., Rodgers, J.D. (1969). "Pareto optimal redistribution". American Economic Review 59, 542–557.
Jones, R. (1982). "Notes on the transfer problem in a three-agent setting". Mimeo.
Kolm, S.-Ch. (1963). Les Fondements de l'Economie Publique, Introduction à la Théorie Economique de l'Etat. IFP, Paris.
Kolm S.-Ch., (1966a). "The optimal production of social justice". In: Guitton, H., Margolis, J. (Eds.). International Economic Association Conference on Public Economics, Biarritz. Proceedings. Economie Publique (CNRS, Paris), 1968, pp. 109–177; Public Economics (MacMillan, London), 1969, pp. 145–200. Reprinted in: Landmark Papers in General Equilibrium Theory, Social Choice and Welfare, The Foundations of 20th Century Economics, selected by Arrow, K.J., Debreu, G., 2001 (Edward Elgar, Cheltenham), pp. 606–653.
Kolm, S.-Ch. (1966b). Les Choix Financiers et Monétaires. Dunod, Paris.
Kolm, S.-Ch. (1969a). "L'exploitation des nations par les nations". Revue économique XX (5).
Kolm, S.-Ch. (1970). L'Etat et le Système des Prix. Dunod, Paris.
Kolm, S.-Ch. (1971a). Justice et Equité. CEPREMAP, Paris (reprint 1972, CNRS); Translation: Justice and Equity, by See, H. MIT Press, Cambridge, MA, 1998.
Kolm, S.-Ch. (1971b). "La taxation de la consommation ostentatoire". Revue d'Economie Politique 1, 65–79.
Kolm, S.-Ch. (1973). La théorie de la réciprocité. CEPREMAP, Paris.
Kolm, S.-Ch. (1984a). La Bonne Economie: La Réciprocité Générale. (General Reciprocity, The Good Economy). Presses Universitaires de France, Paris.
Kolm, S.-Ch. (1984b). "Théorie de la réciprocité et du choix des systèmes économiques". Revue Economique 35, 871–910.
Kolm, S.-Ch. (1985). Le Contrat Social Libéral. (The Liberal Social Contract). Presses Universitaires de France, Paris.
Kolm, S.-Ch. (1987a). "Public economics". In: Eatwell, J., et al. (Eds.), New Palgrave Dictionary in Economics. MacMillan, London, pp. 1047–1055.
Kolm, S.-Ch. (1987b). "The freedom and consensus normative theory of the state: The Liberal Social Contract". In: Koslowski, P. (Ed.), Individual Liberty and Democratic Decision-marking: The Ethics, Economics and Politics of Democracy. JCB, Tübingen, pp. 97–127.
Kolm, S.-Ch. (1987c). Freedom and Public Goods, CERAS, n°62. Paris.
Kolm, S.-Ch. (1987d). Free-Riding and Voluntary Contributions in Large Numbers, CERAS, n°63. Paris.
Kolm, S.-Ch. (1987e). Freedoms, Cores and Public Goods. CERAS, n°66. Paris.
Kolm, S.-Ch. (1987f). Freedom and the Provision of Public Goods with all Degrees of Exclusion. CERAS, n°67. Paris.
Kolm, S.-Ch. (1987g). Freedom, Core, Efficiency with Public Goods in General Interdependence. CERAS, n°68. Paris.
Kolm, S.-Ch. (1989). Cooperative Game Properties of International Cooperation. CERAS, n°77. Paris.
Kolm, S.-Ch. (1990). "Employment and fiscal policy with a realistic view of the social role of wages". In: Essays in Honor of E. Malinvaud. MIT Press, Cambridge, MA, pp. 226–286.
Kolm, S.-Ch. (1995). "The theory of social sentiments: the case of envy". The Japanese Economic Review 1 (46), 63–87.
Kolm, S.-Ch. (1996a). Modern Theories of Justice. MIT Press, Cambridge, MA.

Kolm, S.-Ch. (1998a). "Chance and justice: Social policy and the Harsanyi–Vickrey–Rawls problem". European Economic Review 42 (8), 1393–1411.
Kolm, S.-Ch. (2004). Macrojustice the Political Economy of Fairness. Cambridge University Press, New York.
Kolm, S.-Ch. (2005). "The perplexing joint giving theorem". IDEP, Marseille.
Kotlikoff, L., Summers, L. (1981). "The role of intergenerational transfers in aggregate capital accumulation". Journal of Political Economy 89, 706–732.
Kranish, L. (1998). "Altruism and efficiency: a welfare analysis of the Walrasian mechanism with transfers". Journal of Public Economics 36, 369–386.
Kreps, D., Milgrom, P., Roberts, J., Wilson, R. (1982). "Rational cooperation in the finitely repeated prisoners' dilemma". Journal of Economic Theory 27 (2), 245–252.
Kurz, M. (1977). "Altruism as an outcome of social interaction". American Economic Review 68, 216–222.
Kurz, M. (1978). "Altruism as an outcome of social interaction". Journal of Public Economics 36, 369–386.
Leonard, D., Manning, R. (1983). "Advantageous reallocations of resources: a constructive example". Journal of International Economics 15 (3/4), 291–295.
Leontief, W. (1936, 1967). Explorations in Economics: Notes and Essays. Contributed in honour of Taussig, F.W. Books for Library Press, Freeport, NY, pp. 84–92.
Margolis, H. (1981). Selfishness Altruism and Rationality. Cambridge University Press, Cambridge.
Marshall, A. (1890). Principles of Economics, An Introductory Volume. New edition, 1920. Macmillan, London.
Mauss, M. (1924). "Essai sur le don, forme archaïque de l'échange". Année Sociologique n.s. 1, 30–186; English translation: Mauss, M., The Gift: Forms and Function of Exchange in Archaic Societies. Norton, New York, 1967.
Mill, J.S. (1898). Correspondance inédite (1828–1871). Alcan, Paris.
Mishan, E.J. (1972). "The futility of Pareto-efficient distribution". American Economic Review 62, 971–976.
Morelly (1755). Code de la Nature. Edition of 1953. Editions sociales, Paris.
Musgrave, R.A. (1970). "Pareto optimal redistribution: comment". American Economic Review 60, 991–993.
Olsen, E.O. (1971). "Some theorems in the theory of efficient transfers". Journal of Political Economy 79, 166–176.
Pareto, V. (1913). "Il massimo di utilità per una colletività". Giornale degli Economisti 3, 337–341. Reprinted as a long footnote in Treatise of General Sociology (and in: Mind and Society).
Phelps, E.S. (Ed.) (1975). Altruism Morality, and Economic Theory. Russell Sage, New York.
Piaget, J. (1932). La Naissance du Sentiment Moral chez l'Enfant. Payot, Genève.
Polemarchakis, H.M. (1983). "On the transfer paradox". International Economic Review 24, 749–760.
Postlewaite, A. (1979). "Manipulation via endowments". Review of Economic Studies 46, 255–262.
Postlewaite, A., Webb, M. (1984). "The possibility of recipient harming, donor benefiting transfers with more than two countries". Journal of International Economics 16 (3/4), 357–364.
Proudhon, P.-J. (1853/1857). Le manuel du spéculateur à la bourse. Garnier, Paris.
Rabin, M. (1993). "Incorporating fairness into game theory and economics". American Economic Review 83, 1281–1302.
Radner, R. (1980). "Collusion behaviour in non-cooperative epsilon-equilibria of oligopolies with long but finite lives". Journal of Economic Theory 22, 136–154.
Rawls, J. (1971). A Theory of Justice. The Belknap Press of Harvard University Press, Cambridge.
Rotemberg, J. (1994). "Human relations in the workplace". Journal of Political Economy 102 (4), 684–717.
Safra, Z. (1983). "Manipulation by reallocating initial endowments". Journal of Mathematical Economics 12, 1–18.
Samuelson, P.A. (1947). Foundations of economic analysis. Harvard University Press, Cambridge, MA.
Scott, R.H. (1972). "Avarice, altruism, and second party preferences". Quarterly Journal of Economics 86, 1–18.
Sertel, M. (1989/90). "Predonations resolve prisoners' dilemma, centipedes and the chain store paradox". Bogazici University, Istanbul, Turkey. Mimeo.

Sertel, M. (1994). "Manipulating Lindahl equilibrium via endowments". Economic Letters 46, 167–171.
Silber, J. (Ed.) (2000). Handbook on Income Inequality Measurement. Kluwer, Boston, MA.
Smale, S. (1980). "The prisoner's dilemma and dynamic systems associated to non-cooperative games". Econometrica 48, 1617–1634.
Smith, A. (1759). The Theory of Social Sentiments. Edition of 1966. Kelly, New York.
Smith, A. (1776). An Inquiry into the Nature and Cause of the Wealth of Nations. Edition of 1937. Random House, New York.
Solow, R.M. (1971). "Blood and thunder". Yale Law Journal 80, 1696–1711.
Steedman, I. (1989). From Exploitation to Altruism. Blackwell, Oxford.
Steinberg, R. (1987). "Voluntary donations and public expenditures in a federalist system". American Economic Review 77, 24–36.
Sugden, R. (1984). "Reciprocity: The supply of public goods through voluntary contribution". Economic Journal 94, 772–787.
Swaney, J. (1990). "Common property, reciprocity, and community". Journal of Economic Issues 24.
Thurnwald, R. (1932). Die Gemeinde der Banaro.
Thurow, L.C. (1971). "The income distribution as a pure public good". Quarterly Journal of Economics 85, 327–336.
Titmuss, R.M. (1971). The Gift Relationship. Allen and Unwin, London.
Wicksteed, P.H. (1888). The Alphabet of Economic Science. R.H. Hutton, London.
Wicksteed, P.H. (1906). "Review of Professor V. Pareto Manuale di Economia Politica". Economic Journal 16, 553–557.
Wicksteed, P.H. (1933). The Common Sense of Political Economy. Robbins Edn., London.
Winter, S.J. Jr. (1969). "A simple remark on the second optimality theorem of welfare economics". Journal of Economic Theory, 99–103.
Yano, M. (1983). "Welfare aspects in the transfer problem". Journal of International Economics 15, 277–290.
Zamagni, S. (Ed.) (1995). The Economics of Altruism. Edward Elgar, Cheltenham.
Zeckhauser, R. (1971). "Optimal mechanisms for income transfer". American Economic Review 61, 324–334.

Further reading

Abrams, B.A., Schmitz, M.D. (1978). "The 'crowding-out effect of governmental transfers on private charitable contributions". Public Choice 33 (1), 28–40.
Andreoni, J. (1988a). "Privately provided public goods in a large economy: The limits of altruism". Journal of Public Economics 35, 57–73.
Andreoni, J. (1988b). "Why free ride? Strategies and learning in public goods experiments". Journal of Public Economics 37, 291–304.
Andreoni, J. (1995). "Warm-glow versus cold-prickle: The effects of positive and negative framing on cooperation in experiments". Quarterly Journal of Economics 110 (1), 1–21.
Archibald, G.C., Donaldson, D. (1976). "Non-paternalism and the basic theorems of welfare economics". Canadian Journal of Economics 9, 492–507.
Aristotle. Ethique à Nicomaque. Edition of 1972, Vrin, Paris.
Aronfreed, J. (1970). "The socialization of altruistic and sympathetic behavior: Some theoretical and experimental analyses". In: Macaulay, J., Berkowitz, L. (Eds.), Altruism and Helping Behaviour. Academic Press, New York.
Aronfreed, J., Paskal, V. (1965). Altruism, empathy, and the conditioning of positive affect. Unpublished manuscript, University of Pennsylvania.

Arrow, K.J. (1981). "Optimal and voluntary income distribution". In: Economic Welfare and the Economics of Soviet Socialism: Essays in Honor of Abram Bergson. Cambridge University Press, Cambridge, pp. 267–288.

Banks, S. (1979). "Gift-giving: A review and an interactive paradigm". In: Wilkie, W. (Ed.), Advances in Consumer Research, vol. 6. MI Association for Consumer Research, Ann Arbor, pp. 319–324.

Baron, J.N. (1988). "The employment relation as a social relation". Journal of the Japanese and International Economies 2, 492–525.

Becker, H. (1956). "Empathy, sympathy and Scheler". International Journal of Sociometry 1.

Becker, H. (1956). Man in Reprocity: Introductory Lectures on Culture, Society and Personality. Praeger, New York.

Becker, G.S. (1961). "Notes on an economic analysis of philanthropy". National Bureau of Economic Research.

Becker, G.S. (1976). "Altruism, egoism and genetic fitness: Economics and sociobiology". Journal of Economic Literature 14, 817–826.

Becker, G.S. (1976). The Economic Approach to Human Behavior. University of Chicago Press, Chicago, London.

Becker, G.S. (1981). "Altruism in the family and selfishness in the market place". Econometrica 48, 1–15.

Becker, G.S. (1981). A Treatise on the Family. Harvard University Press, Cambridge, MA.

Bentham, J. (1789). Principles of Morals and Legislation. Clarendon, Oxford.

Bentham, J. (1952–1954). "The philosophy of economic science". In: Stark, W. (Ed.), In: Jeremy Bentham's Economic Writings, vol. 1–3. Franklin, New York.

Berg, J., Dickhaut, J., McCabe, K. (1995). "Trust, reciprocity and social history". Games and Economic Behavior 10, 122–142.

Bergstrom, T.C. (1970). "A "Scandinavian consensus" solution for efficient income distribution among nonmalevolent consumers". Journal of Economic Theory 2, 383–398.

Bergstrom, T.C., Blume, L., Varian, H. (1986). "On the private provision of public goods". Journal of Public Economics 29, 25–49.

Berkowitz, L. (1966). "A laboratory investigation of social class and national differences in helping behavior". International Journal of Psychology 1, 231–242.

Berkowitz, L. (1968). "Responsibility, reciprocity, and social distance in help-giving: An experimental investigation of English social class differences". Journal of Experimental Psychology 4, 46–63.

Berkowitz, L. (1970). "The self, selfishness and altruism". In: Macaulay, J., Berkowitz, L. (Eds.), Altruism and Helping Behavior. Academic Press, New York.

Berkowitz, L. (1971). Social norms, feelings and other factors affecting helping behavior and altruism. Unpublished manuscript, University of Wisconsin.

Berkowitz, L., Daniels, L. (1963). "Responsibility and dependency". Journal of Abnormal and Social Psychology 66, 429–437.

Berkowitz, L., Friedman, P. (1967). "Some social class differences in helping behavior". Journal of Personality and Social Psychology 5, 217–225.

Bernheim, B.D. (1986). "On the voluntary and involuntary provision of public goods". American Economic Review 76, 789–793.

Berthoz, A., Jorland, G. (Eds.) (2004). L'Empathie. Odile Jacob, Paris.

Bianchi, M. (1993). "How to learn sociality: True and false solutions to Mandeville problem". History of Political Economy 25 (2).

Bishop, J. (1987). "The recognition and reward of employee performance". Journal of Labor Economics 5, S36–S56.

Boadway, R., Pestieau, P., Wildasin, D. (1989). "Tax-transfer policies and the voluntary provision of public goods". Journal of Public Economics 39, 157–176.

Bolton, G., Brandts, J., Ockenfels, A. (1998). "Measuring motivations for the reciprocal responses observed in a simple dilemma games". Experimental Economics 1 (3), 207–219.

Bolton, G., Ockenfels, A. (2000). "ERC – A theory of equity, reciprocity and competition". American Economic Review 90, 166–193.

Boorman, S.A., Levitt, P.R. (1980). The Genetics of Altruism. Academic Press, New York.
Boudon, R. (1979). La logique du social. Hachette, Paris.
Boulding, K.E. (1962). "Notes on a theory of philanthropy". In: Conflict and Defense. A General Theory. Harper, New York.
Bowles, S. (1998). "Endogenous preferences: The cultural consequences of markets and other economic institutions". Journal of Economic Literature 36 (1), 75–111.
Bremmer, R.H. (1975). "Private philanthropy and public needs: historical perspective", pp. 89–114, in Research Papers, vol. 1, part. II. Commission on Private Philanthropy and Public Need (Department of the Treasury), Washington, DC.
Brunner, J.K., Falkinger, J. (1999). "Taxation in an economy with private provision of public goods". Review of Economic Design 4, 357–379.
Bryan, J.H. (1972). "Why children help: A review". Journal of Social Issues 28 (3).
Bryan, J.H., London, P. (1970). "Altruistic behavior by children". Psychological Bulletin 73, 200–211.
Bryan, J.H., Test, M.A. (1967). "Models and helping: Naturalistic studies in aiding behavior". Journal of Personality and Social Psychology 6, 400–407.
Buber, M. (1977). "Utopie et socialisme". Aubier-Montaigne, Paris.
Camerer, C. (1988). "Gifts as economic signals and social symbols". American Journal of Sociology 94, 5180–5214.
Campbell, D.T. (1965). "Ethnocentric and other altruistic motives". In: Levine, D. (Ed.), Nebraska Symposium on Motivation. University of Nebraska Press, Lincoln.
Carens, J. (1980). Equality, Moral Incentives and the Market. Chicago.
Coate, S., Ravallion, M. (1993). "Reciprocity without commitment". Journal of Economic Development 40, 1–24.
Coricelli, G., McCabe, K., Smith, V. (2000). "Theory of mind mechanism in personal exchange". In: Hotano, G., Okada, N., Tanabe, H. (Eds.), Affective Minds. Elsevier, Amsterdam.
Cornes, R.C., Sandler, T. (1984). "Easy riders, joint production and public goods". Economic Journal 94, 580–598.
Cornes, R.C., Sandler, T. (1984). "The comparative static properties of the impure public good model". Journal of Public Economics 54, 403–421.
Cornes, R.C., Sandler, T. (1985). "The simple analytics of pure public good provision". Economica 52, 103–116.
Wolfenden Committee Report (1978). The Future of Voluntary Organizations. Croom Helm, London.
Darwin, C. (1981). La descendance de l'homme, et la sélection sexuelle (transl. E. Barbier). Complexe, Brussels.
Davis, J. (1975). "The Particular theory of exchange". Archives européennes de sociologie XVI (2).
Descartes, R. (1897–1910, 1965). In: Adam, C., Tannery, P. (Eds.), Œuvres complètes. Vrin, Paris.
Dickinson, F.G. (Ed.) (1962). Philanthropy and Public Policy. NBER, New York.
Dickinson, F.G. (1970). The Changing Position of Philanthropy in the American Economy. Columbia University Press, New York. (For: Nat. Bur. Econo. Res.)
Doland, D., Adelberg, K. (1967). "The learning of sharing behavior". Child Development 38, 695–700.
Doland, D., Adelberg, K. (1967). "The learning of sharing behavior". Child Development 38, 695–700.
Douglas, J. (1983). Why Charity. The Case for a Third Sector. Sage Publications, Beverly Hills.
Ekstein, R. (1972). "Psychoanalysis and education for the facilitation of positive human qualities". Journal of Social Issues 28 (3).
Elster, J. (1982). Sour Grapes. Cambridge University Press, Cambridge.
Elster, J. (1989). The Cement of Society – A Study of Social Order. Cambridge University Press, Cambridge.
Elster, J. (1998). "Emotions and economic theory". Journal of Economic Literature 36, 47–74.
Falk, A., Fischbacher, U. (2001). "A theory of reciprocity". CEPR n°3014, October.
Fehr, E., Gächter, S. (2000). "Fairness and retaliation: The economics of reciprocity". Journal of Economic Perspective 14 (3), 159–181.
Fehr, E., Gächter, S., Kirchsteiger, G. (1996). "Reciprocal fairness and noncompensating wage differentials". Journal of Institutional and Theoretical Economics 152 (4), 608–640.

Fehr, E., Gächter, S., Kirchsteiger, G. (1997). "Reciprocity as a contract enforcement device: experimental evidence". Econometrica 65 (4), 833–860.
Fellner, C.H., Marshall, J.-R. (1970). "Kidney donors". In: Macaulay, J., Berkowitz, L. (Eds.), Altruism and Helping Behavior. Academic Press, New York.
Foster, V., Mourato, S., Pearce, D., Özdemiroglu, E. (2000). The Price of Virtue: The Economic Value of the Charitable Sector. Edward Elgar, Cheltenham, United Kingdom and Northampton, MA.
Frank, R.H. (1988). Passions Within Reason: The Strategic Role of the Emotions. Norton, New York.
Frank, R.H. (1990). "A theory of moral sentiments". In: Mansbridge, J. (Ed.), Beyond Self-Interest. University of Chicago Press, Chicago, pp. 71–96.
Freuchen, P. (1961). Book of the Eskimos. World Publishing Co., Cleveland and New York.
Frey, B. (1997). Not Just for the Money – An Economic Theory of Personal Motivation. Edward Elgar, Cheltenham.
Friedrichs, R.W. (1960). "Alter versus ego: An exploratory assessment of altruism". American Sociological Review 25, 496–508.
Frisch, D.M., Greenberg, M.S. (1968). "Reciprocity and intentionality in the giving of help". Proceedings of the 76th Annual Convention of the American Psychological Association 3, 383–384.
Gächter, S., Falk, A. (2002). "Reputation or reciprocity? An experimental investigation". Scandinavian Journal of Econometrics 24.
Geanakoplos, J., Pearce, D., Stacchetti, E. (1989). "Psychological games and sequential rationality". Games and Economic Behavior 1, 60–79.
Gergen, K., Gergen, M., Meter, K. (1972). "Individual orientations to prosocial behavior". Journal of Social Issues 28 (3).
Gergen, Greenberg, Willis (Eds.), Social Exchange, Plenum Press, New York and Londres.
Gide, C. (1905). Economie sociale. Librairie de la Société du Recueil général des lois et des arrêts, Paris.
Gintis, H. "Strong reciprocity and human sociality". Journal of Theoretical Biology.
Giving in America (1975). Report of the Commission on Private Philanthropy and Public Need. John H. Filer, Chairman. Washington, DC, Commission on Private Philanthropy and Public Need.
Goodman Committee (1976). Charity Law and Voluntary Organizations. National Council of Social Service, London, Bedford Square.
Goodstadt, M.S. (1971). "Helping and refusal to help: A test of balance and reactance theories". Journal of Experimental Social Psychology 7, 610–622.
Goranson, R.E., Berkowitz, L. (1966). "Reciprocity and responsibility reactions to prior help". Journal of Personality and Social Psychology 3, 227–232.
Greenberg, J. (1978). "Effects of reward value and retaliative power on allocation decisions: Justice, generosity or greed?". Journal of Personality and Social Psychology 36, 367–379.
Greenberg, M.S., "A theory of Indebtedness", In: Gergen, Greenberg, Willis (Eds.), Social Exchange, Plenum Press, New York and Londres.
Greenglass, E.R. (1969). "Effects of prior help and hindrance on willingness to help another: Reciprocity or social responsibility". Journal of Personality and Social Psychology 11, 224–232.
Gui, B. (2000). "Beyond transactions: On the interpersonal dimension of economic reality". Annals of Public and Cooperative Economics 71 (2), 139–168.
Güth, W. (1995). "An evolutionary approach to explaining cooperative behavior by reciprocal incentives". International Journal of Game Theory 24 (4), 323–344.
Güth, W., Yaari, M. (1992). "An evolutionary approach to explain reciprocal behavior in a simple strategic game". In: Witt, U. (Ed.), Explaining Process and Change, Approaches to Evolutionary Economics. University of Michigan Press, Ann Arbor.
Guyer, P. (1993). Kant and the Experience of Freedom. Cambridge University Press, Cambridge.
Hamilton, W.D. (1971). "Selection of selfish and altruistic behavior in some extreme models". In: Eisenberg, J.F., Dillon, W.S. (Eds.), Man and Beast: Comparative Social Behavior. Smithsonian Institution Press, Washington, DC.
Hamilton, W.D. (1972). "Altruism and related phenomena, mainly on social insects". Annual Reviews of Ecology and Systematics 3.

Handlon, B.J., Gross, P. (1959). "The development of sharing behavior". Journal of Abnormal and Social Psychology 59, 425–428.
Hansmann, H.B. (1980). "Role of non-profit enterprise". Yale Law Journal 89 (April), 835–901.
Harris, L.A. (1967). "A study of altruism". Elementary School Journal 68, 135–141.
Harris, M. (1970). "Reciprocity and generosity: some determinants of sharing behavior". Child Development 41, 313–328.
Hartmann, H. (1960). Psychoanalysis and Moral Values. International Universities Press, New York.
Hebb, D.O. (1971). "Comment on altruism: The comparative evidence". Psychological Bulletin 76, 409–410.
Heider, F. (1958). The Psychology of Interpersonal Relations. Wiley, New York.
Heimann, F. (Ed.) (1973). The Future of Foundations. Prentice-Hall, Englewood Cliffs, NJ.
Hochman, H.M., Rodgers, J.D. (1970). "Pareto optimal redistribution: a reply". American Economic Review 60, 997–1002.
Hoffman, M. (1970). "Moral development". In: Mussen, P. (Ed.), Carmichael's Manual of Child Development. Wiley, New York.
Hornstein, H., Fisch, E., Holmes, M. (1968). "Influence of a model's feelings about his behavior and his relevance as a comparison on the observers' I helping behavior". Journal of Personality and Social Psychology 10, 222–226.
Hornstein, H.A. (1970). "Experiments in the social psychology of prosocial behavior". Final report. NSF Grant 1715.
Hume, D. (1902). An Enquiry Concerning the Principles of Morals. L.A. Selby-Bigge, Oxford.
Isaac, M.R., McCue, K.F., Plott, C. (1985). "Public goods provision in an experimental environment". Journal of Public Economics 26, 51–74.
Isaac, M.R., Walker, J.M. (1988). "Communication and free-riding behavior: The voluntary contribution mechanism". Economic Inquiry 26, 585–608.
Isaac, M.R., Walker, J.M. (1988). "Group size effects in public goods provision: The voluntary contribution mechanism". Quarterly Journal of Economics 103, 179–199.
Isaac, M.R., Walker, J.M., Thomas, S.H. (1984). "Divergent evidence on free riding: An experimental examination of possible explanations". Public Choice 43 (2), 113–149.
Isaac, M.R., Walker, J.M., Williams, A.M. (1994). "Group size and the voluntary provision of public goods: experimental evidence utilizing large groups". Journal of Public Economics LIV, 1–36.
Isen, A.M., Horn, N., Rosenhan, D.L. (1971). "Success, failure, and altruistic behavior". Mimeo. Stanford University.
Isen, A.M., Levin, P.F. (1972). "Effect of feeling good on helping: Cookies and kindness". Journal of Personality and Social Psychology 21, 384–388.
Kahneman, D., Knetsch, J.L. (1992). "Valuing public goods: The purchase of moral satisfaction". Journal of Environmental Economics and Management 22 (1), 57–70.
Kahneman, D., Knetsch, J.L., Thaler, R.H. (1986a). "Fairness as a constraint on profit seeking: Entitlements in the market". American Economic Review 76, 728–741.
Kahneman, D., Knetsch, J.L., Thaler, R.H. (1986b). "Fairness and the assumptions of economics". Journal of Business 59, S285–S300.
Kant, I. (1980). Fondements de la métaphysique des moeurs. Delagrave, Paris.
Kant, I. (1991). The Metaphysic of Morals. translated by M.J. Gregor. Cambridge University Press, Cambridge. The first edition in 1797.
Kennett, D.A. (1980). "Altruism and economic behaviour". American Journal of Economics and Sociology 39 (2).
Keynes, J.M. (1949). How to Pay for the War?. Harcourt, Brace, New York.
Kim, O., Walker, M. (1984). "The free rider problem: Experimental evidence". Public Choice 43 (1), 3–24.
Kolm, S.-Ch. (1969b). "Théorie démocratique de la justice sociale". Revue d'Economie politique 1, 138–141.
Kolm, S.-Ch. (1975, 1979). La réciprocité générale. CEPREMAP, Paris.
Kolm, S.-Ch. (1979). Fondements de la théorie du don de la réciprocité, et du choix des systèmes économiques. CEPREMAP, Paris.

Kolm, S.-Ch. (1980). "Psychanalyse et théorie des choix". Social Science Information 19 (2), 269–339.
Kolm, S.-Ch. (1981a). "Altruisme et efficacité: le sophisme de Rousseau". Social Science Information 20, 293–344.
Kolm, S.-Ch. (1981b). "Efficacité et altruisme: le sophisme de Mandeville, Smith et Pareto". Revue Economique 32, 5–31.
Kolm, S.-Ch. (1983b). "Introduction à la réciprocité générale". Social Science Information 22, 569–621.
Kolm, S.-Ch. (1983a). "Altruism and efficiency". Ethics 94, 18–65;
  Reprinted in Zamagni, S. (Ed.), The Economics of Altruism, op. cit.
Kolm, S.-Ch. (1986). "Is only egoism productive?". Development 3.
Kolm, S.-Ch. (1987h). L'Homme Pluridimensionnel. Albin Michel, Paris.
Kolm, S.-Ch. (1992). "Reciprocity". Political Economy of the Good Society Newsletter 2 (Summer), 1–6.
Kolm, S.-Ch. (1994). "The theory of reciprocity and of the choice of economic systems". Investigaciones Económicas 18 (1), 67–95.
Kolm, S.-Ch. (1996b). "Moral public choice". Public Choice 87, 117–148.
Kolm, S.-Ch. (1997b). The Theory of Reciprocity. IEA, Marseille; In: Gérard-Varet, L.-A., Kolm, S.-Ch., Mercier-Ythier, J. (Eds.), The Economics of Reciprocity, Giving, and Altruism. Macmillan, London, 2000, pp. 1115–1141.
Kolm, S.-Ch. (1997a). Introduction to the Economics of Reciprocity, Giving and Altruism. IEA, Marseille; In: Gérard-Varet, L.-A., Kolm, S.-Ch., Mercier-Ythier, J. (Eds.). The Economics of Reciprocity, Giving, and Altruism. Macmillan, London, 2000, pp. 1–44.
Kolm, S.-Ch. (1998b). "Une introduction à la théorie de la réciprocité et du choix des systèmes économiques". In: Mahieu, F.-R., Rapoport, H. (Eds.), Altruisme, Analyses Economiques. Economica, Paris, pp. 17–50.
Kolm, S.-Ch. (2000). "The logic of good social relations". Annals of Public and Cooperative Economics 72 (2), 171–189.
Kolm, S.-Ch. (2005). "The logic of good social relations". In: Gui, B., Sugden, R. (Eds.), Economics and Social Interaction, Chapter 8. MacMillan, London.
Kranton, R. (1994). "Reciprocal exchange: a self-sustaining system". American Economic Review 86 (4), 830–851.
Krebs, D. (1970). "Altruism: An examination of the concept and a review of the literature". Psychological Bulletin 73, 258–302.
Kropotkin, P. (1896–1897). "Co-operation: A reply to Herbert Spencer". Freedom, Dec. 1896–Jan. 1897.
Kropotkin, P. (1892). La conquête du pain. Tresse & Stock, Paris.
Kropotkin, P. (1927). L'éthique. Stock, Paris.
Kropotkin, P. (1902, 1972). Mutual Aid: A Factor of Evolution. Re-edition. Penguin Books, London.
Kurz, M. (1979). "Altruistic equilibrium". In: Balassa, B., Nelson, R. (Eds.), Economic Progress, Private Values and Policy. North-Holland, pp. 177–200.
Latane, B., Darley, J. (1970). The Unresponsive Bystander: Why Doesn't He Help?. Appleton-Century-Croft, New York.
Ledyard, J. (1995). "Public goods: A survey of experimental research". In: Roth, A., Kagel, J. (Eds.), Handbook of Experimental Economics. Princeton University Press, Princeton, pp. 111–194.
Leeds, R. (1963). "Altruism and the norm of giving". Merrill-Palmer Quarterly 9, 229–240.
Lenrow, P. (1965). "Studies in sympathy". In: Tomlins, S.S., Izard, C.E. (Eds.), Affect, Cognition, and Personality: Empirical Studies. Springer, New York.
Leventhal, G., Anderson, D. (1970). "Self-interest and the maintenance of equity". Journal of Personality and Social Psychology 15, 57–62.
Leventhal, G.S., Weiss, T., Long, G. (1969). "Equity, reciprocity and reallocating rewards in the dyad". J. Pers. Soc. Psychol. 13, 300–305.
Lévi-Strauss, C. "The principle of reciprocity". In: Coser, L.A., Rosenberg, G. (Eds.), Sociological Theory. MacMillan, New York.
Levine, D.K. (1997). "Modeling altruism and spitefulness in experiments". Review of Economic Dynamics 1 (3), 593–622.

Lewinsky, H. (1951). "Pathological generosity". The International Journal of Psychoanalysis 32, 185–189.
Lindbeck, A., Nyberg, S., Weibull, J. (1999). "Social norms and economic incentives in the Welfare State". Quarterly Journal of Economics 116 (1), 1–35.
Lindbeck, A., Weibull, J. (1988). "Altruism and time consistency: the economics of the fait accompli". Journal of Political Economy 96, 1165–1182.
Macaulay, J., Berkowitz, L. (Eds.) (1970). Altruism and Helping Behavior. Academic Press, New York.
Mac Kean, R.M. (1979). "Private charity and public policy". Liberty Fund seminar. Miami. April.
Mahieu, F.-R., Rapoport, H. (1998). Altruisme Analyses Economiques. Economica, Paris.
Mandeville, B. (1714). The Fable of the Bees or Private Vices, Public Benefits. Clarendon Press, Oxford, 1988.
Marshall, A. (1890). Principles of Economics. MacMillan, London.
Marwell, G., Ames, R. (1981). "Economists free ride, does anyone else?: Experiments on the provision of public goods, IV". Journal of Public Economics 15, 295–310.
Mavity, J., Ylvisaker, P., "Private philanthropy and public affairs", pp. 795–836, in *Research Papers*, vol. 2, 1975, Commission on Private Philanthropy and Public Need (Department of Treasury), Washington, DC.
Meade, G.H. (1934). Mind, Self and Society. University of Chicago Press, Chicago.
Mercier Ythier, J. (1993). "Equilibre général de dons individuels". Revue Economique, 925–950.
Mercier Ythier, J. (1998). "The distribution of wealth in the liberal social contract". European Economic Review 42, 329–347.
Midlarsky, E. (1968). "Aiding responses: An analysis and review". Merrill-Palmer Quarterly 14, 229–260.
Miller, D. (1988). "Altruism and the welfare state". In: Donald Moon, J. (Ed.), Responsibility, Rights, and Welfare: The Theory of the Welfare State. Westview Press, Boulder and London, pp. 163–188.
Mullin, R. (1980). "Present Alms". Phlogiston, Birmingham.
Nagel, T. (1970). The Possibility of Altruism. Oxford University Press, Oxford.
Nagel, T. (1986). The View from Nowhere. Clarendon Press, Oxford.
Nason, J.W. (1977). "Trustees and the Future of Foundations". Council on Foundations, New York.
Nédoncelle, M. (1942). La réciprocité des consciences. Aubier, Paris.
Nicole, P. (1675). Essais de Morale. Paris.
Niobe Layton, D. (1987). "Philanthropy and voluntarism. An annoted bibliography". The Foundation Center.
Owen, D. (1964). English Philanthropy 1660–1960. Harvard University Press, Cambridge, MA.
Pareto, V. (1916). A Treatise on General Sociology. Dover, New York.
Pareto, V. (1966). "Manuel d'Economie politique, 1906". In: Oeuvres complètes, vol. 7. Droz, Genève.
Pfaff, M. (1972). "Le domaine de l'économie de don". Analyse et Prévision 13 (6), 733–738.
Piliavin, J., Rodin, J., Piliavin, J. (1969). "Good samaritanism: An underground phenomenon?". Journal of Personality and Social Psychology 13, 289–299.
Posnett, J., Sandler, T. (1986). "Joint supply and the finance of charitable activity". Public Finance Quarterly 14, 209–222.
Pruitt, D.G. (1968). "Reciprocity and credit building in a laboratory dyad". Journal of Personality and Social Psychology 8, 143–147.
Pryor, F. (1977). The Origins of the Economy. Academic Press, New York.
Rabin, M. (1998). "Psychology and Economics". Journal of Economic Literature 36, 11–46.
Roberts, R.D. (1984). "A positive model of private charity and public transfers". Journal of Political Economy 92, 136–148.
Rosenhan, D.L. (1969). "Some origins of concern for others". In: Mussen, P., Covington, M., Langer, J. (Eds.), Trends and Issues in Developmental Psychology. Holt, Rinehart & Winston, New York.
Rosenhan, D.L. (1970). "The natural socialization of altruistic autonomy". In: Macaulay, J., Berkowitz, L. (Eds.), Altruism and Helping Behavior. Academic Press, New York.
Rosenhan, D.L., White, G.M. (1967). "Observation and rehearsal as determinants of prosocial behavior". Journal of Personality and Social Psychology 5, 424–431.
Russel, D.R. (1984). "A positive model of private charity and public transfers". Journal of Political Economy 92, 136–147.

Sacco, P.L., Zamagni, S. (1996). "An evolutionary dynamic approach to altruism". In: Farina, F., Hahn, F., Vannucci, S. (Eds.), Ethics, Rationality, and Economic Behavior. Clarendon Press, Oxford, pp. 265–300.
Sacco, P.L., Zamagni, S. (Eds.) (2002). Complessità Relazionale e Comportamento Economico. Il Mulino, Bologna.
Sahlins, M. (1977). The Use and Abuse of Biology (An Anthropological Critique of Sociobiology). Tavistock Publications, London.
Sawyer, J. (1966). "The altruism scale: A measure of cooperative, individualistic, and competitive interpersonal orientation". American Journal of Sociology 71, 407–416.
Scheler, M. (1971). Natures et formes de la sympathie. Payot, Paris.
Schwartz, B. (1967). "The social psychology of the gift". American Journal of Sociology 73, 1–11.
Schwartz, R. (1970). "Personal philanthropic contributions". J.P.E. 78 (6), 1264–1291.
Selten, R., Ockenfels, A. (1998). "An experimental solidarity game". Journal of Economic Behavior and Organization 34 (4), 517–539.
Sertel, M. (1992). "The Nash bargaining solution manipulated by pre-donations is Talmudic". Economic Letters 40, 45–55.
Sertel, M., Chen, F. (1989). "Resolving paradoxical centipedes behavioralistically or by unilateral predonations". In: Partasenathy, I. (Ed.), Game Theory and Economic Applications. Springer-Verlag, Berlin.
Sethi, R., Somanathan, E. (2001). "Preference evolution and reciprocity". Journal of Economic Theory 97, 273–297.
Singer, P. (1973). "Altruism and commerce: A defense of Titmuss against Arrow". Philosophy and Public Affairs 2.
Sorokin, P.A. (1954). Forms and Techniques of Altruistic and Spiritual Growth. Beacon Press, Boston.
Staub, E. (1972). "Instigation to goodness: The role of social norms and interpersonal influence". Journal of Social Issues 28 (3).
Stein, E. (1964). On the Problem of Empathy. Transl. W. Stein. Martinus Nijhoff, Den Haag.
Stotland, E. (1969). "Exploratory investigations of empathy". In: Berkowitz, L. (Ed.), Advances in Experimental Social Psychology. Academic Press, New York.
Sugden, R. (1993). "Thinking as a team: Towards an explanation of nonselfish behavior". Social Philosophy and Policy 10, 69–89.
Sugden, R. (2000). "Team preferences". Economics and Philosophy 16, 175–205.
Sugden, R. (2002). "Beyond sympathy and empathy: Adam Smith's concept of fellow feeling". Economics and Philosophy 18, 63–88.
Thurnwald, R. (1932). Die Gemeinde der Banaro.
Thurnwald, R. (1932). Die menschliche Gesellschaft.
Thurnwald, R. (1969). Economics in Primitive Communities. Oxford University Press, London.
Thurnwald, R. (1973). Black and White in East Africa: the Fabric of a New Civilization. Kraus Reprint, Nendeln (Liechtenstein).
Tognoli, J. (1975). "Reciprocation of generosity and knowledge of game termination in the decomposed Prisoner's Dilemma Game". European Journal of Social Psychology.
Tönnies, F. (1972). Gemeinschaft und Gesellschaft. Wissenschaftliche Buchgesellschaft, Darmstadt.
Tournier, P. (1963). The Meaning of Gifts. John Knox Press, Richmond.
Trivers, R.L. (1971). "The evolution of reciprocal altruism". Quarterly Review of Biology 46, 35–37.
Turner, W.D. (1948). "Altruism and its measurement in children". Journal of Abnormal and Social Psychology 43, 502–516.
Ugurel-Semin, R. (1952). "Moral behavior and moral judgement of children". Journal of Abnormal and Social Psychology 47, 463–476.
Uhlaner, C.J. (1989). "Relational goods and participation: Incorporating sociability into a theory of rational action". Public Choice 62, 253–285.
Vickrey, W.S. (1962). "One economist's view of philanthropy". In: Dickinson, F. (Ed.), Philanthropy and Public Policy. National Bureau of Economic Research, New York.
Walras, L. (1865). Les Associations populaires de consommation, de production et de crédit (Ristampa anastatica della prima od. dol 1865, Paris, Dentu, a cura di Oscar Nuccio, Ed. Bizzarri, Roma, 1969).

Warr, P.G. (1982). "Pareto optimal redistribution and private charity". Journal of Public Economics 19, 131–138.

Warr, P.G. (1983). "The private provision of a public good is independent of the distribution of income". Economic Letters 17, 207–211.

Weisbrod, B.A., "Towards a theory of the non-profit sector", In: E.S. Phelps (Ed.), Altruism, Morality and Economic Theory.

Weisbrod, B.A. (Ed.) (1977). The Voluntary Non-Profit Sector. Heath, Lexington, MA, DC.

Weisbrod, B.A. (1988). The Nonprofit Economy. Harvard University Press, Cambridge, MA.

Weiss, R.F., Buchanan, W., Alstatt, L., Lombardo, J.-P. (1971). "Altruism is rewarding". Science 171, 1262–1263.

Wildavsky, A., Douglas, J. (1978). The Future of Foundations. Change Magazine, New Rochelle, NY.

Wilke, H., Lanzetta, J. (1970). "The obligation to help: The effects of prior help on subsequent helping behavior". Journal of Experimental Social Psychology 6, 466–493.

Wilson, E.O. (1975). "Sociobiology: the New Synthesis". The Belknap Press of Harvard University Press, Cambridge (Mass.), London.

Wintrobe, R. (1981). "It pays to do good, but not to do more good than it pays". Journal of Economic Behavior and Organization 2, 201–213.

Wispe, L. (1968). "Sympathy and empathy". In: Sills, D.L. (Ed.), International Encyclopedia of the Social Sciences, vol. 15. Macmillan, New York.

Wispe, L. (Ed.) (1972). "Positive forms of social behavior". The Journal of Social Issues 28 (3).

Wright, B. (1942). "Altruism in children and the perceived conduct of others". Journal of Abnormal and Social Psychology 37, 218–233.

Wright, D. (1971). The Psychology of Moral Behaviour. Pelican.

PART 1

FOUNDATIONS

1A: SOCIAL VIEW

Chapter 2

THE EMPIRICAL ANALYSIS OF TRANSFER MOTIVES

ERIK SCHOKKAERT

Center for Economic Studies, KU Leuven

Contents

Abstract	128
Keywords	128
1. Introduction	129
2. Some basic insights from the psychological literature	130
2.1. A list of motivations	131
(a) self-interest	131
a.1. material self-interest	131
a.2. social prestige	132
(b) reciprocity	132
(c) norms and principles	133
c.1. dutiful altruism	133
c.2. social pressure	133
(d) pure altruism and empathy	134
2.2. Some broader questions	135
3. Tastes and motivations: Why are economists interested? Why should they be interested?	137
3.1. The empirical predictions of the pure public goods model	138
3.2. Other consequences for government policy	140
3.3. The analysis of philanthropic markets and non-profit organizations	141
3.4. Rationality and egoism: The homo economicus	142
4. Charitable giving and volunteering	144
4.1. Giving as a private good: Tax prices and income	144
4.2. Crowding out and the warm-glow of giving	153
4.3. Status of sociological and demographic variables	157
4.4. Direct evidence on preferences	159
5. Interhousehold and intrafamily transfers of money and time	165
5.1. Altruism versus exchange or reciprocity: A sketch	166
5.2. Motives for interhousehold transfers	168
5.3. Gifts: The deadweight loss of Christmas?	171

Handbook of the Economics of Giving, Altruism and Reciprocity, Volume 1
Edited by Serge-Christophe Kolm and Jean Mercier Ythier
Copyright © 2006 Elsevier B.V. All rights reserved
DOI: 10.1016/S1574-0714(06)01002-5

6. Conclusion 174
Acknowledgements 176
References 176

Abstract

The empirical economic literature covers many different forms of pro-social behaviour going from anonymous charitable contributions to caring for an ageing parent or buying Christmas gifts. The chapter focuses on the meta-questions concerning the motivations underlying this behaviour. While the "public goods"-model of altruism has played a pivotal role in the economic work, the discussion in the chapter is structured around a simple list of motivations, derived from the psychological literature. Altruism (or empathy) is only one of the many motivations leading to voluntary transfers. Transfers may also follow from a feeling of duty or because the donor wants to obey social norms. They may be part of reciprocal arrangements, which finally are in the self-interest of all the parties involved. They may reflect pure materialistic egoism or a desire to gain social prestige.

The survey of the empirical literature makes a distinction between one-way transfers where there is no real social interaction between the donor and the recipient and two-way transfers, i.e. interpersonal gifts that take place in a non-anonymous setting. The former refer to contributions of money and time to charities, the latter refer to interhousehold and intrafamily transfers. It is argued that the simple oppositions between "pure altruism" and "warm glow" or between "altruism" and "exchange" are insufficient, and that we should more explicitly think about how to distinguish the different "warm glow" or "exchange"-interpretations from one another. Traditional economic methods of "indirect testing" for motivational differences will probably be insufficient for this task.

A better insight into the different motivations for pro-social behaviour is important for its own sake. It is also necessary for understanding the consequences of government intervention (the crowding-out effect) or the behaviour of charities.

Keywords

warm glow, pure altruism, dutiful altruism, social norms, social prestige, crowding-out

JEL classification: D10, D64, Z13

1. Introduction

Simple observation shows that non-market transfers of money and time play an essential role in the economy. Despite the existence of welfare states, people contribute money or supply volunteer labour for charities. At Christmas or for special occasions they give each other gifts, which are mainly non-cash. Parents spend money and time on their children, even after they have grown up. Children keep supporting their parents when they grow old. People help other people when these get ill or unemployed. In some pre-industrial societies this has given rise to complicated networks of informal social insurance.

In all of these transactions there is no direct or immediate gain for the donor. Therefore, some people tend to interpret all these acts as indications of "altruism". This simple interpretation does not survive closer scrutiny, however. Although there may be no direct quid pro quo, donors still may gain in the longer run, e.g., because they expect reciprocal action at a later stage when they themselves need help. Since it is very well possible that these delayed gains are the primary motivation guiding behaviour, social scientists distinguish acts of pro-social *behaviour* from the *motivations* lying behind it. The altruistic motivation is only one of the possible motivations explaining pro-social behaviour.

As a matter of fact, many have questioned whether we even need such an "altruistic" motivation to explain pro-social behaviour. Is it not possible to interpret all seemingly altruistically motivated behaviour as basically egoistic? Certainly among economists it seems to be a popular idea that it is the task of science to reason away the existence of or the need for altruism. To quote Frank (1988, p. 21): "The flint-eyed researcher fears no greater humiliation than to have called some action altruistic, only to have a more sophisticated colleague later demonstrate that it was self-serving."

However, this simple strategy of reducing all pro-social behaviour to a more or less sophisticated form of egoism is nowadays much less popular than it used to be. Psychologists have collected convincing evidence for the existence of a genuine feeling of empathy, i.e. concern for others, in human beings. Sociobiologists have created room for pro-social behaviour by showing how selfish genes may induce altruism at the level of the phenotype. Cultural transmission of values plays an important role in the stimulation of such pro-social behaviour. Hoffman (1981) describes how the emotion of empathy can be seen as the main mediator between genetic inclinations and observed behaviour. Evolutionary game theory has shown how altruists may survive in a population together with egoists. Economists have incorporated altruistic motivations in their model of the *homo economicus*.

If the simple research strategy of reducing all pro-social behaviour to egoism does not work, we are facing a much more challenging task. What is the relative importance of altruism and other motivations in explaining pro-social behaviour? Can we devise a reasonable classification scheme for these different motivations? How to distinguish between them? Are the behavioural predictions following from different motivations identical?

In this chapter I will look at the empirical economic literature on pro-social behaviour from this angle. The literature covers many different forms of pro-social behaviour going from anonymous charitable contributions to caring for an ageing parent or buying Christmas gifts. We know from psychological and sociological work that pro-social behaviour is highly context-dependent and that there is much interpersonal heterogeneity in motivations. It therefore does not make sense to try constructing an encompassing approach and it is not at all surprising that the literature contains such a wide variety of models. I will not go into the details of these different approaches, which are discussed in other chapters of this Handbook, but rather focus on the meta-questions concerning the motivations underlying behaviour.

I start in Section 2 with a brief summary of some basic insights from the psychological literature. This summary hinges around an admittedly simplistic list of motivations, which can be used to structure the discussion later on. While economists traditionally have been rather reluctant to introduce taste differences in their models, this is much less so in their work on pro-social behaviour. In Section 3, I suggest some reasons for why this may be the case. This offers me the opportunity to introduce the "public goods"-model of altruism, which has played a pivotal role in the economic work. I then turn to a more concrete discussion of different strands of the literature. I make a distinction between one-way transfers where there is no real social interaction between the donor and the recipient[1] and two-way transfers, i.e. interpersonal gifts that take place in a non-anonymous setting. The former refer to contributions of money and time to charities and are analysed in Section 4. The latter refer to interhousehold and intrafamily transfers. I discuss them in Section 5, which also includes a short section on Christmas gifts. Section 6 concludes.

Throughout the chapter I focus on the empirical work using real-life data. I largely neglect the huge experimental literature on reciprocity, altruism and the voluntary provision of public goods. This is not because I think it is relatively less important. Quite the contrary, I will argue that it is essential if we want to get a better understanding of the motivational structure underlying voluntary transfers. I will illustrate this claim with some examples.

2. Some basic insights from the psychological literature

The question of the identification of motives guiding pro-social behaviour is essentially a multidisciplinary one. Economists tend to accept that other social scientists have a comparative advantage in this field. As a matter of fact, many economists seem to treat the academic literature in the other social sciences as a kind of toolkit from which they can pick at any moment any tool they want in a highly selective way. But, while it is true that almost any economic model can probably be justified by at least one psychological

---

[1] This is the "master–dog" model in the terminology of Archibald and Donaldson (1976).

article, this practice hardly does justice to the richness of the work in the other social sciences. Giving an overview of this work therefore looks like a natural starting point for this chapter. Yet, given that this literature is large and disparate,[2] it would be rather naive to imagine that a simple summary can be given. The main aim of this section is therefore to introduce a framework that may help structuring my review of the empirical work of economists. It may also help in seeing more clearly some of the remaining lacunae in the economic approaches.

I first set up a structured list of different transfer motives. In a second subsection I raise some broader questions related to that list.

2.1. A list of motivations

Neglecting the fine subtleties of the different theories and cutting through the differences in terminology, I propose to distinguish four broad motivations, which seem to cover the classifications used in the literature. I classify them from "more selfish" to more "altruistic", although the use of these terms is sometimes quite confusing.

(a) self-interest

a.1. material self-interest

A first series of motivations is related to pure material self-interest. People give money and time because they hope to derive consumption benefits from it.[3] As Frank (1988, p. 21) remarks: "Sure enough, when we examine membership lists of Rotary Clubs and other "service" organizations, we find a surfeit of lawyers, insurance agents, and others with something to sell, but not many postal employees or airline pilots". The most unambiguous evidence of such motivations can be found in the sphere of volunteering. Volunteers participate more in service organizations when they have an active interest in the good or service produced by the organization. Or they want to invest in their human capital, e.g., when they are not participating in the job market and want to maintain or rebuild their employment skills [Unger (1991), Piliavin and Charng (1990)].

But material self-interest may also be important where one would not expect it *a priori*. Even concern for the fate of the poor in society can be motivated by purely selfish considerations: do not keep the poor too poor or they will steal your car or break your windows [Brennan (1973), Archibald and Donaldson (1976)].

---

[2] Batson (1998) has found in the psychological academic literature since 1973 not less than 538 articles with "prosocial behaviour", "helping" or "altruism" in the title. Another piece of evidence for the multifarious nature of the non-economic literature is the (fascinating) "open peer commentary" following Caporael et al. (1989). A more detailed discussion of the psychological literature can be found in Chapter 7 by Lévy-Garboua et al. in this Handbook. The latter authors work with a slightly different classification of motivations than the one I propose.

[3] The term "material" self-interest is a little problematic because the personal consumption benefits may refer to non-material goods (such as enjoying poetry or music).

a.2. social prestige

Another self-interested motivation is the desire to acquire social prestige. Gift giving or volunteering by themselves may lead to an increase in social prestige in a society where these activities are valued positively. It is possible that the degree of "social prestige" obtained depends on the relationship of one's own gift and the gift of others [Holländer (1990)]. Or charity can be a means of signalling income [Glazer and Konrad (1996)]. What is obviously crucial to acquire social prestige is the fact that others know that the gifts are made and by whom. As we will see later on, the "reporting" behaviour of charities may help in identifying the importance of the social prestige motive [Harbaugh (1998a, 1998b)].

(b) reciprocity

A more sophisticated (because less one-sided) version of the self-interest motivation has always been present in the economic literature. Already in the seventies economists like Hammond (1975) and Kurz (1978) presented simple game-theoretic models showing that pro-social behaviour could be a stable equilibrium in a game of social interaction between purely self-interested players. The more recent literature offers many more sophisticated versions of the same idea. While it could be said that this is only another version of the pure egoism hypothesis, I think it is useful to distinguish the two. In the case of reciprocity all partners in the social interaction gain – and the fact that others gain is a necessary condition for them to keep participating. My self-interest therefore to some extent coincides with the self-interest of others. This is not true in the "material interest" or "social prestige"-motivations. Moreover, in the reciprocal case it is possible that I really do care about others – and that others care about me. It is difficult to differentiate reciprocal altruism and continuous social interactions motivated by egoism. Both the behaviour and the outcomes may be identical in the two cases: the individuals act (apparently) in a pro-social way and they all gain.

The concept of "reciprocity" has been used with many similar but not identical connotations.[4] For some authors "reciprocity" refers in the first place to a pattern of behaviour. Fehr and Gächter (2000) define reciprocity as a behavioural tendency through which the actor is responding to friendly or hostile actions even if no gains can be expected. "Reciprocity means that in response to friendly actions, people are frequently much nicer and much more cooperative than predicted by the self-interest model; conversely, in response to hostile actions they are frequently much more nasty and even brutal. (...) People repay gifts and take revenge even in interactions with complete strangers and even if it is costly for them and yields neither present nor future material rewards" [Fehr and Gächter (2000, p. 159)]. Sugden (1984) uses the term "reciprocity" for the situation in which individuals "match" their own contributions to a public good with the

---

[4] See Kolm (1984, 2000b) for a more elaborate analysis and a more precise definition.

contributions of others. I do not follow these behavioural interpretations and I use the concept of reciprocity in a motivational sense, in which I am referring to "cooperation" in repeated interactions where the actors help each other and at the same time expect to gain from cooperation.

There are obvious links between this "reciprocity"-motivation and the behavioural patterns as described by Fehr and Gächter (2000) and Sugden (1984). But they do not coincide. This brings us in the lively debate about the mechanisms, which can support cooperative behaviour in repeated interactions, and about the further question whether it is possible that behaviour which is "learnt" for prisoner dilemma-type situations then also crops up in other situations. I do not want to go into this debate here. Nor do I want to explore in any depth the role of social norms and emotions in this regard. For my purposes, it is sufficient to remember that one motivation for pro-social behaviour may be the expectation that the recipient will reciprocate this pro-social behaviour.

(c) norms and principles

People may act pro-socially because they want to obey personal principles or social norms, which dictate pro-social behaviour in a given situation. If they obey their own personal principles, we can talk about dutiful altruism; if they follow externally imposed social norms they are sensitive to social pressure.

c.1. dutiful altruism

When norms are internal, we refer to a "sense of duty". People feel committed to pro-social behaviour because they want to follow their "conscience", i.e. a set of internalised moral norms. The dutiful altruist acts pro-socially, even if the recipient does not reciprocate this pro-social behaviour. The literature sometimes talks about "Kantian altruism", referring to the deontological ethics in the work of Kant. However, the use of the adjective "Kantian" may be problematic. "Kantian" conduct follows rational maxims, i.e. norms obtained by reason and definitely not by tradition, education, imitation, and so on.[5] I will therefore use the more general term "dutiful" altruism.

c.2. social pressure

In the second case, the norms are external and social rewards are essential to explain behaviour. A dutiful altruist will (try to) act pro-socially, even in a situation where nobody else can see him. On the contrary, someone who obeys external social norms does so in the first place to avoid blame or to get social approval. In many psychological approaches the motivations c.1 and c.2 are considered to be different stages in moral

---

[5] I owe this remark to Serge-Christophe Kolm.

development. Someone who acts pro-socially because he wants to avoid social disapproval is then situated at a lower stage of moral development than the dutiful altruist, who has internalised the moral principles.

It is obvious that there is some overlap between these motivations and the ones mentioned earlier. Obedience to norms may reflect (dutiful) unconditional commitment. But it is equally clear that norms play an important role in sustaining a reciprocal equilibrium. Although the theoretical difference between the two interpretations is clear, real world actors may not always be able to distinguish the two. The same is true for the desire to acquire social prestige (as an egoistic motivation) and giving in to social pressure in the acceptance of norms. The basic motivating factor may be different – but again they are quite close[6] and it may be very difficult to distinguish them in empirical work.

(d) pure altruism and empathy

Finally we have the truly altruistic motivation of pro-social behaviour, reflecting a genuine concern for the situation of someone else. The psychological literature now accepts rather generally that "empathy" is an important motivating factor, where "empathy" can be described in general terms as "an other-oriented emotional response congruent with the perceived welfare of another person" [Batson (1998)]. This definition is close to the economic modelling of utility interdependency, in which the utility of other human beings, and more specifically of the recipient(s), enters the utility function of the donor.[7] More generally, however, the idea of "altruism" also covers the possibility of what economists would call "paternalistic altruism", in which other aspects of the recipient's situation (e.g., his health situation) enter the donor's utility function. At the level of motivations, the number of potential donors is not really relevant. For the analysis of behaviour, however, it will turn out to be crucial whether there are many potential donors or only one (or a few).

Considerable evidence has been collected to support the idea that feeling empathy for a person in need leads to increased helping of that person.[8] Some have questioned whether this is really "altruism". Mueller (1986) mentions the so-called "hedonistic paradox": if a person is motivated to increase another's welfare, he is pleased to attain this desired goal and therefore his apparent altruism can also be seen as a product of egoism. But this paradox is not really a paradox: even if goal attainment brings pleasure, this does not imply that attainment of pleasure is the ultimate goal of human action [Batson (1998)]. Of course, even after discarding the paradox, there still remains the more basic objection that helping someone for whom one feels empathy could still be instrumental

---

[6] One way to see the difference would be to introduce an asymmetry between going for rewards (social prestige) and trying to avoid punishments (social disapproval). While this asymmetry may be essential for some psychological work [Batson (1998)], it is much less popular among economists.

[7] Note that the utility of the recipient in this sentence refers to her level of happiness. This presupposes a level of measurement which goes beyond what is assumed in the largest part of economic theory.

[8] Batson (1998) gives an overview of the most important studies.

behaviour that is ultimately driven by the motivations described before. Careful experimental work [Batson (1998)] has shown, however, that the empathy-altruism hypothesis can in some cases better explain behaviour than the most evident of these egoistic reinterpretations: (a) that helping behaviour reduces one's empathic arousal, which is experienced as aversive; (b) that it avoids possible social and self-punishments for failing to help; (c) that it promises social and self-rewards for doing what is good and right. Nobody denies that these other motivations may dominate sometimes. But at the same time the recent experimental research strongly suggests that "altruism-acting with the goal of benefiting another – does exist and is part of human nature" [Piliavin and Charng (1990, p. 27)].

Note that we use a narrow definition of "true altruism". The two latter "egoistic" reinterpretations of helping behaviour basically bring us back to the motivations of obedience to social norms and of the sense of duty. Is the dutiful altruist really an egoist? Most ordinary citizens will find it very strange to call a person who is driven by high moral principles an "egoist". After all, someone who would sacrifice his own life out of a sense of duty would then also be called an egoist. While the definition of "pure altruism" is clear and coherent from a "scientific" point of view, at the same time it goes counter to the emotional and moral connotations of the concept of "altruism" among the population. I will therefore keep using the term "dutiful *altruism*", assuming that obedience of moral principles may also be seen as a form of altruism.

Whether we call these motivations "egoist" or "altruist", the basic distinction between "social norms" and "empathy" is clear and is made by different authors, albeit under different names. It is close to the overview of values given in the book by Kolm (1984) or in the articles of the sociologists Piliavin and Charng (1990) and the social psychologist Batson (1998). A learning theorist like Rushton (1982) distinguishes empathy and norms. An "empathy" theorist like Hoffman (1981) distinguishes empathy, social approval and guilt. Oliner and Oliner (1988) find three dispositional factors to predict the activity of people rescuing Jews in Nazi Europe: a proclivity to feel empathy, a sensitivity to normative pressure from social groups and the adherence to moral principles. Elster (1990) distinguishes the motives of love and duty, Sen (1977) talks about sympathy and commitment. Although my list of motivations is admittedly superficial and incomplete, it does reflect the distinctions made in the largest part of the literature.

2.2. Some broader questions

When we observe pro-social behaviour we tend to think in terms of altruism or charity. But what about justice? In the philosophical literature there is often a difficult relationship between justice and charity. Put (too) simply one could say that justice is about the basic institutions in society and about rights, while charity is more about personal behaviour and about compassion. In actual reality, however, many people will not make these philosophical distinctions. In any case, there will be a constant interaction between justice opinions and charitable behaviour. I give two examples.

Take the case of a person who thinks that there should be no poor in a just society (certainly when that society is rich enough). Suppose that person is consistent and votes in favour of political parties or in favour of proposals that support a more equal income distribution. What implications does this have for his charitable giving? Since his ideas about justice reflect a concern for the poor, we could expect a priori that he would also give to charities in a society where his justice ideal is not reached. But it is equally well possible that he argues that justice is a matter of politics and of government intervention and that his egalitarian opinions do not compel him to a specific pattern of personal behaviour.[9] These attitudes do not only reflect differences in moral principles concerning equality and distribution. They are also influenced by attitudes towards the government. Why doesn't the US have a European-style welfare state [Alesina, Glaeser and Sacerdote (2001)]?

A second example can be found in the sphere of helping behaviour. Experimental research has shown that people's helping behaviour may be influenced by their attribution of responsibility. When the need situation can be blamed on the victim's laziness, drunkenness or other irresponsibility, others are less likely to help [Unger (1991), Batson (1998)]. Here again, justice considerations seem to interact with compassion.

In a certain sense one could say that all these justice considerations can be captured in the concept of "principles" and "norms". But then the examples clearly suggest that it may not be easy to derive the structure of these principles directly from observable behaviour. Things get even more complicated when we realize that most people have conflicting and incoherent principles – and that they may use arguments concerning responsibility and justice to hide mere self-interest.

Giving a list of motivations can hardly be seen as an explanation of behaviour. I have noted already that some of these motivations are overlapping. More importantly, in some circumstances they will also be conflicting among each other. It is fairly obvious that there may be a conflict between "empathy" and "material self-interest". Trade-offs will have to be made and different people will make these trade-offs in a different way. Cognitive factors play a role in the complex benefit–cost calculations underlying behaviour. Individual information processing and formation of expectations will influence decisions in any specific situation. Moreover, there is plenty of evidence that human beings react to specific cues in their environment and to specific experiences. People who have themselves been helped or who did get a gift are more likely to help or make a gift themselves, even when the people concerned are different persons. Even more surprisingly, people tend to help someone or make him a gift if they have seen that other person helping or making a gift, even if they were not involved in that previous interaction.[10] All this implies that pro-social behaviour is highly context-dependent.

---

[9] I do not want to raise the philosophical question whether it is consistent to be in favour of a more egalitarian income distribution and at the same time keep the largest part of one's income – see Cohen (2000).

[10] Kolm (1984, 2000a) calls this the Descartes-effect, because it has already been observed and discussed by René Descartes. An overview of the abundant psychological literature on helping behaviour can be found, e.g., in Chapter 10 of Baron and Byrne (2003).

In some cases it may be necessary to take the next step and ask the question: where do these preferences come from? While economists have a tendency to take preferences as given, this may be a serious limitation when preferences are endogenous. There is consensus among psychologists that social learning – through reinforcement or simply through imitation – plays an important role in the process of preference formation [Rushton (1982)]. Therefore social interactions may be crucially important: seeing people giving might increase one's own giving. Moreover, there is also some evidence of a kind of hysteresis-effect [Piliavin and Charng (1990)]: someone who has given in the past is more likely to give in the future (after controlling for personality factors). Certainly a better insight into such learning processes may be important to understand the (optimal) behaviour of charities that want to raise money. It may also help explaining why there is a well-functioning social network with reciprocal transfers in some villages of a country and not in others. Modelling social interactions and taking into account the past may be crucial to understand actual giving.

Many of the questions raised in this section belong traditionally to the realm of other social sciences: sociology, psychology, anthropology and sociobiology. Economists have often been reluctant to think explicitly about motivations. However, this is much less true for the economic literature on charitable giving and monetary transfers. How to explain this unusual interest?

3. Tastes and motivations: Why are economists interested? Why should they be interested?

For a non-economist the question of this section must be very surprising. How could any social scientist *not* be interested in the motivations behind charitable behaviour? Yet the economic tradition is rather suspicious of explanations of behavioural changes or interindividual differences in terms of what is called preference changes or preference differences. These are often seen as ad hoc explanations and *de gustibus non est disputandum* [Stigler and Becker (1977)]. Rather than being interested in motivations, many economists are only interested in rationalizing observed behaviour. They are already happy with an approach in which people behave *as if* they are following a simplified (and therefore easily understandable) model of rational choice. This focus on observable behaviour is defensible. But the main reason for being interested in the motivations behind pro-social behaviour is exactly this: the reactions of economic agents on exogenous changes in the environment will crucially depend on the motivational structure (Section 3.1). This has immediate implications for the analysis of government policy and philanthropic markets (Sections 3.2 and 3.3). Finally, the whole question of pro-social behaviour raises doubts about the basic idea of the homo economicus (Section 3.4). These four sets of reasons explain why the economic literature on charities and gift giving has shown an unusual interest in motivations.

3.1. The empirical predictions of the pure public goods model

The most straightforward approach to model gifts is to start from the idea that the donor is concerned about the utility of the recipient, i.e. to introduce the utility of the recipient into the utility function of the donor. As became already clear in Becker (1974)'s influential article, this straightforward model turns out to have dramatic consequences. Not only is it difficult to reconcile the predictions from the model with the observable facts. In addition the choice of model turns out to have important policy implications.

Let us first consider the simple case of two individuals. Assume that individual i is concerned about j and maximizes the utility function $U_i(x_i, U_j(x_j))$ where x_i and x_j refer to the consumption of i and j respectively. Denote the initial income levels of i and j by y_i and y_j respectively and the possible gift from i to j by g_i. We then can write the budget constraints for i and j respectively as

$$x_i + g_i = y_i, \tag{1a}$$
$$x_j = y_j + g_i, \tag{1b}$$

where the consumption price has been normalized to 1. Combining expressions (1a) and (1b), the maximization problem for individual i becomes

$$\max U_i(x_i, U_j(x_j)) \tag{2}$$
$$\text{s.t.} \quad x_i + x_j = y_i + y_j.$$

This shows immediately that any redistribution of initial income between the two individuals (leaving the sum of the incomes unchanged) will not change the optimal values of x_i and x_j: if individual j gets a larger income, individual i will reduce his gift by the same amount so as to stay in the original optimum, i.e. the original combination (x_i, x_j). This simple intuition has been used to model bequests and intergenerational transmissions between parents and children. It lies at the heart of Barro (1974)'s interpretation of the Ricardian equivalence hypothesis, i.e. the neutrality of debt financing of government expenditures. For understandable reasons, this neutrality assumption has been widely tested.

A similar result has been derived in the case of charitable giving. Again, the most straightforward approach is to say that the donor is interested in the cause for which she is giving. If we call this cause Z, the utility function of individual i is written as $U_i(x_i, Z)$. The good cause Z can refer to the utility of the poor (in which case we are close to the model sketched before), but other interpretations are also possible. In the realistic situation where there are many donors, Z is "produced" by the total amount of gifts, i.e. $Z = z(G)$, where $G = \sum_i g_i$. Introducing this expression for Z in the utility function the specification of $z(\cdot)$ can be merged into the functional form and we get (with some slight abuse of notation and after reformulating the budget constraint (1a))[11]

$$\max U_i(x_i, G)$$
$$\text{s.t.} \quad x_i + G = y_i + G_{-i},$$
(3)

where $G_{-i} = \sum_{j \neq i} g_j$ is exogenously given for individual i. It is immediately obvious that the cause Z (or G) becomes a pure public good in this model. Among others, Andreoni (1988) has shown that this would imply that in large economies virtually no one would contribute. The model therefore predicts the non-existence of what it tries to explain, i.e. charitable donations. Of course, this result is basically an application of the traditional free rider-argument [Samuelson (1954)] and it brings us immediately into the large literature on voluntary provision of public goods.

The public goods-specification leads to some other drastic predictions. Under the traditional Nash assumptions individual i will treat G_{-i} as given and therefore the expression $y_i + G_{-i}$ plays the same role as money income in the traditional consumer model. Taking into account (1a), it is straightforward to derive that

$$\frac{\partial g_i}{\partial G_{-i}} = \frac{\partial g_i}{\partial y_i} - 1.$$
(4)

Sugden (1982) has argued that this is an extremely unrealistic prediction. Take the case of someone giving 100 Euro to a certain charity, which collects 1 million Euros from all kinds of sources. Now suppose the charity gets an additional 100 Euro from another donor. If $\partial g_i/\partial y_i$ is small enough, expression (4) implies that this would be sufficient for donor i to reduce his own gift to almost nothing. This does not seem to be what we observe.

An even more striking prediction is the one of perfect crowding-out of government expenditures. For a complete formal analysis we have to analyse the full Nash equilibrium of the contribution game and take into account the possibility of corner solutions.[12] However, the basic intuition can be grasped with the following less rigorous reasoning. Since for each individual j the budget constraint can also be written as $y_j = x_j + g_j$, we get for the budget constraint of individual i[13]

$$x_i + G = y_i + \sum_{j \neq i}(y_j - x_j).$$
(5)

---

[11] I assume for convenience that the price of charitable gifts is equal to 1. This is not correct if gifts are tax deductible. I will return to that possibility in Section 4.1.

[12] See Roberts (1984) and Bergstrom, Blume and Varian (1986). The analysis can be extended to the case of proportional tax and matching subsidy rates – see Boadway, Pestieau and Wildasin (1989a, 1989b).

[13] Note that this way of writing the budget constraint already suggests that income redistribution will not change the amount of G, a finding which is again similar to the one in the two-person case. This suggestion has also been proven rigorously [Warr, (1982, 1983)].

Now suppose that the government starts contributing G^* to cause Z, financed through taxes τ_k on individuals $k = 1, \ldots, n$. The budget constraint for individual i then becomes

$$x_i + G = y_i - \tau_i + \sum_{j \neq i}(y_j - \tau_j - x_j) + G^*, \tag{6}$$

which under the government budget constraint $G^* = \sum_k \tau_k$ is completely equivalent to (5). Therefore an analogous reasoning holds as in the simple two-person case: if the government contributes G^*, individual i will adjust his own giving behaviour so as to stay in the original (x_i, G) combination. Since the same reasoning holds for all individuals, we can derive a prediction of perfect crowding-out: if the government starts "producing" G^*, it will "crowd out" private gifts completely. Government provision will only influence G after it has fully crowded out all private gifts.

This perfect crowding-out prediction of the public goods model has important policy implications. These were especially relevant at the time during the eighties when governments in the UK and in the US wanted to cut down government expenditures and argued that such a cut would be largely compensated by an increase in private charity. Many authors have tried to test the crowding-out prediction in their empirical analysis of charitable donations. As we will see in Section 4.2, the assumption of perfect crowding-out was usually rejected. Therefore, doubts were raised concerning the basic specification of the altruistic motivation in the public goods-model. This led to the formulation of alternative models, which fitted better the observed facts. More specifically, Andreoni (1989, 1990) argued that the empirical facts with respect to charitable giving and crowding-out can only be explained if one makes the assumption that donors derive a so-called "warm glow" from the act of giving itself, i.e. that the own contribution and the contributions of others cannot be seen as perfect substitutes. The gift g_i then enters the utility function directly and we have to replace model (3) with

$$\begin{aligned} \max\ & U_i(x_i, g_i, G) \\ \text{s.t.}\ & x_i + G = y_i + G_{-i}. \end{aligned} \tag{7}$$

The comparison of (3) and (7) has generated a keen interest among economists. We will return to this debate in Section 4.2.

3.2. Other consequences for government policy

As noted in the previous section one reason for the interest of economists in the neutrality and perfect crowding-out hypotheses is to be found in their drastic policy implications. One cannot model the effects of government debt or government provision of public goods without making explicit assumptions about consumer motivations. The typical agnostic stance of economists concerning tastes does not work here. As a matter of fact, the limitations of such an agnostic stance for the analysis of government policy do not only show up in the debate on neutrality and crowding-out. I give two other examples.

First, as Kaplow (1998) has shown, the optimal tax treatment of gifts will depend on the structure of preferences. This is fairly obvious. If the gift reflects the existence of externalities, these will have to be taken into account in tax policy. And it obviously will matter whether donors derive a warm glow from the gross gift (tax component included) or rather from their net contribution to the charity. Empirical insight into the structure of preferences is then crucial to formulate the optimal tax rules.

Second, the importance of motivations has cropped up in cost–benefit analysis and in the environmental economics literature. Many economists have proposed the use of interview techniques to evaluate non-market goods, which are often of a public nature. There is a whole debate around the exact interpretation of the answers to these so-called contingent valuation questions. Do they really reflect "willingness to pay"? Or are they rather seen by the respondents as charitable contributions? In the latter case they may also reflect a "warm glow" component [Kahneman and Knetsch (1992), Schkade and Payne (1993), Spash (2000), Nunes and Schokkaert (2003)]. It has even been argued that the warm-glow hypothesis explains some seeming anomalies in the contingent valuation responses. The most important of these is the so-called embedding (or adding-up) problem: the fact that the sum of the revealed willingness to pay for two independent projects A and B when the two questions are asked separately, is not identical to the revealed willingness to pay for A and B together when both projects are included in the same question. In its simplest form, the "warm glow" interpretation of this phenomenon rests on the following hypothesis concerning response behaviour:

$$WTP^*_A = WTP_A + WG, \tag{8a}$$

$$WTP^*_B = WTP_B + WG, \tag{8b}$$

$$WTP^*_{A+B} = WTP_{A+B} + WG, \tag{8c}$$

where the asterisk denotes "revealed" willingness-to-pay and WG refers to a warm glow component, assumed identical in the different cases. If the "true" willingness-to-pay values are consistent, i.e. if $WTP_{A+B} = WTP_A + WTP_B$, it will still be true that the "revealed" willingness-to-pay values are not. More specifically,

$$WTP^*_{A+B} < WTP^*_A + WTP^*_B. \tag{9}$$

The specification (8)–(9) is admittedly very simple and a more complete model should incorporate the possibility that the warm-glow component does not necessarily enter in an additive way and may depend on the nature and the size of the contribution. Yet it suffices to make the point that many of the questions treated in the literature on contingent valuation are closely related to the topic of this chapter. Given the methodological and social (including financial) relevance of the contingent valuation techniques, it is not surprising that the debate has been at times rather heated [Hausman (1993)].

3.3. The analysis of philanthropic markets and non-profit organizations

Non-profit organizations play an important role in the economy. Their financing does depend to a large extent on charitable contributions. Moreover, they often use volunteer labour. Even to simply understand the rationale for the existence of non-profit organizations – and why they are crucially important in some sectors and at the same time completely absent in other sectors – it is necessary to understand the motivations of donors and volunteers [Rose-Ackerman (1996)].

At a more concrete level, non-profits will use economic factors of production to collect monetary contributions and to convince people to volunteer. The structure of consumer motivations will influence the efficiency of these fund raising efforts and therefore also the degree of competition on the philanthropic market. The crowding-out effect is relevant here. Does an increase in government subsidies lead to a decrease in the amount of private donations? But again, the scope of the inquiry is broader. The optimal direction of information and advertising efforts will be influenced by the structure of consumer preferences. If potential donors are sensitive to social pressure, direct social contacts (possibly via friends and peers) may be a good strategy. Things are completely different when donors are immune to this kind of pressure and rather want to get objective and reliable information on the good cause supported by the charity. A policy of reporting the names of the generous donors may be successful if people care about social prestige and think they can enhance it by signalling their generosity. However, it may be counterproductive if dutiful donors prefer to remain anonymous.

3.4. Rationality and egoism: The homo economicus

I think that there is still another and more basic reason for the unusual interest of economists in the motivations underlying voluntary transfers. Some social scientists (economists and non-economists alike) have argued that the mere presence of such transfers points to the importance of altruism, and hence to the unacceptability of the traditional paradigm of the *homo economicus*. It is not surprising that many economists then have taken up the challenge and tried to show that pro-social behaviour can be explained with the economic model.

I must admit that I find a large part of this literature very confusing. Many non-economists see the *homo economicus* as a neurotic creature pursuing all the time his own material self-interest. Yet the basic hypothesis of rational behaviour does not refer to the content of the preferences, but rather to the idea that individuals try to do the best they can according to their own subjective ordering of social states. For some, this ordering will be dominated by material self-interest. For others, however, their "self-interest" may consist in the pursuit of a higher moral ideal. The utility function does not have any hedonistic connotation but simply reflects these orderings. Look at model (2) with an individual i that is really concerned about the utility of individual j. This seems an attractive way to model the purely altruistic motivation of "empathy". As a matter of fact, a large part of the psychological discussion about empathy – including the experimental work – can easily be rephrased in terms of "utility functions", *on the condition that* one does not give these functions a hedonic interpretation.

On the other hand, economists have been very keen to show that many instances of apparently pro-social behaviour reflect either immediate material self-interest, a desire for social prestige or at least reciprocal egoism. There can be no doubt that some of the models proposed are really informative in analysing the social mechanisms at work. However, one wonders why some economists seem to be so happy after having constructed another example of an "egoistic" model. What do they want to prove? Nobody is denying that there are many different motivations for pro-social behaviour. And formulating one specific example of an "egoistic" explanation is not at all convincing evidence that real empathic altruism would not exist in the real world (and even less so if the proposed model is not tested with empirical data). In their narrow-minded emphasis on material self-interest many economists have added to the confusion about the *homo economicus* as an artificial construction without any link with the psychological and sociological literature.

This does not dissolve all questions around the usefulness of the economic paradigm. The real challenge consists in investigating whether pro-social behaviour can be explained in terms of a model of a rational actor without having to resort too often to ad hoc-explanations. I think that it has become pretty clear in recent years that the analytical tools of economics have worked very well in explaining (or making sense of) social interactions in general and pro-social behaviour in particular. This is true even for "extreme" cases, such as the tendency for people to give non-monetary gifts at occasions like birthdays or Christmas. I will return to this phenomenon in Section 5.3. At the same time, however, some specific examples of context-dependent behaviour remain to be explained. Why do people react so strongly to specific cues in the environment? Is it possible to explain the Descartes-effect by considerations of merit? Perhaps these specific phenomena are beyond the interest of economics. But certainly much more work about expectations and information processing is needed before we will be able to draw a conclusion about the limitations of the paradigm of economic rationality. In the meantime, it remains an attractive and coherent framework, if only one makes room for a sufficiently broad set of motivations.

The necessity of such a broad framework is well illustrated by the empirical work on motivations for transfers, which is the main topic of this chapter and to which I now turn. I first concentrate on charitable giving and volunteering, i.e. on a situation where people contribute for a more or less anonymous cause. While in the case of some charities it is possible that donors expect something in return, e.g., goods and services produced by the charity, in any case they do not expect reciprocity. The charity or the good cause in general will not reciprocate the gift with a counter gift. In Section 5 I will look at the literature on interhousehold and intrafamily transfers. In these closer relationships reciprocity is possible and in fact it will turn out to be an important motivation.[14]

---

[14] Remember the distinction made before between different definitions of reciprocity. Although reciprocity in our preferred motivational interpretation cannot play a role in anonymous charitable giving, this is not true for reciprocity in the sense of "matching".

4. Charitable giving and volunteering

The empirical work on charitable giving started already in the sixties. In the beginning the focus was mainly on the effects of tax deductibility. Later the scope of the literature has been broadened. Put (too) simply the literature makes use of two kinds of data sources. A first part of the literature works with data at the level of the donors. This approach allows (at least in principle) the introduction of direct motivational information. Much of this research works with the total sum of charitable donations at the level of the individual donor without distinguishing explicitly between different causes. A second part of the literature is more interested in the behaviour of the charities themselves and uses data at the level of these charities. Information about the characteristics of the donors is then more limited. I will include some findings from that latter part of the literature in so far as they are relevant for the purposes of this chapter. Certainly in the United States private donations cover much more than what one usually would classify as charitable giving: the empirical work includes studies on donations to research universities, to radio stations and to religious organizations. I will try to focus on those gifts, which are most closely related to "altruism" in the traditional sense.

From the point of view of pro-social behaviour and giving to charities, decisions about monetary gifts and about supplying volunteer labour are closely linked. While the literature on volunteering is more limited, it still gives some interesting indications about motivations. Moreover, it will turn out that not including volunteering in the model may lead to misleading conclusions. I will therefore include volunteering in my overview.

In Section 4.1 I briefly summarize the older approach, in which giving is seen merely as a private good. The empirical work on the crowding-out hypothesis is discussed in Section 4.2. In Section 4.3, I argue that more attention should be devoted to the modelling of social interactions. Finally, in Section 4.4 I summarize some of the work, which has tried to introduce direct information on motivations.

4.1. Giving as a private good: Tax prices and income

In the first empirical work on charitable giving, gifts were treated as ordinary consumption goods. The (mostly implicit) model behind this work was

$$\max U_i(x_i, g_i)$$
$$\text{s.t.} \quad x_i + p_i g_i = y_i, \tag{10}$$

which can be usefully compared to (3) and (7). While I simplified the model in the previous section by putting the price of the gift equal to 1, this (personalized) price is introduced explicitly in (10). If charitable donations are tax deductible the price is different from 1 and related to the marginal tax rate of individual i. In a certain sense, (10) is an agnostic specification in the spirit of traditional demand analysis. This is not so surprising, since the purpose of the first work on charitable donations was the estimation of price and income effects. Sociological and demographic variables were included only as conditioning variables to control for taste differences. Of course, if either (3) or (7) is the true model the neglect of G_{-i} in the estimating equations may cause an omitted variables-bias.

An overview of some results is given in Table 1.[15] The upper part of the table contains studies with data at the level of the donors. The lower part of the table contains work with data at the level of the charities. Note that in this latter work authors tend to use a richer definition of the price of the gift than in the former work. Since Weisbrod and Dominguez (1986) the price of giving is defined as the monetary cost for the donor of increasing the output of the charity by one monetary unit. This price is equal to $p = (1-t)/[1-(f+a)]$, where t is the marginal tax rate, f is the proportion of total expenditures used by the charity for fund raising and a is the proportion of total expenditure used for administration. The fifth column indicates whether the authors included a variable related to government provision with the intention to test the crowding-out hypothesis. We will return to the interpretation of these results in the next section.

The data used and the variables included in the different papers vary widely. This reflects largely the availability of data. At the same time, the degree of econometric sophistication has grown over time. The original work consisted mainly of simple linear regressions of (the log of) contributions on the available demographic and sociological variables, income and the tax price. Later on, more attention has been devoted to: (a) the *treatment of zero donations*. In a first stage, the use of Tobit regressions became very popular. Later, it was emphasized that the variables explaining the decision whether or not to give could be different from the variables determining the amount of giving (conditional on the fact that one has decided to give). More sophisticated two-stage specifications led to the rejection of the Tobit-restrictions; (b) the *endogeneity of the tax price*, if gifts bring the donors in a different tax bracket; (c) the *dynamics* of income and price effects. Permanent income may be more important than current income. Leads and lags may also be important for a correct estimation of the price effect.

A deeper analysis of these econometric aspects and of the price and income elasticities lies beyond the scope of this chapter. Yet it seems fair to conclude that the price elasticities are significantly negative and considerable in the United States. The European studies yield estimates of the price elasticities, which are much smaller in absolute value. Why is this so? Is the tax awareness larger in the US? It certainly is low in the sample of Schokkaert and Van Ootegem (2000), who asked Belgian respondents explicitly about their own subjective perception of their tax price. Only 30% of the respondents were able or willing to give an estimate of their own individual tax price. Since Schokkaert and Van Ootegem had sufficient information to calculate the correct tax price for all individuals, they could check the accuracy of the subjective estimates of the respondents. The Pearson correlation between the computed tax prices and the

---

[15] This overview certainly is *not* complete. However, it is sufficiently large to allow a fair conclusion about the main findings of the literature.

Table 1
Empirical results on charitable giving

Author	Data	Price elasticity	Income elasticity	Crowding-out	Socio-economic variables	Estimation procedure
			Papers at the level of donors			
Schwartz (1970)	U.S. aggregate time series data 1929–1969 Itemizing taxpayers only	−0.6	0.19 to 0.92[1]			Log-linear
Feldstein (1975a)	U.S. time series of cross-sections 1948–1968 Itemizing taxpayers only	−1.24	0.82			Log-linear
Feldstein (1975b)	U.S cross-section 1962 Itemizing taxpayers only	−0.49 (religious org.) −2.23 (educat. inst.) −2.44 (hospitals) −1.19 (health & welfare)	0.63 1.22 1.08 0.85			Log-linear
Feldstein and Clotfelter (1976)	U.S. cross-section 1963–1964 Itemizing and non-itemizing givers	−1.15	0.87		Community size: + Age: +	Log-linear
Feldstein and Taylor (1976)	U.S. cross-sections for 1962 and 1970 Itemizing taxpayers only	−1.09 (1962) −1.28 (1970)	0.76 0.70		Married[2]: + Age: +	Log-linear
Boskin and Feldstein (1977)	U.S. cross-section 1974 low and middle income	−2.54	0.69		Age: +	Log-linear

(continued on next page)

Table 1
(Continued)

Author	Data	Price elasticity	Income elasticity	Crowding-out	Socio-economic variables	Estimation procedure
Hood, Martin and Osberg (1977)	Canada pooled time series 1968–1973	−0.52 −0.86	0.68 0.52			Log-linear Weighted data to remove heteroskedasticity
Abrams and Schmitz (1978)	U.S. pooled time series of cross-sections (tax returns)	−1.10	0.81	−23 cents per dollar		Log-linear
Reece (1979)	U.S. cross-section 1972–1973 (expenditures)	−1.19	0.88		Age: +	Maximum likelihood Tobit
Clotfelter (1980)[3]	U.S. panel data (itemizers)	−0.39 short run: −0.9 long run: −1.5	0.45 0.42 0.7		Age: + # deps.[4]: +	Log-change model Partial adjustment model
Clotfelter and Salamon (1982)	U.S. cross-section	−1.27 −0.95 to −1.78[5]	0.78 0.39 to 1.09[5]		Married: + deps.[6]: + age: +	Log-linear with constant elasticities Variable elast. over income groups
Abrams and Schmitz (1984)	U.S. cross-section 1979 (itemized tax returns)	−1.48	0.53	−30 cents per dollar	Poverty in resident's state: +	Log-linear
Woodward (1984)	U.S. cross-section 1974	−1.51	0.45		Age: + Assets: +	Loglinear

(continued on next page)

Table 1
(*Continued*)

Author	Data	Price elasticity	Income elasticity	Crowding-out	Socio-economic variables	Estimation procedure
Schiff (1985)		−2.79 (aggregate donations) −4.97 (donations to welfare)	0.76 (aggregate donations) 0.43 (donations to welfare)	Stategov: +34[7] Logov: −66 Cash: −6 Welfare: +5 Locs[8]: +3		Tobit
Reece and Zieschang (1985)	U.S. exp. Survey 1972–1973	−0.85[9]	1.43		Age: + Education: +	Maximum likelihood
Kingma (1989)	U.S. data on public radio contributions	−0.43	0.99	−15 cents per 10,000\$ of government funds	Age: + Education: +	Tobit
Kitchen and Dalton (1990)	Canada exp. Data 1982	−1.07	1.21		Age: +	Tobit
Jones and Posnett (1991a)	U.K. exp. Survey	N/A	0.91 0.53		Education: + House owner: + Regional dummies Regional dummies Self-empl[10]: − House-owner: + Education: +	Standard tobit Generalised tobit
Jones and Posnett (1991b)	UK income survey 1985–1986	Not robust	0.5 to 1.65		Over 65[11]: +	Generalised tobit
Lankford and Wyckoff (1991)	U.S. 1983 tax file data	−2.02 to −1.45	0.2 to 1.03[12]			Box–Cox standard tobit

(*continued on next page*)

Table 1
(Continued)

Author	Data	Price elasticity	Income elasticity	Crowding-out	Socio-economic variables	Estimation procedure
Kitchen (1992)	Canada exp. data 1986	−2.29 (all contributions) Not sign. (religious contr.)	0.91 (all contributions) 1.09 (religious contr.)		Wealth: + Age: + Wealth: + Age: +	Standard tobit
Smith, Kehoe and Cremer (1995)	U.S. cross section on giving to specific charity	−0.94 (not significant)	0.74[13]		Over 65: + Charity[14]: + Business-owner: + Self-employed: + Agriculture[15]: + Hospital visits: +	Heckman 2-step method
Kingma and McClelland (1995)	U.S. data on charitable giving to radio station	−3.25 −3.54 −0.62 (not sign.)	0.57 0.71 0.28	(cts / $ 10,000) −15 −19 −15	Education: + Age: +	Censored regressions –Tobit –Weibull –Generalised logistic
Randolph (1995)	U.S. panel of tax return data 1979–1988	Permanent: −0.51 transitory: −1.55	Permanent: 1.14 Transitory: 0.58		Age: +	Generalised two-stage least squares
Ribar and Wilhelm (1995)	U.S. state level data 1988–1991 Contributions to specific type of charity	−1.71	1.55			Random effects with socio-political controls
Banks and Tanner (1997)	U.K. cross-section 1974–1996	N/A	1.125[16]	No evidence for crowding-out by introduction of National Lottery	Age: + Education: + Wealth: + White collar: +	Heckman two step method

(continued on next page)

Table 1
(Continued)

Author	Data	Price elasticity	Income elasticity	Crowding-out	Socio-economic variables	Estimation procedure
Forbes and Zampelli (1997)	U.S. cross-section 1992; data on religious giving		Tithing Catholics: 0.19 Tithing Protestants: 0.04 Non-tithing Catholics: 0.40 Non-tithing Protests.: 0.02		Unemployed: + Region: significant Proportion of females in hh: + Age: + Church attendance: + Confidence in org.: + tax_ded: +[17][18]	Tobit, with correction for heteroskedasticity[19]
Barrett, McGuirk and Steinberg (1997)	U.S. panel data 1979–1986	−0.47	0.50		Married: +	2-way fixed effects
Andreoni and Scholz (1998)	U.S. cross section of exp. Data 1985	−1.20 to −1.45[20]	0.51 to 0.56[20]		Age: + Educ.: +	Weighted data to take account of interdependent giving
Duquette (1999)	U.S.	−1.30	Itemizers: 0.91 Non-item.: 1.47		# deps: +(item.) −(non-it.) Married: + Age: +	Tobit
Schokkaert and Van Ootegem (2000)	Flanders: 1991 survey with data on individuals' motivation for giving	Not sign. (deductible donations)	0.86 to 1.07 (deductible donations) 0.51 (non-deductible donations)	Evidence for non-perfect crowding-out	Age: +[21] Education: + Importance of religion: +	Tobit

(continued on next page)

Table 1
(Continued)

Author	Data	Price elasticity	Income elasticity	Crowding-out	Socio-economic variables	Estimation procedure
Auten, Sieg and Clotfelter (2000)	U.S. panel data	Persistent: −1.26 Transitory: −0.40	Persistent: 0.87 Transitory: 0.29			Estimation approach that explicitly models the dynamic process determining prices and incomes
Papers at the level of charities						
Weisbrod and Dominguez (1986)		Library: −1.06 Art, museum, zoo: −2.65 Poor & aged: −0.73 (not sign.) Hospital: −1.28 Handicapped: −0.79 Scientific research: −0.81 Education: −1.07				OLS
Posnett and Sandler (1989)	U.K. data	−2.02		Not sign.		OLS with White s.e.
Khanna, Posnett and Sandler (1995)	U.K. panel data 1983–1990	−0.52		+9.4 pence per pound		One-way fixed effects
Payne (1998)	U.S. panel data 1982–1992			OLS: +1 cent per dollar 2SLS: −50 cents per dollar		Fixed effects

(continued on next page)

Table 1
(*Continued*)

Author	Data	Price elasticity	Income elasticity	Crowding-out	Socio-economic variables	Estimation procedure
Wong, Chua and Vasoo (1998)	Pooled time series Singapore 1980–1989	Total donations: −1.87 Direct donations: −2.51		Partial crowding-out (mixed results)		Weighted least squares
Okten and Weisbrod (2000)	U.K. panel data 1982–1994	Hospitals: −0.26 Higher education: −0.21 Scientific research: −2.58		Hospitals: +0.012 (elasticity)		2SLS fixed effects
Khanna and Sandler (2000)	U.K.	−1.00		+0.45 (elasticity)		One-way fixed effects, endogenous government grants
Payne (2001)	U.S. data on donations to universities			+64 cents to +94 cents per dollar of federal research funding[22]		Instrumental variables

[1]Depending on income bracket. [2]Dummy variable equal to 1 if giver is married, 0 otherwise. [3]Reported results are for 1968–1970 period. [4]Number of dependents. [5]Depending on income bracket. [6]Dummy variable equal to 1 if giver has dependents, 0 otherwise. [7]Cents per dollar. [8]STATEGOV: total per capita state expenditures, LOCGOV: total per capita local expenditures, CASH: per capita cash transfers to the needy, WELFARE: other welfare spending (non-cash) to the needy, per capita, LOCSW: local government spending on social welfare, per capita. [9]Based on full tax schedule, not solely on first dollar price. [10]Dummy variable equal to 1 if giver is self-employed. [11]Dummy variable equal to 1 for those who are older than 65. [12]For different price-income combinations. [13]Step 2 coefficient. [14]Charity: dummy set equal to 1 if the household gave to national causes (measures altruistic attitude/motivation). [15]Dummy equal to 1 if household's head is employed in agriculture or forestry (risky occupations). [16]Not corrected for price effect. [17]Dummy equal to 1 if the household intends to use the tax deduction for charitable contributions. [18]These variables are significant only for catholics. [19]OLS confirms previous results that protestants give more than catholics. [20]Depending on type of interdependence weighting matrix. [21]Significant only for deductible donations. [22]Depending on type of university.

answers of the respondents was -0.04. If tax awareness is really that low, it is not surprising that the estimated tax price elasticities are insignificant or small in absolute value.

This hypothesis is based on one study only and it begs the question how to explain the (possible) differences in tax awareness between different countries. Perhaps such differences in tax awareness are themselves related to underlying motivations. Can the different results be explained by the relative size of private giving and of government provision in the US and in Europe? If crowding-out is more important in Europe, the remaining donors may to a larger extent be dutiful altruists. It seems reasonable to hypothesize that donors who give out of a sense of duty may be less sensitive to price variation. But this approach again begs a deeper question: *why* is government intervention so much larger in Europe? I will return to that question at the end of Section 4.2.

Volunteering can be considered as a straightforward extension of the previous model. One can indeed write the consumer problem as

$$\max U_i(x_i, g_i, l_i, v_i)$$
$$\text{s.t.} \quad x_i + p_i g_i = w_i(1 - l_i - v_i) + n y_i \tag{11}$$

in which l_i is leisure time, v_i is volunteering time (and total time available is normalized to one), w_i is the wage and ny_i is non-labour income. Starting from (11) one can then focus on the tax price elasticity of volunteering. It turns out that volunteering and donating are complements [Menchik and Weisbrod (1987), Brown and Lankford (1992)]. This seems to reflect a "taste for giving" in general.[16]

As said already before, however, there are also other aspects to volunteering. Menchik and Weisbrod (1987) therefore propose an alternative "investment" model in addition to the "consumption" model (11). In this model people volunteer because they hope that this activity will raise their future earnings power by providing work experience and social contacts. Their empirical work suggests that this purely egoistic motivation also plays a role in the volunteering decision [see also Unger (1991) and Vaillancourt (1994)].

4.2. Crowding out and the warm-glow of giving

As explained in Section 3, one can derive from the pure altruism model a hypothesis of perfect crowding-out of private donations by government expenditures. The testing of this hypothesis has received much attention in the literature, not in the least because of its important policy implications. Since in model (3) the gift basically becomes a contribution to a public good, the whole question of crowding-out goes far beyond the problem of charitable giving and is in fact related to the much broader question of

---

[16] The results of Freeman (1997), however, are less clearcut in this regard. Moreover as we will see later the complementarity between volunteering and donating is much less clear for the contributions to one specific charity.

voluntary provision of public goods (where these public goods can be anything and not just charities). Strategic considerations are crucial to explain behaviour and there is no consensus among economists about how to model these. The huge experimental literature on provision of public goods therefore also is relevant to understand the pattern of charitable contributions. It is impossible to review this literature here and I will focus on charitable contributions. But one should keep in mind that it might be dangerous to neglect strategic considerations and to draw immediately strong conclusions about motivations from simple empirical tests.

The testing of the crowding-out assumption raises some additional technical problems in addition to the ones already mentioned in Section 4.1. When using data at an aggregate level there is an endogeneity problem: not only may government expenditures influence private donations, the reverse causality may also hold. Things get even more complicated because of the interaction between government expenditures at the central and at the local level [Steinberg (1991)]. More important for our purposes is the requirement of matching perfectly the definition of government expenditures as an explanatory variable with the definition of the cause for which the private donations are given. As was emphasized already by Roberts (1984, 1987) the hypothesis of one-for-one crowding-out rests on the assumption that own donations and public expenditures are perfect substitutes.[17] When one wants to test the crowding-out effect of government expenditures for the poor one should then only use private charity to the poor as the dependent variable. If one uses instead "total charitable giving" one includes also donations for religion, for health, for education. Much of the empirical work has therefore to be taken with a grain of salt, since the match between private donations and public expenditures is far from perfect and/or the data are situated at a very aggregate level.

Taking due account of the technical limitations of some of this work, it still seems fair to conclude that the overall picture one can derive from the results in Table 1 is clear. The individual-level data suggest that crowding-out does exist but that it is far from perfect. There have also been some studies on crowding-out in the volunteering decision. Both Menchik and Weisbrod (1987) and Day and Devlin (1996) find differentiated effects for different forms of government expenditures – but they find only very weak indications of crowding-out. Quite the contrary: in some cases they observe the existence of crowding-in, i.e. the amount of volunteering increases with the amount of government expenditures.

The data with charities in Table 1 also often indicate the existence of crowding-in: the charities that get more government support also get more private donations. Note that here the definitional match is almost perfect. Several explanations for this crowding-in effect have been put forward. The most convincing explanation refers to informational

---

[17] Kingma (1989) distinguishes in addition to the models (3)–(6), (7) and (10) a fourth one in which private donations by others and government provision are not perfectly substitutable [see also Schiff (1985)]. However, in his empirical work he does not find a significant difference between the effects of contributions by others and government contributions. The same result is found by Duncan (1999).

aspects: government subsidies may signal to the donors that the charity is of high quality and, moreover, is well monitored by the authorities. Donors may therefore find it more attractive to contribute to that specific charity. If this is indeed a good explanation, it points immediately to a crucial limitation of the simple models of Section 3.1. They all assumed that the (potential) donors had perfect information. Like the strategic considerations mentioned earlier, the introduction of informational aspects makes the immediate link between observable behaviour and motivations less obvious. It suggests that the indirect testing of motivations may yield misleading results.

That caution is needed in interpreting the indirect tests is also made clear by Duncan (1999). He proposes a model of the public good-variety in which individuals contribute both time and money. In his approach consumers solve the following problem:

$$\max U_i \left[x_i, l_i, Z\left(\sum_j g_j, \sum_j v_j \right) \right]$$
$$\text{s.t.} \quad x_i + p_i g_i = w_i(1 - l_i - v_i) + ny_i. \tag{12}$$

The function $Z(\cdot)$ gives the total supply of the charity and is determined by the total of all gifts and volunteer time by all donors. In model (12) the goals of the donor are perfectly harmonious with the goal of the charity. The charity uses capital and labour as inputs. Duncan (1999) shows that in equilibrium the charity firm will not be capital constrained, i.e. it will not like to sell some of its volunteer labour. But then the only remaining constraint is that it can hire labour and capital for a total amount smaller than the total value of its charitable gifts, which is $T = \sum_i g_i + w \sum_i v_i$ or $T = \sum_i (g_i + w v_i)$. This last expression suggests that for donor i his monetary gift and his volunteer labour supply are perfect substitutes. Duncan proves that this is indeed true in the Nash-equilibrium. His model has implications for the analysis of the supply of volunteer labour. In this approach the fact that charitable contributions of time and money move in the same direction if there is a change in the tax price does *not* imply that they are complements. One minus the marginal tax rate is the price of *total* charitable contributions. If this price increases, quantity demanded will decrease and consumers will accommodate this decrease by reducing money donations, volunteer labour, or both. More importantly for our purposes, Duncan's model also yields a reinterpretation of the crowding-out hypothesis. It suggests that government spending will crowd-out total contributions, not only money contributions. Even in the pure "public good" model, one-for-one crowding out of monetary contributions will only hold if money is the only way to contribute to the public good. Estimates, which focus exclusively on monetary contributions, will therefore underestimate the true crowding-out effect. His own empirical work with US-data from the *National Study of Philanthropy* suggests that the crowding-out parameter in the money equation is 27% smaller in magnitude than the crowding-out parameter for the total value equation. On the other hand, despite this correction, his more sophisticated testing procedure still leads to a rejection of the hypothesis of perfect crowding-out. He therefore concludes that "households derive 'warm glow' utility from the total value of their charitable contributions" [Duncan (1999, p. 238)].

Duncan's quotation in a certain sense is typical for most of the authors who have tested the hypothesis of perfect crowding-out. The rejection of this hypothesis has been seen as support for the alternative hypothesis (7), made popular by Andreoni (1989, 1990). Let us therefore turn now to the interpretation of the latter model. Andreoni himself talks about a "warm glow" – a good feeling that donors derive from the act of giving. He interprets this feeling as an egoistic motivation and uses the terms "pure altruism" for model (3) and impure altruism for model (7). However, this terminology is rather misleading. What is crucial to explain the crowding-out phenomenon is the distinction between the *public* good-character of the good cause in (3) and the *private* good-character of the gift in (7) and (10). Very different interpretations may be given to the motivations underlying these models.

This is immediately clear for the "private" component. Returning to the provisional list of motivations in Section 2, we see that in addition to the warm-glow there may be other reasons why g_i appears directly in the utility function, i.e. why g_i and G_{-i} are not perfect substitutes. People may give out of material self-interest (certainly relevant for volunteering) or to build up social prestige. They may give out of a sense of duty or because of social pressure.[18] I argued already that it is confusing to call all these motivations "egoistic". And similar problems arise with the interpretation of the public good model (3) as reflecting "pure altruism". Some of the charities included in the empirical work "produce" goods and services, which are in the interest of the donors. Even concern for the fate of the poor does not necessarily reflect only altruism. Remember the possibility that such concern follows from a desire to avoid stealing or aggressive behaviour. The conclusion is obvious: the private good–public good distinction, while very useful, does *not* coincide with the egoism–altruism distinction. The empirical rejection of perfect crowding-out therefore does not imply necessarily that donors are not altruistic in the common sense of the word and a finer distinction between different motivations is needed to interpret the "private good" model. Still, there can be no doubt that the literature on testing the crowding-out assumption has really set the stage for such a deeper analysis.

Moreover, the policy implications of these results are less ambiguous. The optimistic hypothesis that a decrease in government provision would automatically be compensated for by private giving is not supported by the facts. Especially striking is the finding of crowding-in with the data of the charities themselves. Government subsidies may signal to the public that the activities of the supported charities are important from the point of view of the community. A reduction in government subsidies may then give to the population at large the opposite signal that this kind of activities is *not* important.[19]

---

[18] Some of these interpretations suggest that it might be useful to work with a specification in which the "private" motivation does not depend only on the level of the gift, but also on the relation between one's own gift and the gift of others.

[19] See also the analysis in Jones, Cullis and Lewis (1998) of the effects of cuts in government activities during the Thatcher-period in the UK.

However, from a broader perspective all these explanations remain incomplete. The real question is why there are such huge differences in the level of government provision in different countries and why this level changes over time. After all, it is the same population that votes for or against given political programs and that decides whether or not to give time and money to charities. Voting for government transfers may be a possible way to give while at the same time avoiding the free rider problem. The interaction between motivations for private giving and attitudes towards distributive justice and government intervention is especially important here. Both are linked to deeper underlying institutional factors. In their analysis of the differences between Europe and the US, Alesina, Glaeser and Sacerdote (2001) focus on the importance of racial heterogeneity in the US. This hypothesis points to the importance of social interactions. Social interdependencies may also play a crucial role in the explanation of the level of charitable giving.

4.3. Status of sociological and demographic variables

One of the most striking findings in the empirical work on charitable giving is the significant effect of the socio-economic and demographic variables included. Data availability plays an important role in the decision which variables to include. Since the estimates of the effects of specific variables may crucially depend on the other variables included (or omitted), we might therefore expect a rather inconsistent pattern for the effects of the sociological and demographic variables. Yet, in general the pattern is surprisingly coherent (see Table 1).[20] To summarize briefly: older and more educated people give more. In addition, empirical work shows significant effects of geographic variables, which are hard to interpret. Why would the Scottish be more charitable than the English [Jones and Posnett (1991a, 1991b)]?

Some authors succumb to the temptation of interpreting the effects of sociological and demographic variables in terms of the degree of "altruism" or "egoism" of the giver. To give an example: if one finds a significantly positive effect of the age of the giver on the amount of giving for old-age provisions, this might be interpreted as an indication that "egoistic" motives play an important role. It is obvious, however, that one should be very careful with this kind of rash conclusions.[21] The sociological variables may capture many different effects.

Economists, focusing on tax prices and income, have spent relatively little attention to the interpretation of these significant effects. In the tradition of conventional consumer theory, they treat the sociological variables as mere controls for taste differences. This really begs the question of this chapter. It also neglects other possibly important

---

[20] This contrasts with Batson (1998, p. 289), who writes about "the highly inconsistent effects on prosocial behaviour of demographic variables such as age and sex". An explanation for the contrast can perhaps be found in the context-dependency of altruistic behaviour. Charitable gift giving is one specific context – and this may explain why demographic variables have a similar influence in the different studies.

[21] See Hudson and Jones (1994) for a similar criticism.

questions. Consider the effect of age. To understand future patterns of charitable giving it is essential to know whether this is indeed an age or rather a cohort effect. If it is the latter the positive "age"-effect suggests that social norms concerning giving are changing over time and that charitable giving may be expected to decrease in the future when younger cohorts grow older. Banks and Tanner (1997) find that the UK-evidence suggests such a cohort effect. Of course, the fact that older and better-educated people give more may also indicate an effect of permanent income, while the current income would capture the transitory effect. Partly because of the lack of data, there is not much research about these questions.

At a deeper level, the significance of the sociological, demographic (and even geographical) variables suggests the existence of social interdependencies. Such social interdependencies are predicted by the bulk of the psychological and sociological literature, that has always emphasized the importance of imitation learning. Among economists also the interest for social interactions has grown in recent years. Manski (2000) distinguishes three different reasons for why members of the same group tend to behave similarly. Let us apply these three hypotheses to the phenomenon that higher educated people give more. A first explanation is the existence of *correlated effects*. Agents in the same educational group behave similarly because they have similar individual characteristics or face similar institutional environments. This interpretation does not imply the existence of social interdependencies and comes close to the simple idea that sociological variables control for taste effects. A second explanation is the existence of *contextual interactions*. Here the propensity to give varies with exogenous characteristics of the group members, e.g., the geographic composition of the educational group. Most important, however, is the third explanation, which refers to *endogenous interactions*. The propensity to give of an individual agent varies with the behaviour of the group. More specifically: individual gifts will vary with the average level of gifts within a group. It is obvious that these different hypotheses have different policy implications. More specifically, endogenous interactions imply the existence of social multiplier effects.

Given the policy relevance of this distinction, it is striking that social interdependencies in charitable giving have received scant attention in the literature.[22] After a first and unsuccessful attempt by Feldstein and Clotfelter (1976), the only coherent approach to the problem is in a paper by Andreoni and Scholz (1998). They start from the concept of a "social reference space" [Van Praag, Kapteyn and Van Herwaarden (1979)] to model the idea that contributions of any one person may depend on those who are similar to that person in age, education and other characteristics. They then estimate a model in which the average contribution of the individual's reference group enters as an explanatory variable. Income turns out not to be an important factor in the definition of reference groups. Depending on the concrete definition of the reference spaces

---

[22] In the non-economic literature on altruism, much attention has been devoted to acts of heroism and self-sacrifice in extreme situations, such as wars. Here also social interactions and group loyalty may be crucial – see the analysis by Costa and Kahn (2003) of soldier behaviour during the American Civil War.

they predict that if contributions in one's social reference space go up by 10% one's own contribution rises by about 2–3%. The induced multiplier effects suggest that the responses to policy changes are about 25% larger than in the conventional approach. At the same time, however, the introduction of social interdependencies does not change the estimates of the price and income effects. There is therefore no immediate need to worry about the estimates of price and income elasticities as summarized in Table 1.

While the findings of Andreoni and Scholz (1998) give a clear indication of the importance of endogenous social interactions, their methodology does not allow discriminating between the different channels of such interactions. As noted by Manski (2000), the concept of endogenous interactions should be further refined. More specifically, it is important to distinguish preference interactions from the effects of observational learning. People may want to give more if they see somebody else giving, either because they want to act like the latter – or because they believe that the other person has superior information about the consequences of giving. Both perspectives have different implications for government policy and for the optimal strategy of charities. If the latter hypothesis holds true, the provision of new information may influence the degree of charitable giving. If the endogenous interaction is mainly a matter of preferences, additional information will have a negligible effect.

4.4. Direct evidence on preferences

While most of the empirical work on crowding-out has rejected the hypothesis of "pure altruism", this is only an indirect test of the motivational structure. As shown by Duncan (1999), the interpretation of this indirect evidence on motivations may be ambiguous. Moreover, it only gives a partial indication about the real motivations guiding behaviour. Even if altruism is not perfect, genuine altruism can still be present. More importantly, the rejection of perfect crowding-out does not give us any clue about what really lies behind the "warm glow". It seems that we need to incorporate more explicit information about preference differences if we want to get a better insight into the motivations of the givers. This is not easy, however, since data combining information on gifts and on psychological characteristics are not regularly collected.

Some studies describe interesting findings, even when their principal aim is *not* to test for different motivations. I give some examples. Menchik and Weisbrod (1987) find that respondents with parents who contributed regularly, themselves supply more volunteer labour. Kingma and McClelland (1995) find evidence for an egoistic motivation: those who use the service more often also donate more. A possible shortcut to the measurement of the degree of altruism is suggested by Smith, Kehoe and Cremer (1995). They show that those who give to national charitable organizations have a higher probability of giving to a specific health care charity. While they interpret this individual "history of giving" as an indicator of altruism, they themselves are well aware of the ambiguity of this interpretation. Apart from the technical problems, quite some psychological and sociological work suggests the existence of a kind of "hysteresis"-effect, with people having given more in the past also giving more in the future [Piliavin and Charng

(1990)]. It makes a big difference whether the significant effect of the history of giving reflects a stable personality trait or rather shows that past behaviour influences future behaviour. The prospects for charities that try to increase charitable giving look much brighter in the latter than in the former case.

A stable finding in the empirical literature is the "importance of being asked". Long (1976) and Keating, Pitts and Appel (1981) find that face-to-face solicitation is much more effective in fund-raising than more impersonal approaches such as advertising. Moreover, the closer the relationship between the solicitor and the donor, the greater the contribution. Freeman (1997) finds a similar effect on the supply of volunteer labour: people volunteer when asked to do so and most volunteers are contacted by either friends or family. He hypothesizes that two factors underlie the response of individuals to requests to volunteer.[23] First, people are only willing to contribute time and money for so-called "conscience goods". They have a latent demand for such goods, which a request brings to the fore. This interpretation is in line with the private good, warm glow paradigm. Second, the request (mainly if it comes from family or friends) induces some "social pressure". Note that this interpretation is a mixture of the "social prestige" and "social norms" hypotheses introduced in Section 2. In the case of the United Way charities, analysed by Keating, Pitts and Appel (1981), pressure from the employer plays an important role – and therefore contributions may even reflect pure material self-interest. Moreover, there is an additional interpretation possible. Being asked also may convey information about the existence of a given charity and the need of the charity to being helped. This may even be important in a public good-interpretation. In the Duncan (1999) model "being asked to volunteer" signals that the charity is not capital constrained and that supplying volunteer labour therefore makes sense. Since "being asked" is a social interaction, it is not surprising that we recover in these various interpretations the crucial distinction between preference interactions and the spread of information.

How then to identify motivations in a finer way? A first possibility in some specific cases is clever modelling of the interaction between the environment and the donor's preferences. A good example is the work of Harbaugh (1998a, 1998b) who focuses on the "warm glow" and on the "social prestige"-motivations. The utility function of the donor is written as $U_i(x_i, P_i, g_i)$, in which the direct inclusion of g_i as before captures a warm-glow effect and P_i is prestige. Social prestige is determined by *reported* gifts. The reporting behaviour of the recipient charity can in general be written as $P_i = f(g_i)$. Substituting the budget constraint into the utility function gives $U_i = U_i(y_i - g_i, P_i, g_i) = V_i(P_i, g_i; y_i)$, where the price of the gift has been put equal to 1 for convenience. The function $V_i(\cdot)$ gives indifference curves in the (g_i, P_i)-space as in Figure 1 where higher curves represent higher utility. We can now compare the

---

[23] Freeman (1997) also mentions the fact that volunteers more often use the services of the charity for which they are volunteering and suggests a possible interpretation as a form of "reciprocal altruism". As I said already in Section 2, the more egoistic motivations often turn up in the explanation of volunteering and I deliberately left them aside here.

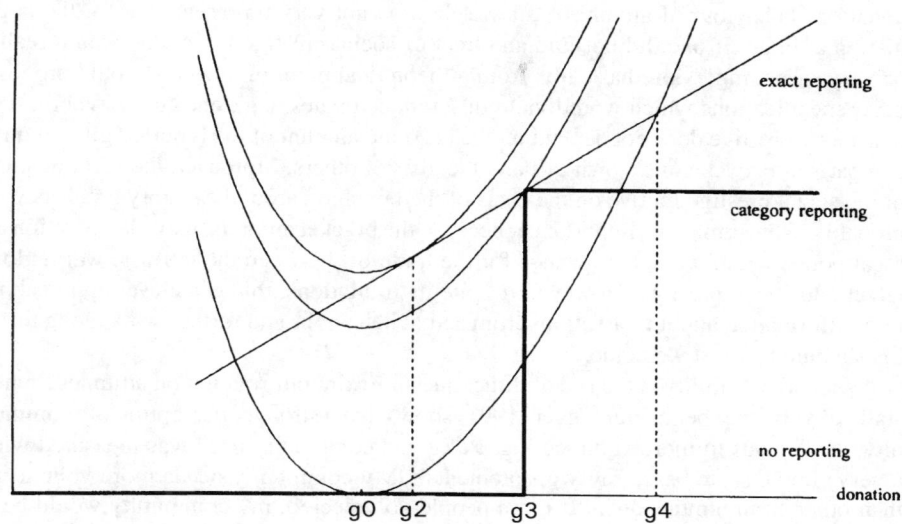

Figure 1. Prestige in the model of Harbaugh (1998a, 1998b).

effects of differences in the reporting behaviour of the charity by drawing $P_i = f(g_i)$ in the figure. If no reports are made the prestige function is a horizontal line and the optimal gift is g_O. If charities report the exact amount of the donation, $P_i = g_i$, and the best the donor can do is to give g_2. An interesting situation occurs when the charity categorizes its report. In the case of one bracket sketched in Figure 1 they report the names of the donors who have given g_3 or more. In that case there will be bunching around g_3. The model explains why so many donors indeed give exactly the minimum amount necessary to get into a category. A person with preferences as given in the figure will donate an amount equal to the lower bracket of the reporting category as long as the latter is smaller than g_4. It is easy to generalize the model to reporting by more than one category.

Harbaugh (1998a) applies this model to analyse the donations by 146 alumni of a law school and estimates the parameters of a Stone–Geary utility function using the methods developed for nonconvex budget constraints. The concentration of observations around the category brackets plays a crucial role in this estimation exercise. To get an estimate of the importance of the prestige motive which is independent of the particular brackets used under category reporting, he uses a simulation procedure and calculates (using the estimated parameters of the Stone–Geary utility function) the difference between what donations would be in the case of no reporting and what they would be under exact reporting. He finds that under exact reporting donations would be 25–33% higher than under no reporting and argues that this can only be due to the social prestige motive.

Harbaugh (1998a) himself mentions some obvious limitations of his exercise. The donations behaviour of alumni of a law school is not very representative for the population at large. If one did not find an effect of social prestige there, this would really be very surprising! More basically, from a theoretical point of view one could propose other specifications which would yield different estimates: e.g., one could hypothesize that social prestige does not depend on the absolute amount of the reported gift but on a comparison between one's own gift and the gifts of others. Moreover, the identification of the social prestige motive on the basis of the bunching around category brackets will probably overestimate its importance, because the bracket amounts may also function as focal points without much relevance for the trade-off between the intrinsic warm glow effect and social prestige. However, despite its limitations, this is a clever approach to infer information about motivations from actual behaviour and further work along these lines would be most welcome.

A second possibility is the use of direct questionnaire information on attitudes. In her study of volunteer behaviour Unger (1991) shows that a stronger perception of "community need" leads to more volunteering. Perceived community need was measured with a very simple scale based on two statements ("My community needs more volunteers than other communities do"; "If more people volunteered, my community would be a better place to live"). This is not a very adequate measure, however. Answers on the second statement could capture attitudes towards social norms and duties which makes the interpretation of the "community need scale" very ambiguous.

In an old and unpublished paper Woodward (1984) distinguishes eight categories of donors on the basis of the answers on a series of attitudinal questions (see Table 2). Introducing dummy variables for these motivational groups increases significantly the explanatory power of a regression of total gifts. Kantian donors[24] give significantly more to charity than the other motivational types. Moreover, the results of interaction variables with the motivational dummies and tax prices and income suggest a great deal of variance among motivational groups. Altruist and Kantian categories are among the groups with the least volatile reactions to prices. This result is consistent with a stronger sense of commitment and sympathy in these groups.

More recently Schokkaert and Van Ootegem (2000) included 32 attitudinal questions in a broader questionnaire on donations submitted to a representative sample of 1013 respondents of the Dutch-speaking population of Belgium. Factor analysis was used to reduce the 32 questions to a set of underlying factors. Four psychological factors emerged:

(a) a sense of principles and duty, closely related to dutiful altruism (a typical item loading on this factor is "I consider it my duty to help wherever I can");
(b) sensitivity to social pressure (with typical item "I will support sooner when I see that others support as well");

---

[24] I follow Woodward's terminology. Remember that I have used the term "dutiful" altruism instead of "Kantian" altruism.

Table 2
Psychological dispositions in Woodward (1984)

ALTRUISTS	Do not feel pressure to give, state that their gifts are made because of a concern for the organization	Give to the organizations which they felt were worth supporting	Consistent
		Do not give to the organizations which they said were worth supporting	Inconsistent
KANTIANS	Either expressed pressure from guilt or obligation or stated that they adhered to a rule in deciding how much to give ("I tithe")	Answered consistently to questions about motives and pressure	Consistent
		Inconsistent in answers to questions about either motives or pressure	Inconsistent
DIRECTLY SELFISH	Explicitly stated that they gave in order to get something back	Do not feel either internal or external pressure to give	Consistent
		Either feel pressure or adhere to a rule	Inconsistent
INDIRECTLY SELFISH	Feel external pressure to give	Consistent in answers to questions about pressure and believed that others are both responsive to pressure and aware of the size of other people's gifts	Consistent
		Either inconsistent in questions regarding explicit motives or answered negatively to one of the questions on others' giving	Inconsistent

(c) narrow altruism, expressing a real concern for the purpose of the gift but with a clear preference for specific uses in the immediate neighbourhood (typical item: "Rather than giving via charity organizations, I'd prefer to give it straight to people who need it");

(d) broad altruism, expressing a keen interest in the outcome of the charitable actions ("Organizations have to tackle problems at their root").

Once these four psychological factors are defined, each individual gets a specific score for each of the factors by averaging the results for the individual items loading on the factors. This means that individuals are not classified in discrete groups but rather characterized by their position on four continuous scales. In general, the respondents agree more with the altruism items (c) and (d) than with the warm glow items (a) and (b).

These psychological scale values are then introduced in Tobit regressions explaining donation behaviour. This leads to a significant improvement in the explanatory power of the regressions. At the same time, the estimates of the effects of income and tax prices hardly change after the introduction of the psychological information.[25] More specifically there is a significantly positive effect of the sensitivity to social pressure and a very strong significantly positive effect of the sense of duty. Again, as in Woodward (1984), the motivation of personal duty turns out to be dominant. At the same time the altruism-components do not have a significant effect. This result can be interpreted in two ways. From a sceptical point of view, one could argue that the measurement of the altruism-factors is weaker than that of the warm glow-factors. From a more ambitious point of view, however, one could also say that this is exactly what we would have expected on the basis of theory. Theory obviously predicts that people who are more sensitive to warm glow considerations will give more. But the same is not true for the altruism motivation. In a situation with huge government intervention, as in Belgium, a large part of the "altruistic" contributions will be crowded out by the taxes used to finance the government intervention. This leads immediately to the hypothesis that interindividual differences in the altruism (or public good) motivations will not necessarily lead to differences in individual donations. The empirical results are perfectly in line with these theoretical hypotheses.

Results like the ones of Woodward (1984) and Schokkaert and Van Ootegem (2000) suggest that direct information on motivations, even if measured in a far from perfect way, can improve the explanatory power of regressions explaining charitable behaviour. The strong effects of the duty motive are in line with what could be expected on the basis of the theory. Future refinement of this work could help in answering some of the questions raised before, e.g., in disentangling the effects of preference interactions and observational learning in social processes. At the same time, caution is needed. The interpretation of the attitudinal questions may be difficult and ambiguous and there is much scope for adhocery. When one tries to explain subjective data with other subjective data there is a real danger of interpreting spurious correlations as causal links. This danger gets very big if the information on donation behaviour and on attitudes is collected from the same respondents with the same questionnaire (as was the case in the previous studies). It is to be expected that someone who is very sensitive to social pressure will also be sensitive to the social pressure in the interview situation and may therefore overestimate his donations. And similar doubts can be raised concerning some of the other motivations.[26] While the traditional scepticism of economists with respect to survey data is strongly exaggerated, there is indeed need for caution and careful interpretation.

Remains the third possibility: the use of laboratory experiments. Laboratory experiments can be designed in such a way that they are perfectly suited to test different motivational assumptions. Without going deeply into this literature, I give some examples. Andreoni (1993) tested the public-goods crowding-out hypothesis in a contribution

---

[25] As mentioned already before the tax price effect is not significant in these regressions.

[26] The practice of tithing has a positive effect on giving independent of the psychological disposition of the giver – see, e.g., Forbes and Zampelli (1997). The inclusion by Woodward (1984) of all who tithe in the "Kantian" category may be an additional explanation for the strong effect of his Kantian dummy.

game and finds that crowding-out is incomplete. Since the behaviour of the subjects in his experiment might be influenced by strategic considerations, it is not possible to derive immediate conclusions about motivations. However, Bolton and Katok (1998) find similar results in a dictator game. In this game one individual decides about the distribution of a sum of money between herself and one recipient. To test for crowding-out they manipulated the initial sum of money, owned by the recipient. Strategic factors do not play any role in this one-person decision task. Therefore, the results may be seen as strong evidence for the existence of a "private" motive of giving.

In another experiment Andreoni (1995) discovers significant framing effects on cooperation in experiments. Cooperation is much larger in a setting where behaviour has a positive externality (when subjects can "do good" to each other) than in a setting with a negative externality (when subjects can refrain from "doing bad" to each other). These results again lead to doubts about the simple pure public-good model. Moreover, they suggest that there is some asymmetry in the way people feel personally about doing good versus not doing bad: the warm-glow must be stronger than the cold-prickle. This is in line with some of the psychological findings described in Section 2.

These and similar experimental results are fascinating and may yield revealing insights in the motivational structure underlying charitable behaviour. At the same time, however, the artificial setting of laboratory experiments has obvious disadvantages. To illustrate, let us start from the finding that both in the experiments of Andreoni (1993) and Bolton and Katok (1998) crowding-out is much larger (more than 70%) than in the field studies summarized in Section 2. When the authors try to explain this difference they introduce a whole bunch of additional factors "such as sympathy, political or social commitment, peer pressure, institutional considerations, or moral satisfactions associated with particular causes" [Andreoni (1993, p. 1326)]. Not all of these motivations can easily be tested in a laboratory setting. Field studies and laboratory experiments are necessarily complementary. Perhaps cleverly designed field experiments may help in bridging the gap.[27]

5. Interhousehold and intrafamily transfers of money and time

In the previous section we considered transfer behaviour in a situation where the recipients remain largely anonymous. In addition to these anonymous gifts, there are many instances of intrahousehold and interhousehold giving in situations where people do know each other. A large majority – but not all – of these gifts is within families, often between different generations. Such relationships within the family are most often immediately connected with altruism. However, here also the predictions of "pure altruism" are rejected by most empirical work and alternative explanations have been

---

[27] There are examples in the literature of the other social sciences, more on volunteering than on charitable giving. See, e.g., the second experiment in Fisher and Ackerman (1998).

provided. We can distinguish at least two (largely unconnected) streams of literature. The first is on intergenerational transmission within families and on the relationship between bequests and *inter vivos* transfers. The second is on informal insurance mechanisms and social networks, mainly in poor countries. In each of these domains the literature is very broad and basically opposes an "altruistic" to a more selfish or strategic or so-called "exchange" interpretation of behaviour. While the use of the term "exchange" is very popular in this literature, in some cases it is preferable to talk about reciprocity. I will sketch these two streams of the literature in Section 5.1. However, I will only give some examples and neglect the finer modelling questions. My main aim is to start from these examples to link this literature in Section 5.2 to the broader question of motivations. In Section 5.3 I will comment on the custom of giving non-monetary gifts at special occasions.

5.1. *Altruism versus exchange or reciprocity: A sketch*

Intrafamily transfers have been the main source of inspiration for the influential articles on altruism by Becker (1974, 1981). It is indeed within the family and in the relationship between parents and children that one would expect altruism *a priori*. However, in Section 3.1 I have already sketched the strong predictions following from the simplest model of pure altruism. Choosing the interpretation that individual i is the parent, Equation (2) shows that for the parent's decision only the sum of the incomes of children and parents matters. Incomes are pooled and changes in the income distribution should not change the consumption levels of parents and children.

More formally, one can derive from (1) that

$$\mathrm{d}x_i = \mathrm{d}y_i - \frac{\partial g_i}{\partial y_i}\mathrm{d}y_i - \frac{\partial g_i}{\partial y_j}\mathrm{d}y_j. \tag{13}$$

Since $\mathrm{d}x_i = 0$ for $\mathrm{d}y_i = -\mathrm{d}y_j$, it follows that

$$\frac{\partial g_i}{\partial y_i} - \frac{\partial g_i}{\partial y_j} = 1. \tag{14}$$

This is a very strong prediction. It has been tested by Cox and Rank (1992) and in a more sophisticated way by Altonji, Hayashi and Kotlikoff (1997). The latter authors find that an increase in parent's income leads to an increase in the transfer and that an increase in the child's income leads to a decrease in the transfer, but the estimates of these effects are much smaller in absolute value than what would be predicted by (14). They therefore reject the assumption of pure altruism. This immediately raises the question of what could be a better explanation. This is not an easy question, as the exact modelling of intrafamily behaviour involves many different aspects. Decisions concerning *inter vivos* transfers interact with decisions (and expectations) on bequests and with decisions to invest in human capital. Taxes may induce shifts from one transmission channel to another. The existence of capital market imperfections plays a crucial role. In this chapter

I do not intend to go into these different aspects. Let me simply illustrate the treatment of "motivations" for *inter vivos* transfers with two examples.[28]

A first approach was formulated by Cox (1987). In this model altruistic parents transfer economic means to their children in exchange for services delivered: attention, companionship and conforming to parental regulations. Children will only accept to participate in this reciprocal exchange if this does not lower their utility. If the parents are sufficiently altruistic, the parent–child transfer is large enough so that the participation constraint is not binding. We are then back in the previous model. An increase in the income of the recipient will lower the probability that she gets a transfer and will also lower the transfer amount. However, things may change when the participation constraint is binding. While it then is still true that the probability of a transfer depends negatively on the income of the recipient, it now becomes possible that the transfer amount itself increases with the recipient's income. If income increases, the threat point of the child also increases and the parent may have to increase his transfer to get the desired services. If such a positive effect is found in the data, this suggests that we are in the "exchange regime". The model has been tested in a long series of papers and for different countries [see, e.g., Cox (1987), Cox and Rank (1992), Cox, Eser and Jimenez (1998), Secondi (1997)]. Most authors find overall support for the exchange hypothesis.

Another hypothesis is the one by Cigno, Giannelli and Rosati (1998). Individuals live for three periods and do not derive utility from anything but their own consumption. Family ties make it possible to reallocate consumption over the life cycle. Such reallocation is governed by a self-enforcing family "constitution" stating that each middle-aged person must transfer a specified amount of income to each of the children and a specified amount of income to each of the parents. The latter obligation only holds, however, if the parent has obeyed the same rules when he was middle-aged. Given that the transfer amounts are fixed by the family constitution, the model predicts only weak effects of income changes on the transfers. It produces clear predictions on the effect of credit rationing, however. Rationing will have as a consequence that some persons switch from a "go it alone" to a "comply with the constitution" strategy, because the latter strategy will allow them a reallocation over the life cycle which they cannot realize without it. Therefore rationing will have a positive effect on the probability of intrafamily transfers. This prediction is different from the one made by both the pure altruism- and the exchange-model: in both these models an increase in rationing would be equivalent to a decrease in the donor's income and would therefore lead to a decrease in the transfer. Cigno, Giannelli and Rosati (1998) find support for their "constitution" model with Italian data.

Interpersonal transfers are not only important as a channel of intergenerational transmission. One also observes an extensive system of gifts and informal loans in the rural environment of pre-industrial societies. These interhousehold transfers act as an informal insurance mechanism in smoothing consumption in the face of risk. Here also the

---

[28] Laitner (1997) gives an overview of the literature on intergenerational and interhousehold economic links. The topic of inheritance is treated in Masson and Pestieau (1997) and Arrondel, Masson and Pestieau (1997).

question has been raised what are the motivations behind this behaviour and it has been popular to oppose the view of a "moral economy" based on altruism with the view of a system of precise and clearly defined (albeit informal) insurance contracts motivated mainly by self-interested reciprocity [Fafchamps (1992)].

As before, the hypothesis of pure altruism leads to strong predictions in the spirit of Equation (14). Reinterpreting the simple model sketched earlier within a context of uncertainty, it is easy to see that a sufficiently high level of altruism would lead to complete risk sharing. Analogous to what we had before, individual negative shocks will then be fully compensated for by the altruistic network. This "efficient risk-sharing hypothesis" has been tested by regressing individual consumption on average consumption and individual income: individual income should be insignificant in these regressions. The evidence [e.g., Ravallion and Dearden (1988), Cox and Jimenez (1990), Altonji, Hayashi and Kotlikoff (1992), Townsend (1994, 1995), Dercon and Krishnan (2000)] suggests that considerable risk sharing takes place, but the hypotheses of pure altruism and efficient risk sharing are most often rejected.

The most interesting contribution of the literature then has been a thorough investigation of the self-enforcing risk-sharing arrangements, which are possible even if individuals are not perfectly altruistic. It has been shown that such arrangements do exist [Coate and Ravallion (1993)]. Recently it has been emphasized that informal credit – bringing in information about past transfers for the determination of current transfers – may play an important role in a situation of limited commitment. Of course, for pure altruists it would be unnecessary to introduce such a credit mechanism. Simple risk sharing (not taking into account the past) would be sufficient. The wide spread of informal credit systems therefore in itself is an argument in favour of a "reciprocal exchange" interpretation of the transfers.

At the same time, family and kinship remain the dominant criteria in the formation of social networks. This may have to do with altruism. It is also possible that the regular contacts within a family help to monitor each other and that reciprocal behaviour is only feasible in such a situation of repeated contacts. A synthetic model has been proposed by Foster and Rosenzweig (2001). They find empirical support for the idea that imperfect commitment indeed substantially constrains informal transfer arrangements, whether kin-based or not. At the same time, however, altruism plays an important role in ameliorating commitment constraints and thus in increasing the gains from income pooling. Their simulation results show that there is an intricate interrelationship between altruism and exchange or reciprocity.

5.2. Motives for interhousehold transfers

Let us now take some distance from this rich and disparate literature in order to link it to the broader question of motivations for income transfers. Most economists working in the field seem to have been mainly interested by the simple question: altruism or exchange? If we provisionally accept that this is an interesting question, the conclusion of bringing all the evidence from very different sources together seems clear: the strong hypothesis of pure altruism has to be rejected. Exchange and reciprocity considerations play an important role in explaining pro-social behaviour. This is not very surprising and completely in line with what was suggested in the previous sections.

The simple focus on altruism versus exchange has its advantages. In so far as reciprocal exchange arrangements will get translated into a set of social norms, the models offer an explanation for the genesis of such norms. Cigno, Giannelli and Rosati (1998)'s family constitution is an explicit example. The literature on informal insurance also offers an explanation for the appearance of social norms with respect to gifts and informal loans in poor rural villages – and a suggestion for why these norms tend to disappear under the influence of external influences changing the economic environment and the social networks of the villages. The literature on interhousehold transfers could be said therefore to make a contribution to a theory of endogenous norms. This is certainly better than introducing social norms as an ad hoc explanation for all kinds of behaviour.

However, one has to remain cautious and remember that most of the tests of "altruism" are indirect tests, based on behavioural predictions within a specific model.[29] It is usually not difficult to respecify the model such that the predictions from an "exchange" or a "reciprocity" model on the one hand and an "altruistic" model on the other hand become observationally equivalent. A recent example is the model by Stark and Falk (1998). They formalize the decision process of an egoistic donor as an optimisation problem that incorporates anticipation of the recipient's gratitude. This gratitude may induce the recipient to help the donor at a later stage. Since gratitude will be larger if the recipient's income is lower, transfers may be larger the lower the recipient's income. Therefore in this case the reciprocity motive and the altruistic motive give rise to types of behaviour that are observationally equivalent and "the ability to infer motive from conduct is jeopardized" [Stark and Falk (1998, p. 271)].

Moreover, while pure altruism can be rejected, there is at the same time plenty of evidence that altruism does matter and that the relationship between "exchange" and "altruistic" motives is a fairly complex one. People who are in need because they get ill or unemployed or because they are confronted with unexpected expenditures have a larger probability to be helped, both in the intergenerational transfers in richer countries and in the systems of informal insurance in the poor countries. Most of the interhousehold transfers – also in systems of social insurance – take place in the setting of larger families or kin. While altruism is perhaps not perfect, it certainly cannot be discarded. As a matter of fact, many of the theoretical models give some role to altruism and model the complementarity between reciprocal exchange and altruism.

At the same time, it is striking that the "intermediate" motivations related to "warm glow" or "moral principles" play a rather minor role in this literature. After all we think about the same individuals deciding at one moment about their charitable contributions

---

[29] Phelps (1988) is an exception introducing explicit information from a psychological testing procedure: the Thematic Apperception Test. "Altruism" is operationalized as the affiliation motive in this TAT. However, she focuses on income formation and on the interrelationship between the effects of personality dispositions in the family and in the market place.

and at another moment about giving to their children or their parents. Certainly one would suppose *a priori* that feelings of "responsibility" and "duty" – and ideas about the equitable treatment of different children – play an essential role in the behaviour of parents. In the context of parent–child relationships these feelings may have deep biological roots. Where are the dutiful altruists, who figured so prominently in the literature on charitable giving? As we have argued before the predictions of a model of "warm glow" and "duty" differ from the predictions of the model of "pure altruism" – if parents get a good feeling from helping their children there is no reason why the extreme prediction (14) would hold. Rejection of (14) therefore does not necessarily mean that one has to resort to an egoistic "exchange" interpretation. In fact, as I argued before, it is too simple to reduce "warm glow" and "duty" to egoism. Gifts may persist in situations where the exchange motive is no longer relevant. Reciprocal relationships may involve pure altruism.

An interesting part of the literature on intergenerational gifts raises the question how parents can compel their children to take care of them when they are old. Again, pure altruism lets the problem dissipate, at least when the altruism is as strong in the children as it is in the parents. A cynical alternative hypothesis is put forward by Bernheim, Shleifer and Summers (1985). In their model parents threaten their children not to leave any inheritance if these children do not deliver the services the parents need. Another approach has been proposed by Becker (1993) and is further worked out in Cox and Stark (1994). Here parents shape the preferences of their children. They teach them the desired behaviour by setting an example, i.e. by helping their own parents. So doing they attempt to inculcate a sense of guilt for misbehaviour in the children. Phrased in somewhat more positive terms, the model endogenises the feeling of "duty" to which I have been referring before. Cox and Stark (1994) generate falsifiable predictions from this approach. First, it should be the case that children who have seen their parents making transfers to their grandparents should be more inclined to giving transfers themselves later in their lives. Second – and more surprisingly – respondents will provide more services to their parents when children are present than when they are not. These predictions are not falsified with US-data from the National Survey of Families and Households. Of course, while Cox and Stark (1994) focus on the deliberate behaviour of the parents in trying to shape the preferences of their children, these parents have been children themselves – so they will be under the influence of the "demonstration effect" induced by their own parents and hence will be characterized also by duty (or guilt). The model therefore gives some insight into the formation of "dutiful altruists".

When reading the literature on intrafamily and interhousehold transfers one cannot escape the feeling that there is a bewildering variety of sometimes highly specific models and a remarkably high correlation between the *a priori*'s of the researchers and their empirical findings. This was perhaps to be expected from the psychological literature. As I mentioned in Section 2, specific pro-social behaviour is highly context-dependent and characterized by intricate person–situation–behaviour interactions. While anonymous charitable giving takes place within a rather well defined setting, this is not true for the behaviour covered by the literature on intrafamily and interhousehold transfers. This behaviour includes both monetary and non-monetary transfers, exchanges of (different) services by children and parents (babysitting and helping ageing parents), informal insurance in the poorest countries of the world and bequests behaviour in the richest. A lot of variation is therefore to be expected and psychologists have collected a mass of evidence showing that the simple one-dimensional opposition "altruism" versus "exchange" does not suffice to make sense of all these different behavioural patterns. A mixture of motivations will be present and, moreover, there is considerable heterogeneity among individuals.

This is definitely not a criticism on the detailed models constructed by economists. Quite the contrary, the main contribution of the economic literature is the careful theoretical analysis of the different forms of pro-social behaviour and the detailed modelling of the constraints imposed by the economic environment. Here are the roots of the economic approach and that is where it is best. It is rather meant to be a criticism of the self-confidence with which some of the empirical work is given a simplistic psychological interpretation. As soon as one accepts that it is not really useful to focus exclusively on the motivation of pure altruism (albeit with the desire to reject it) or on the hypothesis of perfect crowding-out (perhaps for political reasons), it turns out that many of the more interesting models with a richer motivational structure are either observationally equivalent or that the data available are not sufficiently rich to be confident about the results of testing the motivational assumptions. "As if" modelling may be fine if one restricts oneself to predicting behavioural changes following from changes in the environment. One can defend the position that the fine distinctions between different motivations are not really important if the predicted behaviour indeed is identical. However, this also implies that one should not start drawing conclusions about motivations while forgetting that the model is only "as if".

Like for the motivations behind charitable giving, I think that real progress in understanding motivations for intrafamily and interhousehold transfers can be made by using direct questionnaire information and by designing clever laboratory and field experiments. The best hope for scientific progress in this matter seems to reside in a combination of the experimental and survey techniques of the other social sciences with the modelling apparatus of economics. This of course also will require that researchers start setting up their own surveys through which they can collect the most relevant information instead of working with data collected by other agencies for other purposes.

5.3. Gifts: The deadweight loss of Christmas?

While until now I have concentrated mainly on monetary transfers, a large part of relatively smaller gifts is typically non-monetary: only 10–15% of gifts offered at times of celebration are in the form of money. Waldfogel (1993) argues that holiday gift expenditures in the US totalled about 40 billion dollars in 1992. At first sight it is not easy for an economist to understand why people give these non-monetary presents. Why not simply give money so that the recipient can buy whatever he wants according to his own preferences? This in any case avoids the danger (that we are all well aware of) that gifts do not match with the recipients' preferences.

Waldfogel (1993) argues that the problem of mismatch leads to a so-called deadweight loss of Christmas giving. He asked student respondents to describe the gifts they had received and to estimate the value of the gifts as the "amount of cash such that you are indifferent between the gift and the cash, not counting the sentimental value of the gift. If you exchanged the original gift, assess the value of the object you got in exchange for the original gift. If you exchanged the original gift for cash, put the cash amount you received here".[30] He then compared these estimated values to estimates of the prices paid by the giver. The results are striking. The average value of the ratio value/price, which he calls the percent yield, is only 83.9. Moreover, there is a clear pattern according to the relationship between the giver and the recipient: for friends the percent yield is 98.8, for siblings and parents about 86.0, for grandparents only 62.9. And people seem to be aware of this yield: friends give only 6.1% of their gifts in cash, parents 9.6%, grandparents 42.3%. All in all, he concludes that between a tenth and a third of spending on Christmas gifts is wasted. In a later study [Waldfogel (1996)] he finds similar, although less extreme, results.

Waldfogel's article has led to a number of comments, questioning his methodology and his results. Solnick and Hemenway (1996) replicated his study with a broader (non)students sample and with a slight reformulation of the question. They found that more than half of the respondents valued the gift above its cost. While they had some real outliers in their sample, even after trimming the mean percent yield was still 214. Half of the respondents valued the gift very much because it showed a lot of thought, half said that the gift was something "you wanted but felt you shouldn't spend money on for yourself", 22% said that the gift was something they needed but never remembered to get, and 20% said they would not have wanted to shop for the gift themselves [Solnick and Hemenway (1996, p. 1301)].

While Solnick and Hemenway (1996) criticized the unrepresentative nature of Waldfogel (1993)'s sample, an alternative explanation for the differences between the studies was offered by Ruffle and Tykocinski (2000). They focused on the formulation of the valuation question. In the Solnick/Hemenway-study the question reads as follows: "Aside from any sentimental value, if, without the giver ever knowing, you could receive an amount of money instead of the gift, what is the minimum amount of money *that would make you equally happy*" (my emphasis). The underlined part replaces the formulation "the amount of cash such that you are indifferent" in the Waldfogel-study. When asking the two versions of the question to two different samples, Ruffle and Tykocinski (2000) find that valuations given in response to the "equally happy"-question are much

---

[30] For another sample he formulated the question as: "... apart from any sentimental value of the items, if you did not have them, how much would you be willing to pay to obtain them?" One may expect that this willingness-to-pay question will lead to lower estimates of the value than the willingness-to-accept question. I will only concentrate on the latter: this will lead to a lower bound of the estimate of the deadweight loss.

higher than those given in the indifference version. The estimated welfare yield from the "equally happy"-treatment is markedly higher than that from the indifference treatment.

The different answers obtained with the two experimental treatments are a warning for all questionnaire work on motivations and altruism. The framing of the questions may matter a lot. However, in this case the framing effect is indicative of a crucial difference between the "material value" and the "sentimental value" of gifts. The problem is well sketched by Waldfogel (1996, p. 1306), who describes his own result as follows: "The result is *not* that recipients value the receipt of gifts at less than the price paid by the givers. Because of the thought that goes into choosing and giving gifts, recipients may value the receipt of gifts highly, even if they dislike the gift objects themselves. Rather, the result is that recipients generally value the *objects* received as gifts at less than the price paid by the giver. As long as the sentimental value conveyed to the recipient by the gift would also have been conveyed by an equally costly gift that has greater material value to the recipient, the gift with lower material value engenders deadweight loss". A possible explanation for the different results of Waldfogel (1993) and Solnick and Hemenway (1996) is that the formulation "equally happy" makes it much more difficult for respondents to separate the sentimental and the material value of the gift (despite the fact that they were asked explicitly to do so).[31]

As a matter of fact the basic idea that recipients value the *objects* received as a gift at less than the price paid by the giver seems very reasonable. But what does it mean? If it is true, why then does the practice of non-cash gift giving persist? If we take seriously the basic idea of revealed preference, simple observation of facts seems to indicate that donors and recipients prefer in-kind gifts. In fact, there is a large psychological literature showing that in some circumstances or relations cash gifts are not appreciated at all. Pieters and Robben (1999) give an overview of possible reasons. A transfer of money is an ambiguous instance of giving, because of the multiple economic functions of money. It suggests a lack of motivation on the part of the giver. Its fungibility precludes it from future identification with the giver. Money as a gift quantifies the relationship by placing an exact price on it. This is why price tags are removed. All these reasons refer in one way or another to the relationship between the giver and the receiver. It is not surprising then that money gifts are better acceptable if the social distance between giver and recipient is larger and/or if their relationship looks more like an employer/employee relation. In general, common psychological knowledge suggests that it is the sentimental value that really matters and that the sentimental value of a cash gift is very low and sometimes negative.

This of course means that the whole idea of deadweight loss in this context is rather ambiguous or, in any case, that one should avoid the normative connotations that the

---

[31] In yet another comment List and Shogren (1998) focus on the "hypothetical setting" of the original Waldfogel (1993)-study and present the results of an actual random price auction procedure. The yields they obtain are smaller than the ones of Solnick and Hemenway (1996) but larger than the ones presented by Waldfogel (1993, 1996). However, the real offers also contain sentimental values and their procedure to separate the sentimental value of the gifts and the material value is not altogether convincing.

term unavoidably must carry. The individual utility of the recipient does not only depend on the commodity received, but also (and crucially) on the fact that it is given in a non-monetary form. The process of transferring the gift itself enters the utility function – and the way in which it enters depends on the personal relationship between giver and receiver.[32] It would be utterly absurd to say that a prohibition of non-cash gifts would lead to a welfare increase. It is rather meaningless then to speak of a deadweight "loss" if the reference situation of a cash gift used to calculate the "loss" is not ideal at all.[33]

Does this mean that economic theory cannot cope with these psychological insights because "according to economic theory, money is the perfect gift" [Solnick and Hemenway (1996, p. 1303)]? Definitely not. Recently there has been a series of elegant models, which try to capture the considerations from the other social sciences. Camerer (1988) argues that gifts can signal good intentions at the start of a long-term relationship. Carmichael and MacLeod (1997) more explicitly explain why the gift must be inefficient for relationship building. In their evolutionary model, if the partners exchanged money at the beginning of a match, then parasites could immediately enter, give (and receive) the money, cheat, and move on. Ruffle (1999) introduces emotions of surprise, disappointment, embarrassment and pride. Prendergast and Stole (2001) show that inefficient non-monetary gifts will be offered instead of cash because the donor wants to signal the quality of his information about the recipient's preferences. If altruism is high relative to the desire to be known to know the preferences of the other, the deadweight loss argument arises and cash gifts become more common.

These models offer an exceptionally rich framework to think about the "value" of non-cash gifts in relations. They suggest how the existence of such gifts can be explained, despite the "deadweight loss" attached to it. They witness to the flexibility of the economic approach to integrate complex psychological phenomena. Future empirical research should try to go beyond the simple measurement of "deadweight loss" and beyond the focus on the material value of the objects given. It should rather concentrate on the components of the sentimental value of the gift itself. This is important to better understand the processes behind gift giving. It is even more important to correct the misleading conclusion that one could derive from the work on "deadweight losses", i.e. that a society without non-cash gifts would be a better society with people at a higher welfare level. As before questionnaire and experimental techniques are complementary in this effort.

6. Conclusion

Very different motivations may lead to voluntary transfers. Altruism (or empathy) is only one of them. Transfers may also follow from a feeling of duty or because the donor

---

[32] Kolm (1984, 2000a, 2000b) also emphasizes the possibility that in situations of reciprocity and gift-giving the process itself enters the utility function.

[33] Of course one could still say that in comparing different non-cash gifts both the donor and the recipient will prefer a gift with a higher "yield".

wants to obey social norms. They may be part of reciprocal arrangements, which finally are in the self-interest of all the parties involved. They may reflect pure materialistic egoism or a desire to gain social prestige. A mixture of these different motivations probably drives all individuals but the relative trade-offs are different and vary with the concrete circumstances or over time. A better insight into these motivations is important for its own sake. It is also necessary for predicting the consequences of government intervention or for interpreting the results of contingent valuation studies. Nor can the behaviour of charities be understood without a better knowledge of interindividual and intertemporal differences in motivations.

It is not surprising therefore that economists have devoted much attention to these motivations. Two features characterize the mainstream of economic research. In the first place, the model of perfect altruism has played a pivotal role. This model leads to very strong predictions, both in the setting of charitable contributions and in the setting of intrafamily and interhousehold transfers. There is now plenty of evidence from very different sources that these strong predictions are falsified by the data. This is not at all surprising, however, as "the altruistic model is victim of its extreme simplicity" [Laferrère (2000, p. 222)]. Alternatives have been proposed. Yet sometimes they remain rather vague. The popular idea of the "warm glow" of giving is a typical example: it can refer to almost all the motivations described earlier and only little attention is given to a comparison of these alternative interpretations. In the same way, different "exchange" or reciprocity models have been presented in the literature on intrafamily and interhousehold transfers. They all have been tested against the altruistic model, but less attention has been given to a careful comparison of these different "non-altruistic" models against each other. It is as if things are settled once one has rejected the pure altruistic model. I think this is too simple. Now that we have discarded the simple extremes of pure altruism and perfect crowding-out, we should begin to tackle the really challenging questions.

In the second place, the economic literature has tried to derive information about motivations in an indirect way. Clever models have been constructed to derive behavioural predictions from different motivational assumptions. While the theoretical literature on charitable contributions has remained relatively simple, the literature on intrafamily and interhousehold transfers is extremely rich and interesting and testifies for the flexibility of the economic approach to take into account specific features of the economic and social environment in which economic agents take their decisions. We now understand much better the interrelationship between bequests and *inter vivos* transfers and the self-supporting social mechanisms, which may underlie informal social insurance. However, in general economists have not bothered too much about the many cases in which different motivational structures are observationally equivalent. This is in the line of the economic tradition in which an "as if"-explanation is often deemed sufficient. However, while an "as if" approach may indeed be sufficient if preferences or motivations are relatively similar and stable, it is by definition not sufficient to get information about the motivations themselves. And it tends to break down if preferences are heterogeneous and change over time, certainly if these changes are caused by factors endogenous to the economic system.

If one is interested in learning more about motivations, one should more explicitly think about how to distinguish the different "exchange", reciprocity or "warm glow"-interpretations from one another. Moreover, the empirical research should perhaps take into account more explicitly the heterogeneity of preferences and motivations within the population – and their possible changes over time.

I am sceptical that "indirect" methods to test for different motivations will be sufficient for this task. More experimental work certainly will be needed – including cleverly designed field experiments. Moreover, I think that collection of direct subjective information also is necessary. Let me quote Manski: "Rather than try to infer preferences and expectations from observations of chosen actions, why not elicit them directly? Pose this question to an economist, and chances are that one will receive an instant hostile response. Economists tend to be deeply sceptical of subjective statements. Early in their careers, they are taught to believe only what people do, not what they say. Economists often assert that respondents to surveys have no incentive to answer questions about their preferences or expectations carefully or honestly; hence, there is no reason to believe that subjective responses reliably reflect respondents' thinking. As a result, the profession has enforced something of a prohibition on the collection of subjective data. In the absence of data on preferences and expectations, economists have compensated by imposing assumptions" [Manski (2000, p. 121)]. I fully agree with this description of the situation. I also fully agree that this situation is deplorable. If we want to get a better insight into the motivations behind charitable giving, we will have to go for a combination of the modelling techniques of economics with experimental methods and with the data collection techniques of other social sciences.

Acknowledgements

I thank Louis Lévy-Garboua, Serge-Christophe Kolm, Frederic Vermeulen and Jorre Renterghem for their valuable comments. In addition, the help of Jorre Renterghem has been indispensable for the construction of Table 1.

References

Abrams, B., Schmitz, M. (1978). "The 'crowding-out' effect of government transfers on private charitable contributions". Public Choice 33, 29–41.
Abrams, B., Schmitz, M. (1984). "The crowding-out effect of governmental transfers on private charitable contributions: cross-section evidence". National Tax Journal 37, 563–568.
Alesina, A., Glaeser, E., Sacerdote, B. (2001). "Why doesn't the US have a European-style welfare state?". Brookings Papers on Economic Activity 2, 187–254.
Altonji, J., Hayashi, F., Kotlikoff, L. (1992). "Is the extended family altruistically linked? Direct tests using micro data". American Economic Review 82, 1177–1198.

Altonji, J., Hayashi, F., Kotlikoff, L. (1997). "Parental altruism and inter vivos transfers: theory and evidence". Journal of Political Economy 105, 1121–1166.
Andreoni, J. (1988). "Privately provided public goods in a large economy: the limits of altruism". Journal of Public Economics 35, 57–73.
Andreoni, J. (1989). "Giving with impure altruism: applications to charity and Ricardian equivalence". Journal of Political Economy 97, 1447–1458.
Andreoni, J. (1990). "Impure altruism and donations to public goods: a theory of warm-glow giving". Economic Journal 100, 464–477.
Andreoni, J. (1993). "An experimental test of the public-goods crowding-out hypothesis". American Economic Review 83, 1317–1327.
Andreoni, J. (1995). "Warm-glow versus cold-prickle: the effects of positive and negative framing on cooperation in experiments". Quarterly Journal of Economics 110, 1–22.
Andreoni, J., Scholz, J. (1998). "An econometric analysis of charitable giving with interdependent preferences". Economic Inquiry 36, 410–428.
Archibald, G., Donaldson, D. (1976). "Non-paternalism and the basic theorems of welfare economics". Canadian Journal of Economics 9, 492–507.
Arrondel, L., Masson, A., Pestieau, P. (1997). "Bequest and inheritance: empirical issues and France-US comparison". In: Erreygers, G., et al. (Eds.), Is Inheritance Legitimate?. Springer, Berlin, pp. 89–125.
Auten, G., Sieg, H., Clotfelter, C. (2000). "Charitable giving, income, and taxes: an analysis of panel data". American Economic Review 92, 371–382.
Banks, J., Tanner, S. (1997). "The state of donation: household gifts to charity, 1974–1996". Commentary 62. Institute for Fiscal Studies, London.
Baron, R., Byrne, D. (2003). Social Psychology. Allyn & Bacon.
Barrett, K., McGuirk, A., Steinberg, R. (1997). "Further evidence on the dynamic impact of taxes on charitable giving". National Tax Journal 50, 321–334.
Barro, R. (1974). "Are government bonds net wealth?". Journal of Political Economy 82, 1095–1117.
Batson, C. (1998). "Altruism and prosocial behavior". In: Gilbert, D., et al. (Eds.), The Handbook of Social Psychology. Oxford University Press, Oxford, pp. 282–316.
Becker, G. (1974). "A theory of social interactions". Journal of Political Economy 82, 1063–1093.
Becker, G. (1981). "Altruism in the family and selfishness in the market place". Economica 48, 1–15.
Becker, G. (1993). "The economic way of looking at behaviour". Journal of Political Economy 101, 385–409.
Bergstrom, T., Blume, L., Varian, H. (1986). "On the private provision of public goods". Journal of Public Economics 29, 25–49.
Bernheim, B., Shleifer, A., Summers, L. (1985). "The strategic bequest motive". Journal of Political Economy 93, 1045–1076.
Boadway, R., Pestieau, P., Wildasin, D. (1989a). "Non-cooperative behavior and efficient provision of public goods". Public Finance 34, 1–7.
Boadway, R., Pestieau, P., Wildasin, D. (1989b). "Tax-transfer policies and the voluntary provision of public goods". Journal of Public Economics 39, 157–176.
Bolton, G., Katok, E. (1998). "An experimental test of the crowding out hypothesis: the nature of beneficent behavior". Journal of Economic Behavior and Organization 37, 315–331.
Boskin, M., Feldstein, M. (1977). "Effects of the charitable deduction on contributions by low income and middle income households: evidence from the National Survey on Philanthropy". Review of Economics and Statistics 59, 351–354.
Brennan, G. (1973). "Pareto desirable redistribution: the non-altruistic dimension". Public Choice 14, 43–68.
Brown, E., Lankford, H. (1992). "Gifts of money and gifts of time: estimating the effects of tax prices and available time". Journal of Public Economics 47, 321–341.
Camerer, C. (1988). "Gifts as economic signals and social symbols". American Journal of Sociology 94, S180–S214.
Caporael, L., Dawes, R., Orbell, J., van de Kragt, A. (1989). "Selfishness examined: cooperation in the absence of egoistic incentives (+discussion)". Behavioral and Brain Sciences 12, 683–739.

Carmichael, H., MacLeod, W. (1997). "Gift giving and the evolution of cooperation". International Economic Review 38, 485–509.

Cigno, A., Giannelli, G., Rosati, F. (1998). "Voluntary transfers among Italian households: altruistic and non-altruistic explanations". Structural Change and Economic Dynamics 9, 435–451.

Clotfelter, C. (1980). "Tax incentives and charitable giving: evidence from a panel of taxpayers". Journal of Public Economics 13, 319–340.

Clotfelter, C., Salamon, L. (1982). "The impact of the 1981 tax reform on individual charitable giving". National Tax Journal 35, 171–187.

Coate, S., Ravallion, M. (1993). "Reciprocity without commitment: characterization and performance of informal insurance arrangements". Journal of Development Economics 40, 1–24.

Cohen, G. (2000). "If you're an egalitarian, how come you're so rich?". Journal of Ethics 4, 1–26.

Costa, D., Kahn, M. (2003). "Cowards and heroes: group loyalty in the American Civil War". Quarterly Journal of Economics 118, 519–548.

Cox, D. (1987). "Motives for private income transfers". Journal of Political Economy 95, 508–546.

Cox, D., Eser, Z., Jimenez, E. (1998). "Motives for private transfers over the life cycle: an analytical framework and evidence for Peru". Journal of Development Economics 55, 57–80.

Cox, D., Jimenez, E. (1990). "Social objectives through private transfers: a review". World Bank Research Observer 5, 205–218.

Cox, D., Rank, M. (1992). "Inter-vivos transfers and intergenerational exchange". Review of Economics and Statistics 74, 305–314.

Cox, D., Stark, O. (1994). "Intergenerational transfers and the demonstration effect". Mimeo. Boston College.

Day, K., Devlin, R. (1996). "Volunteerism and crowding out: Canadian econometric evidence". Canadian Journal of Economics 29, 37–53.

Dercon, S., Krishnan, P. (2000). "In sickness and in health: risk sharing within households in rural Ethiopia". Journal of Political Economy 108, 688–727.

Duncan, B. (1999). "Modeling charitable contributions of time and money". Journal of Public Economics 72, 213–242.

Duquette, C. (1999). "Is charitable giving by nonitemizers responsive to tax incentives? New evidence". National Tax Journal 52, 195–206.

Elster, J. (1990). Nuts and Bolts for the Social Sciences. Cambridge University Press, Cambridge.

Fafchamps, M. (1992). "Solidarity networks in pre-industrial societies: rational peasants with a moral economy". Economic Development and Cultural Change 41, 147–174.

Fehr, E., Gächter, S. (2000). "Fairness and retaliation: the economics of reciprocity". Journal of Economic Perspectives 14, 159–181.

Feldstein, M. (1975a). "The income tax and charitable contributions I: Aggregate and distributional effects". National Tax Journal 28, 81–99.

Feldstein, M. (1975b). "The income tax and charitable contributions II: The impact on religious, educational and other organisations". National Tax Journal 28, 209–226.

Feldstein, M., Clotfelter, C. (1976). "Tax incentives and charitable contributions in the United States: a microeconometric analysis". Journal of Public Economics 5, 1–26.

Feldstein, M., Taylor, A. (1976). "The income tax and charitable contributions". Econometrica 44, 1201–1222.

Fisher, R., Ackerman, D. (1998). "The effect of recognition and group need on volunteerism: a social norm perspective". Journal of Consumer Research 25, 262–275.

Forbes, K., Zampelli, E. (1997). "Religious giving by individuals: a cross denominational study". American Journal of Economics and Sociology 56, 17–30.

Foster, A., Rosenzweig, M. (2001). "Imperfect commitment, altruism and the family: evidence from transfer behavior in low-income rural areas". Review of Economics and Statistics 83, 389–407.

Frank, R. (1988). Passions within Reason. Norton, New York.

Freeman, R. (1997). "Working for nothing: the supply of volunteer labor". Journal of Labor Economics 15, S140–S166.

Glazer, A., Konrad, K. (1996). "A signaling explanation for charity". American Economic Review 86, 1019–1028.

Hammond, P. (1975). "Charity: altruism or cooperative egoism?". In: Phelps, E. (Ed.), Altruism, Morality and Economic Theory. Russel Sage Foundation, New York, pp. 115–131.

Harbaugh, W. (1998a). "The prestige motive for making charitable transfers". American Economic Review (Papers and Proceedings) 88, 277–282.

Harbaugh, W. (1998b). "What do donations buy? A model of philantropy based on prestige and warm glow". Journal of Public Economics 67, 269–284.

Hausman, J. (1993). Contingent Valuation: a Critical Assessment. North-Holland, New York.

Hoffman, M. (1981). "Is altruism part of human nature?". Journal of Personality and Social Psychology 40, 121–137.

Holländer, H. (1990). "A social exchange approach to voluntary cooperation". American Economic Review 80, 1157–1167.

Hood, R., Martin, S., Osberg, L. (1977). "Economic determinants of individual charitable donations in Canada". Canadian Journal of Economics 10, 653–669.

Hudson, J., Jones, P. (1994). "Testing for self-interest: "the economic person in sociological context" revisited". Journal of Socio-Economics 23, 101–112.

Jones, A., Posnett, J. (1991a). "Charitable donations by UK households: evidence from the Family Expenditure Survey". Applied Economics 23, 343–351.

Jones, A., Posnett, J. (1991b). "The impact of tax deductibility on charitable giving by covenant in the UK". Economic Journal 101, 1117–1129.

Jones, P., Cullis, J., Lewis, A. (1998). "Public versus private provision of altruism: can fiscal policy make individuals 'better' people?". Kyklos 51, 3–24.

Kahneman, D., Knetsch, J. (1992). "Valuing public goods: the purchase of moral satisfaction". Journal of Environmental Economics and Management 22, 57–70.

Kaplow, L. (1998). "Tax policy and gifts". American Economic Review (Papers and Proceedings) 88, 283–288.

Keating, B., Pitts, R., Appel, D. (1981). "United Way contributions: coercion, charity, or economic self-interest". Southern Economic Journal 47, 815–823.

Khanna, J., Posnett, J., Sandler, T. (1995). "Charity donations in the UK – new evidence based on panel data". Journal of Public Economics 56, 257–272.

Khanna, J., Sandler, T. (2000). "Partners in giving: the crowding-in effects of UK government grants". European Economic Review 44, 1543–1556.

Kingma, B. (1989). "An accurate measurement of the crowd-out effect, income effect and price effect for charitable contributions". Journal of Political Economy 97, 1197–1207.

Kingma, B., McClelland, R. (1995). "Public radio stations are really, really not public goods: charitable and impure altruism". Annals of Public and Cooperative Economics 66, 65–76.

Kitchen, H. (1992). "Determinants of charitable donations in Canada: a comparison over time". Applied Economics 24, 709–713.

Kitchen, H., Dalton, R. (1990). "Determinants of charitable donations by families in Canada: a regional analysis". Applied Economics 22, 285–299.

Kolm, S.-C. (1984). La bonne économie. La réciprocité générale. Presses Universitaires de France, Paris.

Kolm, S.-C. (2000a). "The economics of reciprocity, giving and altruism: introduction". In: Gérard-Varet, L.-A., et al. (Eds.), The Economics of Reciprocity, Giving and Altruism. Macmillan, London, pp. 1–44.

Kolm, S.-C. (2000b). "The theory of reciprocity". In: Gérard-Varet, L.-A., et al. (Eds.), The Economics of Reciprocity, Giving and Altruism. Macmillan, London, pp. 115–141.

Kurz, M. (1978). "Altruism as an outcome of social interaction". American Economic Review (Papers and Proceedings) 68, 216–222.

Laferrère, A. (2000). "Intergenerational transmission models: a survey". In: Gérard-Varet, L.-A., et al. (Eds.), The Economics of Reciprocity, Giving and Altruism. Macmillan, London, pp. 207–225.

Laitner, J. (1997). "Intergenerational and interhousehold economic links". In: Rosenzweig, M., et al. (Eds.), Handbook of Population and Family Economics. North Holland, Amsterdam, pp. 189–238.

Lankford, R., Wyckoff, J. (1991). "Modeling charitable giving using a Box–Cox Standard Tobit model". Review of Economics and Statistics 73, 460–470.

List, J., Shogren, J. (1998). "The deadweight loss of Christmas: comment". American Economic Review 88, 1350–1355.

Long, S. (1976). "Social pressure and contributions to health charities". Public Choice 28, 55–66.

Manski, C. (2000). "Economic analysis of social interactions". Journal of Economic Perspectives 14, 115–136.

Masson, A., Pestieau, P. (1997). "Bequests motives and models of inheritance: a survey of the literature". In: Erreygers, G., et al. (Eds.), Is Inheritance Legitimate?. Springer, Berlin, pp. 54–88.

Menchik, P., Weisbrod, B. (1987). "Volunteer labor supply". Journal of Public Economics 32, 159–183.

Mueller, D. (1986). "Rational egoism versus adaptive egoism as fundamental postulate for a descriptive theory of human behavior". Public Choice 51, 3–23.

Nunes, P., Schokkaert, E. (2003). "Identifying the warm glow effect in contingent valuation". Journal of Environmental Economics and Management 45, 231–245.

Okten, C., Weisbrod, B. (2000). "Determinants of donations in private nonprofit markets". Journal of Public Economics 75, 255–272.

Oliner, S., Oliner, P. (1988). The Altruistic Personality: Rescuers of Jews in Nazi Europe. Free Press, New York.

Payne, A. (1998). "Does the government crow-out private donations? New evidence from a sample of non-profit firms". Journal of Public Economics 69, 323–345.

Payne, A. (2001). "Measuring the effect of federal research funding on private donations at research universities: is federal research funding more than a substitute for private donations?". International Tax and Public Finance 8, 731–751.

Phelps, C. (1988). "Caring and family income". Journal of Economic Behavior and Organization 10, 83–98.

Pieters, R., Robben, H. (1999). "Consumer evaluation of money as a gift: a two-utility model and an empirical test". Kyklos 52, 173–2000.

Piliavin, J., Charng, H.-W. (1990). "Altruism: a review of recent theory and research". Annual Review of Sociology 16, 27–65.

Posnett, J., Sandler, T. (1989). "Demand for charity donations in private non-profit markets: the case of the UK". Journal of Public Economics 40, 187–200.

Prendergast, C., Stole, L. (2001). "The non-monetary nature of gifts". European Economic Review 45, 1793–1810.

Randolph, W. (1995). "Dynamic income, progressive taxes and the timing of charitable contributions". Journal of Political Economy 103, 709–738.

Ravallion, M., Dearden, L. (1988). "Social security in a moral economy: an empirical analysis for Java". Review of Economics and Statistics 70, 36–44.

Reece, W. (1979). "Charitable contributions: new evidence on household behaviour". American Economic Review 69, 142–151.

Reece, W., Zieschang, K. (1985). "Consistent estimation of the impact of tax deductibility on the level of charitable contributions". Econometrica 53, 271–293.

Ribar, D., Wilhelm, M. (1995). "Charitable contributions to international relief and development". National Tax Journal 48, 229–244.

Roberts, R. (1984). "A positive model of private charity and public transfers". Journal of Political Economy 92, 136–148.

Roberts, R. (1987). "Financing public goods". Journal of Political Economy 95, 420–437.

Rose-Ackerman, S. (1996). "Altruism, nonprofits and economic theory". Journal of Economic Literature 34, 701–728.

Ruffle, B. (1999). "Gift giving with emotions". Journal of Economic Behavior and Organization 39, 399–420.

Ruffle, B., Tykocinski, O. (2000). "The deadweight loss of Christmas: comment". American Economic Review 90, 319–324.

Rushton, J.P. (1982). "Altruism and society: a social learning perspective". Ethics 92, 425–446.

Samuelson, P. (1954). "The pure theory of public expenditure". Review of Economics and Statistics 36, 387–389.
Schiff, J. (1985). "Does government spending crowd out charitable contributions?". National Tax Journal 38, 535–546.
Schkade, D., Payne, J. (1993). "Where do the numbers come from? How people respond to contingent valuation questions". In: Hausman, J. (Ed.), Contingent Valuation: a Critical Assessment. North-Holland, New York, pp. 271–293.
Schokkaert, E., Van Ootegem, L. (2000). "Preference variation and private donations". In: Gérard-Varet, L.-A., et al. (Eds.), The Economics of Reciprocity, Giving and Altruism. Macmillan, London, pp. 78–95.
Schwartz, R. (1970). "Personal philantropic contributions". Journal of Political Economy 78, 1264–1291.
Secondi, G. (1997). "Private monetary transfers in rural China: are families altruistic?". Journal of Development Studies 33, 487–511.
Sen, A. (1977). "Rational fools: a critique of the behavioural foundations of economic theory". Philosophy and Public Affairs 6, 317–344.
Smith, V., Kehoe, M., Cremer, M. (1995). "The private provision of public goods: altruism and voluntary giving". Journal of Public Economics 58, 107–126.
Solnick, S., Hemenway, D. (1996). "The deadweight loss of Christmas: comment". American Economic Review 86, 1299–1305.
Spash, C. (2000). "Ethical motives and charitable contributions in contingent valuation: empirical evidence from social psychology and economics". Environmental Values 9, 453–479.
Stark, O., Falk, I. (1998). "Transfer, empathy formation, and reverse transfers". American Economic Review (Papers and Proceedings) 88, 271–276.
Steinberg, R. (1991). "Does government spending crowd-out donations? Interpreting the evidence". Annals of Public and Cooperative Economics 62, 591–617.
Stigler, G., Becker, G. (1977). "De gustibus non est disputandum". American Economic Review 67, 76–90.
Sugden, R. (1982). "On the economics of philanthropy". Economic Journal 92, 341–350.
Sugden, R. (1984). "Reciprocity: the supply of public goods through voluntary contributions". Economic Journal 94, 772–787.
Townsend, R. (1994). "Risk and insurance in village India". Econometrica 62, 539–591.
Townsend, R. (1995). "Consumption insurance: an evaluation of risk-bearing systems in low-income economies". Journal of Economic Perspectives 9, 83–102.
Unger, L. (1991). "Altruism as a motivation to volunteer". Journal of Economic Psychology 12, 71–100.
Vaillancourt, F. (1994). "To volunteer or not: Canada, 1987". Canadian Journal of Economics 27, 813–826.
Van Praag, B., Kapteyn, A., Van Herwaarden, F. (1979). "The definition and measurement of social reference spaces". Netherlands Journal of Sociology 15, 13–25.
Waldfogel, J. (1993). "The deadweight loss of Christmas". American Economic Review 83, 1328–1336.
Waldfogel, J. (1996). "The deadweight loss of Christmas: reply". American Economic Review 86, 1306–1308.
Warr, P. (1982). "Pareto optimal redistribution and private charity". Journal of Public Economics 19, 131–138.
Warr, P. (1983). "The private provision of a public good is independent of the distribution of income". Economics Letters 13, 207–211.
Weisbrod, B., Dominguez, N. (1986). "Demand for collective goods in private nonprofit markets: can fundraising expenditures help overcome free-rider behavior?". Journal of Public Economics 30, 83–95.
Wong, C., Chua, V., Vasoo, S. (1998). "Contributions to charitable organizations in a developing country: the case of Singapore". International Journal of Social Economics 25, 25–42.
Woodward, R. (1984). An Empirical Analysis of Philantropic Motivations. Department of Economics, Middlebury.

Chapter 3

ALTRUISTIC BEHAVIOR AND ALTRUISTIC MOTIVATIONS

JON ELSTER[*]

Columbia University, USA

Contents

Abstract	184
Keywords	184
1. Introduction	185
2. The nature and sources of altruistic motivations	185
3. Can interest mimic altruism?	187
4. Can passion mimic altruism?	192
5. Transmutation of motivations	200
6. Is altruism possible and knowable?	202
References	205

[*] I am indebted to Raquel Fernandez, Russell Hardin, Stephen Holmes, Serge-Christophe Kolm, Avishai Margalit, Adam Przeworski, John Roemer and Edna Ullmann-Margalit for comments on an earlier draft.

Handbook of the Economics of Giving, Altruism and Reciprocity, Volume 1
Edited by Serge-Christophe Kolm and Jean Mercier Ythier
Copyright © 2006 Elsevier B.V. All rights reserved
DOI: 10.1016/S1574-0714(06)01003-7

Abstract

Altruism can be understood in a behavioral or in a psychological sense. Motivationally, altruism is the desire to enhance the welfare of others at a net welfare loss to oneself. Behaviorally, altruism is any act that could have resulted from altruistic motivations. The economic literature shows many examples of how altruistic behavior can be generated from self-interested motivations, in iterated games or in reputation-building. The chapter provides further categories and examples, notably from political behavior. Two main examples are taken from the debates at the Federal Convention in 1787 and the elections to the Estates-General in France in 1789. In addition, it is argued that altruistic acts may be caused by the emotions of the agents, notably pride and shame. A distinction is drawn between acts whose performance is conditional on seeing what other agents are doing, corresponding to quasi-moral norms of fairness or reciprocity, and acts whose performance is conditional on being observed by other agents, corresponding to social norms. The operation of quasi-moral norms is observed in experiments where subjects engage in one-shot anonymous interactions. Many subjects not only display cooperative and generous behavior, but are willing to spend resources on punishing those who do not. Since A's punishment of B may induce B to behave cooperatively with C in later interactions, it can be seen as an altruistic act. Experiments by Ernst Fehr and co-workers suggest that the motivation for such altruistic punishment may be non-altruistic, being related instead to a "warm glow" effect. Whether this conclusion is valid for more general forms of reciprocity, such as the tendency for A to punish B when he observes B harming C, remains to be seen. Throughout the chapter there is an attempt to trace the origin of these ideas back to writers such as Montaigne, Descartes, Pascal, Hume and Kant.

Keywords

altruism, reciprocity, emotion, norms, punishment

1. Introduction

I shall understand an "altruistic motivation" as the desire to enhance the welfare of others at a net welfare loss to oneself, and an "altruistic act" as an action for which an altruistic motivation provides a sufficient reason. If I see you giving money to a beggar in the street I call it an altruistic act because it is an action that *could* spring from an altruistic motivation. The topic of this chapter is the problem of sorting out altruistic acts that spring from altruistic motivations from those that do not, that is, from cases in which other motivations mimic or simulate altruism. I do not aim to provide complete coverage, but to fill some gaps in the existing literature.

I shall proceed as follows. In Section 2 I describe some varieties of altruistic motives and discuss how they may be derived from more fundamental motivations. In Section 3 I consider some ways in which *interest* can mimic altruism, and some limits of that approach. In Section 4 I similarly consider how *passion* can mimic altruism, and some limits of that approach. In Section 5 I argue that these two motivations (interest and passion) are also capable of being *transmuted* into altruistic motivations. I conclude in Section 6 by discussing two closely related questions: whether, in the final analysis, genuinely altruistic motivations are possible and, if they are, whether we can know it when they are operating.

2. The nature and sources of altruistic motivations

The full set of human motivations can be classified in many ways. I do not claim that the classification I shall use – the trichotomy of interest, passion and reason – is canonical, but I have found it useful [Elster (1999, Chapter II)]. By interest I shall understand a concern for the absolute level of welfare of the agent, on the assumption that concerns for relative welfare are grounded in emotions such as envy or sympathy. By passion I shall mainly understand emotions such as anger, indignation, fear, shame, contempt, envy, sympathy and love. By reason – not to be confused with rationality [Elster (2004a)] – I shall understand any benevolent and impartial motivation. (Benevolence is needed in the definition, since some people might be impartially malevolent.) Impartiality should typically be understood with reference to a proper subset of humanity. I act impartially in donating to charity that will alleviate the fate of the poor in my country or in risking my life for my fellow-citizens, even when in doing so I disregard the vast majority of humankind.

Although these motivations often operate simultaneously, their mode of interaction is not well understood. In some cases, the agent makes a conscious trade-off between (say) private interest and the general good. In other cases, the agent resolves a motivational conflict by non-compensatory procedures, e.g. by making one motivation lexicographically secondary to another or by making the satisfaction of one goal at a certain level a constraint on maximizing another. In still other cases, causal metaphors such as "a parallelogram of forces" seem more appropriate. Path-dependence may also operate [Elster (1998, pp. 65–66)].

In a given society, these motivations are typically ranked in a normative hierarchy [Elster (1999, Chapter V)]. In ancient Athens, the highest-ranking motive was patriotism; next, revenge, then, self-interest; and at the bottom, envy. The motivation of *hybris*, the deliberate humiliation of another for the sheer pleasure of it, was held in such low esteem that those accused of it might try to explain their behavior as motivated by revenge, drunkenness, or erotic love. Tocqueville (1969, p. 526) claimed that the Americans he observed on 1830 imputed even spontaneous altruistic behavior to self-interested motives, thus showing the privileged place of the latter motivation in the hierarchy [see also Miller (1999)]. Today that ranking is reversed. A reversal has also taken place with regard to the revenge motive, as seen from the fact that people no longer (or less strongly) blame those who do not avenge themselves for insults. In these and similar cases, the hierarchy induces a tendency to *misrepresent* one's motive as better than it actually is. Often, the misrepresentation is addressed to other people. In many cases it also operates on the agent himself, by a motivational alchemy I shall refer to as *transmutation*.

The place of altruistic motivations in this scheme is somewhat indeterminate. On the one hand altruism can derive from an impartial motivation, e.g. from a utilitarian principle in which each counts for one and nobody for more than one, or from a desire to improve the welfare of the worst-off, whoever they might be. On the other hand, it can stem from an emotion-based desire to promote the welfare of close kin and friends at the expense of one's own. Feinberg (1984, pp. 74–75) argues that altruism that is restricted to persons to whom the agent has close emotional relations is actually a "self-interested", although "other-regarding", motivation. According to my definition, this motivation is altruistic (and not self-interested) if the agent is willing to suffer a *net* loss in welfare by the promotion of the welfare of another. Suppose I ask myself whether I want to pay $100,000 to pay for my child's college education, and that my answer is positive if and only if the welfare gains I derive from the welfare of my child are greater than the welfare loss I incur by lowering my consumption. In that case, I am motivated by other-regarding self-interest. If my motivation is genuinely altruistic, I am willing to pay the tuition fees even when this inequality is reversed. In practice, this distinction is obviously going to be hard to draw. In many cases, we may not be able to tell whether we observe altruism or other-regarding self-interest. For practical purposes, therefore, we may define altruism by the willingness to incur a loss of *material* welfare to enhance the welfare (material or not) of others.

Altruism thus defined may, therefore, derive from reason, emotion, or even from (other-regarding) interest. Regardless of its proximate source, however, altruism may ultimately be due to the pressures created by the hierarchy of norms. In many important cases, we may think of human beings as motivated by two aims: their self-interest and their need to see themselves as motivated not only by their self-interest. Similar cases arise if we replace "self-interest" by "emotion" or "vanity" in the preceding sentence. Thus Seneca: "Reason wishes the decision that it gives to be just; anger wishes to have the decision which it has given seem the just decision" (On Anger I.xviii), and la Bruyère: "Men are very vain, and of all things hate to be thought so" (*Characters*

XI.65). The question whether, how and to what extent the first-order and the second-order motivations can be satisfied simultaneously is the topic of Section 5 below.

Altruistic motivations can differ in scope as well as in strength. If induced by reason, they have universal scope (within the relevant community); if induced by emotion or other-regarding self-interest, a more limited scope. The strength of the motivation is naturally measured by the size of the sacrifice one is willing to incur in order to produce a given increment in the welfare of others. It is often assumed that scope and strength are inversely related to each other, an assumption confirmed by the tendency for people to spend more on education for their children than on donations to charity. The fact that many people volunteer for dangerous war service or even for suicide missions suggests, however, a more complicated relationship. The claim that Palestinian volunteers for suicide missions are motivated by the benefits that will accrue to their families is ill-documented and intrinsically implausible [Elster (2005a)].

There is one further issue I want to introduce here, and then return to in the concluding section. Consider again a father who sacrifices net welfare for the sake of his child's education. He derives some welfare from the welfare of the child, but not enough to offset his loss of welfare from reduced consumption. He might, however, receive welfare from a third source, namely the satisfaction he takes from the act of giving. If this satisfaction, sometimes referred to as the "warm glow" effect, is added to the welfare he derives from other sources, he might end up being better off as the result of his material sacrifice. In that case, is his motivation still altruistic? Intuition suggests a positive answer if the warm glow is a mere side effect of the action, but not if it is the aim of the action in the sense that but for the warm glow he would not have undertaken the action. But how can we (or he) tell the difference?

3. Can interest mimic altruism?

Let us first note that if motivation A can mimic (i.e. produce the same behavior as) motivation B, then B can also mimic A. Taking A for prudence (long-term self-interest) and B for reason, some of the founders of modern philosophy offered both arguments. Montaigne (1991, pp. 709–710) wrote that "Even if I did not follow the right road for its rightness, I would still follow it because I have found from experience that, at the end of the day, it is usually the happiest one and the most useful". In other words, if we are moral we shall also end up promoting our self-interest. Montaigne does not suggest any mechanism, however, that might tend to bring about this happy coincidence.

The more common argument is that prudence can mimic morality. In two letters to Princess Elisabeth Descartes affirms more explicitly the extensional equivalence of these two motivations. In the first, he simply asserts it without argument

> [It] is difficult to determine exactly how far reason orders us to interest ourselves in the public; yet that is not something in which one must be very exact; it suffices to satisfy one's conscience, and in doing that, one can grant very much to one's

inclination. For God has so established the order of things, and has joined men together in so connected a society, that even if everyone related only to himself and had not charity for others, a man would nevertheless ordinarily not fail to employ himself on the behalf of others in everything that would be in his powers, provided he uses prudence [Descartes (1978, p. 164); translation slightly modified].

This is little more than a restatement of Montaigne's optimistic view, with the left-hand and right-hand sides of the equation reversed. In the second letter, he also offers a mechanism, the "Descartes effect" [Kolm (1984)], by which this coincidence would be brought about:

The reason that makes me believe that those who do nothing save for their own utility, ought also, if they wish to be prudent, work, as do others, for the good of others, and try to please everyone as much as they can, is that one ordinarily sees it occur that those who are deemed obliging and prompt to please also receive a quantify of good deeds from others, even from people who have never been obliged to them; and these things they would not receive did people believe them of another humor; and the pains they take to please other people are not so great as the conveniences that the friendship of those who know them provides. For others expect of us only the deeds we can render without inconvenience to ourselves, nor do we expect more of them; but it often happens that deeds that cost others little profit us very much, and can even save our life. It is true that occasionally one wastes his toil in doing good and that, on the other hand, occasionally one gains in doing evil; but that cannot change the rule of prudence that relates only to things that happen most often. As for me, the maxim I have followed in all the conduct of my life has been to follow only the grand path, and to believe that the greatest subtlety [*finesse*] is never to make use of subtlety (*ibid.*, pp. 176–177; translation modified).

If we help out a neighbor in a pinch we may benefit him much more, in absolute terms, than what it costs us to help him. If each of two parties to an interaction adopts the strategy of responding to demands for help when helping doesn't cost too much and asking for help when it doesn't cost the other party too much to provide it, both are likely to be better off than if each tried to be self-sufficient. Although the net effect for A in his interactions with B may turn out be negative, if B finds himself in a pinch more frequently than A, the net effect of adopting the strategy in all his interactions with B, C, D, etc. is likely to be positive. Assuming that agents have a reasonably long time-horizon, enlightened self-interest may thus mimic morality. Note that Descartes does not count merely on bilateral reciprocity, as in the iterated Prisoner's Dilemma (PD), since he says that if A helps B he is also likely to receive the help of C, even if the latter has "never been obliged" to him. The argument, obviously, does not satisfy modern demands for rigor, but, as we know from the theory of iterated games and reputation-building, it can be made rigorous.

A different mechanism operates when the presence of some genuine altruists induces other (selfish) persons to mimic them. The argument comes in several varieties. Consider first an argument proposed by Becker (1974), using the example of an altruistic husband and a selfish wife. He likes reading in bed, which disturbs her sleep. Becker claims [but see Bergstrom (1989)] that she nevertheless benefits from his reading because at the higher utility level it induces he will more than compensate her for her loss of sleep. She would, therefore, not take the opportunity to prevent him from reading if it were available to her at no cost. Her behavior is the same as that of a wife who genuinely cares for her husband, but the underlying motivation differs. In real families (but not in Becker's model) a husband would rather be loved than not, i.e. he would prefer that this wife let him read because it benefits him, not because it benefits her. If he takes her altruistic behavior as evidence of an altruistic motivation, he is living in a fool's paradise.

Another variety of the argument arises when selfish individuals behave altruistically because they are afraid of being punished by altruistic interaction partners if they don't, or hope to be rewarded by them if they do [Fehr and Fischbacher (2002)]. The argument relies on an idea of *conditional altruism*, in which the altruist is motivated to reward those who show a cooperative attitude and to punish those who don't. This *strong reciprocity* differs from the "weak reciprocity" of the iterated PD with self-interested actors in that it shows up even in one-shot interactions. At the same time, since strong reciprocity embodies a "normative standard" it also differs from spontaneous or pre-social emotions of gratitude or vindictiveness [Fehr and Fischbacher (2004, p. 65)]. It is thus reducible neither to interest nor to passion. [For further comments, see Section 3 below and Elster (2005b)].

The Ultimatum Game (UG) offers an example of altruistic behavior induced by fear of punishment [Camerer (2003, Chapter 2)]. By themselves, the generous offers made by the typical Proposer in the UG might seem to reflect altruistic motivations. When we compare them with the much less generous offers in the Dictator Game (DG), in which the Responder has no opportunity to punish a stingy Proposer, we can infer that a large part of the generosity is due to non-generous motivations. The logic of the argument is clearly brought out by an intervention by George Mason at the Federal Convention in 1787 in a debate over the terms of accession of future Western states. When Gouverneur Morris and others proposed that these should be admitted as second-rate states, so that they would never be able to outvote the original 13 states, Mason argued strongly for admission with the same rights as the original states. First, he argued from principle: By admitting the Western states on equal terms, the framers would do "what we know to be right in itself" [Farrand (1966, vol. I, p. 578)]. To those who might not accept that argument, he added that the new states would in any case be unlikely to accept a degrading proposal.

> If the Western States are to be admitted into the Union, as they arise, they must be treated as equals, and subjected to no degrading discriminations. They will have the same pride & other passions which we have, and will either not unite with or will speedily revolt from the Union, if they are not in all respects placed on an equal footing with their brethren (*ibid.*, p. 578–579).

Mason refers to the "pride and passions" of the new states, not to their self-interest. Even if it would in fact be in their interest to accede to the union on unequal terms rather than remain outside, they might still, out of resentment, prefer to stay outside. At the same time, he appeals to the self-interest of the old states, not to their sense of justice. He is telling them that because the new states might be motivated by passion rather than by interest, it would be in the interest of the old states to act as if they were motivated by reason rather than by interest.

At the Federal Convention we also find repeated claims that, in Feinberg's terminology, self-interested other-regarding motivations can mimic altruistic motivations. The best-known argument of this kind was made by George Mason when he warned against the danger of overreacting to the abuses and excesses of popular democracy:

> We ought to attend to the rights of every class of people. He [Mason] had often wondered at the indifference of the superior classes of society to this dictate of humanity & policy, considering that however affluent their circumstances, or elevated their situations, might be, the course of a few years, not only might but certainly would distribute their posteriority through the lowest classes of Society. Every selfish motive therefore, every family attachment, ought to recommend such as system of policy as would provide no less carefully for the rights and happiness of the lowest than of the highest orders of Citizens (*ibid.*, vol. I, p. 49).

A similar argument was offered by Gouverneur Morris in the debate over the representation of the states in the Senate:

> State attachments and State importance have been the bane of this Country. We cannot annihilate; but we may perhaps take out the teeth of the serpent. He wished our ideas to be enlarged to the true interest of man, instead of being circumscribed within the narrow compass of a particular Spot. And after all how little can be the motive yielded by selfishness for such a policy. Who can say whether he himself, much less whether his children, will the next year be an inhabitant of this or that State (*ibid.*, vol. I, p. 531).

On another occasion Gouverneur Morris was at the receiving end of the same argument. In response to Gerry's espousal of Gouverneur Morris's proposal to limit the representation of future Western states, Roger Sherman replied that "We are providing for our posterity, for our children & our grand Children, who would be as likely to be citizens of new Western States, as of the old States. On this consideration alone, we ought to make no such discrimination as was proposed by the motion" (*ibid.*, vol. II, p. 3).

Another episode from eighteenth-century politics may be cited to show how interest may be made to mimic a more impartial attitude. In the elections to the French Assemblée Constituante in 1789, the normal pattern was that members of one estate in a given electoral district chose a representative among themselves to represent them. The electoral rules allowed, however, delegates of all three estates to the electoral assemblies to vote jointly on who should represent a given estate. For instance, members of the clergy, the nobility and the third estate would all vote on who should represent the nobility in the National Assembly. A few districts, notably the Dauphiné, took advantage of this possibility. The idea seems first to have been formulated by the Comte de Virieu, who proposed in 1787 that

> in this new election *all* be elected by *all*, so that there is no deputy from one Order that does not also have the support (*voeu*) of the other two. Although each deputy is destined to communicate the interest of the body to which he belongs, he is nevertheless not its special mandatory, and thus is not obligated to embrace exclusively its particular passions and views, but becomes through this mode of election the representative of all [cited after Joubert (1990, p. 349)].

The system was adopted in the fall of 1788 by an assembly of the three estates convened by the King for the purpose of organizing the meeting of the provincial Estates. Mounier – the leading spirit in the reform movement in the Dauphiné – justified it as follows:

> This form offers a precious advantage: that of having all the Orders contribute to the choice of their respective deputies. They all become the mandatories of the people as a whole (*le peuple en corps*), and this union of the various classes of electors will be a new motive for representatives to consult only the interests they have in common [cited after Egret (1942, p. 76)].

Modifying the details of the arrangement in Dauphiné, I shall offer a numerical example to show how such *cross-voting* [Elster (2005c)] may temper the effect of interest. Assume that an electoral assembly of 30 clergy, 30 nobles and 60 commoners has to elect 15, 15 and 30 deputies from the three orders. Assume also, for specificity, that within each estate two thirds want only to promote the particular interests of that estate and one third want to promote the general interest. Suppose finally that the candidates elected are those who receive the largest number of votes. Within (say) the clergy, the 10 members who want to promote the general interest will receive 10 votes from the clergy, 30 votes from the nobility, and 60 votes from the third estate, 100 votes altogether. These 10 candidates between them will receive 1000 votes. The total number of votes to be cast is $15 \cdot (30 + 30 + 60) = 1800$. The remaining 800 votes could in theory be cast for 7 candidates who would each receive more than 100 votes. At worst, therefore, 8 of the 15 deputies from the clergy will represent the general interest. In practice, the votes for those who do not represent the general interest will be so diluted (perhaps for strategic reasons) that all will receive less than 100 votes. In that case, 10 out of 15 deputies from the clergy will represent the general interest. The same reasoning holds for the nobility.

Within the third estate, the 20 members who want to promote the general interest will receive 20 votes from their own estate and 30 votes from each of the other estates, 80 votes altogether. These 20 candidates between them will receive 1600 votes. The total number of votes to be cast is $30 \cdot (30 + 30 + 60) = 3600$. The remaining 2000 votes could in theory be cast for 24 candidates who would each receive more than 80 votes.

On that worst-case assumption, only 6 out of 30 deputies from the third estate would represent the general interest. On the best-case assumption, the 2000 remaining votes would be divided more or less equally among the forty remaining candidates. All would receive less than 80 votes, and ten would be elected. In that case, 20 out of 30 deputies from the third estate would represent the general interest. This outcome would in fact be realized as long as the candidate ranked eleven among the forty candidates received less than 80 votes. It would take considerable coordination to bring the vote of the eleventh-ranked above this threshold.

Needless to say, the numbers are arbitrary. What the exercise shows is that even when two thirds in each group are concerned only with the interests of that group, cross-voting can produce an assembly in which two thirds of the members care only about the general interest. As Tocqueville (2004, p. 531) wrote in his posthumously published notes to the *Ancien régime*, "If the practice of voting in common [rather than separately by orders] were to be adopted, it is to be regretted that one did not everywhere follow the practice of the Dauphiné, so that the deputies from each order would have been chosen by all orders; that would have favored agreement". For an exercise in the same spirit, yielding somewhat similar results, see White (1987, pp. 234–235).

These examples of interest-induced altruistic behavior fall in several categories. (i) Reputation-building. (ii) Investing in the welfare of altruists to induce even larger gifts in return. (iii) Hope of reward from strong reciprocators. (iv) Fear of punishment by strong reciprocators. (v) The fusion of interest and impartiality behind the veil of ignorance. (vi) The emergence of impartiality through mutual checking of interests. This is certainly not an exhaustive list. Yet however many further mechanisms we might want to include, they will not be able to account for all observable altruistic behavior. There is no reason to doubt the sincerity of those framers at the Federal Convention who thought the new states should be admitted on an equal footing because it was "right in itself". At the same time, they tried to persuade others that this policy would be in their interest, either because new states would reject unequal terms or because the descendants of the original framers might be citizens of one of them. Also, when altruistic behavior occurs in situations where people are shielded from the observation by others so that the latter are unable to punish or reward them, it is likely to spring from altruistic motivations (but see Section 6 for some complications). To elicit such motivations experimentally, therefore, it is important that subjects do not engage in face-to-face interaction.

4. Can passion mimic altruism?

Earlier, I noted that emotions (e.g. love or sympathy) can *produce* altruistic motivations. Here I shall discuss whether other emotions (e.g. pride and shame) can *mimic* altruistic motivations, that is, make a non-altruistic agent act as if he cared about the welfare of others.

As a point of departure, let us again consider the importance of anonymity in experimental design. This condition may be important even when others are not in a situation to offer rewards or punishments. Since even a selfish person might feel uncomfortable knowing that another person, who cannot punish him and whom he will not meet again, thinks badly about him, the presence of the other might induce him to act altruistically. Although he may not care about other people's welfare, their thoughts about him may matter to him. Immoral individuals need not be shameless. This is why experimenter anonymity is sometimes imposed (and made known to the subjects) in laboratory studies that try to elicit "pure" motivations, i.e. motivations that are untainted by ongoing social interactions [Fehr and Fischbacher (2002, p. 5; 2003, p. 785)]. Similarly, to provide reliable evidence of altruistic motivations, donations to charity must be unknown not only to the recipient and to outside observers, but to the staff of the charitable organization. However, if people shield their good deeds from the world by dropping money into collection boxes in empty churches, scholars are unlikely to learn about them. I return to this paradox in the concluding section.

The desire to be well thought of by others, independently of their capacity to confer material rewards or punishments, can be a powerful mechanism for mimicking motives that one does not really feel. Equally strong, perhaps stronger, is the desire not to be badly thought of. These desires are linked to the emotions of pride and shame that guide a large part of human behavior. Again I begin with Montaigne, who drew a distinction between true and false motivational "coins" – acting for the sake of what is right and acting for the sake of what other people think about you. As the former motivation is rare, policy makers may have to rely on the latter:

> If that false opinion [a concern for what other people think] serves the public good by keeping men to their duty [...], then let it boldly flourish and may it be fostered among us as much as it is in our power. [...] Since men are not intelligent enough to be adequately paid in good coin let counterfeit coin be used as well. That method has been employed by all the lawgivers. And there is no policy which has not brought in some vain ceremonial honours, or some untruths, to keep the people to their duties [Montaigne (1991, p. 715)].

Napoleon echoed the idea when, defending the creation of the Légion d'Honneur in 1802, he said that "men are led by such baubles". (His old soldiers from the republican army reacted strongly against this invention.) *Approbativeness* [Lovejoy (1961)] – the desire to be well thought of by others – is a false coin that may have to substitute for the true coin of morality. Alternatively, *shamefulness* – the desire not to be thought badly of by others – may serve as the false coin. Social norms may induce people to refrain from actions that they might have otherwise have carried out. Abiding by the norm is not enough to make others think well of them, however. Approbation is reserved for supererogatory acts that go beyond the norm. What is obligatory in one society may be supererogatory in another. In Norway, there is a (mild) social norm that a sibling should donate a kidney if one is needed for transplantation, whereas in France such behavior might be seen as supererogatory [Lorenzen and Paterson (1994, pp. 110–111, 113)]. In certain social circles, donations to charity are mandatory [Posner (2000, p. 61)].

Whether approbativeness or shamefulness can mimic altruism depends on the substantive criteria others apply in assessing behavior. In societies that value disinterestedness highly, the desire for praise might cause people to act as if they did not care for their personal welfare. Among the founding fathers in America, the desire to be *seen* as disinterested [Wood (1987); Adair (1998)] generated behavior that was indistinguishable from that which would have been produced by genuinely disinterested motivations. The self-denying ordinances of the French Assemblée Constituante on August 4 1789 [Elster (2004b)] and May 16 1791 [Shapiro (2002)] were at least in part motivated by the desire of the framers to outdo each other in disinterestedness. It has been said, in fact, that on the latter occasion, they were "drunk with disinterestedness" [Lebègue (1910, p. 261)]. In suicide missions, the desire for posthumous glory may reinforce and perhaps substitute for patriotic altruism [Elster (2005a)]. Contributions to good causes can also owe much to the desire for tangibly expressed praise. In the Art Institute of Chicago, for instance, the relative importance of donors is carefully indicated by the size of the plaques honoring them. In Great Britain, it is sometimes alleged that there are two ways of becoming a peer: by secretly giving a great deal of money to the governing party and by publicly donating large sums to charity.

Other societies may place greater value on – and thus stimulate the expression of – virtues that do not in any systematic way tend to mimic altruism. Napoleon's baubles were intended to encourage soldiers to risk their lives in battles that for the most part were intended to enhance the glory of France, not the welfare of the French. Some individuals may choose a life of self-abnegation because of the praise their society bestows on religious virtuosi, but hermits and monks are often more focused on the rituals of worship than on their fellow beings. As far as I know, there is no tendency for communities that place a high value on education and learning to generate more altruistic behavior than others. The cult of beauty in modern Western societies stimulates self-centered behaviors that would seem to be inimical to the concern for others. Overall therefore, it is hard to say whether the desire for praise by one's fellow beings tends to induce behaviors that also enhance their welfare.

Social norms – based on fear of blame rather than hope of praise – are also ambiguous in this respect. The behavior they dictate may or may not coincide with spontaneous altruistic acts. Consider first how the causal structure of the operation of social norms distinguish them from moral norms (Figure 1).

Although the *content* of social norms may be unconditional ("Don't litter in public parks"), their *efficacy* may be conditional on the presence of observers. (Later I consider the converse phenomenon – norms that are conditional in content but do not require observers for their efficacy.) The presence of others has, in fact, a very strong multiplier effect. There is a consensus among psychologist that the burning feeling of shame is more intensely painful than the pang of guilt [Lewis (1992, p. 77), Tangney (1990, p. 103)]. The contemptuous stare of others is more difficult to ignore or rationalize than the voice of conscience. A person who would feel few or no twinges of guilt by littering if unseen may abstain if observed by others.

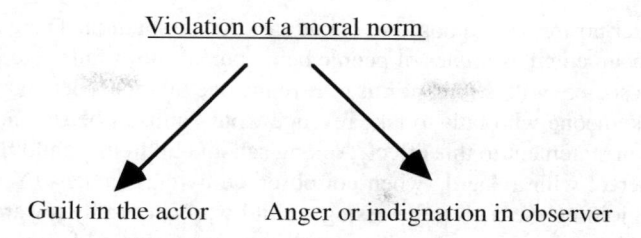

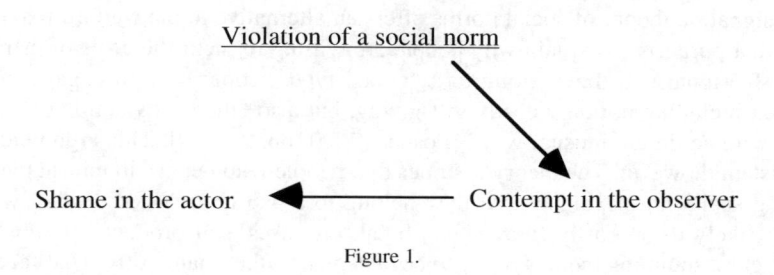

```
          Violation of a moral norm
              /            \
             ↙              ↘
    Guilt in the actor    Anger or indignation in observer



          Violation of a social norm
                           \
                            ↘
    Shame in the actor  ←——————  Contempt in the observer
```

Figure 1.

Many social norms mimic altruism by forbidding behavior with negative externalities, such as littering. The existence and efficacy of the norm enhances aggregate welfare. The most influential current theory of social norms asserts that they exist *because* they have this effect [Coleman (1990), Ellickson (1991)]. The theory also asserts that norms forbidding behavior generating negative externalities are enforced by complementary norms generating positive externalities, viz. second-order norms to punish those who violate first-order norms. When we observe someone littering in the park, we are obliged by the second-order norm to show our disapproval, thus creating an incentive for first-order actors to act to avoid it.

The theory has many problems [Elster (1989a)]. First, there is the unabashed functionalism: norms are explained by their consequences, not by their causes. I shall not dwell on this topic here [see Elster (1983a, Chapter 2)]. Second, there is the poorly supported claim that social norms tend to arise when and only when they enhance aggregate welfare. As I shall argue below, many norms are welfare-reducing rather than welfare-enhancing. Third, there is what is often referred to as the "second-order free rider problem". If people can be made to abstain from littering by sanctions imposed on them by others, the question arises why anyone would take the trouble of creating a positive externality by sanctioning. Since many sanctions involve costs or risk to the sanctioner, while the benefits *to him* of sanctioning are typically very small, it seems that he would be better off acting as a free rider. The problem arises with respect to all social norms, not merely norms to cooperate in PD-situations.

Second-order norms are supposed to counteract this temptation. There are not, however, many documented examples of people being punished for failing to punish norm-violators. In a society with strong norms of revenge one might expect that a person who fails to shun someone who fails to take revenge would himself be shunned, but I have seen no explicit statement to this effect. Among school children, a child might be more willing to interact with a "nerd" when not observed by class mates. (Yet a child who abstains from joining the mob in harassing a child who is friendly towards the nerd is unlikely to be harassed. Hence the third-party harassers are not likely to be motivated by the fear of punishment.) Experimentally, the question might be examined by seeing whether third-parties would punish Responders who, by accepting very low offers in the UG, fail to punish ungenerous Proposers. I would be surprised if they did, and even more surprised if fourth-party observers punished non-punishing third parties.

The signaling theory of social norms offers an alternative to the welfare-maximizing theory that purports to explain why people are willing to incur the costs of ostracizing others. To signal that they belong to a "good" type, people have to engage in costly behavior, including not only costly gift-giving, but also "the costly action of shunning people who act in an unusual way" [Posner (2000, pp. 25–26)]. This argument seems inconsistent, however. The theory assumes that people who behave in unusual ways, by violating social norms, signal that they belong to a bad type. Since dealing with bad types is likely to be costly (they cheat, break promises, sell products of substandard quality, etc.), shunning them is likely to be *beneficial* rather than costly. That fact might, of course, provide a direct reason for shunning them, but this is not what the theory claims.

I believe that these instrumental considerations are misguided. When people shun first-order violators, most of the time they act emotionally and spontaneously, not to avoid punishment or to signal their type. In fact, they may not even be motivated by a desire to *inflict* punishment. Observers may shun violators even when, as is often the case, the shunning is unobservable to the violator or to third parties. As shunning is a non-action, it is intrinsically difficult to observe unless accompanied by direct evidence of rejection. If hosts say about an uncouth guest, 'Let's not invite him again", he may not realize he is being shunned. In this case, the shunning may or may not be costly to the shunner. If the ill-mannered guest is someone who might be able to do one a favor, the decision not to invite him again could have real costs. There will not, however, be the risk of retaliation that can arise when someone understands that he is being deliberately shunned.

In many cases, to be sure, spontaneous avoidance is both observable and costly. School children may reject nerds even when the latter could help them with their homework. (As noted earlier, the rejection may be especially likely in the presence of others.) Novels often refer to "gentlemen" who lose out because they ostentatiously refuse to deal with "upstarts". In *Persuasion*, it is only with great reluctance that the impoverished Sir Walter Elliott – the ultimate snob – is willing to have his house let to a mere naval officer. In the *ancien régime*, many penniless aristocrats were averse to their children marrying rich commoners, although others justified the practice by the condescending phrase that they were "spreading manure on their land" [Droz (1860, vol. I, p. 81)]. Even after an edict of 1701 allowed the French nobility to engage in commerce (only wholesale, not retail), it took more than fifty years before they overcame the norms of their class [Mousnier (1974, vol. I, pp. 154–155)]. What Becker (1957) refers to as a costly "taste" for discrimination reflects the operation of social norms rather than of idiosyncratic individual preferences. Examples could be multiplied to show that because of powerful social norms people are willing to incur substantial losses in order to avoid interaction with those whom they hold to be inferior in one way or another. Such norms obviously do not maximize aggregate welfare.

Other norms, too, are recalcitrant to accounts in terms of welfare-enhancement. Norms against dealing with commoners or members of ethnic minority groups do not create an incentive for members of these categories to act differently, since behavior is strictly irrelevant. Norms against dealing with people who violate rules of etiquette create an incentive to master these rules, but nobody else benefits from the mastery just as nobody is hurt by lack of it. Egalitarian norms ("Nobody shall have what not everybody can have") or codes of honor are equally pointless. Although some have claimed that duels were collectively useful for keeping up the fighting spirit of the nobility [Kiernan (1986)], the proposition is an unverifiable piece of functionalism.

This is not to deny that some norms are capable of mimicking altruism. (i) As noted, donations of money or of an organ for transplantation, which are often seen as supererogatory, may come to be the object of social norms. In the case of organ donation, the norm may be sustained by fear of second-party sanctions (by the potential recipient) or of third-party sanctions (by the doctor). (ii) Norms against littering, spitting in the street and other actions with negative externalities can make non-altruists do what altruists do spontaneously. (iii) In warfare, peer pressure may substitute for patriotism to induce courageous behavior. As Aristotle noted (Nicomachean Ethics 1116), there are in fact three distinct emotions that can mimic altruistic courage: fear (of one's superiors), craving for glory, and avoidance of shame. (iv) Norms of tipping taxi drivers or restaurant waiters in one-shot interactions induce a redistribution of income caused by the desire not to be badly thought of by the other person. Such transfers are induced by fear of second-party reaction, since there are typically no third parties involved. These situations, incidentally, provide a further reason why the signaling theory of norms is inadequate.

I have emphasized that social norms are effective when and because others can observe what the agent is doing. What I shall call *quasi-moral norms* are effective when and because the agent can observe what others are doing. These norms do not enjoin behavior unconditionally, but only contingently on the behavior of others. They include the norm of *strong reciprocity* and the norm of *conditional cooperation* [Fehr and Fischbacher (2002, 2003, 2004)]. The first tells people to help those who have helped them (or others) in the past and hurt those who have hurt them (or others). The second, which has also been called a "norm of fairness" [Elster (1989b, pp. 187–192)] tells them to cooperate in a many-person PD if and only if most others have cooperated in a previous round of the game. These norms may, to be sure, take the form of social norms, that is, be effective only in the presence of second-party or third-party observers. In that case, they are doubly conditional on observing and on being observed. If all the other guests to a garden party are helping to clean up afterwards, I may feel pressured to join them both because it would be unfair for me to act as a free rider and because they would look askance at me if I did. Often, however, people are motivated by quasi-moral norms even when unobserved. Consider the following cases:

(i) The city authorities try to reduce water consumption by getting households to use less water. Since others cannot observe how much water I consume, I cannot be shamed into using less. Since I cannot observe how much others use, there is no scope for quasi-moral norms.

(ii) A person walking in the park may abstain from littering either because he sees that others don't litter or because he knows others could see him if he did. The first observation might trigger a quasi-moral norm, the second the operation of social norms.

(iii) Imagine case (i), with the difference that the authorities regularly announce aggregate water consumption on TV. (This has actually been done in Bogotá, under the imaginative mayorship of Antanas Mockus.) Although there is still no room for social norms, quasi-moral norms can ensure cooperation since each agent can observe whether most others are doing their share.

(iv) Imagine case (ii), with the difference that the person is too shortsighted to see whether others are littering although he can see well enough to notice their presence. He might be influenced by social norms, but not by conditional cooperation.

Quasi-moral norms can obviously be powerful in inducing altruistic behavior. Do they merely *mimic* altruism or *are* they altruistic motivations? The reason I refer to them as quasi-moral and not as moral is also why I lean to the first answer. The norm of reciprocity allows you not to help others in distress unless they have helped you previously. A typical moral norm is to help others in distress unconditionally, even if there is no prior history of assistance. The norm of conditional cooperation obliges you to donate to charity when it does little good (because others are already giving much), but allows you to abstain when it would do a great deal of good (because others are giving little). Morally, a utilitarian norm, creating a stronger obligation to give if others give little seems more appropriate. In both cases, social norms make my appropriate action depend on what others have done, whereas moral norms make it depend on what I can achieve by my action. I am not arguing that morality always is consequentialist, only that it must be capable of identifying a concept of right action that is independent of whether others are acting rightly.

A further reason why strong reciprocity is only a quasi-moral norm emerges when we compare behavior in UG and DG. There is a moral norm that resources should be shared equally unless one of the parties can claim a special entitlement. In both UG and DG, this norm implies that the Proposer should retain half of the amount to be divided and offer half to the Responder (for convenience I use the latter term also for recipients in the DG even though they have no opportunity to respond). While mean offers in the

UG are 30–40% of the total, they are only about 20% in the DG [Camerer (2003, pp. 49, 56)]. About half of the Responders in the UG reject offers of 20% and less (*ibid.*, p. 49). When they do so, it can hardly be because they subscribe to the moral norm of equal sharing. Since Proposers and Responders are chosen at random among the subjects, they will on average have the same motivations. If Responders subscribed to the norm of equal sharing, so would Proposers. If Proposers were so motivated, they would make more generous offers in the DG than they actually do. Instead, Responders subscribe to the quasi-moral norm of strong reciprocity and Proposers, knowing this, make more generous offers than they do when there is no opportunity to respond. Moral norms, one might say, are *proactive*; quasi-moral norms only *reactive*.

Case (iii) is similar to an experiment carried out by Fehr and Fischbacher (2003, p. 787), in which the members of a group decide whether to cooperate or defect in one round of an iterated game on the basis of average group behavior in the previous round. The finding is that cooperation tends to unravel over time, since any level of cooperation short of 100% induces some cooperators to defect, thus reducing the level even more and inducing even more defections until some stable, low but non-zero level is reached. One can also observe the opposite effect – *snowballing* rather than *unraveling* [Elster (1989b, p. 204)]. In a heterogeneous population, the norm of conditional cooperation may be triggered by different proportions of cooperation in the rest of the population. Assume a hard core of unconditional cooperators, making up (say) 10% of the population. In the first round, they are the only who cooperate. In the next round, they are joined by the (say) 5% of the population who need at least 10% of the population to cooperate before they are willing to join. In the third step, they are joined by those who are willing to cooperate at a threshold of 15%, and so on. Depending on the distribution of thresholds in the population, the process could move all the way to universal cooperation or stop short of it. A real-life example of snowballing was observed in the build-up of crowds on successive Sundays in Leipzig prior to the demolition of the Berlin Wall in 1989 [Petersen (2001, pp. 262–269)]. Whether any given case will lead to unraveling or snowballing depends on initial beliefs and on the distribution of thresholds.

By assumption, the motivation of those who assist others merely because of the desire for glory or avoidance of shame is not altruistic, but nor is it in any way malignant. There are, however, cases in which individuals engage in altruistic behavior towards others out a desire to hurt or humiliate them. The Greeks referred to the desire to humiliate as *hybris*, characterized by "the absence of any motive, good or bad, apart from the pleasure of insulting" [Fisher (1992, p. 11)], an example being to urinate on others in public. *Hybristic altruism* is found in gift-giving that is undertaken for the purpose of showing the donor's superiority and the inferiority of the recipient. A statement by La Rochefoucauld may be understood in this light: "A man's ingratitude may be less reprehensible than the motive of his benefactor" (Maxime 96). Why, indeed, show gratitude for an offer intended to humiliate? Why accept such an offer at all?

The last question is not merely rhetorical. In a summary of the cross-cultural studies of behavior in the Ultimatum Game carried out by Henrich et al. (2004), Colin Camerer (2003, pp. 71–72)] refers to two unusual cultures – the Ache headhunters of Paraguay and the Lamelera whalers of Indonesia – who offer more than half [of the total to be shared)] on average. The anthropologists think these hyperfair offers represent either a norm of oversharing because game caught in a hunt cannot be consumed privately or a potlatch or competitive gift-giving. Accepting an unusually generous gift (such as excess meat caught in a successful hunt) incurs an obligation to repay even more, and is *considered something of an insult* (since it implies that the giver is a better hunter than the receiver). Hyperfair offers are often rejected, consistent with the competitive gift-giving interpretation. (Italics added)

These statements are somewhat misleading. The two "unusual cultures" display some hyperfairness, but no rejection of hyperfair offers. A third culture [Henrich et al. (2004, Chapter 8)] showed high rates of rejection, even of hyperfair offers, but the numbers are small. The general idea of gift-giving as a form of deliberate insult is nevertheless a plausible one. In many cases, too, gifts motivated by genuinely altruistic concerns may be *perceived* as insulting by the recipient. Anticipating this reaction, some potential donors may abstain from giving or give less than they would otherwise have done. Whereas standard accounts of the Ultimatum Game emphasize that high offers are made in the anticipation that low offers would be turned down, the opposite pattern could also make sense.

5. Transmutation of motivations

In economic theory, motivations are usually taken for given. Attempts to endogenize preferences, whether by a purely causal mechanism [Von Weizsäcker (1971)] or by an optimizing one [Becker and Mulligan (1997)], do not seem to have entered the mainstream. The idea of a normative hierarchy of motivations suggests a perspective on endogenous preferences that is somewhat different from what these and other writers have offered. The argument, simply stated, is that people have preferences over options, that these preferences are determined by underlying motivations, and that these motivations in turn are influenced by underlying meta-motivations that reflect the normative hierarchy in the given society. Thus an individual might want to lose weight (a preference) out of vanity (a motivation), but represent the motivation to himself and others as a concern for health because of the low status of vanity in the hierarchy of motivations. The idea of meta-motivations is unrelated to the concept of meta-preferences introduced by Sen (1977). An example of Sen's approach would be a person with two *different* preference orderings, one for eating over dieting and one for dieting over eating, and a meta-preference favoring the latter. A meta-motivation, by contrast, amounts to a preference for preferring dieting over eating on grounds of health over having the same preference ordering on grounds of vanity.

Although in principle any motivation could be transmuted into any other [see Elster (1999, Chapter V) for examples], I shall focus here on the transmutation of interest and passion into altruism. For a simple hypothetical case of interest transmuted into reason, consider people's attitude towards charity. As noted earlier, individuals might experience a tension between their self-interest and their desire to see themselves as not motivated only by self-interest. In the case of donations to charity, the tension can be resolved by adopting the appropriate philosophy of philanthropy. If others make large donations, I can adopt a utilitarian philosophy [Margolis (1982)] according to which my obligation to give is lessened. If others give little, I can appeal to a principle of fairness [Sugden (1984)] to argue that I have an obligation to give if and only if others give too. In either case, I can appear as willing to donate my cake – and eat it too.

One might object that the meta-motivation does not do any causal work here, since the upshot is that I simply follow my self-interest. The philosophy of philanthropy is merely icing on the cake that helps me feel good about myself. A response might be that while the meta-motivation does not affect my behavior, it can lead to an increase in utility. It is more relevant, however, to note the existence of a mechanism by which meta-motivations can also affect behavior, viz. what Rabin (1995) calls *moral priming*. Once I have adopted a moral principle, perhaps on opportunistic grounds, I am stuck with it. Even if circumstances change so that another principle would serve my self-interest better, e.g. if other people begin donating less or more than they did previously, the very same need for a non-selfish self-image that dictated my adoption of the principle in the first place will prevent me from discarding it. The work by Linda Babcock and George Loewenstein (1997) on the role of fairness in litigation settlements confirms this idea.

Conceptions of impartiality are not entirely irreversible. They may change under the pressure of changing interest, but the impact is often lagged. In the 1930s, wages of Swedish metal workers lagged behind those of construction workers. The strong dissatisfaction of the metal workers with the existing wage differentials was a major cause of the move towards centralized bargaining with its greater emphasis on inter-industry wage equality [Swenson (1988, pp. 43–45)]. Later, when the metal workers became the high-wage outliers, they were bound by their past appeals to solidarity. As early as "at the beginning of the war, they were already some who thought that Metall had blundered by becoming the standard bearer for the idea of solidaristic wage policy in 1936. Certainly, it had been the underdog then, but now that they were better off, it gave them the moral obligation to show solidarity even when it was to their disadvantage" (Gösta Rehn, cited in *ibid.*, p. 60). It took fifty years for the norm of equality to lose its grip on the metal-workers' union [Elster (1989b, p. 241)].

As noted earlier, emotion-based altruism may induce the agent to attach greater weight to the welfare of some individuals than to others. Under the pressure of the normative hierarchy, this kind of limited altruism may then be presented under the guise of impartiality. The agent may persuade himself that the beneficiaries of his altruism are in fact the most deserving from an impartial standpoint. In a variation on Seneca's statement: love wishes to have the decision which it has given seem the just decision. Alternatively, the agent may recognize his partiality, but defend it as an unbiased response to the costs of gathering information about the relative worthiness of potential beneficiaries. More subtly, he may recognize that he is partial and biased towards those who are close to him, but allow others to be similarly partial towards individuals close to them [Nagel (1995)]. These responses are not necessarily disingenuous, but they can be. Overall, though, the normative pressure to present emotion-based altruism as impartial rather than partial is less strong than the pressure to present self-interest in a disinterested perspective.

6. Is altruism possible and knowable?

A common objection to the claim that people sometimes act to promote the welfare of others at expense of their own is that when they appear to do so they are in reality acting to produce the "warm glow" [Andreoni (1990)] they expect to derive from benefiting others. The idea is not merely that people feel a warm glow when they benefit others, which might arise even when they act from duty, but that production of the glow is the motivating aim of the action. To have any content, the objection would presuppose that one can (i) measure the warm glow and (ii) show that production of the glow is the aim and not merely a side effect of the action. Until recently, these presuppositions were so obviously unrealizable that the objection could hardly be seen as anything but a piece of dogmatic cynicism. With the advent of brain scans that allows one to measure the flux of psychic reward in real time, the situation has changed. I shall briefly describe and discuss an experiment by De Quervain et al. (2004) which uses brain scanning to argue for a distinction between biological and psychological altruism. Even when we observe altruistic behavior in a one-shot experiment with full anonymity, the underlying motivation can be the expectation of a measurable warm glow.

The experiment relies on the idea of "altruistic punishment" developed by Fehr and Fischbacher (2002). In my earlier discussion of the second-order free-rider problem I noted the difficulties associated with the idea that first-order actors respect social norms because they are afraid of being punished by second-order actors, whose incentive to punish stems from their fear of being punished by third-order actors, and so on. The infinite regress can be cut short if people have, as I suggested, a spontaneous tendency to punish free riders, independently of any benefits from doing so or costs of not doing so. Although the idea of altruistic punishment might seem counterintuitive, it makes sense in the context of these experiments. On the one hand, if A punishes B for non-cooperative behavior, B is more likely to cooperate with C in a subsequent game [Fehr and Fischbacher (2002, p. 138)]; hence A's punishment confers a benefit on C. On the other hand, the experiment is designed so that punishment has direct costs for the punisher; moreover, since A is never going to interact with B again he cannot expect any offsetting benefits. In other words, A is conferring a benefit to C at a net cost to himself, thus satisfying the definition of an altruistic act.

In the experiment by De Quervain et al. (2004), subjects who were treated ungenerously in a "trust game" (essentially a sequential PD with full information) had the option of imposing a punishment on their partner. In one condition, the punishment was costless for the punisher; in another, it was costly. In both conditions, subjects were asked to think intensely for one minute about the punishment (if any) to be imposed, during which period their brain was scanned to detect activation of brain circuits. In both conditions there was a correlation between activation of reward-related circuits and the actual monetary punishment. To distinguish between two interpretations of these findings, (i) that the decision to punish induces satisfaction and (ii) that the expected satisfaction from punishment induces the decision to punish, the authors considered 11 subjects who imposed the maximal feasible punishment in the "costless" condition. Among these subjects, those whose reward circuits were more highly activated also imposed more severe punishments in the "costly" condition. This finding, as well as other findings not mentioned here, support (ii). "Biological altruists" punish defectors because they expect it will make them feel good, not because they want to benefit others.

Future research will show whether this claim holds up. Assuming that it does, the implications might be less drastic than they appear to be. In other work, Fehr and Fischbacher (2004) introduce a distinction between second-party punishment in which the punisher has been harmed by the person that is punished, and third-party punishment in which he is not personally affected by the harmful behavior. Two findings stand out: people are willing to impose third-party punishments even when they have to spend resources on it, but they spend less than they do in second-party punishment. The motivation behind first-party punishment is closer to revenge, that behind third-party punishment closer to the desire for justice, corresponding to the emotions of anger and indignation respectively [Descartes (1985, Art. 195)]. While the idea that revenge can be deeply satisfactory – sweet as honey, said Homer, Plato and Aristotle – is not novel, the demonstration that the satisfaction may be the aim rather than a side effect is striking. I conjecture, however, that the pleasure motive may be less important in third-party punishment. In revenge, it is important that the person who has offended me suffer by my agency (and that he knows it). If someone else punishes him for what he did to me, it does not satisfy my craving for revenge. In third-party punishment, it does not matter how the offender's suffering is brought about. This might, for instance, be left to the courts. Thus third-party punishment might (or might not) involve genuine psychological altruism, not merely biological altruism.

Assuming that genuine altruism is possible, can I ever *know* that on a given occasion I acted from genuinely altruistic motives? According to Kant (1996, pp. 61–62)

> it is absolutely impossible by means of experience to make out with complete certainty a single case in which the maxim of an action otherwise in conformity with duty rested simply on moral grounds and on the representation of one's duty. It is indeed sometimes the case that with the keenest self-examination we find nothing besides the moral ground of duty that could have been powerful enough to move us to this or that good action and to so great a sacrifice; but from this it cannot be inferred with certainty that no covert impulse of self-love, under the mere pretense of that idea, was not actually the real determining cause of the will; for we like to flatter ourselves by falsely attributing to ourselves a nobler motive, whereas in fact we can never, even by the most strenuous self-examination, get entirely behind our covert incentives, since, when moral worth is at issue, what

counts is not actions, which one sees, but those inner principles of actions that one does not see.

The origin of this line of thought is probably to be found in Augustine. In more recent times, its most consistent exponent was La Rochefoucauld. Their skepticism went deeper than Kant's, however. Whereas he merely stipulated that we can never know whether moral behavior springs from a moral motivation or from self-love (amour-propre) Augustine and La Rochefoucauld took it for granted that the latter motivation was always at work.

The most obvious but also the most superficial form of amour-propre is the desire to be esteemed by others. As noted above, even when the object of this desire is to be esteemed for one's disinterested behavior, we cannot infer the presence of a disinterested motivation. Thus Hume (1985, p. 86) was surely wrong when he claimed that "To love the glory of virtuous deeds is a sure proof of the love of virtue". Montaigne (1991, pp. 1157–1158) by contrast, asserted "The more glittering the deed the more I subtract from its moral worth, because of the suspicion aroused in me that it was exposed more for glitter than for goodness: goods displayed are already halfway to being sold". At the limit, the only virtuous acts are those that never come to light.

The more profound expression of amour-propre is the desire for self-esteem. People may even be willing to trade esteem by others off against self-esteem. De Montaigne (1991, p. 259) says that "Cato would rather have done a fair and noble deed which brought him shame than to do it for glory". La Rochefoucauld observed that "Pridefulness always finds compensations, and even when it gives up vanity is loses nothing" (Maxime 33). "Hence there is nothing to be surprised at if it [amour-propre] sometimes throws in its lot with the most rigorous austerity and brazenly joins in its own destruction, for the moment of its defeat on one side is that of its recovery on another" (Maxime Supprimée 1). As Lovejoy (1961, p. 101) notes, "those who give alms in secret perhaps gain more in enhanced self-approval than they lose through the repression of their approbativeness". Many charitable and altruistic acts are performed for the sake of the *inner audience*.

The approval of the inner audience does not by itself disprove that the behavior was altruistic. To refute altruism, one would have to show that the behavior was undertaken for the sake of that approval. (These remarks also apply to approval by an external audience.) In trying to determine whether the approval was the aim or the side effect of the action, introspection is not likely to take us very far. We might believe it is the former when it is actually the latter, and vice versa. As Nicole observed, we always risk "mistaking charity for amour-propre and amour-propre for charity" [cited after Lafond (1986, p. 191)]. The striking achievement of De Quervain et al. (2004) is that they enable us to tell the difference, at least in the case they study.

Let me conclude by reconsidering the person who drops money into the collection box of an empty church. What might his motivation be? One possibility is that he is trying to buy salvation. Various theologians tell us that this aim is unattainable, since salvation is essentially a byproduct of actions undertaken for other reasons [Elster (1983b,

Chapter II)]. Yet many believers have tried to attain it, some by donating money and others by choosing martyrdom. Another possibility is that he is trying to gratify the inner audience, not only by his donation but by the apparently virtuous choice of a place for giving where he cannot be observed. A third possibility is that he wants to help others in need, that the collection box was simply a convenient vehicle for the donation, and that he would have chosen it even had others been present to observe him. Until the day scientists can conduct brain scans at a distance, we shall not know.

References

Adair, D. (1998). Fame and the Founding Fathers. Liberty Press, Indianapolis.
Andreoni, J. (1990). "Impure altruism and donations to public goods: a theory of warm-glow giving". Economic Journal 100, 464–477.
Babcock, L., Loewenstein, G. (1997). "Explaining bargaining impasse: the role of self-serving biases". Journal of Economic Perspectives 11, 109–126.
Becker, G. (1957). The Economics of Discrimination. University of Chicago Press, Chicago.
Becker, G. (1974). "A theory of social interaction". Journal of Political Economy 82, 1063–1094.
Becker, G., Mulligan, C. (1997). "The endogenous determination of time preferences". Quarterly Journal of Economics 112, 729–758.
Bergstrom, T. (1989). "A fresh look at the rotten kid theorem". Journal of Political Economy 97, 1138–1159.
Camerer, C. (2003). Behavioral Game Theory. Princeton University Press, Princeton.
Coleman, J. (1990). Foundations of Social Theory. Harvard University Press, Cambridge, MA.
De Montaigne, M. (1991). Essays, tr. Screech, M.A. Allen Lane, The Penguin Press, Harmondsworth.
De Quervain, J.F., et al. (2004). "The neural basis of altruistic punishment". Science 305, 1254–1258.
Descartes, R. (1978). Descartes: His Moral Philosophy and Psychology, tr. Blom, J. Harvester Press, Hassocks, Sussex.
Descartes, R. (1985). "Passions of the soul". In: The Philosophical Writings of Descartes, vol. I. Cambridge University Press, Cambridge.
De Tocqueville, A. (1969). Democracy in America. Anchor Books, New York.
De Tocqueville, A. (2004). Oeuvres, vol. III. Gallimard, Editions de la Pléiade, Paris.
Droz, J. (1860). Histoire du règne de Louis XIV pendant les années où l'on pouvait prévenir og diriger la Révolution française, vols. I–III. Renouard, Paris.
Egret, J. (1942). Les derniers Etats de Dauphiné. B. Arthaud, Grenoble.
Ellickson, R.C. (1991). Order without Law. Harvard University Press, Cambridge, MA.
Elster, J. (1983a). Explaining Technical Change. Cambridge University Press, Cambridge.
Elster, J. (1983b). Sour Grapes. Cambridge University Press, Cambridge.
Elster, J. (1989a). "Social norms and economic theory". Journal of Economic Perspectives 3, 99–118.
Elster, J. (1989b). The Cement of Society. Cambridge University Press, Cambridge.
Elster, J. (1998). "Emotions and economic theory". Journal of Economic Literature 36, 47–74.
Elster, J. (1999). Alchemies of the Mind. Cambridge University Press, Cambridge.
Elster, J. (2004a). "Emotions and rationality". In: Manstead, A.S.R., Frijda, N.H., Fischer, A.H. (Eds.), Feelings and Emotions: The Amsterdam Symposium. Cambridge University Press, Cambridge, pp. 30–48.
Elster J. (2004b). "The night of August 4 1789". Manuscript. Department of Political Science, Columbia University.
Elster, J. (2005a). "Motivations and beliefs in suicide missions". In: Gambetta, D. (Ed.), Making Sense of Suicide Missions. Oxford University Press, Oxford, pp. 233–258.
Elster J. (2005b). "Fehr on altruism, emotions and norms". Forthcoming in Analyse und Kritik.
Elster J. (2005c). "Cross-voting". Forthcoming in Journal of Political Philosophy.

Farrand, M. (Ed.) (1966). Records of the Federal Convention. Yale University Press, New Haven.
Fehr, E., Fischbacher, U. (2002). "Why social preferences matter – the impact of non-selfish motives on competition, cooperation and incentives". Economic Journal 112, C1–C33.
Fehr, E., Fischbacher, U. (2003). "The nature of human altruism". Nature 425, 785–791.
Fehr, E., Fischbacher, U. (2004). "Third-party punishment and social norms". Evolution and Human Behavior 25, 63–87.
Feinberg, J. (1984). Harm to Others. Oxford University Press, Oxford.
Fisher, N.R.E. (1992). Hybris. Aris and Phillips, Warminster.
Henrich, R., et al. (2004). Foundations of Human Sociality. Oxford University Press, Oxford.
Hume, D. (1985). "Of the dignity or meanness of human nature". In: Essays: Moral, Political and Literary. Liberty Fund, Indianapolis, pp. 80–86.
Joubert, J.-P. (1990). "1788 en Dauphiné". In: Chagny, R. (Ed.), Aux origines provinciales de la Révolution. Presses Universitaires de Grenoble, Grenoble, pp. 344–359.
Kant, I. (1996). "Groundwork of the Metaphysics of Morals". In: Immanuel Kant, Practical Philosophy. Cambridge University Press, Cambridge, pp. 37–108.
Kiernan, V. (1986). The Duel in European History. Oxford University Press, Oxford.
Kolm, S.-C. (1984). La bonne économie. Presses Universitaires de France, Paris.
Lafond, J. (1986). La Rochefoucauld: Moralisme et litérature. Klincksieck, Paris.
Lebègue, E. (1910). Thouret. Felix Alcan, Paris.
Lewis, M. (1992). Shame. The Free Press, New York.
Lorenzen, H., Paterson, F. (1994). "Donations from the living: are the French and Norwegians altruistic?". In: Elster, J., Herpin, N. (Eds.), The Ethics of Medical Choice. Pinter Publishers, London, pp. 100–115.
Lovejoy, A.O. (1961). Reflections on Human Nature. Johns Hopkins Press, Baltimore.
Margolis, H. (1982). Selfishness, Altruism and Rationality. Cambridge University Press, Cambridge.
Miller, D.W. (1999). "The norm of self-interest". American Psychologist 54, 1053–1060.
Mousnier, R. (1974). Les institutions de la France sous la monarchie absolue. Presses Universitaires de France, Paris.
Nagel, T. (1995). Equality and Partiality. Oxford University Press, Oxford.
Petersen, R. (2001). Resistance and Rebellion: Lessons from Eastern Europe. Cambridge University Press, Cambridge.
Posner, E. (2000). Law and Social Norms. Harvard University Press, Cambridge, MA.
Rabin M. (1995). "Moral preferences, moral constraints, and self-serving biases". Manuscript. Department of Economics, University of California at Berkeley.
Sen, A. (1977). "Rational fools". Philosophy and Public Affairs 6, 317–344.
Shapiro, B. (2002). "Self-sacrifice, self-interest, or self-defense? The constituent assembly and the 'self-denying ordinance' of May 1791". French Historical Studies 25, 625–656.
Sugden, R. (1984). "Reciprocity: the supply of public goods through voluntary contributions". Economic Journal 94, 772–787.
Swenson, P. (1988). Fair Shares. Cornell University Press, Ithaca, NY.
Tangney, J.P. (1990). "Assessing individual differences in proneness to shame and guilt: development of the self-conscious affect and attribution inventory". Journal of Personality and Social Psychology 59, 102–111.
Von Weizsäcker, C.C. (1971). "Notes on endogenous change of tastes". Journal of Economic Theory 3, 345–372.
White, M. (1987). Philosophy, the Federalist, and the Constitution. Oxford University Press, Oxford.
Wood, G. (1987). "Interest and disinterestedness in the making of the constitution". In: Beeman, R., Botein, S., Carter II, E. (Eds.), Beyond Confederation: Origins of the Constitution and American National Identity. University of North Carolina Press, Chapel Hill, pp. 69–109.

Chapter 4

THE GIFT AND RECIPROCITY: PERSPECTIVES FROM ECONOMIC ANTHROPOLOGY

CHRIS HANN

Max Planck Institute for Social Anthropology, Germany

Contents

Abstract	208
Keywords	208
1. Introduction	209
2. History and theory	210
2.1. Malinowski and Mauss	210
2.2. Polanyi and Sahlins	213
2.3. Recent contributions	214
3. Ethnographic examples	216
3.1. Food sharing	216
3.2. Socialist and postsocialist networking	218
4. Cross-cultural experiments	220
5. Conclusions	221
References	221

Handbook of the Economics of Giving, Altruism and Reciprocity, Volume 1
Edited by Serge-Christophe Kolm and Jean Mercier Ythier
Copyright © 2006 Elsevier B.V. All rights reserved
DOI: 10.1016/S1574-0714(06)01004-9

Abstract

Economic anthropology is a contested area of interdisciplinary research. Although some practitioners define the task as the application of mainstream economic theorizing to the full range of human groups in time and space, many others argue in the light of the ethnographic evidence that it is impossible to generalize Western models, such as those which base themselves on concepts of utility maximization by individual agents. These objections have nowhere been more vociferous than in the domain of exchange. Bronislaw Malinowski identified many kinds of transaction among the Trobriand Islanders; after initially sketching a notion of the 'pure gift', he later modified this and argued instead that reciprocity, in the sense of calculated 'give and take', was the central principle underpinning all social life. A more significant theoretical challenge to the presuppositions of modern economics came in same period from Marcel Mauss, who outlined in his essay *The Gift* an evolutionary process that began with the 'total prestation' and ends in the modern world, dominated by contracts and markets. Only in this modern world do we – arguably – have the possibility of altruism, understood as 'disinterested giving'.

After reviewing some of the more influential later contributions to the anthropological literature on these topics, notably those of Karl Polanyi, Marshall Sahlins and Stephen Gudeman, this paper goes on to present brief ethnographic illustrations. These include examples of food sharing among hunter–gatherers and cultivators, and the hospitality rituals of the contemporary western bourgeois classes. Illustrations from postsocialist societies show the difficulties of predicting economic behavior in this field: some people seem to respond to dislocation by using objects to strengthen their interpersonal networks, while others facing apparently similar conditions prefer to contract their giftgiving. Finally, brief critical note is taken of recent 'ethnographic experiments' in this field.

Keywords

anthropology, experiments, gift, reciprocity, sharing

JEL classification: Z000, Z130

In Cristian, an originally German but now multi-ethnic village in Transylvania, a Romanian peasant gifts her Saxon neighbor few new-born ducklings. *I brought you some ducklings, I have way too many* – the Romanian explains. The Saxon politely refuses. The Romanian insists, and, after a long 'negotiation' the two women agree that the Saxon will pay the countervalue of the ducklings. The Romanian leaves, slightly in doubt, and the Saxon explains to me: *Imagine if I would have accepted! Who knows what she would ask me later on, and we'd keep endlessly going in this manner. But now, in this way we are even!* [Mihailescu (2002, p. 1)]

1. Introduction

Economic anthropology is understood differently by different practitioners [for recent overviews of the field see Wilk (1996), Narotzky (1997), Ensminger (2002a)]. There are 'paradigmatic' differences which have a close bearing on what scholars in this field can contribute to the economic analysis of giving and reciprocity. For some, economic anthropology means the application of mainstream ('neoclassical', rational choice models based on *homo oeconomicus*) economics to anthropological materials, most often – but not necessarily – ethnographic data from 'exotic', non-Western societies. These scholars have been variously labeled 'formalists', 'transactionalists', 'decision theorists', etc. Others in this subdiscipline, including myself, have reservations about the extent to which these mainstream models can be generalized, both outside and inside the West. We question the value of assumptions such as that of stable preferences and rather than stress individual agency we prefer to draw attention to the fundamental *sociality* of human beings. An emphasis on the social and cultural diversity of human economic practices in time and space does not necessarily force us to abandon the search for general patterns and even universals, though many scholars in this camp have a strong tendency to cultural relativism. These scholars, formerly known as 'substantivists', more recently sometimes 'culturalists', are prone to disagree with the majority of economists concerning what is really going on when human beings engage in exchanges, particularly those that do not fit familiar market models.

Stephen Gudeman (2001, p. 81) suggests that economics and anthropology are 'caught in a dialectic' with each other. Gudeman's own effort to transcend this dialectic is an argument that limits economists to neoclassical models of the market and utility maximization. For him, economists cannot contribute to understanding the opposed sphere of community, which is culturally distinctive, morally cohesive, and ultimately sacred. Suspicious of attempts by a school of economists to colonize the 'commons' of a community, e.g. when recommending the privatization of public goods, Gudeman (2001, p. 163) asserts that 'the market can be allowed to exchange (only) what a community does not need'. Similarly, Maurice Godelier (1999) insists on the need to distinguish inalienable objects which must be retained for the (re)production of society both from market commodities and from gift objects. It follows for Gudeman that 'the conversation concerning how to divide our economic life between community and market must take place outside the market discourse' (*idem*).

I shall come back to these arguments at the end. Other influential anthropologists have been similarly critical of attempts to extend 'exchange theory' throughout the social sciences, to indulge in what they see as a 'market-metaphorising' of motives, which is inconsistent with the complexity of the ethnographic evidence [Davis (1992)]. On the other hand, rational choice approaches have recently been taken up again by some anthropologists; there are many strands in our subdiscipline, just as there are in economics. The first part of this chapter will review key developments in the history and theory of economic anthropology over the last century or so, with reference to the central concepts of gift and reciprocity. I shall then turn to some detailed examples and take brief note of a recent interest in the conduct of economic experiments in small-scale societies. Most anthropologists are skeptical of the utility of such games, for reasons which exemplify their dissatisfaction with economics-based approaches in general.

2. History and theory

2.1. Malinowski and Mauss

The topic of exchange was prominent in anthropological theory and field descriptions long before economic anthropology emerged as a more or less coherent subdiscipline in the 1950s. In the nineteenth and early twentieth centuries, ethnographers began to provide useful descriptive accounts of non-European systems of production and trade. The case of 'silent trade', the mythology of which dates back at least to Herodotus, attracted particular fascination [Hamilton Grierson (1903)]. A breakthrough came in the early 1920s, following the 'fieldwork revolution' that was promoted above all by Bronislaw Malinowski in the course of his Trobriand studies. Malinowski's first Trobriand monograph, *Argonauts of the Western Pacific* (1922), paid close attention to the exchange system known as *kula*, through which items circulated in varying directions across a wide region of Melanesia. These armbands and bracelets were the objects of intense individual strategizing, since they brought high status to those who held them (albeit temporarily). Malinowski also showed how, alongside the ceremonial inter-group exchanges associated with *kula*, a separate sphere of barter exchange existed, known locally as *gimwali*. Despite the absence of money, the basic rules in this sphere seemed to resemble the rules of a market, at any rate the sort of market where it is possible to haggle to get the best deal one can. This was quite unlike the formal style of *kula* exchange, though here too individual maximizing behavior dominated 'off-stage'. According to one plausible interpretation, the ultimate rationale of *kula* was to provide an 'umbrella' of security among these stateless peoples, thereby enabling peaceful *gimwali*, which was in turn warranted by the objective desirability of promoting the circulation of goods, some of which were found or produced only in particular communities in this regional system.

Malinowski identified many other types of exchange among the Trobrianders – 80 in all – and his ethnographic accounts have been plundered by many later analysts. His theoretical work has been much criticized, starting with his 1921 contribution to the *Economic Journal* in which he contrasted Trobriand behavior with that of modern entrepreneurs. The Trobriand chief spent much time and energy giving things away, whereas a modern businessman sought, on the contrary, to accumulate. Yet it is easy to gloss this account and conclude that both were in effect maximizing utilities (of course under very different institutional constraints) and that therefore the basic assumptions of modern economics were not challenged. It is interesting to note that Malinowski developed, in *Argonauts*, a category of the 'pure gift' which he retracted in subsequent publications. He eventually settled for a notion of reciprocity, in the sense of 'give and take', which he believed to underlie all human social life. This perspective was carried forward by his distinguished student Raymond Firth, who unlike Malinowski had some training in economics [see in particular Firth (1939, 1966)]. Many later fieldworkers, above all in the non-centralized societies of Melanesia, have confirmed the significance of agonistic 'give and take' in detailed ethnographic studies [Strathern (1971), Young (1971), Sillitoe (1979)].

It is not the detailed fieldwork of Bronislaw Malinowski but a short essay by a French scholar who never himself did any anthropological fieldwork that has dominated the anthropological discussion of this subject ever since its publication in 1924. Marcel Mauss's *The Gift* (*Essai sur le Don*) has been an inspiration to many, including Claude Lévi-Strauss.[1] It has been the subject of many readings and commentaries and two English translations. Even the superior version of W.D. Halls [Mauss (1990)] does not manage to resolve all the ambiguities, mysteries even, of Mauss's text; these are no doubt an element in the enduring fascination of the work.

Drawing on the work of Malinowski and other recent ethnography, including numerous references to the *potlatch*, where subjects channeled resources towards their chiefs, who famously destroyed much of this wealth in orgies of conspicuous consumption, Mauss hypothesized an evolutionary descent from gifts in the form of inter-group 'total services' (*prestations*) to the impersonal, contract-dominated world of modern market economy. Humans in 'archaic' societies were under an obligation to give, to receive gifts, and then to repay them. More adventurously, picking up some local ideas from the Pacific, Mauss suggested that some essence of the donor was transferred with the object, 'the spirit of the gift', which impelled it ultimately back to the original owner. This argument was criticized as dubious metaphysics by Raymond Firth and other Anglophone scholars. Lévi-Strauss was also critical, alleging that Mauss was guilty of confusing *hau*, a specific Maori representation of giving and reciprocity, with the analytic level of universal exchange principles. Nonetheless these postulates have proved endlessly fertile within anthropology – Mauss's own gift to his successors.

---

[1] In the structuralism of Claude Lévi-Strauss (1969), principles of exchange, notably the exchange of women, are crucial in explaining the emergence and evolution of human societies. However stimulating philosophically, these ideas are not always empirically testable and of marginal relevance to the present Handbook.

It is clear that when Mauss turned to ethnographic reports of 'primitive' or 'archaic' societies, he was at least in part concerned to develop a critique of the capitalist society of his time. As a cooperative socialist, he held the perhaps utopian conviction that humanity needed urgently to reaffirm norms of social solidarity. Now, for the first time in history, it could do so with a self-conscious awareness of the importance of giving and reciprocity as the basis of human social life. Mauss was unsympathetic to socialist solutions of the Bolshevik type, and hardly an early advocate of the welfare state. Rather, upholding the principle that 'charity wounds', he had a more subtle understanding of how reciprocity maintains a balance between obligation and freedom in all forms of society. He was arguing for new ways of integrating the individual into society, of reconciling the 'spirit of the gift' with market economy [Hart (2000, pp. 191–196)].

Mauss also offers an evolutionary argument, but this is far from clear. Sometimes he suggests that the key departure from earlier norms of the total prestation was initiated only in post-medieval Europe. At other places, he shows that India and ancient Rome made similar dangerous distinctions between persons and things, as the basis for developing a notion of the autonomous individual agent akin to that of modern capitalist society and modern economic theory. In the persuasive reading of Parry (1986), who pays particular attention to the Indian case, Mauss is concerned to show that only in particular historical conditions, and perhaps only in the context of particular religious doctrines, do we find the emergence of the *concept* of 'disinterested giving'. The problem of altruism simply cannot be posed in the primitive societies. In her *Preface* to the 1990 English translation, Mary Douglas insists that, in terms of social realities, it cannot apply to modern societies either. For her, Mauss offers a simple universal message: 'no free gifts!'

This interpretation has not gone unchallenged. John Davis (1992) shares Douglas's view that the cultural worlds of exchange in modern societies may be every bit as complex or 'thick' as those of the 'archaic' societies. He attaches priority to the way humans create mental order through the use of categories, in economic life as in everything else (1992). For him, this means that 'native' views must be taken seriously. If the natives have a category 'altruism', it behooves us to take that seriously and not assume either an ulterior selfish motivation (as many economists do) or the dictate of a collectivity (as many sociologists do). We may comment that, in a particular case, someone's behavior is not appropriately placed in the category 'altruism', but the term must figure in our general 'repertoire' of exchange acts because we (unlike the archaic peoples) do have this notion of 'disinterested giving'. Like Mauss, Davis pays close attention both to the symbolism of giving and to the material consequences of how exchanges are manipulated and controlled in the world.

Mauss implied that, in some original phase, *all* human societies engaged in total *prestations*, thereby visibly demonstrating the importance of exchange and reciprocity as *essential* features of human sociality. But this too can be challenged. If such patterns of giving are indeed of universal significance, why is their geographical distribution in the ethnographic record largely restricted to societies around the Pacific? Meeker, Barlow and Lipset (1986) posit an underlying materialist logic, given by the distinctive ecological conditions and horticultural techniques of this region. They then develop a culturalist argument to explain the prominence of giving and receiving, both at the level of representations and in the practical organization of social life. This argument views the salience of food exchanges as an outcome of male strategies to maintain their domination. There is no space to pursue details here. The important point to note is that these anthropologists challenge the implicit claim of Malinowski and Mauss (and, following them, of Lévi-Strauss) that giving and reciprocity are everywhere essential features of humanity. In other preindustrial societies (the example explored by Meeker, Barlow and Lipset is that of east African pastoralists) one finds the construction of autonomous individuals along lines more readily familiar to modern Euro-Americans, with little emphasis on giving and receiving as the basic principles of social organization. It follows from this diversity that the investigation of regionally specific cultural histories is a more credible scholarly ambition than attempting to reconstruct a unilineal evolution of exchange practices on a global scale; economists and psychologists should therefore resist the temptation to scour the ethnographic record to identify an original 'essence' of human gift giving.

2.2. Polanyi and Sahlins

In the Anglophone tradition the origins of the subdiscipline of economic anthropology are conventionally traced to Herskovits (1940) and to polemics generated by a research group led by Karl Polanyi at Columbia University in the 1950s. Polanyi was primarily an historian, born and raised in central Europe, and deeply unsympathetic to the unbridled forms of capitalism that he saw there and in Britain, where he lived in the 1930s. His major work was *The Great Transformation* [Polanyi (1944)], a book which has continued to influence scholars in various disciplines in many parts of the world. Polanyi indicted the world's first industrial nation for, in effect, removing the sphere of economy from the social and political controls in which, before the onset of Victorian capitalism, it had always previously been *embedded*. In his later theoretical work he developed a critique of modern economics, which in his view was appropriate for the study of market-dominated societies, but no use for all the others [Polanyi, Arensberg and Pearson (1957), Polanyi (1968)]. His alternative 'substantive' definition of economy emphasized not choice, scarcity and means-ends utility maximization, but obtaining a living in the environment. As methodological tools, Polanyi suggested drawing a distinction between two preindustrial 'modes of integration'. *Reciprocity* was the prime mode in situations such as that of the Trobriands, where there was no dominant central political force. *Redistribution* was the appropriate term for cases such as that of the *potlatch* of the North West Coast, with their much stronger chiefs. Polanyi's third type was market exchange, dominant in modern industrial societies. Here, the substantivists implied, the toolkit of the market economist was fully appropriate, even though both reciprocity and redistribution could continue as subordinate modes of exchange. Many contemporary anthropologists are critical of Polanyi for his apparent willingness to leave the modern economies to the economists; they insist that cultural and social embeddedness is integral to *all* human economies.

Polanyi's substantivist manifesto, published in 1957, soon provoked a vigorous counterattack from those economic anthropologists who basically took the view that the fundamental assumptions of modern economics could, with appropriate modifications according to context, be adapted to any economy in time or space. They alleged that Polanyi and his followers were motivated primarily by an 'obsolete anti-market mentality' [Cook (1966), mimicking a phrase of Polanyi]. More constructively, the 'formalists' tried to show in empirical work how economic models could shed light on, for example, the decision taking of a peasant farmer. Fredrik Barth (e.g. 1966) developed an influential theory of 'transactionalism' to elucidate the behavior of political leaders and economic entrepreneurs. Others extended 'exchange theory' into still broader areas of social life.

Polemics between formalists and substantivists continued vigorously for about a decade. The best known attempt to formulate a more rigorous theory in the substantivist tradition is Marshall Sahlins' essay from the mid-1960s '*On the Sociology of Primitive Exchange*' [see Sahlins (1974)]. Sahlins questioned Polanyi's use of reciprocity as an ideal-type characterizing all societies lacking a political center. He offered a spectrum of forms of reciprocity, ranging from 'negative' (e.g. barter, theft), through 'balanced' (including many forms of gift exchange) to 'generalized' (without calculation of returns – here Sahlins explicitly introduces the term altruism, linking it to the core of the kin group).

Many later commentators have criticized this typology. Does it make sense to classify standard market exchange in the same category as theft, simply because the agent in both cases is trying to get the best deal he can for himself? Countless societies exhibit examples of 'positive reciprocity' in the context of markets and long-term trading relationships, where close personal ties are essential for the generation of trust. On the other hand, use of the term 'generalized reciprocity' to describe resource allocation among egalitarian hunter–gatherer bands has been rejected by James Woodburn (1998), who prefers to speak simply of sharing. Ingold (1986) has pointed out that the negative variant, in the sense of individual utility maximization, can certainly be found within the family. It seems that Sahlins' own ideal types are hardly an improvement on those of Polanyi. John Davis (1992) criticizes him for reducing all exchange to forms of reciprocity in basically the same way that neoclassical economists reduce everything to self-regarding utility maximization.

2.3. Recent contributions

The topic has remained a lively one in recent decades. Neo-Marxist approaches, popular in the 1970s and 1980s, insisted that behavior at the level of exchange could only be explained by reference to the deeper level of the 'mode of production'. Godelier (1977) criticized both formalists and substantivists for failing to address this level; he also contributed a fascinating case study on the production and circulation of 'salt money' in

New Guinea, which showed that the 'labour theory of value' could not account for the exchange rates of this primitive commodity. In a number of thoughtful contributions, Donald Donham (1990; see especially Chapters 1, 4) showed how practices of mutual aid among the Maale of Ethiopia were regulated by inter-generational power relations. 'Working together' was an important cultural institution among these people, but the traditional obligation to give labor could, in changing economic circumstances, facilitate the emergence of new forms of economic exploitation. Donham develops in the course of this analysis a sophisticated theoretical critique of the 'maximization' assumptions of the neoclassical economists. Christopher Gregory (1982) also drew on the Marxist tradition, as well as his ethnographic observations in New Guinea, to construct a sharp opposition between the 'gift economy', made up of reciprocal, interdependent agents, and the 'commodity economy', made up of atomistic individuals. In later work Gregory (1997) responded to critics [such as Appadurai (1986)] by insisting that these were ideal types, which he had never intended to apply as blanket characterizations of particular economies or societies. They are perhaps to be used rather like Polanyi's 'modes of integration', different societies exhibiting different empirical combinations.

Currently, economic anthropology is a highly heterogeneous field, ranging from complex statistical analysis in the service of applied development projects to equally complex studies of the cultural ideas underpinning economic behavior. The American Anthropological Association's 'Society for Economic Anthropology' has an important monograph series, and Barry Isaac is the long-serving editor of an eclectic annual review, *Research in Economic Anthropology*; but one suspects that the partisans of different approaches do not gather regularly to debate their differences – they talk past each other. In the case of exchange theory, Robert Hunt (2002) has called recently for more rigorous distinctions to be made in an often confusing literature. He himself would seem to prefer to abandon the Maussian tradition altogether, on the grounds that it is too ambiguous to supply us with analytic categories. The first distinction he recommends is between exchanges with an economic component, goods or services, and social exchange more generally. Secondly, he urges that exchanges be distinguished from transfers: in the latter there is no flow of goods or services in the opposite direction. For Hunt, altruism and theft mark the poles of a spectrum, but cannot strictly be considered forms of exchange at all.

For John Davis, however, these remain in the frame as two among many other classes of exchange. The social classification of exchange repertoires varies enormously across the globe and Davis is inclined to treat them all in the same way. Thus his own identity as a male Englishman is constituted through his exchanges in essentially the same way as the identity of a Trobriand chief who manipulates *kula* valuables. A more radical cultural relativism is to be found in the position developed by Marilyn Strathern (1988). Where Davis retains a basic concept of a stable individual agent, in Strathern's account the Melanesian person is not an 'individual' at all, but is only constituted in the course of exchanges and therefore constantly changing. This is arguably closer to Mauss, to whom we owe the idea of culturally variable 'personhood' in the first place. Maurice Godelier (1999) has also gone back to Mauss for inspiration in reflecting on the tensions of the contemporary welfare state (in his case the French), which excludes many residents from valued entitlements, whilst continuously appealing to those in a position to do so to donate more to charitable causes.

Among other recent contributions, Caroline Humphrey has reinterpreted barter relationships in Nepal in terms of long-term trading partnerships. Like Parry (1986) she draws attention to the role of religion in establishing the necessary moral framework [Humphrey and Hugh-Jones (1992)]. Even in work on markets, culturalist trends have become very strong [Geertz (1979), Dilley (1992), Carrier (1997)]. To round off this survey, let me return to the recent work of Gudeman, who also claims to offer a return to Mauss. In his view the major error in previous interpretations of the master, carried to its greatest extreme in the work of Lévi-Strauss, is to see in exchange and reciprocity the ultimate origins of human social life. According to Gudeman, Mauss builds his theory on an already constituted community of some sort, and the source and force of this community cannot be reduced to any reciprocating dyad. Reciprocity is, rather, the uncertain, highly tactical activity of extending this community through exchanges with others; Gudeman restricts the term 'gift' to the initial gesture in a tentative initiative to expand community. He draws on the 'practice' theory of Pierre Bourdieu to offer the following assessment: 'Not a rule or norm of social life, not a feature of mind, a function of self-interest, or an essential foundation of society, reciprocity is part of a system of practices in which participants express, conserve, lose and gain position in the sphere of social value' [Gudeman (2001, pp. 89–90)].

3. Ethnographic examples

3.1. Food sharing

After this discussion of theoretical developments in economic anthropology, which must remain inconclusive, it may help to focus more closely on some particular cases. Commensality, the sharing of food and drink, plays an important role in most human societies. Gifts and countergifts of food were the principal objects of exchange in the exchanges analyzed by Marcel Mauss. Let us consider some further examples.

First, let us look at the allocation of meat in societies which live by hunting and gathering (often known as foraging societies). There is typically a division of labor between men and women, and women's economic activities are largely confined to the household or vicinity of the camp. Their contribution to the reproduction of the group may include the bulk of the food supply in calorific terms, e.g. through gathering nuts and wild fruits. Men gather also, but they are also likely to be associated with hunting, moving far away from the group camp in pursuit of game, either alone or with just a few partners.

What happens when a hunter is successful? He may consume some of the meat at once in its raw state, but if it is an animal of any size, then he cannot consume it all. The usual pattern seems to be that the hunter takes the carcass back to the camp. The meat may be distributed in some prescribed way (e.g. according to kinship ties) or it may simply be shared by all those present. In some of the earlier literature it was asserted or assumed that such acts of sharing were grounded in the generosity of the individual, successful hunter. Others have interpreted such sharing in terms of an underlying insurance rationality: meat is scarce, no hunter can be sure of success, and giving meat when one has it is the best insurance policy one has, to ensure that others will give when you have none. James Woodburn (1998) rejects both these lines of explanation. He argues that such sharing is not a form of pooling, reciprocity or exchange at all. It is to be understood as the expression of an egalitarian morality or ideology, very strictly implemented by groups such as the East African Hadza, studied by Woodburn himself. Following Petersen (1993), Woodburn describes hunter–gatherer economic relations in terms of 'demand sharing': the distribution of shares does not take place automatically to all, but anyone who asserts a claim will receive. The skill of successful hunters is played down: it is rather chance or the accident of using a particular arrow to which success is attributed. The question of altruistic giving does not arise.

In the terminology of Robert Hunt (2000), much of the activity taking place in hunter–gatherer food sharing involves 'transfers'; but more or less hidden 'dyadic pathways' of exchange may also be involved. For Hunt, as we have already noted for other anthropologists, the ultimate test is what the 'folk' themselves can tell you about these activities. If they say that, at some point, perhaps quite unspecified, some return will or should be made to the person who gives, then it is legitimate to speak of exchange. When this is not the case, then we should speak of sharing and transfers. Needless to say, the folk may not always agree on such matters, and the same people may suggest different, apparently contradictory explanations. Hunt calls for more empirical research to resolve these issues.

If sharing may be the more appropriate term for many transfers or exchanges of food among hunter–gatherers, societies of cultivators afford more plentiful opportunities to explore the dynamics of giving and receiving at both group and individual levels. As noted above, Melanesian horticulturists provide countless examples of large-scale, ritualized competitive giving and receiving between groups. The gift of ducklings offered by a Romanian peasant to her Saxon German neighbor, described in the quotation at the head of this chapter, illustrates a case of interpersonal tension, possibly related to inter-ethnic difference in a time of rapid social change. According to the ethnographer [Mihailescu (2002)], the Romanian is adhering to traditional norms of generosity, 'generalized' in the terms of Marshall Sahlins, but which in the eyes of the receiver certainly imply an obligation to make a return. The German does not wish to be obligated and prefers to settle the matter with an immediate balancing transaction through the payment of cash. We are given no further information about the development of this relationship, but Mihailescu suggests that we are dealing here with a cultural difference of considerable antiquity that may play a significant role in determining how different groups and regions of Romania adapt to the challenge of the postsocialist market economy.

Elements of tension and competition are evident in hospitality customs in peasant communities all over the world, but they are often disguised or pushed into the background. Among Uighur villagers in Sinkiang, north-west China, it used to be said that if a house went three days without a neighbor or relative stopping by to be entertained, then it would lose its luck. Why did even very poor households give as generously as they could? It is clear that they had – and still have – a strong idea that it is religiously meritorious, *savap*, to do so. More specifically, they believe that such generosity to others pleases the spirits of their own ancestors, who regularly returned to visit their house and its present occupants. Rituals commemorating the dead and other Islamic rituals are all occasions for demonstrative, non-calculated giving by the deceased person's family. Beliefs about the other world seem to underpin the morality of giving and virtually all Uighur sociality [Bellér-Hann (2005)].

Gifts of food and drink have retained at least some of their social significance in industrial and post-industrial societies. The example of the middle class dinner party is often advanced in discussions of giving and reciprocity in contemporary western societies. For Gudeman (2001) this exemplifies his understanding of reciprocity in terms of 'extending the base'. By providing abundant food of high quality, the host family is seeking to impress and at the same time, in some sense, to enlarge community. Expectations are thereby created, and it is embarrassing if a return is not made. It is also usually an embarrassment to attend such a dinner without bringing a counter gift, typically a bottle of wine. Gudeman comments that

> The wine is like an intermediary gift that signals acceptance of the dinner and promises further reciprocation, but is not the full return itself. So we have two cycles; distinct parts of the base – wine and food – are circulated against one another; one is consumed; the other is held. Indeed, I harbor images of a few unopened bottles of wine endlessly circulating among households [Gudeman (2001, p. 87)].

Following John Davis's line of argument, the making and ruining of reputations that takes place through such cycles of dinner parties between putative equals is not inherently different from the egalitarian rivalries found at the inter-group level in Highland New Guinea, or the agonistic competition in hierarchical societies of the North West Coast, or neighborhood tensions in villages in contemporary Transylvania. On the other hand, while each of these cases may be described as equally 'thick' in cultural terms, one must also recognize that they vary considerably in their wider social significance.

3.2. Socialist and postsocialist networking

The distinctive conditions of the state socialist economies and their successors have attracted the attention of numerous anthropologists, some of whom have attempted to draw out general theoretical implications. According to the theory or ideology of socialism, redistribution, rather than market exchange, was the dominant mode of integration of the centrally planned economy. The differences should not be exaggerated, especially in more flexible 'market socialist' countries such as Hungary after 1968, or China after

1978. Nonetheless, it is clear that the combination of economic shortages and political repression had a considerable impact on forms of giving and reciprocity. Western analysts were quick to condemn bribery and corruption. Yet they were also obliged to recognize that even the most repressive regimes, in fact especially those that came closest to the model of 'totalitarianism', also left niches of freedom, in which groups larger than the family – neighbors, allotment holders, dissident cliques etc – exchanged goods and resources in a quite different spirit. For example, key tasks in rural housebuilding were commonly undertaken by large groups of kin, neighbors and friends, without exhaustive calculation of the debts incurred. Some gifts made to individuals could be adequately classified as instrumental: the gift functioned as a payment, and there was no further contact between the parties. Others were offered in a spirit of positive reciprocity, which is not to say that self-interest was ever fully excluded, even when close family and friends were involved. Some transactions intended as simple payments led to long term social ties and the integration of new members into a 'moral community'.

These ambiguities assume different forms in the conditions of postsocialism. Where previously one might have needed to bribe a Communist Party official to secure a privilege of some sort, one might now have to bribe the same person to secure a job in the privatized factory of which the ex-*apparatchik* has become a manager. Large work parties for housebuilding have become less common in rural Hungary, and Gerald Creed (2002) has documented a dramatic contraction in the sums spent by Bulgarian villagers on rituals and feasting, which he attributes to harsh economic conditions. Yet the increased importance of maintaining networks in uncertain economic conditions has led to *higher* incidence of gifting in other postsocialist countries. Cynthia Ann Werner has shown how 'through conspicuous exchange and conspicuous consumption, rural Kazaks manage to recreate their social status and identity through feasting and gift exchange' [Werner (1999, p. 70)]. Lavish wedding banquets sometimes yield a material profit, in terms of the resources given in return by those invited; more importantly, they help poorer families to maintain the ties they need for their survival strategies, and reinforce 'values of cooperation, reciprocity and communal responsibility' (*ibid.*, p. 66). The reasons for such different responses in postsocialist societies coping with very similar economic problems cannot be deduced from general laws, but must be sought in particular histories and ethnographies.

Contemporary China, although strictly speaking not postsocialist at all, provides another very interesting example of how gifting may flourish in the context of market-oriented economic reforms. Following Yan (1996), Susanne Brandtstädter (2003) has shown that it is not possible to oppose the individual to the collective, or the material to the emotional, as in simplistic western dichotomies. Working in one of the most prosperous coastal regions of Southern China in the boom years of the 1990s, she has documented a remarkable efflorescence of family-based rituals. Where the standard modernization paradigm would predict a contraction of expenditure for non-productive purposes, the Chinese have continued to invest heavily in their social relationships. According to Brandtstädter, it is through these wedding and funeral rituals that they 'produce relatedness'. They do so with very rational motives: to establish trust and predictability, to reduce the risks they face in an unstable economic environment, and to fill a legitimacy void in the post-Maoist state. One could say that, through their practices of giving and receiving, people create islands of community, just as they always have in the past. Once again, the elements of individual and community rationality simply cannot be disentangled [cf. Wilk (1993)].

4. Cross-cultural experiments

Given the complexities posed by even the 'simplest' of the ethnographic cases, it is perhaps not surprising that many theoreticians prefer to gather their data in the laboratory. They hope thereby to cut through the levels of belief, culture and ideology, so that the bases of individual decision-taking can be brought into relief. An interesting recent development is the application of 'experimental economics' in ethnographic settings [Ensminger (2002b), Henrich et al. (2003)]. Early results, notably with the ultimatum game, have shown considerable cross-cultural variation in the propensity to be generous to other group members. People such as Hadza hunter–gatherers, with very simple forms of economy and a strong reputation for sharing, turn out to be among the most 'mean' in their offers. This is not inconsistent with Woodburn's (1998) account of the egalitarianism of these people, which made no claims about generosity or altruism. The researchers found that two groups in Papua New Guinea contradicted the model of *homo oeconomicus* by making 'hyper-generous' offers, i.e. giving the responder more than 50% of the sum available. This is of course consistent with the ethos of lavish giving in this region. Should we be surprised that such offers are frequently rejected in the game, as they cannot be in real life?

Some of the variation in the results of these behavioral experiments, notably in the dictator game, can be plausibly accounted for in terms of the importance of cooperation for the social and economic life of the community. However, many anthropologists have profound reservations about these experiments, which invite individual agents to make decisions in a context which abstracts from their real life worlds. They will be sympathetic to the conclusion that 'culture' shapes or modifies economic behavior, but will question whether games such as ultimatum and dictator give genuine access to those differences, or allow inferences about the 'generosity' or 'sociability' of the people invited to play along. Anthropologists will not be surprised to learn that, when the ultimatum game was played at a second Hadza camp, the results obtained were quite different from those obtained at the first (much closer to the behavior of an income-maximizing *homo oeconomicus* on the part of the proposers). Few if any socio-cultural anthropologists would interpret such data in terms of evolutionary speculations.

Despite these reservations, experimental economic anthropology (including research on the internet, with its unprecedented possibilities for impersonal exchange) is clearly an expanding area of interest in the subdiscipline at the present time.

5. Conclusions

In spite of the lengthy history of description and theorizing in anthropological accounts of giving and reciprocity, this remains a contested field. There is still confusion concerning the definition of key terms, including 'exchange' and 'reciprocity'. On the whole, the main thrust of the anthropological tradition goes against that of the mainstream economists. Whereas the latter assume or search for universal foundations, usually in psychology and/or biology, those who study the full range of actual human societies emphasize the diversity of forms of exchange and their motivations, and resist what they consider to be seductive reductionisms. Marcel Mauss (1990) is the founding figure of this countercurrent, even though he himself offered a universalist argument based on questionable if not illusory notions of evolution, 'archaic society' and 'total *prestation*'. Although Bronislaw Malinowski (1922) polemicised against the economists of his day, his own use of reciprocity was quite consistent with economistic insistence on calculation and utility maximization. The Maussian tradition has been continued in myriad ways, among them the insistence of Karl Polanyi (1968) and his Substantivist school on the *embeddedness* of economic activities in preindustrial societies, the 'reciprocity' spectrum developed by Marshall Sahlins (1974), Gregory's (1982) dichotomy between 'commodity' and 'gift' economies, Davis's (1992) concern with social classification (a topic that originates with Durkheim and Mauss), and Strathern's (1988) analysis of the 'dividual' self in New Guinea.

An interesting convergence in recent work [Godelier (1999), Gregory (1997), Gudeman (2001)] has emphasized a distinction between goods that are intended for exchange, and a sphere of what Annette Weiner (1992) has called 'inalienable possessions' on the other. Godelier has built on Weiner's work in suggesting that modern Western societies also have their *sacra*, e.g. in the form of a Constitution, which cannot be sold or gifted, but must be transmitted to future generations. Reciprocity cannot apply in this sphere, which is basic to the construction of community. It is a sphere from which the precepts of utilitarian exchange are either excluded completely or pushed into the background by long-term considerations of morality. This brings us back to Woodburn's understanding of sharing in egalitarian hunter–gatherer societies, grounded in morality and ideology rather than psychology and biology. Few communities in the modern world can hope to emulate forager egalitarianism. Yet Gudeman shows that it remains everywhere possible, indeed necessary, to establish a sphere in which the usual laws governing economic transfers do not apply. The giving and sharing that take place within this sphere, and the reciprocity that is poised on the boundaries between the two spheres, are not susceptible to elucidation by economic analysis alone.

References

Appadurai, A. (1986). "Introduction: commodities and the politics of value". In: Appadurai, A. (Ed.), The Social Life of Things; Commodities in Cultural Perspective. Cambridge University Press, Cambridge, pp. 3–63.

Barth, F. (1966). Models of Social Organization. RAI, London.
Bellér-Hann, I. (2005). Community Matters. Unpublished Habilitation Thesis. Humboldt University, Berlin.
Brandstädter, S. (2003). "The moral economy of kinship and property in southern China". In: Hann, C., The 'Property Relations' Group (Eds.), The Postsocialist Agrarian Question. LIT, Münster, pp. 419–440.
Carrier, J.G. (1997). Meanings of the Market: The Free Market in Western Culture. Berg, Oxford.
Cook, S. (1966). "The obsolete anti-market mentality: critique of the substantive approach to economic anthropology". American Anthropologist 68 (2), 323–345.
Creed, G. (2002). "Economic crisis and ritual decline in eastern Europe". In: Hann, C.M. (Ed.), Postsocialism: Ideals, Ideologies and Practices in Eurasia. Routledge, London, pp. 57–73.
Davis, J. (1992). Exchange. Open University Press, Buckingham.
Dilley, R. (Ed.) (1992). Contesting Markets; Analyses of Ideology, Discourse and Practice. Edinburgh University Press, Edinburgh.
Donham, D. (1990). History, Power, Ideology; Central Issues in Marxism and Anthropology. Cambridge University Press, Cambridge.
Ensminger, J. (Ed.) (2002a). Theory in Economic Anthropology. AltaMira Press, Walnut Creek.
Ensminger, J. (2002b). "Experimental economics: a powerful new method for theory testing in anthropology". In: Ensminger, J. (Ed.), Theory in Economic Anthropology. AltaMira Press, Walnut Creek, pp. 59–78.
Firth, R. (1939). Primitive Polynesian Economy. Routledge, London.
Firth, R. (Ed.) (1966). Themes in Economic Anthropology. Tavistock, London.
Geertz, C. (1979). "The bazaar economy in Sefrou". In: Geertz, C., Geertz, H., Rosen, L. (Eds.), Meaning and Order in Moroccan Society. Cambridge University Press, Cambridge, pp. 159–268.
Godelier, M. (1977). Perspectives in Marxist Anthropology. Cambridge University Press, Cambridge.
Godelier, M. (1999). The Enigma of the Gift. Polity, Cambridge.
Gregory, C. (1982). Gifts and Commodities. Academic Press, London.
Gregory, C. (1997). Savage Money; The Anthropology and Politics of Commodity Exchange. Harwood Academic Publishers, Amsterdam.
Gudeman, S. (2001). The Anthropology of Economy. Blackwell, Oxford.
Hamilton Grierson, P.J. (1903). The Silent Trade; A Contribution to the Early History of Human Intercourse. William Green & Sons, Edinburgh.
Hart, K. (2000). The Memory Bank; Money in an Unequal World. Profile, London.
Henrich, J., et al. (Eds.) (2003). Foundations of Human Sociality: Ethnography and Experiments in 15 Small-scale Societies. Oxford University Press, Oxford.
Herskovits, M.J. (1940). The Economic Life of Primitive Peoples. Knopf, New York.
Humphrey, C., Hugh-Jones, S. (Eds.) (1992). Barter, Exchange and Value; An Anthropological Approach. Cambridge University Press, Cambridge.
Hunt, R.C. (2000). "Forager food sharing economy: transfers and exchanges". In: Wenzel, G.W., Hovelsrud-Broda, G., Kishigami, N. (Eds.), The Social Economy of Sharing. Resource Allocation and Modern Hunter–Gatherers. National Museum of Ethnology, Osaka, pp. 7–26.
Hunt, R.C. (2002). "Economic transfers and exchanges: concepts for describing allocations". In: Ensminger, J. (Ed.), Theory in Economic Anthropology. AltaMira Press, Walnut Creek, pp. 105–118.
Ingold, T. (1986). The Appropriation of Nature; Essays on Human Ecology and Social Relations. Manchester University Press, Manchester.
Lévi-Strauss, C. (1969). The Elementary Structures of Kinship. Beacon Press, Boston.
Malinowski, B. (1921). "The primitive economics of the Trobriand Islanders". The Economic Journal 31 (121), 1–16.
Malinowski, B. (1922). Argonauts of the Western Pacific. Routledge & Kegan Paul, London.
Mauss, M. (1990). The Gift; Forms and Functions of Exchange in Archaic Societies. Routledge, London. (First publication 1924.)
Meeker, M.E., Barlow, K., Lipset, D.M. (1986). "Culture, exchange, and gender: lessons from the murik". Cultural Anthropology 1 (1), 6–73.
Mihailescu, V. (2002). "Between reciprocity and contract? The case of the *Nachbarschaft* in multi-ethnic Transylvania". Paper presented at EASA Conference, Copenhagen.

Narotzky, S. (1997). New Directions in Economic Anthropology. Pluto, London.
Parry, J. (1986). "The gift, the Indian gift, and the "Indian gift"". Man 21, 453–473.
Petersen, N. (1993). "Demand sharing: reciprocity and the pressure for generosity among foragers". American Anthropologist 95 (4), 860–874.
Polanyi, K. (1944). The Great Transformation. Beacon Press, Boston.
Polanyi, K. (1968). Primitive, Archaic and Modern Economies. Anchor Books, Garden City (ed. Dalton, G.).
Polanyi, K., Arensberg, C., Pearson, H. (Eds.) (1957). Trade and Market in the Early Empires. Free Press, Glencoe.
Sahlins, M. (1974). Stone Age Economics. Tavistock, London.
Sillitoe, P. (1979). Give and Take: Exchange in Wola Society. Australian National University Press, Canberra.
Strathern, A. (1971). The Rope of Moka. Cambridge University Press, Cambridge.
Strathern, M. (1988). The Gender of the Gift. University of California Press, Berkeley.
Weiner, A. (1992). Inalienable Possessions. University of California Press, Berkeley.
Werner, C.A. (1999). "The dynamics of feating and gift exchange in rural Kazakstan". In: Svanberg, I. (Ed.), Contemporary Kazaks; Cultural and Social Perspectives. Curzon, London, pp. 47–72.
Wilk, R. (1993). "Altruism and self-interest: towards an anthropological theory of decision-making". Research in Economic Anthropology 14, 191–212.
Wilk, R. (1996). Economies and Cultures; Foundations of Economic Anthropology. Westview, Boulder.
Woodburn, J. (1998). " 'Sharing is not a form of exchange': an analysis of property sharing in immediate-return hunter–gatherer societies". In: Hann, C.M. (Ed.), Property Relations; Renewing the Anthropological Tradition. Cambridge University Press, Cambridge, pp. 48–63.
Yan, Y. (1996). The Flow of Gifts: Reciprocity and Social Networks in a Chinese Village. Stanford University Press, Stanford.
Young, M. (1971). Fighting with Food: Leadership, Values and Social Control in a Massim Society. Cambridge University Press, Cambridge.

1B: OVERALL VIEWS

Chapter 5

THE ECONOMIC THEORY OF GIFT-GIVING: PERFECT SUBSTITUTABILITY OF TRANSFERS AND REDISTRIBUTION OF WEALTH

JEAN MERCIER YTHIER[*]

Université de Metz and Institut d'Economie Publique, France

Contents

Abstract	228
Keywords	229
1. Introduction	230
2. Gift-giving in social equilibrium theory: A preliminary overview	232
2.1. Preferences and rights	232
2.2. Four characteristic properties	236
2.3. Theory and facts	241
3. Perfectly substitutable transfers in a pure distributive social system	243
3.1. Pure distributive social system and equilibrium	244
3.1.1. Pure distributive social systems	244
3.1.2. Distributive equilibrium	245
3.2. Diagrammatic representation	247
3.3. Three studies of pure distributive equilibrium	251
3.3.1. Becker (1974): The theory of social interactions	252
3.3.2. Arrow (1981): Optimal and voluntary income distribution	255
3.3.3. Bergstrom, Blume and Varian (1986): On the private provision of public goods	258
3.4. Existence, determinacy	261
3.4.1. Existence	261
3.4.2. Determinacy	264
4. Perfectly substitutable transfers in a competitive market economy	267
4.1. Interdependent preferences	269
4.1.1. Interdependence of primitive utilities	270
4.1.2. Interdependent preferences on allocations and the fundamental theorems of welfare economics	271
4.2. General equilibrium with benevolent gift-giving and competitive market exchange	275

---

[*] I am indebted to the participants to the authors' conference of Marseilles, but especially to Serge-Christophe Kolm and Louis Levy-Garboua for useful comments and suggestions.

Handbook of the Economics of Giving, Altruism and Reciprocity, Volume 1
Edited by Serge-Christophe Kolm and Jean Mercier Ythier
Copyright © 2006 Elsevier B.V. All rights reserved
DOI: 10.1016/S1574-0714(06)01005-0

4.2.1. Social equilibrium	275
4.2.2. First-order conditions	277
4.2.3. Equivalence of money transfers and in-kind transfers	279
4.2.4. Existence of a social equilibrium	279
4.3. Perfectly substitutable transfers and the transfer problem	282
5. The effectiveness of public redistribution with perfectly substitutable transfers	283
5.1. Neutrality in general Pareto social systems	285
5.2. Neutrality in BBV distributive social systems	288
5.2.1. Neutral lump-sum taxation	289
5.2.2. Neutral distortionary taxation	291
6. Efficient redistribution with perfectly substitutable transfers	296
6.1. General theory	297
6.1.1. Collective gift-giving and social equilibrium	298
6.1.2. Distributive liberal social contract	305
6.1.3. The distributive liberal social contract and the irreversibility of time	317
6.2. Free-riding and population size in BBV distributive social systems	318
6.2.1. Inefficient underprovision of the public good at non-cooperative equilibrium	319
6.2.2. Group size and public good provision level at non-cooperative equilibrium	322
6.2.3. Group size and the suboptimality of non-cooperative equilibrium	323
6.2.4. Free-riding, population size and core solution	326
6.3. Mechanism design in BBV distributive social systems	328
7. Imperfectly substitutable transfers	329
7.1. Logical tests of the perfect substitutability of transfers	329
7.1.1. Perfect competitive markets	329
7.1.2. Non-paternalistic utility interdependence	331
7.1.3. Cournot–Nash behavioral assumption	332
7.2. Empirical tests of the perfect substitutability of transfers	336
7.2.1. Experimental tests of Cournot–Nash individual behavior	336
7.2.2. Measures of the elasticity of substitution of transfers	338
8. Conclusion	341
Appendix A	341
A.1. Proofs	341
A.2. Mechanisms for private contributions to public goods	354
A.2.1. Two-stage mechanisms	354
A.2.2. One-stage mechanisms	356
References	361

Abstract

This chapter reviews the theory of the voluntary public and private redistribution of wealth elaborated by economic analysis in the last forty years or so. The central object of the theory is altruistic gift-giving, construed as benevolent voluntary redistribution of income or wealth. The theory concentrates on lump-sum voluntary transfers, individual or collective, which aim at equalizing the distribution of wealth from altruistic reasons or sentiments (perfectly substitutable altruistic transfers). It implies: (i) the Pareto-inefficiency of the non-cooperative interaction of individual altruistic transfers; (ii) the neutralization of public transfers by individual altruistic transfers; (iii) and the crowding out of private altruistic transfers by Pareto-efficient public redistribution. The chapter is organized as follows. Section 2 presents an informal overview of the general intent and content of the theory. Section 3 gives a first formal version of the theory in a one-commodity setup (pure distributive social system). Non-cooperative distributive equilibrium is characterized, and its fundamental properties of existence and determinacy are analyzed. Section 4 extends the definitions and fundamental properties of pure distributive social systems to general social systems that combine competitive market exchange with the non-cooperative altruistic transfers of individuals endowed with non-paternalistic interdependent preferences. Section 5 states the neutrality property in two versions of the theory successively: the general social systems of Section 4; and the important special case of the pure distributive social systems of Section 3, where the set of agents is partitioned in two subsets, namely, a subset of "poor" individuals with zero endowments and egoistic preferences, and a subset of "rich" individuals altruistic to the poor and indifferent to each other. Section 6 reviews the theory of Pareto-efficient redistribution in pure distributive social systems. Section 7 returns to the fundamental assumption of perfect substitutability of transfers through a selective review of theoretical models of imperfectly substitutable transfers and empirical tests of perfect substitutability.

Keywords

gift-giving, altruism, neutrality, distributive efficiency, liberal social contract

JEL classification: A10, A12, A13, A14, B00, B10, B40, B49, C60, C62, C70, C71, C72, D30, D31, D50, D51, D60, D61, D62, D63, D64, D70, D71, D90, D91, H00, H10, H11, H20, H21, H22, H23, H24, H40, H41, H42, H53, H70, H71, H72, I30, I38, N40, O10, O15, P00, P48

1. Introduction

This chapter reviews the theory of the voluntary public and private redistribution of wealth elaborated by economic analysis in the last forty years or so.

The main feature of the theory, captured in the subtitle of the chapter under the notion of perfectly substitutable transfers, is the existence of a fundamental identity of all voluntary transfers, whether public or private, both in terms of their means (endowment redistribution) and in terms of their ends (making the distribution of wealth more equal).

In formal theory, perfect substitutability translates into a complex set of assumptions which combine, in their most elaborate form, elements from three key constructs: (i) competitive markets; (ii) individual preferences relative to the distribution of wealth; (iii) and Cournot–Nash interactions in transfer activities.

The first two constructs have a long history in economics, whether considered separately or combined.

The idea that human behavior in society can be fruitfully analyzed in a number of autonomous components (such as the "Market", the "Family" and the "State") corresponding to well-characterized differences in the motives of individual action, can be traced at least as far back as the work of Adam Smith, whose psychological explanation of the construction of the (pro-social and altruistic) moral self of individuals in the *Theory of Moral Sentiments* (1759) sharply contrasts with his representation of self-interested market behavior in the *Wealth of Nations* (1776). The first two constructs outlined above can be viewed, in many respects, as workable formal representations of Smith's theories: market exchange as interaction of self-interested individuals resulting in a socially efficient outcome; and the construction of the moral self of individuals as the outcome of acts of imaginative sympathy by which individuals imagine themselves in the position of others and experience, to some limited extent, the feelings associated with these positions.

The contrast between the representations of human behavior conveyed by Smith's two major works was sometimes viewed as a contradiction in nineteenth century controversies on the Economic Man (the "Adam Smith problem"). Two analytical contributions at the beginning of the twentieth century proved particularly useful to overcome this difficulty and to bridge (some of) the gaps between Smith's original insights and a formulation compatible with the stringent methodological demands of modern economic theory. The first one is Wicksteed's characterization of market behavior as "non-tuistic" (1910), that is, a behavior which is neither egoistic nor altruistic but proceeds, rather, from a type of instrumental rationality narrowly adapted to the context of market exchange, and compatible a priori with the large variety of goals that human beings pursue in other contexts. The second analytical contribution, which has proved very useful to the modern economic theory of gift-giving reviewed in this chapter, is Pareto's concept of a "maximum of utility for a collectivity" (1916), that is, in modern terms, a Pareto optimum defined according to (non-paternalistic) interdependent individual utilities. This notion places the Economic Man in the Social Man and, accordingly, market equilibrium in social equilibrium, in such a way that the (social) Pareto-efficiency of the latter entails the (market) Pareto-efficiency of the former.

The third feature of the perfect substitutability of transfers is much more recent than the former two [despite the reference to Cournot's (1838) early contribution]. It proceeds from the systematization of the use of game theory concepts in economics, from the 1950s, and notably from the contributions of Nash (1950) and Debreu (1952).

Combined with individual preferences on the distribution of wealth (distributive preferences, in short), Cournot–Nash interactions result in a public good problem, as: firstly, distributive preferences make the distribution of wealth an object of common concern, that is, a pure (non-rival, non-excludable) public good in the formal sense of modern economic theory [Kolm (1968)]; and secondly, non-cooperative individual contributions to a public good generally result in a socially inefficient (in the sense of Pareto) outcome, which in turn can be analyzed as a coordination deficiency of collective action [Samuelson (1954), Olson (1965)].

The joint assumption of distributive preferences and Cournot–Nash interactions has a second characteristic consequence, the so-called neutrality property, which essentially states that exogenous lump-sum wealth redistribution between agents connected directly or indirectly by operative (that is, positive) equilibrium gifts leaves the equilibrium distribution of wealth unchanged [Becker (1974) and, in an intertemporal setup, Barro (1974)]. Although noticed relatively late, the neutrality property is certainly the most obvious and salient aspect of the theory of redistribution reviewed in this chapter, as the direct translation, in general equilibrium terms, of the perfect substitutability of transfers.

The combination of the public good problem with the neutrality property results in a simple but powerful consequence, which can be viewed as the main prediction of the theory and can serve as a basis for an evaluation of its relevance and scope: the social efficiency of distribution requires the full crowding-out of all equilibrium transfers [Warr (1982)], unless a single agent is willing and able to make gifts to all others [Becker (1974)]. Put another way, the theory implies that if distributive concerns are widespread enough, they result in the socialization of a fraction of aggregate wealth (redistributed wealth) – in other words a redistributive welfare state – as the outcome of a Pareto-efficient social contract on the distribution of wealth [a distributive "liberal social contract": Kolm (1985)].

The chapter is organized as follows.

Section 2 presents a preliminary overview of the general intent and content of the theory.

Section 3 gives a first formal version of the theory in a one-commodity setup (pure distributive social systems). Non-cooperative distributive equilibrium is characterized, and its fundamental properties of existence and determinacy are analyzed.

Section 4 extends the definitions and fundamental properties of pure distributive social systems to general social systems, combining competitive market exchange with the non-cooperative benevolent transfers of individuals acting according to their non-paternalistic interdependent preferences (Pareto social systems).

Section 5 states the neutrality property in two versions of the theory successively: the general Pareto social systems of Section 4; and the important special case of the pure distributive social systems of Section 3, where the set of agents is partitioned in two subsets, namely, a subset of "poor" individuals with zero endowments and egoistic preferences, and a subset of "rich" individuals benevolent to the poor and indifferent to each other [Cornes and Sandler (1985a); Bergstrom, Blume and Varian (referred to as BBV in the sequel) (1986)].

Section 6 reviews the theory of Pareto-efficient redistribution in pure distributive social systems of the general type and of the BBV type.

Section 7 returns to the fundamental assumption of perfect substitutability through a selective review of theoretical models of imperfectly substitutable transfers and empirical tests of perfect substitutability. Special attention is given here to the meaning and degree of relevance of Cournot–Nash interactions and to the basic prediction of the full crowding-out of private redistributive transfers by public transfers.

2. Gift-giving in social equilibrium theory: A preliminary overview

This section briefly reviews, in an informal way, the object of the theory, the elements or determinants it mobilizes, the main solution concepts and results, and their interpretation and confrontation with facts.

The object of the theory is altruistic gift-giving, construed as benevolent voluntary redistribution of income or wealth.[1]

2.1. Preferences and rights

The benevolence of redistribution is understood as an expression of both the individual rationality of the donor(s) and his (their) favorable intentions relative to the beneficiary of his (their) gifts.

Individual rationality (in the usual sense of economic theory) translates into the maximization of well-behaved (that is, reflexive, complete and transitive) ordinal preferences of individuals on the distribution of wealth within a social group. Gift-giving appears, in other words, in the theory, as a "logical action" in the sense of Pareto (1916), designed to maximize donors' preferences on the distribution of wealth within the group; see Chapter 1 of this Handbook and the introduction to Section 4 below. Such preferences are defined directly on the distribution of income or wealth in the one-commodity setup of Section 3, or indirectly, via non-paternalistic interdependent preferences on the allocation of resources (see Footnote 2[2] for a precise formulation) in the setup of Section 4 with multiple market commodities exchanged on competitive markets.

---

[1] Wealth is understood as monetary wealth throughout Section 2.

[2] Following Pareto (1916) we name *ophelimity* the utility that an individual derives from his own consumption of market commodities. The assumption of non-paternalistic utility interdependence supposes that every

The favorable intentions of donors relative to beneficiaries translate into a positive valuation of the wealth of the latter in the preferences of the former, that is, donors' preferences increasing in the wealth of the beneficiaries of their gifts. This positive valuation of the beneficiary's wealth by the donor usually is named altruism in economic theory, notably since Becker (1976), following a long-running tradition in sociology initiated by Auguste Comte.[3] Formal altruism, in the sense just defined, is susceptible to cover various psychological contents in terms of donors' motives, depending on the context of redistribution, and notably on the size of the social group within which redistribution takes place. Three types of social contexts are considered in applications: families, or, by extension, small groups of close relatives; charity networks, where donors and beneficiaries may or may not be (and most frequently are not) in direct individual relation with each other; and general redistribution within large social groups, possibly whole political communities such as states or nations. Formal altruism usually is interpreted, accordingly: in family contexts, as feelings of individual sympathy, such as liking or love; in charity contexts, as philanthropy (sympathy towards mankind[4]), frequently associated with feelings or emotions of pity or compassion; in socio-political contexts, as feelings of solidarity (sympathy towards community members) or fraternity (sympathy towards equals).

Individual rational altruistic preferences on wealth distribution, as outlined above, make a first fundamental class of determinants in the social equilibrium theory of gift-giving. A second fundamental class of determinants, which refers to the voluntary character of gift-giving, consists of the property rights of individuals on income and wealth.

Gift-giving as voluntary wealth redistribution is an expression of the property right of donors. Property right is defined as the possibility, legitimated and protected by society, for the individual owner of a scarce resource, to freely decide on its use or abuse,

---

individual i has well-defined preferences on both: his own consumption of market commodities; and the vectors of individual ophelimities. In the sequel, the former is represented by an individual *ophelimity function*, denoted by u_i, and the latter by an individual *social utility function* of the type $w_i(\hat{u}_1, \ldots, \hat{u}_n)$, where $\hat{u}_j$ denotes an ophelimity level of individual j for all j. In the one-commodity setup, ophelimity is identified with wealth and interpreted as individual consumption expenditure.

[3] Auguste Comte was one of the founders of scientific sociology. He probably coined the neologism "altruism" (or perhaps Andrieux), which, to the best of my knowledge, first appeared in print in his *Cours de Philosophie Positive* (1830). Former authors usually employed such terms as "benevolence", "beneficence", "love" or "sympathy". This notably was the case of Adam Smith, whose *Theory of Moral Sentiments* is deduced from sympathy [defined as "fellow-feeling with any passion whatever", a notion more commonly designated under the name of "empathy" in modern vocabulary (1759, Part First, Chapter I of Section I)] and characterizes benevolence as one of the three fundamental virtues in his classification of the systems of moral philosophy [the other two being the virtues of "propriety" and "prudence" (1759, Part Seventh, introduction to Section II)]. Vilfredo Pareto who, besides his fundamental contributions to economic theory, is also considered, like Auguste Comte, as a founder of scientific sociology, uses the term "humanitarianism" in the *Traité de Sociologie Générale* (1916, Chapter XII, notably Footnote 1 of §2131).

[4] The reader can find an exquisite literary illustration of philanthropic psychology (and so modern!) in the character of Mrs Birdseye in *The Bostonians* of Henry James (1886, notably Chapter IV).

within a conventional list of alternatives which typically consist of own consumption, consumption as input in a production process, disposal, selling and giving. Gift-giving is construed, consequently, as a free act of the donor(s), that is, notably, as a choice within a range of several accessible gifts, including the possibility of giving nothing.

An important extension of the freedom of agents so postulated by the theory lies in the representation of resulting social interactions as, firstly, non-strategic, and as, secondly, open to cooperation by means of explicit or implicit contracts between donors.

Non-strategic interactions, on the one hand, suppose that every individual agent or, in the case of cooperation, every group of cooperating individuals, makes the instrumental choice of taking the actions of others (for example, their gifts) as independent of its own. This corresponds to the so-called Cournot–Nash behavioral assumption, and opposes to strategic interactions, where agents, or at least some of them (called "leaders", "principals", ..., depending on the game under consideration), base their decisions on an accurate prediction of the reactions of others to their own actions. Contractual cooperation, on the other hand, supposes that individuals pool their resources in order to make collective decisions on the actions of the members of the resulting cooperating group (notably their gifts inside and outside this group) when such association is individually beneficial to all members. In the sequel, for the sake of brevity, we name *non-strategic cooperation* the combination of contractual cooperation (if any) with non-strategic interactions of non-cooperating agents or groups. This corresponds, in the formal definitions of Section 6.1.1, to the strong Nash distributive equilibrium.

The social equilibrium theory of gift-giving develops the view that the individual freedom of agents should result in non-strategic cooperation in the context of rational altruism. This view stems, in part, from a priori considerations reviewed in the sequel of this section, and also finds a posteriori justifications in the third and fourth characteristic properties of the theory considered in the next subsection (see notably the last paragraph of Section 2.2).

It seems to be a basic natural presumption that the independent acts of a genuinely free individual cannot be predicted with an objective certainty by the individuals who interact with him. While partly a postulate, as a "natural" consequence of the abstract notion of liberty in action, this proposition nevertheless can be given practical content in a variety of contexts relevant for us. Let us briefly enumerate three such realistic interpretations.

A first interpretation, expressed in terms of the cognitive abilities of any individual non-cooperatively interacting with a free individual agent (that is, more concretely, with a right-holder, such as an individual owner susceptible, for example, to make gifts, or consume them), is that the former knows the past and present acts of the latter or, still more realistically, is able to get such knowledge at sufficiently low cost and with sufficient accuracy to make it useful for his own practical purposes, but is unable to predict the latter's acts at similar practical conditions (that is, to perform by himself sufficiently accurate predictions at sufficiently low cost). In short, the act is known (or can be), the agent is not. This interpretation clearly appears suitable for individual interactions in large social groups.

The second interpretation corresponds to the relativistic variant of the first, where the costs and hazards of non-strategic cooperation (essentially, transaction and enforcement costs and associate uncertainties) appear significantly lower than the costs and hazards of the individual prediction of others' reactions. This might, conjecturally, apply to social groups of any size, although more easily perhaps to groups of intermediate size, as the practical prevision of individual reactions can be presumed less difficult in (stable) micro-social units, and practical impediments to cooperation obviously increase with the size of the cooperation pool.

The third interpretation, finally, applies to situations where the ability of an agent to predict the reactions of another largely follows from his ability to relevantly constrain the latter, that is, relevantly restrain the set of alternatives accessible to his opponent by various means such as credible threats of retaliation in case of "bad conduct", "fait accompli", reliance on social norms etc. This is the interpretation which is most commonly retained, although implicitly, in the theoretical literature on strategic gift-giving reviewed in Section 7.1.3 below, notably models of strategic bequests and Samaritan's dilemma. It seems to apply, most relevantly, to long-lasting interactions, notably (but not only) in social contexts which imply close individual relations between agents. It must somehow contradict, by definition, the full liberty of action of private owners, and also formal altruism (in the sense of the former paragraph) when the use of the means of constraint is due to the donor, because of the characteristics that the donor's psychology then usually takes on. Let us briefly illustrate these points with an informal discussion of strategic bequests and Samaritan's dilemma, to finish with (see Section 7.1.3 for more detailed accounts).

Models of strategic bequest illustrate game situations where a testator, wishing to receive attention and care from "egoistic" heirs, obtains satisfaction, and moreover manages to reap the whole surplus from corresponding interactions, when he is in position to credibly threaten recalcitrants with disinheritance [Bernheim, Shleifer and Summers (1985); and also, putting specific emphasis on the importance of credibility, Hirshleifer (1977)]. Both articles find a nice literary illustration in the misfortunes met by Shakespeare's King Lear (1608) with his heirs. Balzac's *Eugénie Grandet* (1833) develops a similar vein in another historical and sociological context.[5] Both provide us with a lively illustration of a psychological process by which the interests induced by massive wealth transmission shape, and finally determine individual psychologies, expelling or deeply altering the ties of "natural" affection. Such literary archetypes, magnified by talent, and the abstract models above, yield pictures of individual interactions relative to inheritance, from which feelings of affection are not absent, but where they appear dominated by other features of the transmission relation (the various other "interests" of participants, which include material interests, although they do not necessarily reduce to them), and where gift-giving (bequest) notably appears as a powerful mean of constraint over beneficiaries.

---

[5] The first blooming of French bourgeois society, which followed the end of Napoleonic Wars.

Samaritan's dilemma [Buchanan (1975), Lindbeck and Weibull (1988)] refer to game situations where the generosity of the donor is negatively related to some characteristic over which the beneficiary has control, typically the beneficiary's current income or wealth from work and past savings. If the loss of one unit of the beneficiary's income, induced by a decrease in his labor or saving effort, is more than compensated, in terms of the beneficiary's welfare, by the corresponding increase in aid and decrease in disutility of effort, the beneficiary has an incentive to "exploit" the donor by choosing the low levels of effort (lower than in the absence of aid) that maximizes his welfare. Moreover, the resulting equilibrium then generally is Pareto-inefficient, implying the possibility of rearranging individual actions in such a way that all agents end up better off, including aid recipients. These models are contemporary echoes, with considerable attenuations in strength and tone though, of the traditional suspicion of parasitism and general misconduct of the beneficiaries of charity and public aid such as reflected, for example, in the debates which surrounded the British Poor Laws of the seventieth and nineteenth centuries. The essence of the argument in these past and present discussions on the political economy of poverty relief refers to aspects of the reality of aid practices which involve paternalistic motives on behalf of donors (notably the state) and their translation into various forms of control over beneficiaries, with a gradual evolution, over three centuries of economic development, from initial coercion and repression to contemporary policies of education and prevention. Note that, characteristically, in the contemporary models above, the agents who suffer de facto restrictions of their liberty of action are not the beneficiaries of aid as suggested above, but donors, who confront constraining "fait accompli" from beneficiaries (in addition to the obligation of respecting the property of others, sole liberty limitation implied, in principle, by property right). As if increasing economic affluence finally had shifted the burden from aid recipients to donors (this actually is the thesis (and regret) of Buchanan in the quoted reference).

The discussion above emphasizes types of interactions which do not fit in the joint assumption of (non-paternalistic) rational altruism and (full) freedom of action of individual owners outlined in the beginning. This raises in turn the question of the specific relevance, and adequate utilization of the latter in social equilibrium analysis. We return to this question in the third part of the section.

2.2. *Four characteristic properties*

Let us now turn to the characteristic properties of the theory.

For the sake of clarity, we name, from now on: *market optimum* a Pareto optimum relative to individual ophelimities;[6] *distributive optimum* a Pareto optimum relative to

---

[6] This terminology implicitly supposes a market economy that verifies the assumptions of the first and second fundamental theorems of welfare economics. These assumptions will be explicitly made in Sections 4 and 5, where we develop the study of the social systems that combine, on the one hand, non-tuistic (see Section 1 above, and Section 4.1.2 below) exchange of consumption goods and services on complete and perfect competitive markets, with, on the other hand, non-paternalistic altruistic individual transfers.

individual interdependent utilities (for the definitions of individual ophelimities and interdependent utilities, see Footnote 2 above). The associate notions of Pareto-efficiency are named, accordingly, *market* and *distributive efficiency* respectively (the latter sometimes also *social efficiency* in the sequel).

Summarizing, we consider social systems of rational altruists, endowed with property rights, who non-strategically interact, and possibly cooperate, in making voluntary wealth transfers.

The main characteristic properties of such systems, presented below in a logical order, are fourfold: the separability of redistribution by non-paternalistic altruistic transfers, from resource allocation by complete systems of competitive markets [Mercier Ythier (1989)]; neutrality [Barro (1974), and Becker (1974)]; a social aggregation property, which entails the Rotten Kid Theorem as a corollary [Becker (1974)]; and the full crowding out of altruistic transfers at distributive optimum [Warr (1982) and Mercier Ythier (1998a, 1998b)]. They are briefly summarized below.

The first characteristic property specifically applies to the multi-commodity setup, with non-paternalistic interdependent utilities and a complete system of competitive markets for consumption goods and services. The social system then involves the interaction of a subsystem of market exchange and production of the Walrasian type (a Walrasian economy) with voluntary wealth transfers from rational altruists. The property states that the *social equilibrium allocation is a market optimum*, under the usual conditions for the Pareto-efficiency of Walrasian economies. Note that the property notably supposes that altruistic donors non-strategically interact with the market, that is, are price takers, whether they act individually, or collectively by contractual cooperation. As a consequence, the type of non-altruistic gifts involved in the so-called transfer problem or paradoxes are excluded from the field of rational transfers considered by the theory (see Section 4.3).

Neutrality states, notably, that *exogenous lump-sum transfers between any pair of individual agents* (say, agents i and j) *leave equilibrium distribution unchanged if individual agents are linked by a gift at social equilibrium, provided that the gift be at least as large as the exogenous transfer when both transfers* (that is, the exogenous transfer and the gift) *have the same direction* (say, from i to j). Exogenous lump-sum transfers are determined outside the social system under consideration, that is, outside the set of interacting individual agents. They most frequently correspond to public decisions (or their consequences) in applications. The property holds under the basic assumptions of the theory, essentially: rational altruism and non-strategic interactions, complemented, in the multi-commodity setup, with non-paternalism and competitive markets. These assumptions are not only sufficient for neutrality (see Section 5) but also, in general, necessary for it as established by the numerous theoretical cases of non-neutralities reviewed in Section 7.1 below and in other chapters of this Handbook (see notably Chapters 18, 13 and 15 by Andreoni, by Laferrère and Wolff, and by Michel, Thibault and Vidal, respectively). Neutrality merely translates in general equilibrium terms the fact that with the assumptions above, and in general with them only, exogenous lump-sum transfers and equilibrium gifts are perfect substitutes: any variation in the exogenous transfer is exactly ("dollar-for-dollar") compensated by an opposite variation in the corresponding equilibrium gift, decided by the donor in order to keep the distribution of wealth unchanged (the best distribution from his point of view, among those he can attain given his budget constraint and the non-negativity of gifts). A simple and important consequence of the property is that gifts and exogenous (say, public) bilateral wealth transfers between the same pair of individual agents (say agents i and j) should not coexist at social equilibrium, as: if gift and exogenous transfer have opposite directions, then an exogenous transfer motivated by an intention to redistribute wealth between i and j is pointless, since the distributive objective of the donor must prevail on the exogenous distributive objective in such circumstances; and if the gift and the exogenous transfer have the same direction, then the exogenous transfer must crowd out the gift (that is, cancel it) in order to modify the equilibrium wealth distribution between i and j.

The third characteristic property states that *if social equilibrium is such that a single agent* (named family or community "head") *gives to all others, then the equilibrium distribution of wealth maximizes this agent's utility relative to the whole set of socially accessible distributions of wealth* (that is, relative to the set of distributions that verify the aggregate resource constraint of the community). The corresponding specific type of social equilibrium, where a single agent gives to all others, is named Becker's social equilibrium in the sequel. Two notable consequences follow, as simple corollaries, from this third characteristic property. Firstly, the social equilibrium trivially is a Pareto optimum relative to individual preferences on the distribution of wealth, since any socially accessible deviation from equilibrium distribution makes the family head worse off. Secondly, the characteristic property above implies Becker's Rotten Kid Theorem when social interactions are embedded in a two-stage sequential game where: the beneficiaries of the head's gifts play first, by (possibly) undertaking individual actions that increase social wealth at some cost for them (that is, increase the aggregate wealth of others by an amount larger than the individual cost they incur); the family head plays next, by making utility-maximizing gifts to all others, given the distribution of wealth which obtains at the first stage. The Rotten Kid Theorem states that, in such sequential games: if the individual wealth of every community member is a normal good for the head, that is, if the individual wealth which maximizes the head's utility is increasing in social wealth, then the egoistic beneficiaries of the head's gifts (the "rotten kids", who feel concerned only with their own wealth and welfare) seize all opportunities to maximize social wealth, because they know that, due to the altruistic behavior of the family head, this maximizes their individual wealth.

The fourth characteristic property states that *non-strategic cooperation in altruistic gift-giving results in status quo* (that is, in a social equilibrium without any individual or collective gift) *if and only if the initial distribution of wealth endowments is a distributive optimum.* The latter property requires, in general, additional assumptions on preferences. A natural sufficient condition states that: progressive wealth transfers[7] between any pair of agents (say, between individuals i and j) are weakly preferred[8] by all others, that is, are not vetoed by any agent distinct from i and j (this part of the condition is named *non-jealousy* in the sequel, for reasons detailed in Section 6.1.1); and individuals object to any bilateral wealth transfers from themselves to individuals wealthier than themselves (*self-centredness* in the sequel). The condition implies that altruistic gifts, if any, should be progressive (by self-centredness) and therefore weakly preferred to the status quo by non-contributors (by self-centredness and non-jealousy), that is: Pareto-efficient initial distribution implies the status quo. Since, moreover, cooperation implies Pareto-efficiency by definition, the characteristic property above follows from the assumption. A variant of the same reasoning obtains, with identical consequences, when the social system is made of "egoistic poor", only interested in their individual wealth, and "altruistic rich", who feel concerned about the aggregate wealth of the poor and are indifferent to the other rich: charitable gifts, if any, flow from rich to poor, and are preferred to the status quo by non-contributors. Note that the latter social system is formally identical to the standard public good model with additive technology,[9] so that the property above and the social contract solution below apply to the latter as well.

The fourth property provides a firm logical basis for a liberal social contract solution to the public good problem of redistribution (and also, by extension, as just noted, for a social contract solution to the financing of public spending on any set of pure public goods).

A liberal social contract consists of a Pareto-efficient arrangement of individual rights, which is unanimously preferred to an (historical) initial arrangement. Such collective agreements find their raison d'être in the inefficiency of individual or collective interactions, non-strategic or otherwise, notably in the presence of public goods or externalities. The contract necessarily remains implicit in many practical circumstances, due to various sources of contract failure in corresponding contexts, such as informational issues (notably preference revelation problems), transaction costs (for example when the number of concerned individuals is large), and so on. The implementation of corresponding Pareto-improving transfers generally supposes public interventions, therefore, with two main variants for the latter in practice: implementation by the state when the efficiency problem under consideration involves universal common concerns, as in the case of the national provision of a general public good; and, when the efficiency problem concerns a large part of society but can be separately solved in each component of

---

[7] A bilateral wealth transfer between individuals i and j is said to be *progressive* if it reduces, without reverting, the difference in wealth between them.

[8] That is, preferred or indifferent.

[9] With notations which have become standard in the literature, the utility of "rich" i reads $u_i(x_i, G_1, \ldots, G_n)$, where x_i denotes his consumption in the private good (his ophelimity), and G_j the aggregate provision of public good j (for example, the aggregate wealth of the poor of type j). Letting t_{ij} denote i's lump-sum contribution to public good j, which can be voluntary or forced, additive technology reads as: $G_j = \sum_i t_{ij}$ for all j, and most conveniently interprets as the financing of public expenditure by lump-sum transfers from private money wealth.

a partition of it, implementation by a set of public or private collective actions such that each action applies to the relevant social subset and the complete set of actions covers the whole society (as in the case of the national provision of a type of local public good by the autonomous actions of all concerned local authorities). With, in the latter variant, a role of the state which then mainly consists in providing an institutional framework that favors the expression and coordination of decentralized initiatives in favor of the public good.

The specific relevance of the notion in the context of the theory of altruistic gift-giving developed here stems from the public good problem of redistribution, which combines the following interrelated aspects: (i) the common distributive concerns of individuals, embodied in their distributive preferences, make the distribution of wealth a pure (that is, non-excludable and non-rival) public good in the formal sense; (ii) non-cooperative gifts generally yield socially inefficient distribution, notably in the presence of multiple donors (more formally, Nash non-cooperative gift equilibrium with multiple donors generally is Pareto-inefficient: see Section 6.1 and the examples in Section 3.3); (iii) as a first consequence, non-strategic cooperation generally fails to produce any equilibrium with gifts (formally, non-zero strong Nash equilibrium of gifts generally does not exist), with Becker's social equilibrium as sole notable exception; (iv) and, as a joint consequence of the public good problem and neutrality, the achievement of distributive optimum by means of exogenous lump-sum redistributions of initial endowments generally supposes the full crowding-out of private transfers. Except in Becker's equilibrium configuration, the achievement of a distributive optimum therefore supposes a re-arrangement of initial endowments, which, under the additional requirement of unanimous preference, precisely corresponds to a (distributive) liberal social contract. The fourth characteristic property above implies that such liberal social contracts are (status quo) social equilibria relative to the non-strategic interactions and contractual cooperation of rational altruists, when all individuals agree (in the sense of weak preference) that wealth transfers, if any, should flow downwards, from the wealthier to the less wealthy. Several important features of the theory follow from this basic fact, such as the existence and indeterminacy of these Pareto-efficient solutions to the public good problem of redistribution (see Section 6.1.2), and the uniqueness of corresponding social equilibria (see Section 3.4.2).

Note, finally, that the third and fourth characteristic properties provide ex post justifications to the Cournot–Nash behavioral assumption relative to altruistic gift-giving at corresponding social equilibria. In Becker's equilibrium, first, the head has no incentive whatsoever to behave strategically; and the strategic gifts of rotten kids, if any, are strictly self-interested. The status quo equilibrium of distributive liberal social contracts, second, exhaust, by construction, the opportunities of social exchange on the public good (that is, on the distribution of wealth), again leaving no room for strategic deviations of individuals or coalitions in the form of altruistic gifts. Note, nevertheless, that the distributive liberal social contract, like Becker's equilibrium, is potentially compatible with strategic non-altruistic gift-giving, notably through the transfer paradox (see Section 4.3), that is, interactions of voluntary redistribution with market exchange such that: endowment redistribution is substantial enough to significantly alter the system of equilibrium market prices (this presumably supposes large collective gifts); and this change in the terms of trade reveals so beneficial to donors that they end up better off in terms of their own ophelimities (that is, the utility they derive from their individual consumption of market commodities is increased).

2.3. Theory and facts

Let us now address, to finish with, the question of the relations between the theory just outlined and facts.

A characteristic structural feature of the theory is the representation of redistribution by altruistic transfers, and of allocation by the market, as autonomous processes, both operated by the non-strategic or cooperative actions of free rational individuals, and resulting in mutually compatible and Pareto-efficient outcomes, that is, respectively, distributive optimum and market optimum.

The main axiomatic constituents underlying this structural feature are: Walrasian economy; non-paternalistic utility interdependence; lump-sum transfers; Cournot–Nash interactions; and free contracting.

The first four elements of this list of constituents form a general hypothesis of perfect substitutability of transfers, as they are sufficient, and in general necessary for the separability and neutrality properties of social equilibrium (first and second characteristic properties).

When transfers are motivated by universal distributive concerns, and there is a unanimous (weak) preference for redistributing, and also sufficient conformity of individual preferences on redistribution (e.g. self-centredness and non-jealousy), the perfect substitutability of transfers generally implies the full crowding out of all private individual transfers at distributive liberal social contract (fourth characteristic property). In that sense, the theory predicts a redistributive welfare state.

Social contracting also provides partial (that is, ceteris paribus) solutions to social efficiency problems when common concerns are restricted to social sub-groups, as in the case of local public goods or club goods. In such contexts, the perfect substitutability of transfers might permit, possibly in association with other assumptions, to consistently combine the partial social contracts into a universal liberal social contract, by allowing for a separate treatment of all partial efficiency problems at an adequate sub-society level. This trivially is the case, for example, in the one-commodity setup, when distributive concerns partition society in a set of "families" in the sense of Becker (that is, of small groups of closely related individuals, who benefit from the altruistic gifts of a family head, and whose altruistic sentiments, if any, are reserved to group members; note that, in this very simple case, the liberal social contract is implemented without any public intervention, by the altruistic gifts of family heads). Interesting issues concerning such decentralized variants of the liberal social contract relate to the dynamics of public good provision in a context of competition of local public and/or private initiatives for the public good, and, in particular, to the corresponding variants of the Coase conjecture as statements relative to the shape and evolution of social equilibrium in the long run (see notably Sections 7.1.3 and 7.2 below).

The possible sources of gaps between theory and facts are transparent from the list of constituents above. They may consist of: market failures; distortionary transfers; individual motives of non-market transfers distinct from altruistic redistributive motives (that is, from motives of maximization of altruistic non-paternalistic interdependent utilities); and the various conceivable impediments to social contracting on public goods, such as costs of information, transaction or enforcement, and possibilities of strategic manipulations. They can be grouped into two large categories.

One consists of the imperfect substitutability of transfers (see Section 7). This refers to forms of complex interdependency between non-market transfers and market allocation, or between non-market transfers themselves. Imperfect substitutability may notably result in violations of the neutrality property, and also in the non-separability of non-market redistribution from market allocation. Non-separability may stem in particular from imperfections in transfer techniques (distortionary taxes, essentially). It may derive, alternatively, from imperfections in the functioning of markets, which are susceptible, notably, to inefficiently bind altruistic redistributive transfers, by superimposing market exchange motives (that is, ophelimity-maximizing motives) upon their original altruistic motives, in situations where the two types of motives cannot be simultaneously fulfilled (a type of second-best problem). Non-neutralities may follow from the two sources above and also, in addition, from the existence of alternative transfer motives, distinct both from market exchange motives and altruistic redistributive motives, such as: tutelary motives, which imply the use of transfers as a means of control on beneficiaries' behavior or conduct; and the various motives which imply that transfers matter per se, independently of their influence on wealth distribution or market allocation (joy of giving, "warm glow", demonstration effects, reciprocity motives etc). They may also derive, finally, from the existence of strategic transfers, notably when they stem from non-altruistic motives (for example strategic bequests and transfer paradoxes). In all such cases, social interactions generally involve some degree of complementarity between public and private redistributive transfers, which can contribute to explain the lasting coexistence of both types of transfer at social equilibrium in the long run (see Sections 7.1 and 7.2.2).

The second category of potential gaps between theory and facts consists of the practical limits to social contracting on public goods, essentially transaction costs and issues of imperfect information, enforceability and manipulability. These problems remain largely unexplored for redistribution as a public good (see nevertheless the remarks and references of Sections 6.3 and A.2 concerning the design of incentive compatible mechanisms in public good economies). They explain why the distributive liberal social contract is bound to remain partly implicit in many practical circumstances, and generally requires public interventions for its implementation. The efficacy of public action and its limitations in terms of the various administrative costs and other disadvantages associated with it contribute, in turn, to determine the practical size and shape of the transfers of the actual social contract.[10]

3. Perfectly substitutable transfers in a pure distributive social system

This section considers the simplest version of the present theory, where individuals interact non-strategically and non-cooperatively by means of altruistic individual gifts of a single commodity ("money wealth"). That is, we concentrate on the (generalized) Nash non-cooperative equilibrium of individual gifts (Section 3.1.2) of pure distributive social systems (Section 3.1.1).

This simple setup is illustrated in Section 3.3, through three classical applications to family gift-giving [Becker (1974)], Pareto-efficient redistribution [Arrow (1981)], and the private provision of public goods [Bergstrom, Blume and Varian (1986)]. These three studies retain the same non-strategic, non-cooperative scheme of social interactions for altruistic gift-giving. They differ in the nature and scope of the altruistic concerns they consider: *microsocial* family altruism with Becker; "*mesosocial*" charitable altruism from rich to poor with Bergstrom et al.; and altruistic concerns for distributive justice (nevertheless biased by some degree of self-centredness) at *macrosocial* level in Arrow's study. Special attention is devoted, in the presentation of these studies, to the *public good problem of redistribution*. We notably provide several graphical examples, using the geometric device introduced in Section 3.2, which substantiate the contention (formulated in Section 2 above as consequence of the third and fourth characteristic properties, and established in Section 6.1 below) that, except in the specific type of equilibrium configuration considered by Becker, non-trivial (that is, non-zero) gift equilibrium generally is Pareto-inefficient relative to individual distributive preferences.

The last Section 3.4 reviews known results on the existence and determinacy of the non-cooperative equilibrium of individual gifts of pure distributive social systems.

---

[10] Social contract theory traditionally defines the social contract relative to some hypothetical initial position (a hypothetical "state of nature", "original position" etc.), where the contingent obstacles to social contracting are consistently assumed away [the nature of the contingent obstacles so removed depending on the nature of the social contract considered; e.g. Kolm (2003)]. Rawl's theory of justice, for example, uses this type of hypothetical device for abstracting from individual characteristics, as contingent obstacles to the impartiality of individual judgments of justice: individuals are thus placed, by hypothesis, under a "veil of ignorance" relative to their actual position in society. The liberal social contract, likewise, is defined relative to an ideal state of society, where the contingent obstacles which are abstractly assumed away are the impediments to (generalized) exchange per se (mainly, transaction costs and enforcement issues). These *abstract social contracts* define ideal norms for public action. Their implementation by public policies is subject, in turn, to the actual limitations of public action. *Actual social contract* policies then consist of the set of public actions, rational and democratic by construction, which implement the ideal norm of the abstract social contract within the practical limits of actual public action.

3.1. Pure distributive social system and equilibrium

3.1.1. Pure distributive social systems

Pure distributive social systems are defined as abstract social systems where: (i) wealth is measured in money units and divisible; (ii) wealth is shared initially among individual owners; (iii) owners can, individually, consume or transfer to others any amount of their ownership, that is, of their initial endowment increased by the gifts received from others; (iv) owners make their consumption and transfer decisions according to their preferences on the final distribution of wealth, that is, on the vector of individual consumption expenditures; (v) aggregate wealth is fixed, which implies notably that the latter is independent of individual consumption and transfer decisions.

Formally, let individuals be designated by an index i running in $N = \{1, \ldots, n\}$, and choose the money unit so that aggregate wealth is 1.

Individual i's *initial endowment* or *right*, that is, his share in total wealth prior consumption or transfer is denoted by $\omega_i \in [0, 1]$.

A *consumption* x_i of individual i is the money value of his consumption of commodities. A *gift* t_{ij} *from individual i to individual j* ($j \neq i$) is a non-negative money transfer from individual i's property (his initial endowment plus the gifts he received from others) to individual j's. A *gift-vector of individual i* is a vector[11] $t_i = (t_{ij})_{j \in N \setminus \{i\}}$ of $\mathbb{R}_+^{n-1}$.

We ignore alternative individual uses of wealth, like disposal or production, as well as "transaction" costs (including taxes) associated with consumption and transfer activities. The property rights (jus utendi et abutendi) of individuals translate then into the following budget identity, which holds for all individual i, endowment ω_i, and decision (x_i, t_i):

$$x_i + \sum_{j:\ j \neq i} t_{ij} = \omega_i + \sum_{j:\ j \neq i} t_{ji}.$$

A distribution of initial rights $(\omega_1, \ldots, \omega_n)$ is denoted by ω. This is an element of the unit simplex $S_n = \{x \in \mathbb{R}_+^n : \sum_{i \in N} x_i = 1\}$ of $\mathbb{R}^n$. A distribution of individual consumption expenditures $(x_1, \ldots, x_n)$ is denoted by x. It is *feasible* if it belongs to S_n. A *gift vector* t is a vector $(t_1, \ldots, t_n)$. Individuals have ordinal preferences on the final distribution of wealth, that is, on the vectors of individual consumption expenditures, represented by their *distributive utility functions* $w_i : x \to w_i(x)$, defined on the space of consumption distributions $\mathbb{R}^n$. These preferences may express individual moral sentiments such as benevolence, malevolence or indifference to others, but also individual opinions of distributive justice relative, for instance, to the equity or fairness of the distribution of wealth. I will say notably that an individual is benevolent or altruistic (resp.

---

[11] Notations like t, t_i, $(t_{ij})_{j \in I}$ or t_I (where I is a subset of N), will refer to row vectors. The entries t_{ij} of these vectors are ranked in increasing lexicographic order (that is, according to the ordering defined on $N \times N$ by: $(i, j) > (i', j')$ if either $i > i'$ or $i = i'$ and $j > j'$).

malevolent, resp. indifferent or egoistic) to another individual in the neighbourhood of a distribution x if the former's utility is locally increasing (resp. decreasing, resp. constant) in the latter's wealth.

The vector $(w_1, \ldots, w_n)$ of individual utility functions is denoted by w.

A *distributive social system* is a pair (w, ω).

We use the following notations. t^T is the transpose of row vector t. $t_{\setminus i}$ (resp. t_I, resp. $t_{\setminus I}$) is the vector of gifts obtained from t by deleting t_i (resp. t_i for all $i \notin I$, resp. t_i for all $i \in I$). $(t_{\setminus i}, t_i^*)$ (resp. $(t_{\setminus I}, t_I^*)$) is the gift-vector obtained from t and t^* by substituting t_i^* for t_i (resp. t_i^* for t_i for all $i \in I$) in t. $\Delta_i t$ is the net transfer $\sum_{j:\, j \neq i}(t_{ji} - t_{ij})$ accruing to individual i when t is the gift-vector. Δt is the vector of net transfers $(\Delta_1 t, \ldots, \Delta_n t)$. $x(\omega, t)$ is the vector of individual consumption expenditures $\omega + \Delta t = (\omega_1 + \Delta_1 t, \ldots, \omega_n + \Delta_n t)$, that is, given the accounting identity above, the unique consumption distribution associated with the distribution of rights ω and the gift-vector t. $x_i(\omega, t)$ is the ith projection $\mathrm{pr}_i\, x(\omega, t) = \omega_i + \Delta_i t$. $\partial_t x(\omega, t)$ (resp. $\partial_{t_i} x_i(\omega, t)$) is the Jacobian matrix of $t \to x(\omega, t)$ (resp. $t_i \to x_i(\omega, t)$) at (ω, t). Finally, for any pair $(z, z') = ((z_1, \ldots, z_n), (z'_1, \ldots, z'_n))$ of vectors of $\mathbb{R}^n$, we write: $z \geqslant z'$ if $z_i \geqslant z'_i$ for all i; $z > z'$ if $z \geqslant z'$ and $z \neq z'$; $z \gg z'$ if $z_i > z'_i$ for all i.

3.1.2. Distributive equilibrium

This subsection defines the gift equilibrium as a Nash non-cooperative equilibrium of individual gifts, and provides a characterization of gift equilibrium for differentiable social systems.

3.1.2.1. Definition The general notion of social equilibrium according to Debreu (1952),[12] applied to the pure distributive social system, becomes the following: every individual agent takes the transfers of others as fixed, and maximizes his utility with respect to his own gifts, subject to the constraint that his consumption be non-negative. An equilibrium is a gift vector that solves all individual maximization problems simultaneously. Formally:

DEFINITION 1. A *distributive equilibrium* of (w, ω) is a gift-vector t^* such that t_i^* is a maximum of $t_i \to w_i(x(\omega, (t_{\setminus i}^*, t_i)))$ in $\{t_i\colon x_i(\omega, (t_{\setminus i}^*, t_i)) \geqslant 0\}$ for all i.

---

[12] This notion is often labeled "Cournot–Nash" equilibrium, by reference to its early definitions by Auguste Cournot (1838), and John R. Nash (1950) [see for instance Cornes and Sandler (1986, Chapter 5)]. Modern game theory often refers to it as "generalized Nash equilibrium". I will stick to the vocabulary of Gérard Debreu in the sequel, because it fits well the substantive object of the theory reviewed in this chapter, and moreover corresponds to the words (if not the precise notion) of Vilfredo Pareto in the pioneering Chapter 12 of his *Traité de Sociologie Générale* (1916, §2067 to 2078, pp. 1308–1315). Note that Debreu's main application of his general notion was the proof of existence of a competitive economic equilibrium [Arrow and Debreu (1954)].

For a fixed w, I define the following equilibrium sets and correspondences. $T_w(\omega) = \{t: t$ is a distributive equilibrium of $(w, \omega)\}$ is the set of equilibrium gift-vectors of (w, ω); $X_w(\omega) = \{x: \exists t \in T_w(\omega)$ such that $x = x(\omega, t)\}$ is the corresponding set of equilibrium distributions; $\Omega_w(x) = \{\omega: \exists t \in T_w(\omega)$ such that $x = x(\omega, t)\}$ is the set of initial distributions ω supporting x as an equilibrium distribution of (w, ω). $T_w : \omega \to T_w(\omega)$ is then the *equilibrium correspondence* of w, $X_w : \omega \to X_w(\omega)$ is its *equilibrium distribution correspondence*, and $\Omega_w : x \to \Omega_w(x)$ is the *inverse equilibrium distribution correspondence*. The *range* of X_w (and domain of Ω_w) will be denoted by M_w. The *range* of Ω_w (and domain of T_w and X_w) is denoted by Q_w. The subscript w will be omitted in the sequel.

3.1.2.2. First-order conditions The remainder of the chapter is restricted to differentiable distributive social systems[13] that verify the following standard assumptions:

ASSUMPTION 1. For all i: (i) w_i is differentiable (smooth preferences); (ii) w_i is quasi-concave (convex preferences: $w_i(x) \geqslant w_i(x')$ implies $w_i(\lambda x + (1-\lambda)x') \geqslant w_i(x')$ for all real number $\lambda \in [0, 1]$); (iii) w_i is strictly increasing in x_i (utility increasing in own wealth); (iv) and $\omega_i > 0$.

Let $W = \{(w, \omega): (w, \omega)$ verifies Assumption 1$\}$.

The first-order conditions characterizing equilibrium are given in Theorem 1 below.[14] Informally, these conditions state that, at equilibrium, a marginal incremental wealth transfer from i to j is either impossible or does not increase i's utility, and that a marginal incremental wealth transfer from j to i does not increase i's utility whenever the equilibrium transfer from i to j is positive.

THEOREM 1. *Let* $(w, \omega) \in W$. *Then, t is a distributive equilibrium of $(w, \omega) \in W \times S_n$ if and only if for all (i, j): (i) Either $x_i(\omega, t) = 0$ or $-\partial_{x_i} w_i(x(\omega, t)) + \partial_{x_j} w_i(x(\omega, t)) \leqslant 0$; (ii) and $(-\partial_{x_i} w_i(x(\omega, t)) + \partial_{x_j} w_i(x(\omega, t)))t_{ij} = 0$.*

PROOF. Let t^* be a distributive equilibrium of $(w, \omega) \in W \times S_n$. Inequalities (i) and (ii) of Theorem 1 are the first-order conditions for a maximum of $t_i \to w_i(x(\omega, (t^*_{\setminus i}, t_i)))$ in $\{t_i \in \mathbb{R}^{n-1}_+ : x_i(\omega, (t^*_{\setminus i}, t_i)) \geqslant 0\}$. These conditions are necessary by Assumption 1(iv) and Arrow and Enthoven (1961: Theorem 2). They are sufficient by Assumption 1 and Arrow and Enthoven (1961: Theorem 1(b)). □

---

[13] A natural strategy for the study of continuous social systems (that is, social systems with continuous individual preference preorderings) consists of "smoothing" them by means of appropriate approximation techniques, and examining then whether, as is often the case, the properties of smooth social systems extend by continuity to continuous ones. This is done, for instance, in Mercier Ythier (1992), for the existence of a social equilibrium in pure distributive social systems.
[14] Where $\partial_{x_j} w_i(x)$ denotes the partial derivative of w_i with respect to its jth argument, and $\partial w_i(x)$ the Jacobian matrix of w_i at x.

The characterization of M and Ω below is a simple consequence of Theorem 1. Let:

$$g(t) = \{(i, j) \in N \times N \colon t_{ij} > 0\};$$

$$\gamma_w(x) = \{(i, j) \in N \times N \colon -\partial_{x_i} w_i(x(\omega, t)) + \partial_{x_j} w_i(x(\omega, t)) = 0\}.$$

These sets will be viewed as directed graphs or digraphs. The *incidence matrix* $\Gamma_{w,i}(x)$ is the $(n, n-1)$-matrix defined in the following way: the rows of $\Gamma_{w,i}(x)$ are associated with the elements (vertices) of N, ranked in increasing order; the columns of $\Gamma_{w,i}(x)$ are associated with the elements (darts) of $\{(i, j) \in N \times N \colon j \neq i\}$, ranked in increasing lexicographic order; if $(i, j) \in \gamma_w(x)$ is such that $i \neq j$, the entries of the corresponding column of $\Gamma_{w,i}(x)$ are -1 on row i, 1 on row j, 0 on the other rows; if $(i, j) \notin \gamma_w(x)$, the entries of the corresponding column of $\Gamma_{w,i}(x)$ are 0 on all rows. The incidence matrix $\Gamma_w(x)$ of $\gamma_w(x)$ is the $(n, n(n-1))$-matrix: $(\Gamma_{w,1}(x), \ldots, \Gamma_{w,n}(x))$. The subscript w will be omitted in subsequent notations of graphs and incidence matrices.

We have then the following corollary:

COROLLARY 1. *Let w verify Assumption 1, and suppose moreover that $M \subset \mathbb{R}^n_{++}$. Then:* (i) $M = \{x \in S_n \cap \mathbb{R}^n_{++} \colon -\partial_{x_i} w_i(x) + \partial_{x_j} w_i(x) \leqslant 0 \text{ for all } (i, j)\}$. (ii) *For all $x \in M$, $\Omega(x)$ is the convex set* $\{x - \Gamma(x).t^T \in S_n \colon t \in \mathbb{R}^{n(n-1)}_+\} = \{x - \Gamma(x).t^T \in S_n \colon g(t) \subset \gamma(x)\}$, *of dimension* rank $\Gamma(x)$.

PROOF. (i) If $t \in T(\omega)$, then $x(\omega, t) \in \{x \in S_n \colon -\partial_{x_i} w_i(x) + \partial_{x_j} w_i(x) \leqslant 0$ for all $(i, j)\}$ by Theorem 1. Conversely, if $\omega \in \{x \in S_n \colon -\partial_{x_i} w_i(x) + \partial_{x_j} w_i(x) \leqslant 0$ for all $(i, j)\}$, then $0 \in T(\omega)$ by Theorem 1.

(ii) Notice that: $\Gamma(x).t^T = \Gamma(x).(0_{\setminus \gamma(x)}, t_{\gamma(x)})^T$ for all t. Suppose therefore without loss of generality that $g(t) \subset \gamma(x)$. Notice then that $\Gamma(x).t^T = (\Delta_1 t, \ldots, \Delta_n t)$ and apply Corollary 1(i), Theorem 1 and the definition of Ω. □

3.2. Diagrammatic representation

Individual preferences relative to the distribution of wealth make each individual's wealth a public good, at least potentially.

More formally, the consumption x_i of individual i is a public good (or bad) at some distribution x if there exists at least another agent j whose utility is either increasing (public good) or decreasing (public bad) in i's consumption at x, that is, if $\partial_{x_i} w_j(x) \neq 0$ for some $j \neq i$. Individual i's consumption is then a common concern for both i (due to the natural assumption of utility increasing in own wealth: Assumption 1(iii) above) and j. This is a *pure* public good in this setting: its "consumption" by individual j consists of his observation of x_i, which has the two classic properties of non-rivalry (observation by j induces no restriction on observation by k) and non-excludability (x_i is correctly observed by all concerned agents).[15] The public good is local if $\{j: \partial_{x_i} w_j(x) \neq 0\}$ is some relevant ("small") subset of N, general otherwise and notably when $\{j: \partial_{x_i} w_j(x) \neq 0\} = N$ (universal common concern).

The diagrammatic representation of distributive social systems presented below is adapted from a geometric device first used by Kolm (1969, Chapter 9), and since often referred to as Kolm's triangle [Thomson (1999)]. Ley (1996) gives a good account of the use of Kolm's technique in models of private provision of public goods, as well as a presentation of frequently used alternative techniques such as the Dolbear triangle (1967) and the diagrams of Cornes and Sandler (notably 1985a, Figure 6, p. 112, and the Cornes–Sandler box, 1986, Figure 5.3, p. 77).[16] The present application of the diagram to the analysis of voluntary redistribution was developed by Mercier Ythier (1989, 1993).

The choice of this geometric device is essentially related to the fact that the elicitation of the so-called public good problem, that is, in this context, the elicitation of the Pareto-inefficiency of distributive equilibrium, requires the existence of at least three agents. We recall and establish in Section 6.1.1.2 below the simple fact that the distributive equilibrium must be Pareto-efficient when the number of agents is $n = 2$ [Nakayama (1980)].

The set $S_3 = \{x \in \mathbb{R}^3_+ : \sum_{i=1}^3 x_i = 1\}$ of feasible distributions of wealth of a three-agent social system is represented, in the canonical system of Euclidean coordinates of $\mathbb{R}^3$, by the equilateral triangle $O_1 O_2 O_3$ (Figure 1), where O_i denotes the element of $\mathbb{R}^3$ whose ith coordinate is $= 1$ and jth coordinate is $= 0$ for all $j \neq i$. Any point of the triangle reads therefore as a vector of individual shares in the unit of aggregate wealth available for individual ownership or consumption. We abstract from the axes but maintain the Euclidean coordinates in the subsequent representations of S_3, which means that the plane of physical representation is implicitly identified with the Euclidean plane $\{x \in \mathbb{R}^3 : \sum_{i=1}^3 x_i = 1\}$.[17]

The loci of the feasible distributions with a constant $x_i \in [0, 1[$, or isowealth lines of individual i, are the straight lines parallel to $O_j O_k$, where $j \neq i$ and $k \neq i, j$, that is, the straight lines parallel to the side of the triangle opposite to O_i (cf. Figure 2, with $i = 1$; x_1 increases south east, from 0 at segment $O_2 O_3$ to 1 at point O_1).

Figure 3 represents the indifference map of an individual (say, agent 1) whose preferences are convex and benevolent. Distribution x^1 is the best feasible distribution for

---

[15] Non-rivalry is clearly an innocuous feature of the setup. Non-excludability, on the contrary, appears much more demanding, in that it does not take into account interesting situations of the real world, where individuals feel concerned about the wealth of others that they do not observe correctly. In other words, this analytical framework recognizes only two types of agents: those who feel concerned about the wealth of some other agent and observe it correctly; and those who are indifferent to the latter.

[16] See also, among others, Chamberlin (1974) and Danziger (1976).

[17] This makes several differences with the usual definition of Kolm's triangle, notably: there are three agents and, at least potentially, three public goods (and, potentially again, no private good), instead of the two agents, the two private goods and the single public good of the usual versions of Kolm's triangle.

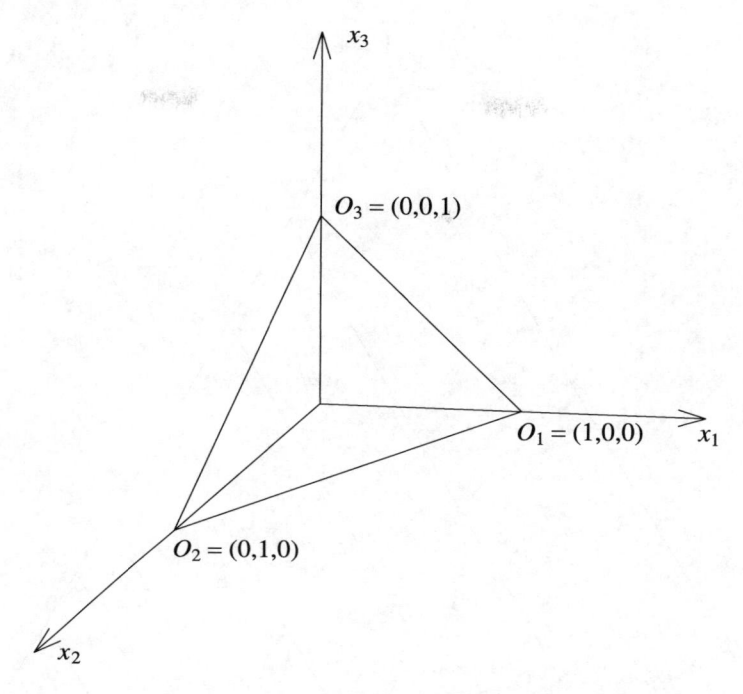

Figure 1. Feasible wealth distributions.

agent 1, that is, the distribution that maximizes $w_1(x)$ in S_3. More generally, the best feasible distribution of agent i will be denoted by x^i in the sequel.

Figure 4 provides the geometric device for the determination of the sign of $-\partial_{x_i} w_i(x) + \partial_{x_j} w_i(x)$ for relevant feasible distributions x, that is, of the sign of the consequence on i's utility of a marginal wealth transfer from i to j at x. We let $i = 1$ and suppose for simplicity that w_1 is strictly quasi-concave. The curve $x^1 m^{1j}$ ($j = 2, 3$) is the locus of tangent points of the indifference map of agent 1 in S_3 with the isowealth lines $\{x \in S_3 : x_k = c, k \neq 1, j\}$ such that $c \geqslant x_k^1$. In view of Assumption 1, $x^1 m^{1j}$ is equivalently the set $\{x \in S_3 : -\partial_{x_1} w_1(x) + \partial_{x_j} w_1(x) = 0;$ and $x_k \geqslant x_k^1, k \neq 1, j\}$, that is, the subset of $\{x \in S_3 : x_k \geqslant x_k^1, k \neq 1, j\}$ where agent 1's utility is stationary with respect to marginal wealth transfers between individual j and himself. The strict quasi-concavity of w_1 readily implies then that $-\partial_{x_1} w_1(x) + \partial_{x_j} w_1(x) < 0$ (resp. > 0) when x is obtained from some distribution of $x^1 m^{1j}$ by means of a wealth transfer from 1 to j (resp. from j to 1), that is, when x is a distribution of the isowealth line $\{x \in S_3 : x_k = x_k^*, k \neq 1, j\}$ such that $x_1 < x_1^*$ (resp. $x_1 > x_1^*$) for some x^* of $x^1 m^{1j}$.

Figure 5 replicates the construct of Figure 4 for all three agents. The range $M = \{x \in S_n \cap \mathbb{R}_{++}^n : -\partial_{x_i} w_i(x) + \partial_{x_j} w_i(x) \leqslant 0$ for all $(i, j)\}$ (Corollary 1(i)) of the correspondence of equilibrium distributions is the area shaded gray. The values of the inverse equilibrium correspondence $\Omega(x)$ are easily represented from the values of the

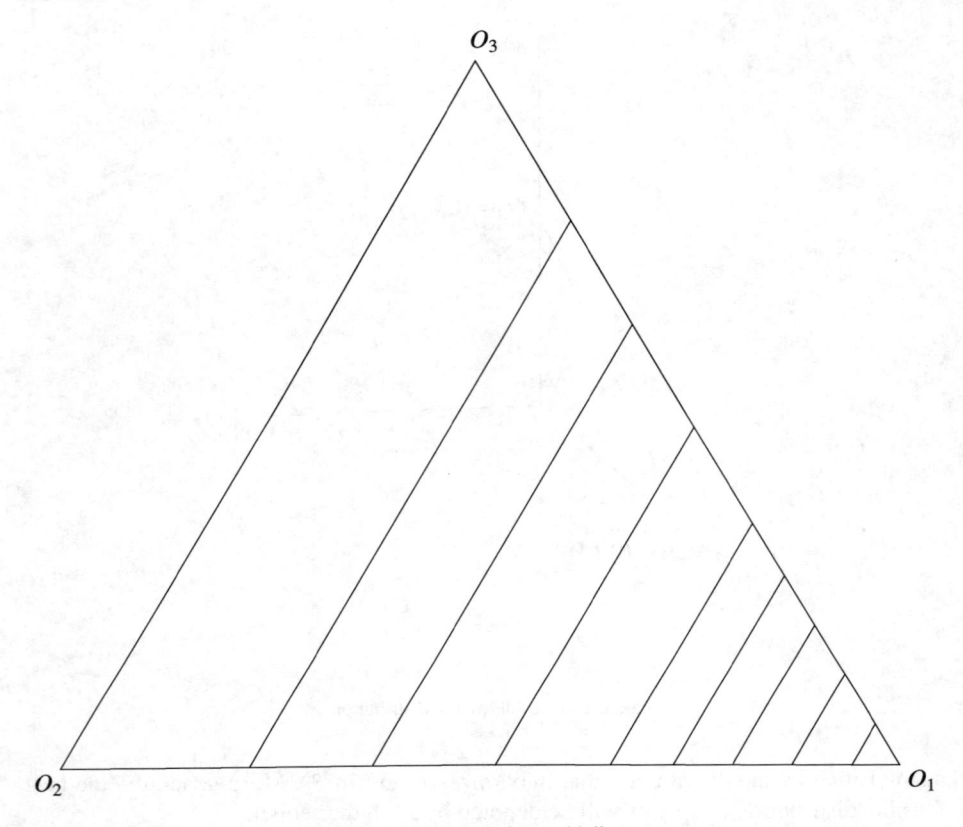

Figure 2. Agent 1's isowealth lines.

digraph $\gamma(x)$ at equilibrium distributions $x \in M$. Recall that $\gamma(x)$ is defined as $\{(i, j) \in N \times N: -\partial_{x_i} w_i(x) + \partial_{x_j} w_i(x) = 0\}$. The subdigraph $\{(i, j) \in \gamma(x): i \neq j\}$ corresponds therefore to the digraph of potential equilibrium gifts at x (potential because t_{ij} and $-\partial_{x_i} w_i(x) + \partial_{x_j} w_i(x)$ can be simultaneously $= 0$ at equilibrium). One verifies then in Figure 5 that: $\gamma(x^i) = \{(i, j): j \in N\}$; $\{(i, j) \in \gamma(z^k): i \neq j\} = \{(i, k): i \neq k\}$; $\{(j, m) \in \gamma(x): j \neq m\} = \{(i, k)\}$ if x is an element of the topological boundary ∂M of M between x^i and z^k; $\gamma(x) = \varnothing$ if x is in the topological interior Int M of M. $\Omega(x)$ is then: $\{x\}$ if $x \in \text{Int } M$; the line segment $\{\omega \in S_3: \omega_i \geqslant x_i \text{ and } \omega_k = x_k \text{ for } k \neq i, j\}$ if $x \in \partial M$ is between x^i and z^j; the triangle $\{\omega \in S_3: \omega_j \geqslant x_j \text{ for all } j \neq i\}$ if $x = z^i$; the parallelogram $\{\omega \in S_3: \omega_j \leqslant x_j \text{ for all } j \neq i\}$ if $x = x^i$. $\Omega(x)$ is, therefore, geometrically, at any $x \in \partial M$, the intersection with S_n of the convex cone generated by the set of half-tangents, outward pointing relative to M, to the indifference curves of the potential donors at x, that is, to the indifference curves of agents i such that $(i, j) \in \gamma(x)$ for some $j \neq i$.

Ch. 5: *The Economic Theory of Gift-Giving*

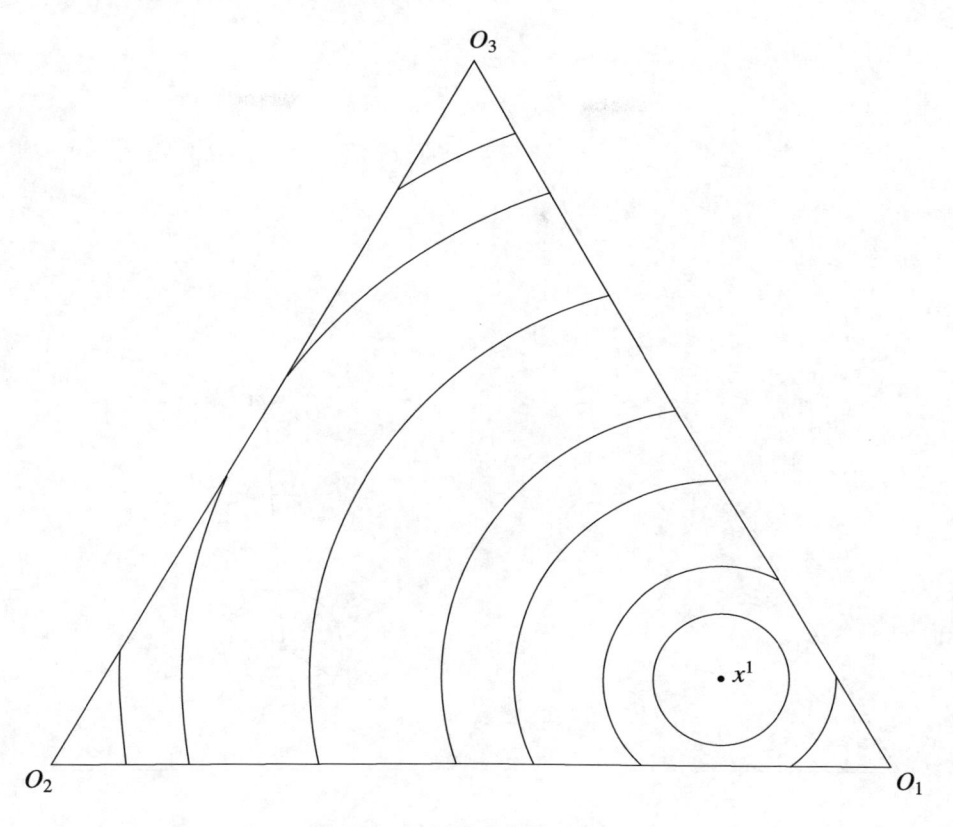

Figure 3. Agent 1's indifference map.

If w_i is the Cobb–Douglas $(x_1, x_2, x_3) \to \beta_{i1} \ln x_1 + \beta_{i2} \ln x_2 + \beta_{i3} \ln x_3$, with $\beta^i = (\beta_{i1}, \beta_{i2}, \beta_{i3}) \in S_3$, then $x^i = \beta^i$ and $x^i m^{ij}$ is the line segment $\beta^i O_k$ such that $k \neq i, j$ (Figure 6).

3.3. Three studies of pure distributive equilibrium

We now examine three classic studies of the distributive equilibrium that were decisive for the elaboration and subsequent popularization of the concept in economic analyses of voluntary redistribution, namely, Becker's "Theory of social interactions" (1974), Arrow's "Optimal and voluntary redistribution" (1981) and Bergstrom, Blume and Varian's "On the private provision of public goods" (1986).

We will show how the three models relate to the general setup of Section 3.1, elicit their particular assumptions with respect to the latter, and recall the salient properties of their respective equilibria, regarding notably their efficiency.

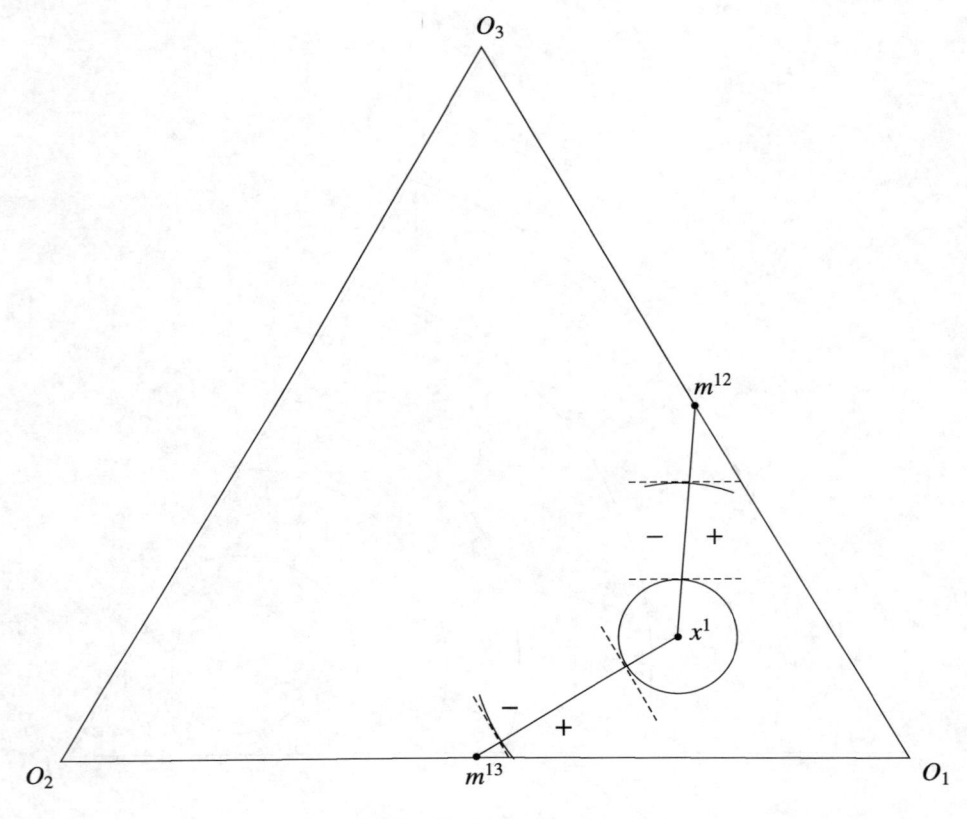

Figure 4. Sign of $-\partial_{x_1} w_1(x) + \partial_{x_j} w_1(x)$.

3.3.1. Becker (1974): The theory of social interactions

Becker's theory concentrates typically on social interactions in small groups, essentially the family. Interactions consist mainly of altruistic wealth transfers, although extensions to merit wants and malevolence are also considered and discussed at some length. The theory concentrates specifically on equilibria where a single agent (the "head") makes altruistic transfers to all other members of the group.[18]

The theory is presented initially in the framework of the household production model, where individual utility depends on a list of basic commodities that are produced from market goods and services, own time, education and the characteristics of others. But this general framework is immediately specialized by assuming a single commodity,

---

[18] This can be viewed as a definition of the social group in Becker's theory. In other words, Becker studies the social groups shaped by the altruistic equilibrium transfers of heads.

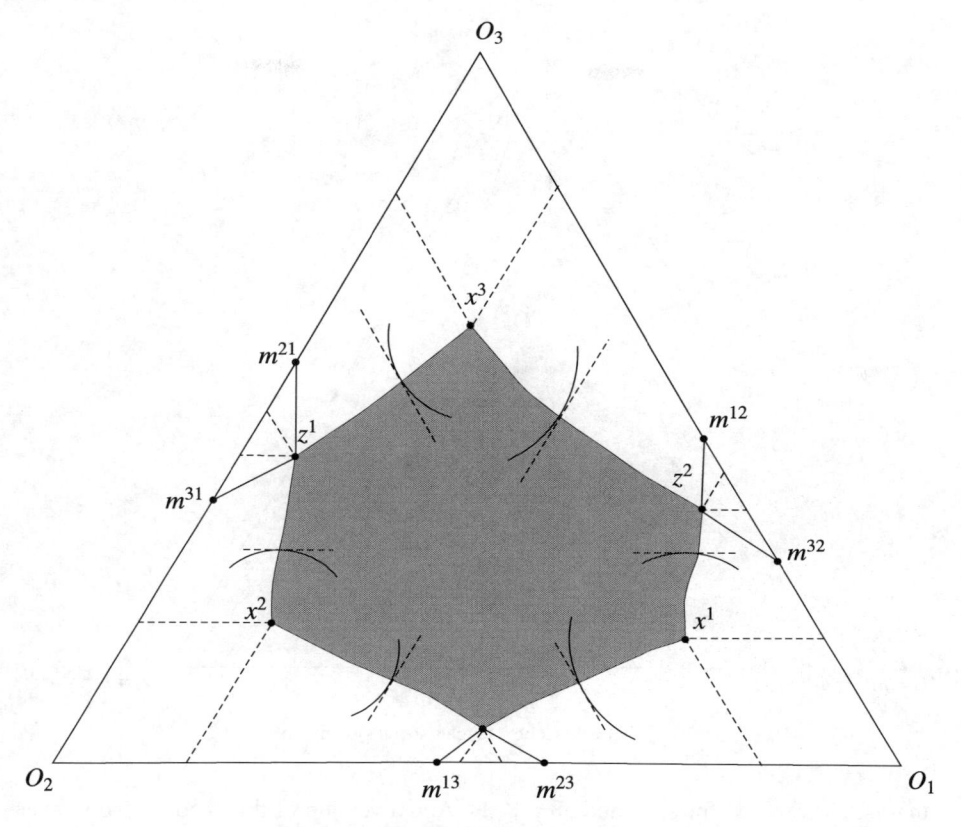

Figure 5. Inverse equilibrium correspondence.

a single market good and a single characteristic of others, so that utility derives from the individual consumption of a single market good and from a single characteristic of others.

The latter is identified in applications (family and charity) to the consumption of market good of the beneficiary of transfers. Let our set $N = \{1, \ldots, n\}$ designate a family in the sense of Becker, that is, the small group made of a head (say, $i = 1$) and the beneficiaries of his altruistic transfers. The utility functions of family members are then of the type $w_i(x_1, \ldots, x_n)$. The head is altruistic to the other members of the family. This translates formally into the strict monotonicity of w_1 (that is, $w_1(x) > w_1(x')$ whenever $x > x'$). Characteristically, Becker does not make any explicit assumption on the distributive preferences of non-heads (but the usual requirements of convexity and utility increasing in own wealth). He only assumes, implicitly, that their altruism, if any, is not strong enough to determine them to make gifts at equilibrium. His "Rotten Kid Theorem" (1974, 3.A, p. 1080; and 1976, p. 820) explicitly assumes selfish beneficiaries

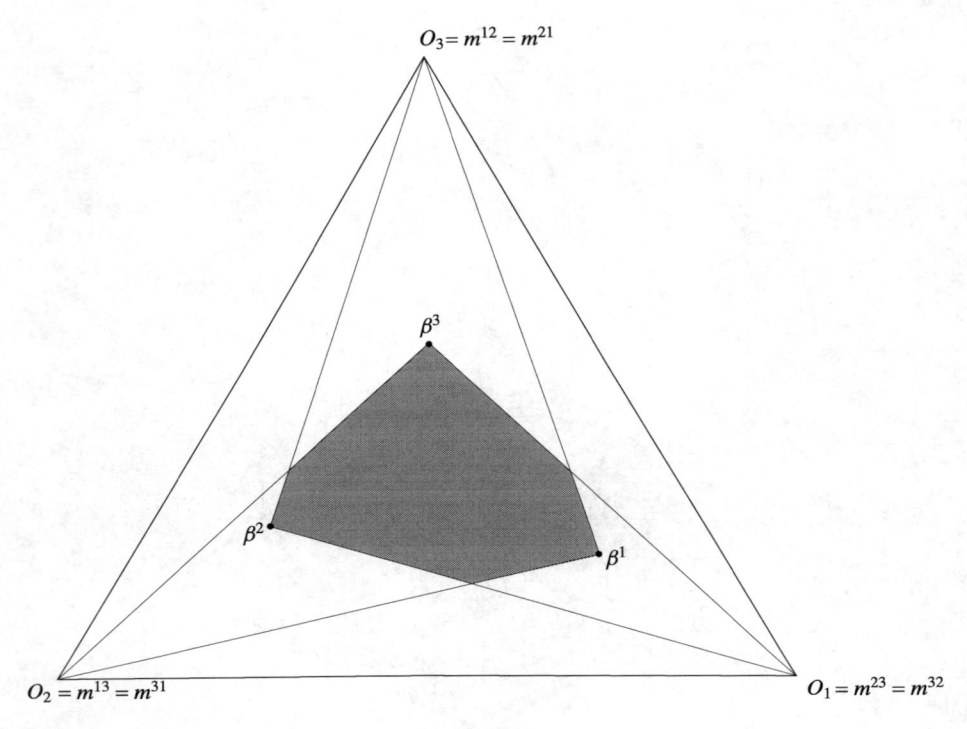

Figure 6. Cobb–Douglas social system.

(that is, $w_i(x) = x_i$ for all x and all $i \neq 1$). And a version of this theorem, in Becker (1981a, corollary, p. 183) or (1981b, p. 7), applies to malevolent ("envious", in Becker's terminology) beneficiaries.

The head chooses his consumption and levels of effort enhancing the characteristics of others so as to maximize the utility function above, subject to the budget constraint for money income: $x_1 + \sum_{j:\, j \neq 1} t_{1j} = \omega_1$.[19] Since the head is the sole donor in Becker's construct, the budget constraint of any other member of the family reads: $x_i = \omega_i + t_{1i}$, or equivalently $x_i - \omega_i = t_{1i}$. Substituting into the head's constraint, one gets the following equivalent formulation of the latter: $\sum_{i \in N} x_i = \sum_{i \in N} \omega_i$, where the right-hand side corresponds to the head's "social income" [Becker (1974, p. 1067)]. The

---

[19] Becker adopts the following more general formulation: $p_x x_i + p_t \sum_{j:\, j \neq i} t_{ij}$, for the left-hand side of the head's budget constraint in Sections 1 and 2, where p_x is the price of own consumption and p_t the price to the head of a unit of wealth of others. Discrepancies between p_x and p_t can stem from transaction costs of transfers (that may include the taxes paid on some types of transfers such as bequests or donations), or fiscal incentives such as the deductibility of charitable transfers from taxable income. They are assumed away in applications, nevertheless, and can be easily accommodated in the general framework presented in Section 3.1.1 above.

positive transfers of the head translate equivalently into the inequalities $x_i > \omega_i$ for the other members of the family.

The equilibrium distribution of Becker's microsocial system, therefore: is the (supposed unique) solution x^1 to $\max\{w_1(x): x \in S_n\}$; and is such that $x_i^1 > \omega_i$ for all $i > 1$. In other words, the equilibrium of his version of the distributive social system defined in Section 3.1.1 above is essentially characterized by the following specific features: redistribution is achieved by a single donor, who gives to all family members, and manages to reach his most favored distribution in the whole set of feasible distributions of the family. These peculiarities of the distributive equilibrium of Becker are illustrated in Figures 7 and 8. Figure 7 represents a social system ("family") of three altruistic Cobb–Douglas agents: Becker's equilibrium obtains, with individual 1 (resp. 2, resp. 3) as family head, if and only if the initial distribution ω lies in the parallelogram $\{\omega \in S_3: \omega_j > x_j \text{ for all } j \neq 1 \text{ (resp. 2, resp. 3)}\}$, that is, geometrically, in the relative interior of $\beta^1 a O_1 b$ (resp. $\beta^2 c O_2 d$, resp. $\beta^3 e O_3 f$) in S_3. Figure 8 represents the social system of the Rotten Kid Theorem (see the third basic property of Section 2), with three Cobb–Douglas agents: one altruistic head (individual 1), and two egoistic kids ($w_i(x) = x_i$, $i = 2, 3$). As in Figure 7, Becker's equilibrium obtains if and only if $\omega \in \{\omega \in S_3: \omega_j > x_j^1 \text{ for all } j \neq 1\} = \beta^1 a O_1 b$.

In summary, Becker's configuration of distributive equilibrium is a perfect illustration of what might be called, paraphrasing Boulding (1973, notably p. 27), the "integrative" virtue of gift-giving: the gifts of the head "make" the family, whose equilibrium happens to coincide in turn with the rational choice of its individual head (individual utility-maximizing behavior).

3.3.2. Arrow (1981): Optimal and voluntary income distribution

Arrow's article, and particularly his charity game (pp. 217–223), is formulated directly in the general framework of Section 3.1.1. Its originality or specificity with respect to the latter lies in the assumptions on distributive preferences. Formally, Arrow supposes that there exist $n + 1$ strictly concave, differentiable and increasing functions $\mathbb{R} \to \mathbb{R}$ $\varphi, \varphi_1, \ldots, \varphi_n$, such that, for all i, all $x \in \mathbb{R}^n$ and all $z \in \mathbb{R}$, $w_i(x) = \varphi_i(x_i) + \sum_{j:\ j \neq i} \varphi(x_j)$ and $\partial \varphi_i(z) > \partial \varphi(z)$. This means that, besides their familiar though non-trivial properties of additive separability and strict convexity, the preferences of Arrow's distributive agents exhibit: benevolence (w_i is monotonic strictly increasing); a (strong) variant of self-centredness,[20] stating that a wealth transfer from i to j makes the former worse off whenever their pre-transfer wealth are identical; and identical impartial-utilitarian views on redistribution affecting others.

---

[20] Arrow uses the word "selfishness" instead of self-centredness. I prefer the latter in order to avoid confusions with common formal definitions of selfishness as indifference to others, i.e. the constancy of utility with respect to the wealth of others [see the account of Becker (1974) above]. The relation between this assumption of Arrow and the similar notions of self-centredness discussed in this chapter (Sections 2.2, 3.4.1.2 and 6.1.1.3) is briefly examined, notably, in Footnotes 23 and 59.

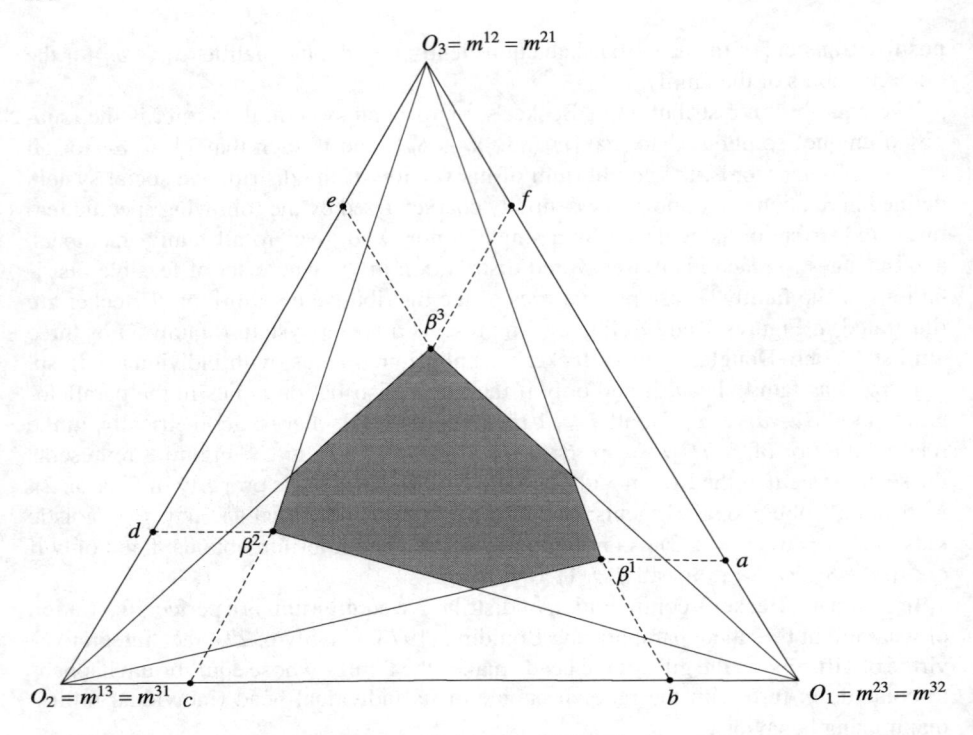

Figure 7. Becker's equilibrium with altruistic family members.

There is a unique equilibrium, which is characterized in the Theorem 5 (p. 221). The characterization relies on the functions $\xi_i : \mathbb{R} \to \mathbb{R}$ defined implicitly by $-\partial\varphi_i(\xi_i(z)) + \partial\varphi(z) = 0$, $i = 1, \ldots, n$. The set of donors is $\{i : \omega_i > \xi_i(\text{Min}_j\, \omega_j)\}$, that is, the set of individuals whose utility is increasing in wealth transfers to the least favored at the endowment point ω. Letting x^* denote the equilibrium distribution, the set of receivers is $\{i : x_i^* > \omega_i\}$, that is, the set of individuals whose equilibrium wealth is larger than their initial wealth. The two sets have an empty intersection, which means that individuals cannot be simultaneously donors and receivers at equilibrium. All receivers have the same equilibrium wealth, which corresponds to the minimum equilibrium wealth $\text{Min}_j\, x_j^*$, denoted by $x_{\min}$ (that is: $x_i^* = \text{Min}_j\, x_j^* = x_{\min}$ for every receiver i). These properties are illustrated in the Cobb–Douglas social system of Figure 9, with log linear utility functions (recall that preferences are ordinal) such that $\beta_{ii} > \beta_{ij} = \beta_{ik}$ for all $i, j \neq i, k \neq i, j$: the minimum endowment is individual 2's; the unique donor is individual 1; the unique receiver is individual 2.

Theorem 6 (p. 222) yields an interesting characterization of Pareto-efficient equilibrium when the latter is not a status quo, that is, when the equilibrium distribution differs from the initial distribution ("non-trivial" equilibrium, in Arrow's terminology). It states that a non-trivial equilibrium is Pareto-efficient if and only if the equilibrium

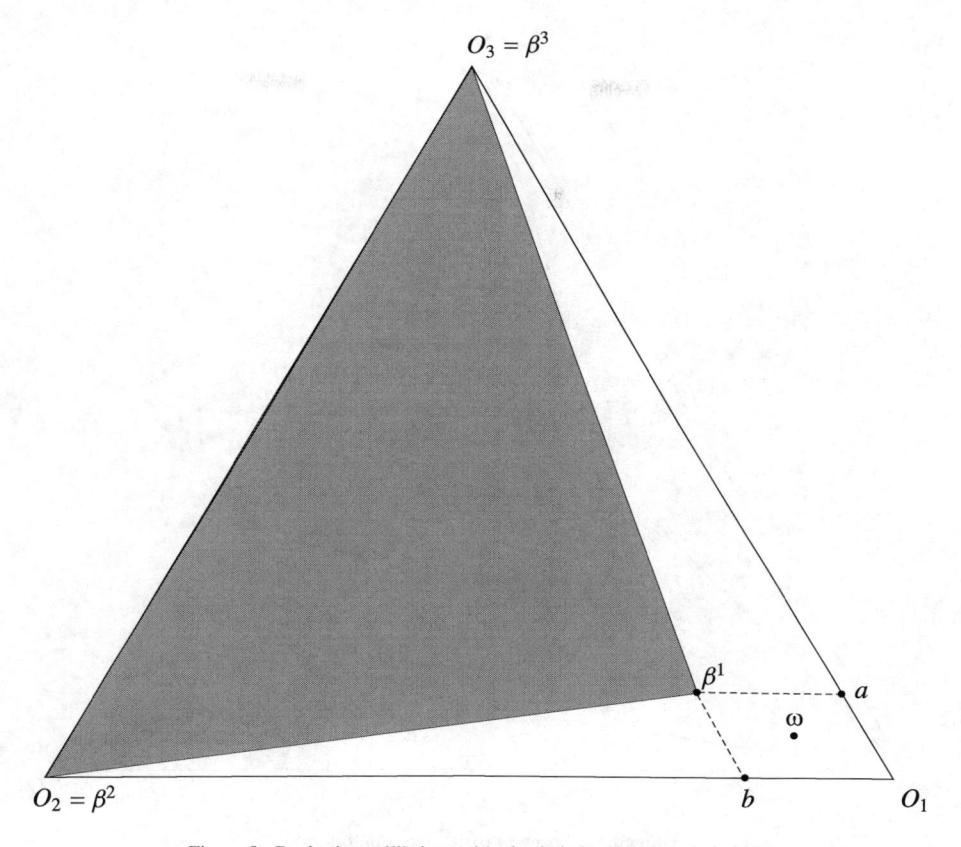

Figure 8. Becker's equilibrium with altruistic head and egoistic kids.

distribution x^* has exactly one individual (say, individual i) above the minimum equilibrium wealth $x_{\min}$. One deduces from the former paragraph that individual i then is the sole donor at equilibrium. And one easily verifies that the equilibrium then is an equilibrium of Becker.[21] In other words, a non-trivial equilibrium of Arrow is Pareto-efficient if and only if it is a social equilibrium of Becker. Figure 10 reproduces the social system of Figures 6 and 7, with the symmetries of distributive preferences that follow from Arrow's assumptions (namely: $\beta_{ij} = \beta_{ik}$ for all $i, j \neq i, k \neq i, j$): the set of Pareto-efficient distributions is the triangle $\beta^1 \beta^2 \beta^3$; its intersection with the set ∂M (the topological boundary of M) of non-trivial equilibrium distributions is the set $\{\beta^1, \beta^2, \beta^3\}$ of Beckerian equilibria; x^i obtains as an equilibrium if and only if the initial distribution is in the parallelogram $\{\omega \in S_3 : \omega_j \geqslant x^i_j \text{ for all } j \neq i\}$.

---

[21] With one minor qualification: the donor needs not make gifts to *all* others, because we might have the coincidental situation where the endowment of an individual is equal to the minimum equilibrium wealth.

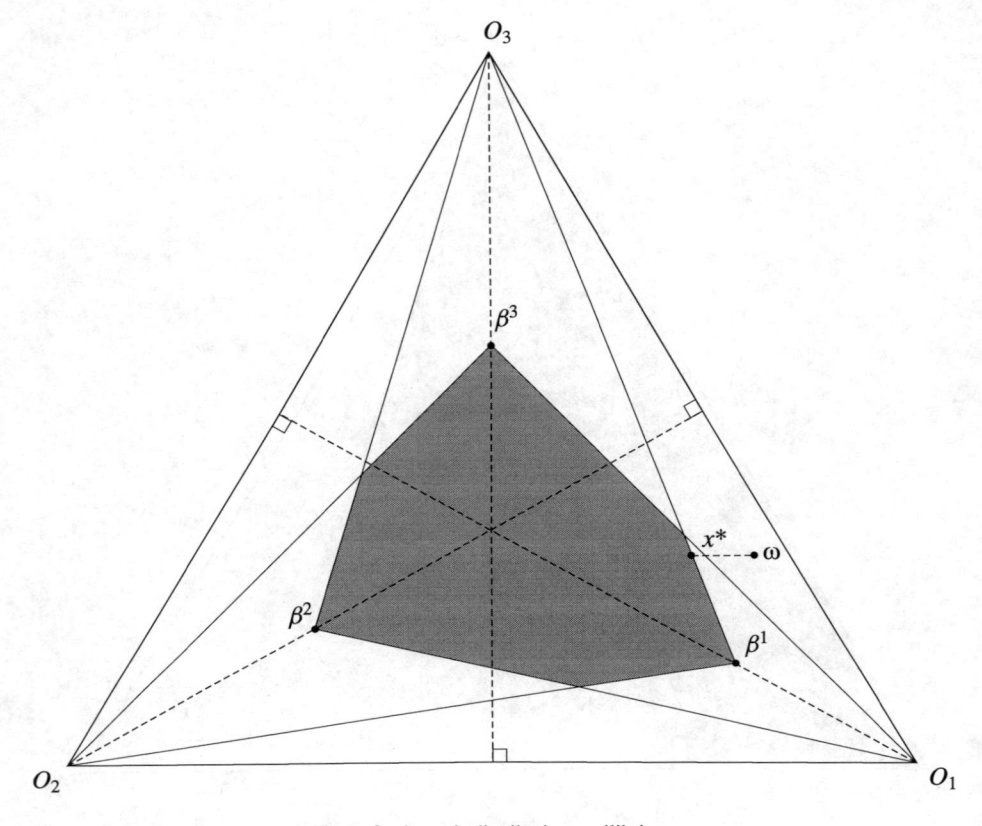

Figure 9. Arrow's distributive equilibrium.

3.3.3. Bergstrom, Blume and Varian (1986): On the private provision of public goods

The model of private provision of public goods of Bergstrom–Blume–Varian (BBV), although formulated in a slightly different setting, can be easily embedded in the framework of Section 3.1.1.

Let the set $N = \{1, \ldots, n\}$ of agents be partitioned in two subsets: the non-poor $\{1, \ldots, m\}$, and the poor $\{m+1, \ldots, n\}$, where $1 \leqslant m < n$. I suppose, accordingly, that $\omega_i > \omega_j$ for all $(i, j) \in \{1, \ldots, m\} \times \{m+1, \ldots, n\}$. The poor have selfish distributive preferences: $w_i(x) = \text{pr}_i\, x = x_i$ for all x for all $i \in \{m+1, \ldots, n\}$, where pr_i denotes the ith canonical projection $x \to x_i$ of $\mathbb{R}^n$. The non-poor are indifferent to the other non-poor and benevolent to the poor: $w_i(x) = \mu_i(x_i, x_{m+1}, \ldots, x_n)$, with μ_i monotonic strictly increasing, for all $i \in \{1, \ldots, m\}$. This implies that the wealth of the poor is a pure (non-rival, non-excludable) public good for the non-poor, while the wealth of the non-poor is a pure private good. An important special case for the shape of non-poor utility functions is $w_i(x) = v_i(x_i, x_{m+1} + \cdots + x_n)$ with v_i monotonic strictly

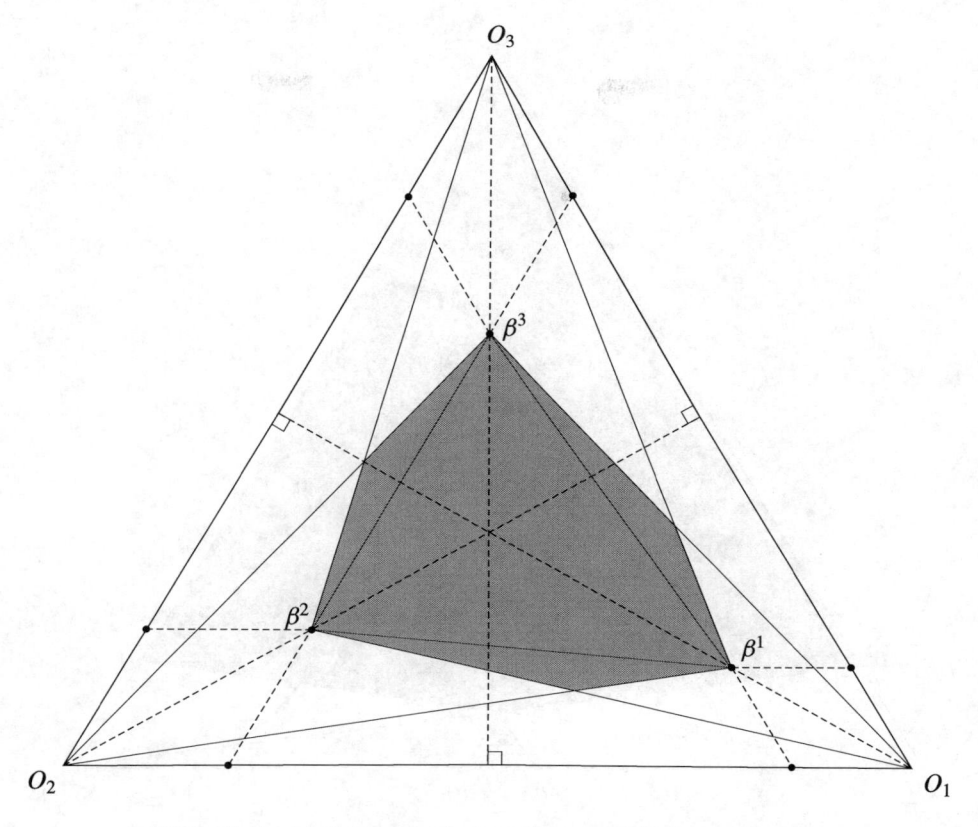

Figure 10. Pareto-efficient redistribution in Arrow's distributive social system.

increasing $\mathbb{R}^2 \to \mathbb{R}$. This is then the aggregate wealth of the poor which appears as the public good.[22]

This setup relates to BBV in the following way. The poor do not contribute to the public good: they choose $t_i = 0$ and consume $x_i = \omega_i + \sum_{j>m} t_{ji}$ for all vector $(t_1, \ldots, t_m)$ of contributions of the non-poor. The contributions of the non-poor, if any, benefit to the poor: non-poor i maximizes $\mu_i(\omega_i - \sum_{j>m} t_{ij}, \omega_{m+1} + \sum_{j \leqslant m} t_{jm+1}, \ldots, \omega_n + \sum_{j \leqslant m} t_{jn})$ with respect to $(t_{im+1}, \ldots, t_{in})$ given $t_{\setminus i}$. A BBV equilibrium of the set

---

[22] The model can be viewed as a crude stylization of traditional charitable redistribution from rich to poor. The assumed preferences of the "rich" and "poor" interpret, most conveniently, as revealed preferences, narrowly conditioned by the specific context of charitable redistribution: agents are endowed with the distributive preferences corresponding to their individual position in this context, as either "donor and rich" or "beneficiary and poor". A more refined and more satisfactory version of the model would assume individual preferences such that the (charitable) altruism of any individual i towards any individual j depend on x_i and x_j (in a natural way: non-decreasing in the former and non-increasing in the latter).

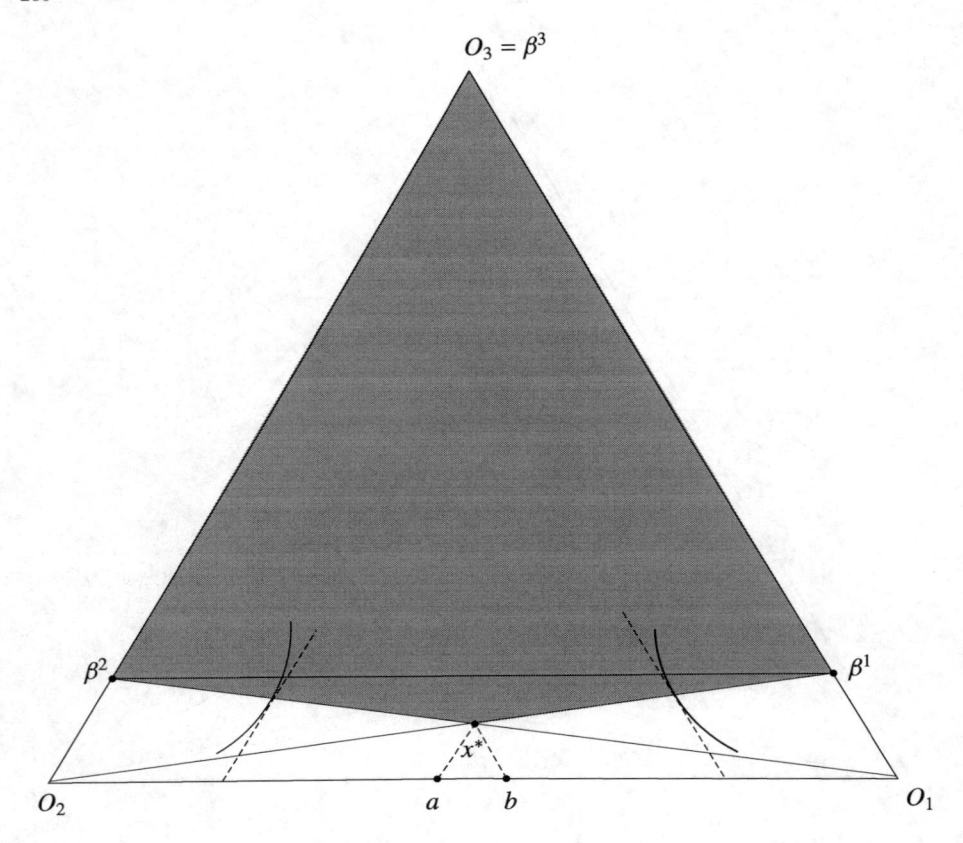

Figure 11. BBV distributive social system.

of non-poor agents $\{1, \ldots, m\}$ [also called Cornes–Sandler equilibrium in the literature, by reference to Cornes and Sandler (1985a), or sometimes also subscription equilibrium] is then a vector of gifts $(t_1, \ldots, t_m)$ such that t_i solves the maximization problem above for each non-poor i. One verifies immediately from the definitions that $(t_1, \ldots, t_m)$ is a BBV equilibrium of $\{1, \ldots, m\}$ if and only if the gift-vector $t = (t_1, \ldots, t_m, 0, \ldots, 0)$ is a distributive equilibrium of $\{1, \ldots, n\}$.

When w is of the type $(\mu_1, \ldots, \mu_m, \text{pr}_{m+1}, \ldots, \text{pr}_n)$, the social system is named a *BBV social system*. When it is of the type $(\nu_1, \ldots, \nu_m, \text{pr}_{m+1}, \ldots, \text{pr}_n)$, it is named a *strong* BBV social system.

The positive and normative properties of the BBV distributive equilibrium will be reviewed later in the chapter. It is sufficient at this stage to illustrate the model by an example. Figure 11 represents a BBV social system. There is a single poor, agent 3, whose utility function is $w_3(x) = x_3$. The non-poor are agents 1 and 2, with Cobb–Douglas utility functions $w_i(x_i, x_3) = \beta_{ii} \ln x_i + \beta_{i3} \ln x_3$. And ω is in the open line segment $]O_1, O_2[$ (that is: $\omega_3 = 0$ and ω_1 and ω_2 are > 0). One verifies easily, using the technique developed in Section 3.2, that: if $\omega \in]O_1, a]$, then agent 1 is the sole donor, and the equilibrium distribution is the projection of ω on the line segment $\beta^1 O_2$ parallel to $O_1 O_3$; if $\omega \in]a, b[$, then both non-poor give to the poor, and the equilibrium distribution is the intersection x^* of $\beta^1 O_2$ and $\beta^2 O_1$; finally, if $\omega \in [b, O_2[$, then agent 2 is the sole donor, and the equilibrium distribution is the projection of ω on the line segment $\beta^2 O_1$ parallel to $O_2 O_3$. The set of Pareto-efficient distributions is the triangle $\beta^1 O_3 \beta^2$, so that none of these BBV equilibria are efficient: it is possible to increase the utilities of the three agents by properly increasing the income support of agents 1 and 2 to the poor. In other words, charity is under-provided by voluntary contributions.

3.4. Existence, determinacy

This section reviews the most fundamental properties of distributive equilibrium. The latter explains the voluntary redistribution of wealth through essentially three types of determinants: individual preferences; initial endowments; and a mode of interaction, namely, the assumption that distributive agents take the transfers of others as fixed when making their own transfer decisions (the conjecture of Cournot–Nash, sometimes called also "zero conjecture" in the literature, and referred to as the "Cournot–Nash behavioral assumption" in this chapter). The study of the existence of equilibrium explores the general conditions under which these determinants are able to generate some equilibrium distribution of wealth from *any* initial distribution. While the study of its determinacy examines the general conditions under which the number of equilibria is finite (local determinacy), or, ideally, equal to 1 (full determinacy). In other words, these studies test the internal consistency and the precision of the determination of the distribution of wealth by the distributive preferences of individuals, their wealth endowments, and the Cournot–Nash behavioral assumption relative to wealth transfers.

The distributive equilibrium shares essentially the same existence and determinacy properties as competitive equilibrium, with only one significant exception: the possibility of logically robust (i.e. generic) non-existence in situations characterized below as "wars of gifts" (Section 3.4.1). Distributive equilibrium is generically locally determinate, and status quo distributive equilibrium is generically unique, as are competitive equilibrium and status quo competitive equilibrium respectively (Section 3.4.2).

3.4.1. Existence

Although the distributive equilibrium is a special case of Debreu's social equilibrium, the corresponding existence theorem [Debreu (1952, pp. 52–53)] does not apply, because the set $\{t: x(\omega, t) \geq 0\}$ of gift-vectors $t = (t_1, \ldots, t_n)$ jointly accessible to the set of all individuals is unbounded above.

We review below examples of non-existence of a distributive equilibrium. The existence problem is characterized as a "war of gifts". We give then a general existence theorem.

3.4.1.1. Non-existence of a distributive equilibrium We consider here examples of distributive social systems which have no equilibrium despite the upper hemicontinuity of individual reaction correspondences. The existence failure stems from the non-compactness of their domain. It is generally robust to small perturbations of utility functions or endowments, that is: existence is *not* a *generic* property of the distributive social systems of W [Mercier Ythier (2004b, 5.2)], and this contrasts with the general existence of market equilibrium in competitive economies with similar characteristics.

The non-existence of a distributive equilibrium implies the presence of a "war of gifts" between two agents or more, that is, more formally, the existence of some distribution and circuit of agents such that the utility of each agent is locally strictly increasing in bilateral wealth transfers from himself to the subsequent other in the circuit (Theorem 2 below). Bilateral wars of gifts are occasionally discussed in the literature as cases of logical inconsistency of models of two-sided altruism [e.g. Abel (1987, Equation (9), p. 1041); or Stark (1993, Footnote 1, p. 1416)]. In the context of two-agent distributive social systems, there is a war of gifts if and only if $x_i^j > x_i^i$ whenever $i \neq j$, when the best feasible distributions for i and j, x^i and x^j, are unique [e.g. Mercier Ythier (1989, P.3.11, p. 103)]. Mercier Ythier (1993) gives an example of a bilateral war of gifts in a three-agent distributive social system (pp. 939–940). And the Cobb–Douglas social system of Figure 12, drawn from Mercier Ythier (1998a, Counterexample 1, p. 340), is the place of generalized, bilateral and trilateral wars of gifts: for instance, agent 1's (resp. 2's, resp. 3's) utility is locally increasing in wealth transfers from himself to agent 2 (resp. 3, resp. 1) in the neighborhood of equal distribution $e = (1/3, 1/3, 1/3)$.

These examples display interesting analogies with the phenomenon known as *potlatch* in anthropology, and conceptualized notably by Mauss in his celebrated *Essai sur le Don* (1924), from the ethnographical works of Boas (1897) and Malinowski (1922), under a comprehensive notion of competitive gift-exchange [see Godelier (1996), for a well documented account of this stream of anthropological literature]. The analogy is formal, not substantial, but it can serve as a starting point for an anthropological interpretation of the abstract social system of Section 3.1. The characteristic features of such abstract systems and of social practices of competitive gift-exchange such as the *potlatch* and the *kula* [e.g. Godelier (1996, 2000)] differ on three articulated aspects. The nature of transferable wealth first: market money wealth for individual consumption, versus symbolic objects for circulation in competitive gift-exchange. The extension of individual property rights on transferable wealth, second: unrestricted *jus utendi et abutendi*, versus the three obligations of giving, accepting, and returning gifts. The motives of gift-giving, third: benevolent correction of wealth inequality, versus competition for rank or fame. In short, the abstract social system conveys a representation of gift-giving as benevolent individual equalization of private wealth, which stands in sharp contrast to the competition for rank or fame that characterizes competitive gift-exchange [Mercier Ythier (2000b, 2.3, pp. 100–101, 2004b, 4.3.3)].

3.4.1.2. Existence theorem The existence theorem presented below is drawn from Mercier Ythier (1993, Theorem 2, p. 941). It states essentially that non-existence im-

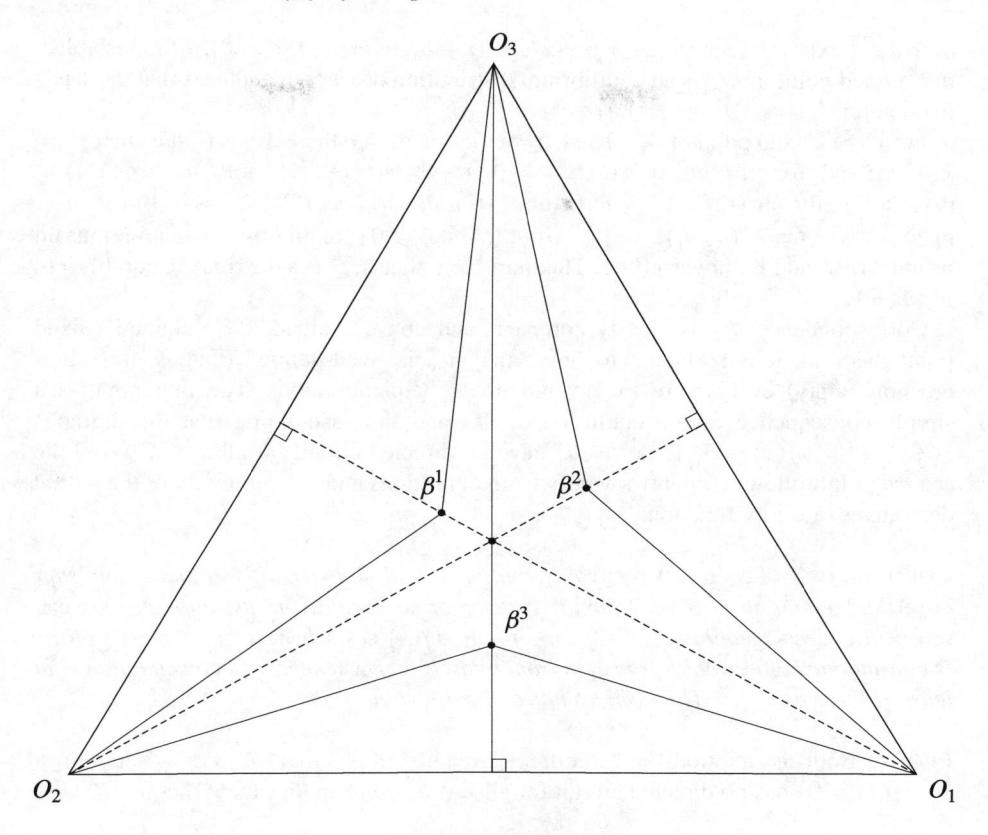

Figure 12. War of gifts.

plies the presence of a war of gifts. It implies (Corollary 2) the existence results of Arrow (1981, Theorem 5, p. 221) or Bergstrom, Blume and Varian (1986, Theorem 2, p. 33); see also Cornes, Hartley and Sandler (1999, Theorem, p. 505).

THEOREM 2. *Let w be twice differentiable and verify Assumptions 1(ii) and 1(iii). Then: if w has no equilibrium for some $\omega \in S_n$, there exists $x \in S_n$ such that the digraph $\{(i, j): -\partial_{x_i} w_i(x) + \partial_{x_j} w_i(x) > 0\}$ has a directed circuit (that is, contains a sequence $((i_k, j_k))_{1 \leqslant k \leqslant m}$ such that $m \geqslant 2$, $j_k = i_{k+1}$ for all $k = 1, \ldots, m - 1$ and $j_m = i_1$).*

PROOF. Suppose that for all $x \in S_n$ the digraph $\{(i, j): -\partial_{x_i} w_i(x) + \partial_{x_j} w_i(x) > 0\}$ has no directed circuit. I want to prove that, then, (w, ω) has an equilibrium for all $\omega \in S_n$.

Let Φ_ω denote the correspondence $S_n \to S_n$ defined by: $\Phi_\omega(x) = \{x(\omega, t) \in \mathbb{R}_+^n: t_{ij} = 0$ whenever $-\partial_{x_i} w_i(x(\omega, t)) + \partial_{x_j} w_i(x(\omega, t)) < 0$; and $x_i(\omega, t) = 0$ whenever there exists j such that $-\partial_{x_i} w_i(x(\omega, t)) + \partial_{x_j} w_i(x(\omega, t)) > 0\}$. I first establish that a fixed point of Φ_ω is an equilibrium distribution of (w, ω), and next that Φ_ω has a fixed point.

Let x^* be a fixed point of Φ_ω. Then, by definition of Φ_ω, there exists t^* such that $x^* = x(\omega, t^*)$ and: for all i, either $x_i(\omega, t^*) = 0$ or $-\partial_{x_i} w_i(x(\omega, t^*)) + \partial_{x_j} w_i(x(\omega, t^*)) \leqslant 0$ for all j; for all (i, j), $(-\partial_{x_i} w_i(x(\omega, t^*)) + \partial_{x_j} w_i(x(\omega, t^*)))t_{ij}^* = 0$. But then t_i^* maximizes $w_i(x(\omega, (t_{\setminus i}^*, t_i)))$ in $\{t_i \colon x_i(\omega, (t_{\setminus i}^*, t_i)) \geqslant 0\}$ for all i by the assumptions on w and Arrow and Enthoven (1961: Theorem 1(c)), that is, t^* is a distributive equilibrium of (w, ω).

Correspondence Φ_ω is clearly compact- and convex-valued. By Kakutani's fixed point theorem, it is sufficient to prove that Φ_ω is: well-defined (that is, its values are non-empty) everywhere in S_n; and upper hemicontinuous. The first point is a simple consequence of the definition of Φ_ω and the assumption that the digraphs $\{(i, j) \colon -\partial_{x_i} w_i(x) + \partial_{x_j} w_i(x) > 0\}$ have no directed circuit for all $x \in S_n$. And the second point follows straightforwardly from definitions and the continuity of the partial derivatives of utility functions. □

COROLLARY 2. *Let (w, ω) verify Assumption 1, with w twice differentiable, and suppose that: either w is a BBV social system; or w verifies the assumption of* weak self-centredness, *meaning that* $-\partial_{x_i} w_i(x) + \partial_{x_j} w_i(x) \leqslant 0$ *whenever $x_j \geqslant x_i$ (i's utility is non-increasing in wealth transfers from himself to j whenever j's consumption is at least as large as i's).*[23] *Then (w, ω) has an equilibrium.*

PROOF. Both assumptions of Corollary 2 readily imply that $\{(i, j) \colon -\partial_{x_i} w_i(x) + \partial_{x_j} w_i(x) > 0\}$ has no directed circuit for all $x \in S_n$. One applies then Theorem 2. □

3.4.2. Determinacy

A detailed formal discussion of the determinacy property of distributive equilibrium is beyond the scope of this chapter. We will provide instead a literary account of the main results of the analysis developed in Mercier Ythier (2004b) and recall the well-known property of uniqueness of the BBV equilibrium.

3.4.2.1. Generic determinacy of distributive equilibrium Generic determinacy is a property of regular distributive social systems. A distributive social system (w, ω) is *regular* if, essentially, the linear system tangent to the subsystem of first-order conditions of the type $-\partial_{x_i} w_i(x(\omega, t)) + \partial_{x_j} w_i(x(\omega, t)) = 0$ (with $i \neq j$) has full rank at equilibrium. Regularity is *generic* in $\{(w, \omega) \in W \times S_n \colon M_w \subset \mathbb{R}_{++}^n\}$, that is,

---

[23] Arrow's notion of self-centredness reads: $-\partial \varphi_i(x_i) + \partial \varphi(x_j) < 0$ whenever $x_i = x_j$. Combined with the concavity of φ_i and φ, it implies that $-\partial \varphi_i(x_i) + \partial \varphi(x_j) < 0$ whenever $x_j \geqslant x_j$, which is clearly stronger than the corresponding assumption of Corollary 2.

verified in an open and dense subset of the latter (Mercier Ythier, 2004b, Theorem 3). In other words, singularity (i.e. non-regularity) is *coincidental*: any linear perturbation of the preferences of a singular distributive social system will almost certainly restore regularity.

I establish the following three consequences of regularity: (i) there is a finite number of equilibria (op. cit: Theorem 5); (ii) status quo equilibrium is unique (op. cit.: Theorem 7); (iii) and the digraph of equilibrium gifts is a forest, that is, has no circuit[24] (op. cit.: Theorem 4).

The finiteness of the equilibrium set is certainly the most familiar, almost trivial implication of regularity. It is the exact analogue of the finiteness of the equilibrium set of finite regular competitive economies established in Debreu (1970).

The second point might appear more intriguing, although the analogous property of uniqueness of autarkic equilibrium is verified by finite regular competitive economies also. This fact usually receives only little attention in the theory of competitive exchange and production, for the simple reason that autarkic equilibrium presents little theoretical and practical interest as a situation of market equilibrium. Distributive equilibrium appears very different from market equilibrium in this respect, because of the public good problem, and particularly the type of inefficiency of equilibrium, encountered in many interesting theoretical cases, that is characterized by insufficient redistribution (see the account of the models of Arrow and BBV above, or Section 6 below). In other words, in many situations of theoretical interest, notably from the viewpoints of normative analysis and policy design, efficient distributive equilibria are status quo equilibria.

The third aspect of determinacy has no equivalent in the theory of competitive market equilibrium. It means, equivalently, that equilibrium gift-vectors and equilibrium wealth distributions are in one-to-one correspondence in regular distributive systems. And it implies that reciprocity, corresponding formally to the presence of a *directed* circuit in the digraph of equilibrium transfers, can appear only by coincidence in the distributive social systems of Section 3.1.

3.4.2.2. Uniqueness of BBV equilibrium We have mentioned already the uniqueness of Arrow's distributive equilibrium. We now recall below a similar property of BBV equilibrium when the aggregate wealth of the poor is the public good.

Let $w_i(x) = v_i(x_i, x_{m+1} + \cdots + x_n)$ be the utility function of non-poor i, $i = 1, \ldots, m$, as in Section 3.3.3 above. For any rich individual i, let $g_i = \sum_{k>m} t_{ik}$ denote the sum of his charitable contributions to the poor, and $G_{-i} = \sum_{j \leq m: j \neq i} g_j$ the aggregate charitable contribution of the other rich. Let $G = \sum_{i \leq m} g_i$ be the aggregate charitable contributions of the rich. If the utility functions v_i of the rich (see

---

[24] A *circuit* of $N \times N$ is a sequence $((i_k, j_k))_{1 \leq k \leq m}$ of pairs of agents (darts) such that, $\{i_k, j_k\} \cap \{i_{k+1}, j_{k+1}\}$ is non-empty for all k (that is, darts (i_k, j_k) and (i_{k+1}, j_{k+1}) have at least one common vertex for all k), with $(i_{m+1}, j_{m+1}) = (i_1, j_1)$ by convention. The circuit $((i_k, j_k))_{1 \leq k \leq m}$ is *directed* if $j_k = i_{k+1}$ for all k, that is, if the head-vertex j_k of dart (i_k, j_k) coincides with the tail-vertex i_{k+1} of dart (i_{k+1}, j_{k+1}) for all k. See also Footnote 45.

Section 3.3.3) are strictly quasi-concave, there exists, for all $i \leqslant m$, a function f_i that solves $\max\{v_i(x_i, \omega_{m+1} + \cdots + \omega_n + G): x_i + G = \omega_i + G_{-i}\}$ with respect to G for any positive value of i's social income $r = \omega_i + G_{-i}$. $f_i(r)$ is i's demand for the public good when his endowment and the contributions of others to the public good add up to r, ignoring the non-negativity constraint on his own contributions. The gift-giving behavior of rich i is then described by the reaction function ρ_i such that $\rho_i(G_{-i}) = \max\{0, f_i(\omega_i + G_{-i}) - G_{-i}\}$. And we have the following property, that synthesizes two independent results of Cornes, Hartley and Sandler [(1999, Theorem, p. 505); see also the former, less general versions of Bergstrom, Blume and Varian (1986, Theorem 3, p. 33), Fraser (1992), and Bergstrom, Blume and Varian (1992)] and Shitovitz and Spiegel (2001, p. 221, §3):

THEOREM 3. *Suppose that v_i is monotonic strictly increasing, and strictly quasi-concave for all $i \leqslant m$, and that the social system verifies one of the following two normality conditions: (i) either, for all $i \leqslant m$, there exists a real number $\alpha_i < 1$ such that, for all G'_{-I} and G''_{-I} satisfying $0 \leqslant G''_{-I} < G'_{-I} \leqslant \sum_{j \leqslant m: j \neq i} \omega_j$, $0 \leqslant \rho_i(G''_{-I}) - \rho_i(G'_{-I}) \leqslant \alpha_i(G'_{-I} - G''_{-I})$ (normality); (ii) or, for all $i \leqslant m$, v_i is C^2, and $\partial_{x_i}(\partial_{x_i} v_i(x_i, y)/\partial_y v_i(x_i, y)) < 0$ and $\partial_y(\partial_{x_i} v_i(x_i, y)/\partial_y v_i(x_i, y)) > 0$ (ordinal normality). Then, there is a unique equilibrium vector $(g_1, \ldots, g_m)$.*

The first normality condition of Theorem 3, due to Cornes et al., is satisfied, in particular, whenever own wealth and the aggregate wealth of the poor are both normal goods for the rich, that is, equivalently, supposing the differentiability of f_i, whenever $0 < \partial f_i(r) < 1$ for all $r > 0$ and all $i \leqslant m$.

The second normality condition (ordinal normality), due to Shitovitz and Spiegel, is essentially equivalent to the (strict) gross substitutability of private goods and the public good at Lindahl prices [see the reference to Gaube (2001) in Section 6.2.3 below]. It states that an individual's marginal rate of substitution between his consumption of the private good and his consumption of the public good, that is, his relative (shadow Lindahl) price of private versus public consumption, is decreasing (resp. increasing) in is his private (resp. public) consumption.

We will omit proofs, and comment instead on the empirical relevance of the first normality assumption, which is by far the most commonly made in the literature. This question is addressed, notably, by Becker (1974, 1981a), whose Rotten Kid Theorem supposes that the wealth of the beneficiary (that is, the public good) is a normal good to the family head, and who argues, on theoretical grounds, that the income elasticity of gift-giving is likely to be positive (1981a, pp. 178–179), but also that it could be larger than 1 in this context of microsocial altruistic redistribution (1974, p. 1072), an empirical conjecture that is at variance with the normality assumption above.

Empirical findings on donors' income elasticities of *inter vivos* transfers were invariably found to be positive, and generally found to be below unity. Altonji, Hayashi and Kotlikoff (1997), for instance, find a 0.05 income elasticity of *inter vivos parental* transfers to children. And most of the 16 estimates of income elasticities of *charitable* giving reviewed in Foster et al. (2000, 6.2, pp. 125–129, notably Table 6.1) and in Schokkaert's Chapter 2 in this volume (Table 1), though much larger than the latter, are below unity also, with a typical value of 0.8 [notable exceptions are Taussig (1967) and Reece and Zieschang (1985)]. The estimates of elasticities of *bequests* relative to parental life resources reviewed in Chapter 14 of Arrondel and Masson in this Handbook, on the contrary, although fairly scattered (ranging from 0.5 to 2.9), are in the majority larger than 1, and in fact much larger than unity for the top quintile of permanent incomes [Menchik and David (1983), Arrondel and Laferrère (1991), and Arrondel and Masson (1991)].The idea that gift-giving is a normal good for donors is therefore supported by the data without ambiguity. The evidence relative to the nature of luxury good of gift-giving, on the contrary, is mixed: the assumption is clearly rejected in the context of inter vivos family gift-giving on the one hand; but, on the other hand, the average income elasticities obtained for charitable gift-giving are often close to 1, usually somewhat lower but sometimes significantly higher, suggesting that this type of transfer could be in fact a luxury good for a significant subsample (top quintile?) of the set of donors; and bequest definitely appears as a luxury good for the top quintile of permanent incomes.

4. Perfectly substitutable transfers in a competitive market economy

We now turn to abstract social systems that involve the simultaneous, non-strategic and non-cooperative interaction of altruistic gift and egoistic or "non-tuistic" [Wicksteed (1910)] competitive market exchange.

The analytical distinction between the motives of human action in market exchange and in other dimensions of social life, at least its conscious and systematic elaboration by Adam Smith in the two major works that span his intellectual life, the *Theory of Moral Sentiments* (1759) and the *Wealth of Nations* (1776), can be viewed as the point of departure for the development of economics as an autonomous social science. Since Smith's work, the difference and potential or actual contradiction between the narrowly self-regarding intentions driving individual market behavior, and other-regarding motives driving individual action in many other circumstances of life (beginning with family life) has been often noted, questioned and criticized as hypothesis and fact, inside economic theory as well as from outside [see for instance the famous "conclusions of morals" of Mauss (1924, Chapter IV), where he expresses his regret of the absence, in modern market exchanges, of the warmth and generosity of potlatch exchanges].

The theoretical constructs reviewed in this section build on the solutions to these questions elaborated by economic theory, and notably those formulated by Edgeworth

(1881), Pareto (1913, 1916) and Wicksteed (1910).[25] Let us examine them briefly, with some of their modern extensions.

Edgeworth emphasizes the abstractness of the representation of human behavior in economic science. Economic theory, at least the hardcore of it, retains from actual human behavior only what is strictly necessary for the understanding of its object, namely, of the determination of market prices and exchanges. This abstract representation of man is characterized as "unsympathetic isolation" (1881, p. 12) rather than substantive egoism. The existence of moral sentiments is actually recognized as a pervasive social fact ["the concrete nineteenth century man is for the most part an impure egoist, a mixed utilitarian": (1881, p. 104)]. To define economic man by abstracting away moral sentiments simply means that the corresponding theory of market exchange *can* dispense with these aspects of human reality (an observation that by no means implies the prescription that it *must* dispense with them).

Pareto (1913, 1916, Chapter 12, notably §2111-38) fits the economic man into the social man, the economic equilibrium into the social equilibrium, and the economic optimum into the social optimum, in the manner of Russian dolls. He distinguishes two types of actions: logical actions, characterized as those actions which involve, both, the adequacy of means to ends, and the coincidence of the objective (that is, real, effective) ends of action with the subjective ends of the agent (his conscious intention when performing his action); and non-logical actions. The economic equilibrium is construed, in the main, as the outcome of a subclass of logical actions, namely, those individual actions that tend to the maximization of individual "ophelimity" defined as the satisfaction derived from individual consumption of market goods and services. The social equilibrium, as an outcome of individual and collective actions, is far from being determined only by logical actions: non-logical actions make up an essential part (e.g. 1916, Chapter 12, §2079). Pareto considers, nevertheless, a broader class of logical actions which is directly interesting for our purposes: the individual actions that tend to the maximization of "utility" defined as the individual satisfaction derived from own ophelimity, the ophelimities (1913) or utilities (1916, Chapter 12, §2115) of others, and other external effects from its membership of a social group. This second class of logical actions makes up a part of the general social equilibrium, that contains economic equilibrium, but is significantly larger than the latter notably because moral sentiments such as altruistic feelings can take place into it.

Wicksteed (1910) notices that the "unsympathetic isolation abstractly assumed in economics" (Edgeworth, op. cit.) can be attenuated considerably without altering the explanation of market exchange provided by economic theory. He observes that all that is required by the latter is "non-tuism", defined as the absence of concern of exchangers for the purposes of their partners in exchange. This minimal notion of self-centredness

---

[25] See also Alfred Marshall's thoughts about the characteristics of individual behavior in modern industrial life, in his *Principles of Economics* (1890), notably §4 in the first chapter of Book I: "It is deliberateness, and not selfishness, that is the characteristic of the modern age".

of traders, strictly limited to the way they conduct their market operations, is compatible with virtually any type of individual behavior outside market exchange, logical or not, selfish, altruistic or otherwise.

Wicksteed's flexible, close to tautological conception of economic man certainly remains the most perfect expression of the abstract representation of human behavior implied by economic theory. Related contributions, such as those of von Mises (1936) and Robbins (1932), have emphasized the individual and social efficiency of non-tuistic market behavior as an explanation of its pervasiveness as individual market behavior and as an explanation of the development of market exchange itself. Becker (1981b) is quite representative of this line of reasoning: he shows (III, p. 11) that a company altruistic to its consumers can generate a greater social surplus, greater profits for itself and greater utilities for its consumers by charging the market price and giving them cash gifts, than by pricing its products below the market price.[26] Kirzner (1990) develops the same type of argument from the perspective of market exchange viewed as a continuous process of learning, with a particular insistence on the role of purposeful non-tuistic behavior in promoting continuous improvements of the mutual awareness of traders. Kolm (1983, 1984, Part III) emphasizes the limits of these arguments: non-tuistic market behavior, as well as market exchange, are not necessarily efficient when information is imperfect or when it proves impossible to constrain agents to respect the rights of others; and the efficiency criterion does not take into account the societal preferences of individuals, and notably their preferences relating to the relative shares of market (non-tuistic) and non-market (e.g. altruistic) behavior in social equilibrium.

The sequel to this review briefly examines the literature on utility interdependence, the subsequent extensions of the fundamental theorems of welfare economics, and the extension of the distributive social system of Section 3 in order to include competitive market economies. It concludes with a brief examination of the transfer paradox.

4.1. Interdependent preferences

Pareto (1913, 1916) suggests two alternative notions of interdependent preferences: in one of them, individual utility depends on the utilities of others (1916, §2115), while in the other one it depends on the ophelimities of others (1913, 1916, §2128[1] and 2131[1]).

The two notions are conceptually distinct. Utility appears, at least a priori, as a primitive notion in the first type of approach, preferences being defined there on mixed objects that combine objective characteristics such as consumption of goods and services with subjective ones, the psychological states of others, reflected by their utility levels. In the second type of approach, on the contrary, interdependent utilities consist solely of preferences on the allocation of resources, that is, on the vector of individual consumption of goods and services. Nevertheless, the first approach reduces to the second one when suitable assumptions are made [see for instance, among many: Becker (1974, Foot-

---

[26] This also is a favorite topic of Maurice Allais.

note 30, pp. 1080–1081); Bergstrom (1970, 1989a, 1999); and Kolm (1968, 2(A)–(F), 1984, Footnote 2, pp. 316–317, or 2000, Chapter 1, 5.2.4)].

4.1.1. Interdependence of primitive utilities

We will assume throughout Section 4 that there are l consumption goods and services, denoted by an index h running in $L = \{1, \ldots, l\}$. The consumption x_i of individual i is reinterpreted as a vector $(x_{i1}, \ldots, x_{il})$ of quantities of his consumption of these goods. x denotes accordingly the allocation $(x_1, \ldots, x_n)$.

Let $\widehat{U}_i$ denote a utility level of individual i, $\widehat{U}$ a utility vector $(\widehat{U}_1, \ldots, \widehat{U}_n)$. A system of interdependent preferences, with utility levels as primitive objects of preferences, consists then of n utility functions of the type $U_i(x_i, \widehat{U})$ that verify the consistency requirement that $\widehat{U} = (U_1(x_1, \widehat{U}), \ldots, U_n(x_n, \widehat{U}))$ for all $(x, \widehat{U})$ of the domain of the product function $U = (U_1, \ldots, U_n)$.

A straightforward application of the implicit function theorem to the functional equation $\widehat{U} = U(x, \widehat{U})$ yields the local existence and uniqueness of a function $\varphi : x \to \widehat{U}$, solving the latter in the neighborhood of any $(x^0, \widehat{U}^0)$ such that $\widehat{U}^0 = U(x^0, \widehat{U}^0)$, provided that U is continuously differentiable on an open domain containing $(x^0, \widehat{U}^0)$ and $I - \partial_{\widehat{U}} U(x^0, \widehat{U}^0)$ has full rank (where I denotes the identity function of $\mathbb{R}^n$). In other words, a system of smooth utility functions "usually" (that is, generically) induces local systems of individual preferences defined solely on allocations (the local functions $x \to \varphi(x)$).

A special case of singularity of $I - \partial_{\widehat{U}} U(x, \widehat{U})$, and a special case of pathology of function φ have received some attention in the literature. They describe situations where individuals are so benevolent to each other that any reasonable connection between utility vectors and allocations is lost, either because there is no function φ (singular $I - \partial_{\widehat{U}} U(x, \widehat{U})$) or because φ is decreasing in all of its arguments: such individuals live, literally, of love and fresh water. Bergstrom (1989a) gives a nice humorous exposition of these paradoxes through the puzzles of Romeo and Juliet grappling with arbitrages between love and (individual consumption of) spaghetti, and in particular: difficulties disentangling love from spaghetti (non-existence of a function φ); and the conclusion that "true lovers hate spaghetti" (a decreasing function φ). Note that these problems are conceptually distinct from the wars of gifts discussed in Section 3.4.1.1 above: the former raise the question of the existence of non-pathological systems of individual preferences on the allocation of resources, while the latter refer to mutually incompatible acts of redistribution derived from well-defined and well-behaved (increasing and convex, notably) individual preferences on the distribution of wealth.

Utility levels and functions, therefore, are not only primitive notions in this version of the interdependence of preferences. They turn out also to be irreducible to preferences on allocations in the presence of singularities of $I - \partial_{\widehat{U}} U(x, \widehat{U})$. Most applications, nevertheless, introduce assumptions that rule out this special case as well as monotonic decreasing preferences on allocations. Bergstrom (1999) provides an extensive discussion of the case where individual utility is weakly separable in own consumption (there is an individual "ophelimity"), increasing in own ophelimity, and non-decreasing in the utilities of others (non-malevolence). Formally, individual i's utility function is of the type $U_i^*(u_i(x_i), \widehat{U})$, increasing in its first argument and non-decreasing in the other ones. He shows (op. cit.: Proposition 3) that such systems of interdependent preferences are reducible to non-malevolent preferences of the type $\varphi_i^*(u_1(x_1), \ldots, u_n(x_n))$, defined on the ophelimity vectors associated with allocations, whenever $I - \partial_{\widehat{U}} U^*(u(x), \widehat{U})$ is dominant diagonal for all $(x, \widehat{U})$ such that $\widehat{U} = \varphi^*(x)$ (with the following notations: $u(x) = (u_1(x_1), \ldots, u_n(x_n))$; $U^*(u(x), \widehat{U}) = (U_1^*(u_1(x_1), \widehat{U}), \ldots, U_n^*(u_n(x_n), \widehat{U}))$, and $\varphi^*(x) = (\varphi_1^*(x), \ldots, \varphi_n^*(x))$). The condition that $I - \partial_{\widehat{U}} U^*(u(x), \widehat{U})$ is dominant diagonal is logically equivalent to the non-singularity of the matrix if, as follows from non-malevolence, $\partial_{\widehat{U}} U^*(u(x), \widehat{U})$ is $\geqslant 0$; its inverse is then the non-negative sum of a geometric series $\sum_{t=0}^{\infty} (\partial_{\widehat{U}} U^*(u(x), \widehat{U}))^t$ (op. cit.: Lemma 1). These results extend to denumerable sets of agents, and apply therefore to the systems of interdependent preferences considered in the literature on intergenerational altruism initiated by Barro (1974) [see notably Kimball (1987), Hori and Kanaya (1989), and Hori (1992)]. In short, benevolent preferences weakly separable in own consumption reduce to well-defined and well-behaved preferences on ophelimity vectors provided that mutual benevolence is not so intense that it implies the divergence of $\sum_{t=0}^{\infty} (\partial_{\widehat{U}} U^*(u(x), \widehat{U}))^t$.

Kolm (1968, 2(F)) states the same type of condition in the language of marginal surplus theory. Let v_{ij} denote the money value to individual i of an additional dollar to individual j ($v_{ii} = 1$). The social value to individual i of an additional dollar to individual j is the sum of its direct individual valuation by i and indirect valuation through i's social valuations of others' individual valuations of the additional dollar to j, that is: $s_{ij} = \delta_{ij} + \sum_{k \neq i} v_{ik} s_{kj}$, where δ_{ij} is the number of Kronecker ($= 1$ if $i = j$, $= 0$ otherwise). Letting S and V denote respectively the n-dimensional matrices (s_{ij}) and (v_{ij}), we have therefore by definition $S = I + VS$. This system of interdependent individual social values is well-defined if and only if $I - V$ is non-singular, and we have then $S = (I - V)^{-1} = \sum_{t=0}^{\infty} V^t$. In other words, individual social valuations are well-defined, and then reducible to combinations of direct individual valuations, provided, again, that mutual benevolence is not so intense that it implies the divergence of $\sum_{t=0}^{\infty} V^t$.

4.1.2. Interdependent preferences on allocations and the fundamental theorems of welfare economics

The alternative approach to the interdependence of preferences considers individual preferences defined directly on allocations. It can be traced back to Pareto (1913, 1916), and was maintained in a French tradition of economists notably by Divisia, and reintroduced in contemporary normative economic theory by Kolm (1968) extending the tradition above, and, independently, by Winter (1969).

This approach distinguishes two types or "levels" of individual preferences: "private" preferences, defined on the private consumption of market goods and services of the individual (Pareto's "ophelimities"); and "social" preferences, defined on allocations

(Pareto's "utilities"). It is frequently assumed, moreover, as a condition of individual integrity, that individual social preferences are weakly separable in own consumption and that the unique preference preordering that they induce on individual consumption coincides with his private preferences.

One defines accordingly, following Pareto (1913, 1916), two notions of allocative efficiency: market efficiency, which is Pareto-efficiency relative to the private preferences of individuals [Pareto's "maximum of ophelimity for a collectivity" (1916, Chapter 12, §2128, p. 1338)]; and distributive efficiency, which is Pareto-efficiency relative to the social preferences of individuals (Pareto's "maximum of utility for a collectivity": ibid, §2131, pp. 1341–1342).[27]

The simplest framework for a precise general formulation of essential ideas is the competitive exchange economy with free disposal. We make therefore, and maintain in the remainder of Section 4, the following assumptions: (i) the total quantity of each good available for individual consumption is given once and for all (exchange economy) and equal to 1 (this is a simple choice of unit of measurement of physical quantities); (ii) an allocation x is feasible if x_i is in the consumption set X_i of consumer i for all i and $\sum_{i \in N} x_{ih} \leqslant 1$ for all h (this definition of feasibility implies free disposal and the perfect divisibility of physical quantities of goods and services). Note that the definitions and properties below (Sections 4.1.2 and 4.2) extend in a straightforward way to full-fledged Walrasian economies with profit-maximizing firms and standard (notably convex) technology.

Denote by: X the Cartesian product $\prod_{i \in N} X_i$; F the set $\{x \in X: \sum_{i \in N} x_{ih} \leqslant 1$ for all $h\}$ of feasible allocations of the economy; $u_i : \mathbb{R}^l \to \mathbb{R}$ the ophelimity function of individual i; u the function $\mathbb{R}^{ln} \to \mathbb{R}^n$ defined by $u(x) = (u_1(x_1), \ldots, u_n(x_n))$; X^i the Cartesian product $\mathbb{R}^l \times \cdots \times \mathbb{R}^l \times u_i(\mathbb{R}^l) \times \mathbb{R}^l \times \cdots \times \mathbb{R}^l$; $W_i : X^i \to \mathbb{R}$ the utility function of individual i, supposed strictly increasing in its ith argument (that is, in i's own ophelimity). A social system is then a list $((W_1, u_1), \ldots, (W_n, u_n))$, and the notions of market and distributive efficiency receive the following precise definitions:

DEFINITION 2. An allocation x is a strong market optimum (resp. strong distributive optimum) of the social system $((W_1, u_1), \ldots, (W_n, u_n))$ if it is feasible and if there exists no feasible allocation x' such that $u_i(x'_i) \geqslant u_i(x_i)$ (resp. $W_i(x'_1, \ldots, x'_{i-1}, u_i(x'_i), x'_{i+1}, \ldots, x'_n) \geqslant W_i(x_1, \ldots, x_{i-1}, u_i(x_i), x_{i+1}, \ldots, x_n))$ for all i, with a strict inequality for at least one i.

This formulation of utility interdependence leads in a natural way to questions on the possibility of extending the first and second fundamental theorems of welfare economics from market to distributive optima, that is, more precisely, to questions of the distributive efficiency of competitive market equilibrium on the one hand, and of the existence of systems of market prices supporting distributive optima on the other hand.

---

[27] For a justification of this terminology, see Section 2.2 (notably Footnote 6).

In view of the first and second theorems of welfare economics themselves [e.g. Debreu, (1954, Theorems 1 and 2)], the issue reduces essentially to the identification of properties of utility functions implying that any market optimum is a distributive optimum (extension of the first theorem) and that any distributive optimum is a market optimum (extension of the second theorem).

The second question received a positive answer for a broad class of systems of interdependent utilities combining two features: non-paternalism, first, which appears by far as the main condition for the extension of the second welfare theorem to distributive optima, and is construed as the respect or endorsement by all individual social preferences of the preferences of others on their own consumption of market goods; and a restriction on malevolence, ensuring that there is always some way of reallocating resources that is preferred to disposal (social non-satiation relative to individual consumption of market goods).

Such properties were first introduced by Winter (1969) with an assumption of non-paternalistic non-malevolence of individual social preferences [Assumption b.3, p. 100; see also Bergstrom (1970, II-A, pp. 385–386)]. Expressed in terms of utility representations, Winter's assumption combines: the existence of functions $w_i : u(X) \to \mathbb{R}$ such that $w_i(u(x)) = W_i(x_1, \ldots, x_{i-1}, u_i(x_i), x_{i+1}, \ldots, x_n)$ for all x; and w_i non-decreasing in j's ophelimity for all i and all $j \neq i$. It generalizes a similar assumption of Edgeworth (1881) and Pareto (1913), where individual utilities are additively separable and strictly increasing in ophelimities, that is, with present notations, where w_i is of the type $\sum_{j \in N} a_{ij} u_j$ with $a_{ij} > 0$ for all i and all j. Non-paternalistic non-malevolence straightforwardly implies that any distributive optimum is a market optimum, and therefore, under classical conditions, that it is attainable as a competitive market equilibrium.

Archibald and Donaldson (1976) and Rader (1980) relax the original assumption of Winter by allowing for malevolence. They simply suppose the existence of the functions w_i above,[28] and prove, essentially, that Winter's result extends to their more general systems of non-paternalistic interdependent utilities, provided that mutual malevolence is not so intense that it induces the disposal of a part of aggregate resources of society at some distributive optima. Rader's main result (1980, Theorem 2, p. 423), which is slightly more general than Archibald and Donaldson's, states precisely that: if the so-

---

[28] Their assumption of utility interdependence is still more general in fact, for they do not assume, as we did above, that utility is increasing in own ophelimity. In other words, their assumption is compatible with an indifference or aversion of an individual to his own satisfaction as a consumer. This introduction of the possibility of a contradiction between individual views on own consumption as a consumer and as a member of society is interesting on logical grounds, notably as a progress in generality, but it does not appear very appealing on more substantive grounds, partly because of the systematic character of this opposition of views, suggesting a severe problem of personal integrity, and partly because of the object of this opposition, own consumption of market goods, which cannot plausibly give rise, as a whole at least, to such an internal debate. For an alternative critique of the same assumption, see Lemche (1986, Remark 1, pp. 272–274).

cial system verifies free disposal,[29] quasi-transferability[30] and local non-satiation of the distributive Pareto preordering,[31] then any distributive optimum is a market optimum.

Lemche (1986) further relaxes the assumptions of Archibald and Donaldson by giving up the weak separability of individual social preferences in own wealth.[32] His notion of non-paternalistic preferences is defined from the conditional preferences on own and on others' consumption sets induced by individual social preferences. It states that whenever an individual is indifferent between any pair of his consumption vectors conditional on some given vector of consumption of others, then all individuals are indifferent between the same pair conditional on the same vector. In order to facilitate the comparison with Rader's result, I will slightly rephrase Lemche's theorem (op. cit.: Theorem 1, p. 278), using the notion of conditional Pareto optimum of Arrow and Hahn[33] (1971, Chapters 6, 2, pp. 132–136) in place of Lemche's essentially equivalent notion of conditional competitive equilibrium. The theorem states that: if individual social preferences are non-paternalistic in the sense above, if the social system verifies Archibald and Donaldson's version of the local non-satiation of the social Pareto preordering,[34] and if conditional individual preferences on own consumption are strictly increasing, quasi-concave and differentiable, then any distributive optimum is a conditional Pareto optimum (op. cit.).

A casual examination of the converse problem relative to the possibility of extending the first theorem of welfare to distributive optima shows that this supposes both non-paternalism and non-benevolence. Even mild benevolence, in particular, will often suffice to exclude from the set of distributive optima the market equilibria that imply situations of extreme poverty for some [see for instance Winter (1969, 5, p. 102)]. Parks (1991) shows that the first theorem extends to the case of non-paternalistic non-benevolence, provided again that malevolence remains limited, although in a different sense than the local non-satiation of the social Pareto preordering. He assumes utility functions of the type $w_i : u(X) \to \mathbb{R}$, strictly increasing in own ophelimity and non-increasing in the ophelimities of others, and shows, essentially, that any market optimum is a distributive optimum whenever the Jacobian matrices $\partial w(\hat{u})$ of the product function $w = (w_1, \ldots, w_n)$ have non-negative inverses (which supposes that the off-diagonal elements of $\partial w(\hat{u})$, that is, the marginal utilities of others' ophelimities, are not "too" negative).

---

[29] That is: $(\{\hat{u}\} - \mathbb{R}^n_+) \cap u(X) \subset u(F)$ for all $\hat{u} \in u(X)$. This notion of free disposal is equivalent to the notion implicit in the definition of the set of feasible allocations as $\{x \in X : \sum_{i \in N} x_{ih} \leqslant 1 \text{ for all } h\}$ whenever ophelimity functions are continuous monotonic increasing and consumption sets are equal to $\mathbb{R}^l_+$.

[30] That is: for all $\hat{u}$ and $\hat{u}'$ in $u(X)$ such that $\hat{u} > \hat{u}'$, there exists $\hat{u}'' \in u(X)$ such that $\hat{u}'' \gg \hat{u}'$.

[31] That is: for all $\hat{u} \in u(X)$ and all neighborhood V of $\hat{u}$, there exists $\hat{u}' \in V$ such that $w(\hat{u}') > w(\hat{u})$.

[32] More precisely, Lemche's notion of non-paternalism implies, and is not implied by, Archibald and Donaldson's notion complemented with the assumption that an individual's utility is strictly increasing in his own ophelimity.

[33] A conditional Pareto optimum is, in our context, a Pareto optimum relative to the conditional preferences of individuals on their own consumption.

[34] Stronger than Rader's (cf. Footnote 31 above) in general, but equivalent to it when ophelimity functions are monotonic strictly increasing.

4.2. General equilibrium with benevolent gift-giving and competitive market exchange

The social system and social equilibrium of Section 3.1 are now extended in order to include competitive market exchange (Section 4.2.1). The corresponding functioning involves the non-cooperative and non-strategic interaction of utility-maximizing individual gifts and ophelimity-maximizing exchanges on competitive markets, of individuals endowed with non-paternalistic interdependent preferences. We name Pareto social system this extension of the pure distributive social system, by reference to Pareto (1916).

It is shown (Section 4.2.2) that the market sub-equilibria of Pareto social systems are competitive equilibria. The first fundamental theorem of welfare economics extends, consequently, to social equilibrium, that is, the equilibrium allocation is Pareto-efficient relative to individual ophelimities (market efficiency). And the characterization and the existence property of the social equilibrium of pure distributive social systems then extend in a natural way to the social equilibrium of Pareto social systems (Sections 4.2.2 and 4.2.4 respectively).

We also establish (Section 4.2.3) the equivalence of in-kind and cash transfers, as a joint consequence of non-paternalism, perfect competitive market exchange and free disposal.

4.2.1. Social equilibrium

The setup of Section 3.1 is amended along the lines of Section 4.1.2 above and Mercier Ythier (1989, 2000a).

Agent i's initial endowment ω_i is now a non-negative element of the space of goods $\mathbb{R}^l$. We consider social systems of private property, where by definition the total endowment of society in all consumption goods is shared initially between its individual members, that is: $\sum_{i \in N} \omega_i = (1, \ldots, 1)$. The vector $(\omega_1, \ldots, \omega_n)$ of individual endowments is denoted by ω.

The agents can use commodities in three different ways: private consumption and individual gift-giving as in Section 3.1; and exchange on competitive markets.

A gift t_{ij} from i to j ($j \neq i$) is a non-negative element of $\mathbb{R}^l$, whose hth coordinate t_{ijh} is a non-negative quantity of consumption good h transferred from i to j. In other words, individuals are allowed to make both "cash" (numéraire) and in-kind transfers. The gift set of individual i is set $T_i = \mathbb{R}_+^{l(n-1)}$. The other notations of Section 3.1 relative to transfers are extended to the multi-commodity setting in the obvious way.

A *net trade* of agent i is a vector z_i of the space of commodities. Its hth coordinate z_{ih} is the net trade of agent i in good h, that is, the difference between his physical purchases and sales of commodity h. We denote by z a vector $(z_1, \ldots, z_i, \ldots, z_n)$ of individual net trades.

A *social state* is then a vector (x, t, z). Since individual uses of commodities are restricted to private consumption, gift-giving, and market exchange, a state (x, t, z) must verify the following physical accounting identities for all i: $x_i = z_i + \omega_i + \Delta_i t$, equating consumption to net physical inflows from trade, gift-giving and initial endowment, for all individuals and commodities.

An *action* of individual i, denoted by a_i, is a pair (z_i, t_i). An *action vector* is then a vector $a = (a_1, \ldots, a_i, \ldots, a_n)$ of individual actions. For all action vector a and all individual action a_i^*, we denote, as above, by: $a_{\setminus i}$ the vector of individual actions obtained from a by deleting its ith component a_i; $(a_{\setminus i}, a_i^*)$ the action vector obtained from a by replacing its ith component a_i by a_i^*. We suppose that every agent considers the actions of others as independent of his own (Cournot–Nash behavioral assumption). It follows from this and the accounting identities above that, given some $a_{\setminus i}$, the choice by agent i of some action $a_i^* = (z_i^*, t_i^*)$ determines the realization of one and only one allocation, namely allocation $x((a_{\setminus i}, a_i^*))$ whose jth component is $z_j + \omega_j + \Delta_j(t_{\setminus i}, t_i^*)$ for all j. We also suppose that every agent perceives market prices as independent from his individual actions (competitive markets). The vector of market prices is denoted by p. The unique social state determined by action vector a is denoted by $(x(a), t(a), z(a))$. The unique action vector associated with (x, t) is $((x_1 - \omega_1 - \Delta_1 t, t_1), \ldots, (x_n - \omega_n - \Delta_n t_n, t_n))$, denoted by $a(x, t)$.

Individuals have interdependent preferences on the allocation of resources that are non-paternalistic in the sense of Archibald and Donaldson (1976), cf. Section 4.1.2 above. We suppose moreover that an individual's utility is strictly increasing in his own ophelimity (cf. Footnote 28). We let, without loss of generality, $u_i(0) = 0$ for all i.

The picture concerning individual behavior is, at this point, the following: each agent chooses his gifts and net trades in order to achieve some allocation of resources according to his non-paternalistic preferences.

We can now complete this description of individual behavior with a specification of the constraints binding individual choices. Consider some price-action vector (p^*, a^*), defining an environment for individual decisions. Individual i will choose his action in the *budget set* $B_i(p^*, a^*) = \{a_i = (z_i, t_i) \in \mathbb{R}^l \times T_i: x_i((a_{\setminus i}^*, a_i)) \in \mathbb{R}_+^l$ and $p^* z_i \leqslant 0\}$, in order to maximize his utility according to the program: $\max\{w_i(u(x((a_{\setminus i}^*, a_i)))): a_i \in B_i(p^*, a^*)\}$.

An *extended distributive social system* is a pair of n-tuples of utility and ophelimity functions $((w_1, \ldots, w_n), (u_1, \ldots, u_n))$, denoted by (w, u). We name an abstract social system of this type a *social system of Pareto*, by reference to the Chapter 12 of his *Traité de Sociologie Générale* (1916). A *Pareto social system of private property* is a triple (w, u, ω). A *Pareto–BBV social system*, likewise, is a pair (w, u) such that society is partitioned into a subset of "egoistic" poor $\{m+1, \ldots, n\}$ with utility functions of the type $w_i(\hat{u}) = \hat{u}_i$ and a complementary subset of non-poor $\{1, \ldots, m\}$ whose preferences are of the type $w_i(\hat{u}) = \mu_i(\hat{u}_i, \hat{u}_{m+1}, \ldots, \hat{u}_n)$, where μ_i is monotonic strictly increasing (non-paternalistic benevolence to the poor).

DEFINITION 3. A social equilibrium of (w, u, ω) is a price-action vector (p^*, a^*) such that: (i) $\sum_{i \in N} z_i^* \leqslant 0$ and $p^* \sum_{i \in N} z_i^* = 0$ (market equilibrium with free disposal); (ii) and a_i^* solves $\max\{w_i(u(x((a_{\setminus i}^*, a_i)))): a_i \in B_i(p^*, a^*)\}$ for all i (everyone is satisfied with his own choice, given prices and the actions of others).

One verifies easily that this definition implies the definition of a pure distributive equilibrium (Section 3.1.2.1, Definition 1) when there is a single commodity (just let, then: $p = 1$, $z = 0$ and u_i be the identity map $\mathbb{R} \to \mathbb{R}$ for all i).

4.2.2. First-order conditions

We will consider differentiable social systems, as in Section 3. The following assumptions on preferences and endowments will be maintained throughout the remainder of Section 4:

ASSUMPTION 2.[35] (i) For all i, $X_i = \mathbb{R}^l_+$ and u_i is: (a) continuous in $\mathbb{R}^l_+$, and differentiable in $\mathbb{R}^l_{++}$ (the interior of $\mathbb{R}^l_+$); (b) monotonic strictly increasing in $\mathbb{R}^l_{++}$ (i.e. $u_i(x_i) > u_i(x'_i)$ for all $(x_i, x'_i) \in \mathbb{R}^l_{++} \times \mathbb{R}^l_{++}$ such that $x_i > x'_i$); (c) and such that $x_i \gg 0$ whenever $u_i(x_i) > 0 (= u_i(0))$. (ii) For all i, w_i is: (a) continuous in $\mathbb{R}^n_+$, and differentiable with respect to its jth argument in $\{\hat{u} \in \mathbb{R}^n_+ : \hat{u}_j > 0\}$ for all j; (b) strictly increasing in its ith argument. (iii) For all i, $w_i \circ u$ is: (a) quasi-concave; (b) and such that $w_i(u(x)) = 0$ whenever $u_i(x_i) = 0$. (iv) For all i, $\omega_i > 0$.

The following theorem extends Theorem 1 to the equilibria of Pareto social systems.

It provides an analogous system of necessary and sufficient conditions for equilibrium.

Its conditions (ii) and (iii) state that *the price system and the allocation of resources induced by a social equilibrium (p, a) of (w, u, ω) make a competitive market equilibrium of the induced exchange economy of private property $(u, (\omega_i + \Delta_i t(a))_{i \in N})$* (see also Footnote 39 below).

In particular, the multipliers λ_i correspond to the marginal ophelimities of wealth of the consumers. Its condition (iv) therefore means the following: *at equilibrium, a marginal incremental wealth transfer from i to j does not increase i's utility* ((iv)(a)), *and a marginal incremental wealth transfer from j to i does not increase i's utility whenever the equilibrium transfer from i to j is positive* ((iv)(b)).

---

[35] Assumptions 2(i)(b) and 2(i)(c) are commonly used in the study of differentiable economies. Together with Assumption 2(ii)(b), Assumption 2(i)(b) implies that prices are positive at equilibrium, while Assumption 2(i)(c) implies that an agent whose post-transfer wealth is positive will consume a positive amount of all goods (thereby eliminating inessential technicalities associated with non-negativity constraints on consumption). Assumptions 2(iii) and 2(iv) ensure that individual behavioral correspondences have the relevant continuity property required for the existence of a social (hence competitive market) equilibrium. Assumptions 2(iii)(b) and 2(iv), together with Assumptions 2(i)(c) and 2(ii)(b), are designed to imply, notably, the seemingly reasonable consequence that every agent will wish and be able to keep a positive post-transfer wealth for all positive price vectors, which ensures in turn the continuity of budget correspondences on relevant domains. The convexity of preferences of Assumption 2(iii)(a) implies then the upper hemicontinuity of behavioral correspondences.

Theorem 4 implies the characterization of Theorem 1, with an interior equilibrium distribution, for pure distributive social systems that verify Assumptions 2(ii) to 2(iv) (just let u_i be the identity map $\mathbb{R} \to \mathbb{R}$ for all i).[36]

THEOREM 4. *Let (w, u, ω) verify Assumption 2. Then, (p^*, a^*) is a social equilibrium of (w, u, ω) if and only if it verifies the following set of conditions*: (i) $p^* \gg 0$; (ii) $\sum_{i \in N} x_i(a^*) = (1, \ldots, 1)$; (iii) *for all i*: (a) $x_i(a^*) \gg 0$; (b) $p^* x_i(a^*) = p^*(\omega_i + \Delta_i t(a^*))$; (c) *and there exist $\lambda_i > 0$ such that $\partial_{x_i} u_i(x_i(a^*)) = \lambda_i p^*$*; (iv) *for all (i, j)*: (a) $-\partial_{u_i} w_i(u(x(a^*)))\lambda_i + \partial_{u_j} w_i(u(x(a^*)))\lambda_j \leqslant 0$; (b) *and* $(-\partial_{u_i} w_i(u(x(a^*)))\lambda_i + \partial_{u_j} w_i(u(x(a^*)))\lambda_j) t_{ij}(a^*) = 0$.

PROOF. See Appendix A.1. □

The next corollary, likewise, extends to Pareto social systems the characterization of the range and inverse of the correspondence of equilibrium distributions of pure distributive social systems given in Corollary 1.

Let the set of market-efficient allocations of (w, u) be denoted by O. Note that, as a classical application of the second fundamental theorem of welfare economics to differentiable market economies, for any (w, u) that verifies Assumption 2, $x \gg 0$ is a market optimum if and only if $\sum_{i \in N} x_i = (1, \ldots, 1)$ and there exists $(p, \lambda) \gg 0$ in $\mathbb{R}^l \times \mathbb{R}^n$ such that $\partial_{x_i} u_i(x_i) = \lambda_i p$ for all i [see for instance Mercier Ythier (2000a, Lemma 3, p. 60)]. The supporting vector (p, λ) of x is unique up to a positive multiplicative constant. We denote by $(p(x), \lambda(x))$ the unique supporting vector of x such that $p \in S_l$.

For any fixed (w, u), denote by: $X(\omega)$ the set $\{x : \exists t$ such that $(p, a(x, t))$ is a social equilibrium of $(w, u, \omega)\}$ of equilibrium allocations of a social system (w, u, ω); M the range of correspondence X; M' the range of the restriction X' of X to $\{\omega : \omega_i > 0$ for all $i\}$; Ω the inverse of X, that is, the correspondence defined by $\Omega(x) = \{\omega : x \in X(\omega)\}$ for all x in M; Ω' the inverse of X'. And for any fixed (w, u) that verifies Assumption 2 and any $x \in O \cap \mathbb{R}_{++}^{ln}$, denote by: $\gamma(x) = \{(i, j) \in N \times N : -\partial_{u_i} w_i(u(x))\lambda_i(x) + \partial_{u_j} w_i(u(x))\lambda_j(x) = 0\}$; $\Gamma(x)$ the incidence matrix of digraph $\gamma(x)$.

Corollary 3(i) states that *the range of the correspondence of equilibrium allocations is the subset of market-efficient allocations such that marginal incremental bilateral transfers evaluated at supporting market prices do not increase givers' utilities*. It implies, notably, that *the first fundamental theorem of welfare economics extends to Pareto social systems*, that is, competitive exchange still yields (market) efficiency in the allocation of resources in the context of such social systems. The corollary is a simple consequence of Theorem 4 and the remark above on the supportability of market optima.

---

[36] Assumptions 2(iii)(b) and 2(iv) imply that the equilibrium distribution is interior, which permits to dispense with the twice differentiability of utility functions in the proof of sufficiency of first-order conditions [Arrow and Enthoven (1961: Theorem 1(b))].

COROLLARY 3. *Let (w, u) verify Assumption 2. Then:* (i) $M' = \{x \in O \cap \mathbb{R}_{++}^{ln}: -\partial_{u_i} w_i(u(x))\lambda_i(x) + \partial_{u_j} w_i(u(x))\lambda_j(x) \leqslant 0 \text{ for all } (i, j)\}$. (ii) *For all* $x \in M'$, $\Omega'(x)$ *is the convex set* $\{\omega: \omega_i > 0 \text{ for all } i; \text{ and } \exists t \geqslant 0 \text{ such that } g(t) \subset \gamma(x) \text{ and } p(x)x_i = p(x)(\omega_i + \Delta_i t) \text{ for all } i\}$.

4.2.3. Equivalence of money transfers and in-kind transfers

A simple but important aspect of social equilibrium is the *equivalence of cash and in-kind transfers* for non-paternalistic individuals operating on the background of perfectly competitive markets. Non-paternalistic utility interdependence implies that gifts of commodities are driven only by, and perceived only through, their consequences on the distribution of wealth. And perfect competition with free disposal implies that any beneficiary of a gift in kind can sell it at non-negative market prices, and freely spend the proceeds, without bearing any transaction cost; that is, the set of alternatives of the beneficiary of a gift is influenced by the market value of the gift, and not by its physical characteristics per se.

To make these statements precise, let $v_i : (\mathbb{R}_+^l \setminus \{0\}) \times \mathbb{R}_+ \to \mathbb{R}$ denote individual i's indirect ophelimity function, that is, $v_i(p, r_i) = \max\{u_i(x_i): x_i \in X_i \text{ and } px_i \leqslant r_i\}$ for all price system $p > 0$ and all (post-transfer) wealth $r_i \geqslant 0$ of individual i. Function v_i is well-defined on $(\mathbb{R}_+^l \setminus \{0\}) \times \mathbb{R}_+$ if u_i is a continuous function $\mathbb{R}_+^l \to \mathbb{R}$. Let: τ_{ij} be a non-negative wealth transfer (money gift) from i to j; $\tau_i = (\tau_{ij})_{j \neq i}$ denote the corresponding vector of money gifts of individual i; $\tau = (\tau_1, \ldots, \tau_n)$ be the vector of money gifts in society; $\Delta_i \tau = \sum_{j: j \neq i} (\tau_{ji} - \tau_{ij})$ be the net transfer of wealth accruing to individual i when the gift vector is τ; and $(\tau_{\setminus i}^*, \tau_i)$ the gift vector obtained from τ^* and τ by substituting τ_i for τ_i^* in τ^*. The social equilibrium can receive then the following alternative definition, essentially equivalent to Definition 3:

DEFINITION 3'. A social equilibrium with money gifts of (w, u, ω) is a vector (p^*, x^*, τ^*) such that: (i) $\sum_{i \in N} x_i^* \leqslant (1, \ldots, 1)$ and $p^*((1, \ldots, 1) - \sum_{i \in N} x_i^*) = 0$; (ii) $x_i^* \in \{x_i \in X_i: p^* x_i^* \leqslant p^* \omega_i + \Delta_i \tau^* \text{ and } u_i(x_i) = v_i(p^*, p^* \omega_i + \Delta_i \tau^*)\}$ for all i; (iii) and τ_i^* solves $\max\{w_i(v_1(p^*, p^* \omega_1 + \Delta_1(\tau_{\setminus i}^*, \tau_i)), \ldots, v_n(p^*, p^* \omega_n + \Delta_n(\tau_{\setminus i}^*, \tau_i))): \tau_i \geqslant 0 \text{ and } p^* \omega_i + \Delta_i(\tau_{\setminus i}^*, \tau_i) \geqslant 0\}$ for all i.

THEOREM 5. *Let (w, u, ω) verify Assumption 2 and suppose moreover that v_i is differentiable in $\mathbb{R}_{++}^l \times \mathbb{R}_{++}$ for all i. Then, (p^*, a^*) is a social equilibrium of (w, u, ω) if and only if $(p^*, x(a^*), p^* t(a^*))$ is a social equilibrium with money gifts of (w, u, ω).*

PROOF. See Appendix A.1. □

4.2.4. Existence of a social equilibrium

Theorem 6 and Corollary 4 below extend Theorem 2 and Corollary 2 (Section 3.4.1.2) to the social equilibria with competitive market exchange. They imply the existence properties of Theorem 2 and Corollary 2 respectively, for pure distributive social systems that verify Assumptions 2(ii) to 2(iv). They imply, also, the existence of a competitive exchange equilibrium for the standard differentiable economies of Assumption 2(i) (just let w_i be the canonical projection $\mathbb{R}^n \to \mathbb{R} : \hat{u} \to \hat{u}_i$ for all i, that is, suppose that all individuals are egoistic).

THEOREM 6. *Let (w, u) verify Assumption 2, and suppose moreover that v_i is differentiable in $\mathbb{R}^l_{++} \times \mathbb{R}_{++}$ for all i. Then: if (w, u) has no equilibrium for some ω such that $\omega_i > 0$ for all i, there exists a market optimum x and a system of market prices p supporting x such that the digraph $\{(i, j): -\partial_{u_i} w_i(u(x))\partial_{r_i} v_i(p, px_i) + \partial_{u_j} w_i(u(x))\partial_{r_j} v_j(p, px_j) > 0\}$ has a directed circuit.*

COROLLARY 4. *Let (w, u, ω) verify Assumption 2, and suppose moreover that: v_i is differentiable in $\mathbb{R}^l_{++} \times \mathbb{R}_{++}$ for all i; and either (w, u) is a Pareto–BBV social system; or (w, u) verifies* extended weak self-centredness, *meaning that $-\partial_{u_i} w_i(v(p, r))\partial_{r_i} v_i(p, r_i) + \partial_{u_j} w_i(v(p, r))\partial_{r_j} v_j(p, r_j) \leq 0$ for all $(p, r) \in \mathbb{R}^l_{++} \times \mathbb{R}^n_+$ such that $r_j \geq r_i > 0$ (where $r = (r_1, \ldots, r_n)$ and $v(p, r) = (v_1(p, r_1), \ldots, v_n(p, r_n))$). Then (w, u, ω) has an equilibrium.*

The proofs of Theorem 6 and Corollary 3 are built on the same pattern as those of Theorem 2 and Corollary 2, but much longer, if only because the former implies the existence of a competitive equilibrium for general exchange economies and the latter refers to the second fundamental theorem of welfare economics (that is, to the existence of price systems supporting the market optima). We will omit them therefore, and refer the reader to Mercier Ythier (2000a, Lemma 6,[37] pp. 63–64, and Theorem 3,[38] p. 52).

The introduction of market exchange generates at least two additional sources of existence failures of the general equilibrium of gifts, besides the altruistic war of gifts already analyzed in Section 3.4.1.1 above: one potentially associated with negative prices of some commodities when disposal is costly, and the other one with paternalistic motives for gift-giving (that is, preferences of the type $W_i(x_1, \ldots, x_{i-1}, u_i(x_i), x_{i+1}, \ldots, x_n)$). The owner of a commodity with a negative market price, for instance, can get rid of it at no cost simply by "giving" it. This will result in the non-existence of equilibrium if individuals are not benevolent enough to refrain from making such damaging gifts: all the temporary owners will try to "give" their bad commodities, thereby generating a non-altruistic war of gifts. Wars of gifts, which involve a direct interaction of individual gifts, are possible also in the presence of paternalistic motives, but the latter are also susceptible to generate a plague of existence failures involving an interaction of

---

[37] A directed circuit of the digraph $\gamma'(x)$ of Lemma 6 is a directed circuit of $\{(i, j): -\partial_{u_i} w_i(u(x))\partial_{r_i} v_i(p, px_i) + \partial_{u_j} w_i(u(x))\partial_{r_j} v_j(p, px_j) > 0\}$ by the Lemma 4(v) of the same article.
[38] Extended weak self-centredness is equivalent to the Assumption 2 of Mercier Ythier (2000a). And digraphs $\gamma'(x)$ have no circuits in Pareto–BBV social systems.

gift-giving with market exchange: paternalistic donors, notably, might relentlessly try to alter the consumption structure of beneficiaries by gifts in kind, and in so doing be systematically frustrated in their attempts, because the latter prefer to sell the gifts and use the corresponding purchasing power to achieve their own, different consumption objectives.[39]

These existence failures are intimately related to the specificities of the Cournot–Nash behavioral assumption in the case of gift-giving. The individuals of the abstract social systems of Sections 3.1 and 4.2 act as if they believed that their gifts were consumed by the beneficiaries (formally, individual i, facing action vector a^* and making gift t_i, views j's consumption as $x_j = z_j^* + \omega_j + \Delta_j(t_{\setminus i}^*, t_i)$). This can be interpreted as non-tuistic behavior in some sense of the latter: donors "believe" that their gifts are consumed by beneficiaries exactly as traders on competitive markets "believe" that they can purchase or sell any quantity at market prices. Both exhibit the same absence of concern for the actual purposes of their partners in gift and exchange, which characterizes non-tuism. An equilibrium of gifts is precisely a social state where donors' conjectures on the use of the gifts they decide to make are all validated by their beneficiaries. The non-existence of the equilibrium of gifts means, consequently, that there is, at any social state, a donor whose conjecture is invalidated by a beneficiary.

The invalidation of a donor's conjecture involves a non-expected use, by the beneficiary of the gift, of his property right on the latter (the gift received is sold, for instance, or given to somebody else, instead of being consumed). The remedy to existence failure with this type of individual giving behavior, therefore, clearly calls for adjustments in the definition of property rights, which will depend on the nature of the existence problem under consideration.[40] A natural remedy to non-paternalistic altruistic wars of gifts, for instance, is the creation of a common property right of the individuals involved, on some adequate fraction of the sum of their private ownerships. Likewise, a simple

---

[39] More precisely, suppose that individuals have paternalistic utilities of the type of functions W_i and define a social equilibrium of (W, u, ω) as in Section 4.2.3 (Definition 3) with obvious adaptations. One establishes straightforwardly that if (p^*, a^*) is an equilibrium, then $(p^*, x(a^*))$ is a competitive equilibrium of $(u, (\omega_i + \Delta_i t(a^*))_{i \in N})$ [Mercier Ythier (1989, P.3.1, p. 83)]. One can generate examples of non-existence of a social equilibrium in the following way: let (u, ω') have exactly one equilibrium for all ω'; and choose W so that, for all ω', there is an individual who wants to deviate from competitive equilibrium allocation by means of a paternalistic transfer to some other agent.

[40] An interesting related issue is the possibility, for the beneficiary of a gift, of *refusing* it. In the context of the present theory of gift-giving, it can happen that a gift impoverishes the "beneficiary", notably when it has a negative market value (this supposes that disposal is costly or impossible) or in the case of a transfer paradox (see Section 4.3). Gift-giving then induces encroachments of the property rights of donors (their right to make gifts) on the property rights of "beneficiaries" (the set of useful alternatives accessible to them). Gift-refusal, as a limit imposed by the beneficiaries on the freedom of action of donors, is one of the possible (spontaneous) means of regulation of such encroachments. Note that, with the assumptions of Section 4.2 (*free disposal*, which implies the non-negativity of market prices; and *individual* gift-giving, which makes the transfer paradox implausible), returning a gift to the donor or transferring it to a third person is a costless and effective way, for the beneficiary of the gift, of "refusing" it. In other words, with these assumptions, a gift can only *enlarge* the set of useful alternatives accessible to the beneficiary.

solution to the non-altruistic wars of gifts of commodities with negative prices will consist either in prohibiting such damaging gifts, or in designing adequate disincentives such as taxes on these transfers that will discourage them or at least permit appropriate compensations for the losses of "beneficiaries". Finally, if the wide spectrum of tutelary motives is incorporated in social equilibrium analysis, the whole range of restrictions on individual property rights will have to be used to solve (if at all possible) the existence problems, from the creation of common property rights to the restrictions on specific types of individual property rights, the design of adequate incentive mechanisms or the command of specific types of individual actions.

Notice, to conclude, that the existence failures discussed informally above are not related to fundamental non-convexities such as discussed by Starrett (1972): an appropriate commodification, as public goods or bads, of the externalities generated by utility interdependence, and the design of corresponding standard Lindahl pricing and equilibrium solve the existence problem, at least as long as there is no local satiation of the Pareto social preordering.[41]

4.3. Perfectly substitutable transfers and the transfer problem

The transfer problem or transfer paradox refers to the logical possibility that an agent or group of agents withholding, destroying or transferring some fraction of their initial endowment ends up better off (and/or the recipients of transfers, if any, worse off) in ophelimity terms, due to the general equilibrium effects of their endowment manipulations on market prices. This was first mentioned by Keynes (1929), and discussed later on mainly in the context of the theory of international trade and aid [see Eichengreen (1987) for a historical overview, and Kanbur's contribution to this Handbook for a well-documented review of the applications to international aid].

Let us briefly summarize here the basis of the argument. It was shown notably that: (i) there is no possibility of a transfer paradox in a Walrasian economy with two agents, two commodities, dynamically stable equilibrium and no administrative costs or waste associated with the transfer [that is, the transfer will necessarily, then, impoverish the donor and enrich the recipient: see for example Johnson (1956)]; (ii) but such a possibility appears when anyone of the former assumptions is relaxed. For example, the possibility of a transfer paradox in the presence of imperfect competition is established by Kolm (1969, pp. 529–548), for stable exchange equilibrium of two commodities (or more) between two agents, one of them (the "monopolistic" nation) able to manipulate the terms of trade with the other (the "exploited" nation) for one pair of traded goods at

---

[41] Local Pareto satiation due to malevolence (Section 4.1.2) does not raise any fundamental obstacle to existence either. The existence result of Theorem 6 notably, which applies to non-paternalistic preferences, supposes no restriction on individual malevolence. If all individuals are non-paternalistic malevolent, for instance, the social equilibrium allocation of (w, u, ω) is simply the competitive equilibrium allocation of the induced exchange economy (u, ω), whose existence is unrelated to the satiation (if any) of the social Pareto preordering.

least. Likewise, the possibility of a transfer paradox at stable Walrasian equilibrium is established, notably, by Bhagwati, Brecher and Hatta (1983) for economies with more than two agents [see also Gale (1974)], and by Kemp and Wong (1993) for two-agent, two-commodity economies with a cost of transfer. General possibility results are derived in Guesnerie and Laffont (1978), and Postlewaite (1979), for pure exchange economies, without explicit reference to Walrasian stability. The former, building on the Debreu–Sonnenschein theorem, establish that "nearly any group of agents can be embedded in a competitive exchange economy in which they could find it profitable to reallocate their initial endowments". And the latter proves, by direct construction of examples, that any Pareto-efficient individually rational mechanism of pure exchange economies (including, therefore, competitive market exchange) can be manipulated, notably by coalitions which could enter general exchange in an improved position by reallocating the initial endowments of their members. Sertel (1994) extends the results of Postlewaite to Lindahl equilibrium of simple public good economies of the strong BBV type.

The transfer paradox is firmly established, therefore, as a logical possibility, stemming essentially from complex interactions of substitution effects and income effects at general equilibrium. This creates in turn new possibilities of non-benevolent (egoistic or malevolent) gift-giving in general Pareto social systems, in addition to the non-altruistic gifts of market bads already discussed in Section 4.2.4. And this opens moreover the possibility of a new class of strategic behavior, where individuals or coalitions "play with the market" (that is, consciously manipulate market prices) in order to achieve their ends, benevolent or not.

The practical importance of such logical possibilities should not be overstated, nevertheless, at least in the context of the Pareto social systems of Sections 4 and 5, where transfer decisions are made by price-taking individuals, with the implicit underlying assumption that individuals are "small" relative to the economy. "Small" agents, in other words, rightfully consider that their transfer decisions have negligible effects on equilibrium market prices; and they are consequently unwilling (and also, in practice, unable) to undertake the sophisticated calculations required to make usable predictions on such effects [see Postlewaite and Roberts (1976) for an elaborate treatment of this matter]. This is not true anymore, naturally, in principle at least, when *collective* gift-giving is considered, as will be the case in the study of Pareto-efficient redistribution developed in Section 6 below. The latter will be formulated, consequently, in the simpler analytical framework of pure distributive social systems (see Footnote 53, in Section 6.1).

5. The effectiveness of public redistribution with perfectly substitutable transfers

An aspect of the perfect substitutability of transfers that has received much attention in the literature is the so-called neutrality property, which specifies general conditions under which the social equilibrium is invariant to exogenous, publicly decided redistribution of wealth.

A derivation of the neutrality property is already implicit in the two-persons bargaining triangle of Shibata (1971), but its first explicit formulations are those of Barro (1974) and Becker (1974), concentrating on the case where the social equilibrium coincides with a rational optimum (the dynastic optimum in Barro's macrosocial system[42] and the family head's optimum in Becker's microsocial system).

The study of neutrality was developed initially in the line of Barro's overlapping generations model [see notably Bernheim and Bagwell (1988), the review of Laitner (1997), and Chapter 15 of Michel et al. in the present Handbook]. Its study in the present setup received a new impulse from the contributions of Warr (1982, 1983). The latter considered a simple distributive social system with three agents, two of them rich and making altruistic gifts to the third one, an egoistic poor (that is, using the terminology of this chapter, a BBV equilibrium with two non-poor giving to a single poor). He observed that: (i) social equilibrium is not Pareto-efficient; (ii) marginal lump-sum redistribution of endowments between rich individuals or from the rich to the poor is compensated dollar for dollar by appropriate changes in equilibrium charitable contributions, and leaves therefore the equilibrium distribution of wealth unchanged as long as charitable gifts remain positive; (iii) the achievement of a Pareto-efficient distribution by means of public transfers requires the complete crowding-out of private charity. Similar contemporary statements were made, in the same basic framework of the public good theory of charity, by Sugden (1982), Cornes and Sandler (1984a), Roberts (1984, 1985), and Kemp (1984).[43]

The present account draws on the general formulations of the property provided by Mercier Ythier (2000a) for the extended distributive social system of Section 4, and by Bergstrom, Blume and Varian (1986) for strong BBV distributive social systems. It concludes with a brief account of the known extensions of the property to cases of neutral distortionary redistribution.

---

[42] The reference to dynasties as representative macroagents aggregating a series of altruistically linked generations remains implicit in Barro's original article but was frequently used in subsequent formulations of his result. The relation between equilibrium and dynastic optimum is partly obscured, in Barro's model, by his formulation of the utility of a generation as a function of its consumption and the *indirect utility* of the subsequent generation. This formulation combines a notion of interdependence of primitive utilities with a notion of dynamic equilibrium. These two features were disentangled in subsequent developments, thanks to the use of subgame perfect Nash equilibrium as explicitly dynamic (and dynamically consistent) equilibrium concept [see notably Bernheim and Bagwell (1988), and Chapter 15 of Michel et al. in this Handbook]. Note that the dynastic optimum need not be an equilibrium or the unique equilibrium in such frameworks, even when all generations are connected by a chain of operative transfers (see Section 4 of Chapter 15 of Michel et al., and notably their Figures 1 and 3).

[43] Sugden elicits the marginal compensation effect "dollar for dollar" with any number of contributors. Cornes and Sandler establish inefficiency and neutrality with any number of identical contributors. Robert's model and conclusions are the same as Warr's, with identical rich and an endogenous determination of public charitable transfers. And Kemp extends Warr's neutrality theorem to the case of multiple public goods.

5.1. Neutrality in general Pareto social systems

The *distributive policies* examined in this section, and in Sections 5.2.1 and 5.2.2 below, consist of *public lump-sum redistributions of individual endowments*. From now on, we let: $\theta_{ij} \in \mathbb{R}_+^{ln}$ denote a vector of public lump-sum transfers of endowments from i to $j \neq i$; $\theta = (\theta_{12}, \ldots, \theta_{1n}, \ldots, \theta_{n1}, \ldots, \theta_{nn-1})$.

Distributive policy is said *locally neutral* if equilibrium distribution is not altered by public lump-sum transfers θ that maintain the resulting distribution of individual endowments $(\omega_1^0 + \Delta_1\theta, \ldots, \omega_n^0 + \Delta_n\theta)$ within some relevant neighborhood of the initial distribution ω^0. It is said *globally neutral* if equilibrium distribution is not altered by any lump-sum transfers. More precisely: public lump-sum redistribution is *locally weakly* (resp. *strongly*) *neutral* at some vector $\omega^0 \in \{\omega: \omega_i > 0 \text{ for all } i\}$ of individual endowments if there exist a neighborhood $V(\omega^0)$ of ω^0 in $\{\omega: \omega_i > 0 \text{ for all } i\}$ and a vector of ophelimity levels u^0 such that u^0 is a (resp. the unique) social equilibrium vector of ophelimity levels for all ω in $V(\omega^0)$. Public lump-sum redistribution, second, is *globally (strongly) neutral* if there exists an ophelimity vector u^0 such that u^0 is the unique social equilibrium ophelimity vector for all ω in $\{\omega: \omega_i > 0 \text{ for all } i\}$.

We know already that, as a simple implication of Theorem 4 or Corollary 3, the set of (interior) decentralisable allocations of a Pareto social system, that is, the set of interior allocations that can be reached by a distributive policy operating by lump-sum transfers, is the set $M' = \{x \in O \cap \mathbb{R}_{++}^{ln}: -\partial_{u_i} w_i(u(x))\lambda_i(x) + \partial_{u_j} w_i(u(x))\lambda_j(x) \leq 0 \text{ for all } (i, j)\}$ of market optima such that donors' utilities are non-increasing in their marginal incremental bilateral gifts evaluated at supporting market prices.

Global neutrality, therefore, *is equivalent to set $u(M')$ being a singleton* (Theorem 7(i) below). A casual examination of the examples of distributive social systems given in Section 3 shows that global neutrality is, consequently, a very strong property, corresponding principally to the case of unanimous agreement on the best accessible distribution (i.e., with the notations of Section 3, $x^i = x^j$ for all i, j).[44]

The *local neutrality* property is stated in parts (ii) and (iii) of Theorem 7, and in the Corollaries 5 and 6 of Theorems 4 and 7 respectively (proofs in Appendix A).

Theorem 7(iii) characterizes local neutrality as *a situation where the digraph of equilibrium transfers is connected*.[45]

---

[44] An interesting special case of singlevaluedness of $u(M)$ is Ramsey's dynastic framework (1928), where the agents are generations and where, using Pareto's vocabulary, their ophelimities are integrated in a single utility function, common to all generations, consisting of the (non-discounted) sum of generations' ophelimities. While very close to Barro's model of 1974 (see Footnote 42 above) in several important respects, it differs nevertheless fundamentally from the latter on the neutrality property. Barro's neutrality property is local in nature: his equilibrium does not coincide, generally, with the dynastic optimum when current generations are not connected to all future generations by a chain of positive transfers.

[45] A digraph γ is *connected* if any pair of its vertices is connected by a path contained in γ (that is, by a sequence of *adjacent* darts of γ, where "adjacent" means "having at least one common vertex"). Note that the path connecting two vertices needs not be directed (a path is *directed* if: either the head-vertex of any of its darts coincides with the tail-vertex of the subsequent dart in the sequence; or the tail-vertex of any of its darts coincides with the head-vertex of the subsequent dart in the sequence).

The first part of Corollary 5 states that equilibrium survives public redistributions of endowments if and only if the corresponding wealth transfers can be *offset* by variations in equilibrium private transfers that leave unchanged the structure of the graph of private transfers which is associated with the equilibrium allocation. Note that, in the important special case of *ceteris paribus* public lump-sum redistributions between any pair of individuals (say i and j) connected by a positive equilibrium wealth transfer (say, from i to j): public transfers in the *direction opposite* to the direction of the private transfer (that is, public redistributions from j to i) *can be offset* by an equal opposite variation in the equilibrium wealth transfer from i to j (as the public transfer from j to i can be used by i to feed his private transfer to j); and public transfers in the *same direction* as the private transfer *can be offset* by an equal opposite variation in the equilibrium wealth transfer from i to j *if and only if* the latter (private transfer) is *at least as large* as the former (public transfer). Such ceteris paribus bilateral public redistributions are neutral, therefore, by Corollary 5, as is, by extension, any distributive policy analyzable in a sequence of such redistributions.

The second part of Corollary 5 states that equilibrium does not survive public redistributions involving net transfers of wealth *between* the components of the graph.[46] This result is intuitively appealing. It draws its logical strength from the fact that there is only one graph of potential equilibrium gifts associated with any potential equilibrium allocation ($\gamma(x)$, associated with $x \in M$). It points to both: a sufficient condition for the non-neutrality of distributive policy, namely, that it performs redistributions of wealth between the connected components of the graph of potential equilibrium gifts; and to its interpretation, that is, that offsetting individual counter-transfers will be incompatible then with the structure of this graph.

Corollary 6 states essentially that an equilibrium allocation survives public lump-sum transfers between the vertices of a connected component of the graph of equilibrium transfers whenever public transfers are *sufficiently small* to be offset by appropriate variations in existing private transfers.

Combining the theorem and corollaries, we end up with the following formulation of the local neutrality property of general Pareto social systems. Public lump-sum transfers *do not alter* equilibrium distribution when the net transfers they imply are *confined to the connected components* of the graph of equilibrium transfers *and can be offset* by appropriate variations in existing private transfers. Public lump-sum transfers *alter* equilibrium distribution: (i) when they imply net transfers of wealth *between the connected components* of the graph of equilibrium transfers at prior equilibrium prices; (ii) or when they imply net transfers of wealth *inside the connected components* of the graph of equilibrium transfers at prior equilibrium prices, *which cannot be offset* by appropriate variations in existing private transfers.

---

[46] A *connected component* of digraph γ is a connected subdigraph of γ that is a proper subdigraph of no connected subdigraph of γ.

THEOREM 7. *Suppose that (w, u) verifies Assumption 2. (i) Distributive policy is globally neutral if and only if set $u(M')$ is a singleton. (ii) For all $x \in M'$, $\Omega'(x)$ is a convex set of dimension $l(n - c(\gamma(x)))$, where $c(\gamma(x))$ denotes the number of connected components of graph $\gamma(x)$. (iii) In particular: distributive policy is locally weakly neutral at an element ω^0 of the interior of $\Omega'(x)$ in $\{\omega\colon \omega_i > 0 \text{ for all } i\}$ if and only if $\gamma(x)$ is connected.*

COROLLARY 5. *Suppose that (w, u, ω) verifies Assumption 2, and let (p, a) be an equilibrium. (i) $(p, x(a))$ is an equilibrium price-allocation vector of $(w, (\omega_1 + \Delta_1\theta, \ldots, \omega_n + \Delta_n\theta))$ if and only if there exists t such that: $g(t) \subset \gamma(x(a))$; and $p(t_{ij} - t_{ij}(a) - (t_{ji} - t_{ji}(a))) + p(\theta_{ij} - \theta_{ji}) = 0$ for all (i, j). (ii) In particular, $(p, x(a))$ is not an equilibrium price-allocation vector of $(w, (\omega_1 + \Delta_1\theta, \ldots, \omega_n + \Delta_n\theta))$ whenever θ implies net transfers of wealth between connected components of $\gamma(x(a))$, that is, whenever there is a connected component γ of $\gamma(x(a))$ such that $\sum_{(i,j) \in V_\gamma \times (N \setminus V_\gamma)} p(\theta_{ij} - \theta_{ji}) < 0$, where V_γ denotes the set of vertices of γ.*

COROLLARY 6. *Suppose that (w, u, ω) verifies Assumption 2, and let (p, a) be an equilibrium. Then, there exists a neighborhood V of 0 in $\{\theta\colon \theta_{ij} = 0 \text{ whenever } i \text{ and } j \text{ are in two distinct connected components of } g(t(a))\}$ such that, for all $\theta \in V$, $(p, x(a))$ is an equilibrium price-allocation vector of $(w, (\omega_1 + \Delta_1\theta, \ldots, \omega_n + \Delta_n\theta))$.*

We conclude this account of the neutrality property of Pareto social systems by three brief remarks.

The first one concerns the structure of the digraph of equilibrium gifts. I established in Mercier Ythier (2004b, Theorems 3 and 4), that the digraph $\gamma'(x) = \{(i, j) \in \gamma(x)\colon i \neq j\}$ of potential equilibrium gifts at an equilibrium distribution x of a pure distributive social system are forests (that is, contain no circuit) generically. In other words, circuits in digraphs of equilibrium transfers are coincidental for pure distributive social systems. A consequence of this is that, generically, $\dim \Omega(x) = \#\gamma'(x)(= n - c(\gamma(x)))$ in such social systems.

Similarly, the set of equilibrium distributions that a distributive policy can reach, from a given (interior) equilibrium distribution x of a distributive social system (w, ω), by operating small lump-sum transfers in the neighborhood of ω, is, generically, a local manifold $V(x)$ of dimension $n - 1 - \#\gamma'(x)$ [that is, generically, $\dim V(x) + \dim \Omega(x) = n - 1 = \dim S_n$, as a simple consequence of Mercier Ythier (2004b, Theorems 3 and 4 and Corollary 2)].

The third remark concerns an issue raised by equilibrium multiplicity. In the presence of multiple equilibria, the same system of public lump-sum transfers can be neutral for one equilibrium and non-neutral for another, that is, *distributive policy can be weakly (locally) neutral and not strongly so*. Figure 13, adapted from Example 4 of Mercier Ythier (2004b), provides a graphical illustration of such a situation. It describes a three-agent pure distributive social system (w, ω) with two equilibrium distributions b and d such that $\gamma(b) = \{(1, 2); (3, 2)\} = \gamma(d)$. Sets $\Omega(b)$ and $\Omega(d)$ are triangles $bb'b''$ and

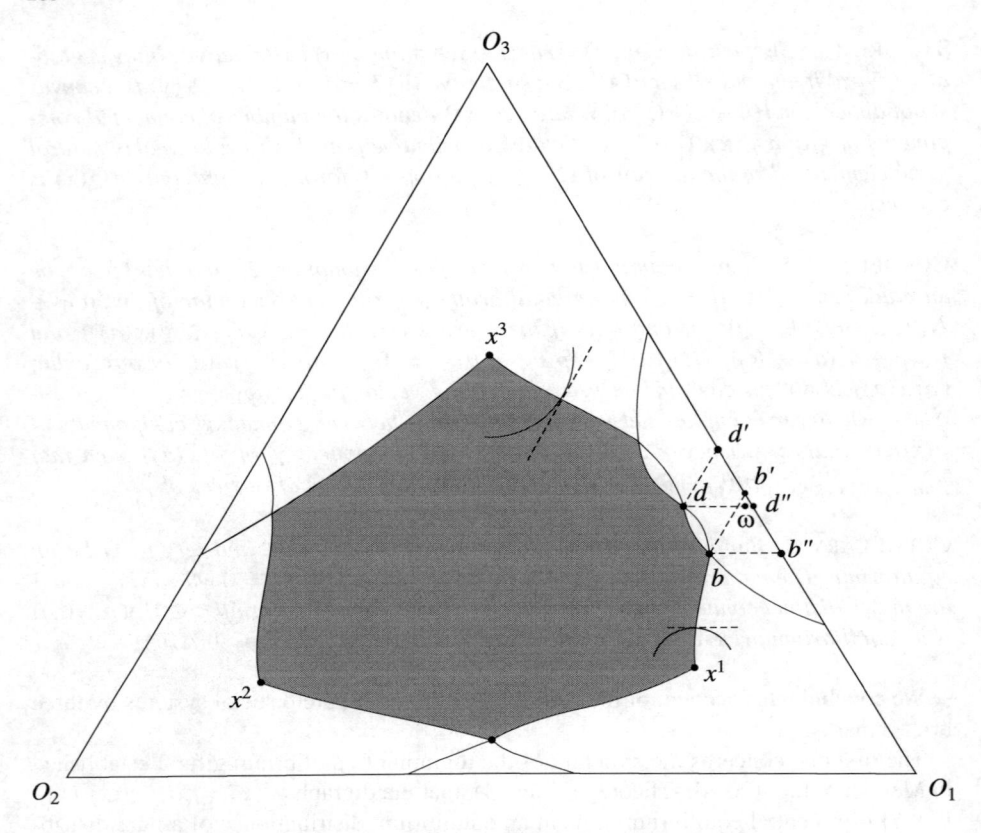

Figure 13. Neutrality with multiple equilibria.

$dd'd''$ respectively. There are two positive equilibrium gifts at b, from agents 1 and 3 to agent 2 (that is, $g(t) = \{(1, 2); (3, 2)\}$ at the associate equilibrium gift vector t), and only one positive equilibrium gift at d, from agent 1 to agent 2 (that is, $g(t') = \{(1, 2)\}$ at the corresponding equilibrium gift vector t'). One verifies easily from the figure that there is local weak neutrality with respect to b, but not with respect to d. For example, distribution d does not survive any public redistribution diminishing ω_3, while distribution b does if the redistribution is not too large. Such examples justify the distinction of a *weak* and a *strong* (local) neutrality property in the formal definitions of neutrality above.

5.2. Neutrality in BBV distributive social systems

The neutrality results above imply the neutrality properties of Bergstrom, Blume and Varian (1986: Theorems 1 and 7), [hence those of Warr (1983), and Kemp (1984)] as special cases, with two additional precisions following from the specificities of BBV distributive social systems.

The first precision follows from the fact that the digraphs of potential equilibrium transfers are always forests in BBV equilibrium, as subdigraphs of $\{(i, j): i$ is non-poor and j is poor$\}$. Consequently, we have dim $\Omega(x) = \#\gamma'(x) = n - c(\gamma(x))$ for all $x \in M$.

The second precision applies to strong BBV social systems where the private good (i.e. individual consumption of non-poor) and the public good (i.e. the aggregate consumption of the poor) are both strictly normal for non-poor. We know that BBV equilibrium is unique then (cf. Theorem 3, in Section 3.4.2.2 above), which implies that neutrality is strong whenever it holds.

Bergstrom and Varian (1985a), show how the neutrality property of strong BBV distributive social systems can be related to a general property of independence of Nash equilibrium from the distribution of agents' characteristics. Their result relies on the resolution of a Pexider functional equations [Aczel (1966, p. 141)], a technique already used to characterize the systems of individual preferences that imply the independence of allocative *efficiency* from distribution in the context of economies with public goods [Bergstrom and Cornes (1983)] and exchange economies [Bergstrom and Varian (1985b)]. They show that the equilibrium of a strong BBV distributive social system with at least 3 agents is independent from distribution if and only if it solves a system of equations of the type: $g_i = \alpha_i(G) + \beta_i(G)\omega_i$, $i = 1, \ldots, n$, where $g_i = \sum_{j>m} t_{ij}$ is i's charitable contribution, $G = \sum_{i \in N} g_i$ denotes total contribution to charity, and α_i and β_i are continuous functions of G. Letting φ_i denote the inverse of i's unconstrained demand for the public good (Section 3.4.2.2), and supposing implicitly that φ_i is well-defined for all i (as this must be the case if charity is a normal good for all agents), Bergstrom and Varian obtain $g_i = \omega_i + G - \varphi_i(G)\omega_i$, $i = 1, \ldots, n$ as a qualifying system.

5.2.1. Neutral lump-sum taxation

The neutrality property of BBV distributive social systems is local in nature. In other words, it does not hold, in general, for *any* system of lump-sum redistributions of endowments. It will generally be possible, notably, to achieve non-neutral public transfers by crowding out some of the equilibrium private transfers. In the BBV social system of Figure 11, for example: equalizing redistributions of endowments between non-poor agents 1 and 2 in segment $O_1 O_2$ are non-neutral whenever $\omega \notin]a, b[$ (the equilibrium distribution runs over the broken line $\beta^1 x^* \beta^2$ when the initial distribution runs over segment $O_1 O_2$); and any distribution of surface $\beta^1 x^* \beta^2 O_3$ (set M) is accessible by fully crowding out private transfers (status quo is the unique equilibrium for all $\omega \in M$).

Bergstrom, Blume and Varian (1986) give results of comparative statics concerning the effects of public lump-sum redistribution (neutral or non-neutral) on the provision of a public good when own consumption and the public good are strictly normal for all potential contributors. We reproduce them below without proof,[47] as Theorems 8, 9 and 10 (corresponding, respectively, to their Theorems 4, 5 and 6), with a few minor adaptations in formulation following, notably, from our interpretation of the public good as the aggregate wealth of the poor (see Section 3.3.3). The notions and notations used in the theorems have been defined above, in Sections 3.3.3 and 3.4.2.2.

Theorem 8 deals with the consequences of *redistributions of endowments among non-poor* individuals on equilibrium total charitable donations ((i), (ii) and (iv)) and on the set of contributors ((iii)).

THEOREM 8. *Let w be a strong BBV distributive social system and suppose that, for all non-poor i, there exists a single-valued (unconstrained) demand function for the public good f_i that is differentiable and such that $0 < \partial f_i(r) < 1$ for all $r > 0$. Then, in an equilibrium: (i) any change in the wealth distribution that leaves unchanged the aggregate wealth of current contributors will either increase or leave unchanged the equilibrium total private donation; (ii) any change in the distribution of wealth that increases the aggregate wealth of current contributors will necessarily increase the equilibrium total private donation; (iii) if a redistribution of income among current contributors increases the equilibrium total private donation, then the set of contributing consumers after the redistribution must be a proper subset of the original set of contributors; (iv) any simple transfer of income from one consumer to a currently contributing consumer will either increase or leave constant the equilibrium total private donation.*

Theorem 9 concentrates on the effects of *equalizing redistributions of endowments among the non-poor* on equilibrium total private donations when the latter have *identical donating preferences* (in the sense of identical demand functions f_i, which must not be confused with, and does not imply identical preferences on wealth distribution[48]).

A redistribution is equalizing in the sense of Bergstrom et al. if it is equivalent to a series of bilateral transfers in which the absolute value of the wealth difference between the two parties to the transfer is reduced.

Identical preferences in the sense above and the assumption of Theorem 8 imply that for any equilibrium total supply G^* of private donations, there is a critical wealth level $\omega^* = \varphi(G^*) - G^*$ (where φ is the inverse of individual unconstrained demand for G) such that every consumer with endowment $\omega_i \leq \omega^*$ contributes nothing and every consumer with endowment $\omega_i > \omega^*$ contributes $g_i = \omega_i - \omega^*$ to the public good [Bergstrom, Blume and Varian (1986, Fact 4); see also Andreoni (1988a, 2.1)]. In

---

[47] Proofs rely on simple properties of a function F defined from inverse demand functions φ_i by $F(G, C) = \sum_{i \in C} \varphi_i(G) + (1 - c)G$ where C denotes a set of contributors and $c = \#C$.

[48] Two non-poor agents i and j with identical demand functions $f_i = f_j$ *cannot* be said to have identical preferences relative to wealth distribution (w_i being definitely distinct from w_j) because each of them values his own wealth positively and is indifferent to the wealth of the other (w_i is increasing in x_i and independent of x_j).

particular: all contributors have greater wealth than (non-poor) non-contributors; and all contributors will consume the same amount of the private good as well as of the public good. Moreover:

THEOREM 9. *Let w be a strong BBV distributive social system and suppose that: for all non-poor i, there exists a single-valued (unconstrained) demand function for the public good f_i that is differentiable and such that $0 < \partial f_i(r) < 1$ for all $r > 0$; and $f_i = f_j \,(= f)$ for all pairs of non-poor agents (i, j). Then:* (i) *an equalizing endowment redistribution among the non-poor will never increase the equilibrium total private donation;* (ii) *equalizing endowment redistributions among current (non-poor) non-contributors or among current contributors will leave the equilibrium supply unchanged;* (iii) *equalizing endowment redistributions that involve any transfers from contributors to non-poor non-contributors will decrease the equilibrium total private donation.*

Theorems 8 and 9 described consequences of endowment redistributions among potential and/or actual contributors to charitable donations (that is, among the non-poor). The last theorem of this section considers the effects of *endowment redistributions from non-poor to poor*, corresponding to the case where public and private actions compete in the achievement of charitable redistribution. Its part (i) characterizes neutral public actions of charitable redistribution, that is, public actions that are offset by variations in private transfers. Effective public actions of charitable redistribution are characterized in the parts (ii) and (iii) of the theorem.

THEOREM 10. *Let w be a strong BBV distributive social system and suppose that, for each non-poor i, there exists a single-valued (unconstrained) demand function for the public good f_i that is differentiable and such that $0 < \partial f_i(r) < 1$ for all $r > 0$. Suppose that starting from an initial position where non-poor consumers supply a public good voluntarily, the government supplies some amount of the public good which it pays for from lump-sum taxes on non-poor individuals. Then:* (i) *if the taxes collected from each non-poor individual do not exceed his voluntary contribution to the public good in the absence of government supply, the government's contribution results in an equal reduction in the amount of private contributions;* (ii) *if the government collects some of the taxes that pay for its contribution from non-contributors, the equilibrium total public and private supply of the public good must increase, although private contributions may decrease;* (iii) *if the government collects some of the taxes that pay for its contribution by taxing any contributor by more than the amount of his contribution, the equilibrium total public and private supply of the public good must increase.*

5.2.2. Neutral distortionary taxation

Bernheim (1986), Bernheim and Bagwell (1988), Andreoni (1988a), and Boadway, Pestieau and Wildasin (1989a), have drawn attention to the surprising fact that the neutrality property extended to a large class of "distortionary" taxes and subsidies, namely, tax-subsidy schemes in which the (net) tax paid by an individual depends on his decisions concerning labor participation (Bernheim, Bernheim and Bagwell), private consumption and saving (Bernheim and Bagwell), consumption of a local public commodity or factor (Boadway et al.) or contribution to a public good (Bernheim and Bagwell, Andreoni, Boadway et al.).

While very close in spirit to the results of Section 5.1, and notably to Theorem 7(iii), the neutrality properties of Bernheim (1986, Theorem 1), and Bernheim and Bagwell (1988, proposition), as well as the variant formulated in Game 3 of Andreoni and Bergstrom (1996, Theorem 5), are not directly comparable to them, being formulated in the dynamic setup of a subgame perfect Nash equilibrium. In Bernheim (1986), and Game 3 of Andreoni and Bergstrom, individuals contribute to a public good as in a Pareto–BBV social system with production, except that individual choices of labor participation and individual choices of gift-giving and consumption are not made simultaneously (labor participation is chosen first). And Bernheim and Bagwell (1988) consider the subgame perfect equilibria of an overlapping generations model with infinite horizon where finite-lived individuals maximize altruistic preferences on the whole stream of consumption and leisure profiles of current and future generations subject to the budget constraint determined by past choices of consumption, saving and gift-giving and by taxes based on the latter. Both setups yield the conclusion that any fiscal policy is locally weakly neutral whenever equilibrium is such that there exists, for any pair of individuals, a chain of operative transfers that connects them.

Andreoni (1988a), Andreoni and Bergstrom (1996), Boadway, Pestieau and Wildasin (1989a), and Brunner and Falkinger (1999) exhibit general properties of neutrality of distortionary taxation for the simultaneous Nash equilibrium of strong BBV social systems. A common feature of these contributions is the assumption that the government has a balanced budget for the public good, tax revenues exactly covering public spending on the latter (public provision, if any, and subsidies on private provision). There remain substantial differences between the models, nevertheless, making direct comparisons of results sometimes difficult. Details are presented in small print below.

Andreoni's (1988a) example of a neutral distortionary fiscal policy is framed in the strong BBV distributive social system, and thus allows direct comparisons with the neutrality properties of Sections 5.1 and 5.2. The present account is based on the version of the example presented as Game 2 in Andreoni and Bergstrom (1996). Let (w, ω) be a strong BBV distributive social system and consider the following three-stage game.

In stage 1, the government chooses a personalized lump-sum tax τ_i for each non-poor individual i and subsidizes private donations at rate β ($0 < \beta < 1$). Thus a non-poor consumer who contributes $g_i (= \sum_{j>m} t_{ij})$ will receive a subsidy of βg_i and will have a net tax obligation of $\tau_i - \beta g_i$. The government spends its net revenue $\sum_{i \leqslant m}(\tau_i - \beta g_i)$ on additional units of the public good. This policy mix combines therefore two instruments of financing of the public good that have contrasted consequences on private donations: the subsidy, that encourages private donations, in the sense notably that an increase in the subsidy rate implies, ceteris paribus, an increase in individual contributions (whenever they exist); and the lump-sum tax, that competes with private donations by the neutrality property of distributive social systems.

In stage 2, individual agents play the gift game of the distributive social system (w, ω), amended to incorporate the fiscal determinants of individual behavior. Non-poor agent i faces budget constraint $x_i + g_i \leqslant \omega_i - \tau_i + \beta g_i$, and views the total supply of charitable contributions as $G = g_i + G_{-i} + \sum_{j \leqslant m}(\tau_j - \beta g_j)$ (he "sees through" the government budget constraint) where he takes $G_{-i} = \sum_{j:\, j \neq i} g_j$ and g_j, $j \neq i$, as independent of his own decisions. For any given $g^* = (g_1^*, \ldots, g_m^*)$, any $\tau = (\tau_1, \ldots, \tau_m)$ and any β, he solves therefore $\max\{v_i(x_i, G + \sum_{j > m} \omega_j):\ G \geqslant G_{-i}^* + \sum_{j \leqslant m}(\tau_j - \beta g_j^*)$ and $x_i + G \leqslant \omega_i + \sum_{j \leqslant m:\, j \neq i}((1-\beta)g_j^* - \tau_j)\}$ where $G_{-i}^* = \sum_{j:\, j \neq i} g_j^*$. With well-defined, continuous (unconstrained) demand functions for the public good[49] and strict normality of the public good and of own private consumption for all the rich, the Cournot–Nash equilibrium exists and is unique for any subsidy rate β such that $0 \leqslant \beta < 1$ and any vector τ of individual lump-sum taxes such that $\tau_i < \omega_i$ for all $i \leqslant m$ [Andreoni and Bergstrom (1996, Theorem 3)].

Finally, in stage 3, the government observes the vector of private donations g, collects taxes $\tau_i - \beta g_i$ from each non-poor i and contributes $\sum_{i \leqslant m}(\tau_i - \beta g_i)$ to the public good.

With continuous, strictly convex preferences and strictly normal public and private goods for all $i \leqslant m$, one gets the following (local strong) neutrality property [Andreoni and Bergstrom (1996, Theorem 4)]:

THEOREM 11. *Let g^* be the vector of equilibrium private contributions if lump-sum taxes and subsidies are zero. If the government introduces taxes and subsidies such that $\tau_i \leqslant g_i^*$ for all non-poor i, then in the new equilibrium with taxes and subsidies, each consumer (poor or non-poor) will have the same private consumption as in the original equilibrium and the total amount of public good will also be unchanged.*

That is, this type of fiscal policy is neutral if (and one can add, using Theorem 10 above, only if) lump-sum taxes crowd out, in the strict sense of the word ($\tau_i > g_i^*$), none of the equilibrium private donations. Note that neutrality is a one-stage property here, corresponding to a notion of simultaneous equilibrium at the second stage of the game.

Boadway, Pestieau and Wildasin (1989a) give two neutrality properties of the simultaneous non-cooperative equilibrium for the same type of linear distortionary tax schemes as Andreoni's. They differ significantly from the latter's neutrality result, nevertheless, in assuming that agents do not see through the government budget constraint, for one of them, or that they see through this constraint but have non-zero conjectural variations, for the second result.

Boadway et al. suppose utility functions of the non-poor of the type $v_i(x_i, y_i, G)$, where y_i is interpreted as the quantity of a local public commodity (with sign convention $y_i > 0$) or factor ($y_i < 0$) consumed by agent ("locality") i. Notice that the corresponding social systems are not Pareto social systems in general, but become so with a few innocuous additional assumptions such as, for instance: utility function of rich i weakly separable in (x_i, y_i) for all $i \leqslant m$; and utility function of poor i of the type $x_i + h_i(y_i)$, that is, egoistic and quasi-linear in x_i, for all $i > m$. Boadway et al. moreover assume that the price of the local public goods is $= 1$ before tax,

---

[49] As implied by the continuity and strict convexity of preferences of the non-poor.

that functions v_i are strictly quasi-concave and twice differentiable, and that the private and local public goods x_i and y_i and national public good G are strictly normal for all $i \leqslant m$.

The authors concentrate on the following class of distortionary, balanced, linear tax schemes. The contributions of a locality i to the national public good are subsidized at constant rate s_i ("matching grant rate") by the government. Agent i also pays a lump-sum tax τ_i, and its consumption in the local public good is taxed at constant rate ρ_i. The balanced budget of the central government reads: $\sum_{i \leqslant m} s_i g_i = \sum_{i \leqslant m}(\tau_i + \rho_i y_i)$ for all $(g_1, \ldots, g_m, y_1, \ldots, y_m)$, where spending consists of the subsidies to localities' contributions (there is no direct contribution of the central government to the public good).

The authors restrict their study to interior equilibria, which implies positive private contributions from all potential donors ($g_i > 0$ for all $i = 1, \ldots, m$).

Their first neutrality result deals with the consequences on equilibrium of a change in lump-sum transfers ($\tau_1, \ldots, \tau_m$). It is derived under the assumption that the implications of the budget constraint of the central government for the net tax liabilities of individual agents are not taken into account by the latter. In other words, localities do not see through the national budget constraint, that is, each i simply solves $v_i(x_i, y_i, g_i + G_{-i})$ with respect to (x_i, y_i, g_i), subject to the individual budget constraint $x_i + (1 + \rho_i)y_i + (1 - s_i)g_i \leqslant \omega_i - \tau_i$, for any given G_{-i}. Under the assumptions above, interior Cournot–Nash equilibrium, if any, must be unique, and the authors establish moreover that any change in lump-sum transfers that respects the budget constraint of the central government leaves unchanged the level of provision of the national public good and the private and local public good consumption of each locality (op. cit.: Theorem 1).

This neutrality property does not extend in general to changes in tax-subsidy rates (($\rho_1, \ldots, \rho_m$), ($s_1, \ldots, s_m$)), whether the agents see through the government budget constraint [Andreoni and Bergstrom (1996, Game 1)] or not [Boadway, Pestieau and Wildasin (1989a, Theorem 2)]. Boadway et al. obtain, nevertheless, a neutrality result for general policy changes, when agents see through the government budget constraint and have adequate non-Nash conjectures on the consequences of the policy change on the contributions of others to the national public good. Conjectural variation is specified as follows: each locality assumes that the others will respond to a change in government policy by adjusting their contributions to the national public good by an amount equal to the opposite of the variation in their individual net tax liabilities. It is proved that, then, any policy changes are fully neutralized at interior equilibrium, and that, moreover, each locality's behavior will conform exactly ex post with the conjecture of the others (op. cit.: Theorem 5).

Brunner and Falkinger (1999), finally, provide a general condition on the tax-subsidy scheme that is sufficient, and in general necessary for neutrality at interior simultaneous equilibrium when individual agents see through the government budget constraint.

They suppose the same type of utility functions as Boadway et al. above, with a different interpretation for y_i, construed as the leisure consumption of individual i. The price of leisure is the market wage rate, which will be set $= 1$ below for notational simplicity. Donors' utility functions v_i are strictly quasi-concave and differentiable. Private consumption x_i and y_i and the public good G are strictly normal for all $i \leqslant m$. The net tax liability of individual i is a differentiable function $\varphi_i(x_i, y_i, (g_1, \ldots, g_m))$ of his private consumption and the whole vector of individual contributions to the public good. It is assumed that the vector of tax functions $\varphi = (\varphi_1, \ldots, \varphi_m)$ verifies the following minimal consistency requirements: aggregate tax revenues $\sum_{i \leqslant m} \varphi_i(x_i, y_i, (g_1, \ldots, g_m))$ are equal to the (non-negative) government provision of the public good for all vectors of individual consumption and contribution; and a ceteris paribus increase in an individual contribution is never more than outweighed by a reduction in tax revenues (that is, $\sum_{i \leqslant m} \partial_{g_j} \varphi_i(x_i, y_i, (g_1, \ldots, g_m)) > -1$ for all j and all vectors of individual consumption and contribution). Finally, individual agents see through the government budget constraint, and maximize therefore $v_i(x_i, y_i, G)$ subject to the individual budget constraint $x_i + y_i + G \leqslant \omega_i + \sum_{j \leqslant m:\ j \neq i}(g_j + \varphi_j(x_j, y_j, (g_1, \ldots, g_m)))$, where G denotes total public and private provision of the public good. It is assumed that φ is such that individual budget sets are convex, a condition that is necessarily verified in the important special case where individual tax functions are linear.

Neutrality is shown to depend in a crucial way, in this setup, on the assumption that ceteris paribus variations in an individual contribution do not affect the aggregate net tax liabilities of others, that is, formally: $\sum_{j \leqslant m:\ j \neq i} \partial_{g_i} \varphi_j(x_j, y_j, (g_1, \ldots, g_m)) = 0$ for all i and all vectors of individual consumption and contribution.

The condition is sufficient for neutrality when all potential donors contribute at equilibrium. Precisely [Brunner and Falkinger (1999, Theorem 3.1)]: (i) if φ^* verifies the assumptions above, then the interior Cournot–Nash equilibria associated with $\varphi = \varphi^*$ and $\varphi = 0$ respectively are identical; (ii) if, in particular, φ_i^* is a function of the sole contribution g_i of agent i for all i, then: (a) there exists a lump-sum φ such that an (interior) equilibrium associated with φ^* is also an equilibrium for lump-sum φ; (b) and if there is a change in the tax function φ_i^* of contributor i, such that agent i keeps contributing after the change, then the associate (interior) equilibrium is unchanged. Note that the part (ii) of this theorem extends Theorem 11 above to the present setup. While the two results are not exactly comparable, due to the introduction of leisure as a strictly normal good and to the technical use of the differentiability of utility functions, the former can be viewed, nevertheless, as implying the latter, essentially at least: labor participation being free of tax by assumption, one can derive any (differentiable) social equilibrium of Andreoni–Bergstrom from some appropriate social equilibrium of Brunner–Falkinger, by making equilibrium leisure consumption fixed parameters in the latter.

The condition that ceteris paribus variations in individual contributions do not affect the aggregate net tax liabilities of others is also necessary, in general, for neutrality (op. cit.: Theorem 4.1). This point is established by means of examples of non-neutrality of linear tax-subsidy schemes (op. cit.: Section 5). The class Φ^L of linear schemes considered there are the linear φ such that $\varphi_i(x_i, y_i, (g_1, \ldots, g_m)) = \tau_i + \sum_{j \leqslant m} \beta_{ij} g_j, \sum_{j \leqslant m: j \neq i} \beta_{ji} \geqslant 0$ and $\beta_{ii} > -1$ for all $i \leqslant m$. Condition $\beta_{ii} > -1$ means, in particular, that individual contributions are not fully subsidized, while condition $\sum_{j \leqslant m:\ j \neq i} \beta_{ji} \geqslant 0$ states that the aggregate net tax liabilities of others is non-decreasing in i's private contributions. These tax-subsidy schemes verify the sufficient condition for neutrality above if and only if $\sum_{j \leqslant m:\ j \neq i} \beta_{ji} = 0$ for all i. The authors prove that (op. cit.: Theorem 5.1): an interior equilibrium associated with a linear $\varphi \in \Phi^L$, if any, must be unique; all linear schemes taken in $\{\varphi \in \Phi^L\colon \sum_{j \leqslant m:\ j \neq i} \beta_{ji} = 0$ for all $i\}$ yield the same (unique) interior equilibrium; and if $\varphi \in \Phi^L$ is such that $\sum_{j \leqslant m:\ j \neq i} \beta_{ji} \neq 0$ for some i, then the associate interior equilibrium, if any, differs from the unique interior equilibrium associated with all elements of $\{\varphi \in \Phi^L\colon \sum_{j \leqslant m:\ j \neq i} \beta_{ji} = 0$ for all $i\}$. In short, the condition that ceteris paribus variations in individual contributions do not affect the aggregate net tax liabilities of others is both necessary and sufficient for the neutrality of the linear tax-subsidy schemes of the class Φ^L with respect to the interior Cournot–Nash equilibria of the associate gift games. With the provision above relative to the assumption of strict normality of leisure, this characterization of non-neutral linear schemes implies the non-neutrality properties elicited in Falkinger (1996) (see Appendix A.2.2 below). With the same provision and the additional and more serious restriction stemming from the fact that the characterization applies to interior equilibria only, this result also implies the non-neutrality property of Game 1 of Andreoni and Bergstrom (1996) (their Theorem 2: see Appendix A.2.2 again). But it does not imply the non-neutrality property elicited by Boadway, Pestieau and Wildasin (1989a) (their Theorems 2 and 3: see Appendix A.2.2), where it is supposed that individual agents do not see through the government budget constraint.

Finally, Brunner and Falkinger provide a neutrality result analogous to the Theorem 1 of Boadway, Pestieau and Wildasin (1989a) relative to lump-sum redistributions in the presence of distortionary taxes and subsidies. They consider tax-subsidy schemes $\varphi_i(x_i, y_i, (g_1, \ldots, g_m)) = \psi_i(x_i, y_i) + \beta_{ii} g_i + \beta_i \sum_{j \leq m: j \neq i} g_j$, additively separable in private consumption and linear in private contributions, such that $\beta_{ii} + \sum_{j \leq m: j \neq i} \beta_j$ is some constant independent of i. They prove (op. cit.: Theorem 4.2) that lump-sum redistribution $(\tau_1, \ldots, \tau_m)$ from such a scheme φ is neutral whenever it verifies $\sum_{i \leq m} \tau_i = 0$ and leaves unchanged the equilibrium set of contributors. Note that the linear scheme of Boadway et al. violates the assumption that $\beta_{ii} + \sum_{j \leq m: j \neq i} \beta_j$ ($= s_i$, agent i's matching grant rate, in their setup) is a constant independent of i, except in the special case where all private contributions are subsidized at the same rate. Though very close in spirit, the two neutrality properties, therefore, are again not directly comparable, because the individual agents of Brunner and Falkinger see through the government budget constraint while the localities of Boadway et al. do not.

6. Efficient redistribution with perfectly substitutable transfers

Section 5 examined the feasibility of lump-sum redistribution when transfers are perfectly substitutable, with the conclusion that such redistributions are effective, essentially, if and only if they crowd out some of the equilibrium transfers. Section 6 will consider the complementary question of the normative justification of such lump-sum redistributions, based on considerations of Pareto-efficiency.

We noticed already in Section 3.2 that wealth distribution (or ophelimity distribution in general Pareto social systems) was, potentially, a pure public good in distributive social systems. Precisely, the wealth (consumption expenditure) or ophelimity (utility from consumption) of an individual is a pure public good or bad for any other individual who feels concerned about it, because the latter's distributive concerns imply that their "consumption" of the former's wealth or ophelimity are both non-excludable and non-rival ("consumption" meaning here simply the accurate perception of the individual wealth or ophelimity that makes the object of common concern). Early formulations of this simple consequence of non-paternalistic utility interdependence were made by Kolm (1968) and Hochman and Rodgers (1969).

Gift-giving generates, in Pareto social systems, two types of non-pecuniary externalities, defined in classical terms [e.g. Laffont (1988, Chapter 1)] as any effect of an individual action on other agents' utility functions or sets of alternatives at fixed market prices, namely: an effect on the budget set of the beneficiary of the gift (expansion of the budget set if the gift increases, contraction if the gift decreases); and the public good effect associated with the consequences of gift-giving on ophelimity distribution given common distributive concerns and the Cournot–Nash behavioral assumption (see Section 3.1.2 above). These external effects, which can be construed, in the manner of Meade (1973) as instances of non-contractual interactions, induce potential difficulties in the functioning of Pareto social systems, notably: the logical possibility of "wars of gifts", which involves the two types of external effects of gift-giving distinguished above (see Sections 3.4.1 and 4.2.4); and the Pareto-inefficiency of equilibrium (see the examples of Section 3.2), which results essentially from the public good externality, and falls therefore under the general class of issues known as "the public good problem" [e.g. Kolm (1964), Olson (1965)].

The sequel reviews the general theory of Pareto-efficient redistribution in pure distributive social systems and related issues relative to the influence of group size on free-riding behavior in that context, and on the design of incentive compatible mechanisms for distributive efficiency.

6.1. General theory

Redistribution has two notable specific characteristics as a public good.

One is its non-materiality, and more precisely the fact that its "consumption" and "production" do not imply, at least in the pure theory of redistribution developed here, any destruction of scarce resources: consumption merely consists of the observation of wealth distribution by concerned individuals; and production is pure and (supposed) costless[50] transfer activity. Distribution is conceptually and practically distinct, in that respect, from allocation, which usually involves, for public as well as for private goods, production and consumption activities relying on a substantial material basis. It is a *pure relational good*,[51] that is, a good (or bad) that consists of moral relations between individuals (moral sentiments, individual senses of distributive justice, ...). It is more naturally construed, consequently, as a part of an autonomous process of social exchange or social justice than as a part of the economic (and even public economic) process of allocation of resources.[52]

The second specificity can be stated as a paradox: the public good here is precisely what is usually meant by individual private wealth or welfare, in the two complementary senses of individual ownership and individual consumption of market goods and services. More precisely, the final destination of wealth in Pareto social systems is individual consumption (as opposed, notably, to collective consumption such as festivals,

---

[50] Real transfer activities do imply the consumption of scarce resources as inputs of a genuine production process, such as, for instance, the services of the departments or financial institutions technically in charge of their implementation. The analytical assumption of costless production is nevertheless approximately verified in practice in the sense that the production costs usually represent only a small fraction of transferred amounts.

[51] For a review of economic analyses of human relations as social "goods", see notably Chapter 9 by Sacco et al. in this Handbook.

[52] This distinction is to be related, of course, to Musgrave's distinction of the allocation and distribution branches of public finance (1959). The formal analogy of redistribution with a type of production is strongly suggested, nevertheless, by the public good theory of redistribution [see for instance its metaphorical use in the title of one of the founding contributions of the theory: "The optimal production of social justice" by Serge Kolm (1968)], and often endorsed literally in the context of BBV social systems [e.g. Cornes and Sandler (1984a), or Posnett and Sandler (1986)]. I argue below that the analogy is generally misleading when the social system is not of the BBV type.

or war effort). And these social systems are social systems of private property in the two complementary senses that: aggregate wealth is owned initially by private agents [that is, $\sum_{i \in N} \omega_i = (1, \ldots, 1)$: we have an economy of private property in the formal sense of Debreu (1959)]; and individuals enjoy a full right of usus (that is, own consumption, selling or gift-giving) and abusus (disposal) of the resources they own (that is, owned initially, purchased, or received as gifts from others). The public good problem of redistribution consists therefore of the Pareto-inefficiency of the distribution of wealth which stems from the spontaneous interaction of donors making use of their basic right of private property, caused by the two types of external effects induced by gift-giving, and notably by the public good externality generated by distributive concerns. And the natural framework for the solution of this problem is, consequently, the liberal social contract [e.g. Kolm (1985, Chapter 19, 1996, V); see also Section 2 above]. We present it below in the simple context of pure distributive social systems.[53]

6.1.1. Collective gift-giving and social equilibrium

This section extends the definition of the social equilibrium of a pure distributive social system (Section 3.1.2.1, Definition 1) to the case of *collective gift-giving of the contractual type*. Precisely, I allow for the possibility, for any subset of agents ("coalition"), to pool their resources (endowments and gifts received from the outside of the coalition) and decide collectively on their consumption and gifts on the basis of the (weak) unanimous preference of members (*cooperative* gift-giving). Formally:

DEFINITION 4. (i) The non-empty subset I (named *coalition*) of the set of agents *blocks* gift-vector t^* in the distributive social system (w, ω) if there exists t_I such that for all $i \in I$: $x_i(\omega, (t^*_{\setminus I}, t_I)) \geqslant 0$ and $w_i(x(\omega, (t^*_{\setminus I}, t_I))) \geqslant w_i(x(\omega, t^*))$ with a strict inequality holding for at least one i. (ii) Gift-vector t is a *strong distributive equilibrium* of (w, ω) if it is unblocked by any non-empty coalition (that is, by any non-empty subset of N).

The strong distributive equilibrium is an application to distributive social systems of a variant of the strong Nash equilibrium of Aumann (1959).[54] Aumann's equilibrium

---

[53] This solution is not written yet in the context of general Pareto social systems. The main difficulty with this extension lies in the basic assumption of price-taking behavior. This assumption is easy to justify in the case of individual donors (see Section 4.3 above), but no longer in the case of collective gift-giving involving agreements between many donors, possibly the population as a whole. Such coalitions of donors cannot ignore a priori the influence of their decisions on market prices and equilibrium, although one can imagine reasons why they could *decide* to do so, for instance normative reasons (if the social system performs better with price-taking behavior, relative to some normative criterion accepted by all) or practical ones (if learning the market equilibrium correspondence costs more than the benefits that can be derived from this knowledge, for example). The exploration of this question certainly is a valuable research program, though seemingly also a demanding one.

[54] Aumann's notion of strong Nash equilibrium requires that a deviation benefits all members of the coalition (strong unanimity), while I only require here that it benefits some of these members and makes none of

notion captures the simultaneous interactions of agents who can freely discuss their strategies but cannot make binding commitments [see for instance Bernheim, Peleg and Whinston (1987) for a discussion of the meaning of the concept].

The Olsonian type of characterization of the public good problem of redistribution as the Pareto-inefficiency of equilibrium in a non-cooperative game of individual gifts extends in a natural way to the case of cooperative gift-giving, namely: individual or collective free-riding on the contributions of others at distributive optimum, where "free-riding" refers to any rational action of individuals or coalitions (that is, any individual or collective action designed to increase agents' own utilities) that results in collective Pareto-inefficiency.[55] The public good problem of redistribution is then logically equivalent to the non-existence of a strong distributive equilibrium (a strong equilibrium distribution being Pareto-efficient by construction since the corresponding transfers are unblocked by the "grand coalition" N).

The right of private property plays a critical role in existence failures of strong distributive equilibrium. I analyze this point below, and recall known existence results for non-status quo and for status quo equilibria.

6.1.1.1. Private property rights and the public good problem of redistribution
Private property rights cover two complementary notions in Pareto social systems, the combination of which determines individual sets of alternatives (individual budget sets). One is the rule that consists of the full right of usus and abusus of individuals over their own resources. Hereafter, it will be referred to as the Right of Private Property (in short: RPP). The other notion is individual endowment or initial right, corresponding to notation ω_i in the formal definition of Pareto social systems, and simply referred to below as individual i's *right*.

Private property rights create the possibility of free-riding in Pareto social systems by making donors' agreements non-binding. Let us make this simple but fundamental point precise.

---

them worse off. The definition of a strong distributive equilibrium in Mercier Ythier (1998a, 1998b, 2000b) embodies the *strong unanimous preference* of coalitions, while the definition used in Mercier Ythier (2004a) relies on *weak unanimous preference*. Strong unanimous preference is usually favored by game theory, because of the explicit causal relation it embodies, from individual incentives to the formation of coalitions. Weak unanimity, on the other hand, is the relevant notion in the liberal social contract for the decisions taken by the "grand coalition", as a normative principle of protection of individuals (or social types, depending on the interpretation that one retains for index i: see Section 6.1.2.2.2), implying an individual right of veto on the decisions of society. I adopt weak unanimity uniformly here for the sake of conceptual homogeneity.

[55] This definition of free-riding implies, naturally, the usual sense, that is, the "action" (in the formal sense of game theory) of consuming a collective good without paying the contractual fare, for instance traveling for free by train or boat without permission. The extended notion in the text is designed to encompass all the various aspects of the public good problem of redistribution, such as inefficient underprovision ("too small" equilibrium transfers, free-riding in the common sense corresponding to a subcase of that type), inefficient overprovision ("too large" equilibrium transfers), or else (some equilibrium transfers "too small" and others "too large", and the cases of non-existence of Nash or strong Nash equilibrium that are related to the public good problem of redistribution, including the "wars of gifts", assimilated to a case of overprovision).

This logical consequence of private property can be understood readily from the formal representation of the right of private property (RPP) through the specification of individual and collective budget sets, namely, sets

$$B_i(t^*) = \left\{ (x_i, t_i) \colon x_i \geqslant 0 \text{ and } x_i + \sum_{j:\, j \neq i} t_{ij} = \omega_i + \sum_{j:\, j \neq i} t^*_{ji} \right\}$$

for individuals, and

$$B_I(t^*) = \left\{ (x_I, t_I)_{i \in I} \colon x_I \geqslant 0 \text{ and } \sum_{i \in I}\left(x_i + \sum_{j:\, j \neq i} t_{ij}\right) = \sum_{i \in I}\left(\omega_i + \sum_{j:\, j \neq i} t^*_{ji}\right) \right\}$$

for coalitions. This specification of individual and collective sets of alternatives, implied by RPP, implies in turn that the corresponding transfer decisions can always be reversed. Formally: if $(x_I, t_I) \in B_I(t^*)$, then any (x_I, t'_I) such that $0 \leqslant t'_I \leqslant t_I$ is also in $B_I(t^*)$. In such a context, an agreement between donors is binding, that is, it makes transfers irreversible for donors, if and only if the corresponding commitments are *embodied* in the individual budget sets of donors and beneficiaries, that is, if and only if the agreement achieves a *transfer of endowments* (implying a change in ω) from the former to the latter. To put it more briefly: *given the right of private property, binding donors' agreements must consist of lump-sum transfers of endowments from donors to beneficiaries.*

Donors' agreements are non-binding, therefore, in strong distributive equilibrium, as the latter represents voluntary redistribution as decisions on variables of the type t_I, which leave the vector of initial endowments ω unchanged by construction. Only exogenous public lump-sum transfers can change ω in this setup.[56]

The non-existence of equilibrium, the public good problem of redistribution, and the individual or collective free-riding on Pareto-efficient gift-giving are, in other words, in this analytical framework, three equivalent expressions of the exercise, legitimate by definition, of individual rights of private property.

6.1.1.2. Sufficient conditions for the existence of a non-trivial efficient distributive equilibrium

The sufficient condition for the existence of non-trivial (that is, $\neq 0$) Pareto-efficient distributive equilibrium corresponds to the distributive equilibrium of Becker. It is derived from a result of Nakayama (1980, Proposition 2, p. 1261), adapted to the

---

[56] Note that the same is true, with some qualifications, for any definition of the distributive core that respects RPP and views initial rights as fixed, such as those that can be derived from Kolm (1987a, 1987b, 1987c, 1987d, 1989) for instance. Kolm's notions differ from Aumann's by allowing for a variety of types of non-cooperative interactions between coalitions involving not only conjectural variations such as Stackelberg's, but also, notably, an explicit modeling of the reactions of coalitions to the defection of some of its members ("splintering" cores, "cooperative" cores and so on). The qualifications follow from the fact that patterns of reaction to defections are susceptible to deter the latter in a variety of contexts, hence facilitating ex post stability of formally non-binding agreements [see the account of Kolm (1987a, 1987b) in Section 6.2.4 below].

present framework in Theorem 13. Nakayama's proposition states essentially that the (Nash) distributive equilibrium is Pareto-efficient whenever there is an agent who gives to all others at equilibrium, and whose utility reaches then its maximum in S_n.

THEOREM 13. *Let (w, ω) be such that for all i: $\omega_i > 0$; w_i is quasi-concave and $w_i(x) > w_i(x')$ implies $w_i(\lambda x + (1 - \lambda)x') > w_i(x')$ for all $\lambda \in]0, 1[$. If t^* is a distributive equilibrium of (w, ω) with a forest graph, and if there exists an agent i who makes positive gifts to all other agents at t^* (that is, $t_{ij} > 0$ for all $j \neq i$), then the associate equilibrium distribution $x(\omega, t^*)$: (i) is a weak distributive optimum of w; (ii) and maximizes i's utility in S_n (that is, $w_i(x(\omega, t^*)) = \max\{w_i(x): x \in S_n\}$).*

PROOF. See Appendix A.1. □

Nakayama's proposition yields a sufficient condition for a non-trivial equilibrium solution to the public good problem of redistribution when gift-giving is individual. The following corollary extends this solution to collective gift-giving.

COROLLARY 7. *Let (w, ω) be such that $\omega_i > 0$ for all i, and $t^* \neq 0$ be a distributive equilibrium of (w, ω). Suppose that: (a) either there exists an agent i, with a strictly quasi-concave utility function w_i (that is, a quasi-concave w_i such that $w_i(x) \geq w_i(x')$ implies $w_i(\lambda x + (1 - \lambda)x') > w_i(x')$ for all $\lambda \in]0, 1[$ and all (x, x') such that $x \neq x'$), who makes positive gifts to all others at t^*, and all others are egoistic ($w_j : x \to x_j$ for all $j \neq i$); (b) or $n = 2$ and all utility functions are strictly quasi-concave. Then t^* is a strong distributive equilibrium and $w_j(x(\omega, t^*)) = \max\{w_j(x): x \in S_n\}$ for every donor j.*

PROOF. See Appendix A.1. □

The condition of Becker–Nakayama is the underlying rationale for the optimism of Hochman and Rodger's original contribution (1969), which concentrates on Pareto-improving redistributions between two agents.

A variant appears also in Arrow (1981, Theorem 6) (see Section 3.3.2 above), stating that a non-trivial equilibrium of his distributive social system is Pareto-optimal if and only if: (i) there is a unique donor i, whose equilibrium wealth x_i is larger than the minimum equilibrium wealth $x_{\min}$; (ii) and the equilibrium wealth of all other agents is that minimum wealth (that is, $x_j = x_{\min}$ for all $j \neq i$, the gift j receives from i then being equal to $x_{\min} - \omega_j$). One verifies readily that the equilibrium distribution then maximizes the donor's utility in S_n, and that Arrow's condition is in fact equivalent to the following: there is a unique donor i, whose utility attains its maximum in S_n.[57]

---

[57] With the notations of Section 3.3.2 above and the assumptions of Arrow (1981), the equilibrium distribution x^*, such that $x_j^* = x_{\min}$ for all $j \neq i$, verifies the necessary first-order conditions: $\partial \varphi_i(x_i^*) = \partial \varphi(x_{\min})$ and $x^* \in \text{Int } S_n$. And the f.o.c. characterize the (unique, interior) maximum of w_i in S_n by Arrow's assumption of strict concavity of utility functions.

Note that this condition does not imply that the donor gives to *all* other members of the social system. Corollary 8 of Section 6.1.1.3 below states that Arrow's condition is in fact necessary and sufficient for the existence of a non-trivial strong equilibrium in Arrow's distributive social systems.

The Becker–Nakayama condition is very sensitive to the number of potential donors and beneficiaries: it breaks down, in general, from two potential (net) donors [see for instance Musgrave (1970), Goldfarb (1970), and Theorem 17(iii) in Section 6.2.1 below]; and it appears very implausible when the number of potential beneficiaries is large. Mercier Ythier (2000b, Theorems 4.1 and 4.2) shows that a subset of three agents, two of them connected by a Nash equilibrium gift, and mild and natural assumptions of common distributive concerns between the three, suffice to imply the non-existence of a strong equilibrium. Such impossibilities, as well as Arrow's characterization of non-trivial efficient equilibria, leave us therefore with a simple alternative, in some respects analogous to the impossibility theorems of the theory of social choice: *either there exist integrative agents, Becker's family heads* (the analogues of the "dictator" of social choice theory), *whose individual optima make the social equilibrium, and this implies notably that distributive concerns are limited to small and closed subsets* (the "families") *of the whole set of agents; or there is no non-trivial strong equilibrium at all.*

6.1.1.3. Sufficient conditions for the existence of a status quo strong equilibrium   The pervasiveness of free-riding in contexts of operative interactions (non-trivial equilibrium) does not extend, at least to the same degree, to status quo equilibrium. Let us introduce two natural assumptions relating to distributive preferences, in order to establish this point.

One is *self-centredness*. A weak variant of the assumption has already been introduced above (Section 3.4.1.2), with differentiable utility functions, as a sufficient condition for the existence of a distributive equilibrium. We now define the following, slightly stronger version, stating that an individual's distributive utility is *increasing* in bilateral progressive wealth transfers (see the definition of the latter in Footnote 7 of Section 2) from any richer individual to himself. Formally, for all (i, j) such that $i \neq j$, let e^{ij} denote the row vector of $\mathbb{R}^n$ whose entries are all $= 0$ except the ith and jth, equal respectively to -1 and 1. We say that the social system w verifies *self-centredness* if: for all (i, j) such that $i \neq j$, function $\mathbb{R}_+ \to \mathbb{R}: \tau \to w_i(x + \tau e^{ij})$ is increasing in $[0, (1/2)(x_j - x_i)]$ whenever $x_j \geqslant x_i$.

The second assumption states that individuals have no objection relative to bilateral progressive transfers as long as they are *not* involved in the transfer as donor or beneficiary. Formally: for all (i, j, k) such that $j \neq k$ and $i \neq j, k$, functions $\mathbb{R} \to \mathbb{R}: \tau \to w_i(x + \tau e^{jk})$ are non-decreasing in $[0, (1/2)(x_j - x_k)]$ whenever $x_j \geqslant x_k$. This excludes, notably, situations where individual i objects to a progressive transfer from individual j to individual k and would enjoy being the beneficiary of j's transfer in the place of k, situations of *relational envy* so to speak, induced by the relational character of wealth distribution as a public good, and where common language and psychology usually recognize a feeling of jealousy (of individual i, relative to j's gift to k).[58] By extension, I will name this second assumption *non-jealousy*, although it excludes, strictly speaking, i's jealousy relative to j's transfers to k only in situations where j is at least as rich as k.

The combination of self-centredness and non-jealousy, while compatible with any degree of individual self-centredness (the social system of the homo economicus, where $w_i : x \to x_i$ for all i, verifies both assumptions), produces a social context favorable to voluntary progressive transfers, in the sense that such transfers are vetoed neither by the beneficiaries (self-centredness), nor by the individuals who are not involved in the transfer (non-jealousy).

The Principle of Transfers, and Arrow's Assumptions 2, 4 and 5 (1981, pp. 204–205), imply them and are not implied by them.[59]

Strong BBV utility functions imply non-jealousy. They do not verify, in general, self-centredness, because each individual donor views his bilateral transfers, essentially, as gifts to a macroagent (the "sum" of all poor), who will be "richer" than him in most practical circumstances; but this does not alter the spirit and fundamental properties of these social systems, which are designed to account for progressive transfers from the rich to the very poor (see Theorem 14 below).

The next theorem shows that status quo strong equilibria abound in social systems that verify self-centredness and non-jealousy, and in strong BBV social systems: in these social systems, *the strong distributive equilibrium is a status quo* ($t = 0$) *if and only if the initial distribution is a (strong) Pareto optimum relative to distributive utilities*.

And the corollary establishes that, in the case of Arrow's distributive social system, the Becker–Nakayama condition is both sufficient *and necessary* for the achievement of a distributive optimum by means of private individual and/or collective transfers.

The (quite simple) intuition underlying the formal proof of Theorem 14 has been given in Section 2 (see the first paragraph of the presentation of the fourth characteristic property, in Section 2.2). The proofs of the theorem and corollary are detailed in Appendix A.[60]

---

[58] Envy is usually construed as the feeling of a person who, considering the position (say wealth, dignity, reputation ...) of another person, prefers the latter's position to his own. The position here envied by i is relational in the sense that it consists of a relation between two individuals (the position of beneficiary of the beneficence of j). Envy, and jealousy as relational envy, reduce to one and the same thing in the important special case where the envied position is a "right" guaranteed by society. These distinctions bear on the general question of the relations between moral sentiments and sentiments of justice. This note points to a conception of the sentiment of justice as a moral sentiment specifically related to comparisons of individual rights.

[59] w verifies the Principle of Transfers if $w_i(x) > w_i(x')$ for all i whenever x can be obtained from x' by a sequence of progressive transfers. Arrow's Assumptions 2 (anonymity) and 5 (convexity) together imply (and are not implied by) non-jealousy, while his Assumptions 4 ("selfishness") and 5 together imply (and are not implied by) self-centredness.

[60] Theorem 14 is adapted from Mercier Ythier (1998a). It differs from the closely similar property established in the latter reference (as Theorem 1) and in Mercier Ythier (1998b) (as Theorem 4) notably because the present chapter retains a notion of blocking coalition that involves the *weak* unanimous preference of its members (see Footnote 54), while the definition of blocking coalitions adopted in the former references

THEOREM 14. *Suppose that w either is a strong BBV distributive social system, or verifies local non-satiation of the distributive Paretian preordering (in short, local non-satiation: cf. Footnote 31), self-centredness and non-jealousy. Then, 0 is a strong distributive equilibrium of* (w, ω) *if and only if* ω *is a strong distributive optimum of w.*

COROLLARY 8. *If w verifies the assumptions of* Arrow (1981) *then a non-trivial distributive equilibrium t of* (w, ω) *is strong if and only if it has a unique donor i, whose utility reaches its maximum in* S_n *(that is,* $w_i(x(\omega, t)) = \max\{w_i(x): x \in S_n\}$).

A simple but powerful consequence of Theorem 14, already noticed by Warr (1982) for individual contributions to a public good in the strong BBV setup, is the *full crowding out of private (individual or collective) transfers by any system of public lump-sum transfers achieving a distributive Pareto optimum.*[61] Likewise, *exogenous lump-sum redistributions of individual endowments within the set of concerned individuals are the only solution to the public good problem of redistribution* when the latter is raised, that is, essentially, when: the initial distribution is Pareto-inefficient (Theorem 14); and the (Nash) distributive equilibrium is non-trivial and does not verify the Becker–Nakayama condition (Section 6.1.1.2, and Corollary 8).

These consequences of Theorem 14, and the pervasiveness of the public good problem of redistribution in the presence of operative transfer motives, substantiate the definition of the distributive core below, as the set of *unblocked initial distributions* [Mercier Ythier (1998b)]. The core, in other words, is conceived here as a set of *initial conditions* (endowments) immune to individual or contractual deviations, and not, as in

---

supposes the *strong* unanimous preference of members. This weakening of the notion of blocking coalition, and the subsequent strengthening of the induced notion of strong distributive equilibrium, mainly result in a strengthening of the relation between status quo strong equilibrium and the Pareto-efficiency of the initial distribution: Theorem 14 establishes that the strong Pareto-efficiency of the initial distribution is *necessary and sufficient* for status quo strong equilibrium (with *weak* unanimous preference in coalitions), while my 1998 theorems establish that the strong Pareto-efficiency of the initial distribution is *sufficient* for status quo strong equilibrium (with *strong* unanimous preference in coalitions). This improvement of the property nevertheless obtains at some cost, in addition to the strengthening of the notion of strong equilibrium itself, namely, the strengthening of the assumption of self-centredness (the 1998 results only require *weak* self-centredness). Note that Theorem 14 and the 1998 results reduce to one and the same property when w is such that *weak* and *strong* distributive efficiency are equivalent. This will be the case, for example, in strong BBV distributive social systems, or in general distributive social systems such that all utility functions are strictly quasi-concave. Note that, in these cases (strong BBV, or strictly quasi-concave distributive preferences), the weak and the strong unanimous preference in coalitions are essentially equivalent (see also Footnote 73 on related subjects).
[61] Consider a social system (w, ω^0) such that ω^0 is Pareto-inefficient and w verifies the assumptions of Theorem 14, and suppose a distributive policy that operates lump-sum transfers from ω^0 in order to reach a distributive optimum ω. By Theorem 14, 0 is a strong Nash (hence Nash) equilibrium of (w, ω). And we know that 0 then is the unique Nash (hence strong Nash) equilibrium of (w, ω), generically (see Section 3.4.2.1). Therefore, the distributive policy crowds out all equilibrium transfers (individual and/or collective) existing in (w, ω^0).

conventional definitions, as a set of actions or action *outcomes* immune to such deviations given initial endowments.[62] It should not be viewed, consequently, as a solution to the public good problem of redistribution, but rather as a set where a solution, if any, must lie.

DEFINITION 5. The *distributive core* of w is the set $C(w) = \{\omega: 0 \text{ is a strong distributive equilibrium of } (w, \omega)\}$.

The set of strong distributive optima of w is denoted by $P(w)$ in the sequel. The distributive core $C(w)$ is contained in $P(w)$ by definition, and identical to it when w verifies the assumptions of Theorem 14 (strong BBV, or local non-satiation, self-centredness and non-jealousy).

6.1.2. Distributive liberal social contract

Summarizing Section 6.1.1, the public good problem of redistribution consists of the non-existence of non-trivial strong (Nash) distributive equilibrium. This notably includes the cases of Pareto-inefficient underprovision of redistributive transfers at (non-cooperative Nash) distributive equilibrium. The public good problem appears, generally, when the initial distribution is Pareto-inefficient relative to individual distributive preferences, and there is no "family head" in the sense of Becker (that is, no individual who is able and willing to give to all others at equilibrium). Its solution supposes exogenous lump-sum redistributions of endowments within the set of concerned individuals. Any Pareto-efficient distribution can be reached by means of such exogenous transfers when

---

[62] Mercier Ythier (2004a, 1.2, notably Theorems 1 and 2) examines the formal relations between the distributive core as defined above, Aumann's strong equilibrium and the notion of core of Foley (1970). Foley's definitions, applied to a pure distributive social system (w, ω), yield: (i) non-empty coalition I "Foley-blocks" gift-vector t^* if there exists t_I such that for all $i \in I$: $x_i(\omega, (0_{\setminus I}, t_I)) \geq 0$ and $w_i(x(\omega, (0_{\setminus I}, t_I))) \geq w_i(x(\omega, t^*))$ with a strict inequality for at least one i; (ii) and the Foley-core of (w, ω) is then $\{x(\omega, t): $ there is no non-empty coalition that Foley-blocks $t\}$. Foley's core presents little interest as a solution concept in the context of general Pareto social systems for two reasons: the Right of Private Property (RPP); and the non-excludable character of distribution as a public good in such systems. Foley's definition implies a violation of RPP by forbidding (logically, if not normatively) individual agents and coalitions to use for their own consumption and transfers the gifts they receive from the outside. And the same "0-conjecture" on off-coalition contributions is usually interpreted as implying that deviating coalitions are able (and willing) to exclude non-members from the consumption of the public good they produce, for only then is the conjecture that non-members will react to a deviation by setting their contribution at 0 fully rationalisable in all circumstances. Note nevertheless that this "0-conjecture" characteristic of Foley's notion is rationalisable, and respects RPP, precisely at the initial distributions ω that make the distributive core in the sense of my Definition 5 (the ω such that 0 is a strong equilibrium of (w, ω)). Note also that, then, Foley's and Aumann's cores boil down essentially to the same notion (since status quo is, generically, the sole equilibrium whenever $\omega \in C(w)$: Section 3.4.2.1), and cannot account for operative redistributions by construction. See Footnotes 69 and 70, and Section 6.2.1 below for further developments on the Foley-core in the important special case of the BBV distributive social systems.

the social system is of the strong BBV type, or when it verifies local non-satiation, self-centredness and non-jealousy. And the exogenous transfers then crowd out all private (individual and/or collective) transfers.

We now endogenise endowment redistributions (the changes in ω), and the corresponding distributive policies, by means of a *distributive liberal social contract*.

General liberal social contracts were characterized, in Section 2, as *Pareto-efficient arrangements of individual rights unanimously preferred to an historical initial arrangement* (see Section 2.2). The general reason for such collective agreements is the Pareto-inefficiency of the social state that would result from individual or group interactions in the absence of them, notably because of pervasive public goods problems or externalities. The agreement can be implicit, and its implementation generally supposes some type of public intervention (see Footnote 10), such as general systems of public transfers (e.g. the Western European welfare states) or general systems of public incentives for private actions of redistribution (e.g. the North American federal systems of tax allowances for charitable contributions).

The precise (axiomatic) formulation of the distributive liberal social contract below combines two ingredients: unanimous agreement, and property rights.

Unanimous agreement (UA) simply characterizes contract as a mode of collective decision-making. It applies to any subset of agents (donors), including the whole set of them. Its formal expression is weak unanimity, corresponding practically either to an individual right to quit a "coalition" (a set of contracting donors) when the latter is a proper subset of the whole set of agents (free exit), or to an individual right of veto on collective decisions when the latter are taken by the whole set of agents.

Property rights are of two species in pure distributive social systems: individual (endowments); and constitutional. Constitutional property rights are of two types themselves: the Right of Private Property (RPP), already defined above; and its extension in the Freedom of Contracting (FC) of donors, that consists of the right of any set of individuals to pool their resources in order to decide contractually the individual consumption and gifts of the members of the resulting "coalition".

The distributive liberal social contract, finally, is required to be self-consistent (SC) in the following sense: its outcome must be immune to individual or contractual deviations of donors making use of their individual and constitutional property rights. That is: the social contract, if any, must redistribute endowments (agreement binding donors), so that the resulting distribution of individual rights lies in the distributive core. The combination of UA, RPP, FC and SC therefore yields [Mercier Ythier (1998a)]:

DEFINITION 6. ω is a distributive liberal social contract of (w, ω^0) if: (i) $w_i(\omega) \geqslant w_i(\omega^0)$ for all i; (ii) and $\omega \in C(w)$.

The remainder of this section examines the characterization, existence and determinacy of the distributive liberal social contract when distributive preferences are self-centered (or strong BBV) and non-jealous. Some fundamental intertemporal issues relative to this type of social contract are also briefly evoked at the end of the section.

6.1.2.1. Characterization, existence As a simple corollary of Theorem 14, *the set of distributive liberal social contracts of a pure distributive social system of private property* (w, ω^0) *that verifies local non-satiation, self-centredness and non-jealousy, or that is strong BBV, is the set of strong distributive optima of w that are unanimously (weakly) preferred to* ω^0. If, moreover, distributive preferences are continuous, there exists a distributive liberal social contract of (w, ω^0) for *any* initial distribution of rights ω^0 [see Mercier Ythier (1998a, Theorem 1 and 2000b, Theorem 4.3) for variants of these results]. Formally, letting $L(w, \omega^0)$ denote the set of distributive liberal social contracts of (w, ω^0):

COROLLARY 9. (i) *If w either verifies local non-satiation of the Paretian preordering, self-centredness and non-jealousy, or is a strong BBV distributive social system, then:* $L(w, \omega^0) = \{\omega \in P(w): w_i(\omega) \geqslant w_i(\omega^0) \text{ for all } i\}$. (ii) *If moreover w_i is continuous for all i, then $L(w, \omega^0)$ is non-empty for all $\omega^0 \in S_n$*.

PROOF. See Appendix A.1. □

Mercier Ythier (1998a) gives three counterexamples to the existence of a distributive liberal social contract: the "generalized war of gifts" reproduced as Figure 12 above (Section 3.4.1.1), involving the violation of self-centredness; a paradoxical "war contract" in a two-agent social system where individuals are so malevolent that distributive efficiency implies the disposal of a fraction of aggregate wealth unless one of them owns the whole of it; and a case of jealousy.

The first two examples stem from an incompatibility of distributive preferences with the right of private property. "Wars of gifts" are suggestive of situations where the good functioning of the social system requires collective ownership of a part of total wealth, associated with collective decision making on individual consumption of collective wealth. Conversely, "war contracts" evoke situations where individual hostility is so intense that individual property rights are susceptible to collapse, because they do not receive sufficient support from the social body (whose existence itself is jeopardized, or at least subject to question in such a context).

The case of jealousy presented in Figure 14 is a variant of the Counterexample 2 of Mercier Ythier (1998a). The example emphasizes a basic problem confronting distributive liberal social contracts, namely, the rejection of welfare transfers to the poor by a sizeable fraction of the working and middle classes, typified here, metaphorically (and somewhat extremely), by the rejection of the abolition of slavery by the poor Whites on the eve of the American Secession War.

EXAMPLE 14. *On the Eve of Secession War*

The example uses a variant of the Cobb–Douglas distributive social system of Section 3.2 with three agents (types), the Abolitionist (agent 1), the poor White (agent 2) and the Slave (agent 3). Slavery is construed as a null endowment for agent 3, and

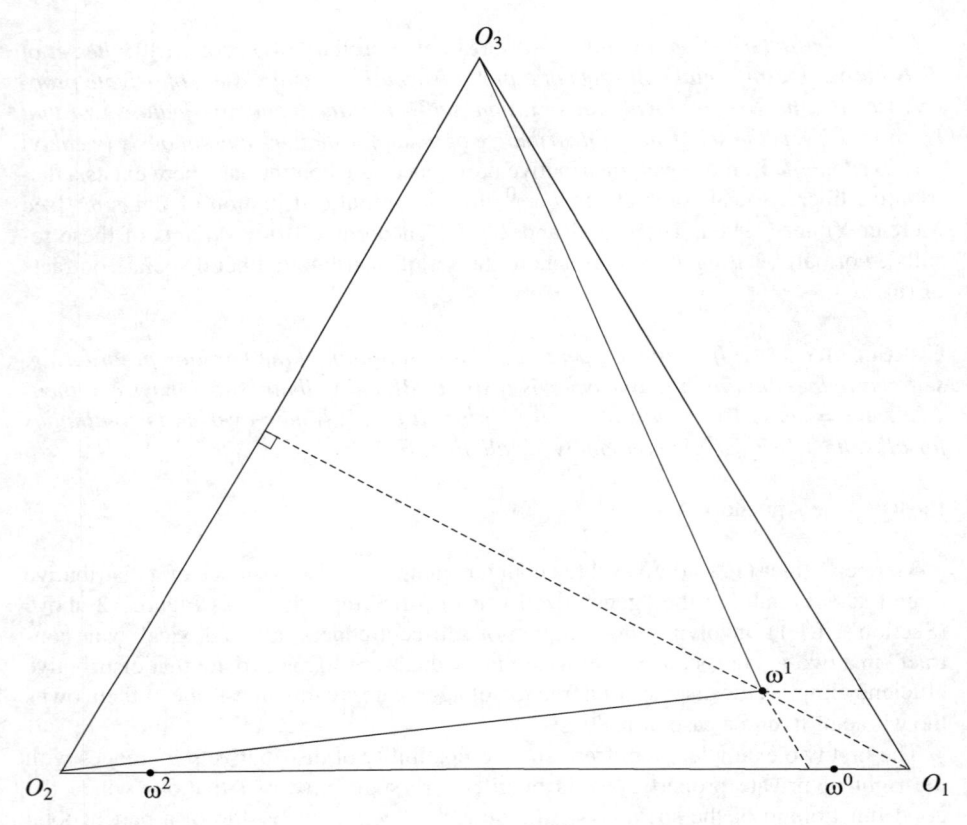

Figure 14. On the eve of the American Civil War.

implies null consumption of the latter in the absence of wealth transfers. The initial distribution of rights in this society is $\omega^0 = (9/10, 1/10, 0)$. The Abolitionist has the self-centered and non-jealous (log linear) Cobb–Douglas utility $w_1(x) = (3/4)\ln x_1 + (1/8)\ln x_2 + (1/8)\ln x_3$, that exhibits an absolute aversion to slavery. The ideal social state for this type (the distribution it prefers in S_3) is $\omega^1 = (3/4, 1/8, 1/8)$, that involves abolition and mildly progressive wealth transfers from itself to the other types, maintaining its relative dominant position and equalizing the positions of the others. The poor White has the following dichotomous utility function: his utility is $-\infty$ at any ω (or x) such that $\omega_3 > 0$, expressing an absolute aversion to abolition; and it is the log linear self-centered $w_2(x) = (1/10)\ln x_1 + (9/10)\ln x_2$ at any x (or ω) such that $x_3 = 0$. This utility function expresses jealousy relative to any wealth transfer from the Abolitionist to the Slave, and also a ("benevolent") envy relative to the (abolitionist) Rich in the sense that the associate social ideal (distribution $\omega^2 = (1/10, 9/10, 0)$) implies the permutation of his initial position with the Abolitionist's. The Slave, finally, is "egoistic": $w_3(x) = x_3$ for all x. The social system so defined verifies local non-satiation and self-centredness. One verifies readily that: $P(w) = \{\omega^2\} \cup [\omega^1, O_3]$; $C(w) = [\omega^1, O_3]$; the set of strongly efficient distributions unanimously preferred to ω^0 reduces to $\{\omega^2\}$; and therefore $L(w, \omega^0)$ is empty. The jealousy of the poor White makes the distributive liberal social contract collapse. Note that there is a unique strong equilibrium in this example, corresponding to the Beckerian equilibrium distribution ω^1: the solution to the collective issue of redistribution goes through a unilateral decision of the dominant agent ("Lincoln's policy", to pursue the metaphor[63]).

6.1.2.2. Determinacy   The set of distributive liberal social contracts $L(w, \omega^0)$ of a locally non-satiated, self-centered and non-jealous social system w has the same dimension as the set of its strong distributive optima $P(w)$ when the liberal social contract induces effective redistributions.[64] It reduces generically to ω^0 otherwise, because of the generic uniqueness of status quo equilibrium. $P(w)$ is itself locally a manifold of the same dimension as S_n [generically: see Mercier Ythier (1997)]. That is, the distributive liberal social contract of Definition 6 is, generally, either fully determinate, when it does not involve any redistribution, or very indeterminate, in the sense of having the dimension of the simplex of feasible distributions, when it does involve effective redistributions (see Figure 15).

In other words, the process of individual and collective interactions of the distributive equilibrium determines fully, hence fully explains wealth distribution at the final agreements of the liberal social contract, while the requirement of weak unanimity that defines a contractual move from the initial distribution to a contractual distribution does not determine fully of course, hence does not fully explain the final agreement.

---

[63] It is needless to say, but nevertheless perhaps better to repeat that this example makes a *metaphorical* use of a historical event, designed to put some flesh on the abstract notions of the theory. It should not be viewed, of course as an *explanation* of the event under consideration, except perhaps through its very crude and simplistic characterization of a situation where collective action (here, the unilateral decision of the dominant agent) must, necessarily, substitute for the uncoordinated interactions of individuals or groups, in the presence of irreducible conflicts on the conception of the public good. A reference to the Secession War, even metaphorical, also makes sense in our context from another point of view: the war was the occasion of the full implementation, in the USA, of the constitutional rule of self-ownership that is a fundamental and in some sense founding part of all definitions of the liberal social contract.

[64] Precisely, we have the following: *If w verifies local non-satiation of the Paretian preordering, self-centredness and non-jealousy, if w_i is strictly quasi-concave for all i, and if $\omega^0 \notin L(w, \omega^0)$, then $\dim L(w, \omega^0) = \dim P(w) \leqslant n - 1$.*

PROOF (SKETCH). If w is locally non-satiated, self-centered and non-jealous, then $C(w) = P(w)$ by Theorem 14, so that the liberal social contract necessarily induces effective redistributions (that is, $\omega^0 \notin L(w, \omega^0)$) if and only if $\omega^0 \notin P(w)$. Set $\{\omega: w_i(\omega) \geqslant w_i(\omega^0)$ for all $i\}$ is convex by quasi-concavity of distributive utility functions. $\omega^0 \notin P(w)$, the strict quasi-concavity of utility functions and the local non-satiation of the Paretian preordering readily imply that $\{\omega: w_i(\omega) \geqslant w_i(\omega^0)$ for all $i\}$ has a non-empty interior in S_n. Hence $\dim\{\omega: w_i(\omega) \geqslant w_i(\omega^0)$ for all $i\} = \dim S_n = n - 1$. And therefore $\dim L(w, \omega^0) = \dim P(w) \leqslant n - 1$. □

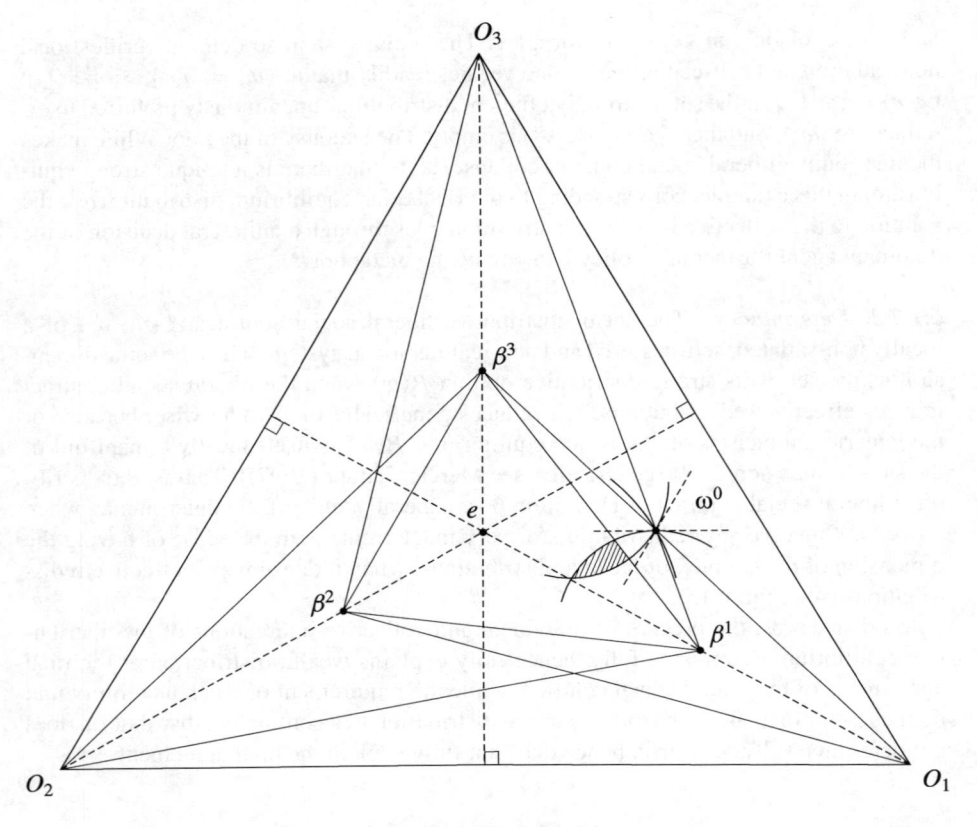

Figure 15. Distributive liberal social contracts.

This opposition between the determinacy of distributive equilibrium and the indeterminacy of distributive social contract parallels the analogous opposition, familiar in the theory market exchange, between the (local) determinacy of competitive equilibrium and the indeterminacy of the core in finite exchange economies. The solution outlined below parallels, likewise, Edgeworth's (1881) solution to core indeterminacy, and its generalization by Debreu and Scarf (1963). It consists of a process of social communication that yields essentially, in large social systems with negligible type diversity, a (generically) finite number of properly defined Lindahl equilibria.

The full description of this solution is beyond the scope of this chapter. We will provide here instead a detailed account of Lindahl equilibrium in the context of pure distributive social systems, and then give a brief literary description of the underlying "causal" process of communication.[65]

---

[65] See Mercier Ythier (2004a) for a precise and complete derivation.

6.1.2.2.1. Distributive Lindahl equilibrium The idea of applying the Lindahl equilibrium to the public good problem of redistribution goes back, at least, to the early precise formulations of the latter. Bergstrom (1970) analyzes in full generality the existence and efficiency properties of such an equilibrium in the context of a competitive exchange economy with non-paternalistic non-malevolent interdependence of utilities [see also Thurow (1971)]. And the fiscal application of Pareto-optimal redistribution developed by von Furstenberg and Mueller (1971) follows from the calculation of the same equilibrium in an example.

Let π_{ij} denote the value (personalized price) to individual i of individual j's consumption x_j, $\pi_i = (\pi_{i1}, \ldots, \pi_{in})$ and $\pi = (\pi_1, \ldots, \pi_n)$.

The sequel defines two variants of distributive Lindahl equilibrium. The first one, given in Definition 7, is designed in such a way that the equilibrium distribution is necessarily unanimously (weakly) preferred to the initial distribution of rights. This property obtains from the (purely instrumental) specification of the right-hand side of individual "budget constraints" as $\pi_i \omega^0$ (the value to i of the initial distribution), which makes the initial distribution of rights accessible to everybody at any system of Lindahl prices. This variant is named, for that reason, a *social contract equilibrium* (Theorem 15(ii)). The second notion, given in Definition 7′, corresponds to the usual version of the concept, used in the references of Bergstrom and von Furstenberg and Mueller above.[66] It is referred to as the *distributive equilibrium of Lindahl–Bergstrom* below. The associate equilibrium distribution is not, in general, unanimously preferred to the initial distribution. We give an example of a three-agent Cobb–Douglas social system that verifies the assumptions of Arrow (1981) where one or even two (that is, the majority of) agents strictly prefer the initial distribution to Bergstrom's equilibrium distribution (Figure 16 below). The two variants are equivalent, nevertheless, in the important special case of BBV social systems (Theorem 16).[67]

---

[66] There are two notable differences between the formal definition of Bergstrom and Definition 7′: Bergstrom's Lindahl prices are assumed non-negative, in the line of the author's assumption of non-malevolent utility interdependence; and his individual budget sets are specified as $\{x \in \mathbb{R}^n_+ : \pi_i x \leqslant \omega_i^0\}$, constraining individuals to choose a non-negative consumption not only for themselves but also for others. The presentation adopted here allows for malevolence, and its possible expressions through negative Lindahl prices and individual choices of negative consumption for others. The equilibrium distribution is non-negative by construction (but some equilibrium prices can be negative) when it exists. The unboundedness of prices and individual budget sets raises, naturally, potential difficulties for the existence of an equilibrium (see the discussion of the existence property at the end of Section 6.1.2.2.1).

[67] A third variant is conceivable, where the right-hand side of i's budget constraint is the *value to i of his own endowment* $\pi_{ii} \omega_i^0$, yielding

DEFINITION 7″. (π, x) is an equilibrium of (w, ω^0) if: (i) $\sum_{i \in N} \pi_i = (1, \ldots, 1)$; (ii) and $w_i(x) = \max\{w_i(z): z_i \geqslant 0 \text{ and } \pi_i z \leqslant \pi_{ii} \omega_i^0\}$ for all i.

This variant has not been studied in the literature. A casual examination suggests that its properties are qualitatively similar to Lindahl–Bergstrom's. Notably, the equilibrium distribution is generally not unanimously preferred to the initial distribution (but is so in the case of BBV social systems, where Definition 7″ is in fact equivalent to the other two).

DEFINITION 7. (π, ω) is a *social contract equilibrium* of (w, ω^0) if: (i) $\sum_{i \in N} \pi_i = (1, \ldots, 1)$; (ii) and $w_i(\omega) = \max\{w_i(x): x_i \geqslant 0 \text{ and } \pi_i x \leqslant \pi_i \omega^0\}$ for all i.

DEFINITION 7'. (π, x) is a *Lindahl–Bergstrom equilibrium* of (w, ω^0) if: (i) $\sum_{i \in N} \pi_i = (1, \ldots, 1)$; (ii) and $w_i(x) = \max\{w_i(z): z_i \geqslant 0 \text{ and } \pi_i z \leqslant \omega_i^0\}$ for all i.

The standard argument, transposed from the classical proof of the Pareto-efficiency of competitive equilibrium by Debreu (1954, Theorem 1), establishes the strong Pareto-optimality of the two variants of distributive Lindahl equilibrium when individual preferences are locally non-satiated at equilibrium [Mercier Ythier (2004a, Theorem 3), and Bergstrom (1970, Theorem 2)]. A social contract equilibrium is, therefore, a liberal social contract when the social system verifies local non-satiation of the Paretian preordering, self-centredness and non-jealousy.

THEOREM 15. *Let (π, ω) (resp. (π, x)) be a social contract equilibrium (resp. Lindahl–Bergstrom equilibrium) of (w, ω^0), such that w_i is locally non-satiated at ω (resp. x) for all i (that is, for all i and all neighborhood V of ω in $\mathbb{R}^n$, there exists $x' \in V$ such that $w_i(x') > w_i(\omega)$). (i) Then, ω (resp. x) is a strong distributive optimum of w. (ii) If, moreover, w is a strong BBV distributive social system, or if it verifies local non-satiation of the Paretian preordering, self-centredness and non-jealousy, then ω is a distributive liberal social contract of (w, ω^0).*

PROOF. See Appendix A.1. □

The Lindahl–Bergstrom equilibrium is not, generally, a distributive liberal social contract, because its equilibrium distributions are not, in general, unanimously preferred to the initial distribution of rights. This point is established through the following example, adapted from Mercier Ythier (2004a, Example 3) [a variant of this example can be found also in Bilodeau (1992), and in Section 4.7 of Bilodeau and Steinberg's Chapter 19 of this Handbook]. Let w be a three-agent Cobb–Douglas social system, with $w_i(x) = \beta_{i1} \ln x_1 + \beta_{i2} \ln x_2 + \beta_{i3} \ln x_3$, $\beta_{ii} = 1/2$ and $\beta_{ij} = 1/4$ for all i and all $j \neq i$. The social system verifies the assumptions of Arrow (1981). In particular, we have: $C(w) = P(w) = \text{co}\{\beta^1, \beta^2, \beta^3\}$, the convex hull of the distributions β^i such that $\beta_i^i = 1/2 = \beta_{ii}$ and $\beta_j^i = 1/4 = \beta_{ij}$ for all i and all $j \neq i$, which maximize the agents' utilities in S_3 (see Figure 16). We let ω^0 run over $P(w)$. The strict quasi-concavity of utility functions in $\mathbb{R}^3_{++}$ readily implies then that the set of feasible distributions unanimously weakly preferred to ω^0 reduces to $\{\omega^0\}$. Therefore $L(w, \omega^0) = \{\omega^0\}$ for all ω^0 in $P(w)$. Bergstrom's equilibrium distribution of (w, ω^0) is $(\sum_{i \in N} \beta_{i1} \omega_i^0, \sum_{i \in N} \beta_{i2} \omega_i^0, \sum_{i \in N} \beta_{i3} \omega_i^0)$ [e.g. Bergstrom (1970, Example, p. 387)]. One verifies easily that this distribution is $\neq \omega^0$, hence not in $L(w, \omega^0)$,[68] and there-

---

[68] It is not a Nash equilibrium distribution (nor of course a strong Nash equilibrium distribution) of (w, ω^0) either: the status quo is the unique Nash and Strong Nash equilibrium of (w, ω^0) for all $\omega^0 \in P(w)$.

fore vetoed by one individual at least, unless $\omega^0 = (1/3, 1/3, 1/3) = e$. In particular, exactly two agents i and j strictly prefer the initial distribution ω^0 to the corresponding Bergstrom equilibrium distribution if and only if their initial endowments are both $> 1/3$, that is, if and only if ω^0 belongs to the interior of the hatched area of Figure 16 (relative interior in $P(w)$). Note that, as a simple consequence of the latter, the theorem of Foley (1970, 6), stating that Lindahl equilibrium, defined in the usual way, must be in the Foley-core, does not apply here.[69]

Lindahl–Bergstrom and social contract equilibrium coincide, nevertheless, in the case of BBV social systems, provided that the initial endowments of the poor are null. In other words, Definitions 7 and 7′ are equivalent when the public good problem of redistribution is framed in the standard setup of public good theory, with a list of pure public goods (consumption of the poor) "produced" from a list of pure private goods (the endowments of the rich).[70]

---

[69] The Foley-core of *any* distributive social system (w, ω^0) (see the definition in Footnote 62 above) is contained by construction in the set of strong distributive optima unanimously weakly preferred to ω^0 (as feasible distribution that is not Foley-blocked by any individual or by the grand coalition). It is a subset therefore [generally proper, see Mercier Ythier (2004a, Example 1)] of $L(w, \omega^0)$ whenever w verifies local non-satiation of the Paretian preordering, self-centredness and non-jealousy (or is a strong BBV social system). Letting $F(w, \omega^0)$ denote the Foley-core of (w, ω^0), we must have, in particular, $F(w, \omega^0) = L(w, \omega^0) = \{\omega^0\}$ for all strongly efficient ω^0 in the social system of Figure 16. Therefore the equilibrium distribution of Lindahl–Bergstrom is not in the Foley-core of these (w, ω^0), in contradiction with Foley's statement. Foley's property fails to hold here for a basic structural reason, already mentioned above as the second specificity of wealth distribution as a public good (see Section 6.1): there is no "private good" (in the formal sense) in Arrow's distributive social systems, because distributive concerns are ubiquitous there (everybody cares about everybody's wealth). It is essential, for Foley's property, that all public goods be "produced" (in a formal sense again) from private goods (and from them only). This structural property is verified, and Foley's property holds, in the BBV social systems where the initial endowments of the poor are $= 0$ (see Theorem 16 and Footnote 70 below).

[70] One proves, also, in the line of Footnote 69, that: *The Lindahl–Bergstrom equilibrium distributions of a BBV social system (w, ω^0) with endowments of the poor $= 0$ are in its Foley-core.*

PROOF (SKETCH). Let (π, ω) be a Lindahl–Bergstrom equilibrium of (w, ω^0), suppose that $x^* = x(\omega^0, (0_{\setminus I}, t_I))$ Foley-blocks ω, and let us derive a contradiction. Note that: $x^* \geq 0$ by construction; $\pi \geq 0$ (BBV implies non-malevolence and utility increasing in own wealth); and I can be viewed without loss of generality as a subset of the set of rich individuals (the poor being egoistic). Note also that $\sum_{i \in I} x_i^* + \sum_{j > m} x_j^* = \sum_{i \in I} \omega_i^0$, since the endowments of the poor are $= 0$ (the Foley-blocking coalition finances its consumption and the total consumption of the poor from its own resources). BBV individual utility functions verifying local non-satiation, $w_i(x^*) \geq w_i(\omega)$ implies $\pi_i x^* \geq \pi_i \omega$, so that $\sum_{i \in I} \pi_i x^* > \sum_{i \in I} \pi_i \omega$. Local non-satiation and the definition of Lindhal–Bergstrom equilibrium imply $\pi_i \omega = \omega_i^0$ for all i. We know from the proof of Theorem 16 that $\pi_{ii} = 1$ and $\pi_{ij} = 0$ for all pairs (i, j) of distinct rich individuals, so that $\pi_i x^* = x_i^* + \sum_{j > m} \pi_{ij} x_j^*$ for any rich i. And $\pi \geq 0$ and the definition of Lindahl prices imply $0 \leq \sum_{i \in I} \pi_{ij} \leq 1$ for all j. Thus:

$$\sum_{i \in I} \omega_i^0 = \sum_{i \in I} \pi_i \omega < \sum_{i \in I} \pi_i x^* = \sum_{i \in I} x_i^* + \sum_{i \in I} \sum_{j > m} \pi_{ij} x_j^*$$
$$= \sum_{i \in I} x_i^* + \sum_{j > m} x_j^* \sum_{i \in I} \pi_{ij} \leq \sum_{i \in I} x_i^* + \sum_{j > m} x_j^* = \sum_{i \in I} \omega_i^0,$$

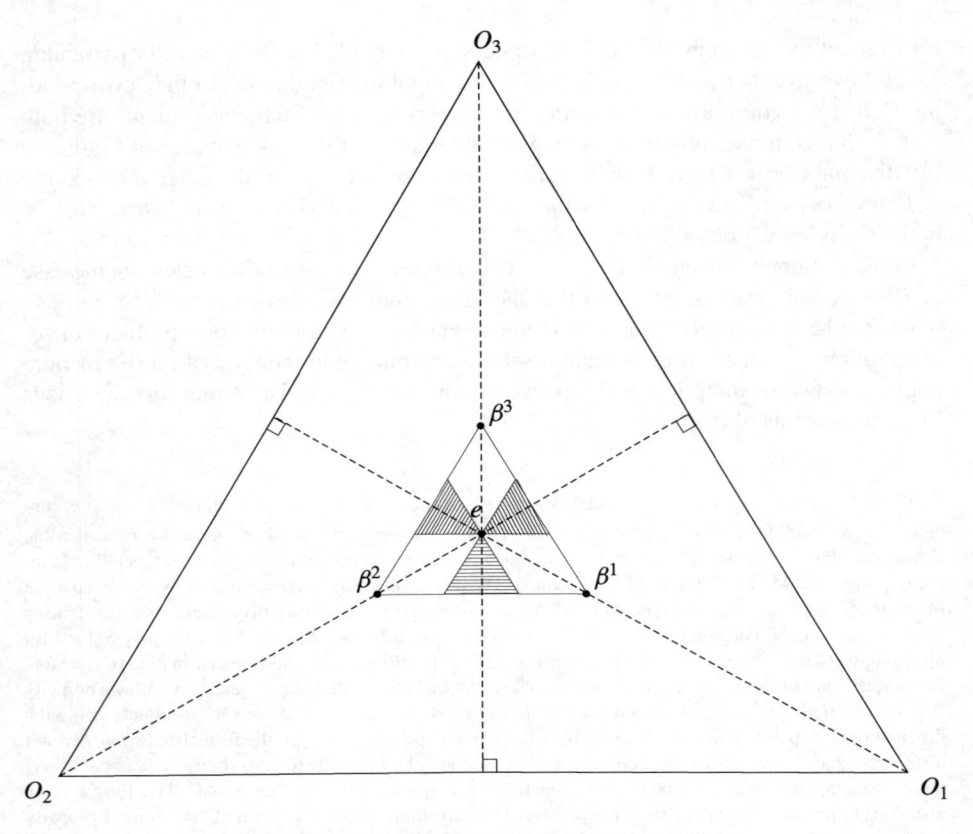

Figure 16. Majority-blocked Lindahl–Bergstrom equilibria.

THEOREM 16. *Let (w, ω^0) be a (weak) BBV social system such that $\omega_i^0 = 0$ for all $i \geqslant m+1$ (that is, for all poor i). (i) (π, ω) is a social contract equilibrium of (w, ω^0) if and only if it is a Lindahl–Bergstrom equilibrium of (w, ω^0). (ii) If, moreover, w is a strong BBV distributive social system, or if it verifies self-centredness and non-jealousy, then the equilibrium distributions of Lindahl–Bergstrom of (w, ω^0) are distributive liberal social contracts of the latter.*

PROOF. See Appendix A.1. □

Bergstrom (1970) and Mercier Ythier (2004a) establish, finally, that the other two fundamental properties of Lindahl equilibrium, namely, the supportability of any Pareto

the wished contradiction. □

optimum as a Lindahl equilibrium [Foley (1970, 3)], and the existence of equilibrium [Foley (1970, 4-B)], extend to distributive social systems.

Establishing these properties is necessary for two reasons. One stems from the specificities of wealth distribution as a public good. I noted above that important structural features and properties of the standard setup of public good theory do not extend to general distributive social systems (see Footnotes 69 and 70). The second reason is that malevolence, that is, the possibility that the wealth of some individuals be a "public bad" for some other individuals, cannot reasonably be discounted from distributive theory. There is of course the flat factual observation that malevolent feelings exist and interact with distributive issues. But one cannot, also, consistently derive an explanation of individual or collective voluntary redistribution from benevolent sentiments and omit taking into account opposite sentiments and their possible influence on the phenomenon under consideration. Malevolence and maleficence are in fact fundamental to this type of approach of redistribution through their potential interactions with the institution of private property. It is important for the logical and normative robustness of the construct to establish that (and to what extent) it can survive and produce reasonable results even in the presence of intense or widespread malevolent feelings [see for instance Mishan (1972) for a critique of Pareto-optimal redistributions founded, notably, on such grounds].

Supportability is established in Bergstrom (1970, Theorems 3 and 4), for convex competitive exchange economies with non-paternalistic non-malevolent distributive preferences, and in Mercier Ythier (2004a, Lemma 4) for differentiable and convex (pure) distributive social systems. The property obtains under standard conditions and minor additional restrictions designed to ensure that individual vectors of prices π_i are all $\neq 0$. As Mercier Ythier (2004a) allows for malevolence, the supportability property supposes moreover, in the latter, a variant of the local non-satiation of the Paretian preordering (differentiable local non-satiation).

Bergstrom (1970, Theorem 1) establishes the existence of distributive Lindahl equilibrium in his setup, under standard technical conditions. Mercier Ythier (2004a, Theorem 4) proves the same for social contract equilibrium in differentiable and convex (pure) distributive social systems. Existence obtains, in spite of the difficulties associated with potential malevolence (see Footnote 66 above), when individual distributive preferences verify the following property of boundedness: (i) marginal valuations of the wealth of others are bounded below, and marginal valuations of own wealth is bounded away from 0 at any solution of $\max\{w_i(x): x_i \geqslant 0 \text{ and } \pi_i x \leqslant \pi_i \omega^0\}$; (ii) and program $\max\{w_i(x): x_i \geqslant 0 \text{ and } \pi_i x \leqslant \pi_i \omega^0\}$ has solutions, contained in a fixed compact set independent of i, for any system of Lindahl prices verifying the boundedness condition (i). Bounded preferences rule out diverging malevolent valuations of the wealth of others, individual satiation, and unbounded choices of x in individual budget sets

$\{x: x_i \geqslant 0 \text{ and } \pi_i x \leqslant \pi_i \omega^0\}$[71] for systems of prices compatible with the boundedness of marginal valuations.

6.1.2.2.2. Dual distributive core   Social contract equilibrium can be formulated, in the manner of Arrow and Debreu (1954), as the outcome of a process of social communication where a central agent, the Auctioneer, announces the systems of Lindahl prices that maximize the sum of individual values of individual distributive choices at any given vector of such choices [Mercier Ythier (2004a, 3.2)]. This subsection presents a brief informal analysis of the causal determination of this centralized social communication from a decentralized communication of the same type, as the field of communication opportunities expands, following the expansion of the number of agents.[72]

Decentralized communication relative to the public good (the distribution of rights ω, or equivalently the vector of net transfers of rights $\omega - \omega^0$) consists of the following process of decentralized auction. Coalitions are allowed to form and block any given strong distributive optimum ω, by proposing a vector of Lindahl shares of their members that increases the value of the public good for them (where value means, for each member i: $\min\{\pi_i z: w_i(\omega^0 + z) \geqslant w_i(\omega)\}$) relative to its value at supporting Lindahl shares, while maintaining their associate utility levels $w_i(\omega)$. Announcements of Lindahl shares by coalitions follow, therefore, the same type of instrumental objective as those of the central Auctioneer, namely, they tend to increase the value of the public good. But, unlike the central Auctioneer's, they embody the particular views of members about the public good, and notably their individual preferences (captured through the dual valuation functions $\min\{\pi_i z: w_i(\omega^0 + z) \geqslant w_i(\omega)\}$).

The *dual distributive core* is made of the strong distributive optima that are unblocked in that sense by any admissible coalition. Admissible coalitions are the coalitions allowed to express their views on the public good by blocking distributive optima. The dual distributive core is identical to: the set of social contract equilibrium distributions when all coalitions are admissible; the set of strong distributive optima when the grand coalition only is admissible (op. cit.: Theorem 5). Decentralized auction, in other words, generates a whole range of solutions to the public good problem of redistribution, from the determinate social contract equilibrium to the (very) indeterminate distributive efficiency frontier, depending on the choice of a set of admissible coalitions.

The expansion of the field of communication opportunities obtains through the replication device of Edgeworth (1881), generalized by Debreu and Scarf (1963): index i

---

[71] Set $\{x: x_i \geqslant 0 \text{ and } \pi_i x \leqslant \pi_i \omega^0\}$ is unbounded below in x_j for all $j \neq i$, and unbounded above in x_j whenever $\pi_{ij} \leqslant 0$. The boundedness of i's choices in such unbounded budget sets appears reasonable, when $\pi_{ii} > 0$, in view of the nature of the object of choice, which can be analyzed in two components: a choice of own consumption, which can be viewed reasonably as unbounded above a priori, but is bounded above by the budget constraint; and the choice of a *relative* distribution of wealth, which can be viewed as essentially bounded (relative shares mattering more than absolute consumption levels), unless of course passionate feelings dominate choices (and then it must be negative passions, for passionate benevolence will be bounded by positive Lindahl prices).

[72] The reader is referred to Mercier Ythier (2004a, 3, 4 and 5) for precise definitions, statements and proofs.

is reinterpreted as a fixed social type, and the number of agents per type is increased evenly, from 1 ("root social system") to infinity. Replication raises specific difficulties with preferences defined on the distribution of individual wealth, because the dimension of the object of preferences expands with the number of agents. They are solved by the application of a variant of the Population Principle, which maintains the structural stability of distributive preferences with expanding populations of agents, essentially by implying that the object of choice is redistribution between social types (identical individuals have identical wealth at any distributive optimum: op. cit., Theorem 6).

It is then shown that *the dual distributive core converges to the set of social contract equilibria* as the number of agents grows to infinity, even when admissible coalitions are required to be "representative", in the sense of containing at least one representative of each social type (op. cit.: Theorem 7).

This causal determination of the distribution of rights through social communication in a large society with finite type diversity faces potential difficulties that are, in many ways, symmetric to the difficulties confronting the causal determination of market prices through private communication in a large economy. The motives of agents for participating in exchange are self-evident in the latter case (participation increases own utility), and impediments to the efficacy of market communication, if any, will come, conspicuously, from informational and other practical limits to contracting and recontracting and the evolution of their relative weight with the expansion of the field of potential exchanges. The expansion of the field of social communication does not seem, symmetrically, susceptible to alter its efficacy to the same degree: convergence obtains despite conditions of representativeness of coalitions that severely restrict the set of admissible coalitions (up to which point is an open question); and the object of social communication, the distribution of rights between social types, is not substantially altered by the expansion of population size (the only significant informational issue being, there, the allocation of individuals between types). The main difficulties, if any, will appear on the motivational side, with the requirement, constitutive of this type of communication, that the relevant representative coalitions participate willingly (coalitions do not increase directly the utility of their members, only the social contract, that is, the final outcome of the participation of all representative coalitions, does) and honestly (by basing their decisions on the true preferences of their members) in social debate.

6.1.3. The distributive liberal social contract and the irreversibility of time

We conclude this review of the general theory with a brief discussion of a fundamental issue raised by the renewal of populations that results from births, deaths and migrations, in relation to the liberal social contract.

Time can be introduced in the formal representation of distributive liberal social contracts above notably by means of an intertemporal exchange economy or, more interestingly for the purposes of the present discussion, by means of an overlapping generations model [e.g. Mercier Ythier (2000b)]. The distributive liberal social contract then becomes susceptible, in principle, to account for redistribution over time, such as redistribution between past, present or future generations.

This extension is facilitated by the putative character of the social contract. The liberal social contract can remain largely imaginary, as an implicit foundation for a variety of institutions or collective decisions that might appear at first sight as expressions of pure public authority (e.g. public assistance) or, conversely, of uncoordinated private initiatives (charities for instance). It can provide, notably, a theoretical foundation for the choice of an optimal level of the public debt, understood as retro-payments from future to present generations: a large subset of concerned individuals, namely children present and future, cannot express any agreement in the present, but the government "foresees" that they will approve the transfers ex post, when they will be at an age to do so [e.g. Kolm (1985)].

This application of the logic of the liberal social contract to long-run redistributions of wealth between generations faces, nevertheless, a basic difficulty if the redistribution under consideration influences, as this actually is the case, the size and individual composition of the population, through the timing and number of births and deaths and through international migrations [e.g. Mercier Ythier (2000b: p. 107) and Footnote 9]. The social states associated with the various patterns of redistribution are not comparable then by definition on an individualistic basis. More precisely, a pattern of redistribution cannot be unanimously preferred to another if the populations of individuals determined by the two patterns differ at some point in time. A liberal social contract can still be defined in principle for this type of decision, but it should be based on the agreement of the sole set of pre-existing individuals, including, as above, relevant predictions of the future opinions of pre-existing young children, but taking due account, also, of the possible (though presumably negligible) influence of the anticipation of social contract redistributions on the size and composition of the set of pre-existing individuals. In the overlapping generations model with an endogenous population of Mercier Ythier (2000b, 4.3), for instance, a distributive liberal social contract is defined at each period of time, for the whole set of agents living at that time (but the object of the contract is instantaneous redistribution of income between social types, not intertemporal redistribution of life-cycle wealth between types or generations).

6.2. *Free-riding and population size in BBV distributive social systems*

One of the basic (and most popular) themes of Olson's *Theory of Collective Action* (1965) is the contention that the public good problem (i.e. the social suboptimality of non-cooperative equilibrium) tends to grow worse as group size increases, essentially because the increase in group size tends to weaken the link between individual contribution to, and individual benefits from, the aggregate social provision of the public good.

This conjecture of Olson has received partial confirmation in the studies of the influence of group size on the non-cooperative equilibrium of BBV social systems. It is shown, notably, that average individual contribution to the public good decreases with group size, but not total contribution, which increases with the number of agents when private goods and the public good are normal goods for donors (Section 6.2.2); and that underprovision of the public good increases with group size, relative to Lindahl equilibrium provision level (Section 6.2.3).

Two studies of Kolm (1987a, 1987b) show, on the other hand, that the increase in population size might actually facilitate the practical emergence of a cooperative solution to the public good problem by making individual benefits from free-riding negligibly small (see Section 6.2.4).

6.2.1. Inefficient underprovision of the public good at non-cooperative equilibrium

We begin this section by synthesizing useful results relative to the basic insight of Olson's theory, namely, the idea that the public good provision level tends to be too low at non-cooperative equilibrium, relative to collectively efficient levels.

Early rigorous expositions of this idea in a general setup were mainly illustrative, relying on graphical comparisons of the non-cooperative equilibria and Pareto-efficient allocations of social systems with a single pure public good produced from private goods by means of the additive technology, that is, in the terminology of the present survey, of strong BBV distributive social systems [see notably the diagram of Cornes and Sandler (1985a, Figure 6, p. 112), for symmetric equilibria and symmetric optima of social systems with any number of identical donors; and the Cornes–Sandler box in Cornes and Sandler (1986, Figure 5.3, p. 77), for general strong BBV distributive social systems with two donors].

Two recent contributions of Shitovitz and Spiegel (1998, 2001) provide general statements that confirm, in the main, Olson's insight within this framework.

Theorem 17, below, reproduces essentially the argument of the main theorem of Shitovitz and Spiegel (2001, 3, pp. 222–223) with slight improvements and an addition of my own. The first proposition (Theorem 17(i)) states that: if a strong BBV distributive social system verifies, notably, ordinal normality (defined in Section 3.4.2.2: Theorem 3), then there is an allocation in its (weak) Foley-core[73] that is unanimously *weakly* preferred by the rich to its unique social (Cournot–Nash) equilibrium. A second proposition (Theorem 17(ii)), that improves slightly upon a similar statement made by Shitovitz and Spiegel in the course of their main proof (p. 223, *Cases* 1 and 2),

---

[73] The weak Foley-core of distributive social system (w, ω) is defined as in Footnote 62, with the sole difference that strong unanimity (see Footnotes 54 and 60) is now required inside coalitions. Formally: (i) non-empty coalition I strongly Foley-blocks gift-vector t^* if there exists t_I such that for all $i \in I$: $x_i(\omega, (0_{\setminus I}, t_I)) \geq 0$ and $w_i(x(\omega, (0_{\setminus I}, t_I))) > w_i(x(\omega, t^*))$; (ii) and the weak Foley-core of (w, ω) is $\{x(\omega, t) \in S_n$: There is no non-empty coalition that strongly Foley-blocks $t\}$. We use these variants to conform the definitions and proof of Shitovitz and Spiegel. Note, nevertheless, that the strict monotonicity and continuity of functions v_i, assumed by these authors and in Theorem 17 below, readily imply the equivalence of weak and strong Foley-blocking and Foley-core in the BBV framework, and that the strict quasi-concavity of utility functions, also assumed here, has the same consequence for general distributive social systems.

states that, moreover: if the social equilibrium distribution is not in the weak Foley-core, then it is *strongly* Pareto-dominated by some distributions of the weak Foley-core, and the provision level of the public good is *strictly larger* in any of the latter. I add, as a third statement (Theorem 17(iii)), a sufficient condition for the (weak) inefficiency of distributive equilibrium that follows in a natural way from my discussion of the Becker–Nakayama condition in Section 6.1.1.2, namely, that there are at least two donors with positive private wealth at equilibrium.

THEOREM 17. *Let (w, ω) be a strong BBV distributive social system, and suppose that, for all i, v_i is C^2, strictly quasi-concave, and verifies ordinal normality. Denote by $(x_1^*, \ldots, x_m^*, y^*)$ its unique equilibrium vector of individual consumption of the rich and aggregate consumption of the poor, suppose that $x_i^* > 0$ for all $i \leqslant m$, and let x^* be any equilibrium distribution (that is, any $x \in S_n$ such that $x_i = x_i^*$ for all $i \leqslant m$ and $x_{m+1} + \cdots + x_n = y^*$). (i) Then, there exists a distribution x in the weak Foley-core of (w, ω) such that $w_i(x) \geqslant w_i(x^*)$ for all $i \leqslant m$. (ii) If moreover x^* is not in the weak Foley-core of (w, ω), then: (a) there exists a distribution x in the weak Foley-core of (w, ω) such that $w_i(x) > w_i(x^*)$ for all $i \in N$; (b) and $x_{m+1} + \cdots + x_n > y^*$ for all such x. (iii) x^* is not in the weak Foley-core of (w, ω), nor is it a weak distributive optimum, whenever $(x_1^*, \ldots, x_m^*, y^*)$ is such that at least two agents contribute whose private equilibrium consumption levels are both > 0 (that is, whenever $0 < x_i^* < \omega_i$ for two distinct $i \leqslant m$ at least).*

PROOF. See Appendix A.1. □

We have argued above (see Footnote 62) that the Foley-core is not specifically relevant as a solution concept in the context of general Pareto social systems, because it does not respect the right of private property and because the distribution of wealth is a non-excludable public good in these social systems. We gave, in particular, in Section 6.1.2.2.1, an example of a distributive social system of Arrow where the initial distribution is preferred to the Lindahl–Bergstrom equilibrium distribution by a majority of agents, and is not, consequently, in its Foley-core.

These remarks do not apply, at least to the same extent, to BBV distributive social systems. When the initial endowments of the poor are $= 0$, Lindahl–Bergstrom and social contract equilibria coincide (Theorem 16(i)) and belong to the Foley-core (see Footnote 70). Moreover the weak (resp. strong) Foley-core of (w, ω) is made, by definition, of distributions that are both weakly (resp. strongly) Pareto-efficient and unanimously weakly preferred to the initial distribution ω. It is contained, therefore, in the set of liberal social contracts of (w, ω) whenever the BBV social system is strong or verifies self-centredness and non-jealousy (Theorem 14).

Two interesting questions, following these remarks and Theorem 17, are then whether the Lindahl equilibrium distributions of a strong BBV social system are or are not unanimously preferred to its Cournot–Nash equilibrium distributions, and whether the corresponding provision levels of the public good are or are not larger than the Cournot–Nash provision levels. Shitovitz and Spiegel (1998) give partial answers to these questions, which are mainly but not entirely positive.

They are unambiguously positive in the important special case of symmetric equilibria of strong BBV distributive social systems with identical "rich" agents [Shitovitz and Spiegel (1998, Theorem 1, p. 5); and Corollary 10 below].

COROLLARY 10. *Let (w, ω) be a strong BBV distributive social system such that the initial endowments of the poor are all $= 0$ and rich individuals are identical (that is, $v_i = v$ and $\omega_i = 1/m$ for all $i \leqslant m$). Let $(z^*, y^*) \in \mathbb{R}^2$ and $(z^{**}, y^{**}) \in \mathbb{R}^2$ be respectively a Cournot–Nash and a Lindahl–Bergstrom (symmetric) equilibrium vector of private consumption of the rich and aggregate consumption of the poor (where symmetry means that the rich make identical gifts at equilibrium, equal to y^*/m and y^{**}/m respectively).* (i) *Then, $v(z^*, y^*) \leqslant v(z^{**}, y^{**})$.* (ii) *If, moreover, v is C^2 and strictly quasi-concave, and if $m \geqslant 2$ and z^* and y^* are both > 0, then: $v(z^*, y^*) < v(z^{**}, y^{**})$; and $y^* < y^{**}$ whenever v verifies the additional assumption of ordinal normality.*

PROOF. See Appendix A.1. □

Theorem 17 stated in essence that inefficient Cournot–Nash equilibria of strong BBV distributive social systems verifying ordinal normality are strongly dominated by some efficient distributions involving higher levels of provision of the public good. Corollary 10 adds the precision that Lindahl equilibria yield such distributions when the social system is made of identical donors. Unfortunately, the latter result extends only partially to strong BBV systems with multiple types of donors. Shitovitz and Spiegel (1998) give an example of a "large" strong BBV distributive social system with potential donors of two different types (one "large" agent, and a continuum of identical "small" agents), where the small donors strictly prefer Cournot–Nash to Lindahl (op. cit.: Example 5, p. 16). The same authors show that, nevertheless, Lindahl equal treatment equilibrium (where equal treatment means that identical individuals have identical private consumption levels) is unanimously preferred to Cournot–Nash equal treatment equilibrium in large social systems, when the relative weight of the set of small donors is important enough. This notably is the case for sequences of replicas of finite strong BBV distributive social systems with a finite number of fixed types of donors and fixed aggregate wealth per type: there exists an integer ι such that Lindahl equal treatment is unanimously strictly preferred to Cournot–Nash equal treatment by the rich for all replicas with numbers of donors per type $\geqslant \iota$ (op. cit.: Theorem 7, p. 12). The same holds for large strong BBV distributive social systems with a continuum of donors and fixed types of donors, including a single type of large donors (atoms) and a finite number of types of small donors (the atomless component): there exists a positive real number ρ such that Lindahl equal treatment is unanimously strictly preferred to Cournot–Nash equal treatment by the rich for all large systems made of these fixed types, such that the weight of the atomless component is $\geqslant \rho$ (op. cit.: Theorem 10: I and III, p. 15).

6.2.2. *Group size and public good provision level at non-cooperative equilibrium*

Chamberlin (1974), McGuire (1974), Andreoni (1988a), Fries, Golding and Romano (1991), and Shitovitz and Spiegel (1998), have studied the effect of group size on the level of individual and aggregate contribution to public good, in the context of strong BBV distributive social systems.

Chamberlin and McGuire concentrate on symmetric equilibria of social systems of identical agents (that is, agents with identical preferences and endowments), the latter in the special case of linear individual reaction functions.[74] They establish that, with fixed individual preferences and endowments (in my terms, fixed identical (w_i, ω_i) for all "rich" i), an increase in group size induces a decrease in equilibrium individual contributions, which converge to 0 as the number of agents grows to infinity. Equilibrium total contribution converges then to a finite value. Moreover, the associate sequence of equilibrium levels of provision of the public good is increasing if (and only if) the public and the private good are both (strictly) normal goods for contributors.

Andreoni (1988a) and Fries, Golding and Romano (1991) extend these results to social systems with multiple types of donors. Types may differ in preferences, endowments or both. It is assumed that individual unconstrained demands for the public good are well-defined differentiable functions (corresponding to functions f_i of Section 3.4.2.2). The private and the public good are both strictly normal. Fries et al. slightly strengthen the normality assumption by supposing moreover that the derivative of the demand for the private good has a positive lower bound for all types of donors (that is, equivalently, that $\partial f_i(r)$ is bounded above by some real number < 1 for all rich i).

The two papers differ principally in the way they model the increase in group size.

Andreoni considers finite independent random draws from a continuous distribution of types, and studies the asymptotic convergence of individual and total equilibrium provision levels as the number of draws grows to infinity, with the following conclusions (op. cit.: Theorem 1, p. 61 and Theorem 1.1, p. 66): (i) the set of contributors to the public good converges to a set containing individuals of a single type; (ii) in particular, the proportion of the population contributing to the public good, and average individual giving, decrease to 0; (iii) if all agents have identical preferences, then only the richest contribute in the limit; (iv) total donations to the public good increase to a finite asymptotic value.

Fries et al. increase the size of the social system by replication in the manner of Debreu and Scarf (1963), that is, by supposing an equal number of individuals of each type and making that number grow to infinity. They establish that: (i) the number of contributing types decreases monotonically with the size of the social system, and there is exactly one contributing type for any size of the social system larger than some well-defined, finite critical level (op. cit.: Proposition 1, p. 152); (ii) individual equilibrium

---

[74] Precisely, with the notations of Section 3.4.2.2, McGuire supposes that $\rho_i(G_{-i})$ is of the type $\max\{0, \alpha - \beta G_{-i}\}$, with α and $\beta > 0$.

contributions decrease monotonically to 0, and total equilibrium provision of the public good grows monotonically to a finite value, as group size grows to infinity (op. cit.: Lemmas 2 and 3, p. 151, and Proposition 1).

Shitovitz and Spiegel (1998), finally, consider large strong BBV distributive social systems with a continuum of donors of fixed types, including a single type of large donors and a finite number of types of small donors (see the last paragraph of Section 6.2.1 above). Their framework differs from Andreoni's in three main respects: it does not suppose the normality of Cournot–Nash individual demands for the private and the public good; it has a finite number of donor types, while Andreoni's has a continuum (but a finite number of types of individual preferences); and it has large donors, that is, donors of non-null relative individual weight, while Andreoni's social system is atomless. They obtain the same qualitative property on free-riding as Andreoni, namely, that only large donors contribute to the public good at Cournot–Nash equilibrium (op. cit.: Theorem 10, II, p. 15). But they do not consider the effects of population size on public good provision level, not surprisingly since they do not make the normality assumption that conditions unambiguous results concerning the latter.

6.2.3. *Group size and the suboptimality of non-cooperative equilibrium*

The contributions above make clear, and on the whole confirm Olson's view that individual free-riding, understood as individual undercontribution to the public good (including the special case of individual non-contribution), increases with population size in a non-cooperative environment. But they also introduce a qualification, by demonstrating that, despite increasing free-riding, the total provision of the public good increases with group size when, as this seems relevant in the context of strong BBV social systems, private goods and the public good are strictly normal for donors.

This qualification raises new questions for the degree of relevance of the collective side of Olson's argument, namely, the idea that social inefficiencies should worsen as population size increases [in Olson's own terms: "...the larger the group, the less it will further its common interests" (1965, p. 2). The latter have been addressed by the contributions of Cornes and Sandler (1986), Laffont (1988), Mueller (1989), Cornes and Schweinberger (1996), and Gaube (2001), which provide precise formulations and give, again, partial confirmations of this aspect of Olson's conjecture in various versions of the BBV social system.

Cornes and Sandler (1986), Laffont (1988), Mueller (1989) and Gaube (2001) share the following common features. They consider strong BBV distributive social systems, and compare non-cooperative provision with Lindahl provision as population size increases. Formally, letting s denote population size, $G(s)$ and $G^*(s)$ the non-cooperative and Lindahl public good production levels respectively, defined consistently for all values of s, these authors consider situations where the ratios $G(s)/G^*(s)$ are < 1 (underproduction of the public good), and exhibit conditions under which they are strictly decreasing in s (relative underproduction getting worse as group size increases).

The case studied by Cornes and Sandler (1986, 5.4, pp. 82–84) is the symmetric (non-cooperative and Lindahl) equilibrium of identical donors endowed with preferences linear in the private good, that is, using my notations, with quasi-linear utility functions of the type $v_i(x_i, x_{m+1} + \cdots + x_n) = x_i + v(x_{m+1} + \cdots + x_n)$. Population size is measured by the number of agents (potential donors, or "rich" individuals: $s = m$). They assume a strictly increasing, strictly concave, twice differentiable function v, and suppose a positive equilibrium provision level of the public good. The strict concavity of v readily implies the uniqueness of interior $G(s)$ as well as the uniqueness of $G^*(s)$.[75] The assumptions on v imply moreover that $G^*(s)$ is strictly increasing in s (op. cit.: p. 84). And the quasi-linearity of preferences and positive equilibrium provision of the public good imply that $G(s)$ is insensitive to population size: the positive wealth effects associated with an increase in the number of donors are entirely absorbed by the increase in individual demands for private goods. Ratio $G(s)/G^*(s)$, therefore, is uniquely defined for all s and decreasing in s.

Laffont (1988, p. 39) and Mueller (1989) analyze an example of symmetric non-cooperative and Lindahl equilibria of identical donors endowed with Cobb–Douglas preferences $v_i(x_i, x_{m+1} + \cdots + x_n) = x_i^\beta (x_{m+1} + \cdots + x_n)^{(1-\beta)}$ ($0 < \beta < 1$). The ratio $G(s)/G^*(s)$, where $s = m$ denotes the number of potential donors, is, again, uniquely determined, equal to $1/(\beta s + 1 - \beta)$, therefore < 1 for all $s > 1$ and strictly decreasing in s. This example differs from Cornes and Sandler's, notably, in that individual non-cooperative demands for the public and private goods are strictly normal [that is, $0 < \partial f_i(r) = 1 - \beta < 1$, while $\partial f_i(r) = 0$ in Cornes and Sandler (1986)]. It verifies, consequently, the property, outlined by Chamberlin (1974) and McGuire (1974), of a non-cooperative provision level of the public good strictly increasing in group size (precisely, one has $G(s) = (1 - \beta)se/(\beta s + 1 - \beta)$, where $e(> 0)$ denotes the identical initial endowments of donors, a function strictly increasing in s). The symmetric Lindahl equilibrium provision level $G^*(s) = (1 - \beta)se$ increases with s also, but faster than non-cooperative provision ($G^*(s) > G(s)$ and $\partial G^*(s) > \partial G(s)$ for all $s > 1$).

Gaube (2001) generalizes the findings of Laffont and Mueller. In my notations and terms, he considers strong BBV distributive social systems with any number m of distinct types of "rich" individuals, strictly quasi-concave, monotonic strictly increasing BBV utility functions $v_i(x_i, x_{m+1} + \cdots + x_n)$, and strictly normal differentiable demands for private goods and the public good. Population size is increased by means of the Debreu–Scarf replication device. Its measure s now denotes the number of individuals per type (that is, the number of individuals per type in the s-replica of root social system $((v_1, \ldots, v_m), (\omega_1, \ldots, \omega_m))$ is s, and the total number of potential donors is

---

[75] Letting $\omega_i = 0$ for all poor i for simplicity, the first-order condition for interior non-cooperative equilibrium reads $\partial v(G) = 1$, which yields a unique equilibrium level for the public good since ∂v is a strictly decreasing function $\mathbb{R} \to \mathbb{R}$. Likewise, if the social system has two distinct symmetric Lindahl equilibrium provision levels of the public good, yielding necessarily the same equilibrium utility level, then any strict convex combination of equilibrium states would induce a feasible Pareto-improvement by the strict concavity of function v, contradicting the Pareto-efficiency of Lindahl equilibrium.

ms).[76] The normality assumption implies that $G(s)$ is well-defined and unique for all s. The comparison of $G(s)$ with optimal provision level is elaborated along the following lines: arbitrary lump-sum transfers are allowed between donors in the root social system, and the resulting initial distribution ω' is then maintained throughout the subsequent replicas; the corresponding Lindahl equilibrium provision level $G^*_{\omega'}(s)$ (here supposed unique for all s for simplicity) is compared with $G(s)$ as above, by means of the ratio $G(s)/G^*_{\omega'}(s)$. This procedure makes the study of relative underprovision independent of the initial distribution of wealth, as appears indispensable in the presence of multiple types of agents. Gaube proves then that: (i) $G(s+1)/G(s) < (s+1)/s$, that is, non-cooperative provision grows at a lower rate than population size (op. cit.: Lemma 1, p. 4); (ii) if the private and the public good are weak gross substitutes[77] at Lindahl equilibrium (that is, if i's Lindahl demand for the private good is non-decreasing in his Lindahl price of the public good for all i), then $G^*_{\omega'}(s+1)/G^*_{\omega'}(s) \geq (s+1)/s$, which means that the Lindahl provision level increases at a higher rate than population size (op. cit.: Lemma 2, p. 5); (iii) ratio $G(s)/G^*_{\omega'}(s)$ is, consequently, strictly decreasing in group size (op. cit.: Proposition, pp. 3–4).

Cornes and Schweinberger (1996), finally, consider general BBV Pareto social systems, with any finite number of private and public goods. Utility functions are strictly quasi-concave, and public goods are produced from private goods by means of concave production functions. Private goods are exchangeable on perfectly competitive markets.[78] The authors define and compare the social (Cournot–Nash) equilibrium and efficient allocation in this Pareto social system for populations that differ in size. A social system is said "more populous" than another if the latter's set of agents is a proper subset of the former's. The main result (op. cit.: Proposition 2, p. 83) states that public goods are more underproduced, at Cournot–Nash equilibrium, in the more populous social system than in the less populous social system, in the following precise sense and circumstances. Suppose that: (a) all agents contribute all factors to all public goods in a Cournot–Nash equilibrium of the more populous social system; (b) the same market value of factors is reallocated from the private to the public goods sectors in the more and in the less populous social systems; and (c) the utilities of the additional households of the more populous social system are kept unchanged in this reallocation by means

---

[76] We may also assume for the sake of completeness that poor types are identical, with null initial endowment, and are replicated in the same way as rich types.

[77] The examples of Laffont and Mueller verify weak gross substitutability, with a price elasticity of the Lindahl demand for the private good = 0. Note that *strict* gross substitutability (that is, positive price elasticity of the Lindahl demand for the private good) implies the uniqueness of Lindahl equilibrium in Gaube's setup.

[78] Their precise formulation fits in the formal definition of Pareto social systems and social equilibrium given in Section 4.2.1, with one mild qualification, and adequate interpretations of production functions. The concave production functions of public goods of Cornes and Sweinberger should be interpreted, in the framework of Section 4.2.1, as concave ophelimity functions of the poor. The qualification comes from the weak separability of donors' preferences in their own consumption of private goods, which is assumed in Section 4.2.1 as a consequence of non-paternalism, and is not supposed in Cornes and Schweinberger (1996). The latter is more general than Section 4.2.1 in this respect, and less general in all other respects.

of appropriate lump-sum taxes. Then, the gains in the more populous social system are greater than in the less populous social system, that is, the social surplus measured in terms of the numéraire in the compensated equilibrium is greater in the more populous social system than in the less populous social system. This result expresses essentially the fact that there are consumption returns to scale associated with the existence of pure public goods, simply because this type of good, by definition, "can be shared among more agents without a utility loss to anyone agent" (op. cit.: p. 83).

6.2.4. Free-riding, population size and core solution

Kolm (1987a, 1987b) examines the same questions in the context of cooperative gift-giving.

The main distinctive feature of the construct is the cooperative solution concept it applies, corresponding to the variant of Kolm's general notions of core with interdependent coalitions where every coalition bases its decisions relative to its own contributions on its anticipation of the best reactions of the complementary coalition (see Section 16.5.3 of the introduction Chapter 1 of the Handbook for a general presentation of the theory). Formally, using the notations of the present chapter, let $\varphi_{\setminus I}(t_I)$ denote the set argmax$\{w_{\setminus I}(x(\omega, (t_I, t_{\setminus I}))): x_{\setminus I}(\omega, (t_I, t_{\setminus I})) \geqslant 0\}$, where $w_{\setminus I} = (w_i)_{i \in N \setminus I}$ is maximized with respect to $t_{\setminus I}$ (which means that if $t_{\setminus I} \in \varphi_{\setminus I}(t_I)$, then there exists no $t'_{\setminus I}$ such that $x_{\setminus I}(\omega, (t_I, t'_{\setminus I})) \geqslant 0$ and $w_{\setminus I}(x(\omega, (t_I, t'_{\setminus I}))) > w_{\setminus I}(x(\omega, (t_I, t_{\setminus I})))$). A gift-vector t^* of a distributive social system (w, ω) is in the core in the sense of Kolm (1987a, 1987b) if, for all non-empty $I \subset \{1, \ldots, n\}$, there exists no t such that: $x_I(\omega, t) \geqslant 0$, $t_{\setminus I} \in \varphi_{\setminus I}(t_I)$, and $w_I(x(\omega, t)) > w_I(x(\omega, t^*))$.[79]

The references above apply this general notion to a simple case, corresponding, in my terms and notations, to the strong BBV distributive social system with identical "rich" donors $i \in \{1, \ldots, m\}$ whose (ordinal) preferences admit a quasi-linear utility representation of the type $w_i(x) = x_i + v(x_{m+1} + \cdots + x_n)$ (with v twice differentiable, strictly increasing and strictly concave). The first reference (1987a) concentrates on the case of a pure public good (the relevant case in the context of the present review) while the second reference (1987b) extends the analysis to excludable public goods with any fixed degree of exclusion.

The core is characterized, in the pure (non-rival, non-excludable) public good case, as the set of Pareto-efficient individually rational states (1987a, p. 10), where individual rationality means that every donor i is satisfied with his own individual contribution given his anticipation of the best reaction of the complementary coalition $N \setminus \{i\}$ to any deviation of himself.

---

[79] This variant of the Kolm-core corresponds, in Kolm's terminology, to the dichotomous core with Cournot group behavior: dichotomous because each coalition I faces the best group response of complementary coalition $N \setminus I$; and Cournot group behavior in the derivation of the best responses of complementary coalitions. See Kolm (1989) for alternative definitions, extensions and refinements, of cores with interdependent coalitions.

There is no room in this construct, by definition, for free-riding as rational individual or collective behavior that would result in a Pareto-inefficient social state (see my definition of free-riding in Section 6.1.1 and Footnote 55), but there remains the possibility of core emptiness, and the possibility that some individuals contribute nothing at some core solution (which must be then a non-symmetric efficient state).

These two possibilities are logically related in the following way.

Suppose without loss of generality that the initial endowments of the poor are null, let individual preferences and endowments be fixed, let the number m of "rich" agents (that is, the number of potential donors) measure the size of the social system, and denote by G_s a provision level of the public good that maximizes the vector of utilities of potential donors in a coalition of size s. Given the quasi-linearity of utility functions, G_s maximizes, equivalently, the sum of the utilities of coalition members $-G + sv(G)$. G_s is, therefore, well-defined and unique for all $s \geqslant 1$ since v is continuous and strictly concave. For any size m of the social system, any element t of its Kolm-core and any potential donor i, let $r_i(m, t) = t_i - v(G_m) + v(G_{m-1})$. When $t_i > 0$, the latter corresponds to i's benefit from "free-riding" in the sense of Kolm, that is, from contributing 0 instead of t_i (the difference between his utility $\omega_i + v(G_{m-1})$ from contributing 0 given that the best response of the complementary coalition of donors is then to provide G_{m-1} of the public good, and his actual utility $\omega_i - t_i + v(G_m)$ at t). A potential donor of a social system of size m contributes nothing at Kolm's core solution t if and only if $r_i(m, t) > 0$. Note that the average benefit from free-riding $(G_m/m) - v(G_m) + v(G_{m-1})$ in the social system of size m only depends on m. Let it be denoted by $r(m)$.

It is notably proved, then, that: (i) the Kolm-core of a social system of size m is non-empty if and only if the associate average benefit from free-riding $r(m)$ is $\leqslant 0$, or, equivalently, if and only if there exists some efficient t that makes individual non-contribution individually non-rational for all $i \leqslant m$ (1987a, p. 15); (ii) the average benefit from free-riding vanishes (converges to 0) as m grows to infinity (1987a, p. 16).

These results state, in other words, that average and individual benefits from individual non-contribution tend to vanish, and with them potential problems of existence of a core solution in the sense of Kolm, as the number of potential (identical, quasi-linear) donors becomes large. They rely in an essential way on the basic assumption that individuals face consistent maximizing reactions of the whole group to their decisions. The point made in these studies is therefore, in many respects, complementary from the point made by Olson and his followers: the latter show how the collective inconveniences from non-cooperative private provision of the public good can increase with group size; and the former how the increase in group size can reinforce cooperative solutions (and make the sharing of cooperative surplus more equitable) when the group reacts consistently to individual defections.

6.3. Mechanism design in BBV distributive social systems

The large body of literature that designs incentive compatible mechanisms[80] in standard finite public goods economies with complete information, reviewed notably in Groves and Ledyard (1987) or Moore (1992), applies immediately, with obvious adaptations, to BBV distributive social systems.

To the best of my knowledge, incentive compatibility has, on the contrary, not yet been studied in the general distributive or Pareto social systems defined in Sections 3 and 4. The extension of known results to the latter is not straightforward, at least at first sight. The optimistic conclusion of Walker (1981), for instance, on the possibility of attaining outcomes unanimously (weakly) preferred to the initial distribution, relies on his construction of an incentive compatible mechanism that implements Lindahl equilibrium. It does not extend as such, therefore, to general Pareto social systems, for the simple reason that standard Lindahl equilibrium is generally not unanimously weakly preferred to initial distribution in such systems (see the social system of Figure 16, in Section 6.1.2.2 above).

I will not review here the general results relative to incentive compatibility in general (BBV) public goods environments. The reader is referred to Groves and Ledyard (1987) and Moore (1992) for such general presentations. I will concentrate instead on the design of mechanisms more specifically related to distributive issues, namely, the tax-subsidy schemes for private contributions to pure public goods.

This body of literature deals with three analytically distinct sets of issues. The first is implementation, which looks for the achievement of Pareto-efficiency by means of an appropriate scheme of taxes and subsidies on private (non-cooperative) actions. The second is treasury efficiency, which designs the tax-subsidy scheme with an objective of minimization of the public budget for a given equilibrium level of provision of the public good. And the third is the comparative evaluation of the distributional consequences of the different tax-subsidy schemes on the equilibrium wealth and welfare of relevant social groups.

These questions are studied in two broad classes of models. In the first one, the state is abstracted: incentive variables and individual contributions are chosen both by individual agents in a two-stage decision process, where incentive variables are determined by simultaneous non-cooperative utility-maximizing decisions in the first stage, and individual contributions to the public good by simultaneous non-cooperative utility-maximizing decisions in the second stage. The second class of models introduces, more realistically, a public authority responsible for the design of the incentive mechanism, and studies the simultaneous determination of efficient tax-subsidy schemes by the state and non-cooperative utility-maximizing contributions by individual agents.

The models and their properties are detailed in Appendix A.2.

---

[80] That is, incentive mechanisms that yield Pareto-efficient social states when all agents play non-cooperative (Nash equilibrium) strategies.

7. Imperfectly substitutable transfers

This section goes back over the basic common features that characterize the stream of theoretical literature reviewed in Sections 3 to 6, and examines how the theory fits to corresponding social reality.

The basic assumption of the theory is a complex set of hypotheses synthesized in a notion of perfect substitutability of transfers, whose main foundations, already enumerated in the introduction to this chapter, consist of: (i) perfect and complete competitive markets; (ii) non-paternalistic utility interdependence; (iii) and the Cournot–Nash behavioral assumption.

The implications of these assumptions which have been mainly studied in the literature are: (i) the separability and neutrality properties, the variants of which have been reviewed in Sections 2 (see Section 2.2), 4 (notably Section 4.2) and 5 above; (ii) the public good problem of redistribution, examined in detail in Section 6, whose most common expression is the Pareto-inefficient underprovision of transfers at non-cooperative equilibrium (an aspect of Olson's conjecture); (iii) and, as a joint consequence of the former two, the full crowding-out of private gifts at distributive optimum.

This theoretical construct has been tested on two complementary grounds. Logical grounds first, with numerous contributions exhibiting counterexamples to the basic properties of the theory, mainly the neutrality property, which follow from selective violations of its basic assumption. And empirical grounds, second, with two substantial streams of literature performing econometric tests of neutrality on the one hand and experimental tests of non-cooperative underprovision of a public good on the other hand.

The review of literature presented below is selective on purpose. We use it mainly as an illustrative support to a general comment on the theory. Most of its aspects are the object of more substantial developments in several chapters of the Handbook, which we will mention when appropriate in the course of the section.

7.1. Logical tests of the perfect substitutability of transfers

The tests reviewed here identify elements of the assumption of perfect substitutability that are essential in the sense that their violation involves in general the refutation of a basic property of the theory, notably the neutrality property. They contribute in eliciting the internal structure of the assumption, and they produce families of constructs derived from the central theory, which can prove useful to understand various aspects of social reality that the latter cannot grasp (see Section 7.2). The presentation below goes through the three foundations of the theory recalled above.

7.1.1. Perfect competitive markets

Papers studying the implications of market imperfections concentrate on capital market failures. The results are formulated, accordingly, in the dynamic setup of infinite horizon economies with finite-lived, altruistically related generations. Two broad classes of constructs are considered.

A first family of models [see notably Altig and Davis (1993), and the models reviewed in Laitner (1997, 3.3, pp. 222–227)] supposes that borrowing constraints impede the programming of individual life cycle consumption and saving. Individual life is divided in three periods (youth, middle age, and old age). Capital market imperfections prevent individuals from borrowing in the first two periods of their life. Parents coexist with children over the last two periods of the life cycle, and are altruistically related to them. Altruism can be one-sided [Laitner (1997)], from parents to children, or two-sided [Altig and Davis (1993)]. The coexistence of generations over two periods of time allows for a variety of patterns of intergenerational transfers, which may notably combine bequests and lifetime transfers such as middle-aged parents paying for the education of their children. It is shown that public intergenerational transfers can foster steady state Pareto improvements in the presence of operative intergenerational transfers, notably when the following conditions hold simultaneously: binding borrowing constraints; and descending intergenerational transfers, which combine null bequests with operative lifetime transfers for the education of the young [see Altig and Davis (1993) for a comprehensive classification of conceivable steady state patterns of intergenerational transfers and their implications for neutrality]. Leaving aside inessential differences associated with the dynamic features of the framework, these types of results clearly involve the violation of two characteristic properties of general Pareto social systems, namely, separability (as implied by Theorem 4) and neutrality (Theorem 7).

The capital market imperfections considered in the second family of models appear more fundamental, as they are related to the time irreversibilities that govern and constrain long-run relationships between generations, already briefly evoked in Section 6.1.3 above. These models consider, accordingly, subsequent generations (instead of overlapping ones) with descending altruism. Their main characteristic feature consists of an institutional constraint forbidding negative bequests. These contributions exhibit (steady state) equilibrium situations where binding non-negativity constraints on bequests result in (market and distributive) Pareto inefficiency. The precise interpretation of the market failure implicit in this finding depends on the type of intertemporal operations involved: credit market imperfections of the type of liquidity constraints in Nerlove, Razin and Sadka (1984, 1987, 1988), and in Becker and Murphy (1988), which concentrate on parental investments in the human wealth of children (fertility decisions and education); insurance market imperfections such as moral hazard or adverse selection problems in Barsky, Mankiw and Zeldes (1986), Feldstein (1988), Sheshinski (1988) or Strawczynski (1994), which view bequests as an insurance device against income uncertainty of current (Barsky et al., Feldstein) or future (Sheshinski, Strawczynski) generations. These sources of market failures can be related, more fundamentally, as suggested above, to the fact that current generations make their decisions at a time when future generations do not yet exist, at least as full-fledged economic agents, and cannot, consequently, enter into contractual relationships with them (a case of "fundamental market incompleteness", so to speak). They imply the possibility of Pareto-improving public redistributions from future to current generations, on both grounds of market and distributive efficiency. Note that this possibility implies a violation of the separability property, but that it implies no violation of the neutrality property since intergenerational transfers are at a corner by assumption. They point to a type of justification of public intervention which appears very important in the context of long-run economic equilibrium,[81] and is ignored by construction in the Pareto social systems above.

7.1.2. Non-paternalistic utility interdependence

Non-paternalistic utility interdependence means essentially, in the context of Pareto social systems, that the sole purpose of gift-giving is the redistribution of market money wealth.

It has been a commonplace from the very beginning of the theory to notice that neutrality does not hold in the presence of other motives of giving, such as merit wants [e.g. Becker (1974, 3.C, pp. 1085–1087)], or anyone in the large variety of motivations implying that gift-giving "matters per se", is a "consumption good" for the donor so to speak, generally of the type of a "status good" or "relational good" such as: (i) renown and prestige [the gifts of the kula ring are a famous example: see Mauss (1924)]; (ii) social rank [as in the potlatch of the Kwakiutl: Mauss (1924)]; (iii) variants of the former more directly adapted to modern individualistic psychologies such as Andreoni's "warm-glow of gift-giving" [Andreoni (1989, 1990)]; (iv) or, at the complementary opposite, the pro-gift feelings fed by modern universalistic ethics, which includes the secular ethics of the multiple variants of socialism, humanitarianism and so on [see Kolm (1984), and his contributions to the present Handbook, for fairly exhaustive pictures of the motives of giving, and notably of the modern universalistic ethics which underlie some of them].

The analysis of gift motives is a central topic of this Handbook, and it is present implicitly or explicitly in virtually all chapters, although detailed more specifically in those of Bowles et al., Elster, Fehr, Hann, Lévy-Garboua et al., Kolm, Schokkaert, Sacco et al. and Thorne. It will suffice, for the limited purposes of the present section, to refer to four early mentions of violation of the neutrality property as an elementary consequence of the assumption that gift-giving matters per se, namely, Cornes and Sandler (1984a), Posnett and Sandler (1986), and Andreoni (1989, 1990).[82] These contributions consider variants of strong BBV distributive social systems, with modified utility functions of donors of the type $v_i(x_i, g_i, G)$, where individual donation g_i appears simultaneously as an individual consumption and as an additive contribution to the public

---

[81] See the last section of Chapter 14 by Arrondel and Masson of this Handbook for a detailed discussion of the policy implications of Becker and Murphy (1988).

[82] The non-neutrality results of Steinberg (1987) are related in some respects with those of Cornes and Sandler and Andreoni, but more complex in structure, as they combine the assumption that gift-giving matters per se with a (non-neutral) linear distortionary tax scheme very close to the tax scheme considered by Boadway, Pestieau and Wildasin (1989a). His results convey, in other words, two independent sources of non-neutrality: warm-glow, and the tax regime (the latter including the implicit assumption that donors do not see through the budget constraint of the government).

good. The utility functions of donors are assumed strictly increasing and strictly quasi-concave. Cornes and Sandler and Posnett and Sandler show that, when private donation and the public good are Hicksian complements, an agent's donation may increase in response to increased donations of others, even when all goods are strictly normal. And Andreoni exhibits non-neutralities which contradict the neutrality properties of Theorem 10(i) above, relative to public lump-sum redistributions (1989, pp. 1454–1457, 1990, Propositions 1 and 2, pp. 467–468), and of Theorem 11 above, relative to his 1988 distortionary tax scheme (1990, Proposition 3, p. 469).

7.1.3. Cournot–Nash behavioral assumption

The Cournot–Nash behavioral assumption (that is, the assumption that the non-cooperative interactions of individuals or groups are of the non-strategic type) is a tautology when status quo is a strong distributive equilibrium, as in the type of configurations considered in Section 6.1 above (liberal social contracts of self-centered (or BBV), non-jealous distributive social systems). The same applies to the Beckerian equilibria of general Pareto social systems with a single altruistic head and $n-1$ egoistic "kids", provided that there is no paradox of transfers, that is, no (practical) possibility of strategic manipulation of market prices by the individual or collective gifts of egoistic kids [see Section 4.3 above, Mercier Ythier (2004b, 4.3.2), and Kanbur's Chapter 26 of this Handbook]. These prima facie justifications of the Cournot–Nash behavioral assumption have been further elaborated in several interesting ways by Sugden (1985), Bergstrom (1989b) and Cornes and Silva (1999).

Sugden considers strong BBV distributive social systems with identical donors, whose utility functions are continuously differentiable, strictly increasing and strictly quasi-concave. He concentrates on the comparative statics of symmetric equilibrium with arbitrary conjectures of donors relative to the individual reactions of others to variations in their own contribution [see also the companion papers of Cornes and Sandler (1984b, 1985b) on the same issue]. Considering an exogenous variation in the contribution of a donor at an interior equilibrium, and supposing that the suitable regularity condition for the application of the implicit function theorem holds, one gets the following value for the derivative of the equilibrium provision of the public good with respect to this exogenous variation of individual contribution: $-\mathrm{MRS}(x, G)/(m-1+\mathrm{MRS}(x, G))$, where $\mathrm{MRS}(x, G) = \partial_x v(x, G)/\partial_G v(x, G)$. If private consumption and the public good are both normal goods, then $\mathrm{MRS}(x, G) > 0$, implying that the derivative lies in the open interval $]-1, 0[$, and therefore that individuals with consistent (i.e. self-fulfilling) conjectures should expect other people to reduce their contributions when they increase their own. Studying the behavior of the derivative as m grows to infinity, the author establishes moreover that consistent expectations of matching contributing behavior (corresponding to a derivative < -1) hold for any m only if private consumption is an inferior good, a highly implausible condition. Sugden's conclusions extend in a simple way to status quo equilibrium, where non-negativity conditions on individual contributions are binding by assumption, yielding a formal justification of

Nash conjectures as the sole plausible type of consistent expectations for this particular type of equilibrium and social system.

In the frameworks of Bergstrom (1989b) and Cornes and Silva (1999), the family head ("social planner") has a non-paternalistic benevolent utility function defined on siblings' ophelimity distribution (one of the siblings interpretable as the egoistic self of the altruistic parent). The arguments of sibling i's (indirect) ophelimity function are the vector $a = (a_1, \ldots, a_n)$ of siblings' actions and the money transfer τ_i received from the head. Equilibrium is defined as subgame perfect Nash equilibrium of the two-stage game where: in the first stage, each sibling i anticipating the head's transfer function $\tau_i(a)$ determined at the second stage, chooses his own action so as to maximize his ophelimity, given the actions of others; in the second stage, the head, observing the vector a of siblings' actions, chooses his transfers so as to maximize his utility subject to the family budget constraint $\sum_i \tau_i(a) = R(a)$, where $R(a)$ denotes the family income associated with a. Bergstrom's definitions allow for (direct) ophelimity functions depending on any number of private goods (including the numéraire) and public goods. Cornes and Silva consider the special case where: sibling i's indirect ophelimity function is the outcome of the maximization of a strong BBV utility function $v_i(x_i, g_i + G_{-i})$ with respect to his individual contribution g_i, in his budget set $\{(x_i, g_i): x_i + g_i = \omega_i + \tau_i, \ x_i \geqslant 0, \ g_i \geqslant 0\}$, given the aggregate contribution of others G_{-i}, and the transfer τ_i he receives from the head; and the family income does not depend on the vector of contributions of siblings to the public good. The Rotten Kid Theorem holds, that is, the subgame perfect equilibrium is the Pareto optimum (relative to ophelimities) which maximizes the head's utility in the set of feasible ophelimity distributions, whenever there is *conditional transferable ophelimity*, that is, whenever the (indirect) consumption preferences of sibling i admit a functional representation of the type $\alpha_i(a) + \beta(a)\tau_i$ for all i [Bergstrom (1989b, Proposition 1)]. The Rotten Kid Theorem holds in the setup of Cornes and Silva also, provided that individual contributions of siblings to the public good are all positive (and that the utility and ophelimity functions are differentiable, quasi-concave and strictly increasing). The assumptions of Cornes and Silva do not imply conditional transferable ophelimity, but Bergstrom establishes, nevertheless, that the latter is essentially implied by the Rotten Kid Theorem when no specific assumptions are made on preferences and technology [Bergstrom (1989b, Proposition 3)]. Conditional transferable ophelimity is verified in a trivial way by our Beckerian distributive social systems with a single altruistic head and $n - 1$ egoistic kids. Bergstrom's Proposition 1 provides therefore a formal justification to the *simultaneous* interactions implied by Cournot–Nash behavior for such contexts, as it states that the agents cannot gain any individual strategic advantage by "playing first" (behaving as Stackelberg leaders) in the altruistic gift game.

There is no such univoqual case for the Cournot–Nash behavioral assumption when: (i) advantageous strategic manipulations of market prices through gift-giving become a practical possibility, as should be the case in general when collective gift-giving is considered; (ii) or Cournot–Nash equilibrium is Pareto-inefficient.

The first type of configuration has been studied in the literature essentially through the transfer paradox (see Section 4.3, Kanbur's Chapter 26, and Section 15.4.3 of the introduction Chapter 1 of the Handbook).

The second type involves a large variety of sources of coordination problems (the so-called "exchange motives" for transfers), including notably: (i) market imperfections, some of them already briefly mentioned in Section 7.1.1 above, such as fundamental market incompleteness, informational and enforcement difficulties for the design and implementation of private contracts (that is, of contracts relative to the private allocation of private commodities), and technological non-convexities; (ii) the analogous impediments to the design and implementation of local or general social contracts, that is, of contracts relative to the treatment of public goods and non-pecuniary externalities by concerned individual agents; (iii) or complex transfer motives such as merit wants (paternalistic preferences), warm-glow, joy of giving and so on.

The analysis of this second type of configurations fed three substantial strands of theoretical literature on voluntary transfers in the last twenty years or so, relative to strategic bequests, the Samaritan's dilemma, and, more recently, the theory of charitable fundraising. This is briefly illustrated in the selective account below (see also Section 2.1 above).

Bernheim, Shleifer and Summers (1985) gave the original impulse to the game-theoretic studies on strategic bequests [see Masson and Pestieau (1997), and Chapter 13 of Laferrère and Wolff of this Handbook for well-documented surveys on this subject]. The social unit ("family") they consider is made of one altruistic head and two or more egoistic children. There are two commodities: consumption, and child care. Head utility is increasing in own consumption, child care and child utility. Child utility is increasing in own consumption and decreasing in attention to head. This specification, simple as it is, implicitly involves some notion of market imperfection: there is no market equivalent for child care from the viewpoint of the head [the same holds in the more general setup of Bergstrom (1989b) above]. The authors show that there is room, then, in general, for Pareto improvements from Cournot–Nash equilibrium, all involving increases in child care and transfers to children. Moreover, the head can capture all corresponding gains from exchange by behaving strategically, namely, by precommitting to a bequest rule. The social conditions of exchange therefore support, in this case, a strategic behavior of the head, as an accessible and individually rational way to reach Pareto-efficiency. The authors show, also, that neutrality does not hold, generally, in such a context.

The "Samaritan's dilemma" [Buchanan (1975)] refers to a type of game configuration which is symmetric, in some respects, to strategic bequeathing, namely, the strategic exploitation, by the beneficiary of a gift, of the benevolence of the donor. Three representative references are the contributions of Lindbeck and Weibull (1988), Bruce and Waldman (1991), and Coate (1995) [see also the examples of the "lazy rotten kid" and the "prodigal son" in Bergstrom (1989b)]. These models have a time structure, which is given a priori, with two periods and a capital market that functions in the first period. There are two types of agents, who coexist in both periods: an altruistic parent and (possibly altruistic) child in Lindbeck and Weibull (1988); altruistic rich and egoistic poor in

Bruce and Waldman (1991) and in Coate (1995). The setup is deterministic in the first two papers and stochastic in the third, uncertainty bearing on the wealth endowment of the poor in the latter. The game is sequential: agents take their investment (i.e. savings or insurance) decisions in the first period, anticipating the second-period optimal transfer schemes of donors. It is shown that interior subgame perfect Nash equilibrium is Pareto-inefficient in general, with first period investments of donees typically too small, and second period equilibrium gifts typically too large, relative to Pareto-efficient levels. The Rotten Kid Theorem fails, therefore. But the neutrality property does not [see notably Bernheim and Bagwell (1988) on the latter]. Summarizing, the Samaritan's dilemma literature differs from the mainstream theory outlined in Sections 3 to 6 only at the margin, by introducing intertemporal strategic interactions as an additional source of inefficiency in public good provision.

Finally, recent theoretical explanations of the role of charities as intermediaries in fundraising activities for the private provision of public goods build on various sources of coordination problems, notably: warm glow [Slivinski and Steinberg (1998)], information costs and competition of donors for social status [Glazer and Konrad (1996)], fix costs in the production of the public good [Andreoni (1998)], and so on. Coordination problems translate into unexploited opportunities of Pareto-improving actions. The models construe the intermediation of charities as the implementation of such opportunities, notably through the design of appropriate fundraising strategies (see Chapter 18 by Andreoni and Chapter 19 by Bilodeau and Steinberg in this Handbook for detailed reviews on this subject). This burgeoning strand of literature shares important features with strategic bequest literature. Both build on the same variant or extension of the Coase conjecture, stating that accessible Pareto improvements should be implemented sooner or later by means of appropriate institutional design, following the initiatives ("strategic" design and move) of individuals, local intermediaries or central authorities interested in capturing for themselves some fraction of the surplus, monetary, symbolic or else, so created. Strategic behavior is generated, in particular, in such contexts, as an endogenous step in the dynamic process of exhaustion of social exchange opportunities. A "corollary" of the conjecture is, consequently, that *Cournot–Nash* (i.e. non-strategic) *behavior should prevail at long-run social equilibrium*, since there remains then, by definition, no room for advantageous strategic deviations, and, notably, no advantage from "playing first".

To finish with this presentation of alternative specifications of individual altruistic behavior, let us briefly mention the so-called "Kantian behavior". This consists of a rational (that is, utility-maximizing) individual behavior which embodies an ethical rule in its specification, namely, the Kantian imperative to "choose that action which would, if also taken by similarly motivated others, result in a good outcome" [Collard (1992); see also the seminal contributions of Laffont (1975) and Collard (1978), and the recent contribution of Bilodeau and Gravel (2004) for generalizations and up-to-date list of references]. Sugden (1984), notably, provides precise definitions and analyzes equilibrium properties in a general model of private provision of a pure public good which encompasses, and allows for direct comparisons with, strong BBV distributive social systems.

We restrict our presentation of his definitions and results to the latter, for notational simplicity. Let g_i^* denote the (supposed unique) maximum of $g \to v_i(\omega_i - g, mg)$, that is, the individual contribution that maximizes i's utility when all donors contribute the same amount. Sugden defines the Kantian rule, which he names an *obligation of reciprocity*, as the (moral) obligation, for any individual i, either to contribute at least g_i^*, or to contribute at least as much as the smallest contribution of others. An equilibrium is then a vector of contributions such that the contribution of each agent i is the smallest contribution compatible with his reciprocity obligation, given the contributions of others. It is shown, under standard assumptions, that: (i) an equilibrium exists (op. cit.: Result 1, p. 778); (ii) equilibrium is generally not unique (op. cit.: IV, p. 778); (iii) an exogenous increase in an individual contribution at equilibrium can induce an increase in the contributions of other individuals, by creating an additional obligation for them (op. cit.: Result 4, p. 780); (iv) the public good is undersupplied at equilibrium, relative to the efficiency criterion of Pareto, if and only if individual equilibrium contributions are not all identical (op. cit.: Result 5, p. 781). Note that point (iii) contradicts the perfect substitutability of transfers. One can establish easily, finally, that the Kantian rule imposes binding constraints on Cournot–Nash free-riding at Sugden's equilibrium.[83] Combined with point (iv) above, the latter statement implies that Kantian behavior improves coordination of individual actions, but not enough to achieve Pareto-efficiency [except in the case of identical individuals studied by Laffont (1975), with the additional provision, then, that only one of the (possibly) multiple equilibria of Sugden is Pareto-efficient: see Sugden (1984, IV)].

7.2. Empirical tests of the perfect substitutability of transfers

An empirical evaluation has been performed on two types of testable implications of the perfect substitutability of transfers, understood as the complex set of hypotheses above (see the beginning of Section 7): the Pareto-inefficient underprovision of the public good at Cournot–Nash equilibrium; and the -1 elasticity of substitution of transfers.

7.2.1. Experimental tests of Cournot–Nash individual behavior

Cournot–Nash free-riding of individuals in public good provision has been the object of a large number of experimental tests [e.g., among many, Andreoni (1988b, 1995), Isaac and Walker (1988), Isaac, Walker and Williams (1994), or Laury, Walker and Williams (1999); see Ledyard (1995), and Fehr's Chapter 8 in this Handbook for a

---

[83] Suppose that individual i makes a positive contribution g_i^* to the public good at Sugden's equilibrium and denote by G^* the equilibrium provision level. Suppose moreover that g_i^* is not a single largest contribution, i.e. that there exists some $g_j^* \geqslant g_i^*$ with $j \neq i$. Sugden's Result 2, standard first-order conditions and the strict concavity of i's utility function imply then together that $\partial_{x_i} v_i(\omega_i - g_i^*, G^*) > \partial_G v_i(\omega_i - g_i^*, G^*)$, which means that i will increase his utility by diminishing his contribution if everyone else's contribution remains unchanged.

comprehensive review], with repeated conclusions that robustly contradict the various aspects of Olson's conjecture.

Experiments are usually built on the following broad common pattern. Participants play a symmetric game of voluntary provision of a pure public good with transferable utility. Cournot–Nash equilibrium and symmetric Pareto optimum are calculable, with an equilibrium provision level of the public good smaller than the Pareto-efficient provision level [the public good equilibrium provision is generally $= 0$; see, nevertheless, Laury, Walker and Williams (1999), for an exception]. Group size is usually small (4 or 5 players), but can rise up to 100 players in some experiments [e.g. Isaac, Walker and Williams (1994)]. The game played by a given group can be single-shot or repeated, with a number of rounds then usually ranging from 10 to 20. Experiments are arranged so that players cannot communicate directly with their group fellows. They receive accurate impersonal information on the past aggregate contributions of others at each round in the case of repeated games.

It is found notably that: (i) actual public good provision is significantly larger than calculated Cournot–Nash provision, and significantly smaller than Pareto-efficient provision, both in single-shot and in repeated games; (ii) there is some tendency for a decrease in public good provision from one round to the next in repeated games, provision remaining nevertheless significantly larger than Cournot–Nash level at all rounds; (iii) actual public good provision does not decrease, and is sometimes even found to increase when group size increases [e.g. Isaac, Walker and Williams (1994)]. Overall experimental evidence tends to support the idea that these results proceed from the widespread conscious propensity of individuals to behave cooperatively in such contexts, rather than from individual misperceptions of game structure or, at the other extreme, from individual strategic sophistication [e.g. Andreoni (1988b, 1995)].

Experimental findings characterize, therefore, a phenomenon of "pure" individual propensity to cooperate in public good provision contexts, where the adjective "pure" refers to the absence, in the experiments, of any interindividual communication between participants, and of any of the various forms of social mediation by which individuals communicate and/or constrain each other in the reality of social life (except, of course, impersonal information on the past contributions of others in repeated-game experiments). A natural interpretation of the results is, then, that cooperative behavior in experiments reproduces some kind of social training:[84] participants have learnt contextual cooperative behavior in their lifelong practice of real social life, which they reproduce without much variation in the artificial (and very short run) context of laboratory experiments (there is some variation though, as pointed out in finding (ii) above).

This raises in turn interesting questions of method, relative to the relevance of such experimental results as empirical tests of the theory. The whole construct developed in

---

[84] A detailed discussion of the social learning of prosocial behavior can be found, for instance, in Rushton (1982). See also Chapters 10, 3, 8, 7, 9 and 2 respectively by Bardsley and Sugden, Elster, Fehr and Schmidt, Levy-Garboua et al., Sacco et al., and Schokkaert in this Handbook.

Sections 2 to 6 above consists, essentially, of a logical reconstruction of social communication and social exchange relative to the redistribution of wealth (a socially highly mediated object indeed, as one of the major objects of the debate between liberalism and socialism, which characterizes, in many respects, modern politics in developed countries), that is, a theoretical explanation of a type of phenomenon which is abstracted, by construction, from the experiments above. The heart of the theory consists of hypothetical statements such as: "The liberal social contracts are the Pareto-efficient distributions unanimously preferred to the initial distribution whenever individuals are self-centered and non-jealous" (Section 6.1.2.1); or the somewhat looser variant of the Coase conjecture stating that "Cournot–Nash behavior should prevail at long-run social equilibrium" (Section 7.1.3). Such statements are not refuted, clearly, by the experiments above, and it is debatable whether they are empirically refutable at all. The next subsection addresses the latter question and proposes, with due provisions and qualifications, a partially positive answer to it.

7.2.2. Measures of the elasticity of substitution of transfers

The most straightforward candidate for an empirical test of the theory is the measure of the elasticity of substitution of transfers.

Theory states that lump-sum wealth transfers between agents connected by private transfers leave, generically, the distribution of wealth locally unchanged (neutrality, see Section 5.1, Theorem 7), implying one-for-one substitution of lump-sum transfers for private equilibrium transfers, that is, an elasticity of substitution of transfers $= -1$.

A related property is the crowding-out of private transfers at distributive optimum first noticed by Warr (1982). An elaborate version states that distributive equilibrium is a status quo equilibrium, generically unique, whenever agents are self-cenetred and non-jealous or are endowed with strong BBV utility functions (see notably Section 6.1.2.1, Theorem 14). The observable consequence is the absence of private transfers at (efficient) social equilibrium.

These properties of the theory are not directly testable, in a strict sense, for two reasons. The first problem is the logical possibility of equilibrium multiplicity, which is coincidental, in the abstract sense of mathematical transversality theory, in the case of status quo equilibrium, but is not coincidental in the general framework of the neutrality property of Theorem 7. The second problem stems from the fact that the assumptions underlying the observable implications are either conspicuously counterfactual idealizations[85] of social reality (perfectly competitive markets and lump-sum taxation, for the neutrality property of Theorem 7) or very difficult to observe (distributive efficiency

---

[85] By idealization I mean, here, a set of features selected in a process of constrained deliberation balancing their adequacy to phenomena with the inner consistency of the system of their relations on the one hand, and with their workable value from the standpoint of the discursive intellectual operations of reasoning and calculation on the other hand.

and the assumptions on individual preferences, for the crowding-out property of Theorem 14).

The "test" will consist, therefore, in a qualitative appreciation of the distance between empirical findings and the "predictions" which follow "naturally" from a good understanding and honest reading of the theory. It will be said, notably, that the theory is refuted if the substitution elasticity of transfers has the wrong sign or is closer to 0 than to -1, or if the share of private transfers in total redistribution is closer to 1 than to 0.

A small number of empirical estimates of substitution elasticities of transfers are available for private donations to charities and family inter vivos transfers for the post-war period.

The estimates calculated from US cross-sectional data on private charitable donations range from -0.15 [Kingma (1989)] to -0.30 [Abrams and Schmitz (1978)]. Posnett and Sandler (1989), working on private charitable donations in the UK, obtain an estimate which is not significantly different from 0 (see Table 1 in Schokkaert's Chapter 2 of this Handbook).

Altonji, Hayashi and Kotlikoff (1997) obtain an elasticity of -0.13 for US panel data on family inter vivos donations. Wolff (1998), following the same methodology on French data, finds a small positive elasticity of $+0.003$.

The studies reported above are narrowly focused in terms of the time-period (the last twenty years or so) and geographic area (Western developed countries) they consider. The picture is significantly altered when the scope of the study is widened so as to situate empirical results in the process of long-run economic development. Evidence relative to the history of economic and social development in the twentieth century elicits a substantial crowding-out of private redistribution by public transfers in relative terms, that is, in proportion of aggregate wealth and redistribution, in relation to the rise of the welfare state.

Roberts (1984) observes an irreversible and almost complete crowding-out of private financial assistance to the poor by public transfers in the United States of the 1930s. Private charitable donations did not disappear of course (and could even have maintained their share in disposable income), but "underwent a fundamental transformation ... away from the relief of poverty toward other activities" such as health services and social counseling.

Lampman and Smeeding (1983) observe that the share of disposable income devoted to private interfamily transfers diminishes slightly in the US from 1935 to 1979, a fact to be contrasted with the considerable rise of the share of public transfer programs in national income during the same period.

And the results of a series of studies conducted by Cox and several co-authors on microeconomic data of Eastern European and other developing countries fit perfect substitutability (the "altruistic model", in the terminology of this literature) much better than the comparable studies on microeconomic data of Western developed countries reported above (see Section 4 of Chapter 14 of Arrondel and Masson and Section 6 of Chapter 13 of Laferrère and Wolff of this Handbook for well-documented reviews of the tests of the altruistic model of family transfers).

While still very imperfect and partial, this set of empirical findings suggests the following scenario for the historical evolution of wealth equalizing transfers during the last century: (i) public wealth equalizing transfers growing much faster than aggregate income over the period, implying a considerable growth of the former both in absolute magnitude and in terms of their share in aggregate income and redistribution; (ii) a stability of, or moderate decline in, the share of private transfers in disposable income, combined with a transformation of their composition, and notably a sharp decline in purely redistributive private wealth transfers such as financial donations to the poor; (iii) and, as a consequence of points (i) and (ii), the present low degree of substitutability (USA) or even the complementarity (Western Europe) of public redistributive transfers and residual private redistributive transfers, with differences between the USA and Western European countries related to such institutional parameters as the share of wealth equalizing transfers in aggregate income (larger in Western Europe) and the tax incentives for private donations (more vigorous in the USA).

The theoretical framework developed in Sections 2 to 6 adjusts to such (presumed) facts through the following three main channels.

The first and principal channel is the introduction of the general class of self-centered and non-jealous distributive preferences, as an ideal representation of the spreading of distributive concerns and of the extension of their object, which seem to go along with economic and social development. This general representation includes notably, but does not reduce to, the traditional concerns relative to the welfare of the poor.

The second channel is the distributive liberal social contract, which predicts the full crowding-out of private redistributive transfers as result of the combination of the public good problem of redistribution and the neutrality property. This prediction of the theory is not refuted, in the main, by the facts above, but it must be adjusted to match the observable remanence of (presumably) residual private redistributive transfers.

Adjustment is performed through the notion of imperfect substitutability of transfers. It is assumed that the bulk of remaining private transfers are complementary of public redistributive transfers. The list of the potential origins of complementarity follows from the analysis of the content of the abstract assumption of perfect substitutability. The latter suggests two main sources of complementarity at long-run social equilibrium. One is the set of the various "imperfections" in the functioning of markets (notably capital markets) and in the administration of the distribution branch of public finance. The other one is the existence of non-redistributive individual motives for transfers, including notably: for charitable donations, the reflection in the preferences of donors of the social valuation (popularity, prestige, ethical appraisal, ...) of voluntary individual participation in public good achievements; and for family gift-giving, the valuation by individuals of the transmission of their individual characteristics, and notably of their human wealth, to their descendants.

8. Conclusion

Summarizing very briefly, the theory reviewed in this chapter contributes to the explanation of the socialization of a fraction of aggregate wealth through the constitution of a redistributive welfare state in the course of long-run economic development. Its prediction of a full crowding-out of private redistributive transfers, notably, can be interpreted as a property of the long-run social equilibrium in the absence of imperfections in market and transfer activities, that is, of a social state where: all opportunities of social exchange relative to wealth distribution as a public good have been exhausted by appropriate public or private initiatives (long-run social equilibrium); and where markets are complete and competitive, and information, transaction and enforcement costs relative to market and social exchanges are negligible.

These conclusions apply to the distribution of market money wealth. Their extension to human wealth confronts many serious difficulties in the theoretical framework above. The most fundamental of them seem to be related to the succession of generations, notably the conspicuous existence of important "non-redistributive" motives of transfers in the intergenerational transmission of human wealth (reflected for example in merit wants), and also the clear case for the incompleteness and other imperfections of capital markets at the corresponding time scale (notably fundamental incompleteness). An increasingly large fraction of modern welfare states correspond to public support to the provision of education, health and social insurance services. New advances in the theoretical analysis of the process of partial socialization of income and wealth which seems to characterize modern economic development certainly require a better understanding of these specificities of human wealth, their causes, and their consequences on development and society.

Appendix A

A.1. Proofs

THEOREM 4. *Let (w, u, ω) verify Assumption 2. Then, (p^*, a^*) is a social equilibrium of (w, u, ω) if and only if it verifies the following set of conditions:* (i) $p^* \gg 0$; (ii) $\sum_{i \in N} x_i(a^*) = (1, \ldots, 1)$; (iii) *for all i:* (a) $x_i(a^*) \gg 0$; (b) $p^* x_i(a^*) = p^*(\omega_i + \Delta_i t(a^*))$; (c) *and there exist $\lambda_i > 0$ such that $\partial_{x_i} u_i(x_i(a^*)) = \lambda_i p^*$*; (iv) *for all (i, j):* (a) $-\partial_{u_i} w_i(u(x(a^*)))\lambda_i + \partial_{u_j} w_i(u(x(a^*)))\lambda_j \leq 0$; (b) *and* $(-\partial_{u_i} w_i(u(x(a^*)))\lambda_i + \partial_{u_j} w_i(u(x(a^*)))\lambda_j) t_{ij}(a^*) = 0$.

PROOF. The set of conditions (iii) and (iv) are the first-order conditions for the solutions to $\max\{w_i(u(x((a^*_{\setminus i}, a_i)))): a_i \in B_i(p^*, a^*)\}$ such that $x_i(a^*) \gg 0$, $i = 1, \ldots, n$. In view of the differentiability and quasi-concavity of functions $w_i \circ u$ implied by Assumption 2, the first-order conditions are necessary and sufficient for such solutions by Arrow and Enthoven (1961: Theorem 1(b) (sufficiency) and Theorem 2 (necessity)). It will be sufficient, therefore, to establish that if (p^*, a^*) is an equilibrium then $(p^*, x(a^*)) \gg 0$. Assumptions 2(i)(b) and 2(ii)(b) imply together that $w_i \circ u$ is monotonic strictly increasing in x_i for all i, which implies readily in turn that all prices must be > 0 at equilibrium. Hence $p^*\omega_i > 0$ for all i by Assumption 2(iv), that is, all individuals have a positive pre-transfer wealth at equilibrium. Assumptions 2(i)(c), 2(ii)(b) and 2(iii)(b) imply then together that the equilibrium allocation $x(a^*)$ is $\gg 0$. □

THEOREM 5. *Let (w, u, ω) verify Assumption 2 and suppose moreover that v_i is differentiable in $\mathbb{R}_{++}^l \times \mathbb{R}_{++}$ for all i. Then, (p^*, a^*) is a social equilibrium of (w, u, ω) if and only if $(p^*, x(a^*), p^*t(a^*))$ is a social equilibrium with money gifts of (w, u, ω).*

PROOF. Notice first that p^* must be $\gg 0$ in both definitions of social equilibrium by Assumptions 2(i)(b) (monotonic strictly increasing ophelimity) and 2(ii)(b) (utility strictly increasing in own ophelimity).

Let $(p^*, x(a^*), \tau^*)$ be a social equilibrium with money gifts. Assumptions 2(i)(c), 2(ii)(b), 2(iii)(b) and 2(iv) imply together that $x(a^*) \gg 0$ and that $p^*\omega_i + \Delta_i \tau^* > 0$ at τ_i^* solution of $\max\{w_i(v_1(p^*, p^*\omega_1 + \Delta_1(\tau_{\backslash i}^*, \tau_i)), \ldots, v_n(p^*, p^*\omega_n + \Delta_n(\tau_{\backslash i}^*, \tau_i)))$: $\tau_i \geqslant 0$ and $p^*\omega_i + \Delta_i(\tau_{\backslash i}^*, \tau_i) \geqslant 0\}$ for all i. The first-order conditions are therefore necessary [Arrow and Enthoven (1961: Theorem 2)] for the solutions of the programs above, and for the programs $\max\{u_i(x_i): x_i \geqslant 0$ and $p^*x_i \leqslant p^*\omega_i + \Delta_i \tau^*\}$. Letting $r^* = (p^*\omega_1 + \Delta_1 \tau^*, \ldots, p^*\omega_n + \Delta_n \tau^*)$ and $v^* = (v_1(p^*, r_1^*), \ldots, v_n(p^*, r_n^*))$, we get: for all i, $x_i(a^*) \gg 0$, $p^*x_i(a^*) = p^*(\omega_i + \Delta_i t(a^*))$, and there exists $\lambda_i > 0$ such that $\partial_{x_i} u_i(x_i(a^*)) = \lambda_i p^*$; for all (i, j), $\partial_{u_j} w_i(v^*)\partial_{r_j} v_j(p^*, r_j^*) \leqslant \partial_{u_i} w_i(v^*)\partial_{r_i} v_i(p^*, r_i^*)$ and $(-\partial_{u_i} w_i(v^*)\partial_{r_i} v_i(p^*, r_i^*) + \partial_{u_j} w_i(v^*)\partial_{r_j} v_j(p^*, r_j^*))\tau_{ij}^* = 0$. A well-known application of the envelope theorem implies moreover that $\partial_{u_i} w_i(v^*)\partial_{r_i} v_i(p^*, r_i^*) = \lambda_i$ for all i. From these conditions and Theorem 4, we deduce therefore that if (p^*, x^*, p^*t^*) is a social equilibrium with money gifts, then $(p^*, a(x^*, t^*))$ is a social equilibrium.

Conversely, let (p^*, a^*) be a social equilibrium. Then $u_i(x_i(a^*)) = v_i(p^*, p^*(\omega_i + \Delta_i t(a^*)))$ for all i as a simple consequence of the definition of equilibrium and the assumption that utility is strictly increasing in own ophelimity. Moreover, it follows readily from definitions and from the fact that $p^* > 0$, that if a_i^* solves $\max\{w_i(u(x((a_{\backslash i}^*, a_i)))): a_i \in B_i(p^*, a^*)\}$, then $p^*t_i(a^*)$ solves $\max\{w_i(v_1(p^*, p^*\omega_1 + \Delta_1(p^*t_{\backslash i}(a^*), \tau_i)), \ldots, v_n(p^*, p^*\omega_n + \Delta_n(p^*t_{\backslash i}(a^*), \tau_i)))$: $\tau_i \geqslant 0$ and $p^*\omega_i + \Delta_i(p^*t_{\backslash i}(a^*), \tau_i) \geqslant 0\}$. Therefore $(p^*, x(a^*), p^*t(a^*))$ is a social equilibrium with money gifts. □

THEOREM 7. *Suppose that (w, u) verifies Assumption 2. (i) Distributive policy is globally neutral if and only if set $u(M')$ is a singleton. (ii) For all $x \in M'$, $\Omega'(x)$ is a convex set of dimension $l(n - c(\gamma(x)))$, where $c(\gamma(x))$ denotes the number of connected components*[86] *of graph $\gamma(x)$. (iii) In particular: distributive policy is locally weakly neutral*

---

[86] See Footnotes 45 and 46 in Section 5.1 for the definitions of connected digraphs and connected components.

at an element ω^0 of the interior of $\Omega'(x)$ in $\{\omega\colon \omega_i > 0$ for all $i\}$ if and only if $\gamma(x)$ is connected.

The proof is adapted from Mercier Ythier (2000a, pp. 65–67). It proceeds in two steps. I establish first the following lemma (the theorem is proved next):

LEMMA. *For all $p \in \mathbb{R}^l_{++}$ and all gift vector t, there is a gift vector t' such that $g(t')$ is a forest*[87] *and $p\Delta_i t' = p\Delta_i t$ for all i.*

PROOF. Consider a circuit $\Gamma = ((i_k, j_k))_{1 \leqslant k \leqslant m}$ of $g(t)$.

Suppose without loss of generality that $pt_{i_1 j_1} = \min_k pt_{i_k j_k}$, and define recursively the following two orientation classes of the darts of Γ: dart (i_1, j_1) has positive orientation; dart (i_{k+1}, j_{k+1}) has positive (resp. negative) orientation if dart (i_k, j_k) either has positive orientation and is such that $j_k = i_{k+1}$ (resp. $j_k = j_{k+1}$), or has negative orientation and is such that $j_k = j_{k+1}$ (resp. $j_k = i_{k+1}$) (with the convention that $(i_{m+1}, j_{m+1}) = (i_1, j_1)$). The adjacent darts (i_k, j_k) and (i_{k+1}, j_{k+1}) thus have identical (resp. opposite) orientations in the circuit if the head j_k of the former coincides with the tail i_{k+1} (resp. head j_{k+1}) of the latter. This orientation is well-defined, for if a dart had simultaneously a positive and negative orientation, then this should be the case of all darts by the recursive definition above, and this would imply in turn that Γ has a single vertex i and a single dart (i, i), which contradicts the definition of $g(t)$.

There exists a gift vector t^1 such that: $pt^1_{i_k j_k} = pt_{i_k j_k} - pt_{i_1 j_1}$ whenever (i_k, j_k) has positive orientation in Γ; $pt^1_{i_k j_k} = pt_{i_k j_k} + pt_{i_1 j_1}$ whenever (i_k, j_k) has negative orientation in Γ; $t^1_{i_k j_k} = t_{i_k j_k}$ whenever i or j is not a vertex of Γ. And one verifies readily that $g(t^1)$ does not contain circuit Γ (dart (i_1, j_1) has been deleted: $pt^1_{i_1 j_1} = 0$ by construction, and $p \gg 0$ by assumption, so that $t^1_{i_1 j_1} = 0$). Moreover $p\Delta_i t^1 = p\Delta_i t$ for all i since: $\Delta_i t^1 = \Delta_i t$ whenever i is not a vertex of Γ; if i is a common vertex of two adjacent darts (j, i) and (i, k) of identical, positive (resp. negative) orientation in Γ, then $p(t^1_{ik} - t^1_{ji}) = pt_{ik} - pt_{i_1 j_1} - pt_{ji} + pt_{i_1 j_1} = p(t_{ik} - t_{ji})$ (resp. $p(t^1_{ik} - t^1_{ji}) = pt_{ik} + pt_{i_1 j_1} - pt_{ji} - pt_{i_1 j_1} = p(t_{ik} - t_{ji})$); if i is a common vertex of two adjacent darts (j, i) and (k, i) of opposite orientations in Γ, the orientation of (j, i) being positive (resp. negative), then $p(t^1_{ji} + t^1_{ki}) = pt_{ji} - pt_{i_1 j_1} + pt_{ki} + pt_{i_1 j_1} = p(t_{ji} + t_{ki})$ (resp. $p(t^1_{ji} + t^1_{ki}) = pt_{ji} + pt_{i_1 j_1} + pt_{ki} - pt_{i_1 j_1} = p(t_{ji} + t_{ki})$). The conclusion follows then from a recursive application of the algorithm above to all circuits of $g(t)$ (in finite number since $g(t)$ is finite). □

PROOF OF THEOREM 7. Part (i) of Theorem 7 is a simple corollary of Theorem 4.

Let $x \in M'$. Part (iii) is a straightforward consequence of part (ii).

Let us establish (ii).

---

[87] A digraph is a forest if it contains no circuit (Section 3.4.2.1).

The convexity of $\Omega'(x)$ is straightforward.

Let $p \gg 0$ be the unique price vector of S_l supporting x. Denote by Ψ the set of spanning forest subdigraphs[88] of $\gamma(x)$, and, for all $\Gamma \in \Psi$, let $\Omega_\Gamma(x)$ be the convex set $\{\omega\colon \omega_i > 0$ for all i; and $\exists t$ such that: $t_{ij} > 0$ if and only if $(i, j) \in \Gamma$; and $px_i = p(\omega_i + \Delta_i t)$ for all $i\}$. We have then $\Omega'(x) = \bigcup_{\Gamma \in \Psi} \Omega_\Gamma(x)$ since, by the lemma above, the wealth transfers associated with any gift vector can be achieved by a gift vector whose associate graph is a forest subgraph of the former. From the definition of a spanning subgraph, we know that $c(\Gamma) \geqslant c(\gamma(x))$ for all $\Gamma \in \Psi$. And from Tutte (1984, Theorem I.36) there exists a $\Gamma \in \Psi$ such that $c(\Gamma) = c(\gamma(x))$. It suffices to prove, therefore, that convex set $\Omega_\Gamma(x)$ has dimension $l(n - c(\Gamma))$ whenever Γ is a spanning forest subdigraph of $\gamma(x)$ such that $c(\Gamma) = c(\gamma(x))$.

Consider thus, from now on, a $\Gamma \in \Psi$ such that $c(\Gamma) = c(\gamma(x))$. By definition of a spanning graph, the set of vertices of Γ is N. By definition of a forest, we must have $i \neq j$ whenever $(i, j) \in \Gamma$ (loop-darts (i, i) are 1-circuits). Let the incidence matrix[89] of Γ be denoted by M_Γ. A well-known result of graph theory is then that matrix M_Γ has full rank $n - c(\Gamma)$, equal to the number of darts of Γ, if and only if Γ is a forest graph [e.g. Berge (1970, Theorem 1)].

For any t such that $t_{ij} > 0$ if and only if $(i, j) \in \Gamma$, denote by t_Γ the vector obtained from t by deleting its coordinates t_{ij} such that $(i, j) \notin \Gamma$. Let pt_Γ denote the vector of bilateral wealth transfers associated with t_Γ. The product $pt_\Gamma \cdot M_\Gamma^T$ of the row vector pt_Γ and the transpose M_Γ^T of the incidence matrix of Γ is then the vector of net transfers $p\Delta t = (p\Delta_1 t, \ldots, p\Delta_n t)$. Denoting $px = (px_1, \ldots, px_n)$, we have therefore $\Omega_\Gamma(x) = \{\omega\colon \omega_i > 0$ for all i; and $\exists t$ such that: $t_{ij} > 0$ if and only if $(i, j) \in \Gamma$; and $px = p\omega + pt_\Gamma \cdot M_\Gamma^T\}$.

Since Γ has exactly $n - c(\gamma(x))$ darts the dimension of convex set $\{t\colon t_{ij} > 0$ if and only if $(i, j) \in \Gamma\}$ is $l(n - c(\gamma(x)))$. From this and the fact that $p \neq 0$ and rank $M_\Gamma^T = n - c(\gamma(x))$, it follows readily that the dimension of $\Omega_\Gamma(x)$ is $l(n - c(\gamma(x)))$. □

COROLLARY 5. *Suppose that* (w, u, ω) *verifies Assumption 2, and let* (p, a) *be an equilibrium.* (i) $(p, x(a))$ *is an equilibrium price-allocation vector of* $(w, (\omega_1 + \Delta_1 \theta, \ldots, \omega_n + \Delta_n \theta))$ *if and only if there exists t such that:* $g(t) \subset \gamma(x(a))$; *and* $p(t_{ij} - t_{ij}(a) - (t_{ji} - t_{ji}(a))) + p(\theta_{ij} - \theta_{ji}) = 0$ *for all* (i, j). (ii) *In particular*, $(p, x(a))$ *is not an equilibrium price-allocation vector of* $(w, (\omega_1 + \Delta_1 \theta, \ldots, \omega_n + \Delta_n \theta))$ *whenever θ implies net transfers of wealth between connected components of* $\gamma(x(a))$, *that is, whenever there is a connected component γ of $\gamma(x(a))$ such that* $\sum_{(i,j) \in V_\gamma \times (N \setminus V_\gamma)} p(\theta_{ij} - \theta_{ji}) < 0$, *where V_γ denotes the set of vertices of γ.*

PROOF. The first part is a simple consequence of Theorem 4. The second part follows from the first part and the simple remark that if θ transfers wealth away from a connected

---

[88] A subdigraph γ' of digraph γ *spans* the latter if it has the same set of vertices.
[89] See Section 3.1.2.2 for the definition.

component γ of $\gamma(x(a))$, this aggregate wealth transfer cannot be offset by any t such that $g(t) \subset \gamma(x(a))$. $\square$

COROLLARY 6. *Suppose that (w, u, ω) verifies Assumption 2, and let (p, a) be an equilibrium. Then, there exists a neighborhood V of 0 in $\{\theta: \theta_{ij} = 0$ whenever i and j are in two distinct connected components of $g(t(a))\}$ such that, for all $\theta \in V$, $(p, x(a))$ is an equilibrium price-allocation vector of $(w, (\omega_1 + \Delta_1\theta, \ldots, \omega_n + \Delta_n\theta))$.*

PROOF. From the lemma in the proof of Theorem 7, we can restrict ourselves to systems of public net transfers θ with forest digraph $g(\theta)$. From the proof of Theorem 7, the convex sets $\{p\Delta\theta: g(\theta)$ is a forest such that $\theta_{ij} = 0$ whenever i and j are in two distinct connected components of $g(t(a))\}$ and $\{px(a) - p\omega - p\Delta t: g(t)$ is a forest subdigraph of $g(t(a))\}$ have the same dimension $n - c(g(t(a)))$. The intersection of their relative interiors contains 0 since $p\omega \gg 0$ and $px(a) \gg 0$ (that is, non-negativity conditions on endowments (resp. consumption) are not binding locally for public (resp. private) transfers). Hence the conclusion. $\square$

THEOREM 13. *Let (w, ω) be such that for all i: $\omega_i > 0$; w_i is quasi-concave and $w_i(x) > w_i(x')$ implies $w_i(\lambda x + (1 - \lambda)x') > w_i(x')$ for all $\lambda \in]0, 1[$. If t^* is a distributive equilibrium of (w, ω) with a forest graph, and if there exists an agent i who makes positive gifts to all other agents at t^* (that is, $t_{ij} > 0$ for all $j \neq i$), then the associate equilibrium distribution $x(\omega, t^*)$: (i) is a weak distributive optimum of w; (ii) and maximizes i's utility in S_n (that is, $w_i(x(\omega, t^*)) = \max\{w_i(x): x \in S_n\}$).*

PROOF. (i) All we have to do to prove (i) is to establish the correspondence between Nakayama's definition of equilibrium and our Definition 1. The distributive game of Nakayama differs from a Pareto social system in one respect only: the agents are not allowed to use the gifts they receive in any way other than consuming them. They cannot, in particular, use them to finance their own gifts. If, therefore, a distributive equilibrium is such that donors are not beneficiaries of gifts (that is, if $t_{ji} = 0$ for all j whenever $t_{ij} > 0$ for some j), it must be also an equilibrium of Nakayama. And this clearly is the case, in particular, if the distributive equilibrium verifies the assumption of Theorem 13. For suppose that an agent, say i, gives to all others, and that a donor j is also the beneficiary of a gift from k: then there must be a circuit connecting agents i, j and k (two of them identical at most) in the digraph associated with t^*.

(ii) Let us prove now that $w_i(x(\omega, t^*)) = \max\{w_i(x): x \in S_n\}$. Suppose the contrary, that is, $w_i(x') > w_j(x(\omega, t^*))$ for some $x' \in S_n$. The convexity assumption on w_i implies then $w_i(\lambda x' + (1 - \lambda)x(\omega, t^*)) > w_j(x(\omega, t^*))$, and the convexity of S_n implies $\lambda x' + (1 - \lambda)x(\omega, t^*) \in S_n$, for all $\lambda \in]0, 1]$. The set of wealth distributions accessible to i is $A = \{x(\omega, (t^*_{\setminus i}, t_i)): x_i(\omega, (t^*_{\setminus i}, t_i)) \geq 0\}$. Since $t^*_{ij} > 0$ for all j, the equilibrium distribution $x(\omega, t^*)$ lies in its relative interior in S_n, so that for any $\lambda > 0$ picked close enough to 0, there exists a gift-vector t_i^λ such that $\lambda x' + (1 - \lambda)x(\omega, t^*) = x(\omega, (t^*_{\setminus i}, t_i^\lambda)) \in A$, a contradiction. $\square$

COROLLARY 7. *Let (w, ω) be such that $\omega_i > 0$ for all i, and $t^* \neq 0$ be a distributive equilibrium of (w, ω). Suppose that: (a) either there exists an agent i, with a strictly quasi-concave utility function w_i (that is, a quasi-concave w_i such that $w_i(x) \geqslant w_i(x')$ implies $w_i(\lambda x + (1-\lambda)x') > w_i(x')$ for all $\lambda \in \,]0, 1[$ and all (x, x') such that $x \neq x'$), who makes positive gifts to all others at t^*, and all others are egoistic ($w_j : x \to x_j$ for all $j \neq i$); (b) or $n = 2$ and all utility functions are strictly quasi-concave. Then t^* is a strong distributive equilibrium and $w_j(x(\omega, t^*)) = \max\{w_j(x): x \in S_n\}$ for every donor j.*

PROOF. Suppose (a). Obviously we must have $t_{\setminus i} = 0$ and $t'_j = 0$ for all $j \in I \setminus \{i\}$ for all t'_I that blocks t. Moreover, $w_i(x(\omega, t^*)) = \max\{w_i(x): x \in S_n\}$ by Theorem 13(ii), and $\mathrm{argmax}\{w_j(x): x \in S_n\}$ reduces to $x(\omega, t^*)$ by the strict quasi-concavity of w_i, so that i does not belong to any coalition blocking t^*. Therefore, t^* is unblocked by any coalition, that is, t^* is a strong distributive equilibrium of (w, ω).

Suppose (b). Applying the lemma of the proof of Theorem 7, we know that there exists a distributive equilibrium t' of (w, ω), with a forest digraph $g(t')$, such that $x(\omega, t') = x(\omega, t)$ (just subtract $\min\{t_{12}, t_{21}\}$ to t_{12} and t_{21}). Theorem 13(i) then implies that the equilibrium distribution is a weak distributive optimum of w. And the strict quasi-concavity of utility functions readily implies the equivalence of weak and strong distributive efficiency. Since $n = 2$, the distributive equilibrium t is strong if and only if the equilibrium distribution is a strong distributive optimum. Finally, the proof of Theorem 13(ii) readily implies that $w_j(x(\omega, t^*)) = \max\{w_j(x): x \in S_n\}$ for every donor j when $n = 2$ and utility functions have the relevant convexity property. □

THEOREM 14. *Suppose that w either is a strong BBV distributive social system, or verifies local non-satiation of the distributive Paretian preordering (in short, local non-satiation: cf. Footnote 31), self-centredness and non-jealousy. Then, 0 is a strong distributive equilibrium of (w, ω) if and only if ω is a strong distributive optimum of w.*

In the proof[90] I establish first the following lemma [adapted from Mercier Ythier, (1998b, Lemma (ii), p. 264); the theorem is proved next]:

LEMMA. *If 0 is blocked by coalition I playing gift-vector t_I in social system (w, ω), then there exist a non-empty coalition of donors $J \subset I$, a non-empty set of receivers $K \subset N \setminus J$, and a gift-vector $t^* \neq 0$ such that: $x(\omega, t^*) = x(\omega, (0_{\setminus I}, t_I))$; $t^*_{jk} > 0$ if and only if $(j, k) \in J \times K$; for all $j \in J$, $\omega_j > x_j(\omega, t^*) \geqslant 0$ (that is, the elements of I are net donors); for all $k \in K$, $x_k(\omega, t^*) > \omega_k$ (that is, the elements of K are net receivers).*

---

[90] Adapted from the proof of Mercier Ythier (1998b, Theorem 4, pp. 271–272). See Footnote 60 above for a comparison of Theorem 14 with my closely similar results of (1998a, 1998b).

PROOF. Suppose that 0 is blocked by coalition I in social system (w, ω), i.e. that there exists a gift-vector t such that, for all $i \in I$, $x_i(\omega, (0_{\setminus I}, t_I)) \geqslant 0$, and $w_i(x(\omega, (0_{\setminus I}, t_I))) \geqslant w_i(\omega)$ with a strict inequality for at least one i. Then, necessarily: $x(\omega, (0_{\setminus I}, t_I)) \neq \omega$; $x_i(\omega, (0_{\setminus I}, t_I)) = \omega_i + \sum_{j \in I} t_{ji} \geqslant \omega_i$ whenever $i \notin I$; and therefore there exist $i \in I$ such that $x_i(\omega, (0_{\setminus I}, t_I)) < \omega_i$ and $i \in N$ such that $x_i(\omega, (0_{\setminus I}, t_I)) > \omega_i$. Denote by: J the non-empty set of agents j such that $x_j(\omega, (0_{\setminus I}, t_I)) < \omega_j$, ($J \subset I$; it is the set of "net givers"); K the non-empty set of agents k such that $x_k(\omega, (0_{\setminus I}, t_I)) > \omega_k$ (K is the set of "net receivers"); $\theta = \sum_{j \in J}(\omega_j - x_j(\omega, (0_{\setminus I}, t_I))) = \sum_{k \in K}(x_k(\omega, (0_{\setminus I}, t_I)) - \omega_k) > 0$ the total amount of redistributed wealth; λ_j the share $\theta^{-1}(\omega_j - x_j(\omega, (0_{\setminus I}, t_I)))$ of agent $j \in J$ in θ; μ_k the share $\theta^{-1}(x_k(\omega, (0_{\setminus I}, t_I)) - \omega_k)$ of agent $k \in K$ in θ; t^* the gift-vector such that $t^*_{jk} = \lambda_j \mu_k \theta > 0$ whenever $(j, k) \in J \times K$, $t^*_{jk} = 0$ otherwise. We have then $x(\omega, t^*) = x(\omega, (0_{\setminus I}, t_I))$, $0 \leqslant x_j(\omega, t^*) = \omega_j - \sum_{k \in K} t^*_{jk} < \omega_j$ for all $j \in J$, $x_k(\omega, t^*) = \omega_k + \sum_{j \in J} t^*_{jk} > \omega_k$ for all $k \in K$, and the lemma is established. $\square$

PROOF OF THEOREM 14. (a) Suppose, first, that w verifies local non-satiation, self-centredness and non-jealousy, and let P denote its set of strong distributive optima and $C = \{\omega: 0 \text{ is a strong equilibrium of } (w, \omega)\}$. We have $C \subset P \subset S_n$ as a simple consequence of the definition of strong equilibrium (that implies that 0 is unblocked by the grand coalition N) and local non-satiation (that implies $P \subset S_n$). It suffices, therefore, to establish that $P \subset C$.

Suppose that $\omega \notin C$, and let us prove that, then, $\omega \notin P$.

By assumption, there exists a coalition I and a gift-vector t_I such that, for all $i \in I$: $x_i(\omega, (0_{\setminus I}, t_I)) \geqslant 0$; and $w_i(x(\omega, (0_{\setminus I}, t_I))) \geqslant w_i(\omega)$, with a strict inequality for at least one i. And by the lemma, there exist a non-empty coalition of net givers $J \subset I$, a non-empty set of net receivers $K \subset N \setminus J$, and a gift-vector $t^* \neq 0$ such that: $x(\omega, t^*) = x(\omega, t)$; $t^*_{jk} > 0$ if and only if $(j, k) \in J \times K$; for all $j \in J$, $\omega_j > x_j(\omega, t^*) \geqslant 0$; and for all $k \in K$, $x_k(\omega, t^*) > \omega_k$. Let $x^* = x(\omega, t) = x(\omega, t^*)$. And suppose, without loss of generality, that $J = \{1, \ldots, m\}$, with $m < n$ and that $K = \{m+1, \ldots, m+p\}$, with $m + p \leqslant n$.

Suppose first that $x^*_j \geqslant x^*_k$ for all $(j, k) \in J \times K$. The positive components of t^*, ranked in increasing lexicographic order (see Footnote 11), make a sequence of bilateral progressive transfers from ω to x^*. Formally: let $x^0 = \omega$; and, for any given $(j, k) \in J \times K$, let $x^{(j-1)p+k-m} = x^{(j-1)p+k-m-1} + t^*_{jk} e^{jk}$. Observe that for all $(j, k) \in J \times K$ and all $x \in [x^{(j-1)p+k-m-1}, x^{(j-1)p+k-m}[$: $x_j > x_k$. Self-centredness implies that w_k is increasing along $[x^{(j-1)p+k-m-1}, x^{(j-1)p+k-m}]$ for all $(j, k) \in J \times K$. Non-jealousy implies that w_i is non-decreasing along $[x^{(j-1)p+k-m-1}, x^{(j-1)p+k-m}]$ for all $(i, j, k) \in N \times J \times K$ such that $i \in N \setminus \{j, k\}$. But $x^{mp} = x^*$ by construction. Therefore $w_i(x^*) \geqslant w_i(\omega)$ for all $i \in N \setminus J$, with a strict inequality for all $k \in K$. Since, moreover, $w_i(x^*) \geqslant w_i(\omega)$ for all $i \in I$ by assumption, and $J \subset I$, we have $\omega \notin P$.

Suppose next that $x^*_j < x^*_k$ for some $(j, k) \in J \times K$ (that is, the bilateral wealth transfer from j to k is "two large" for some net donor j, given the self-centredness assumption).

We reduce this case to the former in two steps. We first proceed to bilateral progressive transfers from social state (x^*, t^*), by diminishing the wealth transfer from j to k whenever $x_j^* < x_k^*$ for some $(j, k) \in J \times K$, until either $x_j \geq x_k$ or $t_{jk} = 0$ at the resulting social state (x, t). We establish next that the latter social state obtains, from $(\omega, 0)$, by a sequence of bilateral progressive transfers which do not decrease the utilities of net donors, that is, the case considered in the former paragraph.

Let $((j_q, k_q))_{1 \leq q \leq \#Q}$ denote the sequence of elements of set $Q = \{(j, k) \in J \times K : x_j^* < x_k^*\}$ ranked in (increasing) lexicographic order. Define the following sequence of bilateral progressive redistributions from x^*: $x^0 = x^*$; for any $q \in \{0, \ldots, \#Q - 1\}$, $x^{q+1} = x^q + t_{j_q k_q} e^{j_q k_q}$, where $t_{j_q k_q} = \min\{t_{j_q k_q}^*, (1/2)(x_{k_q}^* - x_{j_q}^*)\}$. Denote $x^{**} = x^{\#Q}$, and let t^{**} be defined from t^* and the above sequence of progressive transfers $(t_{j_q k_q})_{1 \leq q \leq \#Q}$ by: $t_{j_q k_q}^{**} = t_{j_q k_q}^* - t_{j_q k_q}$ for all $(j_q, k_q) \in Q$; $t_{jk}^{**} = t_{jk}^*$ whenever $(j, k) \notin Q$. By construction: $x^{**} = x(\omega, t^{**})$; and $t_{jk}^{**} = 0$ whenever $x_j^{**} < x_k^{**}$.

We now proceed to the second step, which will conclude this part of the proof.

Self-centredness implies that w_{j_q} is increasing along $[x^q, x^{q+1}]$ for all $q \in \{0, \ldots, \#Q - 1\}$. Non-jealousy implies that w_i is non-decreasing along $[x^q, x^{q+1}]$ for all $(i, q) \in N \times \{0, \ldots, \#Q - 1\}$ such that $i \in N \setminus \{j_q, k_q\}$. Therefore, all elements of J strictly prefer x^{**} to x^*. And there is at least one $j \in J$ who is a net donor at x^{**}, for, otherwise, $x^{**} = \omega$, while $w_j(x^{**}) > w_j(x^*) \geq w_j(\omega)$ for all $j \in J$, a contradiction. In particular: the set $J' = \{j \in N : x_j^{**} < \omega_j\}$ of net donors at x^{**} is non-empty, and its elements all strictly prefer x^{**} to ω.

Let $K' = \{k \in N : x_k^{**} > \omega_k\}$ denote the set of net receivers at x^{**} (a subset of K by construction, which is non-empty since J' is non-empty), and $Q' = \{(j, k) \in N \times N : t_{jk}^{**} > 0\}$ denote the set of pairs of agents linked by a net wealth transfer at t^{**} (Q' is non-empty, and is contained in $\{(j, k) \in J' \times K' : x_j^{**} \geq x_k^{**}\}$ by construction). The positive components of t^{**}, ranked in increasing lexicographic order, make a sequence of bilateral progressive transfers from ω to x^{**}. Formally, let $((j_q, k_q))_{1 \leq q \leq \#Q'}$ denote the sequence of elements of Q' ranked in increasing lexicographic order, and define, as above, the following sequence of bilateral progressive redistributions from ω: $x^0 = \omega$; for any $q \in \{0, \ldots, \#Q' - 1\}$, $x^{q+1} = x^q + t_{j_q k_q}^{**} e^{j_q k_q}$. Observe that for all $q \in \{0, \ldots, \#Q' - 1\}$ and all $x \in [x^q, x^{q+1}]$: $x_{j_q} > x_{k_q}$. Self-centredness implies that w_{k_q} is increasing along $[x^q, x^{q+1}]$ for all $q \in \{0, \ldots, \#Q' - 1\}$. Non-jealousy implies that w_i is non-decreasing along $[x^q, x^{q+1}]$ for all $(i, q) \in N \times \{0, \ldots, \#Q' - 1\}$ such that $i \in N \setminus \{j_q, k_q\}$. But $x^{\#Q'} = x^{**}$ by construction. Therefore $w_i(x^{**}) \geq w_i(\omega)$ for all $i \in N \setminus J'$, with a strict inequality for all $k \in K'$. Since, moreover, $w_i(x^*) > w_i(\omega)$ for all $i \in J'$, we have $\omega \notin P$.

(b) Suppose, finally, that w is a strong BBV distributive social system. One verifies readily from the definitions that BBV social systems verify local non-satiation. It will suffice, therefore, to establish that $\omega \notin C$ implies $\omega \notin P$. By the lemma, combined with the structure of distributive preferences particular to strong BBV social systems (egoistic poor, and individual utility of the rich strictly increasing in own wealth and in aggregate wealth of the poor and independent of the wealth of the other rich), $\omega \notin C$

readily implies the existence of a non-empty subset J of the set of rich individuals $\{1,\ldots,m\}$, and of a gift-vector $t_J > 0$ of coalition J such that, for all $j \in J$: $\omega_j > x_j(\omega, (0_{\setminus J}, t_J)) \geqslant 0$; $w_j(x(\omega, (0_{\setminus J}, t_J))) > w_j(\omega)$; $t_{jk} = 0$ whenever $k \leqslant m$ (the rich do not receive gifts); and, therefore, $\omega_k < x_k(\omega, (0_{\setminus J}, t_J))$ only if $k > m$ (net receivers are poor), and $\omega_j > x_j(\omega, (0_{\setminus J}, t_J))$ if and only if $j \in J$ (the net donors are the members of J). Let: $t^* = (0_{\setminus J}, t_J)$; $x^* = x(\omega, t^*)$; $K = \{k \in N: t^*_{jk} > 0$ for some $j \in J\}$. The assumptions on distributive preferences readily imply then: $w_i(x^*) > w_i(\omega)$ for all $i \in \{1,\ldots,m\} \setminus J$; and $w_i(x^*) \geqslant w_i(\omega)$ for all $i > m$, with a strict inequality whenever $i \in K$. Therefore $\omega \notin P$, and the proof is completed. □

COROLLARY 8. *If w verifies the assumptions of Arrow (1981) then a non-trivial distributive equilibrium t of (w, ω) is strong if and only if it has a unique donor i, whose utility reaches its maximum in S_n (that is, $w_i(x(\omega, t)) = \max\{w_i(x): x \in S_n\}$).*

PROOF. One verifies readily from the definitions that Arrow's distributive social systems verify local non-satiation of the Paretian preordering, self-centredness and non-jealousy. Necessity then immediately follows from the definition of a strong equilibrium, the Theorem 6 of Arrow (1981), and the Footnote 57 of this chapter. Let us establish sufficiency. Let $t \neq 0$ be a distributive equilibrium with a unique donor i ($t_j = 0$ for all $j \neq i$) such that $w_i(x(\omega, t)) = \max\{w_i(x): x \in S_n\}$, suppose that t is blocked by a coalition I playing t_I^*, and let us derive a contradiction. By definition of a blocking coalition, for all $j \in I$, $x_j(\omega, (t_{\setminus I}, t_I^*)) \geqslant 0$ and $w_j(x(\omega, (t_{\setminus I}, t_I^*))) \geqslant w_j(x(\omega, t))$ with a strict inequality holding for at least one j. This implies in turn that coalition I playing t_I^* blocks 0 in the social system $(w, x(\omega, t))$. Let $\omega' = x(\omega, t)$. The maximum ω' of w_i in S_n being unique by strict concavity of w_i, we have $\omega' \in P$, so that $\omega' \in C$ by Theorem 14, the desired contradiction. □

COROLLARY 9. (i) *If w is a strong BBV distributive social system, or if it verifies local non-satiation of the Paretian preordering, self-centredness and non-jealousy, then: $L(w, \omega^0) = \{\omega \in P(w): w_i(\omega) \geqslant w_i(\omega^0)$ for all $i\}$. (ii) If moreover w_i is continuous for all i, then $L(w, \omega^0)$ is non-empty for all $\omega^0 \in S_n$.*

PROOF. (i) follows immediately from Theorem 14, Corollary 8 and the definition of $L(w, \omega^0)$. Let us prove (ii). Set $X(\omega^0) = \{\omega \in S_n: w(\omega) \geqslant w(\omega^0)$ for all $i\}$ is a non-empty ($\omega^0 \in X(\omega^0)$) and closed (by continuity of utility functions) subset of compact set S_n. It is therefore a non-empty compact set. Function $\sum_i \alpha_i w_i$, where α_i denotes a positive real number for all i, is continuous and attains therefore a maximum at some $\omega^* \in X(\omega^0)$. ω^* is a strong distributive optimum by construction, unanimously preferred to ω^0 by definition of $X(\omega^0)$. It is therefore a distributive liberal social contract of (w, ω^0) by Corollary 9(i). □

THEOREM 15. *Let (π, ω) (resp. (π, x)) be a social contract equilibrium (resp. Lindahl–Bergstrom equilibrium) of (w, ω^0), such that w_i is locally non-satiated at ω*

(resp. x) for all i (that is, for all i and all neighborhood V of ω in $\mathbb{R}^n$, there exists $x' \in V$ such that $w_i(x') > w_i(\omega)$). (i) Then, ω (resp. x) is a strong distributive optimum of w. (ii) If, moreover, w is a strong BBV distributive social system, or if it verifies local non-satiation of the Paretian preordering, self-centredness and non-jealousy, then ω is a distributive liberal social contract of (w, ω^0).

PROOF. (i) By Definition 7(ii) (resp. 7'(ii)): $w_i(z) > w_i(\omega)$ (resp. $w_i(z) > w_i(x)$) implies $\pi_i z > \pi_i \omega^0$ (resp. $\pi_i z > \omega_i^0$) whenever $z_i \geq 0$. By local non-satiation of individual preferences: $w_i(z) \geq w_i(\omega)$ (resp. $w_i(z) \geq w_i(x)$) implies $\pi_i z \geq \pi_i \omega^0$ (resp. $\pi_i z \geq \omega_i^0$) whenever $z_i \geq 0$. If, therefore, there exists $z \geq 0$ that is Pareto-superior to ω (resp. x), i.e. such that $w_i(z) \geq w_i(\omega)$ (resp. $w_i(z) \geq w_i(x)$) for all i with a strict inequality for at least one i, then $\sum_{i \in N} \pi_i z > \sum_{i \in N} \pi_i \omega^0$ (resp. $\sum_{i \in N} \pi_i z > \sum_{i \in N} \omega_i^0$), while

$$\sum_{i \in N} \pi_i \omega^0 = \left(\sum_{i \in N} \pi_i \right) \omega^0 = (1, \ldots, 1) \cdot \omega^0 = \sum_{i \in N} \omega_i^0 = 1.$$

Therefore z is not feasible and the first part of the theorem is established.

(ii) We know from the first part of the proof that ω is a strong distributive optimum. It suffices therefore, from Corollary 9, to establish that ω is unanimously weakly preferred to ω^0. But ω^0 belongs to $\{z \in \mathbb{R}^n: z_i \geq 0 \text{ and } \pi_i z \leq \pi_i \omega^0\}$ for all i. We have therefore $w_i(\omega) \geq w_i(\omega^0)$ for all i by Definition 7(ii). □

THEOREM 16. *Let (w, ω^0) be a (weak) BBV social system such that $\omega_i^0 = 0$ for all $i \geq m+1$ (that is, for all poor i). (i) (π, ω) is a social contract equilibrium of (w, ω^0) if and only if it is a Lindahl–Bergstrom equilibrium of (w, ω^0). (ii) If, moreover, w is a strong BBV distributive social system, or if it verifies self-centredness and non-jealousy, then the equilibrium distributions of Lindahl–Bergstrom of (w, ω^0) are distributive liberal social contracts of the latter.*

PROOF. The second part of the theorem is a simple consequence of the first part, Theorem 15(ii), and the obvious remark that BBV social systems verify local non-satiation of the Paretian preordering. Let us prove the first part.

In view of Definitions 7 and 7', it suffices to prove that $\pi_i \omega^0 = \omega_i^0$ for all i when (π, ω) is a social contract equilibrium and when it is a Lindahl–Bergstrom equilibrium of (w, ω^0). Let (π, ω) be either a social contract equilibrium or a Lindahl–Bergstrom equilibrium of (w, ω^0) from now on.

Note first that $\pi_{ii} > 0$ for all i, for if $\pi_{ii} \leq 0$ individual i can increase his utility indefinitely in $\{x \in \mathbb{R}^n: x_i \geq 0 \text{ and } \pi_i x \leq \pi_i \omega^0\}$ and in $\{x \in \mathbb{R}^n: x_i \geq 0 \text{ and } \pi_i x \leq \omega_i^0\}$ simply by increasing his consumption (the utility function of a BBV agent being strictly increasing in his own consumption).

Consider now a pair of distinct agents i and j such that either i is poor or i and j are rich, and let us prove that $\pi_{ij} = 0$. Suppose $\pi_{ij} \neq 0$, let $\varepsilon > 0$ be a positive real number, and define distribution x from equilibrium distribution ω by: $x_i = \omega_i + \varepsilon$; $x_j = \omega_j - (\pi_{ii}/\pi_{ij})\varepsilon$; $x_k = \omega_k$ for all k distinct from i and j. Then $\pi_i x = \pi_i \omega$, so that x belongs to $\{z \in \mathbb{R}^n: z_i \geqslant 0 \text{ and } \pi_i z \leqslant \pi_i \omega^0\}$ if ω is a social contract equilibrium distribution and to $\{z \in \mathbb{R}^n: z_i \geqslant 0 \text{ and } \pi_i z \leqslant \omega_i^0\}$ if ω is a Lindahl–Bergstrom equilibrium distribution. But agent i is indifferent to j (that is, his utility does not depend on j's consumption) by BBV assumptions, so that $w_i(x) > w_i(\omega)$, a contradiction.

From the above result and the assumption that the endowments of the poor are $= 0$, we deduce that $\pi_i \omega^0 = \pi_{ii} \omega_i^0$ for all i. If i is poor, then $\pi_{ii} \omega_i^0 = 0 = \omega_i^0$, so that $\pi_i \omega^0 = \omega_i^0$ as expected. If i is rich, then $\pi_{ji} = 0$ for all $j \neq i$ and the definition of equilibrium Lindahl prices ($\sum_{i \in I} \pi_i = (1, \ldots, 1)$) implies therefore that $\pi_{ii} = 1$, so that $\pi_{ii} \omega^0 = \omega_i^0$, and finally $\pi_i \omega^0 = \omega_i^0$. □

THEOREM 17. *Let (w, ω) be a strong BBV distributive social system, and suppose that, for all i, v_i is C^2, strictly quasi-concave, and verifies ordinal normality. Denote by $(x_1^*, \ldots, x_m^*, y^*)$ its unique equilibrium vector of individual consumption of the rich and aggregate consumption of the poor, suppose that $x_i^* > 0$ for all $i \leqslant m$, and let x^* be any equilibrium distribution (that is, any $x \in S_n$ such that $x_i = x_i^*$ for all $i \leqslant m$ and $x_{m+1} + \cdots + x_n = y^*$). (i) Then, there exists a distribution x in the weak Foley-core of (w, ω) such that $w_i(x) \geqslant w_i(x^*)$ for all $i \leqslant m$. (ii) If moreover x^* is not in the weak Foley-core of (w, ω), then: (a) there exists a distribution x in the weak Foley-core of (w, ω) such that $w_i(x) > w_i(x^*)$ for all $i \in N$; (b) and $x_{m+1} + \cdots + x_n > y^*$ for all such x. (iii) x^* is not in the weak Foley-core of (w, ω), nor is it a weak distributive optimum, whenever $(x_1^*, \ldots, x_m^*, y^*)$ is such that at least two agents contribute whose private equilibrium consumption levels are both > 0 (that is, whenever $0 < x_i^* < \omega_i$ for two distinct $i \leqslant m$ at least).*

PROOF. I first establish parts (i) and (ii) of the theorem, and then turn to the proof of part (iii).

(i) The proof of parts (i) and (ii) follows Shitovitz and Spiegel (2001, 3, pp. 222–223) with minor adaptations. Part (i) is a simple consequence of part (ii). Let us establish the latter.

Let (M, V) be the cooperative non-transferable utility game such that $M = \{1, \ldots, m\}$ and $V(I) = \{v \in \mathbb{R}^m:$ There exists $((x_i)_{i \in I}, y) \in \mathbb{R}_+^{\#I} \times \mathbb{R}_+$ such that $\sum_{i \in I} x_i + y \leqslant \sum_{i \in I} \omega_i$, $x_i \leqslant \omega_i$ for all $i \in I$, and $v_i \leqslant v_i(x_i, y)$ for all $i \in I\}$ for any $I \subset M$. Define the core of (M, V) by: $C(M, V) = \{v \in V(M):$ There is no non-empty coalition $I \subset M$ and $v' \in V(I)$ such that $v_i' > v_i$ for all $i \in I\}$. We know from Shitovitz and Spiegel (2001, 3.1) that $C(M, V)$ has the following external stability property: $v \in V(M) \setminus C(M, V)$ implies that there exists $v' \in C(M, V)$ and a non-empty coalition $I \subset M$ such that $v' \in V(I)$ and for each $i \in I$, $v_i > v_i'$.

One verifies readily, from the definition of strong BBV distributive social systems, that $V(M) \setminus C(M, V)$ contains $\{(w_i(x))_{i \leqslant m}: x \in S_n$ and is not in the weak Foley-core of $(w, \omega)\}$, the set of utility vectors of the rich associated with the feasible distributions that are strongly Foley-blocked.

Since, by assumption, equilibrium distribution x^* is not in the weak Foley-core of (w, ω), there must exist therefore, by the external stability property recalled above, a utility vector $v \in C(M, V)$ and a non-empty coalition $I \subset M$ such that $v \in V(I)$ and, for each $i \in I$, $v_i > w_i(x^*) = v_i(x_i^*, y^*)$. And by the definition of $V(I)$ there exists $((x_i)_{i \in I}, y) \in \mathbb{R}_+^{\#I} \times \mathbb{R}_+$ such that $\sum_{i \in I} x_i + y \leqslant \sum_{i \in I} \omega_i$, $x_i \leqslant \omega_i$ for all $i \in I$, and $v_i \leqslant v_i(x_i, y)$ for all $i \in I$.

I prove that $y > y^*$. Suppose, on the contrary, that $y \leqslant y^*$, and let us derive a contradiction. Since $v_i(x_i, y) \geqslant v_i > v_i(x_i^*, y^*)$ for all $i \in I$, it follows that $x_i > x_i^*$ for all $i \in I$, by strict monotonicity of functions v_i. But then $g_i^* = \omega_i - x_i^* > \omega_i - x_i \geqslant 0$ for all $i \in I$, which implies that all agents in I are contributing to the public good at distributive equilibrium. And therefore y^* is > 0, since I is non-empty. Let i be, from there on, a fixed element of non-empty coalition I. From the first-order conditions for distributive equilibrium (Section 3.1.2.2, Theorem 1), $y^* > 0$ and $\partial_y v_i(x_i^*, y^*) \neq 0 (> 0)$, we have $\partial_{x_i} v_i(x_i^*, y^*) / \partial_y v_i(x_i^*, y^*) \leqslant 1$. Ordinal normality, $y \leqslant y^*$ and $x_i > x_i^*$ imply that $\partial_{x_i} v_i(x_i, y) / \partial_y v_i(x_i, y) \leqslant \partial_{x_i} v_i(x_i, y^*) / \partial_y v_i(x_i, y^*) < \partial_{x_i} v_i(x_i^*, y^*) / \partial_y v_i(x_i^*, y^*)$. Therefore $\partial_{x_i} v_i(x_i, y) / \partial_y v_i(x_i, y) < 1$. And $x_i > 0$ since $x_i > x_i^*$. This implies in turn that there is a real number ε such that $0 < \varepsilon < x_i$ and $v_i(x_i - \varepsilon, y + \varepsilon) > v_i(x_i, y) \geqslant v_i$. Strict monotonicity implies then that $v_j(x_j, y + \varepsilon) > v_j$ for all $j \in I \setminus \{i\}$, while $(x_i - \varepsilon + \sum_{j \in I: j \neq i} x_i) + (y + \varepsilon) = \sum_{i \in I} \omega_i$ by construction. Therefore the utility vector v is not in $C(M, V)$, the desired contradiction.

I now establish that $v_i > v_i(x_i^*, y^*)$ for all $i \in M \setminus I$. Suppose, on the contrary, that $v_i \leqslant v_i(x_i^*, y^*)$ for some $i \in M \setminus I$, and let us derive a contradiction. Inequalities $x_i^* \leqslant \omega_i$ and $y > y^*$ and strict monotonicity clearly imply then $v_i(\omega_i, y) > v_i(x_i^*, y^*) \geqslant v_i$. Since $\omega_i > 0$ (see Section 3.3.3) and v_i is continuous, there exists, therefore, a real number ε such that $0 < \varepsilon < \omega_i$ and $v_i(\omega_i - \varepsilon, y + \varepsilon) > v_i$. And $v_j(x_j, y + \varepsilon)$ is then strictly greater than $v_j(x_j, y) \geqslant v_j$ for all $j \in I$ by strict monotonicity. Let v' be any element of $\mathbb{R}^m$ such that $v_i' = v_i(\omega_i - \varepsilon, y + \varepsilon)$ and $v_j' = v_j(x_j, y + \varepsilon)$ for all $j \in I$. Clearly, $v' \in V(I \cup \{i\})$, and non-empty coalition $I \cup \{i\}$ is such that $v_j' > v_j$ for all j in $I \cup \{i\}$, so that v is not in $C(M, V)$, the desired contradiction.

Since $v \in V(M)$ is $\gg (v_i(x_i^*, y^*))_{i \leqslant m}$, there exists $((x_i')_{i \leqslant m}, y') \in \mathbb{R}_+^m \times \mathbb{R}_+$ such that $\sum_{i \in M} x_i' + y' \leqslant \sum_{i \in M} \omega_i$, $x_i' \leqslant \omega_i$ for all $i \in M$, and $v_i(x_i', y') \geqslant v_i > v_i(x_i^*, y^*)$ for all $i \in M$. Any $((x_i)_{i \leqslant m}, y) \in \mathbb{R}_+^m \times \mathbb{R}_+$ such that $\sum_{i \in M} x_i + y < \sum_{i \in M} \omega_i$ must be blocked, utilities being strictly increasing; therefore we must have $\sum_{i \in M} x_i' + y' = \sum_{i \in M} \omega_i$. One establishes as above that, necessarily, $y' > y^*$. And it follows then immediately from the latter that there exists a wealth distribution of the poor $(x_i')_{i > m}$ such that $x_{m+1}' + \cdots + x_n' = y'$, $x_i' > x_i^*$ for all $i > m$, and $x' \in S_n$. Distribution x', being feasible, must be in the weak Foley-core of (w, ω), for otherwise v would be blocked. And we have $w_i(x') > w_i(x^*)$ for all $i \leqslant m$ by construction, and also $w_i(x') = x_i' > w_i(x^*) = x_i^*$ for all $i > m$ by definition of BBV distributive social systems.

Finally, inequalities $(w_i(x))_{i>m} \gg (w_i(x^*))_{i>m}$ readily imply $x_{m+1} + \cdots + x_n > y^*$, and this remark completes the proof of parts (i) and (ii) of the theorem.

(ii) The result of part (iii) is quite simple and largely independent of the results of parts (i) and (ii). Notably, it does not suppose ordinal normality. Suppose that there are two distinct agents i and j in $\{1, \ldots, m\}$ whose equilibrium contributions verify: $0 < \omega_k - x_k^* < \omega_k$, $k = i, j$. Then y^* must be > 0, and the first-order equilibrium conditions and the monotonicity assumptions on functions v_k imply that $\partial_{x_k} v_i(x_k^*, y^*) = \partial_y v_i(x_k^*, y^*) > 0$, $k = i, j$. Function $\xi_k : \mathbb{R} \to \mathbb{R}$ defined by $\xi_k(\varepsilon) = v_k(x_k^* - (\varepsilon/2), y^* + \varepsilon)$ has derivative $\partial \xi_k(\varepsilon) = -(1/2)\partial_{x_k} v_k(x_k^* - (\varepsilon/2), y^* + \varepsilon) + \partial_y v_k(x_k^* - (\varepsilon/2), y^* + \varepsilon)$, which is continuous by the smoothness assumption on v_k, and > 0 at $\varepsilon = 0$ for $k = i, j$ by the first-order condition above. Therefore, function $\mathbb{R} \to \mathbb{R}^2$ defined by $\varepsilon \to (\xi_i(\varepsilon), \xi_j(\varepsilon))$ is monotonic strictly increasing in an open neighborhood V of 0 in $\mathbb{R}$. Let ε in V be such that $0 < \varepsilon < \min\{x_i^*, x_j^*\}$, and define distribution x such that: $x_k = x_k^* - (\varepsilon/2)$ if $k = i$ or j; $x_k = x_k^*$ if $k \in \{1, \ldots, m\} \setminus \{i, j\}$; and $x_k = x_k^* + (\varepsilon/(n-m))$ for all $k > m$. Obviously, $x \in S_n$. And we have $w_k(x) > w_k(x^*)$ for $k = i, j$ by construction, and $w_k(x) > w_k(x^*)$ for all $k \neq i, j$ by the monotonicity properties of preferences in strong BBV distributive social systems. Therefore x^* is strongly Pareto-dominated, implying that it is neither weakly Pareto-efficient nor in the weak Foley-core of (w, ω). □

COROLLARY 10. *Let (w, ω) be a strong BBV distributive social system such that the initial endowments of the poor are all $= 0$ and rich individuals are identical (that is, $v_i = v$ and $\omega_i = 1/m$ for all $i \leqslant m$). Let $(z^*, y^*) \in \mathbb{R}^2$ and $(z^{**}, y^{**}) \in \mathbb{R}^2$ be respectively a Cournot–Nash and a Lindahl–Bergstrom (symmetric) equilibrium vector of private consumption of the rich and aggregate consumption of the poor (where symmetry means that the rich make identical gifts at equilibrium, equal to y^*/m and y^{**}/m respectively). (i) Then, $v(z^*, y^*) \leqslant v(z^{**}, y^{**})$. (ii) If, moreover, v is C^2 and strictly quasi-concave, and if $m \geqslant 2$ and z^* and y^* are both > 0, then: $v(z^*, y^*) < v(z^{**}, y^{**})$; and $y^* < y^{**}$ whenever v verifies the additional assumption of ordinal normality.*

PROOF. We know from Footnote 70 that the Lindahl equilibrium distributions are in the (strong) Foley-core of BBV (w, ω). Part (i) of Corollary 10 follows readily from this fact, for $v(z^*, y^*) > v(z^{**}, y^{**})$ implies, clearly, that Lindahl equilibrium distribution is strongly Foley-blocked by the coalition of the rich playing the Cournot–Nash equilibrium transfers. Inequality $v(z^*, y^*) < v(z^{**}, y^{**})$, in the second part of the corollary, follows from the same fact and Theorem 17(iii). Combined with ordinal normality, it implies $y^* < y^{**}$ by the reasoning developed in §5 of the proof of Theorem 17(ii). □

A.2. Mechanisms for private contributions to public goods

A.2.1. Two-stage mechanisms

The mechanisms reviewed here develop the original idea of Guttman (1978, 1987). All of them suppose that individual agents are perfectly informed about the preferences and endowments of others.

Guttman sets his mechanism in the framework, already described several times above, of a strong BBV distributive social system of identical ("rich") agents endowed with distributive utility functions that are quasi-linear in the private good, strictly concave in the public good and differentiable. A donor's contribution to the public good is made of two parts: a flat contribution g_i; and a matching grant $s_i \sum_{j \leqslant m: \, j \neq i} g_j$ proportional to the sum of the flat contributions of the other donors. In the first stage of the game, donors choose simultaneously the matching rates s_i that maximize their utility given the matching rates announced by the others and the flat contributions that they anticipate for the second stage of the game as functions of the whole vector of matching rates. In the second stage (subgame), they choose simultaneously the flat contributions that maximize their utility, given the flat contributions of others and the vector of matching rates $(s_1, \ldots, s_m)$ determined in the first stage. Each player's strategy consists therefore of a matching rate and a flat contribution as a function of all matching rates. An m-tuple of strategies is a subgame perfect equilibrium of this sequential game if it makes a Nash equilibrium at both stages of the game. Attention is restricted to symmetric equilibria. Guttman states that the equilibrium provision level of the public good is the (unique) Pareto-efficient provision level. This property is no longer verified in the presence of income effects [Guttman (1987)] or preference heterogeneity. In the latter case, nevertheless, (that is, in the case of heterogeneous quasi-linear preferences), the equilibrium provision level of the public good induced by Guttman's mechanism remains larger than the non-cooperative level.

Danziger and Schnytzer (1991) develop a variant of Guttman's mechanism where donors choose the rate at which they subsidize the flat contributions of others. Formally, let s_i ($\geqslant 0$) denote a subsidy rate chosen by agent i. His total contribution to the public good is made of the following two parts: his subsidies to the other donors $s_i \sum_{j \leqslant m: \, j \neq i} g_j$; and his own subsidized flat contribution $(1 - \sum_{j \leqslant m: \, j \neq i} s_j) g_i$. And the sequential game is specified as the following variant of Guttman's implementation game. In the first stage, donors choose simultaneously the subsidy rates that maximize their utility given the subsidy rates announced by the others and their flat contributions as functions of the vector of subsidy rates. In the second stage, they choose simultaneously the flat contributions that maximize their utility, given the flat contributions of others and the vector of subsidy rates determined in the first stage. Donors have general (strong) BBV preferences, which are assumed differentiable and strictly concave. The private and the public goods are both strictly normal goods for all of them, and the marginal rates of substitution $\partial_{x_i} v_i(x_i, y) / \partial_y v_i(x_i, y) \to \infty$ as $x_i \to 0$. Danziger and Schnytzer prove, in their Theorems 1 and 2 [op. cit.: pp. 59

and 61 respectively; see also the remarks of Althammer and Buchholz (1993)], that interior sequential equilibria exist and are in one-to-one correspondence with interior Lindahl equilibria (and therefore Pareto-efficient) when Pareto-efficiency requires a positive provision of the public good. If, however, the latter condition is verified, there exist also sequential equilibria with zero provision of the public good (therefore inefficient) if and only if there is no pair of individuals who want to make stand-alone positive joint contributions with equal cost-sharing (that is, formally, if and only if $(\partial_y v_i(\omega_i, 0)/\partial_{x_i} v_i(\omega_i, 0)) + (\partial_y v_j(\omega_j, 0)/\partial_{x_j} v_j(\omega_j, 0)) \leqslant 1$ for all (i, j), $i \neq j)$. If, finally, non-provision of the public good is Pareto-efficient, then: all sequential equilibria imply non-provision; there exists at least one such equilibrium; and the sequential equilibria are Pareto- efficient.

Varian (1994a, 1994b), to finish with, designs three alternative variants of Guttman's original mechanism.

The first one is simply the subsidy-setting mechanism of Danziger and Schnytzer above, applied to a context that does not fit in the technical assumptions of the latter, namely, a strong BBV distributive social systems with only two donors, endowed with utility functions quasi-linear in the private good, strictly concave in the public good and differentiable (violating, therefore, notably, the strict concavity and normality assumptions of Danziger and Schnytzer). Varian (1994a, Theorem 1) establishes that the subsidy-setting game of Danziger and Schnytzer has a unique equilibrium in such social systems and that the associate allocation is a Lindahl equilibrium allocation.

In the second mechanism, the rate at which a donor i subsidizes the flat contribution of a donor j ($\neq i$) is chosen by a third agent k picked in $\{1, \ldots, m\} \setminus \{i, j\}$ according to some fixed rule assigning one and only one k to any pair (i, j) (e.g. $k = \min\{1, \ldots, m\} \setminus \{i, j\}$). This supposes, naturally, that $m \geqslant 3$. In order to facilitate exposition, I will suppose, following Varian (1994a), that $m = 3$. Then $\{1, \ldots, m\} \setminus \{i, j\}$ reduces to a single agent, and we can denote therefore, without ambiguity, by s_{kj} the subsidy rate facing agent j as set by agent k (and paid by the single remaining agent in $\{1, 2, 3\} \setminus \{k, j\}$). The total contribution of a donor, say agent 1, to the public good consists of the following two components: his subsidized flat contribution $(1 - s_{31} - s_{21})g_1$; and the sum $s_{32}g_2 + s_{23}g_3$ of his subsidies to the other agents. The sequential game is defined along the same lines as above, with a first stage setting subsidy rates and a second stage setting individual flat contributions. The author establishes (1994a, Theorem 3) that, in a strong BBV distributive social system with continuous convex preferences and locally invertible individual (Lindahl) demand functions for the public good, the subgame perfect equilibria of this subsidy-setting game yield Lindahl equilibrium allocations. Demand functions are locally invertible, in particular, when distributive utility functions verify ordinal normality or are quasi-linear in the private good, differentiable and strictly concave in the public good.

Varian's third mechanism is specified as follows. In the first stage, each agent i announces a number $1 - s_i$, which will turn out, in equilibrium, to be both the rate at which agent i's contributions are subsidized (agent i being paid subsidy $(1 - s_i)g_i$) and the rate at which he subsidizes the contributions of everyone else (agent i paying the subsidy

$(1 - s_i)g_j$ to every $j \neq i$). In the second stage, each agent i chooses his private consumption and flat contribution, given the vector $(s_1, \ldots, s_m)$ and the flat contributions of others, to maximize his utility subject to the budget constraint

$$x_i + \left(1 - \sum_{j \leq m:\ j \neq i} s_j \right) g_i$$
$$= \omega_i - \left(1 - \sum_{j \leq m:\ j \neq i} s_j \right) \sum_{j \leq m:\ j \neq i} g_j - Q(s_1, \ldots, s_m),$$

where $Q(s_1, \ldots, s_m)$ is a quadratic penalty term defined as $(\sum_{j \leq m:\ j \neq i} s_j)^2$. The subsidy rate $\sum_{j \leq m:\ j \neq i} s_j$ facing agent i in the second stage of the game is set by the other agents as in Varian's second mechanism, but each agent announces now a single number as in the mechanism of Danziger and Schnytzer. Varian's third mechanism differs from the latter also by the penalty term introduced in its second stage. If utility functions of donors are differentiable and quasi-concave, and if the subgame perfect equilibrium allocation $(x_1, \ldots, x_m, G)$ is an interior Pareto optimum, then the penalty term must be $= 0$ by Samuelson's first-order conditions for Pareto-efficiency. This implies in turn that $\sum_{j \leq m} s_j = 1$, so the equilibrium budget constraints read $x_i + s_i G = \omega_i$ and we have, clearly, a Lindahl equilibrium. Therefore, any interior Lindahl allocation is a subgame perfect equilibrium allocation of the mechanism [Varian (1994a, 1994b)].

A.2.2. One-stage mechanisms

The interest in one-stage mechanisms was fostered, notably, by an original study of Roberts (1987). This article examines the relative treasury-efficiency and distributional consequences of direct taxation and subsidy as alternative means of financing of a pure public good. The underlying (largely implicit) setup is the strong BBV distributive social system. Two paradoxical statements are made in this context.

A first proposition can be viewed as a simple consequence of the neutrality property of Andreoni (1988a) (see Section 5.2.2 above: an increase in public spending on the public good corresponding to a budget-balanced increase in lump-sum taxes and/or flat subsidy rate on private contributions leaves the equilibrium provision level of the public good unchanged as long as it does not push any existing contribution to 0). Roberts' proposition states that a flat (proportional) subsidy is more treasury-efficient than (lump-sum) direct taxation *irrespective* of the price elasticity of private contributions to the public goods: the neutrality property implies that the equilibrium provision of the public good G is invariant to the tax-subsidy scheme; and the corresponding public spending is G if provision is entirely financed by direct taxation and $\beta G < G$ (where $\beta < 1$ denotes the uniform subsidy rate facing all donors) if the same provision level is financed by subsidies. This property stands in sharp contrast with the conventional statement that the subsidy is more efficient if and only if the price elasticity of the sum of private contributions is larger than 1 (the partial equilibrium condition for an increase in the subsidy rate to prompt an increase in aggregate *net* private contributions).

The second proposition states that an increase in the individual subsidy rate facing a donor i makes him worse off, ceteris paribus, at equilibrium, if the agent's contribution to the public good is price elastic: unchanged provision level of the public good (as implied by the ceteris paribus proviso) and increased individual net contribution (as implied by the elasticity assumption) together result in a fall in i's private consumption x_i and utility $v_i(x_i, G)$. As a consequence, paradoxically, rich donors, whose contributions are more susceptible to be price elastic, will presumably prefer flat subsidy schemes, involving a uniform subsidy rate for all agents, to skewed schemes involving subsidy rates increasing in wealth or contribution. Similarly, rich donors might end up better off with uniform lump-sum taxation than with flat proportional subsidy. Note that, although this is not explicitly stated by Roberts, unchanged G is an assumption here, not a consequence of neutrality (a change in the subsidy rate of a single agent is non-neutral in general: see the account of Boadway, Pestieau and Wildasin (1989a) below).

While essentially correct, Roberts' findings suffer from some imprecision, due to some ambiguity in the way they combine general equilibrium analysis (the neutrality property) and partial equilibrium comparative statics. They were further elaborated in explicit general equilibrium setup, and, moreover, explicitly related to implementation theory, in two broad classes of models, namely, the models where individuals ignore the budget constraint of the government when taking their decisions (they ignore, for instance, that the subsidies they receive individually must be financed endogenously by appropriate taxes), and the models where they fully integrate the consequences of this budget constraint for themselves (they "see through" the government budget constraint: see Section 5.2.2 above).

Models of the first type are studied by Bergstrom (1989a), Boadway, Pestieau and Wildasin (1989a, 1989b), and Roberts (1992) [see also Kaplow (1995)]. The present account follows the elaborate presentation of Boadway, Pestieau and Wildasin (1989a, 1989b). They consider strong BBV distributive social systems,[91] whose main features are briefly summarized as follows (see Section 5.2.2 for details): agent i's budget constraint reads: $x_i + (1 - s_i)g_i = \omega_i - \tau_i$, where s_i is his matching grant rate and τ_i a lump-sum tax; the balanced budget of the central government reads $\sum_{i \leqslant m} s_i g_i = \sum_{i \leqslant m} \tau_i$ for all $(g_1, \ldots, g_m)$; agents do not see through the government budget constraint, and maximize therefore $v_i(x_i, g_i + G_{-i})$ with respect to (x_i, g_i), subject to the individual budget constraint above for any given G_{-i}. Attention is restricted to (Cournot–Nash) equilibria that involve positive contributions of all potential donors (that is, equilibria such that $g_i > 0$ for all $i = 1, \ldots, m$).

---

[91] They suppose, actually, as mentioned already in Section 5.2.2 above, utility functions of the type $v_i(x_i, y_i, G)$, where y_i is a quantity of a local public commodity or factor consumed by agent ("locality") i and taxed at a given fixed rate by the central government. Nevertheless, local public goods and associate taxes play a role only in their analysis of the neutrality property (see Section 5.2.2). Tax rates on local public goods are set $= 0$ and equilibrium levels of y_i can be viewed essentially as fixed parameters in their treatment of non-neutral fiscal policy and related implementation theory. The same remarks apply, essentially, to the article of Brunner and Falkinger (1999), with a change in the interpretation of y_i (the leisure or the labor participation of agent i in their setup).

The authors obtain the following three sets of remarkable results relative to the efficiency and distributional implications of non-neutral changes in matching rates. First, a (marginal) budget-balanced increase in the subsidy rate s_i of a single agent i (financed, therefore, by any appropriate marginal change in lump-sum transfers): (i) increases the equilibrium provision level of the public good; (ii) increases i's equilibrium contribution, and lowers his equilibrium private consumption and welfare; (iii) lowers the contributions of the other agents and increases their private consumption and welfare [Boadway, Pestieau and Wildasin (1989a, Theorem 2 and proof); see also Bergstrom (1989a, Puzzle 2, parts 1 and 3), for the distributional aspects of this property]. Second, a (marginal) budget-balanced increase in a uniform subsidy rate $\beta = s_1 = \cdots = s_m$ raises individual and total contributions to the public good, with ambiguous consequences on individual welfare in general, except in the case of two-agent social systems with identical individual preferences, where individual welfare raises if $\beta < 1/2$ and attains a local maximum at $\beta = 1/2$ [Boadway, Pestieau and Wildasin (1989a, Theorem 3 and proof)]. Third: (i) there is a one-to-one mapping from (interior) Lindahl allocations (hence interior Pareto-efficient allocations) to the vectors of matching rates $(s_1, \ldots, s_m) \gg 0$ satisfying $\sum_{i \leq m} s_i = m - 1$; (ii) the price facing any agent i at the Lindahl allocation associated with such a vector $(s_1, \ldots, s_m)$ is $1 - s_i$; (iii) in particular: (a) the unique uniform matching rate that yields a Pareto-efficient allocation at Cournot–Nash equilibrium is $\beta = s_1 = \cdots = s_m = (m - 1)/m$; (b) and a (marginal) budget-balanced increase in the subsidy rate s_i of agent i, from a vector $(s_1, \ldots, s_m) \gg 0$ satisfying $\sum_{i \leq m} s_i = m - 1$, lowers his Lindahl private consumption and welfare and increases the Lindahl private consumption and welfare of others [Boadway, Pestieau and Wildasin (1989a, Theorem 4, 1989b); see also Roberts (1992), Kaplow (1995) and Brunner and Falkinger (1999, Lemma 6.1), for similar characterizations of Pareto-efficient linear tax-subsidy schemes with positive individual contributions in one-stage equilibrium setups].

A comparison with the results of Roberts (1987) is instructive in two respects.

First, Boadway et al. make full general equilibrium comparative statics, which was not the case of Roberts. The heart of their argument lies in the derivation of the Sultsky equations for equilibrium individual contributions [Boadway, Pestieau and Wildasin (1989a, Equation (13))]. These equations combine exogenous (compensated) substitution effects associated with policy manipulations of matching rates, and endogenous wealth effects associated with the variation in the equilibrium provision level of the public good determined by these manipulations (this second type of effects ignored in Roberts' study). This combination, and the normality assumption which implies that substitution and wealth effects work in the same direction, drive all their other results [including an interesting confirmation, not mentioned above, of a standard result in the literature on grants, namely, that matching grants stimulate private contributions more than lump-sum grants do: Boadway, Pestieau and Wildasin (1989a, Equation (14))].

Second, while the type of policy considered by Boadway et al. is not neutral (notably because their individual agents do not "see through" the government's budget constraint: see Section 5.2.2 above), their statement that the Pareto-efficient level of a uniform matching rate is $\beta = (m-1)/m$ implies, nevertheless, similar conclusions as Roberts' on comparative treasury-efficiency of (flat) matching grants and lump-sum direct taxation, namely: public spending associated with efficient equilibrium provision G is smaller with flat subsidy ($= ((m-1)/m)G$) than with direct taxation ($= G$). Moreover, the relative advantage of flat subsidy in terms of treasury-efficiency decreases in the number of donors and vanishes in the limit as this number grows to infinity, a property that parallels Roberts' remarks that the subsidy rate will be close to 1 in the case of genuine pure public goods such as national defense or public assistance and that the treasury-efficiency advantage of flat subsidy will be negligible then.

We now turn, to finish with, to the class of one-stage implementation models where it is assumed that the agents see through the budget constraint of the government. We will review the contributions of Andreoni and Bergstrom (1996),[92] Falkinger (1996), Kirchsteiger and Puppe (1997), and Brunner and Falkinger (1999) successively. All study variants of the linear tax-subsidy scheme.

We follow more particularly Brunner and Falkinger for the formulation of the analytical framework.[93] General budget-balanced tax-subsidy schemes are specified in the setup of the strong BBV distributive social system with differentiable, strictly quasi-concave utility functions of donors and strictly normal private and public goods. The net tax paid by contributor i when the gift-vector is $(g_1, \ldots, g_m)$ reads: $\tau_i + \sum_{j \leqslant m} \beta_{ij} g_j$, where τ_i is lump-sum, $\beta_{ii} > -1$ is the subsidy rate facing i for his own contribution and β_{ij} is the tax rate facing i for j's contribution, $j \neq i$. It is assumed that taxes levied on any agent's contribution are non-negative on the aggregate (that is: $\sum_{j \leqslant m:\ j \neq i} \beta_{ji} \geqslant 0$ for all i) and that the government balances its budget (that is: $\sum_{i \leqslant m} (\tau_i + \sum_{j \leqslant m} \beta_{ij} g_j)$ covers exactly the direct contribution of the government to the public good). Individual budget constraints read: $x_i + (1 - \beta_{ii}) g_i = \omega_i - \tau_i - \sum_{j \leqslant m:\ j \neq i} \beta_{ij} g_j$. Finally, individual agents see through the government budget constraint, which means that each agent i maximizes $v_i(x_i, g_i + G_{-i} + \sum_{i \leqslant m} (\tau_i + \sum_{j \leqslant m} \beta_{ij} g_j))$ subject to the individual budget constraint above.

Two subclasses of linear schemes are considered and studied in this literature.

The first one is the class of uniform tax schemes, where, by definition, each agent i faces a unique tax rate β_i on the contributions of others (that is: $\beta_{ij} = \beta_i$ for all i and all $j \neq i$). The distortionary tax paid by an individual is then completely determined by the aggregate contribution of others. A non-cooperative equilibrium where all agents contribute is Pareto-efficient if and only if it verifies the condition of Boadway et al. above, that is: $-\sum_{i \leqslant m} \beta_{ii} = m - 1$ [Brunner and Falkinger (1999, Lemma 6.1)]. Each uniform linear tax-subsidy scheme that verifies this condition yields a unique equilibrium allocation $(x_1, \ldots, x_m, G)$, which is efficient and $\gg 0$ (op. cit.: part (a) of Theorem 5.1). If all

---

[92] As already noticed in Section 5.2.2 above, Andreoni and Bergstrom present their games in a multi-stage setting, but the equilibria that they study in their first two games are, actually, simultaneous equilibria played at one of these multiple stages only (at stage 2, to be precise). Their results apply to, therefore, and are actually viewed in the literature as relative to, one-stage implementation theory.

[93] With the provision on the specification of individual utility functions mentioned in Footnote 91 above.

agents contribute, nevertheless, the efficient non-cooperative equilibrium is not unique, for there exists then an infinite number of equilibrium vectors of positive private contributions $(g_1, \ldots, g_m)$ that yield the unique efficient allocation (op. cit.: Theorem 6.1).

Two examples of uniform linear tax-subsidy schemes have been studied in some detail in the literature.

Game 1 of Andreoni and Bergstrom (1996), first, lets individuals be subsidized at a flat rate β and pay taxes proportional to aggregate government subsidies βG at an individual tax rate s_i. Formally, they let $\tau_i = 0$, $\beta_{ii} = -\beta(1 - s_i)$, $\beta_{ij} = s_i \beta$ for all $j \neq i$, and $\sum_{i \leqslant m} s_i = 1$ in the general scheme above, with resulting individual budget constraints of the type: $x_i + (1 - \beta)g_i = \omega_i - s_i \beta G$. They prove that: the Cournot–Nash equilibrium is unique whenever $(\beta, s_1, \ldots, s_m)$ is such that $0 \leqslant \beta < 1$ and $0 \leqslant s_i < 1$ for all i [Andreoni and Bergstrom (1996, Theorem 1)]; moreover, the equilibrium provision level of the public good is then strictly increasing in $\beta (< 1)$ (op. cit.: Theorem 2). Kirchsteiger and Puppe (1997) establish in the same setup, under the additional assumption of continuous differentiability of utility functions, that: there always exists $\beta \leqslant 1$ such that the associate equilibrium supply of the public good is Pareto-efficient; and an efficient equilibrium is interior if and only if $\beta = 1$, the associate individual prices $1 - \beta + \beta s_i = s_i$ then being the Lindahl equilibrium prices, such that $\sum_{i \leqslant m} s_i = m - 1$ [Kirchsteiger and Puppe (1997, Theorem 1)]. The tax-subsidy scheme of Andreoni and Bergstrom, therefore, yields an efficient interior equilibrium that is not unique and implies the full financing of the public good by government budget. This was noticed by Falkinger (1996) who proposed an alternative uniform linear scheme with better treasury-efficiency [see also Falkinger et al. (2000)]. The tax paid by individual i is now proportional to the deviation $g_i - (G_{-i}/(m - 1))$ of his contributions from the average contribution of others. There is a unique tax rate β, so that individual budget constraints read: $x_i + (1 - \beta)g_i = \omega_i - \beta(G_{-i}/(m - 1))$. Falkinger establishes that: the Cournot–Nash equilibrium is unique whenever $0 \leqslant \beta < 1 - (1/m)$, and the associate provision level of the public good is then increasing in β (op. cit.: Proposition 1(i)); an interior equilibrium is efficient if and only if $\beta = 1 - (1/m)$ (op. cit.: pp. 417–418). The interior efficient equilibrium is not unique [op. cit.: Proposition 1(ii), or Brunner and Falkinger (1999, Lemma 6.1)], but the associate supply of the public good is [Brunner and Falkinger (1999, Theorem 5.1)]. The latter can be therefore achieved approximately by a unique non-cooperative equilibrium, by taking $\beta < 1 - (1/m)$ arbitrarily close to $1 - (1/m)$. The Pareto-efficient scheme of Falkinger is more treasury-efficient than Andreoni and Bergstrom's, in relative terms, because the associate public spending covers only a fraction of public good provision.[94]

The second subclass of mechanisms examined by this literature is the class of non-uniform linear tax-subsidy schemes. The linear tax-subsidy scheme associated with the

---

[94] Comparison can only be made in relative terms, that is, on the basis of total public spending per unit of supply of the public good, because the efficient provision levels corresponding to the two schemes will, in general, be different.

family $(\beta_{ij})_{i \leqslant m, j \leqslant m}$ of tax-subsidy rates is non-uniform if, by definition, $\beta_{ij} \neq \beta_{ik}$ for some triplet of distinct agents $i, j \neq i$ and $k \neq i, j$. The tax paid by an agent whose tax rates are non-uniform depends on the whole vector of contributions of others, and not only on their sum. An example is the case of uniformity of the tax rate with respect to a partition of the set of donors, imagined by Falkinger (1996). The set of donors $\{1, \ldots, m\}$ is partitioned first in a family $(I_r)_{1 \leqslant r \leqslant \rho}$ of ρ non-empty subsets, with $\rho \geqslant 2$ and $\#I_r \geqslant 2$ for all r (implying that $m \geqslant 4$). The tax paid by member i of group r is then proportional to the deviation $g_i - ((1/(\#I_r - 1)) \sum_{j \in I_r} g_j)$ of his contributions from the average contribution of the group, with the same tax-subsidy rate β^r for all. Formally, we have, for any pair of distinct agents i and j: $\beta_{ij} = \beta^r (= -\beta_{ii}/(\#I_r - 1))$ if i and j are members of group r; $\beta_{ij} = 0$ otherwise; so the budget constraint of the members of group r read $x_i + (1 - \beta^r) g_i = \omega_i - \beta^r ((1/(\#I_r - 1)) \sum_{j \in I_r: j \neq i} g_j)$. It is then shown that: interior non-cooperative equilibrium is unique whenever $\beta^r \neq 1 - (1/\#I_r)$ for all r [as a consequence of Brunner and Falkinger (1999, Theorem 6.2); see also Falkinger (1996, Proposition 2) as a special case]; it is both unique and efficient, in particular, whenever $\beta^r = (1/(\#I_r - 1))(1 - (1/m))$ for all r [as a consequence of Brunner and Falkinger (1999, Lemma 6.1)]. Kirchsteiger and Puppe (1997), nevertheless, exhibit examples of strong BBV distributive social systems with Cobb–Douglas utility functions, which have a Pareto-inefficient boundary equilibrium, in addition to their unique interior efficient equilibrium (op. cit.: 4, notably Theorem 2 and proof); moreover, the efficient interior equilibrium is unstable in some of their examples. Note, finally, that the Pareto-efficient non-uniform scheme of Falkinger is superior, in terms of relative treasury-efficiency (public spending per unit of equilibrium supply of the public good), to his Pareto-efficient uniform scheme, since $\beta^r < 1 - (1/m)$ for all r.

References

Abel, A.B. (1987). "Operative gift and bequest motive". American Economic Review 77, 1037–1047.
Abrams, B.A., Schmitz, M.D. (1978). "The "crowding-out" effect of governmental transfers on private charitable contributions". Public Choice 33, 29–39.
Aczel, J. (1966). Lectures on Functional Equations and their Applications. Academic Press, New York.
Althammer, W., Buchholz, W. (1993). "Lindahl-equilibria as the outcome of a non-cooperative game". European Journal of Political Economy 9, 399–405.
Altig, D., Davis, S.J. (1993). "Borrowing constraints and two-sided altruism with an application to social security". Journal of Economic Dynamics and Control 17, 467–494.
Altonji, J.G., Hayashi, F., Kotlikoff, L.J. (1997). "Parental altruism and inter vivos transfers: Theory and evidence". Journal of Political Economy 105, 1121–1166.
Andreoni, J. (1988a). "Privately provided public goods in a large economy: The limits of altruism". Journal of Public Economics 35, 57–73.
Andreoni, J. (1988b). "Why free-ride? Strategies and learning in public goods experiments". Journal of Public Economics 37, 291–304.
Andreoni, J. (1989). "Giving with impure altruism: Applications to charity and Ricardian equivalence". Journal of Political Economy 97, 1447–1458.
Andreoni, J. (1990). "Impure altruism and donations to public goods: A theory of warm-glow giving". The Economic Journal 100, 464–477.

Andreoni, J. (1995). "Cooperation in public-goods experiments: Kindness or confusion?". American Economic Review 85, 891–904.
Andreoni, J. (1998). "Toward a theory of charitable fundraising". Journal of Political Economy 106, 1186–1213.
Andreoni, J., Bergstrom, T.C. (1996). "Do government subsidies increase the private supply of public goods?". Public Choice 88, 295–308.
Archibald, G.C., Donaldson, D. (1976). "Non-paternalism and the basic theorems of welfare economics". Canadian Journal of Economics 9, 492–507.
Arrondel, L., Laferrère, A. (1991). "Successions et héritiers à travers les données fiscales". Economie et Prévision 100–101, 137–159.
Arrondel, L., Masson, A. (1991). "Que nous enseignent les enquêtes sur les transferts patrimoniaux en France?". Economie et Prévision 100–101, 93–128.
Arrow, K.J. (1981). "Optimal and voluntary income distribution". In: Economic Welfare and the Economics of Soviet Socialism: Essays in Honor of Abram Bergson. Cambridge University Press, Cambridge, pp. 267–288.
Arrow, K.J., Debreu, G. (1954). "Existence of an equilibrium for a competitive economy". Econometrica 22, 265–290. Reprinted in Debreu, G. (1983). Mathematical Economics. Cambridge University Press, Cambridge, pp. 68–97.
Arrow, K.J., Enthoven, A.C. (1961). "Quasi-concave programming". Econometrica 29, 779–800.
Arrow, K.J., Hahn, F.H. (1971). General Competitive Analysis. Holden-Day, San Francisco.
Aumann, R. (1959). "Acceptable points in general cooperative n-person games". In: Contributions to the Theory of Games IV. Princeton University Press, Princeton, New Jersey.
Balzac, H. (1833). Eugénie Grandet. Flammarion, Paris, 2000.
Barro, R.J. (1974). "Are government bonds net wealth?". Journal of Political Economy 82, 1095–1117.
Barsky, R.J., Mankiw, G., Zeldes, S. (1986). "Ricardian consumers with Keynesian propensities". American Economic Review 76, 676–691.
Becker, G.S. (1974). "A theory of social interactions". Journal of Political Economy 82, 1063–1093.
Becker, G.S. (1976). "Altruism, egoism and genetic fitness: Economics and socio-biology". Journal of Economic Literature 14, 817–826. Reprinted in Zamagni, S. (Ed.) (1995). The Economics of Altruism. Edward Elgar, Aldershot, England and Brookfield, Vermont, pp. 321–330.
Becker, G.S. (1981a). A Treatise on the Family. Harvard University Press, Cambridge, Massachusetts and London, England.
Becker, G.S. (1981b). "Altruism in the family and selfishness in the market place". Economica 48, 1–15. Reprinted in Zamagni, S. (Ed.) (1995). The Economics of Altruism. Edward Elgar, Aldershot, England and Brookfield, Vermont, pp. 209–223.
Becker, G.S., Murphy, K. (1988). "The family and the state". Journal of Law and Economics 31, 1–18.
Berge, C. (1970). Graphes et Hypergraphes. Dunod, Paris. English translation: Graphs and Hypergraphs. North-Holland, Amsterdam, 1976.
Bergstrom, T.C. (1970). "A "Scandinavian consensus" solution for efficient income distribution among non-malevolent consumers". Journal of Economic Theory 2, 383–398.
Bergstrom, T.C. (1989a). "Puzzles: Love and spaghetti, the opportunity cost of virtue". Journal of Economic Perspectives 3, 165–173.
Bergstrom, T.C. (1989b). "A fresh look at the Rotten Kid Theorem – and other household mysteries". Journal of Political Economy 97, 1138–1159.
Bergstrom, T.C. (1999). "Systems of benevolent utility functions". Journal of Public Economic Theory 1, 71–100.
Bergstrom, T.C., Cornes, R.C. (1983). "Independence of allocative efficiency from distribution in the theory of public goods". Econometrica 51, 1753–1765.
Bergstrom, T.C., Varian, H.A. (1985a). "When do market games have transferable utility?". Journal of Economic Theory 35, 222–223.
Bergstrom, T.C., Varian, H.A. (1985b). "When are Nash equilibria independent of the distribution of agents' characteristics?". Review of Economic Studies 52, 715–718.

Bergstrom, T.C., Blume, L.E., Varian, H.R. (1986). "On the private provision of public goods". Journal of Public Economics 29, 25–49.

Bergstrom, T.C., Blume, L.E., Varian, H.R. (1992). "Uniqueness of Nash equilibrium in private provision of public goods: An improved proof". Journal of Public Economics 49, 391–392.

Bernheim, B.D. (1986). "On the voluntary and involuntary provision of public goods". American Economic Review 76, 789–793.

Bernheim, B.D., Bagwell, K. (1988). "Is everything neutral?". Journal of Political Economy 96, 308–338.

Bernheim, B.D., Peleg, B., Whinston, M.D. (1987). "Coalition-proof Nash equilibria". Journal of Economic Theory 42, 1–29.

Bernheim, B.D., Shleifer, A., Summers, L.H. (1985). "The strategic bequest motive". Journal of Political Economy 93, 1045–1076.

Bhagwati, J.N., Brecher, R.A., Hatta, T. (1983). "The generalized theory of transfers and welfare: Bilateral transfers in a multilateral world". American Economic Review 73, 606–618.

Bilodeau, M. (1992). "Voluntary contributions to United Charities". Journal of Public Economics 48, 119–133.

Bilodeau, M., Gravel, N. (2004). "Voluntary provision of a public good and individual morality". Journal of Public Economics 88, 645–666.

Boadway, R., Pestieau, P., Wildasin, D. (1989a). "Tax-transfer policies and the voluntary provision of public goods". Journal of public Economics 39, 157–176.

Boadway, R., Pestieau, P., Wildasin, D. (1989b). "Non-cooperative behaviour and efficient provision of public goods". Public Finance/Finances Publiques 44, 1–7.

Boas, F. (1897). The Social Organization and the Secret Societies of the Kwakiutl Indians. Washington.

Boulding, K.E. (1973). The Economy of Love and Fear: A Preface to Grants Economics. Wadsworth Publishing Co, Belmont, California.

Bruce, N., Waldman, M. (1991). "Transfers in kind: When they can be efficient and non-paternalistic". American Economic Review 81, 1345–1351.

Brunner, J.K., Falkinger, J. (1999). "Taxation in an economy with private provision of public goods". Review of Economic Design 4, 357–379.

Buchanan, J.M. (1975). "The Samaritan's dilemma". In: Phelps, E.S. (Ed.), Altruism, Morality and Economic Theory. Russell Sage Foundation, New York.

Chamberlin, J. (1974). "Provision of collective goods as a function of group size". American Political Science Review 68, 707–716.

Coate, S. (1995). "Altruism, the Samaritan's dilemma, and government transfer policy". American Economic Review 85, 46–57.

Collard, D.A. (1978). Altruism and Economy. Martin Robertson, Oxford.

Collard, D.A. (1992). "Love is not enough". In: Gay Tulip Meeks, J. (Ed.), Thoughtful Economic Man: Essays on Rationality, Moral Rules and Benevolence. Cambridge University Press, Cambridge. Reprinted in Zamagni, S. (Ed.) (1995), The Economics of Altruism. Edward Elgar, Aldershot, England and Brookfield, Vermont, pp. 149–162.

Comte, A. (1830). Cours de Philosophie Positive. Hermann, Paris, 1975.

Cornes, R.C., Sandler, T. (1984a). "Easy riders, joint production and public goods". Economic Journal 94, 580–598.

Cornes, R.C., Sandler, T. (1984b). "The theory of public goods: Non-Nash behaviour". Journal of Public Economics 23, 367–379.

Cornes, R.C., Sandler, T. (1985a). "The simple analytics of pure public good provision". Economica 52, 103–116.

Cornes, R.C., Sandler, T. (1985b). "On the consistency of conjectures with public goods". Journal of Public Economics 27, 125–129.

Cornes, R.C., Sandler, T. (1986). The Theory of Externalities, Public Goods and Club Goods. Cambridge University Press, Cambridge. (2nd edition: 1996.)

Cornes, R.C., Schweinberger, A.G. (1996). "Free riding and the inefficiency of the private production of pure public goods". Canadian Journal of Economics 29, 70–91.

Cornes, R.C., Silva, E.C.D. (1999). "Rotten kids, purity and perfection". Journal of Political Economy 107, 1034–1040.
Cornes, R., Hartley, R., Sandler, T. (1999). "Equilibrium existence and uniqueness in public good models: An elementary proof via contraction". Journal of Public Economic Theory 1, 499–509.
Cournot, A. (1838). Recherches sur les Principes Mathématiques de la Théorie des Richesses. Librairie des sciences politiques et sociales, M. Rivière & cie, Paris.
Danziger, L. (1976). "A graphic representation of the Nash and Lindahl equilibria in an economy with a public good". Journal of Public Economics 6, 295–307.
Danziger, L., Schnytzer, A. (1991). "Implementing the Lindahl voluntary exchange mechanism". European Journal of Political Economy 7, 55–64.
Debreu, G. (1952). "A social equilibrium existence theorem". Proceedings of the National Academy of Sciences 38, 886–893. Reprinted in Debreu, G. (1983). Mathematical Economics. Cambridge University Press, Cambridge, pp. 50–58.
Debreu, G. (1954). "Valuation equilibrium and Pareto optimum". Proceedings of the National Academy of Sciences 40, 588–592. Reprinted in Debreu, G. (1983). Mathematical Economics. Cambridge University Press, Cambridge, pp. 98–104.
Debreu, G. (1959). Theory of Value. Wiley, New York.
Debreu, G. (1970). "Economies with a finite set of equilibria". Econometrica 38, 387–392. Reprinted in Debreu, G. (1983). Mathematical Economics. Cambridge University Press, Cambridge, pp. 179–185.
Debreu, G., Scarf, H. (1963). "A limit theorem on the core of an economy". International Economic Review 4, 235–246. Reprinted in Debreu, G. (1983). Mathematical Economics. Cambridge University Press, Cambridge, pp. 151–162.
Dolbear, F.T. (1967). "On the theory of optimal externality". American Economic Review 57, 90–103.
Edgeworth, F.Y. (1881). Mathematical Psychics. C. Keagan Paul and Co, London.
Eichengreen, B. (1987). "Transfer problem". In: Eatwell, J., Milgate, M., Newman, P. (Eds.), New Palgrave Dictionary of Economics. Macmillan, London, pp. 684–685.
Falkinger, J. (1996). "Efficient private provision of public goods by rewarding deviations from average". Journal of Public Economics 62, 413–422.
Falkinger, J., Fehr, E., Gächter, S., Winter-Ebner, R. (2000). "A simple mechanism for the efficient private provision of public goods: Experimental evidence". American Economic Review 90, 247–264.
Feldstein, M.S. (1988). "The effects of fiscal policies when incomes are uncertain: A contradiction to Ricardian equivalence". American Economic Review 78, 14–23.
Foley, D.K. (1970). "Lindahl's solution and the core of an economy with public goods". Econometrica 38, 66–72.
Foster, V., Mourato, S., Pearce, D., Özdemiroglu, E. (2000). The Price of Virtue: The Economic Value of the Charitable Sector. Edward Elgar, Cheltenham, United Kingdom and Northampton, Massachusetts.
Fraser, C.D. (1992). "The uniqueness of Nash equilibrium in the private provision of public goods: An alternative proof". Journal of Public Economics 49, 389–390.
Fries, T.L., Golding, E., Romano, R. (1991). "Private provision of public goods and the failure of the neutrality property in large finite economies". International Economic Review 32, 147–157.
Gale, D. (1974). "Exchange equilibrium and coalitions: An example". Journal of Mathematical Economics 1, 63–66.
Gaube, T. (2001). "Group size and free-riding when private and public goods are gross substitutes". Economic Letters 70, 127–132.
Glazer, A., Konrad, K.A. (1996). "A signaling explanation for private charity". American Economic Review 86, 1019–1028.
Godelier, M. (1996). L'Enigme du Don. Fayard, Paris. Translated as The Enigma of the Gift. Polity Press, Cambridge, 1999.
Godelier, M. (2000). "Things you don't give or sell but which you keep: Valuable and social objects". In: Gérard-Varet, L.-A., Kolm, S.-C., Mercier Ythier, J. (Eds.), The Economics of Reciprocity, Giving and Altruism. Macmillan, London, pp. 182–195.

Goldfarb, R.S. (1970). "Pareto optimal redistribution: Comment". American Economic Review 60, 994–996.
Groves, T., Ledyard, J. (1987). "Incentive compatibility since 1972". In: Groves, T., Radner, R., Reiter, S. (Eds.), Information, Incentives and Economic Mechanisms. University of Minnesota Press, Minneapolis, pp. 48–111.
Guesnerie, R., Laffont, J.-J. (1978). "Advantageous reallocations of initial resources". Econometrica 46, 835–841.
Guttman, J. (1978). "Understanding collective action: Matching behavior". American Economic Review 68, 251–255.
Guttman, J. (1987). "A non-Cournot model of voluntary collective action". Econometrica 54, 1–19.
Hirshleifer, J. (1977). "Shakespeare vs. Becker on altruism: The importance of having the last word". Journal of Economic Literature XV (2), 500–502.
Hochman, H.M., Rodgers, J.D. (1969). "Pareto optimal redistribution". American Economic Review 59, 542–557. Reprinted in Hochman, H.M. (2002). Economic Behaviour and Distributional Choice. Edward Elgar, Cheltenham, United Kingdom and Northampton, Massachusetts, pp. 5–20.
Hori, H. (1992). "Utility functionals with non-paternalistic intergenerational altruism: The case where altruism extends to many generations". Journal of Economic Theory 56, 451–467.
Hori, H., Kanaya, S. (1989). "Utility functions with non-paternalistic intergenerational altruism". Journal of Economic Theory 49, 241–255.
Isaac, R.M., Walker, J.M. (1988). "Group size in public goods provision: The voluntary contribution mechanism". Quarterly Journal of Economics 103, 179–200.
Isaac, R.M., Walker, J.M., Williams, A.W. (1994). "Group size and the voluntary provision of public goods: Experimental evidence utilizing large groups". Journal of Public Economics 54, 1–36.
James, H. (1886). The Bostonians. Oxford University Press, Oxford, 1998.
Johnson, H.G. (1956). "The transfer problem and exchange stability". Journal of Political Economy 64, 212–225.
Kaplow, L. (1995). "A note on subsidizing gifts". Journal of Public Economics 58, 469–477.
Kemp, M.C. (1984). "A note on the theory of international transfers". Economic Letters 14, 259–262.
Kemp, M.C., Wong, K. (1993). "Paradoxes associated with the administration of foreign aid". Journal of Development Economics 42, 197–204.
Keynes, J.M. (1929). "The German transfer problem". Economic Journal 39, 1–17.
Kimball, M. (1987). "Making sense of two-sided altruism". Journal of Monetary Economics 20, 301–326.
Kingma, B.R. (1989). "An accurate measurement of the crowd-out effect, income effect and price effect for charitable contributions". Journal of Political Economy 97, 1197–1207.
Kirchsteiger, G., Puppe, C. (1997). "On the possibility of efficient private provision of public goods through government subsidies". Journal of Public Economics 66, 489–504.
Kirzner, I.M. (1990). "Self-interest and the new bashing of economics: A fresh opportunity in the perennial debate?". Critical Review 4, 27–40. Reprinted in Zamagni, S. (Ed.) (1995). The Economics of Altruism. Edward Elgar, Aldershot, England and Brookfield, Vermont, pp. 423–436.
Kolm, S.-Ch. (1964). Les Fondements de l'Economie Publique: Introduction à la Théorie du Rôle Economique de l'Etat. IFP, Paris.
Kolm, S.-Ch. (1968). "The optimal production of social justice". In: Guitton, H., Margolis, J. (Eds.), Proceedings of the International Economic Association on Public Economics, Biarritz, Economie Publique. CNRS, Paris, pp. 109–177. (First publication 1966; Public Economics. Macmillan, London, 1969, pp. 145–200.)
Kolm, S.-Ch. (1969). L'Etat et le Système des Prix. Dunod-CNRS, Paris.
Kolm, S.-Ch. (1983). "Altruism and efficiency". Ethics 94, 18–65. Reprinted in Zamagni, S. (Ed.) (1995). The Economics of Altruism. Edward Elgar, Aldershot, England and Brookfield, Vermont, pp. 236–283.
Kolm, S.-Ch. (1984). La Bonne Economie: La Réciprocité Générale. Presses Universitaires de France, Paris.
Kolm, S.-Ch. (1985). Le Contrat Social Libéral. Presses Universitaires de France, Paris.
Kolm, S.-Ch. (1987a). "Freedom, cores and public goods". Discussion Paper 66. Ceras, Ecole Nationale des Ponts et Chaussées, Paris.

Kolm, S.-Ch. (1987b). "Freedom and the provision of public goods with all degrees of exclusion". Discussion Paper 67. Ceras, Ecole Nationale des Ponts et Chaussées, Paris.
Kolm, S.-Ch. (1987c). "Freedom, core efficiency with public goods in general interdependence". Discussion Paper 68. Ceras, Ecole Nationale des Ponts et Chaussées, Paris.
Kolm, S.-Ch. (1987d). "The freedom and consensus normative theory of the state: The liberal social contract". In: Koslowski, P. (Ed.), Individual Liberty and Democratic Decision-Making: The Ethics, Economics and Politics of Democracy. J.C.B. Mohr, Tübingen, pp. 97–127.
Kolm, S.-Ch. (1989). "Cooperative game properties of international coordination". Discussion Paper 77. Ceras, Ecole Nationale des Ponts et Chaussées, Paris.
Kolm, S.-Ch. (1996). Modern Theories of Justice. MIT Press, Cambridge, Massachusetts and London, England.
Kolm, S.-Ch. (2000). The theory of reciprocity. In: Gérard-Varet, L.-A., Kolm, S.-C., Mercier Ythier, J. (Eds.), The Economics of Reciprocity, Giving and Altruism. Macmillan, London, pp. 115–141.
Kolm, S.-Ch. (2003). "Logique et usage du contrat social". Revue de Philosophie Economique 8, 3–17.
Laffont, J.-J. (1975). "Macroeconomic constraints, economic efficiency and ethics: An introduction to Kantian economics". Economics 42, 430–437.
Laffont, J.-J. (1988). Fondements de l'Economie Publique. Economica, Paris. English translation: Fundamentals of Public Economics. MIT Press, Cambridge, Massachusetts.
Laitner, J. (1997). "Intergenerational and interhousehold economic links". In: Rosenzweig, M.R., Stark, O. (Eds.), Handbook of Population and Family Economics. North-Holland/Elsevier, Amsterdam.
Lampman, R.J., Smeeding, T.M. (1983). "Interfamily transfers as alternatives to government transfers to persons". Review of Income and Wealth 29, 45–66.
Laury, S.K., Walker, J.M., Williams, A.W. (1999). "The voluntary provision of a pure public good with diminishing marginal returns". Public Choice 99, 139–160.
Ledyard, J.O. (1995). "Public goods: A survey of experimental research". In: Kagel, J., Roth, A.E. (Eds.), The Handbook of Experimental Economics. Princeton University Press, Princeton, New Jersey.
Lemche, S.Q. (1986). "Remarks on non-paternalism and the second theorem of welfare economics". Canadian Journal of Economics 19, 270–280.
Ley, E. (1996). "On the private provision of public goods: A diagrammatic exposition". Investigaciones Economicas 20, 105–123.
Lindbeck, A., Weibull, J.W. (1988). "Altruism and time consistency: The economics of fait accompli". Journal of Political Economy 96, 1165–1182.
Malinowski, B. (1922). Argonauts of the Western Pacific. Routledge, London.
Marshall, A. (1890). Principles of Economics. Macmillan, London.
Masson, A., Pestieau, P. (1997). "Bequest motives and models of inheritance: A survey of the literature". In: Erreygers, G., Vandevelde, T. (Eds.), Is Inheritance Legitimate?. Springer-Verlag, Berlin.
Mauss, M. (1924). Essai sur le Don: Forme et Raison de l'Echange dans les Sociétés Archaïques, L'Année Sociologique, 1. Translated as The Gift: The Form and Reason for Exchange in Archaic Societies. W.W. Norton, New York and London, 1990.
McGuire, M. (1974). "Group homogeneity and aggregate provision of a pure public good under Cournot behaviour". Public Choice 18, 107–126.
Meade, J.E. (1973). The Theory of Economic Externalities: The Control of Environmental Pollution and Similar Social Costs. Sijhoff, Leiden, Sweden.
Menchik, P.L., David, M. (1983). "Income distribution, lifetime savings and bequests". American Economic Review 73, 672–690.
Mercier Ythier, J. (1989). Equilibre Général et Don. Thèse de Doctorat en Sciences Economiques. Institut d'Etudes Politiques de Paris.
Mercier Ythier, J. (1992). "Existence of a general equilibrium of individual gifts". Discussion Paper. Université de Paris-Panthéon-Sorbonne.
Mercier Ythier, J. (1993). "Equilibre général de dons individuels". Revue Economique 44, 925–950.
Mercier Ythier, J. (1997). "First-order conditions for distributive efficiency". Discussion Paper 98A39. GREQAM, EHESS and Université d'Aix-Marseille II et III, Marseille.

Mercier Ythier, J. (1998a). "The distribution of wealth in the liberal social contract". European Economic Review 42, 329–347.
Mercier Ythier, J. (1998b). "Existence of an equilibrium of property rights". Mathematical Social Sciences 35, 261–272.
Mercier Ythier, J. (2000a). "The effectiveness of distributive policy in a competitive economy". Journal of Public Economic Theory 2, 43–69.
Mercier Ythier, J. (2000b). "Gift equilibrium and the liberal distributive social contract: A tentative synthesis". In: Gérard-Varet, L.-A., Kolm, S.-C., Mercier Ythier, J. (Eds.), The Economics of Reciprocity, Giving and Altruism. Macmillan, London, pp. 96–112.
Mercier Ythier, J. (2004a). "A limit theorem on the dual core of a distributive social system". Social Choice and Welfare 22, 147–174.
Mercier Ythier, J. (2004b). "Regular distributive social systems". Journal of Public Economic Theory 6 (1), 109–141.
Mishan, E.J. (1972). "The futility of Pareto-efficient distribution". American Economic Review 62, 971–976.
Moore, J. (1992). "Implementation, contracts and renegotiation in environments with complete information". In: Laffont, J.-J. (Ed.), Advances in Economic theory: Sixth world congress, vol. 1, pp. 182–281.
Mueller, D.C. (1989). Public Choice II. Cambridge University Press, New York.
Musgrave, R.A. (1959). The Theory of Public Finance. McGraw-Hill, New York.
Musgrave, R.A. (1970). "Pareto optimal redistribution: Comment". American Economic Review 60, 991–993. Reprinted in Hochman, H.M. (2002). Economic Behaviour and Distributional Choice. Edward Elgar, Massachusetts, Cheltenham, United Kingdom and Northampton, pp. 21–23.
Nakayama, M. (1980). "Nash equilibria and Pareto optimal income redistribution". Econometrica 48, 1257–1263.
Nash, J.F. Jr. (1950). "Equilibrium in N-person games". Proceedings of the National Academy of Sciences 36, 48–49.
Nerlove, M., Razin, A., Sadka, E. (1984). "Investment in human and nonhuman capital, transfers among siblings and the role of government". Econometrica 52, 1191–1198.
Nerlove, M., Razin, A., Sadka, E. (1987). Household and Economy: Welfare Implications of Endogenous Fertility. Academic Press, New York.
Nerlove, M., Razin, A., Sadka, E. (1988). "A bequest-constrained economy: Welfare analysis". Journal of Public Economics 37, 203–220.
Olson, M. (1965). The Logic of Collective Action. Harvard University Press, Cambridge.
Pareto, V. (1913). "Il massimo di utilità per una colletività". Giornale degli Economisti 3, 337–341.
Pareto, V. (1916). Traité de Sociologie Générale. Droz, Genève.
Parks, R. (1991). "Pareto irrelevant externalities". Journal of Economic Theory 54, 165–179.
Posnett, J., Sandler, T. (1986). "Joint supply and the finance of charitable activity". Public Finance Quarterly 14, 209–222.
Posnett, J., Sandler, T. (1989). "Demand for charity donations in private non-profit markets: The case of the U.K". Journal of Public Economics 40, 187–200.
Postlewaite, A. (1979). "Manipulations via endowments". Review of Economic Studies 46, 255–262.
Postlewaite, A., Roberts, D.J. (1976). "The incentives for price-taking behaviours in large exchange economies". Econometrica 44, 115–128.
Rader, T. (1980). "The second theorem of welfare economics when utilities are interdependent". Journal of Economic Theory 23, 420–424.
Ramsey, F.P. (1928). "A mathematical theory of saving". Economic Journal 38, 543–559.
Reece, W.S., Zieschang, K.D. (1985). "Consistent estimation of the impact of tax deductibility on the level of charitable contributions". Econometrica 53, 271–293.
Robbins, L. (1932). An Essay on the Nature and Significance of Economic Science. Macmillan, London.
Roberts, R.D. (1984). "A positive model of private charity and public transfers". Journal of Political Economy 92, 136–148.
Roberts, R.D. (1985). "A taxonomy of public good provision". Public Choice 47, 267–303.

Roberts, R.D. (1987). "Financing public goods". Journal of Political Economy 95, 420–437.
Roberts, R.D. (1992). "Government subsidies to private spending on public goods". Public Choice 74, 133–152.
Rushton, J.P. (1982). "Altruism and society: A social learning perspective". Ethics 92, 425–446. Reprinted in Zamagni, S. (Ed.) (1995). The Economics of Altruism. Edward Elgar, Aldershot, England and Brookfield, Vermont, pp. 382–403.
Samuelson, P.A. (1954). "The pure theory of public expenditure". Review of Economics and Statistics 36, 387–389.
Sertel, M.R. (1994). "Manipulating Lindahl equilibrium via endowments". Economics Letters 46, 167–171.
Shakespeare, W. (1608). King Lear. Clarendon Press, Oxford, 1963.
Sheshinski, E. (1988). "Earnings uncertainty and intergenerational transfers". In: Help, E., Razin, A., Sadka, E. (Eds.), Economic Effects of the Government Budget. MIT Press, Cambridge, Massachusetts.
Shibata, H. (1971). "A bargaining model of pure theory of public expenditure". Journal of Political Economy 79, 1–29.
Shitovitz, B., Spiegel, M. (1998). "Cournot–Nash and Lindahl equilibria in pure public good economies". Journal of Economic Theory 83, 1–18.
Shitovitz, B., Spiegel, M. (2001). "Stable provision versus Cournot–Nash equilibrium in pure public good economies". Journal of Public Economic Theory 3, 219–224.
Slivinski, A., Steinberg, R. (1998). "Soliciting the warm glow: An economic model of fundraising". Working Paper. Department of Economics, University of Western Ontario, London, CA.
Smith, A. (1759). The Theory of Moral Sentiments. Edited by Raphael, D.D. and Macfie A.L. Clarendon Press, Oxford, 1976.
Smith, A. (1776). An Inquiry into the Nature and Causes of the Wealth of Nations. Campbell, R.H. and Skinner A.S., general editors; Todd, W.B., textual editor. Clarendon Press, Oxford, 1976.
Stark, O. (1993). "Nonmarket transfers and altruism". European Economic Review 37, 1413–1424.
Starrett, D. (1972). "Fundamental non convexities in the theory of externalities". Journal of Economic Theory 4, 180–199.
Steinberg, R. (1987). "Voluntary donations and public expenditures in a federalist system". American Economic Review 77, 24–36.
Strawczynski, M. (1994). "Government intervention as bequest substitute". Journal of Public Economics 53, 477–495.
Sugden, R. (1982). "On the economics of philanthropy". Economic Journal 92, 341–350. Reprinted in Zamagni, S. (Ed.) (1995). The Economics of Altruism. Edward Elgar, Aldershot, England and Brookfield, Vermont, pp. 224–233.
Sugden, R. (1984). "Reciprocity: The supply of public goods through voluntary contributions". The Economic Journal 94, 772–787.
Sugden, R. (1985). "Consistent conjectures and voluntary contributions to public goods: Why the conventional theory does not work". Journal of Public Economics 27, 117–124.
Taussig, M.K. (1967). "Economic aspects of the personal income tax treatment of charitable contributions". National Tax Journal 20, 1–19.
Thomson, W. (1999). "Economies with public goods: An elementary geometric exposition". Journal of Public Economics Theory 1, 139–176.
Thurow, L.C. (1971). "The income distribution as a pure public good". Quarterly Journal of Economics 85, 327–336.
Tutte, W.T. (1984). "Graph theory". In: Gian-Carlo Rota (Ed.), Encyclopedia of Mathematics and its Applications, vol. 21. Addison-Wesley, Massachusetts.
Varian, H.R. (1994a). "Sequential contributions to public goods". Journal of Public Economics 53, 165–186.
Varian, H.R. (1994b). "A solution to the problem of externalities when agents are well-informed". American Economic Review 84, 1278–1293.
von Furstenberg, G.M., Mueller, D.C. (1971). "The Pareto optimal approach to income redistribution: A fiscal application". American Economic Review 61, 628–637.

von Mises (1936). Socialism: An Economic and Sociological Analysis. Jonathan Cape, London. (Translated from the second revised edition of Die Gemeinwirtschaft, 1932; 1st edition 1922.)
Walker, M. (1981). "A simple incentive compatible scheme for attaining Lindahl allocations". Econometrica 48, 56–73.
Warr, P.G. (1982). "Pareto optimal redistribution and private charity". Journal of Public Economics 19, 131–138.
Warr, P.G. (1983). "The private provision of a public good is independent of the distribution of income". Economic Letters 13, 207–211.
Wicksteed, P.H. (1910). The Common Sense of Political Economy. Macmillan, London.
Winter, S.G. (1969). "A simple remark on the second optimality theorem of welfare economics". Journal of Economic Theory 1, 99–103.
Wolff, F.C. (1998). Altruisme, Echange et Réciprocité. Thèse de Doctorat en Sciences Economiques. Université de Nantes.

Chapter 6

RECIPROCITY: ITS SCOPE, RATIONALES, AND CONSEQUENCES

SERGE-CHRISTOPHE KOLM

Institute of Public Economics, School for Advanced Studies in the Social Sciences

Contents

Abstract	375
Part I: Facts and forms	376
1. Introduction	376
1.1. Evidence, scope, and motives of reciprocity	376
1.2. Social scope and values of reciprocity	378
1.3. Equality and fraternity: The two, three or four types of reciprocity	380
1.4. Reciprocity and the general motives for giving	382
1.5. Reciprocity and reciprocating good or bad	384
1.6. Understanding and explaining reciprocity	385
1.7. Organisation	386
2. The evidence, scope, and pervasiveness of the reciprocity relationship	387
2.1. Society as reciprocity and general respect	387
2.2. Relations of reciprocity	388
2.3. Extended reciprocities	389
2.4. Reciprocity and exchange and markets	391
2.5. Reciprocity and organizations and labour	392
2.6. Established groups, cooperatives, associations	393
2.7. Reciprocity and community	393
2.8. Public aid	394
2.9. Intergenerational reciprocities	395
2.10. Evidence and history	395
3. Reciprocity as the quintessential sociality and social bond	397
4. Definitions, givings and exchanges	398
4.1. Concepts and distinctions	398
4.1.1. Person, agent, actor, individual, etc.	398
4.1.2. Action, conduct, behaviour, motives, preference	398

Handbook of the Economics of Giving, Altruism and Reciprocity, Volume 1
Edited by Serge-Christophe Kolm and Jean Mercier Ythier
Copyright © 2006 Elsevier B.V. All rights reserved
DOI: 10.1016/S1574-0714(06)01006-2

4.1.3. Gift-giving	398
4.1.4. Types and effects of gifts, refusing gifts	399
4.2. Motives for giving, notably in reciprocity	400
4.2.1. A wide variety of motives, from best to worst	400
4.2.2. Benevolent giving	401
4.2.3. Neutral giving	403
4.2.4. Giving, inequality and status	405
4.3. Sequential exchange	408
5. Reciprocities: Forms and structures	411
5.1. Facts and relations	411
5.2. Reciprocal structures	411
5.2.1. Basic structure	411
5.2.2. Extended reciprocities	412
5.2.3. Generalized and general reciprocity	413
5.2.4. Causes of extended and notably general and generalized reciprocities	413
5.2.5. Reverse reciprocity and the Descartes effect	415
5.2.6. Chain reciprocities	415
5.3. Larger reciprocities	416
5.4. Reciprocity as social or economic system	417
5.5. Reciprocity, revenge, reciprocation	418
5.6. Reciprocity as giving or as reciprocation	420
Part II: Motives	421
6. Motives: The three worlds of reciprocity	421
6.1. Three basic reasons	421
6.2. An outlook of the general structure	423
6.3. Comparative, matching, compensatory, or balance reciprocity	424
6.3.1. The propriety of reciprocity	424
6.3.2. The basic motives of balance reciprocity	425
6.3.3. The inconveniences of imbalance	426
6.3.4. A social sentiment	427
6.3.5. Refusing and revenge	428
6.4. Liking reciprocities	429
6.4.1. Introduction	429
6.4.2. Reciprocities in giving and in liking	430
6.4.3. Basic phenomena	430
6.4.4. The various reasons for liking to be given to	430
6.4.5. Causal likings	431
6.4.6. Gratitude	432
6.4.7. The existential value of being the object of attention, approval, and liking	432
6.4.8. Slave or master of one's passions	433
6.4.9. Liking giver	434
6.4.10. Reciprocal liking	434

6.4.11. All liking effects	437
6.4.12. Imitation, contagion, conforming	437
6.4.13. Interdependent and dynamic liking	438
6.4.14. Asymmetry	439
6.4.15. Conclusion	439
6.5. Continuation reciprocity	439
6.6. Comparing the three polar motives of reciprocity	441
6.7. Relational, process, status, or symbolic reciprocities	441
6.8. Imitation and conforming	442
6.9. The graph of reciprocity	442
6.10. The six basic reciprocations	443
6.11. The motives of extended reciprocations	443
7. Reciprocity and other social sentiments	444
7.1. Fairness, equity, justice	444
7.1.1. Balance reciprocity and justice, equality, retribution, compensation	445
7.1.2. Reciprocal fairness	446
7.1.3. From reciprocal fairness to distributive justice	447
7.2. The principle of universalization: the categorical imperative	448
7.3. Other social sentiments	449
8. Reciprocity in the modes of economic realization	449
Part III: Values and reasons	**453**
9. The values of reciprocity	453
9.1. The issues	453
9.2. General respect and sociability from reciprocity	455
9.3. Reciprocal corrections of market failures	456
9.3.1. Reciprocal solutions for correcting market failures	456
9.3.2. Sequential relation	457
9.3.3. Reciprocities and public goods or collective actions	458
9.3.4. Reciprocities as correcting or superficially creating economic or social inefficiencies	463
9.4. Reciprocity in trust, relational capital, and efficiency	465
9.5. The intrinsic values of reciprocity	467
10. Normative uses of reciprocity	468
10.1. The values of reciprocity	468
10.2. Cooperatives	469
10.3. General rules of society	469
10.4. Putative reciprocities	470
10.5. Macrojustice	470
10.6. The Good Society: The classical scientific directing utopia	471
11. How and why? Understanding and explaining reciprocity	472
11.1. Understanding	472
11.2. Biology?	475

11.3. Social and cultural evolution	478
11.3.1. Motives and behaviour	478
11.3.2. Choice and influence	478
11.3.3. Efficiency and values of modes	479
11.3.4. Processes of social selection of modes of relation	479
11.3.5. Education and development	481

Part IV: Formal analysis and interaction — 482

12. Formal analysis of reciprocity	482
12.1. Methodology	482
12.2. Comparative, matching, or balance reciprocities	486
12.2.1. Reciprocitarian comparative sentiments	486
12.2.2. Basic concepts of comparative reciprocity	487
12.2.3. Neutrality	488
12.2.4. Structures of imbalance	490
12.2.5. Choice	490
12.3. Liking-reciprocity	492
12.3.1. Liking-reciprocity and comparative reciprocity	492
12.3.2. The sentiments of liking-reciprocity	492
12.3.3. The interrelations of liking-reciprocity	498
12.3.4. The economics of liking-reciprocity	499
13. Strategic interaction and process preferences: Games of reciprocity and their consequences	504
13.1. Presentation	504
13.1.1. Objects of preferences	504
13.1.2. Interaction and solution	506
13.2. General properties about processes	508
13.2.1. General preferences	508
13.2.2. Dyadic processes	510
13.3. Solutions of the return-gift and reciprocity games	513
13.3.1. The three solution concepts	513
13.3.2. The quantitative case	516
13.4. Comparison of reciprocities with other processes	520

Part V: Reciprocity in economics — 521

14. Reciprocity in economics	522
14.1. A short overview and a corrected bias	522
14.2. Completing economics	526

References	529
Further reading	534

Abstract

Reciprocity is one of the main basic social relations that constitute societies. It consists of being favourable to others because others are favourable to you (and not from an exchange in the strict sense). It rests on three possible rationales: (1) balance (comparison, matching), often related to equality and fairness, or to the desire to avoid moral indebtedness; (2) liking because being purposefully favoured induces liking which induces favouring, or because liking can directly result from being liked; (3) self-sustaining sequences of mutual favours, which can be solely self-interested (and are not in fact proper reciprocity). Reciprocity extends to important cases of aids inducing aids that are not strictly reciprocal. It has essential social roles in permitting general peace in freedom and respect of rights, the decentralized correction of many "market failures", the efficient working of organizations of all types through mutual trust and support, and basic relations between individuals and collectivities and governments. It constitutes the essential relation in families and genuine cooperatives, and it is present in all communities. It explains deviations from competitive equilibria, and it is closely involved in questions of development. The theory of reciprocity shows and compares the various types of solutions of the reciprocity game. Reciprocity is compared with other modes of transfers. Ways of explaining it are proposed. Its normative uses associate efficiency, fairness, and the intrinsic quality of social relations.

Keywords

reciprocity, gift-giving, transfers, altruism, fairness, balance, matching, compensation, liking, social relation, family, market failures

JEL classification: A13, C72, D61, D62, D63, D64, H23, H41, J22, J41, J53, J54, L14, O12, P13, P40, Z13

"Of all the persons, however, whom nature points out for our peculiar beneficence, there are none to whom it seems more properly directed than to those whose beneficence we have ourselves already experienced. Nature, which formed men for that mutual kindness, so necessary for their happiness, renders every man the peculiar object of kindness, to the persons to whom he himself has been kind."

Adam Smith. *The Theory of Moral Sentiments* (VI, 2, 1).

"Give and you will be given to."
Luke

Part I: Facts and forms

1. Introduction[1]

1.1. Evidence, scope, and motives of reciprocity

In his *Essay on the Gift* (1924) – one of the most influential founding works of the social science – Marcel Mauss (calls reciprocity "one of the human rocks on which societies are built". L.T. Hobhouse (1906) sees in reciprocity "the vital principle of society", while, for Richard Thurnwald (1921), "the principle or reciprocity is the basis on which the entire social and ethical life of civilizations rests". And Georg Simmel adds: "Social equilibrium and cohesion could not exist without the reciprocity of service and return service. All contacts among men rest on the scheme of giving and returning the equivalence".

Reciprocity is treating others as they treat you, because of this very fact and not as the result of some agreed upon or expected exchange (this will be explained in detail). This basic, polymorphic, and pervasive pattern of human social conduct is one of the few fundamental interactions that constitute societies, and, although it mobilizes most aspects of human social experience, its elementary forms closely relate to the other basic bonds of fairness, altruism, and joint interest.[2]

---

[1] This chapter draws largely on the translation of sections of the book of 1984 *La Bonne Economie, La Réciprocité Générale*. It intends to be complementary to the other chapters of the present volume concerned with reciprocity, notably Chris Hahn's presentation of the long history of the analysis of reciprocity in economic anthropology, Ernst Fehr's and Klaus Schmidt's presentation of recent laboratory experiments and of a few models different from the one retained here, Luc Arrondel and André Masson's presentation of the new economics of the family, Julio Rotemberg's analysis of the importance and role of reciprocity in the workplace, Louis Putterman's presentation of the economics of cooperatives, and the interpretation and foundation of the welfare state from reciprocitarian sentiments by Christiana Fong, Samuel Bowles, and Herbert Gintis. This chapter also relates to most of the other chapters, even when they are concerned with giving and altruism that are not specifically reciprocities.

[2] The basic logical relations between these social sentiments will be pointed out shortly. Essentially, empathy makes one be interested in the interest of others in altruism (Adam Smith, John Stuart Mill). This also leads

The existence, extent, importance and forms of reciprocity are obvious. Indeed, you tend to give in return when you receive a gift or favour, and to hit back when harmed. You tend to like people who like you (and you need to be so positively considered, especially by people you consider). You tend to respect persons and properties if other people respect your person and your property. You tend to like people who benevolently give something to you or help you, and also to be grateful towards them, and this tends to induce you to aid them or give them gifts in turn. You may also feel morally indebted towards people who give something to you, or help or favour you, and this may induce you to give something in return, sometimes for relieving a situation felt as a burden – a motive thoroughly different from the foregoing one. You generally resent being hurt, and this may lead you to hurt back in revenge (you also tend to dislike people who hurt you, but mere disliking usually does not induce hurting – in contrast to giving because of liking; and in a similar contrast, being disliked does not induce disliking as being liked tends to induce liking). You tend to trust people who trust you (trustful people tend to be trustworthy – because trustworthy people tend to think others are like them).

It is well documented that you tend to be helpful if you have been helped – even by people different from those you help (this classical "helping behaviour" is called "generalized reciprocity"). Symmetrically, the plea that offenders were themselves victims of crime in their youth is one of the most common lines of defence in court cases. Both the philosopher René Descartes and Adam Smith discuss the opposite fact that people who tend to help others tend to be helped by still others (at least, they deserve it) – this is called "reverse reciprocity". This may be implied by "give and you will be given to" (Luke). Similarly, people often tend to treat fair people fairly and rude people rudely.

You may also give in return in order to induce further gifts in your favour, but since a new gift induced in this way is made in expectation of another reward, this has a priori to be the start of a foreseen endless "sequential exchange". This relation can be strictly self-interested, and it is indeed a type of exchange rather than reciprocity proper as the foregoing cases, because you only "give" under the threat of not being "given" to later (then, the terms "give" and "gifts" are not really proper). You may also hit back as retaliation in order to deter further harms; this is motivationally similar to the former case but formally the opposite since it stops the relation rather than extending it.

Reciprocity as *a set of motivationally interrelated gifts* or favours is considered and studied by a long and rich tradition in the social science. Hence, the term *reciprocation* came to be used to also include revenge and retaliation which are only very partially the "harmful" mirror image of reciprocity (liking in return, or giving in return because one came to like the benefactor, have no such negative mirror image, as we will see).[3]

---

to impartiality which, with rationality in its most elementary sense ("for a reason"), requires equity (the Latin word for equality). And altruism and equality entail the two basic pure forms of reciprocity, liking reciprocity and balance reciprocity.

[3] Uses of the concept of reciprocity with mention or consideration of the particular relation, sentiments, or motivations can for instance be found in Morelly (1755, 1953) (the sentiment being gratitude), Proudhon (1853), and Hobhouse (1906). Whether Adam Smith's use of the terms reciprocity and mutuality in *The*

1.2. Social scope and values of reciprocity

Attentive observation of life in society shows how pervasive, important, and sometimes essential reciprocity is in it.[4]

A family is neither a *pater familias* (*à la* Becker) nor an exchange (*à la* Chiappori), but a dense and intense network of various reciprocities in sentiments and conduct, where commands and exchanges are in fact embedded in larger relations of reciprocity.[5]

Communities of all kinds imply reciprocities among their members, and often among members and the community as such. In fact, reciprocity and sense of community (with various possible intensities) are very closely related.

All working groups use reciprocities of mutual services of aid and of information, and often could not function without them. The most efficient teams, firms, and societies are often those where reciprocities are the most developed. Firms have various types of reciprocities among peers and across hierarchies. Reciprocities at the workplace are pervasive and necessary.[6]

The existence of a globally peaceful and free society owes much to reciprocity. People generally respect others and their rights and properties, even when these other persons are weaker and the police is absent (one cannot put a policeman behind each of us). Yet, they would or could not do this if they were not themselves so respected in their person, rights, and properties. In particular, such a general reciprocal respect of rights and properties is necessary for the existence and possibility of a working market. General sociality – politeness, small help, and so on – also results from the same reciprocitarian motives: people would generally not so behave towards others if they were not themselves similarly treated. This is also the case for more intense aid: people help others in need more when they are so aided themselves (this is the much studied "helping behaviour", a classical favourite topic of social psychology).

When, for some reason, the market "fails", the most common correctors and efficient substitutes rely on a variety of reciprocitarian motives such as matching (or balance) reciprocity or reciprocal promise-keeping for paying one's due in the absence of enforceable contracts, reciprocal trust for remedying lack of information and incomplete

---

Theory of Social Sentiments (1759) refers to reciprocity proper or to purely self-interested exchanges has been hotly debated (see Danner, 1973). The emphasis on reciprocity as an economic system is basically due to Thurnwald, the anthropologist student of Carl Menger, in *Die Gemeinde der Banaro* (1921) and a number of later books. This has largely been followed in anthropology. The concept of reciprocity is also much used in sociology (see, for instance, the works of G. Simmel, H. Becker (1956), or A. Gouldner (1960)). Forms of reciprocitarian conduct are favourite topics of social psychology. We will point out that the analysis, modeling, and applications of reciprocity in economics also goes back a long way. Finally, the term reciprocity is, of course, used here as it is by the tradition in the social science, namely a set of motivationally interrelated gifts, a priori different from self-interested exchange, but less scientifically careful uses of terms have used them in all directions (for instance, calling reciprocity a particular exchange or exchange a particular reciprocity).

[4] I can only warmly recommend the excellent and very informed recent survey of the scope of the economy of reciprocity "Between the gift and the market: the economy of regard", by Avner Offer (1997).

[5] See Kolm 1984a and 1997b, and the chapters of Part II of this Handbook.

[6] See Julio Rotemberg (1994) and Chapter 21 in this book.

contracts and markets, or reciprocal joint free contributions to public goods (reciprocity transforms a prisoner's dilemma into a coordination game, and such a contribution is also a gift to the other beneficiaries of the good).[7] In all such cases, owing to the social interaction of reciprocity, failing to pursue self-interest is favourable to self-interest, and, in this sense, it is rational to be irrational.

Vast public transfers are largely accepted in some societies both because they manifest reciprocities in case of need and because they constitute joint contributions for helping the needy (a kind of public good). The same societies often strongly support the "chain reciprocity" of "pay-as-you-go" pension systems where one generation supports ageing people of the previous generation, given that it will itself be so supported later (and pensioners have themselves paid for the pensions of others). Financing the public education of the young has an analogous rationale.

Moreover, reciprocity is commonly seen as one type of economic system – along with market exchange and command –, given that most actual economic regimes are compounds of the three in various proportions and according to various arrangements. Smaller societies work essentially as systems of reciprocity.

Finally, with regard to the overall quality of a society, of relations in it, and of its members themselves, reciprocity is the only alternative to oppressive command, selfish exchange, and the utopia of widespread unconditional altruism. Although social control, social pressure and stringent or oppressive norms can impose one type of reciprocity (balance or matching) in small groups, such obligations are found neither for many cases of this type, nor for other types of reciprocity, and generally not beyond such groups. Hence, reciprocity is necessarily central to genuine social improvement. Indeed, all social philosophers and reformers with some breadth of vision have seen this for millennia. For this reason also, an ideal of a larger role for good reciprocity has been and is the inspiration and the hope (the "directing utopia") of important social movements. However, normative social science can analyse the possibilities of this idea and of its implementation.

Reciprocity thus appears as one of the basic interaction forces that keep a bundle of individuals into a society, along with a shared culture and mutual self-interest (however, they all rest on more basic facts such as interest, imitation, liking, comparison, status, fairness, communication, etc.). This explains why it has been one of the few central concepts of the social science, although with different emphases in the various disciplines. It has been the central concept of anthropology for almost a century. Social psychology has extensively studied important instances of reciprocity, essentially by the means of a variety of experiments. General sociology has commonly considered reciprocity. Economics has analysed the relation of reciprocity and applied the results for a long time, although this has not entered (yet) into the most commonly used tools of the discipline. In this field, the analysis of reciprocity and use of the resulting concepts is a main contribution to the much needed general progress towards a more realistic psychology than that of the caricature called the "economic man".

---

[7] These issues will be analysed in Section 7.3.

1.3. Equality and fraternity: The two, three or four types of reciprocity

This short list of manifestations of reciprocity provides a glimpse of the extent, properties, and varieties of this phenomenon. The variety exists but is limited by the fact that reciprocity rests on basic types of motivations that are quite different but are very few in number. There are in fact two types, *balance-reciprocity* (or *comparative* or *matching* reciprocity) and *liking-reciprocity* which is itself of two different types, *liking the liker* or *reciprocal liking* (a reciprocity of sentiments) and *liking the benevolent giver*. In addition, *continuation reciprocity* leads to the relation of sequential exchange and has retaliation for deterrence as negative counterpart, and both reactions can be purely self-interested. These pure reciprocitarian motives can more or less be jointly present.

In *comparative*, *matching*, or *balance reciprocity*, you (and possibly others) feel that a gift or favour you receive from some agent has broken the balance of some previous state of affairs, and that you should give in return a "return-gift" of similar value so as to restore the balance. This return giving results from a social judgment, felt as being above your own will and desire (Kant's "inclinations"), held by you and also possibly by other people, possibly including the initial giver. You may also be concerned by the judgment of others. This return giving is thus considered something to do or that you should do, proper behaviour, sometimes a duty. This motive is deontic (deontological). Providing this return-gift is often a social norm. It can be backed by a sentiment of justice, fairness, or equity, related to the aspect of equality in value of the two acts or transfers. While this return is not provided, this social sentiment, which you generally endorse or care for, holds that you are morally indebted towards the initial giver. This tends to elicit in you a sentiment of dependency, sometimes of inferiority, and, in "strong" cases, sentiments of shame or guilt. The return gift redeems more or less this moral indebtedness.

In contrast, in *liking reciprocity* the motive of your giving to the initial giver is that you like her – with any degree of liking, from caring about to love. Yet, you may like this person because she gives something to you or because she likes you. This makes two very different cases called gift-induced liking and reciprocal liking, respectively. However, they can be quite intermingled. Indeed, first, these two cases have a common reason in the value you attach to other people's attention towards yourself, especially when this attention is appreciative and kind, due to the fact that this attention fosters your sense of self and of social existence. Second, you really like someone because she gives something to you only if the final intention of this giving is to benefit you, which may result from her liking you. Moreover, in reciprocal liking, giving can be a means to show and prove one's liking in order to be liked in return, by a subtle process that will be considered in detail: in short, the other person tends to like you more if she knows you like her, and you want more to be liked by her the more you like her, and therefore your desire to show your liking proves it. These relations involve various types of liking, issues of responsibility, and questions about the formation of sentiments. They will be analysed in Section 6.3, but can be summarised here.

In *gift-induced liking*, you like the giver as benefactor (and not only as you like a thing or a person for another reason) because she has given you something benevolently, i.e., with the final aim of benefiting you. Then, you may like to receive this gift or favour for several reasons. One is simply the gift or favour you receive. Moreover, you are bound to like the attention shown by the giving, especially since it is appreciative of yourself and kind: this fosters your sense of self and of social existence, a most essential value. And you may also like the kind intercourse in the process of giving. Your liking these facts makes you like the giver who is responsible for them. Then, you are bound to give something to her because you like her.

In contrast, in *reciprocal liking* you tend to like people who like you (a priori irrespective of any giving), this may be reciprocal, and each liking can induce giving. This reciprocity is of sentiments (liking). The process by which you tend to like people who like you is rather subtle. You generally like to be liked, particularly by people you care about and hence, in particular, by people you like, because it is agreeable and, more deeply, because their implied attention towards yourself fosters your essential sense of self and of social existence, especially since it is appreciative of yourself and kind. This tends to make you like people who like you by two categories of effects.

First, you like the person who likes you because you like to be liked and you like the causes of what you like. This causal liking, in itself, is what makes you like the apple tree because of the apples and your coat because of its warmth. In addition, however, this cause is a person. Yet, causally liking a person for a fact makes a particularly large difference if this person both is responsible for the fact and intends to favour you in choosing it. In addition, these conditions make it possible that you are grateful towards this other person for liking you, and your gratitude is favourable to your liking this person. Now, the responsibility of the other person for her sentiment of liking you is ambiguous because it depends on her possibility of avoiding this sentiment or getting rid of it. The classical ways of wilfully influencing one's sentiments by focussing or diverting attention and by reasoning exist but have limits; in fact, the issue of responsibility in this respect is even conceptually thorny (for instance, *akrasia* or weakness of the will is a common obstacle to changing one's sentiments, and you are responsible for it if it is considered outside the will which could overcome it, whereas you are not if it is counted as a given property of the will).[8] Moreover, in so far as the other person is responsible for liking you, hence can wilfully influence this sentiment of hers, she hardly does this because you like it (she is bound to do it more because you like her through the various effects considered here in reversing the roles). Hence your *directly* liking the other person because she likes you exists but is limited.

However, a second series of effects intervene in the same sense. As suggested above, your sense of self and of social existence induced by someone liking you is larger the more you care about this person's view, hence in particular the more you care about this person in general, and notably the more you like her. Moreover, a number of pleasurable effects of being liked are the stronger the more you like the person who likes you.

---

[8] The general question of responsibility for one's tastes, preferences, or sentiments, is analysed in Kolm 2004, Chapter 6.

As a result, by a process which has both unconscious and conscious elements, and involuntary and wilful aspects, implying creation and transfers of attention and emotion, this tends to make you adjust your sentiments towards liking people who like you and – *ceteris paribus* – liking more people who like you more.

In addition, gifts are not only given directly because of liking, but also in order to show and prove liking. They do this because the giver wants all the more to show this, for pleasing the other and most importantly in order to be liked in return by her, that she in fact likes the other in the first place.

There are thus three worlds of reciprocity, *comparison* (*balance*, *matching*), *liking*, and *continuation* (notably for *self-interest*). They can be jointly present with some restrictions – notably, strong liking excludes comparison (love does not count) and self-interest, but milder liking does not (*les bons comptes font les bons amis* – good accounting makes good friends). These three worlds also associate by pairs, each in opposition to the other world. The duty of balance is opposed to the hedonistic or interested consequences of pleasing oneself or people one likes. The altruism of liking is opposed to favouring the interest or the social position (balance) of the ego. And self-interest is opposed to the social concerns of altruistic likings and of balance.

In the end, the three reciprocities respectively relate to the three basic social relations: fairness, altruism, and joint interest.

1.4. Reciprocity and the general motives for giving

Since reciprocity constits of gifts, it should relate to the general motives for giving. The characteristic aspect is that this should be the case for the return gift. The Introduction of this volume (Chapter 1) includes an exhaustive presentation of the motives for giving. These motives divide in two: altruistic giving and non-altruistic giving. The motives for altruism and for non-altruistic giving are presented in Chapter 1 in Sections 13 and 15, and epitomized in Tables 1 and 2, respectively. Liking reciprocity is based largely on altruism and altruistic giving of the hedonistic or natural variety and, in it, on the affective type which is affection or the milder sympathy (in the common sense) or on the pure hedonistic type which is either empathy or emotional contagion. Indeed, being liked or receiving a benevolent gift can elicit affection or sympathy towards the benefactor. Gratitude is an aspect of this. Being liked or given to can also elicit an interest for the giver which may be favourable to feeling empathy towards her. Moreover, being liked tends to elicit a mirror-image emotional contagion in liking the liker. Yet, some normative altruism may also play a role because there may be a moral value, or a non-moral social value, that praises reciprocal liking (liking the person who likes you). Finally, giving in a liking reciprocity can also aim at the social relation, for maintaining it, showing or proving liking or love, or enjoying the very process and intercourse of giving.

Balance-reciprocity results from both altruistic and non-altruistic motives for giving. Its altruistic base refers to a sense of fairness which results from empathy plus rationality. Its non-altruistic base refers to the maintenance of relative social balance and in particular social positions.

This sense of due balance induces the receiver of a gift or favour to give in return for restoring some social balance which is felt as having been disturbed by the initial gift. This motive sees giving in return as a kind of propriety or duty. It is also often considered a social value or a norm. Then, it can in particular be supported by the judgments of other people or of "society in general", which are approval (or simply an absence of disapproval) or praise. Personal sentiment and social opinion can also judge disagreeably situations of moral indebtedness that the return gift can prevent or suppress.

Moreover, empathy towards other people induces you to take an impartial point of view putting them and yourself on the same footing. Then, rationality in the mildest sense of "for a reason" provides a requirement of equality, justice, and fairness.[9] Balance-reciprocity is an application of this sentiment of required equality to interpersonal relations. Note that in the last stage of the moral development of children described by the psychologist Jean Piaget (1932), interaction with peers leads to an empathetic awareness of them which induces a sense of justice and reciprocity. However, empathy is usually only partial (except in the smallest family circle) and, as a result, both impartiality and distinct self-interest are usually present in people's views – they interact in various ways, often relating to different types of actions (e.g., individual and the political implementation of allocative justice), or with some compromise.

It is noteworthy that Adam Smith explains moral sentiments and conducts from a particular phenomenon in the family of reciprocity. Indeed, he sees the person as imagining an external observer who, from empathy for this person, experiences sentiments parallel to hers but weaker. The person then feels in turn empathy for this external observer and, hence, feels her sentiments which parallel her original ones but in a weaker form. This induces the person to act with the corresponding restraint. One can add that the external observer also feels empathy for the other persons, which leads the person in question to take care of others in an actual altruism. This view of the external observer, and, hence, of the person, will in particular be impartial. Smith summarizes his derivation of personal morality from reciprocal empathy and just impartiality as the turning over of the Christian principle "love your neighbour as you love yourself" into "the great precept of nature to love ourselves as we love our neighbour, or what comes to the same thing, as our neighbour is capable of loving us" (*The Theory of Moral Sentiments*, I.i.5.5).

Finally, continuation reciprocity and sequential exchange are typical gift-giving motivated by self-interest.

There results in particular that the full explanation of altruism, sense of justice, and reciprocities essentially rests, after the specification of the psychological mechanisms and taking the motive of self-interest for granted, on the explanation of very general mental facts and capacities such as empathy, emotional contagion, and rationality. If one wants to resort to explanation by evolution (including of biology and of social forms, and selection mechanisms), these general social mental phenomena should be the first objects to explain.

---

[9] See notably Kolm 1971, English translation 1998, Foreword, Section 5.

1.5. Reciprocity and reciprocating good or bad

We have seen that behind the apparent symmetry between reciprocating favourable and unfavourable acts lie, in fact, deep dissymmetries. The similitudes and differences depend primarily on the type of reciprocity, and the most striking is the quasi-absence of negative sentiments, acts and relations that would be symmetrical to liking reciprocities, for two reasons: your disliking someone neither induces you to hurt her nor induces her to dislike you.

Disliking someone does not induce you to hurt her, at least as liking tends to induce you to give or to favour. It may have such an effect in the extreme case of hating, and even in this case the reason generally refers to a cause of the hatred felt and to the harm done that induces it, and the hurting has a dimension of balance such as revenge – which is a different rationale. Hence, you generally dislike someone responsible for a harm you incur, but this disliking *in itself* is generally not a cause of hurting in return. The balance motive of answering harm with harm is something else, although it is then intrinsically accompanied by disliking (this motive is not retaliation for deterrence, which is still another reason).

Moreover, if someone dislikes you, or even hates you, this generally does not induce you to dislike (or hate) her, but, rather, to ignore her. This does not either induce her to hurt you, as with giving in the opposite case of liking. (Indeed, pursuing the comparison, first, she would not enjoy your resulting dislike of her; and second, if this harm is information about her sentiment, her disliking you would not elicit your disliking her, and even if it did she would not enjoy being disliked, even by someone she dislikes.)

As far as sentiments are concerned, resentment towards people responsible for harm you incur has some symmetrical analogy with gratitude, but giving for showing and proving one's gratefulness has no symmetrical counterpart in hurting for showing resentment.

The symmetry is closer with balance reciprocity. The analogue to return-giving is revenge, with vengefulness being the analogue to the sentiment of moral indebtedness. The requirement of balance, of evening out, and the sentiments of duty, desert or merit, and justice, are present in both cases.

We saw that retaliation for deterrence is in the family of continuation reciprocity and can have similar motives. However, successful continuation reciprocity expands the relation, a priori indefinitely, whereas successful retaliation for deterrence stops it (although peace can be seen as sequential gifts consisting of abstention from harming).

Our focus here will be on acts, sentiments or attitudes favourable to others, because they are much more important at the overall social level, they play a crucial role in the constitution of societies, they can underlie social systems, they carry an intrinsic normative value in supporting altruism and implementing fairness, they have a major importance in the working of the economy and of political systems, and they are related to the other topics of this volume, altruism and giving. In its common use, notably as one of the central classical concepts of the social science, the term reciprocity is restricted to these favourable, pro-other, actions, attitudes and relations. We will thus follow this long tradition here, and use the term *reciprocation* for covering both types of relations, favourable and hostile. Hence, reciprocation encompasses reciprocity plus revenge and retaliation for deterrence.

1.6. Understanding and explaining reciprocity

The outline of the social scope of reciprocity presented above shows its overwhelming overall importance. It is thus very important to understand it, for understanding society and notably its economy, possibly for forecasting aspects of it, and certainly for improving it through social design and reform of its institutions and regulation and by way of all forms of education. In Section 1.4, we saw that all of reciprocity is ultimately explained by more basic phenomena such as self-interest and pleasure, sense of self and of social existence, empathy, emotional contagion, and rationality (which notably explain altruism and fairness). However, we also want to know when reciprocity appears, what are its consequences, and the modalities of this social interaction. Then, understanding reciprocity begins with understanding it psychologically, since human conduct and action derive from motivating sentiments and reasons, and reciprocal liking is directly a reciprocity of sentiments. Fortunately, we do not need to study human psychology from the outside, as chemistry (in laboratory experiments) or as animal behaviour, since the permanent contact with ourselves and others whom we understand during the decades of our life has given us the information we need.[10] This field of information is much more than simple "introspection", given the overdeveloped capacity of humans for empathy and compassion. Only our own experience can show us the meaning of basic terms such as liking, gratitude, resentment, moral indebtedness, vengefulness, or the sentiment of unfairness or injustice. Yet, all the information is relevant for knowing when such sentiments appear, under which conditions, how they relate to other sentiments, and what they lead one to do. The relevant analysis of the phenomena under consideration (reciprocities) then results from close and intelligent (as far as possible) consideration of this information, with the relevant distinctions, discernment, thought experiments in imagining oneself (or others) in the relevant situation, and so on. The obtained relations between sentiments, and sentiments and acts, are then fruitfully gathered in a formal model which can analyse their interactions. Individuals' choice of actions – here giving or helping – are often fruitfully considered as resulting from some ordering or ordinal utility function. The analysis of the structure and relevant variables and parameters of

---

[10] Laboratory experiments of reciprocity have a long history, with an upsurge from the 1960's for the analysis of so-called "helping behaviour" (shortly explained). More recent laboratory experiments of reciprocity and more or less related "behaviour" are excellently presented in two contributions to this volume, the chapters by Ernst Fehr and Klaus Schmidt, and by Louis Lévy-Garboua, Claude Meidinger and Benoit Rapoport. Although experiments that solely concluded "there exists reciprocity" added no information, the more developed ones can usefully, or importantly, contribute, although only as complements and means to the psychological analysis that provides the understanding, explanation and meaning of the phenomenon (an analysis that should not be simplistic, arbitrary, or partial, or use undefined or vague concepts).

this ordering or function raises relevant questions about the interactions of the relevant facts. These putatively maximizing individual conducts then permit the analysis of individuals' strategic interactions in the mode of game theory. However, concepts and structures usually absent from game theory will have a foremost importance in such "games of reciprocity", such as preferences about the type of social relation, or various aspects of notions of fairness. One can thus explain reciprocities and their effects, and evaluate their consequences (for instance concerning satisfaction, efficiencies, and equities). The obtained results can then be used for explaining and evaluating a number of social facts, in the field of organizations, economic intercourse, the firm, the family, political systems, social and economic change, and so on.

1.7. Organisation

These ideas are developed in this chapter with the following organisation. The reader need not strictly follow this order of presentation, depending on her interest. For instance, the analysis of reciprocity can focus on its various types and their psychology in Section 6, on their formal analysis in Section 11, and on that of the reciprocitarian interaction in Section 12.

Section 2 presents in greater detail the general evidence about reciprocity, its scope, and its various types, characteristics, conditions, and consequences.

Section 3 notes that reciprocity appears in fact as the main bond and interaction constitutive of a society.

Section 4 presents basic facts and concepts necessary for the analysis of reciprocity, in particular giving and its large variety of motives, and the case of sequential exchange.

Sections 5 and 6 present respectively the structure and forms, and the motives, of reciprocities. Reciprocity is a relation between acts, sentiments or attitudes towards other people, of several individuals. It can have a variety of forms described in Section 5, including direct reciprocity; extended reciprocities such as generalized and general reciprocities, reverse reciprocities, and chain reciprocities; larger reciprocitarian interactions; and reciprocity as social and economic systems. The comparison with "negative" reciprocations is also closely considered.

The central issue of the various motives for reciprocity is the topic of Section 6. The reasons and rationales for reciprocity divide in three very different and contrasting categories which are analysed. One type rests on comparison, matching or balance of the acts (or sentiments), and on avoiding moral indebtedness. A second category rests on liking and can be either reciprocating because of liking or reciprocal liking. Reciprocity of the third type aims at inducing continuation of the relation for a reason which can be purely self-interested. The processes of liking reciprocities rest on particularly subtle – although profound – relations among sentiments.

In Section 7, the motives of reciprocity are compared with and related to other social sentiments, such as fairness and the categorical imperative.

In Section 8, reciprocity is compared with the other modes of economic realization, standard exchange, pure gift giving, and taking by force, with respect to issues of freedom and altruism.

The values of reciprocity are presented in Section 9. They include general respect and sociality. They also include the various ways in which reciprocities palliate market failures, notably in ending sequential relations, in inducing voluntary provision of non-excludable public goods through a series of different rationales, and in replacing information and impossible contracts by the particular reciprocity in trust which is a main source of social efficiency. Finally, the intrinsic value of many reciprocities, due to their properties of mutual liking and fairness, has a major social importance.

For these reasons, reciprocity has an important normative role in the setting of social forms such as genuine cooperatives, in general institutional design, and in moral education, as shown in Section 10.

Section 11 discusses the issue of understanding and explaining reciprocities. Reflection about human experience provides the understanding of motives and the explanation of acts from them. Specific motives are explained by cultural and social evolution (including competition), and one can suggest biological evolutionary explanations for the broad general background. Models of social interaction explain and judge the final outcomes of reciprocities of various types and of other social processes, which intervene in the actual selection of their processes.

Section 12 then constructs the basis of the formal analysis of reciprocity, in distinguishing balance (comparative, matching) reciprocity and the various forms of liking reciprocity. Motives are finally summarised as preferences about choices.

The effects of the interactions of reciprocity are then analysed in Section 13. An important feature is the presence of preference about processes of interaction, along with preferences about allocations and about the acts or transferred items. Various solutions of the game are also considered, some representing procedural fairness. Apparent allocative inefficiencies may be superseded by the intrinsic value of the processes. The effects of various reciprocities and other processes (e.g., exchange) are then compared with respect to the achieved transfers and allocations, and individuals' preferences. These conclusions are notably important for understanding and evaluating processes of "development".

Finally, Section 14 focuses on the relations between reciprocity and economics. It notes the economic analyses of reciprocity, including the recent upsurge of interest, and shows how the consideration of reciprocity is necessary in most fields of economics.

2. The evidence, scope, and pervasiveness of the reciprocity relationship

2.1. Society as reciprocity and general respect

Society is reciprocity. This is one of the deepest and most fruitful way of seeing it, as it emphasises both that society is made up of individuals (and groups) and that these are essentially interrelated by direct, deep, and primary sentiments with the triple dimension of reinforcing mutual affects, reciprocal equity, and joint interest. Rather than putting forward social wholes as holisms do, or the single individuals emphasized by atomisms, this view focuses on relations, relations between relations, and the social sentiments that underlie them. Life in society, indeed, can be seen as being, first of all, a dense network of reciprocities of various kinds. At least, it would and could not exist without this underlying relational structure. This is something you know and feel, sometimes enjoy, resent, or endure, and practice almost all the time. Sufficient awareness of this fact and its scope and modalities is straightforward and needs no more than a few remarks.

You live in various groups of people who, in different ways and degrees of importance, act favourably towards you, and towards whom you similarly act, including your family, your country, your workplace, and other people in general. In most cases, you would not have this favourable attitude if you did not benefit from that of others.

You generally respect people who respect you. Indeed, the result is a fair balance, and their respect makes them deserve yours and elicits *prima facie* benevolent sentiments toward them. Wilfully respecting people who do not respect you has an aspect of rare saintly conduct or of contradiction (or masochism) in supporting offences against oneself. By extension, in a society where people generally respect others, you generally respect others because still others have respected you and because respectful people deserve respect. There results the possibility of a peaceful society, given that people's strengths are quite different and there cannot be a policeman behind each of us. Thanks to reciprocity, a Hobbesian war of all against all and a police state are not the only two alternative possible ways of life in society. Applied to property rights, this reciprocal respect permits in particular the existence of the exchanges of a free market.

2.2. Relations of reciprocity

You like people who like you – most of the time. And you like to be liked by people you like – short of masochism. Being so considered and valued is essential to your sense of self and of social existence, the ontological need which is the most basic of basic needs.

"I will love he who loves me", an old song says.

You act favourably towards people you like and you like people who act favourably towards you when this effect is their final objective.

You are grateful towards people who help you. This makes you prone to help them in turn, and to like them.

You also often feel morally indebted towards people who make you a favour of any kind. You know they and possibly others often feel you are so indebted. You often feel like "paying your debt" to them. You also sometimes think you ought to. And this commonly leads you to return a favour re-establishing the moral balance (moral indebtedness sometimes also entitles the benefactor to ask a favour in return).

Yet, you also like being aided or given to for straightforward reasons: for the result; because this manifests concern and interest about you and in particular benevolent ones – which is good for your ego –; and because it establishes agreeable actual and symbolic social relations. Then, you tend to like the benevolent people so responsible for your pleasure, your social existence or your dignity. Moreover, you want to favour people you like. You like their situation being improved, their pleasure, their satisfaction, often their gratitude, their liking you more, and the relation between you. All this induces you to give or aid in return.

Inuit wisdom, which is expressed in proverbs, has two about giving, one for each base of these two motives for reciprocity. One dictum, the nice "friends make gifts and gifts make friends", only points out the noted positive feedback of altruistic sentiments and action in reciprocity from liking. Yet, a harsh, cold life does not grind out naïve people, as shown by their second giving proverb: "the gift makes the slave as the whip makes the dog".

You don't like being exploited, but you often prefer a fair deal to a good deal. And you tend to be fair towards people who are fair to you, thus transforming conflictual sharing into consensual fairness.

You doubtlessly forgive offences, love your enemy, present the other cheek, and return good for evil. But you know people who don't. You did not invent "an eye for an eye and a tooth for a tooth".

Many people can hardly avoid instinctively hitting back when they are hit. Balance, status, and deterrence are compressed into a spark of nervous influx. They are not so much unconscious but instinctual, although they are provided as explanation when asked. Even dogs bite back. Deterrence and status may have selected their genes for that (status gives a reproductive advantage, and there may also be selection of the trait of liking mates prone to self-defence who will transmit this character to the common offsprings, etc.). On the other hand, it took Alexandre Dumas's Count of Monte-Cristo a whole life of refined strategies to obey this primitive instinct, to take revenge and to do justice. In another kind of sophistication, Axelrod (1981) shows experimentally that tit-for-tat strategies (plus an initial favourable act) entail efficient cooperation; this can probably be explained by strategic rationality with its informational limits, but selection of behaviour of revenge and return-giving can also be imagined.

The return of favours or aid may simply aim at inducing more of them. The return of harm may be retaliation for deterrence. But these narrowly interested strategies are not the only motives for reciprocating. They are not the gut *social* feeling of man in society. The other motives are those properly called reciprocity and revenge.

2.3. Extended reciprocities

Moreover, you tend to be more polite towards polite people, more helpful towards helpful people, more carefully fair towards fair people – even if you are not the beneficiary of their virtue. This may be natural since they deserve it. This "reverse reciprocity" has been discussed for long. For example, both the philosopher René Descartes and Adam Smith think that people who give are given to, even by people who did not benefit from their acts – they even believe that these people will benefit more than the cost of their gift in the end.[11]

You are also more likely to be kind if you have been raised by loving parents. The opposite is the basis of the psychology of crime and the most heard of argument in courtrooms.

More generally, you tend to be more helpful if you have been aided (even if not by the people you aid). At least, this is the overwhelming conclusion of scores of experiments, systematic observations and inquiries by American social psychologists in the sixties and seventies. They focussed on this relation which they called "helping behaviour" after the ordeal of the young Kitty Genovese who, in 1964 in Queens, was stabbed to death and raped in sight of 32 onlookers none of whom tried to intervene or even called for help. This launched a nation-wide self-deprecating and soul-searching collective analysis, and these studies were the social psychologists' contribution (there also was a "public good" aspect: several onlookers thought others would call for help).[12]

Hence, you tend to help others if you have been helped yourself, to be nice if others have been nice to you, and so on, even if the people you help or favour are not those who favoured or helped you in the first place. And this is probably not only by sheer imitation of a behaviour that you have closely watched. This "generalized reciprocity" extends into "general reciprocity" when you see this relation as one between yourself and society, the group of others, or the "generalized other" as G.H. Mead puts it: you tend to treat them well because they (globally) have been nice or kind to you, no matter how instinctual or thoughtful, conscious or unconscious, this relation is.

Indeed, people in this situation commonly feel grateful or morally indebted toward society, the group of others, or the "generalized other". This gratefulness accounts for their favourable attitude toward these entities, and both gratefulness and indebtedness can account for their benevolent conduct.

Any dense society is a closely knit network of reciprocities. So is the family, an integrated complex of intense reciprocities of sentiments, givings and services (economists have often modelled "the household" as a single agent; but would you like to be married to those whose progress consists of seeing the family as an exchange contract between purely self-interested agents?).[13] So also is the workplace, and it would not work without the multifarious reciprocities of services, trust, respect, goodwill, and information

---

[11] R. Descartes, *Works*, IV, and A. Smith, *The Theory of Moral Sentiments*, VI, 2,1.

[12] See in particular the contributions to Macaulay and Berkowitz (1970), Berkowitz (1966, 1968, 1971), Berkowitz and Friedman (1967), Bryan and Test (1967), Doland and Adelberg (1967), Frisch and Greenberg (1968), Gergen, Gergen and Meter (1972), Goodstadt (1971), Goranson and Berkowitz (1966), Greenglass (1969), Handlon and Gross (1959), Harris (1967), Harris (1970), Hornstein (1970), Hornstein, Fisch and Holmes (1968), Latane and Darley (1970), Leventhal, Weiss and Long (1969), Midlarsky (1968), Pruitt (1968), Rosenhan (1969, 1970), Wilke and Lanzetta (1970), Wright (1942), and the more recent works of Hoffmann and Spitzer (1982), and Kaheman, Knetsch and Thaler (1986a, 1986b).

[13] See Kolm 1997a, and Chapter 14 by Luc Arrondel and André Masson in this Handbook.

2.4. Reciprocity and exchange and markets

Adam Smith was convinced by Parisian economists, if not to abandon the "moral sentiments" of his first major study, at least to propose that if you need meat, you should not expect it from your butcher's altruism but from his self-interest in an exchange. However, your best self-interest is not for you to buy his meat but just to take it away without paying, if you are stronger than your butcher (you can gang up for this with the next customer). Among the reasons you have not to behave in this way, your spontaneous tendency to respect the butcher's property is an important one. However, people would tend less to respect others and their property if they were not so respected themselves. You may even have to steal to survive if you are continuously robbed. Hence, general reciprocal respect of property is a necessary condition for a working market. As, more generally, general reciprocal abstention from harming in any way is a condition for a peaceful and free society, a most essential good. The war of all against all interspersed with fragile and diffident truces, or a police state, are the two ugly alternatives to the overall reciprocity of respect of others' lives, quietness and property. Moreover, if your butcher gave you the meat you need, as a gift, you would probably want to give him something in return, and each of you will have what she needs, plus the valuable bonus of a friendly and warm social relationship.

The market thus has essential and ambivalent relations with reciprocity. As a set of purely self-interested agreements, it opposes the usual reciprocitarian sentiments based on liking or a sense of duty. By the same token, giving destroys the logic of markets, and possibly its reasons for implementing economic efficiency. However, pure self-interest leads one to take, not to exchange. Self-defence and the police deter that. Yet, self-defence cannot stop organised predators, and the police would hardly suffice if there is not one policeman behind each (other) individual. Hence, some voluntary respect of others and their property is doubtlessly necessary. And a person would not or could not respect others if she is not similarly respected. Therefore, reciprocity of giving is an alternative to the market in the proper conditions, but reciprocity of respect is a condition of a working market. Moreover, purely self-interested exchanges are also impeded by a number of impossibilities and costs – the classical causes of "market failures" –, which are overcome by reciprocities of various types: reciprocity of transfers, trust, or promise keeping replaces missing contracts or impossible complete contracts; reciprocity of voluntary contribution permits the free production of public goods; in exchanges of items provided alternately, reciprocity motivated by duty or benevolence elicits providing the last transfer and hence also the previous ones; and so on.[15] Furthermore, bargaining that

---

[14] See Julio Rotemberg's Chapter 21 in this book, and the references noted there, including his own previous work (Rotemberg, 1994).

[15] Reciprocitarian corrections of "market failures" are analyzed in Section 7.

is uncertain and costly is often ended and solved by reciprocal concessions seen as fair and which save time, cost of information and of threats, and the risk of seeing threats carried out. Hence reciprocity, sometimes an alternative to exchange and markets, or an impediment to them, also permits or improves them both in general and on specific important and widespread occasions.

2.5. Reciprocity and organizations and labour

Yet, reciprocity is no less widespread, important, and necessary within organisations of all types, including firms, administrations, offices, political parties, and associations of all kinds (even that paragon of hierarchical command, the army, needs to stress spontaneous mutual support among its fighters). In all organisations, mutual goodwill, help, support, or information are common and widespread. Some amount of them is indispensable to the working of the organisation. They are often a major factor of its efficiency and productivity. And they also often provide some of the most important amenities of life in such a structure. These reciprocal services occur among employees or members of the same category, or of different categories, and in particular across hierarchical levels. They concern not only the work, the objectives of the organisation, but also the individuals' position and benefits in it. Moreover, reciprocities are also often common and important between members and the organisation itself. Employees receive various non-contractual favours such as bonuses, promotions, or special personal services, and they provide effort, goodwill and loyalty. This has also been much studied in "oriental firms", but it is quite general with various degrees of importance.

Indeed, the influence of norms, fairness, and gratitude in exchange is particularly frequent in the provision of personal services and its reward, notably as a result of the fact that these "goods" are directly attached to persons. Tipping, a return-gift for the quality of service, shows at least how widespread this view is. But the tip is only a fraction of the pay. The reverse case, where labour reacts to pay, is much more important. You often want to – or think you should – provide labour matching the wage you receive, which you want to deserve (or feel you deserve). This reaction and sense of balance have been studied in many experiments – the famous ones of Adam (1963, 1965) and Adam and Rosenbaum (1964) raised intense discussions – and empirical studies (this has become a rich and important branch of the fields of labour relations and labour economics, which is reviewed, discussed, and used in Kolm 1990).[16] The employer may have similar motives or this may not be the case, and the outcome can be any of the solutions of reciprocity games presented in Section 13.[17] When the employer is strictly self-interested (which may be imposed by competition or by shareholders), she

---

[16] For relatively recent discussions of the empirical evidence of behaviour of this type, see Bishop (1987), Baron (1988), Simon (1991), Levine (1991, 1993), Rabin (1993), Rotemberg (1994), Bewley (1995, 1999), the works reviewed by Fehr and Gächter (1997) and Chapter 7 of this volume by Louis Lévy-Garboua, Claude Meidinger and Benoît Rapoport.

[17] Also presented in Kolm 1984a and 1984b.

exploits in this way the return-gift behaviour of the employee. The "efficiency wages" described by Georges Akerlof (1982) are determined in this manner and they can explain deviations from the competitive equilibrium that resemble involuntary unemployment. However, the issue is in fact qualified not only by the possible prevalence of other solutions of the reciprocity game, but also by the fact that preferences of individuals are affected by the type of relation (see Section 13).

2.6. Established groups, cooperatives, associations

In fact, both some sets of transfers and services, and some organizations, not only include a part of reciprocity, but are essentially kinds of reciprocities in themselves. This is common in the economy of small groups, notably with face-to-face steady relations (even beyond the family), as in villages or other small societies. This is a reason why reciprocity has been the central concept and concern of economic anthropology.[18]

In the field of organisations, the ideology – both a moral and an ideal – of cooperatives and of a number of associations is precisely reciprocity. They claim, and pride themselves, to be "more" than only groups of self-interested exchanging associates and to establish, among their members, a reciprocitarian solidarity with the corresponding attitudes and sentiments (cooperatives often do not have this dimension, and, in some of them, it has been reduced to mere decorum; yet, it is important in other cases).[19]

2.7. Reciprocity and community

Finally, a community of any kind importantly implies reciprocities of sentiments and acts among its members, and also, often, between members and the community as such which can be an object of sentiments and an actor through its institutions. A community is not just a collection of individuals or an association of purely self-interested individuals. It implies some commonness and communion among its members (for instance, it is Tönnies's *gemeinschaft* as opposed to *gesellschaft*). Communities are very varied in scope, in the nature of what is common to their members, and, importantly, in the intensity of the links and relations that they imply. They extend from the nuclear family to all mankind (if you see someone as a person, you feel you have at least a common humanity). Between two members of a community, there can exist sentiments of liking (as a person), status, and justice, fairness and equality. These sentiments happen to be the bases of the two pure reciprocities in the strict sense (see Section 6). Hence, reciprocitarian relations are largely characteristic of a community, and their importance is related to the intensity of the sense of community of the members. Moreover, reciprocities in communities take place not only among members but also, more or less, among each member and the set of others and the community as such, through sentiments and conducts of "general reciprocity" (see Section 5).

---

[18] See Chapter 4 by Chris Hahn in this volume.
[19] See Chapter 22 by Louis Putterman in this Handbook.

National communities are important instances. You doubtlessly "ask what you can do for your country rather than what your country can do for you" (as President Kennedy proposed). But it helps if the country also helps you. In fact, you receive for free benefits from public services which use a large part of GNP. Conversely, apart from your readiness to die for your motherland if necessary, most of us vote for parties that demand only relatively small changes in the system, and hence, notably, most of us vote for the correspondingly high taxes. Note that reciprocities, which are intrinsic if the collectivity is an organic community with a common culture and history, are no less present if the nation is seen as an association as in eighteenth-century or liberal political theory. Indeed, "social contracts", either among citizens or between citizens and the State, have often been found a powerful reason for mutual support or services; however, they are not actual contracts of exchange but only hypothetical or putative ones; therefore, their being felt as more or less compelling probably basically rests on sentiments of reciprocity by which each individual finds it normal to provide her contribution given that the others, or the government, provide their contribution.

2.8. Public aid

In particular, the general concern for the welfare and dignity of other people and for justice need not be pointed out in countries where the people either have some sort of socialist ideal or draw similarly their moral inspiration from Christianity or Buddhism – and which, in the end, redistribute a large part of income. Pure and direct altruism by which several people care for the needs, welfare, situation or income of the same persons can induce "joint or collective giving" which is not reciprocity, but a case of contribution to a non-excludable public good (the beneficiary's situation) which can be sustained by a reciprocity among the contributors.[20] More specifically, however, many of us vote for public transfers towards people who earn little or have particular needs, not only in exchange for our receiving transfers when we are in their situation – which is only standard insurance –, but also when we will certainly never be in their situation – this becomes altruism –, and often with the reasoning that had chance put us in this situation, other people would have similarly helped us – a reasoning of putative reciprocity (or of putative "fundamental insurance" reciprocally accepted among contributors).[21] For

---

[20] As explained in Section 9.3.3 (including the paradoxical and important case of obligations that are necessary although they are not actually binding).

[21] See Kolm 1985. A "fundamental insurance" is a hypothetical self-interested exchange or agreement of mutual insurance about a risk which, in reality, has already occurred, such as, for instance, the natural endowments of individuals or their education induced by the family. This is a theory of the compensation for these facts, justifying and determining it by the imaginary free agreement. It can be shown that this theory is a priori morally dubious from the point of view of justice, because a self-interested choice in uncertainty – that of the persons agreeing about the insurance contract – does not have, a priori, the same structure as a choice of justice – for compensating the relative handicaps. However, this theory has to be accepted if all individuals accept it, and one may accept it given that the others also accept it, hence from a type of reciprocity among people who give (see Kolm 1985, 1996a, 2004, and Chapter 1 in this volume).

this reason, Europeans overwhelmingly vote for a public system of social insurance which includes redistributions of this type towards people a priori endowed with a poor health (contrary to the pure actuarial exchange of private insurance with differentiated premia).[22]

2.9. Intergenerational reciprocities

The same people, generally, vote for collective support of individuals who earn no income because of their place in the life cycle: they favour a system of pensions "by repartition" or "pay-as-you-go" and public financing of education. Yet, this is not justified only by helping people in need, but also by a rationale of open-ended "chain reciprocities", forward and backward. That is, active people pay the pensions of the older people given that they will be paid their own pensions by the next generation, and the elder have paid the pensions of the previous generation. Similarly, active people finance the education of the young given that their education has been paid for by the older generation, and the young will in turn finance the education of the generation to come. These chain reciprocities are particular structures of "extended" ("reverse" and "generalized") reciprocity. Yet, one could also note that people so pay the pensions of the financial purveyor of their education. All these transfers are inter-related gifts but are not exchanges in the strict sense.

These structures correspond in fact to some of the six intergenerational reciprocities at work in families, among which four open-ended chain reciprocities: you take care of your ageing parents given that they have taken care of you and of their parents and that your children will take care of you, and you take care of your children given that they will take care of you and of their children and your parents took care of you. More distant relations enrich the network (you take care of your grandparents who took care of your parents, and so on) – this is relevant for pensions since the system of some countries (Italy, Belgium) is indebted and so people in fact pay for the pensions already distributed to the generation of their grand-parents.[23]

2.10. Evidence and history

These are but a few samples of a conspicuous evidence. You do not need a laboratory experiment to know that reciprocity exists, or to know which factors a priori influence specific reciprocal conducts, and such experiments could hardly analyse the essential steady and complex social relations and strong interpersonal sentiments (not to mention

---

[22] Relatedly, Chapter 23 by Christina Fong, Herbert Gintis and Samuel Bowles in this volume emphasizes the reciprocitarian motivations that support the "welfare state".

[23] See Kolm (1997a). Family reciprocities are analyzed in depth in Chapter 14 by Luc Arrondel and André Masson in this book.

the "total social facts" that Marcel Mauss sees in reciprocities).[24] However, experiments can inform you about the frequencies of elementary reciprocal reactions in particular sub-cultures, a possibly interesting piece of statistical anthropology. They can, moreover, elicit reflection about these relations, and, since the issues are sometimes rather subtle and not obvious, no help is to be discarded.[25]

If, moreover, you are the kind of person interested in the perceptive observations and elaborate reflection of other people, you will find thousands of pages to satisfy your curiosity about reciprocity. Mutual love, the cases where it fails to be mutual, revenge,

---

[24] Michel Foucault said of this kind of conclusions: "there are maniacs of indiscretion who, when they have to see across a glass door, look through the keyhole".

[25] The possible lessons of laboratory experiments are excellently reviewed in Chapters 7 and 8 by Ernst Fehr and Klaus Schmidt, and Louis Lévy-Garboua, Claude Meidinger and Benoit Rapoport in this volume. They present a rather exhaustive survey of laboratory experiments of social psychology about reciprocity in the last few years (but much less the abundant ones of previous decades). The experiments reviewed present specific instances and cases of the more general phenomena considered. They raise at least three kinds of epistemic issues. Their incontestable success as scientific endeavour in the strictest sense is that they do falsify a hypothesis, namely that of the non-existence of the phenomena they study. However, nobody ever suggested this hypothesis in the first place (except, sometimes, a handful of ideologists talking tongue-in-cheek who were not expected to be taken seriously). The existence of these phenomena is obvious to all from numerous observations in life (the fact that these phenomena are absent from a number of theoretical economic models which purposefully simplify reality is something else, the issue being only if and when the models choose the wrong simplification for their purpose, which requires a discussion including this purpose). The other, deeper, contribution of these experiments consists of providing frequencies of the phenomenon in question in the specific case of the experiment. Yet, there are also often commentaries about what can be concluded from such figures, in relation to the various specific aspects of the experiment. Now, in generally presenting and considering these reflections as second and subsidiary to the experiment and the figures rather than the converse, these discussions, feeling secure about precision, distinction, and rigor because of the experimental figures they consider, typically do not find it a priority to, in addition, much emphasise carrying over these characteristics to the concepts they mention. Showing this for all these studies would be too long and beyond the present scope, and may meet exceptions, but, for example, "reciprocity" may not be used with the discernment one may wish, its various very different types may not be distinguished when this may be relevant, it is sometimes confused with fairness (only one type of reciprocity relates to fairness and much of fairness is something totally different), or again with altruism, and so on. Moreover, is the relative importance of prior reflective analysis and of chance and haphazard discussions for choosing the topic to submit to laboratory experiment always the right one? The interested reader is sometimes tempted to suggest an inversion of priority, emphasis and importance of methods, which could be presented as an application, to experimentation, of the famous mathematicians' dictum about efficient sequencing: "first think, then compute". However, considering the set of such studies rather than a single one does show progress in this direction. But how far and how fast compared with different possible uses of means? As far as economics as a whole is concerned, the analysis of reciprocity and of its consequences is an old story. There have been models of reciprocity since the early seventies, a meeting on this topic in Athens in 1974, a session about reciprocity at the meeting of the Econometric society in Oslo in 1975, the consideration of a semi-reciprocity creating wage rigidity by George Akerlof in 1982, a book on reciprocity, its analysis, evidence and applications, and a number of related papers, by Kolm in 1984a, a paper on a special reciprocity for contributing to a public good by Robert Sugden in 1984, an application of the same issue to facing a "tragedy of the commons" in the depletion of a free common resource by Swaney in 1990, before more recent studies related shortly and in the noted chapters of this book.

and gratitude or the lack of it, provide a large part of news headlines and still more of fiction. Reciprocity is one of the few main topics of the social science. It has dominated anthropology for eighty years,[26] whether it explains the economy, the polity, rituals, or kinship (marriages). It has been importantly considered in sociology.[27] It has been a main topic of social psychology – about "helping behaviour" and other relationships –, and it has been considered in numerous socio-psychological laboratory experiments for half a century. It has been analysed with economic models for several decades. In the classical theory of comparative economic systems, reciprocity is one of the three pure types along with exchange (markets) and command. And reciprocal mutuality of services has been the main hope of thinkers about the good society for centuries and even millennia, since it is the only alternative to oppressive command, selfish exchange, or the utopia of widespread unconditional altruism.

3. Reciprocity as the quintessential sociality and social bond

Given that: (1) community implies and entails more or less reciprocity among its members (a shared culture entails some reciprocity in consideration, communication, generally respect, often help, and so on), and reciprocity implies and entails community among its participants through mutual liking or fair comparative balance; (2) market exchange can be seen as not constituting a proper society in itself and requires some reciprocity of respect; (3) pure altruism has a limited scope of possibility; (4) reciprocity and reciprocation manifest most social sentiments (love, liking, friendship, sense of community, balance, fairness, gratitude, respect, self-respect, dignity, duty, conforming, norm, shame, guilt, indebtedness, resentment, vengefulness, envy, jealousy, regard, esteem, admiration, despising, indictment, hatred, and so on); and (5) reciprocity intercourse is in a sense intermediate between solely self-interested exchange (of the market type) and pure altruistic giving, and can be seen as extending to both these limiting cases or to the latter only; then reciprocity can be seen and studied as the main, central, essential, general or archetypical social bond, cement or glue that keeps society together, and also lubricant that permits its smooth working. Basically, reciprocity, mobilizing the deep interpersonal sentiments of interlocked fairness and reinforcing liking (plus mutual interest), fulfils the necessary dual function of joint integration and individuation, in tying up individuals into a society, while keeping them self-consciously distinct and different from their fellow humans.[28]

---

[26] See Chris Hahn's Chapter 4 in this volume.
[27] See, for instance, Alvin Gouldner's (1960) "The norm of reciprocity".
[28] A number of perceptive social scientists have had the intuition of this central role of reciprocity. This has been the case of sociologists Hobhouse, Simmel, H. Becker, or Homans, for instance. This view has dominated anthropology (with, for example, Malinowski, Thurnwald, Mauss, Firth, Lévi-Strauss) although it applies to all societies. The noted studies in social psychology largely support this viewpoint.

4. Definitions, givings and exchanges

4.1. Concepts and distinctions

4.1.1. Person, agent, actor, individual, etc.

We consider entities with these names who can act, perform actions, have conduct resulting in behaviour, be responsible, have feelings, emotions, sentiments, reasons and motives of all kinds, have information, expectations and memory, have attitudes, preferences and desires, have social status, and so on. They will usually be individuals, but they can occasionally be constituted groups or institutional entities (whose consideration as persons in these various respects requires an extended discussion omitted here).

4.1.2. Action, conduct, behaviour, motives, preference

An action is a set of acts (possibly a single act) with an intention (or joint intentions) and a meaning for its actor (and generally also for other members of the society). An action manifests some freedom (though it can be more or less constrained and induced). Hence, it implies some responsibility of the agent. The intention results from motives which can be reasons or sentiments of various possible types. A set of acts is behaviour. A set of actions is conduct. Hence, conduct is behaviour plus the corresponding motives (and meaning). Desires and drives are forms of motives. Preference comparatively evaluates several items with respect to some value. Applied to action, it describes the choice of one rather than of possible alternatives, as a result from the corresponding motives.

4.1.3. Gift-giving

We consider actions that intend to benefit someone else and are in some way costly for the actor. A transfer of a good, or a service, can be such actions. This action is gift-giving, and its result is a gift, if it is not a part of an exchange. "Exchange", here, denotes, and is restricted to for clarity, a set of acts from various actors, accepted by all these actors when this exchange is free, and such that the acts of each actor are compulsory by external obligation when the others are implemented.[29] An obligation is

---

[29] A moral conduct of promise-keeping is to be seen as such an external obligation in the present analysis. It is not a reciprocity, which is not defined by an agreement but is an individually free choice (even if it is influenced by social norms or pressure). Both promise-keeping and matching (balance) reciprocity can be felt as moral obligations and considered so by others, but the motives of these obligations are widely different. Moreover, there can be reciprocity of promise-keeping conduct. Hence, the position described by the statement "I keep my promise given that you keep your promise", referring to the same specific agreement, is the implementation of an exchange by a reciprocity (a reciprocity of the balance type, with often a touch of liking, about promise-keeping). The position that "I keep my promises given that you keep your promises" referring to general patterns of conduct, is only reciprocity, with applications to any type of promise (not only in an exchange). When applied to an ongoing relationship it is often motivated by the desire that promise-keeping continues, and hence it is a "continuation reciprocity" which is in fact a kind of exchange.

"external" when it is not a pure sentiment of moral duty or norm-following alone. Market exchanges are the paradigmatic exchanges. In an exchange, the basic and primary (free) action of a participant is not her doing her part; it is, rather, the previous decision of accepting this binding agreement. Hence, an act that is part of such an exchange is not gift-giving. Note also that since gift-giving is an action, it is by definition free, not thoroughly imposed (although it may be induced). Yet, several gift-givings can be related not by such conditionalities but by motivations. When you have received a gift (by definition without condition), you sometimes want to give something "in return", or think or feel you have to, out of gratitude, for pleasing your benefactor, or for establishing a balance and not carrying a moral debt. But you are not obliged to perform this act by an "external" obligation such as a contractual one or an equivalent sense of duty or propriety to abide by an agreement – another possible moral or social obligation is something different. This is the classical basic gift/return-gift relationship, the prototype and archetype of reciprocity, and the building block of more complex relations of reciprocity.

Moreover, the cost of gift-giving can have a compensation for the giver, but it is not a conditional compensation as in an exchange. For instance, the giver may be pleased to please the receiver, to conform to a duty, norm or custom, to display generosity or a superiority over the receiver – in other's eyes or in her own –, and so on. In fact, one can always trivially explain a gift by the fact that the giver enjoys some sort of compensation exceeding the cost she incurs, since it is a free action. The advantage can occasionally be quite material and self-interested, as with givings that elicit a return gift (for whatever reason) that the initial giver values more than the cost of the gift for her – this is the "half-reciprocity" of exploitation of return-giving conduct and motives –, rewards of various possible other origins, or indirect effects through markets or other social processes.

The case of sequential exchanges is shortly specifically considered. They are sequences of free transfers or services both ways between agents and extending in time, where each transfer is provided for receiving further ones. Hence, each transfer is provided independently freely. However, each full sequence of transfers from one agent to the other is provided under the condition that the other such sequence is also provided. Hence the full process belongs to the category of self-interested exchanges (though other motives can also intervene in addition). One can also simply see that each transfer is provided under the threat that next ones in the other direction are not.

4.1.4. Types and effects of gifts, refusing gifts

Hence, a gift from an agent to another can consist of anything done by the former and favourable to the latter or favoured by her, which has the properties just noted, and can be, for instance, bestowing a gift in the strict sense or a favour, approving or expressing a favourable judgment (if it has some cost, perhaps by its effects or compared to alternative opportunities), and so on. The former agent is the giver or benefactor, and the latter is the receiver or the beneficiary.

Besides providing the gift, giving implies a couple of facts that sometimes have a part in its appreciation. It generally shows that the giver acknowledges the existence of the receiver, pays attention to her, gives her some kind of consideration. This can in itself be valuable for the receiver, notably for a benevolent gift, and notably when it shows that the giver likes the receiver. This appreciation generally results from the fact that this concern is favourable to the social existence and the ego of the receiver, in her eyes or in those of others whose opinion matters for her. This effect can result from the mere giver's consideration or attention, but it is reinforced by her favourable attitude or sentiment towards the receiver, and still more by additional affects of kindness. The valuation and affection can be proven and even more or less measured by the cost incurred for providing the gift. Moreover, giving, receiving, accepting, or refusing constitute in themselves a *social intercourse* which is sometimes important. In addition, the very facts and acts of giving and receiving can constitute, or be the occasion of, a *factual social intercourse*, which is sometimes appreciated in itself by any of the participants and which sometimes has opposite effects. Most gifts actually benefit the receiver, but *symbolic gifts* are symbols of the relation between the agents, or of the giver's favourable sentiments towards the other. A particular gift can jointly have several effects, roles, or functions. Yet, anyone of these effects is sometimes the main or only reason for giving.

A gift can sometimes be refused, or restituted, but this also is sometimes not possible, for two very different types of reasons. The reason can be factual: the service has been provided, the judgment made public, or the act has involved an irreversible physical transformation. But the reasons are also often social, in that refusing or sending back the gift is thought improper, "is not done", or is grossly offensive towards the giver. A gift received may also sometimes be sold (some are directly in money income), or given as a gift (the ceremonial gifts of the Melanesian *kula ring* have to be given in turn to other people), but these uses are improper for other gifts. Symbolic gifts are often submitted to constraints of this type: returning the gift so received means refusing the relation or the homage, but providing a return-gift can mean accepting them, on the contrary.

4.2. Motives for giving, notably in reciprocity

4.2.1. A wide variety of motives, from best to worst

Many motives elicit giving.[30] They include liking, compassion, moral conduct and duty, social value, norm, or praise, the desire to produce various possible social effects, and simple self-interest, with their various modalities. They combine, associate and relate in various ways. For instance, you give to your family because you like or love its members, and to someone in need because of compassion or pity, but giving to these persons is also morally and socially valued or praised or is a duty, and you may seek

---

[30] A full analysis of this topic is presented in Kolm 1984a. Only a short summary is presented here.

the approval or to avoid the disapproval of others or of your own conscience by these acts. Moral and social praise or requirement even attach to the sentiments of liking and compassion or pity themselves. Other norms and traditions lead you to other kinds of giving. And we will shortly discuss giving for inducing other social effects. The reasons to give in return in reciprocity both can mobilize most of these psychological and social phenomena and are more focussed. Apart from the possible interested desire to elicit a further gift, which leads to "sequential exchange" (see Section 4.3), there are two properly reciprocitarian types of motives. Liking the benevolent giver, possibly because she likes the beneficiary, refers to one the most common motive for giving, liking. In contrast, giving in return for maintaining some sort of balance or equality is proper to reciprocity (and relates to the revenge aspect of negative reciprocation). On the other hand, another main motive for giving, namely compassion or pity, is a priori absent from reciprocity. Finally, the classification of general gift-givings that is relevant for understanding reciprocity is according to the social sentiments and attitudes they manifest.

There are three kinds of giving in this respect: it can be benevolent, or neutral towards the receiver, and even hostile towards her in some way, and each category itself encompasses various types. An instance of giving can have several joint motives, but the various motives are more or less compatible. Moreover, besides giving to specifically known people, giving can be to more or less anonymous receivers as with giving through the intermediary of charities or "general giving" to the group of others or to society as a whole. In these cases, many motives can be the same as those of giving in general, but there are also differences – in particular, some motives cannot be present in anonymous givings (notably the worst ones).

4.2.2. Benevolent giving

4.2.2.1. Liking and compassion Benevolent giving is giving that results from a sentiment of benevolence towards the beneficiary. This is to be distinguished from giving accompanied by benevolence towards the receiver but provided for another reason – notably the neutral ones shortly to be noted – (and a gift can have several joint motives). Benevolent giving can have two different types of motives since this benevolence results either from *liking* the receiver – *affection* towards her – or from a *general motive of helping people in need*, which includes solidarity, charity, pity, and compassion. Often, only one of these types of motives is present. They can also both be present, but only if the liking sentiment is in a mild form. Indeed, if you help someone whom you sufficiently like and who needs help in such a way that this would elicit help for a motive of compassion, pity, charity, or solidarity, then your motive for helping is your affection for this person and the resulting pain that her pain induces in you, and not the other altruistic motives. Affection tends to drive away pity and the like.

The psychological phenomena of empathy and emotional contagion can support the two types of motives of benevolent giving.

Moreover, the aim of giving may indeed simply be to *please or satisfy the receiver*, because liking someone implies liking the pleasure, the satisfaction or the joy she feels. It may also be to *do something good* for the receiver independently of the receiver's tastes or preferences (then, it would often not please the receiver as much as it could, or it can even displease her – the possibility or impossibility of refusing the gift is then relevant) – this is often called "paternalism". This type of distinction even occurs sometimes for pity or compassion, which usually induces reducing the other person's pain, but sometimes regrets some other impropriety in her situation by comparison with some norm and may induce trying to remedy it.

Of course, the gift or favour can benefit or please the beneficiary in a variety of ways: by the gift or favour received, in showing appreciation or respect of the receiver to her or to other people – which sometimes enhances the receiver's social status –, for the social intercourse in the relation of giving, and so on.

Finally, giving as a result of liking the receiver in general has itself three possible motives, which are closely interrelated, as we will see: doing something deemed to be good for the receiver and in particular something she likes, giving in order to be liked by the receiver, and the demonstration effect of showing and proving one's liking sentiment.

4.2.2.2. Giving for eliciting the receiver's liking The objective of gift-giving is sometimes to induce the receiver to like the giver. However, this process raises the issue of an opposition between the central motive of the giving and the main reason why it could have this effect. Indeed, the aim in question of the giver is not to please the receiver – or to do something good for her – as an end, because she likes the receiver. Rather, the aim is to be liked by her. The pleasure or appreciation of the receiver, or the improvement in her situation, then is a means to this final aim. And the receiver of a gift tends to like the giver in a particularly specific and genuine way as a consequence, only if the final objective of this giving is to benefit her, which is not the case here. However, the giver a priori likes more to be liked by the receiver, the more she likes her (for a reason to be explained in Section 6), apart from peripheral reasons such as the status one can derive from being liked (even in one's own eyes). Then this giving, accompanied by benevolence if not made directly because of benevolence, and made for a reason (being liked) which practically requires liking the person whose affection is sought, nevertheless elicits some forms of liking the giver, although of an inferior nature and intensity (this will be presented in Section 6). Moreover, since the giver likes the receiver, she enjoys doing something that benefits her, even if this motive, by itself, would not suffice for eliciting giving. In fact, these two objectives are not inconsistent, and they are often jointly present: the giving then aims both at favouring the beneficiary and at inducing her to like the giver.

4.2.2.3. Showing and proving liking Moreover, the object of giving may be to *show or prove* to the receiver that the giver likes her. The giver does this for two possible reasons. First, she may think the receiver will like to know she is liked, and she enjoys the receiver's pleasure or satisfaction because she likes her. Second, the giver may expect that the receiver's knowledge that the giver likes her will induce her to like the giver ("I will love he who loves me") – a reciprocity of sentiments explained in Section 6. And the giver likes to be liked, especially by people she likes. In all this description, "like" can also mean "like more". Giving, then, is a signal of liking sentiment. The sacrifice of the cost of the gift measures the intensity of the liking. It is chosen for showing and proving this intensity. However, this giving only shows and proves that the giver wants the receiver to think that she is liked with this intensity. It does not directly show or prove the actual liking. Nevertheless, for the first effect of pleasing the receiver who likes to be liked, the giver wants more the receiver to think that she is liked, and she wants her to think that she is liked more, the more she herself likes the receiver. Hence, the giving finally reveals the liking, and its cost reveals the intensity of this sentiment. And for the second effect of eliciting the receiver's liking by the reciprocity of sentiments, the giver wants more to be liked, and she wants to be liked more, the more she likes the receiver. Hence, the giving does again reveal the liking, and its cost reveals the intensity of this sentiment.

Moreover, the receiver tends to be grateful towards the giver for actions and choices of the latter that aim at benefiting the receiver as an end – and for which the giver is responsible (which is implied by an action or a choice). This includes such gifts – and the corresponding sacrifices – because the giver likes the receiver, and also gifts or aid for a reason of compassion, pity, charity, or solidarity. It also includes directly the giver's liking sentiments towards the receiver in so far as she can influence this sentiment of hers. Now gratitude can pave the way to liking if other relevant facts intervene, and it can elicit a kind of return-giving for showing and "proving" it.

4.2.3. Neutral giving

The second category, that of giving with sentiments and attitudes that are neutral toward the receiver, includes very different types of motives.

4.2.3.1. Interest In *interested giving* the only objective of the giver is to favour her own interest in a strict sense. Such an effect can have many causes (rewards, economic or other social indirect effects, and so on). Yet, one type of them is directly related to the issue of reciprocity: the intention to benefit from a *return-gift* elicited by the gift. This sometimes includes appreciation of the attention manifested by the return-gift or of the corresponding symbolic or factual relation. Since this giving not motivated by liking does not elicit or increase the receiver's liking of the giver (if the receiver does not mistakenly believe that this giving results from her being liked), the motive for this return-gift (or increase in it) is not this liking but another motive. There are two possibilities (see Section 6). One is comparative or balance reciprocity which elicits a return-gift counterbalancing the gift. The other is that the return-gift is motivated by the desire that the gift be repeated, a case that leads to the sequential exchange described in the next section. However, an interested giver may also hope to receive something from *imitation* of her giving by any agent, or from a *reverse reciprocity* by which a giver is given to by someone other than the receiver, possibly as a reward for her merit (see Section 5.2.4 – this is a "Descartes effect").

4.2.3.2. Duty and propriety A second type of "neutral" giving is that of giving motivated by *duty* or by the conception that it is *proper* or appropriate. Duty generally refers to a moral judgment, whereas propriety only refers to a social value or norm that is not moral. Three types of such motives for giving are noteworthy. One is giving to people in need, as charity or solidarity. This attaches to the needs of the receiver and the means of the giver, or to their relative status. There need not be any corresponding benevolent sentiment of the giver. However, there also is a conception of a duty to have sentiments of compassion, charity or solidarity towards the people in need, which implies that the person has some possibility of influencing her own sentiments (this issue will be discussed in Section 6.3 about other sentiments). The second type of duty-bound or proper giving consists of the return giving motivated by comparative, matching or balance reciprocity. Finally, there are gifts to particular people or relatives in particular occasions, induced by tradition, sometimes routinely performed, sometimes in a particular social setting (often a feast). In all cases, duty or propriety is not only a sentiment of the individual but also a social normative view. Hence, all givings from duty or propriety are bound to be more or less demanded as a norm, and can be more or less induced by social opinion or other forms of social inducement or pressure.

4.2.3.3. Being generous, wanting to be or to appear generous Other categories of motives involve further-order desires and judgments. You give because you *are generous* (or acting properly or from duty). You also sometimes give because you *want to be generous*. You then are generous in acts (this is generally all you want, but if you also want to be generous in sentiment in addition, you may know or have the intuition that the best way to acquire a sentiment is to act as if one had it and acted for this motive – this is explainable by the reduction of a kind of cognitive dissonance). At any rate, wanting to be virtuous is often more praised than acting from a natural, given, effortless generosity. For Kant, for instance, only this type of conduct is moral – spontaneous generosity is only an "inclination", as any other taste is. However, some people also act generously because they want to be *praised*, or *praiseworthy*, for so acting, or for being generous in sentiments (misperceived or induced by the action), or for wanting to be generous. This may be their own judgment about themselves,[31] or the judgment of others about which they care. They thus try to build an image of themselves in their own view or in the view of others (reputation) as someone generous in acts, in sentiments, or in intentions. However, this can be for two reasons. Such givers may want to be praiseworthy or praised in this way because they value generosity, a homage to virtue

---

[31] The case of self-judgment about the act of giving – in fact, the gift – is what Jim Andreoni aptly labels the "warm glow" (see Andreoni (1989, 1990), and his Chapter 18 in this Handbook).

which is in itself half a virtue, and hence they like to appear to be generous in their own view or in the view of others, whether they actually have generous sentiments or not. Or they may want to be praised or praiseworthy in itself, and then they choose the virtue of generosity (in acts, sentiments, or intention or appearance of sentiments) because generosity is valued by a common social sentiment, by other people, or society. They may also desire various possible benefits entailed by this reputation or society's judgment in terms of honour, status, interest, and so on.

The case where people give because they care for the approval or disapproval of other people who value this giving because it would be moral and hence for a moral reason presents a particularly interesting social structure of sentiments and action which applies more generally to all moral conducts. In such cases, indeed, some people value giving and do not give, while others give but do not value giving in itself. More generally, some people are moral in judgment but not in action, while others act morally but have no moral judgment. This nice division of labour is quite common. There is no moral actor, and yet there are actions whose form is moral in the society. However a priori the general situation is that each individual both praises giving by anyone – herself or others –, and gives because of praise by anyone – herself or others. The praise of others may be necessary for her to give (even if she also morally value her own giving). In the end, society as a whole may be much more generous, or moral, than each individual's motives are for her own actions (this society may be any small or large group of persons so interconnected by such judgments).[32]

4.2.4. Giving, inequality and status

4.2.4.1. Status   The third type of giving and of motives for it concerning the effect on the receiver emphasizes the inequality between both parties. The relevant inequalities are of roles, means, wealth, freedoms, positions and, importantly, status in hierarchical relations. Besides the material effects of gifts, the symbolic function of giving will be particularly important. Inequality, status, moral indebtedness, and the like, are a priori social views. They can be so conceived by the receiver, by the giver, or by other members of the society. These views of others may matter for the giver. And they can be enforced on her by the various forms of "social pressure". Most relevant sentiments will be relational and positional, such as sentiments of inferiority and superiority, of subjection and domination or power, of humiliation, or the corresponding pride and shame, or again sentiments associated with an attitude of condescension.

Giving, an asymmetrical relation by nature, is often in itself seen as an inequality. Avoiding or suppressing this effect is a main reason for refusing a gift or for returning a compensatory return-gift. However, this is an inequality of roles, of acts, and in the transformation of situations and in particular of holdings for a material gift. Indeed, in this latter case, the inequality in wealth is diminished – on the contrary – by a gift from

---

[32] See an analysis of this situation in Kolm 1996a, Chapter 14.

a richer person to a poorer one. And this decrease in inequality is obtained in a way that respects freedom and, indeed, thanks to a free act. By the same token, however, this gift makes this inequality in wealth conspicuous, and, since it is voluntary, it displays the giver's generosity. Giving can thus display wealth or means, possibly obtained with effort, or generosity, in absolute terms or comparatively to other persons – in particular the beneficiary. This can thus provide the giver with a desired reputation or status. This status can be in absolute or relative terms. By the same token, the gift can attract attention on the poverty of the receiver and endow her with the corresponding status. Giving sometimes aims at showing a superiority of the giver over the receiver. This gift, and the receiver's acceptance if she has the choice, may moreover elicit a particularly unfavourable image of the receiver. For example, it may suggest that she is unable or too lazy to cater for her own needs (or those of her family). This is sometimes received with severe social judgments which can elicit shame, arouse guilt or entail humiliation. And there exist vicious givings that specifically aim at this result.

4.2.4.2. Power and moral credit If the gift is important for the beneficiary, she can become dependent on it, and hence dependent on the giver's will, which is a loss of freedom. Correspondingly, this is a power of the giver, who may specifically seek it. However, this is before the gift is given, but that is often a recurrent situation.

Yet, receiving a gift often creates a *moral debt* of the receiver toward the giver. Refusing the gift – when this is possible –, or providing an adequate return-gift, often aims at avoiding such a situation. This indebtedness is often disagreable for the receiver, in itself or as a result of the judgment of other people (possibly including the giver) or of society. Redeeming this debt by a return gift is often proper and a norm. This moral debt is sometimes seen as attributing some form of social superiority of the giver over the receiver. The time and manner of redeeming the debt by a return gift is often a choice of the initial beneficiary. However, the moral creditor can sometimes ask the debtor to do various things in appealing to this situation ("you owe me something"). The receiver is the "*obligé*" of her benefactor. In some societies and situations, norms can make such a situation very oppressive, often with the help of other people's judgment and sometimes of social pressure of some kind. Giving sometimes aims at such a moral domination or enslaving, by giving more than the receiver can ever return. This power may be sought for its actual possibilities or in itself, notably as superiority. Giving in return redeems the debt and erases its effect, but this sometimes is a further occasion for showing that the initial gift or service and the ensuing indebtedness have existed. Recall the Inuit proverb: "the gift makes the slave, as the whip makes the dog".

4.2.4.3. Hierarchies The giving relationship constitutes one of the main social bonds, but it uses this property in a large variety of ways. Being both a voluntary sacrifice for a person and a benefit for the other, giving is an adequate ingredient for tightening other bonds. Indeed, givings often accompany an agreement, to seal it in showing goodwill. Established statuses also often use gifts of various kinds. They sometimes require them. These cases are sometimes neutral obedience to tradition. However, statuses often use required giving to remind of and confirm the relation. They sometimes tend to erode when this is not done. This can induce more or less balanced gifts between equals. Yet, such givings are also often important vectors of unequal and hierarchical relations. But gifts both ways are used for this purpose. A very common case is that of a gift from a superior to an inferior. It shows this relation and the comparison, and it produces the corresponding moral indebtedness. In fact, acknowledging superiority and superior status of the giver often is, for the receiver, an implicit way of "paying her debt". The superior so "buys" her status in some sense – although this is not an exchange in the strict sense. However, there are also cases where the inferior gives to the superior. This is also a way of acknowledging acceptance of the status. And yet, when the status corresponds to relative force, such payments are commonly *de facto* forced, although in a steady relationship both parties often find it convenient to pretend that these transfers are a free, voluntary gift or tribute.[33] There can thus be transfers both ways, especially when the nature of the services or gifts differs, in a kind of unequal, hierarchical and hierarchy-strengthening reciprocity.

4.2.4.4. The variety   Hence, giving is the vector of many types of social sentiments, attitudes and relations. Liking the other and generosity constitute its central domain. Yet, even this field encompasses quite different cases. Solidarity is in the sphere of fraternity. But charity is often tainted with condescension. And we have met gifts used for establishing or maintaining superiority or domination, even for humiliating or *de facto* enslaving. However, the important thing for normative uses concerned with the intrinsic quality of social relations, attitudes, and persons, is the existence and the possibility of the former cases.

The foregoing analysis of the variety of motives for giving, and of sentiments and views related to it for the actors or onlookers, have shown that there are essential differences between the case where the receiver is specifically known, notably by the giver, and the case of giving to anonymous beneficiaries. This latter situation is notably the case of giving to or through charitable organisations, or of "general" giving to the group of others or to society as a whole performed in general prosocial behaviour (which can extend, for example, from abstaining to pollute public places to dying for the motherland). Most motives or sentiments that are present in the "anonymous" case can also exist with identified beneficiaries and givers, but many that are present in the latter case do not exist with the former, or exist only in a quite different form. In particular, giving for showing a specific superiority, or for humiliating, does not exist in the case of gifts to anonymous beneficiaries. The superiority that can be exhibited in being generous through charities is different; it is more superiority over other givers or possible givers than superiority over the beneficiaries. And, for general gifts, the corresponding

---

[33] History shows many instances where a tribute is called a voluntary gift (for instance from proud Arabic tribes to the Persian king, or from the "Franc-Lyonnais" who took a toll on all merchandises moving into and out of the city of Lyon to the king of France). This transfer sometimes also is a price for protection, but the same force can protect and threaten, and, in fact, it protects its own source of income.

possible pride or competitive devotion to the public good is something rather different. In particular, the noted particular vices in giving are impossible or much less possible for gifts to anonymous or general others, or to society.

4.3. Sequential exchange

In an important type of situations, there are two agents each of which performs actions favourable to the other and costly for herself, either alternately or when the relative need of the beneficiary or the relative means of the actor are high, or again as a sequence of simultaneous actions (possibly a continuous relation), with purely and narrowly self-interested motives. That is, the motive of each action is that the process continues and hence that the actor benefits from later actions of the other. It is purely "consequentialist". Each action is a condition for later actions and, consequently, has former actions as conditions (except the last and the first actions, respectively). Hence, on the whole each actor provides her set of actions only under the condition that the other provides hers. Therefore, this is in fact an exchange in the retained sense, as shown by the exclusively narrowly self-interested motivations (in spite of the fact that each step can be considered an action, with the continuation of the process as its intention – although this can also be seen as acting under the *de facto* threat that later acts of the other party are withheld). This is not reciprocity in the proper sense, although it may look like it if one considers partial gestures only rather than also their motives and the whole process. Yet, omitting motives leads to the superficial consideration of "behaviour" only, which may be proper for studying animals but misses the essence of the social science. Now, there can indeed also be a similar sequence of similar actions that are actual gift-giving. In particular, each gift can be influenced by the gifts received by the actor, by the gifts she gave, and also by the set of gifts both ways she expects, in a steady reciprocity. Yet, the overall motivations are not the same. In the former, exchange, case, the motive of each other-gratifying action is: "I do this in order that she gratifies me later – and she will be motivated by the same reason". In contrast, in the latter, reciprocity case, the motive rather is: "I gratify her because she has gratified (and will gratify) me". The two cases may present similar behaviour but consist in deeply different and opposite conducts – but behaviour is superficial while understanding and explanation refer to conduct. The difference will in fact show in the specific acts – for instance, quantities handed out to the other –, which have no reason to be the same with the two kinds of motives. This difference, however, may not be large if the reciprocity proper is motivated by a sense of balance (see Section 6), since self-interested handing out will be sufficiently high for inducing the next steps but not higher than necessary for that[34] – yet, reciprocity proper can also have another reason, mutual liking. In addition, however, these two types of motives are often both present and associated, in various possible proportions.

---

[34] Remember, however, that the so-called "folk theorem" suggests that the case of sequential exchange can have a large scope of solutions.

They even tend to be, as a consequence of the protracted interaction of the sequential exchange. Indeed, in this process each pays attention to the other, is aware of her. This may elicit some sentiment of duty or fairness towards her, and possibly some sympathy for her. All the more so that this person benefits from the relationship, and, hence, from the existence and cooperation of the other person. And these sentiments of fairness, with the corresponding sentiment of balance between what each person yields to the other, and of sympathy with the satisfaction from the other's satisfaction it may entail, constitute the two basic motives of reciprocitarian conduct. Moreover, reciprocity may be more sustainable if the participants are aware that it also benefits their self-interest. Of course, the motives may differ for the two participants: one can be self-interested and the other reciprocitarian of one kind or the other, and they also can have several motives in different proportions.

However, even the simple self-interested sequential exchange is not something simplistic. If one participant once provides less than the other expected, the other may react in providing more in order to draw the attention of her partner on the interest of the relationship, or in providing less for the same reason, or because she thinks that her partner has become less interested and wishes to exchange smaller amounts, or because this decrease makes her less confident about the pursuit of the relationship (she may think that her partner loses interest), or, finally, in order to punish her partner. However, a purely self-interested agent is only forward-looking or "consequentialist". For her, therefore, punishing can only aim at showing the other that punishment will occur again if she fails again. Yet, if this partner indeed fails again later, the threat has not worked and hence punishment for showing a threat does not work. Therefore, the agent does not repeat it. The other agent foresees this logical reasoning, and hence the threat is ineffective. The agent understands that, and hence she has no reason to threaten and to punish in the first place. Hence, this initial punishment is not performed. Then, however, the other, failing agent receives no message and has no reason to stop failing. Unless the agent gives less or not at all for the other noted reasons. This may induce the failing agent to give again sufficiently. But this is no longer the effect of an action chosen as a punishment for a simply and strictly self-interested motive. Note that this reasoning is not affected by the idea that the failing and punished agent will abstain from the second failure because she would believe that "the same situation entails the same effect", because the situation is not the same since there has been the threat;[35] the reasoning can also be extended to the case where there can be several successive punishment as a learning process for carrying the message of the threat. In contrast, the threat can work, and hence the punishment can be effective, if the agent is not purely consequentialist and in particular not purely self-interested, and is moved or also moved by motives such as revenge for not being treated as expected, or a sense of duty to punish someone who breaks an implicit contract, or a moral of promise keeping for carrying the threat (even though this is not

---

[35] For a finite process, the passing of time modifies the future prospects at each moment, and hence the conditions, but this often does not affect the noted effects.

a promise of something agreeable) – at least, it suffices that the other believes that she has such motives. This is one of the various cases where self-interest is best served by not solely pursuing it.

The simplest case is that of the last action favouring the other person at some cost for oneself. It cannot be motivated by self-interest. Hence it will not exist if self-interest is the only motive. However, if there is no last action, there can only be no action at all. Hence this process cannot exist. Or else it should last indefinitely. But you don't need a Keynes to tell you that in the infinitely long run, we will all be dead – even for meta-individual institutions such as nations, governments or firms. In fact, both agents can foresee that any considered last action will not take place, hence that the last but one, becoming last, will not occur either, and so on, and they do not begin or they stop. This is sometimes also described by the complicated mental process of "backward induction". That is, the agent who would be last but one foresees that the would-be last one will not act in fact, and hence she will not perform the last-but-one action either; the would-be last one guesses this rational thinking of the other, and deduces she would not take the previous step either; this is understood by the other; and so on; and hence no one acts in the first place.[36] Actually, however, sequential reasonings of this type are not made beyond two or three steps – a case of "bounded rationality". What exists in people's mind in this respect is "unknowledge" (absence of knowledge, which is not uncertainty which refers to clear and conscious lack of certainty between possibilities). Yet, it can work here as uncertainty, and uncertainty of one agent (at least) about the end of the process or about the other's behaviour can suffice for sustaining the existence of the process.[37] Another solution is a binding contract with an enforced last move, but this is another situation and it may not be possible. And an unconditional imposition by force of the last move pushes back the problem to the last but one, and so on. Finally, the only other solution is that the last action would be provided for another motive. It would be a gift. But if it is a simple unconditional gift, the same question as before is raised for the previous actions, which will not be provided. Hence, this last action has to be motivationally conditional on the previous actions. That is, it would be a move of a reciprocity. The motive could be balance (for instance, there should be the same number of actions favourable to the other person from each side, or some equivalence in value), gratitude, or, perhaps, altruism or liking. Yet, if such motives exist, there is no reason why they do not exist during previous actions, and the process is in fact reciprocity, including self-interested motives as usual. Note that the non-strictly self-interested last move requires this motivation for the last actor only; hence only one actor only need to have this motivation and behaviour; the other can remain strictly self-interested. Finally, it is remarkable that sequential exchange can only exist if there is uncertainty, irrationality, or non-self-interested reciprocity. Yet, mechanics also tells us that there would be no walking without friction.

---

[36] See, notably, Peter Hammond (1975) and Mordechai Kurz (1978a, 1978b, 1979), in their description where they enjoy thus showing that "altruism" is in fact self-interested.

[37] See Basu (1977), Radner (1980), Smale (1980), Kreps et al. (1982), and Axelrod (1984).

5. Reciprocities: Forms and structures

5.1. Facts and relations

Reciprocity takes a variety of forms which are more or less close to or distant from the core meaning of the concept. It consists of relations between facts such as actions, sentiments, attitudes or judgments, each belonging to one person and concerning another or others, that are directly related by motivations. In standard cases, these facts concern two persons, they are from one to the other and vice versa. In extensions of the concept, however, only one person is concerned in two facts, or both persons are replaced by two different ones (as explained shortly). The persons are often individuals, but they can also be groups or institutions of various kinds. The various cases depend on the nature of these facts and persons, on the structure of the relationship and the number of persons and of facts involved, and – most essentially – on the types of motives that induce the relation.

The nature of the facts can be varied. They can be actions favourable to the other person, as with the basic gift/return-gift relation, or unfavourable to the other, as with revenge (and retaliation for deterrence). There are also reciprocities of sentiments, as with liking people who like you (explained in Section 6). There are reciprocities of attitudes, which are induced by sentiments or reasons and may denote propensity to action. You can, for instance, be benevolent, kind, polite, fair, hostile, rude, unfair, and so on, towards people who display a similar attitude towards you, or possibly toward others, or again only because still other people have manifested such an attitude towards yourself. Reciprocity can also apply to judgment, to saying something about someone, and so on.

The facts whose relation constitutes the reciprocity must have something in common in their nature and in some concept of their intensity. These relations depend on the specific motives of the reciprocity (balance, liking, or continuation) and on the particular application. The natures of the related facts should have something in common, but they may have to be more or less similar according to the case. For instance, they sometimes have to be of the same nature, while in other cases it is sufficient that they are all favourable or all unfavourable. The "intensities" of the acts or sentiments are also related in various ways. Some sort of equality in intensity is often directly favoured with matching reciprocities motivated by comparison and balance, while other motives lead to different relations – with generally the same sense of variation – or indirectly to some sort of equality (the relation in the case of sequential exchanges has been noted – give enough for the desired continuation but no more than needed for it).

5.2. Reciprocal structures

5.2.1. Basic structure

The structure of the relations between the oriented facts (each from one person towards another) and the number of involved persons and facts depends first of all on two dichotomies: there are two facts or more, and there are two persons or more. Let us denote different involved persons as A, B, C, etc., and a fact of person A toward person B as $A \to B$ (A gives to, likes, favours, hurts, is fair or kind to, praises, etc., B). The influence between facts is that one elicits the other. With only two persons and two facts, the only case is $A \to B$ elicits $B \to A$. The gift/return-gift relationship is such a case. So are liking people who like you, returning benevolence, kindness or fairness, and, on the dark side, revenge. The theory of reciprocity will show how this relation is sometimes associated with the converse one, $B \to A$ elicits $A \to B$, in various possible ways (Section 13). There are also cases of longer sequences of motivationally related givings between the two persons A and B. In fact, the most typical reciprocities are of this type. Each act can be influenced by several past ones in either direction, and possibly by expected ones. There can thus be a dynamics and equilibria of the relation. One act or giving can also be seen as a set or a sequence of elementary acts in one direction.

5.2.2. Extended reciprocities

There are also cases of "extended reciprocity" where more than two actors are involved. They are of various possible types. With only two acts, $A \to B$ can elicit $B \to C$, or $C \to A$, or $C \to D$. The former ($B \to C$) is called "generalized reciprocity" and the second ($C \to A$) is "reverse reciprocity". The basic question is, of course, the motivation of the second act – whatever it is – in relation to the former. Several types of cases have to be distinguished. They depend on the relation between the agents who change from one act to the second, or on the absence of such a relation. With the closest relation, a receiver is replaced by someone she likes or a giver is replaced by someone who likes her: the second act $B \to C$ can be motivated by the fact that A likes C; the second act $C \to A$ can be motivated by the fact that C likes B; and the second act $C \to D$ can be motivated by the fact that C likes B and A likes D. In another type of cases, possibly associated with the former, the participants consider in fact that the relevant actors or objects of the act are social groups: one person is considered as receiving or giving for the groups she belongs to and, possibly, represents (as with inter-clan *vendetta* for revenge).[38] If (AB) denotes the group of persons A and B, the three cases are in fact seen by the deciding participants as $(AC) \to B$ elicits $B \to (AC)$, $A \to (BC)$ elicits $(BC) \to A$, and $(AD) \to (BC)$ elicits $(BC) \to (AD)$. Moreover, the relevant groups usually encompass a larger number of persons than the two directly involved in a specific case. Then, the scope and size of these groups, hence the set of persons who are the potential objectives of actions or actors of an extended reciprocity, constitute an essential issue. In the limiting case opposed to that of simple reciprocity, this is a relation between one individual and all the others, or society as a whole. In all cases all the basic reciprocitarian motives can be at work, that is, liking, balance, or

---

[38] *Vendetta* is the Corsican term (see, for instance, the beautiful short novel *Colomba* by Prosper Mérimée for a very perceptive rendering of the relations, rationales and sentiments involved).

inducing continuation, singly or in association with others, with all the more specific motives such as gratitude, moral indebtedness, deservingness and merit, imitation and conforming, and so on. However, particular aspects or reasons of these motives are emphasized in each structure, and the various types of extended reciprocities are quite different in this respect.

5.2.3. Generalized and general reciprocity

The cases where $A \to B$ elicits $B \to C$ constitute "generalized reciprocity" (or generalized reciprocation for including cases of harmful acts). Examples are the noted famous "helping behaviour", or the fact that people tend to treat their children as they have been treated by their parents. When the reason is that person B sees persons A and C as belonging to the same relevant group, and this group extends in fact to all other people in the society under consideration – possibly the "generalized other" of G.H. Mead –, or, even, is seen as "society as a whole", the case is "general reciprocity". Generalized reciprocity consists of a "transfer of reciprocity" (from A to C, for B), and general reciprocity results from a "generalization of reciprocity" (from A to the group, for B). Sentiments and relations of general reciprocity between a person and a community she belongs to constitute a very important element of a sense of community (which can also rest on a common culture or history, common interest, neighbourhood, kinship, and so on). The largest general reciprocity extends to all mankind and is not inexistent. A specific generalized reciprocity is a result of general reciprocity when person C is helped by the reciprocating person B because she is a member of the relevant group. Yet, general reciprocity can take two polar forms and be any combination of them. In one type, the reciprocal attitude is a general helpfulness or kindness, a general tendency to aid others and, possibly, to like them. In the second case, the sentiment and attitude is more focused towards the group itself, with a propensity to make efforts or incur sacrifices on her behalf, from sentiments of duty or of liking (as with nationalism, for instance).

5.2.4. Causes of extended and notably general and generalized reciprocities

The causes of and reasons for reciprocity will be considered in Section 6. The main ones can be at work for extended reciprocities: balance and matching, liking, continuation and self-interest, and imitation. Yet, a number of particular relations that can be very important in reciprocities between two people are absent in particular extended reciprocities, because of substitution of persons, or because "the group" or "society" is a priori not an individual person comparable with oneself, endowed with a specific will, intention, responsibility, and capacity to like.

Extended reciprocities motivated by likings *among* others have been pointed out (Section 5.2.2). Liking reciprocities can be general and generalized, to some extent. In a general reciprocal liking, you like others in general, or the group, because some others like you and you see them as representative of all others or of the group, or, possibly, because institutions of the group display a favourable attitude towards you. As a result, you are bound to aid others or favour the group. And if you receive aid from others or from the institutions of the group, this tends to enhance your liking of others in general or of the group, which tends to lead you to give to others or to the group. Yet, these possible relations should be explained. Now, reciprocities based on liking result from rather complex psycho-social mechanisms presented in Section 6.3. It turns out that some of them apply to extended and in particular general or generalized reciprocities, whereas important ones do not.

Benefiting from others or from the group also often elicits a sentiment of general indebtedness towards others in general or the group. This can induce return giving to the group or to specific members as representatives of the group, in a general balance reciprocity. Yet, the balance then generally is a rather vague concept, without the precise comparison that is sometimes the case in ordinary reciprocities.[39] The role of general balance reciprocity in the relation between citizens and public finance will be pointed out.

In contrast, continuation reciprocity – giving in return for eliciting another gift – (notably from a motive of self-interest) a priori does not work in a generalized reciprocity where the beneficiary of the return gift is not the initial giver – except if the initial giver wishes to favour the beneficiary of the return gift. Moreover, in a general reciprocity the information that a particular individual gives in return tends to be lost. However, there are general continuation reciprocities with rewards for pro-social acts or for contributions to the collectivity, provided by institutions or otherwise. Finally, giving in return to a giver for inducing another gift can have this effect on onlookers expecting such a reward as well as on the initial giver. Hence, this can be a reason for a reverse reciprocity as well as for a direct one at the next round (the expected reiteration then is a gift to the new giver and not to the initial giver) with the following logic. An onlooker C who sees that $A \to B$ induces $B \to A$ can give $C \to B$ in expecting that this will similarly induce $B \to C$. Then, this $C \to B$ appears in a sense as a reverse reciprocity to the return-gift $B \to A$. Individual B may thus give in return $B \to A$ not – or not only – for eliciting another $A \to B$, but – or but also – for eliciting this gift $C \to B$. Moreover, if individual C thinks that any $A \to B$ is motivated by A's desire to establish a sequential exchange, this may induce her to establish such a relation with A in giving $C \to A$, which appears as a reverse reciprocity to this $A \to B$.

Imitation, and doing what is done and proper to do, commonly play a role in giving and helping, and watching help can constitute a reminder of the duty to help. $A \to B$ can thus induce $C \to D$. If the identity of the beneficiary of the act is included into the object of such an imitation, then $A \to B$ induces $C \to B$. Another fact has the reverse effect: the beneficiary is also a particularly close watcher of the act, and this is favourable to her imitating it; thus, $A \to B$ induces $B \to C$. Moreover, the initial actor

---

[39] This is not always the case, though. In various societies there is a careful accounting of individuals' voluntary contributions to the group (for example in awards of public honours in our societies, or in the representation of pigs given in collective feasts by the wooden pieces of the chest necklace of Papua highlanders).

is, for the beneficiary, readily available for the reciprocation and, thus, $A \to B$ tends to induce $B \to A$.

5.2.5. Reverse reciprocity and the Descartes effect

Reverse reciprocity, where $A \to B$ elicits $C \to A$, is the case formally opposed to generalized reciprocity ($A \to B$ elicits $B \to C$), and it extends more generally to reverse reciprocation. The philosopher René Descartes thought this favouring favourable people to be an important social fact, and Adam Smith emphasizes this idea in almost the same terms.[40] The reasons for reverse reciprocity are found in all types of reasons for reciprocity in general, but in a particular application which is partial and dim for the most typical motives, liking and balance. The standard motives for person C giving to person A who has given to person B have two faces. First, person A's generosity classifies her as a good person, notably in the field of giving and helping, and this is in itself favourable to helping her. Second, person A's good action can be thought of as deserving a reward, and person C volunteers for providing it. Person C's gift also has an aspect of compensatory justice concerning person A. Person C's gift can also intend to induce person A to give again – the continuation motive. However, if receiving such a gift becomes person A's motivation, she is no longer generous and a priori deserving, and these possible motives for giving to her disappear (the generous person becomes person C who helps person B through person A's self interested gift). Of course, if a priori person C particularly likes person B, her giving to person A can simply be a substitution to a return gift of person B, for all possible motives. Finally, there also is a reverse negative reciprocation, but, as usual, for motives of balance or justice but not of disliking: if person A hurts person B, person C may want to punish person A, or avenge person B, or deter person A from doing it again, in hurting person A (but she does not hurt simply because she dislikes person A for her conduct).

5.2.6. Chain reciprocities

Generalized reciprocities and, much more rarely, reverse reciprocities, may induce chain reciprocities $A \to B \to C \to D \ldots$ where each relation entails the next one. The chain is generally open-ended but could be closed (coming back to A). For instance, the various specific chain reciprocities at work in the family have been noted.

---

[40] Descartes, *Works*, IV, and Adam Smith, *The Theory of Moral Sentiments*, Part VI, Section 2, Chapter 1. Both Descartes and Smith even thought that the initial giver will gain in the end, as concerns her self-interest, from the whole process (she finally receives more than she gives). She may thus have this non-altruistic objective. Yet, the others may not give to her if they are aware of this motive. See discussions in Kolm 1984a and in Chapter 3 by Jon Elster in this volume.

5.3. Larger reciprocities

Reciprocities also often involve larger numbers of facts or people. The most standard concept of reciprocity in the social science does not in fact refer to an individual's *reaction*, but to a steady *relation* between people or groups, with a rather large number of acts favourable to the other or to others. For instance, individuals or groups give to others or work for them in turn, or they provide others with their particular type of products or services, or each is aided by others when she particularly needs help and aids others when they need help, or each shares with others exceptional benefits she receives. This can happen between two people or groups or among a larger number of them. This relationship can describe many types of transfers or services provided as a series of gifts in reciprocity rather than as elements of an exchange (in the strict, strictly self-interested sense of exchange defined above). They can be services to the community provided in turn (chores, work, watching over, organizing festivities, and so on), division of labour, mutual "insurance" against particular needs whose nature arouses more benevolent motives than the exchange of commercial insurance does, the sharing of the product of hunting or crops favoured by chance, aid for exceptional building, providing wives to other groups, and so on. One recognizes here the very stuff of social life in groups or communities, such as in durable dyads, families, village societies, many associations, the workplace, as well as, for a part, larger communities, and general sociality.

In such steady relations of reciprocity, each transfer or service is jointly the return-gift of past or foreseen others, and the gift that will initiate others as return-gifts in the future or whose previous anticipation has elicited other gifts in the past. When there are more than two people, the process generally includes extended reciprocities. Of course, a single action can result from several motives intervening jointly, often in a more or less dim or instinctive way. The essential difference with exchange (in the strict sense) concerns the motivations, and, from them, the attitudes towards other people and the types of social relationship that goes with them, but this will also induce a difference in the acts and transfers performed towards others. Each of these transfers or services is first of all a voluntary free gift. There is no explicit or implicit binding contract. Yet, a number of motives different from those that induce this giving can also be present, although the free giving gives the relation its particular nature. Self-interest in the benefit of gifts, aid or services is generally present. Indeed, apart from exclusively symbolic or relational gifts, a gift should have some value and some cost, in terms of self-interest, for the receiver and the giver respectively. However, being helped or given to in the future can be one of the reasons for giving or helping. That is, the relation can be also and in part a sequential exchange as described above. But this is not the only motive, by definition. In particular, the quality of the social relation, through mutual voluntary caring for others, the mutual liking of receiving, of giving, and of others themselves, or the festive aspect of the intercourse, are often very important. They even become the main or the only value in a number of cases. This is in particular manifested when the gifts or services are identical, as with reciprocal givings of drinks, meals, entertainments or feasts. Durable gifts, notably reciprocal ones, are often only valued as reminders or symbols of the relation. An external, purely "behaviourist" observer could hardly explain why people mutually transfer to each other identical wedding rings. But, of course, all the motives proper to reciprocity can be present, hence not only mutual liking and collective high mood but also duty and a sense of fairness, moral obligation or indebtedness, the relevant equality or balances (which can be strict equality or according to need, means or merit), and social opinion, reputation, maintaining or acquiring status, and social pressure of all types.

The use of money or its absence is sometimes relevant. Money is not characteristic of exchange (in the strict sense) since barter, that is, moneyless exchange, does not use it. Gifts can be in money, for aiding or sharing, notably in reciprocities. But the giver means more if she chooses specific goods or services. This sometimes means that she cares for the specific desires and tastes of the receiver, or the nature of the gift obeys a custom or a norm. In both cases, this is bound to make for a stronger social bond (norms that have not degenerated into mere routine are rich in meaning). The receiver can a priori in turn sell the gift, if this is materially possible, but she often ought not to since this would impair the relational value.

5.4. Reciprocity as social or economic system

Reciprocity is also used as the name of a social system, and in particular of an economic system. It has become usual, in particular after Karl Polanyi[41] to distinguish three types of economic systems: exchange, redistribution and reciprocity. Exchange refers notably to market exchange. Redistribution consists of a political central power taking products and redistributing them, or deciding allocations of goods and services. In modern times, this describes the public sector, and, when extended to most of the economy, central planning. The third system is reciprocity as a set or interrelated givings. Of course, the actual economies of whole societies are *regimes* which encompass these three pure *systems* in various proportions. These systems are thus more generally modes of transfers of goods or services: exchange, force and reciprocity. The various relevant properties or aspects of these modes will be compared in Section 8. Their relative importance in a society constitutes an essential feature of this society. They can be measured by the proportion of goods or services transferred using each mode. Of course, such measures require many specifications of what is taken into account and what is not. They can nevertheless be very interesting for comparing societies and studying their evolution. These proportions can in particular be represented in a triangular diagram by a point in an isosceles triangle with these proportions as distance to each of the three sides. This is sometimes quite enlightening for comparing economies and representing their evolution. Clusters of points show economies of the same type in this respect. Some show economies with a dominant system (points close to the corresponding summit).[42]

---

[41] *The Great Transformation* (1944).
[42] Discussion, development and application of this analysis can be found in Kolm 1984a, Chapter 1.

Finally, Marcel Mauss, whose *Essay on the Gift* durably shook the social science and launched its analysis of giving and reciprocity, focusing notably on the great ceremonial givings and return-givings of traditional society, dubbed giving and reciprocity a "total social fact". This also in a sense somewhat applies to more modest levels of reciprocity, given the variety of relations and motives that can be involved (as pointed out in Section 4.2).

5.5. *Reciprocity, revenge, reciprocation*

Favouring and harming give rise to actions and sentiments with symmetrical counterparts, to some extent. We thus have: gift or favour *versus* harm; return-giving for maintaining some balance *versus* revenge; gratitude *versus* resentment; liking benevolent givers *versus* disliking responsible harmers; moral indebtedness *versus* vengefulness; and rewarding giving for eliciting another *versus* retaliation for deterrence. The grand tradition of the social science restricts the term reciprocity to the case of gifts or favours.[43] This is natural since it wants to explain a more or less extended social system of transfers of goods and services, the social bond, the primary integrative forces of society, with sometimes an emphasis on intrinsic values of social relations. Revenge is of limited relevance in this respect (and punishment as purposeful harm by society is another topic – although it is a case of general reverse balance reciprocation). Moreover, as soon as the facts are observed with a minimum of perceptiveness and precision, the symmetry crumbles and the parallel appears to be only very superficial, approximate, and rather misleading. The structures turn out to be basically different, and essential phenomena, sentiments, and relations on each side have no counterpart on the other.

This appears for all three pure motives for reciprocity (see Section 6).

The self-interested return-gift which rewards giving for receiving another gift resembles retaliation to harm incurred, for punishment in order to deter further harms. In both cases, the reaction is self-interested (or it is made by a third party who wants to favour the future beneficiary or victim), it is favourable or harmful according as the action is favourable or harmful, and it intends to show and prove an intention and willingness of being repeated if the action is repeated (since, in the case of giving, it assumes that this reward will induce another giving for obtaining another reward). In both cases, the reaction can also be a message to third parties, for inducing them to give or deterring them from harming. However, the return act intends to induce similar acts in the positive case, and to stop similar acts in the negative case. Consequently, the effects are formally the opposite. Rewarding giving for receiving another gift develops into a sequence of givings (the initial giver gives again for receiving again). This sequence should even be a priori considered endless if this motive is the only one, that is, it should be a pure sequential exchange (see the analysis of this process in Section 4.3). In contrast,

---

[43] The expression "negative reciprocity" has occasionally been used. However, its most famous use is by Marshall Sahlins who basically uses it for fighting (see Chapter 4 by Chris Hahn in this volume).

successful retaliation for deterrence is only one-shot. However, the situation after retaliation can also be seen as becoming a type of positive reciprocity, a positive reciprocity of restraint, characteristic of armed peace: the retaliation has shown the possibility, capacity, and willingness to hurt back, and, then, the "gift" of not hurting is rewarded by the return-gift of not hurting back, with continuation as in a sequential exchange. However, if hurting provides an advantage of any kind to the offender (as with stealing, for instance, or if the offense is a side effect of a beneficial action), and if hurting back is any costly, the issue of the last restraint is raised as with the last gift of a sequential exchange, with similar theoretical detrimental effects on the whole relation, and similar solutions (uncertainty about duration or about the other agent's behaviour, or other motivations inducing respect – but, then, these motives should also exist before).

The motives that lead to reciprocating for establishing or restoring a balance are also superficially parallel but quite different in reciprocity and in negative reciprocation. The possible embarrassment of being "morally indebted" for having received a gift or a favour is usually much milder than the possible anger, humiliation (or shame) that may lead one to hurt back. Anger for being morally forced to give in return is much more rare and indirect. And the instinctual hitting back has no proper equivalent for giving (except, perhaps, in smiling back in many cultures, but this usually entails no cost).

The superficial similarity and deep difference in the result is the most pronounced for the effects of liking and disliking (and love and hate). You tend to like people who benevolently give to you and to dislike people responsible for harm you incur, especially if harming you and your resulting suffering is their final, vicious objective. Note that there is already only an imperfect symmetry, and that such vicious harming is rarer than giving for favouring the receiver as a final objective (because simply disliking someone induces less to enjoy what is bad for her than liking makes one enjoy what is good for her, and still less to cause this harm, as we will shortly see). A parallel can also be made between resentment and gratitude, and resentment is favourable to disliking the person who is the object of it, as gratitude is favourable to liking (yet, for a reason shortly to be pointed out, there is no harming for showing resentment – and disliking – as there is giving for showing and proving gratitude, and when there is harming in such a situation it rather comes from a motive of revenge and balance stemming from an initial previous harming). Now, liking someone who gives you can induce you to provide a return gift, since liking someone implies liking what is good for her, and generally her satisfaction, pleasure or happiness. Disliking someone may similarly lead one to like the bad events or pain she endures. If the disliking comes from having been hurt, this satisfaction is revealed by expressions such as "it serves her right" which, however, refers to a concept of balance. Yet, liking what is bad for people whom one dislikes is in itself bound to be much more restricted than the converse liking what is good for the people one likes, except in the strong case of hatred. Relatedly, *schadenfreude* in general is usually considered a morally condemnable sentiment, and this may tend to limit its extent and its effects.

The main difference, however, lies in the next step. Enjoying things favourable to people one likes can lead one to create such things by favouring or giving. Yet, if you dislike someone and – perhaps reluctantly – like her pain or misfortune, this usually does not in itself lead you to endorse responsibility for creating this pain or any other bad situation for her. Such conducts would rather be abnormal. Inflicting pain for the pleasure of it – sadistic conduct – is a pathology. However, this no longer tends to be the case in the strong case of hatred, but here the sentiment tends to have an aspect of revenge, with close relation with the harm received in the first place. Moreover, you tend to give because this shows and proves your liking, which enhances the other person's liking you – something you appreciate because you like her. There is no symmetrical hurting just for showing your disliking. This hurting may elicit or increase the other person's disliking you, but you are often indifferent towards this sentiment, or you can evaluate it any way. Finally, liking someone directly because she likes you – the essential "reciprocal liking" that will be explained in Section 6 – has no real counterpart: you certainly do not dislike someone because she dislikes you, at least to the same extent.

Still another difference is that punishing harmful actions is more easily socialized than rewarding free favourable ones. There are other differences, and, when closely looked at, all the items of the symmetry in fact have notable differences and the symmetry appears to be only a rough and rather superficial approximation.

5.6. Reciprocity as giving or as reciprocation

Reciprocity, therefore, is at the intersection of two fields of conduct, and its relation with one or with the other can be stressed. Return giving – the elementary reciprocity – can be considered either as giving or as return, and hence be classified with giving of other types or resulting from other motives, or with other reciprocations in revenge or retaliation. If your other concerns are giving and altruism, as in the topic of this volume, you first see this reciprocity as a gift, as a kind of gift. But you can depart from this point of view for two reasons, opposed to one another, but both of which lead you to emphasize the reciprocating obedience. If you tend to think that mere self-interest rules the world, you suspect that the return giving only aims at eliciting another gift (from the initial giver or from other observers), and hence you classify it along with the (partially) symmetrical retaliation for deterrence. Then, however, you can hardly explain revenge, especially when it is costly for the actor, except if you extend your concept of self-interest to caring about one's honour, self-respect, or status. In fact, if, more generally, you consider that strict interest, even extended to others' if you sufficiently like your neighbour, is not the only motive, and hence become puzzled by deontic action, you will associate return giving with revenge and hence again emphasise reciprocation. Only the third of reciprocitarian motives, that based on liking, does not induce you to closely associate return-giving with return-hurting, and this is the motive associated with the other motives considered in this volume.

This holds true for all of reciprocity. On the one hand, it is related to the sphere of giving. It consists of a set of givings. A single gift can be considered as the limiting case of a gift/return-gift where the return-gift vanishes, hence as a case of reciprocity, and then this term encompasses this whole field. On the other hand, reciprocity can be related to revenge and retaliation within the general field of reciprocation (punishment by society's system or norms of justice has a structure symmetrical to that of a "general reverse reciprocity" according to preceding distinctions). The tradition in the social science, the corresponding topics and interests, the relation with gift-giving and altruism (the topic of this volume), the normative aspects, and the important structural differences between reciprocating good or bad, lead to focusing on the analysis of reciprocity proper, with only occasional remarks about revenge and retaliation.

Part II: Motives

6. Motives: The three worlds of reciprocity

6.1. Three basic reasons

If you look attentively within yourself, or draw on your synthesis of the thousands of relevant experiences you have incurred and felt, watched and understood in others, or been told about and explained, during the decades of your life, you see that being favoured by someone – say receiving a gift – can elicit a large number of various sentiments. But you also see that providing a return-gift-can only result from a much smaller number of types of sentiments, although ones which are very different from each other (and which can be jointly present or not).

Indeed, the most important thing about reciprocity is its motives. And the most important thing about the motives of reciprocity is that they belong to three fully different classes, which can be labelled a sense of *propriety*, induced *liking*, and seeking *interest*. The third motive only consists of giving in return in order to elicit another gift, and, in fact, is barely worth the label reciprocity. The second type of motives rests on sentiments of induced mutual liking between the partners. The motives of the first type rest on a sense of social balance and include particular types of fairness. The motives of propriety or fairness and of liking have sub-motives of different kinds. The various motives and sub-motives can more or less be jointly present.

Very briefly, in *comparative*, *matching*, *compensatory*, or *balance reciprocity*, your return giving or favour aims at establishing some balance between what you benefited from and what you provide in return. It "evens out" some inequality in the relation. You think that you ought to do this, that this is the proper thing to do, and you often feel a kind of moral debt towards the initial actor as long as you have not "paid your debt" by this return action.

In a second case – call it *liking reciprocity* –, your providing a return gift or favour results from your liking the initial benefactor. This liking can itself result from two kinds of reasons. On the one hand, you like a giver whose final objective in giving to you is your good as you see it, which can happen from the various advantages you receive from the giving: the gift or favour itself, the appreciative and kind attention towards yourself which supports your sense of self and of social existence, and possibly the very process of receiving the gift. On the other hand, if the giver likes you, you tend to like her for this very fact which is kind, appreciative attention towards yourself with the effects just noted, especially in so far as she can be held responsible for this sentiment. Then, the gift has (also) the effect of revealing, showing, and proving the giver's liking. Moreover, since the giver knows this, she tends to give for this very demonstration effect because she likes to be liked, particularly by people she likes. Such an informational giving then is not altruistic, yet it nevertheless does show and prove the liking, and this in fact is its intention. Moreover, being given to for the final purpose of favouring you, and being liked, both elicit gratitude, which in turn favours liking the giver and the liker, and also may elicit giving as a "proof" of gratitude. These effects will shortly be considered more at length.

In the third case – call it *continuation reciprocity* – the return-gift is a reward meant to induce another gift. This assumes that this latter gift will be motivated by the expectation of another similar reward, which can be given only for inducing still another gift, and so on. Hence, the agents logically should foresee the full sequence of an iterative exchange. The motives can be anything appreciated in receiving the gift. This can simply be the item received (as in the standard sequential exchange), but one can also appreciate the mere attention of being given to (favourable to the sense of self and social existence), some status derived from the relationship, and the relation in itself or the very process of receiving. Pure interest can be a motive of an (apparent) reciprocity only in this way. But motives of the other two types – liking and balance – can also be present in addition. The two parties can have different reasons for appreciating each giving. Their expectation of the whole sequence is implicit in and implied by their choice, although it is generally not clear to their mind (as we have seen, this sequence has to be infinite, or else with uncertainty about the end or the other agent, or it can be associated with reciprocitarian sentiments of the two other types which can put an end to a sequence of gifts). Moreover, such a return gift may be provided as a reward for inducing third persons to give to the giver with the intention to also receive a corresponding reward.

Revenge is akin to balance reciprocity and retaliation for deterrence to continuation reciprocity – the differences have been pointed out.

In addition to these motives aroused by effects or causes of the initial gift that specifically concern the receiver, the latter's reaction can also be motivated by judgments about the initial gift or harm that do not depend on who benefits or suffers from it (as it is the case for the general motives of reverse reciprocity or reciprocation). She can thus notably in general reward merit, like good people, induce to pursue the relation, punish for a reason of desert and retributive justice or of deterrence, and also imitate and conform, and she applies these motives, in particular, to the gift or harm of which she happens to be the beneficiary or victim. These motives are usually much less intense than those induced by being the beneficiary or the victim of the action, but they can have a social importance because they can reflect the opinion of many people, who, therefore, judge favourably the return gift, and the receiver may be sensitive to their opinion. All these various types of motives can be jointly present (either for favourable or for harming actions) in various possible proportions.

We will shortly point out in detail the specific modalities, workings and reasons of these various motives, and relations between them, but we should first emphasize that on the whole they belong to three very different regions of the mind in society.

6.2. *An outlook of the general structure*

There thus are three categories of reciprocitarian motives: *liking, comparative (matching, balance)*, and inducing *continuation* which will be associated with *interest*.

There also are three kinds of dichotomies in the categories of motives: **pleasure** *from satisfying one's interest or that of people one likes versus* **duty** (or propriety, honour, norm, fairness); **altruism** *versus* sentiments based on the *interest or the social situation of the self*; and **self-interest** versus **socially oriented** *sentiments in altruism or comparison*. These classifications and remarks require some explanation shortly provided. They do not tell everything – one can also focus on the fields of manifestation of reciprocal conducts, or on the association of varied sentiments or motives. However, they seem to be indispensable for getting out of confusion in the consideration of reciprocitarian and reciprocal conducts. They lead to the structure represented by Figure 1.

A particular giving or favouring in return can be motivated by one or jointly by several of the noted relations. That is, its motives can be pure or mixed. Denoting the initial gift or favour as g, the return act as r, and the types of motives as respectively a for *altruism*, b for *balance*, and c for *continuation*, the return act, determined by g and by these motives, can be written as the function

$$r = r(g; a, b, c).$$

These motives have different effects on the return act, and in particular on its relation with the initial gift or favour, denoted as g. For instance, balance alone directly tends

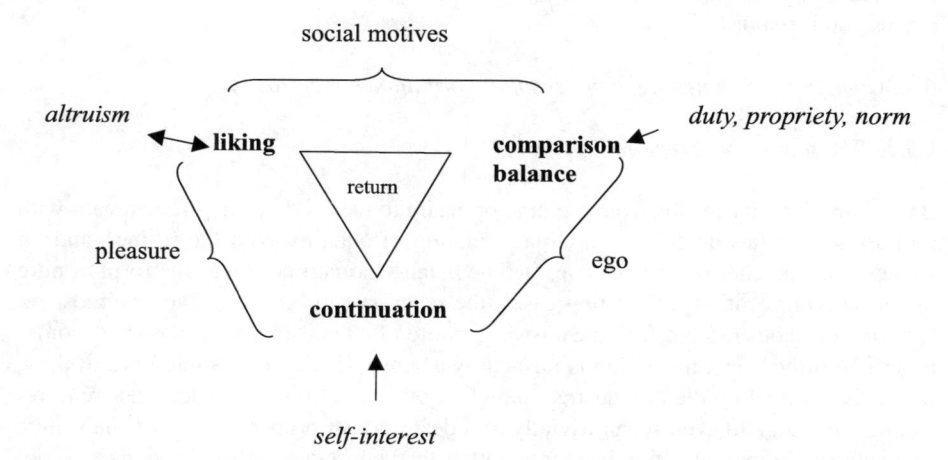

Figure 1. The three spheres of reciprocitarian motives.

to elicit some sort of equality between r and g. Continuation also elicits some equality, but a much more approximate one, and for an indirect reason: giving too little may not suffice for the inducement, while giving more than necessary for it is a waste. As for the effects of altruism, mutual likings often tend to be not too dissimilar and each can induce giving. However, a return-gift induced by liking a benevolent giver varies in the same direction as the initial gift (if relations of more and of less are defined), but with no a priori tendency to an equality.

Moreover, if, in a very rough and impressionistic but possibly suggestive way, one dares to express the relative importance of the three types of motives as proportions, the set of motives at work in a particular reciprocity can be represented by a point in the isosceles triangle represented in Figure 1: the distance of the point to each side roughly represents the proportion of the motive denoted at the opposite summit (the sum of these three distances is constant). Each summit represents the corresponding case of pure motives. Points on a side of the triangle are those where one of the motives is absent (that corresponding to the opposite summit), and hence each side corresponds to one of the considered properties of motives (pleasure, ego, and social). Of course, apart from the possible absence of some motives, this device is only impressionistic since no "quantity" of motive is defined yet. But it sometimes has a qualitative illustrative value for analyzing particular reciprocities or their evolution, for comparing them, and for analyzing or comparing various groups of reciprocities, notably by the clustering or dispersion of the points.

However, these motives in fact interact. Some are incompatible and others mutually favourable, depending on the motives and on their intensity. For instance, love as very strong liking is not consistent with seeking balance in giving in return, and with attributing too large importance to self-interest in the relation. On the contrary, the milder liking of amity and moderate friendship is both favourable to the fairness of balance and favoured by it. Compare the two dictums: "Love does not count" and "Good accounting makes good friends".

6.3. Comparative, matching, compensatory, or balance reciprocity

6.3.1. The propriety of reciprocity

Balance-reciprocity results from the urge or desire to reciprocate the gift or favour with a return-gift or favour that has a certain relation of equality with the former, and, in some sense, matches or compensates it. The balance sometimes takes the form of pure tit-for-tat reciprocation; in limiting cases, the reaction can be instinctive or almost so, with no conscious motive. Yet, the answer is more often conscious and weighed, sometimes carefully. Then, the action is pushed by a sense of *propriety*, sometimes of duty, rather than directly pulled by desire – although one can always consider a desire to restore a balance, and even speak trivially of a desire to act properly or to do one's duty. The balance-reciprocal action is deontic rather than consequentialist – although the actor wants both the consequences of her act (the balance) and to have behaved properly, and may have a desire for social approval (or non-disapproval). At any rate, the motives of balance-reciprocity are thoroughly different from those of other reciprocities: they have nothing to do neither with liking nor – consciously – with interest (although they can be associated with some motives of these types to some degree and in various ways). These other motives of reciprocity are consequences of other sentiments or desires – liking and interest –, and the balance motive is the only directly and specifically reciprocitarian motive. This is, in a sense, "pure reciprocity". The other reciprocities may lead to some relation in the family of equality, but this relation is not primitive and its reasons are very different. For continuation reciprocity, the self-interested return gift should be sufficiently close to the initial gift in value so as to induce another gift, whereas giving too much is a waste; the approximate equality is a consequence and not a primary value. As regards liking reciprocities, a priori the return-gift or the return in liking only increases with the gift or with the other person's liking; and a desire to be liked as much as one likes applies to a sentiment of the other person.

The motive of balance-reciprocity rests on several more basic and elementary sentiments or reasons. They can be jointly present, and each one can be more or less intense, or absent. Some of these sentiments directly induce giving in return. Other sentiments exist when the return gift is not provided or is insufficient, and avoiding them is one of the motives for giving in return. They can include sentiments of failing to do what is proper or required, of moral indebtedness with the possible dependency on the initial giver's future demands, and of inferiority. Moreover, all these sentiments are properly social sentiments in the sense that they are not proper to the beneficiary of the initial gift but represent opinions that are bound to be shared by other people and are "objective" in this sense. The initial giver can be one such person. The initial beneficiary may care for these opinions, and for the judgment about her behaviour that they entail. This may influence her (it may even constitute her only motive).

6.3.2. *The basic motives of balance reciprocity*

A sentiment that can entail balance-reciprocity can focus on several items: the overall situation disturbed by the initial gift, the two transfers or services, and the situation of either of the two agents or of both jointly. The fact that the initial gift is a free and voluntary act – with its implication of responsibility – may be relevant or not. With regard to the overall situation, the sentiment is that the initial gift has disrupted the existing order of things and the *balance* it includes, and the return transfer or service aims at restoring this balance. This return gift then matches the initial gift and compensates its effect with respect to this balance. The focus can also be on the situation of the initial giver: the initial gift constitutes a cost or a loss for her, that the return transfer compensates. This concern about a person's situation for maintaining it in some sense belongs to the realm of *compensatory justice*. Similarly, the initial receiver has benefited from a windfall profit that, a priori, may not be justified by a new particular merit, need, or right. This makes her situation a legitimate source for the transfer compensating the initial giver. Moreover, the required equality in value of the two transfers or favours also results from a sense of equality which results from rationality in its most basic sense.[44]

None of the foregoing considerations rests on the fact that the initial transfer is a gift, hence a free and voluntary act. This fact can have two opposite effects. On the one hand, since the cost of the initial gift is voluntarily incurred, there may be no moral requirement of compensating it. On the other hand, one may think that having voluntarily incurred a cost or a loss for benefiting the other person is a praiseworthy action that deserves a *reward*. This is a concept of *merit* or *desert*, with this possible consequence in the field of *retributive justice*. This reward can be provided by the initial beneficiary. It can also be provided by another agent, thus inducing a "reverse reciprocity" (a "Descartes effect").

However, when the freedom and will of the initial giver intervenes in the motives for the second transfer, her intention is also bound to matter. If, for instance, the initial giver only aims at inducing a return gift for a purely self-interested reason, there can be a compensation for the cost she incurred, but no reward for kindness or benevolence, or from gratitude. If, on the contrary, the initial gift is motivated by the benevolent desire to benefit the receiver, this kind of reward is justified. Then, in particular, the receiver is bound to feel grateful, and gratitude can be a motive for giving in return, alone or along with some other motive. Yet, this situation is also bound to elicit liking the benevolent giver and the corresponding liking reciprocity.

Yet, taking the intent of the initial giver into account can, on the contrary, prevent giving on favouring in return. If the initial giver only wants to obtain a return gift, her selfish behaviour may lead to the conclusion that she does not deserve one, and that she does not even deserve a compensation because she voluntarily parted with what she gave with no benevolent concern about others. Then, self-interestedly trying to extract a return gift is self-defeating. If, on the contrary, the initial giver intends to benefit the receiver as an end in itself, she certainly deserves praise, but giving in return would diminish the favour she provides to the receiver, hence go against her intention, which may have to be respected – all the more so that it is praiseworthy. Then simple thanks are the appropriate return.

6.3.3. *The inconveniences of imbalance*

When the return gift is not provided, or is considered insufficient for matching the initial gift, the initial beneficiary can be considered, by herself and other people, as having a moral debt towards the initial giver. This can entail disagreable sentiments and judgments, and avoiding them can motivate the return gift. These sentiments can have very varied intensities. At the lowest level, the beneficiary is only ill-at-ease because of the situation. With higher intensities, the beneficiary may feel guilty for not giving (or giving sufficiently) in return. When she refers to the social judgment about herself – even

---

[44] See Kolm 1998 (translation of 1971), Foreword, Section 5.

when this judgment is only interiorized and imagined by her – she may feel ashamed. The situation can lead to a dependency towards the giver, which can be quite material when it is admitted that this moral debt entitles the giver to demand in return its reimbursement in the form of services or goods whose nature and dates she can more or less choose. Depending on the case and society, this tends to create a situation of inferiority towards the giver, and also sometimes in comparison with other persons who are not so indebted, with a corresponding lower social status. These lower status and inferiority, and particularly the dependency, can offend the person's pride and, most importantly, her dignity. "I owe nothing to no-one" expresses the dignity of being free from this dependency. Correspondingly, when the gift is not counterbalanced by a return gift, the giver often sees herself as a moral creditor ("she owes me something"). This sometimes elicits in her sentiments of superiority, of power and domination, and sometimes of pride, although they tend to be less intense than the symmetrical sentiments of the receiver. The Inuits' dictum "the gift makes the slave as the whip makes the dog" denotes an extreme form. In the case of harm, vengefulness consists of various sentiments that parallel those of moral indebtedness, often with more intensity as with anger and sentiments of humiliation, shame, or being the victim of an injustice.

Yet, the sentiment of moral indebtedness is not only an inducement to return the gift. It is also, in itself, a social bond which is very important in the constitution of society in many instances – and, then, this situation can last long.

6.3.4. A social sentiment

The sentiment leading to or requiring the reciprocal act, and the sentiment of moral indebtedness when the return gift is not provided, are often shared by members of society other than the beneficiary or victim. The latter is often more or less concerned by these people's view, and this can reinforce her motivation or create it in the first place. This can also induce social pressures of various kinds for properly reciprocating. That is, this sentiment is not a priori incorporated in a specific individual, as for instance a particular liking is. It is a social-moral sentiment (in this sense, and in this sense of the term moral). The demand of this sentiment (the reciprocal action) is bound to be labelled a social "norm", although this labelling in itself explains nothing. Note that there is also a norm for the mere sentiment of gratitude, which appears notably as an indictment of ingratitude or a blame for it. These two aspects of norms are very different, however; the "ought" or "should" of gratitude concerns the sentiment itself (you ought to or should be grateful), while those of giving in return or revenge concerns the fact (you ought to or should return the favour or harm), and moral indebtedness refers to facts. Yet, the final result may be analogous because gratitude may elicit giving first for showing it, and second because it favours liking the benefactor, which can be conducive to giving to her in turn – although none of these effects induces the strict requirement of balance.

6.3.5. Refusing and revenge

A situation of balance-reciprocity can be accompanied by most other effects of the gifts. The gifts or services received and the costs of providing them matter for the self interest of the parties. There can be other sentiments between the parties, although not all sentiments are possible. Notably, strong altruism, and in particular strong liking tend to exclude the accounting comparison of the gifts and moral indebtedness. Yet, the balance is consistent with mild liking and even favourable to it. The total self-interested effects can be favourable or unfavourable to any of the participants. A participant for whom they are unfavourable can accept the relation for other effects. Yet, a participant may find the relation undesirable in taking all aspects into consideration. If she is the initial giver, she can avoid the relation in not giving in the first place (this sometimes implies going against some norm of giving). If she is the initial beneficiary, this avoidance consists of refusing the gift.

Refusing a gift is sometimes possible, and sometimes impossible or costly because the gift cannot be reversed materially or for a social or moral reason which can be more or less compelling: refusing the gift may be impolite, or offensive, or against a norm which can be supported by social opinion or, possibly, by social pressure of any possible kind. The initial receiver may have any possible preference between remaining with this unique giving, refusing it, or providing a return gift, according to the possibilities and everything being considered (the gifts or favours received and provided, the balance or imbalance, the moral indebtedness, and other aspects of the relation). This may lead her to refuse the gift in the first place, if she can. If she accepts the gift while refusing it is possible and costless, she is responsible (coresponsible) for the whole situation, including her moral indebtedness. Similarly, if the initial giver freely refuses a return gift, the beneficiary's moral indebtedness vanishes. Being ready to redeem suffices for this result.

Refusing the gift can sometimes be identical to returning back the gift received, or providing an identical item or service as return gift. Yet, a matching return gift can generally differ from the initial gift, and the initial receiver generally prefers this case. A similar gift or favour in another similar occasion is often suitable, however. With unfavourable acts, taking back something stolen, or a compensation for harm received, is not balance-reciprocation, but revenge or the talion law are – with a new equilibrium with about equal losses for everyone. In this case, providing an identical harm is a possibility and is often favoured ("an eye for an eye..."); the parallel in the "positive" case can only occur when the gifts are ear-marked for their giver and their "exchange" symbolises the relation and the sentiments (e.g., wedding rings) or when the givings are valued for the social relation that occurs during their process (e.g., meals, drinks). Punishment for a reason other than to deter future misdeeds is a type of balance-reciprocation, in the family of generalized or general reciprocation (in the sense of Section 4.2) if the punisher is not the initial victim (as with lawful punishment "in the name of society").

Being angry at some person, or simple resentment towards her, results from this person being responsible for harm or prejudice that disrupts some state of affairs considered as fair, or expected, or hoped for. These sentiments thus often accompany or motivate balance-reciprocation of harm. Resentment presents some symmetry with gratitude, but gratitude also belongs to the field of liking-reciprocity. Resentment does not suffice to motivate hitting back, whereas anger is a standard motive for it. Gratitude usually only favours liking and supports and reinforces liking motives for giving in return, although showing or proving it is sometimes the only motive of some giving. All this shows again that the "symmetry" between "good" and "bad" is only very superficial.

6.4. Liking reciprocities

6.4.1. Introduction

"Friends make gifts and gifts make friends", an Inuit proverb says. This pair of relations proposes a reason for reciprocity in giving when taken in reverse order, and in friendship, or liking one another, when taken in this order. However, not all gifts make friends, only friendly ones. Hence, one may in fact only have "friendship makes friendship", a direct reciprocity in liking, plus the easily understandable "friends make gifts" and a possible role of giving of informing about liking. Staying with folk wisdom, this is what a beautiful old song expresses in saying *j'aimerai qui m'aimera* (I will love he who loves me). Yet, although folk wisdom epitomizes respectable experience, it is no substitute for explanation. If "liking elicits giving" is rather straightforward, "receiving a gift elicits liking the giver" requires closer explanation and analysis of its conditions, and "liking elicits liking" still more so.

These reciprocities based on liking constitute one of the main fields in the realm of reciprocity (with balance reciprocity and self-interested continuation). Moreover, reciprocity in liking is a main social bond, with essential manifestations from general sociality to family love, the constitution of groups, and the nature of communities. And liking reciprocities have a major direct normative value for the quality of society and of relationships and persons in it. Hence, understanding and explaining liking reciprocities is a major task.

We will thus, successively, point out giving from liking; emphasize the distinction between reciprocities in giving and in liking; present the basic relevant phenomena, analyse the various types of "causal liking" and notably "benefactor-liking"; consider gratitude and its various types (for favours or gifts and for sentiments); point out the existential value of being considered (and approved and liked); discuss whether sentiments are given to their holder or can be influenced by her; show how and when receiving a gift entails liking the giver; analyse the mechanisms of reciprocal liking; present the property of the complementarity of mutual liking; analyse informational giving; point out the role of imitation, "contagion", or conforming; consider the consequences of such mutual interactions; observe that there is practically no counterpart in negative reciprocation; and note the factual and normative importance of reciprocities based on liking.

The sentiments of liking considered here can be of various intensities, from simple respect to love.

A basic and characteristic fact of liking-reciprocity is that liking someone is a standard, direct reason for giving to or favouring her. This is indeed the main motive for giving. The reason is simply that if you like someone, you like what you deem to be good for her, and you produce it if it is not too costly otherwise (this is often liked by the receiver – in particular, you are bound to like her satisfaction –, but not necessarily so in the cases called "paternalism", and then the gift depends on whether the receiver can refuse or resell it, which depends on material and social considerations).

6.4.2. Reciprocities in giving and in liking

A crucial point is that there are two kinds of liking-reciprocities: a reciprocity in giving and reciprocity in liking. The former is reciprocity of giving from a motive of liking. The second, also called reciprocal liking, is a reciprocity in sentiments, the sentiments of liking. These likings can then induce givings. These two reciprocities are quite different, although they are related in various ways.

Liking-reciprocity in giving is your giving in return of a gift you received because you like the initial giver, and this liking results from her giving. This latter relation requires that the initial giving has particular motivations such as liking you, as we will see.

The other type, reciprocal liking, consists of the fact that you tend to like people who like you (*j'aimerai qui m'aimera*). Yet, the reason for this tendency is a complex of interrelated effects that will be explained shortly.

6.4.3. Basic phenomena

Understanding and explaining these facts require understanding a few basic facts and relations. Some of these basic issues are present in both types of liking-reciprocity. They are the questions of causal liking (i.e., liking the causes of what one likes), the reason for liking to be the object of attention and consideration, the question of responsibility for one's sentiments, and the issue of gratitude. Liking-reciprocity in giving also rests on the general reasons for liking to be given to. And reciprocal liking also rests on the issues of the allocation of one's capacities for liking, and of giving for informing about liking.

6.4.4. The various reasons for liking to be given to

Remark, to begin with, that you have various different possible reasons to appreciate receiving a gift or benefiting from a favour. You can first enjoy the gift or favour in itself, of course. Yet, the very fact of being an object of attention – which is implied by this situation – can be very valuable *per se*, for reasons discussed shortly. If the giving results from the giver liking you, it shows and proves this sentiment directly and, possibly, also because the giver wants this giving to show that she likes. Indeed, the giver may want to inform you about her liking you because she knows you like to be liked and favours what makes you happy because she likes you. Even if she wants you to know, or to believe, that she likes you in order that you like her in return (by processes shortly explained), she wants this essentially when she likes you and she wants this more, the more she likes you. Hence, this giving again reveals that she likes you. Note that these informational effects can be obtained by simple communication, but the cost incurred in giving proves the intentions and sentiments. And you indeed generally more or less like this liking and the kind attention towards you that it implies (one reason is that they enhance the effects of simple attention towards you). Moreover, in all cases the giver's sacrifice of the cost of the gift reveals the intensity of these attention and liking. The process of giving is also often a type of relationship, a positive or even warm one if liking the beneficiary is the reason, and this is often appreciated in itself. The giving and the gift can in addition have various other effects related to their symbolic value or to establishing or confirming statuses.

6.4.5. Causal likings

The various types of liking the causes of what one likes have an important role in the analysis of liking reciprocity. *Causal liking* is the fact that you tend to like the causes of what you like. Yet, three types of causes have to be distinguished here in this respect. (1) In *simple causal liking*, the cause can be anything. For instance, you can like the apple tree because of the apple and your coat because of its warmth. (2) *Agent-liking* refers to the cases where a cause is an agent's free (freely chosen) act, that is, a part of an action in the proper sense of the term (inaction is a particular case), and hence something this agent is responsible for. This act is a cause of something you like, and this agent (and notably her will) is a cause of this act and hence of the item you like. (3) *Benefactor-liking* is agent-liking when the final motive of the act is specifically to benefit you. Note that this latter case does not include the cases where the giver provides you with a benefit as the result of another motive, even if the final end of this motive is a consequence of your being pleased by the gift and the giving (these other motives can be, for example, inducing a return gift, eliciting liking in return if the giving could have this effect, being or appearing generous and benevolent, or even showing one's liking as shortly discussed).[45] The required benevolence of the final objective of the giver can result from any altruistic sentiment towards the receiver. However, the focus here is

---

[45] A common case is that where the giver gives in order to be liked in return by the receiver, because she likes the receiver, and she likes to be liked by people she likes – for a reason that will be explained shortly. The giver may then rely on two possible reactions. Her giving may directly elicit the receiver's liking. Or her giving shows her liking to the receiver, and this liking elicits the receiver's direct "reciprocal liking" shortly explained. In this latter case, the receiver likes because she is liked and not because she receives (the gift merely shows and proves the liking, either directly or in showing and proving the giver's desire to be liked which may result from her liking). This is not benefactor-liking. However, since benefactor-liking the giver requires a motive of benevolence for the gift, and this can result from the giver liking the receiver, these two reasons for liking the giver are not easily disentangled. Benevolent giving in fact commonly obeys all these

in the family of liking the receiver, which is essentially affection of various possible intensities (sympathy in the common sense of the term is a mild form of it), but can also be one kind of pity or compassion that is accompanied with liking, and can include – as a borderline case – appreciative attitudes leading to respect.

6.4.6. Gratitude

The conditions of the existence of the sentiment of benefactor-liking are also those of the sentiment of gratitude toward the benefactor. Moreover, both these sentiments belong to the same field of sentiments carrying positive affects toward this person. Their intensities can be quite different, however. Yet, gratitude is a priori favourable to liking the person one is grateful to. At least, it seems difficult to both be grateful towards someone and dislike her. Since benefactor-liking and gratitude are sentiments in the same field of positive interpersonal sentiments and with the same cause, reason and protagonists, gratitude tends to induce liking through a kind of classical "halo effect". Gratitude in itself can motivate some giving in return for the particular motive of showing or proving it. Yet, these sentiments are quite different and distinct in themselves, and they have different positions as social sentiments. Indeed, there is a social value and norm about having a sentiment of gratitude towards benevolent benefactors, and, correspondingly, a blame for ingratitude. In contrast, liking one's benefactor is not a normative requirement, although it can be somewhat socially approved. This difference is as if being grateful were considered to be more amenable to voluntary choice than liking. The sentiment of gratitude, and any return-giving it can motivate, have an aspect of deontology and of balance reciprocity. In a sense, they constitute a bridge between the two proper types of reciprocity, liking-reciprocity and balance-reciprocity.

Moreover, there also exists a particular sentiment and mental attitude of "existential gratitude", of being grateful for the simple existence of something one likes or appreciates, a sentiment that is not addressed to a particular person. This can in particular apply to the existence of someone's favourable sentiments towards oneself, or to the existence of someone one likes or who likes oneself (one could be grateful in the standard sense for the other person's sentiment only in so far as she wilfully chooses her sentiment for the purpose of benefiting oneself, a case which usually has only a limited scope).

6.4.7. The existential value of being the object of attention, approval, and liking

You can be the object of attention and consideration, in various possible degrees. This attention can be accompanied by judgment or evaluation of yourself. Moreover, this

---

motives jointly: benefiting the receiver, showing liking from this effect and possibly from showing a desire to be liked, and hence eliciting returns of benefactor-liking and of reciprocal liking. More straightforwardly, note that giving for being praiseworthy or praised elicits no benefactor-liking. The question of giving in order to be liked implies impossibilities and relations that will be considered more closely in Section 13.

attention and evaluation can be accompanied by affects toward yourself (e.g., liking, disliking, hating, loving. despising, and so on).

Being the object of attention is favourable, and probably to some degree necessary, to your sense of self and ego and of social existence. All the more so when this attention is accompanied by an appreciative judgment or evaluation of yourself. And still all the more so when, in addition, it is accompanied by positive affects towards you. Moreover, these effects increase with the intensity (including duration) of this attention, positive judgment, and affection. Such effects are thus elicited by being the object of attention, possibly by being "known", by being the object of consideration, especially if it is with approval such as being esteemed or admired, and particularly if it is with affection (which implies some sort of approval), such as being liked or loved. Kindness implies attention, some approval, and some favourable sentiment in the direction of liking.

This benefit that you derive from these facts is something you may like, favour or prefer; its nature, however, is in fact deeper than is usually implied by these terms, in the realm of existence, being, and "ontology". Lack of these attentions and of their qualities is the most common cause of suicide.

Now being given to implies being an object of attention. Being liked implies being an object of attention with some favourable evaluation and with positive affects.

6.4.8. Slave or master of one's passions

The extent to which one can be held responsible for one's sentiments, and the dynamics of sentiments, are crucial facts in liking reciprocity.

Sentiments tend to be given to their holders. David Hume expresses this in saying that we are "slaves of our passions". Yet, a figure in a play of Jean Racine proclaims "I am master of myself as of the universe". But few of us are Stoician Roman emperors. The reality is often in between, with the largest part on Hume's side. However, we sometimes wilfully, consciously and purposefully influence our sentiments. This is done by reasoning or by more or less indirect devices such as focussing attention or "forgetting about it", or in trying to get used to something. However, these effects and their possibilities are limited. Even if we are not thoroughly "slaves of our passions", they do have an important hold on us. In so far as one can voluntarily influence one's sentiments, and to this extent only, we are responsible for our sentiments, as implied by the very meaning of the concept of responsibility (although defining this possibility can lead to a long analysis).[46] All this applies in particular to liking.

Moreover, it is not uncommon that sentiments adjust more or less involuntarily to interest or other advantages. This mental process involves a number of well-known phenomena such as attention, habit, oblivion, halo effects, reward, conditioned reflexes, compliance, and so on. It is parallel, in the field of sentiments, to cognitive dissonance in the domain of cognition. In fact, both the conscious and unconscious, and the voluntary

---

[46] See the discussion in Kolm 2004, Chapter 6.

and involuntary are often closely interwoven in this process (for instance, a phenomenon such as attention can be both voluntary and involuntary, and it can even be unconscious). Although *l'amour est aveugle* (love is blind) and Cupido is blindfolded, the blindfold is not thoroughly opaque (people generally happen to fall in love with persons of the appropriate social class).

6.4.9. Liking giver

You can appreciate to receive a gift or favour for this gift in itself, for the attention towards yourself this constitutes, and possibly for the relationships established in the very process of giving and receiving and as a result of the gift, or for an effect on your social status. Since giving is a free act, this makes you agent-like the giver. If, moreover, the giving is made with a motive of benevolence towards you, this fosters the positive effect of the attention and possibly of the relationship or status, and it makes you benefactor-like the giver and can induce your gratitude towards her. This latter liking may in turn elicit a gift to the initial giver, which appears as a return gift motivated by the process described. However, this initial giver's liking of the receiver can also have an effect in itself, a priori irrespective of the giving.

6.4.10. Reciprocal liking

6.4.10.1. General presentation After liking the benevolent giver – and hence, possibly, giving to her – the second type of liking-reciprocity is reciprocal liking. This is a direct reciprocity in the sentiment of liking. It consists of the fact that the relation "person A likes person B" tends to entail the relation "person B likes person A". This occurs with any of the possible types or degrees of the relation of "liking". The reverse influence normally tends to also occur, and, therefore, these two relations entail a dynamics of these two sentiments with states of equilibrium. Moreover, there can also be giving which can notably have the effect of informing about liking in various possible ways.

A notable number of psychological phenomena cooperate in a few psychological processes that can lead to reciprocal liking. Although people generally appreciate being liked, reciprocal liking can only be very different from balance reciprocity for several reasons: people do not choose their sentiments except to a limited extent; liking has no direct cost as a gift has (at most, it can have a kind of opportunity cost in allocating attention or affection); people's effort is more for being liked than for liking; and the issue of balance in sentiments, although not thoroughly absent, cannot have the same property as that of gifts and return gifts (notably for the comparison).

The main process inducing reciprocal liking rests on the fact that people benefit more from being liked the more they like the person who likes them – as discussed shortly. This is the *complementarity of mutual liking*. This benefit, indeed, induces, in the sentiments of the liked person, adjustments that make her like her "liker", by a process which is largely involuntary but can include some voluntary elements. This both enhances and allocates the person's "liking capacities" of attention and affection.

Another phenomenon inducing reciprocal liking is that people, who generally like to be liked, like *ipso facto* the main cause of this sentiment towards them, that is, the person who likes them – a "causal liking" of the "liker". However, this liking cannot be of the strong benefactor-liking kind – as with liking a benevolent giver – because the original liking is only limitedly voluntary (if at all), and, at any rate, when it has a voluntary dimension, its intent is not to benefit or please the liked person. This causal liking can only be simple causal liking, and, to the (small) degree to which the liking may be voluntary, agent-liking.

For the same reason, there can be no sentiment of gratitude towards the liker in the usual sense of the term. However, there is often the noted kind of sentiment of gratitude, addressed to nobody, for the existence of the liker's liking sentiment, and hence of the liker as she is, and this sentiment of gratitude has some importance (the importance of the object one is grateful for "compensates", in some sense, the absence of someone to be grateful to).

Finally, the liking person may inform the other of her sentiment in order to please her, by communication or by giving – or giving more than otherwise – as a signal. Even if her objective is to be liked in return, this often reveals her liking since she most often wants to be liked when she likes, and all the more, the more she likes.

The reciprocal liking can be of various intensities, as it is the case for each of its factors. Its absence in unreturned love is one of the most common topics of fiction.

6.4.10.2. Complementarity of mutual liking

Most of the benefits that you derive from being liked by someone are larger, the more you like this person. The sense of self and of social existence provided by being an object of attention, still more of appreciative attention, and more again of appreciative and kind attention is larger the more you care for the other person. Your social status as you see it is correspondingly augmented. And you care for this person in particular when you like her, and the more, the more you like her. Moreover, the warmth of the relation with someone who likes you is larger, the more you like her.

This advantage of liking, or liking more, the person who likes you adds to other effects of liking or liking more, which, however, can affect your satisfaction both ways: if you like someone (more), you are (more) pleased by what is good for her, but you also suffer (more) from what is bad for her.

Yet, the advantage of liking more someone who likes you can elicit your liking her more, by the process described in Section 6.4.8. Most of this effect is bound to come involuntarily, by a kind of mental process akin to cognitive dissonance in the case of cognition. A part of this adjustment can be more or less voluntary, by reasoning and focussing attention. And, in this process, the voluntary and involuntary aspects, and the conscious and unconscious processes are often closely interrelated.

The result is both a creation of affection or positive sentiments, and a reallocation of existing ones. Indeed, liking uses capacities for emotional involvement and for attention which have a dimension of scarcity.[47] Now, from the foregoing you benefit from liking more people who like you more, *ceteris paribus*. Then, the described process of formation of your sentiment realizes this allocation. This process, and notably its voluntary part, can be particularly helped by a material allocation of your attention – you see particular friends, you generally marry only one of the persons you can love.

6.4.10.3. Reactions and interactions A priori and apart from any other effect, if you like someone more, you benefit more from her liking you, she likes your higher liking and you like her resulting higher satisfaction; she also tends to like you more by the described processes of reciprocal liking, and you appreciate her liking you more. A similar reciprocal process is at work for both persons. Both the involuntary and the – usually more indirect – voluntary effects are at work, notably in the complementarity of mutual liking and in causal likings.

Finally, both agents can have a similar set of reaction towards the other. Each liking tends to augment the other by reciprocal liking. A dynamic can develop and there are states of equilibria. However, there can be several equilibria, with both individuals' liking being higher or lower in one state of equilibrium compared to the other.[48] A priori, people prefer equilibria with higher liking, but many phenomena can intervene and possibly qualify this (e.g., suffering from the poor situations of people one likes, the effects of gifts induced by liking, and so on).

6.4.10.4. Information Someone who likes someone else wants her to know it because this sentiment pleases the liked person and because this may induce reciprocal liking. Insofar as this information is provided by the liking person for the purpose of pleasing the other, this entails benefactor-liking in return. Yet, this is benefactor-liking for this action of informing rather than for the sentiment itself (for which, as we have seen, benefactor-liking is usually quite limited – since it implies liking both voluntarily and for the final purpose of pleasing the other person). Insofar as the person who likes informs the other of this fact for the purpose of being liked in return, this entails no benefactor-liking, and yet it generally reveals the initial liking since people benefit more from being liked by someone else, and hence want it more, the more they like her.

Providing this information can use any means of communication. Moreover, if a liking sentiment induces benevolent giving, this act a priori reveals the sentiment to the

---

[47] Both attention and emotional involvement rest on basic human capacities which have limits, and they are necessary to liking. The allocation of your liking capacities is a major aspect of your situation in the world, in particular as regards persons. Another old folksong puts it as "The heart of my sweetheart is so small that there is place for only one good friend". However, Victor Hugo suggests that motherly love is different and is a public good: "A mother's heart is like the bread a God partakes and multiples: each has her share and all have the whole" (however, issues about one being more loved than another are common in families). Moreover, liking capacities can also be increased by training and practice and can present this kind of increasing return to scale.

[48] Such liking dynamics and equilibria are discussed in Kolm 1984a, Chapter 10.

beneficiary. However, there can be liking without giving, and this sentiment can induce reciprocal liking. Yet, there can be a gift or favour for the specific purpose of showing the liking sentiment or of proving it thanks to the cost of the gift for the giver. More generally, the informational effect of giving can be an extra motive which, added to others, induces a gift which would not have taken place otherwise. A message of liking of any kind can prove this sentiment even if it aims at inducing being liked in return, for the reason just noted (one likes more to be liked, the more one likes). This information about one's sentiment tends to be mutual, with reinforcing effects ("I like you, I like you too"), thus favouring the transmutation of these individual sentiments into what is often better described as a kind of collective and joint mutual sentiment of the pair of persons (our friendship, our love).

6.4.11. All liking effects

Giving in order to be liked, one of the most common interpersonal relation, necessarily results in frustration to a larger or smaller extent. It is, indeed, the paragon of self-defeating endeavour. The reason, of course, is that it cannot induce the strong benefactor-liking because the final objective is not to benefit the receiver. Such a gift can only induce the milder agent-liking type of causal liking. Yet, the receiver benefits from the gift for all possible reasons. Moreover, this gift also generally informs her that the giver likes her, although indirectly, because this is generally a condition for desiring to be liked, as we have seen; the cost of the gift for the giver even proves this liking and reveals its intensity; and if this is news for the receiver, this may induce her reciprocal liking; but this possible effect of information is something else. The central issue is that being the object of benefactor-liking cannot be purposefully elicited by giving. It is necessarily a by-product of giving directly because of liking.

Indeed, directly giving to someone or favouring her because one likes her elicits benefactor-liking, and it ipso facto informs about this liking. More specifically, the cost of the gift for the giver provides a measure of the intensity of this sentiment. This information then induces directly some liking in return for the reasons described. And the receiver's liking of the initial giver for all these reasons, possibly supported by gratitude for the gift and for the sentiment, may induce the beneficiary to give in return. This is full liking reciprocity mobilizing all its ways of influence of all types.

6.4.12. Imitation, contagion, conforming

Among the most basic social facts are imitation of acts, attitudes or sentiments, and "contagion" of these items that are not chosen if the term imitation is restricted to wilful acts.[49] This is supported by the sheer pleasure of being in tune with others in sentiments and action. Moreover, other people, or a shared social sentiment, may appreciate

---

[49] Guillaume de Tarde, whose work is often considered the beginning of sociology, sees imitation as the basic social fact.

that you conform with prevalent acts, attitudes, or sentiments, or judge deviations unfavourably, and you may care about this opinion (possibly because of some kind of social pressure). At any rate, the behaviour, conduct and feeling of others provide available patterns whose duplication straightforwardly solves the problem of conscious or unconscious selection of sentiments, attitudes, and acts. These facts tend to be stronger the more the imitator is aware of her models.

Now, being the beneficiary of giving and the object of liking sentiments makes you particularly aware of these acts, motives and sentiments. This awareness is reinforced by the affects carried in the process. And we have seen that liking tends to induce showing this sentiment to the other person, in giving or otherwise. These are the conditions most favourable to imitation or contagion, all the more so that these acts, attitudes, and sentiments receive general social approval. Now, your benefactor or liker is directly available as the object of your giving and liking. And social judgments approve of such grateful conduct. This leads to mirror image imitation which directly constitutes reciprocity or can reinforce its other causes, in attitudes, sentiments, and actions. These reciprocal actions and attitudes can result both from direct imitation (wilful or from an effect of contagion) and from imitation or contagion of the sentiments that induce them. This can thus lead one to give in return, to like the liking giver, and also to emulate her in seeking her liking notably in giving for its direct and demonstration effects.

6.4.13. Interdependent and dynamic liking

All the described relations of reciprocal liking, the related givings for direct or informational reasons, reciprocal giving because of liking and gratitude, and imitation-contagion-conforming, constitute a network of relations which introduces, in situations of mutual liking, a positive feedback in liking (and giving) which produces dynamics and evolution, and also equilibria in liking (and giving).[50] There often are several such liking or giving equilibria, and, indeed, several stable equilibria, some with high likings and others with low likings. People commonly unanimously prefer the former ones (although we have noted some reasons for the opposite preferences, notably because liking someone makes one more sensitive to her misfortune). Hence, one should try to avoid deteriorating dynamics and low stable liking equilibria, and to favour the dynamics of self-improving mutual liking and high stable liking equilibria. This, however, meets two interrelated types of difficulties. One is due to the fact that sentiments are largely involuntary. The other is that giving in the proper sense of the term cannot be an object of mutually conditional exchange or agreement, and cannot be imposed by force. Strategies for reaching high stable mutual likings rather than lower ones are essential both in small group therapy and in choices that influence social structures, relations, and attitudes at all levels of societies, through institutions, organizations, rules, and education.[51]

---

[50] This dynamic interaction is analysed in Kolm 1984a, Chapter 10.
[51] Same reference.

6.4.14. Asymmetry

In these respects, love is intense liking. But it is noteworthy that symmetry of the noted relations with disliking, hating, or hurting, is very limited. As we have seen, being wilfully hurt by someone certainly tends to elicit disliking her, but being disliked or hated does not a priori elicit disliking or hating in return, and disliking – short of hating – does not generally entail liking the other person's harm and hence harming her, or the desire to show one's aversion. Only peripheral phenomena have counterparts. Imitation and contagion can intervene in both types of relationship. Resentment is somewhat akin to gratitude. It favours disliking the person who is object of the sentiment, but this a priori does not tend to induce hurting. Moreover, resentment is not a norm as gratitude is, and giving for showing gratitude has no counterpart. Revenge and retaliation, of course, correspond to the two other types of motives of reciprocity.

6.4.15. Conclusion

Even though we all live immersed in liking reciprocities of various types and intensities, understanding these phenomena turns out to require careful attention, distinction and analysis. They are not prime and basic mental and social facts but the result of interacting deeper psychological phenomena. Although various types of relations often work jointly, two of them should be distinguished in the first place, reciprocal liking and reciprocities in giving where liking motivates the return giving. An important issue concerns the formation of sentiments, with the particular role and ways of action of the will, and, in the other causes, the involuntary processes that nevertheless tend to more or less adjust sentiments to particular situations of their holder (somehow like classical cognitive dissonance does for beliefs). In the end, these analyses, necessary for understanding and, when needed, forecasting, are also the basis of choices and actions aimed at fostering the quality of society at all levels and with regard to most values. These values supported by liking reciprocities, indeed, are not only the direct quality of social relations and of persons in giving and in liking others, but also, as we will see, social and economic efficiency and welfare (see Section 9), and justice and liberty (giving redistributes wealth in respecting freedom and, indeed, thanks to it).

6.5. Continuation reciprocity

Reciprocating to an act, an attitude, or an expressed judgment in order to induce its repetition is common but requires a number of conditions. This act, attitude or judgment is desired by the reciprocator, for instance favourable to her, and the reciprocation is favourable to the initial actor. The repetition should be a possibility. And the initial actor should believe that this new act, attitude or judgment of hers will again be rewarded, for instance again by a reciprocation. This latter act should then be possible and the first actor should think it will be performed. But if the reciprocator is still of the same mind, this new reciprocation will be motivated by the desire to induce again an act she likes from the initial giver. And so on. Hence, with steady motivations of this type, the foreseen process should be endless, which is not realistic.[52] This becomes in fact a sequential exchange previously discussed. The successive acts can occur without further conditions or be triggered by particular needs of the receiver or means of the giver. As we have recalled, a solution to this unrealistic endlessness can be found in uncertainty about the end of the process or the behaviour of the other agent. In fact, the protagonists do not usually consciously foresee the whole future process and this limited rationality intervenes in a sense as such an uncertainty. A solution can also be found in an end by an act, attitude or expressed judgment with a different motivation. It cannot be a simple gift since the problem would remain posed about the previous act. Therefore, it has to be induced by past acts, notably by the last but one. This last act can thus be motivated by sentiments of balance-reciprocity – notably egalitarian fairness –, gratitude, liking-reciprocity from a sentiment induced by previous relations, or sheer imitation. These other motives can be those of one participant only. In the case of balance-reciprocity, the last favourable act, attitude or expression is provided as a reward for previous benefits, bestowed out of a sense of balance or fairness and propriety or duty. In the case of liking-reciprocity, the last act, attitude or expression is motivated by liking the other person. These motives are quite frequent. In particular, both the liking and the sense of fairness can develop in the course of the relationship, from the simple fact that the persons come to consider and know each other, in a relationship profitable to both. However, these sentiments would then be more or less present before the last move. Hence, this is a case of mixed motives, in particular of mixed and evolving motives. This is indeed common.

Of course, each agent may desire the other person's acts in question for any reason. This normally is, or includes, the act itself or its consequences, such as the gift received. But there can also a priori be the fact of being the object of attention, the interaction in the process, a status induced by the relationship, and so on. However, these latter benefits are limited, in the pure continuation case where liking is absent from the motives, by the fact that this absence limits the value of the attention, the warmth of the relation, or the status that can result from being liked. Yet, liking, continuation, and possibly fair balance, are commonly associated in reciprocities of a mixed nature, and continuation of the effects of being liked and of liking may be sought.

As it has been noted, retaliation for deterrence begins like continuation reciprocity but does not develop the same since the aim is to prevent further harm rather than to induce repetition of the initial fact. It builds up a threat, and it makes verbal threats credible. However, continuous mutual restraint from harming because of a threat and a fear of retaliation can be seen as a repetition in time. Yet, two aspects should be pointed out. First, the actors may be sufficiently convinced that retaliation is a possibility and that the other actor is ready to incur the cost of the retaliating act. Second, the case

---

[52] The timing of the acts could accelerate in time in such a way that all their dates remain finite, but, then, the speeds of reactions would have to become irrealistically small.

becomes a standard sequential exchange if the harm for each is in fact a benefit for the other, as is notably the case with stealing, hurting the other as a side effect of a desired action, or, possibly, showing a higher social position or status and humiliating. This can sustain the very important situations of respecting the other persons or their rights or properties.

We have also remarked that simple continuation reciprocity tends to present some property of balance in value, since reciprocating more than is necessary for the inducement is a waste for this agent, while reciprocating too little will not suffice for the inducement. Long sequences of acts can elicit many strategies, but these reasons for the relevant kind of approximate balance will nevertheless also be at work. A similar reason tends to adjust deterrence to the costs and profits of the harm prevented.

6.6. Comparing the three polar motives of reciprocity

We have now seen the three polar motives of reciprocity: *seeking* **balance**, *induced* **liking**, and *inducing* **continuation**. They respectively correspond to three basic fields of sentiments. Balance reciprocity rests on **duty**, **propriety**, and **norm** following. Liking reciprocity lies in the field **affective altruism**. And continuation can be induced by **interest** although one may want the pursuite of various aspects of the relationship. Table 1 has summarized this structure and the three basic dichotomies it implies. **Self-interest** is opposed to both the altruism of liking other people and the duty or propriety of balance and fairness which are **social motives** (moral or not). The **duty** or **propriety** of balance is opposed to the **pleasure** of satisfying one's interests and benefiting people one likes. And **altruism** in liking others opposes the *ego* which requires both the satisfaction of its interest and the protection of its social place in balance-reciprocity.

These are the essential structures. Other relations are adventitious. For instance, one can derive pleasure from doing one's duty (and some hedonist philosophers have said you ought to seek pleasure), find an ego satisfaction in altruistically liking others and still more in being liked by them, seek material interest for acquiring social status or for giving to people one likes, and so on.

6.7. Relational, process, status, or symbolic reciprocities

The focus so far has emphasized the basic pure motives of the acts of reciprocity or reciprocating. However, reciprocity also denotes a relationship. In particular, it often is a more or less steady relationship, and this is an important feature of it. The relationship as such is often the relevant aspect. The reciprocity can then associate various motives in various ways and proportions, although not all such associations are possible (e.g., as we have seen, strong liking or love is generally inconsistent with counting or measuring gifts induced by a reason of balance since "love does not count", whereas balance is possible with milder liking, and its fairness can even be required for it since "good accounting makes good friends"). The relationship can be one aspect of the givings that is appreciated, and whose continuation is sought. Its steadiness is particularly important for the basic sentiment of liking. The appreciation of the relationship can itself have various quite different motives, such as appreciating the social intercourse in itself, the attention or sentiments towards oneself, the social role or status created or exhibited by the relationship, and so on. Such relational reciprocities can thus be process-reciprocities, status-reciprocities, and so on. The gifts of relational reciprocities may matter in themselves, but their intrinsic value often becomes secondary or even vanishes, as they become mere pretexts for or symbols of the relationship. Recall again the cases where people give to one another identical drinks or meals, or wedding rings. This place of reciprocity makes it a central issue in the conception of society that sees it neither as a Durkheimian whole, nor as a heap of individuals at most related by interest, but as a complex of living relations.

6.8. Imitation and conforming

We have seen that imitation – or, rather, contagion – of sentiments can lead to or reinforce liking-reciprocity through a mirror-image duplication of liking the other person. But there can be reciprocation of benefiting the other simply from the imitation of an act, or from acting in conformity with acts of others. The receiver is particularly aware of the act she benefits from, and the giver is straightforwardly available as beneficiary of her replication. Yet, contagion or imitation of sentiments and of acts, or conforming to conduct, can also occur for agents not concerned by the initial sentiments or acts.

6.9. The graph of reciprocity

Figure 2 shows the graph of the influences which constitute reciprocity, epitomizing the previous analysis.

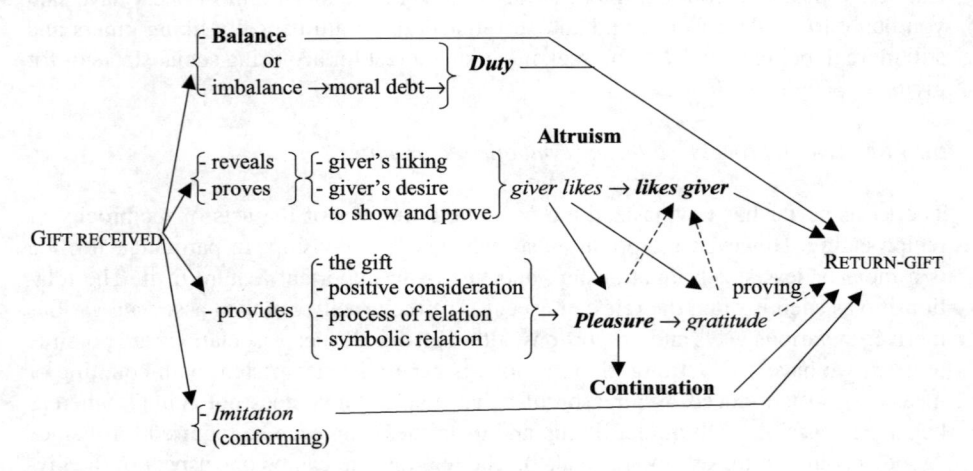

Figure 2. The logic of reciprocity.

6.10. The six basic reciprocations

Adding now "negative" or harmful reciprocations, the most conspicuous fact is the practical absence of negative parallels to reciprocities based on liking, because the tendency to dislike someone because she dislikes you, or to hurt someone because you dislike her, are generally absent (or, at least, without possible comparison with the corresponding "positive" sentiments and actions). This gives, on the whole, the six basic or pure types of reciprocations displayed in Figure 3.

	interest	balance, matching	affects	
positive	sequential exchange	balance reciprocity	gift reciprocity from liking	reciprocal liking
negative	retaliation for deterrence	revenge	✕	✕

Figure 3. The six pure reciprocations.

6.11. The motives of extended reciprocations

Extended reciprocities and more generally reciprocations – generalized, general, and reverse – are important phenomena. Their motives belong (or are akin) to those of ordinary (bilateral) reciprocities and reciprocations, but they cover only a part of these motives. We have seen in Section 1.5 that some explanation rests in the substitution of a person to another because of liking relations or belonging to the same group. Indeed, if the sign $\rightarrow$ denotes either "gives to" or "hurts", $A \rightarrow B$ entails $B \rightarrow C$ because A likes C or B acts towards the group (AC); or $A \rightarrow B$ entails $C \rightarrow A$ because C likes B or acts on behalf of the group (BC). The motives can be liking, balance, continuation, revenge, or deterrence (and imitation can play a role).

More generally, someone who has been well treated often tends, as a consequence, to be favourable to others in general, or to think she owes something to others in general. Conversely, someone who has been hurt by some person sometimes tends, as a result, to be hostile and rough towards others, or to take revenge on society. And someone who is generous and helpful towards someone else is often seen as deserving a reward, notably to be helped when she needs it, which would maintain some balance; moreover, one is prone to like this generous character and this is favourable to helping her when she needs it. This effect remains when you happen to be the beneficiary of this person's generosity, and it adds to the specific reasons you have to appreciate being helped or given to. This reverse reciprocity has classically been emphasized by moralists and even religions, as the source of worldly immanent reward for altruism. It is even often suggested that the return gifts overcompensate the cost of the initial benevolence (e.g., by René Descartes or Adam Smith). When this is the case, the initial giver can come to give for a purely self-interested reason. Yet, she then is self-interested and no longer a generous person deserving a reward. However, she may then be given to in order to induce her to repeat her giving, in a reverse continuation reciprocity, and the benevolent agent is the agent who gives to her and thus, indirectly, favours the final beneficiary. This rewarder of merit or inducer of further actions can be society represented by its institutions.

On the dark side of reciprocation, similar effects exist for such an "anonymous" extension of revenge and of retaliation for deterrence into the motives for punishment. Yet, the liking effect has no such parallel, since, although you are prone to dislike mischievers, you are probably much less to harm people simply because you dislike them (as you tend to give to people you like). These "objective" motives for reciprocation can be present for anyone, in particular the victim in addition to her specific reason as victim, and the standard implementer is society at large represented by its *ad hoc* institutions of justice. Unlawful harm has indeed to be prevented as respect of law and hence by society at large. Punishment for deterrence of such actions constitutes a part of this activity. However, the other motive for punishment, namely the notions of desert and merit which induce seeking some sort of balance, raises a major issue about the progress of civilization. A first step is the socialization of revenge for violence into lawful justice. But this motive remains no less barbarian for being a "motive of society". It even is more so since revenge may in part be excused as a primitive reaction and sentiment whereas social rules should be based on reason. The next progress in this respect will therefore be the suppression of such motives from the reasons of law.

7. Reciprocity and other social sentiments

Understanding and intelligence begin by distinction, and this is particularly true for understanding the mind in general – since it has no directly observable features – and sentiments in particular. Understanding reciprocity requires that it be fully and clearly distinguished from other sentiments and ensuing conducts which are a priori very different, such as, for instance, fairness, equity and justice, altruism and spitefulness, liking and disliking, or envy and jealousy. In particular, lumping various sentiments and conducts together because they are not strictly individualistic self-interest elicits confusion that can thoroughly forbid understanding. However, some of these sentiments have relations with reciprocities, notably crucial roles in them, and the analysis of reciprocity should point them out, in particular in order to make use of the previous analyses of all these sentiments.

7.1. Fairness, equity, justice

Reciprocity and fairness are a priori very different things. However, there are, between them, a number of important relations or possible relations of different types.

7.1.1. Balance reciprocity and justice, equality, retribution, compensation

To begin with, there is a *common structure of ideal equality in both fairness and balance reciprocity* in general. This fairness can *more particularly apply to the items of a balance-reciprocity*: the mutual favours or gifts between agents.

And, indeed, two types of equity are among the basic sentiments that induce balance reciprocity. Yet, they are not the only sentiments leading to this conduct. There also are desires of balance per se, as something proper or required.

These two types of fairness inducing balance reciprocity are applications, to the items of the reciprocity, of two of the types of justice, compensatory and retributive.

This sense of *compensatory justice* says that the gift (favour) should be compensated by a return gift establishing some sort of balance, that this is just or fair.

The sense of *retributive justice* says that the initial giver deserves or merits a reward, a retribution, for her sacrifice on behalf of the other.

These two sentiments of justice are different, although they may lead to the same or similar results. No idea of desert, merit, or reward is present in compensatory justice. Only issues of balance or equality matter. Some idea of balance between the two gifts is also present in retributive justice, but it is a derived concept, the way to reward the desert or merit of the initial giver. In compensatory justice, in contrast, the notion of the appropriate balance or equality is primary, with reference to the initial state and to somehow compensating deviations from it.

In retributive justice, only the initial giver and her responsibility matter. This is why the reward can a priori be provided by a third party, in a typical reverse reciprocity (a "Descartes effect"). In particular, this third party can be a public authority acting on behalf of society as a whole. Yet, the reward of desert or merit can also be provided by the initial beneficiary, in a standard return gift. Then, the notion of duty to reward is often supported by a sentiment of gratitude.

Compensatory justice can have two ways of effects in this respect. The issue is balance, or some sort of equality, between the two gifts. Yet, the compensation can refer to the situation of both individuals, or to that of the initial giver only. In the former case, the return gift is necessarily from the receiver to the initial giver, and hence it is decided by the receiver (who, however, may be influenced by social judgments, morals, norms, or social pressure). In the latter case, by contrast, the initial giver may be compensated by another agent, in a reverse reciprocity. This agent can, for instance, be a public authority acting on behalf of society as a whole. Yet, it can also be the initial receiver concerned with the initial giver's situation.

Negative reciprocation following harm raises similar issues, although not with a symmetry. Retributive justice then is specifically punishment, which can be desired, or felt as being required, for a reason of desert or merit – apart from its possible role of deterring from future similar actions. This punishment can a priori be inflicted by any agent. If the punisher is not the initial victim, this is a case of reverse negative reciprocation. This is for instance a basic role of the public authority, notably because, in a "state of law", it has the monopoly of lawful coercion. Yet, the punisher can in particular be the initial victim. Then, the latter motive is usually not to punish *per se*, but, rather, to take revenge.

Compensatory justice for harm has to distinguish two cases. One case is the compensation of harm done from the point of view of the victim – restitution of things stolen, other compensation, *praetium doloris*, and so on. The focus now is the situation of the victim. The payment – whatever its form – may be demanded from the initial actor, for a reason of responsibility, or of compensation between the two transfers or in the initial actor's situation. Yet, there can also be a desire to balance the harm done to the victim by a punishment of the initial actor irrespective of the compensation of the victim or of desert of the initial actor. Then, the punishment may provide no actual benefit to the victim. The focus is some kind of balance in the situation of the initial actor, between her act and the punishment – this notion of balance can exist *per se* but tends to be associated with the notion of desert, merit, or punishing guilt. Of course, all compensations required or punishment inflicted can be implemented by the judicial system and the public force (the monopoly of lawful coercion).

7.1.2. Reciprocal fairness

A thoroughly different relation between reciprocity and fairness is that the gift or favour of one agent towards another can consist of being fair in any respect towards this agent, in acts, judgments, or the corresponding attitudes, notably at some cost of any kind for the agent who behaves in this manner. Such a fair conduct may elicit a returned favour which can be of the same type, possibly about similar items. This is *reciprocal fairness*.

Reciprocal fairness is amenable to all the extensions of reciprocity: negative reciprocation (not being fair towards unfair people), and, for both positive and negative forms, all the cases of extended reciprocity, for the general reasons – generalized, general, reverse ("Descartes effect"), or chain reciprocal fairness or unfairness.

Reciprocal fairness can be motivated by most of the usual and general motives for reciprocity. This can be any of the motives for balance reciprocity. In particular, the motive can be retributive or compensatory fairness (it may be fair to be fair). Continuation can also play this role: people are fair so that others continue to be fair towards them. Liking someone can also induce being fair towards her, and you tend to like someone who treats you fairly – notably if she actually freely chooses to do it rather than doing it for complying to a strong moral obligation (or under strong social pressure). However, the liking induced by fairness or inducing it is milder than the stronger liking that induces, or may be induced by, favouring the other more than is required by simple fairness.

A fair behaviour towards another person can be one of the gifts in a reciprocity of any type. The tendency of similitude in the gifts can lead to both gifts having this nature (or a larger number in longer reciprocities), and, moreover, to the issues of fairness in each being more or less similar.

7.1.3. From reciprocal fairness to distributive justice

In a particular but particularly important case, all the attitudes and behaviours of fairness in a situation of reciprocal fairness concern the very same issue, such as sharing something between the participants, or choosing a rule for their relations. Then, if the conceptions of fairness of both agents lead to the same result, the outcome is chosen by both agents unanimously. This transforms a situation of conflict into a unanimous choice. The central point here is that fairness or justice implies impartiality from the very nature and definition of these concepts. That is, an agent's impartial view, when it considers her own interest, is not influenced by the fact that this interest is specifically her own (and similarly for the interests of the people she particularly likes or dislikes). Hence, these views can coincide with each other, while this is not possible for interests when they are opposed by the nature of the issue – a distribution or sharing for instance.

This type of situation can apply to several issues of sharing. One is sharing a given resource between the agents. Another is sharing a cost, such as the cost of a public good for these agents, or the payment of a given liability or contribution. Still another case concerns the conclusion of an agreement, possibly the solution of a bargaining: the issue then is sharing the corresponding surplus. The category of justice at stake here is *distributive justice*. This can apply with more than two participants, each behaving fairly towards others, for all these cases of distribution of a given resource, reaching a collective agreement, or contributing to a public good or a given liability.

However, the solution leads to a unanimous choice only if the participants have a congruent conception of the relevant principle of fairness. Now, there are a priori a variety of such possible conceptions. Essentially, the distribution can be equal in some good, according to need, according to merit or desert,[53] or according to some right either acquired or ascribed by social choice or social position. However, when this "substance" of justice is agreed upon with sufficient precision (which good, need, merit, or right), the very nature of the concept of justice, fairness or equity tends to provide a solution unanimously agreed upon. The key property of these concepts is indeed the noted one of impartiality, by which each sees herself on the same footing as others (Thomas Nagel's "view from nowhere"). This leads in particular to equality in the relevant items (such as goods, reward for given merit, the satisfaction of a given need, or the compliance to a given right), from a requirement of pure rationality.[54] When this equality is impossible or too costly in other terms, the same sentiment entails a preference for a lower inequality in the relevant items. Such comparisons of inequalities, and the building of corresponding indexes of inequality, constitute one of the most intensively studied topics in the social science. This analysis consists of the consideration of various sentiments about changes in inequality – and in the underlying unfairness – produced by

---

[53] The difference between merit and desert is that in merit individuals are entitled to – or liable for – the effects of their personal capacities whereas this is not the case with desert.

[54] See Kolm 1998 (translation of 1971), Foreword, Section 5.

various structural changes in the distribution, and of showing the relations among these properties.[55] The agreement about the relevant "substance" of justice (and about the second-best structure of relevant inequality if necessary), can result from reason applied to the issue in question, shared values, social norms, influences among agents in the reciprocal interactions, or influences, imitations (or "contagion") of judgments.

The question of distributive justice is a priori raised everywhere and every when in society: why does this thing belong to this person rather than to any other, or why are not unequal situations compensated by some other transfer? Distributive justice does not give rise to such a permanent universal dispute and debate because of a broad consensus about this topic in a given society. And this agreement has a reciprocal form: each person acknowledges the relevant property of others, and hers is similarly acknowledged. In particular, any encounter between people raises issues of fairness as long as the other is seen as a person – with the implied respect –, and then it implies reciprocal acknowledgment of rights and rules. The issues of justice and fairness thus are pervasive. However, beyond all the cases of "microjustice" are the general rule of society – a reciprocal respect of general rights – and the main distributions concerning basic needs and the allocation of the product of the main resources, notably of given human capacities, which often lead to widespread redistributions. These redistributions follow or should follow principles of justice, some of which are closely related to issues of reciprocity, as will shortly be pointed out (Section 10).

7.2. The principle of universalization: the categorical imperative

When asked why they bother to vote in large elections where their own voice makes no actual difference, most people answer: "what if nobody voted?" And they are immune to the remark that their own voting will not induce other people to vote. In fact, such a popular version of Kant's categorical imperative is a main reason for people to participate in collective actions and freely contribute to public goods. The moral indictment is: "Act in a way such that, if everyone acted the same – or followed the same principle – you would wish the result" (for Kant, if everyone acted according to the same "maxim", you "could wish the result"). This conduct solves prisoner's dilemmas, "coordination dilemmas" in which one coordinated solution is preferred by everyone, and the corresponding dilemmas about free contributions to public goods (see Section 9), because each action obeying this principle does not take care of the possible *actual* choices of the other players. This principle amounts to assuming that the others reciprocate (or duplicate) your act. It is putative reciprocity with each of the others. It is a kind of actual reciprocity only if the others adopt this principle for themselves because you do (then it is a reciprocity in the principle of action rather than in the action itself).

---

[55] See Kolm 1966 and the handbook edited by Jacques Silber (1999).

7.3. Other social sentiments

Comparative, matching or balance reciprocities are motivated by various more basic sentiments. The noted sentiments of justice, fairness, or equity are only some of them, and they are not always present – they seem to be more often present in revenge reciprocation than in (positive) reciprocities. Other sentiments motivating such reciprocities are a sense of duty, or of propriety and adequacy, in particular in following a norm of conduct. Moreover, such reciprocities are often motivated by the desire to avoid moral indebtedness. One often wants to avoid this indebtedness because it can mean dependency, subjection, or inferiority, and this arouses the corresponding sentiments. These sentiments can go as far as undermining dignity and arousing shame or guilt. Symmetrically, this imbalance can put the initial giver in the position of a moral creditor, which can elicit sentiments of pride, or of superiority, domination and power.

Liking and love are also quite apart from reciprocity in themselves, yet they constitute the material and vector of liking-reciprocities, in rather complex processes analysed in Section 6.4. These reciprocities also involve the sense of self and of social existence, and notions of responsibility of the other person. The sentiment of gratitude has aspects of both balance and liking.

Envy and jealousy also are sentiments a priori quite apart from reciprocity. Yet, balance-reciprocity is occasionally motivated by envy or jealousy about a possible superior moral or social position attributed to the initial giver. Jealousy in personal relations can entail specific revenge when its cause is seen as not respecting a promise or something due.

8. Reciprocity in the modes of economic realization

Science – and simple understanding – begin with the distinction and classification of phenomena, in pointing out the critical discriminating properties. Approaching a social process from the point of view of economics means beginning with "transfers". In the strict sense, the term "transfer" denotes the ordinary transfer of a good from one agent to another, but, by extension and for convenience of vocabulary, it will also denote, here, a service provided by one agent to another, and, more generally, any change in the world that is both costly in some sense for an agent and favourable to another. This can be an act of the former agent. Hence, transferring can mean acting favourably; giving can refer to such an act; and taking can mean forcing the other person to perform such an act. The distinction and comparison of the various modalities and modes of transfer is particularly important for understanding society. With respect to types of social relation and motivations, four types of modes of transfer can be distinguished: *taking* by force (forcing); *gift-giving*; *exchange*; and *reciprocity*. As before, exchange is understood here as standard exchange between self-interested agents (as with market exchange); that is, a set of transfers that are mutually conditional by external obligation (or promise keeping, or moral obligation to abide by an agreement). Reciprocity means here reciprocity proper, or "positive" reciprocation, and the corresponding transfers have the nature of gifts. The simplest relations presently considered will be between two agents, but a larger number of agents can be directly involved, as with collective agreements among more than two persons (which are exchanges), contributing to or deteriorating collective concerns or public goods, and extended reciprocities (generalized, general, reverse, chain).

Of course, each transfer can be closely related to others belonging to different modes. For example, a person may take something or acquire it in exchange in order to give it to someone else; or she may buy, or acquire in reciprocity, the services of someone else for robbing or forcing a third person; "bands of brothers" can be bands of thieves or of killers; and so on. The fact that a person can behave selfishly towards some people, notably in markets, with the aim of giving what she obtains to other persons (or of using it for any other non-selfish purpose) was a main concern of the clergyman-economist P. Wicksteed (1888, 1933). He called such a restrictively selfish conduct *nontuism*, in order to distinguish it from general egoism. Note that nontuism violates Kant's dictum of always treating others also as ends, as purely egoistic relations do.

The most elementary property is the smallest *number of transfers* involved in the relations in each mode, which is the number of transfers in the most elementary relations in each mode. Forceful taking and giving need one transfer only, while exchange and reciprocity need at least two interrelated transfers, one in each direction.

The second property – a deeper one – concerns *freedom*. The use of force and taking by force violate the liberty of one agent, while the other three modes respect the freedom of all involved agents. There is, however, a major difference in this respect between the two two-way transfers, exchange and reciprocity. In both cases, the pair – or a larger set – of transfers is freely chosen or accepted by the participants. In addition, however, in reciprocity each single transfer is free by itself. For example, the initial giving of a gift/return-gift relationship is obviously decided by the giver alone, but the receiver is also free to hand out a return gift or not, and to choose this return gift. This latter agent may feel an internal obligation to return the favour, but she is free from external obligations in this respect. An internal obligation can also be felt for the initial giving, or indeed for a single isolated gift, and in all these cases the cost of non-giving may be increased by a requirement of norm following and by social opinion or pressure. Yet, the act is, in the end, a free one, since otherwise it would just not be gift giving but force and constraint. In an exchange, in contrast, each transfer is conditional on the other by an external obligation – where such a "transfer" can mean the set of transfers in one direction. When one transfer is performed, the other has to be completed too. Legal obligation can be used to enforce such a contract, but the enforcement can be any other threat either of use of force (by the other party or still other agents) or of denying further benefits or possibilities, notably of exchanges, for instance in the continuation of a sequential exchange (obeying a moral of promise-keeping or of respecting an agreement is also included in this kind of constraint). Each single transfer is not free by itself. The expression "I give you this if you give me that" cannot refer to "gifts" in the proper sense of the term, but only to the terms of an exchange. On the other hand, "I give you

Coercion	Exchange	Reciprocity	Pure gift-giving
Forced		Globally voluntary	
Individually coerced transfers		Independently voluntary transfers	
Independent one-way transfer	Interrelated two-way transfers		Independent one-way transfer
Self-centred motivation		Other oriented	

Figure 4. The four dichotomies of the four modes of economic transfer.

this because you have given that to me" can refer to the return gift of a previous gift (although most often this sentence will not be uttered and the idea will remain implicit). The fact that the transfers of a reciprocity cannot be mutually conditional by external obligation, and, to a lesser degree, the fact that the acts occur successively (although return gifts of expected gifts may occur in particular cases) will be important features in the theory of reciprocity, both for the possibilities of realization, and for the nature and quality of the social relation.

Finally, the third property – the deepest one – concerns *motivation*. Taking and exchange can be performed by selfish or nontuistic people. In contrast, the givings and reciprocities that differ most from the other modes and are the most interesting for the quality of society are based on positive other-regarding sentiments or reasons, notably altruism, aspects of justice and fairness for balance-reciprocity, and gratitude.

Figure 4 summarizes this discussion. The present volume deals with two of the four modes of economic relations, and hence it covers half of the field in this sense. The modes it focuses on – reciprocity and pure giving – are distinguished from the others by their broader liberty (each single act is free), and by their motivations, which are generally not purely self-centred.[56]

The relative position of these four modes is meaningful and interesting. In the modes with overall freedom, reciprocity is situated between exchange and pure gift-giving. It consists of interrelated two-way transfers, as with exchange, but it shares with pure gift-giving both the other-oriented motivation and the fact that each transfer is individually free. Similarly, exchange is situated between coercion and reciprocity. As reciprocity, it consists of a set of several interrelated and globally voluntary transfers. But as with coercion, these transfers are individually forced and the direct motivation is self-centred (although there can be Wicksteedian "nontuism").

---

[56] Needless to say, this typology of modes of transfers bears a priori no relation to the types of goods (commodities, services) that are transferred. However, particular cultures establish as norms such correlations, some of which commonly are important aspects of the culture (for instance, particular services or goods must be transferred as gifts – perhaps in reciprocity – rather than sold and bought, etc.). These cultural traits can change, and these modifications are often important aspects of overall cultural changes (notably in "modernization" where, typically, more goods become amenable to exchange).

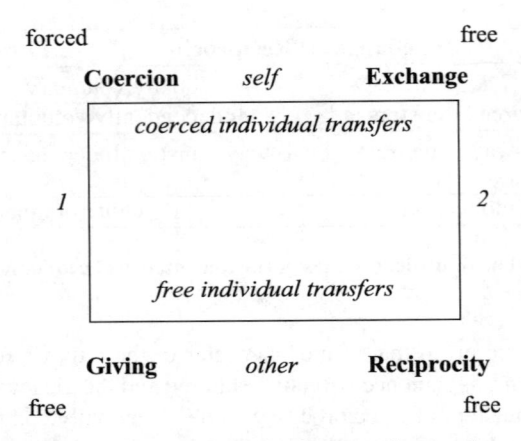

```
                forced                          free
              Coercion      self         Exchange
             ┌─────────────────────────────────────┐
             │     coerced individual transfers    │
             │                                     │
          1  │                                     │  2
             │                                     │
             │       free individual transfers     │
             └─────────────────────────────────────┘
              Giving       other         Reciprocity
                free                          free
```

Figure 5. The quadrangle of economic transfers.

This discussion can also be summarized with the quadrangle diagram of Figure 5. The four corners of the square respectively represent the four modes of transfers: coercion, exchange, giving and reciprocity. The sides containing coercion and gift, and exchange and reciprocity, correspond to smallest numbers of transfers of one and two, respectively. The sides containing coercion and exchange, and giving and reciprocity, correspond to selfish and other-oriented conducts, respectively. They also correspond to transfers that are individually forced and free, respectively. On the other hand, only coercion corresponds to force when all transfers are taken jointly since exchange is free in this respect.

A society of any kind (a nation, a region, an organization of any type) can use several of these modes in proportions which constitute a basic characteristic and can be measured as the proportion of economic values transferred in these modes. The comparison of these proportions across societies is a major aspect of the comparison of these societies, and the evolution of these proportions over time reveals an essential aspect of the transformation of these societies. This has been used, in particular, for providing a general taxonomy and analysis of economies, and for studying the evolution of economies in the processes of modernization and "development" and their various types. Several technical devices have been used for such studies, depending on the issue one wants to emphasize. In all cases, exchange refers to self-interested free exchanges of the market type. One can consider the four modes, or three modes in lumping two of them together.

In important studies, the three modes are exchange (market), the public and command economy with coercion, and (private) reciprocity.[57] Private gifts are included in reciprocity (reciprocity is a set of gift-givings and a pure gift can be seen as a limiting

---

[57] The reciprocities or exchanges that can be at work in the political and public processes are not considered as reciprocity or exchange.

case of a reciprocity where the return gift vanishes). Transfers by the public sector lead to its assimilation to the system of "redistribution" by a central power, as considered by some scholars such as Karl Polanyi (1944). The economy of an actual society is a regime which is a mix of these three systems in various possible proportions. The comparison and evolution of economies are fruitfully illustrated by the representation of the three corresponding proportions in a triangular diagram where each proportion is the distance of a point representing the economy to each side of an isosceles triangle including the point. The summits of the triangle represent each of the pure system, and one system is lacking for the points on a side of the triangle.[58]

The proportions of the four modes in a society can also be represented by a point in the quadrangle of Figure 5: the distance of this point to a side is proportional to the volume or proportion of transfers in the two modes indicated at the corners on the opposite side (the sum of these two volumes or proportions). Hence, points on a side correspond to the case where only the two modes of the corners on this side are present. And the corners correspond to the pure modes. The sides correspond, respectively, to selfishness (upper side) which opposes concern for others (lower side), and to a single agent's decision (left-hand side) which opposes interactive choices (right-hand side). A higher or lower point corresponds to more selfishness and more concern for others, respectively. And a point more on the left or on the right corresponds to more individualistic decisions and more collective choices, respectively. This also corresponds to various classical emphases in the conception of society: Hobbes is obsessed by the top left (coercion, plus a social contract), many economists by the top right (exchange), whereas many anthropologists first see the bottom right (reciprocity), and utopians favour the bottom left (pure giving).

Part III: Values and reasons

9. The values of reciprocity

9.1. The issues

Relations of reciprocity have a number of good consequences – some of which are very important –, and also sometimes bad ones. Very briefly, they permit a general peaceful and free society, they correct "market failures" in various ways, liking-reciprocities are appreciated for liking and balance-reciprocities for social balance or fairness, whereas reciprocities may also take the place of an efficient price system and balance-reciprocity is sometimes imposed by oppressive norms. Understanding these effects is important for two reasons, acting and explaining. Indeed, reciprocity can be more or less favoured or promoted, often indirectly, by collective choices about institutions, rules, and education,

---

[58] See the analyses using such a device in Kolm 1984a.

and by individual choices in choosing a type of relationship with other persons in specific circumstances. These choices then have to evaluate reciprocities and try to foresee and understand their various effects. However, such wilful and conscious decisions are usually only a small part of the causes of reciprocities or of their absence. Indeed, these modes of relation result essentially from a social and psychological process of evolution involving the joint formation of sentiments, culture, traditions, habits, social structures, institutions, and moral and educational views. This process includes conscious choices about many issues, unconscious or partially conscious influences on more or less distant consequences, the formation of views, opinions, sentiments and personalities, and many mechanisms of selection of psychological, cultural, or other social traits (with, in a very distant and general background, genetic selection of overall potentialities). Now, these selections of all types, including direct and indirect choices as probably a minor part, tend to create social forms that favour the thriving of society. In particular, they can install reciprocities because of such effects. Hence, understanding the favourable effects of reciprocity is part of the explanation of this mode of social relation.

Now, both explaining and evaluating for choosing are common questions. Even people who discard explaining for the sake of it may require explanations for making the appropriate choices. As for evaluation, its question is posed by the very fact that we have to choose. Economics has always been particularly concerned by this issue. It has always been a normative science, and it is largely the only normative social science (setting aside law and political philosophy). This is so because it aims at guiding action in evaluating the reasons for it and its consequences (it is a praxeology). The standard question addressed to authors of economic studies is: "what are the conclusions for policy?" The best-known economist – although a special one – has proposed that "the aim is not to know the world but to transform it". Of course, the proper and useful evaluations generally involves more than concern with economic goods in the strict sense. In particular, this is the case concerning the modes of economic interaction.

We thus have to consider the values – including shortcomings – of reciprocities. The overview is as follows. Reciprocity of respect permits the existence and performance of other peaceful social interactions, in particular of otherwise self-interested exchanges and markets. Reciprocity also constitutes a main corrector of "market failures" in taking the place of missing or imperfect markets, ending sequential exchanges, inducing free contributions to non-excludable public goods through various mechanisms, voluntarily internalising externalities, or sustaining mutual trust. These "failures" are cases where self-interest is self-defeating as a consequence of social interactions. Then, the relevant reciprocities are important instances of conducts that, in not pursuing self-interest, promote it in the end. However, reciprocity can also take the place of some allocatively efficient markets and exchanges. This may lead to losses in allocative efficiencies, but reciprocities also have other types of effects.

Indeed, in addition to reciprocity's effects on the distribution and allocation of goods, a very important aspect of this interaction concerns the style of social relations it introduces. These relations are bound to be positive and appreciated with liking-reciprocities, and more ambivalent with balance-reciprocities, where one may like the aspects of social balance and justice, and dislike the moral obligation of a norm if there is one. But the very fact of concern in and of others implied by reciprocities is often important and valued. A priori, in liking and balance reciprocities people consider the other person also as an end in itself;[59] they do not consider her only as a means to their own satisfaction (as with standard exchange or self-interested continuation reciprocity, for instance). In fact, the various types of behaviour and conduct are differently evaluated from a normative or moral point of view, both by the actors and by other people: taking by force, self-interested exchange, benevolent giving, norm-abiding, and so on, are judged very differently in this respect. Finally – and, possibly, most importantly – these actions and relations are related to different types of personality of individuals. Personality determines acts, but conversely, an individual's behaviour can also influence her sentiments, outlook, and preferences through the avoidance of kinds of cognitive dissonance. Moreover, the actions, reactions, opinions, and sentiments of other people, and the examples and arguments they provide, generally strongly influence the individual's judgments, feelings, worldview, attitudes and conduct. There are societies of benevolent, helpful and hospitable people, societies where a price is demanded for every service, and societies where you are happy to lose a cow, or an eye, if your neighbour loses two. Most people think it makes a difference. The good society is made of good people, not only of well-fed or even happy individuals. Most ethics find a progress from feeling good, to doing good, and to being good – indeed, being good induces doing good, which provides a feeling of high quality as by-product and immanent reward.

9.2. General respect and sociability from reciprocity

A society is not a permanent war of all against all. Yet, purely self-interested individuals have no reason to respect others, be polite towards them, or abstain from taking the property of people weaker than them, or enslaving them. Why do most people not behave this way?

Simple sociability in general respect and helpfulness cannot be explained with purely self-interested individuals. There are other motives, be they benevolence, the duty to behave properly, or sheer imitation, obtained with the aid of education and the judgment of others. Yet, people do not behave in this way when they themselves commonly face tougher behaviours towards themselves. And the general situation and motive cannot be sequential exchange when this behaviour is among people who will not meet again. It cannot even be the desire not to disrupt such a beneficial social order when the individual is small among many others. Moreover, the attitude and helpful behaviour of the general sociability in question are not obtained and obtainable by force (private or public). Hence, this is a case of generalized and general reciprocity, from and towards anonymous others although they are specific in each encounter. All the corresponding

---

[59] Except in cases of balance reciprocity where the aim becomes only the norm and the comparison of acts rather than the actors as well.

sentiments and behaviour can intervene: imitation, sense of balance, a priori favourable sentiments towards others, norm of conduct, and the judgment of other people.

This extends to the respect of more important items, such as the property and freedom of others people. Purely self-interested individuals should take the property of others when they can, and even enslave them. The reason why this is not the common situation in steady societies is threefold: self-defence and protection, the fear of the police, and voluntary restraint. These three means exist in various proportions. Self-restraint from harming and robbing others suffices in particular societies. It is never absent in the whole of society, and it is generally quite important (individuals who *fully* lack it are pathological types). It comes about as general morality from education, imitation, "proper" behaviour and probably some "innate" propensity, and it works in close association with the other means using force or the threat of it. However, a person would doubtlessly be less prone to manifest this respect if the others did not also do so, notably towards herself. Hence, generalized and general reciprocity are at work here, in the family of the noted "helping behaviour" but applied to the more straightforward restraint from harming. Again, this conduct cannot result from a purely self-interested sequential exchange since being respected by some sustains or induces respecting others (and a single individual's behaviour has little effect on most others). The outcomes are very important, including notably general social peace (relative scarcity of direct violence), and the possibility of property rights and hence of exchanges.

Similarly, and for the same reason, people do not maximally use fraud, lying and deception in social relations and notably exchanges. This often simply makes these relations and exchanges possible. And generally, it tends to make these exchanges more efficient.

9.3. Reciprocal corrections of market failures

9.3.1. Reciprocal solutions for correcting market failures

The situations of general sociability, respect, peace, and honesty could not be obtained by contracts of mutual agreement and exchange alone because of impossibilities and costs in information and constraining (and the basic fact that sentiments are important per se and cannot be bought). In the case of honesty limiting deceit and fraud, this impossibility of contract is due to asymmetrical information. For general respect of people and property, this agreement would be an overall contract involving everyone (akin to the kind envisioned by Thomas Hobbes). However, such a sufficient *actual* contract is not possible because of costs and impossibilities in information, communication, contact, discussion, transaction, and writing the contract in sufficient detail. Such limitations of exchanges or agreements have many other occurrences. They include what is called "market failures" and extend more generally to agreement failures. Their causes are impossibilities or costs in the domains of information, imagining possible events, writing sufficiently detailed contracts, and, for implementing the contract, checking, monitoring, constraining as required, and in particular specifically excluding from benefits joint with others of the same person or of other people. These "failures" are faced in a number of ways. This is one of the functions of public sectors who, however, have their own difficulties, costs and impossibilities with respect to information and constraining (as well as limitations concerning the motives of their members and the reliability of political processes). Other solutions rely on conducts of the people involved that depart from pure individualistic self-interest. Among the types of conducts leading to this result, reciprocations hold important roles. This is notably the case for sequential actions and for collective action and the provisions of public goods.

9.3.2. Sequential relation

Person A may give something to person B, or abstain from hurting her, for purely self-interested reasons, because she expects person B to reciprocate correspondingly. There can thus be mutual transfers or respect without binding agreement, hence, in particular, when the corresponding binding agreement is not possible or is too costly in any way (a "market failure"). The result may be beneficial to both parties, and in particular to person B, from the point of view of their pure self-interest. If person A may reiterate later her gift or respect, person B's motivation to reciprocate may simply be that of continuation-reciprocity for the sake of her self-interest. This possible reiteration is often not the case, however. At any rate, when this mechanism is at work, it has to assume a continuing sequence, which will have a last move. Now, without the consideration of further reiteration, person B's answer has to have a non-self-interested motivation. This cannot be full liking-reciprocity, or gratitude, aroused by the previous gift, since this giving's final intention was not to benefit person B. Person B's motives should thus be in the family of balance-reciprocity, such as keeping a balance, justice or fairness, or rewarding desert or merit, sustained by conducts of behaving properly, doing one's duty, or even acting according to honour. They are not strict, direct and intrinsic self-interest. Yet, they serve this person's self-interest in permitting this "exchange" or mutual respect (as if by an immanent reward of duty-bound conduct), since self-interested person A would not give in the first place if she knows that person B will not return a gift or do her part because she is purely self-interested.

Both parties benefit from this moral or balance-reciprocitarian conduct of this person, and this explains the various processes that lead to the existence of such motives and conduct. Indeed, the benefit for others (such as person A) leads society to praise this conduct and its motives, and to consider them as moral (in addition to the intrinsic morality of balance-reciprocity due to its properties of impartial equality and rewarding merit). This induces this conduct and motivates it by seeking approval and praise, including in one's own judgment; in particular, moral education is a notable means of this influence. Moreover, the own benefit of the person (B) tends to induce her to adopt these moral or reciprocitarian motivations, which are both profitable and morally valued, by a psychological process which associates effects that are conscious and unconscious, and voluntary and involuntary. These two types of forces for adopting such conduct and motive reinforce one another, and they can finally overcome the narrowly self-interested impulses. One could in addition imagine that genetic selection has paved the way in laying down broad tendencies. They can come from both benefit to others and benefit to the agent herself. However, this makes two very different types of theories. The influence of benefits to others can only play through group selection, whereas that of benefit to oneself rests neither on group selection nor on kin selection which sociobiologists see as the cause of "altruism" (quite simply, moral or reciprocitarian individuals would tend to survive more because of the benefit they derive from relations of the type in question).[60] If the term "rational" is used – as it sometimes is – for serving one's self-interest in a narrow sense, these effects show that it may be rational to be irrational, and they can provide a basis for explaining such irrationalities.

The general logic of sequential exchange has been considered earlier. The case where there are more than only two moves introduces important facts. One is the possibility of punishment and threat of punishment for maintaining the sequence of transfers, services, or contributions. Moreover, a frequent case is that, in a steady relation of mutually favourable acts, some sentiments in the family of liking progressively develop, even if there is no benefactor-liking at the onset, and this sentiment can motivate the last action (this may not be foreseen from the start, however, but we have pointed out that backward induction or other detrimental consideration of the last act does not actually occur beyond a few moves). Finally, we have also recalled the possible role of uncertainty about the end of the process or the other agent's behaviour for sustaining the relation.

9.3.3. Reciprocities and public goods or collective actions

9.3.3.1. Outline It often happens that each of a number of individuals can perform some act, prefers that everyone acts in this way to the case where no one does, but prefers not to do this herself when she takes what the others do as given, whatever it is. This is a typical simple case for contributions to a public good. But the act can also be any kind of collective action or the respect of other people's property and integrity previously discussed – then, general respect and peace can be seen as a public good. A collective binding agreement may solve the problem. However, in important and common situations, such an agreement may not be reachable because of the large number of people concerned or of costs of transaction, and access to the good cannot be sold to each person because of difficulties, costs or impossibilities of exclusion. In these cases, if everybody has a purely individualistic and self-interested reasoning, no one will perform her act, and nothing of the public good is produced (the Cournot–Nash solution of "free-riding"). This is indeed the outcome in a number of cases, but it is not in many others which are conspicuous in life.[61] And, indeed, other reasonings or sentiments by the participants often lead to different outcomes. One type of them refers

---

[60] Another mechanism of natural selection of pro-social traits, based on sexual selection, will be presented shortly.

[61] Taking the trouble to vote in large elections, for people who do not consider the probability that they be the pivotal, decisive voter (others being in a tie), is a case in point, and there are innumerable other cases

to the shortcomings of the purely individualistic reasoning and reactive behaviour that take the actions of others as mere parameters and lead to the Cournot–Nash solution. The common knowledge (in the technical sense) that other solutions are preferred by everyone can lead to such other solutions. Psychologically, this leads to reasons for conduct – generally implicit ones – akin to the very common "folk categorical imperative" that says: "I do this because what if nobody did?" (This is the main reason given by people when asked why they vote in large elections where their own vote makes no relevant difference.) Other reasonings, motives, and sentiments leading to the required action – such as voluntary contribution to a public good or a collective action – belong to various types of reciprocity, based on continuation and sequential exchange, balance or matching and equity, liking and reciprocal liking, or gratitude.

These different motives will be considered successively: strict self-interest, the categorical imperative which is a type of putative reciprocity, matching reciprocity, and liking reciprocity. A notable property will be the role of constraint in matching reciprocity: a constraint is required, and yet it does not actually bind people. Of course, the various individuals can have different motives, and each individual can have mixed motives. Moreover, there is a variety of structures through which individual actions can jointly have the relevant effect, depending on the technology and the number of people. For instance, the contribution of each individual may be favourable to each other – although perhaps only very little when the participants are numerous –; or there has to be several contributions for making a difference – possibly all of them. For analysing the effects of these motives and emphasising the aspects most particular to them, we will often consider the simplest situations where all the individuals have the same motives, and the simplest technical structure (which can be presented as individual contributions to a pure public good, and even sometimes with only two choices for each individual, cooperating or contributing or not).

9.3.3.2. Strict self-interest: a cumulative sequential exchange
People may be strictly self-interested. If they reason individualistically in taking others' behaviour as given parameters, the outcome is a Cournot–Nash equilibrium of free riding: usually, too little action is undertaken or the good is underproduced (except for exceptional indirect or income effects), and nothing is done or produced when the participants are sufficiently numerous and "small". A general agreement can solve the problem, but it may

---

in voluntary participations, abstaining from polluting, and so on. Many laboratory experiments on voluntary contributions to public goods have refined the fact in their special context (see notably Orbel et al. (1978), Ames and Marwell (1979), Schneider and Pommerhene (1981), Güth et al. (1982), Kragt, Orbell and Dawes (1983), Isaac, Walker and Thomas (1984), Kim and Walker (1984), Isaac, McCue and Plott (1985), Dawes, de Kragt and Orbell (1988), Andreoni (1988a, 1988b), Isaac and Walker (1988a, 1988b), a general discussion by Dawes and Thaler (1988), and a general review in Ledyard (1995)). Only motives and reasons for voluntary contribution that belong to the realm of reciprocity are noted here. There are a number of others. For instance, mutual approval or status seeking, in the person's reference group, is beyond the present scope (see, e.g., Holländer 1990), as well as many other social or moral causes of contributing (the specific effects of all possible motives are presented in Kolm 2006).

be prevented by the noted impediments, notably the impossibility to exclude from the benefit of the good, which prevents obtaining a payment in exchange for this benefit. Contributions can then be made compulsory, notably by a public sector.

Yet, there is often still another possible solution, relying on free contributions and self-interest alone: the transformation of the contributions into a sequential exchange and a "continuation reciprocity" if the contributions (the good) are divisible. In this case, people first contribute a fraction of their overall contribution, possibly a small one. Then, other small contributions are provided, each in the hope that other people continue contributing further, and so on in a recurrent or continuing process. Each contributes under the threat that others will stop their own contribution if she does not continue. The common house is thus built stone after stone. This is a *cumulative sequential exchange*. The question of the end of the process, already discussed for the standard sequential exchange, is present here. But the process can theoretically be endless if the successive contributions are decreasing but with a sum converging to a finite amount. Yet, the necessary divisibility of the good and general visibility of the contributions may not be the case.

9.3.3.3. Universalization or "Categorical imperative": A general putative matching reciprocity We have noted that a common answer given by people for explaining their contribution or participation is "I do it because what would happen if nobody does?" This is for instance the main answer received when people are asked why they vote in large elections where their vote makes no relevant difference and they don't imagine being a "pivotal voter" in a tie. People cling to their view and their slogan when it is pointed out to them that this is nonsense from the point of view of their individual action – which does not influence that of others.

This motivating reasoning is a kind of Kantian "categorical imperative": the person acts according to what would be the consequences if all others acted the same. The imaginary condition ("as if") amounts to matching contributions from others – that the agent's own contribution matches in turn. This is a kind of matching reciprocity, only the other person's contributions need not be actual. This motive can be called a putative general matching reciprocity. The other people's contributions become actual if the others hold the same reasoning and act in consequence. This "imperative" is in the realm of duty (Kant's favourite motive). Although this reasoning and the corresponding conduct are widespread, they are also a priori quite demanding in terms of risk to self-interest. This is why they are particularly present when the individual costs of contributing are small (such as voting or individual abstention from polluting public places). But they also exist in other cases. And, of course, everybody's interests are best served when this conduct is widespread.[62]

Yet, other, less demanding, motives in the field of balance reciprocity also exist.

---

[62] A full analysis of this "universalization" principle of conduct is provided in Kolm 2006.

9.3.3.4. Matching reciprocity and the necessary non-binding constraint
A very common position is: "I'll do my share if the other people do theirs". This differs from the categorical imperative by the requirement that others' contributions should be actual. Yet, this goes beyond individualistic self-interest in individual action, which advises defecting in the situation under consideration. This is a typical matching reciprocity based on a sense of fairness in contribution and in sharing the burden of a public good.

This matching reciprocity transforms a game of the prisoner's dilemma type into a coordination game in the sense that all individuals want to act some way if the others act this way. As with typical coordination games, there are several such Cournot–Nash equilibria. There is, however, a major difference. In the standard coordination game, the players are indifferent about these solutions (for instance, they prefer that all drivers drive on the same side of the road, but they are indifferent between it being the right side or the left one). In contrast, in the present "contribution or participation coordination game", all players prefer that all sufficiently contribute to the case where no one contributes. Hence, the willingness to do like others associates with a preference between the alternative (coordinated) solutions. In fact, there often can be various levels of contribution of each and various attitudes in the population, but, in order to focus on the essential phenomena and for simplicity in presentation, the expression will be as if there were only two alternatives, cooperate (contribute) or not, and if all individuals had the same attitude. The fact that individuals all prefer one Cournot–Nash solution to the other makes the choice of one not easier but more difficult. Indeed, in the standard coordination game, a simple sign may rally all actions, since people are indifferent among the coordinated solutions and know the others also are. In contrast, in the present situation, the fact that all participants have the noted ethics and unanimous preferences for one coordinated solution does not suffice to secure the solution. Even if each knows these characteristics of the others, this does not induce her to believe that the others will contribute, and hence to contribute herself, since each follows her interest in defecting if she is not sufficiently ascertained that the others contribute. Hence the solution might not be reached short of a binding agreement or mutual credible promises with mutual trust.

One way of making an individual sure that the others contribute (cooperate, do not defect) is that they be forced to contribute. Since others also make the same reasoning, all individuals should be forced to contribute. This coercion seems to make this situation not a case of reciprocity in the retained sense (which implies that the acts in question are free). However, this may not be the case and this situation is in fact deeply paradoxical. Indeed, each individual is forced to contribute, and yet she voluntarily contributes because she knows the others contribute and she is sure of it. Hence, she is not actually forced. That is, she voluntarily and freely does what the constraint requires her to do. She is forced to do what she wants to do. The constraint is not actually binding. Yet, it is reached by the act and there is no slack, no extra margin of freedom. Since the constraint is not binding, it is redundant in this sense. However, it is not useless: it is, for the others, the guarantee that the individual contributes. Yet, given this person's mentality, this guarantee is not necessary as long as the others contribute. And the others in fact know that this person would freely contribute if they themselves contribute, if they know her motives. In the case where there are two people only and acts are visible, no constraint is needed, since each knows that if she shows she contributes, the other will contribute too. The paradox of the necessary non-binding constraint is only for larger societies (for the same reason as in a pair, no constraint is needed in the variant of the game where each contributes if at least one other contributes). Practically, since the constraints are not actually enforced, they may require only light coercive means. The policeman may in the end practically become a mere symbol or signpost indicating that the cooperative solution is at work (rather than "enforced"). This is the result of the half-moral matching reciprocitarian conduct (full morality would be unconditional contribution, whatever the motive for it – it can be backed by a categorical imperative argument or not).

This matching reciprocitarian motive has variants. In one of them, the individuals want to contribute if the others want to contribute. The focus is on others' intention. The condition is their "goodwill" (in the sense of *bonne volonté*). Someone motivated in this way acts if she can and if the others would have acted if they could. She excuses an individual for not contributing if this person is not responsible for her absence. There can, indeed, be reciprocity of intentions. In a third case, the condition may be that the other people both want to contribute and do contribute, that is, they freely contribute. In this case, an obligation to contribute a priori does not suffice for inducing others to freely contribute. And yet, it may suffice if the individuals foresee that this constraint will not actually be binding. Of course, the free contribution is trivially guaranteed if individuals' conduct is that they contribute when others are in the same state of mind as they are (since this homogeneity is a priori assumed here). Moreover, an individual may require that only a subset or a fraction of the others act as required or intend to, or that they have this property to some extent, while her own action is also sometimes amenable to various forms or degrees. All these interesting and often important cases will not be discussed here.[63]

---

[63] A full analysis of all these cases is proposed in Kolm (1984a). The basic case of individuals willing to contribute if the others do is also presented by Sugden (1984) under the term reciprocity. It is applied by Swaney (1990) in a model of a case of depletion of a common resource, that is, of a "tragedy of the commons" (Hardin, 1968). Laboratory experiments displaying such behaviour have been performed by Croson (1999) and Fishbacher, Gächter and Fehr (1999), with notable results showing proportions of people behaving this way or not, or doing this to some extent, in the population of the experiment. Repeated voluntary contributions introduce the possibility of punishment in contributing less if others contribute less. This is no longer the pure non-excludable public good case, since punishment is a form of exclusion. When there are at least three contributors, a second type of non-excludable public good is then introduced, that of punishing people who do not sufficiently contribute. And further types can similarly be introduced if one iteratively considers punishing agents who fail to punish, and so on. All these aspects of commonness add to the simple question of the rationality of self-interested punishing discussed earlier. A major point is that contributing little in order to punish people who contribute too little also imposes a cost on all others, including fair contributors. Another is that, notably with a large number of "small" participants, the low contribution of a single individual – whether it is due to a failure to contribute or intends to punish others – may not be actually felt by another individual.

Moreover, the ethics in question can be seen as a set of relations in pairs of individuals. Indeed, each individual contribution to the public good benefits each other consumer of it, and hence it is a gift to her if it is voluntary. The balance reciprocity between these two gifts between two individuals amounts to the noted ethics – with the added structure that each such individual contiribution benefits both individuals.

Finally, in a number of situations the beneficiaries of the public good or the participants to the collective action constitute a priori a community of some sort (or, possibly, become one as a result of this collective action). This is favourable to relationships of reciprocity among them. In particular, fairness among them can induce the noted matching or balance reciprocity. Moreover, a sense of community can lead these persons to more or less like one another. This introduces first, a concern of people for the interest of others in the public good and the contributions, and second, the possibility of motivations of reciprocity based on liking.

9.3.4. *Reciprocities as correcting or superficially creating economic or social inefficiencies*

"Market failures" in general, and any such "failures" of exchanges and agreements, are the classical economic reasons for productive inefficiency in a broad sense, which in the end entails Pareto inefficiency (it is possible to satisfy some people better while no one is less satisfied). A classical conclusion is that the public sector should take care of these domains. However, public sectors have their own "failures". Indeed, they have the same two basic causes of failures as markets, exchanges and agreements, namely difficulties, costs, and impossibilities in information and in constraining. Moreover, the

---

The logic resulting from all these phenomena is analyzed in Kolm (1984a). Fehr and Gächter (2000b) and Falk, Fehr and Fischbacher (2000) made experiments with such repeated games and the possibility that participants "punish" non-cooperative others, in order to observe effects of non-strictly self-interested propensities to punish on the outcome. They assume that the same individuals both voluntary contribute if the others do and volunteer for punishing, hence face both the direct public good and the (first order) punishing one with the same non-purely self-interested behaviour. Note, however, that voluntarily contributing if the others contribute has, as parallel, voluntarily punishing if the others punish (except the person object of punishment) rather than unconditionally. Moreover, contributing is a cost while punishing others in contributing less is a direct profit. More importantly, for many people the direct relation established by their action matters. People with pro-other tendencies are often *not* prone to take the initiative of harming for punishment for the sake of it. In fact, there are two types of reciprocitarian characters in this respect: the libertarian *reciprocitarians* contribute if the others do but do not feel like punishing people who do not contribute, and the authoritarian *reciprocators* contribute if the others do and wish to punish people who do not contribute. These are very different – and in a sense opposed – types of socially-minded personalities, the relatively pro-others and the pro-order (who can be the determinant personalities in socialist and fascist societies, respectively). It is for instance well-known that the various European cultures traditionally emphasise different types in this respect (some emphasise punishment, even at individual initiative, more than others; some are "cultures of punishment" more than others). Finally, as already noted, the possibilities of punishment make the situation depart from the pure, non-excludable public good case, in the sense that punishment has the properties of a form of exclusion – possibly more or less partial – (the farmer who shoots to death anyone who has walked through her field has, when this is known with certainty, a way of excluding trespassers from her property).

various motivations of members of the political process and the public sector do not a priori guarantee optimality or efficiency – "benevolent dictators" hardly exist and the "political market" among competing politicians is hardly a perfect one. Now, the various possible individual motivations that are not purely self-interested in intent and not purely individualistic in reasoning provide spontaneous, decentralized, and free solutions and remedies of these failures and inefficiencies in a number of cases. For instance, they participate to the fact that observed voluntary contribution to public goods is often much better – and free riding lower – than predicted for purely individualistic and self-interested participants (this is for instance observed in various voluntary participations, in voting – the public good being the maintenance of electoral democracy –, and in laboratory experiments which are by now numerous).[64] Reciprocities are, in this role, less demanding in terms of motivation than pure altruism, since the self-sacrifices of individuals are lower because they are accompanied by benefits from the self-sacrifices of others. It is noteworthy that these motivations, where people are directly concerned with others' benefits or conduct (for reasons of balance, fairness, justice, respect, liking, and so on), constitute economic "externalities", and externalities are another classical source of market failures. In this case, these particular externalities correct other "failures".

On the other hand, externalities of the altruistic kind can also impair the functioning of the exchange system and its productive efficiency. A transfer by giving, hence at a null price, does not play the game by which the price system efficiently transmits information about possibilities and desires and can secure productive efficiency.[65] The distortion is also direct in any benevolent price rebate. This result also a priori holds for the set of givings that constitute a reciprocity, unless the return-gifts happen to have the same market value as the gift, which sometimes is the case, notably in balance-reciprocities. However, the possible losses may be compensated by the direct preferences about providing and receiving the gifts, due to the various possible sentiments of liking or fairness, the consideration you receive, the pleasure derived from this type of interaction, and so on. This effect and its conditions and consequences will be analysed in Section 13. As an example, George Akerlof's (1982) "efficiency wages", chosen by an employer in order to benefit from the reciprocitarian labour supply of the employees, seem to induce a wasteful involuntary unemployment, but employees' preferences include their preference for this kind of conduct. And givings by transfers that are sufficiently lump-sum, in income or as a gift which can be sold by the receiver, avoid these distortions. We have noted that such issues particularly interested the economist and clergyman Philip Wicksteed, whose concept of *nontuism* can reconcile market efficiency and altruism. Nontuism, indeed, means that when you operate in a classical market, you do not need to disregard the interest of everybody except yours – that is, to be selfish –, but only that of your vis-à-vis in the deal, while you can be altruistic towards everybody else. You can in particular give your profit, and seek profit for giving it.

---

[64] See a previous note.
[65] See the general discussion in Kolm (1984a), and the model presented by Laurence Kranish (1998).

9.4. Reciprocity in trust, relational capital, and efficiency

Conducts and relations of reciprocity are also frequent in the working of most organizations, including firms.[66] They commonly improve this working and are often necessary for it, notably because of the impossibilities and costs of specific information and overall checking. They take the form of mutual aid, including in information and advising. This happens among members of the organization, or between the organization as such and her hired employees, in which case it is a particular case of reciprocity within an exchange or market relationship. These reciprocities within organizations can also have all the extended forms: generalized, general and reverse.

These effects of reciprocities as correcting microeconomic deficiencies of markets and improving or making possible the working of organizations are important causes of economic and social efficiency.

In particular, impossibilities or costs of contracting or enforcing contracts, and of imposing hierarchical command, and resulting uncertainties about the behaviour of others, are corrected by a family of conducts that are largely supported by their being – in these cases – reciprocal, notably keeping one's promises, hence being trustworthy, and also trusting, along with voluntarily paying one's due and doing one's part. These conducts and attitudes can be at work between individuals, within organizations (including firms) between members or bureaus and between the management and other parts, between organizations or organizations and individuals, for social relations of various types and importance. They are essential factors of economic efficiency and social cohesion.

Trust, in particular, can replace impossible or costly contracts, and permit the working of incomplete contracts, and it has a particular importance. It can raise, and rest on, all the mechanisms of reciprocity, and in addition it has a number of very specific characteristics in this respect. The basis of the particular characteristics of the relation of trust is that an individual can have, in this relation, not two positions – as with giving and being given to – but three positions: trusting, being trusted, and being trustworthy. Therefore, first of all, the favourable attitude, the "gift", can be both to be trustworthy and to trust, to be trustful. Hence, the "return-gift" to someone who trusts you, in the same field, can be to trust her, but also to be trustworthy, to deserve her trust. In fact we will see that there is another reason for trusting the "truster". Yet, the "return-gift" to someone whom you can trust should be that she can trust you, since the other alternative, trusting her, is implied by her trustworthy character.

Second, trust, being made of two personal situations, trusting and being trusted, and of the two corresponding attitudes and conducts, trusting and deserving trust (being

---

[66] Julio Rotemberg (1994 and his Chapter 21 in this Handbook) analyses the issue of altruism at the workplace and its effects on productivity. More precisely, he considers mutual altruism. However, these liking sentiments have causes, among which the fact that others like and help oneself, which lead to the two types of liking reciprocity. Moreover, balance reciprocity and continuation reciprocity are also important in this situation, with roles for the various types of extended reciprocities.

trustful and trustworthy), entails a particular structure, raised by the psychological relation between the propensities to these two attitudes and the corresponding actions. This relation comprises two possible effects. The first one is that, other things being equal, an individual tends to attribute to others the properties of mankind she observes in the sample of it of which she has the most intimate knowledge, namely herself. For this reason, if she is trustworthy she tends to think others are and hence to trust them. And if she tends to trust them, this tends to reveal that she herself is prone to be trustworthy. Similarly, if she is not much trustworthy, she tends to think that others are not either and hence to distrust them. And if she is prone to distrust others, this may reveal that she is not much trustworthy herself. However, in the case of distrust and diffidence, another effect can lead to the opposite relation. Indeed, someone who has high standards of morality can tend, for this reason, both to be trustworthy because she applies these standards to her own conduct, and to demand much from others in order to trust them and, therefore, to be frequently diffident and untrustful. If trusting is the "gift", in trusting someone because you think she is trustworthy because she easily trusts others, you practice a "reverse reciprocity" (a "Descartes effect"). Correspondingly, you may distrust someone who tends to be diffident about others because you think this reveals a general disbelief in trustworthiness that reveals her own character in this respect. Yet, you may also trust someone who tends to distrust others because you think that this reveals, in this respect, very high standards that she presumably also applies to herself. The first effect can be a particular cause of direct reciprocity (trusting people who trust you, and distrusting those who distrust you), among the other, ordinary causes.

The general reciprocitarian structures indeed fully work for trust, with again a number of specific particularities in addition. If someone trusts you, balance-reciprocity commonly induces you to trust her – and in addition she probably is trustworthy at any rate as we have seen –; but this also often induces you to be trustworthy towards her in order to "deserve" her trust, which also is in the general family of balance-reciprocity. If you can trust someone, this implies *ipso facto* that you trust her if you are in the appropriate relationship; and balance-reciprocity induces you to be trustworthy towards her, when the occasion comes; moreover, being trustworthy, she is probably also trustful, and you may not want to disappoint her in this respect. By the standard "helping behaviour", you tend to trust if you have been or are trusted, and to be trustworthy if others have deserved your trust, even if they are not the same people, thus leading to generalized and general reciprocities in trust and in trustworthiness.

The standard reciprocities present here are of the balance type. In addition, however, you tend to like someone who trusts you and someone you can trust. This only reinforces the relationships, and it possibly induces side-gifts which also reinforce and symbolise the relationship and express both sympathy and satisfaction. It also emotionalizes the relationship and so reinforces it, although other emotions come when trust is denied – a possible offence – and especially when it is betrayed. Finally, of course, sequential exchange for the continuation of trustworthy conduct is very important, and both sides of trust are of course also heavily influenced by imitation, conforming, previous or a priori knowledge of the other person, hence social proximity and a common culture and education, and the practices, norms and morality of the society.

The effects of the bundle of conducts constituted by reciprocity, trust, promise keeping or doing one's part, on the efficient working of various social systems have been studied for various organizations and in particular for firms. The positive effect of this relational capital on productivity at an overall level and on growth have been the object of a number of important recent empirical studies, notably by Putnam (1993), Berg, Dickhaut and McCabe (1995), Knack and Keefer (1997), Helliwell and Putnam (1999), Glaeser et al. (2000), Alesina and Ferrara (2002), and Zak and Knack (2001).[67]

9.5. *The intrinsic values of reciprocity*

Last but not least, reciprocities have direct social values which are often very important. These values are judged both by the preferences of individuals, notably participants, and from higher standpoints (which are also taken by individuals).

In particular, liking-reciprocities, or the liking dimension of reciprocities, support and promote sentiments of liking other persons, more specifically mutual and reciprocal liking, which are the basis of the most highly valued complex of social sentiments. You generally like being liked, you often like liking, you normally like being liked by people you like, and you probably approve that people like each other, both for their sake and on moral grounds. The social intercourse of the realization of the givings or favours is also often valued. It often is the best of times. Gifts are the standard symbols of liking of all types and intensities, from simple esteem to love.

All kinds of givings, favours and reciprocities whose final aim is to benefit the receiver, or to show and prove that she is liked, promote the social recognition and existence of the beneficiary, in a way that is absent in purely self-interested exchange, and still more in taking by force. This effect is all the more marked as the giver's attention and concern is more respectful, benevolent, or kind.

Balance-reciprocities, or the balance aspect of reciprocities, are quite different from liking-reciprocities or the liking aspect of reciprocities in this respect. Such relationships can be either liked or disliked. They often constitute and entail balanced social relations, in a framework of fairness and justice where dues are paid and merit is rewarded, with dignity and the satisfaction of accomplished duty. However, they also sometimes are a domain for oppressive norms, guilt, shame, and heavy social pressure through opinion or otherwise. When reciprocities are considered in social design, the point is that, although not all reciprocities are valued, there exist types of reciprocities that are highly valued and, indeed, considered among the best of social relations.

Finally the moral praise of being "good" is applied to types of actions, conducts, attitudes, intentions, motives, thoughts, and sentiments of persons addressed to other

---

[67] This topic is somewhat discussed in Chapter 9 of this volume by Pier-Luigi Sacco, Paolo Vanin, and Stefano Zamagni. Note that "relational capital" is to be preferred to the more general "social capital" (see, e.g., Kolm 1966).

persons, such as respect, aid, gift-giving, forgiveness, benevolence, compassion, pity, solidarity, kindness, helpfulness, liking, friendliness, amicability, generosity, consideration, gratitude, fairness, forgivingness, and the like. People who so act and hold such thoughts, sentiments and motives are also praised as being "good" in this sense. Now, the good society is not only a collection of well-fed individuals, of satisfied persons or of free agents. It is not only structured by institutional justice – supposedly its "first vitrue" (Aristotle). It also comprises good acts, actions, attitudes, and intentions. And, ultimately, the good society is made up of good people. This aspect of society cannot be separated from the others. In particular, services and goods cannot be separated from the way they are transferred, acquired and produced. Such conducts, attitudes, motives, and sentiments would also remedy a number of other vices such as miseries, social disregard and discrimination, various injustices, oppositions between distributive justice and individual freedom (giving redistributes in respecting liberty and thanks to it), and many productive inefficiencies for the reasons discussed above. Normative judgments, social and institutional design – and, of course, education – cannot leave out this basic dimension.

10. Normative uses of reciprocity

10.1. The values of reciprocity

Properly reciprocal and notably reciprocitarian conducts result from the appropriate sentiments, and sentiments are more given than chosen. However, there are a number of ways in which relying more or less on reciprocity can be chosen. Such a choice should rest on the values and possibilities of reciprocities, qualified for their possible shortcomings. These choices and instruments include various types of social and institutional design. They rely on the existing or potential relevant social sentiments. Hence, they are also closely associated to ways of shaping and modifying such sentiments, in education both in childhood and in the general culture, including the effect of imitation and psychological and emotional "contagion". At an overall level, both social structures and these formations of social sentiments are closely interdependent (Jean-Jacques Rousseau published simultaneously his work on moral education, *Emile*, and his work on political theory, *Social Contract*, and he considered the second as an appendix to the first).

The values and shortcomings of reciprocities to be considered have been pointed out. They relate to efficiency, justice, and social relations. Reciprocity permits general sociability and social peace, in particular the general possibility of a market system, and it corrects a number of market failures, although it can also somewhat impair strict economic efficiency in not making the best use of the information role of the price system. Balance-reciprocity manifests local justice, and we will see that it can have a basic role in overall distributive justice. Liking-reciprocities have a basic function in the quality of social relations. Balance-reciprocity also has such a function in securing fairness, equity, equality, sometimes dignity or social status; yet, its possible demand by more or less constraining norms or social pressure can have unfavourable effects in restricting both freedom from the interference of society and other people, and mental freedom, by constraints which are either internalized or the effect of social opinion, and which can thus be seen as having a particularly vicious nature. Finally, extended reciprocities, and notably generalized and general reciprocities, have an essential role in maintaining social cohesion and a working community in individual freedom.

10.2. Cooperatives

The most direct institutional impact of an ethics based on reciprocity is in the movement of cooperatives. A cooperative is sometimes a name given to an association of purely self-interested members. Most of the time, however, a cooperative rests more or less on an intrinsic ethic of mutual help and is essentially based on relationships of reciprocity. Liking-reciprocity is then supposed to be present to some degree among members, and balance-reciprocity and the accompanying conception of fairness are also often deemed important. Historically, a number of reciprocitarian cooperatives have failed and disappeared. Others have thrived but have lost most of their initial specific motivations and have become standard firms or associations – although they often keep their founding ideal as ideological decorum. Still other reciprocitarian cooperatives continue and keep their initial ideal or some of it, but, when they are immersed in an economy with a different basic rationale, this is often in relation with particular social or political situations.[68]

10.3. General rules of society

The general rules of society, including its overall distributive system, are demanded and maintained by sentiments that include crucial aspects of reciprocity. General rights, including basic rights and relevant property rights, are generally accepted or desired, which implies that each accepts to respect those of others and to abide by the rule, given that her own rights are similarly respected. This is not the object of an explicit exchange in the strict sense. The logic of this situation has been previously discussed, and the essential role of reciprocity in it has been pointed out. Moreover, present societies engage in large-scale redistribution implementing other ideas and sentiments, notably benevolence and solidarity, and some egalitarian justice. Reciprocity is also very present in the reasonings, sentiments and situations concerning this distributive justice. Two instances are shown in the next two sections.

---

[68] Cooperatives are the topic of the Chapter 22 by Louis Putterman in this Handbook (see also the theoretical analysis and factual study in Kolm 1984a).

10.4. Putative reciprocities

Particular needs of people can be faced by savings or insurance when they can be envisioned ex ante, by others' help in single gifts or in reciprocities, or, when the individual need is repeated without a strong correlation in time among individuals in a population, by alternative mutual aid sustained as a self-interested sequential exchange or by motives of fair balance or of liking and very often by a mix of these motives.

Helping as a single gift – individually, collectively, or institutionally – can be motivated by mere sentiments of compassion, equality, or affection. However, among the various motives people have to help others who have a particular need, an important and frequent one is expresses as: "I help her because she would have helped me if our situations were reversed". This reasoning and motive is a putative, imaginary, or hypothetical reciprocity. If the situation has actually been the reverse one with the reverse help, or if one expects that it could become the reverse one with the reverse help, this would be ordinary reciprocity, sustained by the possible reasons of interested continuation, liking, balance, or fairness; but the reasoning in question is held in cases where an actual reverse situation is not possible. The primary motive of putative reciprocity is a notion of balance possibly accompanied by fairness between the two agents. Other, different sentiments can accompany cases of putative reciprocity, such as compassion or general fairness. There are also putative extended reciprocities, either generalized ("I help her because I would have been helped myself if I needed it, possibly by someone else") or reversed ("I help her because she would have helped others if needed and if she could").[69]

10.5. Macrojustice

However, distributive justice basically demands sharing given resources. For overall distribution, the resource of this type which produces the largest amount of economic value, by very far, consists of the given productive capacities of individuals. Then, it can be shown that properties unanimously adhered to imply that this redistribution should amount to an equal sharing of the incomes that the individuals can earn with the same given labour different from their actual labour (but with their different capacities).[70] This distribution also amounts to each individual yielding to each other the proceeds of the same labour. This has a structure of reciprocity, more precisely of balance reciprocity where the balance is the equality in labour. This equality in sacrifice entails that this redistribution is amenable to support by sentiments of reciprocity.

More generally, in a democracy, implementable policies should be in tune with what people want, or, better, they should implement what people want. They should thus

---

[69] Applications of the concept of putative reciprocity can be found for distributive justice in Kolm 2004 (pages 360 and 447) and for the question of joint giving in Kolm 2006. Note that if reciprocating is following the same rule, putative reciprocation (by any number of other people) leads to the principle of universalization (the categorical imperative).

[70] This is the theory of "macrojustice" (see Kolm 1996a, 1996b, and particularly 2004).

abide by the social-ethical values and preferences of the people. Among these judgments are those that belong to the family of reciprocity. The program presented in the chapter by Christina Fong, Samuel Bowles, and Herbert Gintis in this volume, of basing welfare state policies on people's social-ethical preferences, has much to say for it (in adding the possibility of educating to these views, as Rousseau would emphasize).

10.6. The Good Society: The classical scientific directing utopia

Members of genuine cooperatives often pride themselves of social relations that avoid the selfishness of the market and the hierarchy of firms and administrations. This is related to a long line of normative social thinkers who saw in cooperatives and associations of mutual aid of various types, relying on relations of reciprocity, the way of avoiding both the inequality, domination and unfreedom of hierarchical organizations and the selfishness, hypocritical hostility and alienation of market exchange relations. Indeed, since relying on pure altruism on a large scale and a for long time would doubtlessly constitute an unrealistic and utopian demand on motivations, reciprocity remains the only more or less possible alternative to selfish exchange and hierarchical command. In it, indeed, people give, but given that they are given to. In joining freedom and orientation towards others, liking and fairness, and often a sense of community, reciprocity can provide the needed ingredients of the "good society". It goes without saying that the freedom-reducing aspects of weighty norms and social pressure – present in a number of reciprocities as we know them – are to be avoided. But these are by no means all of reciprocity, and they are absent in many cases of reciprocity. In fact, extensions of reciprocities tend to suppress conditions of some of their vices. For instance, exploiting the return-gift (i.e. giving in order to receive a return-gift) does not work for a generalized reciprocity where the beneficiary of the return-gift is not the initial giver. Or again, the possibilities of social pressures of all kinds present in small-group relations are much diminished at more extended social levels relevant for general reciprocities.

Moreover, the various types of systems of economic and social relations co-exist. The question concerns the scope of each. In particular, their relative importance has a determinant influence on the general *ethos* of the society, that is, on the general style and type of sentiments, attitudes, relations and personalities in it. A society's ethos is a major feature of its quality. There are societies of merchants, societies of bureaucrats or of company men, and societies of brothers. Hence a main issue of social improvement consists of the consideration of the possibilities of qualifying an ethos produced by the association of a pervasive market with a hierarchical organization of production and of government. This can be an important function of a larger scope for reciprocities.

Finally, the noted social thinkers have all been keen on using the scientific knowledge available in their time (see, for instance, Piotr Kropotkin's use of Darwin, Marcel Mauss's ethnographic inspiration of his social remarks, the relation between Saint-Simonians and industry – and their later role in it –,[71] or the general "scienticism"

---

[71] Saint-Simonians cared so much about reciprocity that they used to wear coats buttoned in the back so that each of them needed another to dress and undress.

of nineteenth century socialist thinkers). We should certainly do the same in using all available and obtainable knowledge. Action, being intentional, implies imagining possible worlds. This holds true for social and political action. Yet, the scope of possibility is uncertain. One possible mistake is to see as possible something that is not. But a worse one consists of failing to imagine the possible and better situations. You may achieve the best possible alternative in trying to reach an impossible one, but never in implementing an inferior possibility. Hence, lack of imagination is more dangerous than utopia, notably if the latter is taken as directing utopia, showing a direction for heuristic progress – while how far one can go along this way appears clearly only in practice.

These exercises require using all relevant information in an integrated synthesis. For motives and possible social relations and structure, the basis is a phenomenology of social sentiments, notably those at work in reciprocities, which tells one what we really are talking about. Besides these basic considerations, all the facets of the social science are bound to contribute. Reflective psychology shows relations and interactions. Anthropology displays a variety of existing social forms which both are instances in the domain of the possible and suggest constants which may be characteristic of "human nature" – in so far as such a thing exists. Sociology presents other examples and proposals of explanation. Psychological theories propose still other explanations of various types. Social psychology suggests generally more local explanatory concepts and a wealth of systematic observations either *in situ* or in laboratory experiments which can falsify some proposed psychological explanations, or at least cast doubt about them, and show the proportions of behaviours of various types in specific subpopulations and conditions. Economics can contribute by its description and analysis of various economic systems, its knowledge of the requirements of successful production, its specific concepts for modelling the conducts of individuals in isolation and in interaction, and its analysis of the logic of notions of equity, fairness, equality and inequality. Of course, the disciplinary assignment of these various types of information is thoroughly irrelevant. When considering a question, all the relevant information is to be considered. There is no valid reason to restrict oneself to only one aspect. As the Chinese dictum puts it: "do not care whether the cat is black or white as long as it catches the mouse".[72]

11. How and why? Understanding and explaining reciprocity

11.1. Understanding

The main focus, so far, has been on understanding reciprocity. The term understanding is to be understood here in two senses. The first is the common sense of knowing the

---

[72] Hence, the present volume on the economics of reciprocity, giving, and altruism, although it tries much to relate this viewpoint to those in psychology, anthropology and sociology, is definitely to be seen as only one aspect of the relevant information rather than as a self-contained compendium.

whereabouts, the various elements and types, the workings, the influences, and the reasons for actions. For reciprocity and its various types, clear and explicit awareness and knowledge of all these elements, workings and possibilities are by no means a priori obvious. They should be a posteriori, though, once the descriptive analysis is presented, apart from the specific analysis of the effects of strategic interactions (this will be the object of Section 13). The reason is the reliance on understanding in the second sense, which is the technical sense in which this term is used in the social science (Max Weber's *verstehen*). This refers to the fact that we speak of things about humans, and we ourselves belong to this category. To begin with, the crucial items are sentiments, which cannot be given a definition – they can only be specified. When we mention a sentiment, each of us understands what the term means from her own subjective experience. This refers to our feelings, but this information is supported by our experience of life in society, with watching others, hearing from them, meaningfully interacting with them, experiencing some empathy or compassion towards them, understanding their words, situations, and feelings, and being so understood by them. We can use our memory of these facts. We similarly understand effects and causes of sentiments, and reasons for actions, conducts and in the end behaviours. The large and presumably unique capacity for "compassion" and empathy that characterises humans is at work here. The most important, however, is that each of us is a rather exhaustive sample of mankind.[73] Refusing to use this source of information is not possible concerning meanings of terms denoting sentiments, feelings or emotions. For the rest, this rejection is inflicting on oneself the handicap of attempting to understand behaviour with only a chimpanzee's capacity for that. This may be suitable for understanding chimpanzees.[74]

In fact, we do not only constitute, for ourselves, an impressionistic dictionary of the meanings of sentiments and feelings, a showcase exhibiting their existence and possibilities, and a cellar stocked with previous experiences and information. Each of us also so has at her disposition a portable and flexible laboratory, and an extremely powerful one if one's methodological religion does not cripple its use. Any experiment in an "outside" laboratory is set up after coarse and fugitive observations in this "internal" laboratory and seems to only provide frequencies in populations at the cost of only dealing with quite simplified and primitive aspects of the actual phenomena. The method pointed out here is not only introspection; it is rational, thoughtful, reflective, experimental, duplicable, shared, and in part verbally communicable introspection. Introspection may

---

[73] It is extraordinary how far we can understand the sentiments, reasons and motives of people of cultures thoroughly different from ours, for instance in tribal life, or very distant in time; it is for instance extraordinary that the Bible, ancient Greek tragedies, classical Indian epics or Buddhist scriptures can still serve as relevant reservoirs of meaningful and powerful examples of such sentiments and conducts.

[74] Chimpanzees pass by food in pretending it is not there, so that others do not know it. That is, they lie. Hence, they seem concerned with the knowledge and state of mind of others. However, experiments – for which chimps are the right subjects – seem to have shown that they only do this because it works. They do not seem to have an image of the others' state of mind. That is, they are behaviourists. They also are pragmatist philosophers ("it works").

be "going at the window to watch oneself pass by". However, as far as feelings and sentiments are concerned, the opposite alternative, behaviourism, entails the following exchange when two behaviourists meet: "Hi, you feel great, how do I feel myself?"[75]

Besides understanding, the next epistemological exercise is explaining, that is, giving reasons or answering the question "why?" The preceding analytical description of reciprocities has explained behaviour by motives induced by sentiments (or interest), and it has sometimes explained sentiments by other sentiments, or by feelings, acts, situations, and rationality. These explanations are obvious and clear, once one has become aware of them. One may want to go further, however, and also explain the propensities to experience these sentiments and their very existence. Indeed, the specific instances of existence of these sentiments has been explained, but their general possibility and influencibility has not: why can people like, why can there be pleasure, gratitude, and senses of balance or imbalance, fairness, moral indebtedness, duty, and so on, why are these sentiments influenced and determined as they are? A first and obvious remark is that explanation is never full; after each explanation, one can still address the question "why?" to each of its elements. And if we decide to stop at some point in the regress, why there? An obvious and natural answer consists of asking why we want or need an explanation. The apex of Buddhist wisdom consists in refusing to answer useless "whies". "When you have been hit by an arrow, take care of the arrow and don't ask who threw it" is its most famous aphorism.[76] Is curiosity a naughty vice, or is pure research "the honour of the human mind" (as the mathematician Kantor puts it)? Following Buddhist therapeutic epistemology, we should want to explain only in so far as we need it for improving things. This seems indeed to be a honourable objective and a rational – or reasonable – answer. One of the most famous economists has even asserted: "The problem is not to explain the world but to transform it". We could be more modestly satisfied with trying to contribute to alleviate its miseries. The normative aspects of reciprocity intervene here. A very ancient tradition has seen in the appropriate reciprocity the only potential for avoiding altogether the selfishness of market exchange, the domination of command, the disasters of fighting, and the utopia of a priori general unconditional altruism. Moreover, reciprocity favours social productivity in securing trust, in ascertaining mutual respect that permits benefiting from one's acts and exchanging, and in remedying a number of market and exchange failures (see Section 9). Yet, a policy trying to promote the favourable aspects and effects of reciprocity needs to know which causes of reciprocity it can influence, if any.

Explanations of reciprocity have first of all to face two facts. First, there are several quite different types of reciprocity and of psycho-social processes that lead to it,

---

[75] Only plain, superficial introspection accessible to anyone without training and specific education is considered here. The trained and taught introspection which is the basis of the psychological knowledge of advanced Buddhist studies is something completely different and the only way to know what mind means and is (see Kolm 1982).

[76] The ultimate reference, for Buddhism, is the decrease of suffering. Hence it advises against seeking any explanation that does not contribute to this end. Especially since, being necessarily incomplete, it will create insatisfaction in any "rational" mind.

based, respectively, on a sense of balance or fairness with sentiments of social propriety and moral duty, on liking including a direct reciprocity of sentiments, and on interest. Second, each reciprocity is constituted of elementary mental facts which also exist without it (affection, sympathy, empathy, emotional contagion, understanding of causality, imitation, sense of impartiality, elementary rationality, sense of social balance and of fairness, sense of duty or propriety, gratitude, sense of moral indebtedness, capacity to foresee and reason, capacity to understand other people, and so on). A full explanation should also explain these elementary facts (this is for instance the case for explanation by selection). However, one can also explain specific forms given the more basic and general facts. Several interacting influences then have generally to be considered. The causes of the specific sentiments and conducts intervening in reciprocity can be found in social influence in all its various forms and ways including education, in psychological structures and processes, in sociological evolution, and in the supporting biological material.

Simple psychology sometimes suffices. For instance, people have found that sequential exchange can be beneficial, and their giving in return may have turned into routine and habit, while they forgot about the strategic reasoning that justified it (the more easily so that the complete rational reasoning about the full future sequence is beyond direct and immediate intuitive grasp). This return giving could thus become simply something to do, an instinctual propriety, and hence de facto a balance-reciprocity. The balancing of the return thus results from the initial benefit of giving in return sufficiently for inducing continuation, while giving too much would be a waste. This habit then would be admitted and transmitted, in a sense a norm. Yet, simple personal interest alone cannot explain in this way the balance return giving when it is the end of the relation. However, other mental and social processes can also be involved (for instance, we have seen the role of impartiality and rationality leading to sentiments of equity).

11.2. Biology?

A number of scholars have found an interest in relating altruistic conduct and gift-giving to biology and more specifically to genetic selection. This approach turns out not to be able to provide sufficiently specific and discriminating concepts and hence results to be useful, presently and undoubtedly for a long time to come. Yet, even if it is not a fruitful point of view, it is just a truism that mental facts "come from" chemical reactions and electrical circuits in the brain. In fact, individual experience, culture, including education, "are" even anatomy of the brain, and not only its physiology, because they create interconnections of neurons. However, there exists the relevant biological material, the neurons and the overall structure of their network, built under genetic information. Yet, even this evolution is not independent of culture which influences sexual selection in mating and differential probabilities of death and life duration, and of reproduction rates in the various subpopulations. And human culture is as old as the hominization process of which it is an aspect.

From a practical point of view, however, the biological influence only has a negative interest, in suggesting what cannot be influenced, since we envision, as policy tools, neither neurosurgery, nor a eugenist policy of human selection or mating, nor cloning. And yet, there might be at least a speculative interest in considering reciprocal conduct in neurobiology and in selectional sociobiology. Reciprocity belongs to mechanisms of treatment of emotional information that play a regulating role in life in groups. In humans, as in many animals, this happens in a set of neuronic circuits part of the limbic system and joining the amygdale to the temporal, the cingular, and the orbito-frontal cortexes.[77] It would be informative to find out how these zones differ in the various types of reciprocity and reciprocation, how they relate with zones corresponding to other sentiments such as greed, fear, liking, love, justice and injustice, and so on. But we may also want to explain the brain along with the rest. Unfortunately, natural biological selection, which made us, clearly cannot enlighten us much in this respect.

There exist, of course, several possible genetic selective mechanisms that can favour and lead to this direction for the sentiments and conducts in question. Returning favours is a kind of altruistic behaviour. It is to be noted, first, that the sociobiological literature suggests generally explanations of behaviour, not of sentiments and feelings, whereas our evidence of human conduct is that behaviour is chosen because of sentiments and feelings (even reflex acts often result from habits of conduct driven by feelings or sentiments). Sociobiology has in fact been made for ants (whose sentiments are hard to guess). Human sociobiology thus needs to explain sentiments, or, rather, patterns of sentiments, that lead to conduct and in the end to behaviour. Mating selection can easily propose an a priori explanation of altruism in general. Indeed, other things being equal, individuals should prefer to mate with altruists who will support and defend them and possibly their common offspring – if mating has some duration, a trait which can be similarly selected –, and hence altruists would reproduce more (even if they survive less – with a genetic equilibrium between all effects). It might be suggested that this is why courtship usually implies giving. And the offsprings also inherit this altruism. Moreover, this preference for altruistic mates can itself be selected since it favours the possible survival of people who make such a choice (and of their offspring). This can a priori explain much more than the "selfish gene" alone, and not only altruism towards individuals bearing the same genes and in proportion to the size of the common genetic material (a degree of kinship which animals do not know beyond the closest relations).

This process, however, selects altruism in general rather than reciprocity. Now, the selection of revengeful people might be that they survive more because they hit back irrespective of cost, and hence their threats are credible. That of balance-reciprocity may be that it can induce help or giving from other people expecting a return-gift; the balance would be explained by this genetic selection along lines noted for the individual choice in sequential exchange: giving back too little does not suffice and giving back too much entails a disadvantage; yet, the individual would benefit from these mutual

---

[77] See Adolphs (2000).

transfers. In fact, we know from Axelrod (1981, 1984) that in a repeated relation, the strategy of reward and punishment which is the most prone to elicit cooperation is tit-for-tat (answer good with good and harm with harm) – plus an initial positive move. But tit-for-tat is reciprocation. These reciprocating behaviours thus favour people who practice them and can foster their survival and therefore be selected. All these mechanisms rest on the direct interest of the individual and do not need the standard devices of the sociobiological explanation of altruism, the selfish gene for nepotistic altruism toward kin and group selection for altruism beyond kin (Darwin's own theory of competing tribes). However, the various contributions of reciprocity to social efficiency and to desired qualities of society (see Section 9) could also promote it by group selection. At any rate, reciprocity, giving when one is given to, implies much less self-sacrifice than pure altruistic giving, and hence will be more easily selected.

In fact, reciprocal conducts of various types are observed in all societies, although with varied emphases and frequencies. Behaviours of these types also exist in a number of animal societies. However, close consideration of such human conducts have shown that they mobilize sets of sentiments, emotions, reasons and relations each of which also appears in the motives of other conducts, as with liking other individuals, its reasons or causes and its effects, causal liking, responsibility, the situation of the ego, balance which also appears in other forms of fairness and justice,[78] rationality, anger, the role of others and of culture, duty, propriety, norms, gratitude, moral indebtedness, imitation, and so on. Full explanation should explain both each of these elements and their organization in reciprocal conduct. At any rate, any effect of biology on human conduct is heavily mediated by mental processes, effects of society, culture, education, and so on. Children raised by animals (*wolf-children*) cannot even walk, they of course cannot speak, and they cannot be said to be able to think. Theories using biological selection can only suggest tentative explanations of very rough, general and vague potentialities, which may propose, for instance, why ants support some other ants, but can hardly explain actual forms of human experience as we know them. Their possible mathematical refinement should not hide that they only deal with very rough variables and concepts. These reasonings need not be totally rejected, but they should be considered for what they show, that is, they should be expressed more or less tongue-in-cheek. On the whole, the thrust of Marshall Sahlins' classical pamphlet *The Use and Abuse of Biology* is relevant here. The social use and moulding of the biological material constitute the essential cause and explanation of conduct.[79]

---

[78] There are two reasons for equality in conceptions of justice. In retributive justice, the reason is that one act or fact more or less restores a state of affairs disturbed by another. In distributive justice, the relevant equality is a requirement of rationality in the most general sense of providing a reason (the most developed explanation is in *Justice and Equity*, Kolm 1998 (translation of 1971), Foreword, Section 5).

[79] Possible biological selectionist bases for altruistic behaviour are reviewed or discussed in Chapters 7, 11 and 22 of this Handbook.

11.3. Social and cultural evolution

11.3.1. Motives and behaviour

Cultural and sociological evolutions determine (and explain) much more and much more specifically than biology. They involve individual choices, collective choices, and competitive selection of social forms and processes. Since reciprocal behaviour is obviously explained as deriving from motivational sentiments (plus, possibly, interest), these sentiments should be explained. These sentiments are liking people and its properties (see Section 6.4), and the senses of balance or imbalance, fairness, and propriety and duty. However, it turns out that behaviour, actions and patterns of actions, and the sentiments that induce them are largely determined jointly, and should therefore be explained jointly. This relation between behaviour and sentiments rests on several mechanisms, in addition to the fact that sentiments motivate behaviour. One mechanism is competitive selection among social structures and processes each based on a style of conduct encompassing the corresponding behaviour and sentiments. An other effect is that not only sentiments elicit behaviour, but also, conversely, behaviour tends to induce the corresponding sentiments through a psychological process of avoidance of dissonance. This adjustment is in part spontaneous, but it also uses affecting one's sentiments through reasoning, focussing attention, or habit (see Section 6.3).

11.3.2. Choice and influence

Direct individual choices play a role in the emergence of reciprocities in various ways. A most straightforward case is the elementary interest of giving for eliciting a return gift, continuation reciprocity, or sequential exchange. The effects of being liked and liking and their relations, properties and effects (see Section 6.4) are also quite primitive. Moreover, impartiality and basic properties of rationality lead to valuing equality, which leads to balance-reciprocation (see Section 6.3). Individual choices also associate into collective choices. Finally, one mechanism of competitive selection of social forms and processes rests on individual choices to join one group rather than another (such as one type of firm, of other group, or of general way of behaving). The relevant social forms and processes imply in general different motives and conducts. Hence these individual choices generally imply the more or less wilful influence on one's own sentiments discussed above. This influence is often limited, especially in the short run. However, these psychological adjustments are fostered by imitation, contagion of sentiments, norm following, other people's judgments, social pressure, evidence of dissonance of one's thinking both with one's induced acts and with the social environment, and so on. Moreover, these influences are particularly favoured when these sentiments are those of reciprocity, since they imply, then, both the presence of a vis-à-vis providing a conspicuous example, and judgments, sentiments and acts addressed to the person, in a mutual structure with positive feedbacks. A person even sometimes welcomes these influences of other people on her own view, sentiments and motives, and even uses them by her choice of joining the group, because they achieve changes that she welcomes but cannot realize by herself, that is, for overcoming a weakness of her will.

11.3.3. Efficiency and values of modes

What is to be explained is the scope of the relations of reciprocity in interpersonal social relations. This is a part of the explanation of the scope of the various modes of relations: reciprocity, pure gift-giving, exchange in the strict sense, or the use of force, and their various forms. The explanation uses a number of elements. Some are the specific circumstances (for instance, one of the agents in presence is much stronger than the others – and hence can impose her force – or this is not the case). Other factors are the possible performances of the various modes. Indeed, by various more or less direct or indirect mechanisms, the existence of a social process is fostered by the interests favoured by its productive efficiency and by the direct preferences of individuals about them. For instance, exchange and reciprocity can use decentralized local information which may not be available to a central planner; exchange permits the informational and motivational advantages of the price system; conversely, gift-giving can disrupt the price system and its efficiency; however, exchange and markets have well-known inefficient "failures" which can be remedied by reciprocities or by centralized intervention if information and motivations (and the possibility of coercion for the centralized solution) permit it – these market failures can be, for instance, limits and costs of contracting (writing, checking, monitoring, implementing) and of constraining or excluding from benefits, the noted problem of sequential exchanges, situations of the type of the prisoner's dilemma and of free-riding non-excludable public goods, etc. –; more basically, mutual respect of the rights of others permits peace and property rights and can save the damages and costs of conflicts and the costs of protection, self-defence and police; in addition, giving and liking-reciprocities entail valued social relations which are missing with relations of self-interested exchange or force; and so on. In fact, individuals have also often direct and intrinsic preferences about various types of social relations that characterize modes of realization. For instance, they often prefer reciprocal trust to general diffidence, convivial reciprocity to contractual obligations, and contractual obligation to hierarchical command or to intrusive social pressure by opinion or otherwise. In particular, all the values of reciprocity presented in Section 9 can favour the existence of reciprocity, although mostly not by a direct choice but by more or less indirect – though important – social processes such as the following ones.

11.3.4. Processes of social selection of modes of relation

Indeed, the relative performance and interest of a mode of realization, and individual preferences about it for other reasons, do not explain in themselves the adoption of this mode (since this generally does not result from a single individual's choice). The social mechanism that translates these interest and preferences into this realization has to be pointed out. It can be of many types. Individual choices sometimes suffice. This is for instance the case for continuation reciprocity. There can also be an explicit collective choice. Public actions, or setting up the conditions of a market physically or by regulation, can be decided and realized in this way. This is rather less possible for reciprocity, although rules and laws that are favourable, or not unfavourable, to it can be important (e.g., in taxation). A frequent process for the establishment of such social forms is by social selection resulting from trial and error with maintenance of the successful form by awareness of common interest, agreement which is often tacit, or the social inertia of tradition. This can sustain a competitive social and cultural selection process of modes of realization. Such a selection can operate by economic competition among firms differently managed (for instance using more or less trust and decentralization); by political competition among alternatives that grant a different importance to public, private and cooperative sectors and to various types and rationales of redistribution; or by other interactions of social forms and structures.

In this process, the roles of individuals consist of supporting or joining structures or processes that satisfy them more on material grounds or with respect to their preferences about social relations and freedom, for instance by joining one type of firm or a cooperative, or by supporting a type of change in any organization they belong to, or a type of public policy. In this social evolution, both individuals who make such choices, and those who are more passively submitted to the change, generally undergo a transformation in their behaviour and its direct motives, which is an adaptation to their new environment. This adaptation uses various modes. When joining a group, an individual can adopt the type and style of social relations that are standard in it – when in Rome . . . She may for instance decide to trust others, as they do in this group, rather than demand detailed contracts. In the adaptation, existing reciprocal conducts often play an important role: people tend to face selfishly selfish people, to give when they are given to, to respect when they are respected, to trust when they are trusted, and to like others when they are themselves appreciated. Yet, imitation and following norms or rules – possibly with social pressure of various possible types and intensity – also play important roles.

This adaptation concerns both behaviour and the sentiments that induce it, in a congruent way if excessive dissonance is avoided. Sentiments then are essentially influenced by the social environment and what it expects from the individual. Contagion of emotion and imitation of worldviews and judgments play important roles. Required or favoured behaviour tend to induce sentiments in line with it (cooperation, hostility, and more specific forms) by a kind of psychological dissonance-avoidance. Conscious and wilful influence on one's own sentiments is generally restricted for "slaves of their passions", but it is in fact not absent, by reasoning, getting used to, or focussing attention. In the longer run, of course, education plays a major role in this respect.

However, other processes are at work in society, and a number of them influence and shape behaviours, motivations, and sentiments. In particular, culture and the formation of personality also have an important autonomous dynamics. In this process, there is no proof of overall optimality in any respect, no "invisible hand" theorem. Wars and mass manslaughters would suffice to prove it. Even barring these extreme phenomena, the simple analysis of social processes shows reasons for their normative "social failure" according to any criterion. In particular, this is the case for reciprocities, which inherently imply two related reasons that can induce them to be socially "inefficient", both resulting from the very nature of these processes (with given motives).

First, a relation of reciprocity cannot be an exchange in the strict sense (a mutually conditional exchange by external obligation). In particular, as it will be made precise in Section 13, reciprocal equilibria (solution of reciprocity games) tend to have structures of the classical Cournot–Nash or Stackelberg types (although for a reason different from the one classically proposed in the former case). Hence, there classically seems to be allocations obtainable by exchange that are preferred by all participants. However, explicit, formal and binding agreements of mutual transfers or sevices are incompatible with a relation of reciprocity: the type of relation would differ and the transfers or services would not be gifts. As a consequence, the preferences of the individuals about the outcomes can be different, and there are also in general preferences about the type of relation in itself. For instance, the intrinsic value of a reciprocitarian relation may overcompensate the losses of an otherwise inefficient allocation in the eyes of all participants. Therefore, the existence of a possible result unanimously preferred to the one obtained is ambiguous. Yet, this is a possibility. Although reciprocities commonly correct market failures, they also constitute one, in a sense. The second risk of inefficiency inherent in reciprocity is that the reciprocal relation produces a feedback with the possibility of several equilibria and notably several stable equilibria. And the interaction may well lead to an equilibrium dominated by others that are clearly better (in particular that are preferred by all participants) and remain stuck in it. For these two issues, the problem comes from the fact that people engaged in such a reciprocity are both too altruistic and not altruistic enough. They are too altruistic for performing an exchange in the strict sense, and yet, their conditional altruism traps them into equilibria of particular types. The solution cannot be an intervention by force since this also violates the reciprocitarian relation. Hence, the solution can only be to induce people to take a broader outlook.[80]

This conclusion in fact holds true for most "failures" of social processes. This should be a main concern of institutional design and of general social information and education.

11.3.5. Education and development

In all societies, indeed, the values that underlie social relations constitute a foremost issue in education. Children are jointly strongly taught these values, shown, by the example of adults, how to accommodate them in real life, and provided ready-made explanations that permit one to avoid the schizophrenia that should result from the frequent tension between both. Children are taught the value and duty of gratitude (this

---

[80] Sections 12 and 13 will provide examples of these two inherent possible inefficiencies of reciprocity. These possibilities, their likelihood, and the ways of overcoming them, are amply discussed in Kolm 1984a.

may be the parents' reward and interest), of respect, and of politeness. They are taught the value of giving, but also the excuse that "good charity begins by oneself" – as the proverb says. They are taught the goodness of generosity, and also shown how to keep it as a utopian ideal (in Europe), or for Sundays or tax-deductible contributions (in the United States). In many societies, the same *ethos* both highly values generosity and sees honour in relentless revenge. More generally, social influence in education and otherwise, and the types of social experiences, are prime factors in people's attitudes and conduct towards others. This is confirmed and specified by many systematic observations and experiments noted earlier. They include the studies of "helping behaviour", a number of studies about personality, analyses of the role of imitation, analyses of child development along the lines of Piaget and Kohlberg, other studies on the formation of norms of pro-social behaviour, and so on.[81] In particular, the line of studies about "the birth of the moral sentiment in the child", initiated by Piaget's book with this title, is rather encouraging. There seems to be evidence of a spontaneous individual development from obedience to authority to abiding by a rule, and then to a sense of impartiality among peers and the internalization of their views, which leads to a sense of equality and reciprocity. This later stage is to be explained by the fact that, in the course of interacting with peers, empathy leads to a sense of impartiality which, with minimal rationality, leads to a sense of equality and of balance-reciprocity (see Sections 1 and 7). Empathy in interaction can also create the basis of liking reciprocity. In the end, however, this stage of moral development appears to be limited by education in the name of realism about life in society (or, rather, to be oriented towards charity or ideology and largely confined there). This should be a main field of study and action.

Part IV: Formal analysis and interaction

12. Formal analysis of reciprocity

12.1. Methodology

The previous analysis of reciprocity should be continued by a formal analysis. This permits making the relations in question more precise and finding out the consequences of sets of relations, in particular the consequences of the interdependence among the acts, sentiments and attitudes of agents that concern others.

In the end, we will arrive at the discussion of the form most classical in economic analysis. In this form, there are two individuals indexed by i and j, who, respectively, chose items x_i and x_j and seek the highest value of *ordinal* utility functions $u^i(x_i, x_j, z_i)$

---

[81] The volume on *General Reciprocity* (Kolm 1984a), includes a full referencing of the relevant studies to its date of publication, and a corresponding discussion of these studies and of the conclusions that can be derived from them. In the present volume, Chapter 7 by Louis Lévy-Garboua, Claude Meidinger and Benoît Rapoport contains presentations and discussions of a large number of these studies emanating from psychology.

and $u^j(x_j, x_i, z_j)$, where z_i and z_j denote sets of relevant parameters (they can in particular include a description of the type of relations between these two individuals when they make these choices). These utility functions can be generalized into preference orderings, which is practically relevant when some aspects of the choices have priority. The resulting interaction also depends on other items, besides domains of choice, such as the information of agents, the order of actions in time, and possibilities of communication and agreement.

In such a formulation, x_i or x_j can, for instance, be a gift of any kind, and the other the return-gift (or a harm and the corresponding response). However, such functions u^i and u^j are, as such, mere "black boxes". Their specific structures and properties should be derived in a meaningful and legitimate way from the phenomena one wants to study. This entails a couple of remarks. In particular, the noted structure with u^i and u^j is the basis of game theory. However, our concern is not game theory. It is not, for instance, to "introduce reciprocity, or any other social sentiment, in game theory". The objective is the converse one. It is the analysis of reciprocity (or the consequences of other social sentiments). The only point is that some concepts of game theory may apply to this relation, and if any of them is useful for its analysis, this concept can be used. However, such "games of reciprocity" have two noteworthy types of relation with usual game theory. First, a number of structures that are crucial in such games are absent from usual game theory, such as the importance of the type of social relation which is an object of preferences and influences the preferences about the other items, or the question of fairness about the order of the moves in time. Second, games of reciprocity will also, as an aside, produce a number of contributions to game theory. For instance, the famous Cournot–Nash solutions are well known to have no actual justification (for one- or two-shot games). Now we will see that one concept of reciprocitarian conduct leads to this solution. This is the only justification provided to date for such solutions.

Our concern here is reciprocity. Reciprocity can a priori be with acts (which are parts of actions), attitudes, sentiments, or judgments (giving is an act, a favour can refer to favourable acts, attitudes or expressed judgments, etc.). Now, determination through the highest u^i or u^j (or the same for more general orderings) classically refers to items that are chosen by the corresponding agent. Gifts are chosen. Sentiments are largely unchosen. Yet, they often are more or less influenced by reasonings – for instance in the name of morals or of hedonism (pleasure-seeking) –, or by efforts for "getting used to" something, or by focussing or diverting attention. Attitudes are determined by sentiments and are also more or less chosen. Acts are determined by sentiments, and by attitudes in so far as they imply propensities to act.[82] Hence, if the chosen variables x_i are acts, the corresponding utility functions depend on the relevant sentiments (or attitudes) – and, at a deeper level of analysis, they may not be thoroughly given to the agent.[83]

---

[82] Attitudes and acts are of course also determined by reason, custom, norms, prejudice, and so on.

[83] The fact that acts are determined by given sentiments does not mean that they are not chosen but that the principles of the choice are these sentiments which, for instance, determine the structure of utility functions or preference orderings.

An essential methodological point is that each relevant type of social sentiment should be analysed separately to begin with. They are very different from one another. Mixing them a priori and from the start can only produce confusion. Unfortunately, there are many instances of this in recent studies whose central point is either that "economics forgets about social sentiments" or that game theory so misbehaves. The logic and the structural implications of each sentiment are then analysed by themselves, possibly with a maximizing conduct and utility functions u^i (or orderings), along with self-interested motives about the result for comparison. In a situation where several such sentiments are present, it is then most often straightforward to consider them jointly, notably with the relevant utility function. Yet, some associations of sentiments require careful study. For instance, sentiments and hence attitudes and behaviour of fairness and balance associate well with moderate liking but much less so with stronger liking.

Consider, for example, that a utility function $u^i(x_i, x_j)$ can a priori encompass or represent various types of social sentiments, a number of which lead *qualitatively* to similar results in choices, for instance in inducing making x_i and x_j more similar or more equal in some sense (or the opposite) – u^i increases, *ceteris paribus*, when x_i and x_j become more similar or less unequal. These sentiments can be the following, some of which are comparative:

- equity, fairness, justice,
- preference for equality or inequality-aversion,
- comparative or balance reciprocity,
- liking-reciprocity in giving,
- gifts induced by reciprocal liking,
- gratefulness,
- continuation reciprocity (two steps of it or comparison of the sets of gifts in the same direction),
- imitation (or on the contrary distinction),
- conforming,
- sentiment of inferiority (or on the contrary of superiority),
- envy,
- jealousy (jealousy adds to envy an aspect of self-debasement; moreover, while envy has no opposite – as with the sentiment of superiority for the sentiment of inferiority –, one particular meaning of the term "jealous" constitutes such an opposite – as with "being jealous of one's prerogatives").

Mixing all these possible sentiments, or several of them, from the onset simply constitutes confused thinking and can only induce faulty analysis. It prevents seeing and understanding some of the essential properties of the corresponding conducts. The comparison and its conditions and requirements differ for these various sentiments. The logic of some of these sentiments has been extensively analysed, notably for justice, equity and fairness, for inequalities, for envy, and for reciprocity.[84]

---

[84] The logic of fairness, justice and inequality has been extensively analysed (see, for instance, Kolm 1966, 1971, 1976, 1977, 1996a, 1999, 2004). That of envy is developed in Kolm 1995.

A second essential methodological point is that the utility functions u^i should not be arbitrarily specified. The same requirement holds for any other concept or relation considered or used in the analysis (such as liking, kindness, fairness, and so on). Arbitrariness, lack of justification, is exactly the contrary of scientific analysis. Any specification of any concept used should be fully justified by facts. Moreover, it turns out that, for the phenomena under study, arbitrary specification of concepts do not make the analysis formally simpler. All the properties can be derived with the properly general concepts with more simplicity than with such specifications. And this is the only way to obtain results in knowing the proper scope of their validity. Results obtained with arbitrarily specified concepts are ascertained only for the case of this specification; they can, at most, provide dim suggestions about other cases, which are in fact unnecessary since the analysis with the properly general concepts show exactly the proper results with their scope – and in fact in a simpler way. Moreover, of course, concepts cannot be assumed properties which have no meaning for them (for instance in representing satisfaction, liking, kindness, fairness, etc. by quantities which are added, multiplied, divided, and so on).

The initial endowment of individual i can be described by a vector of quantities of goods X_i (goods of different qualities can be described as different goods). Similarly, gifts x_i and x_j, of any kind of nature, can also be considered as vectors of quantities of goods. Thus, $X_i, x_j, x_i \in X \subseteq R_+^m$ where m is the number of goods, and the restriction to set X can notably represent possible indivisibilities. Then, with a sufficiently large space of goods, individual i, initially endowed with X_i, receiving x_j, and giving x_i, has $X_i + x_j - x_i$ as final endowment. Then, individual i's utility function can be written, more explicitly, as

$$u^i(x_i, x_j) = U^i(X_i + x_j - x_i, x_i, x_j),$$

where the effect of the first argument denotes the purely self-interested and self-centred preferences of individual i about her allocation of goods. The considered social sentiments determine the effects of the last two arguments.[85]

The two following sections analyse respectively the logic of the two genuine reciprocities, comparative, matching or balance reciprocity and liking reciprocities – sequential self-interested exchange is a type of standard exchange rather than genuine reciprocity with respect to the nature of the underlying sentiments and desires, which are the main criteria of distinction here. The formal analyses are preceded by considerations of the relevant basic properties that rest on the presentations of the reciprocities in Section 6 and of the motives for giving in Section 4.2, in completing them notably concerning properties that appear to be critical in the logical analysis.

---

[85] Other social sentiments such as comparative fairness, envy, jealousy, sentiments of superiority and inferiority, and possibly conforming or distinction, can make U^i depend on individual j's final allocation $X_j + x_i - x_j$, in addition to individual j's own $X_i + x_j - x_i$.

12.2. Comparative, matching, or balance reciprocities

12.2.1. Reciprocitarian comparative sentiments

Reciprocity is motivated by comparison when the return-gift is elicited by sentiments based on a comparison between the gift and the return-gift. Such comparative reciprocity contrasts with liking reciprocity (although both are joined in the particular cases where the return-giver wishes to show that she likes the other as much as she is liked by her).

Comparative reciprocities can involve various kinds of sentiments that elicit giving in return. The essential sentiment is the *propriety of balancing* the gift with some appropriate return-gift. It has various different basic motives. Some of them focus on the overall situations and others on the transfers (gifts). Some focus on one of the two agents and others on both of them. Some refer to concepts or sentiments in the family of justice or fairness, whereas this is not the case for others. The sentiments or senses that can be involved are very varied: propriety, adequacy, fairness, justice, equity, equality, desert, merit, moral indebtedness, shame, guilt, duty, or the requirement of a norm. These sentiments can be of the initial receiver who gives in return, or of other people (including the initial giver). The initial receiver may care about these opinions and judgments of other people. Her decision to give in return can depend jointly on her own intrinsic judgment and on her view of other people's or society's judgments and opinions.

To begin with, a most basic concept is that the initial gift has disrupted the initial state, that some balance that existed in this state should be restored, and that this can be done by a transfer from the receiver to the giver that in some sense compensates the initial gift. The notion of restoring balance can also focus on the giver – who has lost – or on the receiver – who has gained. The focus can also be directly on the transfers (gifts) and on their equality in value in some sense. The second transfer then appears as a compensation for the first.

Sentiments of fairness can focus on the situations or transfers only, or also on the fact that the initial gift is a free and voluntary act. Fairness can thus refer to *compensatory justice*, and require a transfer that compensates the loss or cost incurred by the initial giver, or the benefit received by the initial receiver, or both jointly – which can be realized by a transfer from the initial receiver to the initial giver. This latter transfer is also simply a compensation for all effects of the initial gift. This can also be seen as the requirement of the particular distributive justice that takes the initial state as reference (with an idea of maintaining a kind of status quo). Moreover, the initial transfer is free and voluntary (since it is a gift) and benefits the receiver at some cost or loss for the giver. This tends to elicit the notion that *retributive justice* justifies or requires rewarding the initial giver who deserves or merits this retribution. Conversely, if the receiver has thus only received a windfall benefit without particular corresponding merit, need, or right, she may be the right payer of this retribution.

These reasons induce the return gift when they sufficiently motivate the receiver directly or through other people's opinions and judgments about which she cares. These sentiments can indicate what is proper behaviour, duty, or a norm of conduct. Failing to provide the return gift, or a sufficient return gift, can elicit shame or guilt. It can also elicit sentiments induced by the unequal relation created by the initial gift alone, or by an insufficient return gift, between the two persons: moral indebtedness and, sometimes, sentiment of inferiority or lower status with respect to the initial given or in general, or even a feeling of humiliation. Conversely, an insufficient (or absent) return gift can make the initial giver a moral creditor – which can be a power to ask later for a compensation chosen by her – and it may give her a higher social status and a sense of superiority with respect to the receiver or in general.

Similarly, if, in giving sufficiently in return, the initial receiver can avoid impropriety, shame, guilt, moral indebtedness, and sentiments of inferiority, she can also, in giving more, reverse the situation, become a moral creditor and – possibly – acquire the corresponding power of demanding something in return for the excess, and derive pride, a higher status and a sentiment or position of superiority.

This provides a remarkable structure and contrast in the various motives. The sentiment of proper balance tends to elicit a return gift both not lower and not higher in value than the initial gift. In contrast, sentiments of moral indebtedness, inferiority, guilt, or shame only tend to elicit not giving too little in return. However, they have opposite sentiments in the same family, the sentiments of being a moral creditor with the corresponding power or status, of superiority, and of pride. These sentiments may be sought, which can elicit giving in return more than required for balance. Therefore, for an insufficient (or absent) return gift, all the sentiments in question have an effect in the same direction of giving more and reducing the imbalance. In contrast, for a return gift higher than required for balance, the sentiment of proper balance favours its reduction whereas the other sentiments that this situation can elicit, when they are present, have the opposite effect of favouring a higher return gift and imbalance.

12.2.2. Basic concepts of comparative reciprocity

Formally, let X denote the set of possible gifts. Such a gift can be described as a set (vector) of quantities of goods. But there can be indivisibilities. Hence $X \subseteq R_+^m$ where m is the number of goods (any). Individual i receives gift $x_j \in X$ from individual j. She may answer with the return-gift $x_i \in X$. Denote as $x = (x_i, x_j) \in X^2$ the ordered pair of the two gifts x_i and x_j, and as $y = x_j - x_i \in R^m$ the vector excess of the gift over the return-gift. The views in question concerning the pair of gifts x will be those of the receiver i because we seek to explain her return-gift x_i, but they are generally shared by a wider society.

For each initial gift x_j, the return-gifts x_i that are considered as matching gift x_j in an appropriate balance constitute a set that defines the subset B such that $x = (x_i, x_j) \in B \subseteq X^2$. For $x \notin B$, there is an *imbalance* between the two gifts. If the return-gift x_i is deemed insufficient for matching the gift x_j, this imbalance is a *deficit*, and the corresponding pairs $x = (x_i, x_j)$ constitute the set $D \subseteq X^2$. If, on the contrary, the return-gift x_i is deemed excessive for matching the gift x_j, this imbalance is a *surplus* and the corresponding pairs $x = (x_i, x_j)$ constitute the set $S \subseteq X^2$. The three sets B, D, and S are separate, and can be considered as constituting a partition of X^2.

Moreover, imbalance, deficit, and surplus are generally considered as being amenable to comparison by relations of more and less, which generally implies that they are representable by numerical functions $m(x)$, $d(x)$, and $s(x)$, respectively, a priori ordinal (i.e., defined up to any arbitrary increasing function).[86] In addition, one can say that imbalance, deficit, or surplus is zero when there is no imbalance, deficit, or surplus respectively, and positive otherwise. This leads to taking $m(x) > 0$ if $x \notin B$ and $m(x) = 0$ if $x \in B$, $d(x) > 0$ if $x \in D$ and $d(x) = 0$ if $x \notin D$, and $s(x) > 0$ if $x \in S$ and $s(x) = 0$ if $x \notin S$. These functions are now defined up to any increasing, zero-invariant and otherwise arbitrary function. Since the present concepts of deficit and surplus specify that of imbalance in their respective case, one can take $d(x) = m(x)$ for $x \in D$, and $s(x) = m(x)$ for $x \in S$. Finally, one has $m(x) > 0$ for $x \notin B$ and $m(x) = 0$ for $x \in B$; $d(x) = m(x) > 0$ for $x \in D$ and $d(x) = 0$ for $x \notin D$; and $s(x) = m(x) > 0$ for $x \in S$ and $s(x) = 0$ for $x \notin S$.

The sentiment of imbalance and propriety of balance is concerned with index m and tends to favour and elicits its reduction. The sentiments of shame, guilt, inferiority, and moral indebtedness are concerned with index d and favour and tend to elicit its reduction. The sentiments of pride, superiority, and moral credit are concerned with index s and may tend to favour and elicit its augmentation. When a sentiment has a converse, one can associate both into one single generalized or extended sentiment. One thus has sentiments of shame-pride, inferiority–superiority, and moral indebtedness-credit. This leads to considering the extended or *generalised deficit* $\delta(x)$ defined as $\delta(x) = d(x) = m(x)$ for $x \in D \cup B$, and $\delta(x) = -s(x) = -m(x)$ for $x \in S \cup B$. Indeed, these extended sentiments tend to favour and elicit a reduction of the generalised deficit in the entire domain. However, it is common that an individual, for a given question, can have sentiments of shame, guilt, inferiority, and moral indebtedness about a deficit, without having the opposite sentiments in case of surplus.

The variations of indexes m, d, s, and δ with x can be expressed by the fact that δ is increasing in x_j and decreasing in x_i in the sense that it increases when x_j is replaced by $x_j' > x_j$ and decreases when x_i is replaced by $x_i' > x_i$ where the relation ">" between vectors denote this relation between each of their coordinates (quantities of each good). Actual cases are often more specific in that social norms hold that only particular goods matter.

12.2.3. Neutrality

The property of balance or imbalance is said to be *neutral* when the gifts x_i and x_j are the only characteristics of individuals i and j that influence the indexes m, s and d.

---

[86] A priori, the relations of more and less normally imply their transitivity, which only implies the existence of orderings of the x for imbalance, deficit or surplus. These orderings will most often be representable by functions m, s, or d. However, this may not be the case, notably when some criteria for so comparing the x have priority over others which, nevertheless, have a domain of relevance.

Then, the meaning of terms imply
$$s(\xi, \xi') = d(\xi', \xi),$$
for all $\xi \in X$ and $\xi' \in X$.

This logically implies that, for $\xi \in X$ and $\xi' \in X$,
$$s(\xi, \xi') > 0 \Leftrightarrow d(\xi', \xi) > 0$$
and hence
$$(\xi, \xi') \in S \Leftrightarrow (\xi', \xi) \in D,$$
and
$$m(\xi, \xi') = 0 \Leftrightarrow s(\xi, \xi') = d(\xi, \xi') = 0 \Leftrightarrow d(\xi', \xi) = s(\xi', \xi) = 0$$
$$\Leftrightarrow m(\xi', \xi) = 0$$
and hence
$$(\xi, \xi') \in B \Leftrightarrow (\xi', \xi) \in B.$$

It also implies that, for all $\xi \in X$,
$$s(\xi, \xi) = d(\xi, \xi),$$
hence $(\xi, \xi) \in B$ and
$$d(\xi, \xi) = s(\xi, \xi) = m(\xi, \xi) = \delta(\xi, \xi) = 0.$$

In particular, in the absence of gifts, $(0, 0) \in B$, $m(0, 0) = 0$, $\delta(0, 0) = 0$, and there is no imbalance.

Hence, neutrality also implies that, for all $\xi \in X$ and $\xi' \in X$,
$$m(\xi, \xi') = m(\xi', \xi)$$
and
$$\delta(\xi, \xi') = -\delta(\xi', \xi),$$
that is, functions m and δ are respectively symmetrical and antisymmetrical in this sense.

Neutrality is not the case when the concepts of balance or imbalance under consideration find that what should be compared are the gifts relative to specific characteristics of the giver or of the receiver, such as their capacities, their needs, their merit or deservingness (apart from those that can result from the gift in question in itself), their social status or position, the various possible specifications of these notions, or who is the first or the second giver. When there is no neutrality for any such reason, it is generally possible to define gifts relative to the considered characteristics such that neutrality holds for these new items. Such transformations are classical and much discussed and studied in the field of the theories of justice and equality and of measures of inequality.

12.2.4. Structures of imbalance

If both gifts include quantities of the same good, only the net amount transferred of this good may be relevant. That is, functions m, d, s, and δ depend on x_i and x_j only through $y = x_j - x_i \in R^m : m(x_i, x_j) = \tilde{m}(y)$, $\delta = \tilde{\delta}(y)$, $d = \tilde{d}(y)$, and $s = \tilde{s}(y)$. In vector y, each dimension is the *net* quantity of one good transferred from one individual to the other, with the proper sign.

If, moreover, there is neutrality, $\tilde{m}(y) = \tilde{m}(-y)$, $\tilde{\delta}(y) = -\tilde{\delta}(-y)$, $\tilde{s}(y) = \tilde{d}(-y)$.

It sometimes also happens that the money value of the gifts is their relevant measure, $v(x_j)$ and $v(x_i)$, with $\delta(x)$ which can be taken as $\delta(x) = v(x_j) - v(x_i)$, and $m(x) = |\delta(x)|$, $d(x) = \max[\delta(x), 0]$, and $s(x) = \max[-\delta(x), 0]$. This implies neutrality. If, moreover, the case of the foregoing paragraphs holds, $\delta(x) = v(y)$, for instance $\delta(x) = \Sigma p_k y_k$ if y_k is the dimension of y for good k and p_k is the price of good k. These reductions to money value are not the case in many instances, precisely because reciprocity is not in the sphere of exchange in the strict sense.

12.2.5. Choice

Let us now denote as $\mu(x)$ a function that can be $m(x)$, $d(x)$, or $\delta(x)$. Function μ can also represent a concern for comparing x_i and x_j that mixes the sentiments in question in any proportions.

Let us also consider a further motive, the simple, direct, self-interest for one's own endowment. Individual i's initial endowment is X_i, and her final endowment after receiving the gift x_j and giving the return-gift x_i is $X_i + x_j - x_i = X_i + y$. Assume individual i has a preference ordering representable by an ordinal utility function U^i. With the considered sentiments, U^i depends on $X_i + y$ and on $\mu(x)$:

$$U^i = U^i[X_i + y, \mu(x)].$$

The sentiments concerning $\mu(x)$ are such that U^i is a decreasing function of μ. If, given the choice of function $\mu(x)$, its specification changes as it is allowed to, for instance by an increasing sign-preserving function for functions m, d, or δ, function U^i incurs the corresponding contravariant transformation. Moreover, it often happens that these preferences of individual i are lexical (lexicographic), and hence cannot be represented by a unique utility function such as U^i, because individual i achieves balance or absence of deficit with priority, at least in some domain. Then, the maximand writes $U^i(X_i + y)$ given that $x \in B$ (or $x \in B \cup S$).

Consider the three cases of imbalance-aversion with $\mu = m$, deficit-aversion with $\mu = d$, and deficit-aversion plus surplus-seeking with $\mu = \delta$ (the case of surplus-seeking only, with $\mu = s$ and U^i increasing in it, can also be considered but seems quite less frequent). Then, $\mu = 0$ implies that the relevant effects are not present. Hence, for any allocation X'_i of individual i, the function $V^i(X'_i)$ defined as

$$V^i(X'_i) = U^i(X'_i, 0)$$

represents individual i's preferences laundered for her reciprocitarian preferences. Moreover, since U^i is a decreasing function of μ, with $\mu(x) > 0$, in all cases,

$$U^i[X_i + y, \mu(x)] < V^i(X_i + y)$$

and, for surplus-seeking with $\delta(x) = -s(x) < 0$,

$$U^i[X_i + y, \delta(x)] > V^i(X_i + y).$$

Individual i, receiving gift x_j, then chooses the return-gift x_i that maximizes U^i (or, if balance is desired with priority and is possible, she achieves $m(x) = 0$ and chooses the x_i that maximizes $V^i(X_i + y)$ on $x \in B$ if there is a choice). Individual j may more or less foresee this move. This leads to the interactions that will be analysed in Section 13. Her choice may also be described by a maximand U^j. The argument of function U^j that represents this individual's self-interest in the strict sense is $X_j - x_j + x_i = X_j - y$. This is the only argument when the initial giver j only aims at receiving a return gift for a purely self-interested reason – this is the case of self-interested exploitation of the return-gift in such a "half-reciprocity". However, the initial giver may also have other concerns and motives of various possible types. If these motives can be represented with the variables x_j, x_i, $X_i + y$, and $X_j - y$ only, then the initial giver's choice is again a "domination" (of the "Stackelberg" type), although it need not be solely and strictly self-interested. These motives for giving can be any of the types noted in Section 4, including benevolence and any "social effects" (comparison or status for various reasons, and so on). In particular, she may also be concerned about balance, deficit or surplus. These items can have two types of relations with those previously considered. First, the roles of the two agents are reversed: a deficit for one can be a surplus for the other. Second, this being taken into account, the definitions of these items by the two agents may be the same or different ones. When they are the same, this may result from a definition that seems "natural" (a particular case is that where money values are considered) or from a shared social norm. Among her possible conducts, the initial giver may seek superiority, pride, or being a moral creditor, in hoping that the return-gift will be insufficient for reaching balance and will leave a surplus in the initial giver's net gift (this surplus is a priori according to the initial giver's conception, but, if conceptions of others differ from it – in particular that of the receiver –, these other conceptions may be relevant if the initial giver cares for these other persons' views). The initial giver can again act in taking into account the receiver's foreseen reaction, in adding this concern about balances, deficit, or surplus to her pure and strict self-interest. The initial giver may have still other concerns and motives. She may simply give out of benevolence. Then, the return giver may act as described, notably in seeking balance. Yet, she may also come to like the initial giver because of this benevolent gift, attitude or sentiment, and give because of this liking, with a possible role for gratitude. This may be expected by the initial giver and a motive for her action. Such interrelations will be analysed in the next section. The initial giver may also give because this is morally valued or praised or as a norm of conduct. She may also seek to establish a social relation that she appreciates. This social relation may be, rather than the domination previously considered, some more egalitarian relation between peers with, in general, also a material appreciation of the mutual transfers. In this case, the return gift is commonly necessary for establishing a required balance. The aspect of fairness and some equality in the relation is then usually important for its quality. This equality or balance may, notably, be extended to erasing the difference that can arise from one person being the first giver and the other the second one. Such a desire shows in the strategic choice and cannot be solely described by the structure of the utility function (as mere imbalance aversion can be). Section 13 will closely consider and analyse these issues.

12.3. Liking-reciprocity

12.3.1. Liking-reciprocity and comparative reciprocity

Liking-reciprocity is reciprocity where giving in return is motivated by liking. As we have seen in Section 6.4, this liking results either from the initial giving, essentially when it is benevolent towards the beneficiary, or directly from the reciprocity in sentiments of reciprocal liking. In both cases, the motivation of the initial giver is essential. In balance reciprocity, in contrast, the motivation for giving in return is thoroughly different, and the motivation of the initial giving is a priori irrelevant. This motive for returning gifts is a "preference" for balance or matching, or deficit-aversion (and possibly surplus seeking), whereas, in both types of liking reciprocity, giving in return is motivated by liking. These two families of reciprocity are thus inconsistent with one another, at least for strong forms of liking-reciprocities: "love does not count" – the dictum says – and it makes one give without seeking any kind of balance, and one is always "indebted" towards the loved one for her love or for her existence. However, for milder kinds of liking the two reciprocating sentiments and motives can be jointly present in the same person for the same return-gift. There can then be both liking and a preference for balance or for lower deficit – and surplus-seeking may not be absent. In fact, balance may be favourable to friendship (*les bons comptes font les bons amis* – good accounting makes good friends – a French proverb says). There is also a kind of specific deficit-aversion about the other's liking in the frustration of being liked less than one likes in mutual likings; however, this compares sentiments rather than gifts *per se*.

12.3.2. The sentiments of liking-reciprocity

Liking-reciprocity, therefore, has to consider the motives and sentiments not only of the return-giver but of the initial giver too. It associates the following twenty or so families of relations between sentiments and between sentiments and giving.

12.3.2.1. Giving and liking You like what you deem to be good for people you like. Hence, you tend to give to someone you like, and you give her if it is possible and not too costly otherwise for you, for increasing this person's happiness, pleasure, welfare, propriety, status, or anything you deem favourable to her. Other reasons for giving to persons you like, for being liked in return or as information, will shortly be pointed out.

You tend to like to be given to, for several reasons. You often appreciate the gift or favour received in itself. You tend to value favourably the attention towards you that giving with the final aim of benefiting you constitutes or manifests. When this giving results from liking, you value all the more this attention which is appreciative of yourself, kind, and possibly more or less affectionate, and the general appreciation, kindness and liking causing the giving and manifested by it. This attention, this appreciation, and this affection are favourable to your sense of self and of social existence. Moreover, when you like the giver you sometimes appreciate the relation and interaction for which the giving is an opportunity. When the giving aims at eliciting liking in return, the effects are somewhat different: this most often shows and proves that you are liked and hence considered favourably, but this is not the direct cause of the giving.

12.3.2.2. Liking to be liked, and the altruistic basis of individualism   You tend to like to be liked in itself – independently of any gift. Indeed, you commonly appreciate or enjoy the appreciative judgment, the respect, possibly the affection, implied by this sentiment towards yourself. Moreover, this liking implies considering you and paying attention towards yourself. And, as noted, this attention is necessary to your sense of self and of social existence, and it is all the more favourable to it that it is appreciative of yourself, and still all the more so that it is accompanied by some affection.

You tend to like more to be liked in itself by someone when you yourself like this person, and all the more, the more you like her. The importance you attach to being liked by some person tends to be larger, the more you like her. This is the *complementarity of mutual liking*. The basic reason is that you care (more) about people you like (more) and notably about their views and sentiments about you. Insofar as you like to be liked because the implied attention, favourable attention, and appreciation and affection, foster your sense of self and of social existence, this sense is enhanced by your own favourable consideration of the others who like you. You feel you "exist" more – as proven by society – the more you care about these others. However, this complementarity also relates to the fact that friendship or love between persons are in a sense more genuinely social than only a pair of individual sentiments, no matter how interrelated they may be. This is suggested by the very expressions of friendship or love "between" persons, and strongly revealed by expressions such as "our (or their) friendship or love". Symmetrically, you tend to suffer if you are not sufficiently liked by persons you like, especially for strong liking or love, and more so the more you like them. In particular, you sometimes resent a deficit in their liking you less than you like them.

The reasons that make you benefit from being liked intervene at three very different levels of depth, from satisfaction or pleasure elicited by the appreciation of yourself by other people and the more or less warm intercourse, to self-evaluation in the realm of self-respect and dignity, and to the "ontological" sense of self and of social existence. These effects increase when you like more the person who likes you. In particular, the resulting self-evaluation, and sense of self and of social existence, are larger, the larger the importance you attach to the consideration, appreciation, and liking of yourself by others, and hence the more you consider, appreciate, value, or like others. Now the sense of self is the sentiment that founds individualism. Hence, both rest not only on the consideration of the individual by others, but also on the individual's own valuation of others. These mutual other-regarding sentiments are complements in a synergy for each individual. And each of these sentiments so fosters the sense of self at both ends, directly for the person object of the sentiment, and for its holder because it increases the value for her of the other's view of herself. Since, moreover, individuals tend to consider and appreciate more the people who consider and appreciate them more – as we have seen for liking –, the deepest basis of the sense of self, of social existence, and hence in particular of individualism is a reciprocity in which all people are immersed. This shows that superficial oppositions between individualism and altruism miss the most important facts. This intrinsically social basis of individualism is fostered by the tendency to like people who like you and conversely, by the psychological and psychosocial interaction of all these sentiments, and, in the end, by the practically properly social and collective aspects of mutual liking.

12.3.2.3. The two gratitudes and their effects You tend to be grateful towards someone responsible for something you favour, for this fact, if her final motives for acting in this way include favouring you one way or the other. This act can be giving to you with benevolence which can manifest liking you (giving for farvouring someone one likes or for the information effects considered shortly) or the different reasons of pity, compassion, or charity. The specific fact eliciting gratitude in this way can be any aspect of gift-giving such as the gift or favour in itself, the attention towards you, possibly an appreciation of yourself and positive affects, or the relationship in the process of giving and receiving. You also tend to be directly grateful for someone liking you, towards this person.

However, this gratitude for a sentiment and towards its holder is particular both in itself and by its consequences. Normally, you can be grateful towards someone for something she chooses to do with the intention of favouring you or something you like. Now a person who likes you is responsible for holding or keeping this sentiment to an extent which is often quite limited, as with most sentiments (this subtle but important issue, touched upon in Section 6, is fully analysed elsewhere).[87] Moreover, insofar as this sentiment is chosen, the intention of this choice is not to please you. Hence, being grateful towards another person for her sentiment towards you in itself is a particular type of gratitude. In fact, since this sentiment is a part of the person, the gratitude is for the very existence of the person as she is. Hence, this is not gratitude towards someone responsible for a favourable act but gratitude addressed to nobody for the existence of something – the sentiment – and of someone – the person holding it.[88] This kind of

---

[87] Cf. Kolm 2004, Chapter 6.

[88] The sentiment and stance of gratitude in itself, addressed to nobody, is basic in advanced Buddhist philosophy and its practice (see Kolm 1982).

gratitude is very close to directly liking the person who likes you and can be seen as an aspect of it.

The sentiment of gratitude in general is favourable to liking the person one is grateful to. At least, it seems rather contradictory to both be grateful towards someone and dislike her. One could even see gratitude as one particular type of liking. This can directly entail giving in return. Gratitude, and such a consequence, are very different from a sense of moral indebtedness and the return-giving it may induce for reducing imbalance or deficit, although both can coexist as result of the same gift and as motives for the same return-gift. Moreover, being grateful because one is liked is being grateful for a sentiment of the other person, and a sentiment is more a part of the intrinsic self of a person than an act of hers is. This tends to be still more favourable to liking this person – then, there is practically an intrinsic direct reciprocity in liking.

In fact, gratitude is in itself a reciprocitarian sentiment. As an appreciative sentiment towards the giver, it plays some role of a return-gift. In this aspect, its intensity manifests some balance with the initial gift. Yet, this is thoroughly different from balance-reciprocity since gratitude is a priori a spontaneous appreciative sentiment and not the wilful manifestation of a duty or sense of propriety to establish balance, or this sentiment of duty or propriety itself, as are the return-gift and its motive in balance-reciprocity. However, there are also the sentiments of a duty or propriety to be grateful and the corresponding reproach or accusation of ingratitude.

12.3.2.4. Reciprocal liking You tend to like people who like you. This *reciprocal liking* is a basic reciprocity of sentiments. It has been explained in Section 6. In brief, since you like to be liked in itself for the noted reasons of attention, favourable attention, and kind attention towards yourself which foster your sense of self and of social existence, and for the agreeableness of the relation, simple causal liking makes you like the person who likes you. Insofar as she can influence her liking sentiment and hence is responsible for it, you agent-like her. Yet, you do not benefactor-like her for this reason since liking you does not a priori aim at benefiting you (she does not like you because you like it).

Moreover, since you particularly like to be liked by people you like, for reasons just noted, it is your "interest" to particularly like people who like you. This tends to make you like them (more) by a complex but standard process. The largest part of this process is not voluntary and conscious (only its result is conscious). It is akin to cognitive dissonance in the field of cognition. However, a part of this process can be conscious and voluntary. This comes from an adjustment of your sentiments by reasoning, attention, habit formation, and the like (this is supported by material acts such as seeing more people who like you). These processes create or reinforce sentiments, and reallocate the scarce factors of your liking capacities – capacities for attention, affection, and emotional involvement – among the objects of your liking, notably towards the people who like you more.

Other phenomena have an effect in the same direction. One is imitation of sentiments (Spinoza's *imitatio affectuum*), applied in mirror-image imitation towards people who like you, and which is better described as emotional contagion since this process is largely involuntary. Yet, the person's will can also intervene, at least in not blocking the influence. There can thus also intervene a notion of the propriety of reciprocal liking and of having mutual likings that are not too imbalanced. In particular, this reciprocal sentiment can be favoured by social approval about which the person cares.

The particular gratitude for sentiments described in the previous section also fosters reciprocal liking. Being liked is appreciated and may tend to elicit gratitude towards the liker. However, gathering a number of previous remarks shows that this gratitude and liking are quite particular. (1) Ordinary gratitude in this case is limited to the degree to which the person who likes can affect this sentiment. (2) It is furthermore limited because the objective of such an influence is usually not to be favourable to the liked person, for instance to please her. (3) Hence, this gratitude is, rather, simply for the existence of this sentiment – rather than towards someone who wilfully causes it. (4) However, this sentiment is a part of the person who likes. (5) Hence, the gratitude which is not towards this person, is for her existence as she is. (6) Moreover, being liked is essential for self-evaluation, self-esteem, and, by the attention, appreciation, and possibly affection it entails, for the individual's sense of self and of social existence. Finally, in this particular relation, the existence of someone supports the sense of existence of someone else. The corresponding particular gratitude is one of the deepest aspect and basis of liking someone who likes you.

The interrelations and dynamics of these related sentiments are essential. They work at three levels: the psychology of each individual, the interaction between the individuals, and the case of sentiments that are more fruitfully seen as collective and properly social. If you like more someone who likes you, *prima facie* both of you benefit from it. She benefits from your sentiment by all the effects described. But you also benefit because her liking you becomes more valuable for you by all its effects, from agreeableness to self-evaluation and sense of self and of social existence (you also enjoy more what is good for her and her satisfaction, but you may also suffer more from her misfortune or pain). At the level of individual psychology, this increased value of her liking can induce you to like her still more by the described processes which are involuntary for the largest part (this is mostly not a choice). Your sentiments can thus have a dynamics and settle in an affective equilibrium. In the meanwhile, however, the other person reacts to your increased liking in liking you more, with similar effects on her sentiments. This creates an interpersonal positive feedback in liking, with, again, a dynamics and possible stable equilibria. However, such a positive interaction of positive mutual sentiments tends to shift them from the realm of individual sentiments towards that of more specifically collective or social facts. This is indeed how people see it when they speak of "our friendship" or "our love". This primarily social aspect of sentiments that are so basic for the sense of individual existence is the reason for the particular place and importance of this reciprocity.

Finally, and more indirectly, liking tends to elicit giving which can be appreciated for the gift, the attention and consideration that giving constitutes and manifests, their kindness, and the corresponding relation and interaction. This tends to elicit gratitude, which is favourable to liking.

12.3.2.5. Giving for eliciting liking   Giving for being liked is most common. It is also commonly frustrated, for an obvious reason. Indeed, the objective to be liked is not to benefit the person who is given to. This benefit is also sought, but only as a means to being liked. Hence, this action is not properly benevolent giving. It is akin to giving for receiving a return gift (although what is sought is being liked, a sentiment and a fact largely beyond the will of the receiver). This does not induce the receiver to benefactor-like the giver. It can only induce her to like the giver as a cause of the benefit she receives (to agent-like her since the benefit results from an agent's action). This is a much milder sentiment, usually not the one expected by the giver. For the same reason, this act a priori elicits no gratitude from the beneficiary. This lack of gratitude is a common complaint of the giver ("she is not even grateful..."). Yet, it is necessary from the lack of intent to benefit the receiver otherwise than for another objective – to be liked by her. (A truly benevolent giver can be said to give because the receiver's pleasure or other benefit pleases herself in the end, but this cannot be taken to mean that this giver is not genuinely benevolent since this effect defines this benevolence). Therefore, for the essential, to be liked from giving cannot be obtained purposefully. It can only be a by-product of an action with another intent, giving for the sake of the receiver's good or pleasure.

Most of the time, however, the desire to be liked by someone implies that one likes her (exceptions can result from indirect benefits from being liked, such as material ones, status, or political interest). And one generally wants to be liked by someone more, the more one likes her. These relations hold for the giver towards the beneficiary. Then, the situation is that of a person who likes the beneficiary, and gives her something in order to please her, but for another final intent – to be liked by her. The beneficiary is a priori aware of this liking – revealed by this objective. This can induce her to like the giver for a direct reason of reciprocal liking. Moreover, the giver may also give directly because she likes the beneficiary. Then, these two motives coexist. This is indeed a common case. However, the foregoing remarks remain valid, in applying to giving in excess to what is directly elicited by liking the beneficiary.

12.3.2.6. Informational giving   Giving also often aims at revealing that the giver likes the receiver. But if this is its aim, this is not directly benevolent giving. If the giver tries to show the beneficiary that she likes her because she knows the beneficiary likes to be liked, then the intent is genuinely benevolent, yet not in directly pleasing the receiver by the gift, but in pleasing her because of her knowledge that she is liked. The corresponding benefactor-liking exists but is bound to be much milder than for a simple gift because of liking. Yet, this information also permits the receiver to develop the sentiment of reciprocal liking that results from being liked – presented above. However, if the giver wants to show her liking in order to be liked in return, this non-altruistic objective prevents the informational giving from being benevolent, but this generally shows and proves the giver's liking, and the corresponding reciprocal liking remains.

12.3.3. The interrelations of liking-reciprocity

12.3.3.1. The four synthetic relations
For convenience, denote as i, j two individuals, x_i individual i's gift to individual j, and ℓ_i individual i's liking of individual j with the description of its type and intensity, while x_j and ℓ_j similarly denote individual j's gift to, and liking of, individual i. Variables l_i and l_j simply denote sentiments here, without further qualifications for the time being; qualifications and specifications will be introduced below when needed.

The noted influences are synthesized as follows.

Individual j's gift to individual i, x_j, can depend on her liking of individual i, ℓ_j, for the following reasons. Individual j wants to please individual i because she likes her (l_j), by the gift (x_j) and because this giving shows and proves that she likes her (which individual i likes). Moreover, individual j wants more to be liked by individual i the more she likes her (l_j). She tends to elicit this liking by the gift x_j in two ways: by reciprocal liking since the giving can show and prove her liking; and, more or less, by liking the benevolent giver who provides the gift, the attention, and the interaction (even though the aim in question is, ultimately, to be liked). Moreover, individual j's gift x_j, when it aims at influencing individual i's liking of individual j, can depend on the present state of this liking, ℓ_i. All these influences can then be epitomized by the functional relation $x_j = x_j(\ell_j; \ell_i)$. Symmetrically, one can have $x_i = x_i(\ell_i, \ell_j)$.

Moreover, individual j's liking of individual i, ℓ_j, depends a priori on individual i's liking of individual j (reciprocal liking), ℓ_i. However, it more precisely depends on individual j's belief about this liking ℓ_i. And this belief depends, in particular, on messages that individual i sends to individual j in the form of giving gift x_i, which can show or prove individual i's liking of individual j. This belief can in addition depend on actual ℓ_i through information about it which can take various other ways (attitude, communication, and so on). Finally, individual j's liking of individual i, ℓ_j, can also depend on the gift she receives from individual i, x_i, because of the gratification she receives from the intrinsic interest of the gift, the attention of the giving, or the interaction; given that individual i is responsible for this giving and does it notably with benevolence because she likes individual j; and that she gives as a result of this liking either directly or for showing and proving this sentiment for pleasing the other and for eliciting her liking in return. Individual j's liking ℓ_j can also be fostered by gratitude toward individual i for these effects of giving x_i, for the liking ℓ_i, and for the noted effects that induce liking them. In the end, all these effects can be epitomized in the functional relation $\ell_j = \ell_j(\ell_i, x_i)$. Symmetrically, one can have $\ell_i = \ell_i(\ell_j, x_j)$.

This makes four relations for four variables, x_i, x_j, ℓ_i, and ℓ_j. A dynamics can result. For instance, one can start with levels (and types) of ℓ_i and ℓ_j. They induce giving gifts x_i and x_j, which in turn induce new levels of ℓ_i and ℓ_j, and so on. Or one giving may begin, followed by the other. There also are equilibria determined by these four independent relations between these four variables.

A notable particular case is that of *pure reciprocal liking* where each liking only depends on the other, whereas each giving depends on the giver's liking only. Then, discarding also informational giving, $\ell_j = \ell_j(\ell_i)$, $\ell_i = \ell_i(\ell_j)$, $x_i = x_i(\ell_i)$, $x_j = x_j(\ell_j)$. There only is a reciprocity of sentiments and benevolent givings.

12.3.3.2. Synopsis and graphs of the relations The relations discussed above constitute a network represented in Figure 6. Figure 6a represents a dynamic ordered graph, while Figure 6b epitomizes the relation of general interdependence, and Figure 6c shows the case of pure reciprocal liking. Note that an individual can like a person, a sentiment, an act, a gift, a relation, and so on. Also, an individual can show or prove her liking not only spontaneously but also in response to a revelation of this type by the other.

12.3.4. The economics of liking-reciprocity

12.3.4.1. Preferences The foregoing analysis considers that each individual chooses her gift to the other, x_i for individual i. The main characteristic of standard economic analysis consists of a theory of choice as resulting from a previous preference ordering, often representable by an ordinal "utility function" which is so maximized. Such an ordering or function is also commonly deemed to represent levels of "satisfaction" of the individual – sometimes seen as her happiness or pleasure. They also commonly have a normative use. This ordering or function depends on objects of choice and on parameters which may influence the choice (and the satisfaction). This will be written for utility functions because this is the common case and for convenience in presentation and discussion (the extension to more general preference orderings is straightforward).

Again, x_i, x_j, ℓ_i, and ℓ_j denote individuals' i and j gifts to, and liking of, the other, respectively. The x_i and x_j are vectors of quantities of goods, as the individuals' initial endowments of goods X_i and X_j. Variables ℓ_i and ℓ_j can just represent the likings. However, it is commonly considered that an individual can more or less like the other. Then, the ℓ_i and ℓ_j will be ordinal numerical representations of this intensity (ordinal means that each index can be replaced by an arbitrary increasing function of it). It is even sometimes considered that an individual likes more than the other does. In such a case, the two ℓ_i and ℓ_j are assumed comparable by a relation of more or less, with "co-ordinality" (i.e., they can be transformed by the *same* arbitrary increasing function). Yet, such structural assumptions – ordinal representation of intensity and interpersonal comparability – are only assumed in the cases where they are used in the representation of actual conceptions, and are not a priori assumed in the other cases.

Following the general methodology, only the structure of liking-reciprocity and of its basic consequences (such as liking the good of people one likes), and pure self-interest, are considered presently. The various relevant effects of variables and parameters are considered. Then, using the relations among the variables pointed out in the previous section, the utility functions will be reduced to functions of x_i and x_j alone, for introduction in the reciprocity games considered in the next section.

U^i and U^j will denote the direct utility functions of individuals i and j respectively, and the values of these functions for any given specifications of these ordinal utilities.

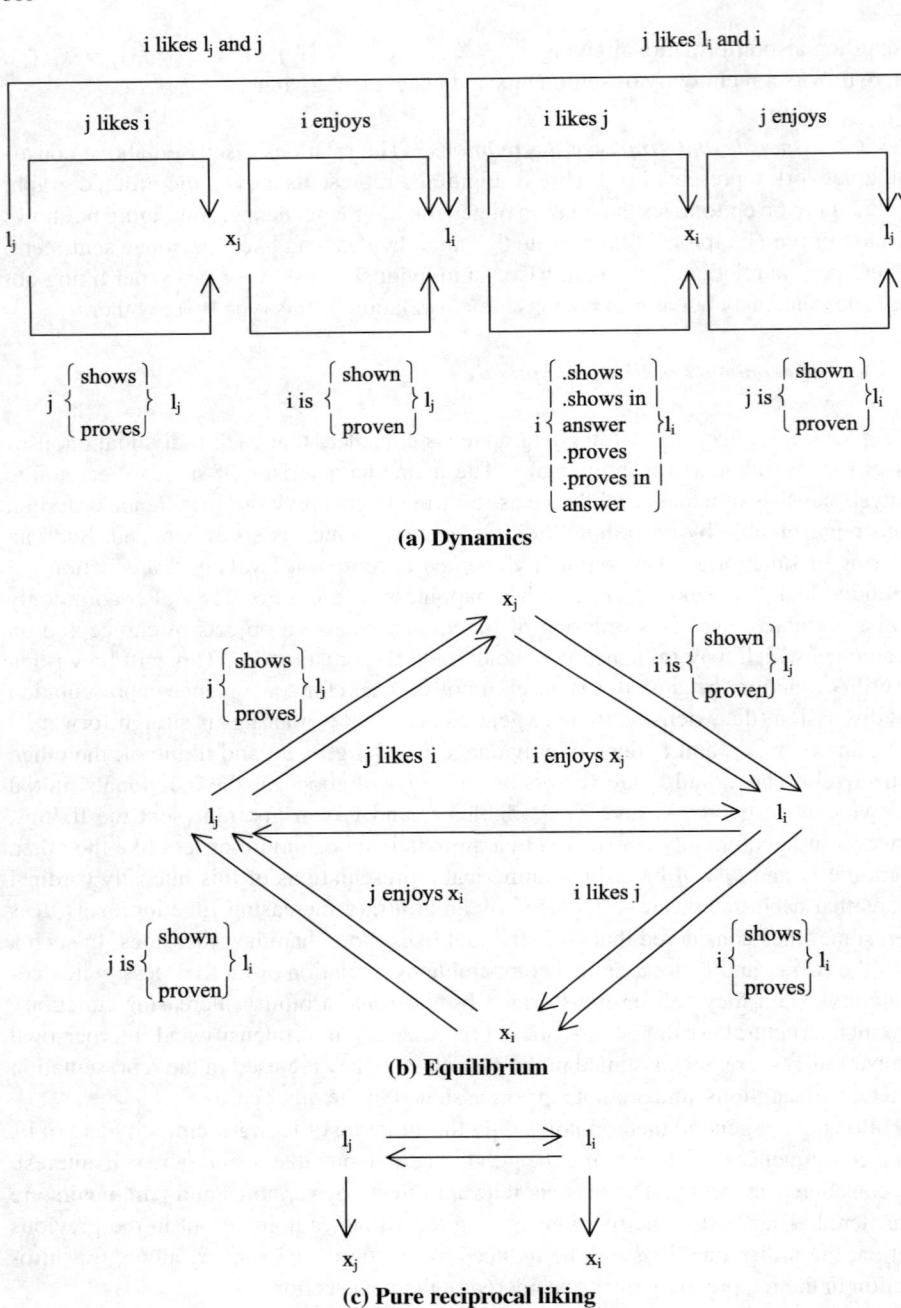

Figure 6. The logic of liking reciprocity.

(a) Dynamics

(b) Equilibrium

(c) Pure reciprocal liking

Then, for individual i,

$$U^i = U^i(X_i + x_j - x_i, U^j, S_j, \ell_j, \ell_i, x_j, x_i), \tag{1}$$

with the following meanings.

The variable $X_i + x_j - x_i$ is individuals i's remaining allocation after the gifts received x_j and given x_i. Its considered effect is pure self-interest (there could also be effects of comparisons with the consumption or incomes of other people).

Individual i liking individual j usually implies that she likes individual j's satisfaction represented by U^j. Hence, U^i is an increasing function of U^j.

More generally, individual i liking individual j implies that she likes what she deems to be good for individual j. This generally includes individual j's satisfaction. Yet, it may also include other items that concern individual j, chosen for reasons that are not only that they satisfy her – and which may sometimes even be disliked by individual j. These items may for instance include individual i's income, general or specific consumption, or anything individual i deems "proper" for individual j. This preference of individual i is usually called "paternalism". These items are the relevant aspects S_j of individual j's situation in a broad sense.

12.3.4.2. The effects of liking and being liked Liking and being liked have important "welfare" effects, or effects on satisfaction, or on the structure of preferences about other items. These effects are of four types: *direct, parametric, comparative* and *inducing*. Indeed, people often enjoy being liked and possibly also liking; liking someone more makes one more sensitive to her satisfaction and situation, and to her liking oneself – hence it makes one happier when they are high or good and less happy when they are insufficient –; mutual likings are sometimes compared; and liking induces giving and other actions. Let us consider these different effects.

Individuals a priori like and enjoy to be liked. A priori especially so when they themselves care about the other person, notably because they like her. Being liked implies being the object of attention and consideration which increase the sense of self and of social existence, especially since this consideration is appreciative of some sort, and still more since it goes with affection. People generally like and enjoy the benevolence and kindness towards them, and the warmth of the relationship. Hence, with the proper representation ℓ_j of individual j's liking, U^i tends to be an increasing function of ℓ_j. Being liked tends to induce liking the other, with the effects, discussed above, of adjustment of one's sentiment, of gratitude, of the extension of the liked object from the other's sentiment (and the resulting attitude) to the person herself, and of imitation (and "contagion").

Liking (or loving) is in itself a positive feeling which is bound to make the individual happier. However, it makes the individual more sensitive to the object of this sentiment, and this effect can either favour or hamper the person's satisfaction, depending on the state of this object. Individual i, liking individual j, is concerned with individual j's satisfaction U^j, possibly with other aspects of her situation S_j, and with individual j's liking of herself, ℓ_j. When individual i's liking ℓ_i increases, these effects make individual i more or less satisfied depending on whether individual j's satisfaction, other relevant aspects of her situation, and her liking of individual i are satisfactory or not. If the other person is happy, otherwise in good situation, and likes you, liking her more tends to make you appreciate these facts more and a priori makes you happier for this reason. But if the other is unhappy, otherwise in a poor situation, or if she likes you too little, liking her more makes you resent more these insufficiencies and lowers your satisfaction. A priori, this implies that there is a critical level for each of these items, such that a higher ℓ_i makes individual i happier if the item is above this level and less happy if it is below. These levels are U_o^j for U^j, ℓ_j^o for ℓ_j, and s_j^o for some other parameter of individual j's situation, s_j, that individual i prefers to be higher. This does not prevent that these representations can be ordinal only, since a corresponding transformation of these indexes (by any increasing transformation) is then also applied to the critical level. If a_j denotes U^j, s_j, or ℓ_j, with a_j^o denoting the corresponding critical level, the increasing curve representing U^i as a function of a_j passes through a point with $a_j = a_j^o$, and, when ℓ_i increases, it becomes higher (larger U^i) for $a_j > a_j^o$, lower (smaller U^i) for $a_j < a_j^o$, while $U^i(a_j^o)$ does not change. The critical levels can a priori depend on all the parameters of the problem, the individuals in question to begin with. They can even depend on the liking parameter ℓ_i itself in the sense that the noted fixed point of the curve $U^i(a_j)$ is replaced by an envelope of this curve. This discussion need not be pursued here.

Moreover, sentiments commonly attach to the comparison of reciprocal likings by more or less. However, the sentiment and its consequences differ depending on whether a surplus or a deficit is faced. Such comparisons a priori imply such a comparability of these likings. People sometimes resent being liked less than they like. This can notably occur in the strong case of love. Then, individual i resents the fact that $\ell_j < \ell_i$, and this reason tends in this case to make U^i increase with ℓ_j, and decrease when ℓ_i is higher. This effect induces individual i to particularly favour acts that tend to increase ℓ_j, and it produces a relief for her when ℓ_i decreases. The converse situation with $\ell_i < \ell_j$ does not elicit the same type of sentiments for individual i. However, it sometimes elicits a sentiment of guilt for not liking the other more, and a sense of duty of liking her more, for diminishing the imbalance, with sometimes some corresponding sentiment of fairness and unfairness. All these effects combine with the other noted reasons and sentiments.

12.3.4.3. Gifts and actions Individual i appreciates the gift she receives x_j for various possible reasons: its effect on her allocation $X_i + x_j - x_i$; its manifestation of individual j liking her, ℓ_j, and its showing and proving its intensity; the attention and consideration giving constitutes; the favourable appreciation it implies; the benevolence and kindness associated with it; the effects of these attention, consideration, and appreciation on her sense of self and of social existence; and the relation established in the process of giving and receiving.

Individual i's basic choice is the gift x_i she gives. With the conception presently retained, she does that with the aim of maximizing U^i. Yet, her motivation in question is her liking individual j (ℓ_i). The resulting effect of x_i on U^i passes through various channels: it increases individual j's allocation $X_j + x_i - x_j$ and hence her satisfaction U^j; it may relevantly improve aspects of individual j's situation S_j; it shows and proves individual i's liking and its intensity – which may augment U^j and induce a higher ℓ_j –; it manifests attention, consideration, appreciation, benevolence and kindness that individual j appreciates – which again tends to augment U^j and ℓ_j –; and it may create a relationship appreciated by any individual or by both in the process of giving. These values are compared with cost in terms of self-interest in $X_i + x_j - x_i$.

Gifts x_i and x_j can also have other effects, for instance demonstration effects of showing liking or being liked to third persons whose opinion may be appreciated by the individuals in question.

Showing one's liking, in particular for eliciting reciprocal liking, is of course mostly done by communication and the appropriate interaction. Moreover, likings are sentiments and common individuals exercise only limited choice over their own sentiments. Yet, such actions more or less exist, through various devices including reasoning, getting used to, meeting or avoiding, focussing attention on sentiments or on their object, or diverting attention from them, and so on.

12.3.4.4. Reduced forms   Considering Equation (1) and the similar one for individual j, the two relations previously discussed $\ell_i = \ell_i(\ell_j, x_j)$ and $\ell_j = \ell_j(\ell_i, x_i)$, relations $S_i = S_i(x_j, x_i)$ and $S_j = S_j(x_i, x_j)$ that express effects of the gifts x_i and x_j, and solving for the levels U^i, U^j, ℓ_i, ℓ_j (and S_i, S_j), one notably obtains $U^i = u^i(x_i, x_j)$ and $U^j = u^j(x_j, x_i)$ for given initial individual allocations X_i and X_j. These reduced forms can then be used for the analysis of the reciprocity game in Section 11.

This is reciprocity in giving for liking-reciprocity. The reciprocity in liking is described by $\ell_i = \ell_i(\ell_j, x_j)$ and $\ell_j = \ell_j(\ell_i, x_i)$. Solving in ℓ_i and ℓ_j would give $\ell_i = \tilde{\ell}_i(x_i, x_j)$, $\ell_j = \tilde{\ell}_j(x_j, x_i)$. In the case of pure reciprocal liking, the relations are $\ell_i = \ell_i(\ell_j)$ and $\ell_j = \ell_j(\ell_i)$, with possible solutions $\ell_i = \tilde{\ell}_i$ and $\ell_j = \tilde{\ell}_j$. However, the cases of multiple solutions, and, if an adjustment process is considered, of multiple equilibria and of multiple stable equilibria, are not rare. There are often dynamics that lead to either mutual high liking or mutual low liking according to the conditions.[89]

12.3.4.5. Group-sentiments   Finally, although reciprocal liking constitutes a close, integrative relationship between the individuals, the foregoing analysis has ultimately considered distinctly individualized items. However, there are limits to this "methodological individualism". Norms and social opinions, notably for comparative reciprocities, already are not always considered in the most fruitful way when they are only seen as related individual views or sentiments. In a different way, but sometimes very

---

[89] This issue is fully analysed in Kolm 1984a.

strongly, mutual liking is not only a pair of individual sentiments but is often more fruitfully seen as a properly collective sentiment of the considered micro-society.[90]

Indeed, we have noted that people consider it this way when they speak of "our friendship", or "our love". However, an analysis from this point of view, possibly based on a phenomenology of intersubjectivity, would take us quite far away from the traditional methods of economics followed here. Yet, from a formal point of view, the full realization of this fusion and commonness of sentiments can be described in writing $\ell_i = \ell_j = \ell$ in the foregoing equations.

13. Strategic interaction and process preferences: Games of reciprocity and their consequences

13.1. Presentation

13.1.1. Objects of preferences

Given possible motives and their relations with actions, there remains, for explaining reciprocity, to consider the effects of the interaction of the participants that leads them to the choice of actions. In so choosing, participants often take into account their anticipation of the others' reaction. They thus consider the thinking of the others, and they may have to consider what others think they themselves think. This gives a game-theoretic form to the interaction leading to the choices of actions. In addition, people also often directly care about the nature of the intentions, attitudes, judgments, and views of others, notably concerning themselves. And they also have judgments about their own intentions, attitudes, judgments, and views towards others. This is notably important for most genuine reciprocities. It is obvious for reciprocities based on liking, but it also holds for the balance or fairness of balance reciprocity. Hence, the strategic game-theoretic dimension of the relation is not only present but also correspondingly enriched by these other concerns. Therefore, beyond the general properties of game theory, there will be large differences with other games, due to the type of motives and concerns. These specific properties of games of reciprocity influence both preferences and concepts of solution (in the sense of game theory) – as will be shortly seen.

These motives refer to social relations, which determine a type of process for the interaction such as, notably, a type of reciprocity, a purely self-interested exchange, or imposition by force. This reciprocity can be of a pure or mixed kind of any type (liking, balance with some liking, normatively oppressive balance, with any kind of combination and of role for self-interest). The definition of the process determines the game and in the end the outcome. It is a parameter of the game and in particular of the preference (utility) functions and of the type of "solution" retained – as will be

---

[90] See Kolm 1984a, and an advocacy of such a viewpoint in Chapters 9 and 10 of this volume.

shortly discussed. Moreover, the comparison of processes and hence of types of social relations, given their intrinsic values or defects and their consequences, is an essential issue. In particular, explaining the existence of processes (and types of social relations), and their choices or the choices that lead to them, is a most important question. As is the normative comparison of the alternatives.

Then, in particular, we have to consider that people have preferences about processes independently of their effects on transfers and the resulting economic allocations. Indeed, a type of process goes along with a type of social relation, and people are generally not indifferent about being liked, appreciated, trusted, treated fairly or instrumentalized, reified, exploited, or forced. When there are two transfers – one in each direction – between two persons, it is not indifferent for these persons (and for many observers) whether these transfers result from a selfish but respectful exchange, a reciprocity induced by mutual liking, a reciprocity motivated by balance or fairness, or a theft or forceful appropriation followed by retaliation. Besides the style of relations, types of processes entail more or less freedom, for the actor, from the acts and choices (and judgements) of others. People often like this freedom in itself, although the costs of choosing, the anguish of choice (as Sören Kierkegaard and Jean-Paul Sartre put it), and a possible aversion for responsibility, can have the opposite effect. These preferences for the type of process in itself are the *intrinsic process preferences*, or "preferences about the process in itself or *per se*". The association of these preferences with the preferences about the effect of the process on the transfers and allocations, that is, the preferences about the process both in itself and because of its consequences, constitute the *full process preferences*, or, for short, simply *process preferences*.

The other relevant variables and objects of preferences are of two kinds: the "transfers" and the "allocations". A "transfer" is a change in the world that is both favourable to an agent and unfavourable to another – this is a transfer from the latter to the former. This can be a physical transfer of a good, or a service from an agent to the other (costly in some sense for the former). The transfers are for instance the gifts or the items exchanged or taken by force. The gifts x_i and x_j of the previous sections are such transfers. The allocation is the resulting allocation of goods and services (for instance, the $X_i + y$ in the previous sections). The transfers influence the allocation. They determine the allocation resulting from the process, given the initial allocation. However, transfers and allocation are relevant in processes for largely different reasons. For instance, in an exchange the transfers both ways are in some sense of the same value. A balance-reciprocity also compares the transfers both ways and induces some sort of balance between them. Giving from liking first aims at the receiver's allocation, but the gifts in themselves sometimes also matter (e.g., for information effects). Of course, the transfers may matter in relation to some aspect of allocation (e.g., giving according to one's means or to the receiver's needs). Preferences so directly concerned by the transfers are *transfer preferences*. They are characteristic of the process considered.

In contrast, the allocation of goods and services (in a sense a stock for which the transfers constitute a flow) elicits preferences for different reasons. Self-interest is a main one, but there are various other reasons, notably reasons that make one individual be concerned with the allocations of goods to others, such as benevolence, views of distributive justice according to needs or comparative and ideally egalitarian, or other comparative sentiments such as envy, jealousy, sense of inferiority or superiority, or preferences for conforming or for distinction. The corresponding preferences are *allocation preferences*. Note that fairness can intervene both among transfers (for instance when it is an aspect of balance reciprocity) and among allocations; then, the concept is more "local" in the former case.[91]

Formally, in the most synthesized (or reduced) form of the presentation, the initial allocations will be given and the only operations considered are the transfers in question. These transfers then determine the final allocation. Therefore, allocation preferences can be described as preferences about them, and allocation preferences and transfer preferences can be considered jointly in a single and aggregate set of preferences called the *allocative preferences*.

In this most reduced form, there thus only remain two basic types of preferences: the intrinsic process preferences and the allocative preferences. The relations between them, for each agent, have remarkable properties that will be presented in Section 13.2.

In addition to individuals' preferences, the game is determined by concepts of "solution" of the strategic interaction – in the sense of game theory. In this respect also, relations of reciprocity bring in something new.

13.1.2. Interaction and solution

In the simplest reciprocity where a gift entails a return-gift, the initial giver may be concerned with the overall reciprocity and, rather than provide a gift irrespective of the reaction it entails, she may also consider the return-gift in choosing her gift. Then, she more or less foresees the other's reaction and chooses accordingly. This Stackelberg-type solution is a *domination*. In so doing, the initial giver may be purely self-interested and hence give in order to receive the return-gift. This is "exploitation of the return-gift". Yet, the initial giver may also perform this domination with any other motive or mix of motives, including altruism, liking and kindness, any of the reasons noted above for being concerned about the resulting allocation, justice and fairness in the comparison of the two gifts, or their proper balance *per se*, and so on.

However, justice, fairness, balance and equality may be among the concerns, and yet, the very fact that there is a first and a second giver, and hence a domination, is in itself an inequality. Hence, the initial giver may want to remedy this basic imbalance in her giving. That is, she is concerned about fairness not only for the transfers or the allocation, but also for the process, in seeking the corresponding *procedural fairness*. This is done when *the initial gift elicits a return-gift such that, if the return-giver were the initial giver and handed out this return-gift as initial gift, the former initial giver would then*

---

[91] See Kolm 2004.

react by a return-gift identical to her initial gift. This leads to a solution formally analogous to a Cournot–Nash solution, yet with the preferences and hence reaction functions corresponding to the type of relation under consideration. Note that Cournot–Nash solutions have no valid justification in usual one-shot or two-move games. Therefore, the described motive of procedural fairness constitutes the only justification proposed so far of a Cournot–Nash solution for one-shot ot two-move games. A solution with this structure will be called an *equilibrium*.

Equilibrium solutions are also interesting because solutions with the same structure result from important cases of longer relations of reciprocity. In these relations, there is a large number of iterative givings, either alternately from each side, or simultaneously at successive dates. The equilibrium structure can notably result from two rationales, the "myopic" and the "cumulative". In the former, each individual gift is the return-gift corresponding to the last gift received by the giver. In the latter case, each individual gift is an adjustment that reacts to the stocks of previous gifts both ways.[92]

Still other solutions with plausible rationales will be pointed out, but the structures of domination and of equilibrium seem to be the main ones and will be particularly considered, and compared. The comparisons will also extend to processes that are not reciprocities, such as standard exchanges or imposition of an outcome.

The usual considerations of situations of such dominations and equilibria in the space of transfers suggest that the outcome is such that other sets of transfers satisfy better both participants, i.e., it is not Pareto-efficient. However, reaching another set of transfers requires another type of process and of social relation, and, hence, other preferences among sets of transfers or utility functions as function of the transfers. For instance, a standard exchange may lead to a Pareto-efficient state, but one with utility functions corresponding to this process and type of social relations. In comparing processes and their outcomes, a seemingly allocatively inefficient reciprocity may be preferred by all participants to an allocatively efficient other process (e.g., exchange or force), if this reciprocity is sufficiently intrinsically preferred because of the social relations it implies (e.g., kindness, liking, fairness, freedom from others' actions, and so on). The logic of this kind of issue will be closely analysed.

Particularly important properties exist when the transfers are quantities of a good (e.g., a good the yielder produces or possesses, possibly her labour, or the value of aid in case of particular needs of the receiver or means of the yielder) – in fact, it suffices, for these properties, that the transfers or favours from the same agent can be ranked by a relation of more or less, and even only that they can be so classified according to their desirability by the receiver. In this *quantitative case*, preferences about processes are related to the fact that more or less of the goods are transferred – an observable property. This leads to a number of notable properties with meaningful and important applications, including counterintuitive logical results that explain some paradoxes observed in processes of social change and development.

---

[92] See Kolm 1984a, 1984b, 1994.

Important applications of the obtained results are found in the comparison of economic systems, and in particular in the properties of the process of "development", since the latter has largely consisted of substituting markets and command systems to economic relations that were essentially based on various types of reciprocity.

The logic of process preferences, notably the relation between intrinsic and full process preferences, and the general resulting properties of interactions between two agents, will be considered in Section 13.2. Section 13.3 then considers the interactions between two agents engaged in some type of reciprocity or other process, and it relates the types of process, preferences about them, their results in transfers and allocations, and the comparisons of the resulting amounts transferred and of participants' satisfaction. In particular, the "reciprocity games" lead to the consideration of specific rationales for the relevant concepts of "solutions" of the game. Reciprocity is compared with other processes in Section 13.4 (in explaining in particular the "paradox of development").

13.2. General properties about processes

13.2.1. General preferences

13.2.1.1. Transfers, process, and preferences Let variable $x \in X$ denote the set of transfers, from and to any agent (these distinctions will come later). As noted, x also entails the final allocation, and the "allocative preferences" can be about both the transfers *per se* and the resulting allocation. Variable $z \in Z$ denotes a type of process, and hence both a type of "mechanism" leading to a solution, and the type of social relations that accompany it. An agent's (overall) preferences are concerned with the pairs (x, z).[93] Classically, these preferences will be assumed to constitute a preordering with pairwise relations denoted as $\succ$ (preference), $\sim$ (indifference), and $\succsim$ ($\succ$ or $\sim$). These preferences are often representable by an ordinal utility function $u(x, z)$, and we will often consider this representation for convenience. These preferences, considered for all involved agents, will be used to explain the outcome x of each type of process z; the emergence of a specific process z; the normative evaluation and comparison of the processes; and the evaluation of the actual social choice among them.

13.2.1.2. Intrinsic process preference and a basic lemma Let us first point out a basic general property. Assume x and $x' \in X$, z and $z' \in Z$, and $(x', z') \succsim (x, z)$. Then, $(x, z) \succ (x, z')$ implies $(x', z') \succ (x, z')$, and $(x', z) \succ (x', z')$ implies $(x', z) \succ (x, z)$. In particular, $(x, z) \succ (x, z')$ and $(x', z) \succ (x', z')$ may result from $(\xi, z) \succ (\xi, z')$ for all $\xi \in \overline{X} \subseteq X$ and $x \in \overline{X}$ and $x' \in \overline{X}$. Hence the following definition and properties.

---

[93] By comparison (full) process preferences are preferences among processes (and the corresponding social relations) z that derive from (overall) preferences among pairs (x, z) in being the preferences among pairs $[x(z), z]$ where $x(z)$ denotes the transfers (and allocation) that are determined by the working of process z.

DEFINITION. Process z is *intrinsically preferred* (or *preferred per se*) to process z' in the relevant domain $\overline{X} \subseteq X$ if $(x, z) \succ (x, z')$ for all $x \in \overline{X}$. Weakly intrinsically preferred (or weakly preferred *per se*) is similarly defined in replacing $\succ$ by $\succsim$.

The domain $\overline{X}$ will usually be kept implicit for simplicity, and hence it will be assumed to be the one relevant for the specific issue under consideration. Intrinsic preference, or preference *per se*, for process z over process z' will be denoted as zPz'.[94]

PROPOSITION 1. *Assume process z to be intrinsically preferred to process z'. Then, $(x', z') \succ (x, z)$ implies both $(x', z) \succ (x, z)$ and $(x', z') \succ (x, z')$; that is, x' is preferred to x with both processes. And $(x, z) \succ (x', z)$ or $(x, z') \succ (x', z')$ implies $(x, z) \succ (x', z')$; that is, the latter relation holds if x' is not preferred to x with either process.*

These properties are particularly meaningful. The former says that for (x', z') to be weakly preferred to (x, z) in spite of the intrinsic preference for z over z', x' should be preferred to x with both processes; this can result, for example, from the fact that the allocation implied by x' is intrinsically much more favourable than the allocation implied by x and this compensates the intrinsic preference for z over z'.[95] For example, z can be a reciprocity that yields x and z' can be a very efficient exchange that yields x'. In the second, converse, property, $(x, \zeta) \succsim (x', \zeta)$ can mean that x is freely chosen by the agent with process ζ while x' is a possibility, and the property implies that if this is the case for ζ being either z or z', then $(x, z) \succ (x', z')$. For example, z can be a reciprocity and z' an exchange, and x can be the choice in either process.

13.2.1.3. Process-dependent allocative preferences Allocative preferences may be the same for different types of processes, but this is certainly not the general case, because a number of reasons for preferences about processes depend on transfers. This notably happens for reasons based on the quality of social relations or on the activity. For example, such reasons are absent if there is no transfer, which will be denoted as $x = 0$. If process preferences rely only on such reasons for the comparison of processes z and z', then $(0, z) \sim (0, z')$. If, furthermore, allocative preferences are the same for processes z and z', and if there exists one $x \neq 0$ such that $(x, z) \sim (0, z)$ (or the same with z'), then $(x, z') \sim (0, z') \sim (0, z) \sim (x, z)$. Hence, process z' cannot be better or worse than process z for x. In particular, none of these processes can be intrinsically preferred to the other for all $x \neq 0$. Of course, when $(0, z) \sim (0, z')$, the case $x = 0$ is to be excluded for Proposition 1 which, hence, considers only situations with transfers.

---

[94] Similarly, x is (weakly) intrinsically preferred to x' in the relevant domain of processes $z \in \overline{Z} \subseteq Z$ if $(x, z) \succ (x', z)$ (or $(x, z) \succ (x', z)$) for all $z \in \overline{Z}$. But this property will be less used. A proposition dual to Proposition 1 but inverting x and z (and x' and z') then holds.

[95] This can result from intrinsic preference for x' over x.

However, other reasons for process preferences may exclude $(0, z) \sim (0, z')$. For example, z may denote some process with much freedom (exchange or reciprocity) which ends up in $x = 0$, while z' may be command that imposes $x = 0$, and preference for freedom may then lead to $(0, z) \succ (0, z')$. In still other cases, the mere attitudes towards others may make the difference between z and z' even when $x = 0$.[96]

13.2.1.4. Preferences and intrinsic preferences among processes If the type of process $\zeta \in Z$ is defined with sufficient specification, it fully determines its outcome $\xi = \xi(\zeta) \in X$. One can say that process z is fully preferred or, for short, preferred, or indifferent, to process z' when $[\xi(z), z] \succ [\xi(z'), z']$ or $[\xi(z), z] \sim [\xi(z'), z']$. Proposition 1 can be written in this case, and it then gives.

PROPOSITION 2. *A process that is intrinsically preferred to another is also preferred to this other if the transfers and allocations it induces are preferred to those induced by the other in either of the two processes.*

If a process is preferred to another although this other is intrinsically preferred to it, then the transfers and allocations it induces are preferred to those induced by the other in both processes.

For instance, if an exchange is preferred to a reciprocity while the latter is intrinsically preferred to the former, then the outcome of exchange is preferred to that of reciprocity with both modes of realization. With exchange, this can be manifested by the choice of this outcome rather than that which would result from reciprocity. With reciprocity, it is regretted that the resulting outcome is not, rather, the one of exchange.

13.2.2. Dyadic processes

13.2.2.1. General concepts Consider now a society made of two agents denoted as 1 and 2. Write $i = 1$ or 2. Agent i's preference, indifference, and ordinal utility function

---

[96] If $(0, z) \sim (0, z')$, system z is said to be intrinsically preferred to system z' if $(x, z) \succ (x, z')$ for all $x \neq 0$, and Proposition 1 becomes the following set of properties:

$(x', z') \succ (x, z) \Rightarrow (x, z') \succ (x, z)$ and $(x', z') \succ (x, z')$,

$(x', z') \succ (x, z) \Rightarrow (x, z') \succsim (x, z)$ and $(x', z') \succsim (x, z')$,

$(x', z') \succsim (x, z)$ and $x' \neq 0 \Rightarrow (x', z) \succ (x, z)$,

$(x', z') \succsim (x, z)$ and $x \neq 0 \Rightarrow (x', z') \succ (x, z')$,

$(x, z) \succsim (x', z')$ results from $(x, z) \succsim (x', z)$ or $(x, z') \succsim (x', z')$,

$(x, z) \succ (x', z')$ results from $(x, z) \succ (x', z)$ or $(x, z') \succ (x', z')$,

or $(x, z) \succsim (x', z)$ and $x' \neq 0$, or $(x, z') \succsim (x', z')$ and $x \neq 0$.

will be denoted as $\underset{i}{\succ}, \underset{i}{\sim}, \underset{i}{\succsim}$ (either $\underset{i}{\succ}$ or $\underset{i}{\sim}$), and $u_i(x, z)$. Write also $j = 1$ or 2 with $j \neq i$. Let x_i denote a transfer from agent i to agent j, and x_j a transfer from agent j to agent i, and write $x = (x_i, x_j) \in X$ (the set of possible x_i may depend on both agents and on x_j, and similarly for x_j).

In a free-transfer process, agent i freely chooses her transfer x_i to agent j, but this can be under various possible conditions. One of these conditions is that x_j is given. The two following concepts will be needed later:

Agent i's *best response* to x_j is

$$r_i(x_j, z) = \arg\max\nolimits_{x_i} u_i(x, z),$$

and this function of x_j is agent i's *best-response or reaction function*.

Agent i's *preferred response of the other agent j* to x_i is

$$p_i(x_i, z) = \arg\max\nolimits_{x_j} u_i(x, z),$$

and this function of x_i is agent i's *preferred response function* of agent j.

The x such that $x_i = r_i(x_j, z)$ for both $i = 1$ and 2 (and $j \neq i$) are formally "Cournot–Nash equilibria" (whether they actually result from process z constitutes a major issue).

The x such that $x_j = r_j(x_i, z)$ and

$$x_i = \arg\max\nolimits_{\tilde{x}_i} u_i\left[\tilde{x}_i, r_j(\tilde{x}_i, z); z\right]$$

are the dominations of agent j by agent i (Stackelberg solutions) – x_i denotes this particular value of the generic $\tilde{x}_i$.[97]

The functions r_i and p_i are written here as single-valued. When they describe an agent's choice (which is always the case for r_i), this can justify this assumption. This assumption also permits a simpler presentation. It will have a consequence only for the r_i for a single particular property.

13.2.2.2. The quantitative case A further specification is the quantitative case where x_i is a quantity of a good, hence $x_i \in \Re^+$, for all i. Then, x_i and x_j are quantities of different goods. For example, each agent can provide to the other services corresponding to their particular skills, endowments, information, or situation in the social structure. Or each good corresponds to the receiver's specific tastes or needs. Or the transfers or services are contingent aid provided in particular cases of need of the receiver or of relatively favourable situation of the giver. Or again the agents may own different resources of any other type.[98] This quantitative case is thus a rather frequent occurrence, and it will be shown to entail particularly remarkable properties (moreover, it suffices,

---

[97] Other solutions are defined by $x_j = r_j(x_i, z) = p_i(x_i, z)$, considered later.

[98] In particular cases where the relational or symbolic value of the transfers predominates, the goods can have, as sole differentiation, the agent who is the origin or the receiver of the transfer, and hence the direction of the transfer.

for these results, that the $x_i \in \Re$ represents an ordering of the transfers in order of desirability for the receiver j). The graph of the reaction function $x_i = r_i(x_j, z)$ in the plane (x_i, x_j) is the *reaction curve* R_i^z of agent i for process z.

DEFINITION. Agent i is said to *appreciate the other's transfer* at (x, z) when the function $u_i(x, z)$ is increasing in x_j.

Mention of this property will implicitly assume it to hold in the domain relevant for the specific issue considered.

PROPOSITION 3. *If agent j appreciates the other's transfer and $x_j = r_j(x_i, z)$, then $(x', z) \underset{j}{\succ} (x, z) \Rightarrow x_i' > x_i$.*

Indeed, if, with the assumptions, $x_i' \leqslant x_i$, then $(x', y) \underset{j}{\precsim} (x_i, x_j'; y) \underset{j}{\precsim} (x, z)$, from agent j's appreciation of the other's transfer and from the definition of r_j.

The same result holds, with agent j's appreciation of the other's transfer, if agent j can dispose of any part of the transfer x_i she receives, that is, with r_j defined as follows with $\xi = (\xi_i, \xi_j) \in X$:

$$r_j(x_i, z) = \{\xi_j : \xi = \arg\max_{\tilde{\xi}} [u_j(\tilde{\xi}, z) / \tilde{\xi}_i \leqslant x_i]\}.$$

The foregoing results entail the following property:

PROPOSITION 4. *If $(x', z') \underset{j}{\succ} (x, z)$, $x_j = r_j(x_i, z)$ and agent j intrinsically weakly prefers process z to process z' and appreciates the other's transfer, then $x_i' > x_i$.*

Indeed, from Proposition 1, the conditions imply $(x', z) \underset{j}{\succ} (x, z)$ and Proposition 3 then provides the result.[99]

There result the following properties which will be applied to the comparison of various types of reciprocities in Section 3 and of reciprocities and other processes (such as exchange or coercion) in Section 4:

PROPOSITION 5. *If a process is unanimously preferred to a Cournot–Nash equilibrium of another where the agents appreciate the other's transfer, although this process is found to be intrinsically inferior to the other by both agents, then it achieves larger transfers than the other does.*

---

[99] Results analogous to Propositions 3 and 4 hold in replacing r_j by p_j.

PROPOSITION 6. *If a process is unanimously preferred to a domination with a nondecreasing reaction function of the dominated agent and where the agents appreciate the other's transfer, although this process is found to be intrinsically inferior by both agents to that which leads to the domination, then this process achieves larger transfers than does the domination.*

PROOF. Proposition 5 directly results from Proposition 4. Let us now prove Proposition 6. Let $x \in R_j^z$ denote the transfers of the domination of agent j by agent i with process z. Denote as x' and z' the transfers and process such that $(x', z') \underset{k}{\succ} (x, z)$ for $k = 1$ and 2, with z' being intrinsically inferior to z for both agents. Then, from Proposition 4 applied to agent j, $x'_i > x_i$. Furthermore, $(x', z') \underset{i}{\succ} (x, z)$ implies $(x', z) \underset{i}{\succ} (x, z)$ from Proposition 1. Denote as ξ the $\xi \in R_j^z$ such that $\xi_i = x'_i$. We have $(x, z) \underset{i}{\succsim} (\xi, z)$ from the domination of agent i. Thus $(x', z) \underset{i}{\succ} (\xi, z)$. Hence, $x'_j > \xi_j$ from agent i's appreciation of the other's transfer. Then, if the function $r_j(x_i, z)$ is non-decreasing in x_i, and since $\xi_i = x'_i > x_i$, $\xi_j \geqslant x_j$. Therefore, $x'_j > x_j$. □

13.3. Solutions of the return-gift and reciprocity games

13.3.1. The three solution concepts

13.3.1.1. Setting In reciprocities, the transfers are gifts. In the simple gift/return-gift processes, there are two agents, and agent i hands out gift x_i to agent j who reciprocates with the return gift x_j to agent i. The x_i and x_j can a priori be of any nature, but we will later consider the "quantitative case" where each gift is a quantity of a good. A notable issue is that of gift refusal, the possibility of refusing a gift in totality or in part, and its consequences. This can apply to the initial gift, to the return gift, or to both. The issue of gift refusal will be forgotten in this section for simplicity and because, in a number of cases, it does not matter, or does not occur, or even cannot occur. (The agents may not refuse because they appreciate the other's gift, or only the gifts offered matter, or refusing the gift or returning it back may not be possible for a material reason or because of a norm internalized or imposed by social pressure, or the giver may be able to refuse the refusal – for instance in not "taking back" something refused –, and so on.)[100] Then, the return gift is the receiver's best response $r_j(x_i, z)$ for the relevant type of process z,

---

[100] There can be many reasons to refuse a gift (including a return gift) in totality or in part: benevolence towards the giver (which can induce refusing or accepting), norm-following in specific situations, dignity and self-respect, avoidance of the requirement to provide a return gift or of moral indebtedness towards the giver, showing the giver or other people that the gift or the return gift is not sufficient (for the sake of it, or in order to induce higher future gifts), humiliating the giver, and so on. And the anticipation of refusal can influence the gift. That of partial refusal may lead one to give more. The gift offered may try to influence the amounts accepted or refused when they depend on the offer. Refusal may lead the giver to offer more so as to appear more generous at no cost, or less (or nothing) so as to avoid the humiliation of rejection. And

and it terminates the game for relevant purposes. A function $r_j(x_i, z)$ is now called a *return-gift function*. Given this function for the return giver and the type of process z, the outcome is fully determined by the initial giver's choice of x_i.

If the return giver were strictly self interested in her allocation, she would return no gift. Then, if the initial giver were similarly self interested, she would not provide a gift in the first place. Both the initial and the return giving can be influenced by the usual motivations for giving such as kind or duty-bound altruism, norm following induced by duty or habit, caring for other people's opinion (or pressure), moral self-gratification, and so on. Moreover, return giving can also be influenced by the initial gift for reasons of gratitude, sense of social balance or fairness, sense of moral indebtedness, imitation, conformity, concern for status, with the same possible role for norms, duties, opinion or pressure, or judging oneself. Hence the initial gift can also be strictly self interested in exploiting the other person's return-giving behaviour (see below). If $x_i = 0$ denotes the absence of gift from agent i, $r_j(0, z)$ is the pure gift of agent j (if agent j, who may return gifts, does not singly give, then $0 = r_j(0, z)$).

13.3.1.2. Solutions The initial giver can follow several possible paths of logic, with three pure rationales and possible compromises between them. Each logic determines a type of process z, and the three pure rationales and the resulting processes will be denoted respectively, when agent i is the initial giver, as δ_i for domination (or exploitation), ε_i for equilibrium, and φ_i for non-frustration.

The formal definitions of these three polar solutions are the following, when the initial giver knows the other's return-gift functions (see the definitions in Section 2.4):

domination-exploitation: $x_i = \arg\max_{\tilde{x}_i} u_i[\tilde{x}_i, r_j(\tilde{x}_i, \delta_i); \delta_i]$;
symmetrical reciprocity equilibrium: $x_i = r_i(x_j, \varepsilon_j)$ and $x_j = r_j(x_i, \varepsilon_i)$; and
non-frustration: $x_j = r_j(x_i, \varphi_i) = p_i(x_i, \varphi_i)$.

But the most important are the reasons for these solutions.

13.3.1.3. Rationales In a *domination* solution, the initial giver is only concerned with obtaining the best pair of the gift and the return-gift given the reaction function of the

---

so on. As a reaction to a gift and towards the giver, gift refusal is in some sense akin to return giving (the refused part is in a sense given back when this is possible and accepted, and refusal is sometimes materially performed precisely in this way), but it is also quite different because the initial receiver is imposed to have to choose explicitly to accept or refuse, and the various modalities may differ (for instance, the initial giver may be unable to refuse the refusal, and so on). With the possibility of gift refusal, agents have two types of acts: giving and refusing or accepting gifts. Each gift is then described by two entities: the offered gift x_i and the corresponding accepted gift $\bar{x}_i$, the latter being limited by the former ($\bar{x}_i \leq x_i$ in the quantitative case). According to the case, one or the other, or both, can matter. A single gift giving now has two moves: giving, and accepting or refusing. And a gift/return-gift has four variables and three moves: the initial giver i offers x_i, the other agent, j, chooses both the accepted gift $\bar{x}_i$ and the offered return gift x_j, and then the initial giver accepts $\bar{x}_j$. This last move renders the game fully strategic if the return giver cares about the accepted $\bar{x}_j$ and not only about x_j. Longer reciprocity processes can also be modelled in taking into account the possibility of gift refusal. The various concepts of solution can be extended to this case.

return giver, without being influenced by any hypothetical choice of the parties. This solution is formally of the Stackelberg type. But, of course, the initial giver's allocative preferences may be concerned with any of the moral, normative, comparative or altruistic reasons, in addition to strict self-interest. However, the initial giver may also be strictly self-interested, and then she can be said to self-interestedly exploit the receiver's return-gift behaviour (then, she is interested in the allocation only, and not in the transfers for any other reason). Such a non-benevolent motive basically prevents liking reciprocity, as we have seen.

In other solutions, the structure of the process itself is also of concern for the initial giver. In particular, the two other polar solutions are more elaborate in being based on rationales of *non-regret*, associated to the rationality of foreseeing the outcome (if possible).

In the case of *symmetrical reciprocity*, the initial giver holds that the solution should be neutral with respect to the order of the gifts. The reason refers to procedural justice, or process fairness, and consists of equality with respect to the roles in the interaction (ideal equality in something is grounded in rationality).[101] If the initial giver i gives x_i and receives in return $x_j = r_j(x_i, \varepsilon_i)$, then she thinks she should have given $r_i(x_j, \varepsilon_j) = r_i[r_j(x_i, \varepsilon_i), \varepsilon_j]$. If this differs from her initial gift, she regrets this initial gift. There is no such regret only if this initial gift satisfies $x_i = r_i[r_j(x_i, \varepsilon_i), \varepsilon_j]$. That is, this solution satisfies both $x_i = r_i(x_j, \varepsilon_j)$ and $x_j = r_j(x_i, \varepsilon_i)$. This outcome is independent of which of the participants is the first giver and which is the second. And the same outcome is reached if both participants play simultaneously this symmetrical non-regret strategy. In this case, furthermore, if any participant knows that the other plays this way, she is justified in choosing the corresponding gift either as a simple reaction or because she also herself plays this way (this holds if there is a single such equilibrium, or otherwise if she knows in addition which equilibrium the other selects, which can be an equilibrium that is better than the others for both agents – see below).

This solution is formally a Cournot–Nash equilibrium, and the foregoing considerations provide *the only reason known to date for reaching a Cournot–Nash equilibrium in a two-move or one-shot game*. In the other views of such an equilibrium, indeed, the fact that it is self-enforcing (in the sense that no agent wishes to depart from it if the other does not) does not suffice to preclude unanimously beneficial correlated deviations. Yet, Cournot–Nash equilibria can also be the convergence states of longer processes (as with Cournot's original theory), and this can also be the case for longer processes of reciprocity (see the corresponding analyses noted in Section 13.1.2).

Moreover, it is likely that when the process and its rationale are such a symmetrical reciprocity, the participants evaluate its intrinsic moral and relational value, referring to its fairness, equity or justice, or to the attitudes and sentiments it involves (equality, respect, concern for other), by comparison with the other types of processes, independently of who initiates the process and chooses it. In these cases, it makes no difference

---

[101] See Kolm 1998, English translation of 1971, Foreword, Section 5.

whether ε_i or ε_j is in the functions u_i, u_j, r_i, r_j, and they can be replaced with the sign ε. The outcome is then a solution of the pair of equations $x_i = r_i(x_j, \varepsilon)$ and $x_j = r_j(x_i, \varepsilon)$.

In the third type of solution (*non-frustration*), the first giver, agent i, knows that if she gives x_i, then the return gift she prefers to receive is $x_j = p_i(x_i, \varphi_i)$. But she actually receives $x_j = r_j(x_i, \varphi_i)$. If these values are not the same, she is frustrated and regrets this divergence. But she can avoid this frustration and regret in choosing a x_i that satisfies the equation $r_j(x_i, \varphi_i) = p_i(x_i, \varphi_i)$, and then the other agent chooses this return gift $x_j = r_j(x_i, \varphi_i)$.

13.3.1.4. The return-gift game The initial giver i chooses her gift x_i and also, by her intention (possibly also manifested by attitudes or otherwise), the type of gift/return-gift process. The receiver a priori cares about the other's intention and attitude, which are crucial for the quality, value and appreciation of the relationship. It may be that the return gift does not depend on these intentions and attitudes, but this is not a priori the general case (recall that a strictly self-interested return giver caring about her allocation only would not provide any return gift at all in such a two-gift game). Issues of information are not discussed here. For example, if the initial giver prefers domination to symmetrical reciprocity equilibrium, then it turns out that she would generally benefit from the other reacting according to symmetrical reciprocity, and she might be able to induce this behaviour in making the other believe that her intention and behaviour correspond to this process (in the quantitative case considered shortly, this benefit results from the relative disposition and the shapes of the return-gift curves in these two cases).

13.3.2. The quantitative case

Let us now consider the specific case where both the gift x_i and the return gift x_j are quantities, each of a given good. They can be the goods that the individuals particularly own or produce, or the durations during which each works for the other, or goods that the receivers particularly enjoy, or gifts contingent on some occurrence of an agent's need or gain, and so on. These quantities will be treated as being divisible. The $x_i \in \Re$ could also more generally represent orderings of the possible gifts in order of desirability for the receiver (only this aspect of quantities will be used). The return-gift functions $x_i = r_i(x_j, z)$ can be represented by graphs R_i^z in the plane (x_1, x_2) – as can be the preferred other's return-gift functions $x_j = p_i(x_i, y)$.

The return-gift functions $x_j = r_j(x_i, z)$ are, in general, increasing functions (or at least nondecreasing functions): if you provide a return gift, you tend to return more (at least no less) if you are given more. This results from the foregoing analyses of the motives of reciprocity, notably of liking reciprocity and balance reciprocity, with the considered effects of induced liking, gratitude, fairness, moral indebtedness, imitation and conformity, norms, duties, and the opinions and – possibly – pressure of others. Of course, several particular reasons can also lead to decreasing return gifts. For example, if the other person gives you little (versus much), this may mean that she is poor (versus wealthy), and hence you will give her much (versus little) out of benevolence – the gift then has this role of information or supposed information. Or, if she gives you little, this may mean that she is a miser, and you may give her much in order to show and emphasize her meanness to herself or to others. And so on. However, increasingness can doubtlessly be considered to be the "normal" case. An agent with an increasing (or, at least, nondecreasing) return-gift function as function of the other's gift is called a "gift-consistent return giver".

"Appreciation of the other's gift" is the application of appreciation of the other's transfer. If an agent can refuse to take part of the other's gift but does not do so, this implies that – everything considered – she appreciates the other's gift. Of course, norms or the opinion of other people may induce someone to accept a gift, or a larger gift, when she would have preferred not to do so, especially if they also demand that she gives in return. However, this is on the whole a secondary phenomenon in the whole field of reciprocity. In particular, it is not present in steady reciprocities, notably related to economic productive or consumptive activities, or to ongoing life in organizations or in collectivities of all types. Now these latter situations will in particular be the ones considered when the present results will be used for comparing economic systems and for considering their transformations.

Of course, individual i's appreciation of the other's gift at (x, z), that is, the function $u_i(x, z)$ is increasing in x_j, implies that the function of x_j defined by $u_i[r_i(x_j, z), x_j; z]$ is also an increasing function of x_j, from the definition of r_i (if u_i is differentiable at (r_i, x_j), $\partial u_i / \partial r_i = 0$ and hence $du_i/dx_j = \partial u_i/\partial x_j > 0$). That is, u_i increases along the curve R_i^z when x_j increases. Therefore, with nondecreasing return-gift functions and appreciation of the other's gift by both agents, if there exist several symmetrical reciprocal equilibria, one is preferred to the others by both agents.

The quantitative case permits further discussion of the existence of solutions. Assume individual k's initial endowment of the good she yields (labelled good k) is quantity X_k. Then, individuals i and j's final endowments of goods i and j are, respectively, $(X_i - x_i, x_j)$, and $(X_j - x_j, x_i)$, and this can be described in an Edgeworth box.[102] All the relevant motivations (and the fact that an individual may already have some amount of the good she receives) may still be present. Consider the return-gift functions and curves $x_i = r_i(x_j, \varepsilon)$ and $x_j = r_j(x_i, \varepsilon)$, defined on $[0, X_j]$ and $[0, X_i]$, respectively. Then, *if these functions are either continuous or nondecreasing, there exists at least one symmetrical equilibrium*.[103]

Proposition 4 entails the following result:

PROPOSITION 7. *If the initial giver of a gift/return-gift chooses a domination while she intrinsically weakly prefers a symmetrical equilibrium, and she appreciates the other's gift, then the return gift is higher than it would be at this equilibrium.*

---

[102] See Kolm 1973, 1984a, 1984b, 1994.
[103] See same references, particularly 1994. If these functions are increasing, there also exists one "stable" such equilibrium.

Indeed, if d^i and e denote the x of this domination when agent i is the first giver and of this symmetrical equilibrium, respectively, then $(d^i, \delta_i) \underset{i}{\succ} (e, \varepsilon)$ from agent i's choice, and $e_i = r_i(e_j, \varepsilon)$ from the definition of e, while agent i intrinsically weakly prefers process ε to process δ_i. Then $d_j^i > e_j$ from Proposition 4.

Agent j is said to be a *gift-consistent return giver* and a *process-consistent return giver* if, respectively,

$$x_i > x_i' \Rightarrow r_j(x_i, z) > r_j(x_i', z) \; (\text{or } r_j(x_i, z) \geqslant r_j(x_i', z)),$$

and

$$zP_j z' \Rightarrow r_j(x_i, z) \geqslant r_j(x_i, z'),$$

where $zP_j z'$ means that agent j intrinsically weakly prefers process z to process z'. These properties hold for a relevant domain of z in the former case and of x_i in the latter. Gift consistency means the increasingness (or nondecreasingness) of the return-gift function, just discussed. Process consistency can result from gratitude for the type of process initiated by the initial giver (and not only for the gift), and from the return-gift being a good complementary to the quality of the social relation (this will be applied for comparing symmetrical reciprocities with dominations). An agent is a *consistent return giver* if she is both gift-consistent and process-consistent.

These definitions imply:

LEMMA. *If agent j is a consistent return giver,*

$$zP_j z' \text{ and } r_j(x_i, z) = r_j(x_i', z') \Rightarrow x_i \leqslant x_i'.$$

Let us, in addition, make it precise that return-gift functions are single-valued, because they describe actual behaviour (this will be used for the function $r_i(x_i, \delta_i)$ as function of x_i at point d^i).

The following result then holds:

PROPOSITION 8. *If both agents intrinsically weakly prefer symmetrical reciprocity to domination, the initial giver appreciates the other's gift, and the return giver is consistent, then the gift is higher in a chosen domination than in an alternative symmetrical equilibrium.*

Propositions 7 and 8 together make up:

PROPOSITION 9. *Both gifts are higher at a chosen domination than at an alternative symmetrical equilibrium if both agents intrinsically weakly prefer symmetrical reciprocity to domination and appreciate the other's gift, and if the return giver is consistent.*

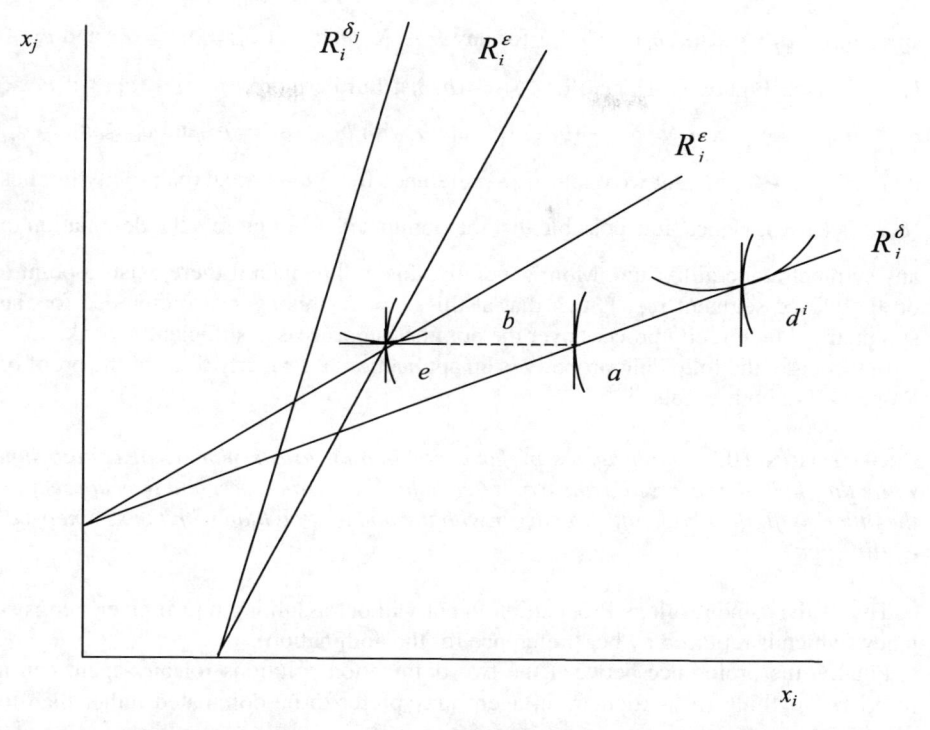

Figure 7. Domination and symmetrical reciprocity solutions of the return-gift game.

This result has the flavour of a paradox, since both agents intrinsically prefer the symmetrical reciprocity to the domination and a noted consistency property (satisfied for at least one of them) tends to make them give more in processes they intrinsically prefer.

PROOF. However, Proposition 7 has obtained $d_j^i > e_j$. Denote as a the x such that $a_j = e_j = r_j(a_i, \delta_i)$ (see Figure 7). Then, if agent j is a consistent return giver and $\varepsilon P_j \delta_i$, $e_j = r_j(e_i, \varepsilon)$ and the lemma implies $a_i \geqslant e_i$. But $d_j^i > e_j = a_j$ (Proposition 7), and the function $x_j = r_j(x_i, \delta_i)$ is increasing or non-decreasing in x_i (gift consistency of agent j), single valued, and satisfied by the coordinates of both a and d^i. Hence $d_j^i > e_i$. □

Let us now turn, in comparing domination and symmetrical equilibrium, from the quantities of gifts to the preferences of agents.

If domination d^i is chosen rather than symmetrical equilibrium, then $(d^i, \delta_i) \underset{i}{\succ} (e, \varepsilon)$. Assume the dominated agent, agent j, appreciates the other's gift. Then, if she is also gift-consistent, $(d^i, \delta_i) \underset{i}{\succ} (a, \delta_i)$ along the dominated return-gift curve $x_j = r_j(x_i, \delta_i)$

since $d_j^i > a_j$. And $(a, \delta_i) \underset{j}{\succ} (b, \delta_i)$ for any $b \in X$ such that $b_j = e_j = a_j$ and $e_i \leqslant b_i < a_i$ (see Figure 7). Hence, $(d^i, \delta_i) \underset{i}{\succ} (b, \delta_i)$. Furthermore, $(b, \varepsilon) \underset{j}{\succ} (e, \varepsilon)$ if $e_i < b_i \leqslant a_i$. Therefore, if $(b, \delta_i) \underset{j}{\sim} (b, \varepsilon)$ for any b with $b_j = e_j = a_j$ and $e_i \leqslant b_i \leqslant a_i$, then $(d^i, \delta_i) \underset{j}{\succ} (e, \varepsilon)$. But weak intrinsic preference for symmetrical reciprocity implies $(b, \varepsilon) \underset{i}{\succsim} (b, \delta_i)$. Hence, it is possible that the dominated agent prefers the domination to any symmetrical equilibrium. More generally, this will happen if there exists a point b on the closed segment $[e, a]$ such that at this $x = b$, this agent's preference for the symmetrical reciprocity process over the domination process is sufficiently weak.

In this case, the following property is an application of Property 5 (or of the proof of Property 7 to both agents):[104]

PROPOSITION 10. *If both agents prefer a domination to a symmetrical equilibrium while they hold the reverse intrinsic preference for these processes, and they appreciate the other's gift, then both gifts are larger with the domination than with the symmetrical equilibrium.*

This is the same result as Proposition 9, but without assuming return giver's consistency (which is replaced by her preference for the domination).

Finally, the preference between the two domination solutions for any agent can a priori be anything (in particular, an agent may prefer to be dominated rather than to dominate).

This choice between gift/return-gift processes is a priori Pareto-efficient among these processes and in considering the whole preferences, because it amounts to a choice by the initial giver.[105] Yet, all these solutions of the reciprocity or return-gift game generally fail to be Pareto-efficient with respect to allocative preferences alone. However, switching from one of these solutions to a unanimously preferred set of transfers requires realization by another process. This, in general, changes the allocative preferences (see Section 13.2.1.3), and it introduces another process (such as exchange or force) which may be considered inferior to reciprocity for its intrinsic value (intrinsic process preferences).

13.4. Comparison of reciprocities with other processes

Reciprocities are often compared with other systems of mutual transfers, such as markets, or coercion and planning. Then, reciprocities are often intrinsically appreciated for the quality of the relations, attitudes and sentiments they embody and that induce them,

---

[104] The results of Proposition 6 would apply to a process intrinsically worse than domination for both agents.
[105] If several possible solutions are equivalent for the initial giver, Pareto-efficiency requires choosing one of them that is preferred by the return giver.

including warmth of the relation, freedom and equity and the free realization of fairness and social balance, sense of community, and so on (although other types of reciprocities can rest on rather oppressive norms and social opinion). However, other systems are often chosen over reciprocity, sometimes – when they are exchanges and markets – apparently freely and by unanimous agreement. Such changes can indeed be said to constitute the essence of the process of economic development and modernization. In these cases, when the change occurs, there often seems to be an increase in the amounts transferred. This increase may seem paradoxical, since people transfer more in the system where the intrinsic social and relational value of the transfers has been lost. But this paradox of the relative "autarky of reciprocity" is waved by the following application of Propositions 5 and 6:

PROPOSITION 11 (the "autarky of reciprocity"). *If two people who transfer to each other all prefer – and possibly freely choose – a system which they deem to be intrinsically inferior to a reciprocity leading to a symmetrical equilibrium or to a return-gift domination, while they appreciate the other's gift and the dominated return-gift function is nondecreasing, then they transfer larger amounts in the former system than in the reciprocity.*

The evaluation of reciprocities by the participants can be influenced by two opposing tendencies: the value of social relations and the possible presence of oppressive norms. Intrinsic preference for reciprocity and appreciation of the other's gift are related to a predominance of the former effect. The foregoing remark and result may suggest that this tends to be the prevailing case for steady reciprocities which can have an important role in ongoing economic life. Many things, however, can occur in historical situations: the choice of some people may induce that of others who lose in the change; people commonly foresee imperfectly their evaluation of another system which is often another world; it may be difficult to compare things as different as commodities and social relations; the nature of the goods and the type of division of labour may radically change; and so on.[106]

---

[106] In fact, in certain cases, switches from gifts and reciprocities to markets restrain transfers. However, in these cases, the previous transfers were often within the extended family (an extreme case is provided by a rather common behaviour in hunting societies where the hunter keeps no share of his take for himself – in Australia, with the Inuits, etc.). However, the main issue is probably the formation of preferences. A type of economic system provides a global experience, which is evaluated by people but also shapes their preferences, and a lack of evaluation of this influence can lead to inconsistent or suboptimal free choices. For example, denote as $U(s', s)$ the ordinal utility function of an individual evaluating system s (both *per se* and for its consequences) when she is in system s'. One can have $U(s', s) > U(s', s')$, thus inducing a change from system s' to system s, and $U(s, s') > U(s, s)$, thus leading one to regret this change and inducing the reverse one. However, the last inequality can also be reversed into $U(s, s) > U(s, s')$, making system s a stable choice, and yet one may have $U(s', s') > U(s, s)$ – that is, this choice may not be the one actually preferred by the individual if she were fully conscious of the effects of systems on her preferences (see Kolm 1984a).

Part V: Reciprocity in economics

14. Reciprocity in economics

Although reciprocity has been emphasized, modelled, and applied for over three decades in economic analysis, there nevertheless is, globally, a sharp contrast between the place it has had in economic studies and the place it should have in them. Sections 14.1 and 14.2 present a few remarks on these two topics, respectively.

14.1. A short overview and a corrected bias

A number of economic studies have analyzed and applied, for long, both the interactions of reciprocity proper and two phenomena related to them, interdependent mutual concern and notably mutual altruism, and sequential exchange. More recent contributions aimed at "introducing reciprocity in game theory" (the converse had been done) or modelling new experimental data (as had been done for more ancient ones). Let us briefly gather here these various trends, some of which are more extensively studied in other sections or in other chapters of this volume.

Section 1 has noted that the analysis of reciprocity in economics began in the early seventies, with an upsurge of developments in the early eighties. This paralleled anthropological and sociological analysis, and numerous experimental and empirical studies in social psychology. Among the latter, a group of studies considered fair labour reaction to pay, such as the famous studies and experiments by Adam (1963, 1965) and Adam and Rosenbaum (1964). Another group is constituted by the very abundant studies of the generalized reciprocity of "helping behaviour" in the sixties and early seventies. General models of reciprocity were presented (Kolm 1973 and in an analysis in book form in 1984a), the notable application to "efficiency wages" was proposed by Akerlof (1982),[107] and the particular but important application to contributions to public goods was developed by Sugden (1984) and applied by Swaney (1990).

The economic modelling of liking reciprocity in Section 13 has led to individuals' utility functions including, as variables, others' utility levels or favourable aspects of others' situations which can be their income or anything else. Now, economists have for very long closely considered individuals' general positive concerns for others, and this implies mutual concerns.[108] However, the theory of liking reciprocity and reciprocal

---

[107] The general influences of relations of reciprocity on wage formation, employment and productivity are presented in Kolm 1990.

[108] Simply considering satisfaction from things that are good for others is very ancient in economics; the mutuality then is only implicit. Adam Smith marvellously describes the pleasure derived from others' pleasure (*The Theory of Moral Sentiments*), but he stops short of considering that you can be pleased from the pleasure that other people derive from your pleasure (or pleased that they derive such a pleasure). Bentham argues that the pleasure you derive from others' pleasure should be added in the utilitarian sum. Individual utilities that depend on the "welfares" or "ophelimities" of all individuals are considered for two individuals and as a

liking does not start with given mutual liking but explains its formation. It belongs to the analyses of the formation of preferences, concerning this mutual altruism. Indeed, in relation (1) of Section 12.3.4, individual i's utility U^i as a function of individual j's utility (or happiness or satisfaction) U^j or of any aspect of her situation S_j depends on individual i's liking of individual j, ℓ_i (moreover, items ℓ_i, x_j and x_i also intervene).

However, the most numerous discussions concerned self-interested sequential exchange, which is not really a reciprocity if the focus is on motivations rather than on gestures and "behaviour". Hammond (1975) and Kurz (1978a, 1978b, 1979) enjoyed showing that "altruism is egoistic", but emphasized backward induction – which, as we have seen, can be solved by uncertainty about the end of the process or the behaviour of the other agent. Axelrod's (1981, 1984) "empirical proof" of the dominance of the tit-for-tat strategy, accompanied an abundant discussion of the "folk theorem" saying that repeated games (and sequential exchanges) can sustain any solution (in which both parties benefit). This prompted a number of analyses such as explanation by evolution by Güth and Yaari (1992) and Güth (1995a), the role of commitment by investment (Prasnikar and Roth, 1992) or by gifts (Carmichael and MacLeod, 1997), the issue of punishment (Bolton and Ockenfels, 2000 and the studies discussed and performed by E. Fehr and Gächter, 2000b), and the question of punishment as a public good in sequential contributions to public goods (Kolm, 1984a, Fehr and Gächter, 2000b, with different emphases on fairness and normative motives – see Section 9.3.3.4).

In application of this kind of process to actual economic issues, a few studies became aware of the possible relational aspect of reciprocities – usually from reading anthropologists – although they do not analyse this aspect. Of course, in reality both cases with and without specific relational value (or disvalue) exist – but the case where it does not exist is a particular case of the general framework. Kimball (1988), and Coate and Ravallion (1993) model mutual insurance where transfers are made to the participant who incurs a particular unforeseen misfortune. Kranton (1994) considers individuals' choices between using market or such a sequential exchange, the resulting sharing of the volume of transfers between both systems, and the dynamics of this situation. This choice and its consequences are essentially determined by information costs. As a consequence, a system is more favourable when it has a larger share of the transfers. There results a tendency to extreme sharings and to the prevalence of an inefficient system. In fact, a number of different phenomena lead to such consequences in the establishment of economic systems,[109] and this study constitutes a precise example of such effects of information facilities and costs.

---

weighted sum by Edgeworth (1881) and generally by Pareto (1913). The general interdependence of utilities that are function of others' utilities or incomes or consumption is analysed in Kolm (1966). The case of incomes is also studied by Hochman and Rodgers (1969) and a subsequent literature (see Kolm (1997a) and the Introduction to this volume (Chapter 1)). These interdependencies imply mutual concerns. Reciprocity of the liking type is one step deeper in constituting a cause of these mutual concerns.

[109] Cf. Kolm 1984a, Chapters 6 and 10.

Let us note here that a number of economists want to explain (and sometimes also to appraise) all social situations from the behaviour of individuals exclusively interested in the "material" outcome concerning solely themselves. This position suggests the following evaluation. If this view denied the existence, or the influence on conduct – indeed, the paramount influence in certain cases – of facts such as love, affection, duty, honour, hatred, revenge, gratitude, faithfulness, fairness and unfairness, status, superiority and inferiority, envy, jealousy, shame, guilt, pride, and so on, then it would only be absurd, as anyone can see in looking around (and, doubtlessly, within herself). On the other hand, this position can be valid if it solely consists of the research program of trying to investigate the scope of what the assumed simplistic motivation can explain, in particular when it is associated with more refined analyses of expectations or of strategic interactions. However, in studying a specific actual case, other motivations should not be discarded when they manifestly exist and are relevantly influential. The fact that actors commonly express reasons for their actions that are not the true ones does not imply that solely the narrowest end-state self-interest is at work in all cases. However, it is also clear that, in many cases, there can be much uncertainty concerning which motivations are the true ones and what is the actual scope of each (individuals are even commonly confused about their own motivations, notably about the relative importance of various motivations that determine a given act). Then, the scientific position requires one to have theories for all the possible cases and not for one only. A priori "parsimony" in hypotheses (or Occam's razor) is not intrinsically epistemologically justified and can rather be intellectual laziness and deficit of scientific imagination – it often also leads to hypotheses different from purely self-interested motives. Finally, the argument that only self-interest in the outcome can be studied by formal models – hence enables one to make use of this powerful tool – is simply erroneous; not only preferences about others' allocations (altruism, envy, etc.), but the whole process can be considered in this way (indeed, can even be studied with the hypothesis of so-called "rational" maximizing behaviour and evaluation, including deontic motives and "process preferences"); the economic theory of reciprocity proves at least this.

Apart from the game-theoretic analyses of reciprocities and gifts/return-gifts with "reciprocity games" and "return-gift games",[110] the bulk of the literature in game theory used to ignore reciprocity and reciprocation. Indeed, it used to shun social sentiments in general and their role in social interaction (with the very occasional exception of altruism). Its ethos was in fact bound to particularly discard deontological behaviour as "irrational". This was but one aspect of an outlook ingrained in a part of economics. This view, however, runs against many cases of clear evidence, and it is in opposition to the central views and concerns of many other perceptive analyses of conduct and society. But there now seems to be the beginning of a reversal – after early observations by Reinhart Selten – starting with works such as those of Matthew Rabin (1993), the Zurich school of Ernst Fehr and his collaborators (1994 and following ones), Claude

---

[110] Kolm 1973, 1979, 1984a, 1984b.

Meidinger, and a number of others.[111] In Rabin's model, two players play a simultaneous one-shot game (while situations of reciprocative conducts are more typically sequential); each has a single-valued belief about the other's action and about the other's belief concerning her own action; each action's "fairness" towards the other agent is the deviation from the average of the best and worst possible payoff it can inflict on the other; and each individual prefers to be fairer when the other is towards herself. Then, Cournot–Nash equilibria are with both agents maximally benefiting or hurting others – an extreme example of a general tendency.

These considerations are of course very welcome (the scandal is that they have not been present decades earlier). They doubtlessly make the literature in game theory more serious and realistic. Some of these studies use laboratory experiments. Because they wanted to criticize widespread practice in economics and game theory by behaviourist scholars who could solely be convinced by experiments, a number of these studies solely concluded from these experiments that certain behaviours exist, while this existence is obvious and common knowledge (and these behaviours had already and for long been the object of experiments and scientific observations in sociopsychology, and of theoretical analysis in psychology, sociology, and economics).[112] However, and more importantly, later developments of this approach go much further and contribute interestingly or importantly to the analysis of these phenomena.[113,114]

---

[111] See Chapters 7 and 8 of this volume.

[112] See the references and analyses in Kolm 1984a.

[113] A number of these theoretical and empirical studies, however, might possibly be perfected on a few grounds and doubtlessly will be. The issues concern both the information about behaviour and its motives or reasons, and, importantly, the modelling. (1) As already noted, conclusions from the experiments are sometimes solely that such and such behaviour exists, or often exists, while this is obvious to (practically) everybody from the common knowledge of life, from introspection, from innumerable expressions in the literature of all times, and from the various psychologies – including numerous laboratory experiments in sociopsychology for decades. This can concern, for instance, sense of fairness or of deservingness, gratitude, revenge or punishment, reciprocity, and so on. For example, the apparent urge to present obvious behaviour in the form of the so-called "ultimatum game" or "dictator game" is interesting, first of all, by what it reveals about the experimenter's assumption concerning the beliefs and epistemology of the people it wants to convince (information only begins with experiments that provide meaningful frequencies of various answers in various cases). (2) Moreover, the various types of motivations are often not sufficiently distinguished (or are confused). For instance, promise-keeping is not reciprocity; inequality-aversion, envy, jealousy, sentiment of inferiority or superiority, and preference for conformity or for distinction, are different sentiments with different structures, conditions, manifestations and consequences; motivations such as gratitude, norm-following, sense of balance or fairness, kindness, etc., are importantly and relevantly different from one another; they differ from egoistic sequential iterative exchange; and all these motivations can yield different results. Probably as an effect of an exclusively behaviouristic methodological ideal, even commonsense knowledge of motivation – from the experience of life or from introspection – is sometimes not used when it is relevant. And different motivations can lead to different models, theories, explanations, and consequences, and also to more discriminating experiments. (3) For theories, these studies generally consider arbitrarily specific models. (4) Moreover, these models use variables having problematic statuses or meanings (such as "amounts" of altruism, goodwill, fairness, or kindness which are mathematically added to other variables, or subtracted, or multiplied between them, etc.) – student in economics, who are so carefully taught about ordinalism and

14.2. Completing economics

A major part of the progress in understanding economic life rests in taking into account more of the relevant psychology of humans in society. This movement should be more ambitious than only pointing out minute and obvious deviations from purely self-interested behaviour and should rather see its aim as: back to Adam Smith and Vilfredo Pareto. At any rate, the integration of reciprocity and reciprocal conduct has a central role in this advance. Its consequences touch almost all fields of economics, in various degrees. Beyond elementary conducts, indeed, it touches many aspects of exchange and the market, and of the life of groups of various types, including, for instance, the economics of the firm and of the family, public economics for the issues of "market failures" and public finance, both the negative aspects of development and the conditions of its success, the causes of economic disequilibria and productivity and hence of macroeconomic problems, and normative economics including economic justice and fairness.

the like, would usually be failed if they proposed such magnitudes. These models might a priori constitute suggestive illustrative devices, but these lacks of meaning a priori stains the meaningfulness of conclusions and limits their scope. In contrast, simple general models, avoiding arbitrary or meaningless variables and properties, happen to illustrate as well, more simply, and more generally, with well-defined scopes of validity of the conclusions (which are properties and not only examples), and they permit the derivation of general properties and conclusions. (5) Some of these studies do not model reciprocity or do not consider the required variables, motives, and behaviour. Some, however, consider half reciprocities where one transactor reacts reciprocally to a conduct of the other who herself has no reciprocitarian motivations and exploits this motivation of the former – the unilateral reaction is the topic of Adam's, Rosenbaum's and others' experiments of decades ago, and a case of this exploitation is Akerlof's "efficiency wage" model. (6) Some of these theories focus on simultaneous one-shot games, whereas the most characteristic situations of reciprocity and reciprocation are sequential. (7) Certain outcomes, such as Cournot–Nash equilibria, are considered without the presentation of a reason why they would be reached. This is in line with the bulk of game theory, but reciprocity analysis precisely can present a justification for such solutions (see Section 13). Moreover, the classical suggestion that Cournot–Nash equilibria have the virtue that they constitute self-sustainable agreements not only does not explain why they would be the outcomes in general, but, in addition, a priori does not apply to reciprocities and reciprocations since they are not agreements. (8) The studies in question do not consider, at least explicitly, that the type of relation – which can for instance be a reciprocity of some type or an ordinary exchange – is bound to constitute an object or a parameter of people's preferences. This omission can be innocuous if the model remains with one type of relations that it does not explain. But it prevents the explanation of behaviour and of preferences that lead to it, the comparison of several types of relations and of their effects, the explanation of the existence of relations, and overall evaluations such as the (Pareto) efficiency of the interaction. (9) When they consider rationality, these studies use this term for meaning materially self-interested consequentialism. But even the standard economists' sense of rational as endowed with transitive evaluations or ordinal utility functions, or as performing maximizing behaviour, can describe deontological or backward-looking reciprocation, as it is shown by the theory of reciprocity. And we have seen in Section 1 that reciprocation itself (of the balance type) is explained by basic properties of social rationality in the general and most common sense of the term. (10) These studies would probably benefit from considering the previous literature on the topic (for example, the voluminous literature in anthropology, sociopsychology, sociology, philosophy, labour relation studies, the existing literature in economics noted above, and the specific extensive positive and normative analyses of reciprocity – see Kolm 1984a, which also includes exhaustive referencing up to this date).

The specific relevance and importance of reciprocity in various economic questions have been shown all along the foregoing pages. Let us gather here the main topics.

For considering reciprocity, the classical economic beginning with "microfoundations" is extended in taking, from the start, a group – at least a dyad – rather than an individual as the relevant elementary unit. There is no reciprocity for Robinson Crusoe (before Man Friday). Evidence, experiments, and the foregoing modelling can have a place here.

As far as exchange and the market are concerned, a basic point is that reciprocity can be an alternative to them (for specific interactions) or a relation permitting their existence, functioning, or efficiency: it can be a *market substitute*, and it also often importantly is *market supporting*.

Mutual transfers can be performed by exchange or by reciprocity (or by command). The role of information about possibilities and desires that a competitive price system can have is not guaranteed by reciprocities in themselves – as it has been analysed for giving in general.[115] However, reciprocitarian relations have an importance in themselves, and are often (not always) valued for reasons related to liking and fairness. This value may overcompensate any economic loss in the strict sense (see the analysis of Section 13.2). Nevertheless, reciprocities can possibly so constitute apparent "market failures". This is for instance the basis of George Akerlof's "efficiency wage" explanation of a kind of "disequilibrium" of the labour market which seems to induce "involuntary unemployment" (in fact, this is only one of the possible kinds of reciprocity solution – of the "domination" type –, which replaces a standard purely self-interested market exchange, and qualifying the situation as one of *involuntary* unemployment is problematic). A vast and very important domain of substitutions between reciprocities and the market is constituted by processes of "development" which largely consist of replacing reciprocities by markets (and command). The normative judgment of these processes cannot be summarized since there are many different cases and the effects are far reaching (not only whole lives are transformed, but civilizations are wiped out). The outcome is the conception and policy of a development that both respects cultures and rests on the rich potential of their solidarities and reciprocities.

---

[114] These important works are interestingly reviewed by Sobel (2005), following excellent reviews by Fehr and Schmidt (2003), Fehr and Gächter (2000a), and early ones by Güth (1995b) and Roth (1995). Levine (1998), after Rabin (1993) noted earlier, models a case of reciprocal liking (although with the modelling problems noted). Various other aspects of concern for fairness and inequity aversion are studied by Fehr and Schmidt (1999), Bolton and Ockenfeld (2000), Charness and Rabin (2002), Falk, Fehr and Fishbacher (2003), Cox (2004), Dufwenberg and Kirchsteiger (2004), Falk and Fishbacher (2005), and Berely-Meyer and Niederle (2005). As we have seen, an important domain of balance-reciprocity motivated by fairness is labour reacting to pay, and this classical topic of social psychology since 1960 and of the field of labour relations (and of Akerlof's (1982) efficiency-wage theory generalized in Kolm (1990)) is experimentally studied by Fehr, Kirchsteiger and Riedl (1993), Fehr, Kirchler, Weichbold and Gächter (1998), Fehr and Schmidt (2000), and Charness and Haruvy (2002).

[115] See Kolm (1984a) and Kranish (1998).

Yet, reciprocities are also market-supporting in essential ways. Reciprocal respect is necessary to property rights. Balanced reciprocal concessions and accepting a fair deal are often necessary for reaching an agreement. Reciprocal views also provide efficient solutions to situations that are initially of the type of the prisoner's dilemma. Incomplete agreements are often completed and maintained by reciprocities. Reciprocities also provide the main decentralized correctors of "market failures" such as permitting sequential exchange or voluntary contributions to non-excludable public goods and collective actions, or replacing difficulties in constraining and information by reciprocal promise-keeping and reciprocal trust. High correlations have been found between the overall productivity of a society and the extent of reciprocities in it, for given technological possibilities.

All these market-supporting effects of reciprocity also play important and sometimes essential roles within constituted organizations. If the theoretical model of the organization is hierarchical command, then these reciprocities correct "command failures" resulting from costs and impossibilities in information and coercion – as with limitations of the possibility of contracts of exchange. Hence, reciprocities in trust or in promise-keeping, or for free mutual services and contributions to collective concerns, play this role. Moreover, the frequent contacts in an organization extend the scope of reciprocal services of all types, both among colleagues and across hierarchical levels including with the management. The frequency of contacts has two effects on the reciprocitarian nature of the relations, which oppose one another in a sense. On the one hand, the recurrence tends to introduce a dimension of sequential exchange (which can be purely self-interested). On the other hand, the frequency and duration is favourable to the development of interpersonal positive sentiments, which is indeed a frequent case.

There are, moreover, specifically reciprocitarian groups, such as families and "genuine" cooperatives. After the *pater familias* economic theory of the family (Becker), and the "new economic theory of the family" that sees it as a self-interested exchange (Chiappori), reciprocity in its various forms is the foundation of the "new new economics of the family" (Arrondel and Masson).[116]

The decentralized correction of "market failures" also makes reciprocity a substitute to the public sector, since a major role of this sector is the correction of these "failures" in a centralized, authoritarian, and political mode. However, the social place and action of the public and political sector itself rests on a number of reciprocities. One can distinguish a basic and general public reciprocity which has various aspects from a number of specific actual or putative reciprocities leading to various specific policies. People receive for free a vast amount of public services, but they can be good citizens in general, law abiding people and taxpayers, and voters who choose governments and taxes. There are corresponding reciprocitarian sentiments in three forms: between society as a whole and individuals (each of whom can also take the "point of view of the society" to which she belongs), between the public administration and the people's general support of the

---

[116] See Chapter 14 in this volume and Kolm 1984a, 1997a.

political/public system, and between politicians on the one hand and voters and political activists on the other hand.

Yet, reciprocity among citizens also intervenes in the normative foundation of a number of policies. For instance, concepts of chain reciprocities induce the acceptance of pay-as-you-go pension schemes or of the symmetrical public financing of education. Concepts of putative reciprocities have also an important role in the basis of distributive policies and of aid. The notion is expressed as: "I will help her because she would have helped me if our situations were reversed" (without the consideration that this hypothetical situation could materialize in the future, which would be a case of sequential exchange, and notably for cases where this reversal is impossible). For instance, Europeans favour public health insurance rather than private one because the support beyond mere actuarial insurance it provides is a transfer to people with given poor health that people in general want to aid basically for a reason of putative reciprocity. Aid relative to other handicaps is justified in the same way. This is, for instance, a notable reason for the support of free public education. Putative reciprocity is also an important motive in aid to victims of disasters. More generally, a larger reliance on reciprocities of various types constitutes the traditional hope for limiting the role, in society, of both coercion and selfish exchange which takes the other person as only a means. This hope can be supported by the perceptive visions of scholars such as Hobhouse, Simmel and Mauss who saw the pervasiveness and central place of reciprocity in social relations. But its actualization requires the specific and precise economic and psychological analysis of reciprocity presently developed.

References

Adam, J.S. (1963). "Wage inequalities, productivity and work quality". Industrial Relat. 3, 9–16.
Adam, J.S. (1965). "Inequity in social exchange". In: Berkowitz (Ed.), In: Advances in Experimental Social Psychology, vol. 2. Academic Press, New York.
Adam, J.S., Rosenbaum, W.E. (1964). "The relationship of worker productivity to cognitive dissonance about wage inequalities". Journal of Abnormal and Social Psychology 69, 19–25.
Adolphs, R. (2000). "Social cognition and the human brain". Trends in Cognitive Science 3, 469–479.
Akerlof, G. (1982). "Labor contract as partial gift exchange". Quarterly Journal of Economics 97, 543–569.
Alesina, A., La Ferrara, E. (2002). "Who trusts others?". Journal of Public Economics 85 (2), 207–234.
Ames, R., Marwell, G. (1979). "Experiments on the provision of public goods: Resources, interest, group size, and the free-rider problem". American Journal of Sociology 84, 1335–1360.
Andreoni, J. (1988a). "Privately provided? Public goods in a large economy: The limits of altruism". Journal of Public Economics 35, 57–73.
Andreoni, J. (1988b). "Why free ride? Strategies and learning in public goods experiments". Journal of Public Economics 37, 291–304.
Andreoni, J. (1989). "Giving with impure altruism: Applications to charity and Ricardian equivalence". Journal of Political Economy 97, 1447–1458.
Andreoni, J. (1990). "Impure altruism and donations to public goods: a theory of warm-glow giving". Economic Journal 100, 464–477.
Axelrod, R. (1981). "Emergence of cooperation among egoists". American Political Science Review 75, 306–318.

Axelrod, R. (1984). The Evolution of Cooperation. Academic Press, New York.
Baron, J.N. (1988). "The employment relation as a social relation". Journal of the Japanese and International Economies 2, 492–525.
Basu, K. (1977). "Information and strategy in iterated prisoners' dilemma". Theory and Decision 8, 293–298.
Becker, H. (1956). Man in Reciprocity: Introductory Lectures on Culture, Society and Personality. Praeger, New York.
Bereby-Meyer, Y., Niederle, M. (2005). "Fairness in bargaining". Journal of Economic Behavior and Organization 56 (2), 173–186.
Berg, J., Dickhaut, J., McCabe (1995). "Trust, reciprocity and social history". Games and Economic Behavior 10, 122–142.
Berkowitz, L. (1971). "Social norms, feelings and other factors affecting helping behavior and altruism". Unpublished manuscript. University of Wisconsin.
Berkowitz, L. (1966). "A laboratory investigation of social class and national differences in helping behavior". International Journal of Psychology 1.
Berkowitz, L. (1968). "Responsibility, reciprocity, and social distance in help-giving: An experimental investigation of English social class differences". Journal of Experimental Psychology 4, 46–63.
Berkowitz, L., Friedman, P. (1967). "Some social class differences in helping behavior". Journal of Personality and Social Psychology 5, 217–225.
Bewley, T.F. (1995). "A depressed labour market as explained by participants". American Economic Review 85, 250–254.
Bewley, T.F. (1999). "Work motivation". Review of the Federal Reserve Bank of Saint-Louis 81 (3), 35–50.
Bishop, J. (1987). "The recognition and reward of employee performance". Journal of Labor Economics 5, S36–S56.
Bolton, G., Ockenfels, A. (2000). "ERC – A theory of equity, reciprocity and competition". American Economic Review 90, 166–193.
Bryan, J.H., Test, M.A. (1967). "Models and helping: Naturalistic studies in aiding behavior". Journal of Personality and Social Psychology 6, 400–407.
Carmichael, H.L., MacLeod, W.B. (1997). "Gift giving and the evolution of cooperation". International Economic Review 38 (3), 485–509.
Charness, G., Haruvy, E. (2002). "Altruism, equity, and reciprocity in a gift-exchange experiment: An encompassing approach". Games and Economic Behavior 40 (2), 203–231.
Charness, G., Rabin, M. (2002). "Understanding social preferences with simple tests". Quarterly Journal of Economics 117 (3), 817–869.
Coate, S., Ravallion, M. (1993). "Reciprocity without commitment". Journal of Economic Development 40, 1–24.
Cox, J.C. (2004). "How to identify trust and reciprocity". Games and Economic Behavior 46 (2), 260–281.
Croson, R.T.A. (1999). "Theories of altruism and reciprocity: Evidence from linear public good games". Discussion paper. Wharton School, University of Pennsylvania.
Danner, P.L. (1973). "Sympathy and exchangeable value: Keys to Adam Smith's social philosophy". Review of Social Economy 34 (3), 317–331.
Dawes, R., Thaler, R. (1988). "Cooperation". Journal of economic Perspectives 2, 187–197.
Dawes, R.M., van de Kragt, A., Orbell, J. (1988). "Not me or thee but we: The importance of group identity in eliciting cooperation in dilemma situations". Acta Psychologica 68, 83–97.
Doland, D., Adelberg, K. (1967). "The learning of sharing behavior". Child Development 38, 695–700.
Dufwenberg, M., Kirchsteiger, G. (2004). "A theory of sequential reciprocity". Games and Economic Behavior 47 (2), 268–298.
Edgeworth, F.Y. (1881). Mathematical Psychics: An Essay on the Application of Mathematics to the Moral Sciences. London School of Economics, London. Reeditions 1888, 1932, 1967, 1981.
Falk, A., Fehr, E., Fishbacher, U. (2000). "Informal sanctions". Working Paper n°59. Institute for Empirical Research in Economics, University of Zurich.
Falk, A., Fehr, E., Fischbacher, U. (2003). "On the nature of fair behavior". Economic Inquiry 41 (1), 20–26.

Falk, A., Fischbacher, U. (2005). "Modelling fairness and reciprocity". In: Gintis, H., Bowles, S., Boyd, R., Fehr, E. (Eds.), Moral Sentiments and Material Interests: The Foundations of Cooperation in Economic Life. MIT Press, Cambridge.

Fehr, E., Gächter, S. (2000a). "Fairness and retaliation: The economics of reciprocity". Journal of Economic Perspective 14 (3), 159–181.

Fehr, E., Gächter, S. (2000b). "Cooperation and punishment in public goods experiments". American Economic Review.

Fehr, E., Kirchler, E., Weichbold, A., Gächter, S. (1998). "When social norms overpower competition: Gift exchange in experimental labor markets". Journal of Labor Economics 16 (2), 324–351.

Fehr, E., Kirchsteiger, G., Riedl, A. (1993). "Does fairness prevent market clearing? An experimental investigation". Quarterly Journal of Economics 108 (2), 437–459.

Fehr, E., Schmidt, K.M. (1999). "A theory of fairness, competition and cooperation". Quarterly Journal of Economics 114 (3), 817–868.

Fehr, E., Schmidt, K.M. (2000). "Fairness, incentives, and contractual choices". European Economic Review 44 (4–6), 1057–1068.

Fehr, E., Schmidt, K.M. (2003). "Theories of fairness and reciprocity–evidence and economic applications". In: Dewatripont, M., Hansen, L.P., Turnovsky, S.J. (Eds.), Advances in Economics and Econometrics: 8th World Congress. Cambridge University Press, Cambridge.

Fischbacher, U., Gächter, S., Fehr, E. (1999). "Are people conditionally cooperative? Evidence from a public good experiment". Working Paper n°16. Institute for Empirical Research in Economics, University of Zurich.

Frisch, D.M., Greenberg, M.S. (1968). "Reciprocity and intentionality in the giving of help". Proceedings of the 76th Annual Convention of the American Psychological Association 3, 383–384.

Gergen, K., Gergen, M., Meter, K. (1972). "Individual orientations to prosocial behavior". Journal of Social Issues 28 (3).

Glaeser, E.L., Laibson, D., Scheinkman, J.A., Sautter, C.I. (2000). "Measuring trust". The Quarterly Journal of Economics CXV, 811–846.

Goodstadt, M.S. (1971). "Helping and refusal to help: A test of balance and reactance theories". Journal of Experimental Social Psychology 7, 610–622.

Goranson, R.E., Berkowitz, L. (1966). "Reciprocity and responsibility reactions to prior help". Journal of Personality and Social Psychology 3, 227–232.

Gouldner, A. (1960). "The norm of reciprocity: A preliminary statement". American Sociological Review 25, 161–178.

Greenglass, E.R. (1969). "Effects of prior help and hindrance on willingness to help another: Reciprocity or social responsibility". Journal of Personality ans Social Psychology 11, 224–232.

Güth, W. (1995a). "An evolutionary approach to explaining cooperative behavior by reciprocal incentives". International Journal of Game Theory 24 (4), 323–344.

Güth, W. (1995b). "On ultimatum bargaining experiments – A personal review". Journal of Economic Behavior and Organization 27 (3), 329–344.

Güth, W., Schmittberger, R., Schwarze, B. (1982). "An experimental analysis of ultimatum bargaining". Journal of Economic Behavior and Organization 3, 367–388.

Güth, W., Yaari, M.E. (1992). "An evolutionary approach to explaining cooperative behavior by reciprocal behavior in a simple strategic game". In: Witt, U. (Ed.), Explaining Process and Change: Approaches to Evolutionary Economics. University of Michigan Press, Ann Arbor, pp. 23–24.

Hammond, P. (1975). "Charity: altruism or egoism?". In: Phelps, E. (Ed.), Altruism, Morality, and Economic Theory. Russel Sage Fundation, New York.

Handlon, B.J., Gross, P. (1959). "The development of sharing behavior". Journal of Abnormal and Social Psychology 59, 425–428.

Hardin, G. (1968). "The tragedy of the commons". Science 162, 1243–1248.

Harris, L.A. (1967). "A study of altruism". Elementary School Journal 68, 135–141.

Harris, M. (1970). "Reciprocity and generosity: some determinants of sharing behavior". Child Development 41, 313–328.

Helliwell, J.F., Putnam, R.D. (1999). "Education and social capital". Working Paper 7121. NBER, Cambridge, MA.
Hobhouse, L.T. (1906). Morals in Evolution: A Study in Comparative Ethics. Chapman and Hall, London.
Hochman, H.M., Rodgers, J.D. (1969). "Pareto optimal redistribution". American Economic Review 59, 542–557.
Hoffman, E., Spitzer, M.L. (1982). "The Coase theorem: Some experimental tests". Journal of Law and Economics XXV, 73–98.
Holländer, H. (1990). "A social exchange approach to voluntary cooperation". American Economic Review 80 (5), 1157–1167.
Hornstein, H., Fisch, E., Holmes, M. (1968). "Influence of a model's feelings about his behavior and his relevance as a comparison on the observers' helping behavior". Journal of Personality and Social Psychology 10, 222–226.
Hornstein, H.A. (1970). "Experiments in the social psychology of prosocial behavior". Final Report. NSF Grant 1715.
Isaac, M.R., McCue, K.F., Plott, C. (1985). "Public goods provision in an experimental environment". Journal of Public Economics 26, 51–74.
Isaac, M.R., Walker, J.M. (1988a). "Communication and free-riding behavior: The voluntary contribution mechanism". Economic Inquiry 26, 585–608.
Isaac, M.R., Walker, J.M. (1988b). "Group size effects in public goods provision: The voluntary contribution mechanism". Quarterly Journal of Economics 103, 179–199.
Isaac, M.R., Walker, J., Thomas, S.H. (1984). "Divergent evidence on free riding: An experimental examination of possible explanations". Public Choice 43 (2), 113–149.
Kahneman, D., Knetsch, J.L., Thaler, R.H. (1986a). "Fairness as a constraint on profit seeking: Entitlements in the market". American Economic Review 76, 728–741.
Kahneman, D., Knetsch, J.L., Thaler, R.H. (1986b). "Fairness and the assumptions of economics". Jurnal of Business 59, S285–S300.
Kim, O., Walker, M. (1984). "The free rider problem: Experimental evidence". Public Choice 43 (1), 3–24.
Kimball, M. (1988). "Farmer's cooperatives as behavior toward risk". American Economic Review 78 (1), 224–232.
Knack, S., Keefer, P. (1997). "Does social capital have an economic payoff? A cross-country investigation". The Quarterly Journal of Economics CXII, 1251–1288.
Kolm, S.-Ch. (1966). "The optimal production of social justice". In: Guitton, H., Margolis, J. (Eds.). International Economic Association Conference on Public Economics, Biarritz, Proceedings Reprinted in (1968). L'Economie Publique. CNRS, Paris, pp. 109–177, and (1969), Public Economics. Macmillan, London, pp. 145–200.
Kolm, S.-Ch. (1971). Justice et Equité. CEPREMAP, Paris; (1972) CNRS, Paris;
  English translation: Kolm, S.-Ch., Justice and Equity. MIT, Cambridge, MA, 1998.
Kolm, S.-Ch. (1973). La théorie de la réciprocité. CEPREMAP, Paris.
Kolm, S.-Ch. (1976). "Unequal inequalities". Journal of Economic Theory I, 12, 416–442. II, 13, 82–111.
Kolm, S.-Ch. (1977). "Multidimensional egalitarianism". The Quarterly Journal of Economics 91, 1–13.
Kolm, S.-Ch. (1979). Fondements de la théorie du don, de la réciprocité, et du choix des systèmes économiques. CEPREMAP, Paris.
Kolm, S.-Ch. (1982). Le Bonheur-Liberté (Bouddhisme Profond et Modernité). Presses Universitaires de France, Paris. (2nd edition 1994).
Kolm, S.-Ch. (1984a). La Bonne Economie : La Réciprocité Générale ("General Reciprocity, The Good Economy"). Presses Universitaires de France, Paris.
Kolm, S.-Ch. (1984b). "Théorie de la réciprocité et du choix des systèmes économiques". Revue Economique 35, 871–910.
Kolm, S.-Ch. (1985). Le Contrat Social Liberal (The Liberal Social Contract). Presses Universitaires de France, Paris.
Kolm, S.-Ch. (1990). "Employment and fiscal policies with a realistic view of the social role of wages". In: Champsaur, P., et al. (Eds.), Essays in Honour of E. Malinvaud. MIT Press, Cambridge, MA, pp. 226–286.

Kolm, S.-Ch. (1994). "The theory of reciprocity and of the choice of economic systems". Investigaciones Económicas 18 (1), 67–95.
Kolm, S.-Ch. (1995). "The theory of social sentiments: the case of envy". The Japanese Economic Review 1 (46), 63–87.
Kolm, S.-Ch. (1996a). Modern Theories of Justice. MIT Press, Cambridge, MA.
Kolm, S.-Ch. (1996b). "The theory of justice". Social Choice and Welfare 13, 151–182.
Kolm, S.-Ch. (1997a). Introduction to the Economics of Reciprocity, Giving and Altruism. IEA, Marseille;
    Kolm, S.-Ch. In: Gérard-Varet, L.-A., Kolm, S.-Ch., Mercier-Ythier, J. (Eds.), The Economics of Reciprocity, Giving and Altruism. MacMillan, London, 2000, pp. 1–44.
Kolm, S.-Ch. (1997b). The Theory of Reciprocity. IEA, Marseille;
    Kolm, S.-Ch.. In: Gérard-Varet, L.-A., Kolm, S.-Ch., Mercier-Ythier, J. (Eds.), The Economics of Reciprocity, Giving and Altruism. MacMillan, London, 2000, pp. 1115–1141.
Kolm, S.-Ch. (1998). "Une introduction à la théorie de la réciprocité et du choix des systèmes économiques". In: Mahieu, F.-R., Rapoport, H. (Eds.), Altruisme, Analyses Economiques. Economica, Paris, pp. 17–50.
Kolm, S.-Ch. (1999). "Rational foundations of income inequality measurement". In: Silber, J. (Ed.), Handbook on Income Inequality Measurement. Kluwer Academic Publishers, Boston, pp. 19–94.
Kolm, S.-Ch. (2004). Macrojustice, the Political Economy of Fairness. Cambridge University Press, New York.
Kolm, S.-Ch. (2006). "The perplexing joint giving theorem". IDEP, Marseilles.
Kragt, A.J.C., Orbell, J.M., Dawes, R.M. (1983). "The minimal contributing set as a solution to public goods problems". American Political Science Review 77, 112–122.
Kranish, L. (1998). "Altruism and efficiency: a welfare analysis of the Walrasian mechanism with transfers". Journal of Public Economics 36, 369–386.
Kranton, R. (1994). "Reciprocal exchange: a self-sustaining system". American Economic Review 86 (4), 830–851.
Kreps, D., Milgrom, P., Roberts, J., Wilson, R. (1982). "Rational cooperation in the finitely repeated prisoners' dilemma". Journal of Economic Theory 27 (2), 245–252.
Kurz, M. (1978a). "Altruism as an outcome of social interaction". American Economic Review 68, 216–222.
Kurz, M. (1978b). "Altruism as an outcome of social interaction". Journal of Public Economics 36, 369–386.
Kurz, M. (1979). "Altruistic equilibrium". In: Balassa, B., Nelson, R. (Eds.), Economic Progress, Private Values and Policy. North-Holland, pp. 177–200.
Latane, B., Darley, J. (1970). The Unresponsibe Bystander: Why Doesn't He Help?. Appleton-Century-Croft, New York.
Ledyard, J. (1995). "Public goods: A survey of experimental research". In: Roth, A., Kagel, J. (Eds.), Handbook of Experimental Economics. Princeton University Press, Princeton, pp. 111–194.
Leventhal, G.S., Weiss, T., Long, G. (1969). "Equity, reciprocity and reallocating rewards in the dyad". Journal of Personality and Social Psychology 13, 300–305.
Levine, D. (1991). "You get what you pay for: tests of efficiency wage theories in the United States and Japan". Institute of Industrial Relations. Working Paper Series 1054, UC Berkeley.
Levine, D. (1993). "Fairness, markets, and ability to pay: Evidence from compensation executives". American Economic Review 83 (5), 1241–1259.
Levine, D.K. (1998). "Modeling altruism and spitefulness in experiments". Review of Economic Dynamics 1 (3), 593–622.
Macaulay, J., Berkowitz, L. (Eds.) (1970). Altruism and Helping Behavior. Academic Press, New York.
Mauss, M. (1924). "Essai sur le don, forme archaïque de l'échange". Année Sociologique n.s. 1, 30–186; English translation in: The Gift: Forms and Function of Exchange in Archaic Societies. Norton, New York, 1967.
Midlarsky, E. (1968). "Aiding responses: An analysis and review". Merrill-Palmer Quarterly 14, 229–260.
Morelly (1755, 1953). Code de la Nature. Editions sociales, Paris.
Offer, A. (1997). "Between the gift and the market: the economy of regard". Economic History Review L (3), 450–476.

Orbell, J.M., Dawes, R.M., van de Kragt, A.J.C. (1978). "Explaining discussion induced cooperation". Journal of Personality and Social Psychology 54, 811–819.
Pareto, V. (1913). "Il massimo di utilità per una colletività". Giornale degli Economisti 3, 337–341. Reprinted as a long footnote in the Treatise of General Sociology (and in Mind and Society).
Piaget, J. (1932). La Naissance du Sentiment Moral chez l'Enfant. Payot, Genève.
Polanyi, K. (1944). The Great Transformation: The Political Origin of our Time. Beacon Press, Boston.
Prasnikar, V., Roth, A.E. (1992). "Considerations of fairness and strategy: Experimental data from sequential games". Quarterly Journal of Economics 107 (3), 865–888.
Proudhon, J. (1853). Manuel du spéculateur à la Bourse.
Pruitt, D.G. (1968). "Reciprocity and credit building in a laboratory dyad". Journal of Personality and social Psychology 8, 143–147.
Putnam, R. (1993). Making Democracy work: Civic Traditions in Modern Italy. Princeton University Press, Princeton.
Rabin, M. (1993). "Incorporating fairness into game theory and economics". American Economic Review 83, 1281–1302.
Radner, R. (1980). "Collusion behaviour in non-cooperative epsilon-equilibria of oligopolies with long but finite lives". Journal of Economic Theory 22, 136–154.
Rosenhan, D.L. (1969). "Some origins of concern for others". In: Mussen, P., Covington, M., Langer, J. (Eds.), Trends and Issues in Developmental Psychology. Holt, Rinehart & Winston, New York.
Rosenhan, D.L. (1970). "The natural socialization of altruistic autonomy". In: Macaulay, J., Berkowitz, L. (Eds.), Altruism and Helping Behavior. Academic Press, New York.
Rotemberg, J. (1994). "Human relations in the workplace". Journal of Political Economy 102 (4), 684–717.
Roth, A.E. (1995). "Bargaining Experiments". In: Kagel, J.H., Roth, A.E. (Eds.), Handbook of Experimental Economics. Princeton University Press, Princeton, pp. 253–348.
Schneider, F., Pommerehne, W. (1981). "On the rationality of free-riding: An experiment". Quarterly Journal of Economics 96, 689–704.
Silber, J. (Ed.) (1999). Handbook on Income Inequality Measurement. Kluwer Academic Publishers, Boston.
Simon, H. (1991). "Organization and markets". Journal of Economic Perspectives 5, 27–44.
Smale, S. (1980). "The prisoner's dilemma and dynamic systems associated to non-cooperative games". Econometrica 48, 1617–1634.
Smith, A. (1759). The Theory of Social Sentiments. Kelly, New York.
Sobel, J. (2005). "Interdependent preferences and reciprocity". Journal of Economic Literature XLIII, 392–436.
Sugden, R. (1984). "Reciprocity: The supply of public goods through voluntary contribution". Economic Journal 94, 772–787.
Swaney, J. (1990). "Common property, reciprocity, and community". Journal of Economic Issues 24.
Thurnwald, R. (1921, 1932). Die Gemeinde der Banaro.
Wicksteed, P.H. (1888). The Alphabet of Economic Science. R.H. Hutton, London.
Wicksteed, P.H. (1933). The Common Sense of Political Economy. Robbins, London.
Wilke, H., Lanzetta, J. (1970). "The obligation to help: The effects of prior help on subsequent helping behavior". Journal of experimental Social Psychology 6, 466–493.
Wright, B. (1942). "Altruism in children and the perceived conduct of others". Journal of Abnormal and Social Psychology 37, 218–233.
Zak, J.P., Knack, S. (2001). "Trust and growth". The Economic Journal 111 (April), 295–321.

Further reading

Alesina, A., La Ferrara, E. (2000a). "Participation in heterogenous communities". The Quarterly Journal of Economics CXV, 847–904.
Alesina, A., La Ferrara, E. (2000b). "Who trusts others?". CEPR Discussion Paper n°2646.

Altman, I. (1973). "Reciprocity of interpersonal exchange". Journal of Theory of Social Behaviour 3, 249–261.
Andreoni, J. (1995). "Warm-glow versus cold-prickle: The effects of positive and negative framing on cooperation in experiments". Quarterly Journal of Economics 110 (1), 1–21.
Archibald, G.C., Donaldson, D. (1976). "Non-paternalism and the basic theorems of welfare economics". Canadian Journal of Economics 9, 492–507.
Aronfreed, J. (1970). "The socialization of altruistic and sympathetic behavior: Some theoretical and experimental analyses". In: Macaulay, J., Berkowitz, L. (Eds.), Altruism and Helping Behavior. Academic Press, New York.
Aronfreed, J., Paskal, V. (1965). "Altruism, empathy, and the conditioning of positive affect". Unpublished manuscript. University of Pennsylvania.
Arrow, K.J. (1972). "Gift and exchanges". Philosophy and Public Affairs 1.
Arrow, K. (1979). "Optimal and voluntary income distribution". Technical Report n°288. The Economic Series, Institute for Mathematical Studies in the Social Sciences, Stanford University, July.
Banks, S. (1979). "Gift-giving: A review and an interactive paradigm". In: Wilkie, W. (Ed.), Advances in Consumer Research, vol. 6. MI Association for Consumer Research, Ann Arbor, pp. 319–324.
Basu, K. (1987). "Modelling finitely repeated games with uncertain termination". Economic Letters 23, 147–151.
Becker, H. (1956). "Empathy, sympathy and Scheler". International Journal of Sociometry 1.
Becker, G.S. (1961). "Notes on an economic analysis of philanthropy". National Bureau of Economic Research.
Becker, G.S. (1974). "A theory of social interaction". Journal of Political Economy 82 (6), 1063–1093.
Becker, G.S. (1976a). "Altruism, egoism and genetic fitness: Economics and sociobiology". Journal of Economic Literature 14, 817–826.
Becker, G.S. (1976b). The Economic Approach to Human Behavior. University of Chicago Press, Chicago, London.
Becker, G.S. (1981). "Altruism in the family and selfishness in the market place". Econometrica 48 (189), 1–15.
Ben-Porath, Y. (1980). "The F-connection: families, friends, and firms and the organization of exchange". Population and Development Review 6, 1–30.
Benabou, R., Tirole, J. (2003). "Intrinsic and extrinsic motivation". Review of Economic Studies 70 (3), 489–520.
Bentham, J. (1789). Principles of Morals and Legislation. Clarendon, Oxford.
Bentham, J. (1952–1954). "The Philosophy of Economic Science". In: Stark, W. (Ed.), Jeremy Bentham's Economic Writings, vols. 1–3. Franklin, New York.
Bergstrom, T.C. (1970). "A "Scandinavian consensus" solution for efficient income distribution among non-malevolent consumers". Journal of Economic Theory 2, 383–398.
Berkowitz, L. (1970). "The self, selfishness and altruism". In: Macaulay, J., Berkowitz, L. (Eds.), Altruism and Helping Behavior. Academic Press, New York.
Berkowitz, L., Daniels, L. (1963). "Responsibility and dependency". Journal of Abnormal and Social Psychology 66, 429–437.
Bernheim, B.D., Shleifer, A., Summers, L.H. (1985). "The strategic bequest motive". Journal of Political Economy 93, 1045–1076.
Bianchi, M. (1993). "How to learn sociality: True and false solutions to Mandeville problem". History of Political Economy 25 (2).
Binmore, K., McCarthy, J., Ponti, G., Samuelson, L., Shaked, A. (2002). "A backward induction experiment". Journal of Economic Theory 104 (1), 48–88.
Boehm, C. (1993). "Egalitarian behavior and reverse dominance hierarchy". Current Anthropology 34 (3), 227–240.
Bolton, G., Brandts, J., Ockenfels, A. (1998). "Measuring motivations for the reciprocal responses observed in a simple dilemma games". Experimental Economics 1 (3), 207–219.

Bolton, G., Ockenfels, A. "Strategy and Equity: an ERC-analysis of the Güth-van Damme game". Journal of Mathematical Psychology 42 (2), 215–226.
Boudon, R. (1979). La logique du social. Hachette, Paris.
Boulding, K. (1973). The Economy of Love and Fear. Wadsworth, Belmont, CA.
Bowles, S. (1998a). "Endogenous preferences: The cultural consequences of markets and other economic institutions". Journal of Economic Literature 36 (1), 75–111.
Bowles, S. (1998b). "Endogenous preferences: The cultural consequences of markets and other economic institutions". Journal of Economic Literature 36 (1), 75–111.
Buchan, N., Croson, R., Dawes, R. (2002). "Swift neighbors and persistent strangers: A cross-cultural investigation of trust and reciprocity in social exchange". Paper presented at the Microeconomic Seminar at Universitat Pompeu Fabra, Barcelona, 17 December.
Camerer, C. (1988). "Gifts as economic signals and social symbols". American Journal of Sociology 94, 5180–5214.
Campbell, D.T. (1965). "Ethnocentric and other altruistic motives". In: Levine, D. (Ed.), Nebraska Symposium on Motivation. University of Nebraska Press, Lincoln.
Cialdini, R.C., Trost, M.R. (1998). "Social influence: Social norms, conformity, and compliance". In: Gilbert, D.T., Fiske, S.T., Lindzey, G. (Eds.), The Handbook of Social Psychology. McGraw-Hill, Boston, pp. 151–185.
Collard, D. (1978). Altruism and the Economy. A Study in Non-Selfish Economics. Martin Robertson, Oxford.
Coricelli, G., McCabe, K., Smith, V. (2000). "Theory of mind mechanism in personal exchange". In: Hotano, G., Okada, N., Tanabe, H. (Eds.), Affective Minds. Elsevier, Amsterdam.
Daly, G., Giertz, F. (1972). "Welfare economics and welfare reform". American Economic Review 62, 131–138.
Darwin, C. (1981). La descendance de l'homme, et la sélection sexuelle. Transl. E. Barbier. Complexe, Brussels.
Dasgupta, P. (2000). "Economic progress and the idea of social capital". In: Dasgupta, P., Serageldin, I. (Eds.), Social Capital: A Multifaceted Perspective. World Bank, Washington, DC, pp. 325–424.
Davis, J. (1975). "The particular theory of exchange". Archives Européennes de Sociologie XVI (2).
de Mandeville, B. (1705). The Grumbling Bees. And (1714), The Fable of the Bees.
Descartes, R. (1897–1910, 1965). Œuvres complètes, Adam, C., Tannery, P. (Eds.). Vrin, Paris.
Durkheim, E. (1958). Professional Ethics and Civic Morals. Translated by Brookfield, C. Glencoe. Free Press, Ill.
Eglar, Z.E. (1958). Vartan Bhanji: Institutionalized reciprocity in a changing Punjab village. Ph.D. thesis, Columbia University.
Ekstein, R. (1972). "Psychoanalysis and education for the facilitation of positive human qualities". Journal of Social Issues 28 (3).
Elster, J. (1989). The Cement of Society – A Study of Social Order. Cambridge University Press, Cambridge.
Elster, J. (1998). "Emotions and economic theory". Journal of Economic Literature 36, 47–74.
Falk, A., Fischbacher, U. (1999). "A theory of reciprocity". Working Paper n°6. Institute for Empirical Research in Economics, University of Zurich.
Falk, A., Fischbacher, U. (2001). "A theory of reciprocity". CEPR n°3014, October.
Fehr, E., Gächter, S. (1997). "How effective are trust- and reciprocity-based incentives?". In: Economics, Values and Organizations. Cambridge University Press, Cambridge.
Fehr, E., Gächter, S. (2002). "Do incentive contracts crowd out voluntary cooperation?". University of Zurich Working Paper 34.
Fehr, E., Gächter, S., Kirchsteiger, G. (1996). "Reciprocal fairness and noncompensating wage differentials". Journal of Institutional and Theoretical Economics 152 (4), 608–640.
Fehr, E., Gächter, S., Kirchsteiger, G. (1997). "Reciprocity as a contract enforcement device: experimental evidence". Econometrica 65 (4), 833–860.
Fellner, C.H., Marshall, J.-R. (1970). "Kidney donors". In: Macaulay, J., Berkowitz, L. (Eds.), Altruism and Helping Behavior. Academic Press, New York.

Firth, R. (Ed.) (1957). Man and Culture: An Evaluation of the Work of Bronislaw Malinovski. The Humanities Press, New York.
Frank, R.H. (1988). Passions within Reason. Norton, New York.
Frank, R.H. (1988). Passions Within Reason: The Strategic Role of the Emotions. Norton, New York.
Frank, R.H. (1990). "A theory of moral sentiments". In: Mansbridge, J. (Ed.), Beyond Self-Interest. University of Chicago Press, Chicago, pp. 71–96.
Freuchen, P. (1961). Book of the Eskimos. World Publishing Co., Cleveland and New York.
Frey, B. (1997). Not Just for the Money – An Economic Theory of Personal Motivation. Edward Elgar, Cheltenham.
Friedrichs, R.W. (1960). "Alter versus ego: An exploratory assessment of altruism". American Sociological Review 25, 496–508.
Gächter, S., Falk, A. (2002). "Reputation or reciprocity? An experimental investigation". Scandinavian Journal of Econometrics 24.
Geanakoplos, J., Pearce, D., Stacchetti, E. (1989). "Psychological games and sequential rationality". Games and Economic Behavior 1, 60–79.
Gergen, K.J., Greenberg, M.S., Willis, R.N. (Eds.) (1980). Social Exchange. Plenum Press, New York and London.
Gide, C. (1905). "Economie sociale". Librairie de la Société du Recueil général des lois et des arrêts, Paris.
Gintis, H. (2000). "Strong reciprocity and human sociality". Journal of Theoretical Biology 206, 169–179.
Goeree, J.K., Holt, C.A. (2000). "Asymmetric inequality aversion and noisy behavior in alternating-offer bargaining games". European Economic Review 44 (4–6), 1079–1089.
Goldfarb, R.S. (1970). "Pareto optimal redistribution: comment". American Economic Review 60, 994–996.
Greenberg, J. (1978). "Effects of reward value and retaliative power on allocation decisions: Justice, generosity or greed?". Journal of Personality and Social Psychology 36, 367–379.
Greenberg, M.S. (1980). "A theory of indebtedness". In: Gergen, Greenberg, Willis (Eds.), Social Exchange. Plenum Press, New York and London.
Greenberg, M.S., Frisch, D. (1972). "Effect of intentionality on willingness to reciprocate a favor". Journal of Experimental Social Psychology 8, 99–111.
Gregory, C.A. (1982). Gifts and commodities.
Gregory, C.A. (1987). "Gifts". In: Milgate, M. et al. (Eds.). The New Palgrave Dictionary of Economics. pp. 524–528.
Gui, B. (2000). "Beyond transactions: On the interpersonal dimension of economic reality". Annals of Public and Cooperative Economics 71 (2), 139–168.
Gui, B., Sugden, R. (Eds.) (2005). Economic and Social Interaction: Accounting for Interpersonal Relations. Cambridge University Press, Cambridge.
Güth, W., Schmitterberger, R., Schwarze, B. (1982). "An experimental analysis of ultimatum bargaining". Journal of Economic Behavior and Organization 3, 367–388.
Güth, W., Yaari, M. (1992a). "An evolutionary approach to explain reciprocal behavior in a simple strategic game". In: Witt, U. (Ed.), Explaining Process and Change, Approaches to Evolutionary Economics. University of Michigan Press, Ann Arbor.
Guttman, J.M. (2000). "On the evolutionary stability of preferences for reciprocity". European Journal of Political Economy 16 (1), 31–50.
Guyer, P. (1993). Kant and the Experience of Freedom. Cambridge University Press, Cambridge.
Hamilton, W.D. (1971). "Selection of selfish and altruistic behavior in some extreme models". In: Eisenberg, J.F., Dillon, W.S. (Eds.), Man and Beast: Comparative Social Behavior. Smithsonian Institution Press, Washington, DC.
Hartmann, H. (1960). Psychoanalysis and Moral Values. International Universities Press, New York.
Heider, F. (1958). The Psychology of Interpersonal Relations. Wiley, New York.
Henrich, J., Boyd, R., Bowles, S., Gintis, H., Fehr, E., McElreath, R., Camerer, C. (2001). "In search of homo œconomicus: Behavioral experiments in 15 small-scale societies". American Economic Review 91 (2), 73–78.

Herold, F. (2003). "Carrot or stick? Group selection and the evolution of reciprocal preferences". University of Munich Discussion Paper.
Hoffman, M. (1970). "Moral development". In: Mussen, P. (Ed.), Carmichael's Manual of Child Development. Wiley, New York.
Holesovsky, V. (1977). Economic System Analysis and Comparison. MacGraw-Hill, Kogakusha, Tokyo.
Holmstrom, B., Milgrom, P. (1991). "Multitask principal-agent analyses: incentive contracts, asset ownership, and job design". Journal of Law, Economics and Organization 7. Special issue: 24–52.
Homans, G. (1958). "Social behavior as exchange". American Journal of Sociology 68, 597–606.
Isaac, M.R., Walker, J.M., Williams, A.M. (1994). "Group size and the voluntary provision of public goods: experimental evidence utilizing large groups". Journal of Public Economics LIV, 1–36.
Isen, A.M., Levin, P.F. (1972). "Effect of feeling good on helping: Cookies and kindness". Journal of Personality and Scocial Psychology 21, 384–388.
Kahneman, D., Knetsch, J.L. (1992). "Valuing public goods: The purchase of moral satisfaction". Journal of Environmental Economics and Management 22 (1), 57–70.
Kant, I. (1790, 1952). "Critique of Judgement". In: Meredith, J.C. (Ed.). Clarendon Press, Oxford.
Kant, I. (1797, 1991). The Metaphysic of Morals, translated by Gregor, M.J. Cambridge University Press, Cambridge.
Keser, C., van Winden, F. (2000). "Conditional cooperation and voluntary contributions to public goods". Scandinavian Journal of Economics 102 (1), 23–39.
Kolm, S.-Ch. (1959). Les hommes du Fouta-Toro. MAS, Saint-Louis.
Kolm, S.-Ch. (1975, 1979). La réciprocité générale. CEPREMAP, Paris.
Kolm, S.-Ch. (1980). "Psychanalyse et théorie des choix". Information sur les Sciences Sociales 19 (2), 269–339.
Kolm, S.-Ch. (1981a). "Altruisme et efficacité : le sophisme de Rousseau". Social Science Information 20, 293–344.
Kolm, S.-Ch. (1981b). "Efficacité et altruisme : le sophisme de Mandeville, Smith et Pareto". Revue Economique 32, 5–31.
Kolm, S.-Ch. (1983). "Introduction à la réciprocité générale". Social Science Information 22 (4–5).
Kolm, S.-Ch. (1983). "Altruism and efficiency". Ethics 94, 18–65. Reprinted in Zamagni, S. (Ed.), The Economics of Altruism, op. cit.
Kolm, S.-Ch. (1986). "Is only egoism productive?". Development 3.
Kolm, S.-Ch. (1987). "Public economics". In: Eatwell, J., et al. (Eds.), New Palgrave Dictionary in Economics. Macmillan, London, pp. 1047–1055.
Kolm, S.-Ch. (1989). "Le devoir général de réciprocité". Les Devoirs de l'Homme, supplément, Revue d'Ethique et Théologie Morale 168, 135–146.
Kolm, S.-Ch. (1992). "Reciprocity". Political Economy of the Good society Newsletter 2 (Summer), 1–6.
Kolm, S.-Ch. (2000). "The logic of good social relations". Annals of Public and Cooperative Economics 72 (2), 171–189.
Kolm, S.-Ch. (2005). "The logic of good social relations". In: Gui, B., Sugden, R. (Eds.), Economics and Social Interaction: Accounting for Interpersonal Relations. Macmillan, London. Chapter 8.
Kolpin, V. (1992). "Equilibrium refinements in psychological games". Games and Economic Behavior 4, 218–231.
Kranton, R.E. (1996). "Reciprocal exchange: A self-sustaining system". American Economic Review 86 (4), 830–851.
Kreps, D.M. (1997). "Intrinsic motivation and extrinsic incentives". American Economic Review 87 (2), 359–364.
Kropotkin, P. (1896–1897). "Co-operation: A reply to Herbert Spencer". Freedom, Dec. 1896–Jan. 1897.
Kropotkin, P. (1892). La conquête du pain. Tresse & Stock, Paris.
Kropotkin, P. (1913). La science moderne et l'anarchie. Paris.
Kropotkin, P. (1902, 1972). Mutual Aid: A Factor of Evolution. Reedition. Penguin Books, London.
Kropotkin, P. (1927). L'éthique. Stock, Paris.

Kropotkin, P. (1970). "Must we occupy ourselves with an examination of the Ideal of a future system?". Letter to Nettlau. In: Miller, M.A. (Ed.). Selected Writings on Anarchism and Revolution. Cambridge, MA.
Landa, J.T. (1994). "Trust, etnicity and identity: Beyond the new institutional economics of ethnic trading networks, contract law, and gift-exchange". Ann Arbor.
Leeds, R. (1963). "Altruism and the norm of giving". Merrill-Palmer Quarterly 9, 229–240.
Lenrow, P. (1965). "Studies in sympathy". In: Tomlins, S.S., Izard, C.E. (Eds.), Affect, Cognition, and Personality: Empirical Studies. Springer, New York.
Leventhal, G., Anderson, D. (1970). "Self-interest and the maintenance of equity". Journal of Personality and Social Psychology 15, 57–62.
Lévi-Strauss, C. "The principle of reciprocity". In: Coser, L.A., Rosenberg, G. (Eds.), Sociological Theory. Macmillan, New York.
Lindbeck, A., Nyberg, S., Weibull, J. (1999). "Social norms and economic incentives in the Welfare State". Quarterly Journal of Economics 116 (1), 1–35.
Lindbeck, A., Weibull, J. (1988). "Altruism and time consistency: the economics of the fait accompli". Journal of Political Economy 96, 1165–1182.
Malinowski, B. (1932). Crime and Custom in Savage Society. Paul, Trench, Trubner, London.
Margolis, H. (1981). Selfishness, Altruism and Rationality. Cambridge University Press, Cambridge.
Marwell, G., Ames, R. (1981). "Economists free ride, does anyone else?: Experiments on the provision of public goods, IV". Journal of Public Economics 15, 295–310.
McCabe, K., Rassenti, S., Smith, V. (1996). "Game theory and reciprocity in some extensive form experimental games". Proceedings National Academy of Science 93 (13), 421–428.
McCabe, K.A., Rassenti, S.J., Smith, V.L. (1998). "Reciprocity, trust, and payoff privacy in extensive form bargaining". Games and Economic Behavior 24 (1–2), 10–24.
Meade, G.H. (1934). Mind, Self and Society. University of Chicago Press, Chicago.
Mercier Ythier, J. (1993). "Equilibre général de dons individuels". Revue Economique, 925–950.
Mercier Ythier, J. (1998). "The distribution of wealth in the liberal social contract". European Economic Review 42, 329–347.
Miller, D. (1988). "Altruism and the welfare state". In: Donald Moon, J. (Ed.), Responsibility, Rights, and Welfare: The Theory of the Welfare State. Westview Press, Boulder and London, pp. 163–188.
Mishan, E.J. (1972). "The futility of Pareto-efficient distribution". American Economic Review 62, 971–976.
Morris, W. (1890). News from Nowhere.
Musgrave, R.A. (1970). "Pareto optimal redistribution: comment". American Economic Review 60, 991–993.
Nagel, T. (1970). The Possibility of Altruism. Oxford University Press, Oxford.
Nagel, T. (1986). The View from Nowhere. Clarendon Press, Oxford.
Neuberger, E., Duffy W. (1976). Comparative Economic Systems. A Decision-Making Approach. Allyn & Bacon.
Nicole, P. (1675). Essais de Morale. Paris.
Olsen, E.O. (1971). "Some theorems in the theory of efficient transfers". Journal of Political Economy 79, 166–176.
Orbell, J., Dawes, R.M., van de Kragt, A. (1983). "The minimal contributing set as a solution to public good problems". American Political Science Review 77, 112–122.
Orbell, J., Wilson, L.A. (1978). "Institutional solutions to the N-prisoners' dilemma". American Political Science Review 72, 411–421.
Ostrom, E., Walker, J.M. (1991). "Cooperation without external enforcement". In: Palfrey, T.P. (Ed.), Laboratory Research in Political Economy. University of Michigan Press, Ann Arbor.
Pantaleoni, M. (1898). Pure Economics. Kelley, Clifton, NJ.
Pareto, V. (1911). Le mythe vertuiste et la littérature immorale. Rivière, Paris.
Pareto, V. (1916). A Treatise on General Sociology. Dover, New York.
Pryor, F. (1977). The Origins of the Economy. Academic Press.
Rabin, M. (1998). "Psychology and Economics". Journal of Economic Literature 36, 11–46.
Rose-Ackerman, S. (1996). "Altruism, nonprofits, and economic theory". Journal of Economic Literature 34, 701–728.

Rosenhan, D.L., White, G.M. (1967). "Observation and rehearsal as determinants of prosocial behavior". Journal of Personality and Social Psychology 5, 424–431.
Sacco, P.L., Zamagni, S. (1996). "An evolutionary dynamic approach to altruism". In: Farina, F., Hahn, F., Vannucci, S. (Eds.), Ethics, Rationality, and Economic Behavior. Clarendon Press, Oxford, pp. 265–300.
Sacco, P.L., Zamagni, S. (2002). Complessità Relazionale e Comportamento Economico. Il Mulino, Bologna.
Sahlins, M. (1968). Tribesmen. Prentice-Hall, Englewood Cliffs, NJ.
Sahlins, M. (1977). The Use and Abuse of Biology (An Anthropological Critique of Sociobiology). Tavistock Publications, London.
Sawyer, J. (1966). "The altruism scale: A measure of cooperative, individualistic, and competitive interpersonal orientation". American Journal of Sociology 71, 407–416.
Schwartz, B. (1967). "The social psychology of the gift". American Journal of Sociology 73, 1–11.
Schwartz, R. (1970). "Personal philanthropic contributions". J.P.E. 78 (6), 1264–1291.
Scott, R.H. (1972). "Avarice, altruism, and second party preferences". Quarterly Journal of Economics 86, 1–18.
Segal, U., Sobel, J. (2004). "Tit for tat: Foundations of preferences for reciprocity in strategic settings". San Diego Discussion Paper. University of California.
Selten, R., Ockenfels, A. (1998). "An experimental solidarity game". Journal of Economic Behavior and Organization 34 (4), 517–539.
Service, E.R. (1966). The Hunters. Prentice-Hall, Englewood Cliffs, NJ.
Sethi, R., Somanathan, E. (2001). "Preference evolution and reciprocity". Journal of Economic Theory 97, 273–297.
Sethi, R., Somanathan, E. (2003). "Understanding reciprocity". Journal of Economic Bahavior and Organization 50 (1), 1–27.
Simmel, G. (1950). The Sociology of Georg Simmel. Translated and edited by Kurt H. Wolff. Free Press, Glencoe, Ill.
Simon, H.A. (1990). "A mechanism for social selection and successful altruism". Science 250, 1665–1668.
Smith, A. (1776, 1937). An Inquiry into the Nature and Cause of the Wealth of Nations. Random House, New York.
Solow, J.L. (1993). "Is it really the thought that counts – toward a rational theory of Christmas". Rationality and Society 5, 506–517.
Solow, R.M. (1979). "Another possible source of wage stickiness". Journal of Macroeconomics 1 (1), 79–82.
Stark, O. (1995). Altruism and beyond: An economic ananlysis of transfers and exchanges within families and groups. Cambridge.
Stein, E. (1964). On the Problem of Empathy. Transl. Stein, W. Martinus Nijhoff, Den Haag.
Stotland, E. (1969). "Exploratory investigations of empathy". In: Berkowitz, L. (Ed.), Advances in Experimental Social Psychology. Academic Press, New York.
Sugden, R. (1993). "Thinking as a team: Towards an explanation of nonselfish behavior". Social Philosophy and Policy 10, 69–89.
Sugden, R. (2000). "Team preferences". Economics and Philosophy 16, 175–205.
Sugden, R. (2002). "Beyond sympathy and empathy: Adam Smith's concept of fellow feeling". Economics and Philosophy 18, 63–88.
Thurnwald R. (1932). Die Menschliche Gesellschaft.
Thurnwald, R. (1969). Economics in Primitive Communities. Oxford University Press, London.
Titmuss, R.M. (1971). The Gift Relationship. Allen and Unwin, London.
Tognoli, J. (1975). "Reciprocation of generosity and knowledge of game termination in the decomposed Prisoner's Dilemma Game". European Journal of Social Psychology.
Tönnies, F. (1972). Gemeinschaft und Gesellschaft. Wissenschaftliche Buchgesellschaft, Darmstadt.
Tournier, P. (1963). The Meaning of Gifts. John Knox Press, Richmond.
Trivers, R.L. (1971a). "The evolution of reciprocal altruism". Quarterly Review of Biology 46, 35–37.
Trivers, R.L. (1971b). "The evolution of reciprocal altruism". Quarterly Review of Biology 46 (1), 35–58.
Uhlaner, C.J. (1989). "Relational goods and participation: Incorporating sociability into a theory of rational action". Public Choice 62, 253–285.

Vickrey, W.S. (1962). "One Economist's View of Philanthropy". In: Dickinson, F. (Ed.), Philanthropy and Public Policy. National Bureau of Economic Research, New York.
von Furstenberg, G.M., Mueller, D.C. (1971). "The Pareto optimal approach to income redistribution: a fiscal application". American Economic Review 61, 628–637.
Waller, W. (1951). The Family: A Dynamic Interpretation. Revised by Reuben Hill. Dryden, New York.
Walras L. (1865). "Les Associations populaires de consommation, de production et de crédit". Ristampa anastatica della prima od. dol 1865, Paris, Dentu, a cura di Oscar Nuccio, Ed. Bizzarri, Roma, 1969.
Warr, P.G. (1982). "Pareto optimal redistribution and private charity". Journal of Public Economics 19, 131–138.
Weisbrod, B.A. (1988). The Nonprofit Economy. Harvard University Press, Cambridge, MA.
Westermarck, E. (1908). The Origin and Development of the Moral Ideas. Vol. 2. Macmillan, London.
Winter, S.J. Jr. (1969). "A simple remark on the second optimality theorem of welfare economics". Journal of Economic Theory, 99–103.
Wintrobe, R. (1981). "It pays to do good, but not to do more good than it pays". Journal of Economic Behavior and Organization 2, 201–213.
Wispe, L. (1968). "Sympathy and empathy". In: Sills, D.L. (Ed.), In: Encyclopedia of the Social Sciences, vol. 15. Macmillan, New York.
Zamagni, S. (Ed.) (1995). The Economics of Altruism. Edward Elgar, Cheltenham.
Zeckhauser, R. (1971). "Optimal mechanisms for income transfer". American Economic Review 61, 324–334.

1C: EXPERIMENTAL SOCIAL PSYCHOLOGY

Chapter 7

THE FORMATION OF SOCIAL PREFERENCES: SOME LESSONS FROM PSYCHOLOGY AND BIOLOGY*

LOUIS LÉVY-GARBOUA, CLAUDE MEIDINGER AND BENOÎT RAPOPORT

Centre d'Economie de la Sorbonne (CNRS), Université Paris I (Panthéon-Sorbonne)

Contents

Abstract	546
Keywords	547
1. Introduction	548
2. The evolutionary emergence of social types	550
2.1. The problem of selection of social behavior in non-cultural species	550
2.1.1. Kin selection	551
2.1.2. Reciprocity selection	552
2.2. From animal societies to human societies	555
2.2.1. Learning and rational decision	556
2.2.2. Cultural transmission	559
3. Social learning	561
3.1. Theoretical perspectives	561
3.2. Empirical findings: The role of the family	563
3.3. The role of other socializers	564
3.4. Cross-cultural differences	565
3.5. Conclusion	565
4. Cognitive theories of moral and pro-social development	566
4.1. How children use the rules of a game and how conscious of these rules they are	566
4.2. How children form moral judgements	566
4.3. Other theories of stages	570
4.4. Cognitive correlates of pro-social development	572
5. Social cognition	573
5.1. Perspective-taking, identification with, and projection of self onto others	573
5.2. Identification with a known other and self-projection onto unknown others	575
5.3. Social cognition and the stages of pro-social development	578
5.4. Choosing and valuing an income distribution	579
6. Social norms and reciprocity	581

---

* We thank Ernst Fehr and the editors for very constructive remarks which helped us to improve the paper.

Handbook of the Economics of Giving, Altruism and Reciprocity, Volume 1
Edited by Serge-Christophe Kolm and Jean Mercier Ythier
Copyright © 2006 Elsevier B.V. All rights reserved
DOI: 10.1016/S1574-0714(06)01007-4

6.1. The fairness heuristic	581
6.2. Social norms of fairness in proposal-response games	583
6.3. Some evidence on social norms	585
6.4. The working of a social norm: Homans' "cash posters"	586
7. In-group favoritism and self-anchored altruism	589
7.1. Categorization and the preference for similarity	589
7.2. In-group favoritism and out-group discrimination in minimal groups	591
7.3. Self-anchored altruism	593
7.4. Comparing behavior in social dilemmas and in social choices	595
8. Social drives and emotions	597
8.1. Social comparison	597
8.2. Reducing inequity	599
8.3. Helping others in need: Is the motivation truly altruistic?	600
9. Some lessons from psychology and biology: A summary	603
References	604

Abstract

The goal of this paper is to draw some lessons for economic theory from research in psychology, social psychology and, more briefly, in biology, which purports to explain the "formation" of social preferences. We elicit the basic mechanisms whereby a variety of social preferences are determined in a variety of social contexts. Biological mechanisms, cultural transmission, learning, and the formation of cognitive and emotional capacities shape social preferences in the long or very long run. In the short run, the built-in capacities are utilized by individuals to construct their own context-dependent social preferences. The full development of social preferences requires consciousness of the individual's similarities and differences with others, and therefore knowledge of self and others. A wide variety of context-dependent social preferences can be generated by just three cognitive processes: identification of self with known others, projection of known self onto partially unknown others, and categorization of others by similarity with self. The self can project onto similar others but is unable to do so onto dissimilar others. The more can the self identify with, or project onto, an other the more generous she will be. Thus the self will find it easier to internalize and predict the behavior of an in-group than an out-group and will generally like to interact more with the former than with the latter. The main social motivations can be simply organized by reference to social norms of justice or fairness that lead to reciprocal behavior, some kind of self-anchored altruism that provokes in-group favoritism, and social drives which determine an immediate emotional response to an experienced event like hurting a norm's violator or helping an other in need.

Keywords

social preferences, preference formation, economics and psychology, economics and biology

JEL classification: B40, D63, D64, D70, D80, Z13

1. Introduction

Adam Smith wrote *The Theory of Moral Sentiments* [Smith (1759)] almost twenty years before *The Wealth of Nations* [Smith (1776)]. The former is a book about other-regarding behavior, while the latter is justly famous for describing individuals as driven by their self-interest in the marketplace. Adam Smith cannot be suspect for ignoring "social preferences" which come into play in interpersonal relations but he likely felt that the concern for others would eventually be superseded by the forces of competition imposed by the efficient functioning of large markets. Adam Smith's intuition has proved to be right. When several experimental players compete for the best offer to a single responder (who may reject all offers, in which case no one gets anything, or accept the best offer without alteration), competition dictates that the responder take the lion's share after only a few repetitions of the game [Roth et al. (1991)]. By contrast, when a single offer is made to the single responder under the same conditions, as in the ultimatum bargaining game [Güth, Schmittberger and Schwarze (1982)], the player who first receives a sum of money to be shared does not exploit her bargaining power and usually gives an equal or almost equal share to the second player. This robust observation, like many others, is plainly inconsistent with the "economic" assumption of selfishness which has become standard – by way of parsimony – since *The Wealth of Nations*. The addition of stable altruistic or envious preferences [Becker (1974)] is not sufficient either to predict behavior observed in many games. For instance, Camerer and Thaler (1995) remark that, in the ultimatum game, "randomly drawn proposers often make generous offers as an altruist would, but randomly drawn responders often reject low offers as an envious person would". Thus, subjects' behavior is role-dependent and cannot be permanently described as either altruistic or envious. In recent years, there have been a few important attempts from economists for reconciling the contrasted behavior appearing in the ultimatum game, the market game and other games as well [Rabin (1993), Fehr and Schmidt (1999), Bolton and Ockenfels (2000), among others]. These papers have generally substituted social utility functions for selfish, money maximizing behavior.

The goal of this chapter is not to review the fast growing economic contributions to social preferences,[1] though, but to draw some lessons for economists from research in psychology, social psychology and, more briefly, in biology, which purports to explain the "formation" of social preferences. In contrast with the standard practice in economics, the biological approach does not assume a given distribution of preferences at the societal level and the psychological approach does not even assume given preferences at the individual level, since the various processes of preference formation constitute their common object of study. Wider access of economists to the important literature in psychology and biology is needed in our view to elicit basic mechanisms whereby a variety of social preferences are determined in a variety of social contexts. For instance, selfish behavior may arise out of selfish preferences (a special case of so-

---

[1] References can be found in Rabin (1998), and Charness and Rabin (2002). See also Chapter 8 in this volume.

cial preferences holding when Self systematically disregards Others in social contexts) but it may also arise out of non-selfish preferences as a result of repeated competition. In a similar fashion, the motives underlying pro-social behavior like helping, sharing or giving, may be altruistic but may also arise from a sense of justice. Given the special emphasis of the present handbook on giving and other pro-social attitudes, rewards are likely to have a greater weight than punishments in our review. This context-dependent bias has been contained but what remains of it should not be taken as neglect of the role of negative feelings and behavior in interpersonal relations.

Although biology and psychology have a definite empirical and experimental orientation, we will be mainly interested in lessons which can be drawn from these disciplines for economic theory. A special effort will be sometimes required of us for putting psychological theories in a choice-theoretic framework while making the least prejudice to the original theoretical ideas. The methodology and content of the work under review is well-suited for raising major questions, like the following: Can the laws of evolution predict the appearance of stable genetically-determined social types? How does the development of children's cognitive abilities and experiences permanently affect pro-social behavior? How does the specific context of social interactions determine social cognition and the "constructed" social preferences [Payne, Bettman and Johnson (1992)], and do the latter follow systematic patterns? Can social preferences arise from emotions as well?

We start this review by examining in Section 2 the evolutionary emergence of stable social types in the very long run. After considering non-cultural species, we move to human societies. In the next two sections, we shift to the intergenerational transmission of social preferences which takes place through learning, cognitive development, and personal experiences of children. Section 3 deals with social learning and Section 4 with the cognitive theories of moral and pro-social development with special emphasis on Piaget. Finally, we study the short run construction of social preferences in the context of interpersonal relations. We suggest that a great many instances of social preference formation reviewed in the social-psychological literature can be articulated with three basic mechanisms of social cognition: identification of self with others, projection of self onto others, and categorization of others by similarity with self. They all have in common to make use of the human ability to take others' perspective. These mechanisms are presented in a simple choice-theoretic framework and serve to synthesize the wide variety of results which can be found in this literature. The first two appear in Section 5, and the third in Section 7. The interplay of these simple mechanisms can generate a number of context-dependent social motivations in the short run, and be either reinforced or inhibited by learning from experience in the long run. The main social motivations, though, can be simply organized by reference to social norms of justice or fairness that lead to reciprocal behavior (Section 6), some kind of self-anchored altruism that provokes both in-group favoritism and out-group discrimination (Section 7), and social drives which determine an immediate emotional response to an experienced event like hurting a norm's violator or helping an other in need (Section 8). Finally, we summarize the main lessons to be drawn from our reading of psychology and biology in Section 9.

2. The evolutionary emergence of social types

The natural evolution of populations in non-cultural species is usually explained by the Darwinian hypothesis of "descent with modification". If the organisms in a population differ in their abilities to survive and reproduce and if the characteristics that affect these abilities are transmitted from parents to offspring, the population will evolve. Within this framework, when one speaks of the ability of an organism to survive and reproduce, one usually refers to the *phenotype* of that organism, i.e. "the observable properties of an organism as they have developed under the combined influences of the genetic constitution of the individual and the effect of environmental factors" [Wilson (1975, p. 591)]. And when one speaks of transmission of these observable properties, one usually considers that these properties are under the control of the *genotype*, i.e. the genetic constitution of an individual organism. Thus, evolution by natural selection works in a remarkable way. Genotypes are mapped onto phenotypes that have different abilities to survive and reproduce. Then, natural selection acting differentially on the phenotypes modifies the composition of the population as it matures to the adult stage. Fitness is a measure of the survival success of the genotypes. The genotype with the highest fitness value will increase its frequency in the population.

Within this approach, one immediately encounters the problem of selection for social behavior. A species is defined as *social* [Boorman and Levitt (1980, pp. 2, 12)] if "its members engage, at any point in the life cycle, in sustained cooperation that goes beyond parental care and the continued association of mated pairs". More specifically, *altruistic* behavior is defined as "any behavior involving the sacrifice of a certain amount of fitness on the part of one organism (the donor) in exchange for augmented fitness on the part of a second con-specific (the recipient)". Social and altruistic behavior offers a challenge to the theory of natural selection since the latter only predicts adaptations that maximize fitness of individuals taken separately.

In what follows, without entering into the complexity of the formal models drawn from mathematical population genetics, we first want to review the different ways which evolutionary models for non-cultural species have tried to solve the problem of selection for social behavior and second to point to what can differentiate human pathways to sociality from animal pathways to sociality.

2.1. The problem of selection of social behavior in non-cultural species

Alternative genetic models of altruism and cooperation are usually divided among group selection, kin selection and reciprocity selection models. For the moment, we neglect the group selection approach. Since the first formulation of this hypothesis by Wynne-Edwards (1959) and its revival as a problem in mathematical genetics by Levins (1970), this approach has received numerous competing formulations distantly related to one another and often without reduction to a common basis. For this reason, escaping from the complexity of these formalisms, the evolutionary approach to animal behavior mostly retains kin selection and reciprocity selection as principal pathways to sociality[2] [Kreps and Davies (1981), McFarland (1985), Smuts et al. (1986)]. Kin selection is selection for altruism toward kin. Reciprocity selection is selection for cooperation between genetically unrelated individuals.

2.1.1. Kin selection

The importance of kin selection for the biological evolution of altruism was first anticipated by Fisher (1930) and Haldane (1953), and fully perceived by Hamilton (1964). The term kin selection [Maynard-Smith (1964)] was used to describe a process by which a behavioral trait is favored owing to its beneficial effects on relatives such as siblings or cousins. Between two full sibs for instance, there is a probability (coefficient of relatedness) of 0.5 that they share a copy of the same gene. Therefore, as an extreme example of altruism, a gene that programs an individual to die in order to save the life of relatives will increase in frequency in the gene pool if on average this altruistic act saves the lives of more than two brothers or sisters. More generally, in a large population of donor-recipient pairs, with each donor giving up a fraction δ units of fitness in exchange of a fitness increment of π to the recipient, Hamilton's theory predicts that an altruist gene will be selected if $-\delta + r\pi > 0$, r being the mean coefficient of relatedness across the population of pairs.

Although the concept of altruism assumes a central position in any discussion of kin selection, behavior that appears to be altruistic at the phenotypic level turns out to be genetically selfish in Hamilton's theory [Dawkins (1976)]. This theory can explain acts of altruism as extreme as suicide or sterility in animal species because the sacrifice of some amount of genetic material in one organism leads on average to the preservation of a greater amount of the same material in another organism. Worker bees who attack predators approaching their nests die as a result of the act of stinging. The evolution of such behavior is explained by the fact that the beneficiaries of the altruistic act are close relatives of the worker [Michener (1974)]. Also sterile castes and helping have evolved in the social insects because sterile workers usually help their mother (the queen) to produce offspring [Brockmann (1984), Wilson (1971)]. Since the rapid development of Hamilton's ideas and the demonstration that a number of cases of sociality outside social insects also involve altruism among close kin, kin selection has become one of the most favored explanations in evolutionary socio-biology.

Kin selection requires an individual to behave differently towards individuals of different degrees of relatedness. In communal animals, this can be simply the result of living near one's relatives. There is also a growing body of evidence showing that individuals can indeed recognize kin and even distinguish close kin from distant kin. For instance, members of a social insect colony identify fellow members by colony-specific pheromones. But it is also clear that, in contrast to Hymenoptera, within social vertebrates' groups for instance most cases of altruism must account for transfers of fitness

---

[2] But see also the Boorman and Levitt (1980) group selection model.

between non-sibs as well as between sibs. Since the strength of kin selection pressure rapidly weakens at a relational distance greater than that of half-sib, there is substantial reason to consider that most social behavior, particularly in vertebrates, has been shaped by the combined effects of more than one selection principle. Therefore, in order to explain how cooperation and altruism evolve among *unrelated* con-specifics, one has to introduce reciprocity selection.

2.1.2. Reciprocity selection

When social evolution is considered, one cannot directly assign fitness to organisms viewed in isolation. As we already argued in the context of kin selection, what needs to be determined is inclusive fitness which goes beyond the physical environment and encompasses the social environment consisting of other con-specifics. Boorman and Levitt (1980) speak of fitness interlocking when the behavior of one individual directly affects the fitness of other individuals. They also note that sociality characteristically imposes fitness tradeoffs between different individuals. Some forms of cooperation, called mutualism by Kreps and Davies (1981), do not involve any altruism because each cooperating individual gains a net benefit from doing so. Pied wagtails joining together to defend a feeding territory enjoy a greater feeding rate than they would by being alone. In other cases, kin selection and mutuality work together. Lionesses in a pride are related so that not only does hunting in packs improve the chances of capturing a zebra but it also confers kin benefit to individuals. More generally, this is also the case with Trivers' (1971) altruism where both participants will gain as long as the help is reciprocated at some later date. However, only in some simple cases of social aggregation is it possible to ascribe a positive value to social participation for *all* members. Advanced cases of sociality impose tradeoffs between benefits to some participants and costs to others. To understand why such cases could be a problem, let us consider here a very simple model of evolution borrowed from Boorman and Levitt's (1980) "minimal model", recast into the framework of the Replicator Dynamics.[3]

---

[3] This "minimal model" can also be recast into the framework of the Evolutionary Game Theory initiated by Maynard-Smith (1982). The concept of an evolutionary stable strategy ESS usually leads to individuals programmed to play mixed strategies and to monomorphic population equilibria. There are known examples of mixed behavior that could be interpreted as an ESS. For instance, Brockmann and Dawkins (1979) studied the female great golden digger wasps (Sphex ichneumoneus) which lay their eggs in underground burrows that they have provisioned with grasshoppers as food for the larvae. The female wasp has two strategies open to her. She can either dig her own burrow, running a small risk of being invaded by another wasp, or she can enter an already dug burrow, saving herself the cost of digging but with the risk that the burrow is being used by the owner. The best strategy depends upon that adopted by other female wasps in the vicinity and clearly digger wasps employ a mixed strategy. This is corroborated by the fact that the success (in terms of the number of eggs laid) of the two pure strategies "Dig" and "Enter" is the same whether the wasp decides to enter an existing burrow or to dig her own. Nevertheless, to restrict ESS considerations to situations in which only a single type (possibly mixed) may exist at equilibrium may be unsatisfactory. In general, one would also like to explain polymorphic population equilibria that could arise in an evolutionary stable way.

Table 1
Payoffs in terms of individual fitness

Individual fitness	social	asocial
social	$1 + \sigma$	$1 - \tau$
asocial	$1 + \sigma_1$	1

Dawkins (1976, 1982) defines a *replicator* as anything in the universe of which copies are made, and considers that evolution is the external and visible manifestation of the differential survival of alternative replicators. A replicator is active if its nature has some influence over its probability of being copied. According to this approach, let us suppose that individuals are vehicles in which two active replicators travel about. The first one is a social replicator that programs individuals to play a pure social strategy S. The second one is an asocial replicator that programs individuals to play a pure asocial strategy A. Social and asocial fitness must now be defined. With each individual randomly paired with another member of the population, the individual fitnesses resulting from such pairwise contests are defined in Table 1 (values in the table are the fitness to an individual hosting the replicator on the left while his opponent hosts the replicator above) In this table, it is assumed that:
– When a social individual meets another social individual, each has fitness $1 + \sigma$ so that σ is the per capita benefit from membership in a partnership between socials
– When a social individual meets an asocial individual, the asocial receives $1 + \sigma_1$ while the social individual has reduced fitness $1 - \tau$
– When asocial individuals meet, both have fitness equals to 1.

Therefore, in a polymorphic p-population (in which there is a fraction p of individuals hosting a social replicator and a fraction $1 - p$ of individuals hosting an asocial replicator), the expected fitness conferred on an individual by the social replicator is $f_S(p) = (1+\sigma)p + (1-\tau)(1-p)$ and the expected fitness conferred on an individual by the asocial replicator is: $f_A(p) = (1+\sigma_1)p + (1-p)$. The Replicator Dynamics is simply determined by the comparison of these two frequency-dependent expected fitnesses. Because the fitness of a host is a measure of how frequently it gets to reproduce its replicator, replicators that confer high fitness to their hosts are going to control a larger share of hosts than those that confer low fitness. In our population, with $\sigma > \sigma_1$ exemplifying the synergistic case in which there is a more than additive advantage of cooperation (as opposed to the opposite case $\sigma_1 > \sigma$ of a Prisoner's Dilemma), the Replicator Dynamics shows that there is a rest point $p^* = \tau/(\tau + \sigma - \sigma_1)$ solution of the equation $f_S(p) = f_A(p)$. But such a rest point which corresponds to a polymorphic equilibrium is unstable, as shown by the fact that for p greater (lower) than p^*, f_S is greater (lower) than f_A. Above p^*, the selection process will lead to social fixation. But below p^*, it will lead to asocial fixation. Therefore, in a population of asocials, a small fraction of social replicators arising by mutation will be counter-selected. Then how is it possible that a social replicator appearing by mutation at a very low initial frequency can ever cross the critical p^* value?

Interestingly, Trivers' (1971) reciprocal altruism can also be reformulated in the framework of the Replicator Dynamics. Whenever the benefit of an altruistic act to the recipient is greater than the cost to the donor, both participants will gain as long as the help is reciprocated at a later date. The problem is of course the possibility of cheating, the recipient being able to refuse to repay the favor at a later date. Axelrod and Hamilton (1981) have shown in a Prisoner's Dilemma framework that a Tit-For-Tat strategy can be an evolutionary stable strategy in a population in which there is always a finite probability that two individuals will meet again, provided this probability is sufficiently large. Such a Tit-For-Tat strategy is simply "be social at the first encounter and then do whatever your opponent did on the previous encounter". This is clearly a strategy of cooperation based on reciprocity. Introduced in a Replicator Dynamics, one can thus consider a population in which there is a positive probability that two individuals will meet again and in which individuals either host an asocial replicator A or a Tit-For-Tat replicator TFT. With the payoffs previously defined in Table 1 for one encounter and with v the probability that two contestants meet again, one gets the following expected fitness[4] conferred on an individual by a Tit-For-Tat replicator and by an asocial replicator in a population with a proportion p of Tit-For-Tat replicators:

$$f_{TFT}(p) = \left(\frac{1+\sigma}{1-v}\right)p + \left(\frac{1-\tau(1-v)}{1-v}\right)(1-p), \qquad (2.1)$$

$$f_A(p) = \left(\frac{1+\sigma_1(1-v)}{1-v}\right)p + \left(\frac{1}{1-v}\right)(1-p). \qquad (2.2)$$

Clearly, $f_{TFT}(p)$ is greater (lower) than $f_A(p)$ if and only if p is greater (lower) than p^*, with: $p^* = \frac{\tau(1-v)}{\tau(1-v)+\sigma-\sigma_1(1-v)}$. Once again, there is a rest point p^* that corresponds to a polymorphic unstable equilibrium if $\sigma - \sigma_1(1-v) > 0$ which means that: $v > \frac{\sigma_1-\sigma}{\sigma_1}$. This is trivially verified when $\sigma > \sigma_1$, the more-than-additive advantage case of cooperation. This could also be verified in the more extreme case of the Prisoner's Dilemma, when $\sigma_1 > \sigma$, provided that the probability v that two contestants meet again is sufficiently large. But also note that in the more-than-additive advantage case of cooperation, p^* is a decreasing function of v. Therefore, the threshold p^* to be crossed before the TFT replicator can invade the population can be low when the probability v is sufficiently large.

---

[4] With v the probability that two contestants meet again: When a TFT plays another TFT, it gets: $(1+\sigma) + v(1+\sigma) + v^2(1+\sigma) + \cdots = \frac{1+\sigma}{1-v}$; whereas when it plays an A, it gets $(1-\tau) + v + v^2 + \cdots = (1-\tau) + \frac{v}{1-v} = \frac{1-\tau(1-v)}{1-v}$. When an A plays a TFT, it gets: $(1+\sigma_1) + v + v^2 + \cdots = (1+\sigma_1) + \frac{v}{1-v} = \frac{1+\sigma_1(1-v)}{1-v}$; whereas when it plays an A, it gets $1 + v + v^2 + \cdots = \frac{1}{1-v}$.

2.2. From animal societies to human societies

According to Hamilton (1964), altruism is expected to be selectively directed toward kin and close kinship is expected to facilitate altruism. As we have seen, there is evidence that kin are responsible for much of the altruism deployed in animal species. To quote some further examples, in primate groups [Silk (1986)] cercopithecine females selectively defend and support maternal kin against aggressive encounters and reserve costly aid for close kin. Also, grooming (the removal of ectoparasites and dirt from skin and hair) is primarily directed to kin. But we also know that there are several examples of altruistic behavior among unrelated individuals [Kreps and Davies (1981), Silk (1986)]. In many cases, such examples are instances of Trivers' reciprocal altruism such as blood sharing in vampire bats, eggs trading in black hamlet fish or alliances in primates (grooming among non-kin increases the probability of future support in aggressive encounters).

We have also seen that in a large randomly mixing population, even if it pays a species to acquire a social or cooperative trait, a frequency threshold has to be crossed that does not seem to permit to achieve the advantageous equilibrium starting from a mutation whose frequency is low. To explain animal social behavior, different evolutionary scenarios are evoked. The first one considers that cooperation could emerge at first between relatives, evolving by kin selection. Because one of the cues favoring the recognition of relatedness could simply be the fact of reciprocation of cooperation, reciprocity cooperation could grow between relatives and thus cross the frequency threshold [Axelrod and Hamilton (1981)]. Independently of such an initial propagation on a kin basis, a second scenario concentrates on clusters of cooperation. This is the *cascade principle* of Boorman and Levitt (1980) according to which, in an appropriately viscous population structure, a local concentration or cluster of the social gene may favor its propagation through interactions which are more frequent than expected from random encounters. More generally, it is quite clear that, by endowing a newly introduced social trait with enough recognition capabilities to enable the socials to recognize each other with great accuracy, one can ensure the successful takeover of such a trait. If individuals hosting *TFT* replicators and individuals hosting *A* replicators are perfectly distinguishable from each other, *TFT* individuals can now interact with one another, getting a payoff: $\frac{1+\sigma}{1-v}$, and asocials are left to interact with one another, getting a payoff: $\frac{1}{1-v}$. This allows *TFT* replicators to invade the population. In many cases, it may be possible for some species to exploit substitutes for innate recognition such as barriers to dispersal, which not only make neighboring con-specifics extremely likely to be kin but also permit the persistence of a local concentration of a social gene.

Thus, as pointed out by Gintis (2000a) using a result from the group selection approach, the usual argument according to which evolution should entail the disappearance of the altruist because such an individual becomes less fit in the process of rendering the group more fit is not necessarily the end of the story. Suppose that in a population there are groups $i = (1, \ldots, n)$, and let q_i be the fraction of the population in group i. In each group, there is a social trait with frequency s_i that contributes to the mean fitness f_i of group i. At a given period, one therefore has $\bar{s} = \sum_i q_i s_i$ the frequency of the social trait in the population and $\bar{f} = \sum_i q_i f_i$ the mean fitness of the whole population. Now, if we consider that from one period to the next, groups grow in proportion of their relative fitness, at the next period one has $q'_i = q_i \frac{f_i}{\bar{f}}$ and $s'_i = s_i + \Delta s_i$ for the frequency of the social trait in the group i at the next period. Therefore, the variation $\Delta \bar{s}$ of the frequency of the social trait in the whole population is determined by: $\Delta \bar{s} = \sum_i q'_i s'_i - \sum_i q_i s_i$, which can easily be rewritten as:

$$\bar{f} \Delta \bar{s} = \sum_i q_i (f_i - \bar{f}) s_i + \sum_i q_i f_i \Delta s_i. \tag{2.3}$$

This is Price equation, well-known in biology. It shows that, despite the fact that the social trait renders individuals bearing it less fit than other group members ($\Delta s_i < 0$), the frequency of the trait in the whole population can nevertheless increase ($\Delta \bar{s} > 0$). With $\Delta s_i < 0$ for all i, the second term in the right member of the equation (the within-group selection effect) is clearly negative. But provided that the first term is positive and sufficiently large, $\Delta \bar{s}$ can be positive. Because $\sum_i q_i (f_i - \bar{f}) \bar{s} = 0$, the first term can also be written as $\sum_i q_i (f_i - \bar{f})(s_i - \bar{s})$ a between-group selection effect represented by the covariance between group fitness and group frequency of the social trait. Thus, with sufficiently high covariance (when groups with above-average frequency of the social trait also have above-average fitness), the social trait can increase in the population. Interestingly, applied to a population of both social and asocial individuals pairing off in each period with payoffs given for instance by a Prisoner's Dilemma defined by Table 1 with $\sigma_1 > \sigma$, the Price equation shows that a small number of socials can invade a population of asocials. This occurs [Gintis (2000a)] if there is a sufficient degree r of assortative interaction (r being the probability that each type meets its own type and $1 - r$ being the probability to meet a random member of the population).

Nevertheless, disregarding the complex of issues and models that can evolutionarily explain social behavior in animal species, the fact remains that empirical and theoretical evidence combine to suggest that there are multiple and often delicate conditions for evolutionary emergence of social adaptation [Boorman and Levitt (1980)]. For perhaps one million of presently existing animal species, at most ten thousand can be considered as social in any significant way. This fact has be related to other factors that have not yet been considered – *learning, rational decision* and *cultural transmission* – the existence of which is generally considered important for explaining social behaviors in the human species.

2.2.1. Learning and rational decision

Evolutionary biologists and ethologists noticed that, as we move up the evolutionary ladder into the higher animals and toward humans, intra-specific variability in social adaptation becomes substantial. Social vertebrates are for instance a more heterogeneous collection of species than social insects. This variability reflects the increasing importance of environmental, as opposed to genetic, factors. Surely, in an uncertain world, genes are more likely to be successful if phenotypes are free to adapt flexibly to the environment in which they find themselves.[5] And, like many other organisms, humans adjust their phenotypes in response to their environment through individual learning and rational calculation.

All organisms appear to possess mechanisms that allow them to modify their phenotypes adaptively in response to environmental contingencies. When an animal learns, it changes its behavioral repertoire forever. Such a change is likely to alter its fitness and therefore is subject to natural selection. From Pavlov's work on conditioning to Thorndike and Skinner's approaches to instrumental learning, it is well known that, given a criterion of reinforcement such as a sense of pain or a taste for rewards, even random errors in behavior can be conditioned to elaborately adaptive behavior. Besides such simple learning, whether animals exhibit intentional behavior that would give them greater flexibility remains a controversial issue. Certainly, as our knowledge of animal behavior has improved, the difference between humans and animals has appeared to diminish [McFarland (1985)]. Nevertheless, even if one can adopt an intentional stance to predict some animals' behavior, treating them as "rational agents with beliefs and desires and other mental stages exhibiting rationality" [Dennett (1987, pp. 15)], it seems that human beings differ not only quantitatively but also qualitatively from animals as far as intentionality is concerned. According to Lumsden and Wilson (1981) for instance, *reification* – a process by which the human mind produces concepts and continuously shifting reclassifications of the world – is a unique activity that fully separates mankind from the most advanced social animal species.[6]

In order to understand the importance of intentionality and rational decision for cooperative behavior, let us return to our society of individuals hosting social and asocial replicators, with payoffs displayed in Table 1. If both types are perfectly distinguishable from one another, we saw that social replicators can interact selectively with another at no cost and invade the population. But suppose now that the two types cannot be distinguished at a glance. An individual has to pay, in terms of fitness, a cost of scrutiny c if he wants to know the type of the individual with whom he randomly meets. If not paid, the two types are indistinguishable. Thus, an individual hosting a social replicator and paying the cost of scrutiny will interact only with another individual of the same

---

[5] Investigating the biological basis of economic behavior and asking the questions: "Why might utility functions exist? Are they adaptive?" Robson (2001, p. 13) notes that "the evolutionary rationale for an hedonic internal evaluation system is to permit an appropriate response to novelty and complexity". With his distinction between homo economicus (who can only be manipulated via his preferences) on one hand and homo behavioralis (programmed directly with behavior that Nature can directly manipulate) on the other hand, Binmore (1994, p. 151) emphasizes the same point. He notes that in a principal-agent problem, with a rapidly changing environment, Nature has to choose homo economicus rather than homo behavioralis because the former adapts more quickly than the latter. This is why she made an expensive investment in brainpower.

[6] This was linked to the enormous increase of the cerebrum of man during a relatively short span of evolutionary time. Over a period of approximately three million years, the brain tripled in size so that no scale has really been invented that can objectively compare the intelligence of man to that of chimpanzees or other primates [Wilson (1975)].

Table 2
Payoffs in a potentially profitable venture

payoff	not cheat	cheat
not cheat	$1 + \sigma$	$1 - \tau$
cheat	$1 + \sigma_1$	1

type and his payoff will be equal to: $1 + \sigma - c$. And if he refuses to pay the cost, his expected payoff will be: $p(1 + \sigma) + (1 - p)(1 - \tau)$, denoting by p proportion of socials in the population. Thus, it is plain that for: $p < p^* = \frac{\sigma + \tau - c}{\sigma + \tau}$, every social will pay the cost of scrutiny and get a payoff: $1 + \sigma - c$ by interacting with another social. Moreover, it will not be in the interest of the asocials to bear this cost because no social will want to interact with them anyway. Therefore, if $\sigma > c$, starting below p^*, a very small proportion of intelligent socials arising by mutation and rationally deciding to pay the cost of scrutiny will expand in the population until they reach a population's share equal to p^*. Above this value, it no longer makes sense to pay the cost of scrutiny. Socials and asocials will then interact at random and the fitness payoff difference will cause the proportion of socials to shrink. The Replicator Dynamics leads here to a stable polymorphic equilibrium characterized by a proportion p^* of socials in the population.

By introducing such a rational decision element in a simple evolutionary model, Frank (1988) wanted to emphasize the fact that rational calculations play only an indirect role in solving social dilemmas. Just consider two self-interested persons who can engage in a potentially profitable venture, but with each having opportunities to cheat. The payoffs are presented in Table 2, similar to Table 1 but with: $\sigma_1 > \sigma$.

In this Prisoner's Dilemma, both persons would profit from making a binding commitment not to cheat. But, once the venture is under way, self-interest guided by material incentives dictates cheating. Suppose now that there are persons in the population who are unable to cheat because of strong feelings of guilt. In order for such a non-cheater to benefit in material terms, she must both be able to be recognized as a non-cheater and to recognize non-cheaters with a sufficiently low cost of scrutiny to make the venture still profitable. Thus, a genuinely trustworthy person must be observably different in a way that is partly insulated from purposeful control in order to solve the commitment problem – to defeat opportunists that could attempt to mimic the symptoms of trustworthiness. Without such a recognition mechanism, rational decision cannot solve the social dilemma except if the venture leads to repeated interactions with a sufficiently high probability. When both persons are involved in repeated interactions, indefinite cooperation is a possibility based on the threat that if someone ever deviates, the opponent will punish him with cheating thereafter. With a discount rate v representing the probability that the venture will remain constituted for at least one more period, this implies: $v > \frac{\sigma_1 - \sigma}{\sigma}$. Therefore, in cases where socials do not have sufficient capabilities to recognize each other or in cases where a venture between self-interested agents disbands with high probability, cooperation among individuals cannot necessarily be sustained. Some research in evolutionary psychology has suggested that humans may be evolutionary predisposed to engage in social exchange using mental algorithms which identify and punish cheaters [Cosmides and Tooby (1992), Hoffman, McCabe and Smith (1998)].[7] And, of course, if intelligence partly evolved from the need to interact with fellow beings, to have a "theory of mind" – a model of the beliefs and preferences of others – can permit a flexible response in strategic situations and so would be evolutionary favored [Robson (2001)].

2.2.2. Cultural transmission

If humans share their proclivity to adjust phenotypes in response to their environment through learning and rational calculation with many other organisms, they are almost unique in their ability to culturally transmit the so acquired phenotypes to the next generation. In non-cultural species, even with a large range of individual learning spanning from trial-and-error to rational choice, variants so acquired and other forms of phenotypic flexibility are lost with the death of the individual because inheritable changes of phenotypical features are only accessible via the one-way road of genotypes. In such species, a given distribution of genotypes G_t in the population gives rise to a distribution of phenotypes F_t through a process of ontogeny (including individual learning). Natural selection, acting on the phenotypic characteristics of individuals, leads to a modified distribution of genotypes G_{t+1} that gives rise to the distribution of phenotypes in the next generation F_{t+1}. However, since all the phenotypic variants acquired by individual learning are lost for the next generation and have to be learned again, one has only to know G_{t+1} to predict the distribution of phenotypes F_{t+1} in a given environment. It is not necessary to know F_t. In cultural species, things are very different [Boyd and Richerson (1985)]. In general, *cultural exchange* is defined as the passage of information capable of affecting individuals' phenotypes from one generation to the next by non-genetic means [McFarland (1985)]. In this case, it is no longer sufficient to know G_{t+1} in order to predict the distribution of phenotypes F_{t+1}. One must also know which cultural traits of F_t are transmitted to the next generation through cultural transmission mechanisms. Vertical (between generations) cultural transmission combined with individual learning thus acts to create a Lamarckian effect by which acquired variation can be inherited.[8] This Lamarckian effect introduces a force of variation in which the origination of novel traits does not result from the play of chance but from "an exercise of will on the part of individuals in actively responding to perceived needs, which they do by initiating constructive adaptations that are subsequently transmissible to offspring" [Ingold (1986)].

---

[7] Barnett (1968) has noted that the use of punishment in the attempt to train their young in anything other than avoidance seems exclusively limited to humans.

[8] Besides vertical cultural transmission, there is also a horizontal cultural transmission (within generations, because adults may copy adults and children may imitate other children) that contributes to the distribution of phenotypes [Cavalli-Sforza and Feldman (1981)].

There is no doubt that biological explanation of cooperation based on kin altruism and reciprocal altruism may apply to human and nonhuman species alike. But there is also no doubt that human cooperation is based in part on capacities that are unique to Homo sapiens. As we have seen, the Price's equation shows that in populations composed of groups characterized by a higher level of interaction among members than with outsiders, the evolutionary process may be decomposed into between-group and within group selection effects. For a social trait whose expression benefits the group, but imposes fitness loss on those who adopt it, it follows that the former effect can offset the latter effect when circumstances heighten and sustain differences between groups relative to within-group differences. Therefore, according to many contributors in this field,[9] if we want to seek an explanation of cooperation that works for humans and does not work or works substantially less well for other species, we must in particular look for distinctive human characteristics than enhance the relevance of group selection for humans. And central to this relevance are psychological and cultural human capacities to suppress within-group phenotypic differences and simultaneously sustain a high frequency of intergroup conflicts.

Cultural transmission leads people to internalize norms of behavior through vertical or horizontal socialization and these norms are followed principally because people value the transmitted behavior for its own sake, in addition to or in spite of its effect on personal fitness or well-being. Thus in cases where cooperation between self-interested people cannot be sustained, an internalized norm of cooperation (individually fitness-reducing but fitness-enhancing at the group level) may be a considerable benefit to a group. Insofar as such norms are largely widespread inside the groups, they contribute (like many other constructed institutional environments) to limit within-group competition and to reduce phenotypic variation within groups. Correlatively, the formation of groups on such non-kin characteristics limits the between-group migration allowing the possibility that group selection pressure can co-evolve with cooperative behaviors because within-group cooperation and hostility toward outsiders co-evolves.

They are some convincing examples of such internalization of norms because recent experimental research has revealed forms of human behavior difficult to explain in terms of self-interest [Fehr and Gächter (2000, 2002), Falk, Fehr and Fischbacher (2005), Fehr, Fischbacher and Gächter (2002)]. Strong reciprocity, for example, is a predisposition to cooperate and to punish those who violate the norms of cooperation, at personal cost and even when it is very implausible to expect that these costs will be repaid. There are many ways to evolutionarily explain strong reciprocity. Using Price equation to chart the dynamics of strong reciprocity, for example, Gintis (2000b) shows that for a sufficient amount of harm which an individual can inflict on non-cooperators at a sufficiently personal low cost of retaliation, a small fraction of strong reciprocators can always invade a population of self-interested agents when group extinction threats are

---

[9] See, for example, Bowles and Gintis (2003), Gintis (2000a, 2000b, 2003), Gintis et al. (2003), Fehr and Gächter (2002).

relatively common. Besides cultural arguments linked to the internalization of norms that point to the decline of cost disadvantage of retaliation as defectors become rare, Gintis points out that, contrary to animal dispute for which victory often involves great cost even to the winner, Homo sapiens has the superior ability to inflict punishment at a low cost to the punisher. This is perhaps one of the most interesting properties that contributes to cooperation inside groups in human societies. Moreover, under assumptions approximating likely human environments over the 1,000,000 years prior to the domestication of animals and plants, agent-based simulations shows that the proliferation of strong reciprocators is very likely [Bowles and Gintis (2003)].

Is it possible to say that, because humans acquire so much of their behavior culturally rather than genetically, the human evolutionary process is fundamentally different from that of other animals? This question is highly controversial. Many examples of cultural exchange and tradition in animal species show that culture and tradition do not necessarily require great intelligence on the part of individuals [McFarland (1985), Nishida (1986)]. Thus, in animal species, individual behavior is certainly under the control of two sets of instructions, genetic and cultural, with culture itself under genetic control. For people who think that individuals are the products of gene pools and cultures, and that humans do not cease to be animals with the advent of culture, this has led to a number of formal models of so-called gene-culture co-evolution [Cavalli-Sforza and Feldman (1981), Lumsden and Wilson (1981), Boyd and Richerson (1985), Gintis (2003)]. These models are designed to show how genetic and cultural evolution can interact through programs of individual developments. Because culture is an inheritance system that makes a pool of cultural traits to co-evolve with the gene pool, one cannot abstract from the details of cultural transmission that are likely to be essential for understanding the social evolution of human behavior. In such a framework, culture may have a variety of structures (patterns of socialization by which a given set of traits is transmitted in a given society) and one has to understand the conditions under which different structures of cultural transmissions might evolve. Cultural transmission leads to the persistence of behavioral traits through time. Because not every individual is equally invented and because experimenting directly with the environment may be dangerous, tradition or culture can be a cheaper and safer way of acquiring information. Thus, "in evolving a reliance on cultural transmission, the human species may well have traded high rates of random error caused by individual learning in variable environments for a lower rate of systematic error (with respect to genetic fitness) due to the partial autonomy of cultural evolution" [Boyd and Richerson (1985, p. 289)].

3. Social learning

3.1. Theoretical perspectives

Pro-social behavior encompasses in social psychology any voluntary action which aims to benefit an other [see Eisenberg (1996)]. Altruistic behavior is generally considered as a subtype of pro-social behavior, and motives underlying pro-social behavior may be altruistic or not. Pro-social behavior includes helping, sharing, giving, and overlaps with moral behavior. This subsection aims to describe the main theories that argue that pro-social attitudes are taught by adults and learned by children. Such hypotheses are not absent from economic literature. For example, Bisin and Verdier (2001) study population dynamics of preference traits in a model of intergenerational cultural transmission. Although their paper is not specially designed to study how altruistic or reciprocal preferences can be sustained in a group, especially when these are not dominant cultural traits, their model can be applied to this kind of preferences. They assume that parents socialize and transmit their preferences to their offspring, who can be socialized either by their parents or by the society (cultural and social environment). The parents are altruistic toward their children, and thus might want to socialize them to a specific cultural model if they think this will increase their children's welfare. However, this altruism is only imperfect, as parents can only use their own preferences to evaluate their children's choices.[10] The authors study the long run stationary state pattern of preferences in the population, assuming that family and society are substitutes in the transmission mechanism. Parents will socialize children more intensively when the set of cultural traits they wish to transmit is common only to a cultural minority of the population. Those parents who belong to a cultural majority will be able to save on their own resources to socialize their children since they anticipate that the latter will adopt with high probability the cultural traits of the majority that they themselves wish to transmit. Bisin and Verdier show that such mechanisms are inefficient because parents invest too many resources to affect their children's preferences.

In the same vein, based on Duesenberry's (1949) work, Cox and Stark [see Stark (1995)] propose to explain how altruistic preferences might be passed on by the parents to their children, by demonstration and imitation. In order to make their children aware that they will have to help them in the future, by means of services or possibly monetary transfers, they conspicuously help their own old parents in front of their children's eyes, that is they demonstrate to their children how they behave with their own parents with the hope that their children will imitate this attitude in the future.[11]

Those economic models are to be related to an important trend among social psychologists: the social learning school. Bandura (e.g., 1986), is probably the most important representative of this school, rooted in behaviorism, that postulates that moral behaviors are mainly induced by modeling and learned by imitation: children learn to behave pro-socially by imitating models (generally adults, but also peers), who behave pro-socially.

---

[10] The terms used by Bisin and Verdier (2001) to designate this form of altruism are paternalistic altruism or imperfect empathy. Anticipating on Section 5, it is a clear case of projection of parents onto their children.

[11] This model has received mixed empirical support, in particular when the probability of imitation is endogenous [see Jellal and Wolff (2005); see also Arrondel and Masson (2001), for other empirical evidence by economists]. See also Chapter 11 of this Handbook for a critical presentation of this hypothesis.

3.2. Empirical findings: The role of the family

These hypotheses have received mixed empirical support. Psychologists have investigated how socialization within and outside the family may induce pro-social behavior among children [see, for instance, Berkowitz and Grych (1998)]. In particular, they have studied the effects of two main parental disciplinary practices: induction (parents give explanations or reasons for requiring the child to change his behavior) and power-assertive or punitive techniques (physical punishment or deprivation of privileges). Punitive techniques appear to be generally unrelated or negatively related to children's pro-social development. In particular, immediate compliance has often been observed, but effects generally disappear over time [see, e.g., Grusec (1981)], although social disapproval, compared to material punishment, may have a positive effect. Researchers have found a positive relation or no relation between parental use of inductions and pro-social responding. When various types of induction are considered separately, there is at least some evidence of a relation between pro-social behavior or sympathy and inductions focused on the state or the feelings of others [see Eisenberg and Fabes (1998) for an extended review of this literature].

Another related point of importance in enhancing pro-social behavior is the quality of the parent–child relationships. Once again, empirical findings are contrasted. Most studies, but not all, have found a positive relation between warm socializers and pro-social children, just as between parental empathy and children empathy. Moreover, support for a positive relation between parental emphasis on pro-social values and children's pro-social responding is mixed [for example, Hoffman (1975b), and Eisenberg et al. (1992)]. Oliner and Oliner (1988) report nevertheless that people who rescued Jews during the Holocaust often recall learning values of caring from parents. In the same way, adults involved in civil rights activities often report that their parents were themselves involved in altruistic or social activities and discussed their altruistic involvement with their children [Rosenhan (1970)]. Thus affection of parents and their altruistic values seem to be determinants of children's acquisition of altruistic behavior, as argued by Hoffman (1975b). For example, Chase-Lansdale, Wakschlag and Brooks-Gunn (1995), investigating the construct of caring, argue that families are instrumental in the promotion of caring through attachment, peer relationships, pro-social behavior, empathy, agency and self-control, and review empirical evidence supporting this hypothesis.

As mentioned above, another way to induce pro-social behavior by socialization is modeling. Most studies involving models are laboratory studies. Experimenters have generally implemented a kind of dictator game under two controls: before donating, the child views or does not view a model. Results indicate that those who view a generous or helpful model are more generous or helpful than children who view no model, as are subjects who view a generous rather than a selfish model. Moreover, multiple models seem more effective than single or inconsistent models, and the more generous the model is, the more effect he or she seems to have. Some researchers have also found that children imitate rewarded models. Besides, some models, in particular those who control valued resources or are perceived as competent, are more imitated than others.

In real life, some evidence has been found that children model on parents' pro-social behaviors, but the data are scarce and correlational [Eisenberg and Fabes (1998)].

Psychologists have also examined the effects of non-disciplinary verbalizations. Statements of intentions appear to have less effect than does directly viewing the model, although they may foster generosity even a few months later. Except in certain situations, preaching and exhortations seem to have little effect, although preaching emphasizing the emotional consequences of the pro-social act seems more effective. Directives are generally effective and often last, but efficiency depends on the nature of the directive, and on the age of the child. Moreover, assigning responsibilities to a child appears to have a positive effect.

Concrete and social reinforcements have often been found to increase children's pro-social behavior at least immediately, although they may have a negative effect in the long run by undermining intrinsic motivations [Lepper (1983)]. Ten-year-old children generalize socially reinforced pro-social actions to new situations, whereas younger children do not [Grusec and Redler (1980)].

Other techniques of fostering pro-social behavior have also been investigated. Provision of internal attribution, for example by telling the children that they are helpful, has a positive effect compared to no provision and to attributing pro-social behavior to the fact that it was expected. Observations generally support the mediation of an enhanced pro-social self-image [Grusec and Redler (1980)]. Moreover, according to Staub (1992), quoted in Eisenberg and Fabes (1998); see also the same review for empirical references), children's participation in pro-social activities seems to enhance pro-social behavior in the long run (learning by doing), although boys sometimes show some reactance in the short run. For Staub (1971), teaching by assigning responsibility first focuses responsibility on the child externally; then the desire to help others in need may be internalized.

3.3. The role of other socializers

Other socializers have received little attention. Children, even 1- to 2-year old, exhibit pro-social behavior toward their siblings, although the findings related to the effect of rank of birth on pro-social behavior are inconsistent. Moreover, mother's behaviors are positively related to pro-social behavior between siblings, although mother's unavailability has also been found positively related to pro-social behavior of older children, specially daughters, toward their young siblings. This influence of peers is complex and may be interpreted in different ways. We will return later on this point.

Next, little is known about the effect of school program, in particular because of the low frequencies of pro-social behavior observed in the classroom and because pro-social behaviors are rarely reinforced or encouraged by teachers. Comparisons between children who attend school and children who don't are equivocal. However, Eisenberg and Fabes (1998) mention a few studies conducted in Israel showing that more pro-social behaviors are observed when there is age heterogeneity in the classroom and when cooperation and individualized learning are encouraged, as in certain kibbutzim.

Some evidence of the effects of the child-teacher relationships has also been found. Last, Eisenberg and Fabes (1998) indicate that some natural experiments, in particular programs to enhance pro-social values, behaviors and attitudes, appear to be partly effective. Staub (1981) also emphasizes the importance of learning by doing or by participation that could be enacted in school.

Last, television can be counted among other "socializers", or at least as displaying models [see, for example, Rushton (1981)]. Most studies have investigated effects of violence on aggressive behaviors, but some have also examined the effect of pro-social models on pro-social behavior. Hoffman (1988) argues that empirical evidence is equivocal and inconsistent, in particular because it takes longitudinal data to conclude on causality.

3.4. Cross-cultural differences

In relation with this family of hypotheses, it is worth investigating cultural factors influencing pro-social development. As asserted by Eisenberg and Fabes (1998), psychological research on this subject is relatively sparse, while societies seem to greatly vary in the degree to which pro-social and cooperative behaviors are normative. In fact, even sub-cultural variations may be important. For example, Eisenberg and Mussen (1989) indicate that, in the United States, children from traditional rural and semi-agricultural communities and from relatively traditional subcultures (Mexican American children) are more cooperative than children from urban and westernized cultures. Other studies by Kagan and Knight [see references in Eisenberg and Fabes (1998)], in which children are asked to share chips, confirm this pattern of results. However, no consistent evidence appears to exist on this subject. Several studies [quoted by Eisenberg and Fabes (1998)] show that Israeli kibbutz children and Israeli city children do not differ in sharing behavior at the age of 5, although fifth-grade Israeli kibbutz boys (but not the girls) share more than their city equivalents. Only few differences in moral reasoning values and beliefs about social responsibilities exist among industrial Western cultures, whereas differences between Western and non-Western cultures have been found [see Turiel (1998), and, for example, comparisons between Indians and Americans by Miller and Bersoff (1992), and Miller, Bersoff and Hartwood (1990)]. Differences may simply reflect differences in degree to which helpfulness and social responsibilities are emphasized [Eisenberg and Fabes (1998)].

3.5. Conclusion

Although learning and enforcement theories have received some empirical support, many psychologists argue that these factors cannot fully explain the acquisition and development of pro-social behavior. As asserted by Krebs and Van Hesteren (1994), "[t]here is relatively little disagreement among developmental psychologists that children construct their social worlds in terms of cognitive structures" (p. 107), and not only by copying "whatever the environment presents to them" [Flavell (1992, p. 998)].

4. Cognitive theories of moral and pro-social development

Jean Piaget was probably one of the first to acknowledge the importance of cognitive factors in the development of moral judgement and moral behavior. However, the most interesting feature of his work appears to be the assumption that children learn to behave pro-socially by interacting with their peers, and not because they have been taught to behave in this way. In his 1932 book [Piaget (1973)], *Le jugement moral chez l'enfant* (*The moral judgement of the child*, 1997), Piaget, before studying how children form moral judgements, showed how the rules of a game are used by the children, and how conscious of the rules they are. In this study, Piaget mainly observed boys playing a game of marbles, and asked them to explain him the rules of the game. Although not directly related to pro-social development, this preliminary step helps to understand how children develop and perceive rules and how they comply with them.

4.1. How children use the rules of a game and how conscious of these rules they are

Piaget distinguished four stages concerning how the rules are put into practice. The first one is purely individual and motor: the child manipulates the marbles according to his desires and motor habits. The egocentric stage appears between the age of 2 and the age of 5, when the child receives from the outside the example of codified rules. He imitates the models, but either plays alone or plays with other children without seeking to win or to standardize the different ways of playing. Around the age of 7 or 8, appears a form of cooperation. Every child tries to win, so that appears the need for mutual control and unification of the rules. Understanding of the rules remains vague and information about the rules given by the children is still different, if not conflicting. By the age of 11 or 12, the rules are fully codified, the games are fixed up in minute detail, and everybody knows the rules.

In the same fashion, Piaget distinguishes three stages in the understanding and respect of the rules. First, the rule is motor, thus not coercive. Then, it is considered as sacred and intangible. It is of adult origin, and unchangeable (from the point of view of the practice of the rules, this stage corresponds to the second half of the egocentric stage and to the first half of the cooperative stage). Lastly, the rules are seen as emanating from mutual agreement. Thus they are compulsory to the children themselves, but can be transformed provided that the modification wins general agreement. In the second stage, the coercive rule is obeyed out of the hierarchical respect that the children have for their parents. In the third stage, the rule is obeyed because of the mutual respect the children have for each other.

4.2. How children form moral judgements

Piaget next studied how children form moral judgements. Although not directly concerned by giving or redistribution, Piaget investigated moral dilemmas like theft, clumsiness, and untruthfulness. Unlike the study of the rules of the marbles game, in which

Piaget was able to observe the children playing the game and to question them on the rules, the analysis on the formation of moral judgements hinges only on discussions with the children, mainly on their reactions and judgements about told stories and situations presented by Piaget and his collaborators. This is an important limitation of his work, but judgements in moral dilemma are of interest even though one cannot be sure that children would act as they prescribe. In fact, Piaget noticed many times that verbal thought and conceptualization are generally behind action, that is children relate that they previously have acted as would prescribe children older than they are. As Piaget studied only children between 6 and 12 (sometimes 13), because younger children may encounter difficulties understanding the stories, no motor stage is observed. Piaget showed quite convincingly that one can observe two stages in moral development, corresponding to two worlds of constraint, and to two types of respect.[12]

According to Piaget, in the first stage of "moral realism", the child is under the adult constraint. The morality is essentially heteronomous. The moral rules are external to the child: the just is what conforms to the rules enacted by the adults. In particular, disobedience is always unfair. Among younger children, intentions are generally not taken into account. Rightness or wrongness of an act is judged only on the basis of the magnitude of its consequences, because any deviation from the rule results in punishment. At this stage, the children obey the rules because they respect their parents (more generally adults), so that this stage is characterized by unilateral respect[13] [see Turiel (1998) for empirical references contrasting the Piagetian view of children's understanding of authority relations, showing that children take into account the nature of act commanded, and the attributes (like social position) of persons giving orders].

In the second stage of "morality of reciprocity", the morality is fully autonomous. As explained by Piaget (1973, p. 157):[14] "The conclusion we will reach is that the feelings

---

[12] Eisenberg (1986) [see also Eisenberg and Mussen (1989)] distinguishes five levels in the development of thinking about pro-social moral questions. Some studies have found a positive relation between the level or the stage of moral reasoning and the tendency to behave pro-socially, among adults [see, for example, Underwood and Moore (1982)] and sometimes among children. Note that empirical evidence may be limited for children, perhaps because the range of moral stages is more limited among them, so that the relation is probably moderated by other factors, like sympathy [Miller et al. (1996)]. Moreover, the correlation appears to be greater when the moral dilemma concerns sharing or helping [see Eisenberg (1986), for a review] and when dilemma and pro-social behavior are similar in content [Levin and Bekerman-Greenberg (1980)]. Among preschoolers, the positive relation was clearer for spontaneous sharing behaviors than for helping or responding to a peer's request behavior. Among elementary or high school students, pro-social behavior involving high costs (donating money or time) has been found more frequently associated with moral reasoning than low-cost behavior (helping). According to Eisenberg and Shell (1986), the reason is that the latter is performed automatically (as discussed in Section 8.3) whereas the former might entail cognitive conflict (as discussed in Section 6.2). In addition, "types of reasoning that clearly reflect a self- versus other-orientation and are developmentally mature for the age-group are likely to predict pro-social responding" [Eisenberg and Fabes (1998, p. 732)].

[13] Piaget drew from Bovet [see Piaget], who proposed two necessary and sufficient conditions for the appearance of the consciousness of the duty: that an individual receives orders from another, and that the former respects the latter. This is in opposition with the Kantian position according to which respect for others follows from the fact that rules are regarded as compulsory.

[14] Our translation. The page numbers refer to the 1973 French edition.

of justice, although they can of course be strengthened by the precepts and the example of adults, are, for a large part, independent of these influences and only need mutual respect and solidarity between children to develop." Piaget distinguished in fact two types of justice: retributive justice, a notion inseparable from the notion of sanction, and distributive justice, which only implies the idea of equality. In the first stage, sanctions are considered by children as just and necessary and the more severe the more just. Among older children, although the first kind of opinion subsists among them and even among adults, Piaget noticed that sanctions are not a moral necessity. Only those which require a "restoration", making the guilty party conscious of the consequences of its act, or which are a reciprocal treatment, are fair.

Piaget argues that those distinctions have important consequences from an educational point of view. Blame and explanations are viewed as more efficient than sanctions. This allows discriminating between expiatory sanctions, which are related to the constraint which presses on the child and are arbitrary, and reciprocal sanctions which emphasize that the social ties have been broken. Piaget showed that younger children referred more frequently to expiatory sanctions, and older children to reciprocal sanctions. These two types of attitudes can be related to the two types of morality. As noticed by Piaget, the first one probably originates from instinctive reactions of the child (the compassion and vindictive tendencies observed among children) but it is first and foremost shaped by the adults. Afterwards, the transition to the second type is a particular case of the general evolution from the unilateral respect to the mutual respect. Hence, even if, at the beginning, the idea of reciprocity appears as a sort of tit-for-tat, the material element of punishment tends to disappear. Thus, as the children begin to interact, mutual respect develops between peers.

When obedience and equality conflict, Piaget showed that the youngest always say the adults are right, whereas the oldest defend equality, even if it is in opposition to obedience. In fact, the unilateral respect seems to raise obstacles to the free development of the feeling of equality even though the parents attempt to instill this feeling into their children, first because no equality is possible between parents and children, and second because equality among children cannot be dictated. Piaget gave an interesting answer to the question of why the democratic practice is so developed in the game of marbles, played by boys of 11 to 13, whereas it is so unfamiliar to adults. For him, an explanation is that these boys have no seniors to impose rules, as the game is generally dropped by the age of 14, whereas adults in many spheres of life are subject to the weight of previous generations. It is also interesting to note with Youniss (1980) that 6 to 14-year-old children define pro-social behaviors as giving, sharing, playing, when directed towards peers, but as being polite, obey, etc. when directed towards adults (parents).

Finally, Piaget distinguished three stages in the development of distributive justice, by differentiating between equality and equity. In the first stage, justice is not differentiated from authority. Then, egalitarianism develops (by the age of 7 or 8), conflicting with obedience. Last, from 11 or 12, children qualify equality and give precedence to equity[15] by taking each particular situation into account. For instance, oldest children agree to favor the youngest when they play together, in order to compensate for the differences in abilities.[16] These three stages in moral development are not clear-cut, though, and the two moral worlds of constraint and cooperation coexist in childhood and persist in adulthood due to the weight of previous generations. In particular, Piaget observes that the different types of morality coexist at a given age, but that the proportion of children who refer to a given type differs across ages. Nevertheless, there is a gradual shift from one to the other, and attitudes of parents and their relationships with their children may favor or delay the development of cooperation and of reciprocal morality.

To summarize, even though adult influence is obviously huge, authority cannot be the source of justice because the development of justice assumes autonomy. Justice can only develop as both cooperation and mutual respect increase, first among children then between children and adults. For Piaget, distributive justice is equivalent to the notions of equality and equity. The notion of distributive justice certainly has individual or biological roots, but according to Piaget, from an epistemological point of view, such concepts can only be *a priori*, in the sense that they are norms "towards which the reason cannot not tend, as it refines" (p. 253). Equity and reciprocity norms are thus an ideal equilibrium. There must exist a collective rule, *sui generis* product of the common life: "The consciousness of a necessary equilibrium that compels and limits both the *alter* and the *ego* must arise out of the actions and reactions of the individuals on others" (p. 254). As stated by Piaget and emphasized by Carpendale (2000), the central element for the development of morality is not the weight of society, as in a Durkheimian perspective, but the existence of social interactions. Hence morality is a social concept, but only insofar justice and reciprocity always concern at least two interacting subjects. For Piaget, Durkheim's error is that "there is no more society as a being than there are isolated individuals. There are only relationships [...]" (p. 290).

---

[15] Some parallels with the psychoanalytic approach can be drawn. According to Freud's theory [see, for example, Freud (1968 [1923])], a newborn is driven by the demands of the id, which require immediate gratification. The dictatorship of the id partly corresponds to the Piagetian egoistic stage. Next forms the ego, which appears with the understanding that immediate gratification is generally impossible, and which acts as a form of repression or a control of the urge. The fear of punishment, in particular by the parents, is a mean used by the ego to repress the urge. Ego can be related to moral realism. By the age of 4 to 6, appears the superego, when the child begins to internalize these external sources of punishment. The superego uses guilt to enforce these internalized rules that may become values. Pro-social behavior may be the consequence of the superego's action. It is worth noting that, for Piaget, the rules are not internalized, but are continuously constructed by the group.

[16] When analyzing distributive justice and equity, Piaget always refers to equity according to needs. According to twelve or thirteen-year old children, equality should be tempered, but only to correct initial inequalities. In particular, they never mention that differences in abilities should be rewarded. It should be noticed that equity is not absent in the world of retributive justice, but it differs from the notion of equity associated to distributive justice. In the domain of retributive justice, equity consists in taking extenuating circumstances into account.

For an economist, the Piagetian theory of pro-social development has interesting consequences. First, pro-social attitudes are not innate, and thus do not seem to be part of individual preferences, at least if preferences are viewed as given. Second, they are not shaped by parents. Third, they ultimately develop while children interact with peers, and follow from mutual respect. Parental authority can only enhance the conditions of the development of pro-social behaviors. Last, it requires that people are able to understand each other, so that cognitive development is a prerequisite to it.

4.3. Other theories of stages

After Piaget, numerous developmental psychologists have proposed theories of stages.[17] The most famous follower of Piaget is Kohlberg [Kohlberg (1984), Colby and Kohlberg (1987); see Campbell and Christopher (1996) for a presentation], who, as noticed by Carpendale (2000), "followed Piaget in rejecting an explanation of moral development as a simple transmission of moral rules from parents to children as incomplete because this view cannot account for how such moral norms arise in first place, and it simply equates morality with conformity to moral rules." Kohlberg distinguished six stages of moral development extending and refining Piagetian stages. At the preconventional level (Stage 1 and Stage 2), subjects do not explicitly understand moral rules and social conventions. At Stage 1, actors base moral judgements on the material consequences of actions for them, and they consider that they behave good when they submit to authority and when they have avoided punishment; at Stage 2, moral judgements are based on what instrumentally satisfies the subject's needs. The conventional level (Stages 3 and 4) is the level of conformity, in which people only strive to conform to the rules of the group, first in order to please others (Stage 3), then in order to maintain the social order (Stage 4). At the post-conventional level, morality is distinguished from social convention. The Stage 5 has clearly a social-contract orientation. Moral rules are necessary to the good functioning of the society, and result from general agreement. At this stage, morality is subjective, and relative. The Stage 6 is characterized by universal ethical principles (justice, equal rights and respect for individual dignity), that concern everyone and thus are not revisable. These principles are those which any perfectly rational agent would choose.

In Kohlberg's views, individuals are supposed to progress orderly through these stages (although Stage 6 is very rare[18]) and this sequence cannot be changed by cultural factors (only speeded up, slowed down or stopped). The six Kohlbergian stages constitute qualitatively different modes of thinking, form structured wholes (a Piagetian concept), develop in an invariant sequence, and integrate previous stage structures in a hierarchical manner ["hard" stages in the words of Krebs and Van Hesteren (1994)]. It

---

[17] See, for example, Krebs and Van Hesteren (1994) who propose a table comparing the stages elaborated by several developmental theorists (Table 1, pp. 114–115). They show that in spite of differences, there is a important degree of correspondence between the stages proposed by these theorists.

[18] This stage is thus generally left out in empirical studies.

follows from these properties that all the moral behaviors of a subject have to be consistent. However, as emphasized by Carpendale, there is much evidence of inconsistency. People do not always use the stage of moral development which they are supposed to have reached [Denton and Krebs (1990)], although the degree of consistency appears to increase with the age of children [see references in Eisenberg and Fabes (1998)]. Children may develop differently[19] in each of the domains (friendship, justice and fairness, obedience and authority, social rules and conventions) and use different concepts to judge or to act [Damon (1977)]. In particular, according to Damon, differential social knowledge in the different domains may enter in conflict.[20]

Developmental psychologists do not unanimously accept the existence of stages, especially of "hard" stages. The evidence points to a softer definition of stages [see Eisenberg and Fabes (1998)]. According to "softer" models (for example, Damon (1977), Eisenberg (1986) or Krebs and Van Hesteren (1994)], development is characterized by the acquisition of increasingly complex forms of thought but stages are defined in terms of the content of thought, affective orientations and behavioral styles. In particular, old stage structures may be retained and invoked [Levine (1979)] after new ones are acquired, so that less consistency in pro-social behavior is expected. How children progress from one stage to another has nevertheless not received much consideration [see, however, Walker, Gustafson and Hennig (2001)]. Empirically, age differences in pro-social behavior appear to be complex and sometimes inconsistent. However, according to a meta-analysis involving 155 studies conducted by Eisenberg and Fabes and presented in their 1998 survey, age is positively related to the likelihood that pro-social behavior occurs. For example, Harbaugh, Krause and Linday (2002) show that bargaining behavior in ultimatum and dictator games clearly changes with age among children between 7 and 18: the older the children, the more generous their proposals. They also found that very young proposers (second graders) earn more in ultimatum games than other age groups; but they also make the smallest offers in dictator games.[21]

---

[19] As recognized by Damon (1977), it raises the problem of the comparison between the advancement in the different domains.

[20] As Damon (1977), Turiel (1983) has argued that moral and pro-social thinking may apply differently in different domains. Turiel (1983) [see Hoffman (1988)] distinguishes between moral and conventional thinking, which are viewed as distinct domains. Moral rules aim to regulate behavior which affects others' rights or well-being whereas conventional rules are used to promote behavioral uniformities that coordinate interactions within a social group. It follows that conventions are context-dependent [Turiel (1998)]. Turiel (1998) reviews studies conducted by several psychologists (in particular, Turiel and Nucci) that support the hypothesis that moral issues are judged by children and adolescents as obligatory, not contingent on authority dictates, rules, consensus or accepted practices within a group. Moreover, judgements about moral issues appear structured by concepts, welfare and rights. On the contrary, certain social judgements are justified based on understandings of social organization, are linked to existing social arrangements, and are contingent on rules. This distinction clearly indicates, according to Turiel, that social judgements are not simply based on acceptance of societal values. Domain theory however lacks of developmental components [Glassman and Zan (1995)].

[21] This result is interpreted by the authors as an indication that the behavioral differences result from differences in preferences for fairness and not in abilities to play strategically.

As argued above, children do not develop autonomous morality as soon as they are exposed to other children. They must first develop cognitive and emotional skills that allow them to understand the needs and the position of others.

4.4. Cognitive correlates of pro-social development

Like Piaget, several theorists have hypothesized that cognitive skills like perspective-taking and moral reasoning foster pro-social behavior [Batson (1991), Eisenberg (1986), Hoffman (1982), Staub (1979)]. Among cognitive skills, some are personal (intelligence), whereas the others concern the relations between individuals.

Probably the most important cognitive skills for the development of pro-social behaviour are perspective-taking skills. The latter are often related with identifying, understanding, and sympathizing with others' distress or need skills, in particular with the capacity to differentiate between own and others' distress and thus to enhance empathy and sympathy. Individuals may acquire information about others' internal states by imagining themselves in another's position. They may also use other processes [see Karniol and Shomroni (1999), for a presentation], like developing a theory of others' psychology and using heuristics such as mental associations to "channel the memory search required for making predictions about other people's thought and feelings in any given context" (p. 148).

Three types of perspective-taking skills have been distinguished [see Underwood and Moore (1982)]: perceptual (the ability to take another's perspective visually); affective (the ability to understand another's emotional state); and cognitive or conceptual (the ability to understand another's cognition). Most empirical studies have reported a positive relation between these three types of perspective-taking and pro-social behavior, although some have found no significant relation. Only a few studies have found a negative relation [for reviews of empirical work on this topic, see Underwood and Moore (1982), Eisenberg and Fabes (1998), Eisenberg, Zhou and Koller (2001)]. Besides, despite Piaget's assertion that children do not acquire the role-taking skills necessary to behave pro-socially because of insufficient cognitive abilities, some studies have shown that even very young children are able of taking roles [Hoffman (1975a), for example].

Higgins (1981) argues that the ability to take an other's point of view into consideration when making judgements and decisions becomes more sophisticated with age, in particular as judgements become more abstract [Miller, Kessel and Flavell (1970)]. Role-taking is a process by which one determines certain attributes of others, but it also involves, according to Higgins, "going beyond the information given" (p. 120), and is thus inference rather than just categorization. Last, as noticed by Eisenberg and Fabes (1998), the use of perspective-taking skills may depend on the context. Moreover, the effect of those skills may be moderated by lack of either relevant social skills or emotional motivation.

Other cognitive skills have sometimes been related to pro-social attitudes, although generally not consistently. Such is the case of intelligence [Bar-Tal, Korenfeld and Raviv (1985)], the level of expressed motives [see however Eisenberg (1986)], sociability or extrovert tendencies [Eisenberg et al. (1996)], social competencies that are nevertheless often correlated to sympathy [Eisenberg and Fabes (1995)] and empathy [Adams (1983)], Eisenberg and Miller (1987), popularity [Hampson (1984)], or self-esteem. However, Eisenberg and Fabes (1998, p. 736) remark that "[g]iven the correlational nature of associations between personality variables and pro-social behavior, causal relations are difficult to prove".

Last, there has been a great debate about gender differences. In particular, Gilligan (1982) distinguished justice (not to treat others unfairly) and care (not to turn away from persons in need), and has argued that, because most of the theory of morality has been formulated by males, the morality of care, supposed to be mainly present among females, has not received enough attention [see Turiel (1998), for a discussion]. Empirical findings are however ambiguous and gender differences in pro-social behavior appear to differ greatly with the situation [see Eagly and Crowley (1986), for a meta-analysis involving older adolescents and adults; and once again the meta-analysis by Fabes and Eisenberg summarized in Eisenberg and Fabes (1998) for children; see also Eisenberg, Zhou and Koller (2001), for recent results and references]. In particular, differences are greater with self-reported and other-reported than with observational measures, in in-the-fields than experimental studies (this effect disappears when controlling for other characteristics of the study),[22] and when the target was an adult or was unspecified than when it was another child.

5. Social cognition

5.1. Perspective-taking, identification with, and projection of self onto others

In this section, we propose a simple theoretical apparatus for describing how people make inferences about others and construct their own social preferences in interpersonal contexts. Social cognition is made possible by the development of the *perspective-taking ability* during childhood, reviewed in Section 4.4. The formation of the perspective-taking ability is probably distinctive of human sociality because it requires sophisticated cognitive abilities and an extended period of development (childhood). Ants and bees, which have a detailed division of labor, have a social life; but they don't have a social mind.

In an attempt to simplify the processes described in a vast social psychological literature for the purpose of economic modeling, we retain essentially three mechanisms that will serve as building blocks for all subsequent analysis: *identification of self with an other, projection of self onto an other, and categorization of others as either similar*

---

[22] Harbaugh, Krause and Linday (2002) found significant differences between boys and girls, but only in dictator game. However, those differences disappear after controlling for height.

or dissimilar to self. These mechanisms rely on the development of the perspective–taking ability. Further elaboration of the third mechanism, i.e. categorization of others into similar and dissimilar others, can be found in Section 7.1.

We first give a short definition of the terms being introduced. We refer to "perspective-taking" as the ability to exchange roles with one another in mental life. Perspective-taking is the basic tool that an individual possesses for making social inferences about others and constructing his own social preferences. Identification and projection are two distinct ways, which we think are the most common, of adopting an other's perspective in specific contexts. They are opposite and extreme processes for making social inferences, since identification can be said to make the maximal use and projection the minimal use of one's perspective-taking ability. Self "identifies" with an other by mentally reincarnating in Other, while Self "projects" herself onto an other by merely imagining what she herself would have done if she played the role of Other.[23] Whenever individuals differ in more than one characteristic, like skills and preferences for example, a combination of these two processes is conceivable along different dimensions.

In what follows, we describe a rational perspective-taking person as viewing all her potential roles or identities as states of the world and ascribing subjective probabilities to each. If she knew nothing about her own future role or identity, she would ascribe equal probabilities to all states. We retain here the latter assumption, not only for convenience, but because it is actually justified by a variety of reasons like the impartiality of judgements, the similarity of group members, and the anonymity of relations in large markets as in experimental conditions. Social judgements of this kind will be reviewed by comparing the division of a given cake of size c between n members of a group both in the "identification" and in the "self-projection" treatment.

In the identification treatment, individual k must behave like an impartial judge à la Harsanyi (1955) who knows the initial distribution of wealth $(w_1, \ldots, w_n)$ and all the individual preferences. If the judge is asked to share a cake between all members of the group, he determines his preferred allocation $(x_1, \ldots, x_n)$ so as to maximize his expected utility

$$W_k = \frac{1}{n} \sum_{i=1}^{n} U_{ki}(w_i + x_i), \tag{5.1}$$

$$\text{s.t.} \quad 0 \leqslant x_1, \ldots, x_n \leqslant c \text{ and } \sum_{i=1}^{n} x_i = c \tag{5.2}$$

with: $U'_{ki} > 0$, $U''_{ki} < 0$ for all i. U_{ki} is the Von Neumann–Morgenstern utility function of k defined over the indirect utility of final wealth that k attributes to i.

---

[23] In our terminology, the self projects her known preferences onto others to determine her own behavior in social contexts. Another meaning of the word in psychology refers to the self projecting her known behavior to guess others' behavior. The problem with the latter concept is that it cannot be used to determine the behavior of self in social contexts.

In the self-projection treatment, individual k must behave as an impartial judge too, but one who, by lack of knowledge of others, evaluates the situation of others by his own standards. When asked to share a cake between all members of a group, this person fails to perceive that the initial wealth and preferences of others will generally be different from his own and merely chooses the allocation that maximizes, subject to the constraints (5.2), his expected utility

$$V_k = \frac{1}{n} \sum_{i=1}^{n} U_k(w_k + x_i) \tag{5.3}$$

as if he were to play himself anyone of the potential roles.

We see the impartial judge's utility functions (5.1) and (5.3) as tractable ways of describing an individual's social preference[24] arising out of either his or her identification with, or self-projection onto, a group. The constrained maximization of (5.1) reduces to the Maximin criterion [advocated by Rawls (1971) in a non-utilitarian framework] when the judge (who runs the risk of reincarnating in the worst identity) has infinite risk aversion. Intermediate forms lying between (5.1) and (5.3) may be relevant for describing the social preferences of an impartial judge who can partially identify with others, say because he merely knows the wealth of others (for an application, see Section 6.4).

These two mechanisms of social inference have two desirable properties. First, they respect Pareto-dominance insofar all participants share the same definition of goods. This is consistent with the fact that a judge's role is ideally to neutralize the inefficiencies caused by the strategic behavior of parties and reach the allocation which could have been reached by themselves had they accepted to use all the possible means of cooperation and exchange [Habermas (1979) comes close to this definition]. Second, they can both generate judgements that do not depend on whether one belongs, or does not belong, to the group. For example, an impartial judge will share a cake alike whether he will eventually eat one of the shares or not.

5.2. *Identification with a known other and self-projection onto unknown others*

Identification and projection have different informational requirements. Identification requires good knowledge of Other while self-projection requires good knowledge of Self. As most people know themselves better than others, self-projection will be more common than identification in social interactions. However, identification should be more frequent with natural groups than experimental groups in which anonymous relations prevail. This is corroborated by a study of Jetten, Spears and Manstead (1996) which compares the same measure of identification for experimental groups (students

---

[24] Although social choice theory seeks to derive society's preference from individual preferences, the derivation of society's preference is beyond the scope of the present paper. Kolm (2001) offers a recent detailed discussion of how individual preferences over distributions may converge towards a unique society-preferred distribution.

from the University of Amsterdam playing anonymously) and natural groups (students from the University of Amsterdam who believed that they were playing anonymously with students from its rival university in Amsterdam, the Free University). A test on the group identification data showed that the degree of identification was significantly higher in the context of natural social groups. Even though the scope for identification seems to be limited in social interactions, it is of the utmost importance in specific circumstances. A young child may identify with a parent along several observable dimensions if he has more limited knowledge of himself than of his parent. A parent may know her child well enough to identify with him even beyond the natural boundaries of her own lifetime [see Becker and Barro (1988)]. The ease of identification of self with an other under complete information reflects the economic definition of pure altruism.

In many situations, though, the informational requirements of identification are too stringent to be met. This point was vividly raised by Adam Smith (1982, pp. 9, 19) who derived one's "sympathy" for others from the faculty of projecting oneself onto the situation of another:

> "As we have no immediate experience of what other men feel, we can form no idea of the manner in which they are affected, but by conceiving what we ourselves should feel in the like situation. [...] Every faculty in one man is the measure by which he judges of the like faculty in another. I judge of your sight by my sight, of your ear by my ear, of your reason by my reason, of your resentment by my resentment, of your love by my love. I neither have, nor can have, any other way of judging about them."

A closely related question raised by the theory of social cognition concerns the mechanisms that are used by self to predict the behavior of others when these are not well known. The same question may be raised about Rabin's (1993) model in which players react to the "kindness" of the intentions of the other player toward themselves. On the basis of what information can the self guess an other's intentions? In the experimental conditions of anonymous relations, numerous psychological studies have shown that individuals rely on self-information and are biased in viewing their own position as normative.

A preponderance of the research on the role of self-knowledge in social prediction has investigated the "false consensus effect" [for reviews, see Mullen et al. (1985), Marks and Miller (1987)], first revealed by the studies of Ross, Greene and House (1977). The false consensus effect refers to the tendency of people to overestimate consensus for their own position, whether the estimated variable concerns an attitude, trait, behavior, or performance. People wrongly anticipate that other people think or behave like themselves in the same role. In a careful study, Alicke and Largo (1995) manipulated the own position variable (thus removing its endogeneity) and were able to assess the direction of the causality unambiguously. Many examples of egocentric biases have been found. For instance, Frankenberger (2000) argues that, when adolescents and young adults start recognizing that other people think thoughts of their own, they anticipate that those thoughts will center on them, which results in adolescent egocentrism. Lind,

Kray and Thompson (1998) noted that people place greater weight on their own experiences of injustice than on the injustice of others when formulating fairness judgements. Van Boven, Dunning and Loewenstein (2000) observed that own perceptions of the endowment effect (i.e., the propensity to over-value an object that one owns and undervalue an object that one doesn't own) contaminate estimates of others' perceptions, even when individuals know or suspect that others' perceptions are systematically different from their own. However, the egocentric biases which affect the prediction of similar others' behavior tend to level-off on average. Charness and Grosskopf (2001, Table 1), asking subjects playing one role to indicate what they would have chosen in another's role, obtained a remarkable similarity of the average hypothetical choices with what another group of subjects actually chose in this role. The same was true when participants in one role were simply asked to estimate the other players' choices. Offerman (2002, p. 1433) made exactly the same observation.[25] Self-projection onto others thus appears to be a statistically unbiased mechanism for predicting the independent behavior of others when the Self lacks knowledge of others.

Alicke and Largo (1995) also demonstrated that people do not ignore case information about another person's position either but do not uniformly over-generalize from the latter information. The score of another individual is particularly valuable when a person has little or no information upon which to base a judgement. People who have similar preferences and values can serve as surrogates when judgements are required about objects or events that we have not experienced. People may also rely more on the opinion of others in estimating consensus when they know that their own opinion is idiosyncratic, or when other people clearly have more expertise in a judgement domain. On the whole, the results which have been obtained on the false consensus effect convey the impression that people use available information consistently while often treating self-information as being more precise than the same information supplied by an other. People rely on the position of others when they think that these detain relatively valuable information. Otherwise, as will often be the case in experimental conditions, people make inferences about others' positions by projecting their own.

The unrestricted use of self-projection would lead to large egocentric biases and costly errors. The purpose of *categorization* is to restrict the use of self-projection as far as possible to those cases for which it yields the more precise inferences. Whenever people lack knowledge of others, they first categorize others with respect to their similarity with self, then they rely on self-information to anticipate similar others' behavior [Dunning and Hayes (1996), Cadinu and Rothbart (1996), Gramzow, Gaertner and Sedikides (2001)]. But they feel unable to project onto the group of dissimilar others. The most natural assumption in the latter case is that they will refrain from making inferences for this category and, as far as possible, take the behavior of dissimilar others

---

[25] The average prediction of second players' behavior by first movers was no longer accurate when first movers predicted how the second players would react to their own intentional move [Offerman (2002, pp. 1433–1434)]. Then first movers underestimated the probability of a reciprocal response, perhaps because they failed to predict the emotional component of the latter (discussed in Sections 8.2 and 8.3).

as given. Categorization and the treatment of dissimilar others will be further examined in Section 7. In Section 6, we focus on self-projection onto similar others.

According to the social cognition story, the concern for others may grow out of three factors: the perspective-taking ability, knowledge of self and/or others, and the perceived similarity of others with self. In this view, an "egoist" is an individual who either lacks a perspective-taking ability or who systematically perceives others as being dissimilar to self. Since the ability to take others' perspective normally develops during childhood (as discussed in Sections 4.4 and 5.3), a young child would be a natural egoist who would not share goods with his playing partners [see Harbaugh, Krause and Linday (2002)]. Adults who were led to believe, through their own experience, education or culture, that most others are not like themselves would form a very different kind of egoists, and one which fits nicely with the current conception of an egoist. The extensive evidence that people have heterogeneous social preferences, some being egoists and many others fair-minded or altruists, is thus wholly consistent with the principles of social cognition mentioned here.

5.3. Social cognition and the stages of pro-social development

In the end of this section, we give two illustrations of the general applicability of the foregoing analysis of social cognition for the development and construction of social preferences. As a first illustration, we use these processes to recover, quite simply, the stages of pro-social development observed by Piaget and Kohlberg (described in Sections 4.1 to 4.3). For making the analysis more concrete, we examine here the four stages of empathic distress considered by Hoffman e.g. (1981) in the face of an other in need. We show that these four stages may simply result from the combined development of perspective-taking skills and empathic concern. Empathy is an affect (see Section 8.3), but it has a cognitive component since one has to use knowledge about others and thus be conscious of the self-other distinction.

Table 3 summarizes the argument along two dimensions, with the three rows describing the development of consciousness of an other by the self and the two columns representing the development of perspective-taking skills. These two dimensions are not independent as pointed out by the two incompatibilities listed in Table 3, which leaves us with four possibilities. The arrow underlines four successive stages of development for empathic distress. Research has shown that even very young children respond to the cry of distress of other babies [Simner (1971)]. During the first year of life, children cannot distinguish the distress of another person from the unpleasant feeling aroused in the self. They experience global empathic distress response ("global empathy"). Then and until 2 or 3 years of age, they are able to differentiate self from others but they still lack the perspective-taking skills to discern the internal states of others ("egocentric empathy"). As they develop perspective-taking abilities, children become increasingly aware that others' feelings may differ from their own. Inevitably, they must realize that they have better knowledge of themselves than they have of others. Thus, in the third stage, they are unable to identify with others and must use the self-projection mechanism to make

Table 3
The development of perspective-taking skills, empathic concern and the four stages of empathic distress

Information of Self about Other:	Perspective-taking skills: No	Perspective-taking skills: Yes
Low Consciousness of Other	Global empathy (babies)	
Consciousness, but little knowledge, of Other	Egocentric empathy (2–3 year old) ⟶	Sympathy
Deep knowledge of Other		Empathy-altruism

sense of others' feelings and behavior. At this stage of their development, they sympathize but do not yet empathize with others. As they acquire enough knowledge of others through the experiences of childhood and adolescence, they will eventually be able to identify with some others[26] and empathize with them. The development of empathy is likely to be gradual and extend to an increasingly wider range of emotions and people.

5.4. Choosing and valuing an income distribution

A second illustration of the self-projection mechanism is offered by the way people choose and value an income distribution and thus resolve the equity-efficiency issue. This problem has been studied by the psychological literature on behavioral justice. Several orientations have been proposed. One is that people acquire stable preferences for equity and efficiency, very much like a conventional economist would state the problem. Rohrbaugh, McClelland and Quinn (1986) have defended this approach and thus sought to measure how much negotiators on a labor-management contract valued both total utility and equity. Total utility was measured by the sum of individual utilities accruing to both parties, while the inequity of a specific contract was defined by the absolute difference between the two individual utilities. In general, utility was shown to be over twice as important as equity in participants' determination of acceptable contract settlements. Yet, equity was treated as such an important value to the participants that Pareto optimality was routinely violated. Fehr and Schmidt (1999) and Bolton and

---

[26] Stinson and Ickes (1992) have shown experimentally that male friends were more able than male strangers to accurately read their partner's thoughts and feelings about imagined events in another place or time.

Ockenfels (2000) have shown that the mere addition to own utility of a concern for equity was sufficient to predict much (though not all) cooperative and reciprocal behavior within an otherwise conventional game-theoretic framework.

Experimental research on behavioral justice leads to the extended assumption that people compromise between these two goals in a *context-dependent* fashion. Mellers (1982) found that subjects used a context-dependent merit rule to set "fair" salaries,[27] but salary levels were constrained by a floor paralleling the stated poverty line. Mellers (1982) found that experimental groups allocated rewards according to a rule that maximizes average income after allowing that no group member fall below a certain income level. To compare these trade-off approaches, Mitchell et al. (1993) had subjects judge the relative fairness of income distribution in hypothetical societies with varying efficiency and equality. Using a hypothetical society paradigm,[28] they manipulated the mean income (representing efficiency) and income variability (representing equality) of distributions of income and the correlation between income and effort within a society. Subjects made all pairwise comparisons of distributions within societies of differing meritocracy. Rawls's (1971) maximin principle of justice received considerable support whenever subjects believed effort and reward were only loosely related. People maximized minimum income within a society. However, a compromise principle best described preferences when income was tightly linked to effort. People then rejected distributions in which some citizens fell below the "poverty line" but maximized efficiency above this constraint.

Differences in the results obtained by various studies are related to the procedures used for eliciting preferences over distributions of income. When people must decide on the highest-valued allocation of income given the contextual distribution of merits [as in Mellers (1982, 1986)], they focus on efficiency and merely soften their evaluation by consideration of the minimum income. By contrast, when they must compare given

---

[27] In Mellers (1986), people choose "fair" allocations of salaries and taxes among hypothetical faculty members on the basis of their merit ratings. They do not follow the rule of proportionality of salaries to merits or contributions [equity theory of Adams (1965), relative ratio model of Anderson (1976)]. A better fit is obtained by asserting that subjects assign salaries in such a way that the relative standing of a person's salary in the distribution of salaries matches the relative position of his or her merit in the distribution of merits (relative equity theory). The relative position of a person's merit in the distribution of merits is assumed to be given by Parducci's (1965) range-frequency compromise. It is a weighted average of the person's subjective value of merit (a cardinal measure taking values of zero for the minimal value and one for the maximal value) and the person's rank in the distribution of merits. Therefore, the relative position of a person's merit is steeply increasing in merit for values where the distribution of merits is highly concentrated. The adjusted function for the subjective value of merit was a cubic function of merit. It was found that the weight of the rank, which measures the sensitivity to the form of the frequency distribution of contextual values of merit, is fairly constant across distributions of merits and budgets. For the salary allocations, the estimated value of the weight is 0.44. In the salary allocation tasks, the minimum living allowance for the lowest merit person ranges from 54% to 69% of the average salary in each condition.

[28] Participants are told that "econometric studies" can accurately determine which effect various policies, emphasizing either efficiency – i.e. the overall standard of living – or equality – i.e. the difference in average income between classes –, would have on the income distribution.

income distributions which unambiguously differ on efficiency and equity grounds and the correlation between income and merit is not salient, many subjects focus on equity and give more emphasis to the lower end of the distribution. As a matter of fact, preference reversals on income distributions parallel those that have been extensively observed on lotteries [e.g., Lichtenstein and Slovic (1971)]. People often choose the lottery yielding a small gain with high probability but set a higher selling price for another lottery of similar expected value which yields a smaller probability of a higher gain. Similarly, in making judgements of distributive justice, people often give a high value to efficiency while they prefer the less efficient but more equal and just society when asked to compare between hypothetical societies. The reference-dependence of inequality aversion has been nicely shown in recent papers of Dolan and Robinson (2001) and Camacho-Cuena, Seidl and Morone (2005).

Therefore preferences on income distribution revealed by opinions of distributive justice support the view that people represent themselves (or a hypothetical self) as being randomly assigned a position in the distribution of income.[29] They take all the different perspectives and project themselves onto each position. In judgements involving lotteries, the lower ranks are often over-weighted in the comparison framing, and the higher ranks are over-weighted in the valuation framing. In judgements about societies alike, the lower ranks – and therefore equity – are over-weighted in hypothetical choices, and the higher ranks – and therefore efficiency – are over-weighted in valuations. Risk-averse people do not wish to imagine themselves at risk of being in the lower ranks of a society who treats the poor badly, but they demand a high price in order to forego the upside risk of being in the upper ranks of a society who treats the deserving nicely.

6. Social norms and reciprocity

6.1. The fairness heuristic

Fairness judgements are essentially needed when one moves into a relationship with other people or with an organization. Fair treatment leads to a shift from responding to social dilemmas in terms of immediate self-interest, which might be termed the "individual mode", to responding cooperatively, which might be termed the "group mode" [Lind (2001)].

Fairness heuristic theory emphasizes the cognitive function of fairness. Fairness gives people prior information as to the extent to which they can trust others not to exploit or exclude them from important relationships and groups. People pay more attention to fairness when such information gets more valuable, that is when they are uncertain

---

[29] This is not to say that people actually maximize a normative expected utility like (5.3), as such behavior would be inconsistent with preference reversals between bids and choices. Our inference is based on the striking similarity of behavioral anomalies concerning judgements over lotteries and over distributions of income.

about things such as the outcome of others [Van den Bos, Vermunt and Wilke (1997)] or an authority's trustworthiness [Van den Bos, Wilke and Lind (1998)].

Fairness heuristic theory was initially concerned, not with the fairness of outcomes but with the fairness of procedures [Folger (1977)]. Lind and Tyler (1988) noted that information about procedures often affects people's fairness judgements more strongly than information about outcomes. For instance, in Tyler and Lind (1992), people want to have information about whether they can trust the authority. When this information is not available, people of bounded rationality will resolve the uncertainty by relying on impressions of fairness and will react more positively toward the outcomes of the authority's decisions if the authority is using fair as opposed to unfair procedures.

To be functional as heuristic, judgements of justice should be used more than they are revised. Once people have established fairness judgements, perceived fairness will serve as a heuristic for interpreting subsequent events. Therefore, fairness heuristic theory suggests that fairness judgements are more strongly influenced by information that is available in an earlier stage of interaction with the authority than by information that becomes available at a later moment in time. Second, in many situations, information about the procedure is available before information about the outcome. For example, the manner in which a court trial is conducted is usually known before the verdict becomes apparent. Thus people form their fairness judgements on the basis of the fairness of the procedure and the perceived procedural fairness positively affects how people later react to their outcome. This "fair process effect" [Folger et al. (1979)] is one of the most replicated findings in social psychology. The fair process effect has been found consistently both in experiments [e.g., Folger et al. (1979), Lind, Kanfer and Earley (1990)] and in survey studies. The Lind, Kanfer and Earley (1990) experiment, for instance, manipulated whether participants were or were not allowed an opportunity to voice their opinion about the number of tasks they were assigned. A fair process effect was found. Those who were allowed to voice their opinions not only judged the procedure as more fair, but also judged their outcome (the tasks assigned to them) as more fair than participants who were not allowed to voice their opinions.

Fairness heuristic theory views fairness judgements as being formed under uncertainty in an early stage of the cognitive process and strongly conditioning behavior. This general argument is not restricted to procedural fairness. Van den Bos, Vermunt and Wilke (1997) tested the prediction that early information sets the stage for the interpretation of the later fairness information. By making outcome information available before or after process information, they found indeed a primacy effect: the first information, whether procedural or distributive, affected people's fairness judgements more strongly than the later one. Lind, Kray and Thompson (2001) conducted a further experiment to show that the primacy effect holds as well with a single type of fairness information. Participants working on a series of three tasks experienced delays caused by equipment failure and always had the possibility of explaining problems to a supervisor. The supervisor refused to consider explanations in one of the three work trials but did consider explanations on the other two trials, and the timing of voice denial was manipulated. Even though all of the participants received the same number of positive and negative fairness experiences, those who encountered the unfair experience early in their relationships with their supervisor viewed the supervisor as much more unfair as did those who encountered the unfair experience later. Roch et al. (2000) further demonstrate the cognitive function of fairness by showing, in a resource-sharing task, that thoughts of anchoring on equality preceded thoughts regarding adjusting from this anchor. They also manipulate high cognitive load[30] and show that the two-stage reasoning only applies to individuals with sufficient cognitive resources. Those subjects with high cognitive load stopped once they applied the equality heuristic, presumably because they were prevented to perceive the self-serving arguments that they would have normally perceived in the second stage.

Even though the fairness heuristic strongly conditions later behavior in social dilemmas, all players don't play fair and systematic deviations are observed. These are important facts which require theoretical efforts in the future. Roch et al. (2000) propose a two-stage model in which individuals first anchor on the equality heuristic and then adjust their requests in a self-serving manner from the amount prescribed by the equality heuristic. Güth (1995) suggested a two-stage process for describing the reasoning of two players involved in an ultimatum game but did not elaborate a formal model. Lévy-Garboua and Rapoport (2006) propose a model of rational behavior under dynamic uncertainty which predicts the formation of fairness norms and allows for individual self-serving deviations from the norm in the second stage.

6.2. Social norms of fairness in proposal-response games

Psychological work on social dilemmas [Dawes (1980), Messick and Brewer (1983), Komorita and Parks (1995)] often attributes to norms the tendency of people to cooperate Kerr (1995). Social norms can be defined as *enforceable tacit coordination rules*. Social norms of fairness are effective in many contexts of interpersonal relations [e.g., Allison and Messick (1990), Allison et al. (1992), Samuelson and Allison (1994), Van Dijke and Wilke (1995)]. As the simplest and most pervasive instance of fairness heuristic is certainly the equality heuristic, we consider here for illustration the social norm of sharing a given cake equally among all members of a party sitting around the table. The purpose of this section is to suggest that the fairness heuristic may be interpreted as a social norm and, further, to relate the emergence of this social norm with the self-projection mechanism spelled out in Section 5.

First of all, the fair division rule cannot arise from players' identification with the group, that is some form of altruism. The maximization of (5.1) under the constraints (5.2) usually entails very unequal sharing. Thus it is unable to explain why most of us will usually divide the cake in equal shares notwithstanding existing differences in

---

[30] A high cognitive load was operationalized by requiring participants to remember an eight-digit number while performing the task, a manipulation successfully used in previous studies investigating the impact of cognitive load.

wealth and preferences. This occurs even if all identities have been given equal weight, except under very special circumstances like all individuals' having identical preferences and initial wealth.

Let us imagine the following thought experiment which, we believe, offers a close description of how thoughts of anchoring on equality first come to mind in a resource-sharing task. Before dividing a cake, the people sitting around the table stand a few seconds in a symmetrical position of not knowing who will be asked to share the cake. At this moment, they play an n-person proposal-response game in which a single player will be given the role of a "proposer" and others will act as "responders". The proposer first offers shares to all players; then, responders react to her offer, say by accepting or rejecting it as in the ultimatum game. The projection mechanism allows one to anticipate (perhaps wrongly) that other proposers behave like self in the same role, as if they shared one's preferences and initial wealth. Each player will choose the whole distribution of shares that she may get depending on whether she will share the cake or not. If she has an equal probability of playing any role, she maximizes her expected utility (5.3) subject to the constraints (5.2). The solution of this simple program is to cut the cake in equal shares notwithstanding the player's risk aversion, initial wealth, and number of players or cake's size.

Two remarkable results come out of the projection mechanism. First, the preference for equality applies to wealth increments, not to final wealth. People may share a cake with their friends, workers may share rents with their co-workers, taxpayers may share their marginal income; but it is certainly uncommon to see a man share his fortune. Second, this solution is independent of the player's index. Thus there exists a *prior common preference* for equality of shares, which all rational players must be aware of before the game begins. A player's prior preference defines his or her *intention*. Thus intentions of other players are common knowledge. Knowing with certainty that all potential proposers intended to share the cake equally, a responder will be entitled to object to receiving a smaller share. This creates in turn the conditions for the *reciprocity* of responses to proposals being common knowledge as well and, therefore, enforceable. In the words of Kahneman, Knetsch and Thaler (1986), "the rules of fairness define the terms of an enforceable implicit contract". If prior intentions are effectively enforced in the actual game, proposers who do not cooperate will incur a sanction by being deprived of an excessive share or, more frequently so, by facing social disapproval for their unkind manners. This unique combination of a prior common reference of all players with an expectation of sanction imposed on deviant behavior fits the definition of a social norm as a tacit coordination rule. The latter fills both a cognitive function, by eliciting others' intentions and making all players feel certain about them, and an incentive function, by driving individuals to respect their prior intentions. However, the incentive provided to one player by the knowledge that other players know their own intentions is weak. In a public good game, for example, social norms may become excessively vulnerable to free riding of a minority of players if the power of social norms exclusively relies on their being common knowledge to all players. The vulnerability of social norms can only be overcome by punishing free riders. In a repeated public good game, the early defection of some players signals to loyal players that the social norm can no longer be trusted and effective punishments are needed to maintain the flow of voluntary contributions in the long run [Fehr and Gächter (2000)]. Even the threat of social disapproval cannot deter defection in the long run if it bears no opportunity cost to free riders [Masclet et al. (2003)].

Social norms and the fairness heuristic seem to provide a promising avenue for positing the role of intentions and reciprocity in proposal-response games and develop the insights so far provided by the recent economic models of reciprocity [Rabin (1993), Levine (1998), Dufwenberg and Kirchsteiger (2004), Falk and Fischbacher (2006), Segal and Sobel (1999), Kolm (2000) and Charness and Rabin (2002)].

6.3. Some evidence on social norms

The results obtained in the ultimatum game and public good game literature give credence to the social norm interpretation. In the ultimatum game, fair sharing is the rule with most proposers giving between 40 and 50% (almost never more) to the responder, almost no offer is found below 20%, and low offers are frequently rejected. These robust findings [Fehr and Schmidt (1999), for instance, derive these quantitative conclusions from ten studies] agree with the social norm of sharing but refute the narrow self-interest (subgame-perfect Nash equilibrium) interpretation. In the public good game, the fact that people's willingness to contribute to a public good depends on their perception that other people are also willing to give provides good evidence that common knowledge of others' intentions to respect the norm of fairness matters [e.g., Gächter and Fehr (1999)]. Finally, based on coordinated ultimatum experiments in 15 small-scale societies, Henrich et al. (2003) found strong support for the enforcement of norms within each group since group level differences explained two-thirds of total variation in ultimatum game offers.

Strong additional evidence of the social norm of equal sharing is indirectly provided by recent experiments of Charness and Rabin (2002). In one experiment, 85% of subjects A gave up a very advantageous but unequal allocation of 900 to self versus 450 to an other B to let B, who had the option of sharing equally (400 to each), make the decisive choice. Since B could also make another choice that would have preserved his share of 400 but would have been damaging to A by only giving her 200, the great majority of A's took the risk of losing 700 for the sake of respecting the social norm. Apparently, the latter exhibited great confidence that B's would in turn respect the social norm when given the opportunity – which about two-thirds did – despite the fact that A's move surely deprived B's of 50. In another experiment, after 61% of A's had let down an allocation (375, 1000) giving 1000 to B, 97% of B's preferred an equal split (400, 400) to the strongly Pareto-dominated allocation (250, 350). Since the latter would have been the way to punish A for "depriving" B of an opportunity to get a much bigger sum, this result means that almost no B's wanted to punish the "unkind" A's. This finding may come as a surprise under an egocentric interpretation of "kindness", but it corroborates the social norm interpretation, because many A's and B's together understand that the fairest allocation among the three alternatives they had is the equal split. Thus the two players manage to coordinate through the use of this social norm. It is not normal for an A subject to punish herself by accepting too small a share when there exist a fair option, and therefore there is no reason for the second player to punish someone who behaved normally (and not unfairly).

Equality of shares is not the only social norm of fairness that people adhere to. Van Dijke and Wilke (1995) demonstrated that, when players possess different endowments and are fully aware of these differences, Resource dilemmas evoke different norms than Public Good dilemmas. Whereas one-shot Resource dilemmas appear to evoke the equality rule, participants to a one-shot Public Good dilemma appear to coordinate behavior through a proportionality rule. According to the latter, each member of the group should contribute to the (fixed amount of) public good in proportion of his or her ability to pay. The use of a proportionality rule does not lead to an equality of final outcomes. Van Dijke et al. (1999) further showed that incomplete information of players as to others' endowments or investment returns had in some cases a profound impact on the norm of fairness. In each case, a single specific rule was followed fairly closely by a great majority of players. Moreover, the players' reported own notion of fair choice was highly correlated with their actual decisions. These results suggest that players use the available information to determine a game-specific norm of fairness and what would be fair behavior for each group member, and that they anchor their own actual behavior on what would be fair for them.

Since it is the presence of (often implicit) social sanctions which ensures the effectiveness of norms, a surprising implication of the functioning of norms is that financial inducements to perform a socially desirable task may undermine the prior willingness to perform this task by signaling to players that the norm is no longer in use. This is one facet of what is called the "crowding-out of an intrinsic motivation" by an extrinsic reward. This phenomenon [Deci (1971), and Frey (1997), for an economic exposition] will occur when the financial inducement is less effective than the norm in driving individuals to perform the socially desirable task. Unexpected interactions between material incentives and non-pecuniary motives are extensively discussed by Fehr and Falk (2002).

6.4. The working of a social norm: Homans' "cash posters"

We end this section on social norms with a formal illustration of their working. We chose to examine the celebrated case of the "cash posters", studied by Homans (1953, 1954), for its extreme clarity and simplicity. This case will be used to demonstrate how the projection/identification mechanism lying at the heart of social judgements may condition the revealed preference for equal hourly wages and a norm of minimal effort within this specific group of workers. Showing the interplay of social preferences and norms of sharing will further help us to reconcile the theoretical intuitions of Homans and Adams

(1963, 1965) and to fit them rather naturally into a unified economic framework when the conditions of perfect competition do not prevail.[31]

Cash posting consisted of recording daily the amounts customers of a utilities company paid on their bills. A group of 10 young women who worked in the same large room were interviewed and observed over a period of six months. The speed at which individual cash posters worked was recorded. Anyone who worked below the rate of 300 per hour received a mild rebuke from the supervisor. The average number of cash postings per hour was 353, well above the company's minimum standard. Only two workers had productivities slightly above the company's norm (namely, 306 and 308), and only two reached more than 400 per hour. In spite of observable differences in their human capital ($h_1, \ldots, h_n$), all the cash posters (e.g., $n = 10$) received the same hourly wage $\bar{w}$.

The firm acts as principal toward its employees. It proposes two enforceable rules for the division of output value, first by setting the labor's share p ($0 < p \leqslant 1$) relative to the firm's profits, second by choosing a pay scheme which allocates wages to workers of varying abilities after the wage bill has been set. Let the allocation of wages result from either of two pay schemes: team compensation, or piece-rate. Assuming that the definition of the equitable share of labor p does not critically depend upon the payment scheme, we normalize p to one. The essential difference between compensation of effort being based on either collective or individual output lies in the revelation of social preferences. All workers have a say in the distribution of wages when output is provided collectively, but each worker is denied voice and property rights on others' outputs when these are singled out. For simplicity, the group of workers is further assumed to determine the group's preferred pay scheme by majority voting.

The social preferences of workers who see their co-workers as forming a homogeneous group with themselves will be captured by assuming that each worker i "socially" choose the distribution of wages ($w_{i1}, \ldots, w_{in}$) and the distribution of efforts ($e_{i1}, \ldots, e_{in}$) for their own team.[32]

Social preferences can be viewed here as a special kind of peer pressure [Kandel and Lazear (1992)]. Since each worker knows the human capital of all members of the group (who accomplish the same task in the same room) but doesn't observe the preferences of others for income and effort, it is natural to assume that worker i makes her personal judgement about all the wages and efforts by both projecting her own preferences onto her co-workers and identifying with their human capital. Worker i's behavior can thus be described by the maximization of a social utility function[33] which is a combination of (5.1) and (5.3), subject to her perception that the sum of wages must equal the labor's share of total output:

$$\max_{(w_{ij}, e_{ij})} \sum_{j=1}^{n} \frac{1}{n}\bigl[u_i(w_{ij}) - c_i(e_{ij})\bigr], \qquad (6.1)$$

---

[31] The reader may also refer to the discussion of Fehr and Falk (2002).
[32] For a purely egoist worker, the perceived size of "team", i.e. group of similar workers, is simply: $n = 1$.
[33] Effort in the workplace is assumed to be separable from home goods and leisure.

$$\text{s.t.} \quad f(h_1 e_{i1}, \ldots, h_n e_{in}) = \sum_{j=1}^{n} w_{ij} \qquad (6.2)$$

with: $u'_i > 0$, $u''_i < 0$, $c'_i > 0$, $c''_i > 0$, human capital and effort taking real positive values, and $f(\ )$ designating the production function. In the cash posters' example, the latter is simply additive: $f(h_1 e_1, \ldots, h_n e_n) = h_1 e_1 + \cdots + h_n e_n$. The first-order conditions are:

$$u'_i(w_{ij}) = \mu_i, \qquad (6.3)$$

$$c'_i(e_{ij}) = \mu_i h_j f'_j. \qquad (6.4)$$

The $2n$ equations (6.3) and (6.4) and the wage-effort constraint (6.2) determine i's social preference for the distributions of efforts and wages, and her positive Lagrange multiplier μ_i. Clearly, these conditions imply the unanimous preference of workers for equal wages and determine the uniform wage and total output preferred by this individual. This conclusion does not rest on the special form of production function which applies to cash posters. It is also worth noticing that the same prediction would derive from a maximin social utility which assumes infinite risk aversion. If most workers are not egoists, the firm knows that uniform wages are the team's norm and that these workers intend to reciprocate the firm's policy to respect this norm in such way that it may be profitable to set uniform wages at the level which is sufficient to attain the desired level of output.

This description of the formation of social judgements predicts the normative preference for equal wages in a not-too-heterogeneous team and associates the norm of minimal production with the expected minimum productivity. The cash posters observed by Homans conform to this description. They formed a roughly homogeneous group and the group's norm was very close to the minimum productivity attained by two of the employees. All workers actually intended to respect this norm and even agreed to produce at a faster rate depending upon their own human capital and preferences. The more productive are willing to help their less productive co-workers if they cannot access to another better group[34] because they still benefit from the cooperation of other productive workers in their own group. The norm of minimal production that we describe is obviously easy to enforce but still needs to be recalled because, once an hourly wage has been set for workers the latter have an incentive to make less effort than they implicitly promised. In actuality, the norm is not restricted to minimal production and extends to all workers since lower-than-expected efforts of anyone are costly to all co-workers with a lower ability than herself. This is made possible by the observability of individual abilities and outputs by co-workers who can thus reward the more productive with a higher social status and prestige among the group, and punish any worker's

---

[34] The cash posters were quite young (21.1 years on average) and had low tenure on the job (with a maximum of 3 years and 5 months). Turnover costs may be an important factor in determining the overall efficiency of team compensation.

negative deviation from their normative expectation by downgrading her status or excluding her from informal relations. Note that each worker's efforts are monitored by lower-ability workers who stand to lose from shirking on the part of their higher-ability co-workers. Only the lowest-ability workers need to be monitored and punished by the firm's supervisor.

Interestingly, team compensation need not be less productive than a piece-rate scheme (assuming that the latter is feasible) when the workers control their own effort. One basic reason is that the piece-rate scheme constrains wages to parallel productivities that will be partly chosen by each worker, whereas team compensation doesn't. For instance, a piece-rate scheme could have been implemented for the cash posters who were all accomplishing the same task independently at an observable rate. Under piece-rate (normalized to one), wages follow individual output: $w_i = h_i e_i$, for all i. With the piece-rate scheme, the wage-effort constraint is automatically verified and worker i merely maximizes her private utility function[35] given that her wage is tied to her own productivity. The corresponding first-order condition is

$$c'_i(e_i) = h_i u'_i(w_i). \tag{6.5}$$

By contrast, under the same production frontier and team compensation, individual efforts would be determined by

$$c'_i(e_i) = h_i u'_i(\overline{w}).$$

More able workers who would be paid higher than average in the piece-rate scheme will end up making more effort under team compensation for lower pay, if the average wage is held constant. To see that this is definitely possible, let us assume identical utility functions of the form: $\ln w_i + \beta \ln(1 - e_i)$, where $\beta > 0$ and $0 < e_i < 1$. Then the solution is easily calculated. Under team compensation, $\overline{w} = \frac{\overline{h}}{1+\beta}$ and $e_i = 1 - \frac{\beta}{1+\beta} \frac{\overline{h}}{h_i}$; and in the piece-rate scheme, $e_i = \frac{1}{1+\beta}$ for all i and $w_i = \frac{h_i}{1+\beta}$. Hence, total output coincides in both regimes ($= \frac{n\overline{h}}{1+\beta}$) and so does the average wage. Since more able workers ($h_i \geqslant \overline{h}$) produce less effort for more pay in the piece-rate scheme, they will tend to favor this regime while the less able workers prefer team compensation. If the distribution of human capital is skewed to the right, as it usually is, team compensation would be chosen over piece-rate under majority voting.

7. In-group favoritism and self-anchored altruism

7.1. Categorization and the preference for similarity

The sharing problem discussed in Section 6 illustrated how the projection of self onto others can generate a social norm of equality, which is often taken for granted. This is a

---

[35] The private utility function is a special case of (6.1) when $n = 1$ and $j = i$.

natural assumption whenever individuals believe that others are "similar" to themselves, for instance because they know their own preferences and have no information about others'. However, subjects tend to categorize others as soon as they receive distinctive information about the latter. Let us assume that others can be classified by an individual as belonging either to her *in-group*, made of similar others, or to her *out-group*, made of dissimilar others. More precisely, it is assumed that individuals can project onto similar others, but can neither project onto nor identify with dissimilar others of whom they have no detailed information. Thus they may reason that similar others behave like self and take the choices of dissimilar others as given.

With this minimal information, an individual and similar others are willing to keep x for themselves if they receive a sum c, give d to their out-group and share the rest equally between other members of their in-group if they play the role of a proposer. Under the same context, out-group members will keep y for themselves, give e to their out-group (i.e. the first individual's in-group), and share the rest equally between all members of their in-group (i.e. the first individual's out-group) if they become proposers. The representative player of the in-group perceives her in-group to be of size I (including herself) and her out-group to be of size O, with: $I + O = n$. She reasons that other players will share her own estimates (given the fact that her in-group may be their out-group). Thus in-group members determine x and d for given values of y and e in order to maximize

$$\max_{x,d} \left\{ \frac{1}{n} U(w+x) + \frac{n-1}{n} \left[\frac{I-1}{n-1} U\left(w + \frac{c-x-d}{I-1}\right) + \frac{O}{n-1} U\left(w + \frac{e}{I}\right) \right] \right\},$$

s.t. $0 \leqslant x \leqslant c,$
$0 \leqslant d \leqslant c.$

Even though in-group members do not know which shares out-group members would keep for themselves or give to them, they do not need this information in order to determine their own behavior thanks to the additive separability of the expected utility function. The solution consists in sharing the cake equally between all members of one's in-group and giving nothing to out-group members, irrespective of the individual's risk aversion and initial wealth

$$x = \frac{c}{I}, \quad d = 0.$$

Since the optimal sharing rule is independent of out-group's behavior and other characteristics of the proposer except which group she belongs to, anyone will eventually be able to infer her out-group's behavior by symmetry. An individual will favor her in-group in order to just compensate for her expectation of being discarded by her out-group. Her expected share of the cake is always c/n and does not depend upon how dissimilar others are effectively. However, out of risk aversion, she would still prefer to play with a group of similar people than with a heterogeneous group because, in the first case, she would be "certain" to receive the share that she only "expects" to receive in the second case. The modal preference for conformity and similarity is a well-known fact in social psychology, pioneered by a famous experiment of Schachter (1951). It is worth noticing that such preference for conformity and similarity does not require that people a priori evaluate themselves positively or prefer their in-group than their out-group. It is only the consequence of the ability to project oneself onto perceived similar others and the inability to do the same on perceived dissimilar others. We manifest a universal preference for sharing with family, friends, and other people we know rather than strangers; and we are inclined to like people who, we believe, are like us.

Consistent with the present analysis, Henrich (2000) found that the Machiguenga of the Peruvian Amazon proposed only 26% of the money in ultimatum games with very few rejections, well below the 40–50% range usually observed. Machiguenga people still primarily rely on their own family for their living but now live in small communities gathering a number of extended families and households. Therefore, Machiguenga proposers probably perceived high responders' heterogeneity because they faced a high probability of being matched with a member of another family. This also provides a potential explanation for the rise of selfishness caused by the expansion of markets, as noted by Adam Smith (1776), which it relates with the necessity to trade with unknown parties of different origins and customs. The emergence and persistence of selfish behavior may have resulted from a feeling of social heterogeneity that did not arise in smaller long-established segments of the society. It may also explain the emergence and persistence of prejudice and social discrimination on the basis of race, ethnicity, nationality, religion, or even gender. In societies visibly divided in two large groups, most members of an in-group who can benefit from economic rents (the "favored" group) will be willing to share rents with similar others and refuse to do it with dissimilar others.

7.2. In-group favoritism and out-group discrimination in minimal groups

Favoritism toward similar others (in-group) and discrimination against dissimilar others (out-group) is a widespread phenomenon which can take the opposite forms of liking or attraction toward in-group members and disliking or aggression against out-group members. One interesting feature of this phenomenon for economists is that discrimination between the in-group and the out-group may arise even when the two groups do not compete for scarce resources. For example, Ferguson and Kelley (1964) showed that participants who had been working independently in two groups judged their own group product more favorably than the other group product, irrespective of any objective differences in output between the two groups. Even more surprising is the finding that in-group favoritism also occurs in a "minimal group" setting, first introduced by Rabbie and Horwitz (1969) and Tajfel et al. (1971).

In the typical minimal group paradigm, subjects are assigned anonymously to one of two novel groups, and there is no direct interaction between or within groups during the experiment [Brewer (1979)]. Group membership is determined by an arbitrary or trivial criterion like being rated as a person preferring the art of Klee versus the art of Kandinski [Tajfel et al. (1971)] or flipping a coin to decide which of the two groups would receive a gift [Rabbie and Horwitz (1969)]. Based on an anonymous categorization into two experimental groups, these studies revealed that members of the novel in-group were better rated [e.g., Rabbie and Horwitz (1969)] and were favored over members of the novel out-group in their reward allocations [e.g., Tajfel et al. (1971)]. Even when researchers describe the groups using objectively identical information, perceivers indicate nevertheless that the in-group possesses more favorable attributes than the out-group [Howard and Rothbart (1980)].

Two leading explanations of in-group favoritism and out-group discrimination successively emerged in the psychological literature. Social identity theory was first proposed by Tajfel and Turner (1979, 1986) who tried to give a theoretical underpinning to one, and certainly the most salient, conclusion of Tajfel et al. (1971). The latter had been surprised to discover that their subjects – young boys of the same age and from the same school-did not hesitate to sacrifice income to their in-group in order to give the latter a winning position relative to their out-group. They wrote: "in a situation in which subjects' own interests were not involved in their decisions, in which alternative strategies were available that would maximize the total benefits to a group of boys who knew each other well, they acted in a way determined by an *ad hoc* categorization". In order to explain this puzzling observation, Tajfel and Turner postulated that individuals have a need for identity which has both a personal and a social component. Social identity is defined by groups one belongs to (in-groups) as opposed to groups one doesn't belong to (out-groups) and the social status of these groups relative to one another. Group members have a need for positive social identity that can be fulfilled by favorable comparisons between in-group and out-group members. By establishing positive in-group distinctiveness, the self-concept can be enhanced. However, social identity theory was not confirmed by a number of recent experiments on minimal groups [e.g., Cadinu and Rothbart (1996), Dunning and Hayes (1996), Otten and Wentura (2001)]. Cadinu and Rothbart (1996) showed that, when almost no information about the groups is available, in-group perception is anchored on self-perception rather than self-perception being based on in-group perception. Cadinu and Rothbart's (1996) self-anchoring theory is a cognitive alternative to the motivational theory of Tajfel and Turner (1986). The self construes the new in-group to be similar to the self. As the self tends to be evaluated positively [e.g., Baumeister (1998)], this self-anchoring process typically implies projecting a positive image onto the in-group.

Our discussion of the last section suggests that the higher ability to project oneself onto an in-group than an out-group is solely responsible for in-group boasting or favoritism. Consistent with this theory is Park and Judd's (1990) observation that perceivers refer more frequently to their own behavior when describing an in-group than when describing an out-group during a "think-aloud" procedure. In a similar vein, the false consensus effect [Ross, Greene and House (1977)] indicates that perceivers use the self to estimate the prevalence of a particular attribute in the general population. Therefore, the behaviors that perceivers rate as typical in the population likely will be those that they consider to be self-descriptive. This implies that self-knowledge serves as an expectancy for the in-group in a minimal group context [Gramzow, Gaertner and Sedikides (2001)]. All of these findings suggest that in-group favoritism and out-group discrimination is largely a function of bolstering the in-group rather than debasing the out-group [also, in Brewer (1979)].

A fatal blow was given to social identity theory by Yamagishi et al. (1999). Following a suggestion of Rabbie et al. (1989), they showed that Tajfel et al.'s (1971) puzzling observation critically depended on their special experimental design in which each subject allocated rewards to two other subjects and, consequently, his own reward was determined by others. When subjects allocated rewards between an in-group member and an out-group member without being the target of other subjects' allocation behavior, they gave on average the same amount of money to the two groups and in-group favoritism vanished. Yamagishi et al. (1999) conclude from a series of clever experiments that, even in minimal group conditions that preclude reciprocal exchanges between two particular subjects, a system of "generalized exchanges" is taking place. In such setting, people receive favors, but not necessarily from the ones to whom they provided favors. Generalized reciprocity of this kind is a direct implication of the prevalence of self-projection[36] onto unknown others in minimal groups.

7.3. Self-anchored altruism

Self-projection with categorization implies a specific form of altruism which is consistent with self-anchoring [Cadinu and Rothbart (1996)] or generalized reciprocity [Yamagishi et al. (1999)] and may thus be called "self-anchored altruism". Let us consider a simple reward allocation problem in which the allocator chooses one distribution of rewards between Self and Other, or between other members of an in-group and an out-group (with a fixed reward for herself, in the latter case). Several economists have recently used the first design to elicit social preferences [e.g., Andreoni and Miller (2002), Charness and Grosskopf (2001), Charness and Rabin (2002)] and Yamagishi et al. (1999) have used the second design to replicate Tajfel et al.'s (1971) in a "more minimal" group condition. Participants in some experiments were explicitly made to view themselves as playing the two roles alternatively. Charness and Grosskopf (2001, study 2) asked them to make decisions as if they were in one role given that, for payment purposes, their actual role would be determined at the end of the session. Charness and Rabin (2002) told their participants that they would be playing the same game a second time in the other role with another anonymous player. In the experimental conditions of anonymous relations and minimal groups, allocators can be described as impartial judges seeking to identify with the beneficiaries of their rewards under incomplete information and choosing the feasible distribution (x_i, x_j) which maximizes their own type (5.1)-social utility function

$$V(x_i, x_j) = \frac{1}{2}EU_i(w + x_i) + \frac{1}{2}EU_j(w + x_j). \tag{7.1}$$

---

[36] As defined in Section 5.1, Yamagishi et al. (1999, p. 181) give another meaning to this word, discussed in Note 10.

Equation (7.1) postulates that the (non-indexed) allocator mentally reincarnates in the identities of her two beneficiaries and projects her own initial wealth onto them. The allocator assesses each beneficiary's similarity with Self on the basis of the information that she received about these identities, and attributes to each beneficiary an expected utility

$$EU_k = \lambda_k U + (1 - \lambda_k)\overline{U}, \tag{7.2}$$

with: $k = (i, j)$ and $0 \leqslant \lambda_k \leqslant 1$. The expected utility of an other's final wealth is a weighted average of one's own concave utility U and a reservation utility level $\overline{U}$ which is out of control to the allocator. λ_k is the subjective probability that beneficiary k be similar to self, and takes value 1 when the beneficiary coincides with Self. If an allocator has no information whatsoever or exactly the same information about the beneficiaries of her rewards, she will infer that $\lambda_i = \lambda_j$ and choose a fair allocation, whatever group they belong to. But if the allocator thinks that beneficiary i is more likely to be an in-group member and j an out-group member, she will infer that $\lambda_i > \lambda_j$, which means that she can project better onto her in-group than her out-group. Consistent with this interpretation, researchers often manipulate empathy-altruism by asking subjects to imagine how the other feels or by making the latter perceive their similarity with the other (see Section 8.3). It is easily derived from (7.1) and (7.2) that the choice of an allocation of rewards by subjects is described (if $\lambda_i \neq 0$) through the maximization of the linear "altruistic" utility

$$W(x_i, x_j) = U(w + x_i) + \lambda U(w + x_j), \tag{7.3}$$

with $\lambda = \dfrac{\lambda_j}{\lambda_i}$ $(0 \leqslant \lambda \leqslant 1)$.

The results obtained for the reward allocation problems in the recent experiments are consistent with the "self-anchored altruism" resulting from incomplete information about others. A person will prefer keeping money for herself than giving it to an unknown other; and she will prefer giving money to an in-group than to an out-group. However, she may sacrifice money to the benefit of an unknown other, or sacrifice her in-group to the benefit of her out-group, if this sufficiently raises the social surplus. The more she can identify with, or project onto, an other the more generous she will be.

What recent experiments show is that a majority of subjects care for others and many are willing to sacrifice money to maximize the social surplus. In sharp contrast with the results reported by Tajfel and his co-authors which gave rise to social identity theory, people do not maximize the difference of rewards between their in-group and their out-group. For instance, denoting an allocation of rewards by (Other, Self), everybody preferred (800, 200) to (0, 0); 89% preferred (600, 600) to (400, 600); and still 66% preferred (900, 600) to (600, 600).[37] This suggests that one-third of subjects at most

---

[37] The first result is given by Charness and Rabin (2002) and the other two by Charness and Grosskopf (2001).

exhibited narrow self-interest (i.e., $\lambda = 0$) or difference aversion (i.e., $\lambda < 0$). Non-negligible degrees of difference aversion are practically ruled out by the unanimous preference for the strong Pareto-improvement (800, 200) over (0, 0), but narrow self-interest is consistent with the occasional rejection of a weak Pareto-improvement which only benefits Other. Subjects who cared for others formed a large majority but exhibited a variable degree of altruism. In Charness and Rabin (2002), 67% preferred (300, 600) to (700, 500), showing that one-third projected themselves onto others to the point of sacrificing 100 to increase an other's reward by 400 and another third at least accepted to sacrifice less than 100 to see an other's reward increase by 400. Another interesting result from the same study is that 54% preferred an equal allocation of 575 to (Other, Other, Self) than the unequal allocation (900, 300, 600) even though, with the second allocation, the inequality concerned the two others and Self was sure to get 25 more than with the first allocation. Equation (7.3) implies for the modal choice:

$$U(575) + 2\lambda U(575) \geqslant U(600) + \lambda \big[U(900) + U(300)\big].$$

This condition will be met with a sufficient combination of risk aversion and altruism. In general, the combination of risk aversion and self-anchored altruism implies that people care more about others who are relatively worse off ("charity") and that they especially have little taste for being themselves at a relative disadvantage. When both implications are tied together, the model's predictions will come close to inequality aversion à la Fehr and Schmidt (1999) without implying, though, that people may engage in Pareto-damaging inequality reduction.

7.4. Comparing behavior in social dilemmas and in social choices

Our review of psychological research clearly reveals that empathy-altruism and equity-fairness are two distinct pro-social motives, even though they may both derive from the same basic mechanisms of social cognition. Moral action is defined by its relation to some evaluative standard or social norm. Empathy-altruism provides no such standard; it provides a partial identification with an other's welfare. Thus altruism and fairness can be in conflict. Batson et al. (1995a) showed experimentally that inducing empathy for one of the individuals a person can help, but only at the expense of others, can lead the person to show partiality toward that individual, consciously violating the moral principle of fairness. In a somewhat less vivid fashion, the experiments of Blount (1995) and Offerman (2002) bring further evidence on this matter. They compare reciprocity-free choices of allocations with reciprocal behavior. Blount only studies negative reciprocity, while Offerman also includes positive reciprocity. The subjects observed by Offerman (2002) responded to an allocation (Other, Self) chosen by a proposer among a set of two possibilities (8, 14) and (11, 6). The first choice by the proposer, which gave 14 to the subject, was relatively "helpful" and the second choice, which gave him only 6, was relatively "hurtful". After receiving one proposal, subjects decided whether they would accept it as it is or modify it. For a small cost of 1, they were entitled to modify the sum received by the proposer by a larger amount of 4 in either direction. Increasing this sum is helpful to the proposer, and decreasing is hurtful. Starting from a helpful proposal (8, 14), subjects could thus make a helpful response $(8 + 4, 14 - 1) \equiv (12, 13)$, maintain the status quo (8, 14), or make a hurtful response $(8 - 4, 14 - 1) \equiv (4, 13)$. Starting from a hurtful proposal (11, 6), the helpful response was (15, 5), the status quo (11, 6), and the hurtful response (7, 5). There were two treatments. In the "Nature" treatment, proposals were randomized. A subject who receives a random proposal should not view himself as responding to an intentional proposal and should take the offer as given by Nature. Thus he should be left with a social choice between three possible allocations. With a social utility function like (7.3), he would never hurt an other who cannot be held responsible for her choice, since this is a dominated option, and he would even be willing to help her if he were sufficiently altruist. In the "Flesh and Blood" treatment, proposals were intentional. A subject who receives an intentional proposal should reason that it was preferred by an other to an alternative proposal. He should thus act like a responder in a modified ultimatum game offering an opportunity to reciprocate in either direction. On getting the helpful proposal (8, 14), he would be sure that the initial proposer respected the social norm. As a result, he would never reject a fair proposal by choosing a hurtful response. He would either opt for the more equal sharing (12, 13), on the ground that the first player did not have the opportunity to give equal shares right away, or for the status quo. After getting the hurtful proposal (11, 6), he might want to hurt back at a small cost by choosing (7, 5), as this is the way of rejecting an initial proposal which violated the norm. He might as well want to accept the offer of 6, but he would not want to help at a cost as this is a dominated option for accepting the offer. The asymmetry of fairness-driven responses after either a helpful or a hurtful proposal in the Flesh and Blood treatment contrasts with the relative independence of reactions of the subjects who were exposed to either a helpful or a hurtful proposal in the Nature treatment. This prediction is consistent with Offerman's (2002) main result: his subjects were 67% more likely to hurt after being hurt by an other than by luck; but they were only 25% more likely to help after being helped by an other than by luck. Another result worth noticing is that, even in the Nature treatment, subjects have a weak tendency to reciprocate. No selfish or difference averse reaction can be found after a helpful unintentional proposal, whereas about one-third of participants to the Charness and Rabin's (2002) experiments seemed to show this type of preferences. On the other hand, a small fraction (17%) of hurtful responses can be found after a hurtful unintentional proposal. One part of the answer lies in the fact that the degree of self-anchored altruism being formed in the Nature treatment depends on the beliefs concerning which group the other belongs to. Both positive and negative surprises are treated as information by subjects and generate both upward and downward revision of the estimated proportion of in-group among participants. For instance, if a helpful proposal indicates a similar other with probability 1, the baseline estimate λ_0 will be revised into: $\lambda_1 = \beta \lambda_0 + (1 - \beta)1 > \lambda_0$. If a hurtful proposal indicates a similar other with probability 0, the baseline estimate will be revised into: $\lambda_1 = \beta \lambda_0 + (1 - \beta)0 < \lambda_0$. This interpretation is suggested by the literature on minimal groups discussed earlier according to which people use even trivial information about others when they lack more relevant information. Knowing that an other has made a helpful or a hurtful move by the toss of a dice is the kind of trivial information which Rabbie and Horwitz (1969) manipulated in the first minimal group experiment.

8. Social drives and emotions

8.1. Social comparison

The tendency of people to judge their own outcome by comparison with some referent is a well-established fact in social psychology [e.g., Crosby (1976), Folger (1986)]. Often, though not necessarily, this referent is another person. Therefore, outcome satisfaction and perceptions of fairness and equity have little to do with own outcome. Rather, they result from the value of one outcome relative to another. Veblen (1934), Duesenberry (1949) and Easterlin (1974) were the first economists to draw attention on this point. For instance, when average Americans are compared to major league baseball players, the players seem to make princely sums. However, the players often feel inequitably treated [Harder (1992)]. Presumably, this is because their referents are other major league baseball players and not "average" Americans. In one of the most influential studies of social sciences, Stouffer et al. (1949) described the adjustment of American soldiers during Army life. They observed that agents outside the Air force had low opportunities for promotion but were nevertheless satisfied with their job; by contrast, Air force soldiers, who had much higher opportunities for promotion, were rather dissatisfied. This result is puzzling because promotion opportunities that would seem to raise income and utility actually brought dissatisfaction. Stouffer and his colleagues reasoned that soldiers were concerned with their relative income. Soldiers outside the Air force were satisfied with their condition because they all followed the same progression and no one was left behind. But soldiers from the Air force who faced greater prospects were often dissatisfied because they could not all be promoted and inevitably some of them would lag behind. In other words, many of those who belonged to the wealthier group were unhappy because they were "relatively deprived" [Davis (1959), Polis (1968), Crosby (1976), Runciman (1966)].

Loewenstein, Thompson and Bazerman (1989) attempted to elicit the individual "social utility functions " by taking the level of self-reported satisfaction as a utility index. They regressed the level of self-reported satisfaction of hypothetical disputants with each of the possible 42 outcomes of the dispute as a function of outcome to self and other. They were able to give within-subjects estimates and found on average a good fit for a function of outcome to self and inequality (the difference between outcome to self and outcome to other) both in quadratic form. They interpreted the satisfaction curve as a "social utility function" which exhibited a strong inequality aversion for disadvantageous inequality and a weaker inequality aversion for advantageous inequality. Subjects always disliked receiving a lower payment than the other party, but their attitude toward advantageous inequality was mixed. They disliked receiving more than friendly people whereas they were satisfied getting more than selfish people. The importance of this work lies in the claim that social utility is indeed observable.[38] More recently, Clark and Oswald (1996) have made a similar claim by showing that job satisfaction is increasing in earnings and decreasing in comparison income, the latter being estimated as the predicted variable of an earnings function. However, Kahneman, Wakker and Sarin (1997) have recently concluded from an "objective" measure of feelings that satisfaction feelings should not be confused with decision-utility, which is the preference index used in modern economics to predict choices. They described satisfaction feelings as "experienced utility", in reference to an alternative concept of utility suggested by Bentham (1789) for measuring pleasure and pain. Now, if the mere observation of satisfaction judgements and feelings does not elicit decision-utility but experienced utility, it is no longer possible to infer from satisfaction data that people make choices that maximize the kind of social utility function exhibited by Loewenstein, Thompson and Bazerman (1989).

There is a simple way of interpreting the role played by social comparisons even if the outcome of other did not enter the utility function of self. Using information about others might as well be an economic way of gathering knowledge about self. This is the thrust of Festinger's (1954) theory of social comparison processes contained in these two important propositions: (i) "When an objective, non-social basis for the evaluation of one's ability or opinion is readily available persons will not evaluate their opinions or abilities by comparison with others" (corollary II B, p. 120); (ii) "Given a range of possible persons for comparison, someone close to one's own ability or opinion will be chosen for comparison" (corollary III A, p. 121). In Festinger's mind, as these two corollaries indicate, comparison to others is essentially a way to acquire self-knowledge when direct information on self is not available or too costly.

It is necessary to understand that social comparisons operate like a *drive* for capturing the role attributed to them by social psychologists in the formation of social preferences. Whatever deviation from their normative expectation people experience in the course of an action operates like a drive. When normative expectations are met by the experienced outcome, people are satisfied with the outcome and feel that they have been treated fairly. As a result, they are more committed and more willing to sacrifice for the social good [Lind and Tyler (1988), Tyler and Lind (1992)]. On the other hand, when experienced outcomes fall short of their normative expectations, individuals are dissatisfied and angry to have been treated unfairly. They are less willing to cooperate and make efforts, and may even engage in hostile demonstrations like theft and aggression [e.g., Greenberg and Scott (1996)]. Following Festinger (1957), people react dynamically to the cognitive dissonance that they perceive when their experience does not conform with their normative expectation [for a further discussion of cognitive dissonance and an economic model of dynamic drives, see Lévy-Garboua and Blondel (2002), Lévy-Garboua and Montmarquette (1996)].

---

[38] The issues of interpersonal comparability and ordinality of satisfaction scales are not raised here.

8.2. Reducing inequity

For Adams (1963, 1965), who explicitly refers to Festinger (1954, 1957), a social exchange between two agents is deemed equitable when the perceived value of outcomes is proportional to the perceived value of inputs. The formula has later been extended to more agents [e.g., Anderson (1976)]. The value of outcome to workers is the offered wage inclusive of non- pecuniary income, and it is balanced with the value of their labor inputs, designated as "effort". Both outcome and input are valued as perceived by workers. The "fair" wage (rate) is *the normative expectation* of the wage rate, i.e. the perceived ratio of wage to effort: $fair\ wage \equiv E(\frac{wage}{effort})$.

However, equity theory does not provide a full description of how this normative expectation is formed. Adams implicitly recognizes that equilibrium wage rates in a perfectly competitive economy would be fair because job inputs (like education, experience, and effort) would then perfectly correlate with outcomes (like pay). "Indeed, it is because they are imperfectly correlated that we need at all be concerned with job inequity" [Adams (1963, p. 424)]. In the experiments supporting his theory, the norm is described by the observable situation of referent others. But such definition raises a reflection problem [see Manski (2000)] since the norm of one person's reference group will generally depend upon this person's situation. It suggests a dynamic adjustment process towards equilibrium, the equity drive. The worker whose wage is lower than that of a comparison worker who works in another accessible firm feels a drive to move into another firm. But the existence of an equity drive does not suffice to determine the norm of fairness. The latter must be given otherwise. We gave a specific example of how the fairness norm might be determined in the previous discussion of Homans' (1953, 1954) cash posters. Another instance is provided by Akerlof and Yellen (1990, Section 4) who assume that the fair wage is a weighted average of the wage received by the reference group and the market-clearing wage. Kahneman, Knetsch and Thaler (1986) designed experiments in which the standard of fairness was simply the reference transaction. Once defined, the fair wage functions like a social norm prescribing agents how to behave in social relations and letting them anticipate others' behavior.

Workers being offered a "low" wage feel inequity because this is dissonant with their normative expectation. The subjects of Kahneman, Knetsch and Thaler (1986) confirm this prediction. They thought that workers were entitled to their current wage and the firm was not entitled to expand its profits by setting lower wages. Only when profits are threatened may firms set lower wages. However, the subjects of these experiments could only express their feelings of unfairness. A worker experiencing enough cognitive dissonance will also find effective ways of reducing effort, like shirking, absenteeism, or quitting the job, in order to maintain her wage rate at a fair level. In some circumstances, she might even force an other to increase his effort until both wage rates level-off. Akerlof and Yellen (1990) have made use of this prediction of equity theory to derive a theory of involuntary unemployment. In their model, there exist one equilibrium type in which the wages of low-paid workers are set at a fair level above the market-clearing level (since low-paid workers compare to the high-paid group), which causes unemployment for this category of workers. Employers adopt this behavior because they fear negative reciprocity from their low-paid employees if the latter felt underpaid. This kind of reciprocal behavior was neatly confirmed by the experimental gift-exchange game of Fehr, Kirchsteiger and Riedl (1993) and by the employers' description of their own wage-setting behavior [Bewley (1999)].

Another prediction of equity theory is even more surprising: workers whose wage rate exceeds the norm also feel inequity. Overpayment too is dissonant with their normative expectation so that they will reduce inequity by increasing effort until the wage rate falls back to a fair level. The reciprocal nature of inequity feelings is suggested by Adams' (1963, p. 427) statement that "whenever inequity exists for Person, it will also exist for Other, provided their perceptions of inputs and outcomes are isomorphic or nearly so".

These two kinds of inequity feelings induce two forms of reciprocal behavior: negative in case of an unfavorable comparison with an other, and positive in case of a favorable comparison. For instance, the worker who feels under-compensated in comparison with a co-worker stands in the position of one responder of a proposal-response game who does not receive her normal share of the surplus. She refuses a proposal that falls short of a prior social agreement and punishes the norm's violator. By contrast, the worker who feels over-compensated in comparison with a co-worker stands in the position of a proposer who committed herself to give a fair share of any surplus she might receive to the responders. She may wish to respect the implicit promise that she made.

We believe that the puzzling observations of Tajfel et al. (1971), discussed in Section 7.2, are a good instance of inequity-reducing behavior. Young boys who knew each other well did not hesitate to sacrifice social surplus and income to their in-group in order to give the latter a winning position relative to their out-group when their own income was determined by the likewise allocation of an unknown other. These observations refute the "self-anchored altruism" assumption expressed by Equation (7.3) and need to be explained. What makes Tajfel et al.'s (1971) experiment interesting is that it provides a rare instance in which subjects are unable to manipulate their own reward, but can manipulate the reward of others. Consequently, whenever maximizing the joint payoff was detrimental to their in-group, Tajfel's boys understood that such behavior would essentially increase their comparison income instead of increasing their own income. Widening the negative gap between own reward and its normative expectation generated feelings of inequity [Adams (1963)] or dissatisfaction [Lévy-Garboua and Montmarquette (2004)] among these boys. The related emotions of envy and anger eventually drove them to reduce the comparison income under their control in order to reduce feelings of inequity or dissatisfaction. Depending on the circumstances, the equity drive may push individuals to hurt an advantaged friend, punish a norm's violator, reward a generous employer or help a stranger in need.

8.3. Helping others in need: Is the motivation truly altruistic?

Do the people who help others in need or distress have an altruistic personality? Answering this question requires a general agreement on the personality measures that should be used. When Staub (1974) and Rushton (1980) first claimed that there is an altruistic personality, the notion of altruism that they used, which only ruled out the individual's quest for external rewards, was criticized for still being too broad and including compliance with internalized social or personal norms. If moral obligation were the reason for helping, the act of helping would not be truly altruistic, many psychologists say, because it would not be ultimately directed toward others [Bar-Tal (1976), Batson and Shaw (1991)]. So the question should be restated: Is there an altruistic personality which goes beyond the disposition to help others for getting peace of mind by avoiding shame and guilt? In other words, those psychologists want to make a distinction between the vicarious emotions of *empathy* (reflecting pure altruism) and *personal distress* (caused by non-compliance to norms).

Empathy is defined as an other-oriented emotional response congruent with the perceived welfare of another person [e.g., Batson et al. (1995a), Hoffman (1988)]. The list of emotions associated with empathy includes adjectives like "sympathetic, moved, compassionate, warm, soft-hearted, and tender". Since the empathic emotion stems from the apprehension of another's emotional state to which it is similar [Eisenberg and Strayer (1987)], it requires at least a minimal awareness of the differences between self and other. Thus empathy implies self-other merging or identification, which we also described as the economic definition of pure altruism in Section 5.1. Contrasting with empathy which is assumed to be truly altruistic, personal distress is a self-oriented emotional response to another person in need or distress. It is usually associated with adjectives like "alarmed, grieved, troubled, distressed, upset, disturbed, worried, and perturbed". The personality measure for empathic concern correlates with the measured disposition for perspective-taking while the personality measure for personal distress correlates with low self-esteem or sadness [Batson et al. (1986)]. As for many emotions [Zajonc (1980)], both empathy and personal distress function like a drive indicating one's current preferences and generating the context-dependent motivation to relieve another person's need. Empathy can be experimentally manipulated by asking subjects to imagine how the other feels (high empathy) versus to take an objective and detached perspective (low empathy) by trying not to get caught up in how the other feels [e.g., Batson et al. (1995a)]. Empathy can also be manipulated by making subjects perceive their similarity (high empathy) or dissimilarity (low empathy) with the other [e.g., Batson et al. (1995b)].

There is extensive evidence that empathy increases helping and other pro-social behavior. However, the empirical significance of this relation seems to depend on how empathy is measured. For instance, using four personality measures of self-esteem, social responsibility, ascription of responsibility, and *dispositional* (i.e., out of context) empathy, Batson et al. (1986) found no evidence that any of these four "altruistic" personality variables was associated with truly altruistic motivation in helping. But Eisenberg and Miller (1987) show by a meta-analysis that this relation is significant for older adolescents and adults [see other references in Eisenberg and Fabes (1998)], when either picture/story or self-report measures of *situational* (i.e., in context) empathy[39] are used (the relation is less clear for children). Similar results using different physiological markers of empathy or personal distress have been obtained by numerous studies, both for children and for adults [see the references in Eisenberg and Fabes (1998)]. Lastly, subjects who are induced experimentally to empathize with an other in need or distress help significantly more than those induced to have an impartial attitude. For example, 62% of Dovidio, Allen and Schroeder (1990) empathy-induced subjects helped versus only 34% for those in the low empathy condition.

In order to distinguish whether the personality measures are associated with a truly altruistic motivation or with compliance to norms, Batson (e.g., 1991) compared helping behavior in two treatments. In one condition, subjects had an easy escape to helping another in need, while escape was difficult in the other condition. An altruist wants to help because she identifies with the other and derives utility from his relief. Making escape easy will not change her motivation. By contrast, a person who just feels morally obliged to help under pressure is less likely to do so when offered an easy escape because she then finds herself in the position of a dictator in a proposal-response game (see the discussion in Section 5.1). Indeed, Batson (1991) found that empathy was more likely related to helping than is personal distress when it is easy to escape contact with the needy person. This is consistent with his "empathy-altruism hypothesis" that empathy is mainly other-oriented, whereas personal distress is self-oriented. For instance, 68% of Batson et al.'s (1995a) participants to the two experiments in the high empathy condition had an altruistic motivation for helping versus only 37% in the low empathy condition.

Although the empathy-altruism hypothesis seems to have gained weight in recent years among psychologists, there is still no consensus about whether the motivation for helping is truly altruistic or "egoistic". Cialdini et al. (1987) exemplify the egoistic approach with their "negative state relief" model. They suggest that negative affects, like sadness, can motivate helping because helping can be perceived as an instrumental act that will relieve these negative feelings. The helping motivation of a "sad" person is egoistic and can be removed by the anticipation of another mood-enhancing event, such as listening to a comedy tape or having the opportunity to help another person [Schaller and Cialdini (1988)]. There is probably no point for a economist in resolving the issue of whether helping others in need is a truly altruistic or an egoistic motivation. The discussions in Sections 6 and 7 demonstrated that norm compliance and unilateral giving are indeed two distinct behaviors arising in different contexts but they both require perspective-taking and anchor in the self. However, there is another lesson to be drawn by economists from psychological research on helping. Whereas giving and

---

[39] A subjective index of empathy is obtained by showing subjects a picture or a story that represents another person in a situation of need or distress and asking them how they feel about it. A subject is supposed to empathize with the other person when his or her reported emotion, either is close to what the picture was meant to convey by the experimenter or scores high on a subjective scale. Objective sympathy indexes using physiological markers like heart rate, skin conductance, or facial reactions can also be found [see Eisenberg and Fabes (1998)].

sharing derived from a cognitive act (reasoning) in previous discussions, helping is an affective response (emotional drive) to the immediate experience of an other in need or distress. Strong emotions work like a cognitive load that inhibits further reasoning and triggers-off the individual's prior attitude in face of the situation. Thus strong emotions elicit pure social preferences which leave no room for opportunistic deviations.

9. Some lessons from psychology and biology: A summary

Which lessons for economic research can be drawn from our survey of the social-psychological and biological literature dealing with the formation of social preferences? The first lesson is that biological evolution can explain the emergence of restricted forms of social preferences like altruism toward close relatives, but multiple and often delicate conditions are found for the evolutionary emergence of social adaptation at large. For perhaps one million existing animal species, ten thousand at most are social in any significant way. As we move up the evolutionary ladder, environmental- as opposed to genetic-factors increasingly come into play and account for an increasing intra-specific variability in social adaptation. Cultural transmission, for instance, is a human-specific type of learning which is transmitted to next generations by making a pool of cultural traits to co-evolve with the gene pool.

Studies on pro-social development conducted by social psychologists since Piaget's seminal work generally confirm that pro-social dispositions are not innate. Although learning and enforcement of pro-social values may seem an obvious explanation, the empirical and experimental evidence is disappointing. Children do a lot more than copying models; they construct their social worlds in terms of cognitive structures. Their pro-social dispositions seem to develop mainly during the first 10 or 12 years of existence, together with cognitive and emotional skills like perspective-taking and empathy. The formation of the perspective-taking ability is probably distinctive of human sociality. Ants and bees, which have a detailed division of labor, have a social life; but they don't have a social mind.

The full development of social preferences requires consciousness of the individual's similarities and differences with others, and therefore knowledge of self and others. The frequent asymmetry of one's knowledge of self and others is the origin of two distinct cognitive processes for generating social preferences: identification of self with known others, and projection of known self onto partially unknown others. These two basic mechanisms of social cognition obviously require perspective-taking skills. They combine with the process of categorizing others with whom an individual interacts into similar others (in-group) and dissimilar others (out-group) to form a variety of social preferences. The self can project onto similar others but is unable to do so onto dissimilar others. Thus the self will find it easier to internalize and predict the behavior of an in-group than an out-group in social interactions and will generally like to interact more with the former than with the latter. The more can the self identify with, or project onto, an other the more generous she will be. Several context-dependent prosocial motives may derive from the same basic mechanisms of social cognition, and the social-psychological literature commonly distinguishes fairness and empathy-altruism. The fairness motive and the empathy-altruism motive are quite different and can even be in conflict.

Fairness is a social norm, present in proposal-response games, that functions like an enforceable implicit contract among a group of players. It brings to all players a precise knowledge of others' intentions and an incentive to respect their own intentions. However, it often needs to be enforced by sanctions. Self-anchored altruism originates from the partial identification of self with an other's welfare, present in a dictator game, by a purely cognitive process. Under incomplete information, Self finds it easier to identify with in-group than out-group.

However, both fairness and empathy-altruism can also arise from the emotional response to the perceived inequity or dissatisfaction of an experienced deviation from one's normative expectation, whether the latter is common to one group or specific to one individual. Disadvantaged responders feel angry and are driven to hurt or punish the norm's violator; symmetrically, many people empathize with the need or distress of another person and are driven to help. Such affective modes of response coexist with the cognitive processes of social cognition to form a rich variety of context-dependent social preferences.

References

Adams, G.R. (1983). "Social competence during adolescence: Social sensitivity, locus of control, empathy, and peer popularity". Journal of Youth and Adolescence 12, 203–211.
Adams, S.J. (1963). "Toward an understanding of inequity". Journal of Abnormal and Social Psychology 67, 422–436.
Adams, S.J. (1965). "Inequity in social exchange". In: Berkowitz, L. (Ed.), Experimental Social Psychology, vol. 2. Academic Press, New York, pp. 267–299.
Akerlof, G.A., Yellen, J.L. (1990). "The fair wage–effort hypothesis and unemployment". Quarterly Journal of Economics 105, 255–284.
Alicke, M.D., Largo, E. (1995). "The role of self in the false consensus effect". Journal of Experimental Social Psychology 31, 28–47.
Allison, S.T., Messick, D.M. (1990). "Social decision heuristics in the use of shared resources". Journal of Behavioral Decision Making 3, 195–204.
Allison, S.T., McQueen, L.R., Schaerfl, L.M. (1992). "Social decision making processes and the equal partitionment of shared resources". Journal of Experimental Social Psychology 28, 23–42.
Anderson, N. (1976). "Information integration theory applied to equity judgements". Journal of Personality and Social Psychology 33, 291–299.
Andreoni, J., Miller, J. (2002). "Giving according to GARP: An experimental test of the consistency of preferences for altruism". Econometrica 70, 737–753.
Arrondel, L., Masson, A. (2001). "Family transfers involving three generations". Scandinavian Journal of Economics 103, 415–443.
Axelrod, R., Hamilton, W.D. (1981). "The evolution of cooperation". Science 211, 1390–1396.
Bandura, A. (1986). Social Foundations of Thought and Action. Prentice-Hall, Englewood Cliffs, NJ.
Barnett, S.A. (1968). "The instinct to teach". Nature 220, 747–749.

Bar-Tal, D. (1976). Prosocial Behavior – Theory and Research. John Wiley and Sons, New York.
Bar-Tal, D., Korenfeld, D., Raviv, A. (1985). "Relationships between the development of helping behavior and the development of cognition, social perspective, and moral judgement". Genetic, Social, and General Psychology Monographs 11, 23–40.
Batson, C.D., Bolen, M.H., Cross, J.A., Neuringer-Benefiel, H.E. (1986). "Where is the altruism in the altruistic personality?". Journal of Personality and Social Psychology 50, 212–220.
Batson, C.D. (1991). The Altruism Question: Toward a Social-Psychological Answer. Erlbaum, Hillsdale, NJ.
Batson, C.D., Shaw, L.L. (1991). "Evidence for altruism: Toward a pluralism of prosocial motives". Psychological Inquiry 2, 107–122.
Batson, C.D., Allison, S.T., Klein, T.R., Highberger, L., Shaw, L.L. (1995a). "Immorality from empathy-induced altruism: When compassion and justice conflict". Journal of Personality and Social Psychology 68, 1042–1054.
Batson, C.D., Turk, C.L., Shaw, L.L., Klein, T.R. (1995b). "Information function of empathic emotion: Learning that we value the other's welfare". Journal of Personality and Social Psychology 68, 300–313.
Baumeister, R.F. (1998). "The Self". In: Gilbert, D.T., Fiske, S.T., Lindzey, G. (Eds.), The Handbook of Social Psychology, vol. 1. Mac Graw Hill, New York, pp. 680–740.
Becker, G.S. (1974). "A theory of social interactions". Journal of Political Economy 82, 1063–1093.
Becker, G.S., Barro, R.J. (1988). "A reformulation of the economic theory of fertility". Quarterly Journal of Economics 103, 1–25.
Bentham, J. (1789). An Introduction to the Principles of Morals and Legislation. Reprinted in 1948. Blackwell, Oxford.
Berkowitz, M.W., Grych, J.H. (1998). "Children's moral development". Journal of Moral Education 27 (3), 371–391.
Bewley, T. (1999). Why Wages Don't Fall During a Recession. Harvard University Press, Cambridge, MA.
Binmore, K. (1994). Game Theory and the Social Contract: Playing Fair. The MIT Press, Cambridge, MA.
Bisin, A., Verdier, T. (2001). "The economics of cultural transmission and the dynamics of preferences". Journal of Economic Theory 97, 298–319.
Blount, S. (1995). "When social outcomes aren't fair: The effect of causal attributions on preferences". Organizational Behavior and Human Decision Processes 63, 131–144.
Bolton, G.E., Ockenfels, A. (2000). "ERC: A theory of equity, reciprocity, and competition". American Economic Review 91, 166–193.
Boorman, S.A., Levitt, P.R. (1980). The Genetics of Altruism. Academic Press, New York.
Bowles, S., Gintis, H., (2003). "The evolution of strong reciprocity: Cooperation in heterogeneous populations", submitted for publication in Theoretical Population Biology.
Boyd, R., Richerson, P.J. (1985). Culture and the Evolutionary Process. The University of Chicago Press, Chicago.
Brewer, M.B. (1979). "In-group bias in the minimal intergroup situation: A cognitive-motivational analysis". Psychological Bulletin 86, 307–324.
Brockmann, H.J., Dawkins, R. (1979). "Joint nesting in a digger wasp as an evolutionary stable preadaptation to social life". Behavior 71, 203–245.
Brockmann, H.J. (1984). "The evolution of social behavior in insects". In: Kreps, J.K., Davies, N.B. (Eds.), Behavioural Ecology: An Evolutionary Approach. Second ed. Oxford, Blackwell, pp. 340–361.
Cadinu, M.R., Rothbart, M. (1996). "Self-anchoring and differentiation processes in the minimal group setting". Journal of Personality and Social Psychology 70, 661–677.
Camacho-Cuena, E., Seidl, C., Morone, A. (2005). "Comparing preference reversal for general lotteries and income distributions". Journal of Economic Psychology 26 (5), 682–710.
Camerer, C., Thaler, R.H. (1995). "Ultimatum, dictators and manners". Journal of Economic Perspectives 9, 209–219.
Campbell, R.L., Christopher, J.C. (1996). "Moral development theory: A critique of its kantian presuppositions". Developmental Review 16, 48–68.
Carpendale, J.I.M. (2000). "Kohlberg and Piaget on stages and moral reasoning". Developmental Review 20, 181–205.

Cavalli-Sforza, L.L., Feldman, M.W. (1981). Cultural Transmission and Evolution: A Quantitative Approach. Princeton University Press, Princeton.
Charness, G., Grosskopf, B. (2001). "Relative payoffs and happiness: An experimental study". Journal of Economic Behavior and Organization 45, 301–328.
Charness, G., Rabin, M. (2002). "Understanding social preferences with simple tests". Quarterly Journal of Economics 117, 817–869.
Chase-Lansdale, P.L., Wakschlag, L.S., Brooks-Gunn, J. (1995). "A psychological perspective on the development of caring in children and youth: the role of the family". Journal of Adolescence 18, 515–556.
Cialdini, R.B., Schaller, M., Houlihan, D., Arps, K., Fultz, J., Beaman, A.L. (1987). "Empathy-based helping: Is it selflessly or selfishly motivated?". Journal of Personality and Social Psychology 52, 749–758.
Clark, A.E., Oswald, A.J. (1996). "Satisfaction and comparison income". Journal of Public Economics 61, 359–381.
Colby, A., Kohlberg, L. (Eds.) (1987). The Measurement of Moral Judgment, vol. 1–2. Cambridge University Press, Cambridge.
Cosmides, L., Tooby, J. (1992). "Cognitive adaptations for social exchange". In: Barkow, J., Cosmides, L., Tooby, J. (Eds.), The Adapted Mind. Oxford University Press, New York, pp. 163–228.
Crosby, F. (1976). "A model of egoistical relative deprivation". Psychological Review 83, 85–113.
Damon, W. (1977). The Social World of the Child. Jossey-Bass, San Francisco.
Davis, J.A. (1959). "A formal interpretation of the theory of relative deprivation". Sociometry 22, 280–296.
Dawes, R.M. (1980). "Social dilemmas". Annual Review of Psychology 31, 169–193.
Dawkins, R. (1976). The Selfish Gene. Oxford University Press, Oxford.
Dawkins, R. (1982). The Extended Phenotype. Oxford University Press, Oxford.
Deci, E.L. (1971). "The effects of externally mediated rewards on intrinsic motivation". Journal of Personality and Social Psychology 18, 105–115.
Dennett, D.C. (1987). The Intentional Stance. The MIT Press, Cambridge, MA.
Denton, K., Krebs, D. (1990). "From the scene to the crime: the effect of alcohol and social context on moral judgement". Journal of Personality and Social Psychology 59, 242–248.
Dolan, P., Robinson, A. (2001). "The measurement of preferences over the distribution of benefits". European Economic Review 45, 1697–1709.
Dovidio, J.F., Allen, J.L., Schroeder, D.A. (1990). "Specificity of empathy-induced helping: Evidence for altruistic motivation". Journal of Personality and Social Psychology 59, 249–260.
Duesenberry, J.S. (1949). Income Saving and the Theory of Consumer Behavior. Harvard University Press, Cambridge, MA.
Dufwenberg, M., Kirchsteiger, G. (2004). "A theory of sequential reciprocity". Games and Economic Behavior 47, 268–298.
Dunning, D., Hayes, A.G. (1996). "Evidence for egocentric comparison in social judgement". Journal of Personality and Social Psychology 71, 213–229.
Eagly, A.H., Crowley, M. (1986). "Gender and helping behavior: A meta-analytic review of the social psychological literature". Psychological Bulletin 100, 283–308.
Easterlin, R.A. (1974). "Does Economic Growth Improve the Human Lot? Some Empirical Evidence". In: David, P.A., Reder, M.W. (Eds.), Nations and Households in Economic Growth. Academic Press, New York, pp. 89–125.
Eisenberg, N. (1986). Altruistic Emotion Cognition, and Behavior. Erlbaum, Hillsdale, NJ.
Eisenberg, N. (1996). "Caught in a narrow Kantian perception of prosocial development: Reactions to Campbell and Christopher's critique of moral development theory". Developmental Review 16, 1–47.
Eisenberg, N., Fabes, R.A. (1995). "The relation of young children's vicarious emotional responding to social competence, regulation, and emotionality". Cognition and Emotion 9, 203–228.
Eisenberg, N., Fabes, R.A. (1998). "Prosocial development". In: Handbook of Child Psychology: Socialization, Personality, and Social Development. Wiley, New York, pp. 701–778.
Eisenberg, N., Fabes, R.A., Karbon, M., Murphy, B.C., Carlo, G., Wosinski, M. (1996). "The relations of children's disposal comforting behavior to empathy-related reactions and shyness". Social Development 5, 330–351.

Eisenberg, N., Miller, P.A. (1987). "The relation of empathy to prosocial and related behaviors". Psychological Bulletin 101, 91–119.
Eisenberg, N., Mussen, P. (1989). The Roots of Prosocial Behavior in Children. Cambridge University Press, Cambridge.
Eisenberg, N., Shell, R. (1986). "Prosocial moral judgment and behavior in children: The mediating role of cost". Personality and Social Psychology Bulletin 12, 426–433.
Eisenberg, N., Strayer, J. (1987). "Critical issues in the study of empathy". In: Eisenberg, N., Strayer, J. (Eds.), Empathy and Its Development. Cambridge University Press, Cambridge.
Eisenberg, N., Wolchik, S., Goldberg, L., Engel, I. (1992). "Parental values, reinforcement and young childrens' prosocial behaviour: A longitudinal study". The Journal of Genetic Psychology 153 (1), 19–36.
Eisenberg, N., Zhou, Q., Koller, S. (2001). "Brazilian adolescents' prosocial moral judgement and behavior: Relations to sympathy, perspective-taking, gender-role orientation, and demographic characteristics". Child Development 72, 518–534.
Falk, A., Fehr, E., Fischbacher, U. (2005). "Driving forces of informal sanctions". Econometrica 73, 2017–2030.
Falk, A., Fischbacher, U. (2006). "A theory of reciprocity". Games and Economic Behavior 54, 293–315.
Fehr, E., Falk, A. (2002). "Psychological foundations of incentives". European Economic Review 46, 687–724.
Fehr, E., Fischbacher, U., Gächter, S. (2002). "Strong reciprocity, human cooperation and the enforcement of social norms". Human Nature 13, 1–25.
Fehr, E., Gächter, S. (2000). "Cooperation and punishment in public goods experiments". American Economic Review 90, 980–994.
Fehr, E., Gächter, S. (2002). "Altruistic punishment in humans". Nature 415, 137–140.
Fehr, E., Kirchsteiger, G., Riedl, A. (1993). "Does fairness prevent market clearing? An experimental investigation". Quarterly Journal of Economics 58, 437–460.
Fehr, E., Schmidt, K.M. (1999). "A theory of fairness, competition, and cooperation". Quarterly Journal of Economics 114, 817–868.
Ferguson, C.K., Kelley, H.H. (1964). "Significant factors in overvaluation of own group's product". Journal of Abnormal Social Psychology 69, 223–228.
Festinger, L. (1954). "A theory of social comparison processes". Human Relations 7, 117–140.
Festinger, L. (1957). A Theory of Cognitive Dissonance. Stanford University Press, Stanford, CA.
Fisher, R.A. (1930). The Genetical Theory of Natural Selection. Clarendon Press, Oxford.
Flavell, J.H. (1992). "Cognitive development: Past, present, and future". Developmental Psychology 28, 998–1005.
Folger, R. (1977). "Distributive and procedural justice: Combined impact of "voice" and improvement on experienced inequity". Journal of Personality and Social Psychology 35, 108–119.
Folger, R. (1986). "Rethinking equity theory: A referent cognitions model". In: Bierhoff, H.W., Cohen, R.L., Greenberg, J. (Eds.), Justice in Social Relations. Plenum, New York, pp. 145–162.
Folger, R., Rosenfield, D., Grove, J., Corkran, L. (1979). "Effects of "voice" and peer opinions on responses to inequity". Journal of Personality and Social Psychology 37, 2253–2261.
Frank, R.H. (1988). Passions Within Reason. The Strategic Role of the Emotions. W.W. Norton and Company, Inc., New York.
Frankenberger, K.D. (2000). "Adolescent egocentrism: A comparison between adolescents and adults". Journal of Adolescence 23, 343–354.
Freud, S. (1968 [1923]). "Le Moi et le Ca". In: Essais de psychanalyse. Petite Bibliothèque, Payot, Paris.
Frey, B.S. (1997). Not Just for the Money. An Economic Theory of Personal Motivation. Edward Elgar, Cheltenham.
Gächter, S., Fehr, E. (1999). "Collective action as a social exchange". Journal of Economic Behavior and Organization 39, 341–369.
Gilligan, C. (1982). In a Different Voice: Psychological Theory and Women Development. Harvard University Press, Cambridge, MA.

Gintis, H. (2000a). Game Theory Evolving. Princeton University Press, Princeton.
Gintis, H. (2000b). "Strong reciprocity and human sociality". Journal of Theoretical Biology 206, 169–170.
Gintis, H. (2003). "The hitchhiker's guide to altruism: Gene-culture coevolution and the internalization of norms". Journal of Theoretical Biology 220, 407–418.
Gintis, H., Bowles, S., Boyd, R., Fehr, E. (2003). "Explaining altruistic behavior in humans". Evolution and Human Behavior 24, 153–172.
Glassman, M., Zan, B. (1995). "Moral activity and domain theory: An alternative interpretation of research with young children". Developmental Review 15, 434–457.
Gramzow, R.H., Gaertner, L., Sedikides, C. (2001). "Memory for in-group and out-group information in a minimal group context: the self as an informational base". Journal of Personality and Social Psychology 80, 188–205.
Greenberg, J., Scott, K.S. (1996). "When do workers bite the hands that feed them? Employee theft as a social exchange process". In: Staw, B.M., Cummings, L.L. (Eds.), Research in Organizational Behavior, vol. 18. JAI Press, Greenwich, CT, pp. 111–156.
Grusec, J.E. (1981). "Socialization processes and the development of altruism". In: Rushton, J.P., Sorrentino, R.M. (Eds.), Altruism and Helping Behavior: Social, Personality, and Developmental Perspectives. Erlbaum, Hillsdale, NJ.
Grusec, J.E., Redler, E. (1980). "Attribution, reinforcement, and altruism: A developmental analysis". Developmental Psychology 16, 525–534.
Güth, W. (1995). "On ultimatum bargaining experiments – a personal review". Journal of Economic Behavior and Organization 27, 329–344.
Güth, W., Schmittberger, R., Schwarze, B. (1982). "An experimental analysis of ultimatum bargaining". Journal of Economic Behavior and Organization 3, 367–388.
Habermas, J. (1979). Communication and the Evolution of Society. Beacon Press, Boston.
Haldane, J.B.S. (1953). "Animal populations and their regulation". Penguin Modern Biology 15, 9–14.
Hamilton, W.D. (1964). "The genetical evolution of social behavior". Journal of Theoretical Biology 7, 1–52.
Hampson, R.B. (1984). "Adolescent prosocial behavior: Peer group and situational factors associated with helping". Journal of Personality and Social Psychology 46, 153–162.
Harbaugh, W.T., Krause, K., Linday, S.G., Jr. (2002). "Children's bargaining behavior". Working Paper. University of Oregon.
Harder, J.W. (1992). "Play for pay: Effects of inequity in a pay-for-performance context". Administrative Science Quarterly 37, 321–335.
Harsanyi, J. (1955). "Cardinal welfare, individualistic ethics, and interpersonal comparisons of utility". Journal of Political Economy 63, 309–321.
Henrich, J. (2000). "Does culture matter in economic behavior? Ultimatum game bargaining among the Machiguenga of the Peruvian Amazon". American Economic Review 90, 973–979.
Henrich, J., Boyd, R., Bowles, S., Camerer, C., Fehr, E., Gintis, H. (2003). Foundations of Human Sociality: Ethnography and Experiments in Fifteen Small-Scale Societies. Oxford University Press, Oxford.
Higgins, E.T. (1981). "Role-taking and social judgement: Alternative developmental perspectives and processes". In: Flavell, J.H., Ross, L. (Eds.), Social Cognitive Development: Frontiers and Possible Futures. Cambridge University Press, Cambridge, pp. 119–153.
Hoffman, M.L. (1982). "Development of prosocial motivation: Empathy and guilt". In: Eisenberg, N. (Ed.), The Development of Prosocial Behavior. Academic Press, New York, pp. 281–313.
Hoffman, E., McCabe, K.A., Smith, V.L. (1998). "Behavioral foundations of reciprocity: experimental economics and evolutionary psychology". Economic Inquiry 38, 335–352.
Hoffman, M.L. (1975a). "Developmental synthesis of affect and cognition and its implications for altruistic motivations". Developmental Psychology 11, 607–622.
Hoffman, M.L. (1975b). "Altruistic behavior and the parent–child relationship". Journal of Personality and Social Psychology 31, 937–943.
Hoffman, M.L. (1981). "The development of empathy". In: Rushton, J.P., Sorrentino, R.M. (Eds.), Altruism and Helping Behavior: Social, Personality, and Developmental Perspectives. Erlbaum, Hillsdale, NJ, pp. 41–63.

Hoffman, M.L. (1988). "Moral development". In: Bornstein, M.H., Lamb, M.E. (Eds.), Developmental Psychology: An Advanced Textbook. Second ed. Erlbaum, Hillsdale, NJ, pp. 497–548.
Homans, G.C. (1953). "Status among clerical workers". Human Organization 12, 5–10.
Homans, G.C. (1954). "The cash posters". American Sociological Review 19, 724–733.
Howard, J.W., Rothbart, M. (1980). "Social categorization and memory for in-group and out-group behavior". Journal of Personality and Social Psychology 38 (2), 301–310.
Ingold, T. (1986). Evolution and Social Life. Cambridge University Press, Cambridge.
Jellal, M., Wolff, F.C. (2005). "Dynamique des transferts intergénérationnels et effet de démonstration". Annales d'économie et de statistique 77, 81–108.
Jetten, J., Spears, R., Manstead, A.S.R. (1996). "Intergroup norms and intergroup discrimination: Distinctive self-categorization and social identity effects". Journal of Personality and Social Psychology 71, 1222–1233.
Kahneman, D., Knetsch, J.L., Thaler, R. (1986). "Fairness as a constraint on profit-seeking: Entitlements in the market". American Economic Review 76, 728–741.
Kahneman, D., Wakker, P.P., Sarin, R. (1997). "Back to Bentham? Explorations of experienced utility". Quarterly Journal of Economics 112, 325–405.
Kandel, E., Lazear, E.P. (1992). "Peer pressure and partnerships". Journal of Political Economy 100, 801–817.
Karniol, R., Shomroni, D. (1999). "What being empathic means: Applying the transformation rule approach to individual differences in predicting the thoughts and feelings of prototypic and non-prototypic others". European Journal of Social Psychology 29, 147–160.
Kerr, N.L. (1995). "Norms in social dilemmas". In: Schroeder, D. (Ed.), Social Dilemmas: Social Psychological Perspectives. Pergamon, New York, pp. 31–47.
Kohlberg, L. (1984). "The psychology of moral development". In: Kohlberg, L. (Ed.), Essays on Moral Development, vol. 2. Harper and Row, San Francisco.
Kolm, S.C. (2000). "The theory of reciprocity". In: Gérard-Varet, L.A., Kolm, S.C., Mercier-Ythier, J. (Eds.), The Economics of Reciprocity, Giving and Altruism. Mc Millan Press Ltd, London, pp. 115–141.
Kolm, S.C. (2001). "Vox Populi, Vox Dei: Endogenous Social Choice and the Rational Original Position". Mimeographed.
Komorita, S.S., Parks, C.D. (1995). "Interpersonal relations: Mixed interaction". Annual Review of Psychology 46, 183–207.
Kreps, J.K., Davies, N.B. (1981). An Introduction to Behavioural Ecology. Blackwell, Oxford.
Krebs, D.L., Van Hesteren, F. (1994). "The development of altruism: Toward an integrative model". Developmental Review 14, 103–158.
Lepper, M.R. (1983). "Social-control processes and the internalization of social values: An attributional perspective". In: Higgins, E.T., Rubble, D.N., Hartup, W.W. (Eds.), Social Cognition and Social Development: A Socio-Cultural Perspective. Cambridge University Press, Cambridge, pp. 294–330.
Levin, I., Bekerman-Greenberg, R. (1980). "Moral judgement and moral reasoning in sharing: A developmental analysis". Genetic Psychological Monographs 101, 215–230.
Levine, C. (1979). "Stage acquisition and stage use: An appraisal of stage displacement explanations of variation in moral reasoning". Human Development 22, 145–164.
Levine, D.K. (1998). "Modeling altruism and spitefulness in experiments". Review of Economic Dynamics 1, 593–622.
Levins, R. (1970). "Extinction". In: Gerstenhaber, M. (Ed.), Some Mathematical Problems in Biology. In: Lectures on Mathematics in the Life Sciences, vol. 2. American Mathematical Society, Providence, pp. 75–108.
Lévy-Garboua, L., Blondel, S. (2002). "On the rationality of cognitive dissonance". In: Grossbard-Schechtman, S., Clague, C. (Eds.), The Expansion of Economics and other Disciplines: Towards an Inclusive Social Science. M.E. Sharpe, Inc., pp. 227–238.
Lévy-Garboua, L., Montmarquette, C. (1996). "Cognition in seemingly riskless choices and judgements". Rationality and Society 8, 167–185.
Lévy-Garboua, L., Montmarquette, C. (2004). "Reported job satisfaction: What does it mean?". Journal of Socioeconomics 33, 135–151.

Lévy-Garboua, L., Rapoport, B. (2006). "A theory of social norms, fairness, and competition". Mimeo. Centre d'Economie de la Sorbonne, Université de Paris I.

Lichtenstein, S., Slovic, P. (1971). "Reversals of preferences between bids and choices in gambling decisions". Journal of Experimental Psychology 89, 46–55.

Lind, E.A. (2001). "Fairness heuristic theory: Justice judgements as pivotal cognitions in organizational relations". In: Greenberg, J., Cropanzano, R. (Eds.), Advances in Organizational Justice. Stanford University Press, Stanford, CA, pp. 56–88.

Lind, E.A., Kanfer, R., Earley, P.C. (1990). "Voice, control, and procedural justice: Instrumental and non-instrumental concerns in fairness judgements". Journal of Personality and Social Psychology 59, 952–959.

Lind, E.A., Kray, L., Thompson, L. (1998). "The social construction of injustice: Fairness judgements in response to own and others' unfair treatment by authorities". Organizational Behavior and Human Decision Processes 75, 1–22.

Lind, E.A., Kray, L., Thompson, L. (2001). "Primacy effects in justice judgements: Testing predictions from fairness heuristic theory". Organizational Behavior and Human Decision Processes 85, 189–210.

Lind, E.A., Tyler, T.R. (1988). The Social Psychology of Procedural Justice. Plenum, New York.

Loewenstein, G.F., Thompson, L., Bazerman, M.H. (1989). "Social utility and decision making in interpersonal contexts". Journal of Personality and Social Psychology 57, 426–441.

Lumsden, C.J., Wilson, E.O. (1981). Genes, Mind and Culture. Harvard University Press, Cambridge, MA.

Manski, C.F. (2000). "Economic analysis of social interactions". Journal of Economic Perspectives 14 (3), 115–136.

Marks, G., Miller, N. (1987). "Ten years of research on the false consensus effect: An empirical and theoretical review". Psychological Bulletin 102, 72–90.

Masclet, D., Noussair, C., Tucker, S., Villeval, M.C. (2003). "Monetary and nonmonetary punishment in the voluntary contributions mechanism". American Economic Review 93, 366–380.

Maynard-Smith, J. (1964). "Group selection and kin selection". Nature 201, 1145–1147.

Maynard-Smith, J. (1982). Evolution and the Theory of Games. Cambridge University Press, Cambridge.

McFarland, D. (1985). Animal Behavior. Pitman Publishing Limited, London.

Mellers, B.A. (1982). "Equity judgements: A revision of Aristotelian views". Journal of Experimental Psychology: General 111, 242–270.

Mellers, B.A. (1986). "'Fair' allocations of salaries and taxes". Journal of Experimental Psychology 12, 80–91.

Messick, D.M., Brewer, M.B. (1983). "Solving social dilemmas: A review". In: Wheeler, L., Shaver, P. (Eds.), Review of Personality and Social Psychology, vol. 4. Sage, Beverly Hills, CA, pp. 11–44.

Michener, C.D. (1974). The Social Behavior of the Bees. Belknap Press, Harvard.

Miller, R.L., Bersoff, D.M., Hartwood, R.L. (1990). "Perceptions of social responsibilities in India and in the United States: Moral imperatives or personal decisions?". Journal of Personality and Social Psychology 58, 33–47.

Miller, J.G., Bersoff, D.M. (1992). "Culture and moral judgement: How are conflicts between justice and interpersonal responsibilities resolved?". Journal of Personality and Social Psychology 62, 541–554.

Miller, P.A., Eisenberg, N., Fabes, R.A., Shell, R. (1996). "Relations of moral reasoning and vicarious emotion to young children's prosocial behavior toward peers and adults". Developmental Psychology 32, 210–219.

Miller, P.H., Kessel, F.S., Flavell, J.H. (1970). "Thinking about people thinking about people thinking about: A study of social cognitive development". Child Development 41, 613–623.

Mitchell, G., Tetlock, P.E., Mellers, B.A., Ordonez, L.D. (1993). "Judgments of social justice: Compromises between equality and efficiency". Journal of Personality and Social Psychology 65, 629–639.

Mullen, B., Atkins, J.L., Champion, D.S., Edwards, C., Hardy, D., Story, J.E., Vanderklok, M. (1985). "The false consensus effect: A meta-analysis of 155 hypothesis tests". Journal of Experimental Social Psychology 21, 262–283.

Nishida, T. (1986). "Local traditions and cultural transmissions". In: Smuts, B.B., Cheney, D.L., Seyfarth, R.M., Wrangham, R.W., Struhsaker, T.T. (Eds.), Primate Societies. The University of Chicago Press, Chicago, pp. 462–474.

Oliner, S.P., Oliner, P.M. (1988). The Altruistic Personality: Rescuers of Jews in Nazi Europe. Free Press, New York.
Offerman, T. (2002). "Hurting hurts more than helping helps". European Economic Review 46, 1423–1437.
Otten, S., Wentura, D. (2001). "Self-anchoring and in-group favoritism: An individual profiles analysis". Journal of Experimental Social Psychology 37, 1–8.
Parducci, A. (1965). "Category judgement: A range-frequency model". Psychological Review 72, 407–418.
Park, B., Judd, C.M. (1990). "Measures and models of perceived group variability". Journal of Personality and Social Psychology 59, 173–191.
Payne, J.W., Bettman, J.R., Johnson, E.J. (1992). "Behavioral decision research: A constructive processing perspective". Annual Review of Psychology 43, 87–131.
Piaget, J. (1973). Le jugement moral chez l'enfant. Presses Universitaires de France, Paris; English translation Piaget, J., "Moral Judgment of the Child". Free Press Paperbacks, New York, 1997.
Pollis, N.P. (1968). "Reference group re-examined". British Journal of Sociology 19, 300–307.
Rabbie, J.M., Horwitz, M. (1969). "Arousal of ingroup–outgroup bias by a chance win or loss". Journal of Personality and Social Psychology 13, 269–277.
Rabbie, J.M., Schot, J.C., Visser, L. (1989). "Social identity theory: A conceptual and empirical critique from the perspective of a behavioural interaction model". European Journal of Social Psychology 19, 171–202.
Rabin, M. (1993). "Incorporating fairness into game theory and economics". American Economic Review 83, 1281–1302.
Rabin, M. (1998). "Psychology and economics". Journal of Economic Literature 36 (1), 11–46.
Rawls, J. (1971). A Theory of Justice. Harvard University Press, Cambridge, MA.
Robson, A.J. (2001). "The biological basis of economic behavior". Journal of Economic Literature 39, 11–33.
Roch, S.G., Lane, J.A.S., Samuelson, C.P., Allison, S.T., Dent, J.L. (2000). "Cognitive load and the equality heuristic: A two-stage model of resource overconsumption in small groups". Organizational Behavior and Human Decision Processes 82, 185–212.
Rohrbaugh, J., McClelland, G., Quinn, R. (1986). "Measuring the relative importance of utilitarian and egalitarian values: A study of individual differences about fair distribution". In: Arkes, H.R., Hammond, K.R. (Eds.), Judgment and Decision Making: An Interdisciplinary Reader. Cambridge University Press, Cambridge, pp. 613–624.
Rosenhan, D.L. (1970). "The natural socialization of altruistic autonomy". In: Macauley, J., Berkowitz, L. (Eds.), Altruism and Helping Behavior. Academic Press, New York, pp. 251–268.
Ross, L., Greene, D., House, P. (1977). "The 'false consensus effect': An egocentric bias in social perception and attribution processes". Journal of Personality and Social Psychology 13, 279–301.
Roth, A.E., Prasnikar, V., Okuno-Fujiwara, M., Zamir, S. (1991). "Bargaining and market behavior in Jerusalem, Ljubljana, Pittsburgh, and Tokyo: An experimental study". American Economic Review 81, 1068–1095.
Runciman, W.G. (1966). Relative Deprivation and Social Justice. University of California Press, Berkeley.
Rushton, J.P. (1980). Altruism, Socialization, and Society. Prentice Hall, Englewood Cliffs, NJ.
Rushton, J.P. (1981). "Television as a Socializer". In: Rushton, J.P., Sorrentino, R.M. (Eds.), Altruism and Helping Behavior: Social, Personality, and Developmental Perspectives. Erlbaum, Hillsdale, NJ, pp. 91–107.
Samuelson, C.D., Allison, S.T. (1994). "Cognitive factors affecting the use of social decision heuristics in resource-sharing tasks". Organizational Behavior and Human Decision Processes 58, 1–27.
Schachter, S. (1951). "Deviation, rejection, and communication". Journal of Abnormal and Social Psychology 46, 190–207.
Schaller, M., Cialdini, R.B. (1988). "The economics of empathic helping: Support for a mood management motive". Journal of Experimental Social Psychology 24, 163–181.
Segal U., Sobel J. (1999). "Tit-for-tat: Foundations of preference for reciprocity in strategic settings. Economics discussion paper". University of California, San Diego.
Silk, J.B. (1986). "Social behavior in evolutionary perspective". In: Smuts, B.B., Cheney, D.L., Seyfarth, R.M., Wrangham, R.W., Struhsaker, T.T. (Eds.), Primate Societies. The University of Chicago Press, Chicago, pp. 318–329.

Simner, L. (1971). "Newborns' response to the cry of another infant". Developmental Psychology 5, 136–150.
Smith, A. (1759). The Theory of Moral Sentiments.
Smith, A. (1776). An Inquiry into the Nature and Causes of the Wealth of Nations. Modern Library, New York.
Smith, A. (1982). The Theory of Moral Sentiments. Reprinted in 1982 from the Oxford University Press edition (1976). Liberty Classics, Indianapolis.
Smuts, B.B., Cheney, D.L., Seyfarth, R.M., Wrangham, R.W., Struhsaker, T.T. (Eds.) (1986). Primate Societies. The University of Chicago Press, Chicago.
Stark, O. (1995). Altruism and Beyond: An Economic Analysis of Transfers and Exchanges Within Families and Groups Oscar Morgenstern Memorial Lectures. Cambridge University Press, Cambridge, MA.
Staub, E. (1971). "Helping a person in distress: The influence of implicit and explicit "rules" of conduct on children and adults". Journal of Personality and Social Psychology 17, 137–144.
Staub, E. (1974). "Helping a distressed person: Social, personality, and stimulus determinants". In: Berkowitz, L. (Ed.), Advances in Experimental Social Psychology, vol. 7. Academic Press, New York, pp. 293–341.
Staub, E. (1979). Positive Social Behavior and Morality, vol. 2: Socialization and Development. Academic Press, New York.
Staub, E. (1981). "Promotive positive behavior in schools, in other educational settings, and in the home". In: Rushton, J.P., Sorrentino, R.M. (Eds.), Altruism and Helping Behavior: Social, Personality, and Developmental Perspectives. Erlbaum, Hillsdale, NJ, pp. 109–133.
Staub, E. (1992). "The origin of caring, helping and non-aggression: Parental socialization, the family system, schools, and cultural influence". In: Oliner, P.M., Baron, L., Blum, L.A., Krebs, D.L., Smolenska, M.Z. (Eds.), Embracing the Other: Philosophical, Psychological, and Historical Perspectives on Altruism. New York University Press, New York, pp. 390–412.
Stinson, L., Ickes, W. (1992). "Empathic accuracy in the interactions of male friends versus male strangers". Journal of Personality and Social Psychology 62, 787–797.
Stouffer, S.A., Suchman, E.A., DeVinney, L.C., Star, S.A., Williams, R.M., Jr. (1949). The American Soldier, vol. I. Adjustment during Army Life. Princeton University Press, Princeton, NJ.
Tajfel, H., Billig, M., Bundy, R.P., Flament, C. (1971). "Social categorization and intergroup behavior". European Journal of Social Psychology 1, 149–178.
Tajfel, H., Turner, J.C. (1979). "An integrative theory of intergroup conflict". In: Worchel, S., Austin, W.G. (Eds.), The Social Psychology of Intergroup Relations. Brooks/Cole Publ., Monterey, pp. 33–47.
Tajfel, H., Turner, J.C. (1986). "The social identity theory of intergroup behavior". In: Worchel, S., Austin, W.G. (Eds.), Psychology of Intergroup Relations. Nelson Hall, Chicago, pp. 7–24.
Trivers, R.L. (1971). "The evolution of reciprocal altruism". Quarterly Review of Biology 46, 35–57.
Turiel, E. (1983). The Development of Social Knowledge: Morality and Convention. Cambridge University Press, Cambridge.
Turiel, E. (1998). "Prosocial development". In: Eisenberg, N. (Ed.), Handbook of Child Psychology: Socialization, Personality, and Social Development. Wiley, New York, pp. 863–932.
Tyler, T.R., Lind, E.A. (1992). "A relational model of authority in groups". In: Zanna, M. (Ed.), Advances in Experimental Social Psychology, vol. 25. Academic Press, San Diego, CA, pp. 115–191.
Underwood, B., Moore, B. (1982). "Perspective-taking and altruism". Psychological Bulletin 91, 143–173.
Van Boven, L., Dunning, D., Loewenstein, G. (2000). "Egocentric empathy gaps between owners and buyers". Journal of Personality and Social Psychology 7, 66–76.
Van den Bos, K., Vermunt, R., Wilke, H.A.M. (1997). "Procedural and distributive justice: What is fair depends more on what comes first than on what comes next?". Journal of Personality and Social Psychology 72, 95–104.
Van den Bos, K., Wilke, H.A.M., Lind, E.A. (1998). "When do we need procedural fairness? The role of trust in authority". Journal of Personality and Social Psychology 75, 1449–1458.
Van Dijke, E., Wilke, H. (1995). "Coordination rules in asymmetric social dilemmas: A comparison between public good dilemmas and resource dilemmas". Journal of Experimental Social Psychology 31, 1–27.

Van Dijke, E., Wilke, H., Wilke, M., Metman, L. (1999). "What information do we use in social dilemmas? Environmental uncertainty and the employment of coordination rules". Journal of Experimental Social Psychology 35, 109–135.
Veblen, T. (1934). The Theory of the Leisure Class. Modern Library, New York.
Walker, L.J., Gustafson, P., Hennig, K.H. (2001). "The consolidation/transition model in moral reasoning development". Developmental Psychology 37, 187–197.
Wilson, E.O. (1971). The Insect Society. Belknap Press, Harvard.
Wilson, E.O. (1975). Sociobiology: The New Synthesis. Belknap Press, Harvard.
Wynne-Edwards, V.C. (1959). "The control of the population density through social behavior: A hypothesis". Ibis 101, 436–441.
Yamagishi, T., Jin, N., Kiyonari, T. (1999). "Bounded generalized reciprocity: In-group boasting and in-group favoritism". Advances in Group Processes 16, 161–197.
Youniss, J. (1980). Parents and peers in social development: A Sullivan–Piaget perspective. Chicago University Press, Chicago.
Zajonc, R.B. (1980). "Feeling and thinking: Preferences need no inferences". American Psychologist 35, 151–175.

Chapter 8

THE ECONOMICS OF FAIRNESS, RECIPROCITY AND ALTRUISM – EXPERIMENTAL EVIDENCE AND NEW THEORIES

ERNST FEHR

Institute for Empirical Research in Economics, University of Zurich, Bluemlisalpstrasse 10, CH-8006 Zurich, Switzerland
e-mail: efehr@iew.unizh.ch

KLAUS M. SCHMIDT

Department of Economics, University of Munich, Ludwigstrasse 28, D-80539 Muenchen, Germany
e-mail: klaus.schmidt@Lrz.uni-muenchen.de

Contents

Abstract	616
Keywords	616
1. Introduction and overview	617
2. Empirical foundations of other-regarding preferences	621
2.1. Other-regarding behavior in simple experiments	621
2.2. Other-regarding preferences or irrational behavior	628
2.3. Neuroeconomic foundations of other-regarding preferences	631
3. Theories of other-regarding preferences	636
3.1. Social preferences	637
3.1.1. Altruism	638
3.1.2. Relative income and envy	639
3.1.3. Inequity aversion	639
3.1.4. Hybrid models	642
3.2. Interdependent preferences	644
3.2.1. Altruism and spitefulness	645
3.3. Models of intention based reciprocity	647
3.3.1. Fairness equilibrium	647
3.3.2. Intentions in sequential games	649
3.3.3. Merging intentions and social preferences	650
3.3.4. Guilt aversion and promises	651
3.4. Axiomatic approaches	652
4. Discriminating between theories of other-regarding preferences	653

Handbook of the Economics of Giving, Altruism and Reciprocity, Volume 1
Edited by Serge-Christophe Kolm and Jean Mercier Ythier
Copyright © 2006 Elsevier B.V. All rights reserved
DOI: 10.1016/S1574-0714(06)01008-6

    4.1. Who are the relevant reference actors? 654
    4.2. Equality versus efficiency 656
    4.3. Revenge versus inequity reduction 660
    4.4. Does kindness trigger rewards? 662
    4.5. Maximin preferences 664
    4.6. Preferences for honesty 666
    4.7. Summary and outlook 667
5. Economic applications 669
    5.1. Cooperation and collective action 669
    5.2. Endogenous formation of cooperative institutions 673
    5.3. How fairness, reciprocity and competition interact 676
    5.4. Fairness and reciprocity as a source of economic incentives 680
6. Conclusions 683
References 684

Abstract

Most economic models are based on the *self-interest hypothesis* that assumes that material self-interest exclusively motivates *all* people. Experimental economists have gathered overwhelming evidence in recent years, however, that systematically refutes the self-interest hypothesis, suggesting that concerns for altruism, fairness, and reciprocity strongly motivate many people. Moreover, several theoretical papers demonstrate that the observed phenomena can be explained in a rigorous and tractable manner. These theories then induced a first wave of experimental research which offered exciting insights into both the nature of preferences and the relative performance of competing fairness theories. The purpose of this chapter is to review these developments, to point out open questions, and to suggest avenues for future research. We also discuss recent neuroeconomic evidence that is consistent with the view that many people have a taste for mutual cooperation and the punishment of norm violators. We further illustrate the powerful impact of fairness concerns on cooperation, competition, incentives, and contract design.

Keywords

behavioral economics, other-regarding preferences, fairness, reciprocity, altruism, experiments, incentives, contracts, competition

JEL classification: C7, C9, D0, J3

1. Introduction and overview

Many influential economists, including Adam Smith (1759), Gary Becker (1974), Kenneth Arrow (1981), Paul Samuelson (1993) and Amartya Sen (1995), pointed out that people often do care for the well-being of others and that this may have important economic consequences. However, most economists still routinely assume that material self-interest is the *sole* motivation of *all* people. This practice contrasts sharply with a large body of evidence gathered by experimental economists and psychologists during the last two decades. This evidence indicates that a substantial percentage of the people are strongly motivated by other-regarding preferences and that concerns for the well-being of others, for fairness and for reciprocity, cannot be ignored in social interactions. One purpose of this chapter is to review this evidence, suggest how it can be best interpreted, and how it should be modeled. We take up this task in Section 2, where we describe the most important experiments that have radically changed the views of many experimental economists over the last two decades. Section 2 also describes recent neuroeconomic experiments that combine the tools of experimental economics with non-invasive brain imaging methods of modern neuroscience to better understand how the brain generates other-regarding behavior.[1]

In hindsight, it is ironic that experiments have proven to be critical for the discovery and the understanding of other-regarding preferences because experimental economists were firmly convinced for several decades that other-regarding motives only had limited impact. They believed that the self-interest assumption provides a good description for most people's behavior. At best, other-regarding behavior was viewed as a temporary deviation from the strong forces of self-interest. Vernon Smith discovered in the 1950s that experimental markets quickly converge to the competitive equilibrium if subjects trade a homogeneous good and all aspects of the good are fully contractible [Smith (1962)]. Hundreds of experiments have since confirmed the remarkable convergence properties of experimental markets [see Davis and Holt (1993), for example]. The equilibrium in these experiments is computed assuming that *all* players are *exclusively* self-interested. Therefore, the quick convergence to equilibrium was interpreted as a confirmation of the self-interest hypothesis.

However, the bargaining and cooperation experiments described in Section 2 below illustrate that this conclusion was premature because a large percentage of the subjects in these experiments – some of which involve fully representative subject pools for whole countries – exhibit other regarding behavior that the self-interest hypothesis cannot rationalize in any reasonable way. Subjects in these experiments have to make simple decisions in situations where the self-interested choice is salient and easy to understand. Thus, if they deviate from the self-interested choice, we can conclude that they

---

[1] Readers who are interested in the role of reciprocity and altruism at the workplace and, more generally, in cooperative endeavours, should consult the excellent Handbook Chapters 21 and 22 by Putterman and Rotemberg. Kolm, provides an interesting discussion of the concept of reciprocity that differs from the preference based theories dealt with in our chapter.

exhibit some form of other-regarding preference. Given this evidence, the real question is no longer whether many people have other-regarding preferences, but under which conditions these preferences have important economic and social effects and what the best way to describe and model these preferences is.

However, the evidence from competitive market experiments remains. How can we reconcile the fact that the self-interest model predicts behavior in competitive experimental markets with fully contractible goods very well while it completely fails in the simple experiments described in Section 2 below? Some of the recently developed models of other-regarding preferences that are described and discussed in some detail in Section 3 provide a solution to this puzzle; they show that competition may completely remove the impact of other-regarding preferences. Thus, the fact that we do not observe other-regarding behavior in certain competitive markets does not mean that other-regarding preferences are absent. Instead, rational individuals will not express their other-regarding preferences in these markets because the market makes the achievement of other-regarding goals impossible or infinitely costly. However, a large amount of economic activity takes place outside competitive markets – in markets with a small number of traders, in markets with informational frictions, in firms and organizations, and under contracts which are neither completely specified nor enforceable. Models based on the self-interest assumption frequently make very misleading predictions in these environments, while models of other-regarding preferences predict much better. These models thus provide fresh and experimentally confirmed insights into important phenomena like the persistence of non-competitive wage premiums, the incompleteness of contracts and the absence of explicit incentive schemes, the allocation of property rights, the conditions for successful collective action, and the optimal design of institutions.

One of the exciting aspects of this development is that the newly developed theories of other-regarding preferences were tested in a new wave of experiments, sometimes before they were even published. This led to important insights into the power and the limits of different models which will be discussed in Section 4. These experiments also show that it is possible to discriminate between different motivational assumptions, answering one important objection to this research program. There has always been a strong convention in economics of not explaining puzzling observations by changing assumptions on preferences. Changing preferences is said to open Pandora's Box because everything can be explained by assuming the "right" preferences. We believe that this convention made sense in the past when economists did not have the tools to examine the nature of preferences in a scientifically rigorous way. However, due to the development of experimental techniques these tools are now available. In fact, one purpose of this paper is to show that the past decade has yielded both progress on and fascinating new insights into the nature of other regarding preferences.

While many people are strongly concerned about others' well-being, fairness, and reciprocity, we consider it equally important to stress that the available experimental evidence suggests that there are also many subjects who behave quite selfishly even when they are given a chance to affect other people's well-being at a relatively small cost. One of the exciting insights of some of the newly developed theoretical models is that the interaction between fair and selfish individuals is key to understanding the observed behavior in strategic settings. These models explain why almost all people behave as if they are completely selfish in some strategic settings, while the same people will behave as if driven by fairness in others.

We describe several examples that show the economic importance of other-regarding preferences in different settings in the final part of the paper, Section 5. Among other things, we provide evidence indicating that other-regarding preferences are decisive for explaining collective action and multi-lateral cooperation. We present, in particular, recent evidence showing that if individuals can choose between an institution allowing mutual punishment of non-cooperative behavior or one which rules out mutual punishment, they converge to a behavioral equilibrium in which the selfish and the other-regarding types unanimously prefer the punishment institution. Moreover, punishment of free riders actually occurs and drives the behavior in the punishment institution towards a state in which full cooperation and no punishment occurs. The threat of punishment alone suffices to generate full cooperation. This experiment constitutes a powerful example suggesting that other-regarding preferences have shaped many of our cooperative institutions. In addition, we document that other-regarding preferences have deep effects on outcomes in markets with moral hazard problems, while the interaction between selfish and fair-minded subjects in markets with fully contractible goods generates outcomes that are close to the competitive prediction. Finally, we report how other-regarding preferences influence voting behavior in taxation games. These examples, although important, provide only a glimpse into the full range of possibilities how other-regarding preferences shape social and economic interactions including, perhaps, some of our most fundamental institutions. The examples also show that the main reason why other-regarding preferences are important lies in the fact that even a minority of other-regarding people may generate powerful cooperation incentives for selfish people.

To set the stage for the discussion of the following sections we give an informal and intuitive definition of several types of other-regarding preferences that received a lot of attention in the recent literature that tries to explain behavior in economic experiments. In Section 3 we define these preferences in a formal and more rigorous way. The theoretical literature on other-regarding preferences has focused on three departures from the standard self-interest model. In addition to the material resources allocated to him a person may also care about: (i) The material resources allocated to other agents in a relevant reference group. (ii) The fairness of the behavior of relevant reference agents. (iii) The "type" of the reference agents, i.e. whether the agents have selfish, altruistic, spiteful, or fair minded preferences.

Consider first the case where the utility function of an individual also depends on the material resources that other agents in a relevant reference group receive. A typical example is *altruism*. Altruism is a form of *un*conditional kindness; that is, a favor given does not emerge as a response to a favor received [Andreoni (1989), Andreoni and Miller (2002), Cox, Sadiraj and Sadiraj (2001), Charness and Rabin (2002)]. In technical terms, altruism means that the first derivate of the utility function of an individual with respect to the material resources received by any other agent is always strictly positive. Thus, an altruist is willing to sacrifice own resources in order to improve the well being of others. The opposite case is *envy* or *spitefulness*. A spiteful person *always* values the material payoff of relevant reference agents negatively. Such a person is, therefore, always willing to decrease the material payoff of a reference agent at a personal cost to himself [Bolton (1991), Kirchsteiger (1994), Mui Vai-Lam (1995)] irrespective of both the payoff distribution and the reference agent's fair or unfair behavior. Therefore, spiteful preferences represent the antisocial version of other-regarding preferences. A conditional form of altruism and/or envy is *inequity aversion* [Fehr and Schmidt (1999), Bolton and Ockenfels (2000), Charness and Rabin (2002)]. An individual is inequity averse if, in addition to his material self-interest, his utility increases if the allocation of material payoffs becomes more equitable. Thus, an inequity averse person may value additional material resources allocated to a reference agent positively or negatively, depending on whether the allocation becomes more or less equitable. Obviously, the definition of equity is very important in these models. In the context of experimental games equity is usually defined as equality of monetary payoffs. However, departures from equality have been defined differently. They can be measured in terms of the income differences between the individual and all relevant reference agents, or in terms of the difference between the individual and the least well-off in his reference group, or in terms of the individual's relative share of the overall surplus.

The case where preferences depend on the fair or unfair *behavior* of other agents has also received much attention in the literature and is often called reciprocity. A reciprocal individual, as we define it here, responds to actions he perceives to be kind in a kind manner, and to actions he perceives to be hostile in a hostile manner [Rabin (1993), Segal and Sobel (2004), Dufwenberg and Kirchsteiger (2004), Falk and Fischbacher (2005)]. Thus, preferences do not only depend on material payoffs but also on intentions, i.e. on beliefs about why an agent has chosen a certain action. This cannot be modeled by using conventional game theory but requires the tools of psychological game theory [Geanakoplos, Pearce and Stacchetti (1989)].

Finally, preferences may depend on the type of opponent [Levine (1998)]. According to type-based reciprocity, an individual behaves kindly towards a "good" person (i.e, a person with kind or altruistic preferences) and hostilely towards a "bad" person (i.e. a person with unkind or spiteful preferences). Note that it is the "type" of a person and not the "intention" of his action that affects preferences in this case. Therefore, type-based reciprocity can be modeled using conventional game theory.

It is important to emphasize that it is not the expectation of future material benefits that drives reciprocity. Reciprocal behavior as defined above differs fundamentally from "cooperative" or "retaliatory" behavior in repeated interactions that is motivated by future material benefits. Therefore, reciprocal behavior in one-shot interactions is often called "strong reciprocity" in contrast to "weak reciprocity" that is motivated by long-term self-interest in repeated interactions [Gintis (2000), Fehr and Fischbacher (2003)].

Readers who are mainly interested in the experimental evidence that documents the existence of other-regarding preferences should first consult Section 2 and then Section 4 of this chapter. In Section 2, we present a list of simple experiments that indicate the existence and the prevailing patterns of other-regarding preferences. In Section 4, we discuss the most recent evidence in the light of the newly developed models of other-regarding preferences. Readers who are mainly interested in the different models of other-regarding preferences and how they perform relative to the available evidence can directly jump to Section 3 and Section 4. Finally those readers who are mainly interested in the economic impact of other-regarding preferences may directly jump to Section 5.

2. Empirical foundations of other-regarding preferences

2.1. Other-regarding behavior in simple experiments

In the introduction, we referred to the previously held belief of many experimental economists in the validity of the self-interest hypothesis. This "commitment" to the self-interest hypothesis slowly weakened in the 1980s, when experimental economists started studying bilateral bargaining games and interactions in small groups in controlled laboratory settings [see, e.g., Roth, Malouf and Murningham (1981), Güth, Schmittberger and Schwarze (1982)]. One of the important experimental games that eventually led many people to realize that the self-interest hypothesis is problematic was the so-called "ultimatum game" by Güth, Schmittberger and Schwarze (1982). In addition, games like the "dictator game", the "power to take game", the "third party punishment game", the "gift exchange game" and the "trust game" played an important role in weakening the exclusive reliance on the self-interest hypothesis. All these games share the feature of simplicity, enabling the experimental subjects to understand them and therefore making inferences about subjects' motives more convincing. In fact, in all these games one player has a strictly dominant strategy if he is self-interested and this selfish strategy is salient and easy to understand in all cases. Therefore, if this player does not choose his or her selfish strategy, we can infer that he deliberately did not do so, i.e., we can make inferences about his motives.

In the ultimatum game, a pair of subjects has to agree on the division of a fixed sum of money. Person A, the proposer, can make one proposal of how to divide the amount. Person B, the responder, can accept or reject the proposed division. In case of rejection, both receive nothing; in case of acceptance, the proposal is implemented. Under the standard assumptions that (i) both the proposer and the responder are rational *and* care only about how much money they get and (ii) that the proposer knows that the responder is rational and selfish, the subgame perfect equilibrium prescribes a rather extreme outcome: the responder accepts *any* positive amount of money and, hence, the proposer gives the responder the smallest money unit, ε, and keeps the rest to himself.

A robust result in the ultimatum game, across hundreds of experiments, is that the vast majority of the offers to the responder are between 40 and 50 percent of the available surplus. Moreover, proposals offering the responder less than 20 percent of the surplus are rejected with probability 0.4 to 0.6. In addition, the probability of rejection is decreasing in the size of the offer [see, e.g., Güth, Schmittberger and Schwarze (1982), Camerer and Thaler (1995), Roth (1995), Camerer (2003) and the references therein]. Apparently, many responders do not behave in a self-interest maximizing manner. In general, the motive indicated for the rejection of positive, yet "low", offers is that subjects view them as unfair. A further robust result is that many proposers seem to anticipate that low offers will be rejected with a high probability. A comparison of the results of dictator games and ultimatum games suggests this. The responder's option to reject is removed in a dictator game; the responder must accept any proposal. Forsythe et al. (1994) were the first to compare the offers in ultimatum and dictator games. Self-interested proposers should allocate nothing to the Recipient in the dictator game. In experiments, proposers typically dictate allocations that assign the Recipient on average between 10 and 25 percent of the surplus, with modal allocations at 50 percent and zero. These allocations are much less than proposers' offers in ultimatum games, although most players do offer something. Comparing dictator with bilateral ultimatum games shows that fear of rejection is *part* of the explanation for proposers' generous offers, because they do offer less when rejection is precluded. But many subjects offer something in the dictator game, so fear of rejection is not the entire explanation. The considerably lower offers in the dictator game suggest that many proposers apply backwards induction. This interpretation is also supported by the surprising observation of Roth et al. (1991), who showed that the modal offer in the ultimatum game tends to maximize the proposer's expected income.[2]

The "power to take game", invented by Bosman and van Winden (2002), is another tool that has proven useful in understanding punishment behavior. Both the proposer and the responder are endowed with some income in this game. Subjects may have earned this income, as in Bosman and van Winden (2002), or the experimenter may have allocated the money to the subjects as in Bosman, Sutter and van Winden (2005). The proposer can set a take or "theft" rate $t \in [0, 1]$ which is the fraction of the responder's endowment that will be transferred to the proposer. The responder is then informed of the take rate and can destroy part or all of his income. Thus, if the responder destroys his or her whole income nothing is transferred to the proposer. If the responder destroys only a fraction d, $d \in [0, 1]$, of his income, the proposer receives a share of $t(1 - d)$ of the responder's pre-destruction income. In contrast to the ultimatum game, the power to take game allows the punishment behavior to vary continuously with the take rate. The evidence indicates that the destruction rate is roughly $d = 0.5$ for take rates

---

[2] Suleiman (1996) reports the results of ultimatum games with varying degrees of veto power. In these games a rejection meant that λ percent of the cake was destroyed. For example, if $\lambda = 0.8$, and the proposer offered a 9 : 1 division of $10, a rejection implied that the proposer received $1.8 while the responder received $0.2. Suleiman reports that proposers' offers are strongly increasing in λ.

around $t = 0.8$, regardless of whether the initial endowment was earned through effort or exogenously allocated by the experimenter. However, the destruction rate is higher for lower take rates if the initial endowment is given to the subjects without effort, whereas the destruction rate is higher for takes rates above 0.8 if the endowment was earned through effort. This indicates that the way the initial endowment is allocated to the subjects matters because it seems to affect their feelings of entitlement. Hoffman, McCabe and Smith (1996b) also reported that feelings of entitlement may be important for punishment behavior in the context of the ultimatum game.

The responders' feelings may be hurt if he or she receives an unfairly low offer in the ultimatum game. Thus, pride or motives to retain self-respect may drive a rejection. Therefore, the question arises whether people would also be willing to punish violations of social or moral norms if they themselves are not the victim of the norm violation. A game that is particularly suited to examine this question is the so-called third party punishment Game [Fehr and Fischbacher (2004)]. The three players in this game are denoted A, B, and C. A and B play a simple dictator game. Player A, the proposer, receives an endowment of S tokens of which he can transfer any amount to player B, the Recipient. B has no endowment and no choice to make. Player C has an endowment of $S/2$ tokens and observes player A's transfer. Player C can then assign punishment points to player A. Player C incurs costs of 1 token and player A is charged 3 tokens for each punishment point player C assigns to player A. Since punishment is costly, a self-interested player C will never punish. However, if there is a sharing norm, player C may well punish player A if A gives too little.

In fact, in the experiments conducted by Fehr and Fischbacher (2004), where $S = 100$, player A was rarely punished if he transferred 50 or more tokens to player B. If he transferred less than 50 tokens, roughly 60 percent of players C punished A and the less A transferred, the stronger was the punishment. If nothing was transferred, A received on average 14 punishment points, reducing A's income by 42 tokens. Thus, if nothing was transferred player A earned (on average) more money in this setting than if he transferred the fair amount of 50. However, if player C was himself the recipient in another dictator game unrelated to that played between A and B, C punished more. All transfer levels below 50 were on average punished so strongly in this case that it was no longer in player A's self-interest to transfer less than 50. It seems that if C is himself a recipient, he is more able to empathize with B if B receives little and thus increase the punishment imposed on A. Finally, if third party punishment is compared to second party punishment (i.e. if B can punish A), it turns out that second party punishment is significantly stronger than is third party punishment. Note that this does not necessarily mean that third party punishment is less effective in sustaining social norms because third parties are often more numerous than second parties.

Dictator games measure pure altruism. Interesting companion games are the trust game [Berg, Dickhaut and McCabe (1995)] and the gift exchange game [Fehr, Kirchsteiger and Riedl (1993)]. In a trust game, both an Investor and a Trustee receive an amount of money S from the experimenter. The Investor can send between zero and S to the Trustee. The experimenter then triples the amount sent, which we term y, so that the Trustee has $S + 3y$. The Trustee is then free to return anything between zero and $S + 3y$ to the Investor. The Investor's payoff is $S - y + z$ and that of the Trustee is $S + 3y - z$ where z denotes the final transfer from the Trustee to the Investor. The trust game is essentially a dictator game in which the Trustee dictates an allocation, with the difference, however, that the Investor's initial investment determines the amount to be shared.

In theory, self-interested Trustees will keep everything and repay $z = 0$. Self-interested Investors who anticipate this should transfer nothing, i.e., $y = 0$. In experiments in several developed countries, Investors typically invest about half the maximum on average, although there is substantial variation across subjects. Trustees tend to repay roughly y so that trust is not or only slightly profitable. The amount Trustees repay increases on average with y if the change in the Investors' transfer is sufficiently high; the Trustees do not necessarily pay back more if the increase in y is modest.

In the gift exchange game, there is again a proposer and a responder. The proposer offers an amount of money $w \in [\underline{w}, \overline{w}]$, $\underline{w} \geqslant 0$, which can be interpreted as a wage payment, to the responder. The responder can accept or reject w. In case of a rejection, both players receive zero payoff; in case of acceptance, the responder has to make a costly "effort" choice $e \in [\underline{e}, \overline{e}]$, $\underline{e} > 0$. A higher effort level increases the proposer's monetary payoff but is costly to the responder. A selfish responder will always choose the lowest feasible effort level $\underline{e}$ and will, in equilibrium, never reject any w. Therefore, if the proposer is selfish and anticipates the responder's selfishness the subgame perfect proposal is the lowest feasible wage level $\underline{w}$. The main difference between the gift exchange game and the trust game is that in the trust game it is the first mover's action that increases the available surplus, while in the gift exchange game it is the second mover who can increase the surplus.

The gift exchange game captures a principal-agent relation with highly incomplete contracts in a stylized way. Several authors have conducted variants of the gift exchange game.[3] All of these studies report that the mean effort is, in general, positively related to the offered wage which is consistent with the interpretation that the responders, on average, reward generous wage offers with generous effort choices. However, as in the case of the ultimatum and the trust game, there are considerable individual differences among the responders. While a sizeable share of responders (frequently roughly 40 percent, sometimes more than 50 percent) typically exhibit a reciprocal effort pattern, a substantial fraction of responders also always make purely selfish effort choices or choices which seem to deviate randomly from the self-interested action. Despite the presence of selfish responders, the relation between average effort and wages can be sufficiently steep to render a high wage policy profitable which may induce proposers to pay wages far above $\underline{w}$. Evidence for this interpretation comes from Fehr, Kirchsteiger

---

[3] See, e.g., Fehr, Kirchsteiger and Riedl (1993, 1998), Charness (1996, 2000), Fehr and Falk (1999), Gächter and Falk (1999), Falk, Gächter and Kovács (1999), Hannan, Kagel and Moser (1999), Brandts and Charness (2004) and Fehr, Klein and Schmidt (2004).

and Riedl (1998), who embedded the gift exchange game into an experimental market.[4] In addition, there was a control condition where the experimenter exogenously fixed the effort level. Note that the responders can no longer reward generous wages with high effort levels in the control condition. It turns out that the average wage is substantially reduced when the effort is exogenously fixed.

The facts observed in the games mentioned above are now well established and there is little disagreement about them. However, questions remain about which factors determine and change the behavior in these games. For example, a routine question in discussions is whether a rise in the stake level will eventually induce subjects to behave in a self-interested manner. Several papers examine this question [Hoffman, McCabe and Smith (1996a), Fehr and Tougareva (1995), Slonim and Roth (1997), Cameron (1999)]; the surprising answer is that relatively large increases in the monetary stakes did little or nothing to change behavior. Hoffman, McCabe and Smith (1996a) could not detect any effect of the stake level in the ultimatum game. Cameron (1999) conducted ultimatum games in Indonesia and subjects in the high stake condition could earn the equivalent of three months' income in this experiment. She observed no effect of the stake level on proposers' behavior and a slight reduction of the rejection probability when stakes were high. Slonim and Roth (1997) conducted ultimatum games in Slovakia. They found a small interaction effect between experience and the stake level; the responders in the high-stake condition (with a 10-fold increase in the stake level relative to the low stake condition) reject somewhat less frequently in the final period of a series of one-shot ultimatum games. Fehr and Tougareva (1995) conducted gift exchange games (embedded in a competitive experimental market) in Moscow. They did not observe an interaction effect between stake levels and experience. The subjects earned, on average, the equivalent amount of the income of one week in one of their conditions, while they earned the equivalent of a ten weeks' income in another condition. Despite this large difference in the stake size, neither the proposers' nor the responders' behavior shows significant differences across conditions.

Of course, it is still possible that there may be a shift towards more selfish behavior in the presence of extremely high stakes. However, the vast majority of economic decisions for most people involve stake levels well below three months' income. Thus, even if other-regarding preferences played no role at all at stake levels above that size, these preferences would still play a major role in many economically important domains.

---

[4] When interpreting the results of gift exchange games it is important to stress that – depending on the concrete form of the proposer's payoff function – gift exchange is more or less likely to be profitable for the proposer. In Fehr, Kirchsteiger and Riedl (1993, 1998), the proposer's payoff function is given by $x^P = (v - w)e$ and effort is in the interval $[0.1, 1]$. With this payoff function the proposer cannot make losses and paying a high wage is less costly if the agent chooses a low effort level. In contrast, in Fehr, Klein and Schmidt (2004) the payoff function used is $x^P = ve - w$ which makes it more risky for the principal to offer a high wage. Indeed, while paying high wages was profitable for the principal in the experiments of Fehr, Kirchsteiger and Riedl, it did not pay off in Fehr, Klein and Schmidt. This difference in performance is predicted by the theory of inequity aversion by Fehr and Schmidt (1999) that is discussed in more detail in Section 3. For a further discussion of gift exchange games in competitive environments see also Section 5.3.

Another important question is to what degree the behavior of students is respresentative for the general population. All the experiments mentioned above were predominantly conducted with students as experimental subjects. Two representative data sets recently addressed this question – one from Germany [Fehr et al. (2002)] and one from the Netherlands [Bellemare and Kröger (2003)]. In both cases, the authors conducted (modified) trust games and in both cases, certain demographic variables affected how the game is played, but these effects do not change the general pattern observed in the experiments with students. In particular, the trustees' back transfers are increasing in the investors' transfer and a large share (79 percent in the Fehr et al. study) of the trustees pays back money. Likewise, 83 percent of the investors transfer positive amounts; roughly 60 percent of them transfer 50% or more of their endowment. Moreover, the proposers' and responders' behavior remains constant, regardless of whether the players' endowment in the trust game is € 10 or € 100.

Among the demographic variables, age seems to be important. Both studies find that people above the age of 60 give less than middle-aged individuals when in the role of an investor. However, both studies also find that the elderly tend to give back more, ceteris paribus, when in the role of a trustee. Fehr et al. also report that subjects who experienced a divorce from their partner during the last year and people who favor none of the parliamentary parties in Germany (i.e. those who feel that they are not represented by the major political parties) pay back significantly less when in the role of a trustee. Furthermore, people who report that they are in good health give back significantly more. The most important result these studies provide, however, is that only very few individual level demographic variables seem to matter for behavior. This suggests that it is possible to detect meaningful behavioral patterns with student subject pools that are representative for a more general subject pool, at least for the trust game.

To what extent does culture affect behavior in these experiments? We define culture in terms of subjects' preferences and their beliefs about others' behavior. For example, in the context of the ultimatum game cultural differences may be reflected in different rejection rates for the same offer or in different beliefs about the rejection rate. In the past, many researchers took subjects' nationality as a proxy for culture. Nationality may be a very imperfect measure for culture in modern nations, however, because different cultures may coexist within the same country. Cohen and Nisbett (1994) provide evidence, for example, indicating that individuals who grew up in the American South have a culture of honour whereas Northerners do not have such a culture. Having said this, comparing subjects' behavior across different continents may nevertheless yield interesting insights. Roth et al. conducted ultimatum games in Japan, Israel, Slovenia, and the USA. Their results indicate somewhat lower rejection rates and lower offers in Japan and Israel compared to the US and Slovenia. Whereas the modal offers remain at 50% of the surplus throughout a ten period experiment with randomly assigned partners in the latter two countries, the modal offer converges to 40% in Israel and to two modes in Japan at 40% and 45%, respectively. The relatively low offers in Israel are also associated with relatively low rejection rates, indicating that a lower proposal in Israel was a rational choice for a self-interested proposer.

Buchan, Croson and Dawes (2002) conducted trust games in China, Japan, South Korea, and the USA. They find significant differences in investors' and in trustees' behavior across countries. American and Chinese Investors transfer significantly more money than do their Japanese and Korean counterparts. Moreover, Chinese and Korean trustees send back a significantly higher proportion of their money than do American and Japanese subjects. Thus, Chinese subjects exhibit relatively high levels of trust (as indicator by investors' behavior) and reciprocation (as indicated by trustees' behavior) whereas Japanese subjects show relatively little trust and little reciprocation. The picture is more mixed for US and Korean subjects. Americans show a relatively high level of trust but a low level of reciprocation, whereas the Koreans show little trust but exhibit high levels of reciprocation.

The study by Henrich et al. (2001) and Henrich et al. (2004) documented the perhaps largest differences across cultures. This study reports the results of ultimatum game experiments conducted in 15 small scale societies located in 5 different continents. The subjects in the cross cultural studies previously discussed were university students; one could therefore argue that, despite national differences, they all share much in common. They probably all have above-average skills, probably stem from higher income families and, perhaps most importantly, share an academic learning environment. This provides a sharp contrast to the Henrich et al. study, where subjects come from vastly different cultures. For example, the Ache from Paraguay practice extreme forms of egalitarianism in which big game is shared equally among the tribe members. Others, like the Au and the Gnau from Papua New Guinea obey norms of competitive gift giving: accepting gifts, even unsolicited ones, obliges one to reciprocate at some future time to be determined by the giver. Acceptance of gifts also establishes a subordinate position between the giver and the receiver. Therefore, large gifts are frequently rejected in this society because of the fear associated with the unspecific commitments.

Henrich et al. observe vastly different proposer behavior across cultures. For example, among the Machiguenga, who live in Peru, the average offer is only 26%, among the Gnau it is 38%, among the Ache it is 51%, while it even reaches 58% among the Lamelara, who are whale hunters on an Island in the Pacific Ocean. Likewise, there are also strong differences regarding rejection rates across several cultures. However, since most offers were around 50% in several societies, few rejections are observed, rendering the analysis of rejection behavior impossible in these societies. Similar to the two representative studies in Germany and the Netherlands, only few, if any, individual level variables predict individual behavior in the experiment. Two group level variables, however, explain a large share of the cross cultural variation in behavior: the more the resources in a society are acquired through market trading and the higher the potential payoffs to group cooperation that are associated with the environment in which the society lives, the higher are the offers in the ultimatum game. For example, groups of 20 and more individuals have to cooperate in order to catch a whale and after the catch, they have to solve a difficult distribution problem: who gets which part of the whale. The Lamaleras have developed an extremely elaborate set of norms that determine in detail who gets what [Alvard (2004)]. These elaborate cooperation and distribution practices may well spill over to the experimental context and induce subjects to make egalitarian offers. In contrast to the Lamelara, the Machiguenga in Peru exhibit little cooperation in production outside narrow family boundaries [Henrich and Smith (2004)]. They are also at the lower end of the spectrum with regard to market integration. It seems plausible that the absence of cooperation norms manifests itself in low offers in the ultimatum game. A third piece of telling evidence comes from the competitive gift giving societies in Papua New Guinea. Among the Au and the Gnau, a significant number of proposers offered *more* than 50% of the surplus, only to have these offers rejected in many cases. Thus, deeply seated social norms again seem to affect behavior in the experiment.

2.2. Other-regarding preferences or irrational behavior

While there is now little disagreement regarding the facts reported above, there is still some disagreement about their interpretation. In Section 3, we will describe several recently developed theories of altruism, fairness, and reciprocity that maintain the rationality assumption but change the assumption of purely selfish preferences. Although opinions about the relative importance of different motives behind other-regarding behavior differ somewhat (see Section 4), it is probably fair to say that most experimental researchers believe that some form of other-regarding preferences exists. However, some interpret the behavior in these games as elementary forms of bounded rationality. For example, Roth and Erev (1995) and Binmore, Gale and Samuelson (1995) try to explain the presence of fair offers and rejections of low offers in the ultimatum game with learning models that are based on purely pecuniary preferences, which assume that the rejection of low offers is not very costly for the responders who therefore only learn very slowly not to reject such offers. The rejection of offers, however, is quite costly for the proposers, who thus quickly realize that low offers are not profitable. Moreover, since proposers quickly learn to make fair offers, the pressure on the responders to learn to accept low offers is greatly reduced. This gives rise to very slow convergence to the subgame perfect equilibrium – if there is convergence at all. The simulations of Roth and Erev and Binmore, Gale and Samuelson show that it often takes thousands of iterations until play comes close to the standard prediction.

In our view, there can be little doubt that learning processes are important in real life as well as in laboratory experiments. There are numerous examples where subjects' behavior changes over time and it seems clear that learning models are prime candidates for explaining such dynamic patterns. We believe, however, that attempts to explain the basic facts in simple games, such as the ultimatum game, the third party punishment game, or the trust game, in terms of learning models that assume completely selfish preferences are misplaced. The responders' decisions, in particular, are so simple in these games that it is difficult to believe that they make systematic mistakes and reject money or reward generous offers, even though their true preferences would require them not to do so. Moreover, the above cited evidence from Roth et al. (1991), Forsythe et al. (1994), Suleiman (1996) and Fehr, Kirchsteiger and Riedl (1998) suggests that many proposers anticipate responders' actions surprisingly well. Thus, at least in these simple two-stage games, many proposers seem to be quite rational and forward looking.

It is also sometimes argued that the behavior in these games is due to a social norm [see, Binmore (1998), for example]. In real life, so the argument goes, experimental subjects make the bulk of their decisions in repeated interactions. It is well known that the rejection of unfair offers or the rewarding of generous offers in repeated interactions can be sustained as an equilibrium among purely self-interested agents. According to this argument, subjects' behavior is adapted to repeated interactions and they tend to apply behavioral rules that are appropriate in the context of repeated interactions *erroneously* to laboratory one-shot games.

We believe that this argument is half right and half wrong. The evidence from the cross-cultural experiments in 15 different small scale societies strongly suggests that social norms of cooperation and sharing have an impact on game playing behavior. Indeed, the very fact that the behavior in the experiment captures relevant aspects of real life behavior is the main reason why such experiments are interesting; if they did not tell us something about how people behave in real life, the external validity of the experiments could be called into question. However, the fact that social norms affect subjects' behavior in the experiment does not at all mean that they are inappropriately applying repeated game heuristics when they play one-shot games. In fact, the evidence suggests that subjects are well aware of the difference between one-shot interactions and repeated interactions where their reputation is at stake. Subjects in the experiments by Andreoni and Miller (1993), Engelmann and Fischbacher (2002), Gächter and Falk (2002), Fehr and Fischbacher (2003), Seinen and Schram (2006) exhibit much more cooperative behavior or punish much more if the probability of repeatedly meeting the same subject increases or if they can acquire a reputation.

Fehr and Fischbacher (2003), for example, conducted a series of ten ultimatum games in two different conditions. Subjects played against a different opponent in each of the ten iterations of the game in both conditions. The proposers knew nothing about the past behavior of their current responders in each iteration of the *baseline condition*. Thus, the responders could not build up a reputation for being "tough" in this condition. In contrast, the proposers knew the full history of their current responders' behavior in the *reputation condition*, i.e., the responders could build up a reputation for being "tough". A reputation for rejecting low offers is, of course, valuable in the reputation condition because it increases the likelihood of receiving high offers from the proposers in future periods.

Therefore, if the responders understand that there is a pecuniary payoff from rejecting low offers in the reputation condition, one should generally observe higher acceptance thresholds in this condition. This is the prediction of an approach that assumes that subjects are rational and not only care for their own material payoff but also have a preference for punishing unfair offers: only the punishment motive plays a role in the baseline condition, while the punishment motive and the self interest motive influence rejection behavior in the reputation condition. If, in contrast, subjects do not understand the logic of reputation formation and apply the same habits or cognitive heuristics to both conditions, there should be no observable systematic differences in responder behavior across conditions. Since the subjects participated in both conditions, it was possible to observe behavioral changes at the individual level. It turns out that the vast majority (slightly more than 80 percent, $N = 72$) of the responders *increase* their acceptance thresholds in the reputation condition relative to the baseline condition.[5] Moreover, the changes in rejection behavior occur almost instantaneously when subjects move from the baseline condition to the reputation condition or vice versa. Thus, the data refutes the hypothesis that subjects do not understand the strategic differences between one-shot play and repeated play.

Therefore, instead of assuming that simple decisions that deviate systematically from self-interest reflect merely a form of erroneous application of rules of thumb, it seems more reasonable to assume that the prevailing social norms affect subjects' preferences. After all, the elaborate cooperation and distribution norms practiced by the whale hunters in Indonesia, or the gift giving norms among the Au and the Gnau in Papua New Guinea have been in place for decades if not centuries. They represent deep seated social practices that are likely to affect subjects' preferences. As these social practices are rather stable, the associated preferences inherit this stability. If a subject rejects a low offer in an anonymous one-shot ultimatum game because he or she is upset by the offer, the subject's emotional reaction to the situation probably drives the behavior. Anger, after all, is a basic emotion and the prevailing fairness norms are likely to be reflected in the emotional response to a greedy offer. Recent papers by Fehr and Gächter (2002), Bosman and van Winden (2002) and Ben-Shakhar et al. (2004) provide evidence for the involvement of anger in punishment behavior.

The view that emotions are important determinants of other-regarding behaviors, however, does not imply that these behaviors are irrational. If I feel bad if I let a greedy proposer go unpunished, and if punishing him makes me feel good, I simply have a taste for punishing a greedy proposer. From a choice theoretic viewpoint, this taste does not differ from my taste for chocolate or lobster. In fact, there is strong experimental evidence suggesting that the demand for altruistic giving and for punishment increases if its price decreases [Eckel and Grossman (1996), Andreoni and Vesterlund (2001) in QJE, Anderson and Putterman (2006)]. In addition, evidence from dictator games [Andreoni and Miller (2002)] also shows that most subjects' preferences for giving in a dictator game obey the generalized axiom of revealed preferences, implying that the preferences can be represented by a utility function. Finally, Andreoni, Castillo and Petrie (2003) have shown that the responder's behavior in a modified ultimatum game, in which the responder could shrink the available pie continuously, can be represented by convex fairness preferences.

---

[5] The remaining subjects, with one exception, exhibit no significant change in the acceptance threshold. Only one out of 70 subjects exhibits a significant decrease in the threshold relative to the baseline. Note that if a subject places a very high value on fairness, the acceptance threshold may already be very high in the baseline condition so that there is little reason to change the threshold in the reputation condition. Identical thresholds across conditions are, therefore, also compatible with a social preference approach. Only a decrease in the acceptance threshold is incompatible with theories of social preferences.

The above arguments suggest that there is no reason for treating other-regarding preferences differently than other types of preferences. This means that we can apply the standard tools of economics and game theory to this area, enabling us to explain a great deal of behavior in the games described above. For example, why do in Forsythe et al. (1994) the proposers give so much less in the DG compared to the UG? Why do the proposers in the control condition with exogenously fixed effort [Fehr, Kirchsteiger and Riedl (1998)] make such low wage offers? Why do subjects punish less if the price of punishing is higher? Why do subjects reject higher offers if they can gain a reputation for being a tough bargainer compared to a situation where no reputation can be acquired? All these questions can be answered if one assumes that subjects are rational and care both for their own *and* others' payoffs. The problem with the alternative approach, which invokes some form of bounded rationality, is that at least so far it cannot explain these important behavioral variations across different games.

Most of the experiments that we consider in the rest of this paper are fairly simple. Therefore, we restrict attention in the following to approaches that maintain the assumption of rationality and ignore the potential role of learning.[6]

2.3. Neuroeconomic foundations of other-regarding preferences

Recently, some experimental economists and psychologists have begun combining non-invasive brain imaging techniques with behavioral experiments. Brain imaging techniques like Positron Emission Tomography (PET) and functional Magnetic Resonance Imaging (fMRI) enable researchers to examine the brain networks involved in decision making. This means, for example, that subjects' empathic feelings for others are not limited to measurement by self-reports or by making inferences about their motives from observed behavior, but are also possible in terms of brain activity. Likewise, if it is true that subjects derive utility from punishing others for behaving unfairly or from mutual cooperation in a trust game, the researcher should find traces of these hedonic rewards by examining the activity in the brain's reward network. Note that this kind of brain evidence may also help discriminate between an approach that assumes that other-regarding motives drives other-regarding behavior and one that assumes that subjects simply do not understand the differences between one-shot games and repeated interactions. If the first approach is correct, we should observe hedonic responses in reward related brain areas when subjects cooperate or punish others for violations of widely accepted social norms. An approach that assumes that subjects are selfish but confuse one-shot with repeated interactions predicts no such activation. In the following we describe several studies which suggest that subjects indeed experience positive hedonic responses when they cooperate or punish norm violators. Some of the studies also indicate that subjects suffer themselves merely by observing others in distress.

---

[6] There are a few models that combine other regarding preferences and learning, e.g. Cooper and Stockman (1999) and Costa-Gomes and Zauner (1999).

Singer et al. (2004a) recently published an intriguing paper on the neural basis of empathy for pain in others. The study of empathy is insofar important as empathic concern for others is likely to be an important determinant of other-regarding preferences. Singer's work is based on a neuroscientific model of empathy suggested by Preston and de Waal (2002). According to this model, observing or imagining another person in a particular emotional state automatically activates a representation of that state in the observer with its associated automatic and somatic responses. The term "automatic" in this case refers to a process that does not require conscious and effortful processing but which can nevertheless be inhibited or controlled. Singer et al. recruited couples who were in love with each other for their study; empathy was assessed "in vivo" by bringing both woman and man into the same scanner environment. More specifically, brain activity was assessed in the female partner while painful stimulation was applied either to her own or to her partner's right hand via electrodes attached to the back of the hand. The male partner was seated next to the MRI scanner and a mirror system allowed her to see both hands, hers and that of her partner, lying on a tilted board in front of her. Flashes of different colors on a big screen behind the board pointed to either hand, indicating which of them would receive the painful stimulation and which would be subject to the non-painful stimulation. This procedure enabled the measurement of pain-related brain activation when pain was applied to the scanned subject (the so-called "pain matrix") or to her partner (empathy for pain). The results suggest that some but not the entire "pain matrix" was activated when empathizing with the pain of others. Activity in the primary and secondary somato-sensory cortex was only observed when receiving pain. These areas are known to be involved in the processing of the sensory-discriminatory components of our pain experience, that is, they indicate the location of the pain and its objective quality. In contrast, the bilateral anterior insula (AI) and the rostral anterior cingulate cortex (ACC) were activated when subjects either received pain or a signal that a loved one experienced pain. These areas are involved in the processing of the affective component of pain, that is, how unpleasant the subjectively felt pain is. Thus, both the experience of pain to oneself and the knowledge that a loved partner experiences pain activate the same affective pain circuits, suggesting that if a loved partner suffers pain, our brains also make us suffer from this pain. These findings suggest that we use representations reflecting our own emotional responses to pain to understand how the pain of others feels. Moreover, our ability to empathize may have evolved from a system which represents our own internal feeling states and allows us to predict the affective outcomes of an event for both ourselves and for others.

The results of the Singer et al. (2004a) study further suggest that the empathic response is rather automatic and does not require active engagement of some explicit judgments about others' feelings. The scanned subjects did not know that the experiment was about empathy; they were merely instructed to do nothing but observe the flashes that indicate either pain to the subject or the loved partner. The analysis also confirmed that the ability to empathize is heterogeneous across individuals; standard empathy questionnaires and the strength of the activation in the affective pain regions (AI and ACC) when the partner received pain were used to assess this heterogeneity. Interestingly, individual heterogeneity measured by the empathy questionnaire was highly correlated with individual differences that were measured by brain activation in those areas that process the affective component of pain (i.e. AI and ACC). Thus, neural evidence and questionnaire evidence on empathy mutually reinforce each other.

Does empathy also extend to unknown persons? The results of three recent studies indicate that empathic responses are also elicited when scanned subjects do not know the person in pain. Activity in the ACC and AI has also been observed when subjects witness still pictures depicting body parts involved in possibly painful situations [Jackson, Meltzoff and Decety (2005)] or videos showing a needle stinging in the back of a hand [Morrison et al. (2004)]. In a new paper Singer et al. (2006) investigated whether the level of empathic response in the ACC and AI can be modulated by the fact whether the subject likes or dislikes the "object of empathy". In this study, actors are paid to pretend to be naive subjects participating in two independent experiments, one on "social exchange" and the other on the "processing of pain". In the first experiment, the two confederates repeatedly play a modified trust game in the position of the trustee with the scanned subject. One actor plays a fair strategy and usually reciprocates trusting first mover choices with cooperation; the other actor plays unfairly and defects in response to first mover cooperation most of the time. Behavioral and neuronal findings of a previous imaging study which revealed aversion and fondness reported verbally as well as emotion-related brain activation in response to faces of people who had previously cooperated or defected [Singer et al. (2004b)] indicate that the subjects like fair players and dislike unfair ones. In the second part of the experiment, all three players participate in a pain study that expands the approach by [Singer et al. (2004a)]. One actor sits on each side of the scanner, enabling the scanned subject to observe flashes of different colours indicating high or low pain stimulation to his/her hand or to those of the fair or unfair players. The evidence from Singer et al. (2006) suggests empathy-related activation in the ACC and AI when observing the unfamiliar but likeable person receiving painful stimulation. However, men who observe that the unfair trustee receives pain do not show any empathy related activation in AI and ACC.

An important prerequisite for neuroeconomic studies is the existence of neuroscientific knowledge about the key components of the brain's reward circuits. Fortunately, many recent studies have shown that an area in the midbrain, the striatum, is a key part of reward-related neural circuits. Single neuron recording in non-human primates [Schultz (2000)] and neuroimaging studies with humans using money as a reward medium [Knutson et al. (2001), Delgado et al. (2003), O'Doherty et al. (2004)] clearly support this hypothesis. This knowledge about the brain's reward network enables neuroeconomists to ask intriguing questions. For example, some men's brains show no empathic concern for an unfair subject who receives pain. Do they perhaps even enjoy this experience? The results of Singer et al. (2006) exactly indicate this. Instead of activating empathy related networks like the ACC and AI, the men (but not the women) show activation in the striatum (the Nucleus Accumbens, NACC)! Moreover, men who reported more anger about others' behavior in self-reports collected after the experiment exhibit higher activation in the NACC. As a higher intensity of anger is probably associated with a higher relief if the unfair subject is punished, this finding further supports the hypothesis that the passive observation of the punishment of unfair subjects is associated with positive hedonic feelings.

This raises the question whether reward related brain areas are also activated if subjects can punish unfair behavior themselves or when they even have to pay for punishing the unfair subject. de Quervain et al. (2004) answered this question in a recent study. These authors modified the trust game by including a punishment opportunity for the investor. In this game, the investor had the opportunity of punishing the trustee after observing whether the trustee reciprocated the investor's trust by assigning up to 20 punishment points to the trustee. The monetary consequences of the punishment depended on the treatment conditions and will be explained below. The investor's brain was scanned with PET when he received information about the trustee's decision and when he decided whether to punish the trustee.

de Quervain et al. (2004) hypothesized that the opportunity to punish an unfair partner will activate the striatum. In particular, if the investor punishes the trustee because he anticipates deriving satisfaction from punishing, one should observe activation predominantly in those reward-related brain areas that are associated with goal-directed behavior. There is strong evidence from single neuron recording in non-human primates [Schultz (2000)] that the dorsal striatum is crucial for the integration of reward information and behavioral information in the sense of a goal-directed mechanism. Several recent neuroimaging studies support the view that the dorsal striatum is implicated in processing rewards resulting from a decision [Knutson et al. (2001), Delgado et al. (2003), O'Doherty et al. (2004)]. The fact that the dorsal striatum also responds to expected monetary gains in a parametric way is of particular interest from an economic viewpoint: if subjects successfully complete a task that generates monetary rewards, the activation in the dorsal striatum increases as the expected monetary gain grows. Thus, if the investor's dorsal striatum is activated when punishing the trustee, one has a strong piece of evidence indicating that punishment is rewarding.

To examine the activation of striatal areas during the decision to punish, subjects' brains were mainly scanned in those trust game trials in which the trustee abused the investor's trust. In the condition termed "costly" (C), the punishment was costly for both players. Every punishment point assigned to the trustee cost experimental $1 for the investor and reduced the trustee's payoff by experimental $2. In the condition termed "free" (F), punishment was not costly for the investor. Every punishment point assigned to the trustee cost nothing for the investor while the trustee's payoff was reduced by $2. In a third condition, which we call "symbolic" (S), punishment had only a symbolic (and no pecuniary) value. The punishment points assigned cost neither player anything. Thus, the investor could not reduce the trustee's payoff in this condition.

The hypothesis that punishment is rewarding predicts that the contrast F–S will show the activation of reward related brain areas after the investor's trust has been abused. The rationale behind this prediction is that the investor is likely to have a desire to punish the trustee both in the F and the S condition because the trustee intentionally abused the investor's trust, but the investor cannot really hurt the trustee in the S condition. Thus, the purely symbolic punishment in the S condition is unlikely to be satisfactory because the desire to punish the defector cannot be fulfilled effectively, and in the unlikely case that symbolic punishment is satisfactory, it is predicted to be less so than punishment in the F condition.

The F–S contrast is ideal for examining the satisfying aspects of effective punishment because – except for the difference in the opportunity to punish effectively – everything else remains constant across conditions. However, costly punishment should also generate satisfaction from an economic viewpoint. If there is indeed a taste for punishing defectors and if subjects actually punish because the cost of punishing is not too high, the act of punishment is analogous to buying a good. Rational subjects buy the good as long as the marginal costs are below the marginal benefits. Thus, an economic model based on a taste for punishment predicts that punishment in the C condition should also be experienced as satisfactory, implying that reward related areas will also be activated in the C–S condition.

Questionnaire and behavioral evidence indicates that investors indeed had a strong desire to punish the defectors. In fact, almost all subjects punished maximally in the F condition, while most subjects still punished in the C condition, albeit at a lower level. This reduction in the level of punishment makes sense because punishment was costly in the C condition. Most importantly, however, the dorsal striatum was strongly activated in both the F–S contrast and the C–S contrast, indicating that punishment is experienced as satisfactory. Moreover, the data show that those subjects in the C condition who exhibit higher activations in the dorsal striatum also punish more. This positive correlation can be interpreted in two ways: first, the higher level of punishment could cause the increased activation of the dorsal striatum, i.e., the higher satisfaction. Second, the greater anticipated satisfaction from punishing could cause the higher level of punishment, i.e., the activation in the striatum reflects – in this view – the anticipated satisfaction from punishing. It would be reassuring from an economic viewpoint if the second interpretation were the correct one because it relies on the idea that the anticipated rewards from punishing drive the punishment decision.

de Quervain et al. (2004) provide two pieces of evidence in favor of the second hypothesis. The first piece of evidence is related to the C–F contrast. Subjects face a nontrivial trade off in the C condition between the benefits and costs of punishing, whereas the decision is much simpler in the F condition because no costs exist. Thus, certain parts of the prefrontal cortex (Brodmann areas 10 and 11), which are known to be involved in integrating the benefits and costs for the purpose of decision-making, should be more strongly activated in the C condition than in the F condition. This is in fact the case. The second piece of evidence is based on the observation that most subjects punished maximally in the F condition. Thus, the differences in striatum activation across these subjects cannot be due to different levels of punishment. However, if different striatum activations reflect differences in the anticipated satisfaction from punishment, those subjects who exhibit higher striatum activations in the F condition (although they punish at the same maximal level) should be willing to spend more money on punishment in the C condition. The data again supports this prediction.

Neuroeconomic evidence also suggests that subjects derive special hedonic rewards from mutual cooperation with other human beings. This finding is insofar relevant as many trustees do reciprocate first mover choices in trust games and many subjects also cooperate in simultaneously played one-shot prisoners' dilemmas. One of the first neuroeconomic studies [Rilling et al. (2002)] reports activations in the striatum when subjects experience mutual cooperation with a human partner compared to mutual cooperation with a computer partner. Thus, despite the fact that the subject's monetary gain is identical in both situations, mutual cooperation with a human partner seems to be experienced as a more rewarding outcome, indicating that extra benefits from mutual cooperation extend beyond mere monetary gain. Unfortunately, however, the Rilling et al. study is based on a repeated prisoners' dilemma. A repeated dilemma game involves a host of other confounding influences which might shed doubt on the interpretation of brain activations in terms of other-regarding preferences. A recent paper based on a simplified trust game solved this problem [Rilling et al. (2002)]. The authors again show that the mutual cooperation outcome with a human partner generates higher striatum activation than does the mutual cooperation outcome with a computer partner. Moreover, the mutual cooperation outcome with a human partner also generates higher activations than does earning the same amount of money in a trivial individual decision-making task. A further study shows that the mere viewing of faces of people who previously cooperated in a version of the trust game activates reward related areas [Singer et al. (2004b)], thus indicating the special hedonic qualities of mutual cooperation. This result suggests that people derive more utility from interactions with cooperative people not just because they can earn more money in these interactions but because these interactions are rewarding per se.

3. Theories of other-regarding preferences

The experimental evidence sketched in Section 2 has provoked several theoretical attempts to explain the observed behavior across different experiments within the rational choice framework. Three different approaches can be distinguished:
1. Models of "social preferences" assume that a player's utility function not only depends on his own material payoff, but may also be a function of the allocation of resources within his reference group, i.e. a player may also be concerned about the material resources other people receive. Furthermore, several models assume that people differ. Some people seem to be quite strongly concerned about how they compare to other people, while others seem to be mainly self-interested. Given these social preferences, all agents are assumed to behave rationally, meaning that the well known concepts of traditional utility and game theory can be applied to analyze optimal behavior and to characterize equilibrium outcomes in experimental games.
2. Models of "interdependent preferences" assume that people are concerned about their opponent's "type". Suppose that each player may be either a selfish type or

a (conditionally) altruistic type. If an altruistic player knows that he interacts with another altruistic player, his preferences are altruistic and he is willing to be generous. If however, he knows that he deals with a selfish opponent, his preferences become selfish, too. Thus, whether player 1's preferences are altruistic or selfish depend on player 2's preferences and vice versa.
3. The third class of models deals with "intention based reciprocity". This approach assumes that a player cares about his opponent's intentions. If he feels that the opponent wanted to treat him kindly, he wants to return the favor and be nice to his opponent as well. If he feels that his opponent has hostile intentions, he wants to hurt his opponent. Thus, a player's interpretation of his opponent's behavior is crucial in this approach. Note that it is not the "type" of a player but rather his *intention* that is kind or hostile. Thus, in a given situation there may be an equilibrium in which a player has kind intentions, but there may also be a second equilibrium in which he has hostile intentions. Traditional game theory cannot capture this phenomenon; the framework of psychological game theory is needed.

Almost all models of these three approaches start out by making some fairly specific assumptions about the players' utility functions. Alternatively, one could start from a general preference relation and ask which axioms are necessary and sufficient to generate utility functions with certain properties. Axiomatic approaches are discussed at the end of this section.

Before we discuss the different approaches in detail, a word of caution is required. Many of the models under consideration here use terms such as "fairness", "equity", "altruism" or "reciprocity" that have been debated for a long time by moral philosophers and economists and that can be interpreted in different ways. Furthermore, some of these models are not entirely clear about what the domain of the theory is and what they want to achieve. In this section we will interpret all of these theories very restrictively. First of all, we view them as *purely positive theories* that try to explain actual human behavior. Thus, we disregard any normative implications the theories may have. Second, we view these models as first attempts *to explain the outcomes of economic experiments*. Typically, subjects enter these experiments as equals, they interact anonymously, and the physical outcome of the experiment is an allocation of monetary payoffs. Thus, for the experiments it is fairly straightforward to give a precise (and hopefully uncontroversial) definition of "altruistic preferences", "equitable allocation", "fair behavior" and the like. Of course, the theories discussed here do have implications for human behavior outside the laboratory as well. In some situations these implications may be very straightforward, but in general there are many important questions that have to be answered before the models can be applied to the "real world". This is a very important next step of this research agenda, but it will not be discussed here.

3.1. Social preferences

Classical utility theory assumes that a decision maker has preferences over allocations of material outcomes (e.g. goods) and that these preferences satisfy some "rationality" or "consistency" requirements, such as completeness and transitivity. However, this fairly general framework is often interpreted much more narrowly in applications, by implicitly assuming that the decision maker only cares about one aspect of an allocation, namely the material resources that are allocated to her. Models of social preferences assume, in contrast, that the decision maker may also care about the material resources allocated to others.

Somewhat more formally, let $\{1, 2, \ldots, N\}$ denote a set of individuals and $x = (x_1, x_2, \ldots, x_N)$ denote an allocation of physical resources out of some set X of feasible allocations. For concreteness we assume in the following that x_i denotes the monetary payoff of person i. The self-interest hypothesis says that the utility of individual i only depends on x_i. We will say that individual i has *social preferences* if for any given x_i person i's utility is affected by variations of x_j, $j \neq i$. Of course, simply assuming that the utility of individual i may be any function of the total allocation is often too general because it yields very few empirically testable restrictions on observed behavior.[7] In the following we will discuss several models of social preferences, each of which assumes that an individual's preferences depend on x_j, $j \neq i$, in a different way.

3.1.1. Altruism

A person is altruistic if the first partial derivatives of $u(x_1, \ldots, x_N)$ with respect to $x_1, \ldots, x_N$ are strictly positive, i.e., if her utility increases with the well being of other people. The hypothesis that (some) people are altruistic has a long tradition in economics and has been used to explain charitable donations and the voluntary provision of public goods.

Clearly, the simplest game for eliciting altruistic preferences is the dictator game (DG). Andreoni and Miller (2002) conducted a series of DG experiments in which one agent could allocate "tokens" between herself and another agent for a series of different budgets. The tokens were exchanged into money at different rates for the two agents and the different budgets. Let $U_i(x_1, x_2)$ denote subject i's utility function representing her preferences over monetary allocations (x_1, x_2).

In a first step, Andreoni and Miller check for violations of the General Axiom of Revealed Preference (GARP) and find that almost all subjects behaved consistently and passed this basic rationality check. Thus, their preferences can be described by (quasi-concave) utility functions. Then Andreoni and Miller classify the subjects into three main groups. They find that about 30 percent of the subjects give tokens to the other party in a fashion that equalizes the monetary payoffs between players. The behavior of 20 percent of the subjects can be explained by a utility function in which x_1 and x_2 are perfect substitutes, i.e., these subjects seem to have maximized the (weighted) sum of

---

[7] One implication, however, is that if a decision maker can choose between two allocations then his decision should be independent on how the two allocations have been generated. This prediction is refuted by some experiments on variants of the ultimatum game, where the proposer either could or could not influence the allocation of resources. See, e.g., Falk, Fehr and Fischbacher (2003) and Blount (1995) and the discussion in Sections 3.2 and 3.3 below.

the monetary payoffs. However, almost 50 percent of the subjects behaved "selfishly" and did not give any significant amounts to the other party. In a different experiment, they find that a sizeable minority (23 percent) of the subjects behaved spitefully by reducing their opponent's payoff if the opponent was better off then they were. Thus, they seem to have preferences that are non-monotonic in the monetary payoff of their opponent. Andreoni and Miller (2002, p. 750) conclude that many individuals seem to have other-regarding preferences and that the individual choice behavior of subjects in dictator games is consistent with rationality. However, individuals are heterogeneous, and only a minority of subjects can be described as unconditional altruists who have a utility function that is always strictly increasing in the payoff of their opponent.[8]

3.1.2. Relative income and envy

An alternative hypothesis is that subjects are not only concerned about the absolute amount of money they receive but also about their relative standing compared to others. The importance of relative income for a person's well being, of envy and jealousy, and of conspicuous consumption has long been recognized by economists and goes back at least to Veblen (1922).[9] Bolton (1991) formalized this idea in the context of an experimental bargaining game between two players. He assumes that $U_i(x_i, x_j) = u_i(x_i, x_i/x_j)$, where $u(\cdot, \cdot)$ is strictly increasing in its first argument and where the partial derivative with respect to x_i/x_j is strictly positive for $x_i < x_j$ and equal to 0 for $x_i \geqslant x_j$. Thus, agent i suffers if she gets less than player j, but she does not care about player j if she is better off herself. Note that this utility function implies that $\partial U_i/\partial x_j \leqslant 0$, just the opposite of altruism. Hence, while this utility function is consistent with the behavior in the bargaining games considered by Bolton, it neither explains generosity in dictator games and kind behavior of responders in trust games and gift exchange games nor voluntary contributions in public good games. The same problem arises in the envy-approach of Kirchsteiger (1994).

3.1.3. Inequity aversion

The preceding approaches assume that utility is either monotonically increasing or monotonically decreasing in the well being of other players. Fehr and Schmidt (1999) assume that a player is altruistic towards other players if their material payoffs are below an equitable benchmark, but she feels envy when the other players' material payoffs exceed this level.[10] For most economic experiments it seems natural to assume that an

---

[8] Another, more specific model of heterogeneous altruistic preferences has been developed by Cox, Sadiraj and Sadiraj (2001). They assume that the marginal rate of substitution between own income and the income of the opponent depends on whose income is higher.

[9] See e.g. Kolm (1995) for a detailed discussion and formalization of "envy" in economics.

[10] Daughety (1994) and Fehr, Kirchsteiger and Riedl (1998) also assume that a player values the payoff of reference agents positively, if she is relatively better off, while she values the others' payoff negatively, if she is relatively worse off.

equitable allocation is an equal monetary payoff for all players. Thus, inequity aversion reduces to inequality aversion in these games. Fehr and Schmidt consider the simplest utility function capturing this idea.

$$U_i(x_1, x_2, \ldots, x_N) = x_i - \frac{\alpha_i}{N-1} \sum_{j \neq i} \max\{x_j - x_i, 0\}$$

$$- \frac{\beta_i}{N-1} \sum_{j \neq i} \max\{x_i - x_j, 0\}$$

with $0 \leq \beta_i \leq \alpha_i$ and $\beta_i \leq 1$. Note that $\partial U_i/\partial x_j \geq 0$ if and only if $x_i \geq x_j$. Note also that the disutility from inequality is larger if another person is better off than player i than if another person is worse off ($\alpha_i \geq \beta_i$).

This utility function can rationalize positive *and* negative actions towards other players. It is consistent with generosity in dictator games and kind behavior of responders in trust games and gift exchange games, *and at the same time* with the rejection of low offers in ultimatum games. It can explain voluntary contributions in public good games *and at the same time* costly punishments of free-riders.

A second important ingredient of this model is the assumption that individuals are heterogeneous. If all people were alike, it would be difficult to explain why we observe that people sometimes resist "unfair" outcomes or manage to cooperate even though it is a dominant strategy for a selfish person not to do so, while fairness concerns or the desire to cooperate do not seem to have much of an effect in other environments. Fehr and Schmidt show that the interaction of the distribution of types with the strategic environment explains why very unequal outcomes are obtained in some situations while very egalitarian outcomes prevail in others. For example, even a population that consists *only* of very fair types (high α's and β's) cannot prevent very uneven outcomes in certain competitive environments (see, e.g., the ultimatum game with proposer competition in Section 5.3) because none of the inequity averse players can enforce a more equitable outcome through her own actions. In contrast, a small fraction of inequity averse players in a public good game with punishment is sufficient to credibly threaten that free riders will be punished, inducing selfish players to contribute to the public good.

Fehr and Schmidt choose a distribution for α and β that is consistent with the experimental evidence of the ultimatum game. Keeping this distribution fixed, they show that their model yields surprisingly accurate predictions across many bargaining, market and social dilemma games.[11]

---

[11] One drawback of the piece-wise linear utility function employed by Fehr and Schmidt is that it implies corner solutions for some games where interior solutions are frequently observed. For example, a decision maker in the dictator game with a Fehr–Schmidt utility function would either give nothing (if her $\beta < 0.5$) or share the pie equally (if $\beta > 0.5$). Giving away a fraction that is strictly in between 0 and 0.5 is optimal only in the non-generic case where $\beta = 0.5$. This problem can be avoided, at the cost of tractability, by assuming non-linear inequity aversion.

Bolton and Ockenfels (2000) independently developed a similar model of inequity aversion. They also show that their model can explain a wide variety of seemingly puzzling evidence such as generosity in dictator, gift exchange and trust games and rejections in the ultimatum game. In their model, the utility function is given by

$$U_i = U_i(x_i, \sigma_i),$$

where

$$\sigma_i = \begin{cases} \dfrac{x_i}{\sum_{j=1}^{N} x_j} & \text{if } \sum_{j=1}^{N} x_j \neq 0, \\ \dfrac{1}{N} & \text{if } \sum_{j=1}^{N} x_j = 0. \end{cases}$$

For any given σ_i, the utility function is assumed to be weakly increasing and concave in player i's own material payoff x_i. Furthermore, for any given x_i, the utility function is strictly concave in player i's share of total income, σ_i, and obtains a maximum at $\sigma_i = 1/N$.[12]

Fehr–Schmidt and Bolton–Ockenfels often yield qualitatively similar results for two-player games, while some interesting differences arise with more than two players. Fehr and Schmidt assume that a player compares herself to each of her opponents separately in this case. This implies that her behavior towards an opponent depends on the income difference towards this person. In contrast, Bolton and Ockenfels assume that the decision maker is not concerned about each individual opponent but only about the average income of all players. Thus, whether $\partial U_i / \partial x_j$ is positive or negative in the Bolton–Ockenfels model does not depend on j's relative position towards i, but rather on how well i does compared to the average. If x_i is below the average, then i would like to reduce j's income even if j has a much lower income than i herself. On the other hand, if i is doing better than the average, then she is prepared to give to j even if j is much better off than i.[13]

---

[12] This specification of the utility function has the disadvantage that it is not independent of a shift in payoffs. Consider, for example, a dictator game in which the dictator has to divide X Dollars. Note that this is a constant sum game because $x_1 + x_2 \equiv X$. If we reduce the sum of payoffs by X, i.e., if the dictator can take away money from her opponent or give to him out of her own pocket, then $x_1 + x_2 = 0$ for any decision of the dictator and thus we always have $\sigma_1 = \sigma_2 = 1/2$. Therefore, the theory makes the implausible prediction that, in contrast to the game where $x_1 + x_2 = X > 0$, all dictators should take as much money from their opponent as possible. Camerer (2003, p. 111) notes a related problem. Suppose that the ultimatum game is modified as follows: If the responder rejects a proposal, the monetary payoffs are 10 percent of the original offer. In this case the relative shares are the same no matter whether the responder accepts or rejects. Hence, Bolton and Ockenfels predict that the responder will always accept any offer, no matter how unequal it is. These problems do not arise in Fehr and Schmidt's model of inequity aversion.

[13] See Camerer (2003, Section 2.8.5) and Section 4.1 for a more extensive comparison of these two approaches.

3.1.4. Hybrid models

Charness and Rabin (2002) combine altruistic preferences with a specific form of inequity aversion that they call *quasi-maximin preferences*. They start from a "disinterested social welfare function" which is a convex combination of Rawls' maximin criterion and the sum of the monetary payoffs of all players:

$$W(x_1, x_2, \ldots, x_N) = \delta \cdot \min\{x_1, \ldots, x_N\} + (1 - \delta) \cdot (x_1 + \cdots + x_N),$$

where $\delta \in (0, 1)$ is a parameter reflecting the weight that is put on the maximin criterion. The first part of the social welfare function represents Rawlsian inequity aversion. The second part reflects altruism based on the idea that each individual's payoff receives the same weight. An individual's overall utility function is then given by a convex combination of his own monetary payoff and the above social welfare function:[14]

$$U_i(x_1, x_2, \ldots, x_N) = (1 - \gamma)x_i + \gamma \big[\delta \cdot \min\{x_1, \ldots, x_N\} \\ + (1 - \delta) \cdot (x_1 + \cdots + x_N)\big].$$

In the two player case this boils down to

$$U_i(x_1, x_2) = \begin{cases} x_i + \gamma(1 - \delta)x_j & \text{if } x_i < x_j, \\ (1 - \gamma\delta)x_i + \gamma x_j & \text{if } x_i \geqslant x_j. \end{cases}$$

Note that the marginal rate of substitution between x_i and x_j is smaller if $x_i < x_j$. Hence, the decision maker cares about the well-being of the other person, but less so if the other person is better off than she is.

Altruism in general and quasi-maximin preferences in particular can explain positive acts to other players, such as generosity in dictator games and kind behavior of responders in trust games and gift exchange games,[15] but it is clearly inconsistent with the fact that subjects try to retaliate and hurt other subjects in some experiments, even if this is costly for them (as in the ultimatum game (UG) or a public good game with punishments). This is why Charness and Rabin augment quasi-maximin preferences by incorporating intention based reciprocity (see Section 3.3.3 below).

Erlei (2004) combines elements of inequity aversion à la Fehr–Schmidt and altruistic preferences à la Charness–Rabin by assuming that

$$U_i(x_1, x_2) = \begin{cases} (1 - \sigma_i - \theta_i R)x_i + (\sigma_i + \theta_i R)x_j & \text{if } x_i \leqslant x_j, \\ (1 - \rho_i - \theta_i R)x_i + (\rho_i + \theta_i R)x_j & \text{if } x_i \geqslant x_j. \end{cases}$$

---

[14] Note that Charness and Rabin do not normalize payoffs with respect to N. Thus, if the group size changes, and the parameters δ and γ are assumed to be constant; thus, the importance of the maximin term in relation to the player's own material payoff changes.

[15] However, altruism has some implausible implications even in these games. For example, altruism implies that if the government provides part of the public good (financed by taxes) in a public good context, then every dollar provided by the government "crowds out" one dollar of private, voluntary contributions. This "neutrality property" holds quite generally [Bernheim (1986)]. However, it is in contrast to the empirical evidence reporting that the actual crowding out is rather small. This has led some researchers to include the pleasure of giving (a "warm glow effect") in the utility function [Andreoni (1989)].

In this formulation, σ_i (ρ_i) represents player i's concern for player j's payoff if player i's payoff is larger (smaller, respectively) than player j's. The term $\theta_i R$ models negative reciprocity explicitly. If player j "misbehaved" by taking an action that violates the norms of fairness, R takes the value -1, otherwise it is 0. The parameter $\theta_i \geqslant 0$ measures the importance of this sort of reciprocity as compared to the other elements of the utility function.

Erlei assumes that there are three different types of players: Selfish players have $\sigma_i = \rho_i = \theta_i = 0$, i.e. they only care about x_i. Inequity averse players are characterized by $\sigma_i < 0 < \rho_i < 1$. Altruistic types always put a positive weight on the payoff of their opponent, so $0 < \sigma_i \leqslant \rho_i \leqslant 1$. Erlei applies this model to the games discussed by Charness and Rabin (2002) and by Goeree and Holt (2001). Obviously, the model offers a better predictive fit than do models that only focus on one type of preference. Perhaps more surprisingly, the author shows that direct negative reciprocity (as captured by $\theta_i R$) does not play a significant role in the games he considers.

Cox, Friedman and Gjerstad (2004) suggest another fairly flexible utility function of the form

$$U_i = \begin{cases} \frac{1}{\alpha}(x_i^\alpha + \lambda x_2^\alpha) & \text{if } \alpha \neq 0, \\ (x_i \cdot x_j)^\lambda & \text{if } \alpha = 0, \end{cases}$$

where $\alpha \in (-\infty, 1]$ reflects the curvature of indifference curves in the (x_i, x_j) space. The marginal rate of substitution between i's income and j's income in i's utility function is given by

$$MRS = \frac{\partial U_i/\partial x_i}{\partial U_i/\partial x_j} = \lambda^{-1}\left(\frac{x_j}{x_i}\right)^{1-\alpha}.$$

Thus, when $\alpha = 1$, preferences are linear (MRS is constant), when $\alpha < 1$, they are strictly convex. Cobb–Douglas preferences correspond to $\alpha = 0$ and Leontief preferences to $\alpha \to -\infty$. Whether preferences are altruistic or spiteful depends on the parameter $\lambda = \lambda(r)$ that is interpreted as the "emotional state" of player i. This emotional state depends on a reciprocity motive r which is defined as[16] $r(x) = \bar{x}_i(s_j) - x_i^0$, where $\bar{x}_i(s_j)$ is the maximum payoff player i can achieve given strategy s_j of player j and x_i^0 is an appropriate reference payoff. If the maximum payoff player i can achieve given the strategy s_j of his opponent is smaller than this reference payoff, $r(x)$ (and λ) are negative and player i wants to hurt player j.[17]

Cox et al. estimate the parameters of their model separately using the existing experimental data for the mini-ultimatum game [Falk, Fehr and Fischbacher (2003)] and for

---

[16] Cox, Friedman and Gjerstad (2004) argue that λ may also depend on the social status s of the players, but this seems to be irrelevant in most experiments and the authors do not make any use of s in the applications they consider.

[17] A similar model has been suggested by Sandbu (2002). In his model the marginal rate of substitution between own income and income of the opponent depends on the sets of actions available to the players.

a Stackelberg duopoly game [Huck, Müller and Normann (2001)]. While the model can fit the data of these two games reasonably well, the authors have yet to show that the parameter estimates derived from one game can also explain the data of other games. Furthermore, the model is quite restrictive because it can only be applied to sequential two-person games of perfect information.

Benjamin (2004) considers a model that allows for different types of social preferences. The main innovation in his paper is that utility is not defined on absolute wealth levels but rather on changes in wealth levels. Furthermore, people are loss-averse over their own changes in payoffs, but they do not weight the losses of others more heavily than the gains of others. Benjamin argues that this may explain why it is often considered unfair if a landlord raises rents for existing tenants but not if he raises rents for new tenants. The point is that raising rents on existing tenants causes a gain to the landlord at the expense of the tenant, while a new tenant enters into a transaction in which both parties gain. In models of social preferences that are defined over absolute wealth levels it would not make any difference whether the tenant is old or new.

Benabou and Tirole (2004) develop a model in which people have different degrees of altruism, but are also concerned about their social reputation and self-respect. Thus, people behave altruistically because they are genuinely altruistic, but also because they want to signal to other people (or to themselves) that they are generous. This model has a rich set of implications. In particular, it can explain why monetary incentives may crowd out altruistic behavior. The reason is that the presence of monetary rewards spoils the reputational value of good deeds. These actions are no longer an unambiguous signal of altruism or generosity with explicit rewards (or punishments), however, because they may have been undertaken for the money at stake. Benabou and Tirole apply this model to charitable giving, incentive provision, and multiple social norms of behavior, but they do not try to explain observed behavior in experimental games.

3.2. Interdependent preferences

Models of social preferences assume that players' utility functions depend only on the final allocation of material resources. Thus, if a player has to choose between different allocations, his choice will be independent of how these different allocations came about. This is implausible in some cases. For example, if I have to decide whether to accept or to reject a very unequal allocation, my decision may depend on whether my opponent chose the unfair allocation deliberately, or whether he had no possibility of affecting the allocation.[18]

A possible solution to this problem is to assume that players may be of different types (e.g., altruistic and spiteful types), and that each player's preferences depend on his opponent's type. In such a model my opponent's action affects my utility in two

---

[18] See, e.g., the experiments on the ultimatum game by Blount (1995) and on the mini-ultimatum game by Falk, Fehr and Fischbacher (2003).

ways. First, it affects my utility directly through its effect on the allocation of material resources. Second, there is an indirect effect if the action conveys information about my opponent's type.

These models are considerably more complex than models of social preferences because they assume that *preferences are interdependent*: my preferences depend on your preferences and vice versa. Several models have been proposed to capture these effects.

3.2.1. Altruism and spitefulness

Levine (1998) considers the utility function

$$U_i = x_i + \sum_{j \neq i} x_j(a_i + \lambda a_j)/(1 + \lambda),$$

where $0 \leqslant \lambda \leqslant 1$ and $-1 < a_i < 1$ for all $i \in \{1, \ldots, N\}$. Suppose first that $\lambda = 0$. In this case, the utility function reduces to $U_i = x_i + a_i \sum_{j \neq i} x_j$. If $a_i > 0$, then person i is an altruist who wants to promote the well being of other people, if $a_i < 0$, then player i is spiteful. While this utility function would be able to explain why some people contribute in public good games and why others reject positive offers in the ultimatum game, it has difficulties explaining why the same person is altruistic in one setting and spiteful in another setting unless the absolute value of a player's a_i is close to zero or the values of the opponent's a_j strongly differs across settings.

Now suppose that $\lambda > 0$. In this case, an altruistic player i (with $a_i > 0$) feels more altruistic towards another altruist than towards a spiteful person. In fact, if $-\lambda a_j > a_i$ player i may behave spitefully herself. In most experiments, where there is anonymous interaction, the players do not know their opponent's parameter a_j and have to form beliefs about them. Thus, any sequential game becomes a signaling game in which beliefs about the other players' types are crucially important for determining optimal strategies. This may give rise to a multiplicity of signaling equilibria.

Levine uses the data from the ultimatum game to calibrate the distribution of a_i and to estimate λ (which he assumes to be the same for all players). He shows that with these parameters the model can reasonably fit the data on centipede games, market games, and public good games. However, because $a_i < 1$, the model cannot explain positive giving in the dictator game.

Rotemberg (2004) suggests a closely related model that focuses on ultimatum and dictator games. He assumes the following utility functions for the proposer and the responder, respectively:

$$U_P = E(x_P + a^P x_R)^\gamma,$$
$$U_R = x_R + [a^R - \xi(\hat{a}^P, \underline{a})] \cdot x_P.$$

Consider first the responder's utility function which depends on his own income x_R and on that of his opponent x_P. However, the weight with which x_P enters his utility function depends on the difference between his own altruism a^R and a function ξ that depends, in turn, on the responder's estimate of his opponent's altruism, denoted by $\hat{a}^P$, and a minimum level of altruism $\underline{a}$. The function ξ is discontinuous and takes only two values: If $\hat{a}^P \geqslant \underline{a}$, ξ takes the value of 0, if $\hat{a}^P < \underline{a}$ there is a discontinuous jump to $\xi = \bar{\xi} = a^R + 1$. Thus, if the responder believes that the proposer does not satisfy some minimal level of benevolence (that may differ across responders), his preferences turn hostile and he enjoys reducing the proposer's payoff.

Consider now the proposer's utility function that also depends on his own income and on that of the responder weighted with the altruism parameter a^P. The proposer moves first, so he does not learn anything about the responder's type before taking his action. This is why the reciprocity term that is part of the proposer's utility function does not play a role here. However, the outcome of the proposer's decision is risky, because he does not know how the responder will react to it. The parameter γ reflects the proposer's risk aversion. In order to explain the distribution of actual offers in the ultimatum game, Rotemberg assumes that the proposer is risk-loving ($\gamma > 1$). Note that the responder does not face any risk, so his attitudes towards risk are irrelevant.

This model can be fit reasonably well to the data of the ultimatum game. The discontinuity of the function ξ may explain why behavior sometimes changes quite quickly from benevolence to hostility if certain standards of behavior are not met by the opponents. However, it is not clear that the parameter estimates for the ultimatum game yield reasonable predictions if the model is applied to other games. Rotemberg considers only one other game, the dictator game. However, here he imposes the additional assumption that the proposer suffers a utility loss of V if he believes that the responder believes that $a^P < \underline{a}$. This additional assumption is not only ad hoc, it also makes the proposer's payoff a function of the responder's *beliefs* about his type, thus turning the game into a psychological game (see Section 2.3 below).

Gul and Pesendorfer (2005) develop a canonical model of interdependent preferences. For example, they consider reciprocity in the ultimatum game and assume that preferences are linear and of the form

$$U_i = x_i + a_i x_j$$

with

$$a_i = c_0 + \sum_{n=1}^{\infty} c_n \cdot t_n^i \cdot t_{n-1}^j.$$

Here $t^i = (t_0^i, t_1^i, t_2^i, \ldots)$, where t_0^i is normalized to 1, is the type of player i which, together with the type of player j and the sequence of parameters $\{c_0, c_1, \ldots\}$, determines the parameter a_i. The interpretation of the vector t^i is that t_1^i is player i's unconditional level of altruism, irrespective of player j's type. The parameter t_2^i captures the strength of the response to player j's kindness, and so on. Gul and Pesendorfer construct an example with just two types that roughly replicates the main features of the mini-ultimatum game. In particular, it explains that an offer of (80, 20) may be rejected if the responder could have chosen (50, 50), but that it will be accepted if the responder had no choice. This model is very general and quite flexible, but it seems difficult to apply to more complicated games.

3.3. Models of intention based reciprocity

The models considered so far do not allow for the possibility that players care about their opponents' intentions. I may be happy to be kind to my opponent if I believe that he intends to be kind to me – independent of what he actually does. In order to evaluate my opponent's intentions, I not only have to form beliefs about what he is going to do, but also about why he is going to do it. But in order to interpret his behavior, I have to form beliefs about which actions my opponent believes I will take. Thus, for a given action of my opponent, it makes a difference for my utility payoff whether I believe that he takes this action because he believes that I will be kind to him or because he believes that I am going to hurt him. Traditional game theory cannot capture this, as it assumes that outcomes (and not beliefs) determine payoffs. However, Geanakoplos, Pearce and Stacchetti (1989) developed the concept of "psychological game theory" that generalizes traditional game theory by allowing for the possibility that payoffs are a function of players' beliefs. All models discussed in this subsection are based on psychological game theory.

3.3.1. Fairness equilibrium

In a pioneering article, Rabin (1993) modeled intention based reciprocity for simple two-player normal form games. Let A_1 and A_2 denote the (mixed) strategy sets for players 1 and 2, respectively, and let $x_i : A_1 \times A_2 \to IR$ be player i's material payoff function.

We now have to define (hierarchies of) beliefs over strategies. Let $a_i \in A_i$ denote a strategy of player i. When i chooses her strategy, she must have some belief about the strategy player j will choose. In all of the following $i \in \{1, 2\}$ and $j = 3 - i$. Let b_j denote player i's belief about what player j is going to do. Furthermore, in order to rationalize her expectation b_j, player i must have some belief about what player j believes that player i is going to do. This belief about beliefs is denoted by c_i. The hierarchy of beliefs could be continued ad infinitum, but the first two levels of beliefs are sufficient for defining reciprocal preferences.

Rabin starts with a "kindness function", $f_i(a_i, b_j)$, which measures how kind player i is to player j. If player i believes that her opponent chooses strategy b_j, then she effectively chooses her opponent's payoff out of the set $[x_j^l(b_j), x_j^h(b_j)]$ where $x_j^l(b_j) (x_j^h(b_j))$ is the lowest (highest) payoff of player j that can be induced by player i if j chooses b_j. According to Rabin, a "fair" or "equitable" payoff for player j, $x_j^f(b_j)$, is just the average of the lowest and highest payoffs (excluding Pareto-dominated payoffs, however). Note that this "fair" payoff is independent of player i's payoff. The kindness of player i towards player j is measured by the difference between the actual payoff she gives to player j and the "fair" payoff, relative to the whole range of feasible payoffs:[19]

$$f_i(a_i, b_j) \equiv \frac{x_j(b_j, a_i) - x_j^f(b_j)}{x_j^h(b_j) - x_j^l(b_j)}$$

with $f_i(a_i, b_j) = 0$ if $x_j^h(b_j) - x_j^l(b_j) = 0$. Note that $f_i(a_i, b_j) > 0$ if and only if player i gives player j more than the "fair" payoff.

Finally, we have to define player i's belief about how kindly player j treats her. This is defined in exactly the same manner, but beliefs have to move up one level. Thus, if player i beliefs that player j chooses b_j and if she believes that player j believes that i chooses c_i, then player i perceives player j's kindness as given by:

$$f'_j(b_j, c_i) \equiv \frac{x_i(c_i, b_j) - x_i^f(c_i)}{x_i^h(c_i) - -x_i^l(c_i)}$$

with $f'_j(b_j, c_i) = 0$ if $x_i^h(c_i) - x_i^l(c_i) = 0$. These kindness functions can now be used to define a player's utility function:

$$U_i(a, b_j, c_i) = x_i(a, b_j) + f'_j(b_j, c_i)[1 + f_i(a_i, b_j)],$$

where $a = (a_1, a_2)$. Note that if player j is perceived to be unkind ($f'_j(\cdot) < 0$), player i wants to be as unkind as possible, too. On the other hand, if $f'_j(\cdot)$ is positive, player i gets some additional utility from being kind to player j as well.

While this specification has some appealing properties, it is not consistent. For example, the utility function adds the monetary payoff of player i (measured for example in Dollars) to the kindness function that has no dimension. Note also that by definition the kindness term must lie in the interval $[-1, 0.5]$. Thus, the kindness term becomes less important the higher the material payoffs are. Furthermore, if monetary payoffs are multiplied by a constant (for example, if we move to a different currency) the marginal rate of substitution between money and kindness is affected. Thus, this utility function has very strong cardinal properties which are unappealing.

A "fairness equilibrium" is an equilibrium in a psychological game with these payoff functions, i.e., a pair of strategies (a_1, a_2) that are mutual best responses to each other and a set of rational expectations $b = (b_1, b_2)$ and $c = (c_1, c_2)$ that are consistent with equilibrium play.

Rabin's theory is important because it was the first contribution that precisely defined the notion of reciprocity and explored the consequences of reciprocal behavior. The model provides several interesting insights, but it is not well suited for predictive purposes. It is consistent with rejections in the UG, but many other equilibria exist as

---

[19] A disturbing feature of Rabin's formulation is that he excludes Pareto-dominated payoffs in the definition of the "fair" payoff, but not in the denominator of the kindness term. Thus, adding a Pareto-dominated strategy for player j would not affect the fair payoff but it would reduce the kindness term.

well, some of which are highly implausible. For example, offers above 50 percent of the surplus are part of an equilibrium even though this is almost never observed in experiments.

The multiplicity of equilibria is a general feature of Rabin's model. If material payoffs are small enough to make psychological payoffs matter, then there is always one equilibrium in which both players are nice to each other and one in which they are hostile. Both equilibria are supported by self-fulfilling prophecies, so it is difficult to predict which equilibrium is going to be played.

The theory also predicts that players do not undertake kind actions unless others have shown their kind intentions. Suppose, for example, that player 1 has no choice but is forced to cooperate in the prisoners' dilemma game. If player 2 knows this, then – according to Rabin's theory – she will interpret player 1's cooperation as "neutral" ($f'_2(\cdot) = 0$). Thus, she will only look at her material payoffs and will defect. This contrasts with models of inequity aversion where player 2 would co-operate irrespective of the reason for player 1's co-operation. We will discuss the experimental evidence that can be used to discriminate between the different approaches in Section 4 below.

3.3.2. Intentions in sequential games

Rabin's theory has been defined only for two-person, normal form games. If the theory is applied to the normal form of simple sequential games, some very implausible equilibria may arise. For example, unconditional cooperation by the second player is part of a fairness equilibrium in the sequential prisoners' dilemma. The reason is that Rabin's equilibrium notion does not force player 2 to behave optimally off the equilibrium path.

In a subsequent paper, Dufwenberg and Kirchsteiger (2004) generalized Rabin's theory to N-person extensive form games for which they introduce the notion of a "Sequential Reciprocity Equilibrium" (SRE). The main innovation is to keep track of beliefs about intentions as the game evolves. In particular, it has to be specified how beliefs about intentions are formed off the equilibrium path. Given this system of beliefs, strategies have to form a fairness equilibrium in every proper subgame.[20] Applying their model to several examples, Dufwenberg and Kirchsteiger show that *conditional* cooperation in the prisoners' dilemma game is a SRE. They also show that an offer from the proposer which the responder rejects with certainty can be a SRE in the ultimatum

---

[20] Dufwenberg and Kirchsteiger also suggest several other deviations from Rabin's model. In particular, they measure kindness "in proportion to the size of the gift" (i.e. in monetary units). This has the advantage that reciprocity does not disappear as the stakes become larger, but it also implies that the kindness term in the utility function has the dimension of "money squared" which again makes the utility function sensitive to linear transformations. Furthermore, they define "inefficient strategies" (which play an important role in the definition of the kindness term) as strategies that yield a weakly lower payoff for all players than some other strategy for all subgames. Rabin (1993) defines inefficient strategies to be those which yield weakly less on the equilibrium path. However, the problem in Dufwenberg and Kirchsteiger (2004) arises with more than two players because an additional dummy player may render an inefficient strategy efficient and might thus affect the size of the kindness term.

game. This is an equilibrium because each player believes that the other party wants to hurt him. However, the equilibrium analysis in this model is very complex, even in these extremely simple sequential games. Furthermore, there are typically multiple equilibria with different equilibrium outcomes, due to different self-fulfilling beliefs about intentions. Some of these equilibria seem highly implausible, but the theory does not offer any formal criteria how to discriminate between "convincing" and "less convincing" equilibria.

3.3.3. Merging intentions and social preferences

Falk and Fischbacher (2006) also generalize Rabin's (1993) model. They consider N-person extensive form games and allow for the possibility of incomplete information. Furthermore, they measure "kindness" in terms of inequity aversion. Player i perceives player j's strategy to be kind if it gives rise to a payoff for player i which is higher than that of player j. Note that this is fundamentally different from both Rabin as well as Dufwenberg and Kirchsteiger, who define j's "kindness" in terms of the feasible payoffs of player i and not in relation to the payoff that player j gets. Furthermore, Falk and Fischbacher distinguish whether player j could have altered an unequal distribution or whether player j was a "dummy player" who is unable to affect the distribution by his actions. The kindness term gets a higher weight in the former case than in the latter. However, even if player j is a dummy player who has no choice to make, the kindness term (which now reflects pure inequity aversion) gets a positive weight. Thus Falk and Fischbacher merge intention based reciprocity and inequity aversion.

Their model is quite complex. At every node where player i has to move, she has to evaluate the kindness of player j which depends on the expected payoff difference between the two players and on what player j could have done about this difference. This "kindness term" is multiplied by a "reciprocation term", which is positive if player i is kind to player j and negative if i is unkind. The product is further multiplied by an individual reciprocity parameter which measures the weight of player i's desire to reciprocate as compared to his desire to get a higher material payoff. These preferences together with the underlying game form define a psychological game à la Geanakoplos, Pearce and Stacchetti (1989). A subgame perfect psychological Nash equilibrium of this game is called a "reciprocity equilibrium".

Falk and Fischbacher show that there are parameter constellations for which their model is consistent with the stylized facts of the ultimatum game, the gift exchange game, the dictator game, and of public good and prisoners' dilemma games. Furthermore, there are parameter constellations that can explain the difference in outcomes if one player moves intentionally or if she is a dummy player. Because their model contains variants of a pure intentions based reciprocity model (like Rabin) and a pure inequity aversion model (like Fehr and Schmidt or Bolton and Ockenfels) as special cases, it is possible to get a better fit of the data, but at a significant cost in terms of the model's complexity.

Charness and Rabin (2002) provide another attempt at combining social preferences with intention based reciprocity. We already described their model of quasi-maximin preferences in Section 3.1.4. In a second step, they augment these preferences by introducing a demerit profile $\rho \equiv (\rho_1, \ldots, \rho_N)$, where $\rho_i \in [0, 1]$ is a measure of how much player i deserves from the point of view of all other players. The smaller ρ_i, the more does player i count in the utility function of the other players. Given a demerit profile ρ, player i's utility function is given by

$$U_i(x_1, x_2, \ldots, x_N | \rho) = (1-\gamma)x_i + \gamma\bigg[\delta \cdot \min\{x_i, \min_{j \neq i}\{x_j + d\rho_j\}\}$$

$$+ (1-\delta) \cdot \bigg(x_i + \sum_{j \neq i} \max\{1 - k\rho_j, 0\} \cdot x_j\bigg) - f \sum_{j \neq i} \rho_j x_j\bigg],$$

where $d, k, f \geq 0$ are three new parameters of the model. If $d = k = f = 0$, this boils down to the quasi-maximin preferences describes above. If d and k are large, then player i does not want to promote player j's well-being. If f is large, player i may actually want to hurt player j.

The crucial step is to endogenize the demerit profile ρ. Charness and Rabin do this by comparing player j's strategy to a "selfless standard" of behavior, which is unanimously agreed upon and exogenously given. The more player j falls short of this standard, the higher is his demerit factor ρ_j.

A "reciprocal fairness equilibrium" (RFE) is a strategy profile and a demerit profile such that each player maximizes his utility function given other players' strategies and given the demerit profile that is itself consistent with the profile of strategies. This definition implicitly corresponds to the Nash equilibrium of a psychological game as defined by Geanakoplos, Pearce and Stacchetti (1989).

The notion of RFE has several drawbacks that make it almost impossible to use for the analysis of even the simplest experimental games. First of all, the model is incomplete because preferences are only defined in equilibrium (i.e., for an equilibrium demerit profile ρ) and it is unclear how to evaluate outcomes out of equilibrium or if there are multiple equilibria. Second, it requires all players to have the same utility functions and agree on a "quasi-maximin" social welfare function in order to determine the demerit profile ρ. Finally, the model is so complicated and involves so many free parameters that it would be very difficult to test it empirically.

Charness and Rabin show that if the "selfless standard" is sufficiently small, every RFE corresponds to a Nash equilibrium of the game in which players simply maximize their quasi-maximin utility functions. Therefore, in the analysis of the experimental evidence, they restrict attention to the much simpler model of quasi-maximin preferences that we discussed in Section 3.1.1 above.

3.3.4. Guilt aversion and promises

Charness and Dufwenberg (2004) argue that people may be willing to help other people because they would feel guilty if they were to let them down. In particular, they would feel guilty if they promised beforehand to help the other party. In order to test this hypothesis, Charness and Dufwenberg conducted several trust game experiments in which one party could send a (free-form) message to the other party before the actual game starts. For example, the second mover could "promise" the first mover that he will reciprocate if the first mover trusts him. The experiments show that these promises significantly increase the probability that the first mover trusts, and second movers who made such a promise are significantly more likely to reciprocate when compared to an experiment without pre-play communication. Of course, pre-play communication is just cheap talk from the point of view of traditional game theory, and should not affect the (unique) equilibrium outcome of this game.

In order to explain the experimental results, Charness and Dufwenberg develop a model of "guilt aversion" using psychological game theory. In this model, players feel "guilt" if they let other players down. More precisely, if player 1 believes that player 2 believes that player 1 will take an action that gives monetary payoff m to player 2, then player 1 feels guilt if he takes an action that gives a payoff of $m' < m$ to player 2. If guilt aversion is sufficiently strong, player 1 may choose an action that is personally costly to him but which benefits player 2 because he does not want to disappoint player 2's belief about his action. As in Rabin's (1993) model, this theory requires that players have second-order beliefs about other players' beliefs and it typically has many equilibria. Pre-play communication and promises can be useful as a coordination device in order to select one of these equilibria. Charness and Dufwenberg also show that guilt aversion can explain tipping behavior, reciprocal effort behavior in the gift exchange game and collusion in oligopolistic markets.

However, the model only focuses on positive reciprocity and cannot explain why people may want to hurt one another. Furthermore, the model shares all of the drawbacks of the other models based on psychological game theory, in particular complexity and multiplicity of equilibria.

3.4. Axiomatic approaches

The models considered so far assume very specific utility functions that are either defined on (lotteries over) material payoff vectors and/or on beliefs about other players' strategies and other players' beliefs. These utility functions are based on psychological plausibility, yet most of them lack an axiomatic foundation. Segal and Sobel (2004) take the opposite approach and ask what kinds of axioms generate preferences that can reflect fairness and reciprocity.

They start by assuming that players have preferences over strategy profiles rather than over material allocations. Consider a given two-player game and let Σ_i, $i \in \{1, 2\}$, denote the space of (mixed) strategies of player i. For any strategy profile $(\sigma_1, \sigma_2) \in \Sigma_1 \times \Sigma_2$, let $v_i(\sigma_1, \sigma_2)$ denote player i's utility function over her own monetary payoff (which is determined by the strategy profile (σ_1, σ_2)), assuming that these "selfish preferences" satisfy the von Neumann–Morgenstern axioms. However, player i's actual preferences are given by a preference relation $f_{i\sigma_j}$ over her own strategies. This preference relation depends of course on the strategy σ_j she expects her opponent to play. Segal and Sobel show that if the preference relation $f_{i\sigma_j}$ satisfies the independence axiom and if, for a given σ_j, player i prefers to get a higher material payoff for herself if the payoff of player j is held constant (called "self interest"), then the preferences $f_{i\sigma_j}$ over Σ_i can be represented by a utility function of the form[21]

$$u_i(\sigma_i, \sigma_j) = v_i(\sigma_i, \sigma_j) + a_{i,\sigma j} v_j(\sigma_i, \sigma_j).$$

In standard game theory, $a_{i,\sigma j} \equiv 0$. Positive values of this coefficient mean that player i has altruistic preferences, negative values of $a_{i\sigma j}$ mean that she is spiteful.

The models of social preferences we discussed at the beginning of this chapter, in particular the models of altruism, relative income, inequity aversion, quasi-maximin preferences, and altruism and spitefulness, can all be seen as special cases of a Segal-Sobel utility function. Segal and Sobel can also capture some, but not all, aspects of intention based reciprocity. For example, a player's utility in Rabin's (1993) model not only depended on the strategy her opponent chose, but also on why he chose this strategy. This can be illustrated in the "Battle of the Sexes" game. Player 1 may go to boxing, because she expects player 2 to go to boxing, too (which is regarded as kind behavior by player 2, given that he believes player 1 will go to boxing). Yet, player 2 may also go to boxing, because he expects player 1 to go to ballet (which is regarded as unkind behavior by player 2 if he believes player 1 to go to ballet) and which is punished by the boxing strategy of player 1. This effect cannot be captured by Segal and Sobel, because in their framework preferences are defined on strategies only.

Neilson (2005) provides an axiomatic characterization of the Fehr and Schmidt (1999) model of inequity aversion. He introduces the axiom of "self-referent separability" which requires that if the monetary payoffs of player i and of all other players increase by some constant amount, then player 1's preferences about payoff allocations should not be affected. Neilson shows that this axiom is equivalent to having a utility function that is additively separable in the individual's own material payoff and the payoff differences to his opponents, which is an essential feature of the Fehr-Schmidt model. Furthermore, he shows that in a one-person decision problem under risk the same axiom of "self-referent separability" implies a generalization of prospect theory preferences [Kahneman and Tversky (1979)].

4. Discriminating between theories of other-regarding preferences

Most theories discussed in Section 3 were developed during the last 5–10 years and the evidence to discriminate between these theories is still limited. As we will show, however, the available data do exhibit some clear qualitative regularities which give a first indication of the advantages and disadvantages of the different approaches.

---

[21] The construction resembles that of Harsanyi's (1955) "utilitarian" social welfare function $\Sigma \alpha_i u_i$. Note, however, that Harsanyi's axiom of Pareto efficiency is stronger than the axiom of self interest employed here. Therefore, the $a_{i\sigma_j}$ in Segal and Sobel may be negative.

4.1. Who are the relevant reference actors?

All theories of other-regarding preferences are based on the idea that actors compare themselves with a set of reference actors or take these actors' payoffs directly into account. To whom do people compare themselves? Who are the relevant reference actors whose payoff is taken into account? There is no ambiguity about who the relevant reference actor is in bilateral interactions; the answer is less clear, however, in multi-person interactions. Most of the theories applicable in the n-person context assume that players make comparisons with all other $n - 1$ players in the game. The only exemption is the theory of Bolton and Ockenfels (BO). They assume that players compare themselves only with the "average" player in the game and do not care about inequities between the other players. In this regard, the BO approach is inspired by the data of Selten and Ockenfels (1998) and Güth and van Damme (1998), which seem to suggest that actors do not care for inequities among the other reference agents. It would greatly simplify matters if this aspect of the BO theory were correct.

One problem with this aspect of the BO approach is that it disenables the theory to explain punishment in the Third-Party Punishment Game [Fehr and Fischbacher (2004)]. Recall that there are three players, A, B, and C in the third party punishment game. Player A is endowed with some surplus S and must decide how much of S to give to B, who has no endowment. Player B is just a dummy player and has no decision power. Player C is endowed with $S/2$ and can spend this money on the punishment of A after he observes how much A gave to B. For any money unit player C spends on punishment the payoff of player A is reduced by 3 units. Note that the total surplus available in this game is $(3/2)S$. Therefore, without punishment, player C is certain to get her fair share $(S/2)$ of the total surplus, implying that the BO model predicts that C will never punish. In contrast to this prediction, roughly 60 percent of the C players punished in this game. This indicates that many players do care about inequities among other players. Further support for this hypothesis comes from Charness and Rabin (2002) who offered player C the choice between the payoff allocations (575, 575, 575) and (900, 300, 600). Because both allocations give player C the fair share of 1/3 of the surplus, the BO model predicts that player C will choose the second allocation which gives him a higher absolute payoff. However, 54 percent of the subjects preferred the first allocation. Note that the self-interest hypothesis also predicts the second allocation, so one cannot conclude that the other 46 percent of the subjects have BO-preferences. A recent paper by Zizzo and Oswald (2000) also strongly suggests that subjects care about the inequities among the set of references agents.

It is important to note that theories of other-regarding preferences, in which subjects have multiple reference agents, do not necessarily imply that the subjects take actions in favor of *all* other reference agents, even if all other reference agents have the same weight in their utility function. To illustrate this, consider the following three-person UG [Güth and van Damme (1998)]. This game includes a proposer, a responder who can reject or accept the proposal, and a passive Receiver who can do nothing but collect the amount of money allocated to him. The proposer proposes an allocation (x_1, x_2, x_3)

where x_1 is the proposer's payoff, x_2 the responder's payoff and x_3 the Receiver's payoff. If the responder rejects, all three players get nothing, otherwise the proposed allocation is implemented.

It turns out that the proposers allocate substantial fractions of the surplus to the responder in this game but little or nothing to the Receiver. Moreover, Güth and van Damme (1998, p. 230) report that "there is not a single rejection that can clearly be attributed to a low share for the dummy (i.e., the Receiver, FS)". BO take this as evidence in favor of their approach because the proposer and the responder apparently do not take the Receiver's interest into account. However, this conclusion is premature because it is easy to show that approaches with multiple reference agents are fully consistent with the Güth and van Damme data. The point can be demonstrated in the context of the Fehr–Schmidt model. Assume for simplicity that the proposer makes an offer of $x_1 = x_2 = x$ while the Receiver gets $x_3 < x$. It is easy to show that a responder with FS-preferences will never (!) reject such an allocation even if $x_3 = 0$ and even if he is very fair-minded, i.e., has a high β-coefficient. To see this note that the utility of the responder if he accepts is given by $U_2 = x - (\beta/2)(x - x_3)$ which is positive for all $\beta \leqslant 1$, and thus higher than the rejection payoff of zero. A similar calculation shows that it takes implausibly high β-values to induce a proposer to take the interests of the Receiver into account.[22]

The above arguments suggest that the "average" player in a game is not an empirically relevant reference agent. This is particularly important for all games in which subjects may want to punish a particular individual for unfair or morally inappropriate behavior. In all these cases, a model, in which the differences (or the ratio) between a player's own payoff and the group's average payoff is the driving force of the punishment, is not able to predict which individual will be punished. A player who just wants to reduce the difference between his payoff and the group's average payoff does not care about the target of the punishment. Any punishment that reduces this difference, even if it is targeted on cooperative or norm abiding individuals, is equally desirable from the perspective of such a player [see also Falk, Fehr and Fischbacher (2005)].

In general, however, very little is known about the outcome of social comparison processes in games. Therefore, our empirical knowledge about what makes a player a relevant reference agent is very limited. The assumption that all players in a game are relevant reference agents to each other should only be taken as a first approximation and may not be true in some games. It seems reasonable to assume that player A is a relevant reference agent for player B if A can affect B's payoff in a salient way. However, there neither seems to be much theoretical work on this question nor persuasive empirical evidence beyond such general statements. Thus, the question "who are the relevant reference agents" is clearly an important unsolved problem.

---

[22] The proposer's utility is given by $U_1 = x_1 - (\beta/2)[(x_1 - x_2) + (x_1 - x_3)]$. If we normalize the surplus to one and take into account that $x_1 + x_2 + x_3 = 1$, $U_1 = (\beta/2) + (3/2)x_1[(2/3) - \beta]$. Thus, the marginal utility of x_1 is positive unless β exceeds $2/3$. This means that proposers with $\beta < 2/3$ will give the responders just enough to prevent rejection and, since the responders neglect the interests of the Receivers, nothing to the Receivers.

4.2. Equality versus efficiency

Many models of other-regarding preferences are based on the definition of a fair or equitable outcome to which people compare the available payoff allocations. In experimental games, the equality of material payoffs is a natural first approximation for the relevant reference outcome. The quasi-maximin theory of Charness and Rabin assumes instead that subjects care for the total surplus ("efficiency") accruing to the group. A natural way to study whether there are subjects who want to maximize the total surplus is to construct experiments in which the predictions of both theories of inequality aversion (BO and FS) are in conflict with surplus maximization. This has been done by Andreoni and Vesterlund (2001), Bolle and Kritikos (1998), Charness and Rabin (2002), Cox (2000) and Güth, Kliemt and Ockenfels (2000). Except for the Güth et al. paper, these papers indicate that a non-negligible fraction of the subjects in dictator game situations is willing to give up some of their own money in order to increase total surplus, even if this implies that they generate inequality that is to their disadvantage. Andreoni and Miller and Andreoni and Vesterlund, for example, conducted dictator games with varying prices for transferring money to the Receiver. In some conditions, the Allocator had to give up less than a dollar to give the Receiver a dollar, in some conditions the exchange ratio was 1 : 1, and in some other conditions the Allocator had to give up more than one dollar. In the usual dictator games, the exchange ratio is 1 : 1 and there are virtually no cases in which an Allocator transfers more than 50 percent of the surplus. In contrast, in dictator games with an exchange ratio of 1 : 3 (or 1 : 2) a non-negligible number of allocators transfer in such a way that they end up with less money than the Receiver. This contradicts the models of Bolton and Ockenfels (2000), of Fehr and Schmidt (1999), and of Falk and Fischbacher (2006) because in these models subjects never take actions that give the other party more than they get in these models. It is, however, consistent with altruistic preferences or quasi-maximin preferences.

What is the relative importance of this kind of behavior? Andreoni and Vesterlund are able to classify subjects in three distinct classes. They report that 44% of their subjects ($N = 141$) are completely selfish, 35 percent exhibit egalitarian preferences, i.e. they tend to equalize payoffs, and 21 percent of the subjects can be classified as surplus maximizers. Charness and Rabin report similar results with regard to the fraction of egalitarian subjects in a simple Dictator Game where the Allocator had to choose between (own, other) allocations of (400, 400) and (400, 750). 31 percent of the subjects preferred the egalitarian and 69 percent the surplus maximizing allocation. Among the 69 percent there may, however, also be many selfish subjects who no longer choose the surplus-maximizing allocation when this decreases their payoff only slightly. This is suggested by the game where the Allocator had to choose between (400, 400) and (375, 750). Here only 49 percent of surplus-maximizing choices were observed. Charness and Rabin also present questionnaire evidence indicating that when the income disparities are greater the egalitarian motive gains weight at the cost of the surplus maximization motive. When the Allocator faces a choice between (400, 400) and (400, 2000), 62 percent prefer the egalitarian allocation.

More recently, Engelmann and Strobel (2004) argued that "efficiency" is an important motive that clearly dominates the desire for equality in 3 player dictator games. For example, the Allocator (who was always player B) could choose between 3 different payoff allocations in one of their games: (14, 4, 5), (11, 4, 6) and (8, 4, 7). Thus B's material payoff was the same in each of the three allocations, but he could redistribute income from the rich person to the poor person. Redistribution has a high efficiency cost in this game because it reduces the rich person's income by 3 units and increases the poor person's income by only 1 unit. Maximin preferences and selfish preferences cannot play a role in this game because the Allocator receives the lowest payoff regardless of the allocation chosen. This game allows, therefore, for a clean examination of how important the equality motive is relative to the "efficiency" motive. Engelmann and Strobel report that 60% of their subjects ($N = 30$) chose the first allocation, i.e., the one with the highest surplus and the highest inequality, and only 33% chose the most egalitarian allocation (8, 4, 7).

However, only students of economics and business administration, which we call for brevity "economists", participated in the Engelmann and Strobel study. These students learn from the very beginning of their studies that surplus maximization is normatively desirable. Therefore, Fehr, Naef and Schmidt (in press) replicated this game with $N = 458$ subjects to examine potential subject pool biases. They find a robust subject pool bias indicating that non-economists ($N = 291$) chose the most egalitarian allocation with the lowest surplus in 51% of the cases whereas economists' probability to choose this allocation was only 26% ($N = 167$). Likewise, the non-economists chose the least egalitarian allocation with the maximal surplus in only 28% of the cases, whereas the economists chose it in 56% of the cases. This result is also important with regard to the interpretation of the results of Charness and Rabin, who also have disproportionately many economists in their subject pool.

Since the evidence in favor of preferences for surplus maximization comes exclusively from dictator games, it is important to ask whether these preferences are likely to play a role in "strategic situations". We define strategic situations to be those in which the potential gift recipients are also capable of affecting the gift givers' material payoffs. This question is important because the dictator game is different from many economically important games and real life situations, because one player is rarely at the complete mercy of another player in economic interactions. It may well be that in situations where *both* players have some power to affect the outcome, the surplus maximization motive is less important than in dictator games or is easily dominated by other considerations. The gift-exchange experiments by Fehr, Kirchsteiger and Riedl (1993, 1998) are telling in this regard because they embed a situation that is like a DG into an environment with competitive and strategic elements.

These experiments exhibit a competitive element because the gift exchange game is embedded into a competitive experimental market. The experiments also exhibit a strategic element because the proposers are wage setters and have to take the responders' likely effort responses into account. Yet, once the responder has accepted a wage offer, the experiments are similar to a dictator game because, for a given wage, the responder essentially determines the income distribution and the total surplus by his choice of the effort level. The gift exchange experiments are an ideal environment for checking the robustness of the surplus maximization motive because an increase in the effort cost by one unit increases the total surplus by five units on average. Therefore, the maximal feasible effort level is, in general, also the surplus maximizing effort level. If surplus maximization is a robust motive, capable of overturning preferences for equality or reciprocity, one would expect that many responders choose effort levels that give the proposer a higher monetary payoff than the responder.[23] Moreover, surplus maximization also means that we should *not* observe a positive correlation between effort and wages because, for a given wage, the maximum feasible effort always maximizes the total surplus.[24]

However, the data supports neither of these implications. Effort levels that give the proposer a higher payoff than the responder are virtually non-existent. In the overwhelming majority of the cases, effort is substantially below the maximally feasible level and the proposer earns a higher payoff than the responder in less than two percent of the cases.[25] Moreover, almost all subjects who regularly chose non-minimal effort levels exhibited a reciprocal effort–wage relation. A related result was observed by Güth, Kliemt and Ockenfels (2003) who also conducted experiments in which dictators face a trade-off between equality and surplus maximization. They report that equality concerns dominate surplus maximization concerns in the sense that dictators never perform transfers such that they earn less than the recipient, even if such transfers would be surplus enhancing. These results are in sharp contrast to the 49 percent of the Allocators in Charness and Rabin who preferred the (375, 750) allocation over the (400, 400) allocation. One reason for the difference across studies is perhaps the fact that it was much cheaper to increase the surplus in the Charness–Rabin example. While the surplus increases in the gift exchange experiments on average by five units, if the responder sacrifices one payoff unit, the surplus increases by 14 units per payoff unit sacrificed in the Charness–Rabin case. This suggests that surplus maximization only gives rise to a violation of the equality constraint if surplus increases are extremely cheap. A second reason for the behavioral difference may be that when both players have some power to affect the outcome, the motive to increase the surplus is quickly crowded out by other considerations. This reason is quite plausible insofar as the outcomes in dictator games themselves are notoriously non-robust.

---

[23] The responders' effort level may, of course, also be affected by the intentions of the proposer. For example, paying a high wage may signal fair intentions which may increase the effort level. Yet, since this tends to raise effort levels, we would have even stronger evidence against the surplus-maximization hypothesis, if we observe little or no effort choices that give the proposer a higher payoff than the responder.

[24] There are degenerate cases in which this is not true.

[25] The total number of effort choices is $N = 480$ in these experiments, i.e., the results are not an artefact of a low number of observations.

While the experimental results on ultimatum games are fairly robust, the dictator game seems to be a rather fragile situation in which minor factors can have large effects. Cox (2004), e.g., reports that *100 percent* of all subjects transferred positive amounts in his dictator games.[26] This result contrasts sharply with many other games, including the games in Charness and Rabin and many other dictator games. To indicate the other extreme, Eichenberger and Oberholzer-Gee (1998), Hoffman et al. (1994) and List and Cherry (2000) report on dictator games with extremely low transfers.[27] Likewise, in the impunity game of Bolton and Zwick (1995), which is very close but not identical to a dictator game, the vast majority of proposers did not shy away from making very unfair offers. The impunity game differs from the dictator game only insofar as the responder can reject an offer; however, the rejection destroys only the responder's but not the proposer's payoff. The notorious non-robustness of outcomes in situations resembling the dictator game indicates that one should be very careful in generalizing the results found in these situations to other games. Testing theories of other-regarding preferences in dictator games is a bit like testing the laws of gravity with a table tennis ball. In both situations, minor unobserved distortions can have large effects. Therefore, we believe that it is necessary to show that the same motivational forces that are inferred from dictator games are also behaviorally relevant in economically more important games. One way to do this is to apply the theories that were constructed on the basis of dictator game experiments to predict outcomes in other games. With the exemption of Andreoni and Miller (2002) this has not yet been done.

Andreoni and Miller (2002) estimate utility functions based on the results of their dictator game experiments and use them to predict cooperative behavior in a standard public goods game. They predict behavior in period one of these games, where cooperation is often quite high, rather well. However, their predictions differ greatly from final period outcomes, where cooperation is typically very low. In our view, the low cooperation rates in the final period of repeated public good games constitutes a strong challenge for models that rely exclusively on altruistic or surplus-maximizing preferences. Why should a subject with a stable preference for others' payoffs or for those of the whole group contribute much less in the final period compared to the first period? Models of inequity aversion and intention based or type based reciprocity models provide a plausible explanation for this behavior. All of these models predict that fair subjects make their cooperation contingent on the cooperation of others. Thus, if the fair subjects realize that there are sufficiently many selfish decisions in the course of a public goods experiment, they cease to cooperate as well (see also Section 5 below).

---

[26] In Cox's experiment, both players had an endowment of 10 and the Allocator could transfer his endowment to the Receiver, where the experimenter tripled the transferred amount. The Receiver made no choice.

[27] In Eichenberger and Oberholzer-Gee (1998), almost 90 percent of the subjects gave nothing. In Hoffman et al. (1994), 64 percent gave nothing and 19 percent gave between 1 and 10 percent. In List and Cherry subjects earned their endowment in a quiz. Then they played the DG. Roughly 90 percent of the Allocators transferred nothing to the Receivers.

4.3. Revenge versus inequity reduction

Subjects with altruistic and quasi-maximin preferences do not take actions that reduce other subjects' payoffs; this phenomenon, however, is frequently observed in many important games. Models of inequity aversion account for this by assuming that the payoff reduction is motivated by a desire to reduce disadvantageous inequality. In models of intention based or type based reciprocity subjects punish if they observe an action that is perceived to be unfair or that reveals that the opponent is spiteful. In these models players want to reduce the opponent's payoff irrespective of whether they are better or worse off than the opponent and irrespective of whether they can change income shares or income differences. Furthermore, intention based theories predict that there will be no punishment in games in which no intention can be expressed. Therefore, a clean way to test for the relevance of intentions is to conduct control treatments in which choices are made through a random device or through some neutral and disinterested third party.

Blount (1995) was the first who applied this idea to the ultimatum game. Blount compared the rejection rate in the usual UG to the rejection rates in ultimatum games in which either a computer generated a random offer or a third party made the offer. Because a low offer can neither be attributed to the greedy intentions of the proposer in the random offer condition nor in the third party condition, intention based theories predict a rejection rate of zero in these conditions, while theories of inequity aversion still allow for positive rejection rates. Levine's theory is also consistent with positive rejection rates in these conditions, but his theory predicts a decrease in the rejection rate relative to the usual condition, because low offers made by humans reveal that the type who made the offer is spiteful which can trigger a spiteful response. Blount indeed observes a significant and substantial reduction in the acceptance thresholds of the responders in the random offer condition but not in the third party condition. Thus, the result of the random offer condition is consistent with intention and type based model, while the result of the third party condition is inconsistent with the motives captured by these models. Yet, these puzzling results may be due to some problematic features in Blount's experiments.[28] Subsequently, Offerman (1999) and Falk, Fehr and Fischbacher (2000b) conducted further experiments with offers generated by a random mechanism but without the other worrisome features in Blount. In particular, the responders knew that a rejection affects the payoff of a real, human "proposer" in these experiments. Offerman finds that subjects are 67 percent more likely to reduce the opponent's payoff when the opponent made an intentional low offer compared to a situation where a computer made the low offer.

---

[28] Blount's results may be affected by the fact that subjects (in two of three treatments) had to make decisions as a proposer *and* as a responder before they knew their actual roles. After subjects had made their decisions in both roles, the role for which they received payments was determined randomly. In one of Blount's treatments deception was involved. Subjects believed that there were proposers, although the experimenters in fact made the proposals. All subjects in this condition were "randomly" assigned to the responder role. In this treatment subjects also were not paid according to their decisions but they received a flat fee instead.

Falk, Fehr and Fischbacher (2000b) conducted an experiment, invented by Abbink, Irlenbusch and Renner (2000), that simultaneously allows for the examination of positive and negative reciprocity. In this game player A can give player B any integer amount of money $g \in [0, 6]$ or, alternatively, she can take away from B any integer amount of money $t \in [1, 6]$. In case of $g > 0$ the experimenter triples g so that B receives $3g$. If player A takes away t, player A gets t and player B loses t. After player B observes g or t, she can pay A an integer reward $r \in [0, 18]$ or she can reduce A's income by making an investment $i \in [1, 6]$. A reward transfers one money unit from B to A. An investment i costs B exactly i but reduces A's income by $3i$. This game was played in a random choice condition and in a human choice condition. It turns out that when the choices are made by a human player A, players B invest significantly more into payoff reductions for all $t \in [1, 6]$. However, as in Blount and Offerman, payoff reductions also occur when a random mechanism determines a hurtful choice.

Kagel, Kim and Moser (1996) provide further support that intentions play a role for payoff-reducing behavior. Subjects bargained over 100 chips in an UG in their experiments. They conducted several treatments that varied the money value of the chips and the information provided about the money value. For example, the proposers received three times more money per chip than the responders in one treatment, i.e., the equal money split required the responders to receive 75 chips. If the responders knew that the proposers were aware of the different money values of the chips, they rejected unequal money splits much more frequently than if the responders knew that the proposers did *not* know the different money values of the chips. Thus, knowingly unequal proposals were rejected at higher rates than unintentional unequal proposals.

Another way to test for the relevance of intention based or type based punishments is to examine behavior in the following two situations [Brandts and Sola (2001), Falk, Fehr and Fischbacher (2003)]. In one treatment, the proposer in a $10 ultimatum game can choose between an offer of (5, 5) and an offer of (8, 2). In the other treatment the proposer can choose between (8, 2) and (10, 0). If responders do not care about whether the proposer has unfair intentions or is an unfair type, the rejection rate of the (8, 2) offer should be the same across both treatments. However, the information conveyed about the proposer's intention or type is very different across treatments. In the treatment where (5, 5) is the alternative to (8, 2), a proposal of (8, 2) is very likely to indicate that the proposer has unfair intentions or is an unfair type. This information is not conveyed by the (8, 2) proposal if the alternative is the (10, 0) proposal. Thus, if the responders care about the proposer's intention or type, the rejection rate for the (8, 2) offer should be higher in the case where (5, 5) is the available alternative. This prediction is nicely met by the data in Falk, Fehr and Fischbacher (2003): if (5, 5) is the alternative, 45% of the responders reject the (8, 2) offer, while if (10, 0) is the alternative, only 9% of the (8, 2) offers are rejected.

Finally, the relevance of intention based or type based punishments can also be examined by ruling out egalitarian motives as follows: If punishment keeps the relative payoff share or the payoff difference constant or even increases them, egalitarian motives, as modeled by Bolton and Ockenfels and Fehr and Schmidt, predict zero punishment.

Falk, Fehr and Fischbacher (2000a) report the results of ultimatum games that have this feature. In the first (standard) treatment of the ultimatum game the proposers could propose a (5, 5) or an (8, 2) split of the surplus (the first number represents the proposer's payoff). In case of rejection, both players received zero. In the second treatment, the proposers had the same options but a rejection now meant that the payoff was reduced for both players by 2 units. The theory of Bolton and Ockenfels and of Fehr and Schmidt predict, therefore, that there will be no rejections in the second treatment while intention based and type based models predict that rejections will occur. It turns out that the rejection rate of the (8, 2) offer is 56 percent in the first and 19 percent in the second treatment. Thus, roughly one third (19/56) of the rejections are consistent with a pure taste for punishment as conceptualized in intention and type based models.[29] This evidence also suggests that payoff consequences alone are a determinant of the responder's rejection behavior. This conclusion is also supported by the results in Blount (1995) and Falk, Fehr and Fischbacher (2003), who report a significant number of rejections even if a third party makes the offer (as in Blount) or if the proposer is forced to make the (8, 2) offer [as in Falk, Fehr and Fischbacher (2003)].

Taken together, the evidence from Blount (1995), Kagel, Kim and Moser (1996), Offerman (1999), Brandts and Sola (2001) and Falk, Fehr and Fischbacher (2000a, 2000b, 2003) supports the view that subjects want to punish unfair intentions or unfair types. Although the evidence provided by the initial study of Blount was mixed, the subsequent studies indicate a clear role of these motives. However, the evidence is also consistent with the view that egalitarian motives play a non-negligible role.

4.4. Does kindness trigger rewards?

Do intention and type based theories of fairness fare equally well in the domain of rewarding behavior? It turns out that the evidence in this domain is much more mixed. Some experimental results suggest that these motives seldom affect rewarding behavior. Other results indicate some minor role, and a few papers find an unambiguous positive effect of intention or type based reciprocity.

Intention based theories predict that people are generous only if they have been treated kindly, i.e., if the first-mover has signaled a fair intention. Levine's theory is similar in this regard because generous actions are more likely if the first mover is an altruistic type. However, in contrast to the intention based approaches, Levine's approach is also compatible with unconditional giving if it is sufficiently surplus-enhancing.

Neither intention nor type based reciprocity can explain positive transfers in the dictator game. Moreover, Charness (1996), Bolton, Brandts and Ockenfels (1998), Offerman (1999), Cox (2000) and Charness and Rabin (2002) provide further evidence that intentions do not play a big role for rewarding behavior. Charness (1996) conducted gift

---

[29] Ahlert, Crüger and Güth (1999) also report a significant amount of punishment in ultimatum games where the responders cannot change the payoff difference. However, since they do not have a control treatment it is not possible to say something about the relative importance of this kind of punishment.

exchange games in a random choice condition where a random device determined the proposer's decision and a human choice condition where the proposer made the choice. Intention based theories predict that the responders will not put forward more than the minimal effort level in the random choice condition, irrespective of the wage level, because high wage offers are due to chance and not to kind intentions. Higher wages in the human choice condition indicate a higher degree of kindness and, therefore, a positive correlation between wages and effort is predicted. Levine's theory allows, in principle, for a positive correlation between wages and effort in both conditions, because an increase in effort benefits the proposer much more than it costs the responder. However, the correlation should be much stronger in the human choice condition due to the type-revealing effect of high wages. Charness finds a significantly positive correlation in the random choice condition. Effort in the human choice condition is only slightly lower at low wages and equally high at high wages. This indicates, if anything, only a minor role for intention and type driven behavior. The best interpretation is probably that inequity aversion or quasi-maximin preferences induce non-minimal effort levels in this setting. In addition, negative reciprocity kicks in at low wages which explains the lower effort levels in the human choice condition.

Cox (2004) tries to isolate rewarding responses in the context of a trust game by using a related dictator game as a control condition. Cox first conducts the usual trust game, which provides him with a baseline level of responder transfers back to the proposer. To isolate the relevance of intention driven responses, he then conducts a dictator game in which the distribution of endowments is identical to the distribution of material payoffs after the proposers' choices in the trust game. Thus, the responders face exactly the same distributions of material payoffs in both the trust game and in the dictator game, but the proposers intentionally caused this distribution in the trust game, while the experimenter predetermined the distribution in the dictator game. The motive for rewarding kindness can, therefore, play no role in the dictator game and both intention based theories as well as Levine's theory predict that responders transfer nothing back. If one takes into account that some transfers in the dictator game are likely to be driven by inequity aversion, the difference between the transfers in the dictator game and those in the trust game measure the relevance of intention based theories. Cox's results indicate that transfers in the trust game are roughly by one-third higher than in the dictator game. Thus, intention based reciprocity plays a significant, but not the dominant, role.

The strongest evidence against the role of intentions comes from Bolton, Brandts and Ockenfels (1998). They conducted sequential social dilemma experiments that are akin to a sequentially played Prisoners' Dilemma. In one condition, the first movers could make a kind choice relative to a reference choice. The kind choice implied that – for any second mover choice – the second mover's payoff increased by 400 units at a cost of 100 for the first mover. Then the second mover could take costly actions in order to reward the first mover. In a control condition, the first mover had to make the reference choice, i.e. he could not express any kind intentions. It turns out that second movers reward the first movers even more in the control condition. Although this difference is not significant, the results clearly suggest that intention-driven rewards play no role in this experiment.

The strongest evidence in favor of intentions comes from the moonlighting game of Falk, Fehr and Fischbacher (2000b) described in the previous subsection. They find that players B send back significantly more money in the human choice condition for *all* positive transfers of player A. Moreover, the difference between the rewards in the human choice condition and the random choice condition are also quantitatively important. A recent paper by McCabe, Rigdon and Smith (2003) also reports evidence in favor of intention driven positive reciprocity. They show that if the first-mover makes a kind decision, two-thirds of the second movers also make kind decisions, while only one-third of the second movers make the kind decision if the first mover is forced to make the kind choice.

In the absence of the evidence provided by Falk, Fehr and Fischbacher (2000b) and McCabe, Rigdon and Smith (2003), one would have to conclude that the motive to reward good intentions or fair types is (at best) of minor importance. However, in view of the relatively strong results in the final two papers, it seems wise to be more cautious and to wait for further evidence. Nevertheless, the bulk of the evidence suggests that inequity aversion and efficiency seeking are more important than intention or type based reciprocity in the domain of kind behavior.

4.5. Maximin preferences

The papers by Charness and Rabin (2002) and by Engelmann and Strobel (2004) show that a substantial percentage of the Allocators in multi person dictator games care for the material payoff of the least well-off group member. The relevance of the maximin motive in these games is, for example, illustrated by the dictator game taken from Engelmann and Strobel (2004), in which player B is the dictator who can choose among the following three allocations: (11, 12, 2), (8, 12, 3) and (5, 12, 4). Both surplus maximization as well as the theories by Bolton and Ockenfels and Fehr and Schmidt predict that B will choose the first allocation in this game, whereas a player with maximin preferences chooses the third allocation. In fact, 53% of the players chose the third and only 27% chose the first allocation, indicating the importance of the maximin motive in these games. This game also shows, however, that nonlinear forms of inequity aversion may come close to maximin preferences. This is, for example, the case if the marginal disutility from advantageous inequality strongly increases in the amount of inequality. In this case also an inequity averse player may prefer the third allocation.

Although the maximin motive plays a prominent role in multi person dictator games, there are several papers that cast doubt on the relevance of this motive in strategic games. A salient example is the three-person experiment of Güth and van Damme (1998) that combines an ultimatum and a dictator game. Recall from Section 4.1 that the proposer has to make a proposal (x, y, z) on how to allocate a given sum of money between himself and players two and three in this game. Then the responder has to decide whether to accept or reject the proposal. If he accepts, the proposal is implemented, otherwise all players get zero. Player 3 remains inactive and cannot affect the final outcome. Güth and van Damme report that the proposer allocates only marginal amounts to the passive Receiver and the responder's rejection behavior is seemingly unaffected by the low amounts allocated to the passive Receiver. These observations contradict maximin preferences while they are consistent with the linear Fehr and Schmidt model and the model by Bolton and Ockenfels [see Bolton and Ockenfels (2000) and Section 4.1].

Frechette, Kagel and Lehrer (2003) provide another striking example of the neglect of the weak player's interests in strategic interactions. One player in a group of five can make a proposal on how to allocate a fixed sum of money among the five players in their experiments. Then the players vote on the proposal under the majority rule, i.e., the support of 3 players is sufficient to implement the proposal. In 65% of the cases, the proposals implied that two of the five players received a zero payoff, completely neglecting the interests of members that are not part of the winning coalition. Moreover, such proposals received the support of the majority in most cases. Thus, maximin preferences seem do play little role in this environment.

Finally, the experiments by Okada and Riedl (2005) also indicate that maximin preferences are of little importance in strategic games. In their three person experiments, a proposer could propose an allocation (x, y) to one responder or an allocation (x, y, z) to two responders. If he proposes forming a three person coalition, i.e., making an offer to two responders, the total amount to be distributed among the three players is 3000 points whereas if he only proposes a two person coalition, the total amount to be distributed is an element of the set $\{1200, 2100, 2500, 2800\}$. However, both responders have to accept the proposal (x, y, z) in the case of a three person coalition, whereas only a single responder has to accept the proposal (x, y) in the case of the two person coalition. If one of the responders rejects a proposal, all players receive zero. If only the two person coalition is proposed, the third player automatically receives a payoff of zero. Therefore, proposers with maximin preferences that dominate their self-interest will always propose a three person coalition with $x = y = z$, regardless of the amount available for the two person coalition. In the case of quasi maximin preferences in the sense of Charness and Rabin (2002) the "efficiency" motive puts even more weight on this proposal because the grand coalition produces a larger surplus.

Okada and Riedl report that 90% of the proposer's went for the two-person coalition when the total amount available for the two person coalition is 2500 or 2800. If the available amount for the small coalition is only 2100 still about 40% of the proposers went for the two person coalition. The grand coalition is favored by almost all proposers only in those cases when the small coalition became very inefficient because the available amount shrank to 1200. These regularities in proposers' behavior are predicted by the Fehr and Schmidt and the Bolton and Ockenfels model of inequity aversion.

Given the evidence from the above mentioned papers, it remains to be shown that maximin preferences play a role in strategic games. It seems that dictator games put players in a different frame of mind than strategic games, where the players can mutually affect each others' payoffs. Players in strategic games seem to be much more willing to neglect weak players' interests and to demand fairness or equity mainly for themselves, whereas the dictators seem to care a lot for the interests of the worst-off players in dictator games. This insight may also help in determining when the maximin motive plays a role in naturally occurring environments. In a competitive environment or in an environment where the players view each other as agents behaving strategically, the maximin motive is likely to be not important. However, the maximin motive may be more or even highly relevant in the context of charitable giving or in the context of referenda or elections with a large number of people, where strategic voting is unlikely to occur.

4.6. Preferences for honesty

Three recent papers indicate that a sizeable share of the subjects also care for honesty. Brandts and Charness (2003) show that subjects are more willing to correct unfair outcomes if these outcomes were reached through a lie. Charness and Dufwenberg (2004) show that the second mover in a sequentially played prisoners' dilemma is more willing to reciprocate trusting first mover behavior if the second mover could send a promise to reciprocate before the sequential prisoners' dilemma started. Gneezy (2005) provides direct evidence for dishonesty aversion in a simple but clever dictator game set up as follows: player B is the dictator who can choose among two alternative actions: action a implements payoff allocation (5, 6) and action b implements allocation (6, 5). However, only player A knows the monetary consequences of the two available actions while player B knows nothing about them. Before B chooses, A must send one of two messages to B. Message a is the honest message. It says: "Action a will earn you more money than action b." Message b is the dishonest message. It says: "Action b will earn you more money than action a." Gneezy shows that the vast majority of player B follows A's message, i.e., they choose the action that gives them the higher payoff according to the message. In addition, the vast majority of players A believes that players B will behave in this way. Thus, most players A believed correctly that they could mislead player B by being dishonest. A could gain $1 at the cost of B by lying.

Gneezy reports that only 36% of the players A were dishonest in the game described above. Moreover, if the monetary consequences of action a were changed to (5, 15), such that A could gain $1 by imposing a loss of $10 on B, the lying rate further decreased to 17%. Finally, if action a implied the allocation (5, 15) whereas action b implied the allocation (15, 5), player A could gain $10 by being dishonest which imposed a cost of $10 on player B. In this case, 52% of the players A send the wrong message. In a dictator game control experiment in which A had to choose between the allocations mentioned above, player A was much more willing to choose the allocation that favored him. If the alternatives were (5, 6) versus (6, 5) 66% of the A's chose the second allocation. Likewise, if the alternatives were (5, 15) versus (15, 5) 90% of the A's chose the second allocation. Thus, if the favorable outcome could be achieved without a lie, much more players A were willing to choose according to their self interest which documents neat evidence in favor of dishonesty aversion. In addition, dishonesty aversion is affected by the private gains from lying and by the harm imposed on the victim of the lie.

4.7. Summary and outlook

Although most models of other-regarding preferences discussed in Section 3 are just a few years old, the discussion in this section shows that there is already a fair amount of evidence that sheds light on the merits and the weaknesses of the different models. This indicates a quick and healthy interaction between experimental research and the development of new theories. The initial experimental results discussed in Section 2 gave rise to a number of new theories which, in turn, have again been quickly subjected to careful and rigorous empirical testing. Although these tests have not yet led to conclusive results regarding the relative importance of the different motives many important and interesting insights have been obtained. In our view the main results can be summarized as follows:

(1) The average payoff in the group is an empirically invalid reference standard for explaining individual punishment behavior. Approaches that rely on this comparison standard cannot explain important aspects of punishment behavior. Evidence from the Third Party Punishment Game and other games indicates that many subjects compare themselves with other people in the group and not just to the group as a whole or to the group average.

(2) Pure revenge as captured by intention based and type based reciprocity models is an important motive for punishment behavior. Since pure equity models do not capture this motive they cannot explain a significant amount of punishment behavior. While the inequality of the payoffs also is a significant determinant of payoff reducing behavior, the revenge motive seems to be more important in bilateral interactions as illustrated in those experiments where responses to a computerized first-mover choice are compared to the responses to human first mover choices.

(3) In the domain of kind behavior, the motives captured by intention or type based models of reciprocity seem to be less important than in the domain of payoff-reducing behavior. Several studies indicate that inequity aversion or maximin preferences play a more important role here.

(4) In dictator games, a significant share of the subjects prefers allocations with a higher group payoff and a higher inequality within the group over allocations with a lower group payoff and a lower inequality. However, this motive only dominates among economists, while the clear majority of non-economists is willing to sacrifice substantial amounts of the group payoff in order to ensure more equality within the group. Moreover, the relative importance of the motive to increase the group's payoff has yet to be determined for strategic games.

(5) In multi person dictator games, a large share of the subjects cares for the least well-off player's material payoff. However, evidence from several strategic games casts doubt on the relevance of this motive in strategic interactions.

(6) Some recent papers report that a substantial share of the subjects has indicated a preference for honesty.

Which model of other-regarding preferences does best in the light of the data, and which should be used in applications to economically important phenomena? We believe that it is too early to give a conclusive answer to these questions. There is a large amount of heterogeneity at the individual level and any model has difficulties in explaining the full diversity of the experimental observations. The above summary provides, however, some guidance for applied research. In addition to the summary statements above, we believe that the most important heterogeneity in strategic games is the one between purely selfish subjects and subjects with a preference for fairness or reciprocity.

Within the class of inequity aversion models, the evidence suggests that the Fehr and Schmidt model outperforms or does at least as well as the Bolton and Ockenfels model in almost all games considered in this paper. In particular, the experiments discussed in Section 4.1 indicate that people do not compare themselves with the group as a whole but rather with other individuals in the group. The group average is less compelling as a yardstick for measuring equity than are differences in individual payoffs. However, the Fehr and Schmidt model clearly does not recognize the full heterogeneity within the class of fair-minded individuals. Section 4.4 makes it clear that an important part of payoff-reducing behavior is not driven by the desire to reduce payoff-differences, but by the desire to reduce the payoff of those who take unfair actions or reveal themselves as unfair types. The model therefore cannot explain punishing behavior in situations where payoff differences cannot be changed by punishing others. Fairness models exclusively based on intentions [Rabin (1993), Dufwenberg and Kirchsteiger (2004)] can, in principle, account for this type of punishment. However, these models have other undesirable features, including multiple, and very counterintuitive, equilibria in many games and a very high degree of complexity due to the use of psychological game theory. The same has to be said about the intention based theory of Charness and Rabin (2002). It is also worthwhile to point out that intention based reciprocity models cannot explain punishment in the third party punishment game because they are based on bilateral notions of reciprocity. The third party was not treated in an unkind way in this game and will therefore never punish. Falk and Fischbacher (2006) do not share these problems of pure intention models. This is due to the fact that they incorporate equity as a global reference standard. Their model shares however, the complexity costs of psychological game theory.

Even though none of the available theories of other-regarding preferences takes the full complexity of motives at the individual level into account, some theories may allow for better approximations than others, depending on the problem at hand. If, for example, actors' intentions constitute a salient dimension of an economic problem, consideration of some form of intention based reciprocity might be advisable, despite the complexity costs involved. Or, to give another example, a type based reciprocity model in the spirit of Levine (1998) may provide a plausible explanation for third party punishment. The essence of third party punishment is that the punisher is not directly hurt but nevertheless punishes a norm violation. While bilateral notions of reciprocity are unable to explain this kind of punishment type based models provide a natural explanation because norm violations are type revealing. However, the most important message of the evidence presented in Section 2 clearly is that there are many important economic problems where the self-interest theory is unambiguously, and in a quantitatively important way, refuted. Therefore, in our view, it is certainly not advisable to only consider the self-interest model, but to combine the self-interest assumption with the other-regarding motive that is likely to be most important in the problem at hand.

5. Economic applications

5.1. Cooperation and collective action

Free-riding incentives are a pervasive phenomenon in social life. Participation in collective action or in industrial disputes, collusion among firms in oligopolistic markets, the prevention of negative environmental externalities, workers' effort choices under team-based compensation schemes or the exploitation of a common resource are typical examples. In these cases the free rider cannot be excluded from the benefits of collective actions or the public good although he does not contribute. In view of the ubiquity of cooperation problems in modern societies it is crucial to understand the forces shaping people's cooperation. In this section we will show that the neglect of other-regarding preferences may induce economists to largely misunderstand the nature of many cooperation problems. As we will see a key to the understanding of cooperation problems is again the interaction between selfish individuals and individuals with other-regarding preferences.

The impact of other-regarding preferences on cooperation can be easily illustrated for the case of reciprocal or inequity averse individuals. First, reciprocal subjects are willing to cooperate if they are sure that the other people who are involved in the cooperation problem will also cooperate. If the others cooperate – despite pecuniary incentives to the contrary – they provide a gift that induces reciprocal subjects to repay the gift, i.e., reciprocators are conditionally cooperative. Likewise, as we will show below, inequity averse individuals are also willing to cooperate if they can be sure that others cooperate. Second, reciprocal or inequity averse subjects are willing to punish free-riders because free-riders exploit the cooperators. Thus, if potential free-riders face reciprocators they have an incentive to cooperate to prevent being punished.

In the following we illustrate the first claim for the case of inequity averse subjects in a prisoners' dilemma who have utility functions as proposed by Fehr and Schmidt (1999). Table 1 presents the material payoffs in a prisoners' dilemma and Table 2 shows how inequity aversion transforms the material payoffs. Recall that in the two-player case the utility of player i is given by $U_i(x) = x_i - \alpha_i(x_j - x_i)$ if player i is worse off than player j $(x_j - x_i \geq 0)$, and $U_i(x) = x_i - \beta_i(x_i - x_j)$ if player i is better off than

Table 1
Representation of prisoners' dilemma in terms of material payoffs

	Cooperate (C)	Defect (D)
Cooperate (C)	2, 2	0, 3
Defect (D)	3, 0	1, 1

Table 2
Utility representation of prisoners' dilemma if players are inequity averse

	Cooperate (C)	Defect (D)
Cooperate (C)	2, 2	$0 - 3\alpha, 3 - 3\beta$
Defect (D)	$3 - 3\beta, 0 - 3\alpha$	1, 1

player j ($x_i - x_j \geqslant 0$). For simplicity, Table 2 assumes that both players have the same preferences so that α and β are identical across players.

Table 1 illustrates that if player 2 (the column player) is expected to cooperate, player 1 (the row player) faces a choice between material payoff allocations (2, 2) and (3, 0). The utility of (2, 2) is $U_1(2, 2) = 2$ because there is no inequality. The utility of (3, 0), however, is $U_1(3, 0) = 3 - 3\beta$ because there is inequality that favors the row player. Therefore, player 1 will reciprocate the expected cooperation of player 2 if $\beta > 1/3$. If player 1 defects and player 2 cooperates the payoff of player 2 is $U_2(3, 0) = 0 - 3\alpha$; if player 2 defected instead the utility would be 1. This means that player 2 will always reciprocate defection because cooperating against a defector yields less money and more inequity. Table 2 shows that if $\beta > 1/3$, there are two equilibria: (cooperate, cooperate) and (defect, defect). In utility terms, inequality averse players no longer face a PD. Instead, they face a coordination or assurance game with one efficient and one inefficient equilibrium. If the players believe that the other player cooperates, it is rational for each of them to cooperate, too.

Inequity averse (and reciprocal) players are thus conditional cooperators. They cooperate in response to expected cooperation and defect in response to expected defection. Theories of other-regarding preferences which imply that subjects are conditionally cooperative are, therefore, also consistent with framing effects in the prisoners' dilemma. Ross and Ward (1996) have shown that players achieve higher cooperation rates if the Prisoners' Dilemma is called a "community game" instead of "Wallstreet game". Many people prematurely argue that these effects of framing on cooperation reflect players' irrationality. However, if the game is framed as "community game" it seems plausible that the players are more optimistic about the other players' cooperation, which induces them to cooperate more frequently than in the case were the game is framed as "Wallstreet game". Therefore, the impact of different frames on cooperation behavior is also consistent with the view that the players have stable other-regarding preferences but exhibit different expectations about others' behavior under different frames.

The transformation of the prisoners' dilemma into a coordination game in the presence of reciprocal or inequity averse players can explain one further fact. It has been shown dozens of times that communication leads to much higher cooperation rates in the prisoners' dilemma and in public good games [Sally (1995)]. If all subjects were completely selfish this impact of communication would be difficult to explain. If, however, the game in material terms is in fact a coordination game, communication allows the subjects to coordinate on the superior equilibrium.

If it is indeed the case that the actual preferences of the subjects transform cooperation games into coordination games, the self-interest hypothesis induces economists to fundamentally misperceive the cooperation problems. In view of the importance of this claim it is, therefore, desirable to have more direct evidence on this. Several studies provided evidence in favor of the existence of conditional cooperation during the last few years [Keser and van Winden (2000), Brandts and Schram (2001), Fischbacher, Gächter and Fehr (2001)]. There is a tricky causality issue involved in this question because a positive correlation between an individual's cooperation rate and the individual's belief about others' cooperation rate does not unambiguously prove the existence of conditional cooperation. Perhaps the individual first chooses how much to cooperate and the belief represents merely the rationalization of the chosen cooperation level. This problem has been overcome by Keser and van Winden in the context of a repeated public goods experiment and by Fischbacher, Gächter and Fehr (2001) in the context of a one-shot public goods experiment. Keser and van Winden (2000) show that many subjects adjust their cooperation in period t to move closer to last period's average cooperation rate. This finding suggests that subjects reciprocate to last period's average cooperation of the other group members. Fischbacher, Gächter and Fehr (2001) elicited so-called contribution schedules from their subjects. A contribution schedule stipulates a subject's contribution to every possible level of the average contribution of the other group members in a one-shot experiment. The parameters of the game ensured that a selfish subject will never contribute anything to the public good regardless of the average contribution of the other group members. The surplus maximizing contribution level was given at 20 which was identical to the maximum contribution.

The results of this study show that 50 percent of the subjects are willing to increase their contributions to the public good if the other group members' average contribution increases although the pecuniary incentives always implied full free-riding. The behavior of these subjects is consistent with models of reciprocity (or inequity aversion). However, a substantial fraction of the subjects (30 percent) are complete free-riders who free ride regardless of what the other group members do. 14 percent exhibit a hump-shaped response. They increase their cooperation rate in response to an increase in the average cooperation of others but beyond a cooperation level of 50% of the endowment they start decreasing their cooperation. Yet, taken together there are sufficiently many conditional cooperators such that an increase in the other group members' contribution level causes an increase in the contribution of the "average" individual.

The coexistence of conditional cooperators and selfish subjects has important implications. It implies, e.g., that subtle institutional details may cause large behavioral effects. To illustrate this assume that a selfish and an inequity averse subject are matched in the *simultaneous* prisoners' dilemma and that the subjects' type is common knowledge. Since the inequity averse subject knows that the other player is selfish he knows that the other will always defect. Therefore, the inequity averse player will also defect, i.e., (defect, defect) is the unique equilibrium. This result can be easily illustrated in Table 2 by setting the inequity aversion parameters α and β of one of the players equal to zero. Now consider the *sequential* prisoners' dilemma in which the selfish player first decides whether to cooperate or to defect. Then the reciprocal player observes what the first-mover did and chooses his action. In the sequential case the unique equilibrium outcome is that both players cooperate because the reciprocal second-mover will match the choice of the first-mover. This means that the selfish first-mover essentially has the choice between the (cooperate, cooperate)-outcome and the (defect, defect)-outcome. Since mutual cooperation is better than mutual defection the selfish player will also cooperate. Thus, while in the simultaneous prisoners' dilemma the selfish player induces the reciprocal player to defect, in the sequential prisoners' dilemma the reciprocal player induces the selfish player to cooperate in equilibrium. This example neatly illustrates how institutional details interact in important ways with the heterogeneity of the population.

Since there are many conditional cooperators the problem of establishing and maintaining cooperation involves the management of people's beliefs. If people believe that the others cooperate to a large extent, cooperation will be higher compared to a situation where they believe that others rarely cooperate. Belief-dependent cooperation can be viewed as a social interaction effect that is relevant in many important domains. For example, if people believe that cheating on taxes, corruption, or abuses of the welfare state are wide-spread, they are themselves more likely to cheat on taxes and are more willing to take bribes or to abuse welfare state institutions. It is therefore important that public policy prevents the initial unravelling of civic duties because, once people start to believe that most others engage in unlawful behavior the belief-dependency of individuals' cooperation behavior may render it very difficult to re-establish lawful behavior.

In an organisational context the problem of establishing cooperation among the members of the organisation also involves the selection of the "right" members. A few shirkers in a group of employees may quickly spoil the whole group. Bewley (1999), e.g., reports that personnel managers use the possibility to fire workers mainly as a means to remove "bad characters and incompetents" from the group and not as a threat to discipline the workers. The reason is that explicit threats create a hostile atmosphere and may even reduce the workers' generalised willingness to cooperate with the firm. Managers report that the employees themselves don't want to work together with lazy colleagues because these colleagues do not bear their share of the burden which is viewed as unfair. Therefore, the firing of lazy workers is mainly used to establish internal equity, and to prevent the unravelling of cooperation. This supports the view that conditional cooperation is also important inside firms.

The motivational forces behind conditional cooperation are also likely to shape the structure of social policies that aim at helping the poor [Bowles and Gintis (2000), Wax (2000), Fong, Bowles and Gintis (2005a, 2005b)]. The reason is that the political support for policies favoring the poor depends to a large extent on whether the poor are perceived as "deserving" or as "undeserving". If people believe that the poor are poor because they do not *want* to work hard the support for policies that help the poor is weakened because the poor are perceived as undeserving. If, in contrast, people believe that the poor try hard to escape poverty but that for reasons beyond their control they could not make it, the poor are perceived as deserving. This indicates that the extent to which people perceive the poor as deserving is shaped by reciprocity motives. If the poor exhibit good intentions, i.e., they try to contribute to society's output, or if they are poor for reasons that have nothing to do with their intentions, they are perceived as deserving. In contrast, if the poor are perceived as lacking the will to contribute to society's output, they are perceived as undeserving. This means that social policies that enable the poor to demonstrate their willingness to reciprocate the generosity of society will mobilise greater political support than social policies that do not allow the poor to exhibit their good intentions. Wax (2000) convincingly argues that an important reason for the popularity of President Clinton's 1996 welfare reform initiative was that the initiative appealed to the reciprocity of the people.

5.2. *Endogenous formation of cooperative institutions*

We argued above that the presence of a selfish subject will induce a reciprocal or inequity averse subject in the simultaneous prisoners' dilemma to defect as well. This proposition also holds more generally in the case of n-person public good games. It can be shown theoretically that even a small minority of selfish subjects induces a majority of reciprocal (or inequity averse) subjects to free-ride in simultaneous social dilemma games [Fehr and Schmidt (1999, Proposition 4)]. In an experiment with anonymous interaction subjects do of course not know whether the other group members are selfish or reciprocal but if they interact repeatedly over time they may learn the others' types. Therefore, one would expect that over time cooperation will unravel in (finitely repeated) simultaneous public goods experiments. This unravelling of cooperation has indeed been observed in dozens of experiments [Ledyard (1995)].

This raises the question of whether there are social mechanisms that can prevent the decay of cooperation. A potentially important mechanism is social ostracism and peer pressure stemming from reciprocal or inequity averse subjects. Recall that these subjects exhibit a willingness to punish unfair behavior or mitigate unfair outcomes and it is quite likely that co-operating individuals view free-riding as very unfair. To examine the willingness to punish free-riders and the impact of punishment on cooperation Fehr and Gächter (2000) introduced a punishment opportunity into a public goods game. In their game there are two stages. Stage one consists of a linear public good game in which the dominant strategy of each selfish player is to free-ride completely although the socially optimal decision requires to contribute the whole endowment to the public good. In stage two, after every player in the group has been informed about the contributions of each group member, each player can assign up to ten punishment points to each of the other group members. The assignment of one punishment point reduces the first-stage income of the punished subject, on the average, by three points but it also reduces the income of the punisher. This kind of punishment mimics an angry group member scolding a free-rider, or spreading the word so the free-rider is ostracised – there is some cost to the punisher, but a larger cost to the free-rider. Note that since punishment is costly for the punisher, the self-interest hypothesis predicts zero punishment. Moreover, since rational players will anticipate this, the self-interest hypothesis predicts no difference in the contribution behavior between a public goods game without punishment and the game with a punishment opportunity. In both conditions zero contributions are predicted.

The experimental evidence completely rejects this prediction.[30] In contrast to the game without a punishment opportunity, where cooperation declines over time and is close to zero in the final period, the punishment opportunity causes a sharp jump in cooperation. Moreover, in the punishment condition there is a steady increase in contributions until almost all subjects contribute their whole endowment. This sharp increase occurs because free-riders often get punished, and the less they give, the more likely punishment is. Cooperators seem to feel that free-riders take unfair advantage of them and, as a consequence, they are willing to punish the free-riders. This induces the punished free-riders to increase cooperation in the following periods. A nice feature of this design is that the actual rate of punishment is very low in the last few periods – the mere threat of punishment, and the memory of its sting from past punishments, is enough to induce potential free-riders to cooperate.

The punishment of free riders in repeated cooperation experiments has also been observed in Yamagishi (1986), Ostrom, Walker and Gardner (1992), Masclet (2003), Carpenter, Matthews and Ong'ong'a (2004), and Anderson and Putterman (2006). In almost all studies the authors report that the possibility to punish causes a strong increase in cooperation rates. Moreover, this increase in cooperation due to punishment opportunities can even be observed in one-shot experiments where the groups are randomly mixed in every period such that no subject ever interacts twice with another subject [Fehr and Gächter (2002)].

More recently, Gürerk, Irlenbusch and Rockenbach (2006) examined whether subjects prefer an institutional environment in which they can punish each other as in Fehr and Gächter (2000) or whether they prefer an institution that rules out mutual punishment by individual actors. In this experiment subjects interacted for a total of 30 periods

---

[30] In the experiments subjects first participate in the game without a punishment opportunity for ten periods. After this they are told that a new experiment takes place. In the new experiment, which lasts again for ten periods, the punishment opportunity is implemented. In both conditions subjects remain in the same group for ten periods and they know that after ten periods the experiment will be over.

and the final period was known by every participant. At the beginning of each period each of 12 subjects had to indicate the preferred institution. Then the subjects who choose the punishment institution played the public goods game with a subsequent punishment stage whereas the subjects who preferred the institution without punishment just played the public goods game. Regardless of how many subjects joined an institution, the members of the institution as a whole earned always 1.6 tokens from each token contributed to the public good. This feature has the important consequence that for larger groups it is much more difficult to sustain cooperation because the free riding incentive is much stronger. For example, if only 2 subjects join an institution each token that is contributed by a subject provides a private return of 0.8 tokens and a group return of 1.6 tokens because the other subject also earns 0.8 tokens from the contribution. However, if 10 subjects join an institution, the group's overall return from a one unit contribution is still 1.6 tokens, that is, each member of the institution earns only 0.16 tokens from the contribution.

Despite the fact that larger groups faced much stronger free-riding incentives Gürerk et al. report convergence to a single institution. At the beginning roughly 2/3 of the subjects preferred to interact without the mutual punishment opportunity. However, after a few periods cooperation rates became very low under this institution which induced subjects to switch to the punishment institution. In fact, over time the percentage of subjects who preferred the punishment institution rose to more than 90 percent from period 20 onwards and remained stable till the final period. Moreover, from period 15 onwards cooperation rates were very close to 100% under the punishment institution whereas under the no-punishment institution cooperation collapsed completely. Although punishment was frequent in the early periods of the punishment institution because many self-interested subjects also joined and attempted to free ride, little or no punishment was necessary to sustain cooperation in the second half of the experiment. The mere threat of punishment was sufficient to maintain nearly perfect cooperation levels.

These results are indeed remarkable because they can be viewed as the laboratory equivalent of the formation of a proto-state. One of the puzzles of the evolution of cooperation concerns the question why humans are such an extremely cooperative species. Humans seem to be the only species that is able to establish cooperation in large groups of *genetically unrelated strangers*. There are several other species (bees, ants, termites, etc.) which show cooperation in large group of genetically closely related individuals but among humans the average degree of relatedness of individual members of a modern society is close to zero. Of course, in modern societies cooperation is based on powerful institutions (impartial police, impartial judges, etc.) that punish norm violations. However, the existence of these institutions is itself an evolutionary puzzle because their existence constitutes a public good in itself. The experiments by Gürerk et al. suggest that deep seated inclinations to punish free riders and the ability to understand the cooperation enhancing effects of punishment institutions are part of an explanation of these institutions.

5.3. How fairness, reciprocity and competition interact

The self-interest model fails to explain the experimental evidence in many games in which only a few players interact, but it is very successful in explaining the outcome of competitive markets. It is a well-established experimental fact that in a broad class of market games prices converge to the competitive equilibrium [Smith (1982), Davis and Holt (1993)]. This result holds even if the resulting allocation is very unfair by any notion of fairness. Thus, the question arises: If so many people resist unfair outcomes in, say, the ultimatum game or the third party punishment game, why don't they behave the same way when there is competition among the players?

To answer this question we consider the following ultimatum game with proposer competition, that was conducted by Roth et al. (1991) in four different countries. There are $n - 1$ proposers who simultaneously offer a share $s_i \in [0, 1]$, $i \in \{1, \ldots, n - 1\}$, to one responder. The responder can either accept or reject the highest offer $s^{\max} = \max_i \{s_i\}$. If there are several proposers who offered $s^{\max}$, one of them is selected at random with equal probability. If the responder accepts $s^{\max}$, her monetary payoff is $s^{\max}$ and the successful proposer earns $1 - s^{\max}$, while all the other proposers get 0. If the responder rejects, everybody gets a payoff of 0.

The prediction of the self-interest model is straightforward: All proposers will offer $s = 1$ which is accepted by the responder. Hence, all proposers get a payoff of zero and the monopolistic responder captures the entire surplus. This outcome is clearly very unfair, but it describes precisely what happened in the experiments. After a few periods of adaptation $s^{\max}$ was very close to 1 and all the surplus was captured by the responder. Moreover, this pattern was observed across several different cultures indicating that cultural differences in preferences or beliefs have little impact on behavior under proposer competition.[31]

This result is remarkable. It does not seem to be more fair that one side of the market gets all of the surplus in this setting than in the standard ultimatum game. Why do the proposers let the responder get away with it? The reason is that preferences for fairness or reciprocity cannot have any effect in this strategic setting. To see this, suppose that each of the proposers strongly dislikes receiving less than the responder. Consider proposer i and let $s' = \max_{j \neq i} \{s_j\}$ be the highest offer made by his fellow proposers. If proposer i offers $s_i < s'$, then his offer has no effect and he will get a monetary payoff of 0 with certainty. Furthermore, he cannot prevent that the responder gets s' and that one of the other proposers gets $1 - s'$, so he will suffer from getting less than these two. However, if he offers a little bit more than s', say $s' + \varepsilon$, then he will win the competition, receive a positive monetary payoff, and reduce the inequality between himself

---

[31] The experiments were conducted in Israel, Japan, Slovenia, and the U.S. In all experiments, there were 9 proposers and 1 responder. Roth et al. also conducted the standard ultimatum game with one proposer in these four countries. They did find some small (but statistically significant) differences between countries in the standard ultimatum game which may be attributed to cultural differences. However, there are no statistically significant differences between countries for the ultimatum game with proposer competition.

and the responder. Hence, he should try to overbid his competitors. This process drives the share that is offered by the proposers up to 1. There is nothing the proposers can do about it even if all of them have a strong preference for fairness. We prove this result formally in Fehr and Schmidt (1999) for the case of inequity averse players, but the same result is also predicted by the approaches of Bolton and Ockenfels (2000), Levine (1998) and Falk and Fischbacher (2006).

The ultimatum game with responder competition provides further insights into the interaction between fair minded and selfish actors. Instead of one responder there are now two competing responders and only one proposer. When the proposer has made his offer the two responders simultaneously accept or reject the offer. If both accept, a random mechanism determines with probability 0.5 which one of the responders will get the offered amount. If only one responder accepts he will receive the offered amount of money. If both responders reject, the proposer and both responders receive nil.

The ultimatum game with responder competition can be interpreted as a market transaction between a seller (proposer) and two competing buyers (responders) who derive the same material payoff from an indivisible good. Moreover, as the parties' pecuniary valuations of the good are public information there is a known fixed surplus and the situation can be viewed as a market in which the contract (quality of the good) is enforced exogenously.

If all parties are selfish, competition among the responders does not matter because the proposer is predicted to receive the whole surplus in the bilateral case already. Adding competition to the bilateral ultimatum game has therefore no effect on the power of the proposer. It is also irrelevant whether there are two, three or more competing responders. The self-interest hypothesis thus implies a very counterintuitive result, namely, that increasing the competition among the responders does not affect the share of the surplus that the responders receive. Fischbacher, Fong and Fehr (2002) tested this prediction by conducting ultimatum games with one, two and five responders under a random matching protocol for 20 periods.[32] In every period the proposers and the responders were randomly re-matched to ensure the one-shot nature of the interactions. All subjects knew that after period 20 the experiment would end.

The results of the experiment show that competition has a strong impact on behavior. In the bilateral case the average share is – except for period 1 – always close to 40 percent. Moreover, the share does not change much over time. In the final period the responders still appropriate slightly more than 40 percent of the surplus. In the case of two responders the situation changes dramatically, however. Already in period 1 the responders' share is reduced by 5 percentage points relative to the bilateral case. Moreover, over time responder competition induces a further substantial reduction of the share and in the final period the share is even below 20 percent. Thus, the addition of just one more responder has a dramatic impact on the share of the responders. If we add three

---

[32] See also Güth, Marchand and Rulliere (1997) and Grosskopf (2003) for experiments with responder competition.

additional responders the share goes down even further. From period 3 onwards it is below 20 percent and comes close to 10 percent in the second half of the session.[33]

The responders' share decreases when competition increases because the rejection probability of the responders declines when there are more competing responders. These facts can be parsimoniously explained if one takes the presence of reciprocal or inequity averse responders into account. Recall that reciprocal responders reject low offers in the bilateral ultimatum game because by rejecting they are able to punish the unfair proposers. In the bilateral case they can always ensure this punishment while in the competitive case this is no longer possible. In particular, if one of the other responders accepts a given low offer, it is impossible for a reciprocal responder to punish the proposer. Since there is a substantial fraction of selfish responders, the probability that one of the other responders is selfish, is higher the larger the number of competing responders. This means, in turn, that the expected non-pecuniary return from the rejection of a low offer is smaller the larger the number of competing responders. Therefore, reciprocal responders will reject less frequently the larger the number of competing responders because they expect that the probability that at least one of the other responders will accept the offer increases with the number of competitors. This prediction is fully borne out by the expectations data. Moreover, these data also indicate that the responders are much less likely to reject a given offer if they believe that one of their competitors will accept the offer.

The previous example illustrates that preferences for fairness and reciprocity interact in important ways with competition. However, this example should not make us believe that sufficient competition will in general weaken or remove the impact of other-regarding preferences on market outcomes. Quite the contrary. In the following we will show that the presence of other-regarding preferences may completely nullify the impact of competition on market outcomes.

To illustrate this argument consider the double auction experiments conducted by Fehr and Falk (1999). Fehr and Falk deliberately chose the double auction as the trading institution because a large body of research has shown the striking competitive properties of experimental double auctions. Fehr and Falk use two treatment conditions: A bilateral condition in which competition is completely removed and a competitive condition. In the competitive condition they embed the gift exchange game into the context of an experimental double auction that is framed in labour market terms. The crucial difference between the competitive condition and the gift exchange game described in Section 2 is that both, experimental firms and experimental workers can make wage bids in the interval [20, 120] because the workers' reservation wage is 20 and the maximum revenue from a trade is 120. If a bid is accepted, a labour contract is concluded and the worker has to choose the effort level. As in the gift exchange game the workers

---

[33] In the study of Roth et al. (1991) competition led to an even more extreme outcome. However, in their market experiments 9 competing proposers faced only 1 responder and the responder was forced to accept the highest offer.

("responders") can freely choose any feasible effort level. They have to bear effort costs while the firm ("proposer") benefits from the effort. Thus, the experiment captures a market in which the quality of the good traded ("effort") is not exogenously enforced but is chosen by the workers. Workers may or may not provide the effort level that is expected by the firms.

In the competitive condition there are more workers than firms and each firm can only employ one worker. In contrast to the double auction firms in the bilateral condition are exogenously matched with a worker and there is an equal number of firms and workers. The bilateral condition implements the gift exchange game as described in Section 2. In each of the ten periods each firm is matched with a different worker. Firms have to make a wage offer to the matched worker in each period. If the worker accepts he has to choose the effort level. If a worker rejects the firm's offer both parties earn nothing. As in the competitive condition a worker who accepts a wage offer has costs of 20 and the maximum revenue from a trade is 120.

The self-interest model predicts that in both conditions the workers will only provide the minimum effort so that the firms will pay a wage of 20 or 21 in equilibrium. However, we know already from bilateral ultimatum games that firms (proposers) cannot reap the whole surplus, i.e., wages in the bilateral gift exchange game also can be expected to be much higher than predicted by the self-interest model. Moreover, since in the gift exchange game the effort is in general increasing in the wage level firms have an additional reason to offer workers a substantial share of the surplus. The question, therefore, is to what extent competition in the double auction pushes wages below the level in the bilateral condition.

The data reveal the startling result that competition has no long run impact on wage formation in this setting. Only at the beginning wages in the double auction are slightly lower than the wages in the bilateral condition but since workers responded to lower wages with lower effort levels firms raised their wages quickly. In the last five periods firms paid even slightly higher wages in the double auction; this difference is not significant, however. It is also noteworthy that competition among the workers was extremely intense. In each period many workers offered to work for wages that are close to the competitive level of 20. However, firms did not accept such low wage offers. It was impossible for the workers to get a job by underbidding the going wages because the positive effort-wage relation made it profitable for the firms to pay high, non-competitive, wages. This finding is consistent with several field studies that report that managers are reluctant to cut wages in a recession because they fear that wage cuts may hamper work performance [Bewley (1999), Agell and Lundborg (1995), Campbell and Kamlani (1997)].

The positive relation between wages and average effort is the major driving force behind the payment of high – non-competitive – wages in the Fehr and Falk (1999) experiments. On average, it was profitable for the firms in this experiment to pay such high wages. In view of the importance of a sufficiently steep effort-wage relation it is important to ask under which circumstances we can expect the payment of non-competitive wages to be profitable for the proposer. There is evidence indicating that reciprocal effort choices are almost absent if the proposer explicitly threatens to sanction the responder in case of low effort choices [Fehr and Gächter (2002), Fehr and Rockenbach (2003), Fehr and List (2004)]. Likewise, if there is a stochastic relation between effort and output, and the proposer is only informed about output but not effort, the effort wage relation is less steep [Irlenbusch and Sliwka (2005)] than in a situation where effort produces output in a deterministic way. In addition, it seems plausible that if responders do not know the profits of the proposer reciprocity is less likely to occur. In the typical gift exchange experiment full information about the payoffs of the proposer and the responder exists. Therefore, the responder has a clear yardstick which enables him to judge the generosity of the proposer's wage offer. If there is no clear reference point against which the responder can judge the generosity of a given wage offer, it seems easier that self-serving biases affect the responder's behavior, implying that reciprocal effort choices are less frequent. Thus, in the presence of explicit sanctioning threats or when there is a lack of transparency it may not pay for the proposer to offer high wages because reciprocation is weak. Finally, as mentioned in Section 2.1 already, the profitability of high wages also depends on the concrete payoff function of the proposer. In many gift exchange experiments [e.g., Fehr, Kirchsteiger and Riedl (1993) or Fehr and Falk (1999)] the proposer's payoff function is given by $x^P = (v - w)e$ and effort is in the interval [0.1, 1] which makes it less risky to offer high wages than in the case where the proposer's payoff function is given by $x^P = ve - w$. Thus, when interpreting the results of gift exchange experiments it is necessary to investigate the conditions of the experiment carefully. Otherwise, it is difficult to make sense of the data.

5.4. *Fairness and reciprocity as a source of economic incentives*

Perhaps the impact of other-regarding preferences on material incentives is the most important reason why they should be taken seriously by social scientists. This is neatly illustrated by the sequential prisoners' dilemma or the gift exchange game: if there are sufficiently many second movers who reciprocate cooperative first mover choices it is in the self-interest of the first mover to make a cooperative choice. However, simple two-stage games underestimate the power of these preferences in shaping material incentives because in games that proceed beyond just two stages the impact of other-regarding preferences on incentives is greatly magnified. This is illustrated by the work of Fehr, Gächter and Kirchsteiger (1997).

In an extension of a simple two-stage gift exchange experiment these authors examined the impact of giving the employers the option of responding reciprocally to the worker's choice of effort e. In addition to the wage offered in the first stage the employer ("proposer") could also announce a desired effort level $\hat{e}$. In the second stage the workers chose their effort level and in the third stage each employer was given the opportunity to reward or punish the worker after he observed the actual effort. By spending one money unit (MU) on reward the employer could *increase* the worker's payoff by 2.5 MUs, and by spending one MU on punishment the employer could *decrease* the worker's payoff by 2.5 MUs. Employers could spend up to 10 MUs on punishment or on rewarding their worker. The important feature of this design is that if there are only selfish employers they will never reward or punish a worker because both rewarding and punishing is costly for the employer. Therefore, in case that there are only selfish employers there is no reason why the opportunity for rewarding/punishing workers should affect workers' effort choice relative to the situation where no such opportunity exists. However, if a worker expects her employer to be a reciprocator it is likely that she will provide higher effort levels in the presence of a reward/punishment opportunity. This is so because reciprocal employers are likely to reward the provision of $e \geqslant \hat{e}$ and to punish underprovision ($e < \hat{e}$). This is in fact exactly what is observed on the average. If there is underprovision of effort employers punish in 68 percent of the cases and the average investment in punishment is 7 MUs. If there is overprovision employers reward in 70 percent of these cases and the average investment in rewarding is also 7 MUs. If workers exactly meet the desired effort employers still reward in 41 percent of the cases and the average investment into rewarding is 4.5 MUs.

The authors also elicited workers' expectations about the reward and punishment choices of their employers. Hence, they are able to check whether workers anticipate employers' reciprocity. It turns out that in case of underprovision workers expect to be punished in 54 percent of the cases and the expected average investment into punishment is 4 MUs. In case of overprovision they expect to receive a reward in 98 percent of the cases with an expected average investment of 6.5 MUs. As a result of these expectations workers choose much higher effort levels when employers have a reward/punishment opportunity. The presence of this opportunity decreases shirking from 83 percent to 26 percent of the trades, increases exact provision of the desired effort $\hat{e}$ from 14 to 36 percent and increases overprovision from 3 to 38 percent of the trades. The average effort level is increased by almost 50% so that the gap between desired and actual effort levels almost vanishes. An important consequence of this increase in average effort is that the aggregate monetary payoff increases by 40 percent – even if one takes the payoff reductions that result from actual punishments into account. Thus, the reward/punishment opportunity considerably increases the total pie that becomes available for the trading parties.

We believe that the material incentives that are provided by reciprocal principals help solving one of the key problems in many agency relations, which is the problem of incentive provision when there are multiple tasks that an agent has to perform. Because of measurement and verifiability problems it is often not possible to give explicit incentives for all tasks that the agent should care about. It is well known [Holmström and Milgrom (1991), Baker (1992)] that in this situation explicit performance incentives may be harmful because they induce the employees to concentrate only on the rewarded tasks and to neglect the non-rewarded tasks. Holmström and Milgrom show that if a task that cannot be explicitly contracted upon is sufficiently important it may even be better to provide no explicit incentives for any task. Yet, this result presupposes a high degree of voluntary cooperation so that employees are willing to spend some effort even in the absence of any monetary incentives. If the agent is not intrinsically motivated this solution is not viable.

The monetary incentives provided by ex-post rewards or ex-post punishments of reciprocal principals often constitute a superior solution to the multi-tasking problem. The reason is that a principal who decides whether to reward or punish the agent ex post will use subjective performance evaluation, i.e., he will take into account the agent's performance in all observable tasks even if some of them are not verifiable and cannot be contracted upon explicitly. To illustrate this point we consider the experiments conducted by Fehr and Schmidt (2004). In these experiments each principal faces ten different agents in ten one-shot interactions. When an agent agrees to the terms of a contract offered by the principal the agent has to choose the effort level e_1 in task 1 and e_2 in task 2. The revenue of the principal is given by $10e_1e_2$ while the agent's effort cost is an increasing and convex function of total effort ($e_1 + e_2$). Effort in both tasks can vary between 1 and 10. This set-up ensures that both tasks are important for the principal because the effort levels are complements in his profit function. Both effort levels are observable for both parties but only effort in task 1 is verifiable while effort in task 2 cannot be contracted upon.

In each period the principal can offer to the agent either a piece rate contract that makes pay contingent on effort in task 1 or a so-called bonus contract. The piece rate contract consists of a base wage and a piece rate per unit of effort in task 1. The bonus contract also consists of a base wage. In addition the principal announces that he may pay a bonus after he observed the actual effort levels e_1 and e_2. However, both parties know that the bonus payment is voluntary and cannot be enforced.

Clearly, selfish principals will never pay a bonus. Furthermore, if agents anticipate that principals are selfish they will always choose the minimal effort in the bonus contract. With a piece rate contract the principal, at least, can induce a selfish agent to work efficiently on task 1. Thus, if all subjects are selfish, the piece rate contract is more profitable and more efficient than the bonus contract, even though the agent will only work on task 1 and completely ignore task 2.

If principals behave reciprocally, however, the result is very different. A reciprocal principal is willing to voluntarily pay a bonus if he is satisfied with the agent's performance. This makes it profitable for the agent to spend effort and to allocate his efforts efficiently across *both* tasks. Thus a preference for reciprocity and fairness is a commitment device for the principal to reward the agent for his efforts, even if this cannot be enforced by the courts.[34]

The experiments by Fehr and Schmidt (2004) show that many (but not all) principals pay substantial bonuses. It turns out that the average bonus is strongly increasing in total effort and decreasing in effort differences across tasks. This creates incentives for the agents to spend high effort and to equalize effort levels across tasks. With a piece rate contract, on the other hand, the average effort is always high in the rewarded task but

---

[34] Note that if the principal is just an efficiency seeker who wants to maximize total surplus he will not pay the bonus. After the agent has chosen his effort levels the bonus is a pure transfer that leaves total surplus unaffected.

close to the minimum level in the non-rewarded task. Thus, the bonus contract induces more efficient effort choices and yields, on average, higher payoffs for both parties. Principals seem to understand this and predominantly (in 81 percent of all cases) choose a bonus contract.

This result also suggests an answer to the puzzling question why many contracts are deliberately left vague and incomplete. Many real world contracts specify important obligations of the contracting parties in fairly vague terms, and they do not tie the parties' monetary payoffs to measures of performance that would be available at a relatively small cost. We believe that the parties often rely on an implicit understanding to reward (or punish) each other that cannot be enforced by the courts but nevertheless works well if the involved parties are motivated by reciprocity and fairness. In an extensive empirical study Scott (2003) provides evidence on deliberately incomplete contracting supporting this claim.

6. Conclusions

The self-interest hypothesis assumes that all people are exclusively motivated by their material self-interest. This hypothesis is a convenient simplification and there are, no doubt, situations in which almost all people behave as if they were strictly self-interested. In particular, for comparative static predictions of aggregate behavior self-interest models may make empirically correct predictions because models with more complex motivational assumptions predict the same comparative static responses. However, the evidence presented in this paper also shows that fundamental questions of social life cannot be understood on the basis of the self-interest model. The evidence indicates that other-regarding preferences are important for bilateral negotiations, for the enforcement of social norms, for understanding the functioning of markets and economic incentives. They are also important determinants of cooperation and collective action and the very existence of cooperative institutions that enforce rules and norms may be due to the existence of other-regarding preferences. The examples that we have given in Section 5 of this chapter do of course not exhaust the potential impact of such preferences on economic and social processes. We did not mention the impact of other-regarding preferences on voting behaviour, tax policy and the demand for redistribution [Fong (2001), Anderhub (2001), Tyran (2004), Riedl and Tyran (2005), Ackert, Martinez-Vazquez and Rider (2004), Fong, Bowles and Gintis (2005a, 2005b), Hahn (2004)] and on various aspects of contract economics, the hold-up problem and the optimal allocation of property rights [Anderhub, Gachter and Konigstein (2002), Ellingsen and Johannesson (2004a, 2004b, 2005), Cabrales and Charness (2003), Fehr, Kremhelmer and Schmidt (2004)]. We also did not mention how other-regarding preferences affect trust and may undermine the impact of incentives [Bohnet and Zeckhauser (2004), Bohnet, Frey and Huck (2001), Gneezy and Rustichini (2000), Fehr and Rockenbach (2003), Fehr and List (2004)]. This long list of examples suggests that other-regarding preferences affect social and economic life in many domains.

If they are neglected social scientists run the risk of providing incomplete explanations of the phenomena under study or – in the worst case – their explanations may be wrong.

However, although in view of the prevailing modelling practices in economics it is natural to emphasize the existence of a substantial share of subjects with other-regarding preferences, one should not forget the fact that many subjects often show completely selfish behaviors. Moreover, many of the examples we have discussed in Section 5 show that the interaction between self-interested actors and actors with other-regarding preferences may play a key role for the understanding of the outcomes of many experiments. Depending on the strategic environment selfish actors may induce actors with other-regarding preferences to behave as if completely selfish but the converse is also often true: actors with other-regarding preferences induce selfish actors to change their behavior in fundamental ways. In order to fully understand the interaction between selfish and non-selfish actors, social scientists need rigorous formal models of other-regarding preferences. In Section 3 we have documented the current state of the art in this domain. While the current models clearly present progress relative to the self-interest approach the evidence reported in Section 4 also makes it clear that further theoretical progress is warranted. There is still ample opportunity for improving our understanding of other-regarding behavior.

References

Abbink, K., Irlenbusch, B., Renner, E. (2000). "The moonlighting game: An experimental study on reciprocity and retribution". Journal of Economic Behavior and Organization 42 (2), 265–277.

Ackert, L.F., Martinez-Vazquez, J., Rider, M. (2004). "Tax policy design in the presence of social preferences: Some experimental evidence". Discussion paper. Department of Economics and Finance, Kennesaw State University.

Agell, J., Lundborg, P. (1995). "Theories of pay and unemployment: Survey evidence from Swedish manufacturing firms". Scandinavian Journal of Economics 97, 295–308.

Ahlert, M., Crüger, A., Güth, W. (1999). "An experimental analysis of equal punishment games". Mimeo. University of Halle-Wittenberg.

Alvard, M.S. (2004). "The ultimatum game, fairness, and cooperation among big game hunters". In: Henrich, J., Boyd, R., Bowles, S., Camerer, C., Fehr, E., Gintis, H. (Eds.), Foundations of Human Sociality. Oxford University Press, Oxford.

Anderhub, V. (2001). "Tax evasion with earned income – an experimental study". FinanzArchiv 58 (2), 188–206.

Anderhub, V., Gachter, S., Konigstein, M. (2002). "Efficient contracting and fair play in a simple principal – agent experiment". Experimental Economics 5 (1), 5–27.

Anderson, C.M., Putterman, L. (2006). "Do non-strategic sanctions obey the law of demand? The demand for punishment in the voluntary contribution mechanism". Games and Economic Behavior 54, 1–24.

Andreoni, J. (1989). "Giving with impure altruism: Applications to charity and Ricardian equivalence". Journal of Political Economy 97, 1447–1458.

Andreoni, J., Castillo, M., Petrie, R. (2003). "What do Bargainers' preferences look like? Experiments with a convex ultimatum game". American Economic Review 93, 672–685.

Andreoni, J., Miller, J. (1993). "Rational cooperation in the finitely repeated prisoner's dilemma: Experimental evidence". Economic Journal 103, 570–585.

Andreoni, J., Miller, J. (2002). "Giving according to GARP: An experimental test of the rationality of altruism". Econometrica 70, 737–753.

Andreoni, J., Vesterlund, L. (2001). "Which is the fair sex? Gender differences in altruism". Quarterly Journal of Economics 116, 293–312.

Arrow, K.J. (1981). "Optimal and voluntary income redistribution". In: Rosenfield, S. (Ed.), Economic Welfare and the Economics of Soviet Socialism: Essays in Honor of Abram Bergson. Cambridge University Press, Cambridge.

Baker, G. (1992). "Incentive contracts and performance measurement". Journal of Political Economy 100, 598–614.

Becker, G.S. (1974). "A theory of social interactions". Journal of Political Economy 82, 1063–1093.

Bellemare, C., Kröger, S. (2003). "On representative trust". Working Paper. Tilburg University.

Ben-Shakhar, G., Bornstein, G., Hopfensitz, A., van Winden, F. (2004). "Reciprocity and emotions: Arousal, self-reports and expectations". Discussion Paper. University of Amsterdam.

Benabou, R., Tirole, J. (2004). "Incentives and prosocial behavior". Mimeo. Princeton University.

Benjamin, D.J. (2004). "Fairness: From the laboratory into the market". Mimeo. Harvard University.

Berg, J., Dickhaut, J., McCabe, K. (1995). "Trust, reciprocity and social history". Games and Economic Behavior X, 122–142.

Bernheim, B.D. (1986). "On the voluntary and involuntary provision of public goods". American Economic Review 76, 789–793.

Bewley, T. (1999). Why Wages Don't Fall during a Recession. Harvard University Press, Harvard.

Binmore, K. (1998). Game Theory and the Social Contract: Just Playing. MIT Press, Cambridge, MA.

Binmore, K., Gale, J., Samuelson, L. (1995). "Learning to be imperfect: The ultimatum game". Games and Economic Behavior 8, 56–90.

Blount, S. (1995). "When social outcomes aren't fair: The effect of causal attributions on preferences". Organizational Behavior and Human Decision Processes LXIII, 131–144.

Bohnet, I., Frey, B.S., Huck, S. (2001). "More order with less law: On contract enforcement, trust, and crowding". American Political Science Review 95 (1), 131–144.

Bohnet, I., Zeckhauser, R. (2004). "Trust, risk and betrayal". Journal of Economic Behavior & Organization 55, 467–484.

Bolle, F., Kritikos, A. (1998). "Self-centered inequality aversion versus reciprocity and altruism". Mimeo. Europa-Universität Viadrina.

Bolton, G.E. (1991). "A comparative model of bargaining: Theory and evidence". American Economic Review 81, 1096–1136.

Bolton, G.E., Brandts, J., Ockenfels, A. (1998). "Measuring motivations for the reciprocal responses observed in a simple dilemma game". Experimental Economics 3, 207–221.

Bolton, G.E., Ockenfels, A. (2000). "A theory of equity, reciprocity and competition". American Economic Review 100, 166–193.

Bolton, G., Zwick, R. (1995). "Anonymity versus punishment in ultimatum bargaining". Games and Economic Behavior 10, 95–121.

Bosman, R., Sutter, M., van Winden, F. (2005). "The impact of real effort and emotions in the power-to-take game". Journal of Economic Psychology 26, 407–429.

Bosman, R., van Winden, F. (2002). "Emotional hazard in a power-to-take-experiment". Economic Journal 112, 147–169.

Bowles, S., Gintis, H. (2000). "Reciprocity, self-interest, and the welfare state". Nordic Journal of Political Economy 26, 33–53.

Brandts, J., Charness, G. (2003). "Truth or consequences: An experiment". Management Science 49, 116–130.

Brandts, J., Charness, G. (2004). "Do labour market conditions affect gift exchange? Some experimental evidence". Economic Journal 114 (497), 684–708.

Brandts, J., Schram, A. (2001). "Cooperation and noise in public goods experiments: Applying the contribution function approach". Journal of Public Economics 79, 399–427.

Brandts, J., Sola, C. (2001). "Reference points and negative reciprocity in simple sequential games". Games and Economic Behavior 36, 138–157.

Buchan, N.R., Croson, R.T.A., Dawes, R.M. (2002). "Swift neighbors and persistent strangers: A cross-cultural investigation of trust and reciprocity in social exchange". American Journal of Sociology 108, 168–206.
Cabrales, A., Charness, G. (2003). "Optimal contracts, adverse selection & social preferences: An experiment". Discussion Paper. Department of Economics, University of Santa Barbara.
Camerer, C.F. (2003). Behavioral Game Theory, Experiments in Strategic Interaction. Princeton University Press, Princeton.
Camerer, C.F., Thaler, R.H. (1995). "Ultimatums, dictators and manners". Journal of Economic Perspectives 9, 209–219.
Cameron, L.A. (1999). "Raising the stakes in the ultimatum game: Experimental evidence from Indonesia". Economic-Inquiry 37 (1), 47–59.
Campbell, C.M., Kamlani, K. (1997). "The reasons for wage rigidity: Evidence from a survey of firms". Quarterly Journal of Economics 112, 759–789.
Carpenter, J.P., Matthews, P.H., Ong'ong'a, O. (2004). "Why punish? Social reciprocity and the enforcement of prosocial norms". Journal of Evolutionary Economics 14 (4), 407–429.
Charness, G. (1996). "Attribution and reciprocity in a labor market: An experimental investigation". Mimeo. University of California at Berkeley.
Charness, G. (2000). "Responsibility and effort in an experimental labor market". Journal of Economic Behavior and Organization 42, 375–384.
Charness, G., Dufwenberg, M. (2004). "Promises and partnerships". Mimeo. University of California at Santa Barbara.
Charness, G., Rabin, M. (2002). "Understanding social preferences with simple tests". Quarterly Journal of Economics 117, 817–869.
Cohen, D., Nisbett, R. (1994). "Self-protection and the culture of honor – Explaining southern violence". Personality and Social Psychology Bulletin 20, 551–567.
Cooper, D.J., Stockman, C.K. (1999). "Fairness, learning, and constructive preferences: An experimental investigation". Mimeo. Case Western Reserve University.
Costa-Gomes, M., Zauner, K.G. (1999). "Learning, non-equilibrium beliefs, and non-pecuniary payoff uncertainty in an experimental game". Mimeo. Harvard Business School.
Cox J.C. (2000). "Trust and reciprocity: Implications of game triads and social contexts". Mimeo. University of Arizona at Tucson.
Cox, J.C. (2004). "How to identify trust and reciprocity". Games and Economic Behavior 46 (2), 260–281.
Cox, J.C., Friedman, D., Gjerstad, S. (2004). "A tractable model of reciprocity and fairness". Mimeo. University of Arizona.
Cox, J.C., Sadiraj, K., Sadiraj, V. (2001). "Trust, fear, reciprocity and altruism". Mimeo. University of Arizona.
Daughety, A. (1994). "Socially-influenced choice: Equity considerations in models of consumer choice and in games". Mimeo. University of Iowa.
Davis, D., Holt, Ch. (1993). Experimental Economics. Princeton University Press, Princeton.
de Quervain, D.J.F., Fischbacher, U., Treyer, V., Schelthammer, M., Schnyder, U., Buck, A., Fehr, E. (2004). "The neural basis of altruistic punishment". Science 305, 1254–1258.
Delgado, M.R., Locke, H.M., Stenger, V.A., Fiez, J.A. (2003). "Dorsal striatum responses to reward and punishment: effects of valence and magnitude manipulations". Cognitive Affective Behavioral Neuroscience 3, 27–38.
Dufwenberg, M., Kirchsteiger, G. (2004). "A theory of sequential reciprocity". Games and Economic Behavior 47, 268–298.
Eckel, C.C., Grossman, P.J. (1996). "The relative price of fairness: Gender differences in a punishment game". Journal of Economic Behavior and Organization 30, 143–158.
Eichenberger, R., Oberholzer-Gee, F. (1998). "Focus effects in dictator game experiments". Mimeo. University of Pennsylvania.
Ellingsen, T., Johannesson, M. (2004a). "Is there a hold-up problem?". Scandinavian Journal of Economics 106 (3), 475–494.

Ellingsen, T., Johannesson, M. (2004b). "Promises, threats and fairness". Economic Journal 114 (495), 397–420.
Ellingsen, T., Johannesson, M. (2005). "Sunk costs and fairness in incomplete information bargaining". Games and Economic Behavior 50 (2), 155–177.
Engelmann, D., Fischbacher, U. (2002). "Indirect reciprocity and strategic reputation building in an experimental helping game". Working Paper No. 132. Institute for Empirical Research in Economics, University of Zurich.
Engelmann, D., Strobel, M. (2004). "Inequality aversion, efficiency, and maximin preferences in simple distribution experiments". American Economic Review 94, 857–869.
Erlei, M. (2004). "Heterogeneous social preferences". Mimeo. Clausthal University of Technology.
Falk, A., Fehr, E., Fischbacher, U. (2000a). "Informal sanctions". Working Paper No. 59. Institute for Empirical Research in Economics, University of Zurich.
Falk, A., Fehr, E., Fischbacher, U. (2000b). "Testing theories of fairness – Intentions matter". Working Paper No. 63. Institute for Empirical Research in Economics, University of Zurich.
Falk, A., Fehr, E., Fischbacher, U. (2003). "On the nature of fair behavior". Economic Inquiry 41, 20–26.
Falk, A., Fehr, E., Fischbacher, U. (2005). "Driving forces behind informal sanctions". Econometrica 73, 2017–2030.
Falk, A., Fischbacher, U. (2005). "A theory of reciprocity", Games and Economic Behavior. Submitted for publication.
Falk, A., Fischbacher, U. (2006). "A theory of reciprocity". Games and Economic Behavior 54, 293–315.
Falk, A., Gächter, S., Kovács, J. (1999). "Intrinsic motivation and extrinsic incentives in a repeated game with incomplete contracts". Journal of Economic Psychology.
Fehr, E., Falk, A. (1999). "Wage rigidity in a competitive incomplete contract market". Journal of Political Economy 107, 106–134.
Fehr, E., Fischbacher, U. (2003). "The nature of human altruism". Nature 425, 785–791.
Fehr, E., Fischbacher, U. (2004). "Third party punishment and social norms". Evolution and Human Behavior 25, 63–87.
Fehr, E., Fischbacher, U., Rosenbladt, B., Schupp, J., Wagner, G. (2002). "A nation-wide laboratory – Examining trust and trustworthiness by integrating behavioral experiments into representative surveys". Schmollers Jahrbuch 122, 519–543.
Fehr, E., Gächter, S. (2002). "Do incentive contracts undermine voluntary cooperation". Working Paper No. 34. Institute for Empirical Research in Economics, University of Zurich.
Fehr, E., Gächter, S. (2000). "Cooperation and punishment in public goods experiments". American Economic Review 90, 980–994.
Fehr, E., Gächter, S., Kirchsteiger, G. (1997). "Reciprocity as a contract enforcement device". Econometrica 65, 833–860.
Fehr, E., Kirchsteiger, G., Riedl, A. (1993). "Does fairness prevent market clearing? An experimental investigation". Quarterly Journal of Economics CVIII, 437–460.
Fehr, E., Kirchsteiger, G., Riedl, A. (1998). "Gift exchange and reciprocity in competitive experimental markets". European Economic Review 42, 1–34.
Fehr, E., Klein, A., Schmidt, K.M. (2004). "Contracts, fairness, and incentives". CESifo Working Paper No. 1215. Munich.
Fehr, E., Kremhelmer, S., Schmidt, K.M. (2004). "Fairness and the optimal allocation of property rights". Mimeo. University of Munich.
Fehr, E., List, J.A. (2004). "The hidden costs and returns of incentives – trust and trustworthiness among CEOs". Journal of the European Economic Association 2 (5), 743–771.
Fehr, E., Naef, M., Schmidt, K.M. (in press). "The role of equality and efficiency in social preferences". American Economic Review.
Fehr, E., Rockenbach, B. (2003). "Detrimental effects of sanctions on human altruism". Nature 422, 137–140.
Fehr, E., Schmidt, K.M. (1999). "A theory of fairness, competition and co-operation". Quarterly Journal of Economics 114, 817–868.

Fehr, E., Schmidt, K.M. (2004). "Fairness and incentives in a multi-task principal-agent model". Scandinavian Journal of Economics 106, 453–474.

Fehr, E., Tougareva, E. (1995). "Do high monetary stakes remove reciprocal fairness? Experimental evidence from Russia". Mimeo. Institute for Empirical Economic Research, University of Zurich.

Fischbacher, U., Fong, C., Fehr, E. (2002). "Fairness and the power of competition". Working Paper No. 133. Institute for Empirical Research in Economics, University of Zurich.

Fischbacher, U., Gächter, S., Fehr, E. (2001). "Are people conditionally cooperative? Evidence from a public goods experiment". Economics Letters 71, 397–404.

Fong, C.M. (2001). "Social preferences, self-interest, and the demand for redistribution". Journal of Public Economics 82, 225.246.

Fong, C.M., Bowles, S., Gintis, H. (2005a). "Behavioral motives for income redistribution". Australian Economic Review 38, 285–297.

Fong, C.M., Bowles, S., Gintis, H. (2005b). "Reciprocity and the welfare state". In: Gintis, H., Bowles, S., Boyd, R., Fehr, E. (Eds.), Moral Sentiments and Material Interests: On the Foundations of Cooperation in Economic Life. MIT Press, Cambridge.

Forsythe, R.L., Horowitz, J., Savin, N.E., Sefton, M. (1994). "Fairness in simple bargaining games". Games and Economic Behavior 6, 347–369.

Frechette, G.R., Kagel, J.H., Lehrer, S.F. (2003). "Bargaining in legislatures: An experimental investigation of open versus closed amendment rules". American Political Science Review 97 (2), 221–232.

Gächter, S., Falk, A. (1999). "Reputation or reciprocity?". Working Paper No. 19. Institute for Empirical Research in Economics, University of Zürich.

Gächter, S., Falk, A. (2002). "Reputation and reciprocity: consequences for the labour relation". Scandinavian Journal of Economics 104, 1–26.

Geanakoplos, J., Pearce, D., Stacchetti, E. (1989). "Psychological games and sequential rationality". Games and Economic Behavior 1, 60–79.

Gintis, H. (2000). "Strong reciprocity and human sociality". Journal of Theoretical Biology 206, 169–179.

Gneezy, U. (2005). "Deception: The role of consequences". American Economic Review 95 (1), 384–394.

Gneezy, U., Rustichini, A. (2000). "A fine is a price". Journal of Legal Studies 29 (1), 1–17.

Goeree, J., Holt, Ch. (2001). "Ten little treasures of game theory and ten intuitive contradictions". American Economic Review 91, 1402–1422.

Grosskopf, B. (2003). "Reinforcement and directional learning in the ultimatum game with responder competition". Experimental Economics 6, 141–158.

Gul, F., Pesendorfer, W. (2005). "The canonical type space for interdependent preferences". Mimeo. Princeton University.

Gürerk, Ö., Irlenbusch, B., Rockenbach, B. (2006). "The competitive advantage of sanctioning institutions". Science 312, 108–111.

Güth, W., Kliemt, H., Ockenfels, A. (2000). "Fairness versus efficiency – An experimental study of mutual gift-giving". Mimeo. Humboldt University of Berlin.

Güth, W., Kliemt, H., Ockenfels, A. (2003). "Fairness versus efficiency: An experimental study of (mutual) gift giving". Journal of Economic Behavior and Organization 50 (4), 465–475.

Güth, W., Marchand, N., Rulliere, J.-L. (1997). "On the reliability of reciprocal fairness – An experimental study". Discussion Paper. Humbold University Berlin.

Güth, W., Schmittberger, R., Schwarze, B. (1982). "An experimental analysis of ultimatum bargaining". Journal of Economic Behavior and Organization III, 367–388.

Güth, W., van Damme, E. (1998). "Information, strategic behavior and fairness in ultimatum bargaining: an experimental study". Journal of Mathematical Psychology 42, 227–247.

Hahn, V. (2004). "Fairness and voting". Discussion paper. Department of Economics, University of Heidelberg.

Hannan, L., Kagel, J., Moser, D. (1999). "Partial gift exchange in experimental labor markets: Impact of subject population differences, productivity differences and effort requests on behavior". Mimeo. University of Pittsburgh.

Harsanyi, J. (1955). "Cardinal welfare, individualistic ethics, and interpersonal comparisons of utility". Journal of Political Economy 63, 309–321.
Henrich, J., Boyd, R., Bowles, S., Camerer, C., Fehr, E., Gintis, H. (2004). Foundations of Human Sociality – Economic Experiments and Ethnographic Evidence from Fifteen Small-Scale Societies. Oxford University Press, Oxford.
Henrich, J., Boyd, R., Bowles, S., Camerer, C., Fehr, E., Gintis, H., McElreath, R. (2001). "In search of homo economicus: behavioral experiments in 15 small-scale societies". American Economic Review 91, 73–78.
Henrich, J., Smith, N. (2004). "Comparative experimental evidence from Machiguenga, Mapuche, Huinca, and American Populations". In: Henrich, J., Boyd, R., Bowles, S., Camerer, C., Fehr, E., Gintis, H. (Eds.), Foundations of Human Sociality. Oxford University Press, Oxford.
Hoffman, E., McCabe, K., Shachat, K., Smith, V. (1994). "Preferences, property right, and anonymity in bargaining games". Games and Economic Behavior 7, 346–380.
Hoffman, E., McCabe, K., Smith, V. (1996a). "On expectations and monetary stakes in ultimatum games". International Journal of Game Theory 25, 289–301.
Hoffman, E., McCabe, K., Smith, V. (1996b). "Social distance and other-regarding behavior". American Economic Review 86, 653–660.
Holmström, B., Milgrom, P. (1991). "Multi-task principal-agent analyses". Journal of Law, Economics, and Organization 7, 24–52.
Huck, S., Müller, W., Normann, H.-T. (2001). "Stackelberg beats cournot: On collusion and efficiency in experimental markets". Economic Journal 111, 749–766.
Irlenbusch, B., Sliwka, D. (2005). "Transparency and reciprocity and employment relations". Journal of Economic Behavior and Organization 56, 383–403.
Jackson, P.L., Meltzoff, A.N., Decety, J. (2005). "How do we perceive the pain of others? A window into the neural processes involved in empathy". Neuroimage 24, 771–779.
Kagel, J.H., Kim, Ch., Moser, D. (1996). "Fairness in ultimatum games with asymmetric information and asymmetric payoffs". Games and Economic Behavior 13, 100–110.
Kahneman, D., Tversky, A. (1979). "Prospect theory: An analysis of decision under risk". Econometrica 47, 263–291.
Keser, C., van Winden, F. (2000). "Conditional cooperation and voluntary contributions to public goods". Scandinavian Journal of Economics 102, 23–39.
Kirchsteiger, G. (1994). "The role of envy in ultimatum games". Journal of Economic Behavior and Organization 25, 373–389.
Knutson, B., Fong, G.W., Adams, C.M., Varner, J.L., Hommer, D. (2001). "Dissociation of reward anticipation and outcome with event-related fMRI". Neuroreport 12, 3683–3687.
Kolm, S.-Ch. (1995). "The economics of social sentiments: The case of envy". Japanese Economic Review 46, 63–87.
Ledyard, J. (1995). "Public goods: A survey of experimental research". In: Roth, A., Kagel, J. (Eds.), Handbook of Experimental Economics. Princeton University Press, Princeton.
Levine, D. (1998). "Modeling altruism and spitefulness in experiments". Review of Economic Dynamics 1, 593–622.
List, J., Cherry, T. (2000). "Examining the role of fairness in bargaining games". Mimeo. University of Arizona at Tucson.
Masclet, D. (2003). "Monetary and nonmonetary punishment in the voluntary contributions mechanism". American Economic Review 93 (1), 366–380.
McCabe, K.A., Rigdon, M.L., Smith, V.L. (2003). "Positive reciprocity and intentions in trust games". Journal of Economic Behavior and Organization 52, 267–275.
Morrison, I., Lloyd, D., die Pellegrino, G., Roberts, N. (2004). "Vicarious responses to pain in anterior cingolate cortex: Is empathy a multisensory issue?". Cognitive, Affective, and Behavioral Neuroscience 4, 270–278.
Mui, V.-L. (1995). "The Economics of envy". Journal of Economic Behavior and Organization 26, 311–336.
Neilson, W. (2005). "Axiomatic reference dependence in behavior toward others and toward risk". Mimeo. Department of Economics, Texas A&M University.

O'Doherty, J., Dayan, P., Schultz, J., Deichmann, R., Friston, K., Dolan, R.J. (2004). "Dissociable roles of ventral and dorsal striatum in instrumental conditioning". Science 304, 452–454.

Offerman, T. (1999). "Hurting hurts more than helping helps: The role of the self-serving Bias". Mimeo. University of Amsterdam.

Okada, A., Riedl, A. (2005). "Inefficiency and social exclusion in a coalition formation game: Experimental evidence". Games and Economic Behavior 50 (2), 278–311.

Ostrom, E., Walker, J., Gardner, R. (1992). "Covenants with and without a sword – self-governance is possible". American Political Science Review 86, 404–417.

Preston, S.D., de Waal, F.B.M. (2002). "Empathy: its ultimate and proximate bases". The Behavioral and Brain Sciences 25, 1–71.

Rabin, M. (1993). "Incorporating fairness into game theory and economics". American Economic Review 83 (5), 1281–1302.

Riedl, A., Tyran, J.-R. (2005). "Tax liability side equivalence in gift-exchange labor markets". Journal of Public Economics 89 (11–12), 2369–2382.

Rilling, J.K., Gutman, D.A., Zeh, T.R., Pagnoni, G., Berns, G.S., Kilts, C.D. (2002). "A neural basis for social cooperation". Neuron 35, 395–405.

Ross, L., Ward, A. (1996). "Naive realism in everyday life: Implications for social conflict and misunderstanding". In T. e. a. Brown, Values and Knowledge 103.

Rotemberg, J. (2004). "Minimally acceptable altruism and the ultimatum game". Mimeo. Harvard Business School.

Roth, A.E. (1995). "Bargaining experiments". In: Kagel, J., Roth, A. (Eds.), Handbook of Experimental Economics. Princeton University Press, Princeton.

Roth, A.E., Erev, I. (1995). "Learning in extensive-form games: Experimental data and simple dynamic models in the intermediate term". Games and Economic Behavior 8, 164–212.

Roth, A.E., Malouf, M.W.K., Murningham, J.K. (1981). "Sociological versus strategic factors in bargaining". Journal of Economic Behavior and Organization 2, 153–177.

Roth, A.E., Prasnikar, V., Okuno-Fujiwara, M., Zamir, S. (1991). "Bargaining and market behavior in Jerusalem, Ljubljana, Pittsburgh, and Tokyo: An experimental study". American Economic Review 81, 1068–1095.

Sally, D. (1995). "Conversation and cooperation in social dilemmas: A meta-analysis of experiments from 1958 to 1992". Rationality and Society 7, 58–92.

Samuelson, P.A. (1993). "Altruism as a problem involving group versus individual selection in economics and biology". American Economic Review 83, 143–148.

Sandbu, M.E. (2002). "A theory of set-dependent fairness preferences". Mimeo. Harvard University.

Schultz, W. (2000). "Multiple reward signals in the brain". Nature Reviews Neuroscience 1, 199–207.

Scott, R. (2003). "A theory of self-enforcing, indefinite agreements". Columbia Law Review 108, 1641–1699.

Segal, U., Sobel, J. (2004). "Tit for tat: Foundations of preferences for reciprocity in strategic settings". Mimeo. University of California at San Diego.

Seinen, I., Schram, A. (2006). "Social status and group norms: Indirect reciprocity in a helping experiment". European Economic Review 50, 581–602.

Selten, R., Ockenfels, A. (1998). "An experimental solidarity game". Journal of Economic Behavior and Organization 34, 517–539.

Sen, A. (1995). "Moral codes and economic success". In: Britten, C.S., Hamlin, A. (Eds.), Market Capitalism and Moral Values. Edward Eldar, Aldershot.

Singer, T., Kiebel, S.J., Winston, J.S., Kaube, H., Dolan, R.J., Frith, C.D. (2004b). "Brain responses to the acquired moral status of faces". Neuron 41, 653–662.

Singer, T., Seymour, B., O'Doherty, J., Kaube, H., Dolan, R.J., Frith, C.D. (2004a). "Empathy for pain involves the affective but not sensory components of pain". Science 303, 1157–1162.

Singer, T., Seymour, B., O'Doherty, J.P., Stephan, K.E., Dolan, R.J., Frith, C.D. (2006). "Empathic neural responses are modulated by the perceived fairness of others". Nature 439, 466–469.

Slonim, R., Roth, A.E. (1997). "Financial incentives and learning in ultimatum and market games: An experiment in the Slovak Republic". Econometrica 65, 569–596.

Smith, A. (1759). The Theory of Moral Sentiments.
Smith, A. (1982). The Theory of Moral Sentiments. (1759) edition reprinted. Liberty Fund, Indianapolis.
Smith, V.L. (1962). "An experimental study of competitive market behavior". Journal of Political Economy 70, 111–137.
Suleiman, R. (1996). "Expectations and fairness in a modified ultimatum game". Journal of Economic Psychology 17, 531–554.
Tyran, J.-R. (2004). "Voting when money and morals conflict: An experimental test of expressive voting". Journal of Public Economics 88 (7–8), 1645–1664.
Veblen, T. (1922). The Theory of the Leisure Class – An Economic Study of Institutions. George Allen Unwin, London. First published 1899.
Wax, A.L. (2000). "Rethinking welfare rights: Reciprocity norms, reactive attitudes, and the political economy of welfare reform". Law and Contemporary Problems 63, 257–298.
Yamagishi, T. (1986). "The provision of a sanctioning system as a public good". Journal of Personality and Social Psychology 51, 110–116.
Zizzo, D., Oswald, A. (2000). "Are people willing to pay to reduce others' income". Mimeo. Oxford University.

1D: HUMAN NATURE

Chapter 9

THE ECONOMICS OF HUMAN RELATIONSHIPS*

PIER LUIGI SACCO

Department of Art and Design, IUAV University, Venice, Italy

PAOLO VANIN

Department of Economics and Business, Pompeu Fabra University, Barcelona, Spain

STEFANO ZAMAGNI

Department of Economics, University of Bologna, Italy

Contents

Abstract	696
Keywords	696
1. Introduction	697
2. 'Communicative' aspects of reciprocity and altruism and the concept of 'socially provided goods'	698
3. The positional side of economic interaction	700
3.1. Positional competition and labor issues	701
3.2. Positional competition and growth	702
4. The relational side of economic interaction	704
4.1. Relational orientation and labor issues	706
4.2. Relational orientation and economic growth	708
4.3. The case of private growth and social impoverishment	711
5. Cultural and economic selection: The evolutionary foundations of altruism and pro-sociality	717
6. Back to the basics in the economic analysis of human interaction?	723
References	726

---

* The ideas expressed in the present chapter owe much to fruitful discussions with Luigino Bruni, Benedetto Gui, Jean Mercier Ythier, Roberto Scazzieri, Amartya Sen and Robert Sugden; we are also grateful to two anonymous referees for very insightful comments and criticisms, with the obvious disclaimer.

Handbook of the Economics of Giving, Altruism and Reciprocity, Volume 1
Edited by Serge-Christophe Kolm and Jean Mercier Ythier
Copyright © 2006 Elsevier B.V. All rights reserved
DOI: 10.1016/S1574-0714(06)01009-8

Abstract

Behind my reciprocation of a friend's gift may lie both instrumental reasons (I expect further future gifts) and 'communicative' reasons (I want to establish or confirm a friendship *per se*). In a theory of rational individual action, such 'communicative' reasons can be incorporated as an argument of an agent's objective function. This chapter starts by reviewing a recent literature that takes this direction and introduces 'relational' concerns through the concept of 'socially provided goods'. From a 'relational' perspective, however, individual intentions are not all that matters: a relation is characterized by the two (or more) persons linked and by the kind of link they have. This perspective, which in our view should complement the more traditional, individualistic one, is particularly suited to embed individual motivations in their social context and to study their co-evolution. In particular, we focus on the conditions under which reciprocity and altruism may survive and even spread over as social norms. Drawing from the literature on the dynamics of social norms, we argue that the combination of individual incentives and the forces of social selection may lead to a contraposition between a society's material success and its well-being, i.e., between its 'vitality' and its 'satisfaction'. Finally, we consider that the recent literature on the economic analysis of human relationships invites to a new reading of the 'classics' of economics and of moral and political philosophy. Both the new and the old literature point at the need to broaden the scope of economic modeling, to lay down the building blocks of a new, up-to-date approach to political economy that is equipped to tackle the challenges posed by advanced industrial societies in their social, cultural and economic selection dimensions.

Keywords

altruism, reciprocity, socially provided goods, evolution of norms

JEL classification: A12, B52, D64, Z13

1. Introduction

Polanyi (1977) identifies three main forms of integration of economic relationships: centralized redistribution, dispersed exchange on a market base and reciprocity based transactions. Economists' attention has been historically more devoted to market and state than to reciprocity, which, in turn, has been at the center of anthropologists' investigations for a long time. As this volume documents, though, several transactions in modern economies are regulated on a reciprocity base and economists' attention to such issues has been sharply increasing for the last few decades. Reciprocity is not just important besides the market and the state, but, even more, it underlies some relevant transactions within those two other spheres.[1] To take just three examples from this Handbook, Fehr and Schmidt (Chapter 8) discuss a wide experimental evidence showing the relevance of reciprocity, Rotemberg (Chapter 21) shows how reciprocity matters for the way how employees react to their employers' decisions, and Fong, Bowles and Gintis (Chapter 23) argue that reciprocity norms are very relevant determinants of both the widespread support for the re-distributive system of the welfare state and of some criticisms to its bad functioning.

In this chapter we are going to focus on the fact that reciprocity entails deep 'relational' aspects, which cannot be entirely captured within a purely individualistic and instrumental approach, and therefore a 'relational' perspective may prove useful. Consider a situation in which I decide to reciprocate another person's action, say a friend's gift. From an individual perspective, I may have both instrumental reasons to do it, for instance because I believe that the other person will reciprocate in turn in the future and I foresee future benefits from this, and I can have 'communicative' reasons, for instance because I am motivated by the desire to establish a reciprocal relation (in this case a friendship) *per se*. In a theory of rational individual action, such 'communicative' reasons can be incorporated as an argument of an agent's objective function. We are going to review a recent literature that takes this direction and introduces 'relational' concerns through the concept of 'socially provided goods'. From a relational perspective, however, individual intentions are not all that matters: a relation is characterized by the two (or more) persons linked and by the kind of link they have. This perspective, which in our view should complement the more traditional, individualistic one, is better suited to discuss the implications of individuals' social identity (and also of groups' identity), because it makes it easy to recognize that establishing a certain kind of link (say, reciprocal, but also altruistic) with a certain kind of person (or group) also affects my own identity, at least in its social component, and, as Akerlof (1997) and Akerlof and Kranton (2000) argue, the choice of one's social identity may be the most relevant economic decision, which then drives all other economic choices. Therefore, after discussing the

---

[1] A convincing example of the contemporary relevance of reciprocity comes from Akerlof's (1982) analysis of efficiency wages as partial gift exchanges. On a similar position is also Blau's (1964) idea of social exchange.

literature on 'socially provided goods', we draw attention to the fact that reciprocity and altruism may be seen as specific social norms, which determine a certain social identity, depending on who adopts them and to whom they are directed. In particular, we emphasize that, while such norms affect traditional economic outcomes in an important way, their evolution is also conditioned by usual economic variables. We illustrate this point by mentioning some contributions on the dynamics of social norms (in particular of altruistic norms). One consequence of this literature is that the dynamics of social norms may lead to a contraposition between a society's material success and its well-being, i.e., between its 'vitality' and its 'satisfaction'. Finally, we discuss at a higher level of generality the scope, the advantages and the limits of an instrumental perspective on reciprocity, based on methodological individualism, on one side, and, on the other side, of a more 'relationally oriented' approach. Our discussion is closely related to the one developed by Bardsley and Sugden in their Chapter 10 of this volume and should be seen as complementary to it.[2]

2. 'Communicative' aspects of reciprocity and altruism and the concept of 'socially provided goods'

A systematic investigation of reciprocity in economics dates back at least to Kolm's (1984) book and Kolm's Chapter 6 in this volume extensively discusses the concept of reciprocity. Its most salient economic feature is perhaps that, unlike market exchange, which occurs at contractually pre-determined prices, reciprocity-based transactions take the form of gifts and counter-gifts (and therefore they are also different from pure altruism, where transfers are uni-directional). As argued by Kolm (1994), reciprocity occupies an intermediate position between self-interest and pure altruism, and as noticed by Zamagni (2004), it is characterized by a peculiar relational orientation.[3]

In a discussion on the birth of modern individualism, Pulcini (2001) focuses on gift giving and argues that its engine is the desire of a link, of a relation. According to her, a gift is neither fully self-interested nor totally altruistic: it starts a game of reciprocity, of material and symbolic exchange which does not take place at pre-determined terms and time, but is rather intrinsically uncertain, expresses trust and recognizes a dimension of non self-sufficiency. In gift giving the other person assumes a special value, since she (or he) gives us back the relational sense of ourselves. A gift is generally driven by both an 'instrumental' concern for the counter-gift and by a non-instrumental intention,

---

[2] They study how the social dimension of human nature has been introduced in economics, first by discussing some 'fathers' of modern economic thought, such as Hobbes, Hume, Rousseau and Adam Smith, and then by considering several contemporary approaches to the introduction of sociality into decision and game theory.

[3] Discussing the economic theory of gift-giving and redistribution, Mercier Ythier points out, in his Chapter 5 in this volume, that the distribution of wealth is a 'pure relational good', in the sense that it 'consists of moral relations between individuals', such as 'moral sentiments' and 'individual senses of distributive justice'. We discuss 'relational goods' and their economic implications below.

corresponding to the desire to shape a relation (and possibly, thereby, one's own identity). The distinction we mentioned above between 'instrumental' and 'communicative' reasons is taken from Habermas' (1981) concepts of 'instrumental action', which just pursues its purposes (and therefore presupposes them, as pertaining to an individual identity), and of 'communicative action', which builds social relations, sense of identity and shared sense of a common world (and therefore, in a way, precedes any instrumental action).

The economic relevance of such 'communicative' aspects is well understood by Akerlof (1997), who recognizes that 'social decisions' affect and are affected by one's social network, are induced and, in turn, determine one's social distance from other individuals and groups, and shape an individual's social identity. It is worth quoting Akerlof at length: "The key difference between social decisions and conventional economic decisions (e.g., the choice of fruits) is that the social decisions have *social* consequences whereas economic decisions do not. [...] All of these activities will affect *who I am* in an important way, and thus how I associate with my friends and relatives, as well as who those friends may be. As a consequence, the impact of my choices on my interactions with other members of my social network may be the primary determinant of my decision, with the ordinary determinants of choice (the direct additions and subtractions from utility due to the choice) of only secondary importance" (1997, p. 1006).[4] In our context, the decision to act reciprocally or altruistically, towards certain individuals or groups and possibly not towards other ones, may be seen a 'social decision' in Akerlof's terms. Bourdieu (1979) in sociology and Akerlof and Kranton (2000) in economics document extensively that, by shaping an individual's social identity, social decisions are a major determinant of his or her future preferences and choices. This means that if we reduce choices of altruism, giving and reciprocity to the maximization of given preferences, we possibly miss some of their most interesting aspects. Of course, depending on the scope of our inquiry, a 'traditional' rational choice perspective on altruism and reciprocity, as can be, for instance, Becker's (1981) analysis of the economics of the family, can be very useful to highlight what we are interested in, but, as Akerlof observes, "a proper theory of social decisions [...] must first spell out their consequences for social exchange" (1997, p. 1007).

One of such consequences, indeed the easiest to introduce in a theory of individual action, is that social decisions provide social rewards. The concept of 'socially provided goods' is a way of specifying such social incentives to action. The peculiar feature of socially provided goods is that they are not provided by either market or state, but rather by social interaction. Examples of socially provided goods include friendship, social approval, social identification, mates and social status. Evidently, such goods differ from standard commodities, since they directly shape human relationships. A consequence of the fact that they are provided by social interaction is that an individual's decision to

---

[4] Akerlof's paper is not focused on the issues of reciprocity, giving and altruism, but his analysis of social decisions is more general than the scope of his applications.

purchase is not sufficient to obtain them, since their enjoyment does not just depend on individual choices, but also on a whole set of characteristics of social interaction, like other people's behavior, identity and motivation, and the norms, relational networks and opportunities available in the social environment. Therefore, by definition, wide externalities are present in the enjoyment of socially provided goods.

We find it convenient to organize our discussion of the literature on 'socially provided goods' by distinguishing two basic motivational orientations towards other people: 'positional' and 'relational'.[5] Essentially, a relational orientation corresponds to the desire to get closer to someone else, whereas a positional orientation corresponds to the desire to gain a better position than other ones on some relative scale. Although both motivations may be seen as oriented to the pursuit of some kind of socially provided goods, it is easy to think of relational orientation as generating altruistic or reciprocal behaviors, and of positional orientation as being rather the source of competitive behaviors. While an interaction based on 'relationality', with its components of altruism and reciprocity, generates 'relational goods', an interaction based on 'positionality', with its prevalence of competitive behaviors, generates 'positional goods'. We therefore consider here positional interaction as opposed to relational interaction, in order to better understand the differences and thus the implications of reciprocal and altruistic behaviors. Moreover, we shall argue that a relational disposition (and the corresponding behaviors) towards a certain group may be the other side of a positional disposition towards other groups, so that, when we acknowledge that altruism and reciprocity may be selectively directed to certain relations and not to other ones, an analysis of social and economic cleavages becomes directly relevant to the issue. While a deep account of the implications of such cleavages would lead us too far, we shall mention a few contributions in which they clearly emerge. Our analysis of relational and positional interaction, which is meant to be illustrative of how the concept of 'socially provided goods' may capture the social incentives that lie behind some forms of altruism and reciprocity, will be focused on their implications for some labor market issues, for growth and for well-being, with a particular attention to social participation, to social capital and to their dynamics.

3. The positional side of economic interaction

As mentioned above, the positional orientation corresponds to the desire to gain a higher relative position along some scale, that is to say, to reduce the distance from those who are above and to increase the distance from those who are below. As pointed out by Hirsch (1976), competition for relative position is a zero sum game, since to somebody's

---

[5] A third basic orientation, which can be called 'neutral', corresponds to the case in which individuals are self-concerned and do not care about others. Since this is the typical assumption in standard economic models, in which individuals care only about own consumption, we do not insist on it. Although the classification of social motivations in terms of positional, neutral and relational is not exhaustive, it offers a framework at the same time articulated and simple.

relative gain corresponds exactly somebody else's relative loss. Therefore, resources invested in this sort of competition are, from the aggregate point of view, a waste that gives rise to an inefficient 'rat-race'.

Social status is the typical example of a positional, socially provided good. The questions of what are the mechanisms according to which social status is attributed and what kind of economic behavior is stimulated by such pursuit have been tackled quite in detail in the recent economic debate. We focus here on two issues analyzed by this literature: the implications of social status concern for labor issues (in particular for labor supply and job satisfaction) and for economic growth.

3.1. Positional competition and labor issues

The desire of a positional advancement may be satisfied in various ways, according to the scale on which one evaluates relative position. Some economically relevant examples of such scales are the distributions of wealth, of income and of human capital. For instance, if relative income is an important social ranking device, the effect of positional competition may be an incentive to work inefficiently too much. Corneo (2002) considers this possibility and draws the policy implication that progressive income taxation may have an efficient side, to the extent that it corrects the over-work distortion and reduces the 'rat-race'.

Neumark and Postlewaite (1998) conduct an empirical study on the relationship between comparison income (i.e., income of a certain reference group) and women's choice whether to work or not. They show that, in taking such decision, women tend to compare their own family income with their relatives' family income: they choose to work if this is necessary to keep a good ranking of their own household in their reference group. This mechanism gives rise to potential chain effects, which are also in very good accordance with empirical findings.

Clark and Oswald (1996) provide an empirical estimation of the relevance of comparison income for job satisfaction. Using UK data for 1991, they find three main results: first, "workers' reported level(s) of satisfaction are at best weakly correlated with absolute income alone"; second, "measures of comparison income are significantly negatively correlated with reported levels of happiness at work"; third, "the higher the level of education, the lower the reported satisfaction level". This last result is explained with the idea that higher education brings about higher aspirations, which are more difficult to be met satisfactorily.[6] The comparison income is specified empirically as "the

---

[6] Aspirations seem to play a crucial role in determining satisfaction, as argued, among others, by Sacco and Vanin (2000) in a simulation model of network interaction. Clark (1997) explains the empirical finding that women report on average a higher job satisfaction than men with the consideration that, mainly because of historical reasons, they have been used to having worse positions and therefore they have on average lower aspirations, which are more easily satisfied. If this explanation is correct, it means that the gender differential in satisfaction is just temporary and will disappear as soon as women's aspirations are adapted and revised upwards.

income of 'typical' employees of given characteristics", as predicted by a standard Mincerian wage regression. The coefficient of this measure in a job satisfaction regression is negative, significant and both higher in absolute value and more significant than that of individual income; moreover, a Chi-square test does not reject the null hypothesis that these two coefficients are equal, thus supporting a pure relative income effect. The same result is confirmed also using different empirical proxies for comparison income. Analogous results are found by Hamermesh (1977), Lévy-Garboua and Montmarquette (1994) and Sloane and Williams (1994), using American, Canadian and British data, respectively.

3.2. Positional competition and growth

Many economists are reluctant to introduce social status into agents' objective functions, because they fear that this might lead to *ad hoc* explanations without explanatory power. One clever way out of such fears, clearly spelled out by Cole, Mailath and Postlewaite (1992) and often adopted in the literature on status seeking, is to recognize that markets are incomplete, so that some private goods are not allocated through the market, but rather through social interaction according to individual social status. Social status is thus interpreted by the authors "as a ranking device that determines how well an agent fares with respect to the allocation of non-market goods", and concern for social status is not exogenously postulated, but rather endogenously generated by private concern for non-market goods (indeed, socially provided goods). They focus on the case in which social status is attributed according to relative wealth: the wealthier you are, the higher your social status and thus the better you are able to enjoy private non-market goods. In their model, differences in social organization, i.e., in the allocation mechanism of non-market goods according to social status, induce different preferences for relative position, and since this depends on wealth, indirectly they induce different preferences for wealth accumulation, and therefore may lead otherwise identical economies to grow at different rates.

An alternative formulation, pursued by Fershtman, Murphy and Weiss (1996), considers status attributed according to relative human capital rather than to relative wealth: the higher your rank in human capital, the more you deserve and may receive social esteem. When human capital is not directly observable, they argue that it may be inferred from an individual's occupational group, and thus they focus on the consequences of status seeking for talent allocation in society. They find in particular that wealthy individuals with low ability may be induced to acquire human capital to gain higher status, thus driving poorer high ability individuals out of the more productive sectors. Consequently, growth might be enhanced by a more egalitarian distribution of wealth, which would reduce the demand for status.

The link between social status, attributed according to relative wealth, and long-run growth is studied in a model *á la* Solow (1956) by Corneo and Jeanne (2001), who show that concern for social status may generate endogenous growth. While in endogenous growth theory *á la* Romer (1986) growth is the result of positive externalities, and thus may be sub-optimally low, an improvement of an individual's relative position imposes a negative externality on others, so that growth resulting from status competition may be sub-optimally high.

The idea that positional competition takes place through a concern for wealth rank is investigated by Corneo and Jeanne (1999a) in a scenario of complete information on wealth distribution and by Corneo and Jeanne (1999b) in one of incomplete information. The first paper shows that, when wealth is perfectly observable, status competition creates an incentive to accumulate wealth and thus fosters growth; moreover, when there is a strong social segmentation, positional competition takes mainly place within each segmented social sphere, since within each of them wealth is more uniformly distributed and thus wealth ranking can be changed more easily through individual effort: under strong segmentation there is a higher incentive to engage in positional competition and therefore there are higher growth rates.

When wealth is imperfectly observable, Corneo and Jeanne (1999b) argue that social status may be attributed on the base of noisy signals, which generate the phenomenon called by Veblen 'pecuniary emulation': lower class people try to over-accumulate in order to be taken for upper class people, whereas upper class people over-accumulate to keep the wealth difference clear and visible. Both too much equality in the distribution of wealth and too much inequality destroy the signaling power of wealth and thus the incentive to accumulate it to gain status. The highest level of pecuniary emulation, and therefore the highest growth rates, correspond to intermediate levels of initial wealth inequality.

While Corneo and Jeanne (1999b) consider noisy signals on wealth in a rather abstract way, two previous contributions by the same authors specify such signals in terms of conspicuous consumption, i.e., consumption of luxury and visible (not necessarily useful) goods. Corneo and Jeanne (1997) derive some unconventional policy implications, related to the fact that the signaling power of conspicuous consumption may be increasing in price, so to generate an upward-sloping demand curve. This means that taxing this kind of goods might increase their demand rather than decreasing it, so that other policy instruments are needed to disincentive this channel of positional competition. Corneo and Jeanne (1998) argue that, while in a static framework conspicuous consumption for status reasons amounts to a reduction of savings, this effect may be reversed in a dynamic framework, if individuals accumulate when young and engage in conspicuous consumption and status competition when old.

One of the interesting aspects of this approach to social status is that it starts with the broad consideration that socially provided goods are not allocated through the market, but rather through social interaction. The next move is to spell such interaction as a competitive game, in which social status is mainly a way to win the competition. The archetype of such interaction, often considered in this literature, is therefore the competition for an individual's mate. Though, it may be observed that not all socially provided goods are allocated through competitive interactions, since participatory dynamics plays a relevant role as well. This leads us to consider a participatory, relational orientation, besides a competitive, positional one.

4. The relational side of economic interaction

The relational orientation corresponds to the desire to increase one's proximity to other people, for instance through friendship, sympathy, sharing of ends, of norms, of group belonging and, at the limit, of life. It is clear that, although we can think of 'positionality' as a desire to go 'above' others and of 'relationality' as a desire to come 'closer' to others, these two motivational orientations are not opposed to one another in a trivial way. For instance, the desire to share life with a certain mate may generate the need to win the social competition to get that mate, and a relational orientation towards the members of the upper class may just be the flip side of a general positional orientation. In other words, both positional competition and relational attitudes may be either pursued *per se* or instrumentally: a good position may serve to gain desired relations and certain relations may serve to gain a higher position. Though, we focus on the 'pure' forms of these two orientations, since an instrumental perspective on either of them already presupposes a clarification of the other one, which constitutes its purpose. In its pure form, 'relationality' reflects a participatory logic, which prompts to solidarity towards other people and fosters identification with them. Since identification with other people is a basic source of altruism towards them, or at least of benevolence, and since norms of solidarity and reciprocity often go together, those environments where a participatory, 'relational' logic may develop are natural sources of reciprocal and pro-social behaviors.

The link between 'relationality' and participation is well understood by Uhlaner (1989), who introduces in the economic literature the notion of 'relational goods'. She argues that traditional rational choice models cannot explain why people are willing to undertake costly actions such as political participation and voting, despite their awareness that the actual influence of their participation or of their vote is indeed negligible in terms of final outcome. On the contrary, such behaviors can be understood as rational once we consider that people are enjoying a relational good. According to her definition, relational goods are a particular type of local public goods, which can only be produced and consumed through the joint action of several individuals, whose identities become relevant. Two peculiar aspects of relational goods are that they cannot be enjoyed alone and that it is mostly very difficult to separate their 'production' from their 'consumption', since they easily coincide.[7] Indeed, not only 'consumers' and 'producers' are the same agents, but social participation 'produces' relational goods at the same time that it puts participants in the condition to 'consume', i.e. enjoy, them.[8] Examples of how social interaction may generate relational goods range from going out with friends to participating to a choir, a football club, a voluntary organization, and so on.

---

[7] The fact that in post-fordist economies production and consumption converge to some extent is observed, among others, by Zamagni and Bruni (2004), Donati (1991) and De Vincenti and Montebugnoli (1997).
[8] Gui (2000) emphasizes affective and communicative aspects of relational goods.

The aspect of joint production, and the fact that they present both private good and public good characteristics, makes relational goods a special case of Cornes and Sandler's (1984) joint production model, of which Andreoni's (1990) theory of 'warm-glow giving' is also a special case.[9] One implication of Cornes and Sandler's mixed private-public good approach is that there is the possibility of crowding in and of multiple equilibria, in the sense that, if everybody else contributes much to the joint production, this may raise my private returns from contribution and therefore lead me to contribute much myself, but if other people's contribution is low, I may have no incentive to contribute much. When Uhlaner emphasizes that, in the case of relational goods, an increase in the number of participants may increase individual utility, she is indeed applying this general result to the case in which the joint production is that of relational goods and individual contributions take mainly the form of some kind of social participation. As we shall see, this aspect opens the possibility that, due to coordination failure, social participation is inefficiently low (or inefficiently high) and a society gets stuck in a Pareto-dominated equilibrium, which, in the case of inefficiently low social participation, may be called a 'social poverty trap'.

Another closely related concept, often used in development economics, is that of 'productive consumption' (for instance, expenditure in food, health and education are consumption activities that raise individual productivity). A consequence of productive consumption is that, contrary to what we are used to think, a higher consumption level may increase production, accumulation and growth, whereas higher savings may result ineffective, as shown, for instance, by Steger (2002). We shall see later that similar surprising results apply to the effects of social participation, but, while Steger considers the effects of joint production on human capital accumulation, social participation may be seen as one of the major forces of social capital accumulation.[10]

A further interesting aspect about relational goods, which also distinguishes them from other kinds of joint production or of productive consumption, is that the identity of the people involved matters. As noticed above, Akerlof and Kranton (2000) emphasize the relevance of identity (a person's sense of self, associated to certain behavioral patterns) for a variety of economic outcomes,[11] and Akerlof (1997) notices that, as far as social decisions are concerned, the main determinant of my choice may be the impact I imagine it will have on the network of my relations with others. What is relevant here is whom I interact with and what is the 'social distance' between us (a special case of

---

[9] Interestingly, Cornes and Sandler already noticed that their theory might be applied to the economics of philanthropy.

[10] Narayan (1999) provides the following general definition: "Social capital is defined as the norms and social relations embedded in the social structures of societies that enable people to coordinate action to achieve desired goals".

[11] They argue that "choice of identity may be the most important 'economic' decision people make. Individuals may – more or less consciously – choose who they want to be. Limits on this choice may also be the most important determinant of an individual's economic well-being".

which is economic inequality). Again, we shall see later that the literature on social capital emphasizes both the theoretical and the empirical relevance of social and economic cleavages for social participation and social capital accumulation.

A common objection to the economic consideration of relational goods is that they would not be economic goods. Such objection takes two main forms. According to the first one, they should not be regarded as economic 'goods', since, while standard consumption goods exist and may be objectively defined before and independently of individual actions concerning them, relational goods come to exist only through social interaction. This distinction is indeed correct; though, its only consequence should be that relational goods are a class of economic goods different from private consumption goods,[12] unless one objects at the same time that relational goods are not 'economic' goods, a much less easily endorsable claim.

This second criticism starts from the conceptualization of 'economic' goods as 'scarce' goods and argues that relational goods are not scarce. Though, besides other possible inputs, enjoyment of relational goods requires participation to some social activities, which are typically time-intensive. Since time is a scarce resource, as already argued by Becker (1965), and since an increased pressure on it may lead to a substitution of time-intensive activities for time-saving ones, relational goods can be considered scarce goods on their own right, and the more so, the higher the pressure on time in a society: in other words, they are scarcer in advanced economies than in less developed ones.

As we did above for positionality issues, we focus again on two specific aspects of the literature on relational orientation: labor issues (in particular, labor supply, productivity and satisfaction) and economic growth (with a special focus on the dynamics of social capital accumulation and on well-being).

4.1. Relational orientation and labor issues[13]

Relational goods may be produced through interaction in any sphere of social life, like family, peer groups, associations and workplace. In each of them, relational and positional attitudes usually appear mixed to some degree, but their relative weight is different in different spheres. As far as relations at workplace are concerned, Rotemberg (1994) studies whether and how firms may benefit from promoting a relational orientation among workers.[14] He argues that workers' solidarity may lead them, depending on the specific situation, either to work harder or to exert a lower effort. This explains why

---

[12] We do not discuss here the difference from standard public goods, since it is not of particular relevance. Generally speaking, relational goods may be regarded as an intermediate case between private and public goods.

[13] For more on this topic see Rotemberg's Chapter 21 in this Handbook.

[14] In particular, he focuses on feelings of altruism among workers and treats them as a choice variable: individuals choose to be altruistic if it is in their own interest.

empirical results on the connection between cohesiveness of the working environment and labor productivity are generally mixed.

In a similar vein are also previous contributions by Holmström and Milgrom (1990) and by Lazear and Rosen (1981), who show that in some circumstances competition (and in particular positional competition) can lead workers to increase effort, whereas the possibility of 'collusion' would reduce labor productivity. In other circumstances, though, and especially when workers are not remunerated on an individual basis but rather on the basis of team performance, a relational orientation among group members would increase productivity, whereas a competitive orientation would easily generate social dilemma situations.

Sugden (1993) sheds further light on this argument, showing that, if individuals interpret themselves as members of a team rather than as competitors, the typical inefficiency of social dilemma situations may be avoided.[15] Rose (2002) argues, moreover, that payment on the basis of individual marginal productivity may be impossible when team synergies arise, so that remuneration on the basis of team performance may become necessary, whereas Holmström (1982) shows that internal competition in teams is worthless per se, and that its only rationale may be the optimal extraction of information about agent characteristics.

Rob and Zemsky (2002) consider that, although workers are not usually directly rewarded for cooperation, they could cooperate because they derive direct utility from doing it, in an amount that depends on firm specific social capital and on firm's direct incentives to cooperation. In this case, a firm might be interested in building social capital among its workers, a concept that we discuss in the next section and that, in the context of Rob and Zemsky, may be interpreted in cultural terms as a norm that prompts cooperation and associates a psychological cost to defection. The degree to which such a norm is effective, they argue, basically depends on the history of past cooperation among workers.

Rob and Zemsky's (2002) contribution captures two phenomena of broad relevance. The first one is the interplay between the psychological incentives provided by relational goods and the material incentives provided by the firm in form of remuneration.[16] The fact that this interplay does not work in an obvious way is highlighted by Frey's (1997) seminal work and by Gneezy and Rustichini (2000), who show through a field experiment that material incentives may crowd out intrinsic psychological incentives, because they change the way people frame a situation and therefore the kind of norm they see as adequate. Therefore, in order to be effective, material incentives have to be strong enough to compensate the psychological incentives crowded out by their introduction. Prendergast (1999) and Frey and Jegen (2001) offer exhaustive reviews of the economic literature on the crowding-out effects of material incentives; whereas Deci, Koestner,

---

[15] Bardsley and Sugden's Chapter 10 in this volume provides a more detailed analysis of team-thinking.
[16] The idea that some interplay of this kind may be relevant goes back, in the economic debate, at least to Akerlof's (1982) consideration that labor contracts may be seen as partial gift exchanges.

and Ryan (1999) discuss the empirical evidence accumulated by social psychology on the crowding-out effects of economic incentives on intrinsic motivation.

The second phenomenon is that there is a two-sided relationship between social capital accumulation and enjoyment of relational goods: on one side, a higher social capital increases returns to cooperation (in terms of relational goods) and therefore fosters it; on the other side, cooperation and enjoyment of relational goods contribute to reinforce cooperative norms and habits, and therefore foster social capital accumulation.

We may summarize the main conclusions of this literature in the following way: while the relationship between relational orientation and productivity is not univocal, but rather depends on the specific context, the contribution of relational orientation to job satisfaction is generally positive. Moreover, it is not subject to the social constraint faced by positional competition, namely, that of being a zero-sum game. Therefore, at least from a static point of view, relational orientation entails a higher potential for aggregate well-being than positional competition. Though, the ambiguity of its impact on productivity raises interesting questions about its dynamic consequences. For instance, one may wonder whether, under certain conditions, a widespread relational orientation may be statically beneficial for well-being but harmful in dynamic terms, or even just statically harmful for well-being, due to the latter effect. To understand such questions more deeply, let us now turn to the analysis of the connection between relational orientation and growth.

4.2. Relational orientation and economic growth

Endogenous growth theory puts a special emphasis on human capital, technology and positive externalities,[17] but at least in its standard versions it tends to disregard social issues. However, the literature on social capital, developed in the last fifteen years, has started to fill in the gap.[18] As Putnam (2000) observes, "The touchstone of social capital is the principle of generalized reciprocity – I'll do this for you now, without expecting anything immediately in return and perhaps without even knowing you, confident that down the road you or someone else will return the favor"[19] (p. 134). The basic reason why "a society that relies on generalized reciprocity is more efficient than a distrustful society" (p. 135) is that it saves on considerable transaction costs. Of course, trusting others is efficient only if they are trustworthy: "*Generalized reciprocity is a community asset, but generalized gullibility is not.* Trustworthiness, not simply trust, is the key ingredient" (p. 136). Indeed, the literature on social capital has proposed a number of theoretical definitions, but most of them focus either on trust and norms of civic

---

[17] See, e.g., Romer (1986), Lucas (1988), Barro and Sala-i-Martin (1995) and Aghion and Howitt (1998).

[18] This literature is by now too wide to review it exhaustively here. Coleman (1988, 1990) and Putnam (1993) are seminal contributions. The World Bank (2006) has an excellent electronic library on social capital.

[19] Putnam provides a number of examples of behaviors inspired to generalized reciprocity: "raking your leaves before they blow onto your neighbor's yard, lending a dime to a stranger for a parking meter, buying a round of drinks the week you earn overtime, keeping an eye on a friend's house, taking turns bringing snacks to Sunday school, caring for the child of the crack-head one flight down" (p. 134).

behavior or on networks of horizontal organizations, and again Putnam observes that "An effective norm of generalized reciprocity is bolstered by dense networks of social exchange" (p. 136).

Knack and Keefer (1997) examine various specifications of the concept of social capital, namely in terms of trust, civic norms and associational activity, and assess their impact on growth on the basis of data from the World Values Survey for 29 market economies between 1981 and 1991. As a proxy for trust (TRUST) they take for each nation the percentage of respondents that most people can be trusted (after deleting the "don't know" answers) to the following question: "Generally speaking, would you say that most people can be trusted, or that you can't be too careful in dealing with people?"[20] To capture the strength of norms of civic cooperation, they construct a variable (CIVIC) on the basis of the answers to various questions about how individuals evaluate some anti-civic behaviors. These two variables are highly positively correlated and both of them are designed to capture generalized trust and cooperative attitudes, rather than social capital at the level of a specific group. Therefore, we can consider them as indicators of society-wide relational orientation. Knack and Keefer's first main finding is that "trust and civic cooperation are associated with stronger economic performance". In particular, they find that one standard deviation change in TRUST is associated with a change in growth of more than half of a standard deviation. This result seems to be quite robust.

The second question they address concerns the effects of associational activities. Theoretically, such effects are ambiguous. Olson (1982) emphasizes that the purpose of some groups is to exert a distributive pressure, i.e. to seek rents, and that active participation to such groups indeed increases the level of distributive struggle in society and decreases social capital. In contrast, Putnam (1993) considers participation in associational networks as the main component of social capital, since it creates the civic engagement that improves both government and economic performance. As a proxy for the density of horizontal networks in a society (GROUPS), Knack and Keefer consider the average number of groups cited per respondent when faced with the question of whether they belong to any of a list of groups of ten kinds. Their second main result is that "associational activity is not correlated with economic performance – contrary to Putnam's (1993) findings across Italian regions". They also split the data to identify the possibly contrasting effects of 'Putnamesque' and 'Olsonian' groups, i.e., of groups that "involve interactions that can build trust and cooperative habits" and of groups with redistributive goals, respectively. The results are contrary to what the theory predicts, but, by admission of the authors, they should be regarded as only preliminary. Their relevance, rather than substantial, is methodological.

Zak and Knack (2001) perform a similar analysis, using the same variable for trust, but with more data. In particular, while Knack and Keefer's investigation concerns 29

---

[20] The variable TRUST exhibits a high cross-country variance and high serial autocorrelation within each country. Glaeser et al. (2000) use two experiments and a survey to address the question of what exactly TRUST measures and argue that it captures trustworthiness better than trust.

OECD countries, Zak and Knack add to the sample 12 additional countries. The effect of the larger sample is basically that it reinforces the statistical impact of trust on investments and growth. Moreover, they investigate the impact of formal institutions and social homogeneity, finding that they "increase growth in part by building trust".

Taken together, this evidence consistently shows that social capital, especially in the form captured by the variable TRUST, has a relevant impact on growth.[21] This raises the question of how social capital is accumulated. Knack and Keefer (1997) find for instance that "trust and norms of civic cooperation are stronger in countries with formal institutions that effectively protect property and contract rights, and in countries that are less polarized along lines of class or ethnicity".

That measures of social capital tend to be positively correlated with property and contract rights protection may appear surprising, since trust and contracts are generally seen as substitutes. Putnam (2000) confirms this result, when he shows that U.S. investment in the legal system (as captured by employment and expenditure measures in police, guards, watchmen, lawyers and judges) remained fairly low for most of the twentieth century, while all measures of social capital were increasing, and started to increase sharply in 1970, in correspondence with the beginning of a marked and prolonged decline in social capital. Nevertheless, one should distinguish between institutional quality, as measured by the extent to which property and contracts are protected in a given institutional setup, and the actual investment of resources in contract enforcement. While trust, saving on transaction costs, is indeed a substitute for the resources invested in contract enforcement, institutional quality provides an environment in which individuals have a further incentive to behave in a trustworthy manner, and it can thus stimulate trust.

The negative impact of class and ethnical polarization on social capital is confirmed by Glaeser et al. (2000), who find that a smaller social distance among people, for instance due to joint group membership or the same 'race' or nationality, increases both trust and trustworthiness; moreover, a person's higher status induces others to behave in a more trustworthy manner toward him or her.[22]

Alesina and La Ferrara (2002) consider both personal experiences and community characteristics as possible determinants of individual trust. Using data from the General Social Survey for the United States from 1974 to 1994, they find that the major causes of low trust are recent traumatic experiences, belonging to a discriminated group, low income, low education, living in a society with strong 'racial' cleavages or in one with high income inequality. Religious beliefs and ethnic origins, in contrast, are found not to affect trust significantly.

Results for social participation are quite similar. Alesina and La Ferrara (2000) study participation in associational activities like religious groups, sport groups, hobby clubs,

---

[21] Another relevant empirical contribution, although a bit harder to interpret, is due to Temple and Johnson (1998), who show that a measure of social capability is a good predictor of long-run growth.
[22] This is one of the ways in which positional and relational issues are linked together.

unions, and so on (they consider participation in a list of 16 different kinds of groups). They analyze data for metropolitan areas in the U.S. from 1974 to 1994, mainly from the General Social Survey, and find the following key results: social participation is higher where income inequality, 'racial' segmentation and ethnic segmentation are lower. This happens in the North/Northwest of the U.S., the opposite features appearing in the South/Southeast. Moreover, looking at participation in different kinds of groups, the authors find that heterogeneity matters less for participation in groups with a relatively high degree of excludability or a low degree of close interaction among members. Finally, they find that, as it could be expected, 'racial' segmentation matters more for individuals more averse to 'racial' mixing.

Helliwell and Putnam (1999) investigate whether and how education determines social capital, specified both in terms of trust and of social participation. They start with the observation that, although average educational levels have risen sharply in the United States in the last half century, the same did not happen to political and social participation. This is somehow puzzling, because individual education is widely acknowledged to be the best predictor of many forms of political and social engagement. Using data from the US General Social Survey from 1972 to 1996 and from the DDB-Needham Life Style surveys from 1975 to 1997, they assess that higher average education increases trust and does not reduce participation. A strong positive correlation between education and social participation is also found by Costa and Kahn (2001). Since such results are based on U.S. data, one should be careful in extending them. For instance, trust appears to be high in some countries with low formal education, but this may be due to a variety of reasons, which are still largely to be explored. One might speculate, for instance, that in some less developed countries the lower educational level is compensated by a higher reliance of the economy on the reciprocity-based transactions rather than on private markets, but this is just a conjecture.

The broad message of this literature is that trust, generalized reciprocity, social participation and relational orientation develop more easily where heterogeneity and social distance among individuals are low, that is to say, in relatively homogeneous groups or societies. Moreover, institutional quality and educational levels also tend to exert a positive impact on social capital.[23]

4.3. The case of private growth and social impoverishment

These considerations constitute the theoretical background of Antoci, Sacco and Vanin's (2002, 2005, 2006) investigation of the dynamics of social capital accumulation in a homogeneous society. They develop two 'neoclassical' models and an evolutionary model, to investigate to what extent such dynamics is related to economic growth and what is the overall impact of different possible development paths in terms of well-being. The basic setup of their models starts from the recognition that individual well-being

---

[23] Many of the quoted studies adopt an instrumental variables approach to tackle reverse causality issues.

depends on satisfaction of both material and relational needs, the first ones mainly addressed through private activities, whose outcome are private goods that enter in the GDP, the second ones mainly through social activities. Such activities yield relational goods, which do not enter in the GDP, to an amount that depends on own and average social participation, as well as on social capital. Besides yielding relational goods, social participation has a positive external effect on social capital accumulation. Individual choices of time allocation between private and social activities may therefore affect at the same time GDP growth and social capital accumulation.

In formal terms, their basic model (2002) considers a continuous population, whose individuals (denoted by subscript $\tau \in [0, 1]$) choose how to allocate their time among social activities (a share s of the entire population), private activities that yield a private 'subsistence' good C (a share l), and private activities that yield a private good C_s (a share l_s), which is a perfect substitute of the relational good B, in order to maximize their lifetime stream of discounted utility:

$$\max_{s_\tau(t), l_\tau(t), l_{s\tau}(t)} \int_0^\infty u_\tau(t) e^{r_\tau t} \, dt,$$

where t denotes time, r_τ is the individual intertemporal discount rate and $u_\tau(t)$ represents instantaneous individual preferences, which, omitting t and τ for notational simplicity, are given by

$$u = U(C, B, C_s) = \ln(C) + b \ln(B + a C_s),$$

where a is the MRS between C_s and B, and b is a strictly positive parameter (equal to 1 in the evolutionary model). It is assumed that the only production factor of private goods is individual labor,[24] whereas the relational good B is produced by own social participation s, aggregate (or average) social participation $\bar{s} = \int_0^1 s_\tau \, d\tau$ and social capital K_s, according to the function

$$B = G(s, \bar{s}, K_s) = \sigma s^\gamma \bar{s}^\delta K_s^\varepsilon,$$

where $\sigma, \gamma, \delta, \varepsilon > 0$ are parameters. Here production and consumption of B are not distinguished.

---

[24] It is not true that work is just a private activity, but it is both theoretically and empirically legitimate to assume that it has a primarily private orientation. Alesina and La Ferrara (2000) argue that, "after controlling for the level of income, the effect of time spent at work could be twofold. On the one hand, a constraint on time may decrease participation; on the other hand, socialization in the workplace may increase social interaction, incentives and ability to participate". Empirically, they find that full-time workers participate more than people out of the labor force, but less than part-time workers: both effects are present, but among working people there is a negative relation between the time spent in social participation and in private production. Corneo's (2001) empirical finding, discussed below, of a positive correlation across countries between the time devoted to watch television and to work is also illuminating.

Besides production technology and the constraints $s_\tau(t), l_\tau(t), l_{s\tau}(t) \geq 0$ and $s_\tau(t) + l_{s\tau}(t) + l_\tau(t) = 1$, individuals have to take into account the dynamics of social capital accumulation. It is assumed that social capital accumulates as social participation brings about relational goods:[25]

$$\frac{dK_s(t)}{dt} = \overline{B} - \eta K_s(t),$$

where $\overline{B} = \int_0^1 B_\tau(t)\,d\tau$ and η is social capital depreciation rate (relations die out if not taken care of). This means that social capital is treated as an accumulated externality. Assuming a homogeneous population (identical individuals), at a symmetric Nash equilibrium the representative individual's instantaneous choice of s depends on K_s. The resulting dynamics of K_s depends on the parameters. The main result is that there exist social poverty traps, i.e., Pareto-dominated fixed points. Along the convergence path to such equilibria the economy may experience at the same time private expansion and social impoverishment. When a social poverty trap exists, its attraction basin depends on the initial level of K_s: economies which are identical in the fundamentals, but differ in their initial stock of social capital, may follow different paths of growth, social development and time allocation between the private and the social sphere.

This basic setup is extended in two ways. First, the (2005) model introduces, besides social capital K_s, individual private capital K_τ, which, omitting τ, is accumulated according to

$$\frac{dK(t)}{dt} = Y(t) - C(t) - C_s(t) - \xi K(t),$$

where ξ is private capital depreciation rate and $Y(t)$ is an individual's total private production, which, omitting t, is given by

$$Y = A(1-s)^\varphi K^{1-\varphi},$$

where φ is a parameter and $A = (1-\bar{s})^\chi K^\psi$ captures possible externalities (χ and ψ are parameters). Even in this setting, where one may expect that private growth is strong enough to more than compensate the negative effects of social impoverishment, still social poverty traps are possible, as well as the simultaneous experience of private growth and social impoverishment along the convergence path. The attraction basin depends now, among other things, on the initial endowment of social capital relative to the representative individual's initial private capital.

The Antoci, Sacco and Vanin (2006) model investigates the same idea in an evolutionary framework. For simplicity, individuals may only choose between two pure strategies: a relational one, in which they produce and consume only C and B, and a private one, in which they spend more time in private activities, in order to produce and

---

[25] This is coherent with Rob and Zemsky's (2002) argument about firm-specific social capital, but is applied to society-wide social capital.

consume also C_s. It is assumed that the fraction x of the population that follows the relational strategy evolves according to the 'replicator dynamics':

$$\frac{dx}{dt} = x[U_R(K_s, x) - \overline{U}(K_s, x)],$$

where $\overline{U}(K_s, x) = U_R(K_s, x)x + U_P(K_s, x)(1 - x)$ is the average payoff and U_R and U_P are the payoffs of the relational and private strategy, respectively. Here only social capital accumulation is considered and it is modeled in the same terms as in the two 'neoclassical' contributions. This model displays two asymptotic attractors: a 'private' one, in which everybody adopts the private strategy and social capital is low, and a 'relational' one, in which everybody follows the relational strategy and social capital is high. Again, along convergence to the 'private' equilibrium, the economy experiences a private expansion based on destruction of social opportunities and on substitution for them with private goods. In some cases the social poverty trap is just the result of a coordination failure, in other ones it is also due to impatience. It is interesting to notice that the effect of impatience changes in the model with both private and social capital, since in that case impatience leads to prefer present socially enjoyed leisure to future private consumption, so that it induces a substitution of social for private activities and thus fosters social capital accumulation.

Apart from the differences, the three models converge as to the main message: they show that, even with a homogeneous population, an economy may get stuck in a social poverty trap. Moreover, they all find that, along the transition path towards the socially inferior equilibrium, an economy may experience at the same time private growth (which is reflected in national accounting statistics), and social impoverishment (which is not): as a consequence, the usual macroeconomic indicators fail to detect this kind of dynamic inefficiency.

The basic engine of this mechanism (a substitution of time-intensive social activities for time-saving private ones) may be self-feeding, since when an economy is experiencing at the same time private growth and a decline in social participation and social capital, the time spent in social activities becomes both more expensive (in terms of opportunity cost) and less 'productive' (in terms of relational goods), so that it becomes even more convenient to shift time towards private activities.[26] A simple intuition of this

---

[26] This perspective on growth is connected to a strand of the environmental economics literature, which focuses on negative externalities. The idea that such externalities might stimulate private activities and therefore foster growth is studied within an evolutionary framework by Antoci and Bartolini (1999) and Antoci and Borghesi (2001). The same idea is further studied within a neoclassical framework by Antoci (1997a, 1997b), Bartolini and Bonatti (1997, 1998, 1999a, 1999b), Antoci, Borghesi and Galeotti (2002) and Antoci (2002). A common point is that growth results from a coordination failure (a failure to internalize negative externalities) and is not necessarily desirable. An implication, shared also by Antoci, Sacco and Vanin (2005), is that, since impatience slows down undesirable growth, it may turn out to increase steady state welfare. The main difference between Antoci, Sacco and Vanin's contributions and this literature is that the former are not focused on natural resources, but rather on social capital accumulation. While (reproducible) natural resources are typically subject to a spontaneous flow of renewal, social capital accumulation rather depends on individual choices of social participation.

mechanism may be provided by the following example: if my friends work too much and do not have time to go out together, or if they do, but the environment does not offer any interesting social opportunity, I may decide to work more myself, in order to earn more, increase my level of private consumption, and therefore rely less on other people and on social environment as relevant sources of my well-being.

Once the possibility of a conflict between growth and social development (in terms of social capital, relational orientation and well-being) is acknowledged, the question becomes whether the mechanism that may lead to it and the conditions under which it emerges are plausible or not. Hirsch (1976) argues: "As the subjective cost of time rises, pressure for specific balancing of personal advantage in social relationships will increase. [...] Perception of the time spent in social relationships as a cost is itself a product of privatized affluence. The effect is to whittle down the amount of friendship and social contact [...]. The huge increase in personal mobility in modern economies adds to the problem by making sociability more of a public and less of a private good. The more people move, the lower are the chances of social contacts being reciprocated directly on a bilateral basis" (p. 80). This means that, in a society with a high degree of mobility, bilateral reciprocity is not enough, in the sense that many interactions take a one-shot form, and therefore people keep cooperating only if their trust is generalized, in the sense that they are ready to make a favor to a stranger with the (quite uncertain and unpredictable) expectation that someone else in the society will return it. This is for instance the case when someone watches a stranger's children and expects other people to do the same in turn. As Putnam (2000) observes, "At this extreme, generalized reciprocity becomes hard to distinguish from altruism and difficult to cast as self-interest" (p. 135).

The relevance of personal mobility for the substitution of private for social activities is also investigated by Schiff (1992),[27] in whose words: "The need to cope with the high degree of isolation caused by the higher degree of geographic labor mobility may lead to the creation of alternative institutions where people who are not as close can interact (e.g., singles' bars, dating services, nursing homes, insurance, and so on). These market activities enter into the gross national product (GNP) but do not necessarily imply higher welfare than in societies where some of these functions are carried out outside the market" (pp. 167–168). Such argument is reinforced by DiPasquale and Glaeser's (1999) empirical finding that homeownership, by reducing mobility, raises investment in social connections.

The issue of whether we should be worried about a process of social impoverishment and decline in social capital has started to receive academic and non-academic attention after Putnam's (1995, 2000) contributions. He documents a rise in U.S. social capital in the first half of the twentieth century, reaching a pick for most of its forms in the Sixties, followed by a marked decline from then on. The general diagnosis on the contemporary U.S. society is therefore that it is becoming more selfish, less altruistic and less able to

---

[27] See also Schiff (1999) for a general equilibrium model of labor mobility in the presence of social capital.

participate and cooperate on a reciprocity base: in one word, that Americans are bowling alone. The main culprits are identified in television and aging of the 'civic generation' of Americans born between 1910 and 1940, with a respective responsibility for up to a quarter and up to half of the decline in social capital.

Corneo (2001) presents striking empirical evidence that the time devoted to watch television and to work are positively correlated across countries and explains this evidence through a model based on the substitution between privately enjoyed and socially enjoyed leisure (i.e., between some private goods and relational goods). His results support the relevance of the mechanism discussed above, namely, of a possible self-feeding shift between social and private activities. Since he displays a static model with multiple equilibria, he focuses on static externalities of social participation and on coordination issues. The models developed by Antoci, Sacco and Vanin integrate such issues into a dynamic framework, which also allows to consider the dynamic externalities of social participation (i.e., time allocation to social activities) on social capital accumulation.

Costa and Kahn (2001) argue that the decline in U.S. social capital has been overestimated by Putnam, although some forms of social participation, like group membership and the time devoted to entertainment and visits with friends, relatives and neighbors, indeed declined in the U.S. from 1952 to 1998. They also cast doubts on Putnam's culprits, showing that the decline in the social capital produced outside the home is mainly due to rising community heterogeneity (especially income inequality), whereas the decline in the social capital produced within the home is mainly explained by women's increased labor force participation rate (always controlling for education). Moreover, they find that, while men mainly substituted social activities for television, women substituted them for work.

This hints at the fact that Putnam's emphasis on the role of television might be more relevant for men's time allocation patterns rather than for women's ones (at least in the U.S., but possibly more generally). At a more general level, it indicates that various dimensions of population heterogeneity play a crucial role for the analysis of social interaction and of social capital accumulation. While the emphasis on such aspects is shared, as we have seen, by Alesina and La Ferrara (2000, 2002) and by Zak and Knack (2001), among others, a sound theory of social capital accumulation in presence of a heterogeneous population is still missing. One of the most interesting analyses from this point of view is due to Narayan (1999), who shows that social capital tends to exert positive aggregate effects when trust, norms and networks that foster cooperation extend beyond primary, ethnic, linguistic or even income groups and form 'bridges' across different groups.[28] The reason is that the same links that keep together the members of a group may also exclude the non-members.

Inequality along some positional scale may be seen as a special example of population heterogeneity. This takes us back to the discussion spelled out at the beginning of

---

[28] He displays an analytical framework to study 'bonding' and 'bridging' (i.e. intra-group and inter-group) social capital at the level of the civil society, together with its connections to the functioning of the state.

this section, where we argued that relational and positional orientations may be simultaneously present but referred to different groups, for instance because solidarity with the members of my group (or of the group to which I aspire to belong) is the flip-side of competition with the members of other groups. While this possibility is explicitly acknowledged in some of the contributions considered so far, for instance in those by Corneo and Jeanne, in most cases it is not.[29] The literature on social capital then tells us that its potential effects in terms of well-being may crucially depend on its ability to 'bridge' heterogeneous groups and, in particular, to contrast the negative effects of positional inequality.

The above discussion has been carried out under the implicit assumption of a given set of dispositions and of corresponding social norms, in order to understand under what conditions certain relational or positional dispositions are stimulated by the economic and social environment, bringing about different possible equilibrium outcomes. The time has come to investigate how such dispositions and social norms may themselves evolve through the action of an underlying, 'deep' social selection dynamics. This issue is dealt with in the next section.

5. Cultural and economic selection: The evolutionary foundations of altruism and pro-sociality

We have emphasized so far either a cultural interpretation of social capital in terms of trust and norms of cooperation, or an interpretation in terms of associations and horizontal networks. The first aspect is the most relevant for our discussion of altruism and reciprocity. Indeed, as we have already noticed, "the touchstone of social capital is the principle of generalized reciprocity" [Putnam (2000, p. 134)]. From a cultural point of view, altruism and reciprocity may be seen as (dispositional counterparts of) specific social norms, and norms are effective when people widely follow them. Therefore, we now focus on reciprocity and altruism as social norms and investigate some of the possible reasons that may induce people to adopt them. As mentioned in the introduction, a relational perspective on social norms is particularly suited to recognize not only their relevance for the determination of individual social identity, but also their evolution through time. We shall consider some recent contributions in evolutionary game theory that shed light on the mechanisms of norms evolution, and then complement them with some reflections on the role and context of altruism and reciprocity from an aggregate point of view, to understand where and how they can develop. As these issues have received considerable attention in the literature, especially in the past decade, this

---

[29] A possible reason is that the reference point of most contributions is constituted by traditional economic models, which are based on agents who are 'neutrally' oriented towards one another so that many scholars have started to introduce, one at a time, either positional or relational orientation in models in which neutral orientation is already present. For instance Corneo (2001) and Antoci, Sacco and Vanin (2002, 2005, 2006) focus on neutral vs. relational.

discussion is not meant to be exhaustive, but rather illustrative. In this volume, a wider discussion of altruism and social norms is spelled out by Elster in his Chapter 3, and a more extensive analysis of the selection mechanisms that drive the evolution of social norms and social behavior is articulated by Bergstrom in his Chapter 11.

The basic idea in the literature on social evolution is that cultural traits, like preferences, values, norms, habits and identities, are not (or not only) innate characteristics of individuals, but are rather endogenous, in the sense of being acquired through, or influenced by, various processes of cultural transmission and of social selection, which, in turn, are influenced by the economic institutions present in a society.[30] A deep account of this perspective, and of old and recent literature on the subject both in economics and in other social sciences, is provided by Bowles (1998).[31] He discusses how markets and other economic institutions may affect individual preferences (conceived in broad terms as reasons for behavior), and identifies several possible channels. He argues that the replication of cultural traits depends, among other things, upon the interplay of two factors: the peculiar mechanism of cultural transmission (for instance from parents or teachers to children, or from peers to peers) and the social selection mechanism that leads to the replication of more rewarding traits (typically studied by evolutionary game theory). On both issues there is by now a considerable literature, which is also combined to the analysis of different models of learning. In the impossibility to review it here, let us focus on a simple example.

To fix ideas, suppose that Betty is following an altruistic norm that prescribes, say, unilateral donations in certain well determined situations. In a cooperative context, her donations may be reciprocated, so that it is easy to imagine possible scenarios where the norm turns out to be both (subjectively) highly satisfactory and (objectively) materially rewarding. There is therefore a good chance that Betty keeps following the altruistic norm and that she is even 'imitated' by other people, so that the norm spreads over. Notice that, in this cooperative context in which there is a straightforward incentive to behave nicely, whether people adopt the norm because of its apparent material convenience or because of the arousal of a deeper commitment to what they perceive to be the underlying disposition, is relatively irrelevant insofar as both possibilities yield the same behavioral prescription. In an opportunistic context, though, the altruist Betty may be materially exploited by others, with the consequence that, due to the undesirable payoff

---

[30] Many models and ideas in this literature come from evolutionary biology. See, among the many possible references, Cosmides and Tooby (1992) for the connections between socio-biology and evolutionary psychology, Dosi, Fagiolo and Marengo (1996) for the issue of learning in evolutionary environments, Weibull (1995) for a theoretical perspective on evolutionary game theory and Basu (1995) for an interesting application to civil institutions. Some contributions go further, boiling social evolution down to genetic evolution, but we do not consider them here.

[31] The general idea that preferences, although quite stable, may be endogenous, is not incorporated in textbook economics and requires a departure from an atomistic version of methodological individualism, to recognize that individual action takes place in social contexts, which may influence it. The methodological reasons for such departure were already clear two decades ago, as shown, among others, by Weintraub (1979), Granovetter (1985), Donzelli (1986) and Boland (1982).

implications of norm compliance, other people are likely to choose not to embrace it. On the other hand, even if she is materially worse off, Betty may gain a high intrinsic satisfaction from donation, because she truly adheres to the norm she abides by, and is happy to see other people well off because of her, even if this does not deliver in material terms. Can then one conclude that, apart from our nice Betty, nobody else will embrace the norm? Not at all: despite the negative material payoff, some people may still find attractive to do the same as Betty, insofar as they either believe that adopting the altruistic disposition their subjective, non-material reward will more than compensate the material loss, or, even more radically, insofar as they choose to abide by the norm whatever its material or psychological implications in terms of well-being.

This simple example calls for some basic distinctions. First, a norm may be either embraced because it corresponds to an intrinsic disposition, as in the case of a true altruist, or instrumentally, because adopting the corresponding behavior turns out to be rewarding even if the individual would behave differently if he had to follow his intrinsic disposition, as in the case of an egoist who – in a context where other people are altruist with seemingly altruist partners and egoist with seemingly egoist ones – finds it egoistically convenient to pretend to be an altruist, and therefore follows an altruistic norm instrumentally. But, as the example suggests, even in the case of an intrinsic commitment to the norm, one has to distinguish between a truly unconditional commitment, i.e. the choice to embrace the norm irrespectively of its consequences of any nature, and a 'rational' one, i.e. the choice to embrace it in view of the favorable tradeoff between the psychological benefit and the material loss. We can therefore speak, respectively, of strong and weak non-instrumentality.

Secondly, in picking up more rewarding traits, social selection may consequently operate at different levels, according to whether the relevant rewards for selection purposes are the material ones or the psychological ones or some combination of the two. As shown in our example, in a cooperative context the selection mechanism may have little or no discriminatory power, whereas in an opportunistic context there is much more scope for discrimination. Clearly, in this latter case, strongly non-instrumental variants of the norm are not affected by the selection process insofar as they are not sensitive to payoff comparisons of any kind, thereby playing the role of a 'drift' factor (which may however bring about important consequences on the selection outcomes as they alter the relative convenience of, say, instrumental vs. weakly non-instrumental altruism vs. egoism).

Thirdly, social selection may not just operate at the individual level, but also the group level, i.e., entire groups may be induced to embrace norms that are highly rewarding when collectively followed, although their individual adoption yields a low payoff.[32] While under individual selection it is easy that Betty remains an isolated exception, under group selection her altruistic norms have much higher chances to spread over, as demonstrated by Sober and Wilson (1998).

---

[32] Convincing examples are provided by Akerlof (1997).

We now consider some papers that investigate various aspects of this manifold set of analytic possibilities.

Sacco and Zamagni (1996) consider the evolutionary implications of several altruistic types[33] in the context of a simple contribution game and focus on 'true' (i.e., weakly non-instrumental) dispositions. They find that each kind of altruistic disposition proves to be (evolutionary) robust against certain player types (or combinations of players) and weak against certain other ones.[34] It follows that, from an evolutionary perspective, the discussion about altruism and its survival possibilities is a subtle one and requires the distinction among different kinds of non-instrumental altruism (e.g., more or less conditional, more or less consequentialistically oriented, etc.).

The possibility that individuals adopt a certain altruistic norm for instrumental reasons is investigated by Menicucci and Sacco (1997), who focus on two alternative types of 'pseudo-altruistic' behavior, namely, what they call 'Rawlsian' and 'Nietzschean' 'pseudo-altruism'.[35] 'Rawlsian' and 'Nietzschean' players act 'as if' they were maximizing, respectively, the lowest and the highest payoff between their own and their opponent's one.[36] The basic idea is that self-interested individuals may find it profitable to act 'as if' they were altruists, since this choice, when shared by enough people, improves their own (selfish) payoff. The evolution of 'pseudo-altruism' therefore depends on its ability to provide higher than average selfish payoffs. It is shown that both kinds of 'pseudo-altruism' are potentially fragile, in the sense that they are able to survive and even spread over in certain contexts but not in other ones, and that 'Rawlsian' altruism can be particularly conducive to efficiency.

While these contributions focus on the evolution of certain kinds of altruism, Sacco and Zamagni (2001) concentrate on reciprocity in a hawk–dove game and consider both the possibility that it is undertaken for instrumental reasons and that it is embraced out of intrinsic motivations.[37] A robust result in their model is that, whatever the initial distribution of player types in the population, the evolutionary dynamics leads to an equal

---

[33] A type here is like a social norm: it specifies the appropriate behavior in several possible situations, it is a rule to decide behavior. The possibility that a norm has a direct behavioral translation is investigated by Sacco (1997), who study the evolution of a cooperative norm in a prisoner's dilemma situation and consider the willingness to enforce cooperation as a meta-norm.

[34] The same result is also found by Antoci, Sacco and Zamagni (2000), who, building on this work, consider the possibility of having three motivational types present in a society at the same time, while Sacco and Zamagni (1996) only allow for two types to be simultaneously present.

[35] They develop the λ-players approach elaborated by Menicucci and Sacco (1996).

[36] As one can easily see, the reference to Rawls and Nietzsche is rather evocative than substantial.

[37] They consider a game in which a given surplus has to be distributed between two players, who can either pretend it for themselves or accommodate. Since distributive conflict is costly, they find it optimal to accommodate if the opponent pretends and to pretend if the opponent accommodates. The authors then study the evolution of different player types. They consider both 'naïve' players, who always play either as hawks or as doves, and 'sophisticated' players, who choose their action according to their opponent's type. Such sophisticated players may have different motivational orientations, namely neutral (traditional self-interested 'Best Reply' players), relational ('Rawlsian' players, who maximize the least advantaged player's payoff) and positional ('Positional' players, who maximize the difference between their own and their opponent's payoff).

split of players acting as 'hawks' and as 'doves' (which corresponds to a mixed strategy Nash equilibrium of the static game), at least as long as either intrinsic or instrumental reciprocity is represented in the population. Allowing for psychological externalities shows that, while 'relational' players may eventually dominate in equilibrium, with beneficial social effects, positional players cannot, precisely because they impose negative externalities on one another.

Although sometimes it may be difficult to identify the precise disposition that prompted an observed action, every day experience and an increasing number of studies[38] show that we indeed care very much about the 'true' intentions of others, and we interpret the same behavior in different ways, and therefore react in different ways, according to our beliefs about other people's intentions. As a matter of fact, a large number of social interactions acquire meaning only in the light of a mutual claim of absence of instrumentality. The meaning of a generous action towards a friend, a child or a business colleague lies precisely in its being gratuitous. If we found out that such action had sprung from an indirect, manipulatory logic, it would be read in a completely different way, and the response by the addressee could differ substantially. That is why it is not only necessary to distinguish between material outcomes and psychological satisfaction, which in general also depends on own and other people's alleged dispositions, but it is also important to understand whether a certain behavior follows from 'intrinsic' or from 'instrumental' motivations.

We have discussed so far a number of evolutionary game theoretic contributions, in which social selection leads to the diffusion of those traits that provide superior rewards. We have distinguished between material rewards and their subjective evaluation and have so far conceded that, in principle, social selection might operate at both levels. Let us now investigate more carefully these two possibilities. The hypothesis that what ultimately matters for social selection are material rewards is coherent with the idea, studied by Björnerstedt and Weibull (1996) and by Schlag (1998), that social selection works through imitation (of other people's successful behavior). Indeed, it is easier to observe, and hence imitate, individuals' relative material success rather than relative psychological satisfaction. In such case, as pointed out by Menicucci and Sacco (1996), social selection tends to attribute a premium to those traits that have a high 'vitality', defined in terms of material (and therefore reproductive) success, over those ones that have a high 'satisfaction' potential, defined in terms of subjective evaluation of the outcomes. If, on the contrary, social selection works through reinforcement of own successful behavior, as studied by Börgers and Sarin (1997), it may well operate directly at the level of subjective utility, since, after experiencing a certain number of behaviors (or of different behavioral norms), individuals may infer which one of them may be most satisfactory and may adopt it with increasing frequency. In this case, social selection might offer a premium to satisfaction over vitality.

---

[38] These studies include part of the experimental evidence discussed by Fehr and Schmidt in their Chapter 8 of this volume.

Joireman et al. (1996) present an interesting contribution in which players with different social value orientations are pair-wise matched to play a random sequence of games. Value orientations are geometrically represented as angles, whose co-sinus and sinus denote the importance attributed to own and other player's material payoffs, respectively. Consequently, if we restrict attention to positive co-sinus and omit pure altruism and pure sadism (corresponding, respectively, to $\pi/2$ and to $(3/4)\pi$), we find at 0 neutral orientation, at $\pi/4$ relational orientation, and at $(7/4)\pi$ positional competition. In this context, the degree of satisfaction of each given type of player depends upon the value orientation of the opponent. For instance, interaction between a pure altruist and a pure egoist is generally satisfactory for both of them, since they both just care about the egoist's material payoff and therefore pursue the same purpose; interaction between two positionally oriented players is unsatisfactory for both, because both try to be better off than the other one and therefore work in opposite directions; interaction between two relationally oriented players is satisfactory for both, since they both equally care about their own and the other player's material payoff. Mixed interaction between different types of players leads to articulated results, which are not easy to summarize here. The authors do not just compare the degree of satisfaction obtained by each motivational orientation in the various combinations, but also their vitality in terms of material success, i.e., accumulation of material payoffs. They find that, from the point of view of single individuals, neutral orientation displays the highest vitality, but from the point of view of the pairs the highest vitality is shown by the pairs of two relationally oriented players.

What is, then, the relevant dimension for selection: the materially-driven one, which creates a natural environment for instrumentality, or the psychological one, which is definitely more conducive to non-instrumentality? The former is clearly what is commonly meant by economic selection, whereas the latter may be phrased as cultural selection. In fact, neither of them is self-sufficient in regulating economic interaction completely. As J.S. Mill put it, culture and competition together are "the two agencies determining the market" [Schlicht (1998, p. 22)]. Apart from extreme circumstances, then, the relevant selection dynamics is likely to result from a combination of the economic and the cultural dimension. Of course, the specific weight of these 'two agencies' is not the same in different historical phases. At a very general level, one may argue that in traditional societies the predominant agency is generally believed to be culture [although someone claims that even in such contexts the apparent prevalence of 'culture' is, in Mill's terminology, nothing but 'competition' in disguise; see e.g. Townsend (1988)]. In industrial societies, the forces of competition take over, in that, by virtue of the increasing productivity of the material side of the economy that marks the various stages of the industrial revolution, the material set of incentives trades off better and better against psychological ones. Finally, in post-industrial societies where saturation effects for material incentives seem to arise as a consequence of the attainment of a generalized, high standard of living in absolute terms [see e.g. Frank (2003)], the cultural dimension strikes back to some degree. This is clearly seen e.g. in the time series of the poll that is conducted on a yearly basis by the Japanese prime minister's cabinet regarding the relative relevance of the material vs. spiritual dimension in determining life satisfaction in Japanese society: after a phase of prevalence of the material dimension up to the early eighties, one notices a steady growth of the relative relevance of the spiritual dimension, which in the past few years has been stably reported to be the primary concern for approximately two Japanese out of three [ACA (2002)].

The alleged inexorability of economic selection as the increasingly relevant dimension governing the evolution of market societies may therefore be questioned to a large extent. The outcomes of the selection dynamics may indeed be quite complex and subtle. Moreover, the relative strength of the various dimensions of selection (e.g., economic vs. cultural) is itself subject to adaptation, clearly on a much slower time scale and at a much deeper level. Therefore, the diffusion of altruism and of other (seemingly anti-economic) pro-social dispositions and behaviors, may be usefully investigated with the tools of co-evolutionary models. Research on these topics is still very preliminary, but is likely to flourish in the close future.[39]

6. Back to the basics in the economic analysis of human interaction?

Notwithstanding the fact that most of the literature reviewed above is very recent, the discussion about positional and relational orientations, and their connections with economic growth, has ancient roots in the early debates among the fathers of political economy and the moral and political philosophers who constituted their natural reference. Two cornerstones of such debates are Hobbes (1996) and Rousseau (1953).[40] For the former, in the 'state of nature' human relations are characterized by violence, and the need of self-preservation from the *bellum omnium contra omnes* drives to a social contract and to the attribution of power to a superior 'artificial person', the State. Therefore, Hobbes might be seen as a modern father of a 'positional' view on human beings. In contrast, Rousseau develops a radical criticism of competitive passions and desire for distinction, based on the fact that they produce a division between being and appearing. His solution lies in the refusal of competition in favor of a re-discovery of the authenticity of the self and of the common good (the 'general will'). Moreover, he thinks that the origin of competitive passions and of false identity lies in social relations, rather than in human nature 'before history'. Hence, the internal transformation of the individual is the prelude to a passage from a society based on competition to a community based on solidarity and *philia*. Therefore, some authors are willing to read Rousseau as a modern interpreter of a 'relational' conception of human beings.[41]

Although stimulating to some extent, straightforward interpretations of this kind risk to be misleading, not only for the over-simplification of the thought of seminal authors

---

[39] For instance, Axelrod (1997) uses simulations with genetic algorithms to provide fascinating insights, but his research essentially calls for further theoretical and empirical studies.
[40] See Bardsley and Sugden's Chapter 10 of this volume.
[41] See Pulcini (2001).

of such caliber, but also because they may induce the idea that relational orientations are intrinsically 'good' and positional ones intrinsically 'bad'. That the matter is more complicated is clear at least since Mandeville (1990), who contrasts two types of society: one is small, peaceful, frugal, homogeneous and close to commercial trade; the other one is large, open and militarily and commercially organized. In the first one there is a direct connection between individual intentions and social effects, because individuals know each other very well, defective behaviors are highly visible, modes of interaction are stable and standardized and the emergence of exotic behaviors and dispositions is unlikely. As a consequence, moral virtues are likely to spread over and are the source of public benefits, but such benefits are intrinsically limited: this closed and virtuous society cannot develop a prosperous and growing economy, scientific progress and political supremacy. In contrast, economic growth and prosperity are favored in the open, large, aggressively oriented society through private 'vices', like pride, ambition, envy and avidity, which are likely to be selected in this environment. Such vices, although morally unacceptable, are the source of public benefits, since they stimulate economic activity, especially through luxury consumption. The 'vicious' society may thus be much more vital than the 'virtuous' one. Mandeville is aware of the potentially disruptive social effects of the egoistic vices that promote economic welfare, but thinks that they are avoided by the fact that individuals learn, opportunistically, to simulate some necessary social virtues. Interestingly, he interprets such learning as taking place because of specific interests dictated by actual life in society and not as dictated by pure rationality in a fictitious state of nature. It is evident that several contributions discussed above articulate and formalize similar ideas, showing under which conditions certain dispositional orientations may be adopted, instrumentally or not, and may spread over, and evaluating the consequences of these dynamics in terms of social well-being.

An interesting aspect of Mandeville's reflection is that, for him, wealth and consumption do not just satisfy material needs, but entail a symbolic element: they attribute social status and distinction. In a similar vein, Adam Smith (2000) too considers the general desire to be admired and approved as one of the strongest and most pervasive human passions, but he derives different implications from Mandeville.[42] At the heart of his vision of human being there are self-love and desire for distinction. As for Mandeville, these are the engines of economic activity in a competitive society, but Smith emphasizes that the desire to be admired does not necessarily lead to private vices. One also desires to be approved by the 'impartial spectator' that is inside each of us, to be worth of admiration besides being admired actually. Social cohesion is not preserved by simulated virtues, but rather by true (i.e., non-instrumental) virtues: self-love is able to generate both growth and social cohesion. The Hobbesian struggle for life becomes, in the Smithian perspective, a more peaceful race for wealth. In contrast to Mandeville's emphasis on luxury expenditure, wealth accumulation is made possible by the virtue of

---

[42] Cole, Mailath and Postlewaite (1992) open their paper with this quote from Smith's *Theory of Moral Sentiments*: "It is not wealth that men desire, but the consideration and good opinion that wait upon riches".

prudence, with its content of foresightedness and sacrifice, whereas the invisible hand composes individual interests into social order.[43]

Both Hobbes' competitive passion and Rousseau's utopia of solidarity seem to play a minor role in the society observed by Tocqueville (2003), i.e., after the advent of democracy.[44] The reason is that democracy increases equality, which, in Tocqueville's view (but contrary to most of the theoretical and empirical evidence discussed in Section 4 above), stimulates an individual sense of self-sufficiency, which tends to erode social ties and to generate atomization, anonymity and massification. One of the consequences is that individuals appear free and independent, but also weak and disoriented, and therefore show a paradoxical need of authority – one of the sources of the possible authoritarian degeneration of democracy.[45] From a slightly different point of view, we might say that Tocqueville anticipates the contemporary widespread social dilemma between the need for security and the restrictions to freedom, through which security should be granted.[46] While aware of democracy's dangers, Tocqueville's way out is in turn entirely internal to democracy and relies on its ability to promote associational activity, that is, it relies on the strength of civil society.

The intellectual stimulation brought about by the reappraisal of the originating thought of modern political economy through the lenses of current analytical tools can hardly be denied. Endorsing Hobbes's rather than Smith's point of view has been for a long time also a matter of ideological positions, e.g. in terms of one's inclinations toward an optimistic vs. pessimistic view of human nature and toward the likely implications that such a fundamental option would deliver. As we have emphasized, the basic lesson we learn from the recent literature reviewed in this chapter is that one should avoid evaluating, say, individual inclinations at their face value, but should rather try to understand the often tricky ways through which they may generate certain instantaneous aggregate outcomes and, even more importantly, the long-run outcomes of social dynamics. We do not want to maintain the naïve position that thanks to the new theoretical developments we can eliminate all ideological elements from political economy debates, but rather that we are now prepared to dig a big deeper into the economic and social implications of certain traits of human nature and of their likely effects in certain environmental contexts, and thus to allow for a more mature and articulate ideological debate on these issues.

---

[43] A criticism of both the contractualistic and the utilitarian approach is developed, after a discussion of Mandeville's thought, by Marina Bianchi (1993), who argues that both approaches use categories that are indeed adequate for a closed and homogeneous society, but not for an open and dynamic one.

[44] See again Pulcini (2001).

[45] From a different perspective, Marx as well emphasizes the fact that economic (capitalistic) development clears all the colorful personal linkages of the Middle Age and leaves individuals only linked through their private economic interests, determined by their production relationships.

[46] The difference is that loneliness and weakness are caused for Tocqueville by the tendency of democratic societies towards atomization and massification, but these factors must at least be complemented with international considerations to explain insecurity and freedom restrictions in contemporary democracies.

The thought of the founding fathers of political economy provides us with a rich array of logical schemes that examine in subtle and complex ways the interplay between individual dispositions and behaviors, institutional settings, social and economic organization, and collective outcomes, often providing insights as to the possible dynamic mechanisms linking all these dimensions. No matter whether one agrees with Tocqueville (or with any of the other scholars cited above), it must be recognized that the recent developments of the literature on the economic analysis of human relationships reviewed in this paper invite to a new reading of these 'classics' and to a substantial broadening of economic modeling to address issues that have been all too often conventionally put outside the scope of economic theory. The re-reading of the classical texts is replete with surprises: there is an impressive number of hints and intuitions that have been disregarded by earlier readers but that now, in the light of the theoretical developments discussed in this paper, may be seen under a new light and may become fresh food for thought and inspiration, and are amenable to theoretical and empirical testing. The issue is clearly not, or not just, that of providing a more sophisticated interpretation of the Good Old Thought, but rather to lay down the first building blocks of a new, up-to-date approach to political economy that is equipped to put in their proper context the new problems posed by the new scenarios of advanced industrial societies and by their cultural and economic selection dimensions. We look forward to a stream of new and exciting research on these issues.

References

ACA (2002). "General circumstances affecting culture in Japan". Agency for Cultural Affairs, http://www.bunka.go.jp/english/English2002/1/I-3.html.

Aghion, P., Howitt, P. (1998). Endogenous Growth Theory. The MIT Press, Cambridge, MA.

Akerlof, G.A. (1982). "Labor contracts as partial gift exchange". The Quarterly Journal of Economics XCVII, 543–569.

Akerlof, G.A. (1997). "Social distance and social decision". Econometrica 65 (5), 1005–1027.

Akerlof, G., Kranton, R. (2000). "Economics and identity". The Quarterly Journal of Economics CXV (3), 715–753.

Alesina, A., La Ferrara, E. (2000). "Participation in heterogeneous communities". The Quarterly Journal of Economics CXV, 847–904.

Alesina, A., La Ferrara, E. (2002). "Who trusts others?". Journal of Public Economics 85 (2), 207–234.

Andreoni, J. (1990). "Impure altruism and donations to public goods: A theory of warm-glow giving". The Economic Journal 100 (401), 464–477.

Antoci, A. (1997a). "Self-protection activities from negative externalities and economic growth". Discussion Paper n. 18/97. Dimadefas, University of Florence.

Antoci, A. (1997b). "Negative externalities, consumption patterns and economic growth". Report n. 9349, M.U.R.S.T. Research Project on Non-Linear Dynamics and Application to Economic and Social Sciences. University of Florence.

Antoci, A. (2002). "Negative externalities as an equilibrium selection device in an economic development model". Mimeo. University of Sassari.

Antoci, A., Bartolini, S. (1999). "Negative externalities as the engine of growth in an evolutionary context". Nota di lavoro 83/99. Fondazione Eni Enrico Mattei, Milan.

Antoci, A., Borghesi, S. (2001). "Working too much in a polluted world: A North-South evolutionary model". Quaderni di Dipartimento n. 334. Department of Economics, University of Siena.

Antoci, A., Borghesi, S., Galeotti, M. (2002). "Economic growth in an economy in which there are private substitutes for environmental goods". Mimeo. University of Florence.

Antoci, A., Sacco, P.L., Vanin, P. (2002). "Participation, growth and social poverty: Social capital in a homogeneous society". Paper presented at the 54th IAES Conference in Washington, DC, October 12, 2002.

Antoci, A., Sacco, P.L., Vanin, P. (2005). "On the possible conflict between economic growth and social development". In: Gui, B., Sugden, R. (Eds.), Economics and Social Interaction: Accounting for Interpersonal Relations. Cambridge University Press, Cambridge.

Antoci, P.L., Sacco, S., Vanin, P. (2006). "Social capital accumulation and the evolution of social participation". Journal of Socio-Economics (forthcoming).

Antoci, A., Sacco, P.L., Zamagni, S. (2000). "The ecology of altruistic motivations in triadic social environments". In: Gérard-Varet, L.-A., Kolm, S.-C., Mercier Ythier, J. (Eds.), The Economics of Reciprocity, Giving and Altruism. Macmillan, London, pp. 335–351.

Axelrod, R. (1997). The Complexity of Cooperation: Agent-Based Models of Competition and Collaboration. Princeton University Press, Princeton, NJ.

Bardsley, N., Sugden, R. (2006). "Human nature and sociality in economics". In: Kolm, S.-C., Mercier Ythier, J. (Eds.), Handbook of Economics of Giving, Altruism and Reciprocity, vol. 1. Elsevier.

Barro, R., Sala-i-Martin, X. (1995). Economic Growth. McGraw-Hill, New York.

Bartolini, S., Bonatti, L. (1997). "Negative externalities as the cause of growth in a neoclassical model". Discussion Paper n. 9. Department of Economics, University of Trento.

Bartolini, S., Bonatti, L. (1998). "Growth as a coordination failure". Discussion Paper n. 5. Department of Economics, University of Trento.

Bartolini, S., Bonatti, L. (1999a). "Endogenous growth and negative externalities". Quaderni di Dipartimento n. 270. Department of Economics, University of Siena.

Bartolini, S. Bonatti, L. (1999b). "Growth and accumulation as coordination failures". Quaderni di Dipartimento n. 271. Department of Economics, University of Siena.

Basu, K. (1995). "Civil institutions and evolution: Concepts, critics and models". Journal of Development Economics 46 (1), 19–33.

Becker, G. (1965). "A theory of the allocation of time". Economic Journal 75 (299), 493–517.

Becker, G. (1981). A Treatise on the Family. Harvard University Press, Cambridge, MA.

Bergstrom, T.C. (2006). "Natural Kantian or *zoo economicus*? Evolutionary theories of selfishess and altruism among men and beasts". In: Kolm, S.-C., Mercier Ythier, J. (Eds.), Handbook of Economics of Giving, Altruism and Reciprocity, vol. 1. Elsevier.

Bianchi, M. (1993). "How to learn sociality: True and false solutions to Mandeville problem". History of Political Economy 25 (2), 209–240.

Björnerstedt, J., Weibull, J. (1996). "Nash equilibrium and evolution by imitation". In: Arrow, K., et al. (Eds.), The Rational Foundations of Economic Behaviour. Macmillan, London, pp. 155–171.

Blau, P. (1964). Exchange and Power in Social Life. Wiley, New York.

Boland, L. (1982). The Foundations of Economic Method. Allen & Unwin, St Leonards, NSW.

Börgers, T., Sarin, R. (1997). "Learning through reinforcement and replicator dynamics". Journal of Economic Theory 77, 1–14.

Bourdieu, P. (1979). La distinction, critique sociale du jugement. Éditions de Minuit, Paris.

Bowles, S. (1998). "Endogenous preferences: The cultural consequences of markets and other economic institutions". Journal of Economic Literature 36 (1), 75–111.

Clark, A. (1997). "Job satisfaction and gender: Why are women so happy at work?". Labour Economics 4, 341–372.

Clark, A., Oswald, A. (1996). "Satisfaction and comparison income". Journal of Public Economics 61, 359–381.

Cole, H.L., Mailath, G.J., Postlewaite, A. (1992). "Social norms, saving behavior and growth". Journal of Political Economy 100 (6), 1092–1125.

Coleman, J. (1988). "Social capital in the creation of human capital". American Journal of Sociology 94S, S95–S120.
Coleman, J. (1990). "Social Capital". In: Coleman, J. (Ed.), Foundations of Social Theory. The Belknap Press of Harvard University Press, Cambridge, MA and London.
Corneo, G. (2001). "Work and television". Discussion Paper n. 376. Institute for the Study of Labor (IZA), Bonn.
Corneo, G. (2002). "The efficient side of progressive income taxation". European Economic Review 46 (7), 1359–1368.
Corneo, G., Jeanne, O. (1997). "Conspicuous consumption, snobbism and conformism". Journal of Public Economics 66 (1), 55–71.
Corneo, G., Jeanne, O. (1998). "Social organization, status, and savings behavior". Journal of Public Economics 70 (1), 37–51.
Corneo, G., Jeanne, O. (1999a). "Social organization in an endogenous growth model". International Economic Review 40 (3), 711–725.
Corneo, G., Jeanne, O. (1999b). "Pecuniary emulation, inequality and growth". European Economic Review 43 (9), 1665–1678.
Corneo, G., Jeanne, O. (2001). "On relative-wealth effects and long-run growth". Research in Economics 55, 349–358.
Cornes, R., Sandler, T. (1984). "Easy riders, joint production, and public goods". The Economic Journal 94 (375), 580–598.
Cosmides, L., Tooby, J. (1992). "The psychological foundations of culture". In: Barkow, J.H., Cosmides, L., Tooby, J. (Eds.), The Adapted Mind: Evolutionary Psychology and the Generation of Culture. Oxford University Press, New York and Oxford.
Costa, D.L., Kahn, M.E. (2001). "Understanding the decline in social capital, 1952–1998". Kyklos 56 (1), 17–46.
Deci, E., Koestner, R., Ryan, R. (1999). "A meta-analytic review of experiments examining the effects of extrinsic rewards on intrinsic motivation". Psychological Bulletin 125, 627–668.
De Vincenti, C., Montebugnoli, A. (1997). L'economia delle relazioni. Laterza, Roma-Bari.
DiPasquale, D., Glaeser, E.L. (1999). "Incentives and social capital: Are homeowners better citizens?". Journal of Urban Economics 45, 354–384.
Donati, P. (1991). Teoria relazionale della società. Franco Angeli, Milano.
Donzelli, F. (1986). Il concetto di equilibrio nella teoria economica neoclassica. La Nuova Italia Scientifica, Roma.
Dosi, G., Fagiolo, G., Marengo, L. (1996). "Learning in evolutionary environments". Working Paper 96-124. International Institute for Applied Systems Analysis (IIASA).
Elster, J. (2006). "Altruistic behavior and altruistic motivations". In: Kolm, S.-C., Mercier Ythier, J. (Eds.), Handbook of Economics of Giving, Altruism and Reciprocity, vol. 1. Elsevier.
Fehr, E., Schmidt, K.M. (2006). "The economics of fairness, reciprocity and altruism: Experimental evidence". In: Kolm, S.-C., Mercier Ythier, J. (Eds.), Handbook of Economics of Giving, Altruism and Reciprocity, vol. 1. Elsevier.
Fershtman, C., Murphy, K.M., Weiss, Y. (1996). "Social status, education and growth". Journal of Political Economy 104 (1), 108–132.
Fong, C.M., Bowles, S., Gintis, H. (2006). "Strong reciprocity and the welfare state". In: Kolm, S.-C., Mercier Ythier, J. (Eds.), Handbook of Economics of Giving, Altruism and Reciprocity, vol. 1. Elsevier.
Frank, R.H. (2003) "Does absolute income matter?". Mimeo. Cornell University.
Frey, B. (1997). Not just for the Money. An Economic Theory of Personal Motivation. Edward Elgar Publishing, Cheltenham, UK.
Frey, B., Jegen, R. (2001). "Motivation crowding theory". Journal of Economic Surveys 15 (5), 589–611.
Glaeser, E.L., Laibson, D., Scheinkman, J.A., Soutter, C.L. (2000). "Measuring trust". The Quarterly Journal of Economics CXV, 811–846.
Gneezy, U., Rustichini, A. (2000). "Pay enough or don't pay at all". The Quarterly Journal of Economics CXV, 791–810.

Granovetter, M. (1985). "Economic action and social structure: The problem of embeddedness". American Journal of Sociology 91 (3), 481–510.
Gui, B. (2000). "Beyond transactions: On the interpersonal dimension of economic reality". Annals of Public and Cooperative Economics 71 (2), 139–168.
Habermas, J. (1981). Theorie des kommunikativen Handelns. Suhrkamp, Frankfurt am Main.
Hamermesh, D.S. (1977). "Economic aspects of job satisfaction". In: Ashenfelter, O.C., Oates, W.E. (Eds.), Essays in Labor Market Analysis. John Wiley, New York.
Helliwell, J.F., Putnam, R.D. (1999). "Education and social capital". Working Paper 7121. NBER, Cambridge, MA.
Hirsch, F. (1976). Social Limits to Growth. Harvard University Press, Cambridge, MA.
Hobbes, T. (1996). Leviathan. The Matter, Form and Power of a Commonwealth Ecclesiastical and Civil. Oxford University Press, Oxford. (Gaskin, J.C.A. (Ed.); first publication 1651.)
Holmström, B. (1982). "Moral hazard in teams". Bell Journal of Economics 13, 324–340.
Holmström, B., Milgrom, P. (1990). "Regulating trade among agents". Journal of Institutional and Theoretical Economics 146, 85–105.
Joireman, J.A., Shalley, G.P., Teta, P.D., Wilding, J., Kuhlman, D.M. (1996). "Computer simulation of social value orientation: Vitality, satisfaction, and emergent game structures". In: Liebrand, W.B.G., Messick, D.M. (Eds.), Frontiers in Social Dilemmas Research. Springer Verlag, Berlin–Heidelberg.
Knack, S., Keefer, P. (1997). "Does social capital have an economic payoff? A cross-country investigation". The Quarterly Journal of Economics CXII, 1251–1288.
Kolm, S. (1984). La Bonne Economie: La Réciprocité Générale. Presses Universitaires de France, Paris.
Kolm, S. (1994). "The theory of reciprocity and the choice of economic systems". Investigaciones Economicas 18, 67–95.
Lazear, E.P., Rosen, S. (1981). "Rank-order tournaments as optimum labour contracts". Journal of Political Economy 89 (5), 841–864.
Lévy-Garboua, L., Montmarquette, C. (1994). "On reported job satisfaction: A test of subjective well-being models and a new interpretation". Mimeo. Université Paris I.
Lucas, R. (1988). "On the mechanics of economic development". Journal of Monetary Economics 22 (1), 3–42.
Mandeville, B. (1990). The Fable of the Bees; Or, Private Vices, Publick Benefits. Liberty Fund, Inc., Indianapolis. (First publication 1714.)
Menicucci, D., Sacco, P.L. (1996). "Evolutionary dynamics with λ-players: Enforcing social outcomes via selective adaptation of individual pseudo-motivations". Quaderni del Centro Interuniversitario per la Teoria dei Giochi e le Applicazioni, n. 19.
Menicucci, D., Sacco, P.L. (1997). "Rawlsian altruism and efficiency". Studi e Discussioni, n. 102. Department of Economics, University of Florence.
Mercier Ythier, J. (2006). "The economic theory of gift-giving: Perfect substitutability of transfers and redistribution of wealth". In: Kolm, S.-C., Mercier Ythier, J. (Eds.), Handbook of Economics of Giving, Altruism and Reciprocity, vol. 1. Elsevier.
Narayan, D. (1999). "Bonds and bridges: Social capital and poverty". Poverty Group, PREM, The World Bank.
Neumark, D., Postlewaite, A. (1998). "Relative income concerns and the rise in married women's employment". Journal of Public Economics 70, 157–183.
Olson, M. (1982). The Rise and Demise of Nations. Yale University Press, New Haven, CT.
Polanyi, K. (1977). The Livelihood of Man. Academic Press, New York.
Prendergast, C. (1999). "The Provision of incentives in firms". Journal of Economic Literature 37, 7–63.
Pulcini, E. (2001). L'individuo senza passioni: individualismo moderno e perdita del legame sociale. Bollati Boringhieri, Torino.
Putnam, R. (1993). Making Democracy Work: Civic Traditions in Modern Italy. Princeton University Press, Princeton.
Putnam, R. (1995). "Bowling alone: America's declining social capital". Journal of Democracy 6 (1), 65–78.

Putnam, R. (2000). Bowling Alone: The Collapse and Revival of American Community. Simon and Schuster, New York.
Rob, R., Zemsky, P. (2002). "Social capital, corporate culture, and incentive intensity". RAND Journal of Economics 33 (2), 243–257.
Romer, P.M. (1986). "Increasing returns and long-run growth". Journal of Political Economy 94, 1002–1037.
Rose, D. (2002). "Marginal productivity analysis in teams". Journal of Economic Behavior and Organization 48 (4), 355–363.
Rotemberg, J.J. (1994). "Human relations in the workplace". Journal of Political Economy 102 (4), 684–717.
Rotemberg, J.J. (2006). "Altruism, reciprocity and cooperation in the workplace". In: Kolm, S.-C., Mercier Ythier, J. (Eds.), Handbook of Economics of Giving, Altruism and Reciprocity, vol. 1. Elsevier.
Rousseau, J.-J. (1953). "The Social Contract". Penguin, London. (First publication 1762.)
Sacco, P.L. (1997). "On the dynamics of social norms". In: Bicchieri, C., Jeffrey, R., Skyrms, B. (Eds.), The Dynamics of Norms. Cambridge University Press, Cambridge.
Sacco, P.L., Vanin, P. (2000). "Network interaction with material and relational goods: An exploratory simulation". Annals of Public and Cooperative Economics 71 (2), 229–259.
Sacco, P.L., Zamagni, S. (1996). "An evolutionary dynamic approach to altruism". In: Farina, F., Hahn, F., Vannucci, S. (Eds.), Ethics, Rationality, and Economic Behaviour. Clarendon Press, Oxford, pp. 265–300.
Sacco, P.L., Zamagni, S. (2001). "Provision of social services: Civil economy, cultural evolution and participatory development". In: Mwabu, G., Ugaz, C., White, G. (Eds.), Social Provision in Low Income Countries: New Patterns and Emerging Trends. Oxford University Press, Oxford, pp. 53–76.
Schiff, M. (1992). "Social capital, labor mobility, and welfare". Rationality and Society 4, 157–175.
Schiff, M. (1999). "Labor market integration in the presence of social capital". Development Research Group, World Bank.
Schlag, K. (1998). "Why imitate, and if so, how? A boundedly rational approach to multi-armed bandits". Journal of Economic Theory 78 (1), 130–156.
Schlicht, E. (1998). On Custom in the Economy. Clarendon Press, Oxford.
Sloane, P.J., Williams, H. (1994). "Job satisfaction, comparison income, and gender differences in earnings". Mimeo. University of Aberdeen.
Smith, A. (2000). The Theory of Moral Sentiments. Prometheus Books, Amherst, NY. (First publication 1759.)
Sober, E., Wilson, D.S. (1998). Unto Others: The Evolution and Psychology of Unselfish Behavior. Harvard University Press, Cambridge, MA.
Solow, R. (1956). "A contribution to the theory of economic growth". The Quarterly Journal of Economics 70, 65–94.
Steger, T.M. (2002). "Productive consumption, the intertemporal consumption trade-off and growth". Journal of Economic Dynamics & Control 26, 1053–1068.
Sugden, R. (1993). "Thinking as a team: Towards an explanation of nonselfish behavior". Social Philosophy and Policy 10, 69–89.
Temple, J., Johnson, P. (1998). "Social capability and economic growth". The Quarterly Journal of Economics August, 965–990.
Tocqueville, A. (2003). Democracy in America. Penguin USA. (First publication 1840.)
Townsend, R. (1988). "Models as economies". The Economic Journal 98 (390), 1–24.
Uhlaner, C.J. (1989). "Relational goods and participation: Incorporating sociability into a theory of rational action". Public Choice 62, 253–285.
Weibull, J. (1995). Evolutionary Game Theory. MIT Press, Cambridge, MA.
Weintraub, E.R. (1979). Microfoundations. The Compatibility of Microeconomics and Macroeconomics. Cambridge University Press, Cambridge.
World Bank (2006). Social Capital Library, http://www.worldbank.org/poverty/scapital.
Zak, P.J., Knack, S. (2001). "Trust and growth". The Economic Journal 111, 295–321.
Zamagni, S. (2004). "Happiness and individualism: A very difficult union". In: Bruni L., Porta, P., (Eds.), Happiness and Economics. Oxford University Press, Oxford (forthcoming).
Zamagni, S., Bruni, L. (2004). Economia civile. Efficienza, equità, felicità pubblica. Il Mulino, Bologna.

Chapter 10

HUMAN NATURE AND SOCIALITY IN ECONOMICS

NICHOLAS BARDSLEY
National Centre for Research Methods, University of Southampton, UK

ROBERT SUGDEN
School of Economic and Social Studies, University of East Anglia, UK

Contents

Abstract	732
Keywords	732
1. Hobbes's asocial model of man	736
2. Convention	738
3. Rousseau and the 'most remarkable change in man'	742
4. Fellow-feeling	745
5. Other-oriented motivations in modern economics	748
5.1. Rational choice altruism	749
5.2. Warm glow	751
5.3. Inequality aversion	752
5.4. Rabin's theory of reciprocity	754
6. Expressive rationality	756
7. Team reasoning	758
8. Sociality and the 'private language' argument	761
9. Conclusions	764
Acknowledgements	765
References	765

Handbook of the Economics of Giving, Altruism and Reciprocity, Volume 1
Edited by Serge-Christophe Kolm and Jean Mercier Ythier
Copyright © 2006 Elsevier B.V. All rights reserved
DOI: 10.1016/S1574-0714(06)01010-4

Abstract

Since *homo sapiens* is a social animal, one might expect human nature – the set of psychological propensities with which our species is naturally endowed – to equip human beings to live in social groups. In this chapter, we consider the implications of this idea for economics and game theory. We begin by discussing four classic accounts of the forces that hold human societies together – those of Hobbes, Hume, Rousseau, and Smith, who focus respectively on rational self-interest, convention, collective reasoning, and natural fellow-feeling. Turning to the modern literature, we review some of the ways in sociality has been introduced into decision and game theory by means of assumptions about non-self-interested preferences – specifically, assumptions about altruism, warm glow, inequality aversion and reciprocity. We identify some of the limitations of these theories as explanatory devices, and suggest that these limitations derive from a common source: that sociality is being represented within a framework of methodological individualism. We then discuss more radical approaches to explaining social interaction, based on the concepts of expressive rationality and team reasoning. Finally, we pose the fundamental question of whether it is possible to explain social interaction all the way down without going beyond the bounds of methodological individualism.

Keywords

human nature, sociality, altruism, sympathy, team reasoning, expressive rationality

JEL classification: D64 (altruism), H41 (public goods), Z13 (social norms and social capital)

Homo sapiens is a social animal. We take this to be a truism: our species, like the other great apes, naturally lives in structured groups, in which each individual's behavior responds to the behavior of the others. What is meant by the crucial term 'naturally' is that we human beings are genetically endowed with emotions, dispositions and ways of reasoning that equip us to live in groups. In more traditional terms, these emotions, dispositions and ways of reasoning are part of *human nature*. In this chapter, we consider the implications of this truism for economics and for decision and game theory.

It is tempting to take it as self-evident that, if man is a social animal, some kind of *sociality* – by which we mean some primitive desire or tendency to participate in society without ulterior motive, or some positive orientation towards other human beings – must be part of human nature. One way of expressing this idea is to picture human society as a network of relations of *mutual assistance*, and to suppose that a desire to assist others on terms of reciprocity is natural to human beings. Just such a conception of society can be found in some pre-Enlightenment traditions of economic thought.[1] But the proposition that man is a social animal does not entail, as a matter of logical necessity, that sociality is part of human nature.

The idea that social relations do not necessarily require sociality has been a guiding principle in economics from at least the time of Adam Smith – a principle summed up in Smith's (1976b, pp. 26–27) remark that it is not from the benevolence of the butcher, the brewer or the baker that we expect our dinner, but from their regard to their own interest. According to Smith, the natural disposition that allows human beings to develop economic relations with one another and so to benefit from the division of labor is the disposition 'to truck, barter, and exchange one thing for another' (p. 25). Economic systems based on property rights and markets – on what Smith calls 'natural liberty' – do indeed organize human activities in ways that are mutually beneficial. In this sense, economic relations are relations of mutual assistance. But this is an emergent property of economic systems: it is not *intended* by individual economic agents. In order for the economic system to function as it does, it may be sufficient that individuals are motivated by rational self-interest.

That social organization does not *necessarily* depend on sociality is now well established in biology. There are many examples of social behavior among animals which *in effect* are relations of mutual assistance, but which close study has shown to rest on the biological analogue of rational self-interest. For example, in many species of birds which feed in flocks, an individual bird which, in the presence of other birds of the same species, becomes aware of a predator (say, a hawk overhead) will make an alarm call; this alerts the other members of the flock, and they all fly away. This behavior pattern has often been interpreted as self-sacrifice on the part of the giver of the alarm call, since it apparently draws the predator's attention to the caller: why not just sneak away and leave the others to be attacked? Various sophisticated explanations of this apparent

---

[1] See, for example, Baeck (1994). Bruni and Sugden (2000) discuss the significance of this conception of sociality in the work of the eighteenth-century Italian economist Antonio Genovesi.

self-sacrifice (for example, kin selection[2]) have been put forward. But many biologists now favor a much simpler explanation. It is very difficult for any predator to capture *any* of a large group of similar-looking prey, all of which are moving rapidly relatively to one another. Thus, having seen a predator, an individual bird has a better chance of escaping if it gives an alarm call and becomes part of a flock of escaping birds than if it tries to escape alone [Skelton (1993, pp. 253–260)]. If this explanation is correct, it is still true that the alarm call is a form of social behavior, just as market exchange is for Smith. But the explanation of the behavior does not require any assumptions about socially-oriented *motivations*.

Whether economics can dispense with assumptions about sociality has never been finally settled. A traditional rhetorical device has been to refer to the mythical species of *homo economicus*, the individual members of which are motivated only by rational self-interest. This device is clearly intended to suggest that economics works with a *model* of human nature which abstracts from some important features of *homo sapiens*. The idea, presumably, is that by isolating certain salient features of real human nature, we can explain the most significant facts about human life that belong to the domain of economic science. Clearly, this is a more ambitious claim, the wider the domain of economics is taken to be.

Even within a narrowly-defined domain of the economic, however, there are significant economic facts which seem not belong to a world populated exclusively by *homo economicus* – for example, the extent to which wealth is transferred through unilateral gifts and bequests. Consider also that even Smith's butcher and baker pursue their own interests within a system of property rights. We might ask why economic agents respect one another's property rights. Of course, there are some theories of politics that claim that social and political order rests on nothing more than a balance of threats; we will discuss some of these theories later. At this stage, we merely point out that conventional economic theory presupposes that property is respected, and that an adequate explanation of why it is respected *might* require assumptions about sociality.

Among economists who accept the model of *homo economicus* as adequate for their purposes, there is disagreement about what subset of human behavior economics is intended to explain. Some of the early neoclassical economists made only modest claims about the domain of their theories. For example, William Stanley Jevons (1970, p. 93) defended his version of the *homo economicus* assumption by saying that economics deals only with 'the lowest rank of feelings'. Vilfredo Pareto (1972) thought that economic theory was suitable only for explaining 'rational actions'. Pareto's concept of rational action seems to involve the existence of a well-defined objective combined with enough repetition to allow agents to correct mistakes.[3] This kind of theoretical

---

[2] Kin selection is natural selection in favor of patterns of behavior which, although self-sacrificing at the level of the individual animal, promote the survival and reproduction of other carriers of the 'altruistic' individual's genes. There is no doubt that *some* patterns of animal behavior are explained by kin selection. Indeed, the whole phenomenon of parental care is explained biologically as a form of kin selection.

[3] Pareto seems to have thought that there was such an objective in the case of consumer behavior: the maximization of utility [Bruni and Guala (2001)].

modesty is now coming back into fashion, in response to experimental evidence of systematic contraventions of conventional economic theory [Plott (1996), Binmore (1999)]. If we are willing to constrain the domain of economics sufficiently, we will probably be able to find *some* definition of economics such that assumptions about sociality are not needed. However, many economists have wanted to claim that their mode of theorizing applies to much more than buying and selling. Gary Becker's (1976, p. 8) manifesto is well known:

> I have come to the position that the economic approach is a comprehensive one that is applicable to all human behavior, be it behavior involving money prices or imputed shadow prices, repeated or infrequent decisions, emotional or mechanical ends, rich or poor persons, men or women, adults or children, brilliant or stupid persons, patients or therapists, businessmen or politicians, teachers or students.

This is perhaps an extreme position, but the aspiration it expresses – the aspiration to explain human behavior in general – is widely shared among economists. If this aspiration is to be sustained, economics may need a richer model of human motivation than *homo economicus*.

Many economists would accept the need to go beyond the assumption of self-interest, but still insist on *methodological individualism* – the principle that explanations of social phenomena should be reducible to rational-choice explanations of the actions of the individual human beings involved. A methodologically individualistic approach to sociality is possible if socially-oriented motivations can be treated as particular kinds of desire or preference which, just like self-interested desires, are acted on by rational individual agents. However, some writers argue that there are social phenomena that cannot be fully explained in methodologically individualistic terms. If this claim is correct, what is needed is something more than a change in the assumptions that are made about preferences.

In the second half of this chapter, we review some of the ways in which sociality can be introduced into decision and game theory by means of assumptions about non-self-interested preferences (Section 5). We then discuss more radical approaches to social interaction which reject what have often been taken to be essential components of methodological individualism (Sections 6 and 7). Finally, we face head-on the question of whether it is possible to explain social interaction all the way down without going beyond the bounds of methodological individualism (Section 8).

We begin, however, by discussing four classic answers to the question of what (to use a common family of metaphors) makes up the social *bond*, the social *glue*, the *cement* of society. We look at the work of four authors who propose different ingredients as essential to this bond: rational self-interest is proposed by Hobbes (Section 1), convention by Hume (Section 2), collective reasoning by Rousseau (Section 3), and natural fellow-feeling by Smith (Section 4).

1. Hobbes's asocial model of man

We start with a classic of rational choice theory which takes methodological individualism to its limits, and which explicitly denies that sociality is part of human nature: Thomas Hobbes's *Leviathan* (1962).

Hobbes rejects the Aristotelian idea that man[4] has a natural desire to participate in society. In a state of nature, he claims, men do *not* find pleasure in one another's company (p. 99). To the contrary, they see one another as potential enemies; the sentiment most reliably associated with natural human interaction is *fear*. Hobbes concedes that his readers may find this hypothesis incredible, on the grounds that since men live in societies, nature must have equipped them with a fundamental desire for social life: 'It may seem strange to some man, that has not well weighed these things; that nature should thus dissociate, and render men apt to invade, and destroy one another' (p. 100). Hobbes's answer is brutally simple: Forget *a priori* reasoning and look at human behavior as it really is. See how little trust men have for one another, how constantly aware they are of the danger that others will take advantage of them. For Hobbes, the state of nature is not an abstract model or a remote era of human history; it is a state into which every society is always in danger of regressing. The motivations which Hobbes ascribes to individuals in the state of nature are motivations which we still have, barely held in check by the forces which secure political order.

Hobbes's model of human behavior is entirely mechanical. Human beings are machines: 'For what is the *heart*, but a *spring*; and the *nerves*, but so many *strings*; and the *joints*, but so many *wheels* ...?' (p. 19). We have an inner sense of the workings of the machines that we are, but we are not the authors of our actions. Action is only motion; desire is only an inner perception of the first stage of one's own motion; will is only the last desire felt before action; what is good for a person is whatever is the object of his desire (pp. 47–54). Reason is identified with arithmetic, which is a 'certain and infallible art' (pp. 41–42). Thought is not dependent on language, which is seen merely as a way of *translating* trains of thoughts into trains of words (pp. 33–34). Through its effects on our trains of thought, reason can have a causal effect on our desires; but it does not make us autonomous actors: we can do only what we desire to do.

None of this implies that we are necessarily self-interested, and indeed Hobbes does not think that we are. On his account, the primary human motivations are desires for self-preservation, delectation (that is, pleasure), security (which in the conditions of the state of nature translates into a desire for power over others), and glory (pp. 98–100). Although the first three of these desires are self-interested, the desire for glory is concerned with one's own position *relative to others*. This is a socially-oriented desire – a desire which is directed towards particular kinds of social relationship – but one which tends to war rather than peace. In the state of nature, men's natural desires lead

---

[4] It is often not clear whether Hobbes is using 'man' to mean 'human being' or 'male human being'. To avoid misrepresenting Hobbes's argument, we use 'man' where he does.

them into a war of all against all. They are able to escape from this state of war through the use of reason, given a natural fear of death and a natural desire for 'commodious living'. Social order – in the form of a common power to keep everyone in awe – is the product of reason, not of natural sociality.

For Hobbes, even the relations of the family are interpreted primarily in terms of rationality. Hobbes allows that there is a 'natural inclination of the sexes, one to another, and to their children'. In the state of nature, natural inclination normally induces mothers to care for their children, rather than to abandon them (as they have the right to do); reason then gives the child the obligation to obey its mother as its protector. (Since the paternity of children is unknown in the state of nature, fathers have no role.) Presumably acting on sexual or parental inclinations, men and women may contract into matrimony, which is modeled as a miniature state. Since, on Hobbes's account, stable order is most effectively supplied by a single ruler, a rational marriage contract will create a tiny monarchy, headed by the man or the woman, depending on the terms of the agreement (pp. 152–153).

At the core of *Leviathan* is Hobbes's list of the nineteen 'laws of nature'. A law of nature is 'a precept or general rule, found out by reason, by which a man is forbidden to do that, which is destructive of his life, or taketh away the means of preserving the same; and to omit that, by which he thinketh it may be best preserved' (p. 103). Hobbes summarizes the content of these laws as 'dictating peace, for a means of conserving men in multitudes' (p. 122). The idea, then, is that a stable social order is made possible by everyone's adherence to these laws, and that rational self-interest gives each individual the motivation to adhere to them. The first two laws direct men to contract their way out of the state of nature, if and only if they can do so safely and on equal terms. The other laws can be roughly divided into two types. One type specifies procedures for resolving various kinds of conflict. The other type is more interesting: it prescribes, on grounds of rationality, dispositions which might otherwise have been interpreted as elements of man's natural sociality.

The most famous of these is the third law of nature, the law of *justice*: 'that men perform their covenants made' (p. 113). But there are also laws prescribing *gratitude* and *complaisance*, and forbidding *contumely* (that is, insolence or contempt for others), *pride* and *arrogance*. To illustrate the logic of these laws, we focus on the law of complaisance, 'that every man strive to accommodate himself to the rest'. Explaining this law, Hobbes tells us that, because of the diversity of their affections, men do not *naturally* get along with one another particularly well. However, a man who makes no effort to accommodate himself to others will be 'cumbersome' to his fellows, and so be in danger of being left out of society. Complaisance – or, which Hobbes treats as a synonym, sociability – is therefore rational. According to Hobbes, then, it is rational to be, or perhaps to appear to be, the sort of person with whom other people want to interact – a person who can be trusted to keep promises, who is sociable, who treats others with respect. These characteristics are not intrinsic to our nature; they are recommended to us by rational self-interest.

Our equivocation over whether Hobbes is recommending men to *be* sociable, to *appear to be* sociable, or just to behave in certain kinds of ways that are called 'sociable', is deliberate. These subtle distinctions presuppose that human beings are autonomous in a way that Hobbes's mechanical model of behavior does not allow. What is clear is that Hobbes interprets sociability as a positive disposition towards others that can consciously be chosen by a rationally self-interested person. Whether this is coherent – whether dispositions of sociability, trustworthiness, gratitude and so on can be the real thing while being chosen for instrumental reasons – is an unresolved question, with (as we shall show later) implications for modern theories of non-selfish behavior.

Few modern philosophers have been willing to go as far as Hobbes in denying outright that sociality is part of human nature. But many Hobbesian echoes can be found in current literature. Among philosophers, David Gauthier (1986) has made the most sustained attempt to reconcile Hobbesian arguments with modern rational choice theory. In an argument which has provoked much debate,[5] he tries to show that a disposition for trustworthiness can be rationally chosen for instrumental reasons. Gauthier is Hobbesian too in his refusal to invoke assumptions about sociality. A just society, he claims, must be one that furthers the interests that people have *as individuals*, independently of any affections they may have for one another. The capacity to feel such affections is characteristic of human beings, Gauthier says, and it 'enriches' social life; but (and here he has feminist thought in mind) 'it becomes a source of exploitation if it induces persons to acquiesce in institutions and practices that but for their fellow-feelings would be costly to them' (p. 11). The implication is that sociality, however real it may be, has no place in the theory of justice.

Among economists, James Buchanan (1975) perhaps comes closest to Hobbes in his account of how social order might be instituted by constitutional contract from a wholly amoral state of nature. Buchanan's opening assertion that 'We live together because social organization provides the efficient means of achieving our individual objectives and not because society offers us means of arriving at some transcendental common bliss' (p. 1) is characteristically Hobbesian in its instrumental view of society and its presupposition that rational individuals are conceptually prior to society.

2. Convention

Contractarian thinkers in the Hobbesian tradition treat social institutions as the products of agreements that have been made, or could have been made, between rational individuals. A different way of thinking about them is to treat them as *conventions* that have gradually emerged out of people's repeated interactions. The philosophical founder of this approach is David Hume.

In the *Treatise of Human Nature* (1978), Hume argues that the rules of justice (understood as rules which assign property to individuals and ensure stability of possession)

---

[5] The issues involved in this debate are discussed by Sugden (1991).

are conventions. The original meaning of 'convention' is 'assembly', and by extension, an agreement reached in an assembly. Hume is conscious that his readers may think he is claiming that justice is the product of agreement, as it is in social contract theory. But, as he makes clear, he is using the term to refer to *tacit* agreements. The convention of justice, he says, 'is not of the nature of a *promise*: For even promises, as we shall see afterwards, arise from human conventions'. So what is it? According to Hume:

> It is only a general sense of common interest; which sense all the members of the society express to one another, and which induces them to regulate their conduct by certain rules. I observe, that it will be for my interest to leave another in the possession of his goods, *provided* he will act in the same manner with regard to me. He is sensible of a like interest in the regulation of his conduct. When this common sense of interest is mutually express'd, and is known to both, it produces a suitable resolution and behaviour. (p. 490)

This convention is not a product of conscious design: it is an unintended consequence of repeated interactions. It 'arises gradually, and acquires force by a slow progression, and by our repeated experience of the inconveniences of transgressing it' (p. 490). To help to explain what he means, he offers three other examples of conventions: the coordinated actions of two men rowing a boat; languages; and the use of gold and silver as currencies.

Thus, for Hume, a convention is a practice which has many of the properties of an agreement between rational individuals, but which in fact no one has ever explicitly consented to. It is a practice which, if followed by all, works in everyone's interests; but individual interest alone is not sufficient to motivate everyone to follow it unconditionally. In order for each individual to be motivated to comply, he must have the *expectation* that enough others will comply too. Such expectations could be generated by explicit agreement; but in most of the cases that Hume is considering, they are generated by *experience* of compliance by others in similar previous situations.

Hume does not explain in any detail how he thinks conventions come into being. At first sight, then, there seems to be a fatal defect in his theory: how, when there is no explicit agreement, are common expectations first generated? How can a convention come into existence unless someone is the first person to follow it? If, as Hume's definition seems to imply, no one has any interest in following a putative convention unilaterally, why would anyone follow it before anyone else did?

To these questions, Hume seems to have two answers.[6] The first answer anticipates Thomas Schelling's (1960) analysis of 'focal points' by two hundred years. It is that certain ways of coordinating individuals' actions are (in modern game-theoretic language) *salient* – that is, they stick out from the rest in some way that is perceived as

---

[6] Hume's analysis of convention, viewed in relation to game theory, is discussed by Sugden (1986) and Vanderschraaf (1998).

'natural' or 'obvious'. Hume construes salience in terms of associations of ideas (a fundamental concept in his theory of mind). In the case of property, Hume argues that familiar natural-law principles for assigning property rights – occupation, prescription, accession and succession – ultimately rest on associations of ideas that human beings are naturally inclined to make (pp. 501–513). The idea seems to be that, even in the absence of specific experience, we are predisposed to expect certain kinds of patterns in other people's behavior. Because these prior expectations are shared by all, they can seed the first stages in the emergence of conventions.

The second answer is that, in trying to explain the origins of conventions, we should not automatically assume that they sprang into being in the forms they now have. If people have come to expect a particular regularity in other people's behavior in one setting, they may expect to find it in other settings that are perceived as similar. Thus, once a convention has begun to emerge, it can spread from one situation to another through the association of ideas; in the process, it may gradually develop new characteristics (just as, to use one of Hume's examples, languages gradually change over time). So the conventions we now see may be very different from the practices from which they evolved; the factors that led people to follow those first practices – perhaps salience, explicit agreement, self-interest, or natural affection – may have little connection with current conventions. For example, Hume speculates that the conventions of justice first emerged in very small societies, perhaps families, and have gradually expanded in scope as societies have grown larger (pp. 498–500).

On Hume's account, once the necessary expectations are in place, conventions are self-enforcing. Although Hume is not so naïve as to suppose that a commercial society can dispense with a criminal justice system, his theory explains how *in principle* social order is possible without a Hobbesian sovereign to keep us all in awe. In this sense, Hume offers a much more harmonious picture of society than Hobbes does. Nevertheless, his assumptions about human motivations, in so far as they bear on justice, are not so very different from Hobbes's. Hume allows that we have sympathetic affections, directed towards our family and friends, and towards anyone whose happiness or misery is 'brought near to us, and represented in lively colours' (p. 481). Sympathy plays an important part in Hume's explanation of why justice is a *virtue*. (Hume's theory of moral sentiments has many similarities with Adam Smith's, which we discuss in Section 4.) But Hume thinks that the 'chief advantage of society' is its capacity to satisfy our material wants, that the main function of justice is to secure this advantage, and that 'the original motive to the establishment of justice' is self-interest (pp. 488, 499). In this sense, Hume's analysis of society is as individualistic as Hobbes's: social order arises out of the interactions of rational, self-interested individuals.

But although Hume's approach does not require socially-oriented *motivations*, it does require certain kinds of common understandings among individuals, sufficient to produce the common conceptions of salience and common associations of ideas that allow conventions to emerge and to reproduce themselves. This aspect of convention is brought out clearly in David Lewis's (1969) game-theoretic reconstruction of Hume's theory.[7]

Lewis focuses on the equilibrium properties of conventions: he asks what it is about these practices that ensures that, once having become established in a population, they continue to be followed. Why do rational individuals act in ways which reproduce conventions? For example, consider the convention that paper currency has value. What makes a British £10 note more valuable than any other elaborately decorated piece of paper? Clearly, the common expectation that these particular pieces of paper will be accepted in return for goods. But this expectation is grounded on nothing more solid than other expectations: if suddenly everyone ceased to expect other people to accept pounds, no one would accept them. Somehow, the fact that everyone has accepted pounds up to now gives us reasons – or what we take to be reasons – to expect that they will continue to do so. This is the force of *precedent*.

But, as Lewis points out, any pattern of observations made in the past can be projected into the future in innumerable different ways. What makes one projection the right one? In a recurrent coordination problem, any projection will turn out to be right if everyone makes it. So the principles that we use to project patterns in other people's behavior – the principles that lie behind the concept of precedent – are themselves conventions. Thus, in order to explain how conventions maintain themselves, we have to appeal to convention at another level. In Lewis's formal model, this idea is represented by the assumption that, within the relevant population, everyone shares the same 'inductive standards' (pp. 52–60). But, if we agree with Hume (1978, pp. 98–106), induction is ultimately grounded in nothing more than customary associations of ideas. Conventions are therefore possible only among people who have some habits of thought in common.

Thus, the theory of social order as convention is not quite so reductionist – not so clearly compatible with the strongest versions of methodological individualism – as Hobbes's contractarianism is. Both Hume (who mentions language only in passing) and Lewis (who devotes several chapters to the topic) treat languages as conventions. However, as we have shown, common habits of thought are conceptually prior to conventions. This raises the contested question of whether thought is essentially linguistic – a topic to which we return in Section 8. If thought is possible without language, one might make a conventionalist theory compatible with methodological individualism by proposing that common habits of thought are ultimately grounded in common human psychology – that some predispositions to think about the world in particular ways are 'hard-wired' into every human being. If, on the other hand, shared habits of thought depend on the prior possession of language, a convention-based theory cannot explain the social phenomenon of language by reference only to non-social concepts. What such a theory can still do is to explain some conventions in terms of others – the more complex in terms of the less, the later in terms of the earlier – just as biological theories explain some life forms in terms of others.

---

[7] Lewis's analysis of convention, viewed in relation to more recent game theory, is examined by Cubitt and Sugden (2003).

3. Rousseau and the 'most remarkable change in man'

For both Hobbes and Hume, social relations are grounded in individual self-interest. This self-interest is treated as a natural property of human psychology, conceptually prior to social relations. Thus, Hobbes and Hume explain social order in terms of desires and modes of reasoning that are ultimately individualistic. Jean-Jacques Rousseau, writing at the same time as Hume, offers the possibility of a very different form of social order.

Like Hobbes, Rousseau contrasts social life with a state of nature. For Rousseau, as for Hobbes, the state of nature is a device which allows the core features of human nature to be revealed. Rousseau's account of human nature is presented most clearly in his *Discourse on Inequality* (1988a). This essay is an attempt to explain the origin of inequality among human beings. Rousseau offers a conjectural history of human life from the earliest times, when (he claims) inequality was unknown. His account of the state of nature is colored by eighteenth-century knowledge about the way of life of the native populations of America, particularly in the vast and thinly populated forests of eastern north America which were presumed to resemble the ancient forests of Europe.[8] However, Rousseau starts his story at a stage of human existence which is far more primitive than that of eighteenth-century native Americans. Whereas Hobbes's state of nature is all too close to modern human life – so close that we are constantly in danger of reverting to it – Rousseau's is an irrecoverable state of innocence.

In Rousseau's state of nature, human beings live almost entirely solitary lives, similar in some ways to those of non-social mammals (such as moles or hedgehogs). Although more intelligent than other animals, Rousseau's natural human beings are not rational in the sense that modern people are: human rationality is presented as a product of social interaction, and societies do not yet exist. Lacking language, natural human beings lack both the conceptual repertoire which underpins rational thought and the means by which discoveries can be passed on from one person to another. They have the basic animal desires for food, water, warmth and sex; they have some simple, unreflective compassion for the sufferings of other members of their own species, perhaps even for those of living beings in general; they have very limited foresight; and mothers have sympathy for their own children, as long as those children are unable to fend for themselves. Apart from the short-lived relationship between mother and child, each individual human being

---

[8] Locke's (1960) social contract theory is similarly grounded in a state of nature modeled on the forests of America. However, Locke's state of nature is governed by a code of natural law, which is taken to be 'plain and intelligible to all rational Creatures' (p. 396). The essential idea is that man is the creation of and the servant of a benevolent deity, whose purpose is that mankind should survive and multiply. The precepts of natural law are principles to be followed by human beings (with ordinary rationality and weaknesses) in the absence of formal government. The content of these laws can be inferred from the presumed purpose of God, and from consideration of the problems of ensuring human survival in the state of nature. In modern terms, Locke's theoretical strategy has some similarities with theories of 'team thinking', in which individuals separately look for rules which, if generally followed, would promote collective ends, and then follow those rules (see Section 7).

lives a self-sufficient life. Sexual relations are brief, motivated only by transient desires. Natural human wants are limited, and can be satisfied easily. Although individuals may occasionally fight over particular resources, it is generally easier for each to seek his own food than to get it by fighting; and natural compassion restrains the inhabitants of the state of nature from gratuitously harming one another. Since natural human beings interact so little, they have no concept of status and so cannot feel the Hobbesian desire for glory. According to Rousseau, Hobbes's mistake was to include in the natural desire for self-preservation, 'a multitude of passions which are the handiwork of society' (p. 27). Rousseau's state of nature is characterized neither by harmony nor disharmony, neither by cooperation nor conflict. It is so deeply asocial that such concepts simply do not apply.

Rousseau's conjectural history describes how, over many generations, human beings develop language, intelligence and social organization. In what he pictures as the happiest epoch of history, 'the true youth of the world', there are simple social structures, but property is still unknown; people live in economically self-sufficient families, supporting themselves through hunting and gathering. But, as a result of social interaction, people gradually come to value 'public esteem'. The first manifestations of this sense of value – admiration for strength, skill, handsome appearance, eloquence – are innocent enough, but: 'From these first preferences vanity and contempt were born on the one hand, and shame and envy on the other; and the fermentation caused by these new leavens finally produced compounds fatal to happiness and innocence' (pp. 38–39).

Decay sets in with the development of property and the division of labor, associated with the invention of agriculture and metallurgy, and the consequent growth of economic inequality. It is only at this stage that the state of nature begins to take on Hobbesian qualities. The final twist in the story is a Hobbesian social contract. But in Rousseau's account, this is nothing more than a crude protection racket, by which the rich and powerful exploit the poor and weak:

> Such was, or must have been, the origin of society and laws, which gave new fetters to the weak and new powers to the rich, irretrievably destroyed natural liberty, established forever the law of property and inequality, made clever usurpation into an irrevocable right, and, for the benefit of a few ambitious individuals, henceforth subjected the whole human race to labour, servitude, and misery. (pp. 44–45)

Once one Hobbesian society has come into existence, it is able to prey on less organized groups of people, whose only defense is to subject themselves to Hobbesian sovereigns too. Thus, the emergence of one politically and militarily organized society sets off a chain reaction which destroys the state of nature.

In *On Social Contract* (1988c), Rousseau tries to find a different form of social contract which could support a legitimate political order. Given his account of human nature, he faces an uphill task. He is starting from a position of alienation from human psychology as we now find it. If the contract is to satisfy his criterion of legitimacy, it must respect the natural liberty of mankind. But natural liberty is natural with respect to a primitive way of life, prior even to rationality and morality, that can never be recovered. The forces which have eroded that natural liberty are construed as unnatural and corrupting, but also as the inexorable consequences of economic and social development. Rousseau's analysis of *actual* human motivation leads to a Hobbesian form of civil society – not as something to be welcomed, but as a long-run equilibrium to which the path of human development leads. The problem is to escape this trap, 'taking men as they are and laws as they can be' (p. 85).

As a solution to this problem, Rousseau proposes a form of democracy in which every citizen participates in the process which determines the 'general will' and, once that general will has been determined, *treats it as his own will*. Thus, after accepting Rousseau's social contract, 'each person, joining forces with all, nevertheless obeys only himself and remains as free as before' (p. 92). For this construction to work, everyone must uphold an austere form of civic virtue. In public life, each individual must act *in the public interest*. When a person casts a vote, he may not express his private interests or his interests as a member of any 'partial association' smaller than the political unit: he must express his judgment about what is 'advantageous to the state'. If the majority opinion is contrary to his own, he concludes that his initial judgment was mistaken (pp. 101, 149, 151).[9] Rousseau expects there to be a sphere of private life within which individuals act on their own interests and judgments, but 'the sovereign' – that is, the citizens acting collectively as a public body – is the sole judge of what may properly be left to the sphere of private life (p. 102).

Rousseau realizes that all this requires 'a most remarkable change in man' (p. 95); but he does not explain how this is compatible with the human psychology of 'men as they are'. In his *Discourse on Political Economy* (1988b), he suggests that public education may solve the problem by training children from an early age 'not to perceive of their own existence, so to speak, except as a part of that of the state [so that] they may finally succeed in identifying themselves in some way with this greater whole' (p. 73). It seems that the 'remarkable change in man' involves some radical shift in each person's perceptions and modes of reasoning such that, when he acts in the role of citizen, he *identifies with* the political unit of which he is a part.

In modern philosophy, Martin Hollis (1998) endorses the spirit of Rousseau's analysis of the relationship between individual and society. Hollis proposes an ideal of a 'liberal community' in which rational individuals are able to identify with the communities of which they are members, and to act as members of those communities rather than as self-interested private individuals. This conception is 'liberal' in that individuals do not submerge their identities in their communities, but maintain a balance of private and public viewpoints, of the perspectives of 'I' and 'we'. Hollis suggests that the 'we'

---

[9] Later in the eighteenth century, this conception of collective decision-making was developed by Condorcet as an application of probability theory. Condorcet's 'jury theorem' presupposes that the propositions about which individuals vote really are either true or false. Each voter expresses a judgment about the truth or falsity of the relevant proposition, recognizing that this judgment, like that of any other voter, may be in error. After everyone has voted, each voter revises his judgment to take account of the information contained in other people's votes. See McLean and Hewitt (1994, pp. 34–40).

perspective of a citizen of a liberal community can be represented in rational choice theory by means of 'collective reasoning' or 'team thinking', an approach we examine in Section 7.

4. Fellow-feeling[10]

In a contemporary review of the *Discourse on Inequality*, Adam Smith argued that Rousseau's analysis rested on a fundamental mistake. While acknowledging the emotional force of Rousseau's writing, which has managed to make an untenable argument appear as 'only the true spirit of a republican carried a little too far', Smith notices that the argument assumes 'that there is in man no powerful instinct which necessarily determines him to seek society for its own sake'.[11] If there is no such principle in human nature, Smith implies, we cannot hope to achieve a stable social order.

It may seem surprising that Smith would make such a criticism. Generations of economists have been influenced by Smith's explanation of economic relations in terms of self-interest. There is no doubt that, for Smith, self-interest is one of the primary human motivations, and that many aspects of social order – particularly in the domain of economics – can be explained on the hypothesis that each individual acts on his or her own interest. Nevertheless, Smith's economics is developed alongside a theory of human nature in which assumptions about sociality are crucial. This theory of human nature has not had a comparable influence, but now that economists are beginning to reflect on the limitations of *homo economicus* as an explanatory model, it is worth looking more closely at what Smith has to say about sociality.

Smith's theory is set out in *Theory of Moral Sentiments* (1976a). The central concept in the theory is *fellow-feeling*. In the language of modern psychology, fellow-feeling is a mechanism which connects individuals' affective states (that is, psychological states which are perceived as pleasurable or painful). Through fellow-feeling, each person's affective states are influenced by his perceptions of the affective states of others. The mechanisms of fellow-feeling are fundamental properties of human nature, not reducible to anything more basic; their intensity depends on the degree to which other people's experiences are (as Smith puts it) 'brought home' to the person who has fellow-feeling for them. There are two main mechanisms.

First, there is a tendency for each person to identify with other people, imaginatively experiencing whatever affective states the other is believed to be experiencing in reality.

---

[10] This section draws on Sugden (2002).
[11] Letter to the editor of the *Edinburgh Review*, 1756; quoted by Ritter and Bondanella (1988, pp. 191–218). Smith's criticism of Rousseau is perhaps over-stated. As we have pointed out, Rousseau assumes a natural instinct for compassion, and sometimes suggests that this instinct underpins such 'social virtues' as generosity and clemency [e.g. Rousseau (1988c, pp. 28–29)]. The importance of sympathy can be seen as a common theme in the work of Rousseau, Hume and Smith – in marked contrast to Hobbes's robust seventeenth-century rationalism.

When one person sympathizes with another in this way, the former experiences feelings which are qualitatively similar to, but typically far weaker in intensity than, the feelings of the latter. These imaginatively-induced feelings are *fellow-feelings*. Thus: 'When we see a stroke aimed and just ready to fall upon the leg or arm of another person, we naturally shrink and draw back our own leg or our own arm; and when it does fall, we feel it in some measure, and are hurt by it as well as the sufferer' (p. 10). Similarly, we feel pleasure when we have a lively consciousness of other people's pleasure. This mechanism of fellow-feeling has some similarities with altruism, as that is modeled in modern economics (see Section 5); but it must be remembered that Smith is analyzing relations between people's affective states and not relations between their preferences.

The second mechanism is what Smith calls 'the pleasure of mutual sympathy' (pp. 13–16). Smith's hypothesis is that human beings derive pleasure from *all* forms of fellow-feeling, whether the fellow-feeling is for another person's pleasure (and hence pleasurable in itself) or for another person's pain (and hence painful in itself). Notice that this mechanism is not a simple reflection of pleasure and pain. From a theoretical point of view, it might seem more natural to propose a model in which all feelings are magnified by mutual sympathy. (Thus, if person A experiences pain, B's sympathy with A is painful to B, A's consciousness of B's sympathetic pain is painful to A, and so on.[12]) Smith considers such a model, but rejects it as inconsistent with what we know about human sympathy:

> The sympathy, which my friends express with my joy, might, indeed, give me pleasure by enlivening that joy: but that which they express with my grief could give me none, if it served only to enliven that grief. Sympathy, however, enlivens joy and alleviates grief. It enlivens joy by presenting another source of satisfaction; and it alleviates grief by insinuating into the heart almost the only agreeable sensation which it is at that time capable of receiving. (p. 14)

Notice that Smith is hypothesizing 'another source of satisfaction', distinct from the pleasures and pains that are constitutive of fellow-feeling. This satisfaction derives from the *correspondence of sentiments* between oneself and another. Smith proposes that all perceived correspondences of sentiment induce feelings of pleasure, and that all perceived dissonances of sentiment induce feelings of pain. He suggests that, in the case of sympathy for pain, the pleasures of mutual sympathy usually outweigh the pains of fellow-feeling, with the consequence that we 'seem to be pleased when we are able to sympathise with [another person's feelings of pain], and to be hurt when we are unable to do so' (p. 15).

One significant implication of this theory is that we have a natural desire for certain kinds of social interaction, independently of any instrumental benefits that society may give us. More precisely, we have a natural desire to engage in activities with other

---

[12] Bernheim and Stark's (1988) theory of altruism among marriage partners, discussed in Section 5, has exactly this property.

people in situations in which their sentiments will be aligned with ours. As an example, Smith discusses the difference between reading alone and reading together with another person:

> When we have read a book or poem so often that we can no longer find any amusement in reading it by ourselves, we can still take pleasure in reading it to a companion. To him it has all the graces of novelty; we enter into the surprise and admiration which it naturally excites in him, but which it is no longer capable of exciting in us; we consider all the ideas which it presents rather in the light in which they appear to him, than in that in which they appear to ourselves, and we are amused by sympathy with his amusement which thus enlivens our own. (p. 14)

If Smith is right, if the mere fact of doing something *together with another person* rather than alone can be a source of pleasure, then he has identified an element of sociality in human nature.

Smith's purpose in analyzing fellow-feeling is to provide the foundations for his theory of moral sentiments. The link between fellow-feeling and morality is the concept of *approval*. According to Smith, we approve of another person's sentiments just to the extent that we have fellow-feeling for them, or (the case of 'conditional sympathy') just to the extent that we are conscious that, were the other person's situation vividly brought home to us, we would have such fellow-feeling (p. 16). And moral sentiments just *are* generalized sentiments of approval. Thus, a person's sentiments have *propriety* – are morally appropriate – to the extent that they tend to induce fellow-feeling in others. An action has propriety to the extent that the motivating sentiment of the actor is in proportion to the cause that has excited it. An action has *merit* to the extent that it is the 'proper and approved object' of gratitude on the part of those who are benefited by it. Conversely, an action has *demerit* to the extent that it is the proper and approved object of resentment on the part of those who are harmed by it (pp. 67–69). In other words, actions have merit and demerit to the extent that the sentiments of gratitude and resentment they evoke tend to induce fellow-feeling.

Given this analysis of approval, Smith's hypothesis about the pleasure of mutual sympathy implies that we have a natural desire for the approval of others. Thus, we naturally have some motivation to act in accordance with prevailing standards of morality. As Smith puts it: 'Nature, when she formed man for society, endowed him with an original desire to please, and an original aversion to offend his brethren. She taught him to feel pleasure in their favourable, and pain in their unfavourable regard' (p. 116). Notice the idea that Nature has *formed man for society*. According to Smith, our natural dispositions for fellow-feeling and mutual sympathy have the effect – indeed, according to his natural theology, have the function – of orienting us to social life. Our moral sentiments can be understood as a complex spontaneous order, the unintended consequence of the interactions of individuals who are equipped with certain simpler, natural dispositions of sociality.

On this account, a code of morality is a certain kind of equilibrium of sentiments. The code specifies which sentiments have propriety in which circumstances. These sentiments have the propriety they do because they tend to evoke fellow-feeling. At the same time, each person's consciousness of the code motivates him to act as if motivated by the sentiments it approves. Consciously or unconsciously, our desire for approval leads us to adapt our sentimental repertoires so as to bring them in line with prevailing norms. This social process – Smith calls it 'the great school of self-command' (p. 145) – imparts a tendency for people who live together in a society to develop similar affective responses to similar stimuli, and to subscribe to norms which give approval to those responses.

In some respects, Smith's approach to understanding the moral character of social relations has been followed in modern economics. Society, as modeled by Smith, is not simply an equilibrium of the forces of self-interest. But it *is* an equilibrium of forces of individual motivation. These forces derive from psychological propensities that are natural to human beings, and which operate whatever kinds of societies people live in. The moral character of social relations derives from the propensity of human beings to be responsive to one another's feelings and interests. This fundamental idea has been developed in a range of modern economic theories of other-oriented motivations, which we discuss in the next section. However, this modern literature differs from Smith by representing other-oriented motivations as exogenously given preferences rather than as sentiments or affective states. As a result, Smith's conception of a spontaneous order *of sentiments* has been lost.

5. Other-oriented motivations in modern economics

Modern economic theory offers various ways of modeling behavior which take some account of sociality, at least in the sense of not assuming self-interest. This body of theory has arisen partly in response to explaining such phenomena as voluntary provision of public goods, the bequest motive, migrants' remittances, and more recently, experimentally generated data inconsistent with selfish maximization.[13] This theory is also partly motivated by a concern with certain puzzles thrown up by game theory, such as the Centipede and Prisoners' Dilemma games, where the strategies it recommends result in outcomes inferior to those induced by alternative strategies which seem reasonable to many real agents. There is generally no departure from individualism, however, the modification being restricted to an expansion of the set of arguments in the individual's utility function. Other-oriented motivations are therefore generally treated as part of an individualistic and instrumental model. We now examine a range of such models.[14]

---

[13] The literature on public goods and public goods experiments is reviewed by Bardsley (2000b).
[14] We make no claim that the models we discuss are historically the original versions of the theoretical strategies they exemplify. Our main aim is substantive rather than historical, to show how social phenomena are modeled in economics. The best way of doing this is to present familiar modern examples.

5.1. Rational choice altruism

Altruism is frequently invoked by economists to explain relations between family members,[15] and is often cited as an explanation of contributions to public goods.[16] The word 'altruism' was originally coined by Auguste Comte (1875), who used it to denote a selfless motivation to act in others' interests (as opposed to a motivation to act in others' interests for an ulterior, selfish reason, such as to cut a good figure). The apparently similar notion that individuals obtain utility from others' well-being dates back to the utilitarianism of Francis Edgeworth's (1881) *Mathematical Psychics*, and to Jeremy Bentham's (1970, pp. 42–44) classification of 'the pleasures of benevolence' as one of the fourteen 'simple pleasures' that human beings can feel. One difference is that Comte's conception does not rule out that people can act in others' interests independently of their own preferences. It is the Edgeworthian notion that is formalized in models of altruism, which we now outline in simplified form.

Let i denote an altruist and j an individual i cares about. Altruism has been modeled in two basic ways. In one type of model, others' *utility* becomes an argument in the utility function, that is, $U_i = U_i(x_i, U_j)$, where U_i is i's utility, x_i is the vector of goods consumed by i, and altruism is represented by the assumption $\partial U_i / \partial U_j > 0$. One then derives a mapping from commodity allocations to utilities. Alternatively, one can start with a mapping from the utility individuals gain from commodities to inclusive utilities. That is, $U_i = U_i(u_i(x_i), u_j(x_j))$, where U_i is the utility function which represents i's overall preferences, u_i is a function which represents i's tastes with respect to his own consumption of goods, and altruism is represented by the assumption $\partial U_i / \partial u_j > 0$. (From now on, in presenting models of other-oriented motivations, we will maintain this distinction between U_i and u_i. Some theories distinguish more simply between 'utility', interpreted as a representation of overall preference, and 'material payoffs', typically interpreted as amounts of money. When presenting such theories, we use U_i to represent the former and u_i to represent the latter.) In the first type of model there are interdependent utility functions, defining a set of simultaneous equations. In the second, there are arguments shared between utility functions. In the first case it is usual to impose restrictions such that one arrives ultimately at a system of functions of the second form.[17]

Altruistic interdependence of utilities can generate some instructively odd predictions concerning interpersonal relations, in just the kinds of context one would think the model most applicable to. First, consider a romantic involvement between persons i and j. Suppose i derives relatively little satisfaction from personal consumption, but cares greatly about the welfare of j. It turns out that i can be better off if j cares little

---

[15] For example, see the intergenerational altruism model of Barro (1974), Becker's (1974) model of the family, and the literature they have spawned.

[16] For example, see McLean (1987) and Elster (1989).

[17] For discussion of the technical issues involved in moving between one formulation and the other see Bergstrom (1999).

about i's well-being relative to his own consumption, since to the extent that j is altruistic, i suffers indirectly from her own low enjoyment of personal consumption – through depressing j. One might regard such cases as interesting possibilities that altruism actually gives rise to, as Douglas Bernheim and Oded Stark (1988) claim in a paper about why 'nice guys finish last'. It is also possible, however, to read them – as Benedetto Gui (2000) does – as a *reductio ad absurdum* of the approach. It seems that i and j do not really relate as partners at all, since the other's concern is generally perceived to be of direct importance for the quality of a relationship. Good partners, then, share each other's misfortunes in a very different manner to that depicted by utility interdependence.

Rational choice altruism also specifies the wrong kind of inter-relatedness between contributors to public goods. It is well known that the economic theory of pure public good provision, in the absence of altruism, yields predictions that are both counter-intuitive and false.[18] It predicts near-zero provision by voluntary contributions. It also yields comparative static predictions of complete crowding-out between individuals' contributions[19] and neutrality of the quantity produced with respect to income distribution and the number of contributors. Also, if incomes are heterogeneous, only the richest will contribute. These implausible comparative static results are not changed by adding the assumption that donors are altruistic towards one another, since individuals' contributions are still perfect substitutes for one another. The same results also extend to cases in which each member of a set of potential donors is altruistic towards a common set of potential recipients, as in a model in which voluntary contributions to famine relief are motivated by altruism. In such models, the assumption of altruism makes the consumption (or utility) enjoyed by recipients into a public good for the group of donors. The theory of voluntary contributions to public goods then applies, and the usual counter-intuitive results are generated.[20]

The difficulties of explaining voluntary contributions to charities as altruism can be illustrated by a simple example. Imagine you are about to give £5 to a charity. Given that you are instrumentally rational, this implies you rank the resulting state of affairs at least as highly as any other you can bring about. Now suppose another individual unexpectedly gives £5 just before you arrive. In terms of the state of affairs that then

---

[18] For the theoretical results referred to in this paragraph, see Bergstrom, Blume and Varian (1986).

[19] Econometric evidence relevant to the crowding-out hypothesis is presented by Paqué (1986), Abrams and Schmitz (1984), Steinberg (1985, 1991), Khanna, Posnett and Sandler (1995) and Connolly (1997). The extent of crowding out is either minimal (the first three studies) or negative (the others). For experimental evidence that there is crowding-in between contributions see Weimann (1994), Croson (1999) and Bardsley (2000c).

[20] One may question the Cournot–Nash assumption of 'zero conjectural variations' in the standard public good model, usually used to derive the free-riding prediction. An alternative approach is to assume that conjectural variations are *consistent*, that is, that each individual's ex ante conjectures are confirmed ex post. But this makes the predictions of the model more counter-intuitive rather than less. Within the standard framework of utility maximization and a pure public good, and given the natural assumption that private consumption is a normal good, consistency of conjectures requires that individuals expect their contributions to be *negatively* correlated. This implies that, in equilibrium, contributions are lower than the predictions of the Cournot–Nash model. See Sugden (1985).

obtains, it is exactly as if you had given your donation and the other person had given £5 to you. If you would not donate all the extra income in the second case, you cannot, consistently with this, give your £5 in the first.[21]

5.2. Warm glow

Another influential approach to other-oriented motivation theory is to depict an agent as deriving utility directly from an act of unselfish behavior, independently of any consequences it gives rise to. The idea is that agents will feel good about themselves – they will experience 'warm glow' – if they act unselfishly, and so act in pursuit of these feelings. This approach is the starting point for James Andreoni's (1990) theory of voluntary contributions to public goods. In this model, an altruist's utility function takes the form $U_i = U_i(x_i, w_i, z)$, where w_i is i's contribution to a public good, and z is the total amount of the public good that is supplied as a result of everyone's contributions; it is assumed that $\partial U_i / \partial w_i > 0$. The idea is i's contribution jointly produces the public good itself and the private good of warm glow (the satisfaction derived from *contributing to* the public good). This model can be interpreted as a special case of the impure public good model of Richard Cornes and Todd Sandler (1984), in which a public good gets provided voluntarily because contributors derive a private by-product by increasing its supply.

The motivation for warm glow theory is in large part to overcome the false predictions of the public good model. As Andreoni notes, however, the prediction in a public good context is still one of crowding-out, albeit to a lesser extent. In fact, there is considerable evidence of crowding-in, particularly from experiments.[22] More fundamentally though, the consistency of the proposition that rational agents are motivated by the prospect of good feelings about their action is highly suspect. There are grounds for claiming that warm glow *presupposes* the rationality of the behavior it is supposed to explain.

Stanley Benn (1978), in a discussion of the rationality of voting, states the basic case. Benn offers the hypothesis that voting is not instrumentally rational, but expressively rational (or *wertrational*) – a concept we consider in Section 6. The 'principle or ideal of conduct' which provides the key to understanding the expressive rationality of an act is not a *consequence* of the act; rather, the act is an *instance* of this principle or ideal, so that the link between the act and its point is conceptual, not causal:

> The point of a wertrational act, if not immediately evident, can be explained only by exhibiting it as an instance of some principle or ideal of conduct. In that sense, it is true, something done for its own sake may be done for the sake of something else: but it would be a caricature to say that it is done for the sake of the satisfaction of having done it. For there would often be no satisfaction either in doing it or

---

[21] The example is borrowed from Margolis (1982). Sugden (1982) uses similar examples in an early critique of rational choice altruism as an explanation of philanthropy.

[22] See Footnote 19 above.

having done it if the agent had no prior belief that it was worth doing apart from the satisfaction. [Benn (1978, p. 8)]

To be satisfied with this argument we would need to establish the 'no satisfaction without prior belief' premise. Let us stay with the public good example. First we may note that without an account of why it is that warm glow adheres to contribution and not to free-riding, it should be equally admissible to have as premise that one can only obtain warm glow from free-riding. Moreover, we can give a reason why this might be so: the standard theory says that, for most potential contributors, only free-riding is rational. A free-rider might then derive self-satisfaction from reflecting on the fact that he has acted rationally, but as contributing is irrational, no such satisfaction is available from donation. Notice that Benn's point would still stand for the non-contributors: the warm glow would add nothing to our understanding of free-riding.

If, as Andreoni's text indicates, warm glow arises from contribution because of people's moral beliefs that donation is either dutiful or good, in contrast with free-riding, this implies Benn's 'prior belief'. To deny this implication one would have to hold that the belief that donation is virtuous does not provide a reason for action. If this were the case one should have to ask why a rational agent should feel good about doing something he has no reason to do. In sum, if warm glow arises from reflecting on an act well done, then it must fall into the class of states Jon Elster (1983) calls 'essentially by-products'. The notion of an act well done implies that there were reasons for which it was done, so warm glow in this sense presupposes the rationality of making a contribution; it cannot found it.

This critique has been framed in terms of a hedonistic interpretation of Andreoni's utility function, in line with Andreoni's (1990) text. Alternatively, one might interpret this function in revealed preference terms, merely as a re-description of the fact that the relevant individual gives voluntarily and intentionally. But then this 'explanation' of giving tells us nothing more than the facts that we are trying to explain. Theories of instrumental rationality can provide *explanations* of behavior only if there is some distinction between actions (the things that individuals choose between, and which the theory is intended to explain) and consequences (the things that are brought about by actions). If warm glow is not an affective state, describable independently of the act of giving, there is no gap between consequence and action, and so there is no conceptual space in which explanation can operate.

5.3. Inequality aversion

Recently, there has been growing interest in models which depict egalitarian motivations. These models are primarily motivated by the need to explain experimental evidence from 'ultimatum' and 'dictator' games, but they have also been used to explain contributions to laboratory public goods. The dictator game is perhaps the simplest imaginable experimental test of the extent of selfishness: a subject is allocated an endowment and has to split it between herself and another subject. Typically, a substantial proportion of subjects choose to give some of the endowment away.[23] The ultimatum game differs in that the recipient has the power to reject the proposed split, in which case the entire endowment is destroyed. Standard game theory predicts the smallest possible offer will be made and accepted, whereas the modal offer in this context is a 50/50 split with inferior offers frequently rejected.[24]

The hypothesis of inequality aversion is that subjects dislike being worse off than others, but also being dislike being better off. In Ernst Fehr and Klaus Schmidt's (1999) version,

$$U_i = u_i + \frac{\psi_i \sum_{j \neq i} \max(u_i - u_j, 0)}{n - 1} + \frac{\varsigma_i \sum_{j \neq i} \max(u_j - u_i, 0)}{n - 1}$$

with $\varsigma_i \leqslant \psi_i \leqslant 0$; n is the number of individuals in the relevant group. Since the second term on the right hand side of the above represents disadvantageous inequality, this amounts to the proposition that agents enjoy consumption but dislike inequality between their own consumption and that of others, with disadvantageous inequality being more disliked than advantageous inequality. Gary Bolton and Axel Ockenfels' (2000) formulation differs in that it assumes that subjects dislike a payoff which diverges from the mean, regardless of the distribution of payoffs amongst others, and does not assume either additively separable utility or linearity. The shared feature is that subjects trade off the enjoyment of personal consumption against a desire to be equal.

Theories of inequality aversion have the merit of having some degree of experimental support. A concern for equity would explain giving in dictator games, rejections of unequal offers in ultimatum games, and the conditionality of one person's contribution on those of others (that is, crowding-in) in a laboratory public good context. However, not all the laboratory evidence can be explained. For example, subjects often sacrifice their own income to make the payoff of another player *higher than their own*, if the opportunity cost of doing so is low enough [Cox (2000), Charness and Rabin (2000)]. Applied outside the laboratory, where endowments and incomes are heterogeneous, these theories have some implausible implications. For example, they imply that only relatively well-off agents contribute to public goods. This is because the only motive to contribute, in either version of the theory, is that one's own payoff is otherwise disproportionately large.

It is possible that a more subtle functional form could increase the explanatory power of the inequality aversion model. But, we suggest, the weaknesses of this approach are more fundamental. The concept of inequality aversion is parasitic on egalitarian concerns about the distribution of income. *In discussions about public policy*, distributional issues are often important; for this reason, distribution is central to welfare economics, which perhaps helps to explain why economists are predisposed to interpret

---

[23] There is some evidence that much of this giving can be eliminated by using a sufficiently impersonal experimental set-up. See Hoffman, McCabe and Smith (1996).

[24] See Roth (1995) for an overview of the evidence.

other-oriented motivations as egalitarian. But concerns about the distribution of income do not appear to play much of a role *in everyday private life*, where voluntary transfers are rare. Most social interactions take place within a framework of socially accepted entitlements, expectations and norms. For example, consider relations between higher-paid and lower-paid colleagues in a workplace. In such a setting, there might be an expectation that the higher-paid workers contribute more than the lower-paid to a public good from which they benefit jointly (say, an office party); but it would be extremely unusual to see the former making unilateral gifts to the latter. Yet such transfers are exactly what we should expect if people were motivated by inequality aversion.

5.4. Rabin's theory of reciprocity

Reciprocity essentially involves doing as one is done by: a reciprocator benefits those whose actions benefit her (positive reciprocity) and/or hurts those whose actions are harmful to her (negative reciprocity). What is now the best known approach to modeling reciprocity is that proposed by Matthew Rabin (1993).

Rabin's theory applies to two-player normal-form games.[25] Consider any such game. Let i be one of the players and let j be the other; let a_i be the strategy chosen by player i; let b_i be player j's beliefs about what strategy player i is choosing; and let c_i be player i's beliefs about what strategy player j believes player i is choosing.[26] Let $u_i(a_i, a_j)$ be i's material payoff if i chooses a_i and j chooses a_j. Now consider i's decision about which strategy to choose, for given beliefs b_j about what j is choosing. For each strategy that i might choose, there is an expected material payoff for each player; thus, i faces a *menu* (or utility-possibility frontier) of feasible payoff combinations (u_i, u_j). Rabin defines i's choice from this menu to be more or less *kind* according to the extent to which i accepts less than the maximum payoff for herself in order to benefit j. More formally, he defines a *kindness function* $f_i(a_i, b_j)$ for each i. This measures the kindness of i's choosing a_i, given his beliefs b_j.

In the most general version of the theory, Rabin assumes that this measure of kindness increases as j's expected payoff increases, and that there is some level of payoff for j at which i's kindness is zero. (This is called the *equitable payoff*.) Except in the trivial case in which i cannot affect j's payoff, it is assumed that there are at least some sufficiently high payoff levels at which i's kindness is strictly positive and other sufficiently low levels at which it is strictly negative. In the restricted version of the theory that Rabin

---

[25] Dufwenberg and Kirchsteiger (2004) extend Rabin's theory to games in extensive form. Falk and Fischbacher (1998) and Charness and Rabin (2000) propose further modifications and to Rabin's original approach.

[26] We state these definitions in Rabin's own words. We interpret a_i as the objective probability distribution over i's pure strategies (thus allowing for randomization by i), b_i as j's subjective probability distribution over i's pure strategies, and c_i as the probability distribution over i's pure strategies that can be derived (by reduction of compound probabilities) from i's subjective probability distribution over the set of possible b_j distributions.

mostly uses, the payoff function (and hence the equitable payoff) is uniquely determined by the formal properties of the menu of payoff combinations. The implication is that 'equity' is defined solely in terms of the distribution of payoffs between the players. Notice that kindness, in Rabin's sense, is the sort of behavior that would result from the instrumentally rational but other-oriented motivations assumed in the theories of rational choice altruism and inequality aversion.

However, Rabin does not assume that players are directly motivated to be kind. Rather, kindness is the standard by which reciprocity is defined. In Rabin's model, the utility function that governs i's behavior is:

$$U_i = u_i(a_i, b_j) + f_j(b_j, c_i) f_i(a_i, b_j).$$

In this formula, $u_i(a_i, b_j)$ is i's expected material payoff, $f_j(b_j, c_i)$ measures j's kindness to i, as perceived by i, and $f_i(a_i, b_j)$ measures i's kindness to j.[27] This functional form has the property that i gains utility both by reciprocating kindness (if $f_j(b_j, c_i)$ is positive, U_i is increasing in i's kindness) and by reciprocating unkindness (if $f_j(b_j, c_i)$ is negative, U_i is decreasing in i's kindness). Rabin then defines equilibrium (on the analogue of Nash equilibrium) as a situation in which, for each player i, the chosen strategy a_i maximizes U_i for given b_j and c_i, and in which beliefs and actions are mutually consistent (that is $a_i = b_i = c_i$).

As a game-theoretic construct, this model is unusual in allowing i's utility to depend *directly* on her beliefs about what j will do and, still more unusually, on her beliefs about what j believes she will do. This requires the use of *psychological game theory*, as proposed by John Geanakoplos, David Pearce and Ennio Stacchetti (1989). As an account of human motivation, Rabin's model arguably represents a more social form of reasoning than do rational choice altruism or inequality aversion, since it makes our attitudes towards others dependent on their intentions towards ourselves. However, Rabin's concept of reciprocity is ultimately based on a standard of 'kindness' which – like the motivations assumed in those other theories – takes no account of expectations, entitlements or social norms.

To see how this feature of the theory limits its explanatory power, notice that the theory does not allow a distinction to be made between harming someone (for example, by breaking a promise to pay for a purchase) and not making a unilateral transfer to that person (for example, by not paying *more* than one has promised). According to ordinary use of the word 'harm', one does *not* harm another person by failing to make such a transfer. It is only in special settings where something of the kind can be maintained. Such a setting is, arguably, implicitly depicted through game theory, since the matter of how a game situation arises, including facts such as the relationship between the individuals and how they come to have their relative positions, is treated as irrelevant

---

[27] Notice that this functional form implies that 'kindness' is measured in the same units as material payoffs, for example, in units of money, and that utility is cardinal. This may strike the modern reader as odd, but it allows the functional form to be simply operationalized in experimental games.

to the analysis of a game once the payoffs have been specified. Another such setting is that of the laboratory experiment in which endowments are generally received as 'manna from heaven', rather than having been earned. It is possible that subjects in the ultimatum game, for example, see the situation as one in which property rights over the endowment are to be decided, rather than one in which they have already been set. It is perhaps this which makes responders so ready to destroy the entire endowment if an uneven split is proposed, and consequently makes proposers wary of making too unequal an offer.

We suggest that Rabin's theory of reciprocity, like the theory of inequality aversion, relies on the implicit assumption that, at the start of a game, players treat the potential payoffs as *unowned* – as resources to which no one has any specific prior entitlement. Thus, these theories describe the effects of certain norms of equality and reciprocity which are specific to a narrow range of social contexts. Moreover, the nature of such norms and their relevance to rational agents represent unexplored dimensions of sociality which the theories take for granted. To make use of these theories, we need to know their domains of applicability; and to identify these domains, we need a deeper account of sociality.

6. Expressive rationality

We now consider some more radical proposals about how sociality should be modeled – proposals which challenge tenets of methodological individualism. We begin with the concept of *expressive rationality*. Rational choice theory is inadequate, proponents of expressive rationality would say, because it overlooks an important type of connection between internal states of the agent and reasons for action. Take the example of futile resistance to an oppressive regime. Even if it is in a consequentialist sense irrational, such action is surely more understandable for someone deeply committed to the cause than it is for someone who does not have strong feelings about it. Rational choice theory offers no insight into this.

Expressive rationality is usually contrasted with *instrumental* rationality – that is, the rationality of choosing an action as a means to some end, which is the picture of rationality embodied in standard, outcome-oriented utility theory. The distinction is articulated originally by Max Weber (1968), whose concept *wertrational* translates literally as 'value-rational'. A clear statement of what it amounts to is offered by Benn (1978, p. 3)

> An action can be rational for a person regardless of its payoff if it expresses attitudes or principles that it would be inconsistent of him not to express under appropriate conditions, given the character which he is generally content to acknowledge as his own. This is what is called being true to oneself.

Hollis (1977, pp. 135–142, 1998, p. 147) gives a similar account.

Appeals to the concept of expressive rationality are frequently coupled with a thesis of the social determination of appropriate expressive actions. The significance of an action, or its connotation(s), does not on this view arise between the agent and it, but is instead dependent on the existence of a shared rule, standard or norm.[28] This is what makes *voting* an appropriate expression of political opinion, for example, rather than singing political songs in the bath or heckling others as they turn out to vote. Agents are concerned with the meanings of their acts, not the consequences of them. This implies a different picture of interaction than obtains in game theory, because, given the social determination thesis, there are *communal* constraints on actions. That is to say, there are constraints and opportunities imposed not through interaction with specific others but by the prevalent attitudes and beliefs of members of a community. In game theory, in contrast, the only relevant attitudes and beliefs of others are those of the specific people an agent is to interact with, and these can be relevant either in predicting what the others will do or because one cares about their approval.

Thus, the role of norms is different in the two kinds of theory. In theories of rational choice, norms govern preferences. In theories of expressive rationality, they govern the appropriateness of acts as expressions of particular meanings. This latter articulation of the relevance of norms for rational agents embodies a deeper conception of sociality.

Some readers may object that expressive rationality can after all be incorporated into rational choice theory, using a suitably broad interpretation of the 'consequences' over which individuals have preferences. Why cannot the expressive content of an act be treated as a property of its consequences, and thus as a source of utility [as in Geoffrey Brennan and Loren Lomasky's (1985) model of the expressive value of voting]? However, there are good reasons to resist such a move.

We have already noted that the characteristic, minimal predictive power of rational choice theory depends on a distinction between actions and consequences. Even the familiar microeconomic prediction of the negative substitution effect of a price increase is lost if we allow utility to flow directly from the action of purchasing goods, rather than from the goods that are bought.[29] Yet an 'expressive consequence' appears to have the notion of (a disjunction of) certain actions built into it. For one can express something only by acting and, if a certain action is performed, it is a matter of logic, given the meaning of that action, whether a certain expressive consequence is instantiated or not. One cannot, logically, express approval for the labor party by voting conservative, for example, since voting conservative does not count as an expression of approval for labor. Whilst if one votes conservative, it follows that one has expressed approval for

---

[28] See, for example, Hargreaves Heap (1997) and Benn's contributions to Benn (1978). Cancian (1975) offers a view of social norms very amenable to their being an element in expressive reasons, in which they are seen as rules mapping actions to character attributes.

[29] We may also ask whether the consistency properties that rational choice theory imposes on preferences are meaningful in the absence of the distinction between action and consequence. That some such properties presuppose this distinction is argued by Sugden (1991).

conservatism.[30] Therefore the incorporation of the expressive dimension of an action into its consequence erodes the act/consequence distinction which gives rational choice theory its predictive power.

Another reason for seeing expressive rationality as inconsistent with utility maximization is that it involves an agent trying to realize an ideal self, or 'identity', thus placing the agent at a distance from at least some of his internal states – his preferences or values – so as to affirm them or modify them [Hargreaves Heap et al. (1992, pp. 22–23)]. This requires a theory with more structure than standard rational choice theory.

7. Team reasoning

In a typical economic model, the collective behavior of a group of people is an unintentional by-product of the maximizing behavior of the separate individuals who make up the group. Really, one could say, there is no collective behavior at all: the individuals behave essentially as they would in isolation, with the presence of other agents merely providing a different opportunity set. There is therefore no genuine sense of *participation* with others, of *joining in*. The alternative thesis of *team reasoning* is that a set of individuals can somehow unite to become a group agent, each individual acting as a part of that agent.

Consider a game between two players, in which each player has two alternative strategies *High* and *Low*. If both players choose *High*, each receives a cash prize of £10; if both choose *Low*, each receives £5; otherwise, each receives nothing. We assume that each player's utility is monotonically increasing in money. What is it rational for the players to do? The answer seems self-evident: that each should choose *High*. But, puzzlingly, the standard theory of rational choice cannot justify this answer. Granted the assumption that the players are perfectly rational and perfectly informed, the most that be proved is that *if* each expected the other to play *High*, then each would be rational to play *High* too. But, equally, *if* each expected the other to play *Low*, then each would be rational to play *Low*.

One might have thought that, for two agents with a minimal degree of social orientation, it would be a trivial problem to coordinate on the unique pair of strategies which together lead to the outcome that is best for both. Yet none of the models of other-oriented motivation presented in Section 5 guarantees this kind of coordination. Because the interests of the players are perfectly aligned, adding the assumption that the players are altruistic would make no essential difference to the coordination problem they face.[31] Whichever strategies are played, each player gets the same payoff as

---

[30] Left-wing voters in France's 2002 presidential elections performed theatrical displays of mock disinfection when voting for Jaques Chiraq, in preference to Jean-Marie Le Pen, presumably because they wanted to negate their expression of approval for him.

[31] The problem of accounting for the rationality of coordinating on a Pareto-dominant equilibrium was first noticed by moral philosophers, who saw it as a problem for act utilitarianism – that is, for a theory in which

the other; so inequality aversion has no bite. In the Pareto-inferior Nash equilibrium of the game (that is, when both players choose *Low*), each player is being as 'kind' to the other as it is possible to be, given the other's strategy; so reciprocity in Rabin's sense cannot detract from the stability of this undesirable equilibrium.

However, if the agents start by asking themselves not 'What should I do?' but instead 'What should *we* do?' the answer 'Play *High*' seems to be immediately evident, without a preliminary excursion into expectation formation. This idea offers a straightforward solution to the problem of explaining why coordination on *High* is so obviously rational: the solution is to conceive of the two players as a collective entity – a *team* – in which each member acts as part of the whole. (We stress: as *part of* the whole, not *in the interests of* the whole. If each acts as a rational individual, separately trying to maximize the sum of payoffs to the two of them, the problem remains.) Sugden (1991, 1993, 2000) and Michael Bacharach (1999) offer models of this mode of team reasoning.

Hollis (1998, pp. 126–142, 150–154) presents team reasoning as an account of 'the bond of society', and suggests that it offers a decision-theoretic formulation of Rousseau's 'most remarkable change in man'. Recall that, for Rousseau, the constraints of social life can be reconciled with the demands of liberty if individuals, when acting in the role of citizen, *identify* with the political unit to which they belong, and treat the collective decisions of that unit – the 'general will' – as *their own*.

To view some of the issues involved in analyzing team reasoning, it is useful to outline Sugden's (1984) 'reciprocity theory', intended as an explanation of voluntary provision of public goods. Sugden proposes a model in which individuals maximize self-interested utility subject to constraints of positive reciprocity. People honor what they perceive to be their obligations to each other, conditional on other people honoring theirs, with obligations being defined relative to ideal levels of contribution. For any agent i, i's obligations are as follows: for any set of people G including i, the ideal level of contribution is that which i would choose to be made by *everyone* in G (himself included), given the actual contributions of people outside G. If the other members of G contribute at least this amount, i is obliged to do so too; otherwise he is obliged only to reciprocate the minimum contribution in the group. (Notice that i has potential obligations to *all* sets of individuals; thus, his obligations to particular subsets of G may require him to contribute more than is required by his obligation to G itself.) The theory is a rational choice theory, not a moral choice theory. It does not assert that the 'obligations' it describes really are morally binding: rather, it assumes that individuals treat these obligations as morally binding constraints on rational action. By virtue of this assumption, the theory predicts under-supply of the public good in equilibrium, positive comparative static relationships between individuals' contributions, and that individuals contribute only to those public goods which benefit them personally.

Reciprocity as represented in this model is significantly different from reciprocity as represented by Rabin. One difference is that reciprocity appears as a moral constraint

---

moral agents treat other people's utility exactly on a par with their own. See Hodgson (1967) and Regan (1980).

on utility-maximization rather than as a source of utility. In this respect the model can be thought of as incorporating aspects of expressive rationality: individuals act on a principle, the principle that free-riding is morally wrong. A second difference is that reciprocity is defined in terms of participation in the collective action of groups, rather than one individual's being 'kind' or 'unkind' to another. Each individual is presented as asking 'What should we do?' In this respect, the model is one of team reasoning.

However, each individual answers this question by looking at which actions by 'us' would maximize *his* utility function. Isomorphism between individual and collective rationality would dictate that what *we* ought to do depends on *our* objective, just as what *I* ought to do depends on *mine*. Later theories of team reasoning have used the notion of *team preferences*. Team preferences, as viewed by an individual team member, represent that individual's conception of the team's goal; they are not necessarily derivable from that individual's personal preferences, or even from the personal preferences of all team members. In this respect, team reasoning is a broader concept than reciprocity: mutual benefit is just one type of goal that the members of a team might work together to achieve [Bacharach (1999), Sugden (2000)].

Thus, accepting the idea of team reasoning seems to commit decision theory to further alien concepts. The isomorphism between individual and team agency appears to commit us to group counterparts to all the concepts used to analyze individual agency: group beliefs, group intentions and group goals. To the extent that one embraces this isomorphism, one then faces the task of explaining how individuals can move between two distinct types of agency. What could make it rational to team reason, or to reason as an individual, in a given context? Even the question 'Should I reason as an individual or a team member?' has an analogue: 'Should we reason as a team or as individuals?' Each of these questions seems ill-formed, since it presupposes a unit of agency before asking what the unit of agency ought to be.

The concept of group intention has received considerable attention, the problem of explaining the determination of the unit of agency rather less.[32] Without an account of this determination, the puzzle posed by the game of *High* and *Low* has not been entirely resolved – if we take team loyalties as given prior to analysis of a game, for instance, the puzzle will be replicated in a game between teams. This perhaps indicates that we have still missed something essential in sociality, for team reasoning without an account of group membership is more *plural* agency than social; it is the rational agency of the individual written across several individuals.

In different ways, Bacharach (1999) and Sugden (2002) suggest that an explanation of how the unit of agency is *in fact* determined has to come from outside the framework of rational choice theory. Bacharach refers to the literature in social psychology which deals with the formation of 'group identity'. His ultimate intention seems to be

---

[32] For discussion of group intentions see Tuomela and Miller (1988), Searle (1990, 1995), Bratman (1992), Gilbert (1989) and Kutz (2000). Only Gilbert (1989) offers an account of group beliefs. Hurley (1989), Sugden (2000) and Bardsley (2000a, Chapter 5) discuss the problem of determining the unit of agency.

to make the specification of team units endogenous in a form of decision theory which takes account of how decision problems are perceived or 'framed' by agents; the perspectives of 'I' and 'we' are to be treated as different frames. The process by which individuals become aware of particular frames can be affected by the payoff structure of the game (for example, the fact that a game offers possibilities for mutual gain may help to prime a 'we' frame), but it may also be affected by contextual factors that are treated as irrelevant in conventional game theory.[33] Sugden discusses Smith's account of fellow-feeling. He suggests that correspondences of sentiment within a group of individuals, induced by the psychological mechanisms explained by Smith, may provide the basis for a sense of group identity and a perception of group preferences.

8. Sociality and the 'private language' argument

So far, we have explored the question of sociality in economics by examining specific historical figures and specific contemporary models of social behavior. We have encountered some problems with this body of literature from the inside, seeing that the models proposed have limited success in dealing with the problems which motivate them. Many of these problems seem to stem from tensions between the methodological individualism that is characteristic of economic theorizing and the social nature of the phenomena that are being explained. It would be a serious omission if we were not also to discuss what many take to be a direct attack on methodological individualism from philosophers of language. At issue in this literature is whether social phenomena can be wholly explained in terms of non-social concepts.

It is interesting that Hobbes himself – the patron saint of methodological individualism – may be read as proposing a view of language according to which it does not arise from interactions between rational, asocial beings. On the origin of language, Hobbes writes: 'The first author of speech was God himself, that instructed Adam how to name such creatures as he presented to his sight; For the scripture goeth no further in this matter' [Hobbes (1962, Part I, Chapter 4)]. Notice that Hobbes states that God *teaches* Adam a language; Adam is therefore introduced to language through a social relationship. Of course, the sincerity of Hobbes' theistic pronouncements is highly debatable, consistency with scripture not being optional for authors in the seventeenth century. But there is at least a *prima facie* case for holding that Hobbes himself is tempted by the social view of language. For so far as consistency with the Bible goes, would it not have been sufficient to say that God gave Adam the gift of speech? Leaving aside this historical matter, it is clear that one may nonetheless interpret Hobbes as having a purely instrumental view of language, in which it functions as a useful tool for thought, with the latter nonetheless capable of working without it.

---

[33] Some of these ideas are only hinted at in Bacharach (1999); they are more fully developed in the manuscript of a book on which he was working when he died in 2002, now forthcoming as Bacharach (2006).

The champion of a social view of language is supposedly Ludwig Wittgenstein, with his celebrated *private language argument* There are two main understandings of what constitutes this argument, as set out in Wittgenstein's (1953) *Philosophical Investigations*. We distinguish them primarily through the conclusion that is drawn from 'the' argument.

The first piece of private language argumentation (which we call PLA1) is centered around §258 of *Philosophical Investigations* and purports to establish the impossibility of a *necessarily* private language, a language which could, in principle, be understood by just one person. One often hears the following kind of query: 'How could I know that the image I have of *red* is not the one you have of *blue*?' This is a natural question to ask if one thinks that perceptions are ideas in the mind, and that others' minds are unobservable. Such a position is the standpoint of the traditional philosophy of mind stemming from René Descartes, according to which the mind is a kind of box of ideas, the contents of which are transparent to its possessor but inaccessible to others and do not necessarily correspond to anything external. The poser of the color question clearly thinks that the same word 'red' could have different meanings for different people, and if the mind cannot be observed it would be difficult to see how anyone could know which meaning it had for another person. PLA1 is intended to show that it does not make sense to say that a word has an incommunicable meaning. Although it has some consequences for economics, in undermining firstly objections to interpreting utility with reference to mental states and secondly an argument against interpersonal comparisons of utility [Peacock (1996)], PLA1 does not bear on the issue of sociality we address here.[34]

In the context of the present paper, we are more concerned with the second version of the private language argument, PLA2. This is a socially holistic interpretation of Wittgenstein, most famously espoused by Saul Kripke (1982, Chapters 2–3), but also proposed by Peter Winch (1958, pp. 24–33) and others.[35] The conclusion of PLA2 is the stronger claim that language is essentially social. That is to say, whilst we can easily think up private uses of words, these always rely ultimately on there being socially established ones. This argument supposedly resides in Wittgenstein's discussion of rule-following preceding §258.

PLA2 stems from a puzzle about how rule-following can be determinate. Wittgenstein's example is of a student attempting to continue a series of numbers. The problem is that any finite series is compatible with an indefinite number of continuations. For example, the series '2, 4, 6, 8, ...' would be continued by any normal reader of this paper '10, 12, 14, 16, ...'. However, it is also possible to conceive the continuation as '9, 11, 13, 15, 16, ...'. The number of possible continuations one can come up with is

---

[34] See Candlish (1980, 1998) for a clear reconstruction of PLA1.

[35] Kripke's version is more extreme than that stated here, in the sense that the argument is presented as one leading to skepticism about the notion of meaning, and its replacement with another notion. This has found little support on the exegetical side, but has generated much debate in its own right. See Boghossian (1989) for a critique of Kripke's skepticism about meaning. For other proponents of PLA2 see Pettit (1996) and Malcolm (1989).

limited only by one's imagination and time constraints: it seems that any continuation is compatible with *some* rule or other. The question then arises how it is possible for there to be a correct application of a rule, such that one can *follow* it or *violate* it. The answer cannot be that there is a formula expressing the rule in question since any such formula needs to be interpreted, and this itself involves the application of rules. Proponents of PLA2 insist that the answer makes essential reference to the agreement of others; only if another person could be brought to the point of making the same continuation automatically can an individual be said to follow a rule. Otherwise, whatever the individual says goes, and the notion of correctness is out of place. This possibility will depend on the other person having received a similar training. Rules are, in Wittgenstein's words, 'practices, customs, institutions'. They presuppose a shared 'form of life'. It follows that *language* is essentially social because to be using language, we must use words in the same way from instance to instance, and to use a word 'in the same way' is equivalent to following a rule governing its use.

If sound, PLA2 supplies the first premise in an argument for holism: we need a society before we can be said to have language. The second premise is that we need a language in order to think. The conclusion is that interaction is logically prior to thought and therefore to rational action, society prior to the fully human individual.

It cannot be a task for this review to decide whether or not PLA2 is sound. That is a vexed issue in the philosophy of language.[36] But the position one takes on PLA2 is highly significant for one's assessment of the arguments we presented in Sections 1 and 2, which represent social arrangements as arising out of explicit or tacit agreements among rational, asocial individuals. If it is incoherent to speak of rationality prior to society, these analyses cannot explain social relations all the way down. (In contrast, Rousseau's account of the social contract is more compatible with PLA2: recall that Rousseau treats rationality as emerging out of social relationships.) In addition to this contradiction of methodological individualism, PLA2 would have consequences for our understanding of expressive rationality, since this concerns the meaning of an action and thereby its linguistic aspect. It implies that if there are expressive constraints on action, these are in general imposed by the practices of members of a community – that is, the social determination thesis mentioned in Section 6.

To illustrate the significance of PLA2, we look again at Lewis's analysis of language as convention, and at whether this analysis succeeds in explaining the social phenomenon of language in terms of non-social concepts.[37] As an example of how a signal might come to have a conventional meaning, Lewis (1969, p. 158) imagines coming across a patch of quicksand, wanting to warn others of the danger, but not knowing of any existing conventional signal. So: 'I put a scarecrow up to its chest in the quicksand, hoping that whoever sees it will catch on'. Although this signal does not yet have any

---

[36] See Footnote 35 above.

[37] Whether Lewis himself claims to offer such an explanation is a matter of dispute. Skyrms (1996, pp. 83–84, 92–93, 102–104) interprets Lewis as making such a claim; Cubitt and Sugden (2003) argue that Lewis's claim that language is conventional does not commit him to any particular position about the genesis of language.

conventional meaning, Lewis says, 'I have done my part of a signalling system in a signalling problem; and I hope my future audience will do its part'. The example seems to establish that an agent could *mean something by* his placement of the scarecrow without its having a prior use in any community. This meaning seems to be established by the agent's intention, and appears to be responsible for its later taking on a conventional meaning, that half-submerged scarecrows *stand for* quicksand.

On a Wittgensteinian view, however, language items have meanings only in view of the fact that 'language games' are played with them. To say that a symbol stands for something is to say nothing unless its role in such an activity is understood. Examples of language games include (amongst a great many other activities) asserting, ordering, asking and answering questions and, as in Lewis's example above, giving and heeding warnings. A Wittgensteinian critic would object that Lewis has presupposed that the agents already know what a warning is, and how to give or heed one; they just lack a warning symbol *for quicksand*. It seems that, if we are to conceive of a *first* convention getting established among previously asocial rational agents, we must suppose that each of these agents has his own conceptual scheme, and that there is some overlap between these schemes. Whether the first supposition is coherent is the issue at the heart of the philosophical debate about private language.

9. Conclusions

Our aim in this chapter has been to review the various approaches that have been proposed to the problem of representing socially-oriented and other-oriented motivations in economics. We have summarized a very diverse literature, in which the differences between rival theories are much greater than is usually the case in economic controversies: fundamental philosophical and methodological issues are at stake.

The variety within the recent literature of sociality is, we suggest, a sign of strength and vitality. We are seeing the early stages of what may turn out to be a theoretical revolution. When the failures of a well-established theoretical approach first begin to be noticed, we should expect to see many different hypotheses being advanced and tested against one another. It is only in the later stages of a revolution that a consensus begins to develop in favor of one particular solution to the problems that prompted the outburst of new theorizing. In this case, the paradigm that is being challenged is that of Hobbes's asocial rational agents, of *homo economicus*. For many years, economists have worked on the assumption that this model of human motivation, perhaps with some minor additions and modifications, was adequate for explaining a broad spectrum of economic and social relations. That assumption is now in question. Some of our own ideas about which theoretical directions are most promising have been expressed in the course of this review, but it has not been our purpose to reach a firm conclusion in favor of one approach rather than another. Let the revolution continue!

Acknowledgements

An early version of this chapter was presented at a conference on the economics of giving, reciprocity and altruism held in Marseille in January 2002. We thank participants in this conference, and Serge-Christophe Kolm and Jean Mercier Ythier as editors, for comments and suggestions. This chapter was drafted while Bardsley was affiliated to CREED, University of Amsterdam.

References

Abrams, B., Schmitz, M. (1984). "The crowding out effect of government transfers on private charitable contributions: cross sectional evidence". National Tax Journal 37, 563–568.
Andreoni, J. (1990). "Impure altruism and donations to public goods: a theory of warm-glow giving". Economic Journal 100, 464–477.
Bacharach, M. (1999). "Interactive team reasoning: a contribution to the theory of cooperation". Research in Economics 53, 117–147.
Bacharach, M. (2006). "Beyond Individual Choice: Teams and Frames in Game Theory". Gold, N., Sugden, R. (Eds.). Princeton University Press.
Baeck, L. (1994). The Mediterranean Tradition in Economic Thought. Routledge, London.
Bardsley, N. (2000a). "Theoretical and empirical investigation of non-selfish behaviour: the case of public goods". PhD Dissertation. University of East Anglia.
Bardsley, N. (2000b). "Interpersonal interaction and economic theory: the case of public goods". Annals of Public and Cooperative Economics 71, 1–37.
Bardsley, N. (2000c). "Control without deception: individual behaviour in free-riding experiments revisited". Experimental Economics 3, 215–240.
Barro, R. (1974). "Are government bonds net wealth?". Journal of Political Economy 82, 1095–1117.
Becker, G. (1974). "A theory of social interactions". Journal of Political Economy 82, 1063–1093.
Becker, G. (1976). The Economic Approach to Human Behavior. University of Chicago Press.
Benn, S. (1978). Political Participation. Australian National University Press, Canberra.
Bentham, J. (1970). An Introduction to the Principles of Morals and Legislation. Athlone Press, London.
Bergstrom, T. (1999). "Systems of benevolent utility functions". Journal of Public Economic Theory 1, 71–100.
Bergstrom, T.C., Blume, L., Varian, H. (1986). "On the private provision of public goods". Journal of Public Economics 29, 25–49.
Bernheim, B.D., Stark, O. (1988). "Altruism within the family reconsidered: do nice guys finish last?". American Economic Review 78, 1034–1045.
Binmore, K. (1999). "Why experiment in economics?". Economic Journal 109, F16–F24.
Boghossian, P. (1989). "The rule-following considerations". Mind 98, 507–549.
Bolton, G., Ockenfels, A. (2000). "ERC: a theory of equity, reciprocity, and competition". American Economic Review 90, 166–193.
Bratman, M. (1992). "Shared cooperative activity". Philosophical Review 101, 327–342.
Brennan, G., Lomasky, L. (1985). "The impartial spectator goes to Washington". Economics and Philosophy 1, 189–211.
Bruni, L., Guala, F. (2001). "Vilfredo Pareto and the epistemological foundations of choice theory". History of Political Economy 33, 21–49.
Bruni, L., Sugden, R. (2000). "Moral canals: trust and social capital in the work of Hume, Smith and Genovesi". Economics and Philosophy 16, 21–45.
Buchanan, J. (1975). The Limits of Liberty. University of Chicago Press.

Cancian, F. (1975). What are Norms?. Cambridge University Press.
Candlish, S. (1980). "The real private language argument". Philosophy 55, 85–94.
Candlish, S. (1998). "Wittgensteins Privatsprachen-argumentation". In: Von Savigny, E. (Ed.), Ludwig Wittgenstein: Philosophische Untersuchungen. Akademie, Berlin.
Charness, G., Rabin, M. (2000). "Social preferences: some simple tests and a new model". Department of Economics Working Paper E00/283. University of California, Berkeley.
Comte, A. (1875). System of Positive Polity. Longmans, Green, London.
Connolly, L. (1997). "Does external funding of academic research crowd out institutional support?". Journal of Public Economics 64, 389–406.
Cornes, R., Sandler, T. (1984). "Easy riders, joint production and public goods". Economic Journal 94, 580–598.
Cox, J. (2000). "Trust and reciprocity: implications of game triads and social contexts". University of Arizona Working Paper.
Croson, R. (1999). "Contributions to public goods: altruism or reciprocity?", University of Pennsylvania Working Paper 96-08-01.
Cubitt, R., Sugden, R. (2003). "Common knowledge, salience and convention: a reconstruction of David Lewis's game theory". Economics and Philosophy 19, 175–210.
Dufwenberg, M., Kirchsteiger, G. (2004). "A theory of sequential reciprocity". Games and Economic Behavior 47, 268–298.
Edgeworth, F. (1881). Mathematical Psychics. Kegan Paul, London.
Elster, J. (1983). Sour Grapes: Studies in the Subversion of Rationality. Cambridge University Press.
Elster, J. (1989). The Cement of Society. Cambridge University Press.
Falk, A., Fischbacher, U. (1998). "A theory of reciprocity". University of Zürich Discussion Paper.
Fehr, E., Schmidt, K. (1999). "A theory of fairness, competition and cooperation". Quarterly Journal of Economics 114, 817–868.
Gauthier, D. (1986). Morals by Agreement. Oxford University Press.
Geanakoplos, J., Pearce, D., Stacchetti, E. (1989). "Psychological games and sequential rationality". Games and Economic Behavior 1, 60–79.
Gilbert, M. (1989). On Social Facts. Routledge, London.
Gui, B. (2000). "Beyond transactions: on the interpersonal dimension of economic reality". Annals of Public and Cooperative Economics 71, 139–169.
Hargreaves Heap, S. (1997). "When norms influence behaviour: expressive reason and its consequences". Paper prepared for the Freiberg Symposium on Abandoning the Hypothesis of Omniscience in Economics, 9–10 January 1997.
Hargreaves Heap, S., Hollis, M., Lyons, B., Sugden, R., Weale, A. (1992). The Theory of Choice. Basil Blackwell, Oxford.
Hobbes, T. (1962). Leviathan. Macmillan, London. (First publication 1651.)
Hodgson, D.H. (1967). Consequences of Utilitarianism. Clarendon Press, Oxford.
Hoffman, E., McCabe, K., Smith, V. (1996). "Social distance and other-regarding behaviour in dictator games". American Economic Review 86, 653–660.
Hollis, M. (1977). Models of Man: Philosophical Thoughts on Social Action. Cambridge University Press.
Hollis, M. (1998). Trust within Reason. Cambridge University Press.
Hume, D. (1978). A Treatise of Human Nature. Oxford University Press. (First publication 1740.)
Hurley, S. (1989). Natural Reasons. Oxford University Press.
Jevons, W.S. (1970). The Theory of Political Economy. Penguin. (First publication 1871.)
Khanna, J., Posnett, J., Sandler, T. (1995). "Charity donations in the UK: new evidence based on panel data". Journal of Public Economics 56, 257–272.
Kripke, S. (1982). Wittgenstein on Rules and Private Language. Basil Blackwell, Oxford.
Kutz, C. (2000). "Acting together". Philosophy and Phenomenological Research 61, 1–31.
Lewis, D. (1969). Convention: A Philosophical Study. Harvard University Press.
Locke, J. (1960). Two Treatises of Government. Cambridge University Press. (First publication 1698.)

Malcolm, N. (1989). "Wittgenstein on language and rules". Philosophy 64, 5–28.
Margolis, H. (1982). Selfishness, Altruism and Rationality. Cambridge University Press.
McLean, I. (1987). Public Choice. Blackwell, Oxford.
McLean, I., Hewitt, F. (1994). Condorcet: Foundations of Social Choice and Political Theory. Edward Elgar, Aldershot.
Paqué, K.-H. (1986). "The efficiency of tax incentives to private charitable giving: some econometric evidence for the Federal Republic of Germany". Weltwirtschaftliches Archiv 122, 690–712.
Pareto, V. (1972). Manual of Political Economy. Macmillan. (Translated by Schweir, A.S. First publication 1909.)
Peacock, M. (1996). "Interpersonal comparisons of utility: some lessons from Wittgenstein". Review of Political Economy 8, 279–290.
Pettit, P. (1996). The Common Mind: an Essay on Psychology, Society, and Politics. Oxford University Press.
Plott, C.R. (1996). "Rational individual behaviour in markets and social choice processes: the discovered preference hypothesis". In: Arrow, K.J., Colombatto, E., Perlman, M., Schmidt, C. (Eds.), The Rational Foundations of Economic Behaviour. Macmillan, Basingstoke.
Rabin, M. (1993). "Incorporating fairness into game theory and economics". American Economic Review 83, 1281–1302.
Regan, D. (1980). Utilitarianism and Cooperation. Clarendon Press, Oxford.
Ritter, A., Bondanella, J.C. (1988). Rousseau's Political Writings. Norton, New York.
Roth, A. (1995). "Bargaining experiments". In: Kagel, J.H., Roth, A.E. (Eds.), Handbook of Experimental Economics. Princeton University Press, pp. 258–348.
Rousseau, J.-J. (1988a). "Discourse on the origin and foundations of inequality among men". In: Ritter and Bondanella (1988). (First publication 1755.)
Rousseau, J.-J. (1988b). "Discourse on political economy". In: Ritter and Bondanella (1988). (First publication 1755.)
Rousseau, J.-J. (1988c). "On social contract". In: Ritter and Bondanella (1988). (First publication 1762.)
Schelling, T. (1960). The Strategy of Conflict. Harvard University Press.
Searle, J. (1990). "Shared cooperative activity". In: Cohen, P.R., Morgan, J., Pollack, M.E. (Eds.), Intentions in Communication. MIT Press, Cambridge, MA.
Searle, J. (1995). The Construction of Social Reality. Allen Lane, Penguin Press, Harmondsworth.
Skelton, P., et al. (1993). Evolution: A Biological and Palaeontological Approach. Addison-Wesley.
Skyrms, B. (1996). Evolution of the Social Contract. Cambridge University Press.
Smith, A. (1976a). The Theory of Moral Sentiments. Oxford University Press. (First publication 1759.)
Smith, A. (1976b). An Inquiry into the Nature and Causes of the Wealth of Nations. Oxford University Press. (First publication 1776.)
Steinberg, R. (1985). "Empirical relations between government spending and charitable donations". Journal of Voluntary Action Research 14, 54–64.
Steinberg, R. (1991). "Does government spending crowd out donations? Interpreting the evidence". Annals of Public and Cooperative Economics 62, 591–617.
Sugden, R. (1982). "On the economics of philanthropy". Economic Journal 92, 341–350.
Sugden, R. (1984). "Reciprocity: the supply of public goods through voluntary contributions". Economic Journal 94, 772–787.
Sugden, R. (1985). "Consistent conjectures and the voluntary provision of public goods: why the conventional theory does not work". Journal of Public Economics 27, 117–124.
Sugden, R. (1986). The Economics of Rights, Co-operation and Welfare. Basil Blackwell, Oxford.
Sugden, R. (1991). "Rational choice: a survey of contributions from economics and philosophy". Economic Journal 101, 751–785.
Sugden, R. (1993). "Thinking as a team: towards an explanation of non-selfish behavior". Social Philosophy and Policy 10, 69–89.
Sugden, R. (2000). "Team preferences". Economics and Philosophy 16, 175–204.
Sugden, R. (2002). "Beyond sympathy and empathy: Adam Smith's concept of fellow-feeling". Economics and Philosophy 18, 63–87.

Tuomela, R., Miller, K. (1988). "We-intentions". Philosophical Studies 53, 367–389.
Vanderschraaf, P. (1998). "The informal game theory in Hume's account of convention". Economics and Philosophy 14, 215–247.
Weber, M. (1968). Economy and Society. Bedminster Press, New York. (First publication 1922.)
Weimann, J. (1994). "Individual behaviour in a free-riding experiment". Journal of Public Economics 54, 185–200.
Winch, P. (1958). The Idea of a Social Science and its Relation to Philosophy. Routledge and Kegan Paul, London.
Wittgenstein, L. (1953). Philosophical Investigations. Basil Blackwell, Oxford.

1E: SPECIAL TOPICS

Chapter 11

NATURAL KANTIAN OR *ZOO ECONOMICUS*? EVOLUTIONARY THEORIES OF SELFISHNESS AND ALTRUISM AMONG MEN AND BEASTS

THEODORE C. BERGSTROM*

University of California at Santa Barbara, USA

Contents

Abstract	772
Keywords	772
1. Selfishness and group selection	774
2. Games and social interactions	777
2.1. What is the game and who is playing?	777
2.2. Prisoners' dilemma games	778
2.2.1. Multi-player prisoners' dilemma	778
2.2.2. The linear public goods game	778
2.3. Stag hunt games	779
2.4. Evolutionary dynamics and altruism	780
2.4.1. Prisoners' dilemma in a freely mingling population	780
3. Haystack models	781
3.1. Maynard Smith's mice	781
3.2. General haystack models and assortative matching	783
3.3. Cohen and Eshel's generalized haystack models	784
3.3.1. Linear public goods games in haystacks	785
3.3.2. Mutation in the haystacks	786
3.3.3. Nonlinearity and polymorphic equilibria	786
3.3.4. Congested resources	787

* Theodore C. Bergstrom is the Aaron and Cherie Raznick Professor of Economics, University of California at Santa Barbara, Santa Barbara, California. A subset of the contents of this paper can be found in the *Journal of Economic Perspectives* under the title: "Evolution of social behavior" [Bergstrom, T.C. (2002). "Evolution of social behavior: Individual and group selection". Journal of Economic Perspectives 16 (2), 67–88]. The current paper includes a lot of discussion cut out of the JEP paper to meet that journal's standards for brevity. Readers who seek a terse discussion of the main issues are likely to prefer the JEP paper. I hope that some may enjoy the more leisurely and thorough discussion that is attempted here. This paper also includes discussion of some interesting work that has appeared since the earlier paper was written.

Handbook of the Economics of Giving, Altruism and Reciprocity, Volume 1
Edited by Serge-Christophe Kolm and Jean Mercier Ythier
Copyright © 2006 Elsevier B.V. All rights reserved
DOI: 10.1016/S1574-0714(06)01011-6

3.4. The iron rule of selfishness　　　　　　　　　　　　　　787
　　　　　3.4.1. Where *not* to look　　　　　　　　　　　　　　788
　　　3.5. Haystacks and the iron rule　　　　　　　　　　　　　788
　　　3.6. Migration and stochastic extinction　　　　　　　　　　789
　　　3.7. Relative and absolute payoffs　　　　　　　　　　　　　790
　　　3.8. "Too stringent to be realistic?"　　　　　　　　　　　　791
4. Assortative matching　　　　　　　　　　　　　　　　　　　794
　　　4.1. Measures of assortativity　　　　　　　　　　　　　　794
　　　4.2. Hamilton's kin selection theory　　　　　　　　　　　　795
　　　　　4.2.1. Index of assortativity for relatives　　　　　　　　797
　　　4.3. Evolutionary dynamics with assortative mating　　　　　798
　　　　　4.3.1. The linear public goods game　　　　　　　　　　798
　　　　　4.3.2. Dynamics with nonlinear payoff functions　　　　　799
　　　4.4. Assortative matching with partner choice　　　　　　　　801
　　　4.5. Assortative matching induced by spatial structure　　　　803
5. Repeated games and group selection　　　　　　　　　　　　　806
　　　5.1. Group selection from multiple Nash equilibria　　　　　　806
　　　5.2. How can costly punishment survive?　　　　　　　　　　807
　　　5.3. Evidence from psychology and anthropology　　　　　　　811
6. Conclusion　　　　　　　　　　　　　　　　　　　　　　　　813
　　　6.1. Further reading　　　　　　　　　　　　　　　　　　　813
References　　　　　　　　　　　　　　　　　　　　　　　　　814

Abstract

This paper addresses the question of whether our evolutionary history suggests that humans are likely to be individually selected selfish maximizers or group selected altruists. It surveys models from the literature of evolutionary biology in which groups are formed and dissolved and where the reproductive success of individuals is determined by their payoffs in a game played within groups. We show that if groups are formed "randomly" and reproductive success of group founders is determined by a multi-person prisoners' dilemma game, then selfish behavior will prevail over maximization of group payoffs. However, interesting models can be found for which "group selection" sustains cooperative behavior. Forces that support cooperative behavior include assortative matching in groups, group longevity, and punishment-based group norms.

Keywords

group selection, altruism, selfishness, evolutionary games, cooperation, biology, haystack model, punishment, reciprocity, linear public goods game, generalized prisoners' dilemma, assortative matching

JEL classification: C70, C73, D60, Dl

1. Selfishness and group selection

What can our evolutionary history tell us about human motivations and social behavior? The genes that influence our own behavior are inherited from ancestors who themselves managed to reproduce successfully. Could it be that there are evolutionary foundations for the selfishness that economists assume is characteristic of *homo economicus*?

Richard Dawkins (1989), a leading expositor of evolutionary theory, believes this is the case:

> If we were told that a man lived a long and prosperous life in the world of Chicago gangsters, we would be entitled to make some guesses as to the sort of man he was. ... Like successful Chicago gangsters, our genes have survived, in some cases for millions of years, in a highly competitive world. ... If you look at the way natural selection works, it seems to follow that anything that has evolved by natural selection should be selfish. (pp. 2–4)

Another well-known biologist, Michael Ghiselin (1974), states this view even more emphatically:

> Where it is in his own interest, every organism may reasonably be expected to aid his fellows ... Yet given a full chance to act in his own interest, nothing but expediency will restrain him ... Scratch an "altruist" and watch a "hypocrite" bleed.

But the view that evolution must lead to selfishness is not universally shared. Alexander Carr-Saunders (1922), a sociologist and pioneer in the study of demography and social evolution, observed that prehistoric humans were clustered into groups who inhabited well-defined areas, and that migration between groups was infrequent. These groups, he maintained, typically managed to avoid overpopulation and the attendant scourges of war, famine, and disease. Carr-Saunders argued that ethnographic evidence from existing primitive societies indicates that fertility is deliberately restrained by means of abortion, infanticide, and long-term sexual abstinence. Thus, he claims, these societies managed to maintain population at roughly constant levels close to those that would maximize per capita food consumption. He argued that this outcome is inconsistent with reproductive selfishness and must somehow be explained by "group selection".

Carr-Saunders believed that group selection operates for humans "who have achieved sufficient social organization", but not for more primitive animals. He was an early proponent of the view that "group selection" operates on the evolution of social norms toward those that serve the group interest.

> Now men and groups of men are naturally selected on account of the customs they practise just as they are selected on account of their mental and physical characters. Those groups practising the most advantageous customs will have an advantage in the constant struggle between adjacent groups over those that practise less advantageous customs. Few customs would be more advantageous than those which limit the number of a group to the desirable number ... There would grow up an idea

that it was the right thing to bring up a certain limited number of children and the limitation of the family would be enforced by convention. [Carr-Saunders (1922, p. 223)]

V.C. Wynne-Edwards, a leading ecologist of a generation ago, proposed that group selection has far more ancient roots, and applies to much of the animal kingdom. His book, *Animal Dispersion in Relation to Social Behavior* [Wynne-Edwards (1962)] includes an encyclopedic collection of data and descriptions of group behavior and territoriality among a huge variety of species of insects, fish, birds, and mammals. Wynne-Edwards maintained that the Darwinian tradition emphasized natural selection at either the level of individuals or the level of species as a whole, while paying insufficient attention to powerful selective forces that act at the level of the social group. Like Carr-Saunders, he further suggests that not only genetic material, but social norms or conventions may be subject to natural selection. Wynne-Edwards documents the importance of relatively stable localized social groups for the evolution of animal behavior and suggests that for many species, groups have evolved systems of hereditary property rights that strongly shape individual behavior.

According to Wynne-Edwards:

It has become increasingly clear in recent years, not only that animal (and plant) species tend to be grouped into more or less isolated populations ... but that this is a very important feature from an evolutionary standpoint ... The local stock of any given animal species, exploiting its resources, consequently tends to adopt many conventions of a strictly localized or topographical character – for example the traditional sites of breeding places. Other conventions rely equally strongly on a procession of mutual relationships among the individual local inhabitants. Above all the local stock conserves its resources and thereby safeguards the future survival of its descendants; and no such conventional adaptation could have evolved if the descendants did not naturally fall heirs to the same ground. Thrifty exploitation today for the benefit of some randomly chosen and possibly prodigal generation of strangers tomorrow would make slow headway under natural selection.... it is of the greatest importance in the long-term exploitation of resources that local populations should be self-perpetuating. If confirmation were needed of this conclusion, it could be found in the almost incredible facilities of precise navigation developed in all long-distance two-way migrants whether they are birds, bats, fish, or insects, to enjoy the advantages of two worlds, and still retain their life-long membership in the same select local stock. Ideally, localisation does not entail complete reproductive isolation however; we have to consider later the pioneering element also – in most species relatively small – that looks after colonisation and disseminates genes. [Wynne-Edwards (1962, pp. 19 and 20)]

Wynne-Edwards also believed that animals do not reproduce as rapidly as they would if individuals were attempting to maximize their own fertility. He cited examples of species in which large gatherings assemble just before breeding time. These gatherings, he claimed, allow individuals to determine the existing population density and to adjust their reproductive decisions in such a way as to maintain a relatively constant population. In Wynne-Edwards view, animal species are able to solve the "tragedy of the commons" and to maintain population densities at an "optimal level for each habitat that they occupy". In Wynne-Edwards (1962), he asserts that:

> Where we can still find nature undisturbed by human influence ... there is generally no indication whatever that the habitat is run down or destructively overtaxed. On the contrary the whole trend of ecological evolution seems to be in the very opposite direction, leading towards the highest state of productivity that can possibly be built up within the limitations of the inorganic environment. Judging by appearances, chronic over-exploitation and mass poverty intrude themselves only as a kind of adventitious disease, almost certain to be swiftly suppressed by natural selection. (p. 8)

In the opinion of many biologists, Wynne-Edwards' conclusions represented a profound misunderstanding of evolutionary theory. According to Richard Dawkins (1989),

> being wrong in an unequivocal way, Wynne-Edwards is widely credited with having provoked people into thinking more clearly about selection. (p. 297)

An eminent ornithologist, David Lack (1966) and a leading evolutionary biologist, George C. Williams (1966) presented trenchant rebuttals of Wynne-Edwards group selectionist views. Lack presented detailed explanations of how the observations that Wynne-Edwards claimed as support for group-selection could be as well explained by the theory that individuals maximize their own reproductive interests or those of close relatives. Lack pointed out evidence from field studies and experiments that indicates that "in the Starling, the Swift, and usually the Great Tit the most frequent clutch-size is the same as that brood size from which, on average, most young are raised per brood". Lack disputed Wynne-Edwards' claim that reproductive self-regulation eliminates "over-exploitation and mass poverty". He cites one of his own studies that finds that "in many species of song-birds, nearly half of the adults and more of the juveniles die each year, probably mainly from starvation". Williams (1966) went on to list many examples of animal behavior that contribute to individual survival at the expense of the survival prospects of the group.

Williams and Lack both argued that in a fluctuating environment, reproductive restraint in times of abundance is likely to be in an individual's long term reproductive interest. Individuals who have fewer offspring and take better care of each are more likely to have descendants strong enough to survive when hard times arrive. Similarly, it may be in an individual's reproductive self-interest to defend territory that is larger than the minimum territory necessary for successful reproduction in good years because this territory will be essential for success in bad years.

Wynne-Edwards did not present a coherent theory to support his view that social groups rather than individuals might be the units of evolutionary selection. More recently, evolutionary theorists have attempted to provide formal underpinnings for group selection. Sober and Wilson (1999) offer a stimulating and detailed account of these efforts. John Maynard Smith (1976), the father of evolutionary game theory and a key contributor to this effort, concludes that:

> the argument is quantitative, not qualitative. Group selection will have evolutionary consequences: the only question is how important these consequences have been.

2. Games and social interactions

2.1. What is the game and who is playing?

To understand the conflict between the individual and group selection views, it is useful to model social interaction as a game in which the players and the payoffs are explicitly specified. In the language of game theory, the two polar positions can be stated as:
- *Individual selection theory:* To predict social outcomes, we need to examine the game in which the players are individual animals and the payoff to each animal is its expected number of progeny. The outcomes that we expect to see are the Nash equilibria for this game.
- *Group selection theory:* To predict social outcomes, we need to examine the game in which the players are geographically semi-isolated communities of individuals and the payoff is the community's expected reproductive rate. The outcomes we expect to see are Nash equilibria where the players are communities.

A third alternative game formulation is suggested by the work of William G. Hamilton (1964) on *kin selection theory*. As Dawkins (1989) suggests, individuals can be thought of as *survival machines* programmed to make copies of their programmers, the genes. The organisms that we observe are machines that were built by those genes that have in the past been most successful in getting themselves reproduced. Selfish organisms are not typically the best vehicle for genes to use in their own reproduction. Machines that are designed to care for their offspring and to help their close relatives (who are likely to carry the same genes as their own) will typically do better.
- *Kin selection theory:* To predict social outcomes, we need to examine the game in which the players are genes that operate according to Mendelian rules of replication and that carry specific instructions to the organisms that carry them. The payoffs to these genes are their replication rates.

We shall return to the discussion of kin selection theory later in this paper. In the next sections, we examine the competing models of individual and group selection theory and points between. Taken at face value, these theories have radically different implications for the evolutionary nature of men and beasts.

Individual selection theory suggests a world populated by resolutely selfish *homo economicus* and his zoological (and botanical) counterparts. By contrast, in a world shaped by group selection we would expect to see impeccable socialists with an instinctive "Kantian" morality toward other members of their group. Of course the localism that leads to group selection would also be likely to produce some unsavory impulses towards xenophobia and intertribal warfare.

When the game being played within communities is prisoners' dilemma, the contrasting predictions of the two theories are particularly stark and simple. Since the payoff from playing *defect* is always higher than that of playing *cooperate*, individual selection theory predicts a population of defectors. But since every member of a community of cooperators gets a higher payoff than any member of a community of defectors, group selection theory predicts a population of cooperators.

Using prisoners' dilemma as a research vehicle, biologists, game theorists, and anthropologists have found much interesting territory between the two poles of individual selection and group selection. Although neither of the polar theories would be supported by modern research, the tension between the forces of individual and group selection continues to be the focus of interesting research. The use of prisoners' dilemma to explore this tension has been very instructive and will play an important part in this survey. However, as we argue in later discussion, most of the really important (and problematic) social interactions in the world are probably not games with unique Nash equilibria, let alone dominant strategies, but games that have many distinct Nash equilibria among which societies somehow select.

2.2. Prisoners' dilemma games

2.2.1. Multi-player prisoners' dilemma

A multi-player prisoners' dilemma is a game in which individuals may take actions that are, in the words of J.B.S. Haldane (1932), "socially valuable but individually disadvantageous". Specifically, we consider a game that has two possible strategies for each player, *cooperate* and *defect*, where the payoff to each player depends on her own strategy and the number of other players who play cooperate. In a game with N players, where K of the *other* players cooperate, let $\Pi_C(K, N)$ and $\Pi_D(K, N)$ denote the payoffs to a cooperator and a defector, respectively.

DEFINITION 1 (N-player Prisoners' Dilemma Game). A game is an N-player prisoners' dilemma game if the payoff functions satisfy the following:
- All players are better off if all play *cooperate* than if all play *defect*; that is, $\Pi_C(N-1, N) > \Pi_D(0, N)$.
- Regardless of what other players do, an individual gets a higher payoff from playing defect than from playing cooperate; that is, $\Pi_D(K, N) > \Pi_C(K, N)$, for all K between 0 and $N-1$.

2.2.2. The linear public goods game

It is customary to credit game theorists, Merrill Flood and Melvin Dresher of the Rand Corporation, with inventing the prisoners' dilemma game in about 1950. But this game has an earlier history. In 1932, J.B.S. Haldane, one of the founders of modern population biology, introduced and analyzed an N person generalized prisoners' dilemma game in which each player's payoff depends linearly on the number of players in the game who cooperate. Economists will recognize Haldane's game as formally equivalent to the linear "voluntary contribution to public goods" game, much studied in experimental economics [see Ledyard (1995) for a good survey of this work]. Thus we will refer to Haldane's linear N-player prisoners' dilemma as the *linear public goods game*.[1]

DEFINITION 2 (The Linear Public Goods Game). The linear public goods game is an N player game in which each player can play either cooperate or defect. Where x is the fraction of all players who cooperate, the payoff to each cooperator is $bx - c$ and the payoff to each defector is bx.

In a linear public goods game with N players, if K other players cooperate, a cooperator will get

$$\Pi_C(K, N) = b\frac{K+1}{N} - c = b\frac{K}{N} - c' \qquad (1)$$

where $c' = c - \frac{b}{N}$ and a defector will get

$$\Pi_D(K, N) = b\frac{K}{N}. \qquad (2)$$

The linear public goods game can be seen to be an N-player prisoners' dilemma if $b > c > \frac{b}{N}$. If all players cooperate, each gets a payoff of $b - c$; if all defect, each gets a payoff of 0. Therefore when $b > c$, all players are better off if all cooperate than if all defect. For all K, $\Pi_D(K, N) - \Pi_C(K, N) = c - \frac{b}{N} = c'$. Thus if $c > \frac{b}{N}$, an individual always gets a higher payoff by defecting rather than cooperating.

In a linear public goods game with N players, a cooperator confers a benefit of $\frac{b}{N}$ on every player, including himself, so that the net cost of cooperating is $c - \frac{b}{N}$. Some writers, such as David S. Wilson (1975), analyze a variant of this game in which a cooperator confers expected benefits of $\frac{b}{N}$ on every player *other than himself* at a cost of c to himself. Results for either of these two games translate easily into corresponding results for the other, since Wilson's formulation of the game with costs c is isomorphic to a linear public goods game with costs $c + \frac{b}{N}$.

2.3. Stag hunt games

In one-shot prisoners' dilemma games, the socially optimal action is never a best response for selfish individuals. But in many social interactions, the action that best serves one's self-interest depends on the actions taken by others. This suggests the usefulness of a second exploratory vehicle, a simple two-person game, known as the stag hunt. This

---

[1] Haldane (1932, pp. 207–210 of the Appendix) presents this model in an early discussion of group selection. The notation used here is that of Cohen and Eshel (1976) rather than that of Haldane.

Table 1
A stag hunt game

	Cooperate	Defect
Cooperate	4	0
Defect	3	3

game formalizes a story told by Jean Jacques Rousseau (1950, p. 428), of two hunters who could cooperate by jointly hunting a stag or defect by individually hunting hare.[2] Table 1 is a game matrix for a stag hunt game, where entries represent payoffs to the row player.

The stag hunt has two equilibria, one where both players cooperate and one where both defect. In later discussion, we consider the question of when one or the other equilibrium is likely to be reached.

2.4. Evolutionary dynamics and altruism

2.4.1. Prisoners' dilemma in a freely mingling population

Let us consider the evolutionary dynamics of a population in which all individuals are "programmed" (perhaps genetically, perhaps by cultural experience) to play one of two strategies, *cooperate* or *defect* in a symmetric multi-person prisoners' dilemma game played by the entire population. We will assume that the dynamics satisfy *payoff-monotonicity* [Weibull (1995)], which means simply that the proportion of the population that plays the strategy with the higher payoff will increase.[3] If the game is prisoners' dilemma, the payoff to cooperators will necessarily be lower than to defectors, so the proportion of cooperators in the population must decline over time and eventually converge to zero.[4]

Gorret Hardin, in *The Limits of Altruism* (1977) explained this result and suggested that the replacement of tribalism and parochialism by a more cosmopolitan society is not likely to enhance cooperation.

---

[2] An engaging paper by Brian Skyrms (2001) makes a strong case that social thinkers should pay more attention to the stag hunt game.

[3] A much-studied special case of payoff monotone dynamics is *replicator dynamics* in which the growth rate of the population share using a strategy is proportional to the difference between the average payoff to that strategy and the average payoff in the entire population [Weibull (1995)]. The results found in this paper do not require the special structure of replicator dynamics.

[4] The result that the proportion of cooperators will decline monotonically is obvious. The result that it must converge to zero is less obvious. A proof can be found in Weibull (1995). Weibull credits this result to John Nachbar (1990).

Competition is severe and total whenever members of the same species are brought together in One World ... Conceivably some conscientious members of the community might eat less than their share of the food, but the resources they thereby released would soon be absorbed by others with less conscience. Some animals might refrain from reproducing, but the space so freed would soon be occupied by those who were less conscientious.... Adapting a phrase of the economist David Ricardo, we can speak of the Iron Law of the Overwhelming Minority. It is silly to dream dreams of a heaven on earth that presume a value of zero for the size of the disruptive minority.

3. Haystack models

Two of the founders of modern population biology, J.B.S. Haldane (1932) and Sewall Wright (1945), proposed that altruistic behavior is more likely to evolve in a population where group interaction takes place within relatively small subpopulations, (sometimes called *demes*) between which there is occasional, but relatively infrequent migration.

3.1. Maynard Smith's mice

John Maynard Smith (1964) produced the first formal model of group selection in which seemingly altruistic behavior prevails, even without assortative matching. Maynard Smith motivates this model with a charming story of "a species of mouse who lives in a hayfield".

The setting for Maynard Smith's haystack model is a meadow. In early summer, a farmer builds several haystacks, each of which is colonized by exactly two mice. These two mice and their descendants interact and reproduce asexually for the entire season, until the haystacks are removed.[5] When the haystacks are cleared, the dislodged mice scramble out into the meadow, mingling freely with the mice displaced from other haystacks. In the next year, when new haystacks are built, exactly two mice from the population resident in the meadow are randomly selected to colonize each new haystack. If the number of surviving mice is more than twice the number of haystacks, the extra mice are consumed by predators.

There are two types of mice in the population at large, timid mice and aggressive mice. Descendants of either type of mouse will be of the same type as their ancestors. Timid mice play the role of "altruists" by pursuing a strategy that is socially valuable but individually disadvantageous. Thus, within any haystack, the timid mice reproduce less rapidly than the aggressive mice, but at the end of the season, haystacks that are made

---

[5] Maynard Smith presented his model as one with sexual diploid reproduction. But he contrived special assumptions that make his model mathematically equivalent to a model with asexual reproduction. To simplify exposition and to make this model directly comparable with the later extensions by Cohen and Eshel, I present an asexual haystack model that is formally equivalent model to his sexual diploid model.

Table 2
The haystack game

	Timid	Aggressive
Timid	$r(1+K)/2$	0
Aggressive	r	$r/2$

up entirely of timid mice will have more inhabitants than those that include aggressive mice.

In a haystack settled by two timid mice, all descendants are timid and in a haystack settled by two aggressive mice, all descendants are aggressive. In a haystack settled by one mouse of each type, the descendants of the aggressive mouse eliminate the descendants of the timid mouse, and the number of its descendants at harvest time is the same as the number in a haystack colonized by two aggressive mice.

Although timid mice do poorly when matched with aggressive mice, haystacks inhabited entirely by timid mice produce more surviving offspring at harvest time than haystacks inhabited by aggressive mice. Thus a haystack colonized by two timid mice produces $1+K$ times as many descendants as a haystack with aggressive mice.

Since the reproduction rate enjoyed by a founding mouse depends on its own type and that of its co-founder, these rates can be represented as the payoffs in a game between the two mice who colonize each haystack. If two aggressive mice colonize a haystack, they will have a total of r descendants, half of whom are descended from each founder. Thus each mouse has $r/2$ descendants. If an aggressive mouse and a timid mouse colonize a haystack, the timid mouse will have no descendants and the aggressive mouse will have r descendants. If two timid mice colonize a haystack, they will have a total of $r(1+K)$ descendants and each will have $r(1+K)/2$ descendants. In the game played by cofounders, payoffs to the row player are shown in Table 2.

If $0 < K < 1$, the haystack game is a prisoners' dilemma, since regardless of its cofounder's type, an aggressive mouse will have more offspring than a timid mouse. If $K > 1$, the haystack game is not a prisoners' dilemma but a stag hunt. If matched with a timid mouse, a mouse will have more offspring if it is timid than if it is aggressive. But if matched with an aggressive mouse, a mouse will have more offspring if it is aggressive than if it is timid.

For the prisoners' dilemma case with $K < 1$, the only equilibrium is a population made up entirely of defectors. For the stag hunt case, with $K > 1$, there are two distinct stable equilibria, one in which all mice are timid and one in which all are aggressive. We demonstrate this as follows. Let the proportion of timid mice in the population at time t be x_t. Since matching is random, any mouse is matched with a timid co-founder with probability x_t and with an aggressive co-founder with probability $1 - x_t$. Given the payoffs in Table 2, the expected reproduction rate of an aggressive mouse is $x_t r + (1 - x_t)r/2$, and the expected reproduction rate of a timid mouse is $x_t r(1+K)/2$. Subtracting the latter expression from the former, we find that the difference between the expected

Equilibria when $K > 1$ (Stag Hunt Case)

Equilibrium when $K < 1$ (Prisoners' Dilemma Case)

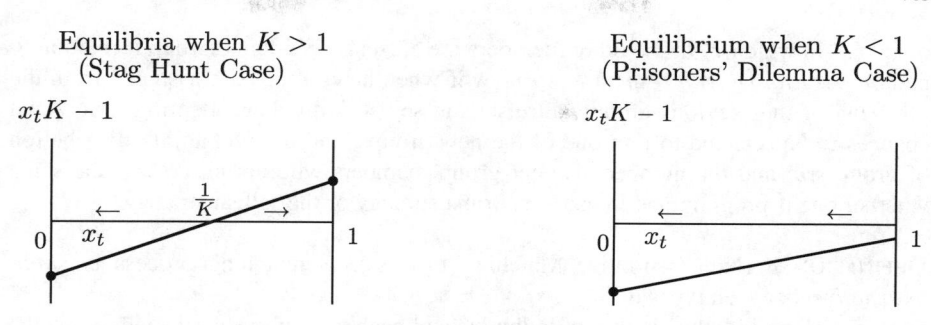

Figure 1. Dynamics of the haystack model.

reproduction rates of timid mice and of aggressive mice is proportional to $x_t K - 1$. Therefore timid mice reproduce more rapidly than aggressive mice if $x_t K > 1$ and aggressive mice reproduce more rapidly if $x_t K < 1$. These dynamics are illustrated by Figure 1. The graph on the left shows that where $K > 1$, there are two stable equilibria, one in which all mice are timid and one in which all are aggressive. (There is also an unstable equilibrium where the fraction $1/K$ of mice are timid.) The graph on the right shows that where $K < 1$, there is a unique equilibrium in which all mice are aggressive.

THEOREM 1 (Haystack Dynamics). *In Maynard Smith's haystack model with random mating:*
- *If haystacks of timid mice produce more than twice as many mice as haystacks of aggressive mice, there will be two stable monomorphic equilibria, one in which $x = 0$ (all mice are aggressive) and one in which $x = 1$ (all mice are timid), as well as one unstable polymorphic equilibrium where $x = 1/K$.*
- *If haystacks of timid mice produce fewer than twice as many mice as haystacks of aggressive mice, the only stable equilibrium is a monomorphic population of aggressive mice.*

3.2. General haystack models and assortative matching

Let us define a *generalized haystack model* to be a model with a large population of individuals, who are programmed for one of two strategies, altruist or selfish. At the beginning of each time period, these individuals are randomly partitioned into groups (possibly of different sizes). Each member produces (asexually) a number of offspring equal to her payoff in a game that she plays with other members of her own group. Offspring are programmed to use the same strategy as their parent. At the end of each time period, all groups are disbanded and new groups are randomly selected from the combined population of the disbanded groups.

Let $p_A(K, N)$ be the probability, conditional on being an altruist, that a player is assigned to a group of size N in which K of the *other* group members are altruists. Let $p_S(K, N)$ be the probability, conditional on being selfish, that one is assigned to a group of size N in which K of the other members are altruists. We define group formation to be *non-assortative with respect to strategy* if when new groups are assigned from the offspring of the previous groups, altruists and selfish individual offspring have equal chances to be selected to join one of the new groups, and the probability distribution of group size and the number of other group members who are altruists is the same whether one is programmed to use the altruist strategy or the selfish strategy.

DEFINITION 3 (Non-assortative Matching Process). A matching process is *non-assortative* between types if
- In each period, the number of individuals of each type who are selected to join the new groups is proportional to the total number of offspring of that type who were produced in the previous period.
- In each period, for all K and N, $p_A(K, N) = p_S(K, N)$.

A simple example of a non-assortative matching process is an urn model in which there is a fixed number of locations, each with a given capacity, and where each location is populated by independent random draws from the total population.

If group formation is assortative, so that an altruist is more likely to have altruist neighbors than a selfish individual, then it is easy to see that altruism can be maintained in the population. For example, in the extreme case where group formation is perfectly assortative so that groups consist either entirely of altruists or entirely of selfish, altruists will always receive higher payoffs than selfish individuals and altruists would eventually constitute the entire population.

But is it possible for altruism to be sustained in a haystack model if new groups are formed at random from the population? When groups are formed by independent random draws, the proportions in each group will not mirror the proportions in the population at large. Random selection results in some groups that have disproportionately many altruists and some that have disproportionately many selfish individuals. Within each group, the altruists get lower payoffs and hence reproduce less rapidly than the selfish. But there is a countervailing effect. Groups that contain more altruists grow more rapidly. Can this between-group effect overwhelm the within-group effect and cause the proportion of altruists *in the overall population* to increase over time? Or does Hardin's "Iron Law" extend to populations randomly selected into groups? The next sections offer a partial answer to this question.

3.3. Cohen and Eshel's generalized haystack models

Dan Cohen and Ilan Eshel (1976) produced a series of interesting generalized haystack models. In these models, there are two types of asexually reproducing individuals, "altruists" and "selfish". As in the haystack model, individuals group into distinct colonies where they live and breed. After some fixed length of time, all colonies are disbanded and new colonies are formed by individuals randomly selected from the population at large. In the Cohen–Eshel model, the number of individuals in the founding population is N. They assume that reproduction takes place continuously over time and that within any haystack, the reproduction rate of both types of individuals is an increasing function of the proportion who are altruists. However, the reproduction rate of altruists is lower than that of the selfish.

Cohen and Eshel focus on determining the stability of each the two possible monomorphic populations, all altruists and all selfish. This investigation is simplified by the following observation. With random group formation, when invaders are rare, almost all invaders will be selected into groups in which all other members are normal. Thus a monomorphic population of either type can be invaded by an initially small influx of the other type only if the reproduction rate of a single invader who joins $N-1$ normal individuals in founding a colony is larger than that of a normal individual among a group made up entirely of the normal type.

3.3.1. Linear public goods games in haystacks

One model that Cohen and Eshel analyze is Haldane's linear public goods game. In the Cohen–Eshel formulation, if $x(t)$ is the fraction of a group that are altruists at time t, then the reproduction rate of selfish group members is $a + bx(t)$, while that of altruists in the same group is $a + bx(t) - c$. Cohen and Eshel find the ranges of parameter values in the linear public goods game for which each kind of monomorphic equilibrium is stable.[6] The length of time T for which communities remain intact before dispersing is of critical importance.

THEOREM 2 (Cohen–Eshel). *In the Cohen–Eshel haystack model, where reproduction rates are determined by the linear public goods game and where T is the length of time for which groups remain intact:*

- *For small T, if $b/N < c$, the only stable equilibrium is a population of selfish individuals and if $b/N > c$, the only stable equilibrium is a monomorphic population of cooperators.*
- *If T is sufficiently large, and $b > c > 0$, there exist two distinct stable monomorphic equilibria; one with selfish players only and one with altruists only.*

The most surprising result is that if T is large enough, there exists a stable equilibrium with a population made up of altruists, even though groups are formed by an independent random matching process, and even though the game that determines instantaneous reproductive rates is an N-player prisoners' dilemma game. To see why this happens, recall that a population of altruists will be stable if the expected number of descendants of a single selfish individual who joins $N-1$ altruists in founding a community is higher than the expected number of descendants of an altruist who is among a founding group consisting entirely of altruists. The number of altruists in a group consisting

---

[6] They are able to find closed-form solutions for the reproduction rates of a mutant cooperator in a population of defectors and of a mutant defector in a population of cooperators.

entirely of altruists grows at the rate $a + b - c > a$. The descendants of the selfish invader will reproduce more rapidly than the *altruist members of the group which she joins*. But to invade the population, her descendants must reproduce more rapidly than *altruists who live exclusively among altruists*. As T is large, the descendants of a selfish invader will eventually comprise almost the entire group to which they belong. Hence the growth rate of the invader population will approach a. Thus when T is large enough, the growth rate of normal altruists is higher than that of the invading selfish. Moreover, this difference in growth rates does not diminish over time. It follows that there exists some survival period T such that if groups persist for longer than T, a monomorphic population of altruists is a stable equilibrium.

3.3.2. Mutation in the haystacks

Cohen and Eshel's Theorem 2 assumes the absence of mutation within haystacks. Indeed, their conclusion that a population of altruists will be stable if the time between haystack dispersals is sufficiently long is not in general true if there is a non-zero probability of mutation at each moment in time. Eshel and Cohen's result depended on the observation that a haystack that initially consists entirely of cooperators will remain uninfected by defectors and will if the haystack remains intact long enough reproduce faster than groups of defectors. But with mutation and very long-lasting haystacks, the haystacks that start out with cooperators only are likely to be infected at some time by mutant defectors. Once infected, their growth will slow as the defectors within the group reproduce more rapidly than the cooperators.

A recent paper by Ben Cooper and Chris Wallace (2001) runs simulations of a haystack model with mutations. In their simulations, altruism does not survive either if haystacks are dispersed after a very short time or after a very long time. However in their simulations, altruism can prevail if the number of generations from the formation of haystack groups until their dispersal is of intermediate size.

3.3.3. Nonlinearity and polymorphic equilibria

The Haldane linear public goods model assumes that a community's growth rate depends linearly on its proportion of altruists. This implies constant returns to altruism in the sense that an additional altruist makes the same contribution to growth regardless of the number of other altruists. Cohen and Eshel show that without this linearity, monomorphic equilibrium do not always exist. They define a "generalized Haldane model" in which the reproduction rate of selfish individuals is $a + b\psi(x)$ when x is the proportion of altruists in their community; where $\psi(\cdot)$ is an increasing function such that $\psi(0) = 0$ and $\psi(1) = 1$. They show that if there is diminishing returns to the addition of altruists to the community, it can happen that the only equilibria are polymorphic, with both types being present in equilibrium.

3.3.4. Congested resources

Cohen and Eshel (1976) also study a version of the haystack model in which growth within each community is constrained by the amount of resources available. There are "selfish" individuals who reproduce more rapidly than "altruists", but consume more resources. At the end of a fixed period of time, T, the original communities are dispersed and new communities are founded by groups who are randomly selected from the entire population. In this model, a community whose founders are mainly altruists will produce more offspring because each uses less resources. On the other hand, the selfish members of a community produce more offspring than an altruistic member. For fixed growth rates and resource exhaustion parameters, if founding populations are small enough, there will be a stable equilibrium with altruists only, if populations are large enough, there will be a stable equilibrium with selfish only, and for intermediate sizes of population, there will be two distinct stable equilibria; one with altruists only and one with selfish only.

3.4. The iron rule of selfishness

David S. Wilson (1975), in a pioneering study of group selection, showed that for his particular model, "random" formation of groups must result in the elimination of altruism. In a survey article called "Natural, kin and group selection" (1984), Alan Grafen states that "with random grouping there is no selection for altruism". However, Maynard Smith (1964, 1976), Eshel (1972), Cohen and Eshel (1976), and Matessi and Jayakar (1976) seem to have contrary results. Although mating is random in Maynard Smith's haystack model, for some parameter values, there is a stable equilibrium in which the entire population consists of altruists. Eshel (1972) asserts that "for any altruistic trait, there is a critical level of demographic mobility under which selection would always operate for the establishment of the altruist". In Cohen and Eshel's models (1976), there is "random distribution of altruist and selfish in small founder groups" and it turns out that if groups remain together long enough before being dispersed, there exists a stable equilibrium consisting entirely of altruists (as well as another stable equilibrium consisting entirely of selfish.)

To establish the circumstances under which Grafen's claim of no-altruism-with-random-sorting is correct, we need to specify the reproductive dynamics that we have in mind, as well as what we mean by altruism, and by random mating. In this section altruism is defined as playing altruist in an N-person prisoners' dilemma game in which a player's payoff is her reproduction rate. As we will later discuss, this does not exhaust the forms of behavior that might reasonably be called altruistic.

THEOREM 3 (Iron Rule of Selfishness). *In a generalized haystack model, if groups are formed by a matching process that is non-assortative and if the game that determines reproduction rates is an N-player prisoners' dilemma played with members of one's* *own group, then the proportion of altruists (cooperators) in the population will approach zero as the number of periods gets large.*

PROOF. In each period at the time when new groups are formed, the expected numbers of offspring produced by each selfish individual and each altruist of the previous generation are, respectively:

$$\sum_N \sum_{K=1}^{N-1} p_S(K,N) \Pi_S(K,N) \quad \text{and} \quad \sum_N \sum_{K=1}^{N-1} p_A(K,N) \Pi_A(K,N). \tag{3}$$

The difference between the growth rate of the number of altruists and the growth rate of the number of selfish individuals is proportional to the difference between these two rates. Since matching is non-assortative, $p_A(K,N) = p_S(K,N)$. Therefore the difference between the two reproduction rates in (3) is

$$\sum_N \sum_{K=1}^{N-1} p_S(K,N) \big(\Pi_S(K,N) - \Pi_A(K,N) \big). \tag{4}$$

Since the game is an N-player prisoners' dilemma game, it must be that $\Pi_S(K,N) - \Pi_A(K,N) > 0$ for all K and N, and hence the expression in (4) must be positive. It follows that the growth rate of the population of selfish individuals exceeds that of the population of altruists at all times. Therefore, the limiting value of the proportion of altruists in the population is zero. □

3.4.1. *Where* not *to look*

It is important to understand that this "Iron Rule" does not tell us that evolutionary selection must eliminate altruistic behavior. The usefulness of Theorem 3 is that it tells us where *not* to look for the evolutionary foundations of such behavior. If we are looking for environments in which cooperative behavior is sustained by group selection, we should expect that at least one of the following is NOT true.
- The game that determines long term reproduction rates is an N-person prisoners' dilemma.
- The matching process that forms groups is "random".

3.5. *Haystacks and the iron rule*

In the haystack models of Maynard Smith and of Cohen and Eshel, communities are formed by independent random draws and the game played by individuals within each community seems to be an N-person prisoners' dilemma. Nevertheless, we have seen that in these models a population of altruists can survive evolutionary selection. How do these populations escape the reach of the "Iron Rule of Selfishness?"

The game that is specified in the Iron Rule is the game played between community founders, in which the payoffs are measured by the number of descendants at the time when the community is dissolved. For Maynard Smith's mice, the payoff matrix for this game is given in Table 2 above. In the case where $K < 1$, this game is a prisoners' dilemma and, as we have seen, cooperators will eventually disappear. If $K > 1$, then the game is not a prisoners' dilemma, but a stag hunt. Thus the conditions of the Iron Rule are not satisfied, and indeed its conclusion does not follow.

The way in which Cohen and Eshel's linear public goods model eludes the strictures of the Iron Rule is especially instructive. In this model, group formation is non-assortative. Furthermore, the number of offspring that any individual produces is the payoff in a multi-player prisoners' dilemma game played among contemporaries in the same group. Nevertheless, cooperative behavior can be sustained if groups spend sufficient time together before dispersal.

The reason that the Iron Rule is not violated is that if time to dispersal is long, the relevant game is not a prisoners' dilemma. In a group where all others are cooperators, a single defecting founder's defecting descendants would slow the growth of the group so that it would eventually be overtaken by a group consisting only of cooperators.

But why can't the Iron Rule be applied at times shortly before dispersal to individuals within a group? If the time to dispersal is short, then the game in which payoffs are descendants at dispersal time will be a prisoners' dilemma. But this game is played between individuals in the same group who are all descendants of the initial population. Matching among these individuals is decidedly not non-assortative. Thus, for the players who are matched non-assortatively, the game is not a prisoners' dilemma, while for the players for whom the game is a prisoners' dilemma, matching is not non-assortative.

Another instructive way of looking at the Cohen–Eshel game is to note that if we measure payoffs of each individual by the number of her own offspring, then the game is a multi-person prisoners' dilemma. But current rates of reproduction are not a proper measure of reproductive success. One's long run reproductive success depends not only on the number of one's own offspring, but on the rate at which these offspring, in turn, will reproduce. In the Cohen–Eshel model, the long-term reproductive value of an additional offspring depends on the proportion of altruists that are expected to be in one's group for the duration of survival of this group. In a population of altruists, an individual could increase her current reproduction by switching to the selfish strategy. But over time, her selfish descendants will slow the rate of reproduction for each other and if groups are sufficiently long-lived, the number of her descendants at the time her group disperses will be lower than it would have been had she remained an altruist.

3.6. Migration and stochastic extinction

Haystack models are artificial in that they assume that groups persist in perfect isolation until they are simultaneously disbanded. More realistic models would allow some migration between groups and would have asynchronous extinctions and resettlement. Such models have been studied, with results that are qualitatively similar to those of the haystack models. Ilan Eshel (1972), R. Levins (1970), Bruce Levin and William Kilmer (1974) and Scott Boorman and Paul Levitt (1980) consider stochastic dynamic models of group selection, in which selfish individuals reproduce more rapidly than altruists within their own group, but where groups face a probability of extinction that increases with the proportion of their members who are selfish. Locations in which extinction has occurred are reoccupied by the descendants of a random selection from the population at large. In the Levins and Boorman–Levitt models, monomorphic populations of altruists are not stable, but polymorphism is favored if the difference in extinction rates between altruistic and selfish groups is large enough relative to the selective pressure within groups. Eshel adds random migration between groups to his model and finds that if the migration rate is sufficiently small, then with probability one, the population will fix at a monomorphic population of altruists, and for larger migration rates the population will fix at a monomorphic selfish population. Levin and Kilmer (1974) conducted Monte Carlo simulations of a model similar to that proposed by Eshel[7] and found that altruism emerged when founding populations were no larger than 25 individuals and migration rates no larger than 5% per generation.

3.7. Relative and absolute payoffs

Some confusion in the debate on group selection has resulted from the fact that there exist games in which, paradoxically, *cooperate* is a dominant strategy, even though *defectors* always receive higher payoffs than cooperators. For example, consider N-player linear public goods game in which x is the fraction of cooperators in the population, the payoffs are bx for each defector and $bx - c$ for each cooperator. Thus defectors always get higher payoffs than cooperators. But suppose that $b > \frac{b}{N} > c > 0$. If this is the case, then given the action of other players, any player will get a higher payoff if she cooperates than if she defects. To see this, notice that if K other players cooperate, a player will get $\Pi_C(K, N) = b\frac{K+1}{N} - c$ if she cooperates and $\Pi_D(K, N) = b\frac{K}{N}$ if she defects. Thus we have $\Pi_C(K, N) - \Pi_D(K, N) = \frac{b}{N} - c > c$ and so *cooperate* is a dominant strategy.

David S. Wilson (1979) noticed this interesting case and argues for its significance. Wilson suggested that someone who cooperates when $b > c > \frac{b}{N}$ be called a *strong altruist* and someone who cooperates $\frac{b}{N} > c$ but not when $\frac{b}{N} < c$ be called a *weak altruist*.[8] Thus, in Wilson's terms, a strong altruist will cooperate even if doing so reduces both his *absolute* payoff and his relative payoff. A weak altruist will cooperate if doing so increases his absolute payoff, even if doing so reduces his payoff relative to that of other members of his group. Wilson maintains that "many, perhaps most, group-advantageous traits such as population regulation, predation defense, and role differentiation" may be explained by weak altruism. Wilson argues that individual selection models will incorrectly predict that weak altruistic behavior will be selected

---

[7] Eshel's model has asexual reproduction. The Levin–Kilmer model, like those of Levins and of Boorman–Levitt models has sexual diploid reproduction.

[8] As remarked in Section 2.2.2, Wilson formulates the game slightly differently. The conditions stated here are equivalent to his when Wilson's game is recast as an equivalent linear public goods game.

against, while properly constructed group selection models will predict selection *for* such behavior.

Alan Grafen (1984) suggests that Wilson's use of the term weak altruism for behavior that is consistent with maximization of absolute payoffs is misleading. According to Grafen,

> Another source of misunderstanding arises from the use of the word 'altruism'. As we noted earlier, altruism will not evolve in simple one-generation groups that are formed at random from the population ... (Wilson, Cohen and Eshel and others) ... redefined altruism to refer to relative success within the group rather than absolute success. ... Under the 'relative' definition, 'altruism' can spread. Wilson calls the acts that are altruistic under the relative definition, but not under the 'absolute' definition, 'weakly altruistic'. An alternative I prefer is 'a self-interested refusal to be spiteful'.

The question of what to call the pursuit of absolute benefit at the expense of relative benefit is of some interest, but a more important question is whether such behavior will prevail under evolutionary dynamics. Cohen and Eshel (1976) answered this question for the case of haystack models. The answer is that in haystack models, where relative and absolute benefit are in conflict, absolute benefit tends to prevail. A more careful statement can be found as part of Cohen and Eshel's Theorem 2 above. In a generalized haystack model in which the linear public goods game is played within localities, if $\frac{b}{N} > c$ then if the length of time T between founding and dispersal groups is short, there will be a unique stable equilibrium and it is a population of cooperators only. If, however, T is sufficiently large, then there will be two distinct stable equilibria, one populated by cooperators only and one by defectors only.[9] Thus Cohen and Eshel's result as applied to "one generation groups formed at random from the population" is in full agreement with Grafen's statement. In equilibrium, individuals will "cooperate" if and only if the direct benefits that they get for themselves exceed the cost. In Wilson's language, strong altruism will be driven out, but weak altruism will prevail. In Grafen's language, altruism will not survive, but the surviving population will show a self-interested refusal to be spiteful. Somewhat more surprisingly, Cohen and Eshel also find that if groups have long persistence, there will exist two equilibria, one where all cooperate and one where all defect, even where cooperation is a dominant strategy in terms of absolute payoffs in the single-shot game.

3.8. "Too stringent to be realistic?"

There seems to be broad agreement with Maynard Smith's (1976) statement that the argument about the significance of group selection for altruism is "not quantitative, but

---

[9] Wilson (1979) claims that theoreticians, including Cohen and Eshel, "tend to lump" the cases of weak altruism and strong altruism since neither is selected for in standard population models. In the case of Cohen and Eshel, I believe that Wilson is mistaken. As we see from Theorem 2, Cohen and Eshel find sharply divergent results for the cases of "weak" and "strong" altruism.

qualitative". At least for some time, there also appeared to be agreement that conditions under which group selection could work were not plausible.

David S. Wilson 1975 said that

> recent models ... make it plausible that (group selection) can occur – the main question is to what extent the conditions for its operation (small group size, high isolation, high extinction rates) are met in nature. The current consensus is that the proper conditions are infrequent or at least limited to special circumstances ...

In his survey of the theory of group selection and kin selection, Alan Grafen (1984) asserted that

> the final consensus on these models was that the conditions for (them) to be successful were too stringent to be realistic.

Even the beleaguered V.C. Wynne-Edwards called it quits, at least temporarily.[10] In a 1978 article Wynne-Edwards reports that

> in the last 15 years, many theoreticians have wrestled with it and in particular with the specific problem of the evolution of altruism. The general consensus of theoretical biologists at present is that credible models cannot be devised by which the slow march of group selection could overtake the much faster spread of selfish genes that bring gains in individual fitness. I therefore accept their opinion. [Wynne-Edwards (1978)]

Levin and Kilmer (1974) seem to have been the first to explore the plausibility of the parameter values under which models of group selection with random matching can lead to altruism. They conducted Monte Carlo simulations of a model similar to Eshel's extinction model (1972) and report that

> Interdemic selection favoring an allele was able to override the effects of Mendelian selection operating against it and led to maintenance of this allele in either fixed or polymorphic states. However, with potentially realistic deme survival functions and significant levels of Mendelian selection, restrictive conditions were necessary for this result to be obtained. In our simulated population, genetically effective deme sizes of less than 25 and usually closer to 10 were required, and the rate of gene exchange, through flow migration could not be much greater than 5% per generation.

Wilson (1987) ran Monte Carlo simulations of a model similar to Maynard Smith's haystack model, with founding populations of two individuals, and with dispersal and rematching of the population at the end of a fixed length of time. Wilson drops Maynard Smith's assumption that in populations with some genes for aggressive behavior,

---

[10] In a (1986) book, Wynne-Edwards attempts to reestablish his group-selectionist arguments on firmer theoretical ground.

all carriers of the gene for timidity are eliminated before the haystack population is dispersed. In Wilson's simulation, in each generation, an altruist reduces its own reproduction rate by c and contributes $b > c$ to the reproduction rate of a randomly selected other member of the group. As in the Eshel–Cohen model, a group stays together for a fixed, finite number of periods before dispersing and mating at random. But while reproduction is asexual in the Eshel–Cohen model, Wilson has sexual diploid reproduction. Wilson points out that if communities disperse after a single period, then the model is the same as Hamilton's model of kin-selection (1964), and Hamilton's rule applies; there will be a unique stable equilibrium, which will be populated by altruists if $b > 2c$ and by selfish individuals if $b < 2c$. When the number of generations is 5, his simulation results that indicate that with $b/c = 2.2$, there are two distinct equilibria, a stable polymorphic equilibrium with a population of 80% altruists and a stable monomorphic equilibrium where the entire population is selfish.

Theoretical considerations may help us to recognize circumstances under which Maynard Smith's haystack model and its generalizations would plausibly support a population of altruists. In the Maynard Smith model where each haystack population gets genetic material from just individuals, we find that a monomorphic population of altruists will be a stable equilibrium if at season's end, the number of mice produced in haystacks of altruists is more than twice the number of mice produced in haystacks of selfish mice. In the Cohen–Eshel extension, with N co-founders, in order for a monomorphic population of altruists to be a stable equilibrium, it must be that a single selfish individual in a community of altruists will have fewer descendants within that community at the time of dispersal than the *per capita* number of descendants of a community consisting entirely of altruists. Thus, if at the time the group disperses, the descendants of the selfish individual constitute the fraction s of its community, then it must be that groups consisting entirely of altruists have more than sN times as many inhabitants as groups that included a selfish individual among their founders. If, much as in Maynard Smith's model, descendants of a selfish individual dominate the population of their community quickly and thoroughly, then the purely altruistic groups would have to produce more than N times as many descendants as groups that included a selfish cofounder.

In haystack models, with durable groups, we have seen that when there is a stable equilibrium of cooperators, there typically exists another equilibrium comprised entirely of defectors. We need to be concerned about whether and how the system could move into the basin of attraction of an equilibrium of cooperators. One possibility is that payoffs to particular actions are likely to shift across time and space. As Wilson (1979) suggested, actions that are "strongly altruistic" in the current environment may have emerged as equilibrium actions in an environment where costs were smaller or benefits were greater so that these actions were once individually rational in single shot games. These equilibria might survive changes in costs or benefits such that self-interested play in single shot games no longer supports cooperation.

4. Assortative matching

In prisoners' dilemma games, everyone gets a higher payoff from playing with a cooperator than with a defector, but in any encounter, playing *defect* yields a higher payoff than playing *cooperate*. In a population where both types are equally likely to play with cooperators, defectors will enjoy higher expected payoffs. But if matching is assortative, so that cooperators have better chances of meeting cooperators than do defectors, the cost of cooperation may be repaid by a higher probability of playing a cooperative opponent.

4.1. Measures of assortativity

Suppose that a population is made up of two types of individuals and each of these individuals is matched with a partner. Let $x = (x_1, x_2)$ where x_1 is fraction of the population that is of type 1 and x_2 the fraction that is of type 2. Let $p_{ij}(x)$ be the conditional probability that an individual is matched with a type j, given that she, herself, is of type i. Since an individual is matched either to its own type or to the other type, it must be that $p_{11}(x) + p_{12}(x) = 1$ and $p_{21}(x) + p_{22}(x) = 1$. These equations imply that $p_{22}(x) - p_{12}(x) = p_{11}(x) - p_{21}(x)$. This equality allows us to define a useful measure of assortativity.

DEFINITION 4 ((Pairwise) Index of Assortativity). Let there be two types of individuals i and j and let $x = (x_1, x_2)$ where x_i is the proportion of type i's in the population. If individuals are matched in pairs, the index of assortativity $a(x)$ is the difference between the probability that an individual of type i is matched with its own type and the probability that an individual of type j is matched with a type i. That is, $a(x) = p_{11}(x) - p_{21}(x) = p_{22}(x) - p_{12}(x)$.

Sewall Wright (1921) defined assortativeness of mating with respect to a given trait as "the coefficient of correlation m between the two mates with respect to their possession of the trait". Cavalli-Sforza and Feldman (1981) interpret Wright's correlation as follows. "The population is conceived of as containing a fraction $(1 - m)$ that mates at random and a complementary fraction m which mates assortatively". With this interpretation, if the population frequency of a type is x, then the probability that an individual of that type mates an individual of its own type is $p(x) = m + x(1 - m)$. Wright's definition and that of Cavalli-Sforza and Feldman are seen to be equivalent where we take Wright to mean that m is the coefficient of correlation between indicator random variables for possession of the trait by mates.[11] It turns out that the definition of assor-

---

[11] Let I_i be an indicator variable that takes on value 1 if mate i has the trait and 0 otherwise. Wright's definition of the correlation coefficient between mates 1 and 2, is the correlation between the random variables I_1 and I_2. Thus we have $m = (E(I_1 I_2) - E(I_1)E(I_2))/(\sigma_1 \sigma_2)$ where σ_i is the standard deviation of I_i. Now $E(I_1 I_2) = xp(x)$, and for $i = 1, 2$, $E(I_i) = x$ and $\sigma_i = \sqrt{x(1-x)}$. Therefore $m = (xp(x) - x^2)/x(1-x)$. Rearranging terms, we find that this expression is equivalent to $p(x) = m + x(1 - m)$.

tativeness proposed by Wright and by Cavalli-Sforza and Feldman is equivalent to the special case of our definition where $a(x)$ is constant.

REMARK 1. Where there are two types of individuals and $a(x)$ is the index of assortativity,
- $p_{ii}(x) = a(x) + (1 - a(x)) x_i$ for each i.
- $p_{ji} = a(x)(1 - x_i)$.

PROOF. The fraction of all partnerships in which a type i is matched to a j is $x_i p_{ij}(x)$ and the fraction of all partnerships in which a type j is matched to a type i is $x_j p_{ji}(x)$. Since these are just two different ways of counting the same encounters it must be that $x_i p_{ij}(x) = x_j p_{ji}(x)$. From the definition of $a(x)$, we have $p_{ii}(x) = a(x) + p_{ji}(x)$. We also have $p_{ij}(x) = 1 - p_{ii}(x)$ and $x_1 + x_2 = 1$. Simple manipulations of these equations yields the claimed results. □

The simplest, and perhaps most useful, way to generalize the index of assortativity from groups of two members to groups of arbitrary size is to simply restate the pairwise definition in terms of expected proportions. Thus for an individual of type i, let p_{ij} to be the *expected proportion of other group members* who are of type j. Where group size is two, this expected proportion is simply the conditional probability that one's partner is a type j, given that one's own type is i. It remains the case, as with pairwise matching that $p_{11}(x) - p_{21}(x) = p_{22}(x) - p_{12}(x)$.

DEFINITION 5 ('Generalized' Index of Assortativity). Where there are two types of individuals and groups are of size N, for an individual of type i, let $p_{ij}(x)$ be the expected proportion of the $N - 1$ other group members who are of type j. The index of assortativity is defined as $a(x) = p_{11}(x) - p_{21}(x) = p_{22}(x) - p_{12}(x)$.

Where there are more than two possible types, we could define an index of assortativity between any two types as previously. In general, the index of assortativity between one pair of types need not be the same as that between another.

4.2. Hamilton's kin selection theory

Families are among the most conspicuous examples of non-randomly formed groups. William G. Hamilton (1964) developed a theory that predicts the strength of benevolent interactions between relatives based on their degree of relatedness. Maynard Smith (1964) conferred the name *kin selection theory* on this theory, while Dawkins (1989) gave it the evocative name *theory of the selfish gene*.

Biologists define the coefficient of relatedness between two individuals to be the probability that the alleles found in a randomly selected genetic locus in the two individuals are inherited from the same ancestor. In a population without inbreeding, the coefficient of relatedness is one half for full siblings, one fourth for half siblings, and

Table 3
Hamilton's help game

		Player 2	
		C	D
Player 1	C	$b-c$	$-c$
	D	b	0

one eighth for first cousins. According to Hamilton's theory, evolutionary dynamics selects for individuals who are willing to help a genetic relative if (and only if) if the increase in reproductive value, b gained by the beneficiary, multiplied by the *coefficient of relatedness r* between the two relatives exceeds the cost in reproductive value c to the helper. The following "maxim" has come to be known as *Hamilton's rule*.

DEFINITION 6 (Hamilton's Rule). Help someone whose coefficient of relatedness to you is r if and only if $br > c$.

Hamilton's work on kin selection came almost 10 years before Smith and Price (1973) introduced formal game theory to biologists. Therefore he did not think of the interaction between relatives as a game, but it is instructive to model Hamilton's interactions as a two-person game. In Hamilton's model, each player can choose whether to "cooperate" by helping the other or to "defect" by not helping. A player who helps the other player reduces her own reproductive success by an amount $c > 0$, but increases that of the other player by $b > c$. The payoff matrix for this game is as in Table 3. When $b > c > 0$, we see that Hamilton's help game satisfies the conditions for a two-person prisoner's dilemma. Since $b - c > 0$, both players are better off when both cooperate than when both defect. Given the other player's action, a player is always better off defecting than cooperating, since $b > b - c$ and $0 > -c$. As later discussion will show, Hamilton's help games are *special cases* of a prisoners' dilemma. There is a large class of prisoners' dilemma games which have quite different evolutionary dynamics from this special class.

A two-person linear public goods game might appear to be qualitatively different from Hamilton's help game. In a linear public goods game a cooperator incurs a cost to produce benefits for the other player *as well as himself*, while in the Hamilton game the other player is the only beneficiary of a helper's efforts. But a one-to-one linear transformation of payoffs allows every Hamilton game to be expressed as a linear public goods game and *vice versa*. A Hamilton's help game with benefit b and cost c is seen to be equivalent to a two-person linear public goods game in which a cooperator bears a cost of c', while conferring benefits of b' on both players; where $b' = b/2$ and $c' = c + b/2$. The Hamilton game is a prisoners' dilemma if $b > c > 0$ and the linear public goods game is a prisoners' dilemma if $c' > b' > c'/2$.

4.2.1. Index of assortativity for relatives

In later work, Hamilton (1975) recognized that his theory of kin selection could usefully be understood as a special case of assortative matching of partners in social interactions. It is helpful to see just how this is done by calculating the index of assortativity between prisoners' dilemma playing siblings who inherit their type by copying one of their parents.

We follow Hamilton (1964) in considering a simplified version of genetics, known to biologists as *sexual haploidy*. Most animals, including humans, are sexual diploids. A sexual diploid carries two alleles in each genetic locus, one of which is inherited from its mother and one from its father. These two alleles jointly determine those individual characteristics governed by this locus. A sexual haploid has only one allele at each locus. This allele is a copy of the allele in the corresponding locus of one of its parents, chosen at random. Sexual haploidy occurs as a genetic process among some living organisms, but is of special interest in the theory of cultural transmission since it is formally identical to a theory in which for a specified behavior, a child randomly selects one of its parents to copy.[12]

Suppose that individuals can adopt one of two possible strategies, cooperate or defect, in games played with their siblings. Each child is able to observe the type of its father and of its mother and copies one or the other with probability 1/2; independently of the choice made by its siblings. Suppose further that parents mate monogamously and independently of their strategy in games with siblings.

Let x be the proportion of cooperators in the entire population. If a child is a cooperator, then with probability 1/2 its sibling will have copied the same parent. In this case, the sibling must be a cooperator. With probability 1/2, the sibling role will have copied the other parent. Since parents are assumed to mate independently of their strategies, the probability that the other parent is a cooperator is x. Therefore the probability that a randomly chosen sibling of a cooperator is also a cooperator is

$$p_{cc}(x) = \frac{1}{2} + \frac{1}{2}x. \tag{5}$$

If a child is a defector, then its sibling will be a cooperator only if the sibling's role model is different from the defector's. With probability 1/2, the two siblings will have different role models, and given that they have different role models, the probability that the other parent is a cooperator is x. Therefore the probability that a randomly chosen sibling of a defector is a cooperator is

$$p_{dc}(x) = \frac{1}{2}x. \tag{6}$$

---

[12] Similar techniques can be applied and similar results obtained in the study of monomorphic equilibria in kin selection models with diploid sexual reproduction. For details, see Bergstrom (1995) or Boorman and Levitt (1980).

Notice that in a family of N siblings, $p_{cc}(x)$ and $p_{dc}(x)$ are equal to the expected proportion of an individual's siblings who are cooperators, conditional on that individual being a cooperator or a defector, respectively. Therefore the index of assortativity between full siblings is

$$a(x) = p_{cc}(x) - p_{dc}(x) = \frac{1}{2}. \tag{7}$$

Thus we see find that with non-assortative monogamous mating, the index of assortativity between siblings is constant and equal to their coefficient of relatedness, $r = 1/2$.

Similar calculations show that the index of assortativity between other related individuals is equal to their degree of relatedness. For example, the index of assortativity between half-siblings is $1/4$ and the index of assortativity between first cousins is $1/8$. Bergstrom (2001) calculates the index of assortativity for siblings under a variety of more general assumptions. For example, if parents mate assortatively, with an index of assortativity of mating m, then the index of assortativity between full siblings is $(1+m)/2$. If with some probability v a child copies neither of its parents, but a randomly chosen stranger, the index of assortativity is $v(1+m)/2$. That paper also calculates indexes of assortativity for children of polygamous marriages, and for cases where children preferentially copy the mother or the father.

4.3. Evolutionary dynamics with assortative mating

4.3.1. The linear public goods game

We can now investigate the evolutionary dynamics of populations of prisoners' dilemma players under assortative mating. The effect of assortative mating on expected payoffs is particularly easy to calculate when payoffs depend linearly on the proportion of cooperators in the group as in Haldane's N-player linear public goods game. Let x be the fraction of cooperators and $1 - x$ the fraction of defectors in the entire population. Define $p_{cc}(x)$ as the expected proportion of cooperators that a cooperator finds among other members of her group and $p_{dc}(x)$ as the expected proportion of cooperators that a defector finds in her group. Recalling Equations (1) and (2), the expected payoff of a cooperator is $p_{cc}(x)b - c'$ and the expected payoff of a defector is $p_{dc}(x)b$. Therefore the difference between the expected payoff of cooperators and that of defectors is just

$$p_{cc}(x)b - c' - p_{dc}(x)b = a(x)b - c' \tag{8}$$

where $a(x)$ is the index of assortativity.

Equation (8) generalizes Hamilton's rule from linear pairwise interactions to the N player linear public goods game with voluntary provision of public goods. In this generalization, the index of assortativity plays the same formal role that the coefficient of relatedness plays in kin selection theory. In the case of kin selection theory, the index of assortativity $a(x)$ is constant for all x and equal to the coefficient of relatedness r between any two players.

If $a(x) = a$ is constant, then except for the knife-edge case where $ab = c$, there will be a unique stable equilibrium. If $a > b/c$, then so long as both types are present, the proportion of cooperators will grow relative to that of defectors. If $a < b/c$, the reverse is true. Thus the unique stable equilibrium is a population made up entirely of cooperators if $a > c/b$ and a population made up entirely of defectors if $a < b/c$.

If $a(x)$ is variable, then it is possible that there may be more than one equilibrium, or there may be a polymorphic equilibrium with some individuals of each type. In Section 4.4 we analyze an interesting example in which $a(x)$ is variable and where there is a stable polymorphic equilibrium.

4.3.2. Dynamics with nonlinear payoff functions

Alan Grafen (1979) and Gordon Hines and Maynard Smith (1979) show that Hamilton's rule is not correct in general for the wider class of games in which the costs of helping and the benefits of being helped may depend on the actions taken by both players. Bergstrom (1995) classifies two-player non-linear games according to whether there is complementarity or substitutability between actions and shows the way that equilibrium is altered from the Hamilton's rule predictions in each of these cases.

We follow Rappaport and Chammah (1965), in denoting the payoffs (Table 4) in a general prisoners' dilemma game by R (reward) for mutual cooperation, P (punishment) for mutual defection, T (temptation) to a defector whose opponent cooperates, and S (sucker's payoff) to a cooperator whose opponent defects.

This game is a prisoners' dilemma whenever $T > R > P > S$.[13] In the case of Hamilton's help game, described by Table 2 in Section 4.2, we have $T = b$, $R = b - c$, $P = 0$, $S = -c$. It follows that for Hamilton's game, $R + P = T + S = b - c$. Not every prisoners' dilemma game has this property. There are prisoners' dilemma games in which $R + P > T + S$ and some in which $R + P < T + S$. The evolutionary dynamics of each of these prisoners' dilemma games are qualitatively different from those of Hamilton's help game.

Table 4
Payoff matrix

		Player 2	
		C	D
Player 1	C	R	S
	D	T	P

---

[13] Some writers use a definition that adds the additional restriction that $2R > T + P$ which ensures that mutual cooperation yields a higher *total* payoff than the outcome where one player cooperates and the other defects.

(a) Two Stable Boundary Equilibria

(b) A Stable Interior Equilibrium

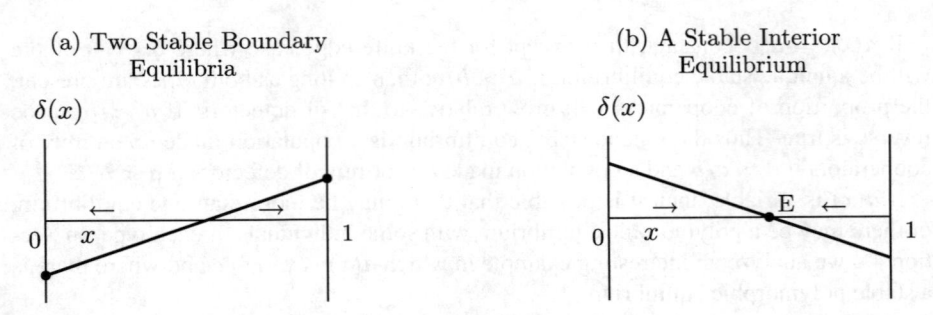

Figure 2. Dynamics of prisoners' dilemma.

Let x be the fraction of cooperators in the population, $p_{cc}(x)$ the probability that a cooperator is matched with a cooperator and $p_{dc}(x)$, the probability that a defector is matched with a cooperator. Then the expected payoff to a cooperator is:

$$p_{cc}(x)R + \bigl(1 - p_{cc}(x)\bigr)S = S + p_{cc}(x)(R - S)$$
$$= S + a(x)(R - S) + x\bigl(1 - a(x)\bigr)(R - S) \qquad (9)$$

where the latter equation follows from Remark 1.

The expected payoff to a defector is:

$$p_{dc}(x)T + (1 - p_{dc})P = P + p_{dc}(T - P)$$
$$= P + x\bigl(1 - a(x)\bigr)(T - P) \qquad (10)$$

where again the latter equation follows from Remark 1. If we subtract the expression in Equation (10) from that in Equation (9), we can express the difference between the expected payoff to a cooperator and that to a defector as a function of x:

$$\delta(x) = S - P + a(x)(R - S) + x\bigl(1 - a(x)\bigr)\bigl(R + P - (S + T)\bigr). \qquad (11)$$

Equation (11) can be used to characterize the equilibria, under the assumption of monotone dynamics (see Section 2.4.1), of any symmetric two-player, two-strategy games with assortative matching.[14]

Where $a(x) = a$ is constant, we see from Equation (11) that the difference between the payoffs to the two strategies is linear in the proportion x of cooperators in the population. In this case, we see that $\delta(0) = aR + (1-a)S - P$ and $\delta(1) = R - (aP + (1-a)T)$. A simple calculation shows that $\delta(1) - \delta(0) = (1-a)(R + P - S - T)$. Thus the graph of $\delta(x)$ slopes upward if $R + P > S + T$, downward if $R + P < S + T$, and is horizontal if $R + P = S + T$. It could happen that $\delta(0)$ and $\delta(1)$ are both positive, in which case there is a unique stable equilibrium

---

[14] Though most of our discussion focusses on prisoners' dilemma, this formula applies as well to games without a dominant strategy, such as *chicken*, and the *stag hunt*.

populated entirely of cooperators or both negative, in which case there is a unique stable equilibrium populated entirely by defectors. But there are also two other interesting cases. In Figure 2(a), where $\delta(0) < 0$ and $\delta(1) > 0$, there are two distinct "monomorphic" equilibria, one consisting of cooperators only and one consisting of defectors only. In Figure 2(b) where $\delta(0) > 0$ and $\delta(1) < 0$, neither monomorphic population is stable and there is a unique stable "polymorphic" equilibrium at the point E.

4.4. Assortative matching with partner choice

We can expect to see assortative matching if individuals have some evidence of each others' types and some choice about with whom they match. In a multiplayer prisoners' dilemma game, everyone would rather be matched with cooperators than with defectors. If players' types were perfectly observable and if groups are able to restrict entry, then groups of cooperators would not admit defectors, and so the two types would be strictly segregated. But suppose that detection is less than perfectly accurate.

Bergstrom (2001) presents a model in which players are labeled with an imperfect indicator of their type. The indicator might be a reputation based on partial information or a set of behavioral cues, or perhaps the result of a psychological test. Assume that with probability $\alpha > 1/2$, a cooperator is correctly labeled as a cooperator and with probability $1 - \alpha$ is mislabeled as a defector. Assume that with probability $\beta > 1/2$, a defector is correctly labeled and with probability $1 - \beta$ is mislabeled as a cooperator.

Everyone sees the same labels, so that at the time when players choose partners there are only two distinguishable types: players who appear to be cooperators and players who appear to be defectors. Although everyone realizes that the indicators are not entirely accurate, everyone prefers to match with an apparent cooperator rather than an apparent defector. Therefore, with voluntary matching, there will be two kinds of groups, those made up entirely of apparent cooperators and those made up entirely of apparent defectors.

In this model, in contrast to the case of kin selection, the index of assortativity varies with the proportion of cooperators in the population. If we graph $a(\cdot)$ as a function of x, the graph looks qualitatively like Figure 3.[15]

There is a simple intuitive explanation for the fact that $a(0) = a(1) = 0$. In general, a cooperator is more likely to be matched with a cooperator than is a defector because a cooperator is more likely to be labeled a cooperator than is a defector. But if x is small, so that actual cooperators are rare, the advantage of being matched with an apparent cooperator is small because almost all apparent cooperators are actually defectors who have been mislabeled. Similarly, when x is close to one, defectors are rare, so that most apparent defectors are actually cooperators who have been mislabeled. In the latter case, even if a defector is labeled a defector, his chance of getting matched with a

---

[15] In Bergstrom (2001), I exhibit a closed form expression for $a(x)$ and show that $a(0) = a(1) = 0$, $a'(0) > 0$, $a'(1) < 0$ and $a''(x) < 0$ for all $x \in [0, 1]$.

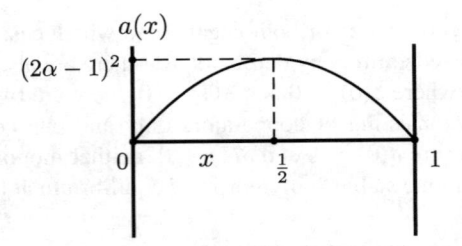

Figure 3. Graph of $a(x)$ where $\alpha = \beta$.

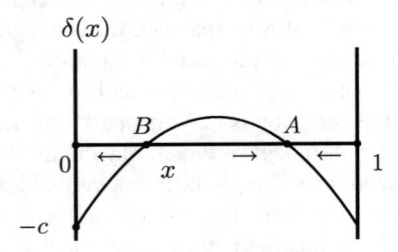

Figure 4. Graph of $\delta(x)$ for additive prisoner's dilemma.

cooperator are good. Thus in the two extreme cases, where x approaches zero and where x approaches one, the chances of being matched with a cooperator are nearly the same for a defector as for a cooperator.

Recall from Equation (8), that in the Haldane linear multiperson prisoners' dilemma game, the difference between the expected payoff of cooperators and that of defectors is simply $\delta(x) = a(x)b - c$ where x is the fraction of cooperators in the population and $a(x)$ is the index of assortativity. Figure 4 shows the graph of $\delta(x)$ for a case in which $\delta(x)$ takes some positive values. As we see from the graph, under monotone dynamics there are two locally stable equilibria. One of these equilibria occurs where $x = 0$ and the other is at the point marked A. For any level of x to the left of the point B or to the right of the point A, $\delta(x) < 0$ and so x, the proportion of cooperators in the population, would decline. For any level of x between the points A and B, $\delta(x) > 0$ and so in this region x would increase.

For Prisoners' Dilemma games with additive payoffs, $\delta(x) = a(x)b - c$. We have shown that $a(0) = a(1) = 0$, $a'(0) > 0$, $a'(1) < 0$, and $a''(x) < 0$ for all x between 0 and 1. It follows that $\delta(0) = \delta(1) < 0$, $\delta'(0) > 0$, and $\delta'(1) < 0$, and $\delta''(x) < 0$ for all x between 0 and 1. The fact that $\delta''(x) < 0$ on the interval $[0, 1]$ implies that the graph of $\delta(x)$ is "single-peaked" as in Figure 4. Where this is the case, and if $\delta(x) > 0$ for some x, there must be exactly one stable polymorphic equilibrium and one stable monomorphic equilibrium with defectors only.

An earlier model by Robert Frank (1987) also explores the evolutionary dynamics in a population of cooperators and defectors.[16] In Frank's model, each member of each type projects a "signal of trustworthiness" that is a random draw from a continuous signal distribution. The two types draw from different distributions, whose supports overlap, but where the higher one's signal is the more likely it is that one is a cooperator. Each individual has the option of matching with a partner or of having no partner. Partners play a game of prisoners' dilemma. Those who choose to have no partner are assumed to receive the same payoff as that received by a defector matched with a defector. Players understand the game, including the payoff values and statistical distributions of payoffs and can rationally calculate their own optimal responses. Since each player prefers those who project higher signals, every individual will be matched with someone who projects approximately the same signal. In equilibrium, cooperators who project a signal lower than some critical value realize that the partners that they can attract are so likely to be defectors that it is better to stay unmatched. Frank shows that for this model there is a unique stable equilibrium and it occurs with a polymorphic population that includes both cooperators and defectors.

Skyrms and Pemantle (2000) explicitly model the dynamic formation of group structure by reinforcement learning. Individuals begin to interact at random to play a game. The game payoffs determine which interactions are reinforced and a social network emerges. They report that social interaction groups that tend to form in their model consist of small interaction groups within which there is partial coordination of strategies.

4.5. Assortative matching induced by spatial structure

The reason that evolution selects for individuals who value their siblings' well-being is that two siblings have a high probability of carrying the same genetic program. Hence an individual who is programmed to be kind to his brother is likely to be the beneficiary of a kind brother. Similarly, if neighbors have a significant probability of sharing the same role model, those who cooperate with neighbors may enjoy a higher likelihood of benefiting from neighborly cooperation than those who act selfishly.

Evolutionary biologists have stressed the importance of spatial structure on the spread of mutations, genetic variation and the formation of species. Wright (1943) studied the degree of inbreeding in a model in which a population is distributed uniformly over a large area, but individuals are more likely to find mates who live nearby. Kimura and Weiss (1964) studied genetic correlations in a one dimensional "stepping stone model" in which there is an array of colonies along a line and where "in each generation an individual can migrate at most 'one step' in either direction" and extended this model to colonies located on two and three dimensional lattices.

More recent authors have explored the dynamics of a population of agents located on a spatial grid, who repeatedly play a game with their neighbors and who may switch

---

[16] Frank calls them "honest" and "dishonest" types.

their strategies either deterministically or stochastically in response to their observations of the payoffs realized by themselves and their neighbors. Nowak and May (1993) ran computer simulations with a deterministic model of prisoners' dilemma playing agents located on a two-dimensional grid. The grid is initially populated with some assortment of cooperators and defectors. In each round, each individual uses its preassigned strategy in a game of prisoners' dilemma with each of its immediate neighbors. After this round, each site is occupied by its original owner or by one of its neighbors, depending on who had the highest score in the previous round. Their simulations show that this process can generate chaotically changing spatial patterns in which the proportions of cooperators and defectors fluctuate about long-term averages.

Bergstrom and Oded Stark (1993) model a population of farmers located on a road that loops around a lake. Each farmer plays prisoners' dilemma with his two adjacent neighbors, using one of the two strategies cooperate or defect. The farmers' sons observe the strategies and payoffs of their fathers and their immediate neighbors and imitate the most successful of these individuals. For this setup, it turns out that any arrangement of cooperators and defectors will be stable if cooperators appear in clusters of three or more and defectors in clusters of two or more. Bergstrom and Stark show that if the sons do not pay attention to their fathers, but copy the more successful of their father's neighbors, then some patterns of behavior will "move in a circle" around the lake. For example, if there are at least eight farmers on the road, a pattern of the form *CDCCC* would move clockwise around the lake, moving by one farm in each generation. Thus a long-lived chronicler, who observed behavior at a single farm would see "cyclic behavior" in which spells of cooperation are interrupted by defection according to a regular temporal pattern.

Eshel, Larry Samuelson and Avner Shaked (1998) present a thorough analysis of the circular setup considered by Bergstrom and Stark. For the nonstochastic case, they show that in addition to an equilibrium with defectors only, there are stable equilibria in which some cooperators and some defectors survive and that in all such equilibria, at least 60 per cent of the population must be cooperators. They also show that if the initial distribution of cooperators and defectors is determined by independent random draws, then as the size of the population gets large, the probability that the initial distribution is in the basin of attraction of one of the equilibria that includes cooperators approaches unity.

Surprisingly, Eshel et al. were able to show that when there is a positive probability of mutations, in the limit as the mutation rate becomes small, the only stationary states that have positive probability are the ones in which at least 60 percent of the population are cooperators. As the authors explain:

> One's initial impression might be that mutation should be inimical to Altruists because a mutant Egoist will thrive and grow when introduced into a collection of Altruists, while a lone Altruist will whither and die when introduced into a collection of Egoists. ... Altruists can thus invade a world of Egoists with only a local burst of mutation that creates a small string of Altruists, which will then subsequently grow to a large number of Altruists. Mutations can create small pockets of

egoism, but these pockets destroy one another if they are placed too close together, placing an upper bound on the number of Egoists that can appear.

Although the structure of equilibrium sets in the Bergstrom–Stark model and in the Eshel–Samuelson–Shaked model seem too complicated and diverse for a simple measure of assortativity to be of any use, Eshel, Emilia Sansone and Shaked (1999) constructed a model of prisoners' dilemma players on a line in which, quite remarkably, the dynamics depend on the index of assortativity for a specific critical configuration of cooperators and defectors. The model starts with an initial configuration of cooperators and defectors. In each period, each individual plays a prisoners' dilemma game with each of her k nearest neighbors. A player will not change strategies from one period to the next if her two nearest neighbors use the same strategy that she uses. But one of these neighbors uses a different strategy, she will observe the average realized payoffs of cooperators and of defectors who are within n positions of herself. She will randomly adopt a strategy for the next period, where the probability that a strategy is adopted is proportional to the average payoff of those whom she observes using that strategy. The authors show that the long run fate of this system depends entirely on what happens at a frontier between long strings of individuals of each type. From this configuration, one can calculate the probability that a defector situated at the boundary will switch to cooperation and the probability that a cooperator situated at the boundary will switch to defection. These two probabilities depend on comparisons of the average payoffs of cooperators and of defectors who are located within n positions of the boundary between a long strong of cooperators and a long string of defectors. The dynamics is a simple random walk in which the limiting outcome is a population of cooperators or of defectors, depending on whether defectors are more likely to switch than cooperators or *vice versa*.

In the Eshel, Shaked, Sansone model the critical observers on the frontier see their own payoffs and the payoffs to their n neighbors. Each observed individual plays prisoners' dilemma with her k nearest neighbors. Since the observed defectors are located somewhere in a string of defectors and the observed cooperators are located somewhere in a string of cooperators, the cooperators enjoy the advantage of a larger proportion of encounters with cooperators than that experienced by defectors. If k, the number of opponents played in each direction is large and if n the distance over which the boundary individuals observe payoffs, this advantage will be slight since both the cooperators and defectors that are observed will be near the boundary and will play nearly equal numbers of cooperators and defectors. On the other hand, if n is large relative to k, then the average payoff of the observed cooperators will be close to the payoff in a community of cooperators only and the average payoff of the observed defectors will be close to the payoff in a community of defectors only.

The defectors would of course get higher payoffs if they played against the same number of cooperators as did the cooperators, but in this spatial setup, the defectors will be matched with more defectors than the cooperators and individuals living further from the frontier will have larger proportions of their neighbors being of their own type. The larger n is relative to k, the greater the proportion of observed neighbors who play their own type. The authors find expressions for the proportions of cooperators and of defectors encountered by those members of each type who can be observed by the frontier individual. From these calculations they produce an explicit function $r(k, n)$ that corresponds exactly to the *index of assortativity* as we have defined it. In the special case where the prisoners' dilemma game has the linear payoffs that we have earlier described as the linear public goods game, they observe that the outcome is exactly as would be predicted by Hamilton's rule where the coefficient of relatedness is $r(k, n)$. That is to say, cooperation will prevail if $r(k, n)b > c$ and defection will prevail if $r(k, n)b < c$.

5. Repeated games and group selection

5.1. Group selection from multiple Nash equilibria

"Punishment allows the evolution of cooperation (or anything else) in sizeable groups" by Robert Boyd and Peter Richerson (1992) is one of those rare scholarly titles that nudges readers' minds toward a productive line of thought.[17] In an earlier paper, Boyd and Richerson (1990) noticed that group selection is a highly plausible evolutionary mechanism where games with more than one Nash equilibrium are played within relatively distinct subpopulations. They suggested that group selection is likely to be effective "if processes increasing the frequency of successful strategies *within* groups are strong compared to rate of migration among groups" and if "individuals drawn from a single group make up a sufficiently large fraction of newly formed groups". In (1990), Boyd and Richerson succinctly explain the essence of group selection among alternative local Nash equilibria in the following words. "Viewed from the within-group perspective, behavior will seem egoistic, but the egoistically enforced equilibria with the greatest group benefit will prevail". In (1992), they strengthen the case for group selection by noting that within stable groups where individuals encounter each other repeatedly and can punish defections from a group norm, an extremely diverse range of results can be sustained as Nash equilibria.

Ken Binmore (1994b) observed that "If our Game of Life were the one-shot Prisoners' Dilemma, we should never have evolved as social animals". Binmore argues that the "Game of Life" is best modeled as an indefinitely repeated game in which reciprocal rewards and punishments can be practiced. As Binmore reminds us, this idea is not new. In the seventh century before Christ, Hesiod stated [Waugh (1929)] the maxim "Give to him who gives, and do not give to him who does not". David Hume (1978) says in language that is suggestive of modern game theory:

> I learn to do service to another, without bearing him any real kindness, because I foresee, that he will return my service in expectation of another of the same kind,

---

[17] Dawkins' *The Selfish Gene* is another member of this class.

and in order to maintain the same correspondence of good offices with me and others. And accordingly, after I have serv'd him ... he is induc'd to do his part, as foreseeing the consequences of his refusal. (p. 521)

Several game theorists in the 1950's nearly simultaneously discovered the *folk theorem*, which informs us that in indefinitely repeated games, almost all possible patterns of individual behavior can be sustained as Nash equilibria. For example, in the simple case of repeated prisoners' dilemma between two players, almost any intertemporal pattern of cooperation and defection on the part of each players can be maintained as a Nash equilibrium. The logic of the folk theorem is that in repeated games, almost any behavior can be induced as a Nash equilibrium by the threat of punishment for deviant actions. Individuals can be coordinated on a configuration of strategies by a stable, self-policing norm. Such a norm prescribes a course of action to each player conditional on the actions of the others and it includes instructions on how to punish any deviant player who violates his prescribed course of action. The punishments for each deviation must be sufficient to ensure that each individual takes the prescribed action.

Where the game is single-shot prisoners' dilemma, the theory of individual selection almost inevitably predicts universal defection, but in repeated games, even repeated prisoners' dilemma, individual selection theory leaves us an embarrassment of Nash equilibria and essentially no predictive power. As Boyd and Richerson (1992, 2001), Binmore (1992, 1994a, 1994b), and Sober and Wilson (1999) suggest, the stage is set for group selection to play a mighty role. Consider a population in which individuals are clustered into semi-isolated groups within which most of their social interactions occur. Within groups, these individuals play a repeated game that has many equilibria, some of which are better for all members than others. Binmore (1994b) suggests that we can expect groups using Pareto-superior equilibria to grow in size and number relative to the rest of the population and that eventually the groups that coordinate on Pareto-inferior equilibria will disappear. The transmission process may be speeded either by migrants who move to more successful groups and adopt local ways or by imitation. Boyd and Richerson (2001) propose that in geographically structured populations, imitation of behavior in successful neighboring groups is likely to greatly speed the spread of Pareto-superior equilibria.

5.2. How can costly punishment survive?

While the *folk theorem* goes a long way toward explaining the power of norms and punishment threats for maintaining a great variety of possible outcomes as Nash equilibria within communities, there remain some troubling details to be resolved in determining whether plausible evolutionary processes will sustain the punishment strategies needed to support all of the outcomes that folk theorem postulates. As Henrich and Boyd (2001) put it

Many students of human behavior believe that large-scale human cooperation is maintained by threat of punishment. ... However, explaining cooperation in this way leads to a new problem: why do people punish noncooperators?... Individuals who punish defectors provide a public good, and thus can be exploited by non-punishing cooperators if punishment is costly.

The standard game theoretic answer to this conundrum is that equilibrium strategies include instructions to punish others if they are "supposed to punish" and fail to do so. These instructions include a requirement to punish those who won't punish others when they are supposed to do so. In equilibrium, if you fail to perform your obligation to punish someone who doesn't do his task, you will be punished by someone else who in turn would be punished if he did not punish you, and so on *ad infinitum*. From an evolutionary point of view, this resolution seems unsatisfactory. Can we really expect that people or animals will keep track of their obligations to do nth order punishment for n greater than one or two? Moreover if the society is really in an equilibrium, deviations that require punishment will be rare and usually the result of a "mistake". Selection is likely to be very weak in such circumstances.

As Rajiv Sethi and R. Somanathan (2003) point out in their survey paper "Understanding Reciprocity", "(The) problem of reciprocity being undermined by the gradual encroachment of unconditional cooperation is pervasive in the literature". Not only is it likely that punishment is costly in terms of direct payoffs. A strategy that involves unused punishments is, by any reasonable measure, more complex than a strategy that dictates the same actions in a world of cooperators but omits the punishment branch. Binmore and Samuelson (1992) present a model in which strategies are modeled as finite-state automata and complexity is measured by the number of states. They postulate that a mutant that gets the same payoff as the incumbents but is less complex will invade a population. This assumption eliminates the possibility that 'nice' strategies, such as tit-for-tat will be stable monomorphic equilibria.

Nowak and May (1998) introduce an evolutionary model in which individuals accumulate reputations. In each generation, a large number of pairs of individuals are selected randomly. One member of each pair is given a chance to play donor and the other is the potential recipient. Those who choose to donate reduce their wealth by c, while the recipient's wealth increases by $b > c$. Each player has an *image score* that starts out at 0 at the beginning of life and is incremented by one unit every time that she makes a donation. A strategy for any individual i takes the form of a threshold k_i, such that if given a chance to donate to a recipient with image score s, i will do so if and only if $s \geqslant k_i$. After the interactions for the current generation have taken place, members of this generation are replaced by their offspring, who inherit the strategies of their parents (but not their image scores). The number of offspring that a parent has is proportional to the wealth that she accumulates during the course of her life. Nowak and Sigmund run computer simulations of this model. They find that when the model is run for about 150 generations, almost all population members adopt a strategy of donating to everyone with an image score of 0 or higher. When these strategies are played out, this means that almost everyone donates at every opportunity. When Nowak and Sigmund add a very small rate of mutation to new strategies, the results are very different. According to Nowak and Sigmund, with mutation the population, long term simulations with mutation ... show endless cycles. ... defectors are invaded by discriminators, who only help players whose score exceeds some threshold. Next discriminators are undermined by unconditional cooperators. The prevalence of these indiscriminate altruists subsequently allows the return of defectors.

The Nowak–Sigmund model does not follow the course suggested by game theoretic constructions of punishment strategies. In their model, one's reputation improves whenever one makes a donation, regardless of whether the potential recipient has been generous or not. The kind of punishment strategy that the folk theorem suggests would be more like the following. Initially, everyone is in *good standing*. After each play, a person is in good standing if and only if she donated whenever she had a chance to donate to a person in good standing and she refused to donate whenever she had a chance to donate to a person not in good standing.

Bowles and Gintis (2000) build an evolutionary model of a population that includes some *shirkers* and some *reciprocators* who don't shirk and who, despite the fact that it is costly, will punish shirkers when they catch them shirking. Equilibrium in their model has a mixed population of workers and shirkers. However, they evade the problem of the evolutionary stability by not allowing the possibility of an invader who neither shirks nor punishes.

In "The viability of vengeance", Dan Friedman and Nirvikar Singh (1999) present a good discussion of the evolutionary stability of costly punishment. Friedman and Singh distinguish between punishment of group members and of outsiders. They suggest that within groups, one's actions are observed and remembered. A reputation for being willing to avenge actions harmful to oneself may be sufficient compensation for the costs of retribution. They propose that in dealing with outsiders, one is remembered not as an individual but as a representative of one's group. Accordingly, a willingness to avenge harm done by outsiders is a *public good* for one's own group since it deters outsiders from uncooperative behavior to group members. They propose that a failure to avenge wrongs from outsiders is punished (costlessly) by one's own group, through loss of status.

In their paper "Why punish defectors: Weak conformist transmission can stabilize costly enforcement of norms in cooperative dilemmas",[18] Henrich and Boyd (2001) present an ingenious theory of the viability of expensive vengeance. The authors suggest that "the evolution of cooperation and punishment are plausibly a side-effect of a tendency to adopt common behaviors during enculturation". They argue that since it is not possible to analyze and "solve" the complex social games that we play, imitation plays a large role in decision-making. Since observation of the realized payoffs of others is not always possible, much of this imitation takes the form of 'copy-the-majority' rather than 'copy-the-most-successful'.

---

[18] This paper is a contender with the earlier cited Boyd–Richerson paper for an "informative title award".

Henrich and Boyd test this idea on a multi-stage game. The first stage of this game is a "Haldane" game in which each individual can choose whether to make a contribution to the group at a cost of c to himself and with a total benefit of b divided equally among all group members. Those who don't contribute share the benefits but don't pay the cost. With a small probability, individuals who intend to contribute mistakenly do not. The game has a second stage in which each individual decides whether or not to punish those who defected in the first stage. Punishing costs ϕ to the punisher and ρ to the punished, where $\phi < \rho < c$. There is a second punishing stage in which individuals decide, with the same cost structure, whether to punish those who have not punished the malefactors of the first stage. And a finite number of additional stages is constructed recursively. At each stage the authors suppose that there is some small probability of mistakes.

At each stage of the game, there are two possible strategies, cooperate or defect. In the first stage, cooperate means to contribute. In later stages, cooperate means to punish those who defected in the previous stage. The population evolves according to "replicator dynamics" applied separately to the strategy used in each stage. In particular the difference between the growth rate of cooperators and the growth rate of defectors for this stage is a weighted average of two differences: the difference between the average payoffs of cooperators and defectors in that stage and the difference between the fraction of the population who are cooperators and the fraction who are defectors. The latter difference reflects the force of conformism.

If the weight placed on conformism is sufficiently large, then of course any strategy, including cooperate and don't punish can be maintained, simply because an invader's payoff advantage would be overwhelmed by the conformist advantage of the incumbent strategy. But while placing some weight on copying the majority is plausibly adaptive, placing such a large weight does not seem likely to be so. The authors stress that

> ... stabilization of punishment is from the gene's point of view a maladaptive side-effect of conformist transmission. If there were genetic variability in the strength of conformist transmission and cooperative dilemmas were the *only* problem humans faced, then conformist transmission might never evolve.

The key to Henrich and Boyd's result is that it takes only a very small weight on conformity to maintain an equilibrium that supports punishment strategies. To see why, let us look at a version of the Henrich–Boyd model with only one punishment stage. Suppose that the population is initially one in which everyone tries to cooperate at the first stage and also in the punishment stage. Then the only defections observed will be mistakes (or possibly actions of a few mutants). Individuals who defect in the first stage will get lower payoffs than those who cooperate in the first stage because almost everyone is cooperating in the punishment stage by punishing first-stage defectors. Individuals who defect in the punishment stage by not punishing first stage defectors *will* get higher payoffs than those who cooperate by punishing first stage defectors, but only slightly higher since there are very few defections in the first stage. Since almost everyone is observed to cooperate in the second stage, even a very small coefficient on conformism will be sufficient to overcome this small payoff difference. Henrich and Boyd show that when higher levels of punishment are accounted for, an even smaller coefficient on conformism is sufficient to maintain cooperation at all stages.

The Henrich–Boyd argument leaves some room for skepticism. If defections on the first round are rare, isn't it likely that in realistic models few individuals would observe a defection? But if that is the case, then conformists who observe a defection might not be able to determine that first-order punishment is the social norm. Perhaps a polymorphic equilibrium that has just enough defectors to make the prevalence of punishment observable to conformists could be obtained in this setting.

There is room to question whether the visceral, seemingly irrational anger that people feel when they are cheated or otherwise violated can really be explained as a result of cultural transmission rather than as genetically hard-wired.

A recent paper by Florian Herold (2003) proposes another interesting explanation for the survival. Herold studies a "haystack model" in which individuals are randomly assembled into groups where they interact and reproduce. The number of offspring that a player has will be her payoff in an n-player prisoners' dilemma game in her group. Players can observe the play of others and are able to inflict punishment, but at a cost to themselves. Individuals have a hard-wired inclination either to punish defectors or not, but make a calculated choice of whether to cooperate or defect. All in the group will cooperate if and only if the number of punishers exceeds some threshold. Otherwise they will all defect. Herold shows that with monotone selection dynamics, there is an evolutionarily stable equilibrium in which all players are programmed to engage in costly punishment and where everyone therefore cooperates. In Herold's model, if almost everybody in the population at large is a punisher, then in almost all groups, there is a preponderance of punishers and so everybody chooses to cooperate. In this case, punishers don't have to bear the costs of punishing. The only way that a non-punisher could have a different payoff from a punisher would be if the random matching process selects a number of punishers that is below the cooperation-inducing threshold. Herold noticed the important fact that if non-punishers are rare, then conditional on the event that a group does not achieve the threshold number of punishers, the probability is very high that the number of punishers in the group is just one below threshold, so that each non-punisher in the group is "pivotal" to whether the group exhibits cooperation or defection. This implies that when they are rare, non-punishers will get lower expected payoffs than punishers.

5.3. Evidence from psychology and anthropology

Leda Cosmides, a psychologist and John Tooby, an anthropologist, offer [Cosmides (1989), Cosmides and Tooby (1989)] experimental evidence indicating that people are much better at solving logical problems that are framed as "cheater-detection" problems than at solving equivalent problems in other frameworks. In their view, this is evidence that individuals have evolved special modules in their brains for solving such problems.

There is interesting experimental evidence that cultural transmission plays an important role in determining when people get angry. Richard Nisbett and Dov Cohen (1996) conducted experiments in which male college students are subjected to rude and insulting behavior in the laboratory. Using questionnaires, behavioral responses, and checks of testosterone levels, they find that students who were raised in the American South become much angrier and more ready to fight than those who were raised in the North. The authors attribute this difference to the existence of a "culture of honor" in the South that is not present in the North.

Economists and anthropologists have recently conducted a remarkable series of experimental studies of how people in different cultures play the *ultimatum game*. In an ultimatum game, two players are matched and there is a fixed sum of money to be allocated. The first player, "the proposer" offers a portion of the total to the second player, "the responder". The responder can either accept or reject the offer. If the responder accepts, the division is that proposed. If the responder rejects, both players receive nothing. If this game is played by rational players who care only about their money payoff, then equilibrium in this behavior is for the proposer to offer the responder a very small share, which the responder will accept. In actual experiments with laboratory subjects in the United States, it was discovered that typically proposers offered a share of nearly one half, and this was accepted. When proposers attempted to capture a significantly larger share, responders would usually reject the proposal, thus acting as if they were willing to forego the small share that they were offered in order to "punish" a greedy proposer. In 1991, Alvin Roth and his coworkers (1991) did a "cross-cultural" conducted in which they compared the results from running the experiment in the U.S., and in Israel, Japan, and in Slovenia. They found very similar results in all four countries. In 2000, Joe Henrich (2000), published a study of an ultimatum game performed with the Machiguenga of Peru. The Machiguenga live in mobile, single-family units and small extended-family hamlets scattered throughout the tropical forests of the Amazon, where they practice hunting, fishing, gathering, and some horticulture. According to Henrich, among the Machiguenga, "cooperation above the family level is almost unknown". Henrich found that in sharp contrast to the results in the Western countries, where the modal offer was usual fifty percent, the modal share offered by the Machiguenga was only fifteen percent. Moreover, although the Machiguenga responders were offered a much smaller share than their counterparts in the developed world, they accepted these offer about 95 percent of the time – a higher acceptance rate than the average in the developed world. A recent study [Henrich et al. (2001)] reports on game experiments that have been conducted in a total of 15 "small-scale societies", including hunter–gathers, pastoralists, and farmers, and villagers. The studies found a great deal of divergence among these societies. In some of them results strongly suggested an equal-split norm and in others most proposers made offers much less generous than equal splitting and were not punished for doing so.

6. Conclusion

6.1. Further reading

The literature on social evolution is large, diverse, and multi-disciplinary. There is a great deal of good work that I have failed to discuss. Some of the omissions are simply due to my ignorance. Some work that I admire and intended to include, didn't find its way into the survey because I had to narrow my focus to limit its length. Fortunately, the seriousness of these omissions is diminished by the fact that much of the omitted work is beautifully presented in other sources.

For a survey article that partially overlaps this material, but also examines a lot of good work not covered here, I recommend Rajiv Sethi and R. Somanathan's (2003) lucid and insightful article, "Understanding reciprocity".

There are several books that I strongly recommend to anyone interested in the subject of social evolution. These books tell their stories better than I could, so I confine my remarks to brief descriptions and hope that readers will find and enjoy them in undiluted form.

Cavalli-Sforza and Feldman's book, *Cultural Transmission and Evolution* (1981) pioneered formal modeling of this subject. Their introductory chapter is richly endowed with examples and presents a clearheaded formulation of the way that the implications of mutation, transmission, and natural selection can be extended from the study of genetically transmitted characteristics to that of culturally transmitted characteristics. Their formulation of the contrasting effects of *vertical transmission*, (from parent to child) and of *oblique* and *horizontal* transmission is insightful and provocative. They illustrate this formulation with fascinating examples such as he spread of linguistic patterns, the introduction of birth control methods, the spread of the kuru virus, which is contracted by ceremonial ingestion of dead relatives, in the Fore tribe of New Guinea. There is also a very interesting empirical study of the transmission from parents to children of such cultural behavior as religious beliefs, political affiliation, listening to classical music, reading horoscopes, and high salt usage.

Robert Trivers' book, *Social Evolution* (1985) is a stimulating and attractive treatise on the evolution of social behavior of animals (including humans) and plants. It is full of interesting examples from the natural world, thought-provoking bits of theory, and delightful photographs and drawings.

Brian Skyrms' short book, *Evolution of the Social Contract* (1996), is a beautifully written and highly accessible application of the methods of evolutionary dynamics to behavior in bargaining games and the evolution of notions of fairness and "the social contract".

My own thinking about matters related to the evolutionary foundations of social behavior has been strongly influenced by Ken Binmore's two volume work, *Game Theory and the Social Contract* (1994a, 1994b). This book combines social philosophy, political theory, evolutionary theory, anthropology, and modern game theory with great depth and subtlety.

Sober and Wilson's book *Unto Others* is written in advocacy of a modern version of the group selectionist view. It contains an extensive and interesting history of theoretical controversies between group selectionists and individual selectionists. There are also reports on interesting empirical work with group selection as well as a useful survey of group norms in a sample of twenty-five cultures that they selected *randomly* from the anthropological literature.

H. Peyton Young's *Individual Strategy and Social Structure: An Evolutionary Theory of Social Institutions* (1998) contains a remarkably accessible introduction to the mathematical theory of stochastic dynamics and to its applications in the study of the evolution of social institutions. Almost all of the work discussed in the present review uses deterministic dynamics to approximate the outcomes in a stochastic model. Heuristically, the justification for doing so is that if an equilibrium that is locally stable under deterministic dynamics receives a small, one-time stochastic shock, then as the shock wears off, equilibrium will be restored.[19] Young observes that the difficulty with this argument is that occasionally, *albeit* extremely rarely, the system may receive a sufficiently large number of shocks to knock it out of the basin of attraction of any locally stable equilibrium that is not globally stable. Thus, Young argues, a proper treatment of the very long run must directly incorporate the stochastic process into the laws of motion. He shows that in models with multiple equilibria, "long run average behavior can be predicted much more sharply than that of the corresponding determinate dynamics".

Those seeking clear, mathematical presentations of the major technical issues in evolutionary game theory will do well to look at Jörgen Weibull's *Evolutionary Game Theory* (1995) and Larry Samuelson's *Evolutionary Games and Equilibrium Selection* (1997).

References

Benaim, M., Weibull, J. (2000). "Deterministic approximation of stochastic evolution in games". Technical Report 534, IUI Working Paper Series. Stockholm.
Bergstrom, T.C. (1995). "On the evolution of altruistic ethical rules for siblings". American Economic Review 85 (1), 58–81.
Bergstrom, T.C. (2001). "The algebra of assortative encounters and the evolution of cooperation". International Game Theory Review. (To appear).
Bergstrom, T.C. (2002). "Evolution of social behavior: Individual and group selection". Journal of Economic Perspectives 16 (2), 67–88.
Bergstrom, T., Stark, O. (1993). "How altruism can prevail in an evolutionary environment". American Economic Review 83 (2), 149–155.
Binmore, K. (1992). Fun and Games. D.C. Heath, Lexington, MA.
Binmore, K. (1994a). Game Theory and the Social Contract I: Playing Fair. MIT Press, Cambridge, MA.
Binmore, K. (1994b). Game Theory and the Social Contract II: Just Playing. MIT Press, Cambridge, MA.

---

[19] Michel Benaim and Jörgen Weibull (2000) have developed a careful formal treatment of the circumstances in which deterministic approximation of stochastic dynamic evolutionary processes is justified.

Binmore, K., Samuelson, L. (1992). "Evolutionary stability in repeated games played by finite automata". Journal of Economic Theory 57, 278–305.
Boorman, S.A., Levitt, P.R. (1980). The Genetics of Altruism. Academic Press, New York.
Bowles, S., Gintis, H. (2000). "The evolution of reciprocal preferences". Technical Report. Santa Fe Institute, Santa Fe, NM.
Boyd, R., Richerson, P. (1990). "Group selection among alternative evolutionarily stable strategies". Journal of Theoretical Biology 145, 331–342.
Boyd, R., Richerson, P. (1992). "Punishment allows the evolution of cooperation (or anything else) in sizeable groups". Ethology and Sociobiology 113, 171–195.
Boyd, R., Richerson, P. (April 2001). "Group beneficial norms can spread rapidly in structured populations". Technical Report. UCLA anthropology department. Los Angeles, CA.
Carr-Saunders, A.M. (1922). The Population Problem: A Study in Human Evolution. Clarendon Press, Oxford.
Cavalli-Sforza, L.L., Feldman, M.W. (1981). Cultural Transmission and Evolution: A Quantitative Approach. Princeton University Press, Princeton, NJ.
Cohen, D., Eshel, E. (1976). "On the founder effect and the evolution of altruistic traits". Theoretical Population Biology 10, 276–302.
Cooper, B., Wallace, C. (2001). "Group selection and the evolution of altruism". Technical Report. Economics Department, Oxford University.
Cosmides, L. (1989). "The logic of social exchange: Has natural selection shaped how humans reason". Cognition 31, 187–276.
Cosmides, L., Tooby, J. (1989). "Evolutionary psychology and the generation of culture ii: A computational theory of exchange". Ethology and Sociobiology 10, 51–97.
Dawkins, R. (1989). The Selfish Gene. (New edition.) Oxford University Press, Oxford.
Eshel, I. (1972). "On the neighbor effect and the evolution of altruistic traits". Theoretical Population Biology 3, 258–277.
Eshel, I., Samuelson, L., Shaked, A. (1998). "Altruists, egoists, and hooligans in a local interaction structure". American Economic Review 88, 157–179.
Eshel, I., Sansone, E., Shaked, A. (1999). "The emergence of kinship behavior in structured populations of unrelated individuals". International Journal of Game Theory 28, 447–463.
Frank, R.H. (1987). "If homo economicus could choose his own utility function, would he want one with a conscience". American Economic Review 77 (4), 593–604.
Friedman, D., Singh, N. (1999). "The viability of vengeance". Technical Report. U.C. Santa Cruz, Santa Cruz, CA.
Ghiselin, M. (1974). The Economy of Nature and the Evolution of Sex. University of California Press, Berkeley, CA.
Grafen, A. (1979). "The hawk–dove game played between relatives". Animal Behaviour 27 (3), 905–907.
Grafen, A. (1984). "Natural selection, group selection, and kin selection". In: Kreb, J.R., Davies, N.B. (Eds.), Behavioural Ecology, Chapter 3, 2nd edn. Blackwell, London, pp. 62–80.
Haldane, J.B.S. (1932). The Causes of Evolution. Harper & Brothers, New York and London.
Hamilton, W.D. (1964). "The genetical evolution of social behavior, Parts i and ii". Journal of Theoretical Biology 7, 1–52.
Hamilton, W.D. (1975). "Innate social aptitudes in man: An approach from evolutionary genetics". In: Fox, R. (Ed.), Biosocial Anthropology. Malaby Press, London.
Hardin, G. (1977). The Limits of Altruism. Indiana University Press, Bloomington, IN.
Henrich, J. (2000). "Does culture matter in economic behavior? Ultimatum game bargaining among the Machiguenga of the Peruvian Amazon". American Economic Review 90 (4), 9730979.
Henrich, J., Boyd, R. (2001). "Why people punish defectors". Journal of Theoretical Biology 208, 79–89.
Henrich, J., Boyd, R., Bowles, S., Camerer, C., Fehr, E., McElreath, R. (2001). "In search of homoeconomicus: Behavioral experiments in 15 small-scale societies". American Economic Review 91 (2), 73–78.
Herold, F. (2003). "Carrot or stick: Group selection and the evolution of reciprocal preferences". Technical Report. Munich University.

Hines, W.G.S., Smith, J.M. (1979). "Games between relatives". Journal of Theoretical Biology 79, 19–30.
Hume, D. (1978). A Treatise of Human Nature, 2nd edn. Clarendon Press, Oxford. (Edited by Selby-Bigge, L.A., revised by Nidditch, P.; first published 1739.)
Kimura, M., Weiss, G.H. (1964). "The stepping stone model of population structure and the decrease of genetic correlation with distance". Genetics 49, 561–576.
Lack, D. (1966). Population Studies of Birds. Clarendon Press, Oxford.
Ledyard, J.O. (1995). "Public goods: A survey of experimental research". In: Kagel, J., Roth, A. (Eds.), The Handbook of Experimental Economics, Chapter 2. Princeton University Press, Princeton, NJ, pp. 111–181.
Levin, B.R., Kilmer, W.L. (1974). "Interdemic selection and the evolution of altruism". Evolution 28 (4), 527–545.
Levins, R. (1970). "Extinction". In: Gerstenhaber, M. (Ed.), Some Mathematical Problems in Biology. American Mathematical Society, Providence, pp. 77–107.
Matessi, C., Jayakar, S.D. (1976). "Conditions for the evolution of altruism under Darwinian selection". Theoretical Population Biology 9.
Nachbar, J. (1990). "Evolutionary selection dynamics in games: Convergence and limit properties". International Journal of Game Theory 19, 59–89.
Nisbett, R.E., Cohen, D. (1996). Culture of Honor: The Psychology of Violence in the South. Westview Press, Boulder, CO.
Nowak, M.A., May, R.M. (1993). "Evolutionary games and spatial chaos". Nature 359, 826–829.
Nowak, M.A., May, R.M. (1998). "Evolution of indirect reciprocity by image scoring". Nature 393, 573–577.
Rappaport, A., Chammah, A.M. (1965). Prisoner's Dilemma. University of Michigan Press, Ann Arbor, MI.
Roth, A.E., Prasnikar, V., Okuno-Fujiwara, M., Zamir, S. (1991). "Bargaining and market behavior in Jerusalem, Ljubljana, Pittsburgh, and Tokyo, an experimental study". American Economic Review 81 (5), 1068–1095.
Rousseau, J.J. (1950). Discourses on the Origins and Foundation of Inequality Among Men (Second Discourse). Everyman's Library, Dutton, NY. (First publication 1755).
Samuelson, L. (1997). Evolutionary Games and Equilibrium Selection. MIT Press, Cambridge, MA.
Sethi, R., Somanathan, E. (2003). Understanding reciprocity. Journal of Economic Behavior and Organization 50 (January), 1–27.
Skyrms, B. (1996). Evolution of the Social Contract. Cambridge University Press, Cambridge.
Skyrms, B. (2001). "The stag hunt". Proceedings and Addresses of the American Philosophical Association 75 (2), 31–41.
Skyrms, B., Pemantle, R. (2000). "A dynamic model of social network formation". Proceedings of the National Academy of Science 97 (16), 9340–9346.
Smith, J.M. (1964). "Group selection and kin selection". Nature 201, 1145–1147.
Smith, J.M. (1976). "Group selection". Quarterly Review of Biology 51, 277–283.
Smith, J.M., Price, G.R. (1973). "The logic of animal conflict". Nature 246, 15–18.
Sober, E., Wilson, D.S. (1999). Unto Others. Harvard University Press, Cambridge, MA.
Trivers, R. (1985). Social Evolution. Benjamin Cummings, Menlo Park, CA.
Waugh, H.E. (Ed.) (1929). Hesiod: The Homeric Hymns and Homerica. Heineman, London.
Weibull, J. (1995). Evolutionary Game Theory. MIT Press, Cambridge, MA.
Williams, G.C. (1966). Adaptation and Natural Selection. A Critique of Some Current Evolutionary Thought. Princeton University Press, Princeton, NJ.
Wilson, D.S. (1975). "A theory of group selection". Proceedings of the National Academy of Sciences 72 (1), 143–146.
Wilson, D.S. (1979). "Structured demes and trait-group variation". American Naturalist 113, 157–185.
Wilson, D.S. (1987). "Altruism in Mendelian populations derived from sibling groups". Evolution 41 (5), 1059–1070.
Wright, S. (1921). "Systems of mating". Genetics 6 (2), 111–178.
Wright, S. (1943). "Isolation by distance". Genetics 28, 114–138.

Wright, S. (1945). "Tempo and modes in evolution: A critical review". Ecology 26, 415–419.
Wynne-Edwards, V.C. (1962). Animal Dispersion in Relation to Social Behaviour. Oliver and Boyd, Edinburgh and London.
Wynne-Edwards, V.C. (1978). "Intrinsic population control: An introduction". In: Ebling, F.J., Stoddart, D.M. (Eds.), Population Control by Social Behaviour. Institute of Biology, London, pp. 1–22. (Volume *Population Control by Social Behaviour*.)
Wynne-Edwards, V.C. (1986). Evolution through Group Selection. Alden Press, Oxford.
Young, H.P. (1998). Individual Strategy and Social Structure. Princeton University Press, Princeton, NJ.

Chapter 12

SOLIDARITY NORMS AND INSTITUTIONS IN VILLAGE SOCIETIES: STATIC AND DYNAMIC CONSIDERATIONS

JEAN-PHILIPPE PLATTEAU

University of Namur, Belgium

Contents

Abstract	820
Keywords	820
1. Introduction	821
2. Other-regarding norms in agrarian societies	823
3. The customary system of land tenure	829
3.1. Land access and guaranteed livelihoods	829
3.2. The commons as embodiment of the community	833
4. Erosion of the social security function of customary land tenure	835
4.1. The transformation of the commons	836
4.1.1. Governance costs and inherited cooperative traits as critical determinants of the evolution of land property systems	836
4.1.2. Reduced economic significance of the commons: The income effect	840
4.1.3. Reduced economic significance of the commons: The insurance effect	843
4.2. Individualization of land tenure rights	846
4.2.1. Deepening individualization in the form of permanent use rights	846
4.2.2. Deepening individualization in the form of increased transfer rights	848
4.2.3. Restrictions on land markets and social security concerns	850
5. Voluntary reciprocal contingent transfers	854
5.1. General considerations	854
5.2. A short survey of the economic theory of informal insurance mechanisms	856
5.2.1. Informal insurance models with stationary strategies	856
5.2.2. Informal insurance models with non-stationary strategies	858
5.2.3. Altruism with non-stationary strategies	861
5.2.4. Social norms	862
5.3. Empirical evidence	863
5.3.1. The extent of risk-sharing	863
5.3.2. Altruism in risk-sharing arrangements	867
5.3.3. Broad balanced reciprocity as a guiding principle in village societies	869

Handbook of the Economics of Giving, Altruism and Reciprocity, Volume 1
Edited by Serge-Christophe Kolm and Jean Mercier Ythier
Copyright © 2006 Elsevier B.V. All rights reserved
DOI: 10.1016/S1574-0714(06)01012-8

6. Conclusion: Institutional change and solidarity mechanisms in village societies 874
References 878

Abstract

The purpose of this essay is to argue that process-regarding preferences or social norms are pervasive in traditional village communities, yet are subject to gradual erosion under the influence of new forces, particularly population growth and market penetration. This is illustrated with respect to norms regarding the allocation of locally controlled natural resources, such as land, forest, pastures and water spaces. As a matter of fact, a communal system of land rights, together with the accompanying set of norms and preferences, is conceivable only under conditions of high land–man ratios resulting in extensive land use patterns. When land becomes intensively exploited, the efficiency costs of equity-oriented arrangements increase significantly. On the other hand, informal insurance arrangements relying on voluntary state-contingent transfers tend to be less effective under the pressure of market integration and the emergence of alternative income-earning opportunities accessible to at least a segment of rural populations.

Keywords

social norms, altruism, reciprocity, land access, common property, informal insurance

JEL classification: D10, O10, O17, Q15

1. Introduction

There is increasing recognition among economists that human behavior cannot be accounted for exclusively in terms of the standard neo-classsical model of strictly self-interested individuals. For example, it has been recently argued that human actions are not only governed by the usual *self-regarding* preferences but also by *other-regarding* and *process-regarding* preferences. While other-regarding preferences concern the consumption and outcomes of other individuals, "process-regarding preferences concern the manner in which the individual in question and the others behave, including the ways in which they attain outcomes of interest". In other words, process-regarding preferences refer to values and sometimes also to codes of behavior, mores, and social norms [Ben-Ner and Putterman (1998, p. 7)].[1] In the analytical scheme of many authors, moreover, norms and codes of conduct are seen primarily "as rules that are socially functional, and that are consciously adopted because people recognize the value of those functions" [Sugden (1998, p. 84)].

Traditional village communities are commonly considered as societies where predispositions toward altruistic or norm-following behavior are pervasively present. This characterization echoes a popular picture favored by some anthropologists and social philosophers who tend to picture these societies as havens of harmony where concern for others is overwhelming present and has not yet been corrupted by the individualizing forces of the modern market. On the other hand, it is interesting to note that some social scientists have construed solidarity arrangements in such societies as essentially motivated by self-interested considerations. This is especially evident in the case of so-called gift exchanges interpreted as systems of mutual insurance in which, according to one well-known anthropologist, "it is scarcity and not sufficiency that make people generous, since everybody is thereby insured against hunger ... in a community where everyone is likely to find himself in difficulties from time to time ... he who is in need today receives help from him who may be in like need tomorrow" [Evans-Pritchard (1940, p. 85); in the same vein, see also Belshaw (1965), Service (1966), Epstein (1967), Sahlins (1968), Bourdieu (1990), Gregory (1982), Wiessner (1982), Cashdan (1985, 1989)].

Following in the wake of these anthropologists, economists have favored insurance-based explanations of voluntary reciprocal transfers characteristic of agrarian societies. In game-theoretical terms, mutual insurance can be sustained as a equilibrium of a repeated game of infinite or indeterminate duration because in such a setup promises to help fellow villagers when the need arises can be made credible. Apparently, only self-interested motivations are invoked in the framework used by economists, even though it is sometimes admitted that social norms, pressures or sanctions may exist that have the beneficial effect of increasing the cost of non-cooperation – direct penalties against breach are then combined with the threat of future exclusion

---

[1] Such a distinction between other-regarding and process-regarding preferences is essentially similar to the distinction between altruism and manners suggested by Camerer and Thaler (1995).

from insurance possibilities to sustain risk-pooling arrangements [Fafchamps (1994), Ligon, Thomas and Worrall (1997)].

Upon a more careful look, however, economic theorizing of contingent reciprocal transfers in agrarian societies does not genuinely rule out the role of norms and codes of conduct. As is well-known, indeed, in repeated games of indeterminate or infinite duration, cooperation is only one possible equilibrium among many others. The emergence of equilibrium strategies that favor cooperation actually depends on the institutions available in the society, and "these institutions include anything and everything that helps individuals learn about what others do, from customs, norms, and laws to common frames of reference and focal points" [Ben-Ner and Putterman (1998, p. 12); see also Dasgupta (1988)]. For example, moral norms may provide the kind of 'friction' required to make the 'good' equilibrium more likely [Dasgupta (1988, pp. 70–71)].

In addition, practices may exist whereby villagers come to the help of people in distress although the latter are not related to them through kinship or friendship ties. This tends to happen when strong redistributive norms prevail in the rural society. Moreover, in lineage-based societies, which may be quite stratified in many respects, probably the most important form taken by solidarity arrangements consists of rules of access to land and other natural resources which guarantee the livelihoods of all the members. The scope of these rules is not limited to local common property resources since they actually encompass the whole land domain situated in the community territory.

The purpose of this essay is to argue in the light of the available literature that other- and process-regarding preferences or social norms are pervasive in agrarian societies, and that they are reflected in mutual insurance arrangements as well as in land allocation rules and redistributive practices aimed at social protection and maintenance of social order. Such arrangements and practices, however, are subject to gradual erosion under the influence of new forces, particularly population growth and market penetration. This is illustrated with respect to norms regarding the allocation of locally controlled natural resources, such as land, forest, pastures and water spaces, and also with respect to informal voluntary reciprocal transfers. In particular, it is shown that, as a shift occurs from extensive to intensive land use patterns, the efficiency costs arising from equity- or insurance-motivated rules and practices increase to such an extent that these rules and practices are called into question. This said, equity-driven restrictions on free land sale transactions may well persist if the community fabric remains sufficiently strong. Likewise, the effectiveness and vulnerability to modernizing forces of informal insurance networks will also be discussed.

The outline is therefore as follows. In Section 2, the implications of the highly personalized relationships that exist among community members in agrarian societies are carefully drawn with a view to highlighting the critical role of other-regarding preferences and codes of conduct, including redistributive norms backed by powerful external sanction mechanisms. In the next two sections, customary land tenure arrangements typically found in lineage-based societies are depicted as well as their evolution as pressure increases on the resources available at village level as a result of both population growth and market integration. In Section 3, the operation of customary rules of access to vital resources is described and the social insurance and redistributive motives underlying them are highlighted. Section 4 is then devoted to the analysis of the dynamic evolution of these rules and the associated norms as the value of natural resources increase under the joint impact of market development and population growth. In this perspective, the transformation of the village commons and the individualization of land tenure arrangements are discussed at some length. Section 5 shifts attention to informal mutual aid arrangements through state-contingent reciprocal transfers, and attempts to assess their importance in the light of the available empirical literature. Their likely evolution under the influence of market integration is also assessed. Section 6 concludes by summarizing the main results of the analysis, and by drawing attention to newly emerging institutional forms that may be the source of both optimism and concern. Optimism is warranted because these new forms seem to be well adapted to many modern challenges and opportunities. Yet, concern arises in so far as they are likely to increase inequality and vulnerability.

2. Other-regarding norms in agrarian societies

When interactions among people are close and continuous, they are inevitably characterized by a high degree of personalization. Such features are typically observed in close-knit village communities, yet are especially evident in tribal societies where the clustering of rural dwellings tends to be more dense than in the peasant societies of Asia and Latin America. One immediate implication is that the spheres of private and social life are not neatly separated as they are in modern societies based on wider and more anonymous interactions. As a consequence of this, any disagreement about a rule or a decision is bound to spill over into the sphere of private relations and to generate personal antagonisms. On the other hand, the wrangles that occur in the sphere of private relations are likely to percolate through to the social sphere where decisions may prove difficult to reach owing to the interference of ill-feelings at the level of interpersonal relations.

This kind of situation creates vast opportunities for tensions, frustrations and conflicts that are susceptible of poisoning the social climate prevailing in the community. Because interpersonal conflicts in small-scale settings can easily get out of control and threaten to undermine the whole social fabric of the community, mechanisms must be devised to prevent them from arising or to contain them as much as possible.

A central feature of lineage-based societies is that other-regarding values are inculcated in every individual from early childhood and carefully nurtured all throughout his or her life. Hence their characterization as 'group-focused' societies by Alfred Hirschman (1958). In Gambia, for example, the concept of *badingya*, which represents harmony, cooperation, and shared progress (or shared decline), is continuously emphasized in contrast to the concept of *fadingya*, which refers to selfish ambitions and competitiveness. Individualistic proclivities are accepted only to the extent that they are considered as necessary for the advancement of the group as a whole [von Braun and Webb (1989, pp. 515–516); see also Sylla (1994, pp. 170–176), for the Wolof in Senegal; and Ortiz (1967), for the Paez Indians of Columbia]. Unlike what we find in the 'Invisible Hand' doctrine, which is at the root of the market-based view of the economic system, the presumption is that the pursuit of selfish ends runs counter to the collective good. Evidence to the contrary must therefore be adduced before exceptions to this rule can be granted.[2] This cognitive orientation has been called "the image of the static economy" or "the image of limited good" by the anthropologist Foster (1964, 1965), and it is formally equivalent to the economic concept of a zero-sum game.[3]

Other-regarding values and codes of conduct are emphasized not only on each and every possible moment of ordinary life but also under exceptional circumstances. Rituals and ceremonies in the course of which the unity and harmony of the group are strongly asserted and celebrated provide these exceptional moments [see, e.g., Godelier (1974)]. They are privileged occasions during which social norms and values stressing the collective good and the necessity for the individual to sacrifice his own self-interest for the benefit of the community are put in the foreground and intensely felt through dances, songs in unison and the sharing of abundant food and drinks. During such events, all participants are called upon to manifest regularly and openly their concern for the collective good and their willingness to contribute to it. What is being thereby instilled is a strong sense of communal identity that influences behavior in many ways: it guides beliefs, it directs the formation of habits, and it affects what is salient to the individual [Alkire and Deneulin (2002, p. 63)]. In particular, reference to self-centered considerations tends to be suppressed from consciousness so that community members can think of themselves as moral individuals [Polanyi (1977, p. 60), Wright (1994)].

It is useful at this stage to recall Karl Marx's characterization of ancient societies. According to him, indeed, members of these societies are completely immersed in the social totality to which they belong, as a result of which they are unable to think of themselves as autonomous beings who view the world as an entity external to them. There prevails an "undifferentiated unity of individual and society" that "arrests the individual's power to disengage himself from the generality of society and establish a self-interest distinct from the general interest of society" [Avineri (1968, p. 113), Deleplace (1979, p. 203)].

Internalization processes are never complete, however, and this is why external reward and sanction mechanisms are needed to complement the work of collective rituals and education. Severe sanctions are thus meted out in case individuals promote their own interest at the presumed expense of the group. Among these sanctions, social ostracism often plays an important role. It is grounded in the 'embedded' nature of many village societies. As a matter of fact, life in such societies can be conceptualized as a series of 'linked games', more particularly as the linking of a 'social exchange game'

---

[2] For a fascinating parallel with the moral economy of pre-industrial Europe, see Thompson (1991).
[3] A natural explanation for the rising economic prosperity of an individual is thus that he "has encroached upon the shares rightfully belonging to others" [Foster (1964, p. 40)].

with particular games occurring in various spheres of the village economy [Aoki (2001, Chapter 2)].

In the 'social exchange game' of the community, which is played repeatedly, each family can contribute to the production of social goods with some costs, and enjoy the benefit from the consumption of social goods. At the beginning of each stage game any family can be excluded from participating in the production and consumption of social goods by other families, if it has not cooperated in another game the outcome of which is vital for the local economy (let us call it the economic game). It can then be shown that the threat of the conditional social ostracism is credible and cooperation among a minimum number of families in the linked (economic) game can become an equilibrium outcome even if there is a strong incentive for free-riding in the stand-alone economic game. That happens if the saving of the cost of effort by shirking in the latter game is smaller than the present-value sum of the sacrifice of future benefits arising from ostracism. It is therefore evident that some strategies that are not an equilibrium (and are not self-enforceable) in an isolated (economic) domain can become profitable strategies for agents, when that domain is 'embedded' in a community social exchange domain [Aoki (2001, pp. 48–49, 53)].

Fear of public humiliation is a related mechanism for punishing deviance. Based on observations among the *Mossi*, the dominant ethnic group in Burkina Faso, Badini thus writes:

> Activated by social rebuke and the accompanying public humiliation, the feeling of shame appears as the most formidable weapon in the service of the traditional *Moose* pedagogy (the *moaga*). Above the individuals, indeed, this feeling asserts the supremacy of social judgment and constitutes a powerful regulating mechanism to which everybody submits ... Since a person can exist only through collective opinion, it is collective opinion that rates people and rare are those who are willing to incur the risk to defy it. The point is that its verdict is merciless and without appeal. [Badini (1994, pp. 146–147) – my translation; see also Foster (1965, pp. 303–305), Ndiaye (1998, p. 183)]

For social ostracism and public humiliation to be effective mechanisms of disciplining individuals into behaving in other-regarding ways, it is essential that members of the community share a common system of beliefs about what would happen if they should behave selfishly. Hence the name 'community norm' chosen by Masahiko Aoki to designate any standard of cooperative behavior supported by the shared beliefs of collective punishment of shirking [Aoki (2001, p. 49); see also Basu (2000, pp. 87–88)]. Ideological intimidation exercised through the nurturing of beliefs regarding the causes and cures of illnesses, accidents and other misfortunes, constitutes another sanctioning mechanism designed to drive people into compliance with cooperative modes of behavior. In tribal societies, in particular, unfortunate events which befall particular individuals are often ascribed to violations of other-regarding social norms that aroused the anger of supernatural powers overseeing human affairs. The implication is that more altruistic behavior must be followed to appease these powers and eventually cure the illness or prevent new accidents from occurring.

Finally, a lot of attention and efforts are devoted by elders and specialized mediators to arbitrating and settling interpersonal conflicts so that they do not disrupt the social order of the community and undermine its collective activities and decision-making processes. Conciliatory attempts, repeated reminders of the group's tenets and values and pressing invitations to behave reasonably, compensatory payments, and judgments allowing all the parties involved to save their face play an important role in traditional village societies, especially in the tightly-knit societies based on lineage. Face-saving is an essential characteristic of conflict-settlement in so far as people are expected to live continuously in close contact with each other[4]. If resentment and frustrations are not adequately tamed or suppressed, there is a serious risk that pent-up interpersonal tensions will one day reappear and perhaps erupt into overtly aggressive acts. Yet, in case soft methods do not succeed, beating and fining the culprits may be the ultimate way to bring them back to their senses [see, e.g., Bourdieu (1990, p. 129)]. Sheer demonstration of force is then resorted to by the persons endowed with the required status and power.

As has been already pointed out, the above is a good description of the formation and maintenance of preferences in traditional lineage-based societies. In other agrarian societies where class differentiation is marked (the so-called peasant societies), many of the aforementioned mechanisms are also at work even though they are typically not as effective. The following characterization, which applies to Japanese village communities of the Tokugawa era, can be readily extended to other peasant societies of Asia and Latin America:

> Tensions were more quickly and intimately felt, but overt expression of them was more resolutely suppressed in favor of an appearance of community harmony – and they were the more explosive for that reason. Deep beneath the everyday appearance of propriety and friendliness there were in many Japanese villages suppressed hatreds that merely needed some shock, some momentary lapse of customary restraint, to send them boiling to the surface. Perhaps it had always been this way; perhaps when the village had been more tightly knit and harmonious the secret antagonisms had gone even deeper and been more powerful. But if so they had also been more effectively suppressed, and it was only as village organization loosened that they were given vent. [Smith (1959, p. 172)]

---

[4] Tackling conflicts in a vicarious manner, using the mediation of supernatural agencies representing the ancestors' souls or acting on their behalf, is a particularly effective method of face-saving. As a matter of fact, when supernatural agencies are the apparent negotiators in charge of settling scores, the losing party, if there is one, does not have to suffer the humiliation of defeat at the hands of the winning party. All what he has to do is obey a verdict meted out by supernatural powers to which all humans have to submit in one way or another. Vengeful feelings arising from an humiliating posture can therefore be avoided or mitigated.

Whenever issues of wealth distribution arise, other-regarding values and social norms prescribing other-regarding behavior assume special importance in agrarian societies, particularly tribal communities.[5] As a matter of fact, when people continuously interact in close proximity to each other, they have a spontaneous inclination to look at the situation of their neighbors or acquaintances to assess their own situation. Invidious comparisons are thus a constant feature of small groups and tightly-knit societies. When social and economic differentiation is low, such as is commonly observed in tribal societies, such comparisons, by arousing jealous and envious feelings, create a highly charged emotional climate that can easily lead to serious conflicts and eventually to the implosion of the group itself. To counter such an ominous threat, these societies do not rely only on the sort of other-regarding values and associated preferences to which the previous subsection has paid much attention.

They also have recourse to redistributive norms that enjoin enriched individuals to share their surplus with their brethren. Such norms, which are often strictly enforced, are justified on the grounds that solidarity is the cement tying all the members of the community together and enabling them to survive in the long run. On the contrary, inequality and competition have the opposite effect of causing enmity between them. As one old Bosnian saying goes: "If the whole society is prosperous, each of its members gains from it, but when one individual is too powerful, he harms his fellow members, whether he likes it or not. When a hand is too big, swollen and painful, it is because it has been bitten or invaded by bad spirits. In order to restore the health of the hand's owner, the swelling must be reduced or the hand will need to be cut off" [Karahasan (2000, p. 191) – our translation].

As a rule, generosity and hospitality are highly praised behavioral traits in traditional rural communities and successful individuals therefore gain social prestige and esteem when they redistribute their surplus.[6] Upon a careful look, there are two mutually reinforcing motives that drive members of tribal communities to put pressure on successful

---

[5] We stick to the distinction between preferences and behavior typical among economists.

[6] Note that, in differentiated, class-based agrarian societies like in lineage-based societies, generosity is a highly valued behavior. Yet, the display of generosity in agrarian societies is of a different nature precisely because it takes place in a context where wealth differences are well-established and may not be leveled. Carried out within the purview of vertical patron–client ties, generosity appears as the duty of the patron acting as a benevolent superior (a kind of 'father' or 'godfather') towards his dependent workers for whose subsistence he is responsible. The patron's generous gestures constitute his part in an asymmetric deal where the clients are always in an inferiority position, which is mostly reflected in the fact that they are 'at the beck and call' of their patron [Breman (1974), Scott (1976)]. To put it otherwise, the generosity of the patron is only apparent and reflects his commitment to ensure the decent survival of his clients (his gifts are in fact a disguised wage with an important insurance element) rather than his willingness to transfer income for the sake of redistribution. How does the behavior of chieftains in tribal societies compare with that of patrons in agrarian societies? Chieftains redistribute wealth and it is in fact one of the main attributes of their chiefly function to do so: they possess in order to give but they also possess by giving, as Bourdieu put it vividly (1990, p. 126). True, redistribution takes place only to an extent compatible with the preservation of predetermined rank differentials. Yet, at the same time, chieftains are not allowed to accumulate private wealth as they wish since economic differentiation may not exceed the rigid limits set by the prevailing social norms.

individuals to share. First, if a prosperous individual were allowed to stop making gifts to fellow villagers, the size of the informal insurance pool formed by the community (about which more will be said in Section 5) would be reduced and the group's ability to spread risks would be correspondingly diminished. Private wealth accumulation is actually perceived as an anti-social behavior precisely because it is an attempt to break away from traditional solidarity networks [Fafchamps (1992, pp. 160–163, 1999), Platteau (1991, pp. 160–161, 2000, Chapter 5)]. According to Guy Hunter, we are dealing with "leveling societies, in which attempts by equals to gain individual advantage are constantly suspected and bitterly resented". At the root of this suspicious atmosphere is the "fear that the fundamental security of the village will slowly be lost if one individual after another can reach a platform of prosperity from which he might not need the help of the community and could therefore excuse himself from helping them" [Hunter (1969, p. 40)].

'Forced mutual help', as Raymond Firth (1951) has called it, is then used to maintain the status quo, which has the potential effect of discouraging exceptional individual performances on the grounds that they can only take place "at the expense of other members and of the cohesiveness of the group" [Hirschman (1958, p. 23)]. "People who have more than they manifestly need are put under relentless pressure to share", writes the anthropologist Woodburn (1998, p. 52) on the basis of his observations of Hadza hunter–gatherers in Tanzania. If great stress is laid on sharing as a moral principle, which is contrasted with "the individualistic wickedness of outsiders", the notion that sharing is virtuous is narrowly linked with this another notion that "accumulation is deeply objectionable and unacceptable" (ibidem: p. 54).

This actually takes us to the second motive underlying social norms of sharing: since the effort of any individual to improve his lot generates positional externalities that negatively affect the welfare of fellow villagers, redistributive norms that enjoin economically successful individuals to share their surplus appear as a form of taxation designed to curb positional race for status. In other words, the presence of sharing norms prevents a chain reaction of emulating efforts from being triggered off. This is a happy outcome in so far as efforts to improve one's lot are mutually offsetting (everyone wants to 'keep up with the Johneses') and inefficient equilibria arise precisely because investment in status enhancement is more attractive individually than collectively [Congleton (1980), Frank (1995, 1998)].

That the insurance-based explanation is insufficient to account for sharing norms in tribal societies is evident from the fact that the hierarchy of ranks may not be called into question. In point of fact, the chief or the elders do not accept that commoners rise above them by acquiring old or new symbols of wealth and status (like cocoa plantations, mechanical devices, or roofs made of corrugated iron). All efforts to accumulate such symbols are unavoidably viewed as conscious attempts to compete with traditional leaders and to overturn the existing social order. As a consequence, they are strongly condemned and the prosperous commoner is immediately coerced into handing over to the chief his newly acquired riches [see, e.g., Geschiere (1995, p. 210), Woodburn (1998, p. 51)].

There is actually a counterpart to these advantages of the chiefly function. Indeed, the source of the chief's power mainly lies in the special economic responsibilities which he has towards his people [see, e.g., Malinowski (1922, 1937), Sahlins (1963, 1968, 1972)]. In particular, it is his recognized duty to provide sufficient productive resources to them so as to ensure a decent livelihood and to use his own wealth for redistributive purposes within the limits set by the need to maintain rank differences. "A good chief is one that is capable of ensuring that his people do not go hungry", as one West African saying goes.

This is not sheer generosity, as it might appear at first sight, since by acting thus he precisely establishes his power over his subjects. In the words of Pierre Bourdieu: "A man possesses in order to give. But he also possesses by giving. A gift that is not returned can become a debt, a lasting obligation; and the only recognized power – recognition, personal loyalty or prestige – is the one that is obtained by giving" [Bourdieu (1990, p. 126)]. Or: "The important man is the one who gives and not the one who possesses; the one who spends and not the one who keeps things for himself" [Nicolas (1968, p. 411) – our translation]. Redistribution of wealth is therefore an essential attribute of the chiefly function, an attribute that both justifies and consolidates his power position. In addition, and of more direct concern to us in the following section, the chief or some specialized elite member is responsible for the just allocation of land among his subjects, meaning that land rights must be awarded in such a way that everybody in the community can make a decent living.

3. The customary system of land tenure

3.1. Land access and guaranteed livelihoods

In the light of the above, traditional village communities appear as micro-societies shaped and cemented by social or community norms. A central function of these norms is to drive members into behaving in other-regarding ways in many life circumstances. In the previous section, the importance of other-regarding behavior for group cohesion and collective survival has been especially stressed. In this section as well as in Section 5, emphasis is instead placed on the role of community norms for the subsistence of individual members. In lineage-based societies, individual livelihoods are protected through two main methods: guaranteed access to productive resources, and reciprocal transfers. In this section, we are concerned with the first method, while discussion of the second method is postponed to Section 5 devoted to informal insurance arrangements.

In tribal societies, a social norm commands that every household, by virtue of being a member of the community, be granted access to the amount of productive resources, land in particular, that it requires to meet basic needs [see, e.g., Cohen (1980, p. 353)]. Since this right of access is associated with the social identity of rural dwellers, the corresponding social norm is especially powerful. It is a 'general right' that is "an inseparable element of the status as member of the tribe", and can only be lost through formal expulsion from the group [Boserup (1965, p. 79)]. Paraphrasing Karl Marx, Shlomo Avineri thus writes that tribal property "appears as a relationship signifying social identification" [Avineri (1968, p. 112)]. No wonder, therefore, that land and other natural resources are held under a system of corporate ownership in many customary land tenure systems.

The relationship between membership and access to land is actually reciprocal: on the one hand, group membership is the basis of social rights and identity and, on the other hand, access to a share of the corporate productive assets serves to validate or confirm membership in the group [Berry (1984, p. 91)]. The term 'member', it must be pointed out, includes not only those who can claim descent, actual or putative, from the founding lineages but also strangers and migrants who have been accepted as members of, and reside with, the group [Popkin (1979, p. 43), Noronha (1985, p. 182)]. As a matter of fact, members of late-arrived people have to obtain prior authorization of local land authorities to have access to land [Breusers (2001, pp. 54–58)]. Such authorization is refused if the 'stranger' is known to be a bad character and is withdrawn if he behaves incorrectly, typically if he violates the local rules and customs. Clearly, rights and obligations that form "a guarantee of relational existence" are deeply associated with land: land is "the basis of social networks that enable people to access a whole series of material and nonmaterial resources" [Ng'weno (2001, p. 118)].

The land system in tribal communities is characterized by multiple tenure, meaning the coexistence of different tenure rights corresponding to various modes of exploiting the land. In particular, individualized use rights may exist side by side with common property resources, and the extent of individualization of private tenure rights also may vary between different portions of the village resource base. The mix of land rights depends on the balance of benefits and costs of land tenure individualization. More precisely, we expect a common property regime to prevail when or where partition of the village natural resources would involve large transaction costs (because these resources are highly spread out, and/or of a low quality or value), or large opportunity costs in terms of lost scale economies and/or foregone insurance benefits. Insurance benefits arise whenever the returns to a common property resource (CPR) are highly variable across time and space. In such circumstances, indeed, a common property system offering access to a large area within which rights-holding users (think of herders or fishermen) can freely move appears as a desirable arrangement from a risk-reducing perspective [Dasgupta (1993, pp. 288–289), Baland and Platteau (1998a, 1998b), Platteau (2000, Chapter 3), Breusers (2001)].[7]

---

[7] Note that parceling out the resource could apparently solve the above problem if users would have access to a wide portfolio of resource patches with different ecological characteristics. The problem, however, is that such a solution would be prohibitively costly to enforce as it is obviously difficult to monitor individualized rights over such highly dispersed and infrequently visited resource patches. The high unpredictability of a resource's returns is therefore not sufficient to account for common property: it must be complemented by the high exclusion costs of a spread resource base [Platteau (2000, p. 88)].

At the other extreme, highly fertile or well located lands tend to be subject to a comparatively high degree of individualization. Contrast, for example, the intensively cultivated garden lands situated near dwellings and over which households have close to permanent rights, on the one hand, and lands devoted to slash-and-burn cultivation over which rights granted are only temporary, on the other hand. In slash-and-burn agriculture, indeed, since the period of fallow is so long that all traces of previous cultivation are lost, a household does not automatically return to the same parcel [Boserup (1965, pp. 79–80), Ault and Rutman (1979, p. 172), Stevenson (1991)].[8] This illustrates that, if community members have a general right of guaranteed access to local natural resources, their rights over particular portions of such resources may be 'specific' (to use Boserup's term), implying that they can be reshuffled according to circumstances.

Access rights granted to all members of the village community are defined in a manner that takes into account the different tenure regimes prevailing over the various portions of the village territory, which are themselves determined by cost–benefit considerations easily amenable to economic analysis. Thus, rights over valuable parcels of land are apportioned in a rather definitive manner among the households and the sharing of these lands aims at enabling each of them to make a decent living. On the other hand, plots of land over which rights are more temporary tend to form an ideal pool that the community can use to meet the fluctuating livelihood requirements of member households across the various stages of their life cycle.

It bears emphasis that, when land is of variable quality, a frequent custom consists of partitioning it in such a way that all rightsholders have equal income opportunities and a guarantee to earn a decent livelihood. For example, in the irrigation communities of the Ziz valley in the eastern High Atlas mountains (Morocco), "when a group decided to settle, whether on virgin lands or not, ... conquered land was divided into as many shares as there were families to settle. These shares of land were generally made up of several fields perpendicular to the valley ... Each share contained one field in the upstream, another in the middle stream, and a third in the downstream so as to guarantee an equal distribution of water and good quality land among the members of the group" [Mezzine (1987, p. 202) – quoted from Ilahiane (2001, p. 105)]. By thus maximizing each household's chances of benefiting from the scarce and variable supply of water, the system aims at providing the subsistence requirements for each of them [Ilahiane (2001, p. 102)].

A similar arrangement has been observed in the *Zanjera* irrigation communities of the Philippines where apportionment of land along a lateral canal ensures that each shareholder has parcels of various distances from the water source. As a result, all farmers have some land in the most advantageous location near the head of the irrigation system, and some near the tail [Ostrom (1990, p. 83)]. In Sri Lanka, likewise, the *Bethna*

---

[8] By abandoning land under cultivation, an individual actually forsakes his right to cultivate it. This is a rational step to take so long as the net return from newly cleared land exceeds the net return from cultivating previously cleared land. This happens when the fertility of the land has been exhausted and "is restored by allowing the land to remain fallow while newly cleared land is cultivated" [Ault and Rutman (1979, p. 172)].

system provides that the rice areas are divided into a number of sections at varying distances from the dam so that in periods of water shortage participants in the water-sharing schemes may decide to restrict the area irrigated to the sections nearest to the dam and thereby gain a sufficient livelihood [Quiggin (1993, pp. 1133–1134)].

It would be wrong to infer from the above that access to land is necessarily equal in lineage-based societies. In point of fact, rights of access are usually qualified by rules relating both to the period of residence in the area and the member's ancestry: thus, members who are recent residents are likely to be entitled only to marginal lands while those who can trace back their ancestry to the founders of the village often get the best lands (whenever they are in scarce supply) or parcels of greater size [Noronha (1985, p. 182)]. In the village's hierarchy of control and access rights to land, relative 'strangers' therefore occupy a low position.[9] In more unequal lineage-based societies, internal socio-economic differentiation takes place along the lines of rather rigid caste distinctions that also get reflected in unequal rights of land access. Thus, in the traditional villages of Vietnam, under the so-called 'equal-field land system', all male inhabitants "from the officials down the lowest social categories such as orphans, the disabled, and destitute, and the wives and children of those who were exiled and banished" were given land which was called 'personal share land'. Yet, "the size of the shares depended on the ranks of the officials and the social levels of the various beneficiaries" [Phan Huy et al. (1993, p. 168)].

By contrast, access to village CPRs is typically defined in ways that do not usually differentiate between households of various social levels: all member households tend to have equal rights regarding use of the commons. Of course, this does not imply that they take identical advantage of such rights in actual practice. In point of fact, village CPRs can benefit all members of the community or mainly the local poor, and they can be used either on a permanent or a transient basis.

Use is permanent when these resources are a vital resource that all or some households depend upon for everyday livelihood. And use is transient when the commons serve as fall-back resources that provide partial protection in times of unusual economic stress. It is evident that the more aggregate the risks, or the more common the (downside) shocks hitting the community, the larger the externalities created in the use of the commons and the lower the (average) return extracted by the villagers. If risks are idiosyncratic rather than collective, it is important that people in the community are left free to access the commons depending upon their needs of the moment. In such conditions,

---

[9] Among the Moose of the North-Central region of Burkina Faso, for example, strangers are entitled only to land not wanted by any member of an earlier arrived kin group [Breusers (2001, pp. 58–60)]. It is actually inconceivable that a 'stranger' fares better, in the long run at least, than a member of the autochtonous population. Still, it remains possible for latecomers to gradually enlarge their claims over local plots through prolonged presence and use of the land – "Consolidating their presence at a particular place is their only way to ever root territorially in the village" – and through ritual collaboration and the establishment of kin relations with founding lineages (ibidem: pp. 60–62). Breusers uses the expression *autochtonisation* to characterize this process of gradually securing tenure rights in a village in which a kin group has been a latecomer.

the absence of exclusive property rights means that risks are more effectively pooled [Bromley and Chavas (1989, p. 730)].

On the other hand, there is abundant evidence that poor villagers (say, farmers who have recently settled in the village) tend to derive a substantial fraction of their permanent incomes from local CPRs. In this case, the CPRs have a clear social security function in the sense of providing protection against the risk of chronic poverty [Jodha (1986), McKean (1986), Das Gupta (1987), Hecht, Anderson and May (1988), Humphries (1990), Agarwal (1991)].

Note that the above-discussed principles essentially apply to herder societies as well: here, members are entitled to own a stock of animals deemed sufficient for subsistence and, when any of them falls into destitution, he can rely on his community to have his ownership position restored and thus escape the poverty trap. In Somali traditional pastoral communities, for example, poor or destitute individuals (known as *maskiin* or *ceer*) are given a collection of animals by members of their lineage (the *reer*) so that they can re-enter the pastoral economy as full-fledged owners [Nunow (2000, p. 151)].

3.2. The commons as embodiment of the community

We have already stressed that the feeling of togetherness or belonging to the same group is carefully nurtured and reinforced through various emotional expressions in members of lineage-based societies (see supra, Section 2). Such feeling or emotion shapes the way in which they view their natural environment. More precisely, they perceive the surrounding natural resources as a super-natural being that presides over their destiny as a collective entity not only by providing or withdrawing essential foods, but also by giving good health or sending illnesses and the possible means of curing them (medicinal plants). Nature is thus 'anthropomorphized', and the relationship between man and nature is conceived in the personal mode [Godelier (1974)]. People look at their natural environment and behave towards it as though it were a human being, admittedly of an exceptional type: deities or cosmic forces, often construed as the spirits of dead ancestors [Bourdieu (1990)]. Another related characteristic is that, far from considering themselves as agents able to act externally on an objectified nature, people in lineage-based societies feel deeply immersed in it.

In such circumstances, local inhabitants are understandably eager and even anxious to maintain harmonious relationships with the personalized deity deemed responsible for any manifestation of natural forces [see Baland and Platteau (1996)]. The natural and the social universes are seen as isomorphic: they obey the same kind of rules and they work in similar manner. This is not surprising since nature is viewed as an active partner that continuously intervenes in human affairs. Unsurprisingly, any disruption occurring in one universe is thought to be related to some serious problem plaguing the other. Causality actually runs from the social to the natural domain: as a matter of fact, troubles arising from social discord and personal conflicts are bound to provoke the anger of (super)natural forces, and thereby lead to ominous physical disturbances (for instance, a prolonged drought or a flood). To keep these forces satisfied, social cohesion must therefore be preserved which implies, in particular, that no open competition for access to vital resources can be tolerated [see, e.g., Godelier (1974), Carrier (1987), Brightman (1987)]. Hence the importance of granting access rights which enable all member households to make a decent living.

The village commons are a powerful symbol of the sense of collective identity that community values and rituals strive to inculcate and reinforce in the people. This follows from the fact that, forming an undivided portion of the village territory to which all members enjoy equal access whether they belong to high or to low strata, and whether their private landholdings are large or small, they represent the common interests of the community. No wonder, then, that in village life the commons are perceived as one of the privileged planes where community-level solidarity is being displayed. It also provides a unique opportunity to manifest community identity feelings and to create tight social relationships among members. When privatization of the commons causes their disintegration, therefore, the strength of communal ties is reduced, especially so when the strong take possession of the largest chunks or the best parts of the commons to the exclusion of the other [for an illustration, see Chakravarty-Kaul (1996, p. 118)].

Unlike what we shall observe for informal risk-sharing arrangements (see infra, Section 5), norms of solidarity regarding access to the lands of the community are not self-enforcing, if only because rights over corporate land property must be reshuffled when circumstances change, new claimants appear, etc. This explains why formal authority to allocate community land and to arbitrate land disputes is vested in the heads of collectives, or trustees, typically ward or village chiefs, earth priests, masters of fire or masters of the ax (or water masters, for aquatic resources). These trustees are expected to act in the interests of the group as a whole and to grants rights in accordance with the aforementioned logic of subsistence. In the villages of Niger, for example, there exists a pool of community land entrusted to the village chief, known as *hawjou* land, which he has the right to put at the disposal of farmers who are short of land [Gavian and Fafchamps (1996)].

In Bechuanaland (presently Botswana), the chief, with the support of the tribal assembly and the notables (among whom the headmen of 'wards' figure prominently), used to act as a trustee for his tribe. He determines "what land shall be used for dwellings, for grazing, for cultivation, and what land shall be temporarily or permanently withdrawn from usage; also, what land shall be used in common by the tribe and what should be parceled out for use to families. The land to be distributed is allocated to the wards, and the headmen of the wards then assign the plots to individuals. From the headman every married man in the ward can claim enough land for residence and cultivation to accommodate his family. Once land has been taken for cultivation, the family to which it has been assigned remains in possession as long as it continues the use" [Landauer (1964, p. 497), quoting Schapera (1943, p. 44)].

In stratified village societies, local land authorities are also charged with maintaining the local hierarchy, which may also necessitate continuous interventions in land allocations. Thus, in the aforementioned case of the Moose of the North-Central region of Burkina Faso, we learn that, "if a 'stranger' obtains high yields or if rainfall circumstances during the past seasons favored for example farming on lowland, the (low)land can be withdrawn for use by a *tengbiiga* [that is, an elder of the village's founding kin group]" and the 'stranger' "will be asked to choose another plot to farm in the village territory" [Breusers (2001, p. 56)]. In the Zorgho region, to take another example, some areas of suitable land were developed under the auspices of the PDLG (Projet de Développement Local du Ganzourgou) and, with the agreement of local land authorities, they were granted to immigrant farmers who were interested in irrigated agriculture. Local farmers preferred to continue their traditional rainfed agricultural practices and did not show any interest in new agricultural methods. Yet, when the land improvement scheme proved successful, they modified their attitude and reacted by opportunistically claiming back what they consider as their own 'ancestral' lands. Local authorities demanded that all stranger farmers be expelled from the improved lands (personal communication of Hubert Ouedraogo).

4. Erosion of the social security function of customary land tenure

The picture presented above is not the end of the story. Lineage-based societies are not static structures bound to persist indefinitely. In the words of Philip Woodhouse: "The conceptualization of rural resource users as fixed in cohesive rural village communities ... is widely acknowledged as a fiction ... This narrative of rural communities appears wholly inappropriate in the light of the empirical evidence presented here that rural resource users are highly mobile, migrating to take up opportunities to use land or water" [Woodhouse (2003, p. 1716); see also, in particular, Berry (1993)].

Tribal societies do evolve and their evolution is essentially shaped by changes in resource endowments. In point of fact, the societies described in Section 3 are societies with a long tradition of extensive land use patterns associated with high land–man ratios. When population grows rapidly and when market integration proceeds at a significant pace, such as we have observed in Africa especially during the postcolonial period, land being in shorter supply acquires more value. This new situation is bound to cause substantial transformations in the indigenous system of land tenure.

Observation of evolving arrangements in many African regions amply confirm the economic prediction that the nature of property rights in land must change in the direction of increased privatization and that allocation processes must increasingly resemble market mechanisms [see Platteau (2001, Chapters 3–4), for detailed references]. The institutional trajectory of many countries therefore suggests that the African land tenure system begins to evolve towards the Asian model. The implication is a gradual erosion of the traditional role of land tenure arrangements as a provider of social security, and the concomitant necessity to rely on alternative mechanisms to protect livelihoods. This said, it will be argued that the transition to more individualized land rights does not involve the complete demise of social safeguards. The village commons need not always disappear under the combined pressures of population growth and market integration. As a result, they may continue to perform their traditional role of a fall-back option for the most deprived sections of the population. On the other hand, the operation of land markets may remain constrained by various limitations arising from social security considerations. Such restrictions, it must be noted, are not necessarily imposed by an authority structure but may result from endogenously evolved behaviors that are other-regarding. This is especially likely to be the case when restrictions aim at protecting the interests of vulnerable members of the kinship group.

Our analysis proceeds in two stages corresponding to the two issues referred to above: the transformation of the village commons (Section 4.1), and the increasing individualization of land tenure rights with a special focus on transfer rights (Section 4.2). In both cases, we examine the ongoing changes as well as the possible persistence of practices evoking customary solidarity.

4.1. The transformation of the commons

4.1.1. Governance costs and inherited cooperative traits as critical determinants of the evolution of land property systems

When pressure is exercised on the commons, either because of population growth or the emergence of new commercial opportunities resulting from greater market integration, growing competition leads to an increasing incidence of externalities among users. On the one hand, this rising pressure causes the average return from the use of the CPR to fall, and in so far as users do not properly internalize the effect of their effort decision on other users, overexploitation ensues, complementary resources are wasted, and rent is dissipated. On the other hand, degradation of the resource base over time is likely to happen in so far as users have no incentive to conserve it for fear that other users will free ride on their restraint. The above is the classic description of the Tragedy of the Commons when the commons are under open access. Yet, the characterization of the commons as the embodiment of the community, which has been proposed in the previous section, suggests that such pessimism may be unwarranted. As a matter of fact, thanks to their belonging to the same community, CPR users can possibly coordinate their actions and jointly regulate the commons with a view to preventing the wasteful use of complementary inputs and the depletion of the resource base.

Things are not so simple, however. For one thing, the physical domain of the resource may not coincide with the social domain of the community, with the result that community regulation is not able to internalize all or even most of the externalities. For another thing, the regulatory capacity of the community ought not to be taken for granted. The feeling of collective identity certainly serves the purpose of defining and strictly enforcing membership rules, which has the beneficial effect of restricting access to the commons contrary to what is assumed in the parable of the Tragedy of the Commons. However, if the community of users expands due to population growth, the level of exploitation of the CPR will tend towards the open-access inefficient equilibrium as the number of rightful users becomes very large [see Platteau (2000, pp. 113–115), for a formal proof]. To counter that ominous threat, it is essential that the community succeeds in laying down and enforcing rules aimed at regulating the way the CPRs are used by its members.

Obviously, that is not an easy task. Feder and Feeny thus write that, when population increases and land becomes scarce, village communities become larger with the consequence that "the mechanisms for imposing restrictions on individuals' land use patterns which are harmful to the group's interest" are increasingly deficient [Feder and Feeny (1991, p. 140)]. Governance costs are unavoidably associated with collective regulation. Such costs include all the expenses incurred to reach a collective agreement and to organize a community of users. They tend to be higher when the group is larger, or when its membership is more heterogeneous [Libecap (1989), Baland and Platteau (1998a), Platteau (2000, p. 79)]. In particular, it can be shown that common property regulation (through taxes, subsidies, and quotas) is all the more difficult to achieve as inequality in wealth among users is greater. In fact, wealth inequality tends to make the regulated outcome less efficient and to amplify the distributive effects of regulation, thereby increasing the likelihood that some agents will be hurt in the process. Conversely, if we require that the regulated outcome Pareto-dominates the unregulated one, the efficiency gains from regulation decrease with inequality [see Baland and Platteau (1998b, 2003, 2006), Bardhan and Dayton-Johnson (2006)]. Aside from wealth inequality, user heterogeneity as reflected in diversity of interests and objectives in the use of the commons makes their collective management more difficult to achieve.

Also included in governance costs are all the expenses required to control the opportunistic tendencies of CPR users. They may, indeed, be tempted to violate or circumvent collective rules, and to eschew efforts to create collective mechanisms of decision-making and enforcement. Several arguments can be adduced to the effect that incentives to free ride on others' efforts diminish with group size. A first argument is derived from a fundamental result of repeated game theory. When a group is small, members are better informed about each other's behavior and observation of others' past actions is easier. As a consequence, reputation effects are possible and repeated actions may significantly reduce the attractiveness of opportunistic behavior [see, e.g., Sethi and Somanathan (1996)]. Moreover, as pointed out in Section 2, through a linking of the commons' game with a 'social exchange' game, incentive constraints can be pooled with the result that incentive constraints are lessened.

The second argument is the so-called 'incentive dilution' argument put forward by Mancur Olson (1965). Free riding is a strategy whereby an individual trades a reduction in his own effort, from which he alone benefits, for reductions in the income of the whole group, which are shared among all members. As the size of the group increases, the terms of exchange become increasingly favorable to the free rider (since shares are diluted), and the opposite is true when the size of the group decreases. Therefore, the cost of free riding rises (falls) when the size of the group is reduced (increased) while the benefit remains constant.

Third, communication is relatively easy when members are few and, as experimental social psychology has shown, communication facilitates collective undertakings not only by allowing verbal exchanges but, more importantly, by encouraging the formation of identity feelings that drive people to better internalize the consequences of their own behavior on others [Frank (1988, pp. 223–225), Dawes and Thaler (1988, pp. 194–195), Ostrom, Gardner and Walker (1994)]. In other words, and unlike what is conventionally assumed in game theory, communication matters and exchanges of promises may influence game outcomes even though fulfilling promises may appear to be against the actor's interest.

In the light of the above considerations, it is difficult to escape the conclusion that collective regulation is bound to remain imperfect as it is difficult to eliminate all the inefficiencies arising from a collective mode of exploitation. The remaining inefficiencies must therefore be considered as genuine costs of maintaining the commons. A direct implication is that people's ability to cooperate in the management of common access resources determines the relative profitability of these resources and those that are individualized and, therefore, affects the allocation of resources held by households to one use or the other. It has thus been shown that in Mexico, when cooperation fails in the management of collectively grazed pastures, more land is allocated to crops than under successful cooperation and less to pastures, while the stocking rate on pastures is increased. This results in too much land in extensive crops and too many animals per hectare of pasture [McCarthy, De Janvry and Sadoulet (1998)].

Since the efficiency losses resulting from the externalities (of both the rent-dissipating and the ecological types) obviously grow with the value of the natural resource, we expect, other things being equal, that resources will be managed relatively inefficiently under collective regulation when their unit value is high as a result of strong demand for the produce extracted from them [Dasgupta (1993, pp. 288–289)]. Privatization of such resources is therefore more likely unless the direct and indirect costs of privatization are comparatively large. By direct costs, we mean the costs of negotiating, defining and enforcing private property rights while, by indirect costs, we refer to opportunity costs resulting from lost advantages in terms of insurance benefits or scale economies [Platteau (2000, pp. 84–89)].

Does this suggest that we propose a rather deterministic explanation of the institutional trajectory of village societies? Not at all. As argued by Aoki, "technological and ecological factors may not be the sole, albeit important, determinants in the selection of an equilibrium outcome of a particular type but historical and social factors may also matter". Almost by definition, institutions and social norms cannot be a simple mechanical transformation of technological and ecological characteristics [Aoki (2001, p. 50)]. There are at least two other kinds of determining factors that are at work behind the choice of the property regime.

First, economic opportunities shape the way in which alternative insurance mechanisms (say, in the form of income diversification) become available to replace the social protection traditionally afforded by the commons. The more attractive are these new possibilities the more efficient is privatization of a CPR, other things being equal.

Second, governance costs are ultimately dependent on economic, social and historical factors that determine the degree of social cohesiveness of particular village societies.

For example, governance costs are likely to be high if the opening of a village economy to the broader market environment results in increased socio-economic differentiation as well as increased heterogeneity in educational, occupational and cultural backgrounds amongst community members. As explained above, agreements are then more difficult to reach and, consequently, collective regulation may be highly imperfect, prompting privatization of village CPRs or their gradual depletion under conditions that may increasingly resemble an open-access situation. On the basis of this argument, it can be predicted that physically remote communities are more likely to retain collective organizations inherited from the past (e.g., collective management of jointly held resources) than communities located closer to markets and important communication ways. This prediction is actually borne out by many empirical observations.

History matters because a society which has acquired a strong collective identity and has evolved well-accepted social norms over time – that is, a society which has accumulated a substantial amount of social capital, – is more likely to have low governance costs for collective organization than a society with the opposite characteristics. This is because, being constrained by social norms and shaped by values emphasizing the collective good, behaviors tend to be more other-regarding. Incentives to free ride on the efforts of others are thus dampened and there is less need to put into place costly mechanisms to discipline individual actions. The experience of village communities during the Tokugawa era in Japan attests that, when such conditions are fulfilled, local CPRs may be efficiently managed by user groups acting as collectives [Smith (1959), McKean (1986), Hayami and Kikuchi (1981, p. 22), Hayami (1997, p. 92)]. As a result, the insurance benefits obtainable from them continue to accrue to the people who are most in need.

Moreover, in accordance with above-stated predictions of economic theory, institutional adjustment towards stronger collective regulation under the growing pressures of population growth and market integration may involve the reorganization of village societies around smaller and more homogeneous social groups, delegating to them as much regulatory power as possible. An excellent illustration of this possibility is given by Wilson and Thompson (1993) in their analysis of the transformation of the *ejidos* in Mexico. Owing to the excessive size of herding groups, pastoral management at community level (the *ejido*) proved to be a failure. In a significant number of cases, this led to the formation of grazing coalitions within smaller groups where cooperation is assured and benefits are enjoyed under very severe ecological conditions. It is noteworthy that the most effective of these (smaller) grazing associations are based upon the extended family. They practice intensive grazing management with short grazing periods and hoof action contributing to a more sustainable and productive range resource. Outside these short periods, interestingly, multiple families combine their livestock into one large herd (200–600 animals) and move the entire grazing operation to range camps situated in remote areas less subject to population pressure [Wilson and Thompson (1993, pp. 300, 310–312)].

Whether the above example provides indirect evidence that altruism or norm-shaped behavior is more likely to be encountered in family or in neighborhood and friendship circles than in larger social set-ups [see, e.g., Uphoff (2000, pp. 222–223)] remains an open question. As a matter of fact, there is an alternative explanation that has been mentioned earlier, namely that information circulates better and communication is easier in small groups of intensely-related people. In a context of repeated interactions, even self-regarding actors can behave in socially beneficial ways. This being said, one cannot rule out the possibility that both explanations are simultaneously true. This problem of measurement of altruistic predispositions in conditions where informational conditions cannot be properly controlled will surface again in Section 5.

Finally, it bears emphasis that a rather long time may possibly elapse before collective regulation is put into place. This is not only because people may have a poor understanding of the causal links between their harvesting behavior and the state of the natural resources [Baland and Platteau (1996, Chapter 10)], but also because they usually prefer to rely on exclusionary practices that allow them to buy time by postponing regulatory efforts [Berry (1993), Noronha (1985), Downs and Reyna (1988), Bassett and Crummey (1993), Laurent, Mathieu and Totte (1994)]. In the case of the Orma pastoralist communities of northeastern Kenya, for example, elders responded to increasing land pressure by prohibiting nomadic (Somali and other Orma) herders from grazing their herds on the village common pasture. Over the years, they strengthened this prohibition by gradually extending the period during which the local common pasture is made inaccessible to outsiders. Eventually, the restricted zone was declared out of bounds to the outsiders year round. Interestingly, however, Orma villagers continued to use the common pasture as much as they liked and this lack of restrictions applied to insiders was not seen by them as problematic in spite of the quick degradation of the resource that ensued [Ensminger (1990, pp. 667–669)].

4.1.2. Reduced economic significance of the commons: The income effect

If a CPR is efficiently managed, it must be the case that aggregate effort is set at its social optimum value, implying that rent is maximized. When the number of claimants rises, maintaining the optimum effort requires that the average amount of effort put in by each claimant is correspondingly reduced with the result that the income derived from the commons is also smaller than before. As population growth proceeds, the average income derived from a CPR therefore declines continuously. If collective regulation fails or is plagued by inefficiencies, the average income also becomes smaller with population growth, but at lower absolute levels than those obtained under an efficient management of the resource. Since the supporting capacity of the CPR is thus impaired by population growth, one can say that its economic significance is reduced whether the resource is efficiently managed or not. On the other hand, increasing market integration may mitigate and even outweigh the negative effect of population growth on average incomes.

To illustrate these simple results, consider a situation in which two income sources are available to community members: farming incomes derived from privately-held land, on the one hand, and incomes obtained from a common property resource, say a fish-

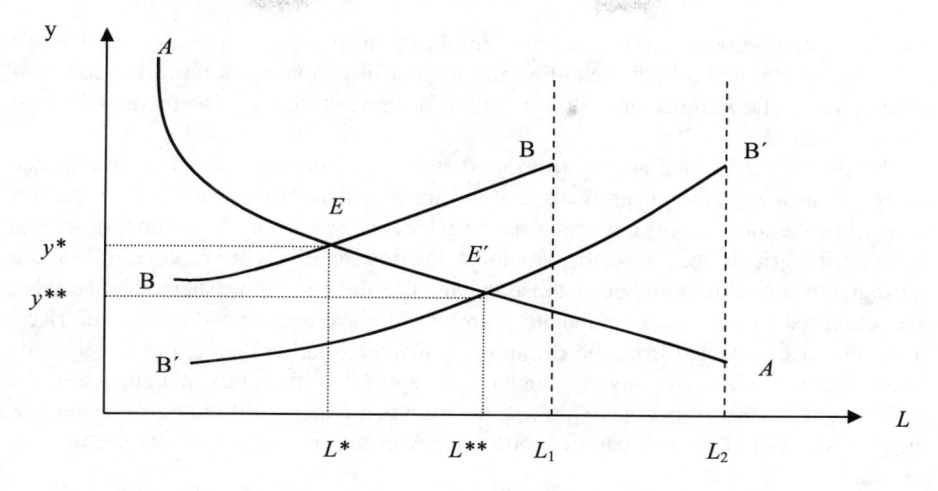

Figure 1. Impact of population growth and market integration on average incomes.

ing space, on the other hand. To begin with, we assume that all households are equally endowed in privately-held land. For the sake of simplicity, we make the additional inconsequential assumption that the two activities, farming and fishing, are exclusive in the sense that a given individual cannot be simultaneously engaged in both. All households choose the proportion of their workforce that is going to work on the commons and, since they are equally endowed, this proportion is identical across all households. Furthermore, all villagers operating on the commons are assumed to be equivalently productive and to receive the average product.

This situation is depicted in Figure 1 where the average income earned per individual, denoted by y, is measured along the vertical axis while the total number of individuals occupied on the common fishery, denoted by L, is measured along the horizontal axis. The number of individuals remaining to work on the family farms is measured residually from right to left as the distance between the initial size of the population, L_1, and L^*, the equilibrium number of individuals engaged in the common fishery in the initial situation. This initial equilibrium is derived by intersecting the downward-sloping curve AA with the upward-sloping curve BB. The curve AA describes the way the average income derived from the fishing sector falls as the number of workers involved increases. As for the curve BB, its shape reflects the fact that the marginal and also the average productivity of labor in agriculture are decreasing with the number of farmers actively working the land. (For the sake of simplicity, all non-labor costs are assumed to be negligible.) Corresponding to the intersection point E is y^*, the average equilibrium individual income in the initial situation.

Comparative statics enables us to highlight the effects of population growth and market expansion. The first effect is depicted by a shift rightwards of the perpendicular to the horizontal axis corresponding to population size, now set at L_2. As a result of this move, the upward-sloping curve shifts downwards from position BB to position B'B'.

The new intersection point, E′, therefore implies a lower equilibrium average individual income, y^{**}, and a higher equilibrium number of people working in the common fishery, L^{**}. The number of people working in agriculture has also increased, from $(L_1 - L^*)$ to $(L_2 - L^{**})$.

The second effect, that arising from market integration, may consist of an increase in the price of agricultural products that get translated in an upward shift of the BB curve. The outcome of this change is, as expected, an increase in the number of people engaged in agriculture, the sector which has become relatively more attractive, and a subsequent fall of the number of those engaged in the common fishery. Unlike what was observed in the case of population growth, the average individual income rises. If the produce collected from the commons is marketed rather than being largely self-consumed, the AA curve may also undergo an upward shift and the net change in the equilibrium number of people exploiting the common fishery will of course depend on the relative sizes of the two parallel shifts. In any event, the individual average income increases.

More interesting is the case where both population growth and market penetration occur at the same time. In such circumstances, two opposite forces are in operation and their net impact on the average individual income is impossible to predict a priori. Thus, if price increases affect only the agricultural sector, the curve BB undergoes a downward shift as a result of population growth and an upward shift as a result of market penetration. Bear in mind that increased rates of use of the village commons following a shift in the internal terms of trade in favor of the products extracted from them (relative to the price of agricultural products) imply a particular risk, namely that of causing their gradual degradation over time. Note that in all the above reasoning dynamic effects in the form of ecological externalities caused by biological overfishing have been assumed away. If they are taken into account, we must allow for the possibility that curve AA is continuously shifting downwards as a result of excessive pressure on the fish stock (pressure beyond the level of fishing effort corresponding to the point of maximum sustainable yield). Other things being equal, incomes from fishing then decline over time and labor is re-allocated towards agriculture.

We may now relax the simplistic assumption according to which all community members are equally endowed in private landholdings. Adopting the formalization used by Baland and François in their aforementioned paper, let us consider a continuum of agents each of whom is endowed with one unit of labor. Each agent i can allocate labor to his private farm, with returns θ_i, or work in the common fishery. Returns to labor on the farm, θ, are continuously distributed over $[0, \infty]$, by the density $f(\theta)$. The fixed amount of the common property resource is denoted by R while, as above, L is the aggregate labor used in the common fishery. The commons' production function, $Y(R, L)$, is homogeneous of degree one, strictly increasing and concave in L. It is then easy to see that an equilibrium allocation of labor in this sector is given by

$$L^0 : \frac{Y(R, L^0)}{L^0} = \theta^0 \quad \text{with} \quad \int_0^{\theta^0} f(\theta)\,d\theta = L^0.$$

With such an allocation, all agents i, for whom $\theta_i \leqslant \theta^0$, work in the common fishery and receive $Y(R, L^0)/L^0$ while all agents with $\theta_i > Y(R, L^0)/L^0$ work on their private landholdings obtaining payment θ_i.[10]

Equilibrium allocations on the common property resource therefore imply that those villagers with smallest land endowments obtain a larger proportion of the rents generated by this resource. As pointed out by Baland and François (1999), a commons "thus provides a form of income targeting to the poor", in line with the empirical evidence reviewed in Section 3.1. A presumed effect of population growth is that the absolute number of community members with $\theta_i \leqslant \theta^0$ increases, putting added pressure on the commons and causing a fall in the average product. The allocation of labor to the common fishery, L^0, rises in the new equilibrium and the incomes of the poor are lower. On the other hand, if it causes the value of incomes from private landholdings to rise relatively to those obtained on the common property resource, market integration reduces the pressure on this resource and the situation of the poorest members of the community improves. If prices rise in both sectors, that pressure may not be relieved, yet the poor are still better than before.

4.1.3. Reduced economic significance of the commons: The insurance effect

In addition to causing a decline in average incomes, rising numbers of rightsholders may erode the insurance capacity of the CPR in the sense that the vulnerability or exposure to risk of the individuals depending on it may become larger. As for increasing market integration, if it may mitigate and even outweigh the negative effect of population growth on average incomes, it is likely to fail to mitigate the negative effect of population growth on income variations.

In order to illustrate the insurance effect of the evolution of the commons, a convenient method is to posit a resource characterized by a fixed number of exploitable spots that are continuously occupied as soon as population pressure begins to bear. Think, for example, of a beachseine fishery. Beachseining is indeed a fishing technique which requires a substantial water space located close to the shore to operate. This requirement follows from the fact that the beachseine is a large bag-shaped net with coir-wings of extensive length which, although it necessitates the help of a boat to be put out at sea, is essentially handled from the shore itself. Note that the sea bottom must be sandy and free from rocks and other obstructions so that the net can be dragged smoothly. These two constraints have the obvious effect of limiting the number of fishing spots that are available to any given coastal community [Alexander (1980, 1982), Platteau, Murickan and Delbar (1985), Amarasinghe (1989)].

Let n be the number of community members who need to work on the resource to earn a living, m the number of available fishing spots, y_i the (certain) daily return yielded

---

[10] By assumption, the distribution of θ is such that $L^* > 0$. Concavity of $Y(\cdot)$ in L ensures that the equilibrium allocation, L^*, is unique.

by spot i, and $\text{Var}(y_i)$ the variance of such returns. Let us also have that $p = n/m$, the number of users per available resource spot. When p exceeds one, there is a queuing problem resulting from an effective pressure of the user group on the commons. The value of p can therefore be construed as a measure of the intensity of that pressure. We are essentially interested in the way household vulnerability to hunger evolves as population pressure increases. Household vulnerability, denoted by V, is defined here as the proportion of annual time during which the income earned by the household falls below an accepted standard of minimum consumption. It obviously varies between a minimum zero value and a maximum unitary value. Incomes are assumed to be earned on a daily basis. Finally, the distribution of location-specific yields is such that the yield falls short of the minimum subsistence level, labeled c, in some fishing sites but not in others. Let us denote by F the relative number of sites such that $y_j < c$ ($0 \leqslant F \leqslant 1$).

The general formula describing household vulnerability as a function of population pressure is:

$$V = \frac{n - (m - mF)}{n} = 1 - \frac{1}{p}(1 - F).$$

In accordance with the anthropological literature, a rotation rule has been posited to exist that allows the limited locations available on each fishing day to be equally shared among the rightsholders.[11] More precisely, the rule provides that fishermen with access rights should be shifted from day to day from one spot to another so that income-earning opportunities are perfectly equalized [see Baland and Platteau (1996, pp. 199–209)].

Polar cases obtain when (i) $p = 1$ and $F = 0 \Rightarrow V = 0$ (all fishermen can be continuously occupied and returns are uniform across all fishing spots at a rewarding level); (ii) $p > 1$ and $F = 0 \Rightarrow V = 1 - (1/p)$ (fishermen are deprived of income on certain days owing to a lack of available spots); and (iii) $p = 1$ and $F > 0 \Rightarrow V = F$ (there are enough spots yet some of them do not provide enough yield to allow subsistence). The general case obtains when the number of claimants exceeds that of the available fishing spots and the quality of these spots varies significantly, so that fishing incomes vary on a double count. This is the situation described by Alexander in his study of beachseine fishing communities in Sri Lanka (1982), by Berkes in his inquiry about Alanya fishermen in Turkey, or by Bene, Bennett and Neiland (2002) with reference to Ghanaian small-scale fisheries. The signs of the first derivatives are straightforward:

$$\frac{dV}{dp} > 0 \quad \text{and} \quad \frac{dV}{dF} > 0.$$

---

[11] Note that, if no rotation rule exists and access to fishing locations is anarchic, welfare losses are likely to occur because fishermen will tend to flock in the most promising spots (those with the best income prospects) while a more balanced distribution of them among the available sites would have been more socially efficient [see Platteau and Seki (2001, pp. 397–399), for a proof]. Moreover, the costs of large congregations of boats in the best locations (collisions entailing damages and injuries) will have to be borne.

Table 1
Evolution of household vulnerability as population grows under two different assumptions regarding the variation of location-specific yields

n ($m = 4$, given)	V with $F = 1/4$	V with $F = 1/2$
6	4/8	8/12
8	5/8	9/12
12	6/8	10/12

Furthermore,

$$\frac{d(dV/dp)}{dF} < 0.$$

In Table 1, we present a simple numerical example that illustrates the aforementioned results. We assume that $m = 4$ while n takes on three different values and F two different ones.

If we now consider the possibility that over time growing population pressure on the common-property resource causes its gradual degradation, we must recognize the existence of a relationship of the form $F = f(p)$, with $f'(p) > 0$. The impact of population pressure on household vulnerability then includes both a direct and an indirect effect:

$$\frac{dV}{dp} = \frac{(1-F) + pf'(p)}{p^2} \geq 0,$$

where $pf'(p)$ corresponds to the indirect effect.

Instead of assuming that yields of the resource vary from one location to another, we could alternatively assume that yields are identical yet fluctuate seasonally. To the problem of unemployment is now added the risky prospect that fishermen will have their turn during the lean season when yields are uniformly low. In the aforementioned work by Alexander (1982), only 25% of the beachseines thus received turns during the flush period in 1970–1971. It is true that over the medium or long term incomes are expected to even out as the rotation rule ensures that every fisherman will operate his net during the flush period if a sufficiently long period is considered. In the short term, however, the pressing question remains as to how fishermen will succeed in buffering the year-to-year fluctuations in income that are the direct result of their growing numbers [Platteau (1991, pp. 125–129)].

In the most complex case, inter-seasonal fluctuations in yields are added to variations between locations. Household vulnerability is likely to be quite large in such circumstances in so far as there is no reason to expect that the different types of risks will cancel each other out.

A last and important remark is in order. If the expansion of market opportunities is accompanied by a process of socio-economic differentiation that is reflected in unequal asset endowments, and if rights to have turns in a rotation scheme are defined on the basis of asset units (in this instance, fishing units) rather than of household units or individuals, the rich will improve their ability to insure in the commons at the expense of the poor. Indeed, by raising the number of their turns in the sequence of access rights and by spreading them over the entire net cycle, the former can stabilize their incomes. The latter find themselves in the opposite situation in so far as their shares or participation rates in the sequence of net turns are more diluted than before, thereby causing an erosion of their insurance capacity. For the poor, increasing inequality has actually the same effect as population growth. This is exactly the story told by Alexander (1982) for the village of Gahävalla in south Sri Lanka [see Bardhan et al. (2006), for a similar story about forestries in Nepal].

Clearly, the old rotational arrangement aimed at equalizing income-earning opportunities is perverted under the joint impact of rising pressure on the resource and private accumulation strategies by the rich. When so perverted, it may quickly become inferior to the private property outcome from the standpoint of the poor.

4.2. Individualization of land tenure rights

Under conditions of growing land pressure, land rights become increasingly individualized. Such a process is reflected in the fact that individual possessors enjoy not only more permanent use rights over the land but also rights to transfer it relatively freely. These two sorts of prerogatives are mentioned in the following statement of Robert Bates who draws a pessimistic picture of their effects on social security, a picture which leaves no room for any form of norm-guided or other-regarding behavior:

> ... membership in the community is no longer sufficient to guarantee access to land; nor is it a necessary condition. Thus, land can be alienated to persons outside the community. Moreover, land that is not in use does not revert to the community; it can be held for purposes of speculation, transferred to other private individuals, or bequeathed to persons of the owner's choosing. It is a consequence of this system, of course, that even in the presence of abundant land, people may starve for want of access to it; primary attraction of a communal system of land rights is that under similar circumstances such deaths would not occur. [Bates (1984)]

In the remainder of this sub-section, we will examine the claim made by Bates by looking at the impact of the two aforementioned components of tenure individualization on the effectiveness of social security via land access rules.

4.2.1. Deepening individualization in the form of permanent use rights

In the first place, regarding use rights, an immediate consequence of population pressure on land resources is the shortening of the fallow period. When this period becomes sufficiently short, actual cultivators are prompted to claim the continued possession of their parcels. They thereby call into question the erstwhile practice according to which the land once fallow must return to the community to be reallocated later when its fertility will have been naturally restored. To enforce their claim, as noted by Boserup, they may even "wish to begin to recultivate a given plot before the normal period of fallow has elapsed ... lest the cultivation right be forfeited by desuetude". As a result, smaller amounts of land will be available for redistribution by the chief, and "valuable land for redistribution will become available mainly when a family dies out or leaves the territory ... Redistribution of land thus becomes a less important and less frequently exerted function of the chief, and in the end it disappears altogether ... [Boserup (1965, pp, 79–81); see also Cohen (1980, p. 359)].

Since less land returns periodically to the village pool, there are also fewer possibilities to adjust the endowments of community members when the need arises. The scope of the social security mechanism that operates through such adjustments is correspondingly reduced to eventually vanish when all land plots are under the permanent control of their individual possessors.

In addition, the establishment of more permanent use rights means that such rights become exclusive. This often implies the demise of secondary or derived rights of access to land that were usually recognized under the customary system of land tenure. With land becoming increasingly scarce, derived rights thus tend to be denied to secondary rightsholders, such as herders, for fear that they might stake ownership claims and/or simply because continuous cultivation practices are being introduced with a view to making land exploitation more intensive [see, e.g., Coldham (1978), Ault and Rutman (1979), Noronha (1985), Bruce (1986), Green (1987), Bruce and Fortmann (1989), Barrows and Roth (1989), Mackenzie (1993), Atwood (1990), Platteau (1992, 1996, 2000, Chapter 4)].

In West Africa, for example, gradual demarcation of parcels for cultivation in what were communal pastures previously arouses the anger of those groups such as the Tuaregs and the Fulanis who primarily depend on animal grazing for their daily livelihood [see, e.g., Lund (1998)]. The outcome, of course, depends upon the configuration of power relations, including possible alliances with state authorities. In actual fact, "the farmers often have the upper hand in conflicts over pastures", and "the extension of cultivated fields into the pastoral areas is the main trend" (ibidem: pp. 142, 145). Revealingly, access to grazing lands is more easily open to influential and wealthy farmers who know with whom to forge tactical alliances, how to approach and mobilize authorities, how to read a sequence of contingent opportunities, and how to use economic resources at their disposal to influence the result of an arbitration or litigation.[12]

Stranger farmers are especially vulnerable to exclusionary practices initiated by indigenous inhabitants confronted with actual or anticipated land scarcity. Their rights of access to plots of relatively high quality are especially likely to be denied. In the

---

[12] As Christian Lund points out, "... some money always change hands during an audience. Economic resources, therefore, play a central role. While the difference between a token of respect, a fee and a bribe can be difficult to discern since the gesture holds several meanings depending on the position of the 'giver', the 'receiver' and the 'onlooking opposing litigant', money or other tangible goods are necessary prerequisites for accessing the politico-legal institutions" [Lund (1998, p. 161)].

Senegal river valley, for example, the local Haalpulaar (Toucouleur) communities have become concerned that land will not be available in sufficient amounts for their children and grandchildren. As a result, they have started closing access to the good inundable lands (known as *waalo*) located near the river for all strangers and immigrant farmers, confining them to the poor-quality drylands (the *jeeri* soils) which are still plentiful [Rodenbach (1999)]. Similar events have occurred in many places in SubSaharan Africa and violent conflicts have resulted in not a few cases (like in Côte d'Ivoire, in the Senegal river valley, in Guinea, in the Kivu state in Congo, etc.).

Finally, on the basis of four case studies conducted in Kenya, South Africa, Botswana, and Mali, Philip Woodhouse has reached a broadly similar conclusion. He thus writes that: "When competition for land intensifies, the inclusive flexibility offered by customary rights can quickly become an uncharted terrain on which the least powerful are vulnerable to exclusion as a result of the manipulation of ambiguity by the more powerful" [Woodhouse (2003, p. 1715)].

4.2.2. *Deepening individualization in the form of increased transfer rights*

An important feature of indigenous land systems in SubSaharan Africa is the existence of extremely tight restrictions on transfer rights. In particular, possessors are not allowed to alienate the land which belongs to the community considered as a corporate entity (see supra). Land gifts and land loans may be permitted when individual use rights to specific plots are established but only provided that the donee or the loanee belongs to the same community (of common descent or residence) as the donor or the lender. As for land sales, they are strictly forbidden as a matter of principle, and prohibitions against them have been frequently backed by curses and taboos.

As land becomes more scarce and therefore more valuable, however, prohibitions against land transfers are gradually relaxed. At one end of the spectrum, concomitantly with the establishment of more permanent rights over the land, the right to bequeath land to children is increasingly asserted. At the other end, the right to sell the land individually held remains circumscribed, although in a less strict manner than before. There are thus several steps through which prescriptions concerning land sale prerogatives evolve as land scarcity increases.

At first, any land parcel sold is redeemable by the seller as soon as he gets the wherewithal to repurchase it [see, e.g., Ault and Rutman (1979, p. 170)]. Indeed, as possession becomes more individualized, land is increasingly viewed as part of a family patrimony and it forms the substance of its social identity and prestige. As a result, it is an asset that may not be parted with: it belongs to the sphere of gifts – or, in the words of Godelier (1999), the sphere of "inalienable possessions" – as opposed to commodity exchanges [Gregory (1982)], implying that it can only be temporarily entrusted, but never really given away, to another individual or family. Moreover, sales are sanctioned only among members of the local community. Indeed, being members of a common social network governed by solidarity norms and proper enforcement mechanisms, only they can be expected to keep their promise to give back the plot of land acquired if the above possibility arises.

Thereafter, sales become subject to a right of preemption by the seller (or his family): in the event that the present owner wants to dispose of the land purchased in the past, the land must go back to the original owner (or his family) provided that the latter is willing and able to repurchase it. If he is unwilling (say, because he has emigrated with his family) or unable to do so, the land may be sold but only with the approval of village elders. As a matter of fact, the elders have the responsibility to ensure that nobody within the group wants to acquire the land proposed for sale before allowing its disposal.

Finally, a stage is reached when all prohibitions fall into decay and land sales become completely free [see, e.g., Bruce (1986, pp. 38–40, 1993, p. 42)]. When the right to sell thus includes sales to members outside the community and the individual possessor of the land does not need any approval, "the last vestiges of general cultivation rights are lost and private property rights are complete. General rights survive only as grazing and collection rights on communal grazing areas and forests, whose soils are usually unsuitable for crop or intensive pasture production" [Binswanger, Deininger and Feder (1995, p. 2669)].

It bears emphasis that allowing the land to fall into the hands of outsiders is generally a consequence of the fact that land markets are often activated through distress sales [Andre and Platteau (1998)]. As has been pointed out by Bohannan and Dalton (1962), indeed, villagers would feel bad if they were to take advantage of the plight of their neighbors or kin in order to enlarge their own farms. As indicated above, it is only under the understanding that they would immediately release the plots to the distress seller would he become able to repurchase them (at the original selling price) that farmers would accept to buy plots disposed of under duress by another member of their community.

If farmers want to make permanent acquisitions (an expected feature given the increasing scarcity of land and the necessity to undertake long-term land improvements), and if there is no hope that the distress seller can retake possession of his land in a foreseeable future, the passing of village lands into the hands of outsiders is a likely outcome. Note incidentally that distress sales are a natural way in which a land market can establish itself despite customary prohibitions. This is because such prohibitions are generally suspended in cases of emergency [Dalton (1962)], and rule violations become the norm when emergency conditions tend to persist.[13]

A similar evolution can be detected for land alienations through mortgaging. To begin with, what is permitted are traditional land pledges whereby a household obtains credit against temporarily foregoing the use of the land offered as a security to the lender. Upon repayment of the loan, the land is automatically redeemed to the pledger. Revealingly, there is a common understanding that, even if the repayment is repeatedly postponed

---

[13] Traditional prohibitions against land sales are more easily subverted when the land and money exchanged are in the form of gifts and counter-gifts rather than trade, as observed by Espen Sjaastad (1998) for Zambia.

or delayed (sometimes over successive generations), ownership of the land is never transferred to the credit-giver, only the right to collect the proceeds derived from its exploitation. Later, this intrinsic right of the pledger to retrieve his land is called into question and lenders, – first discreetly and almost shamefully, then more openly, – assert their willingness to set a time limit beyond which they can claim the right to keep the pledged land in full ownership (as I could observe in the highly populated district of Anloga, Ghana; or in the high value lands of the irrigation schemes of Yalogo, Burkina Faso).

With a mortgage, the lender does not have the right to use the land offered as security but, precisely for that reason, he will be all the more keen to exercise his right to seize upon it if the debt is not cleared in due time. The main question is how long the borrower may delay his loan repayment before the threat of foreclosure becomes effective. Like in the case of land pledges, evolution towards free alienability of land assets is reflected in the shorter grace periods granted to the borrower, in the diminished role of the group in negotiating such grace periods in order to rescue him, and in the increasingly recognized right of the lender to stipulate precise terms regarding repayment conditions.

On the other hand, since the same kind of prohibitions as found in the case of land sales also traditionally applied to land mortgages, the individualization of land rights also gets reflected in the gradual relaxation of these prohibitions. Yet, given the enormous stake involved in such an evolution, it is not surprising that loans are often taken against other securities than the land itself, e.g. the security of standing crops. It may nevertheless happen, as has been observed on irrigation schemes in Burkina Faso (Yalogo region), that the credit-giver reserves to himself in the event of crop failure the right to take hold of his borrower's land if the latter is unable to return the loan after a more or less protracted span of time [Baland, Dubuisson and Platteau (1998)]. In such circumstances, the risk of crop failure is entirely borne by the borrower and loans are ultimately secured by his land.

4.2.3. Restrictions on land markets and social security concerns

There is an evident rationale behind restrictions on free land sales or free land mortgaging by individual rightsholders and this rationale is based on obvious social security considerations. As a matter of fact, heads of a lineage or a family, and elders in general, are concerned that if land becomes freely disposable they will have eventually to bear the negative consequences that can follow from the granting of such a freedom. In Kenya, for instance, we learn that it is mainly elders who reject the idea of land mortgage while younger men tend to be more attracted by the prospect of ready cash and, as a result, they are more liable to have their lands foreclosed [Shipton (1988, pp. 106, 120)]. 'Urgent' consumption needs which elders may well regard as luxury can easily drive young people into landlessness, whether inadvertently or not [Green (1987, p. 7), The Economist, 21–27 January (1995, p. 49)]. Attractive but risky investment projects may have the same effect.

Once deprived of their land assets, since there is no state social security system to fall back on and since alternative employment opportunities are rare and labor markets risky, the venturesome or myopic youngsters are tempted to rely on the elders for their subsistence needs. To avoid being involved in such rescue operations, elders prefer that land sales by youngsters be made subject to their approval. In other words, restrictions on the free play of land markets eventually arise from the absence of a centralized social security mechanism as well as from all sorts of market imperfections (including risky labor markets and imperfect credit and insurance markets) that make people dependent on their native community or social group for a guaranteed livelihood.

It is interesting to point out that in Kenya (the only country in SubSaharan Africa with several decades of experience with systematic registration and titling of rural lands), District Land Control Boards in charge of approving land sales are frequently reluctant to permit transactions which would leave families (and their descendants) landless and destitute. That is why they insist that all adult members of the household (including women) of the title-holder are to be present at the hearing to indicate their agreement with the sale. The government has actually sanctioned this de facto situation since a presidential directive aimed at minimizing land disputes requires the agreement of family members in addition to that of the title-holder prior to any sale or use of land as collateral [Haugerud (1983, p. 84), Mackenzie (1993, p. 200), Pinckney and Kimuyu (1994, p. 10)].

In Zimbabwe, likewise, a proposal by a land tenure commission appointed by the government (October 1994) provides that individual farmers should be given the right to own their land, but their right to buy and sell it should be subject to the approval of the traditional village council (the *sabuku*) which in pre-colonial days used to be vested with the prerogative of allocating local lands [The Economist, 21–27 January (1995, p. 49)].

The lesson to draw from the above evidence is that, although there is an unmistakable trend towards the assertion of the right to permanently transfer land in African rural areas, resistance is still pervasive against uninhibited land sale and mortgage transactions [see Platteau (2000, Chapter 4)], for a more detailed account). This is apparently because of the social security risk involved. Revealing of the resistance that people can put up against such unfettered transactions is the fact that in Kenya lenders have had great difficulty foreclosing on land mortgages chiefly because "the presence of many kin around mortgaged land makes it politically unfeasible to auction the holdings of defaulters" [Shipton (1988, p. 120)]. In urban peripheries, notes another study, "although some banks have accepted titled land as collateral and auctioned it off in cases of default, in some cases purchasers were not able to take occupation of the land for fear of reprisals" [Migot-Adholla et al. (1991, p. 170)].

In a recent study conducted by Baland et al. (2001) in 36 villages of East-Central Uganda, two results are particularly relevant to our discussion. On the one hand, rural land markets are remarkably active as indicated by the fact that almost half of the total land area owned has been purchased. (Uganda is probably the African country with the strongest tradition of land market activity, a feature which is to be partly ascribed to an active policy of freehold establishment during colonial times.) And, on the other hand, people who are native of a given location and did not inherit any land from their father have a good access to the local land sales market: other things being equal, they are able to purchase significantly larger areas than other residents, which enables them to eventually hold an amount of land roughly equal to that afforded by indigenous villagers who inherited positive amounts of land from their parents.

The key question is, of course, how the landless got the wherewithal to buy land in the local market. What the study by Baland and co-authors suggests is that the unequal distribution of family land assets among male children is matched by the unequal distribution of non-land assets, particularly cattle, in the opposite direction. This is reflected in the fact that children who did not inherit land yet purchased parcels in the local market (which is the case for a majority of them) tend to own more cattle heads than those who did inherit positive quantities of family land. It is true that the difference is not statistically significant. What matters, however, is that children who were initially landless own (at least) as much livestock as those who were not, even after they have made compensatory land purchases.

Now, it also appears that migrants – who, by definition, arrived in a landless state in the host village – are able to buy land and become landowners. Nonetheless, they are doing less well than the native landless in the sense that their landholding is much smaller than that of the native inhabitants (4.6 acres as against about 7.2 acres for native residents whether they initially inherited land or not). The average area purchased in the local market is 6.3 acres for native farmers who did not inherit any land, 2.4 acres for those who did, and 4.0 acres for migrants.

There might thus be a preference for the local "sons of the soil" in the land sale market. Such a preference can easily be manifested insofar as land sale transactions are typically subject to restrictions in the form of requirement of prior notification or approval by lineage authorities. Revealingly, a recent study done in the same region has concluded that "despite the high proportion of parcels that had been acquired through purchase, the unfettered individual right of sale is relatively uncommon" [Place, Ssenteza and Otsuka (2001, p. 219)]. Such restrictions are usually driven by social security considerations, meaning concretely that (i) land may not be sold by people who may later need it, and (ii) priority is given to land-hungry people when parcels are disposed of.[14]

In the survey area, it is only in a minority of villages (in maximum one-third of them) that prior approval of a land sale to an outsider is formally required. It can therefore be concluded that the positive distributive effects of the land sale market are generated with a small measure of customary regulations, yet this could happen only because parents are eager to treat all their (male) children equally during the inheritance process. Since

---

[14] For a reason explained above, this priority is more easily given when the land sale is caused by the owner's emigration (a frequent occurrence in Uganda) or his desire to consolidate his land assets in the village than when it is caused by distress conditions.

they are also keen to avoid the fragmentation of family land into non-viable plots, equal treatment is achieved in terms of the overall distribution of all assets.

It bears emphasis that customary restrictions do not necessarily work in favor of the poor, especially in in inegalitarian village societies such as caste-based communities. The erosion of these restrictions is then likely to lead to a more equitable distribution of land. Thus, in the Ziz valley (Morocco, see above), by contrast, customary restrictions on land transactions were aimed at barring people with a low and subservient status (the *Haratine*, of dark complexion) from acquiring land.[15] There, liberalization of the land sales market caused by the inflow of foreign remittances in the hands of the *Haratine* and the multiplication of distress sales by traditional landowners had beneficial effects on the distribution of land assets [Ilahiane (2001, pp. 104–108)].

That free land sale transactions can well have the opposite effect of concentrating land in the hands of an elite is evident from the in-depth study of a Rwandan village by Andre and Platteau (1998). In this case, the unequalizing effect of the market is a direct result of the fact that only a minority of people could purchase land because they enjoyed privileged access to the few non-agricultural employment opportunities available. Others, who did not have the required political connections to get access to these scarce jobs, have often been forced to resort to distress sales of land parcels in order to make ends meet. In Rwanda, customary restrictions on land sale transactions have completely collapsed, giving rise to extremely bitter reactions on the part of landless people towards those who have purchased significant amounts of land thanks to their discriminatory access to ample non-agricultural incomes. The centrifugal tendencies operating in the Rwandan countryside are so strong that one can no more speak of 'village communities' and 'village customs', a consequence of extreme and continuing land pressure combined with an acute dearth of off-farm employment opportunities. These accumulated resentments, frustrations, and hatred manifested themselves in the crudest manner on the occasion of the 1993 civil war since there was a selective killing of large landowners even after controlling for ethnic affiliation.

The obvious lesson from the above case studies is that rural land sale markets, freed from customary restrictions, are susceptible of either mitigating or accentuating inequalities in initial endowments. Whether the former or the latter outcome obtains depends upon the existence of imperfections in other markets, particularly the financial and labor markets, and upon prevailing inheritance rules.

It is time to recap our central argument. When a household head is allowed to sell land to another member of his community, it is because he can thus tide over a difficult period and is expected to redeem his land in the future. And it is because it wants

---

[15] The concept of *shafa'a* – preemption rights in favor of the Berber clans or lineages – ensured that land would remain in their hands "because a lineage member's price and blood negated those of a stranger or a *Haratine*". As a matter of fact, "in the Berber villages, any land transactions or selling of trees had to be made public so that the right of *shafa'a* could be applied by distant clan and lineage members who might be away from the village during the sale" [Ilahiane (2001, p. 104)].

to ensure that such repurchase will indeed be feasible that the social group does not approve land sales to people outside of its confines. Only upon its own members can it exercise the necessary pressure to prevent any reneging on the promise to give back the land purchased when the seller will be in better straits. Yet, beyond a point, presumably, land becomes such a valuable asset that promises to part with the land purchased once the seller is able to buy it again become non-credible, even when they have been made by fellow community members.

At this stage, the granting to the land seller of a preemption right to later repurchase his land if offered for sale constitutes the expected next step in the gradual emergence of a free land sale market. The rule according to which landless members of the community should have priority access to the local land sale market whenever parcels are offered for sale participates in the same logic of providing whatever feasible support to deserving community members. This said, in so far as the social group does not really provide the landless or the land-hungry or the distress seller with the wherewithal needed to buy land, the above rules constitute only an imperfect mechanism. Witness to it is the fact that distress sales do occur in the first place. Incidentally, the fact that poor people sell land under duress also attests to the imperfection of mutual insurance networks based on state-contingent reciprocal transfers, or to the presence of important aggregate risks.

In this section, the point has been made that, as land becomes more scarce, distress sales tend to be more frequent and landless people are not necessarily able to repurchase the parcels which they have lost under duress. The inference drawn from this observation is that inter-individual mutual aid transfers are not (or no more) sufficient to ensure community members against the risk of subsistence crises. In the forthcoming section, attention is therefore focused on the literature dealing with such transfers in order to seek a possible confirmation of such an inference.

5. Voluntary reciprocal contingent transfers

5.1. General considerations

The central problem with a decentralized risk-pooling mechanism is that rational selfish people may join a risk-pooling network because welfare gains can be derived from their participation, yet they are tempted to defect afterwards when they realize they have to make a positive contribution to the network. Some anthropologists have nevertheless argued, and economists have shown, that rural communities can solve this commitment problem even though they have no means to enforce commitments to share (written and legally binding contracts are not possible), and their members do not behave altruistically. This is because continuous and personalized relationships among community members help create an interaction framework resembling a repeated game of indeterminate or infinite duration. In such a game, reputation effects are at work and punishments can be meted out to willing free riders, thereby ensuring that promises to help fellow villagers hit by adverse economic events are self-enforcing [Posner (1980, 1981), Sugden (1986, Chapter 7), Kimball (1988), Foster (1988), Coate and Ravaillon (1993), Udry (1990, 1993, 1994), Platteau (1991), Alderman and Paxson (1992), Fafchamps (1992), Coate and Ravaillon (1993), Ligon (1993), Dasgupta (1993, pp. 201–217), Townsend (1994), Kocherlakota (1994), Wang (1994), Alderman and Paxson (1992), Besley (1995), Hoff (1996), Bardhan and Udry (1999, Chapter 8), Ray (1998, Chapter 15)].

Mutual insurance can thus be sustained as an equilibrium of a repeated game, thereby escaping the trap of a one-period insurance contract that obviously has no risk-pooling equilibrium (since it corresponds to a prisoner's dilemma where the unique Nash equilibrium is autarky). Of course, it is also necessary that risks are not completely synchronized among agents, at least during some of the succeeding periods. Furthermore, informational problems are unimportant: thanks to close relations, agents can perfectly observe each other's income to spot defections.[16] Interestingly, as early as in the eighteenth century, David Hume had remarkably anticipated the possibility of informal risk-pooling arrangements based on selfish behavior:

> We can better satisfy our appetites in an oblique and artificial manner, than by their headlong and impetuous motion. Hence I learn to do a service to another, without bearing him any real kindness; because I foresee, that he will return my service, in expectation of another of the same kind, and in order to maintain the same correspondence of good offices with me or with others. And accordingly, after I have served him, and he is in possession of the advantage arising from my action, he is induced to perform his part, as foreseeing the consequences of his refusal ... After these signs [i.e., promises] are instituted, whoever uses them is immediately bound by his interest to execute his engagements, and must never expect to be trusted any more, if he refuse to perform what he promised. [Hume (1888, Book III, Part II, Section V, pp. 521–522)]

Altruism is therefore not a necessary condition for making mutual insurance work in the form of reciprocal transfers. This does not mean, however, that selfish behavior is as good as altruistic behavior in the case considered here. Altruism can, indeed, increase the gains from income pooling, for example, because it helps mitigate the commitment problem that constrains informal insurance arrangements. The same conclusion also holds when social norms prevail and, in this case, the effect is even less ambiguous than when agents have altruistic preferences.

In Section 5.2, in which the theory of informal insurance arrangements is briefly surveyed, I therefore proceed in four successive steps. In the first two steps, I look at the main results obtained by modeling reciprocal transfers as exclusively guided by selfish motives, first in the context of stationary strategies, thereafter in the context of more

---

[16] An important exception is the recent attempt by Karla Hoff (1996) in which the author assumes away the enforcement problem to focus her attention on the information issue. In her model, only certain income flows, not exogenous luck or individual inputs, are observable. Like in all other models, participation in risk-pooling schemes is voluntary, yet she innovates by assuming that the extent of income-pooling is determined by a majority voting rule among the participants.

complex, non-stationary strategies. In the third step, the assumption of selfishness is abandoned and the influence of altruism is considered when agents are not confined to stationary strategies. Finally, in the fourth step, the effect of social norms on the effectiveness of reciprocal transfers is brought to light. Section 5.3 is entirely devoted to an examination of available empirical evidence. First, I look at the empirical findings about the extent of risk-sharing. Thereafter, I deal more specifically with the incidence of altruism in informal insurance arrangements. Finally, I draw attention to the logic of broad balanced reciprocity that seems to prevail in village societies.

5.2. A short survey of the economic theory of informal insurance mechanisms

5.2.1. Informal insurance models with stationary strategies

The natural point of departure is a family of models in which players' strategies are restricted to stationary strategies that do not permit past history to bear upon current decisions except when defections and punishments are concerned. Consider the oft-cited model of Coate and Ravaillon (1993). It is directly inspired by that of Kimball and is grounded on the assumption that each household makes a state-contingent decision on the amount of transfer. Such decision is made at any date they receive incomes. After the true state of income is revealed, households with relatively high incomes pay to those with relatively low incomes the promised amount of transfer. When a participant to the network free rides on his obligation, he is detected and expelled from the group (no graduate punishments are allowed for).[17]

Since individuals cannot rely on the advantage of explicit, complete and legally enforceable contracts that stipulate transfer payments contingent on certain events occurring, an incentive compatibility or participation constraint is introduced to ensure the self-enforceability of the risk-pooling mechanism. This condition stipulates that the difference between each individual's expected utility under continued participation and the status quo is always greater than the gain from current defection.

Formally, the participation constraint of individual i can be written thus:

$$U_i(y^i_{s'}) - U_i(y^i_{s'} - q^i_{s'}) \leqslant \frac{\partial}{1-\partial} E[U_i(y^i_s - q^i_s) - U_i(y^i_s)], \tag{1}$$

where ∂ is the discount factor with $\partial \in (0, 1)$; y^i_s the income accruing to individual i ($i \in N$) in state of nature s ($s \in S$); q^i_s the amount of the conditional transfer from or to individual i in state of nature s (it is positive when i gives the transfer and negative when he receives it); $U_i(\ )$ is the utility function of individual i which depends on the amount consumed in each period (bear in mind that the good produced cannot be stored and there is no savings in the economy considered); and E is the expectation operator. Note

---

[17] Moreover, it is assumed that a deviant is forced into autarky, i.e., is unable to form another alliance for risk-sharing purposes after a defection. In addition, since no saving is possible in the model, a defecting individual is prevented from self-insuring [Besley (1995, p. 2166)].

that $EU_i(y_s^i)$ is i's autarky payoff, that the conditions $0 \leqslant q_s^i \leqslant y_s^i$ and $\sum_{i \in N} q_s^i = 0$ apply, and that $U_i' > 0$, $U_i'' \leqslant 0$ for all i's while $U_i' > 0$, $U_i''' < 0$ for some i's (at least some people are risk-averse). Obviously, in states of nature for which q_s^i is negative, the above participation constraint is never binding.

Equation (1) therefore means that, for any realization of the state of nature s', the short-run gain from deviation is smaller than the long-run gain from cooperation. If social norms, pressures or sanctions exist that have the effect of increasing the cost of non-cooperation (direct penalties against breach are then combined with the threat of future exclusion from insurance possibilities to sustain risk-pooling arrangements), a new variable representing the corresponding utility loss, say $L_s^i \leqslant 0$, can easily be added to the left-hand side of the equation [Fafchamps (1994), Thomas and Worrall (1994)]. Yet, L_s^i should not be too large lest there should not be any enforceability problem (see supra).

People can thus cooperate informally and their mutual insurance arrangements can be self-enforcing if the framework of their interactions allows reputation effects to come into play: free riding on assistance obligations will be punished at later stages and, given these punishments, people find it in their long-run interests to meet their informal obligations so as to remain entitled to assistance in case they in turn fall into distress.

Since individuals are unable to make binding commitments, they cannot credibly commit to full sharing of risks and only second-best solutions are possible – the incentive compatibility constraint is binding and therefore impose limits on the degree of risk-sharing and Pareto efficiency that can be achieved – even in the absence of any problem of asymmetric information [Coate and Ravaillon (1993, pp. 20–21), Fafchamps (1994)].[18] By investigating the properties of the second-best solution, Coate and Ravaillon are able to identify a number of factors that determine the extent to which informal risk-sharing arrangements diverge from first-best risk-sharing (corresponding to full income pooling), which can be construed as a measure of their effectiveness. Like Kimball (1988), they find that the amount of transfer when state-contingent contracting is not legally enforceable gets nearer to the first-best amount when the discount rate is lower, the degree of relative risk aversion is higher, and income differences between participants are smaller [for several qualificatory comments on these propositions, see Fafchamps (1994)].[19]

Low discount rates (corresponding to high ∂'s) that are favorable to cooperation may mean different things: that individuals are not impatient (they do not have a strong

---

[18] Bear in mind that complete insurance occurs when the set of state-contingent transfers which maximizes average expected utility has the property that each individual's final wealth depends only on the aggregate wealth of the insurance group in the realized state [Coate and Ravaillon (1993, pp. 7–8), Eeckhoudt and Gollier (1995, p. 227)]. As is well known, the first-best sharing contract is characterized by the equality of marginal utilities at all points in time and in all states of the world. In the particular case of isoelastic utility functions, such a contract specifies that all incomes should be simply pooled in every period and then divided according to some fixed distribution rule [Foster and Rosenzweig (2001, p. 392)].

[19] Note that Kimball as well as Coate and Ravaillon get rid of the multiplicity of equilibria characteristic of repeated games of infinite or indeterminate duration by positing that a social planner picks the allocation that maximizes the unweighted sum of individual utilities subject to participation constraints [Fafchamps (1994, p. 6)].

preference for current payoffs), that they think there is a high probability that interactions among them will continue (that the game will continue to be played), or that the frequency of random shocks (e.g., the frequency of income draws) is high [Coate and Ravaillon (1993, p. 14)]. If the expected length of time between realizations of the natural hazard is rather long, the participation constraint is likely to be violated or, if risk-pooling is established, its extent will strongly diverge from the first-best situation of full sharing.

As pointed out by Tim Besley, the result according to which consumption smoothing through risk-pooling is very effective for incomes that are very close is counter-intuitive: it is when individuals in the network face large differences in their incomes that they should help each other [Besley (1995, p. 2167)]. The agents' inability to commit is responsible for this result since agents will be reluctant to pay high transfer amounts when income differences are large. Besley has actually proposed an extension of the Coate–Ravaillon model that, by assuming imperfect information, also changes the counter-intuitive result of the original model. In his own words: "If individuals' incomes depend upon effort and luck, but effort is hard to observe, then under certain conditions, it will be reasonable to infer that very bad draws are due to bad luck and good ones due to good luck. The incentive consequences of helping individuals in the tails of the income distribution will thus not be as severe as helping out around the mean" (ibidem: p. 2168).[20]

5.2.2. Informal insurance models with non-stationary strategies

Another, more recent family of informal insurance models allows for history dependent decisions. So far, it must be noted, the players' strategy space has been restricted to strategies that are affected by the past history of play only inasmuch as defection and punishments are concerned (the so-called stationary strategies). As a consequence, conditional transfers between agents along any equilibrium path depend only upon the current state of nature [Fafchamps (1994, p. 7)]. In the alternative modeling to be contemplated now, players can adopt non-stationary strategies that are much more complex than the simple strategies allowed in, for example, the Coate–Ravaillon model: bear in mind that in the latter two-agent framework where each of the participants may have either a high (h) or a low (l) income, stipulation of transfer payments simply amounts

---

[20] By dropping the interpretation of voluntary participation as a state-contingent decision constrained by an incentive problem, Myriam Wijaya (1996) has also succeeded in showing that large differences in incomes are what motivates villagers to mutually insure. Her basic idea is that voluntary reciprocity is the result of a non-state-contingent decision taken in a state-contingent stationary environment. More precisely, in her model, agents decide whether to participate or not in the insurance network and how much to transfer *after the contingency is revealed*. Even though they thus hold common information about their income states by the time they decide to pay a transfer, they ignore how long they can stay in that income state. The necessary condition for the existence of voluntary reciprocity shows that agents are all the more likely to make reciprocal transfer payments if their discount rate is lower, their degree of relative risk aversion is higher, and the differences between their respective incomes are larger.

to choosing a single transfer to be made in states hl and lh from the agent with a good realization to that with a bad one.

When the transfers are history dependent, the participation constraints that must be satisfied along any equilibrium path *after* s is revealed cannot be written in such a simple form as before. For individual i, this constraint is[21]

$$U_i(y^i_{s'}) - U_i(y^i_{s'} - q^i_{s'}) \leqslant \partial \sum_{t=0}^{\infty} \partial^t EU_i(y^i_{s,t} - q^i_{s,t}) - \frac{\partial}{1-\partial} EU_i(y^i_s), \qquad (2)$$

where the subscript t is introduced to allow for history dependence effects. (Note in particular that the transfer $q^i_{s,t}$ does not depend only on s but also on the time period t.)

Jonathan Thomas and Tim Worrall (1994) have thus developed a general model which admits aggregate and idiosyncratic risks as well as serial correlation of incomes (yields are assumed to follow a finite-state Markov process), and where players are allowed to follow non-stationary strategies. Agents make their decisions after the state of nature is revealed to them. Through a recursive procedure, the authors have derived a complete characterization for constrained-efficient contracts in the bilateral exchange case, assuming complete information but limited commitment.[22] Such characterization takes on the form of a simple updating rule that can be construed as a debt contract with occasional debt forgiveness.

In the words of the authors, "the household that receives a bad shock receives income from the other household, but thereafter 'repays' this 'loan' at a constant rate until another bad shock is received by one of the households. At this point the resemblance to a standard debt contract ceases. The household suffering the latest bad shock receives a 'loan' of the same size as before, and starts repaying the following period. The previous history is *forgotten*, so it doesn't matter who had previously 'borrowed' from whom; all that matters is who was the last to receive a loan. If both households simultaneously receive bad shocks then the repayments continue, except they are reduced for that period, proportionately to the fall in aggregate income" [Thomas and Worrall (1994, pp. 16–17)].

The simplest framework that can be used to see the working of this constrained-efficient updating rule is one in which there are three possible states of nature, i.e. (l, h), (h, l), and a symmetric state, say (l, l), or (h, h), or (m, m) with m standing for middle income. If the first state is realized, agent 1 who obtained the low income receives a transfer from agent 2 who earned a high income. Assume now that the state (m, m) occurs twice in succession during the second and third rounds. The updating rule characterizing the constrained-efficient arrangement requires that agent 1 pays to agent 2 a given fraction of the amount he was given in the first round. If, afterwards, the

---

[21] This formulation is adapted from Fafchamps (1994, p. 6).
[22] As we know, the arrangement cannot be Pareto optimal since, given imperfect commitment, agents may renege on their promises to give a transfer if the benefits from doing so outweigh the costs, hence the operation of participation constraints.

state (l, h) is again realized, agent 1 will be entitled to the same transfer amount that he received in the first round of the sequence and his past debt to agent 2, assuming it has not been completely repaid during the two intermediate rounds, will be forgiven. If, contrariwise, it is the state (h, l) that is realized in the fourth round, the rule requires that agent 1 starts 'lending' to agent 2 while his own outstanding debt vis-a-vis the latter will be forgiven.

It is easy to understand why the above-described rule is optimal given imperfect commitment. As a matter of fact, the promise of future repayments induces the lucky agent to lend more to the unlucky agent than would be the case if no such repayments could be anticipated, as under the stationary arrangement characterized by Coate and Ravaillon. This said, "the drawback to such repayments is that while they achieve significant insurance at a particular date, it is at the cost of variable consumption over time, as the level of consumption will be higher when a household is in a 'creditor' position than in a 'debtor' position in the symmetric states" [Thomas and Worrall (1994, p. 17)].

What about more conventional debt contracts (or sequence of debt contracts) with fixed, state independent repayments? The problem with them is that they 'remember' all previous loans: "if a household which already has built up debt is supposed to lend to the other household when the latter has a bad shock, then it will not anticipate future repayments if its overall debt is still positive, and so the default option may be preferable to sacrificing current income". The result obtained by Thomas and Worrall says that "a contract which forgets the previous debt altogether allows a larger transfer to be made for insurance purposes", which follows from the fact that, if the debtor is forgiven any repayment in the state where it is due to lend again, then only the beneficial effect of anticipated repayments remains Thomas and Worrall (1994, pp. 17–18)]. In addition, the above feature of the standard debt contract is responsible for it being unable to improve upon the stationary contract proposed by Coate and Ravaillon (a single transfer of given amount is to be made from the lucky to the unlucky agent in states (l, h) and (h, l)).

In short, it is because Thomas and Worrall allow the distribution rule to be shifted in favor of the better-off household that the latter's incentive to renege on his promise by withholding his transfer when he does particularly well can be removed. By allowing both current and future distribution of incomes to be affected by the participation constraints when they bind, the loss relative to the first-best risk-sharing contract is kept to a minimum.[23]

It may finally be noted that the debt contract with occasional forgiveness defined by Thomas and Worrall is clearly not incentive compatible when information is imperfect (income shocks are not observable). Claiming to have a bad shock is then an attractive strategy not only because a positive transfer can be currently received, but also because previous debts are forgotten, and consequently an opportunistic agent would make this claim each period Thomas and Worrall (1994, p. 17)].

---

[23] Note that assuming that the first-best, full risk-sharing contract is implementable comes down to assuming that the participation constraints never bind.

5.2.3. Altruism with non-stationary strategies

In a recent paper, Andrew Foster and Mark Rosenzweig (2001) have examined whether risk pooling is more advantageous among altruistic compared to selfish agents in a framework where individuals cannot make binding commitments. In theory, the answer is rather straightforward: to the extent that agents entering into a risk-sharing arrangement care about each other's welfare, they should gain more from insurance than they would otherwise and the scope of risk-sharing contracts should be greater. Even the one-shot game can actually support some transfers if agents are altruists. Intuitively, the better-off household will make a positive transfer to the worse-off household in the static Nash equilibrium when he cares sufficiently about that household that he is better off doing so than he would be by accepting the autarchic allocation. In a repeated framework, too, altruistic agents are more likely to engage in a risk-pooling arrangement since their altruism has the effect of ameliorating the commitment constraint arising from the impossibility to legally enforce the contract.

Adapting Thomas and Worrall's two-agent model to the case where each agent cares about the other,[24] and then using simulations to assess the impact of combinations of different degrees of altruism, imperfect commitment, and income covariances, Foster and Rosenzweig have reached interesting conclusions. As expected, they show that history matters in the sense that past transfers affect current transfers net of contemporaneous shocks: a household that has recently received transfers is less likely to receive subsequent transfers than is a household that has recently provided transfers. Moreover, the degree of history dependence is affected both by the degree of altruism and income correlation. As a matter of fact, history dependence is less for higher levels of altruism and when those levels are so high as to correspond to those in which full risk-sharing is achieved, there is simply no history dependence. On the other hand, the degree of history dependence is positively related to the degree of income correlation at high levels of altruism, but negatively related to the degree of income correlation for low levels of altruism.

A second finding concerns the extent of risk-sharing which appears to be facilitated both by low levels of income correlation and high degrees of altruism between transfer partners. Finally, for each level of correlation, the surplus generated by the optimal implementable risk-sharing contract – that is, the expected discounted utility gain of such a contract relative to that obtained under the fall-back position represented by a sequence of static Nash equilibria corresponding to autarchy or limited transfers – rises sharply with altruism and then levels off. Beyond a certain threshold, the surplus also declines, reflecting the fact that autarchy is no more a credible threat when the partners are sufficiently altruistic [Foster and Rosenzweig (2001, pp. 390–394)].

---

[24] This adaptation not only requires the specification of altruistic utility functions, but also a change in the specification of the consequences for the two parties of violating the contract. Indeed, at sufficiently high levels of altruism, partners may be less able to penalize deviant behavior, so that the credibility of the threat of autarchy is being reduced.

On the assumption that altruism is more likely among family than non-family members, Foster and Rosenzweig predict that the family will play a primary role in the provision of insurance (since a higher surplus is thereby generated for a given income correlation). However, the family cannot be expected to provide all the insurance because the number of potential family partners is small and income correlation among them is likely to be comparatively large. Households will therefore also establish insurance relationships with non-family partners, "selecting from the set of potential non-family partners those with which they have relatively low income correlations" (ibidem: p. 394).

To sum up, altruism facilitates risk-sharing on a double ground. For a given degree of income correlation, reciprocal transfers exhibit not only a weaker negative dependence on past transfers but also a more positive relationship with own income shocks when transfer partners are altruistic than when they are selfish. On the other hand, however, too much altruism may be problematic in so far as the threat to relegate the insurance partner to an autarchic position loses a great deal of its credibility when an agent cares a lot about his partner. As has been argued elsewhere [Platteau (2000, pp. 261–263)], indeed, sanctioning may be especially difficult in the context of kin-based relationships in which altruism is usually thought to prevail. Because of face-saving considerations, in particular, such relationships can give rise to strains and tensions that are not easily handled, making free riding rather hard to discipline. Yet, this characteristic has to be balanced out against the fact that information tends to better circulate among kin than among non-kin, with the result that punishing deviance is more effective: in the insurance context, the threat of relegation to the limited risk-sharing state is more credible, as the family member whose transfer arrangement is discontinued will find it more difficult to be accepted by another altruistic partner [Foster and Rosenzweig (2001, p. 391, Footnote 5)].

5.2.4. Social norms

More in tune with the argument developed in Section 2, villagers may follow social norms that prescribe obeisance to rules governing contracts in general, and insurance arrangements in particular. Violation of such norms would be followed by serious punishment, often in the form of a credible threat of ostracizing the opportunistic household from participating in various spheres of the social, political, and economic life of the village. For example, as observed in Tokugawa, Japan, village families can refuse to cooperate with a shirker by excluding him from labor exchange networks and from participation in social events such as ritualistic village parties and seasonal festivals [Aoki (2001, p. 46)]. The important feature of this sanctioning mechanism is that the punishment is meted out by the whole village community and not only by the partner who has been taken advantage of. As a result, the threat of punishment is much more effective in inducing villagers to comply with rules of fair dealing in bilateral transactions such as risk-sharing arrangements.

Because of the presence of powerful social norms that have the effect of increasing the cost of shirking (as pointed out earlier, direct penalties against breach are then combined with the threat of future exclusion from insurance possibilities), the commitment problem that potentially plagues reciprocal transfers is significantly reduced. The direct consequence of this fact is that the extent to which such transfers diverge from first-best risk-sharing is concomitantly and unambiguously lessened. In the case of altruism, as we have seen above, the conclusion is not so clear-cut inasmuch as the threat to relegate the failing partner to the autarchic position is less credible owing to altruistic feelings.

It must be finally recalled that repeated games are characterized by a 'profusion' (to use Kreps' word) of possible (Nash) equilibria, and non cooperative equilibria are as likely as cooperative ones [Kreps (1990, p. 512)]. Informal risk-sharing, even if incomplete, is therefore only one among many possible self-sustaining equilibria, and the question as to which one will eventually get established depends on the agents' expectations which are themselves influenced by the prevailing social (or community) norms. The cooperative equilibrium necessarily rests on beliefs selected at the community level, and these beliefs have to be shared in a self-sustaining manner among village families regarding what would happen to them if they ever shirk (see supra, Section 2).

In other words, it is wrong to think that because mutual insurance may be sustained as an equilibrium of a repeated game even with selfish agents, it can be the product of purely decentralized decisions occurring outside the purview of a community and its history. As a matter of fact, one thing that melds people together into a community is precisely the fact that they share common beliefs that are reflected in converging expectations. And it is an important function of social norms to make people converge on the right kind of expectations and strategies, or to punish deviations. The relationship between beliefs and expectations actually establishes a link between the ideology of a society and its social institutions (Knight (1992, pp. 77–82)].

5.3. Empirical evidence

5.3.1. The extent of risk-sharing

A simple test exists to check whether the economic theory of informal risk-sharing is borne out by the facts. This test boils down to whether or not coefficients on income and income growth are statistically significant in explaining patterns of household-level consumption once regional consumption aggregates are controlled for. If the hypothesis is strictly valid, we should find that the marginal propensity to consume out of idiosyncratic income changes should be zero whereas, if there is no insurance at all, the coefficient should be equal to one [Morduch (1999)]. Using data from rural South India, Townsend (1994) found that the evidence does not support the full risk-pooling hypothesis (any unpredicted event is fully covered by a state-contingent transfer from other members in the group) yet comes remarkably close: the marginal propensity to consume is nowhere greater than 0.14. On the contrary, using the same data set as Morduch

(1991), Ravaillon and Chaudhuri (1992), and Ligon, Thomas and Worrall (1997) concluded otherwise: informal mutual insurance exists but is only partial.

The latter finding has actually been confirmed by all subsequent empirical studies, such as those carried out by Udry (1990, 1993, 1994) for northern Nigeria, Townsend himself (1995a, 1995b) for Thailand, Deaton (1997) and Grimard (1997) for the Côte d'Ivoire, Jalan and Ravallion (1999) for China, or Dercon and Krishnan (2000) for Ethiopia, Fafchamps and Lund (2000) for the Philippines.[25] Kurosaki and Fafchamps (2002) reach the same conclusion for Pakistan on the basis of a more roundabout test. As a matter of fact, they infer the absence of complete insurance against village-level shocks through informal risk sharing from the fact that production choices made by farmers can be shown to depend on risk.

Other evidence is available to show that informal insurance mechanisms have only a restricted scope in village societies. To begin with, state-contingent transfers may represent only a low proportion of the income shocks in bad periods. For example, Gertler and Gruber (2002) found that in Indonesia households can protect their consumption levels against only less than half of low-frequency shocks (such as health shocks) that seriously impair performance over the long term. More precisely: "Households are able to fully insure the economic costs of illnesses that do not affect physical functioning, insure 71 percent of the costs resulting from illnesses that moderately limit an individual's ability to function physically, but only 38 percent of the costs from illnesses that severely limit physical functioning" (p. 67).

Despite the importance of large weather shocks, most of the variation in measured household incomes over time is idiosyncratic to particular households. Just to give an idea of the lost benefits of mutual insurance, Morduch (1991) has estimated that within-village state-contingent transfers could in principle reduce the variability of household post-transfer income to as little as 9–57% of variability under autarky,[26] yet actual transfers amount to only 10% of typical income shortfalls [as estimated by Rosenzweig (1988); for a similar conclusion, see Udry (1993)]. coping mechanisms therefore consist mainly of private actions such as borrowing and saving.

Platteau (1997) came to a similar conclusion when studying informal sea rescue mutual groups in communities of artisanal fishermen in Senegal: if fishermen do not hesitate to go to the help of a fellow fisherman in trouble out at sea, and to make a free gift of the time spent and the fuel expenses incurred in the search trips, they show a lot of reluctance for transferring resources aimed at indemnifying the accident's victim for the equipments lost or damaged. As a matter of fact, the indemnity paid represents only a small portion of the cost of the damages suffered.

---

[25] Even this evidence must be taken cautiously, though. This is because it can be attributed to other informal methods of consumption smoothing than to group-based insurance *per se*, such as lending and borrowing, or saving and dissaving [Ravaillon and Chaudhuri (1992)].

[26] In this study, Morduch shows that 75–96% of the variance of the logarithm of household income remains after removing variation due to changes in average village income over time and to average household income over the period (1976–1982).

Moreover, informal insurance networks may involve only a limited fraction of the village population and, in particular, they may be unreliable in protecting the poorest households. Thus, Jalan and Ravallion (1999) observed that in rural China the lower a household's wealth, the less well insured is its consumption to income risk. While the bottom 10% of households can protect themselves from just 60% of an adverse income shock, the top 10% can cope with as much as 90% of such shocks on average. The conclusion holds for both total consumption and food consumption, although the latter is better protected from idiosyncratic income risk. Using data on adult nutrition in Ethiopia, Dercon and Krishnan (2000) show that poorer households are not able to smooth their consumption over time and within the household. In addition, they do not engage in complete risk-sharing, and women in these households bear the brunt of adverse shocks. For rural Tanzania, likewise, De Weerdt (2002) concludes that poor households have less dense risk sharing networks compared to rich households.

On the other hand, Goldstein, De Janvry and Sadoulet (2001) reached the conclusion that inability to rely on mutual insurance to face cash shortages is "surprisingly pervasive" in rural Ghana: "mutual insurance works for some, but not for many". Social exclusion of many community members with specific individual, household, and community characteristics thus makes for very imperfect insurance at village level. This said, mutual insurance is equally accessible to the poor and non-poor. Nonetheless, "low wealth endowments are more likely to be associated with an initial cash shortage for both personal and household items". In addition, "the poor utilize different alternate mechanisms when they are rejected from mutual insurance support or do not seek this assistance, relying more on credit or accepting not to buy the [household] item and to defer consumption". In point of fact, individuals who are asset poor are more likely to be short of cash for household and personal items and are more likely to ask their spouse for assistance with the household item.

One evident reason why informal risk-sharing schemes tend to work unsatisfactorily for the poorest households is the following: relations within insurance networks are likely to be tense when all the members are down on their luck as a result of a collective shock. In such circumstances, indeed, holding onto whatever income is available is especially tempting and the promise to share with others may be easily broken. This holds true, in particular, for poor members who are close to their subsistence margin and therefore run a relatively high risk of being excluded from the network [Morduch (1999)]. Another reason is that state-contingent transfers may take place within the framework of rotating credit-and-savings associations (ROSCAS) which require regular contributions from members: in such a case, the sequence of assignment of the 'pot' (i.e., the pool periodically allotted to each participant in turn) takes account of the relative needs of group members. If the poor do not earn regular incomes, they will not have a sustainable access to such associations [see, e.g., Andre and Platteau (1998)].

Finally, it is important to notice that considerable variations in the prevalence and effectiveness of informal insurance arrangements may be observed across villages even within a limited area. For example, Townsend (1995b, p. 97) points out that, in his sample of Thai villages, "One village is replete with village institutions and is very 'organized'. A second village has problems with its institutions and appears less successful in credit and insurance arrangements. A third has virtually no institutions, but instead has a lively within-village credit market". The same observation has been made for Thailand: even though deaths and funerals certainly do elicit mutual concern and cooperation, it is puzzling to note that funeral societies are confined to no more than 20 or 30 percent of villages [Shigetomi (1998, Table 5.1) – cited from Bryant and Prohmmo (2002, p. 70)]. This failure is ascribed by Bryant and Prohmmo (2002) to pervasive worries about cheating in virtually all Thailand's village organizations. Explaining the above-reported variations across villages is a difficult challenge since they probably arise from the peculiar institutional history of different village communities.

Clearly, the evidence of risk-pooling in the village societies of the southern hemisphere is not very compelling, and some may even say that it is frankly disappointing. A measurement problem nevertheless exists in so far as most empirical studies have actually tested the theory of risk-pooling against data pertaining to entire villages, while mutual insurance may be practiced over networks of individuals other than the community as a whole: in other words, informal insurance relations are not randomly established between households in a village [Goldstein, De Janvry and Sadoulet (2001), La Ferrara (2003)]. Studies looking at more disaggregated evidence came to the conclusion that a good amount of transfers take place among people belonging to narrower networks.

For example, Grimard (1997) shows that in Côte d'Ivoire there appears to be some partial insurance performed by individual households with other members of the same ethnic group, particularly in the regions least likely to have access to formal financial arrangements. Yet, it bears emphasis that his data lead him to reject the hypothesis of complete risk-sharing even within ethnic groups [see also La Ferrara (1997)]. In rural Tanzania, Dercon and De Weerdt (2002) evaluated the efficiency of clusters of friends, neighbors and relatives, in providing insurance against health shocks, and they found that even within smaller networks of self-selected households, risk is not fully shared. Likewise, referring to the Philippines, Fafchamps and Lund (2000) show that risk-sharing takes place largely among small clusters of relatives and friends yet, again, there is no evidence of perfect insurance against shocks.[27]

As for Goldstein (2000), he concludes that in Ghana women tend to insure outside the household and the family, doing so instead with other women: for them, therefore, insurance networks in the villages run by gender rather than by kinship. The afore-mentioned study by Platteau (1997) of informal insurance in Senegalese coastal communities indicates that fishermen form rather small groups to help each other in sea rescue operations,

---

[27] Note that, as pointed out by Dercon and De Weerdt (2002), imperfect risk-sharing at the level of small networks may be due to the fact that households are members of several networks, in which case full insurance would imply that a household is able to insure its network partners against claims laid upon them from other networks. Since insurance of such claims (which amounts to a reinsurance arrangement) is likely to be limited, full insurance should not be expected to be attained in small clusters with lots of overlap.

and these groups are typically based on close kinship and friendship relations. But protection against the risk of damages is highly imperfect (see supra). Finally, in her study of rural Zimbabwe where villages have been purposely selected on the basis of different initial social dynamics, Dekker (2004) comes to the conclusion that each village differs from the other with respect to the specific social relationship that matters for informal risk-sharing (clan ties, membership in church groups, sport associations, etc.).

At this stage, it is worth referring to the study of Murgai et al. (2002), which made a pioneering effort to endogenize the size of the risk-pooling group and simultaneously explain the choice of insurance partners and the quality of insurance within the risk pool. In their model, the number of partners in an informal insurance arrangement as well as the degree of risk-pooling achieved are a function of different types of transaction costs which are themselves influenced by such things as the specific purpose of the insurance system, the community characteristics, etc. Such costs comprise *association costs*, that is, the costs of establishing associations (searching for potential partners, establishing relationships and coordinating activities) which depend on the number of members in an insurance cluster but not on the degree of risk-pooling within the group, and *extraction costs* to implement income transfers that vary with the level of transfer requested from the partner and are therefore a function of the quality of insurance. The authors succeed in demonstrating that, in particular, high association costs combined with low extraction costs will lead to small clusters with full insurance, while low association costs with high extraction costs will lead to community-level partial insurance. This hypothesis finds support in their empirical study of water transfers in Pakistan, which indicates that the size of the mutual insurance cluster decreases with association costs while the intensity of exchanges decreases with extraction costs.

5.3.2. Altruism in risk-sharing arrangements

Foster and Rosenzweig (2001) have attempted to determine empirically whether altruism facilitates risk-sharing in the manner suggested in the previous subsection. Since altruism is assumed to be more prevalent among family than non-family members, this comes down to assessing whether imperfect commitment effects are less important when partners have family links than when they are strangers. The testing strategy followed by these two authors works as follows. They estimate econometrically an equation that is an approximation to the transfer function derived from the above-cited work of Thomas and Worrall, that is, a function that allows for non-stationary strategies. It has the following form:

$$\tau_{it} = \alpha_0 + \alpha_1 T_{it} + \alpha_2 y_{it} + \alpha_3 y_{-it},$$

where τ_{it} denote the net transfers out by household i at time t, y_{it} is the income earned by household i at time t, y_{-it} is the income at time t earned by the household with which i is contracting to provide insurance, and T_{it} is a summary measure of the history of transfers at time t for household i. The latter variable, which can be interpreted as the "stock of transfer assets", is simply defined as the sum of past transfers, so that

$T_{it} = \sum_{t=0}^{t-1} \tau_{it}$. This transfer function is estimated separately for family and for non-family transfers. Moreover, to control for the problem that correlations between family and non-family transfer partners are unlikely to be the same on average, Foster and Rosenzweig focus on within-village transfers. As a matter of fact, income correlations across partners within the same village are likely to be more similar than are income correlations across partners who reside in different villages. Differences in information sharing is also minimized by this procedure.

Applying the model to Indian village data, they find that, in conformity with the imperfect-commitment framework, altruism between partners reduces the commitment problem. Indeed, the within-village family-based transfers are less history dependent, and substantially more responsive to income shocks than are the within-village non-family transfers. In formal terms, the absolute value of α_1 is smaller, and that of α_2 is larger, for family than for non-family transfers. Note that, as expected, α_1 is negative, reflecting imperfect commitment, and α_2 is positive, indicating that transfers play an insurance role. The same result obtains when the model is estimated on a sample of Pakistan village data. In the authors' words, the following conclusion can be drawn from their econometric work: "Despite the fact that, in theory, altruism may lessen the extent of risk-sharing, the empirical evidence also indicates that the commitment constraint is attenuated, but not eliminated, among altruistically linked households" [Foster and Rosenzweig (2001, p. 405)].

The above conclusion is not necessarily warranted, however. As a matter of fact, what the authors have shown, strictly speaking, is that intra-family relationships enhance the effectiveness of risk-sharing. Whether this is because altruism permeates such relationships or because of any other reason is not subject to test but is decided in the *a priori* mode. As the authors themselves recognize, another plausible explanation for the above finding is the informational advantage of family networks. Thus, if family partners can better monitor effort than non-family members, we would also expect insurance arrangements to be facilitated.

Another interesting finding of the same study is that, when transfers are compared across the two partner types (family and non-family) and the two locations (within the village and outside), it is found that non-family, within-village transfers are the most prevalent, and non-family, external village gross transfers the second-most prevalent and the highest in magnitude. On the one hand, this result suggests that problems of income correlation within villages are quite important. On the other hand, it runs counter to the expectation that the family should play a dominant role in providing informal insurance owing to its advantage in terms of higher-level motivations (altruism) and better information sharing.

Finally, it must be emphasized that the effect of altruism in informal insurance arrangements ought not to be measured only by considering the extent to which it relaxes the problem of imperfect commitment in actually observed transfers (through a look at levels and history dependence of those transfers). It ought also to be assessed in terms of the outreach of insurance transfers, which involves the question as to whether more people are hedged against subsistence risks, especially the poor, than would be the case if selfish behavior had prevailed. Facts in this regard are not very encouraging, as attested by evidence of widespread exclusion resulting from segmentation of village communities and marginalization of poor or very poor people. The formation of small clusters of people for insurance (and other) purposes, indeed, does not ensure that everybody is included in one cluster or another. As pointed out above, significant numbers of people with identifiable individual, household, and social characteristics are frequently excluded from insurance networks.

Using a series of economic experiments designed to gauge the norms of altruism and trust within rural communities that had been devastated by the hurricane Mitch in Honduras in 1998, Carter and Castillo (2004) came to the following conclusion. While there is evidence that "moral norms can enhance the effectiveness of mutual insurance, they do not resolve the thorny question of inclusion and exclusion within communities". As a matter of fact, trust and altruism appear to work best "for only a subset of communities or individuals within communities". If it is true, therefore, that "mutual insurance underwritten by altruistic norms offer the basis for substantial self-help even in the face of an environmental shock, social and market isolation, and ineffective risk coping, is a reality for many households" (p. 20).

It can also be the case that people who are initially included in a reciprocal transfer network see their insurance ability decrease over time as members with better access to new opportunities pull out of the risk pool. This happens when these better-off participants are being presented with good opportunities to accumulate savings (including the possibility of asset depletion and replenishment), which provides them with a good degree of self-insurance free of obligation to neighbors and kin. When incomes of participants grow at different rates, richer households are thus tempted to opt out rather than face the possibility of systematically redistributing to others, hardly a reflection of altruistic predispositions [Platteau and Abraham (1987, 2001, Chapter 5), Alderman and Paxson (1992), Hoff (1996), Morduch (1999), Fafchamps (1992, 1999)]. Increasing mobility and urbanization are an especially powerful dynamic force that may likewise hinder the functioning of informal insurance arrangements. This happens if, in moving away, households are able to 'default' on their obligations to relatives and neighbors, and this shortcoming outweighs the advantage of greater diversification of incomes that has the effect of enhancing the value of reciprocal relationships [Morduch (1999), Platteau (2000, Chapter 5)].

5.3.3. Broad balanced reciprocity as a guiding principle in village societies

Risk characteristics are an important determinant of the feasibility of group- or community-based informal insurance. In particular, low frequency events as well as repeated shocks (shocks strongly correlated over time) and covariate risks are difficult to insure against on a local level (see supra). The latter carries the unfortunate implication that informal village mechanisms may be particularly fragile when needed most [Morduch (1999)]. Regarding the former, just contrast Platteau and Abraham's study (1987) of a fishing village in South India (Kerala state), with Platteau's aforementioned survey of sea rescue associations in the coastal communities of Senegal (1997). Evidence of effective state-contingent reciprocal transfers appears to be stronger in the former case where what are insured against are fluctuations in daily fishing incomes that are barely correlated across individuals, than in the latter case where low-frequency sea accidents are the hazards to be covered.

An especially striking finding in Platteau (1997) concerns the motivation of group-leavers: when fishermen want to leave sea rescue mutual aid groups, indeed, they stress the unbalanced character of a situation in which some people have contributed while others have benefited from their contributions. Still more revealing is that, upon leaving their group, they typically ask for their past money contributions to be returned to them (they do not ask to be compensated for their labor contributions as it is not the practice to compute the money equivalent of labor time spent in assisting others), and, moreover, other participants see no problem in acquiescing in such demands which they consider entirely legitimate [Platteau (1997)].

Likewise, in Kibera slum, Nairobi (Kenya), when individuals decide to leave a mutual health group, it is because they consider that they have been too long on the giving side. And, upon departure, they are again being paid back all the contributions they have previously made to the group. Moreover, even when members are expelled for repeated misconduct (e.g., throwing unjustified suspicion on the executive committee's management, causing vicious rivalries among members, attending general assemblies in a drunken state), their entire contributions are returned to them as a matter of principle (personal field observations). Evidence of similar behavior has been reported in the case of mutual insurance groups in rural Albania (personal communication of Anne-Claude Creusot from CIRAD, Paris).

Even in the case of high-frequency events, such as daily income variations, transactions are not genuine transfers but interest-free loans with flexible repayment conditions (yet no system of debt forgiveness as predicted in Thomas and Worrall's model). The point can be made that there is a fine line between mutual aid or reciprocal transfer payments, on the one hand, and state-contingent loans that are free of interest, on the other hand. A difference still persists between these two types of transactions in so far as loans must be returned when the debtor's position has sufficiently improved to allow repayment, even though the creditor is not in distress. This runs counter to the principle of mutual aid where reciprocation takes place only when the donor is in need of help. As Platteau (1997) has argued at length on the basis of his interviews with Senegalese fishermen, the fact that people favor insurance schemes relying on credit transactions points to the importance of balanced reciprocity as a guiding behavioral norm in interindividual relations: reciprocal transfer payments are possible only if an implicit pattern of more or less balanced accounts is followed.

In India, for example, transfers have been found to be not only frequent but also relatively balanced for many households, which is consistent with a high degree of symmetry among transfer partners [Foster and Rosenzweig (2001, p. 399)]. It must nevertheless be stressed that the balancing of debits and credits often occurs over a wide range of accounts pertaining to diverse domains of individual and social life. As a matter of fact, small groups or communities are generally characterized by the multiplex pattern of their members' interrelationships, a feature that follows from their socially 'embedded' nature. The implication is that the sectors of social life in which individuals interact are numerous and can never be neatly separated in the minds of the members. Thus, speaking of social life in a rural county in present-day California, Ellickson (1991) has recently captured this essential characteristic of village communities in a vivid manner. We can not resist the temptation to quote him at some length:

> Shasta County norms entitle a farmer ... to keep track of those minor losses in a mental account, and eventually to act to remedy the imbalance. A fundamental feature of rural society makes this enforcement system feasible: rural residents deal with one another on a large number of fronts, and most residents expect those interactions to continue far into the future. (...) They interact on water supply, controlled burns, fence repairs, social events, staffing the volunteer fire department, and so on. (...) Thus, any trespass dispute with a neighbour is almost certain to be but one thread in the rich fabric of a continuing relationship. A person in a multiplex relationship can keep a rough mental account of the outstanding credits and debits in each aspect of that relationship. Should the aggregate account fall out of balance, tension may mount because the net creditor may begin to perceive the net debtor as an over-reacher. But as long as the aggregate account is in balance, neither party need be concerned that particular subaccounts are not. For example, if a rancher were to owe a farmer in the trespass subaccount, the farmer could be expected to remain content if that imbalance were to be offset by a debt he owed the rancher in, say, the water supply subaccount. [Ellickson (1991, pp. 55–56)]

The in-depth study of agricultural villages of northern Nigeria by Udry (1990, 1993, 1994) is suggestive in several respects. In conformity with the above observations, people are informally insured against a wide variety of production and consumption random shocks (such as flooding, wind damage, and infestation by insects or various household emergencies comprising medical problems, rain damage to houses, etc). Risk-pooling is possible in so far as 42 percent of the variation in farm yields across households results from idiosyncratic shocks [Udry (1993, pp. 100–101)]. In addition, given the repetitive nature of the above random shocks, everyone can expect to have his contributions reciprocated within a reasonably short span of time: at each moment, a participant household can expect to be hit by at least one of the misfortunes covered by the multi-purpose insurance scheme.

Like in the Indian fishing villages studied by Platteau and Abraham, credit transactions allow risks to be pooled over time, yet the loans that serve as state-contingent commodities carry positive interest rates. A telling feature of such loans, however, is that they are renegotiable after the realization of any random shocks and their adjustment can be in favor of either the borrower or the lender depending on whom is in difficulty. Moreover, the date of repayment of the loans is also flexible, meaning that loans are repaid later when the borrower has a bad shock or earlier when it is the lender who faces an adverse circumstance [Udry (1993, pp. 98–99)]. In other words, the amount that a borrowing household has to repay and the time when it will have to do it will be indexed or adjusted according to both its own income draw and that of the lending household. Note that the interest discount which a lender grants his borrower when the latter suffers an adverse production or consumption shock can be construed as a risk premium which he is willing to pay in order to be able to benefit from an interest bonus if he is himself struck by a misfortune in the future.

The fact that assistance takes on the form of repayable contributions assures the giving household that the relationship with the receiving household is likely to be roughly balanced. True, there is a crucial difference between state-contingent loans and conventional credit. Access to conventional loans allows a household to spread the consumption effects of an unexpected shock to income (and therefore to wealth) over time, yet does not enable it to avoid consuming its permanent income. In contrast, insurance-motivated loans provide a mechanism through which both borrowers and lenders can neutralize or at least mitigate the unexpected shock itself so that it has a reduced effect on wealth [Udry (1993, p. 100)]. Nonetheless, the insurance aspect of emergency loans tends to vanish from sight due to the prominent character of *quid pro quo* typical of a loan transaction. This is all the more so as the insurance element of state-contingent loan transactions turns out not to be important quantitatively.[28] In particular, differences in repayment periods, although statistically significant, are not large: the lender does not wait much longer to be repaid by an unlucky borrower and, conversely, the borrower does not have to pay back his loan much earlier if his lender had a bad shock. We are therefore a long way from the constrained-efficient non-stationary rule according to which debts should be completely forgiven in certain stages of the sequence of hazard occurrences.

In a more recent study devoted to the Philippines, Fafchamps and Gubert (2002) have only partially confirmed Udry's findings. More precisely, they show that the form contingent repayment takes is not a reduction in the amount repaid. Debt rescheduling actually turns out to be the dominant form of contingency: when they are hit by a shock, borrowers are given more time to pay and allowed to pay part of the loan in labor while the remainder is paid in cash at a later date (conversely, borrowers accelerate repayment

---

[28] Udry's evidence shows that on average a borrower who experienced a good shock repays 20.4% more than he borrowed but a borrower who had a bad shock repays 0.6% less than he borrowed. In addition, a lender with a good realization receives on average 5% less than he lent, but a lender with a bad realization receives 11.8% more than he lent. On the other hand, even though repayment periods are significantly longer for debtor households which have had bad fortunes or significantly shorter for creditor households which have encountered similar difficulties, the differences are not very large. Thus, the average repayment period when the borrower did not receive any adverse shock is 67 days while it is 72 days when the borrower did suffer a misfortune. Likewise, the average repayment period when the lender did not face any random shock is 89 days to be compared with 80 days in the opposite situation. Differences are actually smaller when only loans between relatives are considered: 69 as against 72 days and 84 as against 80 days, respectively [Udry (1993, Tables 5.3 and 5.5, pp. 100, 102); see also Udry (1990, 1994)]. Loans in the state-contingent informal credit market are typically of a scale and timing associated with short-term consumption and working capital needs [Udry (1993, p. 91)].

when the lender is hit by a shock). Yet, when the debt is eventually paid, the difference between the amount contracted and the amount repaid is in general small and does not depend on shocks. Debt forgiveness can however take on the form of a reduction in interest charges. Rather than force a borrower into bankruptcy or debt peonage by accumulating interest charges, Filipino lenders thus choose to reduce interest ex post.

As pointed out by the authors, such a practice is a priori incompatible with pure profit seeking motive. One plausible explanation is that contractual interest is not enforceable owing to the informal nature of the contract. The fact of the matter is that insisting on full interest charges is likely to be counterproductive whenever repayment is voluntary and based on an implicit long-term relationship. Such an hypothesis receives some partial support from the data at hand. Another possibility, as suggested in Section 2, is that lenders and borrowers follow redistributive norms of behavior and that the former are thereby prevented from abusing their power. Another finding is that lenders tend to refrain from granting new loans to borrowers who have failed to repay old loans, or taken a long time to repay them. We are clearly far away from the idealized picture describing a world where all insurance takes place through contingent repayment [e.g. Townsend (1994), Udry (1994)].

In this connection, it is interesting to notice that there is no agreement among anthropologists about the incidence of insurance-motivated gift exchange. Thus, in an aforementioned paper, Woodburn (1998) challenges the widespread view that sharing of meat in hunter–gatherer societies obeys a logic of mutual insurance [see, e.g., Wiessner (1982)]. According to him, the hunter has very limited control over who gets the meat and "the meat cannot, in general, be directed to past donors or potential future donors": "It has to be given to everybody in the camp, whether or not they are effective hunters with the capacity to give in future". Relatedly, "receiving meat does not bind the recipient to reciprocate. Many men are ineffective hunters because they are lazy or lack the necessary abilities or skills. They never, or almost never, reciprocate with meat or in other ways ... Donors tend to remain on balance donors over long periods". As a consequence, "donation establishes no significantly greater claims on future yields than would be the case without donation". In addition, generosity is not stressed and people actually believe that they are entitled to their share: "the whole emphasis is on donor obligation and recipient obligation ... typically the donor is not thanked" [Woodburn (1998, p. 49)].

The practice of meat sharing among the Hazda obeys distributive norms that prescribe strict sharing rules: the obligation to share "is a product of a system of values, indeed a political ideology, backed by sanctions positive and negative" [Woodburn (1998, p. 50)]. And even though Woodburn writes that "equality is what matters and the threat of inequality is of more concern than the threat of hunger" (ibidem), it is clear from his own description that the hierarchy of ranks must be respected when apportioning the meat. As a matter of fact, the initiated men are granted exclusive rights over the best parts of the meat, which they share on an equal basis amongst themselves (ibidem: p. 51). As explained in Section 2, the main function of such redistributive norms is to ensure that the social and political structure of the society is preserved and that private wealth accumulation by dynamic individuals is duly held under check.

Moreover, like the system of land tenure described in Section 3, these norms ensure that everybody in the community can make a daily living. Hence, the importance of rules guaranteeing access to food for old and sick persons, pregnant women, destitute children, etc. Woodburn thus tells us that the pregnant women have "the strongest claim of all to shares of meat and of other foods" among the Hazda [Woodburn (1998, p. 52)]. In Senegal, to take another example, a certain share of fish landings, known as the *ndawal* among the communities of Lebou fishermen, must be handed over to the old, the sick and the poor members of the extended family. More generally, in many Asian and African fishing communities, children belonging to families in distress are entitled to take a handful of fish from every catch brought ashore [Platteau (1991, p. 131)].

In other words, redistributive norms are part of a genuine social security system that operates at the community level. In so far as internalization of other-regarding preferences is insufficient to ensure effective enforcement, an authority structure is required to make people obey the prescribed rules of sharing. The immediate implication is that any force undermining the prestige and authority of this structure, whether it acts from within or from without, is bound to cause an erosion of the community-level social security system. The threat comes from within when traditional village leaders transform themselves into greedy patrons, eager to devote a growing part of their energies to the pursuit of private wealth accumulation [Baland and Platteau (1996, pp. 275–277)]. In the process, they powerfully contribute to shake off the old social order and to call customary redistributive norms and practices into question.

6. Conclusion: Institutional change and solidarity mechanisms in village societies

Norm-guided behavior is pervasive in traditional village societies, especially in lineage-based societies where the sentiment of collective identity is especially strong. Prevalent social norms are typically geared towards ensuring the subsistence needs of all members and maintaining social order in a context of highly personalized relationships. In particular, such norms serve to govern redistributive arrangements and land allocation rules within the community.

Communal systems of land rights, together with the accompanying set of norms and preferences, have evolved under conditions of relatively high land–man ratios (see, e.g., Boserup (1965), Johnson (1972, p. 271), Ault and Rutman (1979, pp. 171–178)].[29] When land becomes scarce and a shift from extensive to intensive land use patterns is observed, these systems are bound to undergo important transformations. Scarcity,

---

[29] Thus, "As long as a tribe of forest–fallow cultivators has abundant land at its disposal, a family would have no particular interest in returning to precisely that plot which it cultivated on an earlier occasion. Under these conditions a family which needed to shift to a new plot would find a suitable plot, or have it allocated by the chief of the tribe . . ." [Boserup (1965, p. 79)].

indeed, gives rise to growing externalities, both static and dynamic, so that institutional innovations are required to overcome them. A tendency to privatize the village commons, increasing individualization of the tenure rights held over private landholdings, and a concomitant decline of the role of communal authorities form different aspects of the ongoing evolution.

Regarding the village commons, the growing incidence of externalities that results from rising land scarcity has the effect of raising the cost of insurance provided through a guaranteed access to local natural resources. The cost may rise so much as to exceed the benefit and rightsholders may therefore wish to divide the commons amongst themselves. This is all the more likely to happen if self-insurance opportunities have become available to them, for example, under the form of non-agricultural incomes. Moreover, growing scarcity of cultivable lands may tempt powerful people or the rural elite to privately appropriate the more valuable commons at the expense of other members of the local community. With respect to non-divisible common-property resources, the following risk must be emphasized: by accumulating capital assets functioning as entry tickets, richer rightsholders are able to increase their relative share of the product flows at the expense of poorer participants, thereby perverting the old rotational arrangements.

On the count of land tenure individualization, several trends are observable. First, secondary or derived rights are called into question and exclusive ownership is claimed by members or groups of members who enjoy higher status and wield more power at village level. In fact, insurance benefits ensuing from the flexibility of a multiple tenure system are gradually outweighed by the growing efficiency costs entailed by that system, especially dynamic efficiency costs. Indeed, long-term land improvements tend to be discouraged at a time when they are increasingly needed to counteract the negative effects of land pressure on yields. Second, as the fallow period is being continuously shortened as a consequence of population pressure, there is a smaller pool of land available for (periodic) redistribution in favor of those currently in need of land. Third, increasing land scarcity unavoidably causes the emergence of an enlarged scope of transfer rights. As a result, marginalization processes through distress sales or foreclosure of mortgaged land are set into motion.

Not surprisingly, these structural changes in land relations are accompanied by parallel transformations of individual preferences and social norms. On the level of preferences, references to self-centered concerns are increasingly allowed to reach consciousness and to guide behavior even though unavoidable tensions are thereby created between the young and the old generations. On the level of norms, moreover, rules prescribing redistribution of wealth and assistance to unfortunate members of the village community tend to fall into disarray as individualization of land rights and farm management practices takes place.

The foregoing account offers only a partial view of the ongoing transformations, however. As a matter of fact, technological and ecological factors are not the sole factors contributing to shape the newly emerging institutions. Economic and social factors also come into play and, depending on the way they determine the governance costs associated with different institutional arrangements, a greater or a smaller measure of tenure individualization and privatization of natural resources will characterize the adjustment process.

Thus, a society which has acquired a strong collective identity and has evolved well-accepted social norms over time will generate comparatively low governance costs for collective organization. As a result, collective regulation of jointly held resources is more likely to succeed and persist in this type of society than in other societies exhibiting opposite characteristics. On the other hand, there is no doubt that the multiplication of economic opportunities that arise in the wake of growing market integration results, first, in greater occupational, educational, and income diversification and, second, in greater economic and geographic mobility of rural inhabitants. Consequently, heterogeneity among users of village resources increases and collective action becomes more difficult or costly to organize. On that basis, it can be predicted that physically remote communities are more likely to retain collective organizations inherited from the past than communities located closer to markets and important communication ways. This prediction is actually borne out by many empirical observations.

Concerning the emergence of more complete private property rights over individualized parcels of land, what must be stressed is that transfer rights may be more or less limited by customary rules aimed at protecting the interests of the weaker sections. Since such constraints on the unfettered operation of land sales markets are typically the outcome of strong social norms, their countervailing force also depends on various social and economic factors partly shaped by the history of the society concerned.

On the whole, the channels through which land pressure makes itself felt compound their effects to cause equity and insurance considerations to recede into the background. As for market integration, it can also be expected to threaten customary insurance arrangements, mainly because, by making new risk diversification opportunities available, it tends to enhance the self-insurance capacity of the elite. By stimulating increases in the value of land and other natural resources, it also accelerates the process of land tenure individualization and possibly intensifies the pressure on the commons so that the risk of their eventual degradation is augmented (if the internal terms of trade turn against the products harvested on private landholdings). Finally, the opening up of new market opportunities, by inducing the village elite to follow a path of individualist capital accumulation, may lead them to call traditional sharing norms into question and to favor asymmetrical patron–client relationships.

The central conclusion emerging from the above is that redistributive and insurance concerns are predominant in the land allocation rules applied in rural societies as long as the resulting efficiency costs are moderate or insignificant. Once efficiency costs associated with corporate ownership increase significantly following a shift from extensive to intensive patterns of land use, major transformations take place in land relations. Such transformations tend to ignore equity and insurance concerns unless strong community norms and institutions have been inherited from the past. As emphasized by Woodhouse, where there is competition for land and investment in increasing agricultural productivity, access to land for the poor tends to be reduced irrespective of the formal tenure regime in place. In other words, "customary tenure acts neither as an obstacle to investment and increased productivity nor as an inalienable safety net for the poor" [Woodhouse (2003, pp. 1714, 1717)].

It is also evident that, even if a community exercises a control on land sales so that the local poor are given priority rights of purchase, the problem is not completely solved. Indeed, inasmuch as it does not provide unlucky members with financial resources in order to help them avoid distress sales of land assets or repurchase lost parcels of land, the community cannot be considered as an effective provider of social security: preemption rights of repurchase to the benefit of the previous owner can be ineffective. The implication is that inter-household transfers have a major complementary role to play. This holds especially true of reciprocal, risk-sharing arrangements which have been amply documented in the recent literature and appear to be pervasive in certain village societies.

A careful look at the evidence available nevertheless shows that mutual insurance is noticeably imperfect, not only because only a (low) proportion of idiosyncratic income variations is effectively buffered, but also in the sense that informal insurance networks generally involve a limited fraction of the village population and may be unreliable in protecting the poorest households. Furthermore, reciprocal transfers tend to fall apart when insurance is most needed. On the other hand, the fact that balanced reciprocity is a pervasive behavioral norm in many agrarian societies (on average, accounts must balance out over a reasonable period of time) partly explains the unsuitability of state-contingent reciprocal transfers as a way of covering low frequency hazards (unless they are mixed up with many other risks so as to transform low frequency into high frequency occurrences), as well as the fact that such transfers often resemble credit transactions.

Redistributive norms that are enforced through a strong authority structure at community level and rest on largely internalized other-regarding preferences form part of a local social security system that probably play a more important role to protect the poor than voluntary state-contingent transfers. The problem with this mechanism is that it is highly vulnerable to any weakening of local authority structures and other-regarding norms and patterns of behavior. New economic opportunities and significant changes in values following the opening up of village societies to the external world tend to cause an erosion of these structures and preference patterns.

Voluntary reciprocal transfers may moreover be expected to dwindle under the pressure of market integration. This is so because market integration generally creates opportunities to accumulate savings and adopt other self-insurance strategies that are probably less costly than informal mutual insurance arrangements given pervasive incentive problems of the kind that plague standard insurance markets. In addition, when socio-economic differentiation processes are set into motion, richer households generally choose to opt out of insurance networks, thereby undermining the latter's ability to spread risks. Owing to the erosion of redistributive social norms, customary barriers that prevent community members from leaving a risk pool tend to be less effective.

The picture drawn above is probably too bleak. Paralleling the decline of old institutional arrangements, new forms of collective endeavors tend to emerge. Because they are defined on the basis of new membership criteria rather than along traditional lines, they are likely to be better adapted to modern challenges and opportunities. Abundant evidence actually exists to show that new types of informal initiatives, such as savings clubs, rotating savings and credit societies, professional associations, self-help and women's groups, water users' associations, religious organizations, etc., have sprung up that are quite varied and innovative. In addition, the new organizational forms are generally small and their membership is rather homogeneous because members are self-selected according to precise needs and objectives. As we know, these two traits are conducive to effective collective action. It is true that new groupings often turn out to be short-lived and transient. But this may be a desirable feature in so far as it imparts to them a good amount of required flexibility.

This being said, as pointed out above, traditional social norms emphasizing other-regarding behavior are less operative in the new context than in conventional village setups: members tend to follow the drive of own particular interests in a more unconstrained manner. Greater inequality is therefore likely to result from the institutional evolution under way. In the words of Sara Berry: "Internal mobility and permeable boundaries also leave room for considerable inequality within and among social networks. Such networks do not tend to redistribute resources equally among their members. Not only do individual members of networks gain or lose influence according to their individual successes or failures in mobilizing resources and followers, but culturally constructed categories of members may be systematically relegated to subordinate positions..." [Berry (1993, p. 163)].

Eventually, the main problem with many of the new forms born of the institutional dynamism of village societies is that social security and protection of the poor are no more a central concern. In actual fact, self-selection processes tend to regroup members according to their initial levels of income and well-being. Consequently, the poor and the weak are either excluded from all new informal associations, or they are left to fend for themselves by organizing without the cushioning support of better-off members. The conclusion is therefore hard to escape that, under the new circumstances, the protection of the poor will not be adequately provided until centralized systems of social security such as they exist in many advanced countries are put in place and run effectively.

References

Agarwal, B. (1991). "Social security and the family: Coping with seasonality and calamity in rural India". In: Ahmad, E., Drèze, J., Hills, J., Sen, A. (Eds.), Social Security in Developing Countries. Clarendon Press, Oxford, pp. 171–244.

Alderman, H., Paxson, C.H. (1992). "Do the poor insure? A synthesis of the literature on risk consumption in developing countries". Policy Research Working Papers, WPS 1008. The World Bank, Washington, DC.

Alexander, P. (1980). "Sea tenure in Southern Sri Lanka". In: Spoehr, A. (Ed.), Maritime Adaptations – Essays on Contemporary Fishing Communities. University of Pittsburgh Press, Pittsburgh, pp. 91–111.

Alexander, P. (1982). Sri Lankan Fishermen – Rural Capitalism and Peasant Society. Australian National University Press, Canberra.

Alkire, S., Deneulin, S. (2002). "Individual motivation, its nature, determinants, and consequences for within-group behaviour". In: Heyer, J., Stewart, F., Thorp, R. (Eds.), Group Behaviour and Development – Is the Market Destroying Cooperation?. Oxford University Press, Oxford, pp. 51–73.

Amarasinghe, O. (1989). "Technical change, transformation of risks and patronage relations in a fishing community of South Sri Lanka". Development and Change 20 (4), 701–733.

Andre, C., Platteau, J.P. (1998). "Land relations under unbearable stress: Rwanda caught in the Malthusian trap". Journal of Economic Behavior and Organization 34 (1), 1–47.

Aoki, A. (2001). Toward a Comparative Institutional Analysis. MIT Press, Cambridge, MA and London.

Atwood, D.A. (1990). "Land registration in Africa: The impact on agricultural production". World Development 18 (5), 659–671.

Ault, D.E., Rutman, G.L. (1979). "The development of individual rights to property in tribal Africa". Journal of Law and Economics 22 (1), 163–182.

Avineri, S. (1968). The Social and Political Thought of Karl Marx. Cambridge University Press, Cambridge.

Badini, A. (1994). Naître et grandir chez les Moosé traditionnels. Sépia-A.D.D.B., Paris and Ouagadougou.

Baland, J.M., Platteau, J.P. (1996). Halting Degradation of Natural Resources: Is There a Role for Rural Communities?. Clarendon Press, Oxford.

Baland, J.M., Platteau, J.P. (1998a). "Dividing the commons – a partial assessment of the new institutional economics of property rights". American Journal of Agricultural Economics 80, 644–650.

Baland, J.M., Platteau, J.P. (1998b). "Wealth inequality and efficiency on the commons – Part II: The regulated case". Oxford Economic Papers 50 (1), 1–22.

Baland, J.M., Platteau, J.P. (2003). "Institutions and the efficient management of environmental resources". In: Mähler, D., Vincent, J. (Eds.), Handbook of Environmental Economics. North-Holland, Amsterdam, pp. 127–190. (Chapter 4).

Baland, J.M., Platteau, J.P. (2006). "Collective action and the commons: The role of inequality". In: Baland, J.M., Bardhan, P.K., Bowles, S. (Eds.), Inequality, Cooperation and Environmental Sustainability. Princeton University Press for the Russell Sage Foundation, Princeton, NJ. (In press.)

Baland, J.M., Dubuisson, D., Platteau, J.P. (1998). "Dynamique des mécanismes informels d'assurance en milieu rural: Le cas du Burkina Faso". Research Report for the General Administration of Development Cooperation. Centre de Recherche en Economie du Développement (CRED), University of Namur, Belgium.

Baland, J.M., François, P. (1999). "Commons as insurance and the welfare impact of privatization". Mimeo. Centre de Recherche en Economie du Développement (CRED), Department of Economics, University of Namur, Belgium.

Baland, J.M., Gaspart, F., Place, F., Platteau, J.P. (2001). "The distributive impact of land markets in central Uganda". Mimeo. Centre de Recherche en Economie du Développement (CRED), Department of Economics, University of Namur, Belgium.

Bardhan, P.K., Dayton-Johnson, J. (2006). "Inequality and the governance of water resources in Mexico and South India". In: Baland, J.M., Bardhan, P.K., Bowles, S. (Eds.), Inequality, Cooperation and Environmental Sustainability. Princeton University Press for the Russell Sage Foundation, Princeton, NJ. (In press.)

Bardhan, P.K., Udry, C. (1999). Development Microeconomics. Oxford University Press, Oxford.

Bardhan, P.K., Baland, J.M., Das, S., Mookherjee, D., Sarkar, R. (2006). "Household firewood collection in rural Nepal: The role of poverty, population, collective action and modernization". In: Baland, J.M., Bardhan, P.K., Bowles, S. (Eds.), Inequality, Collective Action and Environmental Sustainability. Russell Sage Foundation and Princeton University Press. (In press.)

Barrows, R., Roth, M. (1989). "Land tenure and investment in African agriculture: Theory and evidence". LTC Paper No 136. Land Tenure Center, University of Wisconsin-Madison.

Bassett, T.J., Crummey, D.E. (Eds.) (1993). Land in African Agrarian Systems. The University of Wisconsin Press, Madison, WI.

Basu, K. (2000). Prelude to Political Economy – A Study of the Social and Political Foundations of Economics. Oxford University Press, Oxford.

Bates, R.H. (1984). "Some conventional orthodoxies in the study of agrarian change". World Politics 26 (2), 234–254.

Belshaw, C. (1965). Traditional Exchange and Modern Markets. Prentice-Hall, Englewood Cliffs, NJ.
Bene, C., Bennett, E., Neiland, A.E. (2002). "The challenge of managing small-scale fisheries with reference to poverty alleviation". In: Neiland, A.E., Béné, C. (Eds.), Small-Scale Fisheries, Poverty and the Code of Conduct for Responsible Fisheries. Center for the Economics and Management of Aquatic Resources (CEMARE), University of Portsmouth, UK.
Ben-Ner, A., Putterman, L. (1998). "Values and institutions in economic analysis". In: Ben-Ner, A., Putterman, L. (Eds.), Economics, Values, and Organization. Cambridge University Press, Cambridge, pp. 3–69.
Berry, S. (1984). "The food crisis and agrarian change in Africa: A review essay". African Studies Review 27 (2), 59–112.
Berry, S. (1993). No Condition is Permanent – The Social Dynamics of Agrarian Change in SubSaharan Africa. The University of Wisconsin Press, Madison.
Besley, T. (1995). "Savings, credit and insurance". In: Behrman, J., Srinivasan, T.N. (Eds.), In: Handbook of Development Economics, vol. 3A. Elsevier, Amsterdam, pp. 2123–2207.
Binswanger, H.P., Deininger, K., Feder, G. (1995). "Power, distortions, revolt and reform in agricultural land relations". In: Behrman, J., Srinivasan, T.N. (Eds.), In: Handbook of Development Economics, vol. III. North-Holland, Amsterdam, pp. 2659–2772.
Bohannan, P., Dalton, G. (Eds.) (1962). Markets in Africa. Northwestern University Press, Evanston.
Boserup, E. (1965). The Conditions of Agricultural Growth: The Economics of Agrarian Change under Population Pressure. Allen and Unwin, London.
Bourdieu, P. (1990). The Logic of Practice. Stanford University Press, Stanford, CA.
Breman, J. (1974). Patronage and Exploitation: Changing Agrarian Relations in South Gujarat. University of California Press, Berkeley.
Breusers, M. (2001). "Searching for livelihood security: Land and mobility in Burkina Faso". Journal of Development Studies 37 (4), 49–80.
Brightman, R.A. (1987). "Conservation and resource depletion – the case of the Boreal Forest Algonquians". In: McCay, B.J., Acheson, J.M. (Eds.), The Question of the Commons – The Culture and Ecology of Communal Resources. University of Arizona Press, Tucson, AZ, pp. 121–141.
Bromley, D., Chavas, J.P. (1989). "On risks, transactions and economic development in the Semiarid Tropics". Economic Development and Cultural Change, 719–736.
Bruce, J.W. (1986). "Land tenure issues in project design and strategies for agricultural development in Sub-Saharan Africa". LTC Paper No. 128. Land Tenure Center, University of Wisconsin-Madison.
Bruce, J.W. (1993). "Do indigenous tenure systems constrain agricultural development?". In: Bassett, T.J., Crummey, D.E. (Eds.), Land in African Agrarian Systems. University of Wisconsin Press, Madison, WI, pp. 35–56.
Bruce, J.W., Fortmann, L. (1989). "Agroforestry: Tenure and incentives". LTC Paper No. 135. Land Tenure Center, University of Wisconsin-Madison.
Bryant, J., Prohmmo, A. (2002). "Equal contributions and unequal risks in a North-East Thai village funeral society". Journal of Development Studies 38 (3), 63–75.
Camerer, C., Thaler, R.H. (1995). "Ultimatums, dictators, and manners". Journal of Economic Perspectives 9 (2), 209–219.
Carrier, J.G. (1987). "Marine tenure and conservation in Papua New Guinea". In: McCay, B.J., Acheson, J.M. (Eds.), The Question of the Commons – The Culture and Ecology of Communal Resources. University of Arizona Press, Tucson, AZ, pp. 142–167.
Carter, M.R., Castillo, M. (2004). "Morals, markets and mutual insurance: Using economic experiments to study recovery from hurricane Mitch". Mimeo. Department of Agricultural and Applied Economics, University of Wisconsin-Madison.
Cashdan, E. (1985). "Coping with risk: Reciprocity among the Basarwa of Northern Botswana". Man 20 (3), 454–474.
Cashdan, E. (1989). "Hunters and gatherers: Economic behavior in bands". In: Plattner, S. (Ed.), Economic Anthropology. Stanford University Press, Stanford, CA, pp. 21–48.
Chakravarty-Kaul, M. (1996). Common Lands and Customary Law – Institutional Change in North India over the Past Two Centuries. Oxford University Press, Delhi.

Coate, S., Ravaillon, M. (1993). "Reciprocity without commitment: Characterization and performance of informal insurance arrangements". Journal of Development Economics 40 (1), 1–24.
Cohen, J.M. (1980). "Land tenure and rural development in Africa". In: Bates, R.H., Lofchie, M.F. (Eds.), Agricultural Development in Africa – Issues of Public Policy. Praeger, New York, pp. 349–400.
Coldham, S. (1978). "The effect of registration of title upon customary land rights in Kenya". Journal of African Law 22 (2), 91–111.
Congleton, R. (1980). "Competitive process, competitive waste, and institutions". In: Buchanan, J., Tollison, R., Tullock, G. (Eds.), Toward a Theory of the Rent-Seeking Society. Texas A&M Press.
Dalton, G. (1962). "Traditional production in primitive African economies". Quarterly Journal of Economics 76 (3), 360–378.
Das Gupta, M. (1987). "Informal security mechanisms and population retention in rural India". Economic Development and Cultural Change 36 (1), 101–120.
Dasgupta, P. (1988). "Trust as a commodity". In: Gambetta, D. (Ed.), Trust-Making and Breaking Cooperative Relations. Basil Blackwell, Oxford, pp. 49–72.
Dasgupta, P. (1993). An Inquiry into Well-Being and Destitution. Clarendon Press, Oxford.
Dawes, R.M., Thaler, R.H. (1988). "Anomalies cooperation". Journal of Economic Perspectives 2 (3), 187–197.
Deaton, A. (1997). The Analysis of Household Surveys. World Bank/Johns Hopkins University Press, Baltimore.
Dekker, M. (2004). "Risk, resettlement and relations: Social security in rural Zimbabwe". PhD Thesis. Tinbergen Institute Research Series, Vrije Universiteit, Amsterdam.
Deleplace, G. (1979). Théories du capitalisme – Une introduction. Presses Universitaires de Grenoble et Maspero, Grenoble and Paris.
Dercon, S., Krishnan, P. (2000). "In sickness and in health: Risk-sharing within households in Ethiopia". Journal of Political Economy 108 (4), 688–727.
Dercon, S., De Weerdt, J. (2002). "Risk sharing networks and insurance against illness". CSAE WPS/2002-16. Centre for the Study of African Economies, Oxford University, Oxford.
De Weerdt, J. (2002). "Risk sharing and endogenous network formation". Mimeo. Center for the Study of African Economies (CSAE), Department of Economics, University of Oxford.
Downs, R.E., Reyna, S.P. (Eds.) (1988). Land and Society in Contemporary Africa. University Press of New England, Hanover and London.
Eeckhoudt, L., Gollier, C. (1995). Risk – Evaluation Management and Sharing. Harvester Wheatsheaf, New York.
Ellickson, R.C. (1991). Order without Law – How Neighbors Settle Disputes. Harvard University Press, Cambridge, MA and London.
Ensminger, J. (1990). "Co-opting the elders: The political economy of state incorporation in Africa". American Anthropologist 92, 662–675.
Epstein , S. (1967). "Productive efficiency and customary systems of reward in rural South India". In: Firth, R. (Ed.), Themes in Economic Anthropology. Tavistock Publications, London, pp. 229–252.
Evans-Pritchard, E.E. (1940). The Nuer: A Description of the Modes of Livelihood and Political Institutions of a Nilotic People. Clarendon Press, Oxford.
Fafchamps, M. (1992). "Solidarity networks in preindustrial societies: Rational peasants with a moral economy". Economic Development and Cultural Change 41 (1), 147–174.
Fafchamps, M. (1994). "The enforcement of mutual insurance contracts". Mimeo. Food Research Institute, Stanford University, Stanford, CA.
Fafchamps, M. (1999). "Rural poverty, risk and development". FAO Economic and Social Development Paper No 144. Rome.
Fafchamps, M., Lund, S. (2000). "Risk-sharing networks in rural Philippines". Mimeo. Department of Economics, University of Oxford.
Fafchamps, M., Gubert, F. (2002). "Contingent loan repayment in the Philippines". Mimeo.
Feder, G., Feeny, D. (1991). "Land tenure and property rights: Theory and implications for development policy". The World Bank Economic Review 5 (1), 135–153.

Firth, R. (1951). Elements of Social Organization. Watts, London.
Foster, A. (1988). "Why things fall apart: A strategic analysis in repeated interactions in rural financial Markets". Mimeo. Department of Economics, University of California at Berkeley, Berkeley, CA.
Foster, G. (1964). "Treasure tales, and the image of the static economy in a Mexican peasant community". Journal of American Folklore 77, 39–44.
Foster, G. (1965). "Peasant society and the image of limited good". American Anthropologist 67, 293–314.
Foster, G., Rosenzweig, M. (2001). "Imperfect commitment, altruism, and the family: Evidence from transfer behavior in low-income rural areas". The Rewiew of Economics and Statistics 83 (3), 389–407.
Frank, R. (1988). Passions within Reason: The Strategic Role of Emotions. Norton, New York.
Frank, R. (1995). The Winner-Take-All Society. Martin Kessler Books at the Free Press, New York.
Frank, R. (1998). "Social norms as positional arms control agreements". In: Ben-Ner, A., Putterman, L. (Eds.), Economics, Values, and Organization. Cambridge University Press, Cambridge, pp. 275–295.
Gavian, S., Fafchamps, M. (1996). "Land tenure and allocative efficiency in Niger". American Journal of Agricultural Economics 78, 460–471.
Gertler, P., Gruber, J. (2002). "Insuring consumption against illness". American Economic Review 92 (1), 51–70.
Geschiere, P. (1995). Sorcellerie et politique en Afrique – La viande des autres. Editions Karthala, Paris.
Godelier, M. (1974). "Anthropologie et économie. Une anthropologie économique est-elle possible?". In: Godelier, M. (Ed.), Un domaine contesté: l'anthropologie économique. Mouton, Paris, pp. 285–345.
Godelier, M. (1999). The Enigma of the Gift. Polity Press, Cambridge.
Goldstein, M. (2000). "Intra-household allocation and farming in Southern Ghana". Ph.D. Dissertation. University of California at Berkeley.
Goldstein, M., De Janvry, A., Sadoulet, E. (2001). "Is a friend in need a friend indeed? Inclusion and exclusion in mutual insurance networks in Southern Ghana". In: Dercon, S. (Ed.), Insurance Against Poverty. Clarendon Press, Oxford. (Forthcomming.)
Green, J.K. (1987). "Evaluating the impact of consolidation of holdings, individualization of tenure, and registration of title: Lessons from Kenya". LTC Paper No. 129. Land Tenure Center, University of Wisconsin-Madison.
Gregory, C.A. (1982). Gifts and Commodities. Academic Press, London and New York.
Grimard, F. (1997). "Household consumption smoothing through ethnic ties: Evidence from Cote d'Ivoire". Journal of Development Economics 53 (2), 391–422.
Haugerud, A. (1983). "The consequences of land tenure reform among smallholders in the Kenya Highlands". Rural Africana 1516, 65–89. (Winter–Spring.)
Hayami, Y. (1997). Development Economics – From the Poverty to the Wealth of Nations. Clarendon Press, Oxford.
Hayami, Y., Kikuchi, M. (1981). Asian Village Economy at the Crossroads. University of Tokyo Press, Tokyo. (And Baltimore, Johns Hopkins University Press.)
Hecht, S., Anderson, A.B., May, P. (1988). "The subsidy from nature: Shifting cultivation, successional palm forests and rural development". Human Organization 47.
Hirschman, A.O. (1958). The Strategy of Economic Development. Yale University Press, New Haven and London.
Hoff, K. (1996). "Informal insurance schemes: An equilibrium analysis". Mimeo. Department of Economics, University of Maryland.
Hume, D. (1888). A Treatise of Human Nature. Clarendon Press, Oxford. (Selby-Bigge, L.A. (Ed.); first publication 1740.)
Humphries, J. (1990). "Enclosures, common rights, and women: The proletarianization of families in the late eighteenth and early nineteenth centuries". Journal of Economic History 50 (1), 17–42.
Hunter, G. (1969). Modernizing Peasant Societies: A Comparative Study in Asia and Africa. Oxford University Press, New York and London.
Ilahiane, H. (2001). "The ethnopolitics of irrigation management in the Ziz oasis, Morocco". In: Agrawal, A., Gibson, C.C. (Eds.), Communities and the Environment. Rutgers University Press, New Brunswick, NJ, and London, pp. 89–110.

Jalan, J., Ravallion, M. (1999). "Are the poor less well-insured? Evidence on vulnerability to income risk in rural China". Journal of Development Economics 58 (1), 61–82.
Jodha, N.S. (1986). "Common property resources and rural poor in dry regions of India". Economic and Political Weekly 21 (27), 1169–1182.
Johnson, O.E.G. (1972). "Economic analysis, the legal framework and land tenure systems". Journal of Law and Economics 15 (1), 259–276.
Karahasan, D. (2000). L'âge de sable. Robert Laffont, Paris.
Kimball, M.S. (1988). "Farmers' cooperatives as behavior toward risk". American Economic Review 78 (1), 224–232.
Knight, J. (1992). Institutions and Social Conflict. Cambridge University Press, Cambridge.
Kocherlakota, N.R. (1994). "Efficient bilateral risk sharing without commitment". Mimeo. Department of Economics, University of Iowa.
Kreps, D.M. (1990). A Course in Microeconomic Theory. Harvester Wheatsheaf, New York.
Kurosaki, T., Fafchamps, M. (2002). "Insurance market efficiency and crop choices in Pakistan". Journal of Development Economics 67 (2), 419–453.
La Ferrara, E. (1997). "Ethnicity and reciprocity: An analysis of credit transactions in Ghana". Mimeo. Department of Economics, Harvard University.
La Ferrara, E. (2003). "Kin groups and reciprocity: A model of credit transactions in Ghana". American Economic Review 93 (5), 1730–1751.
Landauer, C. (1964). Contemporary Economic Systems – A Comparative Analysis. J.B. Lippincott Cy, Philadelphia and New York.
Laurent, P.J., Mathieu, P., Totte, M. (1994). "Migrations et accès à la terre au Burkina Faso". Cahiers du Cidep No 20. Louvain la-Neuve.
Libecap, G.D. (1989). Contracting for Property Rights. Cambridge University Press, Cambridge.
Ligon, E. (1993). "Risk sharing under varying information regimes: Theory and measurement in village economies". Mimeo. Department of Economics, University of Chicago.
Ligon, E., Thomas, J., Worrall, T. (1997). "Informal insurance arrangements in village economies". Mimeo. Department of Economics, Warwick University.
Lund, C. (1998). Land, Power and Politics in Niger – Land Struggles and the Rural Code. Lit Verlag, Hamburg.
Mackenzie, F. (1993). "A piece of land never shrinks: Reconceptualizing land tenure in a smallholding district, Kenya". In: Bassett, T.J., Crummey, D.E. (Eds.), Land in African Agrarian Systems. University of Wisconsin Press, Madison, WI, pp. 194–221.
Malinowski, B. (1922). Argonauts of the Western Pacific – An Account of Native Enterprise and Adventure in the Archipelagoes of Melanesian New Guinea. Routlege, London. (Reprinted 1999.)
Malinowski, B. (1937). "Anthropology as the basis of social sciences". In: Cohen, C., Travers, O. (Eds.), Human Affairs. Macmillan, London.
McCarthy, N., De Janvry, A., Sadoulet, E. (1998). "Land allocation under dual individual–collective use in Mexico". Journal of Development Economics 56 (2), 239–264.
McKean, M.A. (1986). "Management of traditional common lands (iriaichi) in Japan". In: National Research Council. Proceedings of the Conference on Common Property Resource Management. National Academy Press, Washington, DC, pp. 533–589.
Mezzine, L. (1987). Le Tafilalet: contribution à l'histoire du Maroc aux XVII et XVIIIème siècles. Publications de la Faculté des Lettres et des Sciences Humaines, Rabat, Morocco.
Migot-Adholla, S.E., Hazell, P., Blarel, B., Place, F. (1991). "Indigenous land rights systems in Sub-Saharan Africa: A constraint on policy?". World Bank Economic Review 5 (1), 155–175.
Morduch, J. (1991). "Income smoothing across space". Mimeo. Department of Economics, Harvard University.
Morduch, J. (1999). "Between the market and the state: Can informal insurance patch the safety net?". World Bank Research Observer 14 (2), 187–207.
Murgai, R., Winters, P., Sadoulet, E., De Janvry, A. (2002). "Localized and incomplete mutual insurance". Journal of Development Economics 67 (2), 245–274.

Ndiaye, M. (1998). Les Moodu Moodu ou l'éthos du développement au Sénégal. Presses Universitaires de Dakar, Dakar.
N'Gweno, B. (2001). "Reidentifying ground rules – community inheritance disputes among the Digo of Kenya". In: Agrawal, A., Gibson, C.C. (Eds.), Communities and the Environment. Rutgers University Press, New Brunswick, NJ and London, pp. 111–137.
Nicolas, G. (1968). "La société africaine et ses réactions à l'impact occidental". In: Merle, M. (Ed.), L'Afrique noire contemporaine. Armand Colin, Paris.
Noronha, R. (1985). "A review of the literature on land tenure systems in Sub-Saharan Africa". Report No ARU 43. Research Unit of the Agriculture and Rural Development Department, The World Bank, Washington.
Nunow, A.A. (2000). "Pastoralists and markets – livestock commercialization and food security in North-Eastern Kenya". Ph.D. Thesis. University of Amsterdam.
Olson, M. (1965). The Logic of Collective Action. Harvard University Press, Cambridge, MA.
Ortiz, S. (1967). "The structure of decision-making among Indians of Colombia". In: Firth, R. (Ed.), Themes in Economic Anthropology. Tavistock Publications, London.
Ostrom, E. (1990). Governing the Commons – The Evolution of Institutions for Collective Action. Cambridge University Press, Cambridge.
Ostrom, E., Gardner, R., Walker, J. (1994). Rules, Games, and Common-Pool Resources. The University of Michigan Press, Ann Arbor.
Phan Huy, Lê, et al. (1993). The Traditional Village in Vietnam. The Gioi Publishers, Hanoi.
Pinckney, T.C., Kimuyu, P.K. (1994). "Land tenure reform in East Africa: Good, bad, or unimportant?". Journal of African Economies 3 (1), 1–28.
Place, F., Ssenteza, J., Otsuka, K. (2001). "Customary and private land management in Uganda". In: Otsuka, K., Place, F. (Eds.), Land Tenure and Natural Resource Management: A Comparative Study of Agrarian Communities in Asia and Africa. The Johns Hopkins University Press, Baltimore and London, pp. 195–233.
Platteau, J.P. (1991). "Traditional systems of social security and hunger insurance: Past achievements and modern challenges". In: Ahmad, E., Drèze, J., Hills, J., Sen, A.K. (Eds.), Social Security in Developing Countries. Clarendon Press, Oxford, pp. 112–170.
Platteau, J.P. (1992). "Land reform and structural adjustment in SubSaharan Africa: Controversies and guidelines". FAO Economic and Social Development Paper No. 107. FAO, Rome (324 pp.)
Platteau, J.P. (1996). "The evolutionary theory of land rights as applied to SubSaharan Africa: A critical assessment". Development and Change 27 (1), 29–86.
Platteau, J.P. (1997). "Mutual insurance as an elusive concept in traditional rural communities". Journal of Development Studies 33 (6), 764–796.
Platteau, J.P. (2000). Institutions, Social Norms, and Economic Development. Harwood Academic Publishers.
Platteau, J.P., Abraham, A. (1987). "An inquiry into quasi-credit contracts: The role of reciprocal credit and interlinked deals in small-scale fishing communities". Journal of Development Studies 23 (4), 461–490.
Platteau, J.P., Abraham, A. (2001). "Two cultural approaches to the problem of women's land inheritance". Mimeo. Centre de Recherche en Economie du Développement (CRED), Department of Economics, University of Namur, Belgium.
Platteau, J.P., Seki, E. (2001). "Coordination and pooling arrangements in Japanese coastal fisheries". In: Aoki, M., Hayami, Y. (Eds.), Community and Market in Economic Development. Clarendon Press, Oxford, pp. 344–402.
Platteau, J.P., Murickan, J., Delbar, E. (1985). Technology, Credit and Indebtedness in Marine Fishing – A Case Study of Three Fishing Villages in South Kerala. Hindustan Publishing Co, Delhi.
Polanyi, K. (1977). The Livelihood of Man. Academic Press, New York and London.
Popkin, S.L. (1979). The Rational Peasant: The Political Economy of Rural Society in Vietnam. University of California Press, Berkeley and Los Angeles.
Posner, R. (1980). "A theory of primitive society, with special reference to law". Journal of Law and Economics 23, 1–53.

Posner, R. (1981). The Economics of Justice. Harvard University Press, Cambridge, MA and London.
Quiggin, J. (1993). "Common property, equality, and development". World Development 21 (7), 1123–1138.
Ravaillon, M., Chaudhuri, S. (1992). "Tests of risk-sharing in three Indian villages". Mimeo. The World Bank.
Ray, D. (1998). Development Economics. Princeton University Press, Princeton, NJ.
Rodenbach, E. (1999). "La transformation des droits fonciers dans la vallée du fleuve Sénégal: Etude de trois villages". Unpublished M.A. Thesis. Department of Economics, University of Namur, Belgium.
Rosenzweig, M. (1988). "Risk, implicit contracts, and the family in rural areas of low-income countries". Economic Journal 98, 1148–1170.
Sahlins, M. (1963). "On the sociology of primitive exchange". In: Banton, M. (Ed.), The Relevance of Models for Social Anthropology. Tavistock Publications, London, pp. 139–227.
Sahlins, M. (1968). Tribesmen. Prentice-Hall, Englewood Cliffs, NJ.
Sahlins, M. (1972). Stone Age Economics. Aldine De Gruyter, New York.
Schapera, I. (1943). Native Land Tenure in the Bechuanaland Protectorate. The Lovedale Press, Lovedale.
Scott, J.C. (1976). The Moral Economy of the Peasant – Rebellion and Subsistence in Southeast Asia. Yale University Press, New Haven and London.
Service, E.R. (1966). The Hunters. Prentice-Hall, Englewood Cliffs, NJ.
Sethi, R., Somanathan, E. (1996). "The evolution of social norms in common property use". American Economic Review 86 (4), 766–788.
Shigetomi, S. (1998). Cooperation and Community in Rural Thailand. Institute of Developing Economies, Tokyo.
Shipton, P. (1988). "The Kenyan land tenure reform: Misunderstandings in the public creation of private property". In: Downs, R.E., Reyna, S.P. (Eds.), Land and Society in Contemporary Africa. University Press of New England, Hanover and London, pp. 91–135.
Sjaastad, E. (1998). "Land tenure and land use in Zambia". Unpublished Ph.D. Thesis. Agricultural University of Norway, Department of Forest Science.
Smith, T.C. (1959). The Agrarian Origins of Modern Japan. Stanford University Press, Stanford, CA.
Stevenson, C.G. (1991). Common Property Theory: A General Theory and Land Use Applications. Cambridge University Press, Cambridge.
Sugden, R. (1986). The Economics of Rights, Co-operation and Welfare. Basil Blackwell, Oxford.
Sugden, R. (1998). "Normative expectations: The simultaneous evolution of institutions and norms". In: Ben-Ner, A., Putterman, L. (Eds.), Economics, Values, and Organization. Cambridge University Press, Cambridge, pp. 73–100.
Sylla, A. (1994). La philosophie morale des Wolof. IFAN, Université de Dakar.
Thomas, J.P., Worrall, T. (1994). "Informal insurance arrangements in village economies". Mimeo. Department of Economics, University of Warwick.
Thompson, E.P. (1991). Customs in Common. Penguin Books, Harmondsworth.
Townsend, R.M. (1994). "Risk and insurance in village India". Econometrica 62 (3), 539–591.
Townsend, R.M. (1995a). "Financial systems in Northern Thai villages". Quarterly Journal of Economics CX (4), 1011–1046.
Townsend, R.M. (1995b). "Consumption insurance: An evaluation of risk-bearing systems in low-income countries". Journal of Economic Perspectives 9 (3), 83–102.
Udry, C. (1990). "Credit markets in Northern Nigeria: Credit as insurance in a rural economy". World Bank Economic Review 4 (3), 251–269.
Udry, C. (1993). "Credit markets in Northern Nigeria: Credit as insurance in a rural economy". In: Hoff, K., Braverman, A., Stiglitz, J.E. (Eds.), The Economics of Rural Organization. Oxford University Press, Oxford, pp. 87–108. (Published for the World Bank).
Udry, C. (1994). "Risk and insurance in a rural credit market: An empirical investigation in Northern Nigeria". Review of Economic Studies 61, 495–526.
Uphoff, N. (2000). "Understanding social capital: Learning from the analysis and experience of participation". In: Dasgupta, P., Serageldin, I. (Eds.), Social Capital – A Multifaceted Perspective. The World Bank, Washington, DC, pp. 215–249.

von Braun, J., Webb, P.J.R. (1989). "The impact of new crop technology on the agricultural division of labor in a West African setting". Economic Development and Cultural Change 37 (3), 513–534.
Wang, C. (1994). "Dynamic insurance between two risk averse agents with bilateral asymmetric information". Mimeo. University of Iowa.
Wiessner, P. (1982). "Risk, reciprocity and social influences on kung san economics". In: Leacock, E., Lee, R.B. (Eds.), Politics and History in Band Societies. Cambridge University Press, Cambridge, pp. 61–84.
Wijaya, M.L. (1996). "Voluntary reciprocity as an informal social insurance mechanism – a game theoretic approach". Ph.D. Thesis, No 108. Faculty of Economics and Business Management, Katholieke Universiteit, Leuven, Belgium.
Wilson, P.N., Thompson, G.D. (1993). "Common property and uncertainty: Compensating coalitions by Mexico's pastoral Ejidatorios". Economic Development and Cultural Change 41 (2), 299–318.
Woodburn, J. (1998). "Sharing is not a form of exchange: An analysis of property-sharing in immediate-return hunter–gatherer societies". In: Hann, C.M. (Ed.), Property Relations – Reviewing the Anthropological Tradition. Cambridge University Press, Cambridge, pp. 48–63.
Woodhouse, P. (2003). "African enclosures: A default mode of development". World Development 31 (10), 1705–1720.
Wright, R. (1994). The Moral Animal: Why We Are the Way We Are: The New Science of Evolutionary Psychology. Pantheon Books, New York.

AUTHOR INDEX OF VOLUME 1

n indicates citation in a footnote.

Abbink, K.   661
Abel, A.B.   262
Abraham, A., *see* Platteau, J.P.   835, 869
Abrams, B.A.   147, 339, 750n
Ackerman, D., *see* Fisher, R.   165n
Ackert, L.F.   683
Aczel, J.   289
Adair, D.   194
Adam, J.S.   27, 88, 107n, 392, 522
Adams, C.M., *see* Knutson, B.   633, 634
Adams, G.R.   573
Adams, S.J.   580n, 587, 599, 600
Adelberg, K., *see* Doland, D.   390n
Adolphs, R.   476n
Agarwal, B.   833
Agell, J.   679
Aghion, P.   708n
Ahlert, M.   662n
Akerlof, G.A.   27, 93, 107n, 393, 396n, 464, 522, 527n, 599, 697, 697n, 699, 705, 707n, 719n
Alderman, H.   855, 869
Alesina, A.   38n, 136, 157, 467, 710, 712n, 716
Alexander, P.   843–846
Alicke, M.D.   576, 577
Alkire, S.   824
Allen, J.L., *see* Dovidio, J.F.   602
Allison, S.T.   583
Allison, S.T., *see* Batson, C.D.   595, 601, 602
Allison, S.T., *see* Roch, S.G.   583
Allison, S.T., *see* Samuelson, C.D.   583
Althammer, W.   355
Altig, D.   330
Altonji, J.G.   166, 168, 266, 339
Alvard, M.S.   627
Amarasinghe, O.   843
Ames, R.   459n
Anderhub, V.   683
Anderson, A.B., *see* Hecht, S.   833
Anderson, C.M.   630, 674
Anderson, N.   580n, 599

Andre, C.   849, 853, 865
Andreoni, J.   110, 139, 140, 150, 156, 158, 159, 164, 165, 202, 290–294, 296, 322, 331, 332, 335–337, 356, 359, 360, 404n, 459n, 593, 619, 629, 630, 638, 639, 642n, 656, 659, 705, 751, 752
Antoci, A.   711–713, 714n, 717n, 720n
Antoci, P.L.   711, 713, 717n
Aoki, A.   825, 838, 862
Appadurai, A.   215
Appel, D., *see* Keating, B.   160
Archibald, G.C.   11n, 130n, 131, 273, 276
Arensberg, C., *see* Polanyi, K.   213
Arps, K., *see* Cialdini, R.B.   602
Arrondel, L.   167n, 267, 562n
Arrow, K.J.   38, 107, 110, 243, 245n, 246, 251, 263, 264, 274, 278n, 301, 301n, 303, 304, 311, 312, 316, 341, 342, 349, 617
Atkins, J.L., *see* Mullen, B.   576
Atwood, D.A.   847
Ault, D.E.   831, 831n, 847, 848, 874
Aumann, R.   298
Auten, G.   151
Avineri, S.   824, 830
Axelrod, R.   88n, 389, 410n, 477, 523, 554, 555, 723n

Babcock, L.   201
Bacharach, M.   759, 760, 761n
Badini, A.   825
Baeck, L.   733n
Bagwell, K., *see* Bernheim, B.D.   284, 284n, 291, 292, 335
Baker, G.   681
Baland, J.M.   830, 833, 837, 840, 843, 844, 850, 851, 874
Baland, J.M., *see* Bardhan, P.K.   846
Balasko, Y.   87
Balzac, H.   235
Bandura, A.   562
Banks, J.   149, 158
Bar-Tal, D.   572, 601

Bardhan, P.K.   837, 846, 855
Bardsley, N.   698, 748n, 750n, 760n
Barlow, K., *see* Meeker, M.E.   212
Barnett, S.A.   559n
Baron, J.N.   392n
Baron, R.   136n
Barrett, K.   150
Barro, R.J.   47, 50, 106, 138, 231, 237, 271, 284, 708n, 749n
Barro, R.J., *see* Becker, G.S.   576
Barrows, R.   847
Barsky, R.J.   330
Barth, F.   214
Bartolini, S.   714n
Bartolini, S., *see* Antoci, A.   714n
Bassett, T.J.   840
Basu, K.   88n, 410n, 718n, 825
Bates, R.H.   846
Batson, C.D.   131n, 134, 134n, 135, 136, 157n, 572, 595, 601, 602
Baumeister, R.F.   592
Bazerman, M.H., *see* Loewenstein, G.F.   597, 598
Beaman, A.L., *see* Cialdini, R.B.   602
Becker, G.S.   33, 49, 106, 110, 138, 166, 170, 189, 197, 200, 231, 233, 237, 243, 251, 253, 254, 255n, 266, 269, 284, 330, 331, 331n, 548, 576, 617, 699, 706, 735, 749n
Becker, G.S., *see* Stigler, G.   137
Becker, H.   378n
Bekerman-Greenberg, R., *see* Levin, I.   567n
Bellemare, C.   626
Bellér-Hann, I.   218
Belshaw, C.   821
Ben-Ner, A.   821, 822
Ben-Shakhar, G.   630
Benabou, R.   644
Benaim, M.   814n
Bene, C.   844
Benjamin, D.J.   644
Benn, S.   751, 752, 756, 757n
Bennett, E., *see* Bene, C.   844
Bentham, J.   598, 749
Bereby-Meyer, Y.   527n
Berg, J.   467, 623
Berge, C.   344
Bergson, A.   12
Bergstrom, T.C.   13n, 139n, 189, 232, 243, 251, 263, 266, 270, 273, 284, 288–290, 311, 312, 314, 315, 332–334, 357, 358, 718, 749n, 750n, 771n, 797n, 798, 799, 801, 801n, 804

Bergstrom, T.C., *see* Andreoni, J.   292–294, 296, 359, 360
Berkowitz, L.   390n
Berkowitz, L., *see* Goranson, R.E.   390n
Berkowitz, L., *see* Macaulay, J.   390n
Berkowitz, M.W.   563
Bernheim, B.D.   170, 235, 284, 284n, 291, 292, 299, 334, 335, 642n, 746n, 750
Berns, G.S., *see* Rilling, J.K.   636
Berry, S.   830, 835, 840, 878
Bersoff, D.M., *see* Miller, J.G.   565
Bersoff, D.M., *see* Miller, R.L.   565
Besley, T.   855, 856n, 858
Bettman, J.R., *see* Payne, J.W.   549
Bewley, T.   392n, 600, 672, 679
Bhagwati, J.N.   87, 283
Bhagwati, J.N., *see* Brecher, R.   87
Bianchi, M.   725n
Billig, M., *see* Tajfel, H.   591–593, 600
Bilodeau, M.   312, 335
Binmore, K.   557n, 628, 629, 735, 806–808, 813
Binswanger, H.P.   849
Bishop, J.   392n
Bisin, A.   562, 562n
Björnerstedt, J.   721
Blarel, B., *see* Migot-Adholla, S.E.   851
Blau, P.   697n
Blondel, S., *see* Lévy-Garboua, L.   598
Blount, S.   595, 638n, 644n, 660, 662
Blume, L.E., *see* Bergstrom, T.C.   139n, 232, 243, 251, 263, 266, 284, 288–290, 750n
Boadway, R.   139n, 291–294, 296, 331n, 357, 358
Boas, F.   262
Boghossian, P.   762n
Bohannan, P.   849
Bohnet, I.   683
Boland, L.   718n
Bolen, M.H., *see* Batson, C.D.   601
Bolle, F.   656
Bolton, G.E.   165, 523, 527n, 548, 579, 580, 620, 639–641, 656, 659, 662, 663, 665, 677, 753
Bonatti, L., *see* Bartolini, S.   714n
Bondanella, J.C., *see* Ritter, A.   745n, 767
Boorman, S.A.   550, 551n, 552, 555, 556, 789, 797n
Börgers, T.   721
Borghesi, S., *see* Antoci, A.   714n
Bornstein, G., *see* Ben-Shakhar, G.   630

Boserup, E. 830, 831, 847, 874, 874n
Boskin, M. 146
Bosman, R. 622, 630
Boulding, K.E. 108, 255
Bourdieu, P. 699, 821, 826, 827n, 829, 833
Bowles, S. 560n, 561, 673, 718, 809
Bowles, S., *see* Fong, C.M. 673, 683, 697
Bowles, S., *see* Gintis, H. 560n
Bowles, S., *see* Henrich, J. 585, 627, 812
Boyd, R. 559, 561, 806, 807
Boyd, R., *see* Gintis, H. 560n
Boyd, R., *see* Henrich, J. 585, 627, 807, 809, 812
Brandstädter, S. 219
Brandts, J. 624n, 661, 662, 666, 671
Brandts, J., *see* Bolton, G.E. 662, 663
Bratman, M. 760n
Brecher, R. 87
Brecher, R., *see* Bhagwati, J.N. 87
Brecher, R.A., *see* Bhagwati, J.N. 283
Breman, J. 827n
Brennan, G. 131, 757
Breusers, M. 830, 832n, 835
Brewer, M.B. 591, 593
Brewer, M.B., *see* Messick, D.M. 583
Brightman, R.A. 834
Brockmann, H.J. 551, 552n
Bromley, D. 833
Brooks-Gunn, J., *see* Chase-Lansdale, P.L. 563
Brown, E. 153
Bruce, J.W. 847, 849
Bruce, N. 334, 335
Bruni, L. 733n, 734n
Bruni, L., *see* Zamagni, S. 704n
Brunner, J.K. 292, 294, 295, 357n, 358–361
Bryan, J.H. 390n
Bryant, J. 866
Buchan, N.R. 626, 627
Buchanan, J.M. 49, 236, 334, 738
Buchholz, W., *see* Althammer, W. 355
Buck, A., *see* de Quervain, D.J.F. 634, 635
Bundy, R.P., *see* Tajfel, H. 591–593, 600
Byrne, D., *see* Baron, R. 136n

Cabrales, A. 683
Cadinu, M.R. 577, 592, 593
Camacho-Cuena, E. 581
Camerer, C.F. 174, 189, 199, 548, 622, 641n, 821n
Camerer, C.F., *see* Henrich, J. 585, 627, 812
Cameron, L.A. 625

Campbell, C.M. 679
Campbell, R.L. 570
Cancian, F. 757n
Candlish, S. 762n
Caporael, L. 131n
Carlo, G., *see* Eisenberg, N. 573
Carmichael, H.L. 174, 523
Carpendale, J.I.M. 569, 570
Carpenter, J.P. 674
Carr-Saunders, A.M. 774, 775
Carrier, J.G. 216, 834
Carter, M.R. 869
Cashdan, E. 821
Castillo, M., *see* Andreoni, J. 630
Castillo, M., *see* Carter, M.R. 869
Cavalli-Sforza, L.L. 559n, 561, 794, 813
Chakravarty-Kaul, M. 834
Chamberlin, J. 248n, 322, 324
Chammah, A.M., *see* Rappaport, A. 799
Champion, D.S., *see* Mullen, B. 576
Charness, G. 527n, 548n, 577, 585, 593, 594n, 595, 596, 619, 620, 624n, 642, 643, 650, 651, 654, 656, 662, 664–666, 668, 753, 754n
Charness, G., *see* Brandts, J. 624n, 666
Charness, G., *see* Cabrales, A. 683
Charng, H.-W., *see* Piliavin, J. 131, 135, 137, 159, 160
Chase-Lansdale, P.L. 563
Chaudhuri, S., *see* Ravaillon, M. 864, 864n
Chavas, J.P., *see* Bromley, D. 833
Cheney, D.L., *see* Smuts, B.B. 551
Cherry, T., *see* List, J. 659
Chichilnisky, G. 87
Christopher, J.C., *see* Campbell, R.L. 570
Chua, V., *see* Wong, C. 152
Cialdini, R.B. 602
Cialdini, R.B., *see* Schaller, M. 602
Cigno, A. 167, 169
Clark, A.E. 598, 701, 701n
Clotfelter, C. 147
Clotfelter, C., *see* Auten, G. 151
Clotfelter, C., *see* Feldstein, M. 146, 158
Coate, S. 168, 334, 335, 523, 854–857, 857n, 858
Cohen, D. 626, 779n, 784, 787, 791
Cohen, D., *see* Nisbett, R.E. 812
Cohen, G. 136n
Cohen, J.M. 829, 847
Colby, A. 570
Coldham, S. 847
Cole, H.L. 702, 724n

Coleman, J.   195, 708n
Collard, D.A.   11n, 108, 335
Comte, A.   233n, 749
Congleton, R.   828
Connolly, L.   750n
Cook, S.   214
Cooper, B.   786
Cooper, D.J.   631n
Corkran, L., *see* Folger, R.   582
Corneo, G.   701–703, 712n, 716, 717n
Cornes, R.C.   232, 245n, 248, 260, 263, 266, 284, 297n, 319, 323–325, 325n, 331–333, 705, 751
Cornes, R.C., *see* Bergstrom, T.C.   289
Cosmides, L.   559, 718n, 811
Costa, D.L.   158n, 711, 716
Costa-Gomes, M.   631n
Cournot, A.   231, 245n
Cox, D.   166–168, 170
Cox, J.C.   527n, 619, 639n, 643, 643n, 656, 659, 662, 663, 753
Creed, G.   219
Cremer, M., *see* Smith, V.   149, 159
Crosby, F.   597
Croson, R.T.A.   462n, 750n
Croson, R.T.A., *see* Buchan, N.R.   626, 627
Cross, J.A., *see* Batson, C.D.   601
Crowley, M., *see* Eagly, A.H.   573
Crüger, A., *see* Ahlert, M.   662n
Crummey, D.E., *see* Bassett, T.J.   840
Cubitt, R.   741n, 763n
Cullis, J., *see* Jones, P.   156n

Dalton, G.   849
Dalton, G., *see* Bohannan, P.   849
Dalton, R., *see* Kitchen, H.   148
Daly, G.   13n
Damon, W.   571, 571n
Danner, P.L.   28n, 378n
Danziger, L.   248n, 354
Darley, J., *see* Latane, B.   390n
Das, S., *see* Bardhan, P.K.   846
Das Gupta, M.   833
Dasgupta, P.   822, 830, 838, 855
Daughety, A.   639n
David, M., *see* Menchik, P.L.   267
Davies, N.B., *see* Kreps, J.K.   551, 552, 555
Davis, D.   617, 676
Davis, J.   210, 212, 214, 221
Davis, J.A.   597
Davis, S.J., *see* Altig, D.   330

Dawes, R.M.   459n, 583, 838
Dawes, R.M., *see* Buchan, N.R.   626, 627
Dawes, R.M., *see* Caporael, L.   131n
Dawes, R.M., *see* Kragt, A.J.C.   459n
Dawes, R.M., *see* Orbell, J.M.   459n
Dawkins, R.   551, 553, 774, 776, 777, 795
Dawkins, R., *see* Brockmann, H.J.   552n
Day, K.   154
Dayan, P., *see* O'Doherty, J.   633, 634
Dayton-Johnson, J., *see* Bardhan, P.K.   837
De Janvry, A., *see* Goldstein, M.   865, 866
De Janvry, A., *see* McCarthy, N.   838
De Janvry, A., *see* Murgai, R.   867
De Montaigne, M.   187, 193, 204
De Quervain, D.J.F.   634, 635
De Quervain, J.F.   202, 204
De Tocqueville, A.   186, 192
De Vincenti, C.   704n
De Waal, F.B.M., *see* Preston, S.D.   632
De Weerdt, J.   865
De Weerdt, J., *see* Dercon, S.   866, 866n
Dearden, L., *see* Ravallion, M.   168
Deaton, A.   864
Debreu, G.   231, 245, 261, 265, 273, 298, 310, 312, 316, 322
Debreu, G., *see* Arrow, K.J.   245n, 316
Decety, J., *see* Jackson, P.L.   633
Deci, E.   707, 708
Deci, E.L.   586
Deichmann, R., *see* O'Doherty, J.   633, 634
Deininger, K., *see* Binswanger, H.P.   849
Dekker, M.   867
Delbar, E., *see* Platteau, J.P.   843
Deleplace, G.   824
Delgado, M.R.   633, 634
Deneulin, S., *see* Alkire, S.   824
Dennett, D.C.   557
Dent, J.L., *see* Roch, S.G.   583
Denton, K.   571
Dercon, S.   168, 864–866, 866n
Descartes, R.   188, 203
DeVinney, L.C., *see* Stouffer, S.A.   597
Devlin, R., *see* Day, K.   154
Dickhaut, J., *see* Berg, J.   467, 623
die Pellegrino, G., *see* Morrison, I.   633
Dilley, R.   216
DiPasquale, D.   715
Dixit, A.   87
Dolan, P.   581
Dolan, R.J., *see* O'Doherty, J.   633, 634
Dolan, R.J., *see* Singer, T.   631–633, 636

Doland, D. 390n
Dolbear, F.T. 248
Dominguez, N., *see* Weisbrod, B. 145, 151
Donaldson, D., *see* Archibald, G.C. 11n, 130n, 131, 273, 276
Donati, P. 704n
Donham, D. 215
Donzelli, F. 718n
Dosi, G. 718n
Dovidio, J.F. 602
Downs, R.E. 840
Droz, J. 197
Dubuisson, D., *see* Baland, J.M. 850
Duesenberry, J.S. 562, 597
Dufwenberg, M. 527n, 585, 620, 649, 649n, 668, 754n
Dufwenberg, M., *see* Charness, G. 651, 666
Duncan, B. 154n, 155, 159, 160
Dunning, D. 577, 592
Dunning, D., *see* Van Boven, L. 577
Duquette, C. 150

Eagly, A.H. 573
Earley, P.C., *see* Lind, E.A. 582
Easterlin, R.A. 597
Eckel, C.C. 630
Edgeworth, F.Y. 11, 76, 267, 268, 273, 310, 316, 523n, 749
Edwards, C., *see* Mullen, B. 576
Eeckhoudt, L. 857n
Egret, J. 191
Eichenberger, R. 659, 659n
Eichengreen, B. 282
Eisenberg, N. 561, 563–565, 567n, 571–573, 601, 602, 602n
Eisenberg, N., *see* Miller, P.A. 567n
Ellickson, R.C. 195, 871
Ellingsen, T. 683
Elster, J. 135, 185–187, 189, 191, 194, 195, 197, 199–201, 204, 718, 749n, 752
Engel, I., *see* Eisenberg, N. 563
Engelmann, D. 629, 657, 664
Ensminger, J. 209, 220, 840
Enthoven, A.C., *see* Arrow, K.J. 246, 264, 278n, 341, 342
Epstein, S. 821
Erev, I., *see* Roth, A.E. 628
Erlei, M. 642
Eser, Z., *see* Cox, D. 167
Eshel, E., *see* Cohen, D. 779n, 784, 787, 791

Eshel, I. 787, 789, 792, 804, 805
Evans-Pritchard, E.E. 821

Fabes, R.A., *see* Eisenberg, N. 563–565, 567n, 571–573, 601, 602, 602n
Fabes, R.A., *see* Miller, P.A. 567n
Fafchamps, M. 168, 822, 828, 855, 857, 857n, 858, 859n, 864, 866, 869, 872
Fafchamps, M., *see* Gavian, S. 834
Fafchamps, M., *see* Kurosaki, T. 864
Fagiolo, G., *see* Dosi, G. 718n
Falk, A. 463n, 527n, 560, 585, 620, 624n, 638n, 643, 644n, 650, 655, 656, 660–662, 664, 668, 677, 754n
Falk, A., *see* Fehr, E. 586, 587n, 624n, 678–680
Falk, A., *see* Gächter, S. 624n, 629
Falk, I., *see* Stark, O. 169
Falkinger, J. 295, 359–361
Falkinger, J., *see* Brunner, J.K. 292, 294, 295, 357n, 358–361
Farrand, M. 189
Feder, G. 837
Feder, G., *see* Binswanger, H.P. 849
Feeny, D., *see* Feder, G. 837
Fehr, E. 132, 133, 189, 193, 197, 199, 202, 203, 463n, 523, 527n, 548, 560, 560n, 579, 585, 586, 587n, 595, 600, 620, 623, 624, 624n, 625, 625n, 626, 628–631, 639, 639n, 653, 654, 656, 657, 669, 673, 674, 677–680, 682, 683, 697, 721n, 753
Fehr, E., *see* de Quervain, D.J.F. 634, 635
Fehr, E., *see* Falk, A. 463n, 527n, 560, 638n, 643, 644n, 655, 660–662, 664
Fehr, E., *see* Falkinger, J. 360
Fehr, E., *see* Fischbacher, U. 462n, 671, 677
Fehr, E., *see* Gächter, S. 585
Fehr, E., *see* Gintis, H. 560n
Fehr, E., *see* Henrich, J. 585, 627, 812
Feinberg, J. 186
Feldman, M.W., *see* Cavalli-Sforza, L.L. 559n, 561, 794, 813
Feldstein, M.S. 146, 158, 330
Feldstein, M.S., *see* Boskin, M. 146
Ferguson, C.K. 591
Fershtman, C. 702
Festinger, L. 598, 599
Fiez, J.A., *see* Delgado, M.R. 633, 634
Firth, R. 211, 828
Fisch, E., *see* Hornstein, H. 390n
Fischbacher, U. 462n, 671, 677

Fischbacher, U., *see* de Quervain, D.J.F.   634, 635
Fischbacher, U., *see* Engelmann, D.   629
Fischbacher, U., *see* Falk, A.   527n, 560, 585, 620, 638n, 643, 644n, 650, 655, 656, 660–662, 664, 668, 677, 754n
Fischbacher, U., *see* Fehr, E.   189, 193, 197, 199, 202, 203, 560, 620, 623, 626, 629, 654
Fishbacher, U., *see* Falk, A.   463n
Fisher, N.R.E.   199
Fisher, R.   165n
Fisher, R.A.   551
Flament, C., *see* Tajfel, H.   591–593, 600
Flavell, J.H.   565
Flavell, J.H., *see* Miller, P.H.   572
Foley, D.K.   97, 305n, 313, 315
Folger, R.   582, 597
Fong, C., *see* Fischbacher, U.   677
Fong, C.M.   673, 683, 697
Fong, G.W., *see* Knutson, B.   633, 634
Forbes, K.   150, 164n
Forsythe, R.L.   622, 628, 631
Fortmann, L., *see* Bruce, J.W.   847
Foster, A.   168, 854
Foster, G.   824, 824n, 825, 857n, 861, 862, 867, 868, 870
Foster, V.   267
François, P., *see* Baland, J.M.   843
Frank, R.H.   129, 131, 558, 722, 803, 828, 838
Frankenberger, K.D.   576
Fraser, C.D.   266
Frechette, G.R.   665
Freeman, R.   153n, 160, 160n
Freud, S.   569n
Frey, B.S.   586, 707
Frey, B.S., *see* Bohnet, I.   683
Friedman, D.   809
Friedman, D., *see* Cox, J.C.   643, 643n
Friedman, M.   17
Friedman, P., *see* Berkowitz, L.   390n
Fries, T.L.   322
Frisch, D.M.   390n
Friston, K., *see* O'Doherty, J.   633, 634
Frith, C.D., *see* Singer, T.   631–633, 636
Fultz, J., *see* Cialdini, R.B.   602

Gächter, S.   585, 624n, 629
Gachter, S., *see* Anderhub, V.   683
Gächter, S., *see* Falk, A.   624n
Gächter, S., *see* Falkinger, J.   360

Gächter, S., *see* Fehr, E.   132, 133, 463n, 523, 527n, 560, 560n, 585, 630, 673, 674, 680
Gächter, S., *see* Fischbacher, U.   462n, 671
Gaertner, L., *see* Gramzow, R.H.   577, 592
Gale, D.   87, 283
Gale, J., *see* Binmore, K.   628
Gale, W.G.   8n, 33
Galeotti, M., *see* Antoci, A.   714n
Gardner, R., *see* Ostrom, E.   674, 838
Gaspart, F., *see* Baland, J.M.   851
Gaube, T.   266, 323, 324
Gauthier, D.   738
Gavian, S.   834
Geanakoplos, J.   620, 647, 650, 651, 755
Geanakoplos, J.D.   87
Geertz, C.   216
Gérard-Varet, L.-A.   108
Gergen, K.   390n
Gergen, M., *see* Gergen, K.   390n
Gertler, P.   864
Geschiere, P.   828
Ghiselin, M.   774
Giannelli, G., *see* Cigno, A.   167, 169
Giertz, F., *see* Daly, G.   13n
Gilbert, M.   760n
Gilligan, C.   573
Gintis, H.   555, 556, 560, 560n, 561, 620
Gintis, H., *see* Bowles, S.   560n, 561, 673, 809
Gintis, H., *see* Fong, C.M.   673, 683, 697
Gintis, H., *see* Henrich, J.   585, 627
Gjerstad, S., *see* Cox, J.C.   643, 643n
Glaeser, E.L.   467, 709n, 710
Glaeser, E.L., *see* Alesina, A.   38n, 136, 157
Glaeser, E.L., *see* DiPasquale, D.   715
Glassman, M.   571n
Glazer, A.   132, 335
Gneezy, U.   666, 683, 707
Godelier, M.   209, 214, 215, 221, 262, 824, 833, 834, 848
Goeree, J.   643
Goldberg, L., *see* Eisenberg, N.   563
Goldfarb, R.S.   13n, 302
Golding, E., *see* Fries, T.L.   322
Goldstein, M.   865, 866
Gollier, C., *see* Eeckhoudt, L.   857n
Goodstadt, M.S.   390n
Goranson, R.E.   390n
Gouldner, A.   29n, 378n, 397n
Grafen, A.   787, 791, 792, 799
Gramzow, R.H.   577, 592
Granovetter, M.   718n

Gravel, N., see Bilodeau, M.   335
Green, J.K.   847, 850
Greenberg, J.   598
Greenberg, M.S., see Frisch, D.M.   390n
Greene, D., see Ross, L.   576, 592
Greenglass, E.R.   390n
Gregory, C.A.   215, 221, 821, 848
Grimard, F.   864, 866
Gross, P., see Handlon, B.J.   390n
Grosskopf, B.   677n
Grosskopf, B., see Charness, G.   577, 593, 594n
Grossman, P.J., see Eckel, C.C.   630
Grove, J., see Folger, R.   582
Groves, T.   328
Gruber, J., see Gertler, P.   864
Grusec, J.E.   563, 564
Grych, J.H., see Berkowitz, M.W.   563
Guala, F., see Bruni, L.   734n
Gubert, F., see Fafchamps, M.   872
Gudeman, S.   209, 216, 218, 221
Guesnerie, R.   87, 283
Gui, B.   704n, 750
Gul, F.   646
Gürerk, O.   674
Gustafson, P., see Walker, L.J.   571
Güth, W.   459n, 523, 527n, 548, 583, 621, 622, 654–656, 658, 664, 677n
Güth, W., see Ahlert, M.   662n
Gutman, D.A., see Rilling, J.K.   636
Guttman, J.   354

Habermas, J.   575, 699
Hahn, F.H., see Arrow, K.J.   274
Hahn, V.   683
Haldane, J.B.S.   551, 778, 779n, 781
Hamermesh, D.S.   702
Hamilton, W.D.   551, 555, 777, 793, 795, 797
Hamilton, W.D., see Axelrod, R.   554, 555
Hamilton Grierson, P.J.   210
Hammond, P.   88, 132, 410n, 523
Hampson, R.B.   573
Handlon, B.J.   390n
Hannan, L.   624n
Harbaugh, W.T.   132, 160–162, 571, 573n, 578
Harder, J.W.   597
Hardin, G.   462n, 780
Hardy, D., see Mullen, B.   576
Hargreaves Heap, S.   757n, 758
Harris, L.A.   390n
Harris, M.   390n
Harsanyi, J.   574, 653n

Hart, K.   212
Hartley, R., see Cornes, R.C.   263, 266
Hartwood, R.L., see Miller, R.L.   565
Haruvy, E., see Charness, G.   527n
Hatta, T., see Bhagwati, J.N.   87, 283
Haugerud, A.   851
Hausman, J.   141
Hayami, Y.   839
Hayashi, F., see Altonji, J.G.   166, 168, 266, 339
Hayes, A.G., see Dunning, D.   577, 592
Hazell, P., see Migot-Adholla, S.E.   851
Heal, G., see Geanakoplos, J.D.   87
Hecht, S.   833
Helliwell, J.F.   467, 711
Hemenway, D., see Solnick, S.   172, 173, 173n, 174
Hennig, K.H., see Walker, L.J.   571
Henrich, J.   220, 585, 591, 627, 628, 807, 809, 812
Henrich, R.   199, 200
Herold, F.   811
Herskovits, M.J.   213
Hewitt, F., see McLean, I.   744n
Higgins, E.T.   572
Highberger, L., see Batson, C.D.   595, 601, 602
Hines, W.G.S.   799
Hirsch, F.   700, 715
Hirschman, A.O.   823, 828
Hirshleifer, J.   235
Hobbes, T.   723, 736, 761
Hobhouse, L.T.   28, 28n, 107n, 376, 377n
Hochman, H.M.   13, 296, 523n
Hodgson, D.H.   759n
Hoff, K.   855, 855n, 869
Hoffman, E.   390n, 559, 623, 625, 659, 659n, 753n
Hoffman, M.L.   129, 135, 563, 565, 571n, 572, 578, 601
Holländer, H.   132, 459n
Hollis, M.   744, 756, 759
Hollis, M., see Hargreaves Heap, S.   758
Holmes, M., see Hornstein, H.   390n
Holmström, B.   681, 707
Holt, Ch., see Davis, D.   617, 676
Holt, Ch., see Goeree, J.   643
Homans, G.C.   586, 599
Hommer, D., see Knutson, B.   633, 634
Hood, R.   147
Hopfensitz, A., see Ben-Shakhar, G.   630
Hori, H.   271

Hornstein, H.A.   390n
Horowitz, J., *see* Forsythe, R.L.   622, 628, 631
Horwitz, M., *see* Rabbie, J.M.   591, 592, 597
Houlihan, D., *see* Cialdini, R.B.   602
House, P., *see* Ross, L.   576, 592
Howard, J.W.   592
Howitt, P., *see* Aghion, P.   708n
Huck, S.   644
Huck, S., *see* Bohnet, I.   683
Hudson, J.   157n
Hugh-Jones, S., *see* Humphrey, C.   216
Hume, D.   204, 738, 741, 806, 855
Humphrey, C.   216
Humphries, J.   833
Hunt, R.C.   215, 217
Hunter, G.   828
Hurley, S.   760n

Ickes, W., *see* Stinson, L.   579n
Ilahiane, H.   831, 853, 853n
Ingold, T.   214, 559
Irlenbusch, B.   680
Irlenbusch, B., *see* Abbink, K.   661
Irlenbusch, B., *see* Gürerk, O.   674
Isaac, M.R.   336, 337, 459n

Jackson, P.L.   633
Jalan, J.   864, 865
James, H.   233n
Jayakar, S.D., *see* Matessi, C.   787
Jeanne, O., *see* Corneo, G.   702, 703
Jegen, R., *see* Frey, B.S.   707
Jellal, M.   562n
Jetten, J.   575
Jevons, W.S.   734
Jimenez, E., *see* Cox, D.   167, 168
Jin, N., *see* Yamagishi, T.   593, 593n
Jodha, N.S.   833
Johannesson, M., *see* Ellingsen, T.   683
Johnson, E.J., *see* Payne, J.W.   549
Johnson, H.G.   282
Johnson, O.E.G.   874
Johnson, P., *see* Temple, J.   710n
Joireman, J.A.   721, 722
Jones, A.   148, 157
Jones, P.   156n
Jones, P., *see* Hudson, J.   157n
Jones, R.   87
Joubert, J.-P.   191
Judd, C.M., *see* Park, B.   592

Kagel, J.H.   661, 662
Kagel, J.H., *see* Frechette, G.R.   665
Kagel, J.H., *see* Hannan, L.   624n
Kahn, M.E., *see* Costa, D.L.   158n, 711, 716
Kahneman, D.   141, 390n, 584, 598, 599, 653
Kamlani, K., *see* Campbell, C.M.   679
Kanaya, S., *see* Hori, H.   271
Kandel, E.   587
Kanfer, R., *see* Lind, E.A.   582
Kant, I.   203
Kaplow, L.   141, 357, 358
Kapteyn, A., *see* Van Praag, B.   158
Karahasan, D.   827
Karbon, M., *see* Eisenberg, N.   573
Karniol, R.   572
Katok, E., *see* Bolton, G.   165
Kaube, H., *see* Singer, T.   631–633, 636
Keating, B.   160
Keefer, P., *see* Knack, S.   467, 709, 710
Kehoe, M., *see* Smith, V.   149, 159
Kelley, H.H., *see* Ferguson, C.K.   591
Kemp, M.C.   283, 284, 288
Kerr, N.L.   583
Keser, C.   671
Kessel, F.S., *see* Miller, P.H.   572
Keynes, J.M.   282
Khanna, J.   151, 152, 750n
Kiebel, S.J., *see* Singer, T.   633, 636
Kiernan, V.   197
Kikuchi, M., *see* Hayami, Y.   839
Kilmer, W.L., *see* Levin, B.R.   789, 790, 792
Kilts, C.D., *see* Rilling, J.K.   636
Kim, Ch., *see* Kagel, J.H.   661, 662
Kim, O.   459n
Kimball, M.S.   271, 523, 854, 857
Kimura, M.   803
Kimuyu, P.K., *see* Pinckney, T.C.   851
Kingma, B.R.   148, 149, 154n, 159, 339
Kirchler, E., *see* Fehr, E.   527n
Kirchsteiger, G.   359–361, 620, 639
Kirchsteiger, G., *see* Dufwenberg, M.   527n, 585, 620, 649, 649n, 668, 754n
Kirchsteiger, G., *see* Fehr, E.   527n, 600, 623, 624, 624n, 625, 625n, 628, 631, 639n, 657, 680
Kirzner, I.M.   269
Kitchen, H.   148, 149
Kiyonari, T., *see* Yamagishi, T.   593, 593n
Klein, A., *see* Fehr, E.   624n, 625n
Klein, T.R., *see* Batson, C.D.   595, 601, 602

Kliemt, H., *see* Güth, W.   656
Kliemt, H., *see* Guth, W.   658
Knack, S.   467, 709, 710
Knack, S., *see* Zak, J.P.   467
Knack, S., *see* Zak, P.J.   709, 716
Knetsch, J.L., *see* Kahneman, D.   141, 390n, 584, 599
Knight, J.   863
Knutson, B.   633, 634
Kocherlakota, N.R.   855
Koestner, R., *see* Deci, E.   707, 708
Kohlberg, L.   570
Kohlberg, L., *see* Colby, A.   570
Koller, S., *see* Eisenberg, N.   572, 573
Kolm, S.-Ch.   8n, 10n, 11n, 12, 12n–14n, 23n, 25n, 27n, 28n, 47n, 51n, 53n, 68n, 69n, 87, 88, 88n, 91n, 92n, 93, 95n, 97n, 99n–102n, 105n, 107n, 108, 110, 132n, 135, 136n, 174n, 188, 231, 243n, 248, 269–271, 282, 296, 297, 297n, 298, 300n, 318, 319, 326, 326n, 327, 331, 378n, 381n, 383n, 390n, 392, 392n, 394n–396n, 400n, 405n, 415n, 417n, 426n, 433n, 436n, 438n, 447n, 448n, 453n, 459n, 460n, 462n–464n, 467n, 469n, 470n, 474n, 477n, 481n, 482n, 484n, 494n, 503n, 504n, 506n, 507n, 515n, 517n, 521n, 522, 522n, 523, 523n–528n, 575n, 585, 639n, 698
Kolm, S.-Ch., *see* Gérard-Varet, L.-A.   108
Komorita, S.S.   583
Konigstein, M., *see* Anderhub, V.   683
Konrad, K.A., *see* Glazer, A.   132, 335
Korenfeld, D., *see* Bar-Tal, D.   572
Kotlikoff, L.J.   8n, 33
Kotlikoff, L.J., *see* Altonji, J.G.   166, 168, 266, 339
Kovács, J., *see* Falk, A.   624n
Kragt, A.J.C.   459n
Kranish, L.   51n, 464n, 527n
Kranton, R.   523
Kranton, R., *see* Akerlof, G.A.   697, 699, 705
Krause, K., *see* Harbaugh, W.T.   571, 573n, 578
Kray, L., *see* Lind, E.A.   576, 577, 582
Krebs, D.L.   565, 570, 570n, 571
Krebs, D.L., *see* Denton, K.   571
Kremhelmer, S., *see* Fehr, E.   683
Kreps, D.M.   88n, 410n, 863
Kreps, J.K.   551, 552, 555
Kripke, S.   762
Krishnan, P., *see* Dercon, S.   168, 864, 865
Kritikos, A., *see* Bolle, F.   656
Kröger, S., *see* Bellemare, C.   626

Kuhlman, D.M., *see* Joireman, J.A.   721, 722
Kurosaki, T.   864
Kurz, M.   88, 132, 410n, 523
Kutz, C.   760n

La Ferrara, E.   866
La Ferrara, E., *see* Alesina, A.   467, 710, 712n, 716
Lack, D.   776
Laferrère, A.   175
Laferrère, A., *see* Arrondel, L.   267
Laffont, J.-J.   296, 323, 324, 335, 336
Laffont, J.-J., *see* Guesnerie, R.   87, 283
Lafond, J.   204
Laibson, D., *see* Glaeser, E.L.   467, 709n, 710
Laitner, J.   167n, 284, 330
Lampman, R.J.   339
Landauer, C.   834
Lane, J.A.S., *see* Roch, S.G.   583
Lankford, H., *see* Brown, E.   153
Lankford, R.   148
Lanzetta, J., *see* Wilke, H.   390n
Largo, E., *see* Alicke, M.D.   576, 577
Latane, B.   390n
Laurent, P.J.   840
Laury, S.K.   336, 337
Lazear, E.P.   707
Lazear, E.P., *see* Kandel, E.   587
Lebègue, E.   194
Ledyard, J.O.   336, 459n, 673, 779
Ledyard, J.O., *see* Groves, T.   328
Lehrer, S.F., *see* Frechette, G.R.   665
Lemche, S.Q.   273n, 274
Leonard, D.   87
Leontief, W.   87
Lepper, M.R.   564
Leventhal, G.S.   390n
Lévi-Strauss, C.   211n
Levin, B.R.   789, 790, 792
Levin, I.   567n
Levine, C.   571
Levine, D.K.   392n, 527n, 585, 620, 645, 668, 677
Levins, R.   550, 789
Levitt, P.R., *see* Boorman, S.A.   550, 551n, 552, 555, 556, 789, 797n
Lévy-Garboua, L.   583, 598, 600, 702
Lewis, A., *see* Jones, P.   156n
Lewis, D.   741, 763
Lewis, M.   194
Ley, E.   248

Libecap, G.D. 837
Lichtenstein, S. 581
Ligon, E. 822, 855, 864
Lind, E.A. 576, 577, 581, 582, 598
Lind, E.A., *see* Tyler, T.R. 582, 598
Lind, E.A., *see* Van den Bos, K. 582
Linday, S.G., *see* Harbaugh, W.T. 571, 573n, 578
Lindbeck, A. 236, 334
Lipset, D.M., *see* Meeker, M.E. 212
List, J. 173n, 659
List, J.A., *see* Fehr, E. 680, 683
Lloyd, D., *see* Morrison, I. 633
Locke, H.M., *see* Delgado, M.R. 633, 634
Locke, J. 742n
Loewenstein, G., *see* Babcock, L. 201
Loewenstein, G., *see* Van Boven, L. 577
Loewenstein, G.F. 597, 598
Lomasky, L., *see* Brennan, G. 757
Long, G., *see* Leventhal, G.S. 390n
Long, S. 160
Lorenzen, H. 193
Lovejoy, A.O. 193, 204
Lucas, R. 708n
Lumsden, C.J. 557, 561
Lund, C. 847, 847n
Lund, S., *see* Fafchamps, M. 864, 866
Lundborg, P., *see* Agell, J. 679
Lyons, B., *see* Hargreaves Heap, S. 758

Macaulay, J. 390n
Mackenzie, F. 847, 851
MacLeod, W.B., *see* Carmichael, H.L. 174, 523
Mailath, G.J., *see* Cole, H.L. 702, 724n
Malcolm, N. 762n
Malinowski, B. 210, 221, 262, 829
Malouf, M.W.K., *see* Roth, A.E. 621
Mandeville, B. 724
Mankiw, G., *see* Barsky, R.J. 330
Manning, R., *see* Leonard, D. 87
Manski, C.F. 158, 159, 176, 599
Manstead, A.S.R., *see* Jetten, J. 575
Marchand, N., *see* Güth, W. 677n
Marengo, L., *see* Dosi, G. 718n
Margolis, H. 108, 201, 751n
Marks, G. 576
Marshall, A. 46, 268n
Martin, S., *see* Hood, R. 147
Martinez-Vazquez, J., *see* Ackert, L.F. 683
Marwell, G., *see* Ames, R. 459n

Masclet, D. 585, 674
Masson, A. 167n, 334
Masson, A., *see* Arrondel, L. 167n, 267, 562n
Matessi, C. 787
Mathieu, P., *see* Laurent, P.J. 840
Matthews, P.H., *see* Carpenter, J.P. 674
Mauss, M. 5, 28, 211, 221, 262, 267, 331, 376
May, P., *see* Hecht, S. 833
May, R.M., *see* Nowak, M.A. 804, 808
Maynard-Smith, J. 551, 552n
McCabe, K.A. 664
McCabe, K.A., *see* Berg, J. 467, 623
McCabe, K.A., *see* Hoffman, E. 559, 623, 625, 659, 659n, 753n
McCarthy, N. 838
McClelland, G., *see* Rohrbaugh, J. 579
McClelland, R., *see* Kingma, B.R. 149, 159
McCue, K.F., *see* Isaac, M.R. 459n
McElreath, R., *see* Henrich, J. 627, 812
McFarland, D. 551, 557, 559, 561
McGuire, M. 322, 324
McGuirk, A., *see* Barrett, K. 150
McKean, M.A. 833, 839
McLean, I. 744n, 749n
McQueen, L.R., *see* Allison, S.T. 583
Meade, J.E. 296
Meeker, M.E. 212
Mellers, B.A. 580, 580n
Mellers, B.A., *see* Mitchell, G. 580
Meltzoff, A.N., *see* Jackson, P.L. 633
Menchik, P.L. 153, 154, 159, 267
Menicucci, D. 720, 720n, 721
Mercier Ythier, J. 237, 246n, 248, 262, 264, 265, 275, 278, 280, 280n, 281n, 284, 287, 299n, 302, 303n, 304, 305n, 306, 307, 309, 310n, 312, 313n, 314–316, 316n, 317, 318, 332, 343, 346, 346n, 698n
Mercier Ythier, J., *see* Gérard-Varet, L.-A. 108
Messick, D.M. 583
Messick, D.M., *see* Allison, S.T. 583
Meter, K., *see* Gergen, K. 390n
Metman, L., *see* Van Dijke, E. 586
Mezzine, L. 831
Michener, C.D. 551
Midlarsky, E. 390n
Migot-Adholla, S.E. 851
Mihailescu, V. 209, 217
Milgrom, P., *see* Holmström, B. 681, 707
Milgrom, P., *see* Kreps, D. 88n, 410n
Mill, J.S. 104n
Miller, D.W. 186

Miller, J.G. 565
Miller, J.G., *see* Andreoni, J. 593, 619, 629, 630, 638, 639, 659
Miller, K., *see* Tuomela, R. 760n
Miller, N., *see* Marks, G. 576
Miller, P.A. 567n
Miller, P.A., *see* Eisenberg, N. 573, 601
Miller, P.H. 572
Miller, R.L. 565
Mishan, E.J. 13n, 315
Mitchell, G. 580
Montebugnoli, A., *see* De Vincenti, C. 704n
Montmarquette, C., *see* Lévy-Garboua, L. 598, 600, 702
Mookherjee, D., *see* Bardhan, P.K. 846
Moore, B., *see* Underwood, B. 567n, 572
Moore, J. 328
Morduch, J. 863–865, 869
Morelly, 28, 377n
Morone, A., *see* Camacho-Cuena, E. 581
Morrison, I. 633
Moser, D., *see* Hannan, L. 624n
Moser, D., *see* Kagel, J.H. 661, 662
Mourato, S., *see* Foster, V. 267
Mousnier, R. 197
Mueller, D.C. 134, 323, 324
Mueller, D.C., *see* von Furstenberg, G.M. 13n, 311
Mui, V.-L. 620
Mullen, B. 576
Müller, W., *see* Huck, S. 644
Mulligan, C., *see* Becker, G.S. 200
Murgai, R. 867
Murickan, J., *see* Platteau, J.P. 843
Murningham, J.K., *see* Roth, A.E. 621
Murphy, B.C., *see* Eisenberg, N. 573
Murphy, K.M., *see* Becker, G.S. 330, 331n
Murphy, K.M., *see* Fershtman, C. 702
Musgrave, R.A. 13n, 297n, 302
Mussen, P., *see* Eisenberg, N. 565, 567n

Nachbar, J. 780n
Naef, M., *see* Fehr, E. 657
Nagel, T. 202
Nakayama, M. 248, 300
Narayan, D. 705n, 716
Narotzky, S. 209
Nash Jr., J.F. 231, 245n
Ndiaye, M. 825
Neiland, A.E., *see* Bene, C. 844
Neilson, W. 653

Nerlove, M. 330
Neumark, D. 701
Neuringer-Benefiel, H.E., *see* Batson, C.D. 601
N'Gweno, B. 830
Nicolas, G. 829
Niederle, M., *see* Bereby-Meyer, Y. 527n
Nisbett, R., *see* Cohen, D. 626
Nisbett, R.E. 812
Nishida, T. 561
Normann, H.-T., *see* Huck, S. 644
Noronha, R. 830, 832, 840, 847
Noussair, C., *see* Masclet, D. 585
Nowak, M.A. 804, 808
Nunes, P. 141
Nunow, A.A. 833

Oberholzer-Gee, F., *see* Eichenberger, R. 659, 659n
Ockenfels, A., *see* Bolton, G.E. 523, 527n, 548, 579, 580, 620, 640, 641, 656, 662, 663, 665, 677, 753
Ockenfels, A., *see* Güth, W. 656, 658
Ockenfels, A., *see* Selten, R. 654
O'Doherty, J.P. 633, 634
O'Doherty, J.P., *see* Singer, T. 631–633
Offer, A. 378n
Offerman, T. 577, 577n, 595, 596, 660, 662
Okada, A. 665
Okten, C. 152
Okuno-Fujiwara, M., *see* Roth, A.E. 548, 622, 628, 676, 678n, 812
Oliner, P.M., *see* Oliner, S.P. 135, 563
Oliner, S.P. 135, 563
Olsen, E.O. 13n
Olson, M. 231, 297, 318, 323, 709, 837
Ong'ong'a, O., *see* Carpenter, J.P. 674
Orbell, J.M. 459n
Orbell, J.M., *see* Caporael, L. 131n
Orbell, J.M., *see* Dawes, R.M. 459n
Orbell, J.M., *see* Kragt, A.J.C. 459n
Ordonez, L.D., *see* Mitchell, G. 580
Ortiz, S. 824
Osberg, L., *see* Hood, R. 147
Ostrom, E. 674, 831, 838
Oswald, A.J., *see* Clark, A.E. 598, 701
Oswald, A.J., *see* Zizzo, D. 654
Otsuka, K., *see* Place, F. 852
Otten, S. 592
Özdemiroglu, E., *see* Foster, V. 267

Pagnoni, G., *see* Rilling, J.K.   636
Paqué, K.-H.   750n
Parducci, A.   580n
Pareto, V.   11, 230, 232, 232n, 233n, 245n, 268, 269, 271–273, 275, 276, 523n, 734
Park, B.   592
Parks, C.D., *see* Komorita, S.S.   583
Parks, R.   274
Parry, J.   212, 216
Paterson, F., *see* Lorenzen, H.   193
Paxson, C.H., *see* Alderman, H.   855, 869
Payne, A.   151, 152
Payne, J., *see* Schkade, D.   141
Payne, J.W.   549
Peacock, M.   762
Pearce, D., *see* Foster, V.   267
Pearce, D., *see* Geanakoplos, J.   620, 647, 650, 651, 755
Pearson, H., *see* Polanyi, K.   213
Peleg, B., *see* Bernheim, B.D.   299
Pemantle, R., *see* Skyrms, B.   803
Pesendorfer, W., *see* Gul, F.   646
Pestieau, P., *see* Arrondel, L.   167n
Pestieau, P., *see* Boadway, R.   139n, 291–294, 296, 331n, 357, 358
Pestieau, P., *see* Masson, A.   167n, 334
Petersen, N.   217
Petersen, R.   199
Petrie, R., *see* Andreoni, J.   630
Pettit, P.   762n
Pfaff, M., *see* Boulding, K.E.   108
Phan Huy, Lê   832
Phelps, C.   169n
Phelps, E.S.   33, 46, 108
Piaget, J.   53, 383, 566, 567
Pieters, R.   173
Piliavin, J.   131, 135, 137, 159, 160
Pinckney, T.C.   851
Pitts, R., *see* Keating, B.   160
Place, F.   852
Place, F., *see* Baland, J.M.   851
Place, F., *see* Migot-Adholla, S.E.   851
Platteau, J.P.   828, 830, 830n, 835–838, 843, 844n, 845, 847, 851, 855, 862, 864, 866, 869, 870, 874
Platteau, J.P., *see* Andre, C.   849, 853, 865
Platteau, J.P., *see* Baland, J.M.   830, 833, 837, 840, 844, 850, 851, 874
Plott, C., *see* Isaac, M.R.   459n
Plott, C.R.   735
Polanyi, K.   213, 221, 417n, 453, 697, 824

Polemarchakis, H.M.   87
Pollis, N.P.   597
Pommerehne, W., *see* Schneider, F.   459n
Popkin, S.L.   830
Posner, E.   193, 196
Posner, R.   854
Posnett, J.   151, 297n, 331, 339
Posnett, J., *see* Jones, A.   148, 157
Posnett, J., *see* Khanna, J.   151, 750n
Postlewaite, A.   87, 283
Postlewaite, A., *see* Cole, H.L.   702, 724n
Postlewaite, A., *see* Neumark, D.   701
Prasnikar, V.   523
Prasnikar, V., *see* Roth, A.E.   548, 622, 628, 676, 678n, 812
Prendergast, C.   174, 707
Preston, S.D.   632
Price, G.R., *see* Smith, J.M.   796
Prohmmo, A., *see* Bryant, J.   866
Proudhon, P.-J.   28n, 377n
Pruitt, D.G.   390n
Pulcini, E.   698, 723n, 725n
Puppe, C., *see* Kirchsteiger, G.   359–361
Putnam, R.D.   467, 708, 708n, 709, 710, 715, 717
Putnam, R.D., *see* Helliwell, J.F.   467, 711
Putterman, L., *see* Anderson, C.M.   630, 674
Putterman, L., *see* Ben-Ner, A.   821, 822

Quiggin, J.   832
Quinn, R., *see* Rohrbaugh, J.   579

Rabbie, J.M.   591–593, 597
Rabin, M.   107n, 201, 392n, 524, 527n, 548, 548n, 576, 585, 620, 647, 649n, 650, 652, 653, 668, 754
Rabin, M., *see* Charness, G.   527n, 548n, 585, 593, 594n, 595, 596, 619, 620, 642, 643, 650, 651, 654, 656, 662, 664, 665, 668, 753, 754n
Rader, T.   273
Radner, R.   88n, 410n
Ramsey, F.P.   285n
Randolph, W.   149
Rank, M., *see* Cox, D.   166, 167
Rapoport, B., *see* Lévy-Garboua, L.   583
Rappaport, A.   799
Ravallion, M.   168, 864, 864n
Ravallion, M., *see* Coate, S.   168, 523, 854–857, 857n, 858
Ravallion, M., *see* Jalan, J.   864, 865
Raviv, A., *see* Bar-Tal, D.   572

Rawls, J. 70, 575, 580
Ray, D. 855
Razin, A., *see* Nerlove, M. 330
Redler, E., *see* Grusec, J.E. 564
Reece, W.S. 147, 148, 267
Regan, D. 759n
Renner, E., *see* Abbink, K. 661
Reyna, S.P., *see* Downs, R.E. 840
Ribar, D. 149
Richerson, P.J., *see* Boyd, R. 559, 561, 806, 807
Rider, M., *see* Ackert, L.F. 683
Riedl, A. 683
Riedl, A., *see* Fehr, E. 527n, 600, 623, 624, 624n, 625, 625n, 628, 631, 639n, 657, 680
Riedl, A., *see* Okada, A. 665
Rigdon, M.L., *see* McCabe, K.A. 664
Rilling, J.K. 636
Ritter, A. 745n, 767
Rob, R. 707, 713n
Robben, H., *see* Pieters, R. 173
Robbins, L. 269
Roberts, D.J., *see* Postlewaite, A. 283
Roberts, J., *see* Kreps, D. 88n, 410n
Roberts, N., *see* Morrison, I. 633
Roberts, R.D. 139n, 154, 284, 339, 356–358
Robinson, A., *see* Dolan, P. 581
Robson, A.J. 557n, 559
Roch, S.G. 583
Rockenbach, B., *see* Fehr, E. 680, 683
Rockenbach, B., *see* Gürerk, O. 674
Rodenbach, E. 848
Rodgers, J.D., *see* Hochman, H.M. 13, 296, 523n
Rohrbaugh, J. 579
Romano, R., *see* Fries, T.L. 322
Romer, P.M. 702, 708n
Rosati, F., *see* Cigno, A. 167, 169
Rose, D. 707
Rose-Ackerman, S. 142
Rosen, S., *see* Lazear, E.P. 707
Rosenbaum, W.E., *see* Adam, J.S. 27, 88, 392, 522
Rosenbladt, B., *see* Fehr, E. 626
Rosenfield, D., *see* Folger, R. 582
Rosenhan, D.L. 390n, 563
Rosenzweig, M. 864
Rosenzweig, M., *see* Foster, G. 168, 857n, 861, 862, 867, 868, 870
Ross, L. 576, 592, 670

Rotemberg, J.J. 43n, 378n, 391n, 392n, 465n, 645, 697, 706
Roth, A.E. 527n, 548, 621, 622, 628, 676, 678n, 753n, 812
Roth, A.E., *see* Prasnikar, V. 523
Roth, A.E., *see* Slonim, R. 625
Roth, M., *see* Barrows, R. 847
Rothbart, M., *see* Cadinu, M.R. 577, 592, 593
Rothbart, M., *see* Howard, J.W. 592
Rousseau, J.-J. 723, 742–744, 745n, 780
Ruffle, B. 172, 174
Rulliere, J.-L., *see* Güth, W. 677n
Runciman, W.G. 597
Rushton, J.P. 135, 137, 337n, 565, 601
Rustichini, A., *see* Gneezy, U. 683, 707
Rutman, G.L., *see* Ault, D.E. 831, 831n, 847, 848, 874
Ryan, R., *see* Deci, E. 707, 708

Sacco, P.L. 701n, 720, 720n
Sacco, P.L., *see* Antoci, A. 711–713, 714n, 717n, 720n
Sacco, P.L., *see* Menicucci, D. 720, 720n, 721
Sacco, S., *see* Antoci, P.L. 711, 713, 717n
Sacerdote, B., *see* Alesina, A. 136, 157
Sadiraj, K., *see* Cox, J.C. 619, 639n
Sadiraj, V., *see* Cox, J.C. 619, 639n
Sadka, E., *see* Nerlove, M. 330
Sadoulet, E., *see* Goldstein, M. 865, 866
Sadoulet, E., *see* McCarthy, N. 838
Sadoulet, E., *see* Murgai, R. 867
Safra, Z. 87
Sahlins, M. 214, 221, 821, 829
Sala-i-Martin, X., *see* Barro, R. 708n
Salamon, L., *see* Clotfelter, C. 147
Sally, D. 671
Samuelson, C.D. 583
Samuelson, C.P., *see* Roch, S.G. 583
Samuelson, L. 814
Samuelson, L., *see* Binmore, K. 628, 808
Samuelson, L., *see* Eshel, I. 804
Samuelson, P.A. 87, 139, 231, 617
Sandbu, M.E. 643n
Sandler, T., *see* Cornes, R.C. 232, 245n, 248, 260, 263, 266, 284, 297n, 319, 323, 324, 331, 332, 705, 751
Sandler, T., *see* Khanna, J. 151, 152, 750n
Sandler, T., *see* Posnett, J. 151, 297n, 331, 339
Sansone, E., *see* Eshel, I. 805
Sarin, R., *see* Börgers, T. 721
Sarin, R., *see* Kahneman, D. 598
Sarkar, R., *see* Bardhan, P.K. 846

Sautter, C.I., *see* Glaeser, E.L.   467
Savin, N.E., *see* Forsythe, R.L.   622, 628, 631
Scarf, H., *see* Debreu, G.   310, 316, 322
Schachter, S.   591
Schaerfl, L.M., *see* Allison, S.T.   583
Schaller, M.   602
Schaller, M., *see* Cialdini, R.B.   602
Schapera, I.   834
Scheinkman, J.A., *see* Glaeser, E.L.   467, 709n, 710
Schelling, T.   739
Schelthammer, M., *see* de Quervain, D.J.F.   634, 635
Schiff, J.   148, 154n
Schiff, M.   715, 715n
Schkade, D.   141
Schlag, K.   721
Schlicht, E.   722
Schmidt, K.M., *see* Fehr, E.   527n, 548, 579, 585, 595, 620, 624n, 625n, 639, 653, 656, 657, 669, 673, 677, 682, 683, 697, 721n, 753
Schmittberger, R., *see* Güth, W.   459n, 548, 621, 622
Schmitz, M.D., *see* Abrams, B.A.   147, 339, 750n
Schneider, F.   459n
Schnyder, U., *see* de Quervain, D.J.F.   634, 635
Schnytzer, A., *see* Danziger, L.   354
Schokkaert, E.   145, 150, 162, 164
Schokkaert, E., *see* Nunes, P.   141
Scholtz, J.K., *see* Gale, W.G.   8n, 33
Scholz, J., *see* Andreoni, J.   150, 158, 159
Schot, J.C., *see* Rabbie, J.M.   593
Schram, A., *see* Brandts, J.   671
Schram, A., *see* Seinen, I.   629
Schroeder, D.A., *see* Dovidio, J.F.   602
Schultz, J., *see* O'Doherty, J.   633, 634
Schultz, W.   633, 634
Schupp, J., *see* Fehr, E.   626
Schwartz, R.   146
Schwarze, B., *see* Güth, W.   459n, 548, 621, 622
Schweinberger, A.G., *see* Cornes, R.C.   323, 325, 325n
Scott, J.C.   827n
Scott, K.S., *see* Greenberg, J.   598
Scott, R.   683
Scott, R.H.   13n
Searle, J.   760n
Secondi, G.   167
Sedikides, C., *see* Gramzow, R.H.   577, 592

Sefton, M., *see* Forsythe, R.L.   622, 628, 631
Segal, U.   585, 620, 652
Seidl, C., *see* Camacho-Cuena, E.   581
Seinen, I.   629
Seki, E., *see* Platteau, J.P.   844n
Selten, R.   654
Sen, A.   135, 200, 617
Sertel, M.R.   88, 88n, 283
Service, E.R.   821
Sethi, R.   808, 813, 837
Seyfarth, R.M., *see* Smuts, B.B.   551
Seymour, B., *see* Singer, T.   631–633
Shachat, K., *see* Hoffman, E.   659, 659n
Shaked, A., *see* Eshel, I.   804, 805
Shakespeare, W.   235
Shalley, G.P., *see* Joireman, J.A.   721, 722
Shapiro, B.   194
Shaw, L.L., *see* Batson, C.D.   595, 601, 602
Shell, R., *see* Eisenberg, N.   567n
Shell, R., *see* Miller, P.A.   567n
Sheshinski, E.   330
Shibata, H.   284
Shigetomi, S.   866
Shipton, P.   850, 851
Shitovitz, B.   266, 319, 321–323, 351
Shleifer, A., *see* Bernheim, B.D.   170, 235, 334
Shogren, J., *see* List, J.   173n
Shomroni, D., *see* Karniol, R.   572
Sieg, H., *see* Auten, G.   151
Silber, J.   14n, 448n
Silk, J.B.   555
Sillitoe, P.   211
Silva, E.C.D., *see* Cornes, R.C.   332, 333
Simner, L.   578
Simon, H.   392n
Singer, T.   631–633, 636
Singh, N., *see* Friedman, D.   809
Sjaastad, E.   849n
Skelton, P.   734
Skyrms, B.   763n, 780n, 803, 813
Slivinski, A.   335
Sliwka, D., *see* Irlenbusch, B.   680
Sloane, P.J.   702
Slonim, R.   625
Slovic, P., *see* Lichtenstein, S.   581
Smale, S.   88n, 410n
Smeeding, T.M., *see* Lampman, R.J.   339
Smith, A.   7, 50, 230, 233n, 267, 378n, 548, 576, 591, 617, 676, 724, 733, 745
Smith, J.M.   777, 781, 787, 791, 795, 796
Smith, J.M., *see* Hines, W.G.S.   799

Smith, N., see Henrich, J.   628
Smith, T.C.   826, 839
Smith, V.L.   149, 159, 617
Smith, V.L., see Hoffman, E.   559, 623, 625, 659, 659n, 753n
Smith, V.L., see McCabe, K.A.   664
Smuts, B.B.   551
Sobel, J.   527n
Sobel, J., see Segal, U.   585, 620, 652
Sober, E.   719, 776, 807
Sola, C., see Brandts, J.   661, 662
Solnick, S.   172, 173, 173n, 174
Solow, R.M.   107, 702
Somanathan, E., see Sethi, R.   808, 813, 837
Soutter, C.L., see Glaeser, E.L.   709n, 710
Spash, C.   141
Spears, R., see Jetten, J.   575
Spiegel, M., see Shitovitz, B.   266, 319, 321–323, 351
Spitzer, M.L., see Hoffman, E.   390n
Ssenteza, J., see Place, F.   852
Stacchetti, E., see Geanakoplos, J.   620, 647, 650, 651, 755
Star, S.A., see Stouffer, S.A.   597
Stark, O.   169, 262, 562
Stark, O., see Bergstrom, T.C.   804
Stark, O., see Bernheim, B.D.   746n, 750
Stark, O., see Cox, D.   170
Starrett, D.   282
Staub, E.   564, 565, 572, 601
Steedman, I.   52n, 108
Steger, T.M.   705
Steinberg, R.   110, 154, 331n, 750n
Steinberg, R., see Barrett, K.   150
Steinberg, R., see Slivinski, A.   335
Stenger, V.A., see Delgado, M.R.   633, 634
Stephan, K.E., see Singer, T.   633
Stevenson, C.G.   831
Stigler, G.   137
Stinson, L.   579n
Stockman, C.K., see Cooper, D.J.   631n
Stole, L., see Prendergast, C.   174
Story, J.E., see Mullen, B.   576
Stouffer, S.A.   597
Strathern, A.   211
Strathern, M.   215, 221
Strawczynski, M.   330
Strayer, J., see Eisenberg, N.   601
Strobel, M., see Engelmann, D.   657, 664
Struhsaker, T.T., see Smuts, B.B.   551
Suchman, E.A., see Stouffer, S.A.   597

Sugden, R.   107n, 132, 133, 139, 201, 284, 332, 335, 336, 396n, 462n, 522, 707, 738n, 739n, 745n, 750n, 751n, 757n, 759, 760, 760n, 821, 854
Sugden, R., see Bardsley, N.   698
Sugden, R., see Bruni, L.   733n
Sugden, R., see Cubitt, R.   741n, 763n
Sugden, R., see Hargreaves Heap, S.   758
Suleiman, R.   622n, 628
Summers, L.H., see Bernheim, B.D.   170, 235, 334
Summers, L.H., see Kotlikoff, L.   8n, 33
Sutter, M., see Bosman, R.   622
Swaney, J.   107n, 396n, 462n, 522
Swenson, P.   201
Sylla, A.   824

Tajfel, H.   591–593, 600
Tangney, J.P.   194
Tanner, S., see Banks, J.   149, 158
Taussig, M.K.   267
Taylor, A., see Feldstein, M.   146
Temple, J.   710n
Test, M.A., see Bryan, J.H.   390n
Teta, P.D., see Joireman, J.A.   721, 722
Tetlock, P.E., see Mitchell, G.   580
Thaler, R.H., see Camerer, C.F.   548, 622, 821n
Thaler, R.H., see Dawes, R.M.   459n, 838
Thaler, R.H., see Kahneman, D.   390n, 584, 599
Thomas, J.P.   857, 859, 860
Thomas, J.P., see Ligon, E.   822, 864
Thomas, S.H., see Isaac, M.R.   459n
Thompson, E.P.   824n
Thompson, G.D., see Wilson, P.N.   839
Thompson, L., see Lind, E.A.   576, 577, 582
Thompson, L., see Loewenstein, G.F.   597, 598
Thomson, W.   248
Thurnwald, R.   28n, 376
Thurow, L.C.   13n, 311
Tirole, J., see Benabou, R.   644
Titmuss, R.M.   38
Tocqueville, A.   725
Tooby, J., see Cosmides, L.   559, 718n, 811
Totte, M., see Laurent, P.J.   840
Tougareva, E., see Fehr, E.   625
Townsend, R.M.   168, 722, 855, 863–865, 873
Treyer, V., see de Quervain, D.J.F.   634, 635
Trivers, R.L.   552, 554, 813
Tucker, S., see Masclet, D.   585
Tuomela, R.   760n

Turiel, E.   565, 567, 571n, 573
Turk, C.L., *see* Batson, C.D.   601
Turner, J.C., *see* Tajfel, H.   592
Tutte, W.T.   344
Tversky, A., *see* Kahneman, D.   653
Tykocinski, O., *see* Ruffle, B.   172
Tyler, T.R.   582, 598
Tyler, T.R., *see* Lind, E.A.   582, 598
Tyran, J.-R.   683
Tyran, J.-R., *see* Riedl, A.   683

Udry, C.   855, 864, 871, 872, 872n, 873
Udry, C., *see* Bardhan, P.K.   855
Uhlaner, C.J.   704
Underwood, B.   567n, 572
Unger, L.   131, 136, 153, 162
Uphoff, N.   840

Vaillancourt, F.   153
Van Boven, L.   577
van Damme, E., *see* Güth, W.   654, 655, 664
van de Kragt, A., *see* Caporael, L.   131n
van de Kragt, A., *see* Dawes, R.M.   459n
van de Kragt, A.J.C., *see* Orbell, J.M.   459n
Van den Bos, K.   582
Van Dijke, E.   583, 586
Van Herwaarden, F., *see* Van Praag, B.   158
Van Hesteren, F., *see* Krebs, D.L.   565, 570, 570n, 571
Van Ootegem, L., *see* Schokkaert, E.   145, 150, 162, 164
Van Praag, B.   158
van Winden, F., *see* Ben-Shakhar, G.   630
van Winden, F., *see* Bosman, R.   622, 630
van Winden, F., *see* Keser, C.   671
Vanderklok, M., *see* Mullen, B.   576
Vanderschraaf, P.   739n
Vanin, P., *see* Antoci, A.   711–713, 714n, 717n
Vanin, P., *see* Antoci, P.L.   711, 713, 717n
Vanin, P., *see* Sacco, P.L.   701n
Varian, H.R.   355, 356
Varian, H.R., *see* Bergstrom, T.C.   139n, 232, 243, 251, 263, 266, 284, 288–290, 750n
Varner, J.L., *see* Knutson, B.   633, 634
Vasoo, S., *see* Wong, C.   152
Veblen, T.   597, 639
Verdier, T., *see* Bisin, A.   562, 562n
Vermunt, R., *see* Van den Bos, K.   582
Vesterlund, L., *see* Andreoni, J.   630, 656
Villeval, M.C., *see* Masclet, D.   585
Visser, L., *see* Rabbie, J.M.   593

von Braun, J.   824
von Furstenberg, G.M.   13n, 311
von Mises,   269
Von Weizsäcker, C.C.   200

Wagner, G., *see* Fehr, E.   626
Wakker, P.P., *see* Kahneman, D.   598
Wakschlag, L.S., *see* Chase-Lansdale, P.L.   563
Waldfogel, J.   171–173, 173n
Waldman, M., *see* Bruce, N.   334, 335
Walker, J.M., *see* Isaac, M.R.   336, 337, 459n
Walker, J.M., *see* Laury, S.K.   336, 337
Walker, J.M., *see* Ostrom, E.   674, 838
Walker, L.J.   571
Walker, M.   328
Walker, M., *see* Kim, O.   459n
Wallace, C., *see* Cooper, B.   786
Wang, C.   855
Ward, A., *see* Ross, L.   670
Warr, P.G.   139n, 231, 237, 284, 288, 304, 338
Waugh, H.E.   806
Wax, A.L.   673
Weale, A., *see* Hargreaves Heap, S.   758
Webb, M., *see* Postlewaite, A.   87
Webb, P.J.R., *see* von Braun, J.   824
Weber, M.   756
Weibull, J.W.   718n, 780, 780n, 814
Weibull, J.W., *see* Benaim, M.   814n
Weibull, J.W., *see* Björnerstedt, J.   721
Weibull, J.W., *see* Lindbeck, A.   236, 334
Weichbold, A., *see* Fehr, E.   527n
Weimann, J.   750n
Weiner, A.   221
Weintraub, E.R.   718n
Weisbrod, B.   145, 151
Weisbrod, B., *see* Menchik, P.   153, 154, 159
Weisbrod, B., *see* Okten, C.   152
Weiss, G.H., *see* Kimura, M.   803
Weiss, T., *see* Leventhal, G.S.   390n
Weiss, Y., *see* Fershtman, C.   702
Wentura, D., *see* Otten, S.   592
Werner, C.A.   219
Whinston, M.D., *see* Bernheim, B.D.   299
White, M.   192
Wicksteed, P.H.   52, 230, 267, 268, 450
Wiessner, P.   821, 873
Wijaya, M.L.   858n
Wildasin, D., *see* Boadway, R.   139n, 291–294, 296, 331n, 357, 358
Wilding, J., *see* Joireman, J.A.   721, 722
Wilhelm, M., *see* Ribar, D.   149

Wilk, R.   209, 220
Wilke, H.   390n
Wilke, H., *see* Van Dijke, E.   583, 586
Wilke, H.A.M., *see* Van den Bos, K.   582
Wilke, M., *see* Van Dijke, E.   586
Williams, A.W., *see* Isaac, R.M.   336, 337
Williams, A.W., *see* Laury, S.K.   336, 337
Williams, G.C.   776
Williams, H., *see* Sloane, P.J.   702
Williams Jr., R.M., *see* Stouffer, S.A.   597
Wilson, D.S.   779, 787, 790, 791n, 792, 793
Wilson, D.S., *see* Sober, E.   719, 776, 807
Wilson, E.O.   550, 551, 557n
Wilson, E.O., *see* Lumsden, C.J.   557, 561
Wilson, P.N.   839
Wilson, R., *see* Kreps, D.   88n, 410n
Wilson, T.F., *see* Boulding, K.E.   108
Winch, P.   762
Winston, J.S., *see* Singer, T.   633, 636
Winter, S.G.   271, 273, 274
Winter Jr., S.J.   11n
Winter-Ebner, R., *see* Falkinger, J.   360
Winters, P., *see* Murgai, R.   867
Wittgenstein, L.   762
Wolchik, S., *see* Eisenberg, N.   563
Wolff, F.C.   339
Wolff, F.C., *see* Jellal, M.   562n
Wong, C.   152
Wong, K., *see* Kemp, M.C.   283
Wood, G.   194
Woodburn, J.   214, 217, 220, 828, 873, 874
Woodhouse, P.   835, 848, 877
Woodward, R.   147, 162–164, 164n
Worrall, T., *see* Ligon, E.   822, 864
Worrall, T., *see* Thomas, J.P.   857, 859, 860
Wosinski, M., *see* Eisenberg, N.   573

Wrangham, R.W., *see* Smuts, B.B.   551
Wright, B.   390n
Wright, R.   824
Wright, S.   781, 794, 803
Wyckoff, J., *see* Lankford, R.   148
Wynne-Edwards, V.C.   550, 775, 776, 792, 792n

Yaari, M.E., *see* Güth, W.   523
Yamagishi, T.   593, 593n, 674
Yan, Y.   219
Yano, M.   87
Yellen, J.L., *see* Akerlof, G.A.   599
Young, H.P.   814
Young, M.   211
Youniss, J.   568

Zajonc, R.B.   601
Zak, P.J.   467, 709, 716
Zamagni, S.   46n, 108, 698, 704n
Zamagni, S., *see* Antoci, A.   720n
Zamagni, S., *see* Sacco, P.L.   720, 720n
Zamir, S., *see* Roth, A.E.   548, 622, 628, 676, 678n, 812
Zampelli, E., *see* Forbes, K.   150, 164n
Zan, B., *see* Glassman, M.   571n
Zauner, K.G., *see* Costa-Gomes, M.   631n
Zeckhauser, R.   13n
Zeckhauser, R., *see* Bohnet, I.   683
Zeh, T.R., *see* Rilling, J.K.   636
Zeldes, S., *see* Barsky, R.J.   330
Zemsky, P., *see* Rob, R.   707, 713n
Zhou, Q., *see* Eisenberg, N.   572, 573
Zieschang, K.D., *see* Reece, W.S.   148, 267
Zizzo, D.   654
Zwick, R., *see* Bolton, G.   659

SUBJECT INDEX OF VOLUME 1

Abrams 750
access rights 831
access to food 874
access to land 846, 847
accumulation 5
action 398
activist 36
Adam 27, 88, 392, 522
Adam and Rosenbaum 27, 88, 392, 522
Adam Smith/Smith 5, 10, 16, 36, 51, 59, 77, 104, 230, 377, 389, 443, 733, 734, 740, 745–748, 753, 761
Adam Smith. *The Theory of Moral Sentiments* 376
Adam Smith's problem xvi, 50, 230
admiration 18
advanced industrial societies 726
affection 4–6, 9, 54, 56, 59, 382
affective 56
affective altruism 6
agent-liking 431
aggregate risks 832
agreement 6
Akerlof 393, 522
Akerlof's efficiency wages 464
akrasia or weakness of the will 381
alarm call 733, 734
Alesina and Glaeser 38
alienability of land assets 850
allocation preferences 506
allocative preferences 506
altruism 9, 56, 212, 233, 376, 383, 385, 551, 616, 619, 638, 746, 749, 750, 755, 780, 839, 855, 861, 862, 867, 868
altruism and fairness in conflict 595
altruism and justice xvi, 71
altruism and uncertainty xvi, 105
altruist 9, 17, 751
altruistic 185, 269, 749, 750, 758
altruistic and egoistic helping 602
altruistic behavior 550
altruistic gift-giving 228
altruistic giving xv, 8
altruistic joint giving xv, 16

altruistic norms 869
altruistic personality 600
altruistic predispositions 840, 869
Andreoni 110, 459, 751, 752
anonymity 192
anthropology 207, 379
anti-social behavior 828
approbativeness 193
approval 747, 748
approve 747
Aristotle 77, 197
Arrow 38, 107, 110
Assemblée Constituante 190, 194
association costs 867
associational activities 709
associations xv, 5, 42, 393
assortative interaction 556
assortative matching 794
assumed empathy 58
autarchic allocation 861
autarchy 861
authority 568
authority structure 877
Axelrod 389, 410, 477, 523

Bacharach 759–761
backward induction 410
bad draws 858
bad luck 858
bad shock 860, 871, 872
Baeck 733
balance 4, 18, 30, 382, 397
balance reciprocity 25, 29, 377, 380, 382, 421, 424, 425, 445
balanced accounts 870
balanced reciprocity 856, 870, 877
bankruptcy 873
Bardsley 748, 750, 760
Barro 47, 749
basic needs 10
BBV distributive social systems 288
BBV equilibrium 265
Becker 26, 33, 49, 110, 189, 735, 749

Becker's social equilibrium 238
behavioral justice 579
behavioral norm 870
bellum omnium contra omnes 723
benefactor-liking 429, 431
beneficence 233
benevolence 20, 233
benevolent giver 4
Benn 751, 752, 756, 757
Bentham 12, 77, 749
bequest(s) 4, 6, 8, 47, 166
Bergson 12, 15, 105
Bergstrom 749, 750
Bernheim 746, 750
between-group selection 560
between-group selection effect 556
bilateral anterior insula (AI) 632
binding commitments 857, 861
Binmore, 1999 735
Birth of the Moral Sentiment in the Child 53
blood and the efficiency of giving xvi, 107
Blume 750
Boghossian 762
Bolton 753
Boulding 108
bounded rationality 410
bowling alone 716
Bratman 760
Brennan 757
Bruni 733, 734
Buchanan 49, 738
Buddhism 394
burden of taxation 25

Cancian 757
Candlish 762
capital accumulation 8
cascade principle 555
categorical imperative 386, 448
categorization xxii, 577, 589, 592
categorization of others as either similar or dissimilar to self 574
causal liking(s) 429, 431
causing market failures 93
Centipede 748
centralized systems of social security 878
chain reciprocity(ies) 25, 379, 386, 395, 415
charity(ies) xv, 4–6, 8, 37, 144, 155, 159, 201, 233, 595
charity game 255
Charness 754

Charness and Rabin 753
cheap talk 652
chiefly function 829
children 5
choice and valuation of an income distribution 580
choosing and valuing an income distribution xxi, 579
Christmas giving 172
civil servants 37
civility xv, 40
classical scientific directing utopia 471
close relations 855
clubs xv, 42
cluster(s) 867, 869
clusters of friends 866
co-evolution 561
Coase conjecture 241
cognitive development 570
cognitive dissonance 598
cognitive factors 566
cognitive skills 572
Collard 108
collective action 231
collective agreement 16, 837
collective gift-giving 283, 298
collective good 824
collective identity 834, 836, 874
collective regulation 837, 838, 840
collective rules 837
collective shock 865
collusions 6
commitment constraint 861, 868
commitment problem 854, 863
common beliefs 863
common distributive concerns 240
common fishery 842
common good 5
common property regulation 837
common property resources 830
communal identity 824
communal system 846
communal ties 834
communication 837, 840
communicative action 699
community(ies) xvi, 9, 56, 89, 378, 393
community heterogeneity 716
community land 834
community norm(s) 825, 876
community values 834

comparative, matching, or balance reciprocities 486
comparative justice 11
comparative or matching reciprocity 380
comparative reciprocity 380, 421, 424
comparison 379, 382
comparison and measures of inequalities 13
comparison income 701
comparison of reciprocities with other processes 520
comparisons 17
compassion 4–6, 8, 54, 56, 59, 385
compensatory justice 425, 445
compensatory reciprocity 421, 424
competition 18
competitive market exchange 229
competitive markets 11
complaisance 737
complementarity of mutual liking 434, 435, 493
Comte 9, 52, 75, 77, 104, 233, 749
conditional cooperation 649
Condorcet 744
conduct 398
conforming 14, 18, 397, 429, 437
Connolly 750
consensus 13
consequentialist 408
consideration 31
constrained-efficient contracts 859
constraining 41
constructed social preferences 549
consumption smoothing 858
contagion 429, 437
contagion of emotions 9
contempt liking 82
context-dependent rules of fairness 580
contingency 872
contingent opportunities 847
contingent repayment 872, 873
contingent valuation 141
continuation 382
continuation reciprocity 25, 380, 383, 384, 422, 439
contract design 616
contribution 4, 24
contribution game 165
contribution schedule 671
convention xxiii, 738–741, 763
conventional 763
conventional credit 872

conventional debt contracts 860
conventional level 570
cooperate 778
cooperation 197, 234
cooperative 566
cooperatives xv, 42, 376, 393, 469
coordination dilemmas 448
coordination game 379
coping mechanisms 864
core with interdependent coalitions 96
Cornes 751
corporate ownership 876
correspondence of sentiment 746, 761
Cournot–Nash 31, 49
Cournot–Nash behavioral assumption 332
Cournot–Nash equilibrium 293
Cox 753
credible threat 862
credit and insurance markets 851
credit transactions 870
crop failure 850
Croson 750
cross-voting 191
crowd out 49
crowd psychology 58
crowding-out 6, 139, 142, 153, 229
crowding-out of an intrinsic motivation by an extrinsic reward 586
Cubitt 741, 763
cultural and economic selection 726
cultural and social evolution 387
cultural exchange 559
cultural majority 562
cultural species 559
cultural transmission 559, 718
culture 561
culture of honor 812
cultures of punishment 463
cumulative sequential exchange 459
curing market failures 93
customary rights 848
customary rules 876
customary solidarity 836
customary tenure 876

Darwin 33
Das Adam Smith Problem 50
Davis 210, 212
debt forgiveness 859, 870, 873
debt peonage 873
debt rescheduling 872
default 869

default option 860
defect 778
deficit 487
degradation 836
democracy xv, 8, 16
demonstration and imitation 562
deontic (deontological) 380
Descartes 18, 21, 187, 203, 377, 389, 443, 762
Descartes effect 136, 143, 415, 445, 466
desert 384, 426
deserving poor 49
deservingness 18
determinacy 229
deviance 862
dictator game(s) 165, 189, 621, 623, 752, 753
differentiable social systems 277
dignity 397
direct empathy 58
directing utopia 379
disapproval 82
discrimination 197
disinterestedness 194
(dis)similarity of others with self 578
(dis)similarity with others 601
(dis)similarity with self 590, 594
distinction 14, 18
distress 857, 870
distress sales 849, 853, 854, 875, 877
distress seller 849
distribution 9, 229
distribution as a public good xvi, 101
distribution of resources 11
distributional preferences 13
distributive core 305
distributive efficiency 237
distributive equilibrium 245
distributive justice 9, 16, 78, 568
distributive liberal social contract 305
distributive Lindahl equilibrium 311
distributive optimum 236
distributive policy 285
distributive preferences 231
distributive social system 229
distributive surplus xvi, 101
District Land Control Boards 851
domination 506
domination reciprocity 31
domination solution 514
donation 873
donations to charity 193
drives: emotional drives 601

drives: equity drive 599, 600
drives: social drives 598
dual distributive core 316
duels 197
Dufwenberg 754
dutiful altruism 133, 135, 162
dutiful altruists 153, 170
duty 82, 156, 384, 397, 424
dyad 14
dyadic processes 510
dynamics of social norms 698

ecological characteristics 838
economic anthropology 376, 393
economic development 236
economic experiments 869
Economic Man / economic man 230, 379
economics and altruism xvi, 103
economics of liking-reciprocity 499
Edgeworth 5, 51, 104, 523, 749
education 8
effects of liking and being liked 501
efficiency 8
efficiency costs 875, 876
efficiency gains 837
efficient 670
egocentric bias 576
egoism 578
elders 828, 850
elicitation of social utility functions 597, 598
Elster 749, 752
emotional contagion 4, 6, 9, 54, 56, 58, 382, 383, 385
emotions 9
empathic distress 578
empathy(ies) 4, 6, 9, 10, 54, 56, 58, 129, 134, 142, 233, 376, 382, 383, 385, 579
empathy and personal distress 601, 602
empathy-altruism 595
empathy-altruism hypothesis 602
endogenous interactions 158
endogenous social choice 14, 103
enforceable contracts 856
enforcement mechanisms 848
environmental shock 869
envy 8, 14, 18, 303
equality 383
equilibrium 507, 836
equilibrium path 859
equilibrium reciprocity 31
equity 377, 444
equity-efficiency 579

equity and efficiency issue 579
equity theory 599, 600
equity-fairness 595
Essay on the Gift 28
Essays on Moral 50
esteem 6, 18, 82
ethic 58
ethics of economics xvi, 90
ethnic group 825, 866
evolution 383
evolutionary dynamics 780
evolutionary stable strategy ESS 552
exchange(s) 4, 166, 398
exclusion 869
exclusive ownership 875
existence 229
existence failures 280
existential gratitude 432
existential value 432
expectations 863
experiments 220
expiatory sanctions 568
expressive rationality xxiii, 756–758, 760, 763
expressively rational 751
extended 395
extended family 15, 874
extended reciprocities 25, 30, 386, 412
external obligation 31
externalities 41, 832, 836, 838, 875
extraction costs 867

face-saving 826
fair division rule 583
fair division (sharing) rule with perceived heterogeneity 590
fair process effect 582
fair wage 599
fairness xvi, 4, 5, 9, 18, 20, 29, 30, 80, 92, 201, 376, 379, 383, 385, 397, 444, 616
fairness concerns 616
fairness equilibrium 648
fairness heuristic xxi, 581–583
fairness norm 599
fairness of outcomes 582
fairness of procedures 582
Falk 754
false consensus effect 576, 577, 592
family(ies) 4, 5, 56, 233, 386
family constitution 167, 169
family networks 868
Federal Convention 189

Fehr 753
Feinberg 186
fellow-feeling xxiii, 31, 54, 745–748
first Leontief paradox 87
fiscal transfers 6
Fischbacher 754
fishing villages 871
fitness 550
focal points 739
folk theorem 807
food sharing 216
foreclosure 850, 875
forgiveness 860
formal analysis of reciprocity 482
four modes of economic transfer 451
framing 165, 173
free contracting 241
free disposal 272
free land sale market 854
free riders 202
free-riding 20, 326, 669, 837
free-riding behavior 297
freedom xvi, 92
Friedman 17, 23
friends 56
friendship 6, 18, 19, 397
full risk-pooling 863
full risk-sharing 861
functional Magnetic Resonance Imaging (fMRI) 631
fundamental insurance 70, 101, 394
fundamental reciprocity 34
fundamental theorems of welfare economics 271
future generation 4

games of reciprocity xv, 30, 386, 504
Gauthier 738
Geanakoplos 755
gemeinschaft as opposed to gesellechaft 393
general benevolence 80
general putative matching reciprocity 460
general reciprocity(ies) 25, 386, 390
general respect and sociability from reciprocity 455
general will 744, 759
generalization ethics 42
generalized 217, 395
generalized and general reciprocity(ies) 413, 466
generalized other 390
generalized putative reciprocity 68

generalized reciprocity(ies) 21, 25, 377, 386, 390, 593
generosity 18, 827, 829, 873
genotype 550, 559
Genovesi 733
geographic mobility 876
George Mason 189, 190
gift 4, 207, 829
gift exchange game 621, 624
gift exchanges 821
gift game 293
gift-giving 229, 398, 449
gift-induced liking 380
gift-refusal 281
gifts 141, 171, 377
Gilbert 760
giving 15, 420
global neutrality 285
Godelier 209, 214
good persons 4
good social relations 4
good society xv, 45, 471
goodwill 6, 82, 83
Gouverneur Morris 189, 190
governance costs 837, 839, 875
graph of reciprocity 442
gratitude 6, 18, 29, 30, 82, 169, 382, 384, 385, 397, 432
grazing associations 839
great economists 4
group cohesion 829
group selection 550, 555, 719, 774
group selection theory 777
group size 322
group-sentiments 503
groups 839
growth 5, 8, 702, 708
Guala 734
guaranteed access 829, 875
Gudeman 209
Gui 750
guilt 9, 55, 194
guilt aversion 652

habit 82
half-reciprocity 399
Hamilton's help game 796
Hamilton's rule 796
happiness 7
Hargreaves Heap 757, 758
Harsanyi 69, 70

haystack models 781
hazard occurrences 872
health shocks 866
hedonistic 56
hedonistic altruism 6, 60
hedonistic or natural altruism 4, 6, 9, 54
help xv, 5, 40
helping xxii, 6, 600
helping behaviour 25, 30, 136, 377, 390, 466
helping externalities 48
heterogeneity 876
Hewitt 744
hierarchical respect 566
hierarchies 406
hierarchy of ranks 828, 873
high-frequency events 870
higher status 6
history dependence 861
history dependent 859, 868
Hobbes 736–738, 740–745, 761
Hodgson 759
Hoffman 753
Hollis 744, 756, 759
Homans' cash posters 588
homo behavioralis 557
homo economicus 33, 103, 142, 557, 734, 735, 745
Homo sapiens 561
homogeneous 839
honesty 20
horticulturists 217
hospitality 217, 827
household emergencies 871
household vulnerability 844, 845
Hume 58, 204, 738–742, 745
humiliating 19
hunter–gatherer 214, 217, 873
Hurley 760
hybris 186, 199
hysteresis 137, 159

identification xxi, 575
identification of self with an other 573
identification of self with others 594
identity feelings 838
ideological intimidation 825
ideology 863, 873
idiosyncratic 832
idiosyncratic income risk 865
idiosyncratic income variations 877
image 17, 55, 89
image score 808

imbalance 426
imbalance between the two gifts 487
imitatio affectuum 9, 58
imitation 18, 379, 404, 437, 721
imitation of affects 58
impartial 10
impartial altruism xvi, 71, 74, 76
impartial judge(s) 574, 575, 593
impartial spectator 10, 28
impartiality 6, 56, 377, 383
imperfect commitment 861, 867
imperfect contracts 20
imperfect substitutability of transfers 242
imperfectly substitutable transfers 229
implementable risk-sharing contract 861
in-group favoritism xxii, 591, 592
in-group/out-group 590, 594
in-kind transfers 279
inalienable possessions 221
incentive compatibility 856
incentive compatible mechanisms 242
incentive dilution 837
incentives 616
inclinations 60
inclusion 869
inclusive fitness 552
income correlation 861, 862
income elasticity of gift-giving 266
income risk 865
income shocks 864, 868
incomplete contract(s) 41, 624
incomplete markets 20
indebtedness 397
index of assortativity 794
indifference 8
indirect effect 82
individual perspective 697
individual rationality 232
individual selection 719
individual selection theory 777
individualization 846
individualization of land rights 875
individualization of the tenure rights 875
individualized land rights 835
individualized use rights 830
individuals' preferences 14
ineffective risk coping 869
inefficiency xv, 23
inefficient equilibrium 670
inequality 9, 56, 405
inequality aversion xxiii, 752–756, 759

inequality of opportunity 10
inequity aversion 620, 639
informal insurance 166, 167, 169, 855, 868, 869
informal insurance arrangements 865
informal insurance mechanisms 864
informal insurance models 858
informal insurance networks 865, 877
informal mutual insurance 864
informal obligations 857
informal risk-sharing 867
informal risk-sharing arrangements 834
information 41
informational advantage 868
informational giving 497
informational problems 855
institutional trajectory 835, 838
institutions 4, 838
instrumental action 699
instrumental rationality 752, 756
instrumentally rational 751, 755
insurance 861
insurance ability 869
insurance considerations 876
insurance contract 855
insurance groups 870
insurance mechanisms 838
insurance networks 865, 866, 869
insurance partner 862
insurance scheme(s) 870, 871
insurance transfers 868
insurance-motivated gift exchange 873
intention 584, 596
intention based reciprocity 637, 647
intentionality 557
inter-household transfers 877
interactions 15
interdependence of utilities 10
interdependences 6
interdependent giving xvi, 106
interdependent utilities xvi, 5, 104, 106
interest 185, 200, 376, 421
interest-free loans 870
interested giving 403
intergenerational altruism 271
intergenerational cultural transmission 562
intergenerational reciprocities 26
intergenerational transfers 6
internalization processes 824
international aid 282
interpersonal conflicts 823, 826

interpersonal relations   823
interrelations of liking-reciprocity   498
intertemporal giving   xvi, 47
intrinsic disposition   719
intrinsic motivation   708
intrinsic preferences among processes   510
intrinsic process preference   508
intrinsically normative (non-altruistic) giving   xvi, 84
introspection   385
intuitive moral values and norms   6
intuitively moral altruism   60
investment   8
invidious comparisons   827
iron rule of selfishness   787
irrational behavior   628

jealousy   14, 18, 303
Jevons   734
job satisfaction   701
joint altruism   23
joint giving   xvi, 4, 8, 94, 95
joint giving theorem   xv, xvi, 23, 108
joint or public giving   xv, 23
joint production model   705
judgment(s)   4, 17
justice   4–6, 9, 56, 68, 80, 135, 157, 383, 384, 444, 738–740

Kaheman   390
Kant   50, 60, 203
Kant categorical imperative   18
Kantian altruism   133
Kantian behavior   335
Kant's reciprocity   6
Khanna   750
kin   851, 862
kin selection   551, 734
kin selection theory   777
kinship   867
Kirchsteiger   754
Kitty Genovese   390
knowledge of other   575, 577
knowledge of Self   575
knowledge of self and others   587
Kohlberg   53
Kohlbergian stages   570
Kolm   522, 523
Kolm's triangle   248
Kranich   51
Kripke   762

Kropotkin   33
kula ring   400
Kutz   760

La Bonne Economie, La Réciprocité Générale   376
la Bruyère   186
La Rochefoucauld   199, 204
labor force participation   716
laboratory experiments   376
labour relations   xv, 43
Lamarckian effect   559
land alienations   849
land allocation rules   874
land assets   853
land disputes   851
land gifts and land loans   848
land markets   836
land mortgages   850
land pressure   876
land relations   875
land rights   846
land system   830
land tenure   835
land tenure commission   851
land tenure individualization   876
land use patterns   835, 874
land–man ratios   835
landlessness   850
landmarks   5
lands foreclosed   850
language   736, 739, 741–743, 761–764
last action   410
learning   556
learning models   628
leisurely equivalent income   13
leveling societies   828
Lévi-Strauss   211
Lewis   741, 763, 764
lexical egoism   103
liberal social contract(s)   xvi, 16, 94, 95, 229
liking   6, 9, 18, 82, 379, 385, 421
liking-reciprocity   25, 28, 377, 380, 421, 430, 492
liking-reciprocity and comparative reciprocity   492
likings   382
limited commitment   859
Lindahl–Bergstrom equilibrium   312
lineage-based societies   832
linear public goods game   778
linked games   824

livelihoods   835
local neutrality   285
Locke   742
logic of liking reciprocity   500
logical action   232
Lomasky   757
love   5, 18, 82
low frequency events   869
low frequency hazards   877
lower status   6
lump-sum transfers   241

macrojustice   470
Malcolm   762
maleficence   315
malevolence   8, 13, 273
malice   8, 13
Malinowski   210
marginalization   869
Margolis   108, 751
market development   823
market efficiency   272
market failures   6, 20, 41, 42, 387, 391, 463
market integration   835, 839, 840, 842, 843, 876, 877
market opportunities   845
market optimum   236
market penetration   842
market substitute   527
market supporting   527
martyrdom   205
matching   379, 382
matching reciprocity   378, 380, 421, 424, 461
material loss   719
mating selection   476
Mauss   5, 28, 210, 376
McCabe   753
McLean   744, 749
mechanism design   xix, 328
mental algorithms   559
merit   18, 56, 384, 426
meta-motivations   200
meta-preferences   200
methodological individualism   735, 736, 741, 756, 761, 763
methodologically individualistic   735
microjustice   448
migration   789
Mihailescu   217
militant   36
Mill   5, 10, 16, 51, 52, 77, 104

Miller   760
minimal group(s)   xxii, 591–593, 596
miseries   5
missing agreements   20
missing market   41
modeling   563
money transfers   279
Montaigne   187, 193, 204
moral   60
moral akrasia   66
moral altruism   55, 61
moral behavior   562
moral conduct(s)   4, 20
moral credit   406
moral debt   19, 406
moral hedonistic   56
moral hedonistic altruism   6
moral indebtedness   385
moral individuals   824
moral intuition   55, 56
moral norms   194
moral or social properness   9
moral principle   828
moral risk   69
moral sentiments   xv, 7
moral time-sharing   69
moral values   55
morality: autonomous   567
morality: heteronomous   567
morally indebted   377
morals   8, 9
Morelly   28
mortgage   850
motivation   185, 451
motive(s)   5, 17, 38, 421
multi-player prisoners' dilemma   778
multiple families   839
multiple selves   14
multiple tenure   830
multiple tenure system   875
multiplex   871
mutual aid   854
mutual aid and trust   5
mutual assistance   733
mutual concern   10
mutual cooperation   616
mutual health group   870
mutual insurance   821, 855, 857, 863–866, 869
mutual insurance networks   854
mutual kindness   31
mutual respect   566, 568

mutual sympathy 746, 747
mutualism 552

Nagel 74
Napoleon 193
Nash equilibria 861
nation(s) 14, 15
natural 56
natural altruism 6
natural or hedonistic altruism xvi, 57, 80
necessary non-binding constraint 461
need 4, 56
need of authority 725
needy people 10
negative externalities 195
negative reciprocation 445
networks 866
neutral distortionary taxation 291
neutral lump-sum taxation 289
neutrality 229
new economics of the family 376
Nicole 50
non-altruistic giving 6
non-assortative matching process 784
non-cooperation 857
non-cooperative distributive equilibrium 231
non-cooperative equilibrium 319
non-cooperative game 299
non-disciplinary verbalizations 564
non-excludable public goods 387
non-invasive brain imaging techniques 631
non-jealousy 239
non-kin 862
non-moral 4
non-moral social norms 9
non-moral social rules 9
non-moral social values 55
non-moral social values and norms 6
non-paternalism 237
non-paternalistic 275
non-paternalistic interdependent preferences 229
non-profit organizations 141
non-stationary rule 872
non-stationary strategies 859
non-strategic cooperation 234
non-strategic interactions 234
non-tuism/nontuism 15, 33, 52, 103, 268, 450, 464
non-tuistic 236, 269
non-uniform linear tax-subsidy schemes 360

nonaltruistic giving xv, 18
norm 4, 397
norm of fairness 586
norm of giving 55
norm violators 616
norm-guided behavior 874
norm-shaped behavior 839
normality 266
normative 56
normative altruism(s) xvi, 4, 6, 9, 29, 54, 60, 61, 80
normative economics xv, 5, 45
normative economics of altruism and giving xvi, 90
normative non-altruism 82
normative non-altruistic giving 81
normative opinions 4
normative uses of reciprocity 468
norms 20, 56, 560
norms of conduct 6
norms of fairness xxii, 9, 56, 583
Nucleus Accumbens, NACC 633

Ockenfels 753
one-stage mechanisms 356
open-access 836
ophelimity 11, 232
opinion 81, 82
opportunistic agent 860
opportunistic behavior 837
opportunistic household 862
opportunistic tendencies 837
optimal tax 141
ordinal normality 266
ordinal utility function 7
organizations 5
ostracism 825
other-regarding behavior 829
other-regarding norms 877
other-regarding preferences 874
other-regarding values 823
out-group discrimination xxii, 591–593
outcome satisfaction 597, 600
own empathy 58

Papuan pig-feasts 19
Paqué 750
parental disciplinary practices: induction, assertive technique, punitive technique 564
parental disciplinary practices: induction, power-assertive techniques, punitive techniques 563

Pareto   5, 11, 51, 52, 232, 523, 734
Pareto efficiency   25
Pareto social systems   285
Pareto-dominance   575
Pareto-efficiency   231
Pareto-efficient income distributions   12
Pareto-efficient redistribution   229
partial insurance   867
partially original position   100
participation   704
participation constraint(s)   856, 859, 860
partners   867
party member   36
Pascal   50
passion   185, 201
paternalism   57
paternalistic   11, 55
paternalistic altruism   134
paternalistic motives   236
patron–client relationships   876
patrons   874
pay-as-you-go   395
"pay-as-you-go" pension systems   379
payoff-monotonicity   780
peace   6
peaceful intentions   82, 83
Peacock   762
Pearce   755
pensions   395
perfect substitutability of transfers   xviii, 227
perfectly substitutable transfers   243
permanent use rights   847
personal mobility   715
personalized relationships   854, 874
perspective role-taking   593
perspective taking   581
perspective-taking ability(ies)   573, 578
perspective-taking skills   572, 578
Pettit   762
pharisian   10
pharisianism   35
pharisians   35
Phelps   46, 108
phenotype   550, 559
philanthropy   xv, 37
Piaget   53
pity   4, 6, 8, 54, 56, 59
Plato   77
Plott, 1996   735
Polanyi   213
political   4

political action   5
political and public sector   xv, 34
political systems   386
politicians   37
polymorphic   553
polymorphic equilibrium   558, 786
poor   10
population growth   823, 835, 839, 842, 843, 846
population growth and market expansion   841
population pressure   845, 846
positional orientation   700
Positron Emission Tomography (PET)   631
Posnett   750
post-conventional level   570
postsocialism   219
potlatch   19
poverty   4
poverty relief   236
power to take game   621, 622
praetium doloris   446
praise   6, 17, 18, 82
preconventional level   570
preemption rights   877
preference about processes   387
preference for conformity   590
preference reversals on income distributions   581
pressure on the commons   876
Price equation   556
pride   193
primacy effect of fairness information   582
principal-agent relation   624
principle of universalization   448
priority access   854
prisoner's dilemma   188, 379, 553, 558, 748, 778
private contributions to public goods   354
private language   762
private language argument   xxiii, 761, 762
private language argumentation   762
private property rights   299, 838, 876
private provision of public goods   243
private 'vices'   724
privatization   834, 838
privatization of natural resources   876
privatize   875
pro-social behavior   561
pro-social conduct(s)   xv, 4, 32
pro-social development   xxi, 578
procedural fairness   506
process of giving   82

process preferences 504, 505
process reciprocity 441
process-dependent allocative preferences 509
process-liberal justice 78
process-liberal public debt xvi, 98
production or consumption shock 872
productive consumption 705
progressive wealth transfers 239
prohibitions 849
projection mechanism 584
projection of self onto an other 573
promise-keeping 15, 20, 31, 378, 450
properties 6
propriety 424
propriety of balancing 486
propriety of reciprocity 424
protection of the poor 878
Proudhon 28
provision of internal attribution 564
proximity 56
psychological benefit 719
psychological game theory 755
public aid 5
public benefits 724
public debt 6, 47
public fund-raising 19
public good(s) 8, 16, 41, 95, 231, 379, 748–753, 759
public good game 585
public good model with additive technology 239
public good problem of redistribution 299
public humiliation 825
public indebtedness 4
public interest 5
public sector 4
public services 34
public transfers 4, 8
punish 409, 463
punishing 409
punishment 202, 616
pure altruism 166, 576
pure gift giving 387
pure hedonistic 56
pure hedonistic altruism 6
pure public 750
pure public good 4
pure public goods model 138
putative reciprocity(ies) 6, 18, 56, 68, 101, 470

quadrangle of economic transfers 452
quality of insurance 867
quality of the parent–child relationships 563
quantitative case 511, 516
quasi-maximin preferences 642
quasi-moral norms 197, 198

Rabin xxiii, 754–756, 759
random shocks 858, 871
rank differences 829
rational 56, 60
rational altruism 60, 67
rational calculations 558
rational decision 557
rational moral principles 6
rationality 185, 377, 383, 385
Rawls 70, 77
Rawls' maximin criterion 642
reason 4, 55, 185
receiver's situation 56
reciprocal altruism 555
reciprocal corrections of market failures 456
reciprocal fairness 446
reciprocal fairness equilibrium 651
reciprocal liking 28, 380, 381, 430, 434, 495
reciprocal relationships 869
reciprocal sanctions 568
reciprocal transfer network 869
reciprocal transfer payments 870
reciprocal transfers 822, 829, 862, 863, 877
reciprocating 384, 755
reciprocation 26, 377, 385, 418, 420, 870
reciprocators 463
reciprocitarian comparative sentiments 486
reciprocitarians 463
reciprocities and public goods or collective actions 458
reciprocity xxiii, 20, 25, 26, 132, 166, 189, 197, 207, 211, 377, 380, 395, 418, 584, 616, 620, 697, 733, 754–756, 759, 760
reciprocity equilibrium 650
reciprocity in economics 522
reciprocity in trust 465
reciprocity selection 550–552
reciprocity: negative and positive 595, 596, 600
rectifiant 14
redistribution 6, 12
redistribution of land 847
redistribution of wealth xviii, 227
redistributive arrangements 874
redistributive norms 827, 828, 873, 874, 877

redistributive social norms 877
redistributive taxes 16
refusing 428
refusing gifts 399
Regan 759
reification 557
reinforcement 721
(rejection of) Pareto-dominance 580, 595
relation xv, 43, 81, 83
relational capital 465
relational envy 303
relational good(s) 297, 704
relational orientation 700
'relational' perspective 697
relational reciprocity 441
relationality 704
relations 4, 56, 867
relative deprivation 597
relative income and envy 639
repeated actions 837
repeated game(s) 806, 821, 855, 863
repeated interactions 840
repeated shocks 869
replicator 553
reputation 18, 89
reputation effects 837, 854, 857
resentment 30, 384, 385, 397
reservation wage 678
respect xv, 6, 20, 31, 40, 397
responsibility 380
responsible 381
restraint from harming 40
retaliation 26, 377, 419
retaliation for deterrence 380, 384
retributive justice 426, 445, 486, 568
retro-gift(s) xvi, 4, 47, 98, 99
retro-payments 99
retro-transfers 99
return-gift(s) 6, 18, 82, 380
return-gift game 516
revenge 26, 186, 377, 418, 428
reverse 395
reverse putative reciprocity 68
reverse reciprocity(ies) 18, 21, 29, 377, 386, 389, 404, 415, 466
reward(s) 6, 18, 82, 418, 426
Ricardian equivalence 47, 138
right of private property 300
rights 5, 6
rights of access 847
rightsholders 847

risk aversion 857
risk characteristics 869
risk diversification 876
risk pool 867, 869
risk sharing 168, 864
risk sharing networks 865
risk-pooling 858, 866, 871
risk-pooling equilibrium 855
risk-pooling group 867
risk-pooling mechanism 854, 856
risk-pooling network 854
risk-sharing 856, 857, 862, 865–868
risk-sharing arrangement(s) 861, 862, 877
risk-sharing contracts 861
risks 832
rituals 218
rostral anterior cingulate cortex (ACC) 632
rotating credit-and-savings associations 865
rotating savings 878
rotational arrangement(s) 846, 875
Roth 753
Rotten Kid Theorem 237
Rousseau xxiii, 36, 37, 67, 742–745, 759, 763
rule violations 849
rule-following 762
rules 5
rules of sharing 874

Sahlins 213, 217, 477
Saint Martin 75
sale and mortgage transactions 851
salience 740
salient 739
Samaritan's dilemma 49, 236
sanctioning 862
sanctioning mechanism 825, 862
sanctions 824
Sandler 750, 751
satisfaction 721
savings 8
savings clubs 878
schadenfreude 8, 14
Scheler 9, 58
Schelling 739
Schmidt 753
Schmitz 750
school programs and socialization 564, 565
Schur-concave 14
sea accidents 870
sea rescue associations 870
sea rescue mutual groups 864
sea rescue operations 866

sealing an agreement 83
Searle 760
second-order free rider problem 195
second-party punishment 203
segmentation 869
self 15
self-anchored altruism xxii, 593, 594, 600
self-anchoring theory 592
self-centredness 239
self-defence 6
self-enforceability 856
self-help 869
self-image 66
self-insurance 869
self-insurance opportunities 875
self-interest 5, 81, 82, 382
self-interest hypothesis 616
self-interested 4
self-interested giving xvi, 84
self-interested preferences 14
self-love 724
self-other distinction 578
self-projection xxi, 575, 578, 581, 593, 595
self-projection mechanism 579, 584
self-respect 397
self-selection processes 878
self-sufficiency 725
selfish 56
selfish altruism xvi, 99
selfish behavior 591
selfish motives 855
selfishness 774
Seneca 186, 201
sense of community 397
sense of justice 5, 7, 383
sense of propriety 421
sense of self and ego and of social existence 433
sense of self and of social existence 385
sentiments 5
sentiments of inferiority or superiority 14, 18
sentiments of liking-reciprocity 492
separability 237
sequential exchange(s) 4, 25, 30, 377, 380, 383, 399, 408
sequential game 354
"Sequential Reciprocity Equilibrium" (SRE) 649
sequential relation(s) 387, 457
sexual haploidy 797
shame 9, 19, 55, 193, 194, 199

sharing 214
sharing norms 828
Sherman 190
shirking 863
shock 860
showing off 24
signaling 196
simple causal liking 431
situation(s) 4, 81, 83
situation or status 82
six basic reciprocations 443
Skelton 734
Skyrms 763
small-scale settings 823
Smith, *see* Adam Smith
social 60
social altruism 60, 61
social and cultural evolution 478
social and economic change 386
social bond 397
social capital 707, 839
social capital accumulation 708, 711
social choice xvi, 5, 104
social cognition xxi, 573
social communication 316
social comparison xxii, 597
social comparison: theory 598
social contract 739, 743, 744
social contract equilibrium 311
social contracting 241
social decisions 699
social distance 15, 710
social effects xvi, 81, 82, 89
social effects of the gift 81
social efficiency 41, 231, 237
social equilibrium 232
social ethical judgments 14
social ethical views 14
social evolution 552
social exchange game 825, 837
social exclusion 865
social freedom 6, 78, 90
social giving xv, 43
social goods 825
social identity theory 592
social interdependencies 158
social learning school 562
social multiplier 158
social norm 56, 584, 829
social norm of minimal production 588
social norm of sharing 585

social norm of wage uniformity 588
social norm: Homans' "cash posters" xxii, 586
social normative motives 64
social norms 169, 193, 194, 585, 717, 821, 828, 838, 839, 857, 863, 875, 876
social norms and values 824
social or community norms 829
social order 828, 874
social ostracism 824, 825
social participation 712
social poverty traps 713
social preferences 637
social preferences: of coworkers 587
social pressure 133, 156, 160, 162
social prestige 132, 156, 160
social prestige and esteem 827
social proximity 80
social psychology 25, 30, 379
social relation(s) xvi, 6, 81, 82, 89
social safeguards 835
social security 835, 846, 874
social security considerations 850, 852
social security function 833
social security mechanism 847
social security system 877
social selection 718
social selection of modes of relation 479
social sentiment(s) 4, 427, 444
social situation(s) 6, 81, 82
social specie 550
social status 702
social utility function(s) 233, 597
social value orientations 722
social welfare functions 12
sociality xv, 40
socialization 560
socially provided goods 697, 699
socio-economic differentiation 845, 877
solidarity xv, 34, 37, 49, 51, 723
solidarity arrangements 822
solidarity networks 828
solidarity norms 848
Solow 107
solutions of the return-gift and reciprocity games 513
somato-sensory cortex 632
Sophie de Condorcet 104
spatial structure 803
Spinoza 9, 58
Spinoza's *imitatio affectuum* 495
spite 13

spread risks 877
Stacchetti 755
Stackelberg equilibrium 49
stag hunt games 779
stage: cooperative 566
stage: egocentric 566
stage: individual and motor 566
standard debt contract 860
Stark 746, 750
state of nature 736, 742, 743
state-contingent 823
state-contingent commodities 871
state-contingent contracting 857
state-contingent decision 856
state-contingent loans 872
state-contingent reciprocal transfers 854, 870, 877
state-contingent transfers 864
statesmen 37
stationary strategies 856, 858
status xv, 18, 20, 43, 82, 89, 379, 405, 828
status reciprocity 441
Steedman 52, 108
Steinberg 110, 750
stochastic extinction 789
stochastic relation 680
stranger farmers 847
strangers 867
strategic bequest 235
strategic environment 684
strategic interaction(s) 234, 504
striatum 633
strong altruist 790
strong distributive equilibrium 298
strong Nash distributive equilibrium 234
strong Nash equilibrium 298
strong reciprocity 560, 620
structures 6
structures of imbalance 490
subgame perfect Nash equilibrium 292
submission 19
subsidy 292
subsidy-setting game 355
subsistence risks 868
substitution 56, 58, 68
substitution elasticity of transfers 339
suffering 56
Sugden 522, 733, 738, 739, 741, 745, 750, 751, 757, 759–761, 763
suicide missions 187, 194
superego 63

supernatural powers 825
supporter 36
surplus 487
symbol xv, 43
symbolic gifts 400
symbolic reciprocity 441
symbols 19
symmetric equilibrium 332
symmetric states 860
symmetrical reciprocity 515
symmetry 14
sympathy 4, 6, 9, 54, 56, 59, 230, 233, 382, 576, 579, 740
synopsis and graphs of the relations 499

targeting to the poor 843
tax prices xvii, 144
tax-subsidy scheme 328
taxes 5
team performance 707
team reasoning xxiii, 758–760
team thinking 742, 745
television 716
television and socialization 565
tenure individualization 875
tenure regimes 831
tenure rights 830, 836
Theory of Moral Sentiments 50, 77, 104, 230
third party punishment game 621, 623
third-party punishment 203
Thomson 49
three worlds of reciprocity 421
Thurnwald 28
tipping 197
Tit-For-Tat 554
titled land 851
Titmuss 38, 107
to be praised 18
to be praiseworthy 18
Tocqueville 192
tradition 18, 561
tragedy of the commons 776, 836
transaction cost(s) 41, 830
transfer function 867
transfer paradox 282
transfer partners 862
transfer payments 856
transfer preferences 505
transfer problem 282
transfer rights 848
transfers 823

transmutation 186, 200
transplantation 193, 197
treasury efficiency 328
tribal societies 823
trust 20, 377, 708
trust game 621, 623
Trustee 623
trustful 377
trustworthiness 20, 708
trustworthy 377
truth-telling 15, 20
Tuomela 760
two gratitudes 494
two-stage mechanisms 354
types and structure of altruism 56

ultimatum 752
ultimatum game 189, 199, 585, 621, 753, 756, 812
ultimatum game with perceived heterogeneity 591
understanding and explaining reciprocity 472
undeserving poor 49
unequal asset endowments 845
uniform linear tax-subsidy schemes 360
unilateral respect 567
universalization 6, 18, 56, 71
universalization or "Categorical imperative" 460
updating rule 859
Use and Abuse of Biology 477
utilitarian 12, 186, 198, 201

vainglory 24
values of reciprocity 453, 468
Vanderschraaf 739
Varian 750
vengeance 397
vengefulness 385
verstehen 473
village commons 834–836, 875
village communities 823
village council 851
village pool 847
village-level shocks 864
violent conflicts 848
virtue 82
virtuousness 6
vitality 721
voluntary provision 387
voluntary reciprocal transfers 877
voluntary redistribution 228

volunteer 162
volunteer labour 155, 160
volunteering 131, 144, 153
voter 36
voting 5, 15

Walras 5, 16, 51, 52, 77
Walrasian economy 237
war of gifts 262
warm glow xxiii, 140, 153, 156, 159, 169, 175, 187, 202, 751, 752
water transfers 867
weak altruist 790
weak reciprocity 620

Wealth of Nations 230
Weber 756
Weimann 750
welfare state 38, 231, 376
Wicksteed 5, 15, 33, 52, 230, 450, 464
willingnesses to pay 13
Winch 762
within-group selection 560
within-group selection effect 556
Wittgenstein 762–764
women's 716
workplace xv, 43

Zamagni 46, 108